ALSO BY MARTIN DAUNTON

State and Market in Victorian Britain: War, Welfare and Capitalism

Wealth and Welfare: An Economic and Social History of Britain,
1851–1951

Just Taxes: The Politics of Taxation in Britain, 1914–1979

Trusting Leviathan: The Politics of Taxation in Britain, 1799–1914

Progress and Poverty: An Economic and Social History of Britain,
1700–1850

The Economic
Government of the World

The Economic
Government of the World
1933–2023

MARTIN DAUNTON

Farrar, Straus and Giroux
New York

Farrar, Straus and Giroux
120 Broadway, New York 10271

Copyright © 2023 by Martin Daunton
All rights reserved
Printed in the United States of America
Originally published in 2023 by Allen Lane, Great Britain
Published in the United States by Farrar, Straus and Giroux
First American edition, 2023

Library of Congress Cataloging-in-Publication Data
Names: Daunton, M. J. (Martin J.), author.
Title: The economic government of the world : 1933–2023 /
 Martin Daunton.
Description: First American edition. | New York : Farrar Straus and
 Giroux, 2023. | Includes bibliographical references and index.
Identifiers: LCCN 2023021274 | ISBN 9780374146412 (hardcover)
Subjects: LCSH: International economic relations—History. | Economic
 policy—International cooperation—History. | Financial institutions,
 International—History. | Economic history—1918–1945. | Economic
 history—1945–
Classification: LCC HF1359 .D3786 2023 | DDC 337—dc23/
 eng/20230512
LC record available at https://lccn.loc.gov/2023021274

Our books may be purchased in bulk for promotional, educational,
or business use. Please contact your local bookseller or the Macmillan
Corporate and Premium Sales Department at 1-800-221-7945, extension
5442, or by email at MacmillanSpecialMarkets@macmillan.com.

www.fsgbooks.com
www.twitter.com/fsgbooks • www.facebook.com/fsgbooks

9 8 7 6 5 4 3 2 1

'Economic diseases are highly communicable. It follows, therefore, that the economic health of every country is a proper matter of concern to all its neighbors, near and distant. Only through a dynamic and a soundly expanding world economy can the living standards of individual nations be advanced to levels which will permit a full realization of our hopes for the future.'

United Nations Monetary and Financial Conference. Statement by the President, 29 June 1944, *Department of State Bulletin* vol XI, no. 262, 13

'When a country (USA) is losing many billions of dollars on trade with virtually every country it does business with, trade wars are good, and easy to win. Example, when we are down $100 billion with a certain country and they get cute, don't trade anymore – we win big. It's easy!'

Donald J. Trump @realDonaldTrump, 10.50 a.m., 2 March 2018

'The multilateral trade system has transformed our world over the past generation. But that system of rules and shared responsibility is now in danger of being torn apart. This would be an inexcusable, collective policy failure.'

Christine Lagarde, Managing Director of the IMF, Hong Kong, 11 April 2018, quoted in the *Financial Times*, 12 April 2018

Contents

Acknowledgements   ix
List of Figures   xii
Abbreviations   xiii
Introduction   xvii

PART ONE
Responding to the Great Depression

1 'The establishment of a sound national economy':
   The Politics of the Great Depression   5

2 'Barren harvest': The World Monetary and Economic
   Conference, 1933   29

3 'Beggar my neighbour': The Failures of the World
   Economy, 1933–39   59

4 'Escaping from backwardness': Strategies of Economic
   Development   89

PART TWO
The Bretton Woods Era

5 'Handling the English': Lend Lease, Commercial Policy
   and Sterling Balances   121

6 'A firm foundation': Reforming the Monetary System   143

7 'An integrated program': Food, Employment and
   Commodities   169

8 'The threshold of the future': The Bretton Woods Agreement   189

9 'A financial Dunkirk': The United States, Britain and Germany   213

10 'Happier relations between all countries': The Failure of the
   International Trade Organization   241

11 'Convertible currencies in the free world': Sterling and Europe   275

12 'Damn it, we're a bank': Contesting Development   307

13 'A common detestation of colonialism': Development,
   Nationalism and the Cold War   337

14 'Competitive cooperation': The Kennedy Round,
    the United States and the Common Market   365

15 'Progress towards self-sustaining growth':
    The Development Decade   399

PART THREE
Washington Consensus

16 'Trying to live with an anomaly': The Limits of Bretton Woods   431

17 'Benign neglect': Closing the Gold Window   461

18 'Music without any Middle C': The Floating World   493

19 'A trade union of the poor': The New International
    Economic Order and the Limits to Growth   533

20 'Expansion of economic freedom': The Rise of Market
    Liberalism   567

21 'Market fundamentalism': The Washington Consensus
    and Financial Liberalization   593

22 'Rules-based system': Creating the World Trade Organization   631

23 'Setting the bird free': Economies in Transition   659

24 'Eurofantasies': From Economic and Monetary
    Union to the Euro   697

PART FOUR
Beyond Neo-Liberalism

25 'Behaving badly': The Global Financial Crisis   731

26 'Messy multilateralism': Nationalism versus Globalism   771

27 Fair Capitalism and Globalization: The Way Ahead   791

    List of Illustrations   835
    Notes   839
    Index   945

Acknowledgements

This book has had a long gestation period. It was conceived as long ago as 2004 as a third-year, source-based special subject in the Faculty of History at the University of Cambridge on 'The political economy of globalization, 1939–1973' that covered the genesis, implementation and demise of the Bretton Woods regime. I was joined by Richard Toye whose doctoral thesis dealt with Labour's post-war economic policies; he was also writing the official history of the United Nations Conference on Trade and Development. I learned much from Richard before he departed for a post at the University of Exeter. I continued to teach the course until 2011/12 – a rewarding experience with argumentative and stimulating students. The ideas from this course informed the four annual lectures I gave as President of the Royal Historical Society on 'Britain and globalization since 1850', which appeared in the Society's *Transactions*. By the time I delivered the fourth lecture in November 2008, we were living through the aftershocks of the global financial crisis.

Current politics caught up with history, and I was interested in the ways that the past was being used in debates about the policy response to the global financial crisis, whether it be appeals not to repeat the Great Depression, unrealistic demands for a new Bretton Woods, or historical data on the threat of high levels of public debt. I put the idea of a wider book that came up to the present and set current concerns in a longer historical perspective to Stuart Proffitt, and I am grateful to him for his support and patience. The task of finishing the book took longer than either of us expected, in part because of my commitments in the University, and also because 'stuff happened' – the impact of austerity, the British vote in 2016 to leave the European Union, the election of Donald Trump as President and the threat he posed to the post-war multilateral order, a more assertive China, a fragile and resentful Russia – all had to be taken into account. The book was virtually complete by early spring 2020, when Covid-19 created the worst health and economic crisis since the influenza epidemic of 1918/19 and the Great Depression. Then Russia's invasion of Ukraine, and the shock of high energy prices, threatened a return to the stagflation of the 1970s or, worse, to large-scale conflict. We are at a crucial moment similar to the emergence of the New Deal and social democratic policies after the Second World War, and the rise of market liberalism in the 1970s. Will we now see a new set of assumptions about the government of the world economy on a par with the emergence of the multilateral institutions during and after the Second World War, and in the 1970s with the rise of neo-liberalism? We live in a world of what Mervyn King and John Kay have called radical uncertainty. The future is difficult to predict – though there is one certainty: there has been a fundamental shift in the balance of economic power toward Asia in general, and China in particular.

I am grateful to many people for their help and support during the long gestation of the book. At Trinity Hall, I had excellent administrative support from Ginny Swepson, Anthea Bain, Anna Walford, Louise Ovens and Mary Richmond. In the Faculty of History, I was fortunate to have outstanding graduate students who were working on related topics with whom I could explore ideas – Colin Chamberlain, Benjamin Choo, Kieran Heinemann, Kiyoshi Hirowatari, Seung-Woo Kim, Tae Hoon Kim, Adrian Leonard, Craig McMahon, Marta Musso, Paolo Natali, Duncan Needham, David Paulson, Charles Read, Sabine Schneider, Hiroki Shin and Adrian Williamson. I discussed ideas with Amrita Narlikar, now Director of the German Institute for Global and Area Studies in Hamburg, with whom I co-taught a Masters' course in the Faculty of History and Department of Politics and International Studies which allowed me to engage with ideas from political science. Some of my thinking developed through a conference that she organized and a jointly edited volume. My thoughts appeared in 'From Bretton Woods to Havana: multilateral deadlocks in historical perspective', in Amrita Narlikar, ed., *Deadlocks in Multilateral Negotiations: Causes and Solutions* (Cambridge University Press, 2010) and 'The inconsistent quartet: free trade versus competing goals', in Amrita Narlikar, Martin Daunton and Robert M. Stern, eds., *The Oxford Handbook on the World Trade Organization* (Oxford University Press, 2012). I am grateful to friends and colleagues – Edoardo Altamura, Marc Buggeln, Martin Chick, Leslie Chung, Julian Hoppit, Jamie Martin, Vanessa Ogle, Ramandeep Singh, Jim Tomlinson, and many others for conversations over the years. Frank Trentmann and Patricia Clavin provided detailed and helpful comments as readers for Allen Lane. I was able to try out ideas in two public lectures at the University of Melbourne; I am very grateful to Peter Griffin and Charles Goode who funded the lectures and showed that businesspeople realize the importance of history, as well as to Tony Pagone for providing hospitality. I also presented my ideas in the R. H. Tawney Lecture to the Economic History Society, in lectures at Gresham College in London, in seminars in Aberystwyth, Berlin, Harvard (where Jamie Martin offered insightful comments), Helsinki, Hong

Kong, Manchester, Turin, and the German Historical Institute in both London and Munich. The conference organized by Ian Shapiro and Naomi Lamoreaux at Yale University in 2015 was an opportunity to meet many leading scholars in the field. My contribution appeared as 'Nutrition, food, agriculture, and the world economy', in Naomi Lamoreaux and Ian Shapiro, eds., *The Bretton Woods Agreement* (Yale University Press, 2019) and I am grateful to the editors for permission to draw on this material. The referendum of 2016 meant that the history of trade policy became a topic of interest in Whitehall: I presented papers at the Treasury, the Department of International Trade, and the Department for Business, Energy, Innovation and Skills.

The research for the book required frequent visits to The National Archives in Kew – a model of well-organized efficiency from which the National Records and Archives Administration in College Park, Maryland, has much to learn. The presidential libraries of Franklin Delano Roosevelt, Harry S. Truman, John F. Kennedy, Lyndon B. Johnson, Richard Nixon, Gerald Ford, Jimmy Carter and Ronald Reagan were helpful and welcoming. Rhys Jones, Sean Bottomley and Sameer Khan provided some archival assistance; Hiroki Shin assisted with work on Japan, and Konstantin Bosch on Germany. Funding was provided by the University of Cambridge and the British Academy. The University of Cambridge library was, as always, an astonishing resource.

At home, Claire has lived with the book for too long. When we met, she was working at the European Commission and writing a report on the establishment of its archive – much of it now digitized and used in my discussion of European monetary integration. At Allen Lane, the editorial input of Candida Brazil, Stuart Proffitt and Alice Skinner led to many improvements. Their engagement with the content, style and design of the book was of the highest order. The copy editing of Charlotte Ridings was meticulous and saved me from error; and the index of Auriol Griffith-Jones was, as in my previous books, excellent. Richard Duguid handled the production with care and efficiency. In New York, the team at Farrar, Straus and Giroux oversaw the American edition, and I thank Eric Chinski and Tara Sharma.

Martin Daunton
Little Wilbraham
November 2022

List of Figures

1. World trade and production, 1926–38
2. Average tariff levels 1925, 1931 and 1952
3. US balance of payments, 1946–73
4. GATT trade rounds, 1947–93
5. US interest rates and short-term financial flows, 1960–72
6. Currency composition of globally disclosed foreign exchange reserves, 1947–2013
7. Currency fluctuations after the end of pegged rates: yen and DM/euro against the dollar, 1950–2019
8. Real crude oil price (West Texas Intermediate), 1970–2022
9. Gross rates of return for all business and manufacturing for selected OECD countries, 1960, 1973 and 1982
10. Inflation in developed countries, 1960–2020
11. Net household saving rate of selected countries, 1985 and 2005
12. IMF lending during economic crises, 1952–2013
13. Global merchandise exports as a % of GDP, 1830–2014
14. Purchasing power parity by GDP per adult, 1960–2020
15. Households and NPISHs final consumption expenditure (% of GDP), China and US, 1960–2020
16. US Treasuries owned by China, 2000–2021
17. US trade deficit in goods with China, 1985–2020
18. Real income growth at various percentiles of global income distribution, 1988–2008
19. a) World industrial production, months after the peaks of June 1929 and April 2008
    b) Volume of world trade, months after the peaks of June 1929 and April 2008
20. Central bank dollar swaps net outstanding, December 2007–December 2009
21. Relative gain in real per capita income by global income level, 1988–2008 and 1988–2011
22. Income shares of percentiles 90–95, 95–99 and the top 1 per cent in the US, 1913–98
23. CEO-to-worker compensation ratio in top 350 US firms, 1965–2019
24. Top 2,000 transnational corporations' profit and the global labour income share, 1995–2015
25. Inheritance tax rates, US, Britain, Germany and France, 1900–2020
26. Aggregate external public debt owed by developing and emerging market economies to official creditors, 2000–2017
27. Growth of world trade in goods and services, 1960–2020

Abbreviations

AAA	Agricultural Adjustment Act
ABA	American Bankers' Association
AES	Alternative Economic Strategy
AFL	American Federation of Labor
AIIB	Asian Infrastructure Investment Bank
ASEAN	Association of South-East Asian Nations
ASP	American Selling Price
BIS	Bank for International Settlements
BJP	Bharatiya Janata Party
C20	Committee of Twenty
CAP	Common Agricultural Policy
CCP	Chinese Communist Party
CEA	Council of Economic Advisers
CIA	Central Intelligence Agency
CIEP	Council on International Economic Policy
CIO	Congress of Industrial Organizations
CIS	Center for International Studies
COMECON	Council for Mutual Economic Assistance
DAFP	*Documents on Australian Foreign Policy*
DCER	*Documents on Canadian External Relations*
ECA	Economic Cooperation Administration
ECB	European Central Bank
ECJ	European Court of Justice
ECLA	United Nations Economic Commission for Latin America
ECLAC	United Nations Economic Commission for Latin America and the Caribbean
ECOSOC	United Nations Economic and Social Council
ECSC	European Coal and Steel Community
EEC	European Economic Community
EFO	Economic and Financial Organization of the League of Nations
EMS	European Monetary System
EMU	Economic and Monetary Union
EPU	European Payments Union
EU	European Union

FAO	Food and Agriculture Organization
FOMC	Federal Open Market Committee
FRUS	*Foreign Relations of the United States*
FSA	Financial Services Authority
FSOC	Financial Stability Oversight Council
FTA	free trade agreement
GAB	General Agreement to Borrow
GATT	General Agreement on Tariffs and Trade
GSP	Generalized System of Preferences
IBRD	International Bank for Reconstruction and Development
IET	Interest Equalization Tax
IFC	International Finance Corporation
IIA	International Institute of Agriculture
ILO	International Labour Organisation
IMF	International Monetary Fund
ISI	Import-Substituting Industrialization
ITO	International Trade Organization
LSE	London School of Economics
MIT	Massachusetts Institute of Technology
NAFTA	North American Free Trade Agreement
NARA	National Archives and Records Administration (US)
NATO	North Atlantic Treaty Organization
NEP	New Economic Policy
NIEO	New International Economic Order
NPC	National Planning Commission
NSC	National Security Council
NTB	non-tariff barrier
OECD	Organization for Economic Co-operation and Development
OEEC	Organization for European Economic Co-operation
OMT	outright monetary transaction
OPEC	Organization of the Petroleum Exporting Countries
PRI	Partido Revolucionario Institucional
QE	quantitative easing
QR	quantitative restrictions
RFC	Reconstruction Finance Corporation
RTAA	Reciprocal Trade Agreements Act
SDR	Special Drawing Right
SUNFED	Special United Nations Fund for Economic Development
TEA	Trade Expansion Act
TNA	The National Archives (UK)

TPP	Trans-Pacific Partnership
TRIMS	trade-related investment measures
TRIPS	trade-related intellectual property rights
TTIP	Transatlantic Trade and Investment Partnership
TUC	Trades Union Congress
TVE	town and village enterprise
UNCTAD	United Nations Conference on Trade and Development
UNESCO	United Nations Educational, Scientific and Cultural Organization
USAID	United States Agency for International Development
WHO	World Health Organization
WTO	World Trade Organization

Introduction

In April 2009, the leaders of the world's major developed and emerging economies – the Group of 20 – met in London under the chairmanship of the British prime minister, Gordon Brown. At a critical time, a year after the global financial crisis, Brown turned to the past for inspiration and warning: 'There was a world economic conference in 1933, and it took place in Britain. People came to London to get agreement, partly on trade, partly on other aspects of the economy. It failed. And partly as a result of that failure the rest of the Thirties was blighted by protectionism.'[1] It was excellent rhetoric with which to urge co-operation and prevent a repetition of the downward spiral into trade and currency wars that had marred the 1930s. In 1933 and 2009, politicians gathering in London faced the two largest economic crises thus far in the twentieth and twenty-first centuries, respectively.

In 1933, leading politicians from sixty-six nations brought radically different perceptions of the causes of the crisis and its solution, and they left in disarray. The new American president, Franklin Delano Roosevelt, sent a delegation to London that was itself riven by disagreement. He stayed at home and tried to make up his mind what to do. In 2009, a smaller group of twenty nations assembled in London. The new US president, Barack Obama – somewhat reluctantly – travelled to London and announced that America would take an active role. 'Leaders of the Group of 20 have a responsibility to take bold, comprehensive and co-ordinated action that not only jump-starts recovery, but also launches a new era of economic engagement to prevent a crisis like this from ever happening again.'[2] The geopolitics of 2009 gave more cause for optimism than 1933 when Mussolini was in power in Italy, Hitler had recently become Chancellor of Germany, Stalin had embarked on a forced march to industrialization in the Soviet Union, China was in a state of chaos, and Japan had invaded Manchuria. By contrast, in 2009 Paul Kennedy – a leading historian of international relations – remarked that 'I don't think anyone is busy with revengeful, pre-war militaristic feelings. Certainly not any in the G20.'[3] At the end of the G20 summit, Brown and Obama proclaimed success, and the *Financial Times* predicted that 'historians will record the summit as the moment when a world in the throes of economic and geopolitical upheaval took a first, hard look in the mirror', helping to preserve multilateralism and avoiding a headlong rush towards 'economic Armageddon'.[4]

By 2022, such optimism had dissipated. The world again faced economic crisis after the pandemic of 2020 and Russia's invasion of Ukraine. Revengeful feelings once more threatened war and the ability of the world to respond to economic crisis and the existential threat of climate change. Rather than hope of a better outcome than in 1933, by 2022 there was danger that geopolitical tensions and economic problems could not be resolved by the nations of the world.

TURNING POINTS

In both 1933 and 2009, the nations of the world gathered to ask not only how to avoid a crisis but how to govern the world economy, above all how to balance national interests with international co-operation. This book explores how the nature of global economic government has changed over the past ninety years by considering how the legitimacy of one economic order was lost, leading to a period of uncertainty during which new ideas were formulated and contested. This interregnum between different ways of thinking about the world economy was followed by a third stage, when new institutions emerged or the policies of existing institutions changed, which then evolved in the light of circumstances until a new crisis of legitimacy again challenged the existing order.[5] During the twentieth and twenty-first centuries, there have been two full cycles and a third, through which we are now living, that is still incomplete, with uncertainty about how it will be resolved.

The first cycle starts with the breakdown of the economic order that existed before the First World War that many countries tried to restore after 1918. Its main features – in an idealized form – were captured by John Maynard Keynes in *The Economic Consequences of the Peace*, his devastating critique of the Versailles treaty of 1919. He famously imagined an inhabitant of London in 1914 who

> could order by telephone, sipping his morning tea in bed, the various products of the whole earth, in such quantity as he might see fit, and reasonably expect their early delivery upon his doorstep; he could at the same moment and by the same means adventure his wealth in the natural resources and new enterprises of any quarter of the world, and share, without exertion or even trouble, in their prospective fruits and advantages ... But, most important of all, he regarded this state of affairs as normal, certain, and

permanent, except in the direction of further improvement, and any deviation from it as aberrant, scandalous, and avoidable.

To this resident of London – not so far removed from Keynes and his circle of upper-middle-class intellectuals – the 'internationalisation' of social and economic life was 'nearly complete in practice'.[6] After the First World War, it no longer worked and there was uncertainty whether it could be restored or should be replaced.

To understand the London Conference of 1933, we need to appreciate the economic system that was failing – a system in which most of the participants had grown up and accepted as the natural order. It rested on a trade-off in what economists term a trilemma or 'impossible trinity'. It is necessary to choose two out of three possible economic policies: fixed exchange rates, free movement of capital across national boundaries, and an active domestic monetary policy. In the world described by Keynes, exchange rates were fixed by membership of the gold standard and the inhabitant of London could invest capital anywhere in the world. An active domestic monetary policy was therefore impossible. If the Bank of England cut interest rates to stimulate the domestic economy and employment, capital would seek a better return overseas by investment in, say, Argentina or Canada. This outflow of funds would put pressure on the exchange rate – but the exchange rate was fixed so that interest rates would need to be raised. We must not be too deterministic, for countries that issued the key reserve currency (above all the United States after the Second World War) had the 'exorbitant privilege' – the phrase used in 1965 by the French finance minister Valéry Giscard d'Estaing – of issuing the currency that the rest of the world needed. And countries could push the boundaries of the trade-off to take account of domestic politics and international concerns.[7] Nevertheless, the concept of the trilemma provides a useful framework for understanding policy choices.

Before the First World War, the government of this highly globalized economy did not rest on formal institutions and rules to ensure the smooth operation of international economic relations. The bodies that existed were of little significance. An International Telegraph Union was established in 1865 to co-ordinate the international telegraph network and the Universal Postal Union was created in 1874 to co-ordinate postal services, replacing a cumbersome system of bilateral treaties between countries. In 1905, the International Institute of Agriculture was created in Italy to collect information on agricultural legislation, production, diseases and organization.[8] There was no body to co-ordinate international monetary relations. The gold standard had been adopted by most major developed economies in the later nineteenth century and supposedly operated auto-matically. Bullion flowed out of countries with a balance of payments deficit to countries with a surplus, so changing their relative price levels and restoring equilibrium in the world economy. Exchange rates were determined by the physical quantity of gold in coins, so there was no opportunity to engage in competitive devaluation of currencies. Similarly, there was no international organization to handle trade relations between nations, which could set their own tariffs or use subsidies and restrictions as they wished. Countries could negotiate bilateral trade deals that could be extended in an interconnected network, but there was no over-arching international body to establish and enforce rules. At most, international public law laid down rules on the rights of neutrals during war – and private trade disputes across national boundaries were mat-ters of private international law and arbitration. As a result, global economic government before 1914 lacked formal institutions or rules to ensure co-operation and enforce the collective good.

Tensions were already apparent before 1914. Integration of the global economy with the growth of trade and capital flows, the expansion of empire, and the movement of large numbers of people from Europe to the Americas had the potential to create both prosperity and disruption. Competition from foreign goods could lead to a loss of employment; for-eign investment could restructure economies in a way that harmed some and benefitted others; and the gold standard had differential impacts on those who gained and those who lost from falling prices in the late nine-teenth century when the absence of gold discoveries restricted the monetary supply. In the mid-west and south of the United States, for example, indebted farmers protested against low prices for their crops, and argued that bankers were gaining from the higher real value of loans. Similarly, countries with silver-based currencies – above all India and China – complained that depreciation of abundant silver against scarce gold increased the costs of servicing debts. Meanwhile, the flow of labour from Europe to the Americas, and the return flow of food, led to rising wages in the Old World and pressure on wages in the New World, and to a fall in the value of land and farmers' profits in Europe and a rise in the Americas. These trends led to a backlash and different political outcomes – the adoption of protective tariffs on food in France, demands for immigration restriction in the United States.[9] Globalization and dynamic capitalism created political and social tensions that increasingly powerful nation states mitigated by securing tax revenues to provide a social safety net, build institutions that were vital for economic success, invest in the physi-cal infrastructure and raise standards of education and health to create a productive workforce. The danger, barely perceived at the time, was that the nation state could also become a vehicle for destructive nationalism, as it did in 1914.[10]

Economic government started to change during the First World War when the allied nations co-operated in the control of shipping and food-stuffs, and with the decision at the Versailles Peace Conference to create the League of Nations. The League started its work in 1920 and co-ordinated financial assistance to central Europe, offered technical assistance in developing countries, collated statistics, exchanged informa-tion, and discussed policy options. The International Labour Organization (ILO) was also created at Versailles, and in 1930, the Bank for Inter-national Settlements (BIS) was set up to co-ordinate the work of central bankers. More international organizations were emerging, with perma-nent staff, to consider how to manage the global economy and establish common rules.[11]

The failure to re-establish the global economic order after the First World War led to a loss of legitimacy and a search for new solutions. The London conference of 1933 was held under the auspices of the League which tried to produce an agenda – an impossible task given the depth of disagreement on monetary and trade policy, and on war debt and repara-tions. It marked the failure of attempts to create international order since the war and to balance regionalism with internationalism.[12] The result was economic nationalism and regional blocs – imperial preference sys-tems in Britain and France, autarchic economic policies in Germany and Italy, the co-prosperity sphere of Japan, and the state-controlled economy of the Soviet Union. In 1933, some countries remained on gold as a source of stability and order, others abandoned it as a cause of rigidity and defla-tion. Above all, the British government made a new trade-off in the trilemma: the abandonment of the gold standard in 1931 meant that exchange rates could be managed and capital movements were controlled, which allowed interest rates to be held down to stimulate the domestic economy. In 1933, Roosevelt was undecided whether to follow Britain's example: he soon opted to abandon gold. The world collapsed into cur-rency and trade warfare as one country tried to gain an advantage over another by undervaluing its currency and turning away from open multi-lateral trade. There was no international co-ordination to prevent 'beggar-my-neighbour' policies that aimed to help individual countries and ended up harming everyone. By looking at the disagreements that destroyed the conference, we can understand the reasons for this move to economic nationalism and collapse of the global economic order.

During the 1930s, leading liberal capitalist democracies came to realize that national self-interest required co-operation, not least in response to the challenge of authoritarian regimes. Initial steps were taken to stabilize exchange rates between the dollar, pound and franc, and to restart talks on trade deals. During this interregnum, new approaches to global economic government were emerging which crystallized during the Second World War. International institutions laid down rules for the global economy – the International Monetary Fund (IMF) and International Bank for Reconstruction and Development (IBRD) at Bretton Woods in 1944, the Food and Agriculture Organization (FAO) in 1945, and the General Agreement on Tariffs and Trade (GATT) in 1947. The second part of the book turns to the creation of these new bodies to overcome beggar-my-neighbour policies and to establish a balance between nationalism and internationalism. It entailed a shift in the trilemma of exchange rates, capital movements and domestic economic policies. Now, exchange rates were pegged, though (unlike the period when they were on the gold standard) with an element of flexibility that allowed devaluation and reduced the need to deflate the domestic economy to remain on a completely fixed rate. By permitting controls on capital movements, countries could pursue an active domestic monetary policy: a reduction in interest rates to stimulate the domestic economy would not lead to an outflow of capital and pressure on the exchange rate. A return to internationalism was linked with the pursuit of domestic welfare. The outcome has been defined by the economist Dani Rodrik as 'shallow multilateralism' and by the political scientist John Ruggie as 'embedded liberalism' – it allowed the pursuit of multilateral trade and economic globalization without surrendering domestic welfare, embedding these aims within formal, rules-based institutions.[13]

What was embedded was largely the assumptions and interests of the leading capitalist and imperialist economies. The new institutions came to define 'the West'. The pursuit of internationalism, as expressed by the post-war institutions, was in effect another form of national interest. Of course, there were differences between these capitalist countries. The United States was more likely to define multilateralism in terms of free-market economics than Britain's post-war Labour government which was committed to planning at home and abroad. The differences were still more marked with the 'state trading' economy of the Soviet Union. Initial hopes that the Soviet Union could be included within the new system, so as to continue the wartime alliance, were disappointed with the onset of the Cold War, and the new institutions became part of an ideological battle between Communist and capitalist views of the economy. Although the less developed countries of Latin America and the newly independent countries of Asia and Africa were members, they complained, with justice, that shallow multilateralism allowed the survival of a world economy based on the interests of the advanced industrial economies and ignored the primary producers' demand for structural change in the world economy.

The new institutions and their rules did not emerge fully formed at the conference at Bretton Woods in 1944, and there was a complex process of adaptation and implementation in the ten to fifteen years after the war. Recovery in Europe required both assistance by the United States and a response from European countries. Currencies were only convertible in 1958 – and not long afterwards, serious strains started to appear in the Bretton Woods regime.

The third part of the book turns to the legitimacy crisis in the institutions that had been created during the war and modified in the process of implementation. During the 1960s, there were tensions between the developed economies as the relative economic weight of the United States declined and Europe and Japan recovered. There were also challenges from a more assertive Third World or Global South. Crisis hit in the early 1970s, with the decision of President Richard Nixon on 15 August 1971 to suspend the Bretton Woods system of exchange rates. Demands from the developing world for a New International Economic Order that would give a better deal to primary producers and low-income countries were expressed in the oil shock of 1973, which led to hopes of distributive justice. Meanwhile, the developed economies faced economic stagnation and inflation. The final abandonment of pegged rates in 1973 removed monetary discipline and the need for wage restraint: if a country became uncompetitive, the exchange rate could depreciate; if the economy faced recession, monetary policy could be loosened. The result was stagflation: low growth and inflation.

This crisis of embedded liberalism was followed by a hiatus as new ideas were formulated and a new global economic order emerged. There was not an obvious event such as the conference at Bretton Woods, but the new order was symbolized by the elections of Margaret Thatcher in 1979 and Ronald Reagan in 1980. The challenge of the New International Order was contained; inflation was brought under control by tight monetary policy and recession; and in 1989, the Soviet Union collapsed. The result was economic transition in the former Soviet bloc with a turn to a market economy – though China took a different path of ensuring that markets remained under the control of the Communist Party. Embedded liberalism and shallow multilateralism gave way to 'neo-liberalism', a contested term that is here taken to mean the pursuit of market

liberalization and financialization, with a negative view of state intervention and priority given to internationalism over national economic
policies. A new generation of government officials, economists and politicians positively welcomed the restoration of capital mobility, which had
started during the 1960s and now expanded greatly, with global institutions changing their approach to encourage financialization. This new
world of mobile capital, and encouragement of multilateral trade, overturned the balance between domestic and international priorities that had
been forged in the war and immediate post-war period and led to a new
form of hyper-globalization that sacrificed domestic priorities to the pursuit of open international trade and financialization.

We are now living through a third cycle. In the last quarter of the twentieth century, global integration of supply chains and the movement of
capital around the world reached levels not seen since before the First
World War. The result was considerable gains for the emerging middle
class in developing countries and for the wealthy elite in both developing
and developed countries. The losers – from de-industrialization as much
as globalization – were the working class and middle class in the developed
world. The world economy was becoming more susceptible to financial
crises, with a shock in 1997–8 followed by the global financial crisis of
2007–8 that exposed the dangers of financialization. The reaction to the
global financial crisis – above all in Europe and the United States – brings
us to the fourth part of the book. Potentially, the shock of 2007–8 was a
legitimacy crisis of neo-liberalism with the power to reshape economic
policy and create a new structure of global economic government. In fact,
change was slight and existing problems remained or were even intensified. The policy response after 2008 rescued the economy in the short
term by bailing out bankers and embarking on austerity. The result was
growing inequality and a failure to remove the fundamental causes for
crises, creating political and social problems that were exposed when
Covid hit in 2020. The hold of neo-liberalism had not yet been broken.

One reaction was a turn to populism and economic nationalism. President Donald Trump tweeted on 2 March 2018 that 'trade wars are good,
and easy to win'. His reaction was, in part, a response to the emergence
of China as the world's second-largest economy through the pursuit of
authoritarian capitalism. Another possible response – better than either
clinging to neo-liberalism or retreating into economic nationalism – would
be a turn to a progressive economic policy based on moving away from
financialization and inequality to a more inclusive and fairer capitalism.
Maintenance of the status quo threatens economic and social stability.
The impact of Covid in 2020, the energy crisis caused by Russia's invasion

of Ukraine, and the challenge of climate change should provide the motivation for a change in economic policy. Unlike at Bretton Woods, when two countries – Britain and the United States – could devise a plan, the world is now multipolar with different political systems. Finding a common approach to the urgent problems of the collective good of the world is more difficult than ever. The ultimate outcome of this third cycle is unclear – but there is no doubt that the world is at a critical moment.

METHOD

The analysis of these changes takes us into the heart of national governments and international institutions. The participants were officials – both national and international – government ministers, central bankers and economists, all of them operating in finance ministries and international institutions, and meeting in ways that were often shielded from public view. My aim is to understand how they reached their decisions, how they were shaped by the structure of the economy, considerations of geopolitical strategy, and the role of economic ideas. I will not be considering the reactions of the press, public opinion and interest groups directly, which would require another book with a different methodology. Rather, they are considered through the responses of officials and politicians. These actors were overwhelmingly male. A few women appear in the first decades, but the first significant women were Indira Gandhi in India and Margaret Thatcher in Britain. By the end of the period, women were more important – Angela Merkel in Germany, Christine Lagarde and Kristalina Georgieva at the IMF, Ngozi Okonjo-Iweala at the World Trade Organization (WTO). This gender bias was also apparent in the work of development economists who rarely considered the gendered dimensions of policies, such as the nature of women's work and family structures. Even the debate over population growth after the Second World War gave little attention to female agency.[14] What we can consider, however, is the challenge of Asia, Africa and Latin America to global institutions and their demands for distributive justice from the so-called developed world – a culturally loaded term that reflected the thinking of development economics. Although the terms developed or advanced, under-developed and less developed are used throughout the book, as they were at the time, I am acutely conscious of the assumptions that they embody.

This book offers a different approach to most accounts of globalization. It deals above all with the political responses to the global economy and considers why choices were made as they were. Unlike most accounts, which focus on one policy area, it considers trade, money, capital, development, population and food and their interrelationship with each other and with geopolitical strategy. It seeks to combine the perceptions of the advanced industrial economies, the 'state trading' economies of the Communist world, and the emerging economies. It aims to analyse the management of the global economy since the Great Depression in order to place current discussions in a historical perspective, not least because of the way the past is used in contemporary debate. Politicians – and economists – use history for their own purposes, to justify policy prescriptions by drawing analogies with the past. Their purpose is rhetorical rather than an objective historical account. For example, the frequent calls for a 'new Bretton Woods' misunderstand the circumstances, which are not replicable, under which the original meeting was held – and ignore the way that the agreement of 1944 was only adopted (and adapted) over more than a decade. Similarly, historical data on the level of debt were used to justify austerity after the global financial crisis without asking how previously high levels of debt had been accumulated, how they had been reduced, and whether they had been as harmful as assumed. Economists looked to the 'lessons' of the Great Depression through ideological filters, so that some saw the solution as monetary policy and austerity; others looked to a return to Keynesianism and the use of state capacity to help poorer members of society.

Dani Rodrik drew the lesson that the pendulum in the 1930s swung too far towards economic nationalism and destroyed the international economy with devastating results. The task after the Second World War was to strike a balance between nationalism and internationalism. His lesson from the global financial crisis was that the pendulum had swung too far in the opposite direction from the 1970s, towards hyper-globalization. The need became a rebalancing of national welfare and internationalism.[15] This book provides historical detail that both supports and complicates Rodrik's interpretation. Above all, I argue that globalization ended in the early twentieth century in part because economic inequality led to a backlash. The multilateral institutions and recovery after 1945 rested on a reduction of inequality and a turn to inclusive growth in the Global North, based on a contract between labour, capital and the state. The emergence of gross disparities within those economies in the recent past has provoked another backlash that needs to be urgently redressed.

Policy choices emerged from the specific circumstances of the Second World War and Cold War, decolonization and the transition of Communist societies, and the power of labour or capital. The mode of economic analysis also framed understandings, and the book will consider the role of economic ideas that embody cultural meanings and ideological assumptions. The role of the historian is to tease out these different influences and constraints, to explain how change occurred and why particular solutions were adopted. The form of the international institutions that emerged during and after the war was not preordained, and we should understand how they were contested by contemporaries who considered many possibilities. They – like everyone at all times, including us in the present – were uncertain about what the future would bring and what might work. They struggled to create a new international institutional architecture to resolve the problems of the global economy, to repair the failures of the Great Depression, and to devise a system that would ensure that it was not repeated. They naturally responded to the problems of the 1930s in ways which arose from particular circumstances and ways of thinking. The almost inevitable result was that institutions which emerged in the conditions of the 1940s then persisted and shaped responses to new problems and circumstances, opportunities and approaches, until the structure they had created was overturned. My aim is to show why the international institutions took the form they did because of the circumstances of the 1930s and 1940s, and how far they could cope with new crises of legitimacy in 1971 and 2008, or whether they were trapped by the circumstances of their creation.

THEMES

The story of global economic government from the World Monetary and Economic Conference of 1933 to the present is shaped by some general questions that run throughout the book.

First, what was the process by which different national interests were, or were not, balanced and reconciled? A major issue in economic life is how to secure collective action, preventing one country from pursuing policies that it considers to be in its own best interests, but which will harm the world economy if adopted by everyone. The temptation for any country facing economic depression is to adopt a self-interested policy of 'beggar my neighbour', attempting to maintain domestic employment and welfare at the expense of others by devaluing its currency or imposing trade restrictions. First movers might have some advantage in such competitions, but the benefit does not continue long if other countries follow in a bidding war. The pursuit of individual national self-interest will often mean that everyone eventually suffers. A major theme in global economic government is, therefore, how to create a mechanism to prevent one country from seeking to gain at the expense of the rest of the world. Can credible commitments and rules be created to prevent the onset of currency and tariff warfare that would harm everyone?

This 'collective action' problem is central to many social interactions and is captured by the notion of the 'tragedy of the commons'.[16] It is in the interest of each farmer to graze as many sheep as possible on the common land of a village, but if all the farmers do the same, the result will be over-grazing from which all will lose. Individual rationality cannot guarantee the highest aggregate income, and rules are needed for the governance of common resources. Creation and enforcement of such rules are no easy matter. One sheep farmer might be less efficient than another so that awarding each a quota might keep inefficient farmers in operation and overall output would be lower. Should quotas be confined to existing farmers and follow the existing distribution of resources, or should newcomers be allowed to enter and quotas adjusted? If so, on what basis should the changes be made? These issues have to be addressed in designing international institutions, whether it be the control of commodities, trade, or carbon emissions. If rules are too rigid, they might be ignored. Some flexibility is therefore needed through 'escape clauses' that allow countries to deal with unforeseen eventualities without permitting them to fail completely in complying with the agreement. This balance between compliance and flexibility is a complicated and sensitive issue in international negotiations.[17]

A related problem is how to ensure that pursuing international economic policies is not at the expense of domestic welfare, and vice versa. As we have seen, a central feature of the globalized world economy before the First World War was the gold standard and open capital markets. When they ceased to provide prosperity after the war, there was a backlash against the domestic burdens of the international economy. The choice between the pursuit of economic globalization, democratic politics, and national determination varied between countries.[18] In the 1930s, for example, globalization was dropped in favour of the nation state and democracy in Britain, the United States and France. In Germany, Italy and the Soviet Union globalization was dropped in favour of the nation state and authoritarianism. These trade-offs are linked with the trilemma – whether to give priority to an active domestic monetary policy or to capital flows and fixed exchanges. These choices have distributional consequences at home as well as in the international economy. What was needed was a set of policies and institutions that allowed a balancing of domestic and international concerns. A major theme of the book is understanding why and how these trade-offs shifted.

The representatives of any country at an international meeting are playing two games.[19] They have to make concessions to other participants in order to strike a deal, but at the same time they are aware that they cannot make a sacrifice that will jeopardize acceptability at home. The task is not easy, for winning one part of the game may lose it on the other. At one extreme, negotiators might welcome a breakdown in talks in order to return home as valiant defenders of the national interest. At the other extreme, negotiators might sacrifice so much to secure an international agreement that they lose acceptance at home. The relationship between the two parts of the game is mediated by domestic political structures. It is easier for a government to strike a deal at the international level and secure domestic agreement in a parliamentary system: the executive is drawn from the party with the largest number of seats and has confidence that a deal will be accepted. The situation is more difficult in presidential systems such as the United States, where there is often a stand-off between the executive that negotiates an international agreement and Congress that might be controlled by another party and where representatives are more concerned with extracting benefits for constituents. The negotiators at international conferences need to be sensitive to domestic politics and be aware of the political systems of their counterparts.

A common assumption is that the world needs a hegemon for stability. Charles Kindleberger, an economist with wide experience at the Federal Reserve Bank of New York, the BIS and the US State Department, argued that the first period of globalization up to 1914 was successful because Britain acted as the stabilizer of the world economy through the dominant position of sterling, the scale of its capital exports, and its open market. In his view, the tragedy of the 1930s arose from the lack of a hegemonic power as Britain lost its dominant position in the world economy and the United States failed to provide international leadership – until it acted to restore order and stability after the Second World War as the undisputed hegemonic power. Problems arose – so the argument continues – in the 1960s and 1970s as American domination was challenged by competition from Germany and Japan, by the hostility of Communist powers and the Global South, and by domestic political resistance to the burdens of leadership. Kindleberger believed that the international order needed a leader, and that the danger was not that one country had too much power but that it had too little.[20] As we will see, 'hegemonic stability' is a flawed interpretation. Despite the economic and military power of the United States, it could not always get its way. After 1945, it failed to force Britain to give up its preference for imperial goods, and it engaged in post-war construction in Europe on terms that did not reflect its priorities.[21] In any case, hegemony did not mean economic stability and order. Rather, it was an attempt to shape the global economy in American or western interests. Economists who continue to regret the loss of hegemonic stability miss the point: we now live in a multipolar world and the question is how to ensure that its members can co-operate rather than retreat into mutual hostility.

Multilateral institutions provoked nationalism in countries which had less of a voice. Groups of developing countries formed coalitions, such as the Non-Aligned Movement or Group of 77 developing countries, to win concessions from more powerful countries. Such coalitions can coalesce around shared economic interests, such as the production of primary products, or around ideology such as 'Third Worldism' and the demand for a New International Economic Order. These coalitions fractured if some members accepted concessions from the developed world, or could hold together in a way that blocked agreement. The outcome was shaped by patterns of voting and representation. Until 1989, these shifting coalitions took place within the context of the Cold War and a battle for influence in less developed countries between the United States, the Soviet Union and, to a lesser extent, China, which gave developing countries some room for manoeuvre.

The government of the global economy cannot be separated from the geopolitical interplay of great powers. In negotiating the creation of the IMF, the Americans wished to break Britain's imperial preference, hoped to work with the Soviet Union, and thought it was necessary to disarm and de-industrialize Germany. Matters changed with the Cold War, when the new international institutions helped define the 'West' against the Soviet Union, and with decolonization increasing the voice of the Third World. In some cases, economic aid was linked with military intervention to prevent or encourage the spread of Communism; in other cases, they were held apart. The struggle for influence in the Third World was not only between capitalism and Communism, for there were differences in both camps, between China's anti-imperialism and the Soviet Union's emphasis on class, and between the United States and Europe over co-operating with the Third World. The collapse of the Soviet Union marked, to some American commentators, the end of history and the triumph of western liberal capitalism – a delusion, as the world moved to a new geopolitical conflict between China and the United States, and with the aggression of a resentful Russia. Economic issues were, and remain, vital to wider geopolitical considerations.

A second set of questions is procedural, dealing with the nature of negotiations, the rules of the game and the structure of international organizations. International negotiations may attempt to reach agreement on a wide package of issues at the same time or proceed issue by issue. The agreement at Bretton Woods in 1944 concentrated on technical monetary issues and left more contentious matters of trade, commodities and development for another occasion. By contrast, the World Monetary and Economic Conference of 1933 or the World Trade Organization's Doha Development Agenda after 2001 attempted (and failed) to combine a large number of contentious issues. The narrower approach is more effective but can be criticized for avoiding fundamental issues of equity and distributive justice, so undermining the legitimacy of any agreement and provoking opposition. Setting the agenda for negotiations, and so the order for consideration of issues, is therefore vitally important.

International bodies take a variety of forms, and their governance and rules are contested. Should they provide an intergovernmental forum for domestic politicians to meet and discuss issues, such as the G20 that met in London in 2009, or larger gatherings to discuss climate change such as in Glasgow in 2021? Large-scale gatherings often produce declarations of good intent without formal means of enforcement, though this is not to say they are valueless because action often results. By contrast, 'supranational' institutions exist apart from individual nation states, with powerful secretariats and binding rules. Even so, it is one thing to have rules and quite another to ensure that there is a credible commitment to compliance, with realistic penalties for failure. Members of an organization hope that everyone will follow the spirit as well as the letter of agreements, but electoral calculations sometimes lead a government to ignore an international agreement, confident that it cannot be enforced or that any sanctions would be worth the price. Political calculation can also lead politicians to use international organizations as a convenient scapegoat for unpopular policies, by calling in an IMF mission to provide a cover for what the government wished to do anyway, for example.

Enforcement can be achieved by financial assistance as well as legal rulings. The IMF's provision of assistance to countries facing balance of payments crises, or the World Bank's loans to developing economies, come with conditions on economic policies, often reflecting a particular ideology. Countries that do not seek support are largely exempt from oversight. By contrast, the General Agreement on Tariffs and Trade could not enforce rules by financial assistance or penalties, and it was not until the creation of the World Trade Organization in 1995 that there was a formal legal machinery to adjudicate between countries. The nature of rules and their enforcement therefore differ between institutions and over time.

Supra-national bodies are open to criticism that they threaten national sovereignty, whether complaints from some Americans that they are succumbing to a form of world government or from less developed countries that the institutions are agents of American neo-colonialism and neo-liberalism.[22] These concerns raise another point: the structure of voting within international organizations. The operation of international organizations varies according to who has a voice. The BIS was created in 1930 as a gathering of central bankers meeting in secret, and is easily portrayed as democratically unaccountable. The formal organizations created during and after the Second World War – the IMF, IBRD, GATT and FAO – raised major questions about representation. They were formally under the auspices of the United Nations, whose General Assembly operated on the principle of one country, one vote. Whether this principle should apply to all international organizations was not clear. The International Labour Organization drew representation from governments, trade unions and business that did not vote as national blocs. Votes in the IMF were determined by the amount of money or 'quota' a country provided, which gave the United States a dominant voice. By contrast, the International Trade Organization (ITO) that was proposed in 1948 would have had one country, one vote regardless of the scale of their trade. The less developed nations remained deeply sceptical about the IMF and worked through more democratic channels, such as the UN's Economic and Social Council (ECOSOC) or the United Nations Conference on Trade and Development (UNCTAD). Equally, the developed countries turned to smaller groups where their voices were dominant, such as the Organization for Economic Co-operation and Development (OECD) or the 'groups' of leading economies. The architecture of global government was complicated by the proliferation of regional bodies – the United Nations Economic Commission for Latin America (ECLA), regional development banks in Latin America and Asia, and trade blocs such as the European Economic Community, Mercosur in Latin America, the Association of South-East Asian Nations (ASEAN) and the North American Free Trade Agreement (NAFTA), and China's Asian Infrastructure Investment Bank. Internationalism and regionalism were in uneasy relation.

The post-war international institutions were devised in a somewhat ad hoc manner, with overlapping and uncoordinated functions. The IMF lost most of its role in overseeing international exchange rates from the early 1970s. It then started to move into the sphere of the IBRD in making loans. On one view, the two organizations should have merged in the 1970s. Similarly, the relationship between the GATT and the IMF was never clear, though a country's balance of payments was affected both by trade restrictions and by exchange rates, and less developed countries criticized both bodies for ignoring wider structural explanations of inequalities between developed and less developed economies. In principle, all these bodies were agencies of the United Nations; in practice, they were largely independent and uncoordinated, with tensions between their staffs in Washington (the IMF and IBRD), Geneva (GATT/WTO and UNCTAD), and the General Assembly in New York.

International negotiations were sometimes deadlocked until a resolution was reached at the last minute, as in the Kennedy Round of trade talks in 1967, or the talks collapsed in acrimony and exhaustion, as with the Doha Round of trade talks which dragged on from 2001 to 2015. A major theme is what causes deadlocks and why they are sometimes broken. A deadlock will occur if some participants think that there is a good or even better alternative so there is no incentive to make a concession. Major trading partners might prefer a bilateral deal to the high costs of a multilateral settlement. Negotiators might misjudge the situation, wrongly believing that they could call their opponents' bluff. The chances of deadlock are also affected by the balance of power. A deal is more likely to be achieved where a club of a few countries dominated, as in the IMF where the United States held most votes, or in GATT which was controlled by the 'Quad' of the European Union, Canada, Japan and the United States. Deadlock is likely where power is more evenly balanced and no party can impose its will, and where the authority of the club breaks down with the arrival of more diverse interests and ideologies. The persistence of deadlocks and the likelihood of agreement are also affected by institutional structures, by voting systems or the need for consensus; and whether agreement is needed on all issues in a comprehensive package so that a minority interest can block a deal.[23]

Finally, there is an ethical question: the nature of distributive justice in the world economy. The institutions created during and after the Second World War were criticized by less developed countries for maintaining the existing distribution of resources in the world economy rather than creating a fairer and more equitable allocation. The structure of the world economy seemed to condemn Latin America, Africa and Asia to supplying primary commodities to the advanced industrial economies on unfavourable terms, leading to poverty, instability and dependence. Equity therefore required not merely regulating the global economy to create stable exchange rates and free trade, but a fundamental structural change in the relationship between primary producers and industrial nations. Obviously, such a policy was contentious and was at the heart of many of the tensions in the government of the global economy. It could also be exploited in the Cold War, as the Americans, Soviets and Chinese vied for influence and the Third World played them off against each other. Wealthy nations in the Global North had to balance making concessions to secure their influence in the developing countries against the costs imposed on their own electors. At the same time, poorer nations of the Global South sometimes refused partial deals that offered some benefits on the grounds that they did not respond to central issues of equity and fairness.

These themes inform my analytical narrative of attempts to manage the risks and opportunities of the global economy from the failure of the World Monetary and Economic Conference to the creation of embedded liberalism, its demise and replacement by neo-liberalism, to attempts to recover after the global financial crisis of 2007–8, and to challenges to the global economy and multilateralism brought about by the election of President Trump in 2016, the arrival of Covid-19 in 2020, and the Russian invasion of Ukraine in 2022. We now turn, in the first part of the book, to the crisis of the global economy of the Great Depression and the attempts to find a solution in London in 1933.

PART ONE

Responding to the Great Depression

The World Monetary and Economic Conference of 1933 offers a vantage point to look both backwards and forwards. We can look back to the global order that existed before the First World War – one that lacked formal institutions and rules of global economic government, based on the supposedly automatic operation of the gold standard, free movements of capital, and trade treaties between countries. In the 1920s, many countries sought a restoration of the global economy by returning to the gold standard, but also by creating rules-based trade at the League of Nations. By 1933, in the midst of depression, it was clear that this had failed and that many countries had embarked on policies that would beggar their neighbours in a downward spiral of trade and currency warfare. The conference met under the aegis of the League of Nations, where new approaches to understanding an interconnected global economy and the need for rules had started to emerge. In this Part, we consider how different countries viewed the crisis of the interwar economy, and why they could not reach agreement in 1933.

Governor Franklin D. Roosevelt shakes hands with a mine worker during his presidential campaign trip to West Virginia, October 1932.

I

'The establishment of a sound national economy'

The Politics of the Great Depression

'Practices of the unscrupulous money changers stand indicted in the court of public opinion, rejected by the hearts and minds of men ... They only know the rules of a generation of self-seekers. They have no vision, and when there is no vision the people perish.

'The money changers have fled from their high seats in the temple of our civilization. We may now restore that temple to the ancient truths. The measure of the restoration lies in the extent to which we apply social values more noble than mere monetary profit.'

Inaugural address of President Roosevelt, 4 March 1933

Franklin Delano Roosevelt addressed these words to a nation in the grip of the worst depression of the modern age. It was a critical time both for the United States and the world. Since 1929, commodity prices and output had collapsed, destroying the livelihood of farmers across the globe. In the United States, the price of wheat fell from a peak of $2.16 a bushel in 1919 to $1.03 in 1929 to 84 cents in 1934, and to 69 cents in 1939. Over the same period, the price of cotton dropped from 35.3 cents to 16.8 cents, 12.4 cents and 9.1 cents.[1] Similarly, Australian sheep farmers selling merino fleeces in Britain received 35.4 (old) pence a pound in 1929 and only 15 pence in 1932.[2] Across the world, from coffee growers in Brazil to wheat farmers in Canada, farmers suffered a fall in their income that was exacerbated by a drop in production (Figure 1). Many primary producing economies suffered from balance of payments deficits and difficulties in servicing their debts, which led to a mixture of currency devaluation, the imposition of trade barriers and debt defaults.

As a consequence, primary producers cut their consumption of industrial goods, which compounded depression in the developed economies. World industrial production fell even more than primary production, by around 30 per cent from the peak of 1929 to the trough of 1932 – a drop that was particularly serious in Germany where industrial output fell by 39 per cent, compared with 18 per cent in the United States and 11 per cent in Britain. Unemployment in the major industrial economies rose and remained stubbornly high. In the United Kingdom, unemployment among workers over the age of sixteen who were covered by state insurance rose from 11 per cent in 1929 to 22.5 per cent in 1932, and it remained at 13.3 per cent in 1938. In the United States, unemployment rose, on one estimate, from 3.2 per cent in 1929 to a peak of 25.2 per cent in 1933 and was still over 19 per cent in 1938. The level of unemployment was even higher in Germany, where it reached 30.1 per cent in 1932.[3] The fall in production of both primary and industrial goods led to a collapse of world trade by about a quarter between 1929 and 1932, and a failure to regain its previous levels before the Second World War (see Figure 1).

These economic problems were an integral part of the geopolitical crisis of the early 1930s. The world faced conflict between fascism and Communism. Mussolini had been in power in Italy since 1922, and Hitler became Chancellor of Germany in January 1933 in part because the Weimar Republic had failed to resolve the financial crisis that hit Germany in 1931.[4] In Asia, the Japanese army embarked on military incursions in China in 1931, launching a new era of imperial expansion that was pursued by Italy in Ethiopia in 1935 and Germany in eastern Europe. These imperial projects created the conditions that led to global war, with the

Figure 1: World trade and production, 1926–1938 (1929 = 100)

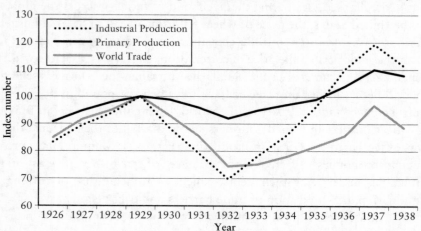

Sources: League of Nations, *World Production and Prices, 1938/39* (Geneva 1939) appendix III Barry Eichengreen and Douglas Irwin, 'The slide to protection in the Great Depression. Who succumbed and why?', NBER Working Paper 15142 (2009), 45.

German invasion of Poland in 1939 and the Japanese attack on Pearl Harbor in 1941.[5] In the Soviet Union, Stalin had embarked on agricultural collectivization and rapid forced industrialization. In hindsight, we know that the Soviet economy failed, but at the time (and despite the devastating impact of famine and terror) it appeared to many observers in depression-ridden states to be a success. Liberal democracies and capitalism did not look secure, and both fascism and Communism offered plausible alternatives. These thoughts were in Roosevelt's mind as he delivered his inaugural address. His ambition was to overcome 'fear itself' and to rescue American democratic capitalism from its opponents.

An inaugural presidential address is an occasion for high-minded generalities rather than specific policies, and Roosevelt was undecided precisely how to deal with the depression. He called for a change in ethics, the rejection of material wealth as the standard of success, an end to 'callous and selfish wrongdoing' in banking and business. He also called for action by the government to put people to work through the planning of transport and other public utilities, the supervision of banking, an end to speculation with other people's money, and the creation of 'an adequate but sound currency'. By such means, he would put 'our own national house in order'. The major issue that puzzled the new team in the White House was whether putting the 'national house in order' meant economic nationalism or internationalism. In his address, Roosevelt was less concerned about the international situation:

> Our international trade relations, though vastly important, are in point of time and necessity secondary to the establishment of a sound national economy. I favor as a practical policy the putting of first things first. I shall spare no effort to restore world trade by international economic readjustment, but the emergency at home cannot wait on that accomplishment.[6]

After the First World War and the Versailles Peace Conference of 1919, America's position in the world had remained uncertain. President Woodrow Wilson's vision at Versailles was national determination, with an end to great power and imperialist rivalry between France, Britain, Germany, Italy, Russia and Japan. Unlike European powers, America – with a few exceptions – did not seek colonial possessions. Wilson's aim was to ensure that other countries did not intervene in the American sphere of influence in Latin America, and that American goods and capital had equal access to world markets without discrimination. On that basis, American productive efficiency would allow national success without the need for militarism and imperialism. Although the Republicans were more inclined to combine equal or open access in foreign markets with protection of the domestic market, Wilson and the Democrats were willing to reduce protective duties. Beyond such generalities, Wilson and his successors lacked an effective strategy to stabilize the world economy or to create collective security after the war. Despite emerging from the war as the world's largest economy, greatest financial power and central player in world politics, the federal government of the United States lacked the administrative and fiscal capacity to provide leadership. Instead, it turned to a conservative vision of 'normalcy' that minimized the role of the federal state. Meanwhile, the collapse of imperial structures in central Europe and the Middle East led to a power vacuum in Eurasia. America failed to provide leadership, yet the prospect of its future dominance impelled Italian Fascists, German National Socialists, Soviet Communists and Japanese militarists to take radical action.[7]

Roosevelt served in Wilson's administration and attended the Versailles conference. He shared Wilson's hostility to imperialism and believed that American security required a liberal world order; however, he differed from Wilson's inflexible and dogmatic approach, as we will see when he turned to the construction of a new world order during the Second World War.[8] In 1933, he was more concerned with pressing problems at home. During the election campaign of 1932, the Republicans supported tariffs to protect American markets and to preserve standards of living.[9] The Democrats were divided. At one extreme were free traders – largely Southerners such as Cordell Hull, a senator from Tennessee, who believed that tariffs led to retaliation, international economic hostility, the destruction of trade, loss of export markets for farmers, and increased costs of production. By contrast, liberal international trade allowed the advance of civilization through prosperity, peace and cultural exchange. Not everyone in the Democratic Party agreed. Al Smith, the Democratic presidential candidate in 1928, saw protection as a way of securing support from agricultural and industrial workers.[10]

During the campaign, Roosevelt had to create a coalition of inconsistent views and interests, which required ambiguity and the hope that he would not need to resolve his dilemma before winning the election. The Democratic platform proposed 'a competitive tariff for revenue with a fact-finding tariff commission free from executive interference, reciprocal tariff agreements with other nations, and an international economic conference designed to restore international trade and facilitate exchange'. It offered some reassurance to all views.[11] As the campaign proceeded, Roosevelt distanced himself from Hull's internationalism, both because of his reading of public opinion and because of the influence of his advisers or 'Brains Trust' that grew up around economists Raymond Moley and Rexford Tugwell.

Roosevelt's dilemma did not disappear after the election. The academics of the Brains Trust lacked a political constituency, whereas Hull was a significant politician with a large electoral base. Hours after the inaugural speech in which Roosevelt pledged himself to create a 'sound national economy', he swore in Hull who, as Moley remarked, had a 'burning faith that the salvation of the world depended upon the revival of international laissez-faire capitalism' as Secretary of State. Moley complained that Roosevelt had no sense of 'the fundamental conflict between his New Deal and the beliefs of the older Democrats, the basic incongruity of his own program and Hull's Adam Smith economics'.[12] Tugwell ruefully remarked that 'there is no one who can say whether the Roosevelt mind changed or whether it was never made up'.[13] More plausibly, Roosevelt used ambiguity to hold together competing visions. He was wary of taking positions, preferring an 'evasive liberalism' that allowed him 'to shelter himself from controversy and keep to generalizations calculated to offend no one'.[14] Henry L. Stimson, the secretary of war from 1940 to 1945, likened a conversation with the president as 'very much like chasing a vagrant beam of sunshine around a vacant room'.[15] Roosevelt was, in the memorable phrase of Richard Hofstadter, 'the patrician as opportunist'.[16] The president admitted to being devious and disingenuous – as he put it, 'I am a juggler, and I never let my right hand know what my left hand does.' This trait drove his colleagues to distraction, but allowing different departments and officials to have responsibility for the same tasks and to devise competing solutions meant he had the final say. Competitive administration meant that power was concentrated in the White House.[17]

The difficulty in bringing diverging views together also applied to monetary policy. Populists had long argued for rising prices to inflate away the debt of farmers by monetizing silver to increase the money supply, which at the time was pegged to the gold standard. On the other hand, financial interests wanted 'sound' money, and workers would benefit from falling prices. The Democratic platform of 1932 again tried to offer reassurance to both sides: 'We advocate a sound economy to be preserved at all hazards and an international monetary conference … to consider the rehabilitation of silver and related questions.'[18] The Brains Trust believed that recovery should start at home by raising prices. The drastic fall in prices during the depression meant that the real burden of debt rose, and purchases of goods were delayed in the expectation that prices would fall still further. Rising prices were needed to break the cycle of debt and deflation, and to stimulate demand. The Brains Trust was also committed to a policy of planning. Moley was responsible for Roosevelt's 'Forgotten Man' speech of April 1932 that blamed the depression on rural poverty and low commodity prices, which meant that farmers did not have the ability to buy industrial goods. His emphasis on internal domestic causes and solutions did not mean a return to an old vision of America as 'a nation of small proprietors, of corner grocers and smithies under spreading chestnut trees'. It meant preventing destructive competition by 'concentrated economic power' through regulation and planning. Moley developed a programme of domestic reforms and economic policies, including social insurance, public works, and the restoration of prices and wages to their pre-depression level.[19] The programme might entail abandoning the gold standard, which limited a country's ability to devalue its currency or to raise the overall price level. Roosevelt's reference in his inaugural address to a currency that was 'adequate but sound' hinted that the gold standard was too limited, and that the monetary supply might need to be increased to end the downward pressure on prices. But could a currency be sound if it cut free from gold and was consciously managed? Roosevelt's financial advisers included James Warburg, a Republican Wall Street banker and son of Paul Warburg, a founding father of the Federal Reserve system. Warburg Jnr was willing to accept occasional devaluations by reducing the gold content of the dollar in agreement with other countries. However, he insisted that the gold standard rather than a managed currency was vital for sound currency and stability.[20]

Roosevelt came to office at a critical time of intense uncertainty both at home and abroad. During his first hundred days, he pushed legislation through Congress to expand the power of the executive and the federal government, with a commitment to act without delay even if it meant breaking with normal governmental procedure.[21] His focus was on immediate domestic concerns. Prevarication and uncertainty continued in international economic policy where three outstanding problems – of trade, money and debt – were causing deep divisions between the major economies.

TRADE WARFARE

Prior to the First World War there was no formal institution of global governance to set, let alone enforce, rules on trade. Disputes were covered by public international law, in the case of the trading rights of neutrals in times of war, and by private international law between traders through national courts or arbitration. Sovereign states set their tariffs and other forms of trade restrictions or subsidies as they wished, according to their needs for revenue, their wish to maintain employment or encourage economic development, and in response to domestic political pressures. They would be alert to the possibility of retaliation from other countries, but there were no international rules or institutions to prevent unfair competition.

What did emerge in the second half of the nineteenth century were bilateral trade treaties between countries that incorporated the 'most favoured nation' principle, which became Article 1 of the General Agreement on Tariffs and Trade in 1947: 'any advantage, favour, privilege or immunity granted by any contracting party to any product originating in or destined for any other country shall be accorded immediately and unconditionally to the like product originating in or destined for the territories of all other contracting parties.'[22] At first sight, 'most favoured' suggests that a country would have special treatment from another. In fact, it means that the signatories of a trade agreement are committed to treat each other as well as they treat a third party who has also signed a trade treaty. Hence if countries A and B negotiate an agreement, any concession in an agreement between A and C would be extended unconditionally to B – and any agreement between B and D would be extended unconditionally to A and C in an interlocking set of agreements. By this means, no country would be treated worse than the country that is treated best in any bilateral agreement. Such unconditional, automatic extension of benefits was open to the criticism that it gave something for nothing, and until 1922 the United States adopted a conditional form of the most favoured nation principle, which extended concessions negotiated by A and B to C only after a further round of negotiations with C.[23]

Before 1914, networks of bilateral treaties based on the most favoured nation principle led to the construction of trade blocs rather than to more general multilateral trade. An initial trade bloc of interconnected treaties emerged from the Cobden–Chevalier Treaty between Britain and France in 1860. It did not last, for France and Britain did not renew the treaty in 1880 because of political pressures in both countries. The Anglo-French network broke down and was replaced after 1892 by another network based on Germany, which aimed to build a central Europe bloc. The challenge from German and American competition and protectionism started to cause alarm in Britain by the end of the nineteenth century, when the question arose whether Britain should abandon its policy of unilateral free trade and retaliate by increasing its tariffs, create a preferential trade bloc within the empire, or maintain and reshape free trade.[24]

In 1903, Joseph Chamberlain – the social reforming former Lord Mayor of Birmingham who was now Colonial Secretary – proposed import duties with preference for the empire. He came to this policy through a commitment to social reform. His proposal for 'Tariff Reform', according to the slogan of the movement, 'Means Work For All'. Its supporters claimed it would create full employment and end poverty, with income from tariffs financing welfare reform. Imperial preference would still allow imports of cheap food from the empire, so domestic consumers would not suffer. The result – so its supporters argued – would be a strong domestic market supplemented by a prosperous imperial market, creating a large economic unit to rival Germany and the United States.[25]

Chamberlain did not convince all his colleagues in the Conservative Party, let alone in the Liberal Party, which portrayed tariff reform as a ruse by landed aristocrats to increase food prices and by selfish industrialists to protect the home market. Free trade was more than an economic policy – to Richard Cobden, leader of the movement for free trade in Britain that secured the repeal of the protective corns laws in 1846 (and signatory of the Anglo-French treaty of 1860), it was also about peace, civilization and morality. Free trade would bring nations together in harmony through comparative advantage, joining them in civilizing commerce rather than the militarism of protectionist Prussia. It purged politics of vested interests, so sparing Britain the pork-barrel politics of the United States. By sweeping away monopolies, it allowed the free association of citizens in co-operative societies, friendly societies and trade unions, and permitted an economy of independent firms rather than American and German trusts and cartels. At the time of the centenary of Cobden's birth in 1904, the future Liberal prime minister Henry Campbell-Bannerman expressed the stark choice facing Britain: 'One road ... leads to Protection, to conscription, to the reducing of free institutions to a mere name ... And the other leads to the consolidation of liberty and the development of equity at home.'[26]

Political mobilization against tariff reform led to free-trade victories in the elections of 1906 and 1910. But if social welfare and employment could not be provided by tariff reform, they would have to be funded through a progressive income tax that might alienate middle-class electors. The Labour Party supported free trade and made common cause with progressive 'new Liberals' in redefining trade as 'free' on condition that it rested on fair conditions of production and employment both at home and abroad. Above all, John Hobson – a leading Liberal thinker and unorthodox economist – argued that huge disparities of income and wealth meant under-consumption by workers and excess savings by the rich, so that excess goods and capital were exported and thus fuelled imperialism. Free trade should therefore be combined with redistribution of income and the taxation of unearned wealth arising from the increase in land values or profits generated by society as a whole and appropriated by individuals. Support for free trade moved from a simple attack on 'food taxes' to positive action against the social problems of unfettered exchange and in support of balance in society.[27]

The First World War marked a further shift in the culture of free trade in Britain to international co-ordination of production and markets. The Allies came together to co-ordinate the use of scarce resources through bodies such as the Wheat Executive of 1916 and the Allied Maritime Transport Council of 1917. They were crucial to the operation of the war and were part of the shift from Cobdenite free trade to international planning and co-ordination of markets and resources. At the Maritime Transport Council, Arthur Salter, an experienced British civil servant, worked with a French official, Jean Monnet. Both went on to work in the League of Nations after the war. The pursuit of Cobdenite international-ism shifted from free trade to a greater interest in organization and planning that could blur the line with imperial preference as a form of planned, co-ordinated trade. Although some Liberals clung to unilateral free trade, a growing belief in the international regulation of markets by rules and institutions began to mutate into an assumption that protection-ism could save undeveloped countries from exploitation, and that co-ordination by international organizations would avoid disruptive eco-nomic fluctuations and apportion resources by need. A new economic internationalism of collective agreements was needed.[28]

The shape of internationalism to be taken after the war was a matter for dispute. At the Paris Economic Conference of 1916, the French min-ister of commerce and industry, Étienne Clémentel, proposed the continuation of wartime bodies to control the supply of raw materials, and the imposition of a post-war blockade of Germany and its allies in central Europe. It would be the continuation of war by other means. In his nightmares, Clémentel envisaged a politically and economically integrated customs union of Germany and the Austro-Hungarian empire, and the only way to prevent such a disaster was by using new international bodies to control the supply of raw materials. The Allies supported the proposal in 1916, and at Versailles Clémentel and his assistant Monnet proposed a new economic order of European co-operation or 'organized peace'. The idea was rejected by President Wilson, who feared a collapse into trade blocs; he wanted an open-door policy and equality of treatment.[29]

The Versailles Treaty removed Germany's status as a most favoured nation for five years, and also dismembered the Austro-Hungarian empire. This situation created a serious problem. Germany remained the most important economy in Europe, at a time when the three major empires to the east – those of Russia, Austria–Hungary and the Ottoman Turks – were weak and divided, with smaller, fragile powers in central and eastern Eu-rope. In the 1920s, competing proposals for the new European economic order were put forward, from a 'Danubian' trade zone in central Europe that would limit German access to markets, to Germany's plans for Mittel-europa. The French countered with a plan for a wider European customs union that would contain German influence. In 1929, Aristide Briand, the former president and current foreign minister of France, proposed to the League of Nations the creation of a European economic union.[30]

Despite their differences in scale and membership, and their different geopolitical ambitions, these schemes all needed an institutional and legal structure provided by the League to define the operation of the most favoured nation principle, and the relationship between regional and international trade. Members of a free-trade area can reduce tariffs between themselves and retain their own external tariffs without making concessions to non-members with whom they can still negotiate bilateral treaties on the unconditional most favoured nation principle. By contrast, members of a customs union, with a single external tariff, lose indepen-dent authority to make treaties with non-members; the customs union as a whole negotiates external treaties. Both approaches needed a legal or institutional structure to codify bilateral treaties and most favoured nation rules. This task was taken up by the League's Economic Commit-tee, and the League's World Economic Conference at Geneva in 1927 endorsed the unconditional most favoured nation principle as the stan-dard against which national and imperial trade policies should be judged.[31]

The conference was followed by a short-term increase in bilateral trea-ties, but the League's efforts could not prevent the collapse of mutual understanding with the onset of the Great Depression. The different approaches to European trade blocs reached a crisis in 1931 when the Ger-man and Austrian governments announced that they had agreed to a customs union. The initiative was blocked by Czechoslovakia, which feared a loss of markets, and by France which feared a revanchist Germany. The proposal was, in the opinion of France, a breach of Austria's commitment to independence in return for a stabilization loan in 1922, and this view was upheld by the International Court at The Hague. The plan for an Austro-German customs union was a challenge to the settlement of 1919 and marked the beginning of a downward spiral into mutual animosity.[32]

Trade policy was a source of international friction and mutual recrimi-nation. The Americans were widely seen as the initiators of a spiral of protectionism with the Smoot–Hawley Tariff Act of 1930 – a measure denounced by the economist Sumner Slichter in 1932 as 'an act of almost incredible economic folly'. Arthur Salter felt that it was 'a turning point in world history'. The tariff remains a symbol of what was wrong in the 1930s; during debates on the North American Free Trade Agreement (NAFTA) in 1993, Vice-President Al Gore likened its opponents to Reed Smoot (a

Republican Senator from Utah and chairman of the Senate Finance Committee) and Willis Hawley (a Republican member of the House of Representatives and chairman of the House Ways and Means Committee) who persuaded Congress to protect American jobs by imposing higher import duties. Gore insisted that the tariff 'was one of the principal causes . . . of the Great Depression in this country and around the world'.[33] The issue reappeared when President Trump's imposition of tariffs led the *Washington Post* to warn that 'one crucial lesson of Smoot–Hawley is to leave trade policy alone . . . Protectionism may make things worse and, possibly, much worse. The Trump administration hasn't absorbed this history.'[34]

The origins of the Act went back to the 1928 presidential election, when the Republican Herbert Hoover campaigned for tariffs to protect American farmers from the worldwide collapse of commodity prices. In reality, tariffs on imports did little to help American farmers, who were major food exporters, and would not solve the main problem of low world prices caused by over-production. Hoover did not intend higher tariffs to apply to industrial goods, but his initially modest proposal was widened in the Republican platform for 1928. Support for protection rested on the belief that it was fundamental to American prosperity, preventing competition from foreign suppliers with low wages, and offering employment and the highest standard of living in the world. On this view, everyone gained. American farmers had good markets for their foodstuffs and raw materials; industrialists had affluent consumers; and foreigners benefitted from the prosperity of the American market. Consequently, ending protection would have the dire consequence of reducing Americans to the standard of living of Europe.[35]

Hoover won the presidential election, and Congress turned to the revision of duties as the boom of the 1920s gave way to depression. The Smoot–Hawley Tariff Bill started its passage through Congress in an atmosphere of crisis. Although the vote for and against the bill as a whole was on party lines, support for individual duties was influenced by local economic interests, with members of Congress making deals to support each other's pet duty.[36] Blatant vote trading undermined the reputation of Congress as a tariff-setting body. Robert La Follette, the progressive Republican Senator from Wisconsin, was horrified at the behaviour of his colleagues in creating a tariff act that was 'the product of a series of deals, conceived in secret, but executed in public with a brazen effrontery that is without parallel in the annals of the Senate . . . this Congress has demonstrated how tariff legislation should not be made.' La Folette's opposition to the bill did not come from a commitment to internationalism so much as from the belief that it was a distraction from genuine solutions to the depression, such as restoring domestic consumption through public works and federal relief for the unemployed.[37]

The Smoot–Hawley Bill only passed by a narrow margin, against the advice of as many as 1,028 economists and of leading industrialists and financiers with international business interests, such as Henry Ford and Thomas Lamont of J. P. Morgan. Although Hoover felt the duties were excessive, he realized that using the presidential veto would have been politically difficult at a time when the American economy was facing serious problems. In any case, the 'flexible tariff' authority allowed him to modify tariffs by 50 per cent in either direction if the Tariff Commission found that a duty did not equalize the cost of production between the United States and a foreign country.[38] Further, the impact of the tariff was not as serious as Gore claimed. Only a third of the 40 per cent drop in American imports between 1929 and 1932 can be explained by higher tariffs, and dutiable imports were only 1.4 per cent of GDP in 1929. The impact on the American economy was therefore modest and tariffs were not a major cause of the Great Depression. What the passage of Smoot–Hawley did show was that any future adoption of lower tariffs would require limiting the ability of Congress to engage in log-rolling.[39]

The Smoot–Hawley Tariff Act was just the latest battle in a long war between Democrats and Republicans over trade policy. On several occasions, the Democrats had reduced tariffs when they had unified control of the Presidency, House of Representatives and Senate, most recently in 1913 when tariffs were cut to the lowest levels since the Civil War. Woodrow Wilson favoured lower tariffs, and Cordell Hull was one of the most vocal supporters of this approach. Hull had been instrumental in securing a federal income tax that year, in part to replace the loss of revenue from import duties. Initially, he supported lower tariffs to raise domestic prosperity and prevent monopolies and trusts. In 1916 he came to see that free trade was vital for peace. Hull explained his conversion:

> unhampered trade dovetailed with peace; high tariffs, trade barriers, and unfair economic competition, with war . . . I reasoned that, if we could get a freer flow of trade – freer in the sense of fewer discriminations and obstructions – so that one country would not be deadly jealous of another and the living standards of all countries might rise, thereby eliminating the economic dissatisfaction that breeds war, we might have a reasonable chance for lasting peace.[40]

The experiences of the First World War convinced him that 'wars were often largely caused by economic rivalry conducted unfairly' and his proposal for a post-war international trade conference to remove 'destructive commercial controversies' was taken up in Wilson's Fourteen Points of 1917. Hull's views would have been familiar to Richard Cobden, though, as we have seen, opinions in Britain had moved beyond Cobden by 1914.[41]

Hull was often derided for naivety in thinking that his approach would work with Hitler and other dictators in the 1930s. Henry Morgenthau, Treasury Secretary from 1934 to 1945, complained that Hull 'failed to realize that Japanese militarism and European fascism had released new and ugly forces which ... could not be controlled politely'.[42] Hull was unrepentant, insisting that the collapse of international friendship started when the Republicans raised duties in 1922, and that the descent into conflict would not have occurred if the United States had persisted with free trade. He was adamant that

> Economic warfare ... offers constant temptation to use force, or threat of force, to obtain what could have been got through normal processes of trade.
>
> A people driven to desperation by unemployment, want, and misery is a constant threat of disorder and chaos, both internal and external. It falls an easy prey to dictators and desperadoes.[43]

Hull's idealistic belief that freer trade was the solution to economic and political difficulties meant that he was regarded patronizingly by members of the political class in Washington. Herbert Feis, an official at the Department of State who worked with him at the World Monetary and Economic Conference, 'wondered whether his mind would be incisive enough and his will strong enough to deal with the harsh forces that were gathering around us'. He had a 'ruminative mind' that lacked flexibility on international economics and was vague on other issues. 'He no longer gathers ideas from others, and when confronted with the obstacles and difficulties to his good intentions, does not analyze them and figure out ways of licking them; he preaches against them.'[44]

Hull's political base was in Tennessee, and the South was vital in trade policy. It was committed to open international markets as an exporter of raw cotton and other primary products, and as an importer of manufactures from the northern United States and Europe. Import duties were perceived as boosting the profits of northern industrialists, financing government at the expense of the poor and harming the ability of foreign countries to buy Southern commodities in an open world economy. Further, Southern poverty led to support for welfare and investment in infrastructure funded by federal spending, largely from income tax paid by the north. A commitment to free trade – as well as more stringent regulations for bankers and finance – was therefore more likely when Southern Democrats had a voice in Congress, as in 1933.

This Southern influence meant that an open world trade system and liberal capitalism were linked with a hierarchical racial order to which Wilson and Hull were committed. In the words of Ira Katznelson, 'the Jim Crow South was the one collaborator America's democracy could not do without.' The South was vital to the early years of the New Deal, until the alliance weakened as Roosevelt turned to trade unions and black voters in northern cities and as Southern racial views came to be associated with Nazi racial ideology. Then, Southern Democrats were more likely to ally with Republicans in a conservative coalition, fearing that federal policies and public works might undermine the Southern racial order. But in the 1930s, the Southern Democrats in Congress were crucial to Roosevelt.[45]

The Smoot–Hawley Act was not the first shot in a trade war so much as a useful piece of political propaganda that allowed other governments to point an accusing finger at the United States as the guilty initiators of a trade war. However, the adoption of tariffs – or imperial preference – in Britain in 1932 arose from long-standing internal debates that went back to Joseph Chamberlain in 1903 and to the introduction of duties in the First World War as a defensive strategy to save foreign exchanges and to 'safeguard' strategic industries. By 1930, Britain's leading bankers, industrialists and economists were more generally in favour of protection, independently of Smoot–Hawley.[46] The converts included John Maynard Keynes, who had been a staunch free trader before the war. In 1932 and 1933, he argued that national self-sufficiency was vital for a 'balanced' society, allowing British people to express their aptitudes for all sorts of activities. Further, the benefits of comparative advantage had declined, for most countries could adopt mass production with equal efficiency, and as wealth increased so agriculture and manufactured commodities became less important than housing, personal services and local amenities, which were not traded between countries. Free trade and capital mobility were just as likely to cause war as to maintain peace:

> I sympathise ... with those who would minimise rather than with those who would maximise economic entanglement between nations. Ideas, knowledge, art, hospitality, travel – these are the things which should of their nature be international. But let goods be homespun whenever it is reasonably and conveniently possible; and, above all, let finance be primarily national.

In a situation of economic crisis, each country should seek its own salvation, rather than being 'at the mercy of world forces working out, or trying to work out, some uniform equilibrium according to the ideal principles of *laissez-faire* capitalism'.[47]

In February 1932, Neville Chamberlain, Joseph Chamberlain's son and

Chancellor of the Exchequer in the 'National' coalition government, introduced a general tariff of 10 per cent on finished and semi-manufactured
goods, with imperial preference, an exemption for goods from the Dominions (the self-governing white colonies of Canada, Australia and New
Zealand), introduced at the Ottawa conference of July–August 1932.
Many Americans – and above all Hull – felt that preferences were worse
than tariffs that applied to everyone; what was so bad about British policy
was the discrimination that breached equal access through the 'open door'.
Although Roosevelt was less concerned with trade than Hull, he agreed on
a desire to end colonialism. Recent studies by economic historians have
downplayed the destructive impact of imperial preference on the grounds
that it promoted trade within the British Commonwealth as a result of
transport links and investment, without significantly diverting trade from
non-members.[48] At the time, the American embassy in London took a
jaundiced view of imperial preference, reporting that 'the group which
negotiated and backed the Ottawa agreements are working to achieve
what the average Britisher still considers to be England's right, namely, a
position of supremacy in the world of finance and trade; at least within the
so-called sterling block of countries.'[49] The stage was set for twenty years
of mutual recriminations.

CURRENCY INSTABILITY

In the chaotic aftermath of the 1914–18 war, many commentators looked
back with nostalgia to the globalized economy that had expanded so rapidly in the late nineteenth century. At its heart was the gold standard,
which had been adopted by most advanced countries in the later nineteenth century, abandoning silver or bimetallic currencies: Germany in
1872, the Netherlands in 1875, France in 1878, the United States in 1879,
Italy in 1884, Japan and Russia in 1897. They were joining the world's
largest trading bloc, avoiding the potential disruption of currency fluctuations, and hoping to secure more favourable terms for borrowing on
international financial markets.[50]

The gold standard was often portrayed as a self-regulating, automatic
mechanism that did not require formalized rules and institutional oversight. Rather, it depended on countries making a credible commitment to
follow the unwritten 'rules of the game' that gold should move freely in
and out of reserves. The relative value of currencies was fixed by the
amount of gold in a dollar, pound, franc or Reichsmark coin, and paper
currency was freely convertible into gold. As a result, there was limited

scope for competitive devaluation between currencies or for manipulation of currencies by bankers or politicians for their own ends. To James Grigg – a Treasury official who advised Winston Churchill on the return to gold in 1925 – the system was 'knave proof'. In theory, the gold standard created international equilibrium through the price–specie flow mechanism. A country with a balance of payments deficit would lose gold and the money supply would be reduced and prices would fall; the country with a balance of payments surplus would receive gold, its money supply would increase and prices would rise. As a result, the competitive advantage of the two countries would be reversed and trade balances restored.[51]

Reality was more complicated, for central bankers co-operated to manage the system – or manipulated it for national political advantage.[52] Further, the gold standard had the potential to affect different groups in society, with serious political ramifications. In the late nineteenth century, gold was in short supply and prices fell. Urban workers in the northern industrial American states and in Britain benefitted from falling prices and had an unprecedented improvement in their standard of living. On the other hand, falling prices in the later nineteenth century hit indebted farmers in the South and western areas of the United States, and increased the real burden of their debts. In the United States, the People's Party urged the monetization of silver as a means of increasing the money supply and raising prices to assist debtors and farmers. The campaign reached its apogee in 1896 when William Jennings Bryan, the presidential nominee of both the Democratic and People's parties, denounced the gold standard in biblical terms: 'You shall not press down upon the brow of labour this crown of thorns. You shall not crucify mankind upon a cross of gold.' Prices started to recover after 1896, and Bryan lost the presidential elections of both 1896 and 1900 to a Republican candidate, William McKinley, who supported the gold standard and tariffs as a better way of securing prosperity. Demands to monetize silver returned when commodity prices fell between the wars – and attitudes also started to shift in Britain as it prepared to return to the gold standard after the war.[53]

The gold standard was a 'contingent rule' that allowed countries to suspend gold in a crisis, such as the First World War, and stop the convertibility of paper currency into bullion.[54] Most countries tried to return to gold after the war. The automatic mechanism of gold would, so many economists and politicians believed, restore order and stability. In Britain, preparations for a return to gold started in 1919, and in 1925 Churchill, as Chancellor of the Exchequer, had to decide whether to continue the suspension. Keynes was the leading opponent of return. In his *Tract on Monetary Reform* of 1923, he suggested that independently managed national monetary systems would produce long-term stability. At the very least, the return to gold should be delayed and should not be attempted through a deliberate policy of deflation to restore the pre-war exchange rate of £1 to $4.86 by forcing down British costs and wages. Opinion generally was in favour of return, on the grounds that gold would prevent inflation, impose discipline upon government spending and require wage discipline. It would return power over monetary policy to the Bank of England, so removing the ability of politicians to subvert sound money. Despite the over-valuation of the pound and loss of export competitiveness, the supporters of a return to gold believed it would restore the world economy – and that any over-valuation would soon be corrected by the automatic operation of the price–specie flow mechanism. In his budget speech of 20 March 1925, Churchill accordingly announced that Britain would return to gold.[55]

Keynes went on the offensive, publishing his swingeing critique *The Economic Consequences of Mr Churchill*. He warned that the return to gold would require an attack on wages to reduce costs and bring prices into line with the exchange rate. Defence of the fixed exchange rate of the pound by credit restriction and high interest rates meant a reduction of wages

> *[i]n no other way than by the deliberate intensification of unemployment* . . . until the workers are ready to accept the necessary reduction of money wages under the pressure of hard facts . . . Deflation does not reduce wages 'automatically'. It reduces them by causing unemployment. The proper object of dear money is to check an incipient boom. Woe to them whose faith leads them to use it to aggravate a depression!

Workers would be victims of 'the theory of the economic juggernaut', a machine that crashed along 'with regard only to its equilibrium as a whole, and without attention to the chance consequences of the journey to individual groups'. The gold standard, he argued, was 'an essential emblem and idol of those who sit in the top tier of the machine' and believed that nothing serious would happen. Keynes warned that one day something *would* happen – and his prediction came true with the General Strike of 1926. Gold no longer offered workers higher real wages, as in the later nineteenth century, but led to deflation and unemployment. A central figure on the union side was Ernest Bevin, the leader of the Transport and General Workers' Union who became Minister of Labour in the wartime Coalition and Foreign Secretary in the post-war Labour government. Keynes's and Bevin's experience of the gold standard shaped attitudes to international monetary reform during and after the Second World War.[56]

In reality, the gold standard did not operate as predicted by the price–specie flow mechanism. Prices in the United States did not rise as expected as gold left Britain for the United States, because it was neutralized in the vaults of Fort Knox – and wages in Britain were 'sticky' and could not be 'adjusted' (i.e., reduced) without serious political risks. At the same time, the Bank of England realized that interest rates could no longer be set merely to defend the external value of the pound, for industries such as cotton borrowed heavily in the post-war boom and had difficulties in servicing loans when export markets collapsed, with a potential threat to over-exposed banks.[57] This growing concern for the domestic impact of interest rates was associated with a greater concern about capital exports.

By the outbreak of the First World War, about a third of all British capital was held outside the country, with a peak outflow between 1905 and 1914.[58] Before the war, a minority of critics, led by John Hobson and radical 'new Liberals', complained that the result was to depress domestic investment. Attitudes shifted after the war.[59] Controls on capital exports were needed during the war but they were not entirely removed on the return to peace given the need to fund the government's major house-building programme and to convert short-term government debt into longer-term bonds. The Bank of England and Treasury recognized that the City could no longer have the freedom to export capital without considering the impact on investment at home. In 1924, an embargo on both foreign and colonial loans was introduced to prevent an outflow of funds, which would threaten depreciation of the pound and make a return to gold more difficult. Otto Niemeyer at the Treasury and Montagu Norman at the Bank of England – both strong supporters of the gold standard – doubted the ability to maintain capital exports, above all to the Dominions, now that the British balance of payments was weaker than before the war. Voluntary restraint by the Dominions would be better than putting up interest rates which might discourage recovery of the economy. Others continued to argue that capital exports secured foreign markets and increased employment – a view that had support in the Treasury in the 1920s, which thought capital exports would be more beneficial than the scheme for public works advocated by Keynes in the general election of 1929. Nevertheless, embargoes on colonial and foreign loans continued, and attitudes were changing even in bastions of orthodoxy in the Treasury and Bank of England. Before the First World War, they accepted fixed rates on gold and free movement of capital; now they saw that capital flows at a time of domestic depression and a weaker balance of payments might put strain on the exchange rate. An increase in interest rates to discourage capital exports and maintain the pound would be more harmful than adopting capital controls.[60]

Problems with the functioning of the gold standard came to a head in

Britain in 1931. Short-term capital left London because of a lack of confidence in the policies of the minority Labour government. The Bank of England raised interest rates to defend the pound, which hit industry and increased unemployment. Financiers felt that the Labour government needed to take firm action to control public spending, and the chancellor welcomed their concern as a way of strengthening his hand in Cabinet. But confidence in the pound was lost and the gold standard was suspended on 21 September 1931.[61] Abandonment of the gold standard in favour of a managed floating rate turned out to be a relief rather than a defeat. The pound fell in value, fluctuating between $3.75 and $3.28 in 1932; its rate was managed by a new Exchange Equalization Account. Devaluation stimulated exports and made imports less competitive, so reinforcing tariff protection. Now that interest rates were no longer needed to protect the fixed exchange rate of the pound, 'cheap money' could be used to stimulate the domestic economy and reduce the cost of servicing the national debt. Instead of exporting capital, Britain now became a net importer.[62]

In Britain, the return to gold had led to deflation and labour unrest in the 1920s, and abandoning gold led to recovery. The outcomes in France and Germany were different. Inflation and political disorder in the 1920s meant that gold was seen as re-establishing order and monetary stability. When France left the gold standard in 1914, the Banque de France made advances to the government to fund the war. After the war, high levels of spending for reconstruction, failure to reform the tax regime, and the inability to repay wartime advances or reduce money in circulation meant that the Bank was drawn into politics – above all, against the government of the Cartel des Gauches of 1924–26. In 1926, the franc was stabilized and taxation reformed, and in 1928 France returned to gold – not at pre-war parity but at a fifth of its pre-war rate, which led to economic recovery. The gold standard seemed to have worked in replacing economic and political instability, inflation and budget deficits with order and prosperity. Similarly, in Germany the hyperinflation of 1921–23 created an obsession with monetary stability. In America, President Hoover retained the gold standard, despite opposition from the silver lobby and populists. To these countries, the British government was manipulating its currency and threatening the stability of the world economy by triggering currency wars. Although some countries had abandoned gold prior to 1931, they were mainly primary producers and international debtors who were hit by a fall in prices and problems in servicing debt. Critics complained that Britain lacked the same justification: it was not a primary producer and sterling's role as a major international currency demanded a firmer resolve to stay on gold. It is true that abandoning gold did work for Britain and other countries that moved off the standard early, but devaluation was not co-ordinated as countries responded to crises, when confidence was lost in one country after another, reducing the benefits to the world economy.[63]

An attempt had been made at the co-ordination of the international monetary system in 1919. The future of the financial system had not been discussed at Versailles, and the British government therefore proposed an international conference to consider the issue. A group of economists and bankers, including Keynes and Paul Warburg, also urged financial co-operation to ensure that loans to European countries did not fail and provoke a financial crisis. The conference was held in Brussels in 1920 under the auspices of the League of Nations, reflecting a new approach of open discussion of international finance rather than agreements between central bankers. Although it made little progress, one outcome was an Economic and Financial Committee of independent experts nominated by the League's council, which became the Economic and Financial Organization (EFO) in 1923. In 1927, the United States agreed to participate, despite not being a member of the League.[64]

The future of the gold standard was discussed by a group set up by the League in 1929 that produced its final report in June 1932. This 'Gold Delegation' was divided. On one side, the orthodox majority supported 'automaticity' – the operation of the gold standard without political intervention or the pursuit of inflationary policies. More sceptical members included Henry Strakosch, a friend of Keynes and financial supporter of Churchill, and the Swedish economist Gustav Cassel, who produced notes of dissent in favour of management of the gold standard. In their view, a major problem was the 'relentless struggle for gold' by central banks and, above all, its accumulation in the reserves of France and the United States, where prices were not allowed to rise and liquidity was withdrawn from the world economy. The maldistribution of the world's monetary stock led to falling prices, a growing burden of debt, pressure to cut wages, postponement of investment and consumption, and economic depression. Cassel castigated 'deflationists' who 'disregard the great social evils, labour struggles, and political disturbances, unavoidably connected with a restrictive policy of such severity'. The problem was not so much the gold standard as its 'flagrant mismanagement'. The solution was international agreement to settle debts and reparations, an end of protectionism, the restoration of a free flow of gold so it was not withdrawn into reserves, a more efficient use of gold by revising the 'cover ratio' – the amount of gold needed to back paper money – and monetary expansion by central bankers who should 'supply the world so abundantly with means of payment that no further fall in prices will be possible'. The dissenters were arguing for reform rather than rejection of gold.[65]

The British government had already abandoned gold and might have been expected to throw itself behind the minority view. But the government was anxious to minimize hostility and tried to create consensus by focusing on another issue: reparations and war debts. At the final meeting, and in the absence of the Americans, the Delegation agreed that 'political debts' were a major cause of the depression. The final report attempted to paper over the cracks. The result was a muddled compromise that largely reflected the majority view in favour of gold, surrounded by notes of dissent. It recommended the settlement of reparations and war debts as a condition for the return of the gold standard – a point readily accepted by the British.[66]

DEBTS AND REPARATIONS

At the end of the First World War, Keynes warned that the decision to collect reparations from Germany would cause economic disruption and political instability. Early in 1919, he produced a scheme for 'the rehabilitation of European credit and for financing relief and reconstruction'. Germany would sell interest-bearing bonds and use the funds to pay reparations to the Allies and to buy food and raw materials for reconstruction. He realized that bonds issued by a defeated country would not be appealing, so he suggested they should have priority over all other German obligations, and that other enemy states would provide an international guarantee enforced by the League of Nations, failing which the Allies would be the next in line to guarantee the bonds. Since the United States was the major creditor, it would have an interest in ensuring that the bonds would be paid, encouraging the Americans to engage in the reconstruction of Europe and the international economy. The British government was attracted by the scheme and assured Woodrow Wilson that its adoption would allow Europe to buy American goods, restore international credit and trade, and contain the menace of Bolshevism. Wilson saw that an American guarantee of European bonds would not be accepted in Congress and he agreed with his adviser, Thomas Lamont, that reconstruction should be financed by private bankers. The proposal was dropped, and Keynes left the peace conference at Versailles in a state of despair, resigning from the Treasury in 'misery and rage'.[67]

In this state of mind, Keynes wrote a book that made him a public figure: *The Economic Consequences of the Peace*. He embarked on a 'violent attack' on the Treaty and reparations. He argued that Germany was at the centre of Europe's economic system before 1914, for only by using its productive capacity continuously and at full blast, could she find occupation at home for her increasing population and the means of purchasing their subsistence from abroad ... Round Germany as a central support the rest of the European economic system grouped itself, and on the prosperity and enterprise of Germany the prosperity of the rest of the Continent mainly depended.

In Keynes's opinion, the Treaty would upset the economic system at a time when it was already threatened by the Russian Revolution. Keynes was unsparing in his account of the failings of the main participants at the peace conference. Georges Clemenceau, the prime minister of France, had only one aim – 'to crush the economic life of his enemy'. To Keynes, the French desire to reduce Germany to the size of 1870 and to restore the European balance of power was impracticable. He was just as damning of Wilson's idealistic self-deception and failure to engage with reality. By contrast, the British prime minister, David Lloyd George, lacked principle and was of 'final purposelessness, inner irresponsibility ... mixed with cunning, remorselessness, love of power'. Lloyd George opted to take strong action against Germany for domestic political reasons, contrary to the advice of the Treasury. The Germans accepted that they would have to pay for the devastation of northern France; more controversially, the British wanted recompense to cover the less tangible impact of the war on its capital stock, borrowing from America to finance the Allied war effort, and the cost of war pensions. The result was a treaty that imposed reparations on a scale that Keynes felt was unsustainable. Above all, he realized that even in Britain, capitalism 'which engages many local sympathies, which plays a real part in the daily processes of production, and upon the security of which the present organisation of society largely depends', was not very safe. Would

the discontented peoples of Europe be willing for a generation to come so to order their lives that an appreciable part of their daily produce may be available to meet a foreign payment, the reason of which, whether as between Europe and America, or as between Germany and the rest of Europe, does not spring compellingly from their sense of justice or duty?[68]

Keynes's 'vicious' attack on Wilson was long held against him and soured relations with Wilsonian Democrats in the Second World War.[69] Both at the time and later, the French were not convinced, arguing that Keynes underestimated both German capacity to pay and the costs inflicted on France.[70]

The issue of reparations was closely connected with inter-Allied debts. The British had lent money to France, and the United States had lent to both countries. In February 1922, Allied debts to the United States amounted to $10,512m, of which $4,427m was owed by Britain and

$3,555m by France.[71] The best hope for France to repay its debts was by securing reparations from Germany – and to make matters still more complicated, the Americans made a loan to Germany to pay reparations. This web of liabilities was the cause of endless negotiations and tensions. In 1929, an attempt was made to resolve the issue by the Allied Reparations Committee, which appointed a group chaired by Owen Young, an American businessman. The Young report was adopted in 1930 and reduced the level of reparations: a third would be repaid and the remaining two-thirds postponed, but with payment of interest. The scheme was funded by a consortium of American banks.

The Young plan was well intentioned but failed to resolve the political and economic crises of the Weimar Republic. Hyperinflation had written off debts in the early 1920s, but by the late 1920s American bankers believed new loans would be safe and provide higher returns. German central, state and local governments borrowed heavily from American banks because of the weakness of Germany's capital markets. When recession hit in 1929, Chancellor Heinrich Brüning had difficulties paying both debts and reparations, and he made repeated cuts in wages and spending, and increased taxes. This policy of austerity exacerbated the recession, and difficulties in securing support in the Reichstag led him to rely on emergency decrees that undermined democratic legitimacy. Brüning was caught between his need to secure domestic political support and to retain the confidence of foreign investors. In 1931, he attempted to reconcile the two issues by adopting austerity to satisfy financial markets, while warning that the German people would not tolerate any more hardship and that action was needed on reparations. He satisfied neither group. Hitler exploited the situation by blaming Germany's economic difficulties on foreigners and international finance, and it was difficult for other parties to counter his appeal when they shared much of the same belief. As the crisis deepened, Germany's creditors became ever more alarmed. Eventually, in June 1931 President Hoover realized that the situation was untenable; he offered a moratorium on war debts and reparations for a year and suggested a world economic conference. It was too late, and the next month Germany was hit by a banking crisis that deepened the economic recession and led to an international liquidity crisis which contributed both to the American banking crash and to the run on sterling that led to Britain's abandonment of gold.[72]

The idea of a world economic conference was not pursued, but a conference was held in Lausanne in July 1932 to find a long-term solution for reparations. Neville Chamberlain saw an opportunity to counter hostility to the devaluation of the pound and imperial preference by tackling the issue of debts and reparations. As Patricia Clavin remarks, 'war debts created lines of disagreement that ran across, rather than parallel to, divisions over monetary policy and were criss-crossed again by varying perspectives on trade, commodity agreements and public works.' Chamberlain reached a deal with the French prime minister, Edouard Herriot, to replace German reparations with bonds to the value of 3 million Reichsmarks. The United States did not welcome this secret agreement, which needed American ratification – and the British and French wanted a settlement of their debts to America that was not part of the discussions at Lausanne. In order to break through the impasse, the League of Nations agreed to convene a conference to consider war debts and other economic and financial issues. The League was well aware that it had been placed in a difficult position by the French and British, and hoped that the wider, more structured, forum would help.[73]

The Democratic election platform of 1932 had suggested an international conference as a way of restoring trade and settling the monetary question. The line to be adopted at the conference was left open – whether Hull's free trade or the Brains Trust's stress on domestic recovery, whether Warburg's support for gold or a looser monetary policy favoured by the silver lobby. The World Monetary and Economic Conference was to meet in London between 12 June and 23 July 1933 to deal with major issues at a time when American policy had not yet crystallized. It was a critical time. The global world economy of the late nineteenth century had been overturned: trade and production were in serious decline; unemployment was at high levels; prices were falling; financial markets were in disarray; international capital movements were at a low ebb; and the gold standard had been abandoned by leading countries. The world was moving to economic nationalism, and the priority had shifted from sustaining the international economy to domestic recovery. In Britain, the 'trilemma' of exchange rates, capital movements and domestic monetary policy had been reshaped. Instead of fixed exchange rates on gold and free capital movements at the expense of domestic monetary policy, the government was now managing exchange rates, limiting capital movements, and adopting a domestic monetary policy of low interest rates to stimulate recovery, complemented by the adoption of imperial preference. Other countries – including the United States, France and Germany – still remained on gold. The World Economic and Monetary Conference met to deal with a toxic mixture of trade warfare, currency instability and the overhang of debt from the First World War. Each was extraordinarily difficult to resolve on its own; together, they promised to be intractable.

2

'Barren harvest'

The World Monetary and Economic Conference, 1933

'Are the statesmen prepared to make the necessary changes in their individual policies and to take the long view which realises that an apparent momentary gain at the expense of others will in nine cases out of ten react in time on their own prosperity?'

'Yay or nay', *The Economist*, 10 June 1933

The World Monetary and Economic Conference was convened by the League, with the Economic and Financial Organization responsible for agreeing an agenda and providing information. When Arthur Salter left the League in 1930, he was replaced by two men – the Italian Pietro Stoppani at the Economic Section and Alexander Loveday at the Financial Section. Loveday had taught economics in Cambridge before the war and served in the War Office between 1915 and 1919 before joining the League, and he now had the unenviable task of reconciling highly divergent views, not least between countries on and off the gold standard.[1] The League also involved other organizations in the conference, such as the International Labour Organization (ILO) that brought together trade unions, employers and states, the International Chamber of Commerce and, above all, the Bank for International Settlements (BIS), which was created in 1930 by Germany, France, Britain, the United States, Italy, Belgium, Switzerland and Japan to facilitate the payment of reparations. After the suspension of reparations, the BIS continued to co-ordinate the activities and policies of central bankers, who met in secret in Basel. The BIS was an important innovation in global governance – an unaccountable and undemocratic club of central bankers. It was committed to 'sound finance' and the gold standard, so that representatives of countries with floating currencies had little voice in its deliberations.[2]

The task of agreeing an agenda for the conference would be extraordinarily difficult given the deep disagreements over trade, monetary policy and

Ramsay MacDonald addresses the World Monetary and Economic Conference at the Geological Museum in London, 12 June 1933.

debt. Countries disagreed on which was most important, and the issues were interconnected so that failure on one would lead to a breakdown on the others. The result was a low point of international collaboration.

PREPARING FOR THE WORLD MONETARY AND ECONOMIC CONFERENCE

The Preparatory Commission of Experts met in October 1932 and January 1933. It was pulled in different directions, and its difficulties were intensified by the French decision to default on its debt to America in December 1932, by the crisis in Germany which brought Hitler to power, by anger at British abandonment of gold and adoption of imperial preference, and by the lack of clarity in America. There was no single topic from which it was possible to build an agreement. The commission was chaired by the governor of the central bank of the Netherlands, L. J. Trip, who was also vice-chairman of the BIS and a voice of orthodoxy on the League's Gold Delegation. The commission was divided into two subcommissions. The monetary subcommission was chaired by James M. Cox, a Wilsonian Democrat whose main qualification was having been the unsuccessful presidential candidate in 1920 when Roosevelt was his running mate. The economic subcommission was chaired by Hendrikus Colijn, a former soldier involved in brutal warfare in the Dutch colonies who became a politician in the Dutch Anti-Revolutionary Party. As prime minister in 1925–26 and from 1933 to 1939, he pursued a strict fiscal policy, supported the gold standard, opposed protectionism and backed colonialism. Both these subcommissions were further divided. The monetary subcommission had two subcommittees, to consider immediate measures for financial reconstruction and 'permanent measures for the re-establishment of the international gold standard', respectively. The economic commission had three subcommittees. One considered trade policy, which was difficult to reconcile with a second group considering primary commodities, where producers pressed for protection. A third subcommittee considered international public works, which gave a voice to the ILO and was potentially in conflict with the fiscal orthodoxy of other committees. The structure was a recipe for confusion.[3]

It was difficult to create consensus given disagreements between countries, domestic divisions between politicians and central bankers, and a motley collection of experts with little or no experience of working together and without a common understanding of the problems facing the world economy or the solutions to be adopted. Some experts were officials with an inside track to their governments and direct political accountability. On the monetary committee, the British representatives were experienced senior Treasury officials, and most European representatives came from the leading ministries and central banks. The Americans were chosen for their economic expertise but lacked authority to speak for the administration – not least because after the election of November 1932 Hoover was a 'lame duck' president and Roosevelt had not formulated a clear position. One American expert – Edmund Day – had expertise in economic statistics and was the director of the Division of Social Sciences at the Rockefeller Foundation, with scant knowledge of international or monetary issues. By contrast, John H. Williams was a monetary economist at Harvard and vice-president of the Federal Reserve Bank of New York, with clear views on the need for stable, though not fixed, rates between a number of 'key currencies', backed by appropriate domestic policies.[4]

The British and French were divided on gold. The French government was fragile and caught between right-wing opposition to tax increases and socialist opposition to budget cuts, leading to continued deficits which could only be funded with the help of the Banque de France – on condition the gold standard was retained. In Britain, leaving the standard stimulated recovery, and a Treasury official on the monetary committee thought 'the countries which are still attached to gold [did] not realise the dangers . . . The machinery is not working. Some essential parts seem to be missing, radical reconstruction is required, involving perhaps a reversal of existing policies.'[5]

The BIS made the running on monetary policy and formulated the 'Basel consensus' – named after its home city – of gold with limited flexibility in exceptional circumstances. The report on permanent re-establishment measures was largely drafted by the economic adviser of the BIS, Per Jacobsson, who was an advocate of the gold standard, an opponent of economic controls, and a supporter of balanced budgets and a small state. He later commented that 'sound monetary relations' were 'a prerequisite for freedom of trade, and, maybe, for freedom also in a more spiritual sense'. He believed that monetary stability would stimulate the flow of goods and capital, leading to an international division of labour and to prosperity. He admitted that monetary stability could in theory be achieved by 'a system of international paper money managed by "a single international body"' but rejected it as impracticable. Although gold lacked flexibility in response to price shocks and limited the possibility of domestic monetary policies, public support for gold as a known and trusted monetary system meant it was the only realistic option. He recommended a return to an international gold standard, which would rest on domestic policies of sound public finances, flexibility in markets, central bank independence, and a greater role for the BIS in dealing with foreign exchange reserves. He doubted the wisdom of increasing prices that might maintain excess production and block readjustment.[6] What was at stake was not just monetary policy but whether it should be controlled by elected governments or central bankers. Jacobsson was sure it should be bankers.

The proposed conference agenda gave 'qualified approval' to 'a direct attack upon the world price level' to break the deflationary spiral that was harming trade and monetary stability, provided that 'a rise of prices can be accomplished consistently with balanced budgets and sound monetary measures'. It urged overturning 'defensive measures' of devaluation and restraints on trade. The American experts understood that this approach would require implausible shifts in policy: Britain should stabilize the pound and aim to restore the gold standard; Germany should relax exchange controls adopted to defend the gold standard; and France should relax its controls on trade. Williams and Day thought that the main contribution of the United States would be to reach a settlement of tariffs and war debts. They realized that Europe 'profoundly believes that American high tariff policy is one of the root causes of the world's economic difficulties, and that any action looking toward a relaxation of this policy would enhance the possibilities of international cooperation'. An agreement with the British on debts would also provide space for bargaining:

> A debt settlement which formed a part of the fulfilment of a general program of reconstruction toward which each of the leading countries made an important contribution ... would probably gain stronger public support in all the countries concerned, and lead to broader constructive results, than a debt settlement without the background of this wider setting.[7]

No part of this programme stood the remotest chance of success.

The preparation of an annotated agenda for the conference was passed to the secretariat of the EFO. Stoppani rejected ambitious plans in favour of achievable targets that would stabilize trade and currency and prevent further deterioration before turning to future improvements. His caution was justified, but could there be agreement on even modest targets? The agenda tried to square the circle between the French and British by suggesting a reduction in the gold 'cover ratio', which would combine adherence to the gold standard with reflating the world economy. It reflected the 'Basel consensus' and the thinking of the BIS, which hoped to become 'an essential agency for central bank action designed to harmonise conflicting views and for joint consultations', balancing the rules of the gold standard with the need for countries to follow their own interests.[8]

In January 1933, President Roosevelt set up a committee to consider American policy at the conference, chaired by the Wall Street banker and supporter of the gold standard James Warburg. It also included Raymond Moley and Rexford Tugwell, whose commitment to increase prices and break the deflationary spiral took priority over international considerations. Disagreement was built into the committee – and the delegation to the London conference would be led by Cordell Hull, whose thinking was dominated by trade. Roosevelt also invited representatives of fifty-three governments to Washington to exchange views, on a one-by-one basis, on trade, monetary stabilization and debts, including the British and French prime ministers Ramsay MacDonald and Édouard Herriot. Before their arrival, Roosevelt secured authority in March 1933 for a gold embargo that required any holder of gold to hand it to the Treasury in return for coin or currency, and on 5 April an Executive Order required all gold holdings to be sold to the government by 1 May at the official price of $20.67 an ounce. The aim was to stop the hoarding of gold and so increase monetary circulation, improve credit and raise prices. At a press conference on 19 April, Roosevelt took another radical step: a ban on exporting gold. The president claimed that the United States had come off the gold standard, and the Committee for the Nation to Rebuild Prices and Purchasing Power – an organization of leading businessmen that pressed for higher prices – agreed. 'We should celebrate April 19 as a Second Independence Day because it is one of the few important dates in our history.' It was only partial independence. Although dollars were no longer convertible into gold, gold still backed the currency and its official price remained $20.67, which limited the amount of currency in circulation and the ability to increase prices. Nor did the move devalue the dollar against other currencies. However, authority to change the price of gold was proceeding in Congress as an amendment proposed, with Roosevelt's blessing, by Senator Elmer Thomas (a Democrat from Oklahoma) to the Agricultural Adjustment Act (AAA).[9] As MacDonald and Herriot headed for Washington, American policy was in flux.

During the Preparatory Commission's deliberations, the Americans had been closer to France's 'hard' money policy than to the British management of a managed floating rate. It was not clear what Roosevelt would decide. His advisers included supporters of hard money such as Warburg and Dean Acheson, a New York corporate lawyer who became Under-Secretary of the Treasury. There was also a long tradition of hostility in the South and western states to east-coast financiers, from Andrew Jackson's bank war of the 1830s through to the populists of the later nineteenth century. The collapse of prices in the early 1930s gave new force to William Jennings Bryan's claim that the American people were being crucified on a cross of gold. Agrarian interests felt that 'hard' money benefitted creditors by reducing prices and increasing the real burden of debts. One response was the old nostrum of monetizing silver. In January 1933, Senator Burton Wheeler (D: Montana) proposed an amendment to the AAA that would require the Treasury to coin silver. Roosevelt saw that there was growing support for action to raise prices, but realized that the monetization of silver would lock him into one partisan solution. Farm organizations were calling for 'monetary reform to definitely raise price levels', and in Iowa farmers dragged a judge from his court and threatened to lynch him to stop foreclosures on loans which they could not repay as prices dropped. The issue extended beyond farmers. Charles Edward Coughlin was a Catholic priest from Detroit whose weekly broadcast on national radio – the 'Golden Hour of the Little Flower' – attracted a large following for his attacks on 'predatory capitalists', and in particular financiers and the 'tyranny of the gold standard'. In a broadcast in February 1933, he denounced bankers and the Federal Reserve as an 'undeserving group who, without either the blood of patriotism or of Christianity flowing in their veins, have shackled the lives of men and of nations with the ponderous links of their golden chain'. His solution was reform of the monetary system, though he was uncertain whether this meant printing dollar bills, monetizing silver, or nationalizing banks. Coughlin argued that control over money was a public duty rather than a personal property right, and should therefore be removed from Wall Street bankers. He warned Roosevelt to ignore 'the whining of these high priests of international finance ... who have prostituted their citizenship, betrayed their leadership and made out of the temple of the Most High God a common market place filled with the dung of animals, crowded with the slaves of gold!'[10] Roosevelt's comment in his inaugural address that the money changers had fled from the temple echoed Coughlin's more extreme language. When Wheeler's amendment attracted thirty-three votes in the Senate in April 1933, the political commentator Walter Lippmann saw that 'resort to a definite plan of controlled inflation cannot be delayed much longer'.[11]

At this point, Senator Thomas proposed his alternative amendment. He was concerned by the low prices of farm goods in Oklahoma, a marginal area that had expanded production during the period of high wartime prices and was devastated by the dust-bowl drought that had hit in the early 1930s. Thomas believed that the solution to the depression was higher commodity prices. The AAA took a supply-side approach by restricting output and holding stocks of commodities. By contrast, Thomas's amendment offered a demand-side response by increasing the amount of money and ensuring an 'honest dollar' that was fair to both creditor and debtor.

When the president wanted monetary expansion, he should authorize the Federal Reserve to purchase $3 billion of government bonds using 'open market operations'. The result would be an increase in the money supply and a drop in interest rates that would stimulate consumption and invest- ment. If monetary easing proved ineffective, the president could authorize the Treasury to issue $3 billion of bank notes or reduce the gold content of the dollar by up to 50 per cent – that is, from $20.67 an ounce to anything up to $41.34. As a concession to Senator Key Pittman (D: Nevada) – a lead- ing advocate of the monetization of silver – the government would also accept silver for the payment of war debts. On 18 April 1933, Roosevelt supported the Thomas amendment – to the horror of Warburg who argued that the proposal was 'completely hare-brained and irresponsible' and would lead to 'uncontrolled inflation and complete chaos'. Lewis Douglas, Director of Budget, went still further: 'this is the end of western civilization.' They scolded Roosevelt as 'a perverse and particularly backward school- boy', but the president ignored the warnings with his usual insouciance. The amendment passed the Senate by fifty-five votes to thirty-five on 28 April 1933.[12] Moley realized that things had changed, and that 'for the first time in history, talk of a cheaper dollar was not the monopoly of populistic farmers . . . This time it came from urban politicians, college professors and even some of the more prominent businessmen.'[13]

At the time, some commentators suspected that Roosevelt accepted the Thomas amendment reluctantly to contain demands by Congress for inflationary action. A more plausible explanation is that Roosevelt used Burton Wheeler to create fear of uncontrolled inflation and then claim that he was containing the risk with the Thomas amendment, which gave him the control over the money supply that he wanted.[14] In their later, hostile accounts, Moley and Tugwell presented Roosevelt as vacillating and indecisive, listening to an eclectic mix of advisers without consistency. In fact, Roosevelt had a long-standing interest in monetary issues, particu- larly the ideas of William Trufant Foster and Waddill Catchings. In the late 1920s, they argued for monetary policy and public spending in response to recessions. They rejected the assumption of classical econom- ics that supply created its own demand, and instead argued that there could be under-consumption and hence over-capacity and depression. Their interpretation differed from the British under-consumptionist John Hobson, to whom the issue was the distribution of income and wealth with the proposed solution of redistributive taxation. To Foster and Catchings, the major issue was a lack of co-ordination between decisions to save and decisions to invest. Savings disrupted the flow of money by extracting it from circulation; they claimed that if firms used it to invest rather than paying dividends, consumers would not have the means to purchase the increased volume of goods. The solution to this 'dilemma of thrift' was to increase the supply of money to ensure 'consumers somehow obtain enough money, year in and year out, to buy the goods as rapidly as they are produced'. Decisions to save and invest would remain in the hands of individuals, with the government filling the gap by public works and injecting the right amount of new money into the economy to sustain prices and employment. In their view, public debt was not a serious concern, for it meant the American people collectively owed themselves money and secured more public assets. Although professional economists were sceptical, this analysis appealed to Roosevelt.[15]

During his term as Governor of New York from 1929 to 1932, Roosevelt was also interested in the ideas of Irving Fisher, an economist at Yale, and of George Warren, a specialist in agriculture and dairy farming who advised him and Henry Morgenthau on their estates in the Hudson valley. Fisher stressed the role of money in stabilizing the economy. Central bankers should provide sufficient money to prevent prices falling and triggering a vicious circle of debt-deflation. As prices and wages fell, people were less able to pay their debts, so that they cut other spending, leading to distress selling and default which could eventually undermine the financial system. Here was the reason for the depth of the depression. If the Federal Reserve had instead reflated prices back to the average level at which debt had been contracted, the debt-deflation cycle could have been broken. Fisher argued that the gold standard meant it was not possible to maintain constant purchasing power at home through an active use of monetary policy; it should be abandoned in favour of floating exchange rates.[16] Warren took a similar line. He claimed that commodity prices rose during times of gold discoveries and fell when commodity output exceeded gold production. There were only two ways out of the depression: deflation, by waiting for debts to be written off so that debt levels came down to the price level; or reflation, by raising prices to the debt level. At a time of falling prices, and in the absence of gold discoveries, he advocated raising the price of gold, using controlled inflation to overcome prolonged deflation, without any need for increasing the government bureaucracy.[17]

Felix Frankfurter, an adviser to Roosevelt and later member of the Supreme Court, realized that the approach implied 'a managed currency along the lines of Maynard Keynes'. Warburg sneered that Keynes's ideas provided 'a scientific backing, if Keynes can be called scientific'. More significant than any direct influence from Keynes, Roosevelt could see that leaving gold had helped recovery in Britain and he was under domestic pressure to act on prices. He was willing to give the new monetary policy a try – arguably something he had been hinting at when he referred in his inaugural address to 'adequate but sound currency'.[18]

The meetings with MacDonald and Herriot coincided with this shift in American policy. MacDonald was less concerned about the turn of events and his joint statement with Roosevelt on 26 April expressed their 'like purpose and a close similarity of method' for the World Monetary and Economic Conference. They felt that 'the necessity for an increase in the general level of commodity prices was recognized as primary and funda-mental', to be followed 'when circumstances permit' by an international monetary standard that would not depress prices. They found 'reassur-ance of unity of purpose and method'. Roosevelt was never one for consistency, and the joint statement with the Italian finance minister on 6 May said that 'a fixed measure of exchange values must be re-established in the world and we believe that this measure must be gold'. When Roosevelt made vague proposals to Herriot to stabilize the pound, dollar and franc, the French feared that he would stabilize at a low rate that would be inflationary – and the British did not wish to abandon their abil-ity to set the exchange rate of the pound. The opportunity passed and the joint statement issued by Herriot and Roosevelt only referred to the 're-establishment of a normal financial and monetary situation'.[19] As we will see, the idea of stabilization of the three currencies reappeared during the conference and was finally agreed in 1936.

Hitler did not accept the invitation to travel to Washington, and sent Hjalmar Schacht, president of the Reichsbank and his chief economic adviser. Schacht took control of Germany's preparations for the confer-ence and was steering a middle course between the concern of the foreign minister, Konstantin von Neurath, for international approval and the aggressive economic nationalism of Alfred Hugenberg, the economics minister and leader of the National People's Party. Schacht's role in sta-bilizing the German monetary system after hyperinflation and his wide foreign experience meant that he was welcomed in Washington, where he soon gained an advantage. His priority was to find a solution to Ger-many's large debts. In public, he claimed that he had no intention of defaulting on the debt to the United States, but he informed Hull and Roosevelt that Germany's large trade deficit with the United States caused by American protectionism made it impossible to earn dollars to service the debt. Schacht used Hull's commitment to free trade to claim tacit accep-tance of a debt moratorium. The Americans had a different understanding, for excusing German debt would be unpopular at a time when farmers and homeowners were threatened with foreclosure on their debts and mort-gages. Berlin retreated from a public announcement of a moratorium, but

Schacht had created a clear impression that it was the only option. On his return to Berlin, he said that no foreign exchange was available for obligations existing at the time of the banking crisis of July 1931. By claiming that the suspension was temporary, Schacht could use resumption of payment as a political and economic lever in talks with the United States.[20]

Roosevelt failed to provide a clear lead for the conference as options were debated in Washington and he concentrated on domestic policies. He selected a delegation that covered most views and did not consult Hull – the leader of the delegation – on its membership, which he was alleged to have chosen in a 'light-hearted mood'. On one side were Hull and the State Department, who were 'little concerned about the domestic policy but who want to keep the rest of the world sweet-tempered'. Hull set off for London with a draft bill to facilitate trade agreements and reduce tariffs, and he was reassured by the temporary truce on tariffs that had been recommended by the commission of experts and accepted for the duration of the conference. However, Roosevelt realized that he could not introduce the bill at the same time as controversial legislation on the National Recovery Administration and AAA. On the way to London, Hull received a message from Roosevelt in which he said that he fully supported the proposal but that the political situation prevented its submission to Congress. Hull's mood was not helped by Roosevelt's appointment of Moley to the post of Assistant Secretary of State in March 1933, without a salary and reporting directly to the president. Moley's presence in London was a source of friction as the two battled for authority, for the Brains Trust gave precedence to domestic policy. Other members of the delegation represented a variety of views that were not easily reconciled. The vice-chairman, James Cox, had some experience as a member of the Preparatory Commission. He was in favour of low tariffs but orthodox on monetary issues. Senator James Couzens of Michigan, a 'self-made and pernickety millionaire', wanted high tariffs and 'soft' money, as did Pittman, chairman of the Senate Foreign Relations Committee, who spent most of the conference drunk, at one point chasing the State Department's Herbert Feis in a rage, brandishing a knife. Roosevelt's intentions were unclear. Was he prevaricating, misleading Hull, or realistically delaying until the Congressional situation allowed him to support action on trade? Was he trying to make the delegation inclusive – or so divided that the conference in London could not interfere with his room for manoeuvre in Washington?[21] H. G. Wells captured the puzzlement felt by those hoping that the new president

would speak plainly to all mankind . . . But the one thing he failed to do was to speak plainly . . . Was it wise to be tactical when all the world was in need of plain speech and simple directive ideas? . . . He listened, it seemed, to his advisors, but was he not also listening to everybody?[22]

Moley later commented that even 'a collection of the political geniuses of all the ages' would have had difficulties in the circumstances of 1933 – and 'the odds were a million to one that the delegation Roosevelt chose could not negotiate satisfactorily on the basis of these confused, confusing, shifting purposes.'[23] Hull had little chance of success. The French were dubious about even the temporary truce on tariffs, given that other countries had secured an advantage by devaluing their currencies, and the British were committed to imperial preference.[24] Tugwell complained that Hull's 'rambling, lisping speeches on the evils of protection, and his extolling of the old *laissez faire* liberal internationalism have become harder and harder to bear'.[25] Moley dismissed Hull as a man with a 'mush mind' and went so far as to tell Roosevelt that Pittman was 'the only member of the delegation able intellectually and aggressively to present your views to the conference'. When Hull saw the message, he exploded: 'That piss-ant Moley! Here he curled up at my feet like a hunting dog and then he goes and bites me in the ass!'[26] Feis, one of the most perceptive officials in London, was sympathetic to Hull, but had doubts about his ability to handle the conference. He was 'kindly, reflective and idealistic', operating 'in a vacuum of his own making, repeating his generalities'. He recalled that the 'confusion over jurisdiction and policy was incessant'.[27] Hull could not cope with the dissension in London and confused messages from Roosevelt, who spent most of the conference on his yacht in Nantucket Harbor. Not surprisingly, Hull seemed 'old and tired and worn . . . pretty overwhelmed with the magnitude of the task'.[28]

THE WORLD MONETARY AND ECONOMIC CONFERENCE, 1933

The conference opened on 12 June 1933 and expired on 27 July. It was a huge affair, with representatives from 66 countries filling 708 seats in the central hall of the Geological Museum in London. Discussions were aided – or hindered – by a bar below the conference hall where delegations listed their preferred drinks – though one British newspaper thought there was less chance of agreeing on 'world restoratives'. Henry Morgenthau Snr, who had served as ambassador to the Ottoman empire during the war, had little confidence: 'This is not a congress of free minds working to solve the world problems'; every delegation had instructions to pursue national advantage, and few could proceed without consulting their home government.[29]

The conference got off to an inauspicious start. In February 1933, the British had submitted a memorandum to Hull that insisted that progress rested on settlement of war debts, which were 'an insuperable barrier to economic and financial reconstruction, and there is no prospect of the World Economic Conference making progress if this barrier cannot be removed'.[30] The Americans believed that the issue had already been resolved by the settlement reached at Lausanne the previous year and that further concessions would be unfair to the American taxpayer. The French and British had a different view. They had reluctantly accepted an end to reparations at Lausanne on the understanding that there would be no further demands for inter-Allied debt repayment – but in December 1931, Congress had passed a resolution rejecting the idea 'that any of the indebtedness of foreign countries to the United States should in any manner be cancelled or reduced'.[31] This clear statement did not stop the British government from continuing to press the issue. The American embassy in London reported that

> while [the British] recognize the desirability and importance of cooperating as closely as possible with us in dealing with world problems as a whole they have had only one real preoccupation in their economic and financial relations with us, namely, the war debt issue ... [T]hey are trying to persuade the world ... that war debts are ... the chief cause of our economic difficulties. The consequence they draw from this is that debts are the primary question to be solved if the Economic Conference is to be successful and that our failure to cooperate in a solution – and to them a solution means only one thing, namely, substantial cancellation – we will bear the onus for any failure of the Conference.[32]

The prediction was correct.

Ramsay MacDonald started his opening speech on 12 June by referring to the disruption of international commerce – without commenting on Britain's adoption of imperial preference – before turning to war debts. He admitted they were not on the agenda but insisted that they 'must be dealt with before every obstacle to the general recovery has been removed, and it must be taken up without delay by the nations concerned'. A few days later, Neville Chamberlain – the Chancellor of the Exchequer – announced that he would make only a token payment of $10m, paid in silver secured from the Government of India, on the next instalment of the war debt to America – a decision that would create problems given Congress's resolution of December 1931. Roosevelt agreed to accept the 'token' payment as an indication that the debt would be honoured and not to treat it as a default. The deal had cross-party support in Britain, and Churchill welcomed Roosevelt's 'sagacious and far-seeing courage'. To many Americans, it was a warning against dealing with mendacious Europeans and the perils of international involvement. Will Rogers, the popular American journalist and actor, captured the American sense of frustration: the conference was a plot to cancel debts owed to America, to reduce American tariffs and to stabilize the dollar above European currencies. 'If things don't pick up in their own countries, they'll think up something else to blame America for, and have another conference.'[33]

Hull was horrified – and his demeanour was not improved by Chamberlain's defence of both imperial preference and devaluation of the pound. The British government had no desire to return to the gold standard associated with deflation in the 1920s, and argued that currency stability was not possible until the world economy returned to prosperity. Chamberlain explained Britain's decision to leave gold because of the difficulties of cutting costs and the damage it caused; and he stressed the virtues of cheap money and credit that reduced debt service, stimulated recovery and encouraged a return to rising prices. Although there was a need for a satisfactory international standard, he laid down onerous conditions for a return to gold: an increase in prices to bring them into line with costs; the removal of reparations, war debts and restrictions on trade that led to economic breakdown; and reform of the gold standard by limiting gold to international settlements, reducing gold reserves, and co-operation between central bankers.[34]

Hull's response was an emotional speech, 'shot with piety in the best American tradition', in which he called for co-operation between nations to resolve the economic problems facing the world:

> If we are to succeed, narrow and self-defeating selfishness must be banished from every human heart within the council chamber. If – which God forbid! – any nation should obstruct and wreck this great Conference, with the short-sighted notion that some of its favoured local interests might temporarily profit, while thus indefinitely delaying aid for the distressed in every country, that nation will merit the execration of mankind.
>
> Ignoring all realities, all nations have pursued the policy of economic isolation – each futilely and foolishly striving to live a hermit's life.

Domestic policies, such as those adopted by Roosevelt, might help if linked with the restoration of international trade as a way of raising prices and prosperity. 'All excesses in the structure of trade barriers should be removed. All unfair trade methods and practices should be abandoned.' Hull then strayed into monetary issues, where he called for an immediate policy which will give the greatest possible measure of stability for the period during which the groundwork will be laid for enduring reform. Simultaneously all the nations must stimulate the natural sources of employment, restart the wheels of industry and commerce, and so build up consumer power that a rise of the price level will of necessity follow.

Then the Conference must face the vexed problem of a permanent international monetary standard and lay down the proper function of the metals, gold and silver, in the operations of such a standard in the future.[35]

Hull was passionate in denouncing economic nationalism – but was he speaking for the president? Feis thought that 'Hull was listening to his own heart, not to the pulse of Washington.'[36]

Hull had good reason to be overwhelmed. Messages from Washington were difficult to interpret, and Feis likened the atmosphere of the conference to 'a cafeteria crush rather than a cohesive gathering with determined common purposes and roughly similar ideas about the ways in which they might be achieved'.[37] Hull knew what his heart was telling him – but did Roosevelt know his own mind? When Tugwell looked back on 1933, he was puzzled by Roosevelt's indecision between Hull's pursuit of free trade and the Brains Trust's 'program of domestic recovery which depended utterly on non-interference from outside. We were temporary isolationists.' Roosevelt, he thought, was 'not then defending any policy; he was trying to arrive at one.'[38]

Matters were not helped when Moley arrived after the conference started and announced he would handle the delegation. Feis complained that Moley treated everyone, including Hull, in an off-hand manner and acted like 'a triumphant political general'. Feis confided in his diary that Moley possessed 'a mind which does no systematic solutions or even systematic procedure, but catches at ideas ... He sometimes asks others to think through; he does not do so himself. He is too blithe on important matters, too disposed to pass them over with a jest.'[39] For his part, Moley was in an invidious position, and claimed to sympathize with Hull over his treatment by Roosevelt whose 'half-encouragements and half-disavowals had left Hull and the rest of the world completely bewildered'.[40] Walter Lippmann's assessment was depressing. The delegates did not know what Roosevelt wanted; no one understood monetary questions properly; they were divided, and 'so frequently repudiated that they were demoralized'. 'How can a delegation which lacks authority, which lacks technical competence, which lacks unity, which lacks contact with the President, hope to undertake the kind of difficult negotiation for far-reaching reforms which the President desires? It cannot be done.'[41]

The World Monetary and Economic Conference was a model of what not to do. It dealt with too many issues at one time, with too many participants, no sense of priorities, and no clear proposals to reconcile different positions. Each country pursued its own interests and beggared their neighbour in hostile trade blocs and competitive devaluation. Hull put the matter well in his reflections on the conference: 'We moved in vicious circles. I wanted tariff reductions but could offer nothing satisfactory myself. France and the gold-bloc countries wanted currency stabilization before they would consider tariff reductions, but I could not talk about it. Britain and others wanted debt settlement, but I could not discuss it.'[42] The negotiations were deadlocked before they started, for each participant would only move if another surrendered something that was non-negotiable. The major participants lacked a shared conceptual understanding of the problems. The British were wedded to a managed float of the pound, imperial preference and settlement of war debts. The Americans wished to avoid discussion of war debts and disliked imperial preference. The French were committed to gold and had defaulted on war debts; they welcomed Mac-Donald's intervention but opposed British currency policy. The French government insisted that currency stabilization was vital before considering trade policy, and farmers' support for agricultural protection meant that concessions on tariffs were out of the question. The German delegation was attempting to reduce foreign anxiety about the new government's intentions, not least about its stance in the Disarmament Conference being held in Geneva. Hitler's ambition to rearm required German economic recovery. He had no intention of reducing tariffs or losing control over monetary policy, for he wanted a nationalist economy unconstrained by international diplomacy. His aim in London was to avoid provoking more hostility on economic issues and to allay concerns about German intentions. The attempt of von Neurath to pursue this line was undermined by Hugenberg, who had insisted on joining the German delegation. The nationalist demanded *lebensraum* in eastern Europe and the restoration of colonies in Africa – a claim that was disavowed by Berlin. Although Schacht was not a member of the delegation, he was in London to discuss a settlement with Germany's British creditors. He reached a deal with London bankers that he would service debt owed to countries with which Germany had a trade surplus, i.e., Britain and not the United States. The result was to divide Britain and the United States, and to strengthen the Nazi regime. To Hitler, Anglo-American co-operation was a threat; by contrast, a powerful British empire could complement a strong German Reich. Despite Hugenberg's intervention, Germany secured an advantage outside the deliberations of the World Monetary and Economic Conference.[43]

As the conference started, the American attitude on monetary policy was still in flux. The AAA with the Thomas amendment became law on 12 May 1933, and Roosevelt had the power – if he wished – to devalue the dollar. Montagu Norman, the governor of the Bank of England, was horrified at the turn in American policy. Britain had left the gold standard because of its weak financial position; there was no reason for America – a major creditor with a strong balance of payments – to abandon gold and provoke currency warfare. Uncertainties over American intentions towards the dollar cast a shadow over the conference. The British and French pressed Roosevelt to take action to stabilize the dollar, at least for the duration of the conference – an opportunity they had spurned a few months previously. They now suggested a separate tripartite meeting, and Roosevelt agreed to send George Harrison of the Federal Reserve Bank of New York and Oliver Sprague, special adviser to the Treasury, to negotiate stabilization. James Warburg, who was in London as financial adviser to the American delegation, saw an opportunity to prevent the devaluation of the dollar. Shortly before the main conference opened, the central bankers met at the Bank of England where differences of opinion were apparent. Norman realized that the British Treasury was in favour of holding down the pound. By contrast, Clément Moret, the governor of the Banque de France, wished to retain gold and rightly pointed out that his counterparts were trying to do 'two things at the same time, namely to get the benefits of inflation and yet have exchange stability'. Nevertheless, on 15 June agreement was reached by Harrison, Norman and Moret to stabilize currencies for the duration of the conference at a median rate of £1 to $4; the British and Americans would not allow the exchange rate to rise above $4.12 or fall below $3.88. It was also agreed that 'the ultimate objective' was to return to gold. The deal seemed to be a conspiracy of central bankers meeting in private at the Bank of England, without regard to the wishes of all their governments, and in breach of the open diplomacy of the League.

The agreement provoked worries in Washington that the policy of raising prices would be reversed. Indeed, seventy-five congressmen and ten senators petitioned Roosevelt to send Father Coughlin to the conference. Roosevelt was concerned that the conference was falling into the hands of bankers and told Hull to concentrate on the main issues, rather than demands for 'exchange stability by banker-influenced cabinets'. The agreement started to unravel with an American statement that temporary stabilization was 'untimely' and that a rise in American prices would be more beneficial. Moley had been instructed to reach an agreement provided that nothing was done to constrain price increases: it was finalized on 30 June, with the aim of preventing a collapse of the conference and allowing central banks to co-operate in stopping currency speculation.[44]

Roosevelt responded with his 'bombshell' of 3 July 1933 – a blunt, angry wireless message. He argued that the agreement was 'unwise from political and psychological standpoints to permit limitation of our action':

> I would regard it as a catastrophe amounting to a world tragedy if the great Conference of Nations, called to bring about a more real and permanent financial stability and a greater prosperity to the masses of all Nations, should, in advance of any serious effort to consider these broader problems, allow itself to be diverted by the proposal of a purely artificial and temporary experiment affecting the monetary exchange of a few Nations only. Such action, such diversion, shows a singular lack of proportion and a failure to remember the larger purposes for which the Economic Conference originally was called together.

He called for the rejection of the 'old fetishes of so-called international bankers', for 'the sound internal economic system of a Nation is a greater factor in its well-being than the price of its currency'. The younger Morgenthau, who had been pressing Roosevelt to follow George Warren's proposals and to devalue, was delighted. 'We were tied up hand and fist at the London conference. We had to break it. He broke it.'[45]

The president set out the basis for future discussions. 'The government of the United States sees no inconsistency between its program for economic recovery and international cooperation for the purpose of restoring prosperity throughout the world.' In reality, his priorities lay at home and not with Hull's internationalism:

> The measures taken in the United States involve: lifting the price level to restore a more equitable relationship between debtors and creditors; provision of a medium of exchange which shall be substantially equal in purchasing power from one generation to another; stimulation of business activity and reemployment of idle millions through an immediate program of public works and reorganization of relations between government and business; managing of production to meet actual needs for farm products; creation of new purchasing power by a concerted effort to raise wages and to spread employment through restriction of hours of work; and a genuine effort to balance current expenditures and current receipts so that the credit of the government can be maintained.

Such policies were 'desirable not only for the United States but for other countries as well', for by a united effort, 'the firmest basis would be laid for world-wide recovery, and international cooperation would immediately become possible. A substantial similarity of standards and of programs for recovery would remove any necessity which may exist for closing our borders to the goods of other nations and for most currency discrepancies and fluctuations.'[46] In other words, if each country took action to stimulate its domestic economy, the world would be saved.

Keynes was delighted by Roosevelt's bombshell and announced that the president was 'magnificently right' in his statement, which provided an opportunity 'to achieve something better than the miserable confusion and unutterable waste of opportunity in which an obstinate adherence to ancient rules of thumb has engulfed us'. He felt that Roosevelt was asking the conference to create 'the managed currency of the future'. Rather than following Europeans who 'cling fanatically to their gold perches' and 'see no virtue in a rising price level', Roosevelt offered a way to save capitalism by putting 'men to work by all the means at our disposal until prices have risen to a level appropriate to the existing debts and other obligations fixed in terms of money'. Keynes was unduly optimistic, for the conference ended without any achievement – though he was a partial exception, for he made a profit of £314 on a gala performance of the ballet *Coppélia* at the Royal Opera House, with his wife, Lydia Lobokova, dancing in public for the last time.[47] MacDonald was reduced to a state of distress and nervous collapse, veering between anger towards Roosevelt and despair at the failure of the conference which would bring the world to ruin.[48] 'There was an element of Greek tragedy in the killing of the London conference,' remarked Moley, 'for Roosevelt destroyed something of which he was one of the parents.'[49]

For more than a month, the conference had engaged in largely fruitless discussion that lacked focus and coherence. After seven plenary sessions, it broke into meetings of the Monetary and Financial Commission, chaired by Cox, and the Economic Commission chaired by Colijn. The Monetary and Financial Commission's subcommission on immediate measures was divided between countries on and off gold, and between debtors and creditors. The second subcommission was itself divided into two subcommittees on silver, where Pittman secured an agreement to stabilize its price, and gold, which was stymied by Roosevelt's intervention. The Economic Commission was no more successful. One subcommission turned to commercial policy, including the use of the most favoured nation principle, reduction of tariffs, and abolition of exchange controls and trade restrictions. Agreement to remove 'excessive' tariffs and 'in principle' to remove trade restrictions were, as Hull realized, 'little more than verbal' given that each country argued for the removal of barriers against its own trade while defending its own restrictions. Another subcommission on the co-ordination and marketing of commodities reached no conclusion by the end of the conference, other than a hope to continue discussion. A third subcommission on the use of subsidies and bounties, and indirect protective measures such as veterinary standards or trademarks, was no more successful, as countries criticized others and defended their own practices. In the final days of the conference, Hull proposed an agreement to reduce tariffs by the unconditional most favoured nation principle, and to continue the tariff truce. His report to Roosevelt attempted to put a positive spin on the conference as indicating that the major countries understood 'there must be world economic rehabilitation' by removing extreme trade barriers. He hoped that the work of the conference would continue with an executive committee representing the commissions and a bureau of the most important countries, with meetings to deal with particular topics or regions, or even to hold a further full session.[50] In reality, the initiative came to nothing, and the delegates spent their time talking past each other.

The world drifted into currency blocs based on gold, the dollar and the British sterling area comprising countries, mainly in the empire, that kept most of their reserves in sterling – to which their currencies were pegged – in return for access to British capital markets. Although the French had kept their distance from other gold standard countries during negotiations with the British and American central bankers, in July they came together with Italy, Switzerland, Belgium, the Netherlands and Poland in a formal commitment to gold, with co-operation between their central banks, which had five of the nine board members at the BIS. Unlike imperial preference, the gold bloc failed to promote trade between its members and depressed trade with the rest of the world. Meanwhile, Germany stayed on gold without joining the bloc. Schacht wished to maintain monetary independence through the use of exchange controls and calculated that German reserves were sufficient provided that agreement was reached on commercial debts. A number of other countries in central and eastern Europe similarly adopted exchange controls and strict regulation.[51]

Where Britain did agree with France and Germany was in suspending debt payments to America. Naturally, the Americans saw self-interest. Senator Hiram Johnson, an isolationist Republican, had opposed Hoover's moratorium as an incentive to irresponsibility in Europe that only benefitted Wall Street. The Europeans, and above all Britain, were accused of avoiding payment and shifting the costs to the American taxpayer. In 1934, the Foreign Securities (or Johnson) Act demanded full rather than token payments and closed the New York money and securities markets to any country that was behind on its payments. Roosevelt's position was ambiguous. Did he reluctantly accept the Act to prevent a more serious confrontation with isolationists? Or did he support it, as the State Department argued, 'as a weapon in dealing with these European welchers'? Johnson had supported Roosevelt's presidential candidacy in return for a promise not to reduce debts at the conference in 1933. Political calculations meant it was sensible for Roosevelt to support the Johnson Act and avoid any responsibility for negotiating with Europeans over the debt.

In Britain, the question was what should the government do in response? The British ambassador favoured paying in full, in the hope that a more realistic settlement could be reached in the future. He reported to London that, 'I detest spending the hard earned millions of my Government and I am afraid that all of you over there will say that I only want to pitch good money after bad ... [but] the money would be well spent taking the long view of policy.' The advice from the British Treasury was 'lie low and say nuffin', in the hope that Washington would be realistic and accept partial payment. Faced by a choice between resuming full payment or making no payment, the government announced in June 1934 that Britain would cease payments as a matter of altruism: to continue to pay would undermine the financial system and, as MacDonald noted, 'be treason to the whole world. We have to take upon ourselves the thankless task of putting an end to the folly of continuing to pay.' To Chamberlain, the Americans 'played a mug's game in depriving themselves of $40 million which they would have pouched if they hadn't given themselves the pleasure of passing the Johnson Act'. It is certainly plausible that the British government had the capacity to pay. The real concern, as in the United States, was public sentiment: the demand for full payment was seen as unreasonable in London, just as failure to pay was seen as irresponsible in Washington. The stand-off was to cause problems as war became more likely. The Johnson Act banned further loans to any country in default and the Neutrality Act of 1935 prohibited the export of 'arms, ammunition and implements of war' to foreign nations who were at war. When the latter Act was renewed in 1937, Roosevelt secured a concession of 'cash and carry' so that, at presidential discretion, countries could acquire from the United States any items except armaments on condition they were paid for at once and carried in non-American ships.[52]

ROOSEVELT DECIDES AT LAST

The World Monetary and Economic Conference marked the end of Moley's career at the State Department, for he was implicated in the agreement on currency stabilization that was rejected by Roosevelt, and he had deeply offended Hull. He was exiled to the Department of Justice and soon resigned.[53] James Warburg also resigned and started a vitriolic campaign against Roosevelt. In *The Money Muddle* (1934), he likened Roosevelt's monetary policy to an incompetent doctor, for 'in seeking to cure an infected toe, he has come perilously close to amputating the whole leg'. He went still further that year in *It's Up to Us* when he compared the New Deal to European totalitarianism, and in 1936 he claimed that Roosevelt had 'substituted for the platform of the Democratic party a strange mixture of Socialist and Fascist principles'.[54] Most orthodox economists and bankers agreed, even if their language was more temperate. Bankers doubted Fisher's view that the quantity of money directly affected prices and pointed to other factors such as harvests and technological change. Edwin Kemmerer, the 'money doctor' to indebted countries in Latin America, supported the gold standard. He felt that the real issue was not the quantity of money, for there was sufficient currency and credit. Rather, loss of business confidence led to a fall in the velocity of circulation of money so that prices fell. The solution was to restore confidence by remaining loyal to gold, sound money and fiscal responsibility.[55]

Roosevelt removed opponents of his monetary policy at the Treasury and the Federal Reserve and pressed ahead with an aggressive policy of devaluation. In August 1933, Warren reported to the Treasury that 'I believe there is only one way to end the depression, and that is an adequate devaluation of the dollar. Other things may help, but they cannot succeed without a reduction in the gold value of the dollar.' He returned from a visit to Europe convinced that it was 'a choice between a rise in prices or a rise in dictators'. Hitler was the product of deflation that undermined domestic institutions; by contrast, the British had successfully raised prices by devaluing. Politicians from the cotton South agreed that prices needed to rise. In September 1933, one Democrat warned that unless the administration took action, farmers would change the form of government, and Elmer Thomas predicted a protest march of a million men. These threats were bluster, but Roosevelt worried about an agrarian revolt if he did not increase prices. He decided to act.[56]

On 29 August 1933, Executive Order 6261 authorized the Treasury to buy new minted gold for sale to foreigners at 'the best price obtainable in the free gold markets of the world'. The intention was to increase the price of gold and hence raise domestic prices – but the limited amount of gold available for purchase within the United States would not affect the world price of gold, the exchange rate of the dollar, or the price of commodities. After a couple of months, it was clear that the plan was not working, and Roosevelt decided to take drastic action by setting the price of gold. In his 'fireside chat' of 22 October 1933, he announced his new gold policy:

> Our dollar is now altogether too greatly influenced by the accidents of international trade, by the internal policies of other Nations and by political disturbance in other continents. Therefore the United States must take firmly in its own hands the control of the gold value of our dollar. This is necessary in order to prevent dollar disturbances from swinging us away from our ultimate goal, namely, the continued recovery of our commodity prices.[57]

He had to circumvent the Gold Act of 1900, which set the official price of gold at $20.67 and made it illegal for the government to buy gold at a higher price. He turned to the Reconstruction Finance Corporation (RFC), a body set up by President Hoover in 1932 to provide liquidity to banks. Roosevelt set a price for gold and the RFC offered debentures at a discount which the Treasury then bought at face value. By this means, gold was nominally bought at the official price, with the higher price secured by the price difference on the debentures. The ruse did not convince Dean Acheson at the Treasury who thought it 'a sham and a violation of law'. He resigned and was replaced by Morgenthau Jnr as Under-Secretary of the Treasury and who soon became Secretary of the Treasury – a post he held until July 1945.[58]

For the next three months, Jesse Jones of the RFC met the president, Morgenthau and Warren daily over breakfast to buy gold at whatever price they decided that morning. There was an air of levity about the exercise. One day Roosevelt proposed – presumably in jest – that a rise of 21 cents would bring luck as three times seven.[59] The purpose was serious: to force the dollar down and increase prices. It did not work as well as expected. Jacob Viner, an economist at the University of Chicago who joined the Treasury, pointed out that modest purchases by the RFC did not change the international price of gold, and that Roosevelt's setting the price for gold purchases was causing uncertainty and speculation. He urged a move from Warren's and Fisher's programme of monetary expansion and devaluation. Keynes agreed: the existing policy was a 'game of blind man's bluff with exchange speculators' that undermined confidence. The solution was to abandon attempts to influence prices by buying gold and to use the Thomas amendment to make a one-off change in the gold value of the dollar. Establishing a definite price for gold would have the virtue of stabilizing the dollar rather than continuing Warren's aggressive policy of increasing prices, which led to speculation and political difficulties with creditors. In January 1934, the Gold Reserve Act gave Roosevelt the power to fix the dollar at between 50 and 60 per cent of the current value of $20.67 for an ounce of gold. He immediately set the new price of gold at $35, which was to be maintained by an Exchange Stabilization Fund on the British model. The dollar was devalued to 59.06 per cent of its pre-1933 value, and stayed at the same gold price until 1971.[60]

Roosevelt's monetary policy faced a constitutional challenge. Unlike in Britain, most contracts contained a clause that payments could be requested in gold. If the gold clause were honoured, private firms would be obliged to pay about $100bn of debts in gold, which would lead to bankruptcy. Similarly, repayment of about $20bn of government debt in gold would require higher taxes or cuts in spending. In both cases, the outcome would be a massive transfer of wealth from debtors to creditors which was not politically appealing. Warren believed that Congress could invalidate the gold clause or, failing that, tax the profits of creditors. In his view, 'ten million unemployed is far more serious matter than the gold clause'. Roosevelt argued that the debt could not be repaid in gold, for there was only about $3bn to $4bn-worth of gold in the world – missing the point that the debt could be repaid in dollars equivalent to the new price of gold. It was far from clear how the courts would rule and whether their decisions would be consistent.[61]

In June 1933, Congress agreed to the administration's request to pass a joint resolution abolishing the gold clause for past and future contracts, both public and private. Senator William Borah (R: Idaho) urged that 'we must cease to pay tribute to the gold standard at the expense of the citizens . . . these contracts were taken by the purchaser with the understanding that the government had the right to change the monetary system. The citizen must take the loss, must accept whatever Congress says is money.' Roosevelt's critics did not agree and insisted that changing the price of gold was a violation of contracts and an expropriation of wealth. In November 1934, the government decided to seek a ruling from the Supreme Court. The case was heard in January 1935. A ruling to enforce the gold clause would cause economic disaster and political unrest. The possible responses were not appealing. To abandon devaluation and the economic policy of rising prices would have a serious impact on economic recovery. The alternative was to appeal to the people against the Supreme Court. Roosevelt prepared a statement that 'If the policy of the government . . . is to be irrevocably fixed by decisions of the Supreme Court . . . the people would have ceased to be their own rulers' and 'would so imperil the economic and political security of this nation that the legislative and executive officers of the Government must look beyond the narrow letter of contractual obligations'. The result would be a serious constitutional crisis.[62]

The government's case rested on two contentions: it had the constitutional power to coin money and regulate value; and the gold clause was 'contrary to public policy' and would lead to public disorder and financial chaos from which everyone, including bondholders, would suffer. The Supreme Court decided by a narrow margin that private debt could be paid in legal currency, and that the gold clause interfered with the powers granted to Congress. It then ruled, also by a small margin, that abrogating the gold clause was unconstitutional for public debts. However, there was no remedy given that bondholders suffered no loss: prices had fallen so that payment of the full amount would be 'unjustified enrichment'. The argument of necessity was accepted, and a constitutional crisis or a forced return to gold by judicial decision was narrowly averted. The result, as Lippmann commented, was victory but not vindication. The Treasury retained its authority to manage the currency and credit and, as Morgenthau put it, 'the 1934 model gold bullion standard . . . streamlined . . . air flow . . . and knee action . . . It's the one which suits our own need.'[63]

Roosevelt's action meant that sterling was more overvalued against the dollar than it had been before 1931. The British were aggrieved that the president had acted unilaterally without concern for the international consequences.[64] There was also new hope that stabilization might provide the basis for international co-operation. Keynes had welcomed Roosevelt's 'bombshell' in 1933, but he soon worried that the gold-buying programme was creating a gold standard 'on the booze'. He welcomed the decision to stabilize the dollar in January 1934 as a middle course between orthodoxy and Warren's extreme inflation. He hoped that the adoption of a stable gold value of the dollar could permit an international conference on money to 'aim for the future not at rigid gold parities, but at provisional parities from which the parties to the conference would agree not to depart except for substantial reasons arising out of their balance of trade or the exigencies of domestic price policy'. Here was the kernel of Keynes's proposals for a new international monetary system that led to Bretton Woods.[65] In 1934, the leading American architect of the Bretton Woods agreement – Harry Dexter White – joined the US Treasury and recommended a managed currency based on a stable value for the dollar that could be changed if circumstances dictated, with international co-operation to co-ordinate shifts in the value of currencies.[66]

Roosevelt's use of monetary policy to increase prices and break the spiral of debt, deflation and depression had the greatest impact on international economic relations, but it was only one element of his efforts to alleviate the Great Depression. The Agricultural Adjustment Act aimed to control output to increase agricultural prices. The central figure was

Henry Wallace, Secretary of Agriculture from 1933 to 1940 and Vice-President from 1941 to 1945. He advocated an 'ever-normal granary' system to store basic commodities in order to balance demand and supply and create price stability – an idea that went back to the Granger movement of the late nineteenth century. The AAA introduced voluntary production controls to reduce output, with compensation for lost production. In addition, farmers were given 'non-recourse loans' on the security of crops stored with the Commodity Credit Corporation: the farmer forfeited the commodity and kept the loan if the price fell below the support level, or reclaimed the crop for sale if the price rose. This attempt to raise prices was in the interest of farmers, but not of urban consumers.[67] Similarly, the industrial codes of the National Recovery Administration were designed to increase prices and the profits of industrialists and traders.

Higher prices might boost the income of farmers and industrialists, and reduce the real burden of debt, but they would squeeze urban consumers and alienate shoppers (mostly women at this time). The New Deal's aim of increasing prices was in tension with the ambition of boosting purchasing power to overcome under-consumption. An attempt had to be made to reconcile the two ambitions. In 1933, the Home-Owners Loan Corporation offered support to distressed borrowers by giving them a lower interest rate over a long term. The 'codes' of the National Recovery Administration for different industries and trades included consumer representation, and created a Consumer Advisory Board, so that women were co-opted to use their purchasing power to ensure fair prices and labour standards. In the opinion of Gardiner Means, an economist who both served on the Board and advised Wallace, consumer representation 'may well be the key that will open the way to a truly American solution of the problem which is leading other countries in the direction of either fascism or communism'. Wallace's advisers, Mordecai Ezekiel and Paul Appleby, made him realize that agricultural prosperity rested on industrial production, employment and consumption. In May 1939, Wallace introduced food stamps as a way of providing surplus food to unemployed and poor workers on relief, so assisting both consumers and farmers.[68]

Means collaborated with lawyer and economist Adolf Berle in a major study of the modern corporation, which argued that ownership by passive shareholders gave power to a small group of managers. In large, monopolistic firms, wages had been held down in the boom years of the 1920s, and 'administered prices' protected profits even as costs fell, resulting in reduced purchasing power which led to depression. The solution was greater social responsibility by corporations, action to break the power of monopolies, and measures to ensure fair wages for workers and fair prices

THE WORLD MONETARY AND ECONOMIC CONFERENCE, 1933   55

for consumers. Such ideas were central to the Brains Trust. As Tugwell remarked, 'those individuals who insist upon the right to make profits fail to accept the responsibility of stabilizing private investment and of maintaining the continuity of society's producing, selling and consuming operations'. Such sentiments informed Roosevelt's Commonwealth Club speech of September 1932, written by Berle: it called for action to ensure that 'purchasing power is well distributed throughout every group in the Nation'.[69]

The call to redistribute wealth to increase purchasing power by poor members of society came not only from academics in the Brains Trust. It was also taken up by the Democratic populist Senator Huey Long of Louisiana, whose Share our Wealth Society in 1934 soon had 7 million members. In June 1935, Roosevelt responded with a speech to Congress in which he argued that

> The transmission from generation to generation of vast fortunes by will, inheritance or gift is not consistent with the ideal and sentiments of the American People . . . Such accumulations amount to the perpetuation of great and undesirable concentrations of control . . . over the enjoyment and welfare of many, many others. Such inherited economic power is as inconsistent with the ideals of this generation as inherited political power was inconsistent with the ideals of the generation which established our Government.

By 1935, the inheritance tax rate on the largest estates was 70 per cent. The aim was not to maximize revenue, which would have been achieved by a higher rate on smaller estates – it was to break up dynastic wealth. Further, purchasing power was extended by encouraging union recognition and collective bargaining under the National Labor Relations Act of 1935. Organized workers could increase wages and consumption, with a continued role for women consumers to ensure fair wages and standards. The aim was to link higher wages with fair prices that would create a coalition of labour and consumers. Senator Robert Wagner, the sponsor of the Act, saw that unions could correct the 'failures of consumer demand' and offer 'democratic self-help by industry and labor instead of courting the pitfalls of an arbitrary or totalitarian state'.[70]

This 'second New Deal' marked the beginning of a major shift in the distribution of wealth that was taken much further in the Second World War (see Figure 22, page 766). These shifts in the distribution of economic power within the United States were crucial to the rebuilding of the international economic order. Global co-operation had a greater chance of success when economic benefits were more widely shared.

*

The World Monetary and Economic Conference, in the opinion of H. G. Wells, 'became by imperceptible transitions a World Economic Conflict ... Never did so valiant a beginning peter out so completely.'[71] Neville Chamberlain complained that 'there has never been a case of a Conference being so completely smashed by one of the participants'.[72] The result was a 'barren harvest', to use the title of The Economist's devastating summary of the conference's inadequacies: 'Faced with the greatest economic crisis of recent history, the effective solution of which can by general consent only be achieved by international action, the assembled statesmen have patently failed to deal with any one of the major issues with which they were directly concerned.' Nothing had been achieved on trade and tariffs, on debt, or on monetary stabilization:

> It is perhaps a small redeeming feature of this mournful catalogue of negatives that no one country can be cast for the role of scapegoat; for though the uncertainty of the American situation has unquestionably been the greatest stumbling-block to effective work, one country after another has by its attitude placed obstacles in the way of the formulation of an international plan and displayed a lack of willingness to subordinate its preconceived ideas to a general plan. No great power has in fact done more than hover at the threshold of a new international world without the courage and resolution to push open the door.[73]

Keynes was equally dismissive of the conference: there was 'no cat in the bag, no rabbits in the hat – no brains in the head'.[74] To a greater or lesser degree, countries turned to economic nationalism – to Latin American import substituting industrialization, British imperial preference, American domestic recovery, Soviet socialism in one country, or to the expansionary, militaristic self-sufficiency of Italian Fascists, Japanese militarists and the Third Reich.

The experience of the World Monetary and Economic Conference provided an object lesson for any future conference. In 1925, Arthur Salter had warned the League of the likelihood of deadlock in any conference of politicians rather than experts. The result would be resolutions 'so limited, tortuous, qualified by exceptions and weakened by reserves as to be useless and almost unintelligible – in fact, perhaps worse than useless as tending to crystallize and give some kind of international acceptance to a retrograde stage of world policy'. E. O. G. Shann, an Australian delegate at the conference, agreed. A gathering of politicians allowed enthusiasts to claim they were 'doing something', with experts hand-picked to provide support for their schemes. Further, the American abandonment of gold meant participants 'had to continue the discussions of crucial issues with the whole world looking in at the windows'. In his view, 'the public discussion of unresolved discords' was likely to lead to deadlock.[75] The lesson was learned. In discussions leading to Bretton Woods, technical consideration of a single major issue replaced all-encompassing, overlapping discussion of many difficult questions, where failure on one topic would jeopardize agreement on any.

The World Monetary and Economic Conference was a low point from which some progress might be made. Roosevelt contributed to the cycle of beggar-my-neighbour policies, yet gave some hope for Hull's internationalist ambitions. Devaluation allowed attention to turn to the stabilization of the dollar, pound and franc. It also meant that tariff protection was less necessary, for Secretary of Commerce Daniel Roper saw that 'dollar devaluation has put the American tariff on such a heightened level that the United States is now in a better position than it has been for a long time to make partial reductions in duties . . . without inducing destructive competition through enlarged imports'.[76] In addition, the AAA and National Recovery Administration supported domestic agriculture and industry so that the case for protection was less compelling. As we will see in the next chapter, Cordell Hull secured a breakthrough with the Reciprocal Trade Agreements Act (RTAA) of 1934, and Henry Morgenthau secured the stabilization of the dollar, sterling and franc in 1936. Together, these measures started to create a coalition of democratic capitalist societies against authoritarian regimes and to lay the basis for the recreation of a multilateral world economy.

Hjalmar Schacht, president of the Reichsbank, with Adolf Hitler,
at the ceremony to lay the foundation stone for its new building, 5 May 1934.

3

'Beggar my neighbour'

The Failures of the World Economy, 1933–39

'... nations have been taught that their interest consisted in beggaring all their neighbours. Each nation has been made to look with an invidious eye upon the prosperity of all the nations with which it trades, and to consider their gain as its own loss. Commerce, which ought naturally to be, among nations, as among individuals, a bond of union and friendship, has become the most fertile source of discord and animosity.'

Adam Smith, *An Inquiry into the Nature and Causes of the Wealth of Nations*, 1776[1]

The eighteenth century has been characterized as an age of mercantilism in which countries engaged in trade warfare and sought to accumulate bullion, with the gain for one trading partner being a loss for another. In 1936, Keynes remarked that such mercantilist policies offered 'avowedly national advantages and are unlikely to benefit the world as a whole' – though he had advocated protectionism a few years earlier.[2] In the 1930s, trade and currency wars between countries were spilling over into warfare. Japan looked for markets and raw materials in Manchuria; Italy embarked on colonialism in Ethiopia; and Germany constructed a trade bloc in south-eastern and central Europe. Mercantilism was given a new identity – Schachtianism, named after the president of the Reichsbank and economics minister in the Third Reich. Hjalmar Schacht's doctoral thesis had been on mercantilism and in the 1930s he turned his academic study into practical politics. At times, Keynes flirted with Schachtianism as a response to the dire economic position of Britain during the Second World War, though he was by temperament a supporter of multilateralism. Above all, the case for multilateral trade was made by Cordell Hull, to whom it was a moral crusade as much as an economic policy.

Hull returned to Washington from the World Monetary and Economic

Conference with his plans for a reduction of tariffs apparently abandoned by a president who was more concerned about domestic economic recovery, and with few potential partners in other countries. Nevertheless, Roosevelt had not completely rejected internationalism or, perhaps more accurately, the extension of the New Deal and American social, economic and political liberalism to the rest of the world. This ambition became more obvious as the United States grew into the dominant military and economic power in the Second World War, but it was already apparent in the 1930s. Hull was useful to the president as a Southern Democrat with long experience on Capitol Hill but was usually kept away from negotiations with the great powers, where Roosevelt took the lead. Nevertheless, Hull did not survive as Secretary of State for eleven years simply because of domestic electoral expediency. Despite some wavering, Roosevelt largely gave Hull responsibility for reducing trade barriers, which became possible with the passing of the Reciprocal Trade Agreements Act in 1934 – a major legislative achievement. The extension of American values and creation of a stable, prosperous world would start within the western hemisphere. More generally, Hull hoped that extending trade agreements to the liberal capitalist democracies of Europe would be a barrier against authoritarian regimes. A similar strategy was pursued by Morgenthau at the Treasury who, with Roosevelt's support, returned to the stabilization of the dollar, franc and sterling that had been rejected in London in 1933. Rather as Hull looked to trade deals to create a bloc of liberal democracies against authoritarian fascists, Communists and militarists, so Morgenthau hoped that currency stability would have a similar result. In 1936, the United States, Britain and France reached a Tripartite Agreement to stabilize their currencies.[3]

Although 1933 had been a disaster for economic co-operation, within a few years Hull and Morgenthau – with the president's more-or-less consistent support – were taking pragmatic steps to create order and stability. The grand ambitions of 1933 gave way to incremental progress that started to devise some of the principles that were formalized and generalized at Bretton Woods in 1944 and in the General Agreement on Tariffs and Trade in 1947. These developments both reflected an international geopolitical strategy to respond to the challenge from authoritarian regimes, and a solution to political difficulties within the United States by limiting the ability of self-interested domestic players to block international economic policy. Success in international economic government was only possible by creating a new domestic alliance of consumers, labour and the middle class – a task that was at the heart of Roosevelt's second New Deal.

HULL AND THE RECIPROCAL TRADE
AGREEMENTS ACT, 1934

Hull's reputation and confidence soon recovered from the London conference. In December 1933, a Pan-American conference was held in Montevideo to consider the construction of a highway the length of the continents. Hull turned this meeting into a platform for internationalism. He developed a friendly relationship with the Argentinian foreign minister Carlos Saavedra Lamas, who was anxious to secure American support for the anti-war treaty that had been signed in Rio de Janeiro earlier in the year, and Lamas reciprocated by backing Hull's policies.[4]

At first sight, the Montevideo convention was merely a well-meaning statement of the right of a sovereign state to exist without any interference in its affairs and to settle differences by peaceful means. In fact, it was a major shift in policy. The Americans were abandoning the 'Platt amendment', a provision in the treaty of 1903 with newly independent Cuba that specified that the country was not to make a treaty that would impair its independence; that it should not incur any public debt that could not be serviced from its ordinary revenues; and 'that the United States may exercise the right to intervene for the preservation of Cuban independence, the maintenance of a government adequate for the protection of life, property and individual liberty'.[5] Although the amendment seemed to limit Cuban independence, to the American government it applied the Monroe Doctrine of non-intervention by European creditors in the western hemisphere. In contrast, America could intervene in defence of its investments on the pretext of defending independence and good government, as it did in Cuba, Haiti, the Dominican Republic and Nicaragua. The policy both fomented political unrest in the region and led to 'moral hazard' on the part of American financiers, who could invest and avoid the consequences of their risk-taking in the expectation of intervention.

The issue came to a head with the ambitious public works of Gerardo Machado, President of Cuba from 1924, which were funded by overseas borrowing and budget deficits. Despite the parlous condition of Cuban finances, American bankers continued to lend in the expectation of intervention. They were mistaken; in 1929, Secretary of State Henry Stimson declared a policy of non-intervention. The result was a wave of defaults on foreign-owned bonds after 1931, which the American government condoned or even encouraged. The depression hit Latin American exports and tax revenues with the result that paying interest to bondholders would entail increasing taxes and imposing austerity. Bondholders were a diffuse group that was difficult to organize. Their interests were sacrificed to protect direct investment by American business, which would suffer from local unrest caused by higher taxes and reduced spending. The new direction of policy was confirmed by Roosevelt's pledge in his inaugural address to 'the policy of the good neighbor – the neighbor who resolutely respects himself and, because he does so, respects the rights of others'. The Good Neighbor policy led to the replacement of the Platt amendment by the pursuit of influence through public loans, aid and access to markets. The Roosevelt administration was willing to use pressure to ensure that direct investment was adequately compensated, as in the dispute with Mexico over the nationalization of the oil industry in 1938, but the policy had shifted from military intervention and coercion that failed to create stability, to the use of persuasion. In the 1930s, the Good Neighbor policy extended the Monroe Doctrine to exclude Germany from the western hemisphere, and this pursuit of regional leadership laid the basis for wider internationalism. Warren Kimball, the historian of Roosevelt's wartime foreign policy, sees that 'Roosevelt's Good Neighborhood reformation of the Monroe Doctrine was, by the end of the Second World War, part and parcel of his broad scheme for creating a peaceful world where the great powers worked separately, but together.' Latin America provided the template for spreading the American vision of a free society based on open commercial and monetary policies that was adopted at Bretton Woods.[6]

After his success at Montevideo, Hull pressed ahead with restoring free trade. His ideal policy was a multilateral agreement by which all nations reduced tariffs by the same amount at the same time, an approach that would have 'sweeping results with a minimum of effort'. It was not possible in the 1930s, given the complex mix of high tariffs, quota restrictions, exchange controls and preferences, particularly when negotiated simultaneously between many countries. Instead, Hull turned to the next best method: bilateral trade agreements. Two countries were more likely to reach a settlement, which could then be extended to other countries through the 'most favoured nation' principle. In the 1920s, as we saw in Chapter 1, different models of the international economy were contested at the League of Nations; the result, by the World Monetary and Economic Conference, was a retreat into trade blocs. At the League, the secretariat now saw that Hull's approach was the only model to pursue in creating a united front against totalitarianism – and he reciprocated by adopting the League's most favoured nation clause as the basis for trade agreements and drew on its work on trade rules in preparations for the post-war General Agreement on Tariffs and Trade.[7]

Leo Pasvolsky, a Russian-born journalist and economist based at the Brookings Institution who played a significant role in planning the post-war order, was a leading advocate of multilateralism and a key adviser to Hull at the State Department. He saw that the conditional most favoured nation principle would not lead to a cumulative liberalization of trade, for concessions to third parties needed to be compensated. Liberalizing trade therefore required the use of the unconditional most favoured nation principle in its 'broader and more constructive' form – that is, insisting on 'non-discrimination as the test for the extension of equality of treatment'. Clearly, this approach would create difficulties for Britain's imperial preference.[8] Further, this procedure had to be enshrined in legislation to prevent the log-rolling that led to Smoot–Hawley and to create a cumulative process of tariff reduction purged of special interests.

The economic nationalists in Washington remained sceptical, and Roosevelt – in another exercise of his style of competitive administration – appointed George Peek, his special adviser on foreign trade, to run a committee to co-ordinate foreign trade relations. Hull was horrified: 'If Mr Roosevelt had hit me between the eyes with a sledge hammer he could not have stunned me more.'[9] Peek was a protectionist who rejected unconditional most favoured nation policies as an opportunity for countries to 'free ride' by securing concessions from the United States without reciprocity.[10]

Meanwhile, the cross-departmental executive committee on commercial policy developed proposals to restore trade, and saw that progress depended on reducing the power of Congress and transferring tariff authority to the president.[11] Hull explained to the House Ways and Means Committee that

> it is manifest that unless the Executive is given the authority to deal with the existing great emergency somewhat on a parity with that exercised by the executive departments of so many other governments for purposes of negotiating and carrying into effect trade agreements, it will not be practicable or possible for the United States to pursue with any degree of success the proposed policy of restoring our lost international trade.[12]

A decision by Congress to voluntarily surrender its powers to the executive would be a remarkable change, amounting in the words of one Republican legislator to 'a betrayal of our representative form of government'.[13]

The experience of negotiating the Smoot–Hawley duties had been bruising for many congressmen, and it might be thought to show that narrow localism harmed the national interest. Senator Arthur Capper from Kansas explained in 1934 that

our experience in writing tariff legislation . . . has been discouraging. Trading between groups and sections is inevitable. Logrolling is inevitable, and
in its most pernicious form. We do not write a national tariff law. We jam
together, through various unholy alliances and combinations, a potpourri
or hodgepodge of section and local tariff rates, which often add to our
troubles and increase world misery.[14]

In fact, few congressmen learned a lesson. Only nine of ninety-five members of Congress who voted for the Smoot–Hawley tariff in 1930 and
were still legislators in 1934 supported delegation of power to the president. More significant was the general sense of crisis that allowed Hull to
argue that 'support is only urged as an emergency measure to deal with a
dangerous and threatening emergency situation'.[15]

Delegation of authority to the president was possible because the
Democratic Party had control of both Houses, with Southern members
committed to free trade. The region exported cotton, tobacco and other
crops and imported manufactures from the northern United States and
Europe, so that high tariffs increased the relative cost of its purchases and
harmed its export markets. Over the period 1933 to 1945, 86.6 per cent
of Republicans voted against the trade agreements programme; by contrast, 94.8 per cent of Southern Democrats and 84.1 per cent of
non-Southern Democrats voted for it.[16] Democratic control of Congress
was a rare opportunity. Since the end of the Civil War, the Democrats had
unified control of both the House of Representatives and the Senate for
only four of thirty-three congresses, and the tariff reductions they achieved
in 1894 and 1913 were soon reversed. Hull's experience after the First
World War made him realize that passing an Act to reduce tariffs was not
enough, and that low tariffs needed to be entrenched by removing authority from a future Congress. Senator Frederick Steiwer (R: Oregon) was
right: the Reciprocal Trade Agreements Act 'was not drawn by novices. Its
very structure indicates that it was carefully formulated by someone who
knew what he was doing, and it is difficult to attribute to the authors of
this bill anything other than the deliberate design to accomplish [the abolition of protective tariffs].'[17] Hull was more than an idealistic preacher of
the eternal truth of free trade: he was a shrewd operator on Capitol Hill.

The carefully crafted provisions of the Reciprocal Trade Agreements
Act of 1934 entrenched low tariffs in three ways. Authority was delegated
from Congress to the president, who was less likely to be concerned about
specific local interests and more with wider national interests. Trade
agreements would no longer need a 'super majority' of two-thirds of the
Senate. In future, all that was needed was a simple majority to renew the

RTAA every three years. The change in the success rate of trade agreements was striking. Between 1844 and 1909, when the president did not have delegated authority, twenty-one trade agreements were proposed to the Senate and only three were accepted. By contrast, twenty-seven trade agreements were successfully negotiated between 1934 and 1946, and another twenty-four in 1947-48. The RTAA changed the balance of power between protectionists and free traders by requiring agreements to be reciprocal. Smoot–Hawley set tariffs unilaterally by the United States, which gave protectionists more power. Support for a high duty on a specific commodity was concentrated in particular firms and locations. Reciprocity meant that any increase in American import duties would immediately lead to higher duties on American exports, so exporters could only secure better terms by supporting lower American import duties. Opposition to unconditional most favoured nation agreements on the basis that they allowed free riding by other countries was removed by the 'principal supplier' rule devised by Harry Hawkins, the head of the trade agreement programme at the State Department. America would offer to negotiate with the country that supplied the largest proportion of imports of a particular commodity. This procedure prevented the generalization of a concession to a small supplier of a particular commodity and ensured that the maximum concession was obtained from the country that was most dependent on the American market. This approach struck a balance between the expansion of trade and protection of domestic interests.[18]

Protectionist Republicans were alarmed that the RTAA changed the dynamics of trade policy. Senator William Borah wondered 'what kind of a miserable politician would I be, having been selected by my people to represent them here, to barter away my power and surrender my influence in such matters?' Allen Treadway, a Republican on the House Ways and Means Committee, feared that 'it would surrender the taxing power of Congress to the President and his subordinates in violation of both the letter and spirit of the Constitution'. However, Roosevelt's technique of sending out mixed signals minimized the influence of opponents. The appointment of Peek to a key position meant that critics of the RTAA were mollified by a protectionist in a senior position as a moderating influence on Hull's ideological commitment to free trade. Above all, opposition was disarmed by limiting the delegation of power to three years. The risk was that Republicans might reverse the RTAA when it came up for renewal, either by rejection or by inserting conditions to increase the influence of Congress, and the danger grew as Republican numbers in Congress increased. The survival of institutional 'lock-in' depended on several other developments. By giving more power to the executive – and especially the State Department – the RTAA created more expertise and administrative capacity that could counter congressional lobbying. Reciprocity gave more incentives to export sectors to mobilize in favour of trade liberalization, and the recovery of world trade meant that they became a larger sector in the American economy: though never so large as in Britain, exports of goods grew from 3.4 per cent of GDP in 1934 to 6.4 per cent in 1947. More significantly, a longer-term change occurred in perception during and after the war. The wartime boom in the American economy and the collapse of major competitors meant that imports were no longer a threat to American producers and workers, and there was a greater realization that increased exports would maintain output and employment after the war.[19]

Hull pressed for the RTAA's renewal in 1940 as 'a cornerstone around which the nations could rebuild their commerce on liberal lines when the war ended'. For the first time, he felt that he had the full support of Roosevelt, who sent a message to Congress that the RTAA was 'an indispensable part of the foundation of any stable and durable peace'.[20] In 1934, fifty-three Democrat senators had voted for the measure and five against; by contrast, six Republicans voted for and thirty against. The Republican position changed to greater support for renewal, so that in the vote in 1945, Democrat senators split forty-five to seven with fifteen Republicans now voting for and twenty-one against. The RTAA survived after the Republican Party took control of Congress in 1946. In 1948, 98 per cent of Republicans in the House and Senate voted for renewal, though only for one year and on condition that 'peril points' were introduced – that is, the point at which a reduction in duties would cause serious harm to an American industry. Senator Arthur Vandenberg, a supporter of Smoot–Hawley and opponent of the RTAA, nevertheless warned against returning power to Congress to set tariffs: 'Tariff-rate making in Congress is atrocious. It lacks any element of economic science or validity.' In 1949, with a return of a Democrat majority, the RTAA was renewed for three years without peril points, and with the support of 57 per cent of Republicans in the House and 45 per cent in the Senate.[21]

The RTAA was a major success for Hull and for the post-war reconstruction of the world economy. The pursuit of internationalism required the reform of domestic economic governance, and liberalization of trade would not have gone so far without the president's securing executive power. Nevertheless, in 1934 Hull had little reason to be optimistic, for economic nationalism was in the ascendant in Britain – and even more so in Germany.

SCHACHT AND THE GERMAN ECONOMY

Hjalmar Schacht had been a banker at the Dresden Bank and the German National Bank, and he helped stabilize the Reichsmark in 1923. He became President of the Reichsbank from 1923 to 1930 and again from 1933 to 1939. He was a founder of the German Democratic Party in 1918, but disillusionment with the Weimar government led him to look to 'a strong government based on a broad national movement . . . to regain Germany's sovereignty and equality as a world power'. In 1932, he joined a number of businessmen in urging President Hindenburg to appoint Hitler as Chancellor, and he was plenipotentiary for the war economy and Minister of Economics from 1934 to 1937, where he launched his 'new plan' to create an autarkic German economy. Although Schacht did not join the Nazi Party, he was made an honorary member and served as minister without portfolio until 1943.[22]

When Hitler became Chancellor in January 1933, Germany was facing a serious economic crisis. The balance of payments was in deficit, partly because imports were rising as the economy recovered from the worst of the depression, though mainly because exports had collapsed. Consequently, the Reichsbank's foreign currency reserves were falling to an alarmingly low level. Schacht blamed protectionism elsewhere in the world, but the problems were as much the result of German policies. Germany defaulted on debt payments in 1933 and made agreements with European creditors to use future export earnings to service the debt – a policy that seriously harmed multilateral trade. Income from German exports to France (for example) was used to pay interest on the debt and could not be used to purchase food and raw materials from the rest of the world. Above all, the collapse of German exports arose from the over-valuation of the Reichsmark because of the devaluation of sterling in 1931 and the dollar in 1933.[23]

The obvious solution was to devalue the Reichsmark. Hitler and Schacht refused. German politicians were scarred by the hyperinflation of the early 1920s and feared that devaluation would reignite inflation by increasing the costs of imported food and materials. Further, devaluation of the pound and dollar had reduced Germany's interest payments and Schacht had no wish to increase the burden by devaluing the Reichsmark. His reasoning was questionable, for devaluation would make German exports more competitive and so increase production and employment; it would improve the balance of payments so that servicing the debt would become easier. But Schacht could not afford to take a gamble: the balance of payments would take time to respond, whereas his problems were immediate. In any case, Schacht followed other central bankers in a commitment to monetary discipline which he had learned from his experience in stabilizing the Reichsmark.[24]

Schacht had to devise some other way to boost exports. The political and economic problems of the Nazi government meant that German bonds fell to around 40 per cent of their face value. Schacht's scheme exploited this fact. An exporter who received $50 from the sale of goods in the United States could buy a bond with a face value of $100 (or 350 Reichsmarks) for $50 (175 RM) and sell it to the Reichsbank for a sum closer to the face value. This device was more attractive than devaluation for it did not increase the price of imports or the costs of debt service, and it could apply to export sectors most in need of assistance. The scheme was both imaginative and inadequate. The reserves of the Reichsbank continued to fall, with importers receiving as little as 5 per cent of the amount of finance they had in July 1931. Consequently, industry had difficulty in purchasing raw materials, which hit production and led to rising unemployment, shortages of goods, higher prices and mounting discontent. The government responded with calls for resilience and sacrifice, and a search for scapegoats. Goebbels, the Nazi propaganda chief, warned that the 'hatred and anger and desperation of the German people would direct itself first of all against those we can get our hands on at home' – above all, the Jews.[25]

The regime faced a choice, whether to increase exports or to use available reserves to ensure essential imports for either civilian consumption or for rearmament. Kurt Schmitt, the minister of economics, wished to sustain civilian consumption. Schacht disagreed and at a critical meeting with Hitler in March 1934 supported rearmament – a policy that alarmed international creditors. Foreign exchange allocations to importers collapsed; rationing schemes were introduced for imports; and on 14 June 1934, Schacht suspended foreign currency payments on international debt. The result was mutual recriminations. The British government authorized the Treasury to seize the earnings of German exporters to meet the claims of British creditors, and the German government authorized the Ministry of Economics to retaliate. This stand-off was worrying, for Britain was Germany's major export market and source of foreign currency for purchases in other countries; the British empire was the major supplier of raw materials to Germany; and London supplied credit for German trade. On 28 June 1934, Schmitt started to deliver a speech on the alarming economic situation, only to collapse at the point where he asked what was to be done. Schacht became acting Minister of Economics, in addition to his post at the Reichsbank.[26]

Schacht's was now the dominant voice in German economic policy, and he pressed ahead with economic nationalism based on self-contained trade blocs and the bilateral exchange of goods. In August 1934, Schacht announced his 'new plan', a 'monstrosity' that he claimed was forced on him by hostile external creditors. More accurately, it was the result of his rejection of devaluation. It entailed the imposition of controls that were, as Adam Tooze remarks, 'unprecedented in peacetime history'.[27] The 'new plan' created a highly regulated economy, with the Reichsbank controlling the allocation of foreign exchange. It set aside what was needed for debt repayments and gave importers 'exchange certificates' based on national priorities, primarily for rearmament. Although production increased, the collapse of imports led to shortages of raw materials, and exports did not recover sufficiently to earn enough foreign exchange. The ruse of repurchasing bonds was no longer affordable. Economic collapse was only averted because other countries accepted the 'new plan', including the British government, which signed a bilateral Anglo-German Payments Agreement in November 1934. As at the time of the London conference in 1933, Schacht adopted a policy of divide and rule. He could discriminate against American creditors, for Germany was less dependent on American markets and he was less concerned about reprisals. Hull was not impressed and removed Germany's most favoured nation status. Schacht devised a further way of subsidizing exports: a tax on the turnover of industries benefitting from rearmament which could be recycled to support exporters. This scheme averted disaster and allowed a modest growth in imports with a bare minimum of foreign exchange reserves. The system needed tight controls over the economy to allocate scarce materials and foreign exchange; it meant producing as many goods as possible at home; and it sacrificed domestic consumption and resources to rearmament.[28]

The 'new plan' came under pressure in 1936 when Hermann Göring was appointed Special Commissioner for foreign exchange and raw materials, with his still greater commitment to rearmament. Göring reopened the question of devaluation and in August 1936 he commissioned a report on policy options from Carl Goerdeler, a member of the German National People's Party. Goerdeler believed that the Weimar Republic was a failure, and that democracy should be replaced by a restored monarchy in a right-wing revolution. He was initially a supporter of Hitler, but he refused to join the Nazi Party, opposed Nazi racial laws (despite his anti-Semitism), and criticized the attacks on the rule of law and the Church. In November 1934, he was appointed Price Commissioner to control inflation, and in a memorandum to Hitler in October 1935 he argued for a shift from rearmament to exports, a rejection of autarky, and a return to free markets. At first, he had opposed devaluation, but his report to Göring concluded that it was the only option and that it would require co-ordination with America and Britain to ensure that they did not follow in a new round of competitive devaluations. He also expected that co-operation in stabilizing currencies would require a change in Nazi policies towards the Jews and the Church, with a return to the rule of law to secure international acceptance. Goerdeler miscalculated. The ideology of the party would not change, and his proposals would produce a short-term increase in unemployment before the onset of recovery. The report was immediately rejected by Göring, who informed Hitler that 'it reveals the complete confusion and incomprehension of our bourgeois businessmen. Limitation of armaments, defeatism, incomprehension of the foreign policy situation alternate.' The proposals were, he sneered, suitable for the mayor of Leipzig (the post Goerdeler had held since 1930) and not for the Führer.[29]

Hitler's memorandum of August–September 1936 accepted that the economy must be subordinated to rearmament and 'the self-assertion of our nation'. He ordered the army and economy to be ready for war in four years' time, and in pursuit of this policy Schacht developed closer trade links with south-east Europe and Latin America on a bilateral basis. The problem was that these areas of the world could provide food and raw materials but, being less prosperous, could buy fewer German goods. As we have noted in Chapter 1, British imperial preference promoted trade between members without significantly diverting trade from non-members. By contrast, Schacht's trade bloc was intended to create self-sufficiency rather than to promote trade. Its members did not have extensive trade with each other in the past, and the result was to curtail trade with non-members without creating trade between the members. This policy was complemented by that of military conquest to integrate the economies of western Europe as a prosperous market for German goods, and, in the east, to remove the Jewish and Slavic populations so that eastern Europe could supply food and raw materials. Once Germany's trading position recovered and the Reichsbank had adequate foreign exchange reserves, controls over the economy could be removed and negotiations could resume with America from a position of strength. In October 1936 Göring was given absolute authority as plenipotentiary for the four-year plan.[30]

Goerdeler, like other members of the conservative upper class, lost patience with the Nazi regime. He resigned as mayor of Leipzig in 1937 and joined Bosch – a major industrial company – as head of foreign sales, which allowed him to travel and urge foreign politicians and officials to take action against Hitler. He stressed that the German economy was close to collapse and that a policy of containment would lead to Hitler's downfall and replacement by a right-wing military dictatorship. The British were sceptical of the army's willingness to mount a putsch and of the strength of anti-Nazi feeling. At the same time, Goerdeler proposed international conferences on disarmament, the stabilization of currencies, and Germany's legitimate grievances. He believed that Hitler's refusal to attend would lead to his downfall. Although Hull offered to set up a conference chaired by Roosevelt, nothing came of the idea. Eventually, Goerdeler's opposition to Hitler and his complicity in the assassination plot of July 1944 led to his execution.[31]

Schacht was in a difficult situation, for retaliation and an end to the Anglo-German Payments Agreement would lead to a collapse of exports. He realized that rearmament would require more imports and would boost domestic demand, with the result that exports would fall. He urged a slower pace of rearmament to reduce the need for imports and to release capacity for exports. In November 1937, Göring forced him to resign as Minister of Economics, and in January 1939 he was dismissed as President of the Reichsbank for a memorandum protesting against inflationary policies. His international reputation meant that Hitler kept him as minister without portfolio until January 1943. After the war, he was tried at Nuremberg for conspiring to bring about war and participating in the preparation for war, though not for crimes against humanity. He claimed to be a patriot rather than a Nazi and was acquitted. It is true that he was hostile to Kristallnacht in 1938, and that he proposed an alternative plan of holding Jewish property in trust as security for loans to finance Jewish migration. He also had some modest involvement with the resistance to Hitler and was arrested after the attempt on the Führer's life in July 1944. Above all, Schacht used the memorandum of January 1939 and his dismissal from office as proof of his moral condemnation of the Third Reich and principled objection to war. In reality, the memorandum was a purely financial case against the inflationary consequences of further rearmament. In post-war West Germany, its signatories – not only Schacht but also Wilhelm Vocke and Karl Blessing, who were presidents of the Bundesbank in 1957 and 1958–69 respectively – became 'monetary martyrs' who stood up for the independence of the central bank and sound money. This reading of the memorandum was 'monetary mythology', for Schacht had in fact used the power of the Reichsbank against the Weimar Republic in a way that endeared him to the Nazis. After his first resignation in 1930, he supported Hitler, and on his return to the Reichsbank in 1933 he worked closely with the regime as a member of the Cabinet, where his efforts were crucial in preventing a collapse of the German economy. After his acquittal in 1946, he was tried by a German court and sentenced to eight years' hard labour – only to be released in 1948. By 1953, he was running a bank to advise developing countries and in the 1960s he emerged as a critic of the Bundesbank, which he claimed was returning to inflation.[32]

In the United States, opinion was divided on how to respond to the economic policies of the Third Reich. Hull was negotiating a deal with Brazil on the basis of trade liberalization and the unconditional most favoured nation principle – yet at the same time Roosevelt agreed to negotiate a bilateral deal with Germany. Peek and Schacht reached an agreement that Germany would buy American cotton above the world price, on condition that the United States reduced the interest rate on German bonds and purchased more German goods. Hull was outraged by this breach of multilateral trade and was convinced that the Nazi regime was close to economic and political collapse. Once again, Hull faced down Roosevelt and insisted that his liberalization agenda be followed. At the end of 1934, Roosevelt rejected Peek's agreement.[33] Nevertheless, American firms entered into secretive barter agreements of dubious legality, and the imposition of 'countervailing duties' on Germany was also contentious. The Smoot–Hawley Act required the Treasury to impose duties if another country subsidized exports, and the State Department and Treasury disagreed on whether this provision applied to Germany's policy of paying exporters above the world price in 'registered Marks' that could only be used to buy German goods. The State Department argued that Germany was in effect devaluing its currency to make exports more competitive, and that countervailing duties were not imposed on countries that devalued. The Treasury disagreed and imposed countervailing duties. The dispute simmered up to the war.[34]

Britain was a much more substantial trading partner with Germany and was similarly divided on its response. In April 1934, Robert Vansittart – the senior civil servant at the Foreign Office – saw that German rearmament and autarky would make its economy less vulnerable to blockade than in the First World War. He was also morally repelled by the Nazi regime. What was less clear was how to respond. Should moderate elements in Germany be encouraged by building economic links, restoring prosperity, and tying Germany into liberal capitalism? Or should links be severed in the hope that economic hardship would delay rearmament or create a crisis that would undermine the Nazi regime? Goerdeler was in touch with Vansittart and stressed the likelihood of economic collapse. The British government was in two minds. The Foreign Office was concerned by German rearmament; the Board of Trade and Bank of England worried about the impact of a German economic collapse on British industrial recovery and the financial role of the City. The Anglo-German Payments Agreement followed the line of the Board of Trade and the Bank – a decision that can be portrayed as appeasement. A more generous interpretation is that concern for the international economy was understandable, and that a more aggressive stance was adopted when the agreement failed to convert Germany from autarky.[35]

Hull continued to argue that international co-operation based on trade agreements and a liberal world economy would create peace. He urged the British to abandon protectionism:

> if a great trading country like Great Britain and another great trading country like the United States should become static and inert and undertake further self-containment alone, such countries as Japan, Germany, and Italy, with their armies and navies would, within two or three years . . . dominate nearly every square foot of trade territory other than that under the immediate ownership or control of Great Britain and the United States, and that would leave our two countries in an amazingly disadvantageous situation.[36]

Anglo-American co-operation 'would probably make the difference between war and peace in Europe', and he pressed for a joint statement of principle in favour of liberal trade. '[T]he moral effect of a pronouncement so urgent and so sound would inspire confidence in the industrial and business world as it would also quiet much of the high tension in both the economic and political situations.'[37] The foreign secretary, Anthony Eden, half-heartedly agreed. He was overruled by Chamberlain at the Treasury and Walter Runciman at the Board of Trade, who feared an attack on imperial preference and insisted that the United States start by reducing its own tariffs and settling war debts.[38]

By the end of 1936, the British government saw that an Anglo-American reciprocal trade agreement might 'persuade the United States . . . that the frontier of democracy lies somewhere in the North Sea'. Runciman agreed to preliminary talks, though he still feared a threat to imperial preference and bilateral deals that would be vital in securing food and raw materials in the event of war. Runciman visited Washington in January 1937 and pressed Roosevelt to accept 'cash and carry' of supplies from a neutral United States in the event of war. Hull had a different idea. Trade liberalization would prevent war, and Britain should take the lead in Europe 'in proclaiming a program of liberal economic relations, on a basis of world order under law':

the economic approach should be the spear point of the approach to peace. First, get all the commercial nations in agreement on liberalizing and increasing trade, removing trade restrictions and eliminating discrimination. And then, with nearly forty nations banded together on economic grounds, show recalcitrant nations like Germany and Italy the undoubted benefits of joining in the same movement . . .

The United States had taken the lead in the trade agreements program, but I felt that Britain should take the lead in this concerted economic movement. This because she had been moving in the opposite direction, toward economic nationalism, and because her commercial relations with most of the nations of Europe were closer than those of other countries.

Hull assured Runciman that his aim was not the abolition of imperial preference, but reform to prevent the diversion of trade into 'unnatural' channels. Runciman, however, was not interested in the grand scheme, and Hull complained that Britain was 'moving backward toward the extremes of economic nationalism, instead of forward toward economic recovery'.[39]

Runciman returned to London unconvinced by the wider political argument and stressing the need to concentrate on the economic case for security in war. Talks with the United States became more feasible when Congress accepted 'cash and carry' in 1937, and when the London Imperial Conference of 1937 – a gathering of the Dominions – agreed in principle to modify imperial preference. Surprisingly, Neville Chamberlain, a long-term supporter of imperial preference who became Prime Minister in May 1937, backed an Anglo-American trade agreement. Chamberlain reasoned that 'it would help to educate American opinion to act more and more with us, and because I felt sure it would frighten the totalitarians. Coming at this moment, it looks just like an answer to the Berlin-Rome-Tokyo axis.' By the time an Anglo-American trade agreement was reached in November 1938, it was clear that Hull's response to German aggression was doomed and that, in Roosevelt's words, little could be achieved by selling 'a few barrels of apples here and a couple of automobiles there'. Trade treaties were, he informed Morgenthau, 'just too goddamned slow. The world is moving too fast.'[40]

Hull's schemes failed in their broader purpose, and Britain declared war on Germany after the invasion of Poland in September 1939. Nevertheless, Hull's efforts to open talks on trade agreements had a beneficial effect. He had tried to construct an alliance of liberal capitalist democracies against authoritarian regimes, and the procedure laid down in the RTAA was used after the war to rebuild a multilateral world economy and undo Schachtianism. The RTAA marked a tentative step away from 'beggar my neighbour' trade policies. Similarly, the tripartite agreement signed between the United States, Britain and France in 1936 marked another attempt to bring these three liberal capitalist democracies together. It started to re-establish order in exchange rates that paved the way for the Bretton Woods conference.

THE TRIPARTITE AGREEMENT, 1936

As Hull pressed ahead with trade agreements, steps were being taken to stabilize the dollar. The Treasury adviser Jacob Viner was concerned that currency instability was delaying recovery in Europe. He challenged the influence of Fisher and Warren, and urged Morgenthau to stabilize exchange rates, for only by ending exchange rate risk and creating 'a habitual and unqualified confidence in the wisdom and financial conservatism of the currency authorities' would trade and investment recover.[41] Similarly, Alvin Hansen, the chief economic analyst at the State Department before his move to Harvard, reported in March 1935 that uncertainty was undermining confidence in investment, provoking countries to adopt quotas and exchange controls, and leading to deflation in the gold bloc. At the Federal Reserve, George Harrison worried that the further depreciation of other currencies would lead to an increase in the value of the dollar, and that it was 'a selfish policy to sit back and watch the other currencies go to pieces without taking any steps either to correct the situation or to find out what was the policy of other nations in the matter'. Morgenthau and Roosevelt were sceptical. They did not wish to surrender the use of monetary policy for domestic purposes, and currency stabilization was associated with the gold standard, deflation and the interests of Wall Street bankers. It might even provoke a revival of congressional demands for mandatory inflation. Roosevelt thought that Hansen should be sacked, and Morgenthau denounced his report as 'one of the most stupid and anti-New Deal memoranda that I have seen in a long time'. Nevertheless, opinion was starting to shift. Roosevelt was cautious about a wider scheme for stabilization, for many countries would reject it until they were content with their internal price levels. He did, however, hope to avoid another round of devaluations, and allowed Morgenthau to test the water with France and Britain.[42]

In a radio talk in May 1935, Morgenthau laid out a careful approach that balanced freedom for domestic monetary policy with international stabilization:

So far from engaging in a competitive race with other nations, we hold out
to them a currency of such steadiness that the normal tendency may very
well be for the rest of the world to move gradually toward practical exchange
stabilization . . . The world should know that when it is ready to seek foreign
exchange stabilization, Washington will not be an obstacle . . . However, if
the great trading nations elect to continue under the present absence of rules
we are no longer at a disadvantage. We revalued our currency no more than
was necessary and we can go either way. Our hands are untied.[43]

Officials at the British Treasury were not impressed. They complained that
'by continuing to mask itself in the trappings suitable to a debtor nation
the United States with its tariff policy, its monetary policy and its refusal to
take steps to adjust an excessively favourable balance of payments, is itself
now the principal obstacle to world stabilisation'. Roosevelt was suspected
of playing a double game, with no intention of stabilizing the dollar and an
expectation that the British would reject his approach. Consequently, he
'would keep his hands free but would be able to throw the blame for the
continued instability of the world on to the United Kingdom'.[44]

The British knew that holding down the value of the pound stimulated
exports, discouraged imports, and allowed lower interest rates which
helped domestic recovery. Chamberlain would not abandon the policy
and he argued that stabilization was impossible so long as the franc and
dollar were out of alignment.[45] When Harry Dexter White of the US
Treasury visited Europe in May 1935 to assess the situation, he tried (and
failed) to convince his British counterparts that a general arrangement
would prevent 'new maladjustments' and retain some of Britain's competitive advantage.[46] The British Treasury did agree to conversations with
France on the condition that it could pursue recovery through its 'liberal
and consistent monetary policy'. These tentative conversations soon
ended, for the British were concerned that stabilization would undermine
management of the pound, and the French were committed to the gold
standard and fearful that the pound might be devalued. In the absence of
co-operation, the French prime minister turned to America, which offered
support for the franc in May and June 1935. But Morgenthau was wary
of being drawn in. When he visited Paris in October 1935 to discuss monetary issues, he insisted that responsibility lay with the Europeans.[47]

The French tried to use the League of Nation's Economic and Financial
Organization to consolidate the gold bloc. At the League, Pietro Stoppani
and Alexander Loveday were cautious, however, for the Economic Committee was supporting policies closer to the American position of
liberalizing the world economy through multilateral co-operation between

liberal capitalist states – an approach that they hoped would save both the League and the world economy. Against this line, Joseph Avenol, the economically conservative Frenchman who was Secretary General of the League, opposed what he considered to be a partisan approach. Despite Avenol's concern, the solidarity of the gold bloc was weakening and the French were marginalized. By 1936, Stoppani feared that the economic and political conditions in Europe would lead to war, and that a political deal was needed to recreate normal monetary, financial and commercial relations. Consequently, exchange rates between the dollar and pound should be stabilized, with new parities for currencies such as the franc, and there should be an end to exchange controls in countries in monetary difficulties such as Germany. This approach would require an agreement between America, Britain and France with Germany and Italy. There was little prospect of success, but a more limited scheme for currency stabilization became feasible when the French government started to consider the devaluation of the franc on condition that the dollar and sterling did not embark on further depreciation.[48]

In France, the gold standard had been associated since the war with a restoration of stability and prosperity, and it gave the Banque de France more autonomy from the government. This belief was questioned as other countries left gold, and as domestic pressure mounted for a reconsideration of policy. The Bank hoped to sustain a gold bloc to deliver stability against the monetary adventurism of Britain and the United States. Its position was challenged when the Popular Front government came to power in June 1936. The left attacked the Bank for interfering in politics. As one tract put it, 'economic fascism exists now. Its leaders have set up their "command post" in the Bank of France. So long as they occupy it, there will be neither freedom nor prosperity in this country.' In 1936, the Bank was reformed to give more voice to domestic economic interests. The new government offered domestic recovery, an end to deflation, public works, the nationalization of the banks and heavy industries, and reductions to the working week. It hoped to achieve these ambitious plans without devaluation but, predictably, the franc came under pressure because of alarm at the alliance between Socialists and Communists, social unrest caused by deflation, and the costs of the social programme. In the absence of devaluation, the government supported exchange controls – a solution that had been adopted in Germany. Emmanuel Mönick, the financial attaché in Washington and subsequently London, argued that France could not act like Hitler. Opinion started to turn to devaluation as the better option, and Mönick was despatched to Washington in June to sound out Morgenthau. The risk was that devaluation of the franc might be followed by devaluation of the dollar and pound, with further disruption of the international monetary system. An agreement was needed to stabilize exchange rates.[49]

Morgenthau sensed an opportunity. If he could reassure France that the Americans and British would not devalue, the French would have the confidence to make a 'clean-cut devaluation' which would bring about stabilization between the three countries.[50] Morgenthau approached the British, arguing that 'it is perfectly silly for the two countries to be doing business together in the dark with a big wall between us, each country slipping the other country a note under the wall but not being willing to talk ... I want to open a channel of communication.' Despite initial caution, Chamberlain accepted that 'the closest and most friendly contact between the two Treasuries is desirable'.[51] The British agreed that if the franc were devalued, the value of the pound would be held – on condition that the gold value of the dollar did not change. Morgenthau felt that this was 'horse sense, sensible thing to do'.[52]

For domestic political reasons, the French government wanted to avoid the impression of being forced into unilateral devaluation and the abandonment of gold. The solution was to present the decision as an achievement by the French government. Mönick asserted that 'We must give the feeling in France that the battle is over, and that it is the beginning of monetary peace and some form of collaboration between the stable currencies.' A complicated (and unrealistic) plan was devised by Vincent Auriol, the finance minister. The value of currencies should be set by a common measure such as world prices and could only be changed with the consent of other countries. Auriol argued that the scheme should be implemented by the United States approaching each country separately and informally to stabilize against the dollar – and when each agreed, to announce a general international monetary truce that could be presented as more than just the devaluation of the franc. Roosevelt and Morgenthau refused. After the experience of 1933, they were wary of multilateral negotiations, and Morgenthau remarked that 'I would no more sit in on a world monetary conference than jump out of this window.' In any case, specified rates and narrow margins of fluctuations would limit the use of monetary policy for domestic reasons. Roosevelt realized too that a deal based on the dollar would alienate the British by implying that the City of London was no longer the centre of the world's financial system. The French should therefore maintain British *amour propre* by a simultaneous approach to Washington and London.[53]

The French proposed that America and Britain should maintain the value of their currencies after a French devaluation, with the three central banks and treasuries co-operating to maintain rates determined by world prices, within narrow margins that would only be modified by mutual consent. There were worrying elements in the proposal, for the final objective was a return to the gold standard. The Americans and British were willing to consider stabilization; they were wary of a loss of domestic autonomy by returning to gold or to specified rates with narrow margins. They realized that adopting world prices as the metric implied a large devaluation of the franc and a revaluation of the pound and dollar. Morgenthau reported Roosevelt's reaction to Auriol's document: 'It's terrible! It gives me a pain!', as he went through it shouting 'OUT' in a loud voice.

The compromise finally agreed was a statement of co-operation or 'gentlemen's agreement', to be issued separately by each government, that would allow the French to claim they were restoring international monetary peace without committing the United States and Britain to return to gold. The agreement aimed for 'the greatest possible equilibrium in the system of international exchanges', with the right to 'take into full account the requirements of internal prosperity'. The statements were issued on 26 September 1936. On 1 October the franc was devalued, without setting a specific gold value.[54]

Morgenthau welcomed the Tripartite Agreement as a sign that nations could co-operate and as a warning to Japan, Italy and Germany that 'we won't stand any monkey business'. He assured Chamberlain that it was

> the greatest move taken for peace in the world since the World War . . . It may be the turning point for again resuming rational thinking in Europe. It may be just the thing to again bring reason back to these perfectly mad people. Let's hope so . . . After all, we are the only three liberal governments left . . . And the beauty of the thing is – there are no signatures. It is good faith. We have confidence in each other, and I would ten times rather shake hands than have all the signatures in the world. Signatures haven't been worth much.[55]

Walter Lippmann welcomed the agreement as an opportunity to 'feel our way to a sound currency for the world as a whole'. He pointed out that the gold standard created stability of currencies abroad at the cost of deflating domestic purchasing power. Conversely, managed currencies without international co-operation led to stability at home and uncertainty abroad. He saw that the Tripartite Agreement created stability at home *and* abroad by allowing countries to co-operate in striking a balance between international stability and domestic flexibility. Even James Warburg was willing to support Roosevelt's re-election on this new commitment to monetary stability.[56] Here, it seemed, was a way of ensuring that national self-interest did not destroy the general good. The principles of the Tripartite Agreement were incorporated into the Bretton Woods agreement of 1944 – to reject competitive devaluation, to encourage exchange rate stability, and to balance international commitments with domestic welfare. As we will see, Bretton Woods also went beyond the Tripartite Agreement, for it covered many more countries who were to set parities that would vary only by 1 per cent either way, with formal rules and the creation of an institution to provide funds to members that were in difficulties.[57]

In September 1936, a further agreement restored a role for gold in the 'twenty-four-hour gold standard'. The pound and franc did not have a fixed gold value, unlike the dollar which was set at $35 an ounce. Each country had its own stabilization fund to buy and sell currencies to maintain the value of its currency. The British Treasury was concerned at the scope for speculation, and the Bank of England and Banque de France agreed that they would set the price for the exchange of gold on a daily basis. This agreement was extended to the United States in October, which offered the same deal to other countries. As a result, the price of each currency was fixed in terms of gold daily by consultation between central bankers and the stabilization funds, except for the dollar which remained at $35 an ounce as a point of stability in a flexible system. Morgenthau welcomed this new 'currency club' as

> a divorcement of the control of the foreign exchange market from the few individual international speculators. The responsible governments of the people will now cooperate to assure a minimum exchange fluctuation. Businessmen with merchandise to sell abroad, or businessmen who are importing merchandise, will be free to operate through their respective banks in regular and normal exchange operations. The international speculator, responsible to no one, and recognizing no flag in the conduct of his business, will in the future not be able by rapidly shifting his fund from market to market, to reap private advantage through stimulating chaos in foreign exchange.

Rates of exchange entailed multilateral consultation rather than unilateral action, and were a matter for governments rather than central bankers at the BIS. The agreement restored some role for gold while offering greater flexibility than the traditional gold standard. After the debacle of 1933, a first step had been made to restore the international monetary system as co-operative rather than competitive – an approach that later influenced Keynes and Harry Dexter White as they negotiated the Bretton Woods agreement.[58]

At the League, Stoppani welcomed the Tripartite Agreement as achieving stabilization by international collective action – and it was soon extended to Belgium, the Netherlands and Switzerland, with Germany, Italy and Japan remaining outside. It was a means of uniting liberal capitalist democracies to safeguard peace. But Stoppani's and Loveday's hopes that an economic conference would follow came to nothing. The Economic Committee instead turned to policies to raise the standard of living of individuals through 'positive security', and to develop new ways of thinking about the world economy. Even in the dark days of the 1930s, a counter-current of internationalism and co-operation was emerging among economists at the League, many of whom would be central to wartime and post-war initiatives.[59]

ECONOMISTS AT THE LEAGUE OF NATIONS

At the end of the First World War, the League was involved in the financial stabilization of a number of countries, above all Austria and also Hungary, Greece, Bulgaria, Poland, Romania and Czechoslovakia.[60] In the 1920s and 1930s, the initiatives of the financial and economic committees of the League were disappointing, for little came of the Gold Delegation of 1928–32 or the expert commissions prior to the World Monetary and Economic Conference.[61] There was some success in devising rules on the most favoured nation principle, though even so the world retreated into trade blocs. The secretariat's response to these failures of economic co-operation and the threat of League irrelevance was to focus on new ways of thinking about the international economy, and of assessing state policies in response to the depression in collaboration with economists with strong links with ministries, universities, banks and businesses. At the Financial Section, Loveday brought together some of the leading young economists of the day, such as Gottfried Haberler, Jan Tinbergen, J. B. Condliffe and Ragnar Nurkse. At the Economic Section, members included James Meade, Bertil Ohlin and Jacques Rueff. They came from different intellectual traditions rather than forming a single epistemic community. Ohlin was associated with the Stockholm School of economics, which anticipated Keynes's use of the budget to stabilize the economy; by contrast, Haberler was associated with the Austrian School with its stress on individualism and free markets. Despite their differences, these economists had something in common – a desire to develop an alternative to both fascism and Communism that could rescue liberal capitalism. Although they lacked authority to make policy recommendations, their reports and memoranda gave priority to transnational interests over those of their own countries, and they developed an agenda for international co-operation independent from the deliberations of the Assembly and Council of the League.[62]

In 1930, the Assembly asked the EFO to study the causes of the depression. Loveday realized that the Gold Delegation report marked the end of monetary approaches, and that more attention should be paid to the business cycle and the connections between national economies that resulted in deep depression. Analysis of business cycles was already in progress in several institutions, often with the support of the Rockefeller Foundation, which, like other American philanthropic bodies, pursued an internationalist agenda.[63]

The history of economics in the 1930s and 1940s is often presented as a battle between orthodoxy and Keynesian use of budgets to restore equilibrium to national economies. However, Keynes's *General Theory of Employment, Interest, and Money* of 1936 was mostly concerned with a closed national economy and his main interest was the balance between domestic consumption and production. He considered global issues in terms of a managed international monetary system and, to a lesser extent, stabilization of commodity prices, with little attention to the world economy as an interconnected system. By contrast, economists at the League were concerned with the processes by which prosperity, depression and recovery spread around the world beyond the individual nation state.

The Austrian Business Cycle Research Institute had been established in 1926 at the Vienna Chamber of Commerce and involved economists who were leading figures in the emergence of neo-liberalism in the 1970s. Ludwig von Mises became secretary of the chamber of commerce in 1918 as the Austro-Hungarian empire imploded. He was joined by Friedrich von Hayek, who ran the business cycle institute. Both men were shaped by hostility to the Austrian socialist government of 1919 and by the conflict between capital and labour in Red Vienna. To Mises, the (relatively modest) welfare reforms of the government were 'Bolshevism' that would lead to starvation and terror. He worried that 'plundering hordes would take to the streets and a second bloodbath would destroy what was left of Viennese culture'. His solution was to cut corporate taxes, balance the budget, repress unions to allow the efficient use of labour, cut welfare and reduce wages to restore competitiveness. Mises welcomed Mussolini as the saviour of European civilization, and 'the merit that Fascism has thereby won for itself will live on eternally in history'. In 1934, he argued that workers' talk of 'universal, equal and direct voting rights' was a cover for 'terror and intimidation'. By contrast, the capitalist market economy was a democracy in which 'every penny constitutes a vote' – a 'consumer plebiscite' where the rich depended on 'the will of the people as consumers'. To the Austrian School of economics, the crash of 1929 was the result of loose monetary policy and over-investment, with high wages and welfare costs leading to depression.[64]

Mises and Hayek shaped a new internationalism in the 1930s. Loveday invited Hayek to Geneva in 1931, and Mises moved to the Graduate Institute of International Studies in the city in 1934. The Graduate Institute was directed by William Rappard, a Swiss economist trained at Harvard and Vienna who was involved with both the International Labour Organization and the League. He was committed to internationalism, free trade and free markets, and was a supporter of classic liberalism against both fascism and Communism. The Graduate Institute was funded – like the Viennese institute – by the Rockefeller Foundation, and work on business cycles was now concentrated in Geneva. At the League and Graduate Institute, a cluster of Austrian School economists – including Lionel Robbins from the London School of Economics (LSE) and the German émigré Wilhelm Röpke, as well as Mises and Hayek – developed a distinctive 'Genevan liberalism'. In 1938, many of them attended the Walter Lippmann Colloquium in Paris to discuss Lippmann's *Inquiry into the Principles of the Good Society* (1937) and to consider how to create a new form of liberalism in place of collectivism and socialism – a precursor to the Mont Pèlerin Society convened by Hayek in 1947 that continued to argue for market liberalism against growing state intervention in the economy.[65]

The initial response to the League's request for a study of the causes of the depression was Ohlin's report of 1931, which was followed in 1934 by the EFO's inquiry into public works programmes. It culminated in 1938 with the appointment of a Depression Delegation to analyse the range of national policy responses. The Depression Delegation built on work on business cycles that stressed the interconnection between national economies and the impossibility of insulating themselves from global forces. Ohlin gathered economists to report on national business cycles – a task that entailed compiling comparable national statistics and understanding global interdependence in a 'world economy of numbers'. Haberler pursued this approach in analysing economic connections that linked 'the ups and downs of the business cycle in different countries' as the 'bacillus of boom or depression' moved from country to country. Above all, he pointed to over-investment and unstable bank credit, which led to a divergence between long- and short-term rates of interest that distorted capital investment – a central theme in the Austrian School's approach. Jan Tinbergen was hired to produce econometric analysis of business cycles, and he was succeeded by Jacques Polak to produce a model of how fluctuations spread between parts of the economy and around the world, especially through fluctuations in the value of currencies and capital movements. Depression was transmitted around the world by reduced demand for primary commodities that led to a steep fall in their price, trade deficits and reduced purchasing power; by international capital movements; and by protectionism and currency depreciation.

This work on trade cycles informed the Depression Delegation's report and its concern for the complex interrelationship of global monetary and economic systems; a need for balance between manufactures and primary products; and for action to remove fluctuations in prices that could transmit depression. A more sophisticated understanding of interdependencies in flows of trade and finance went beyond the price–specie flow models of the gold standard, or Cordell Hull's emphasis on trade barriers in preventing automatic adjustment of the world economy. The Depression Delegation viewed the world economy as a system in constant flux in which defensive, nationalistic recovery programmes harmed the international economy. They could agree on the need to consider the world economy as an interconnected whole, and the need for international agencies to establish rules for a co-operative approach. They disagreed over how to proceed. At one extreme, Rueff, of the Banque de France, wished to return to the gold standard and classic liberal economic policies. Others supported deficit finance to stabilize national economies. Ohlin praised the Swedish Unemployment Commission's approach to public works; Loveday agreed that it provided a model and that the Delegation 'should concentrate on educating public opinion to understand that a deficit in bad times was not necessarily a bad thing'. James Meade went further in advocating 'consumer credits' when unemployment increased above a certain level and in stressing the problem of unequal wealth distribution.[66]

The Delegation's concern for consumption was taken in another direction by the Australian Frank McDougall, who emphasized the need to reshape the world economy to increase consumption and improve nutrition in a programme of 'positive security'. Nutrition was linked to proposals for a radical change in world agriculture to solve the problems of depression and instability, both in primary-producing and in advanced-industrial economies. Stanley Melbourne Bruce – the Australian representative on the League's Council and its president from 1936 – and his confidant, McDougall, linked nutritional science with agriculture, poverty reduction and economic recovery. Agricultural protection led to high prices, shielding inefficient producers at the expense of consumers and reducing the income of exporters. Cheaper food and income redistribution were needed so that the poor could buy food needed for their health. 'Protective' food (eggs, vegetables, fruit, dairy products and meat) that contained vitamins and minerals should be supplied locally; staple 'energy' food such as wheat should be supplied by the most efficient, low-cost producer. Many people were suffering from malnutrition because they did not eat enough protective foods due to paying the higher prices for imported energy foods designed to support domestic farmers. The problem could be solved if European farmers concentrated on protective foods and large-scale exporters (such as Australia) supplied energy foods, which would increase their income to buy manufactures. Over-production and malnutrition could be resolved, and at the same time political stability would be re-established by raising the standard of living.[67]

These ideas were pursued by the League's 'mixed committee' with the International Institute of Agriculture (IIA) and ILO. McDougall was a vocal member of the mixed committee and the main author of its final report that supported 'economic appeasement', that is policies – above all on nutrition – to remove economic problems that were causing political difficulties. 'No single policy is more likely to assist towards economic appeasement than the adoption of nutrition policies by a considerable number of the more advanced countries.' 'Positive security' was a liberal capitalist approach that would 'demonstrate that democratic countries can achieve for their people greater comfort and well-being than can the Fascist and Communist states'. Better pay and conditions of labour would spread purchasing power and ensure economic stability, by minimum wages, social insurance, income redistribution, and through direct assistance to supplement diets such as school meals and milk. Nutrition was linked with international action by the ILO on pay and conditions, and with national policies on pensions, family allowances, and distribution of food to the poorest. Nutrition policies 'could bring about an expanding need for the products of international trade in which all countries may find full outlets for their energies and full employment for their peoples'.[68] Such an approach did not reject Hull's desire for trade agreements, nor Morgenthau's for stabilization of currencies, but they were secondary to the task of restoring the world economy by adjusting agriculture.

Alexander Loveday saw that 'the fate of democratic and liberal societies might be determined by the success or failure in mitigating the consequences of economic depressions, and thus providing at least a minimum of social security for the masses.' He pointed to an intellectual shift in

our whole economic outlook. Ever since the time of Adam Smith economic thought has centred around the art of production or the conditions of citizens as producers. The nutrition movement reflects the first serious endeavour, certainly on an international scale, to consider the economics not of production but of consumption.[69]

The Bruce–McDougall approach was not accepted by all the members of the mixed committee. The IIA, established in Rome in 1905, largely represented European farmers who favoured protection over the interests of consumers. The IIA criticized McDougall's approach on the sensible grounds that changes in diet were slow and major adjustments to agricultural output would be complicated, expensive, and not necessarily more profitable. There was also an ideological split over policy. The IIA was influenced by Fascist corporatism in which employers came together with non-unionized workers to run the economy in the interests of the nation and under the guidance of the state.[70] The difference of approach surfaced in 1931 when the League agreed to provide advice to China. The League's experts saw rural co-operation rather than Soviet collectivization as a solution to peasant backwardness. British officials with experience in India argued that co-operatives should consist of small farmers coming together to achieve more than they could as individuals. By contrast, Carlo Dragoni, the Fascist head of the IIA, wanted local co-operatives to be part of a hierarchy of associations leading up to national bodies that would bring together the interests of farmers, workers and capitalists in a corporatist system, working with the state.[71] The solution to the problems of peasant agriculture was therefore contested within the League until Italy withdrew from the organization after the imposition of sanctions in 1937, in response to its invasion of Abyssinia.

'Genevan liberals' such as Mises and Hayek were uneasy about these developments, which subverted their work on business cycles and the measurement of the economy. Statistics were being used in the service of managing and planning the economy at the level of the nation state. In a lecture at the Graduate Institute, Röpke pointed out that 'planning on a national scale and the disorder on the international scale are not only parallel, but causally connected phenomena'. To Mises and Hayek, the global economy was an open space apart from national politics that distorted the free market by protection or planning. The task of international institutions – preferably supranational bodies that were above the state rather than intergovernmental organizations – was to create enforceable rules that would limit national sovereignty so that nationalism and democratic pressures did not undermine the global economy or limit the freedom of capital to work across state lines. They rejected planning or prevention of depression that threatened stagnation and a loss of liberty – steps on *The Road to Serfdom* (the title of Hayek's book of 1944).

Depression was intrinsic to economic change, and the correct response was to mitigate its impact when a crisis inevitably came. Rather than measuring the economy, Hayek now argued that it was unknowable and based on ignorance, yet it produced a distribution of resources 'which can be understood as if it were made according to a single plan, though nobody has planned it'. The liberals viewed the economy as a spontaneous phenomenon operating within a framework of laws and institutions that should serve the market by guarding 'providential planlessness' from the delusions of planners who thought they knew the economy and were therefore tempted to adopt 'totalitarian methods of economic management'.[72] To them, international organizations should set rules and not extend state planning to the international level.

This approach entailed suspicion of the nation state as a threat to the efficient operation of the global economy. William Rappard emphasized the need for world unity against the 'wicked folly of absolute national sovereignty', and the Genevan liberals saw that the maintenance of the liberal world economy needed concerted political effort. Although nation states could not be replaced, they could be prevented from becoming destructive forces. Lionel Robbins and Hayek (whom he recruited to the London School of Economics) proposed supranational government based on loose federations on the lines of the Habsburg or British empires, which (supposedly) combined multiple national identities within a free economic space. Individual states would preserve the cultural identity that was demanded by their population and should abandon controls over trade and capital. By this means, national borders would be complemented by a borderless regional or world economy. In lectures at the Graduate Institute, Robbins argued that a 'liberal world federation' would allow 'the maximum scope for international division of labour; and any restriction of trading between governmental areas would be totally alien'. Federation would assist 'de-planning'. Tariffs would not be needed, labour could move freely within its territory, and prosperity would rely on the global economy rather than the security of the nation state. In 1938, Robbins and Hayek became founder members of the Federal Union, which urged political federation to preserve an open world economy against the lure of national protectionism and planning. In their view, electors in a single nation state might be willing to adopt protection to assist their own industry; in a federation, French voters would oppose tariffs that protected a British industry and imposed a cost on French consumers. By this logic, a superior political power could protect the global economy from the misuse of sovereignty by nation states that harmed prosperity in general. To these economists, the international order that emerged after 1945 was a disappointment. The international institutions and rules that they advocated were associated with continued – even strengthened – nation states that could pursue domestic policies and, if they wished, plan their economies.[73]

The crisis of legitimacy provoked by the Great Depression was followed by a period of uncertainty during which new ideas were formulated. As yet there were no international agencies or formal rules to enforce good behaviour and the step of creating new institutions was yet to be made. Questions posed at the start of this book came into play: how many issues should be negotiated at any time, and in what order? Who should be invited to participate, and how should they be represented? And the most fundamental question of all – what should be the nature of distributive justice in the world economy? A deal between the leading economies to stabilize their currencies or open their markets would not help undeveloped countries, whose concerns could be excluded from consideration. In the next chapter, we turn to these other voices.

4

'Escaping from backwardness'

Strategies of Economic Development

'... the production of primary commodities after the [First World] war was somewhat in excess of demand. It was this which, by keeping the terms of trade unfavourable to primary producers, kept the trade in manufactures so low, to the detriment of such countries as the UK, even in the twenties, and it was this which pulled the world economy down in the early thirties ... '

W. Arthur Lewis, *Economic Survey, 1919–39*, 1949[1]

Economists at the League of Nations concerned with global interconnections of the business cycle had little to say about structural conditions that led to poverty and dependence. Arthur Lewis had a lot to say. He grew up in the West Indies, studied economics at the London School of Economics and worked for the British government in the Second World War, where he encountered racism and became active in opposition to colonialism. After the war, his lectures on the Great Depression at the LSE stressed how the First World War stimulated production of primary products and how excess capacity led to falling prices. Lewis argued that 'it was this insecurity in the markets for primary commodities that was so decisive in converting the crisis of 1929 into a major depression'. The situation would have been better if primary product prices had been stable, 'for it was the violent fall of prices that was deflationary, and the prices of manufactures are not as subject to violent change as are those of primary commodities.'[2]

Unlike economists who stressed monetary influences on the fall in prices, Lewis's explanation was the structural relationship between industrial and primary producers. His emphasis on the terms of trade was taken up in under-developed countries pressing for policies to raise primary product prices. Above all, Raúl Prebisch, the head of the central bank in Argentina in the 1930s, would make the case after the Second

Russian peasants who were to work on new collective farms carrying a banner reading 'Immediately exterminate the kulaks as a class', Soviet Union, January 1930.

World War at the United Nations Economic Commission for Latin America (ECLA) and the United Nations Conference on Trade and Development (UNCTAD). Latin American countries were major exporters of primary commodities and their experience of falling prices between the wars shaped their responses to post-war reconstruction. Similarly, Australian economists and politicians developed a distinctive approach in response to the Great Depression. They insisted that freer trade required full employment of the resources of the world – an approach that influenced thinking in the League and debates on the new international institutions. India was less reliant on exports and was a vital part of the British empire; here, debates over economic development were linked with nationalism and planning of the domestic economy for development. Not least, the Soviet Union challenged capitalist development with its command economy and rapid industrialization. Meanwhile, China experienced internal turmoil and Japanese invasion, and adopted a strategy for national development with international support. An understanding of the institutions of world economic government that emerged after the Second World War must take these alternative experiences and voices into account.

THE SOVIET MODEL: COLLECTIVIZATION AND PLANNING

In 1917, the Russian Revolution overthrew the Tsarist regime – a largely peasant society with pretensions to be a great power that had expanded its territory until it reached from the Black Sea to the Pacific Ocean. By the Second World War, the Union of Soviet Socialist Republics that covered this vast territory had transformed itself into a major industrial power. In the 1930s, the Soviet Union seemed to many observers – often deluded or ignorant of the horrors of famine and terror – to offer an alternative path to modernity from that taken by western industrial powers. Britain and the United States faced deep depression as the Soviet Union embarked on rapid industrialization – a source of envy to some, of fear to others.[3]

The new regime faced fundamental questions about the transition to a socialist economy. Marx had assumed a shift from feudalism based on the land to capitalism with an industrial bourgeoisie before capitalism collapsed under its internal contradictions and gave way to socialism. His main focus was on capitalist accumulation by the expropriation of 'surplus value' from workers by the bourgeoisie – but how was capital secured to start the process? The transition from feudalism to capitalism required 'primitive accumulation' of capital by 'the expropriation of the agricultural producer, of the peasant, from the soil'. Marx thought that in England the free peasantry was destroyed by forcible expropriation and 'reckless terrorism' to create large, landed estates with capitalist tenant farms, which appropriated the surplus value of landless labourers who moved into industrial employment and provided a market for both agricultural and industrial goods. In Marx's analysis, the unplanned transformation of English rural society over several centuries was a precondition for industrialization, by accumulating capital, creating a workforce and establishing a market.[4]

The Soviet Communists had to decide how to bring about this initial accumulation of capital for industrialization, and whether it was possible to move straight from a feudal society to socialism without passing through a bourgeois-capitalist stage. There were two main schools of thought. On the one side was the evolutionary approach of Alexei Rykov, Nikolai Bukharin and the majority of the Politburo. They favoured industrialization by developing the internal market, raising the standard of living of the peasantry and industrial workers, accumulating resources for industry through the state sector, gradually improving peasant agriculture, and allowing the market to play a role. Nikolai Kondratiev, a leading Russian economist, favoured a 'developing strata' of efficient peasant farms with freedom to rent land and hire labour, encouraged by the availability of consumer goods. Alexander Chayanov, an agrarian economist, took a different, though still evolutionary, approach. Peasant households produced for their own consumption needs and not for profit. Consequently, it would be difficult to force peasant farmers to provide a surplus for the growth of industry and towns. His solution was co-operatives to market and process agricultural products.[5] By contrast, the Left Opposition, associated with Leon Trotsky and Grigory Zinoviev, opposed concessions to kulaks – the more prosperous peasants – and argued for the rapid development of industry by holding down the prices received by peasants compared with those of industrial consumer goods. Yevgeni Preobrazhensky, a major political figure and writer on economics, thought that the Soviet Union needed to undertake 'primary socialist accumulation' through appropriation of the agricultural surplus by taxes and price controls within a market economy. Others preferred to use force and collectivization.[6]

Lenin's New Economic Policy (NEP) of 1921 rested on 'state capitalism' – a mixed economy of small private enterprises in artisan production and peasant agriculture, with a role for markets and incentives alongside state control over banks, foreign trade, and large-scale industry using advanced technology.[7] Lenin died in 1924, after being incapacitated for the previous two years, which led to a power struggle between Rykov, Bukharin and Joseph Stalin, General Secretary of the Communist Party since

1922. Stalin and Bukharin supported the continuation of the NEP, which was reaffirmed at the Party Congress in December 1927. The problem was that the small, mainly subsistence peasant farms of the NEP could not provide enough food for the army, towns and industrialization. In 1925 and 1926, the party stressed the need to press ahead with industrialization so that the country could avoid 'capitalist encirclement' and protect the revolution from its enemies, which meant concentrating on investment in capital goods. In 1925, Stalin called for an increase from about 4 million to 15–20 million industrial proletarians – but feeding the growing towns was not easy.[8] The peasants preferred to store their grain rather than sell it to the state at low, fixed prices, and they had little motivation to increase output in the absence of consumer goods. By 1928, the result was food scarcity and urban unrest. Bukharin and Rykov urged a restoration of the balance between agriculture and industry by slowing the pace of industrialization and offering incentives to peasants to increase their marketable output. Stalin broke with Bukharin, rejected the NEP, and favoured rapid industrialization to remove bottlenecks in production, with coercive collection of grain from the peasants, rigid price controls and rationing, and the destruction of kulaks with a reorganization of the countryside through *sovkhozy* (state-owned farms) and *kolkhozy* (collective farms). The problem, in Stalin's view, was not the rapid pace of industrialization, vital to economic independence in a hostile capitalist world. Rather, the market and peasants must be subordinated to the needs of the state.

The result was a dramatic shift in policy in the winter of 1929–30 to accelerate industrialization and remove constraints, by the full socialization of agriculture to break the power of the kulaks. Stalin announced that 1929 was to be the 'year of the great break-through' by the 'decisive offensive by socialism'. 'We are going full steam ahead to socialism along the road of industrialisation, leaving behind our traditional "Russian" backwardness. We are becoming a country of metal, a country of the automobile, a country of the tractor.' He embarked on 'a tremendous break-up of the old and a feverish construction of the new'. Stalin's vision was a new world that 'destroyed illusions about the omnipotence of capitalism in general and North-American capitalism in particular'. The Soviet Union would replace the chaos of the market and under-consumption by 'organised human will' and allocation of goods by 'socialist product exchange'. Stalin feared that the crisis of capitalism in the Great Depression might provoke the bourgeoisie to a 'new imperialist war'. Rapid industrialization was therefore vital to overcome backwardness. He was convinced that industrialization, based on heavy industry and machine-building rather than consumer goods, was essential if the Soviet Union were not to be 'unarmed in the face of the capitalist encirclement'. China offered a warning. Its lack of heavy industry and armaments meant it was 'nibbled at by anyone who feels like it'. A new socialist society must be created in 'an offensive against the capitalist elements along the whole front' to produce a 'huge break-through in the psychology of the masses'. The transformation of the Soviet Union was a patriotic, revolutionary duty to be carried out by a new type of Soviet citizen:

> With a passionate effort of will it is possible to achieve anything, to over-come all obstacles ... To slacken the pace means to lag behind. And those who lag behind get beaten. And we do not want to be beaten ... That is the law of the exploiters – beat and rob the backward and the weak. The jungle law of capitalism. You are backward, you are weak – and therefore you are in the wrong, therefore you can be beaten and enslaved. You are powerful, therefore you are right, therefore we must handle you carefully. That is why we must no longer lag behind.

Anyone who expressed doubts was denounced as an unpatriotic, defeatist class enemy in waves of purges and terror.[9]

The rapid growth of heavy industries required changes in agricultural production to release labour from the land and feed urban workers. Large collective farms for entire administrative districts were assumed to lead to economies of scale and higher productivity, and they would have further gains – so it was hoped – through fleets of tractors and agricultural machinery.[10] The process entailed the brutal destruction of the kulaks and the end of peasants' private property rights. However, collectivization and de-kulakization failed to produce the predicted benefits, which was not surprising given the upheaval of replacing about 25 million individual peasant households by about 250,000 socialized collective farms without administrative expertise to run such large units. Peasants saw collectivization as a second serfdom and mounted passive and active resistance. The authorities diverted blame from their unreal-istic plans to class enemies, traitors and saboteurs, with show trials, the forced resettlement of whole villages to remote districts, expulsions to forced labour camps, and executions. Economics was a matter of life and death. Kondratiev and Chayanov were arrested in 1930 and charged with membership of the non-existent Peasants' Labour Party. Kondra-tiev was convicted as a 'kulak professor' and sentenced to eight years' imprisonment; he was re-arrested in 1938 and shot. Chayanov was sen-tenced to five years in a labour camp in 1932 and was executed in 1938. Preobrazhensky was sent into internal exile in 1933 and executed in 1937. Bukharin and Rykov were arrested on charges of treason in 1937 and executed in 1938.[11] Meanwhile, Soviet citizens died in their millions as a result of the policies pursued by Stalin.

The plans of 1929–30 failed. Bottlenecks in agriculture and industry were not broken, and the expanded production of capital goods led to serious shortages of consumer goods. In March 1930, Stalin's article 'Dizzy with success: problems of the *kolkhoz* movement' blamed local officials for proceeding too quickly. In the summer of 1930, collectivization resumed with smaller units on the scale of the village, with peasants retaining a small plot and animals. Instead of wages, collective farmers were paid for the amount and quality of their work by distributing what remained after meeting the needs of state agencies, taxes and the collective farm. Tractors and agricultural machinery were transferred from the large *kolkhoz* to state Machine Tractor Stations. In practice, the farms were under state control with limited independence, and a large part of production was appropriated by the state at low prices. They were not able to offer decent returns to workers who preferred to spend time on their own small plots that continued to supply a large portion of the food supply at market prices.[12]

Industrialization proceeded without regard to financial stability. The aim was to dispel the 'magic of banks' so that 'the shell of credit falls off and the clear features of the process of production and circulation in physical terms are emerging'. This socialist planned economy based on 'cashless accounting' had serious defects. Payments were made against the plan, whether or not it was fulfilled and regardless of the quality and quantity of the goods. It was not clear whether enterprises were in debt, and there was a lack of capacity to administer the new system.[13] When rapid industrialization led to bottlenecks, the response was not to reduce targets but to force open the bottlenecks. The result was absurdly unrealistic targets based on the belief that socialist production was inherently more efficient.[14]

The five-year plan was modified in 1931 and 1932 to allow an element of wage incentives, the provision of more consumer goods, and permission for peasants and collective farms to sell food at market prices after the demands of the state were met.[15] These reforms were too late and too minor to avert disaster. A poor harvest in 1931 led to reductions in food rations in towns, near famine in the countryside, and social unrest. Peasants had little motivation to supply produce at a market price, for there were few consumer goods to purchase; and the collective farms received low prices from the state. Diverting consumer goods to the countryside left fewer goods for the towns, which were facing shortages of food, with rapidly rising prices for anything that was available through the market. Urban discontent mounted and kulaks were denounced as class enemies.[16]

Critics of Stalin's policy called for a reduction in the pace of change and a redress of the balance between industry and agriculture. In their view, expropriation in the countryside by the compulsory collection of food 'led the whole country to a most profound crisis, appalling impoverishment of the masses and famine in both village and town'.[17]

Disaster struck in 1932–33. The poor harvest of 1932 led to devastating famine and the death of perhaps 5 to 6½ million people, above all in Ukraine where around 4 million people died – precise figures are impossible. Stalin pursued absurdly optimistic economic policies of agricultural reform in the hope of securing more grain. He suspected that peasants were hoarding food, which he aimed to force them to surrender – and suspicion and paranoia of attacks from foreign capitalists and from kulak 'class enemies' meant that efforts continued even when the peasants had no grain for their own survival or for the next harvest. Stalin's pursuit of a rigid and ill-conceived economic policy had appalling humanitarian consequences. In the case of Ukraine, the impact of the famine was particularly devastating thanks to Stalin's desire to destroy Ukrainian national identity. The failure of grain requisitions was blamed on Ukrainianization. A lack of loyalty to the Soviet Union, demonstrated by the existence of the Ukrainian language and culture, led – so it was believed – to subversion of collective farms and sabotage of the harvest, which justified draconian searches for food. The result was a purge of the Ukrainian Communist Party and an onslaught on Ukrainian culture and identity.[18]

The crisis led Stalin to strengthen his hold on the party by a campaign of terror and to accept greater realism. By proclaiming the success of collectivization and industrialization, the pace of change could be moderated, for it was no longer necessary to 'whip and spur on the country'. Instead, there was more emphasis on financial stability by reducing capital investment to the level dictated by the supply of food. The Soviet Union created a socialist economy based on the collectivization of agriculture supplemented by a free peasant market; the end of private hire of labour for profit; and a planned economy with state enterprises.[19] Agriculture was transformed. In 1928, 96.2 per cent of the sown area was held by peasants with a further 1.1 per cent in household plots, and only 1.5 per cent in state farms and 1.2 per cent in collective farms. By 1940, peasant holdings were down to 9.5 per cent, with a further 3.5 per cent in household plots; state farms accounted for 8.8 per cent, and collective farms 78.2 per cent.[20]

This transformation led to immense human suffering in famine and terror. Fellow travellers and supporters in Europe and the Soviet Union turned a blind eye to the Gulag, purges and famine, and celebrated the metamorphosis of a backward peasant society into a dynamic, modern industrial economy and military power that made a major contribution, at huge cost, to the defeat of Nazi Germany. Even ideological opponents of Communism and the Soviet Union saw a threat to capitalism rather than the flaws of planning and control. During the Second World War, the Soviets were a crucial part of the grand alliance against Germany and Roosevelt expected them to be one of the 'four policemen', along with the United States, Britain and China, who would ensure post-war peace and stability. Many American officials hoped the Soviet Union would play a full part in the new institutions of global economic government, a sentiment that extended beyond Harry Dexter White – a Soviet agent who passed on secret information – to Treasury Secretary Morgenthau and President Roosevelt. The question was whether the 'state-trading' Soviet economy could be integrated into a system that relied on capitalist market-based economics and multilateral trade. It soon became clear that it could not, and the new institution became a bloc of capitalist economies – the West – aligned against Communist economies.

In the Cold War, two models of modernization vied for influence – or, more accurately, three models, with Communist China competing with the Soviets in many parts of the world. The Communist Party took over China in 1949, but in the 1930s their success was not preordained. The nationalist Chinese government had one of the largest delegations at Bretton Woods, with a distinctive view of the role of international institutions that went back to the Treaty of Versailles.

CHINA: NATIONALISM AND INTERNATIONALISM

Although China avoided direct colonization in the nineteenth century, major European powers controlled 'treaty ports' and ran the customs service so that the Chinese government had limited control over economic policy. When the Boxer Rebellion of 1899–1901 threatened the European presence in China, the response was military intervention, the humiliating sacking of the Summer Palace in Beijing, and the imposition of an indemnity. The ruling Qing dynasty was soon replaced by a republic that was unstable from the start. In 1912, the nationalist leader Sun Yat-sen was proclaimed provisional emperor in Nanjing, before he stepped down in favour of Yuan Shikai, who was based in Beijing. The attempt by a new political party – the Chinese Nationalist Party or Kuomintang – to overthrow Yuan was defeated in 1913 and Sun went into exile in Japan, where he created a new Chinese Revolutionary Party. Yuan's rule came to an end in 1916, the republic was restored, and Sun returned from Japan. He formed a military government in part of China and in 1919 re-established the Kuomintang.[21]

Sun Yat-sen devised a development strategy that rested on the 'three people's principles': nationalism based on the descent groups that comprised China; democracy or the people's rights; and socialism or the people's livelihood. National sovereignty should be regained by taking control over tariffs, for 'just as forts are built at the entrance of harbours for protection against foreign military invasion, so a tariff against foreign goods protects a nation's revenue and gives native industries a chance to develop.' Sun realized that China could not modernize without international assistance, so nationalism and protection should be complemented by an 'international development organization' that would provide foreign capital and expertise to modernize the Chinese economy and improve the 'people's livelihood'. State intervention should be linked with international financial assistance from 'the various governments of the Capital-Supplying Powers' who would enter into a contract with the Chinese government rather than (as in the Soviet Union) by 'primitive accumulation' from peasants. The industries and infrastructure created by this investment would be owned by the state in a 'Great Trust' managed for the mutual benefit of the Chinese people.[22] Agrarian reform was less radical than in the Soviet Union: farmers should own and operate small and medium-sized farms, with a limited amount of waged labour.

Sun Yat-sen's approach to modernization was partly inspired by Japan, the only Asian power to achieve modernization and maintain independence through its own endeavours. Japan had only limited engagement with foreign traders, from the early seventeenth century until the arrival of the 'black ships' of the American fleet in 1853. In 1868, Japan adopted a new policy to avoid the fate of China: rapid modernization by adopting western institutions in the fields of law, education, the military and business, as well as western ideas in economics, science and politics. At the same time, Japan incorporated religion and its imperial past into its cultural identity. The result was its transformation from a feudal, agricultural society to a modern industrial and military power that defeated Russia in the war of 1904–5 and started to build its own empire. Yet China was different: it was larger and more ethnically and religiously diverse, and it did not experience the swift regime change that allowed the Japanese Meiji government to embark on reform. Another model was the transformation of Turkey by Kemal Atatürk after the collapse of the Ottoman empire. Like China, Turkey emerged from the collapse of an existing regime, and

Atatürk adopted a policy of secularism and, in effect, a one-party state that was close to the ambitions of Sun and the Chinese nationalists.[23]

When Sun's proposals for his country were rejected at Versailles, he made an alliance with the small Chinese Communist Party (CCP) and turned to the Soviets for assistance – though they thought that China was too backward for a Communist revolution. At first, the Kuomintang and Communist parties co-operated in a National Revolutionary Army with the aim of securing control over the whole of China. The attempt was short-lived. When Sun died in 1925, the Kuomintang split between those who supported the Communists and a right wing under Chiang Kai-Shek, who purged Communists from areas under his control. The situation was chaotic, with rival governments alongside the internationally recognized government in Beijing, as well as powerful provincial warlords. By 1928, Chiang had gained support from the rival Kuomintang faction, struck deals with warlords, and secured international recognition for his government in Nanjing. Nevertheless, his control of the country remained uncertain, with unstable agreements with local warlords, a revival of Communism, and the Japanese invasion of Manchuria in 1931.[24]

In these difficult conditions, the Nationalist government in Nanjing revived Sun's development strategy to create economic modernity and build a republican nation. Control over tariffs was regained between 1928 and 1930, and in 1936 these duties provided 43.7 per cent of central government tax revenue that was crucial to meeting obligations to foreign creditors, modernizing the Chinese economy, and financing war against the Japanese.[25] The leading figure behind the revival was Soong Tse-ven, a Harvard- and Columbia-educated economist and businessman who was Minister of Finance from 1928 to 1933. At the World Monetary and Economic Conference, he pointed out that China offered a solution to the economic crisis by absorbing excess capital. He sought to reschedule loans and raise foreign capital through a committee representing China, the United States, Britain, France, Germany and Italy, headed by the former League official Jean Monnet. The proposal failed, for J. P. Morgan and the Hong Kong and Shanghai Bank refused to co-operate for fear of offending Japan. However, in 1932 Monnet accepted an invitation to move to China where he set up the Chinese Development Finance Corporation.[26]

Soong also turned to the League of Nations. Ludwik Rajchman, its expert on public health, advised China from 1926, and in 1931 the League entered into an agreement to supply technical advice on water, public health, education and transport. This advice soon widened to cover economic development and especially agriculture, with a National Economic Council as recommended by the League to develop a three-year plan. The

League's advice came from different ideological positions. In the case of agrarian reform, experts argued for rural co-operatives that were close to Chayanov's ideas. They disagreed on the form they should take. The British expert W. K. H. Campbell had worked in the Indian Civil Service and argued that co-operatives would allow small farmers to be more successful. Carlo Dragoni, the Fascist head of the IIA, wanted a corporative approach that brought together different interests in a hierarchy building from local co-operatives to national bodies, and his approach had sympathizers in China. The German social democratic Max Brauer saw co-operatives as a way for peasants to compete with large capitalist concerns and individualistic economic interests. China's nationalists could choose between these different voices in pursuit of their own agenda. To them, co-operative societies offered a way of mobilizing peasants to supply food and good quality raw materials, and to extend the nationalists' hold over the villages against Communist influence. This international involvement came to an end in 1934 when Joseph Avenol, the new secretary-general of the League, imposed greater control from Geneva in the hope that Japan would resume its membership.[27]

In 1935, the Nationalist government turned to a new economic policy based on the development of heavy industries for rearmament – an approach that reflected Chiang's more authoritarian approach and the subordination of the economy to military needs. The situation was deteriorating. The government had to abandon Nanjing in 1937 and revenues from tariffs, crucial for development plans, collapsed with the loss of major ports to the Japanese invaders.[28] The strategy of modernization was also undermined by currency reform. China's currency was silver-based, and problems arose when Senator Pittman and the American silver lobby secured the Silver Purchase Act of 1934, which required the American government to purchase silver and raise its price. As a result, the yuan increased in value and Chinese exports became less competitive and imports cheaper. Further, silver was exported to secure a higher price in the United States. The Chinese government pressed Washington to confine its purchases to American silver – a course forbidden by the Act – or to provide financial support for currency reform.

Opinion in Washington was divided. The State Department felt that China was incapable of reform and that support would offend Japan. Hull therefore insisted that action should be international and include the British. At the Treasury, Morgenthau criticized the State Department for its servility to Japan and realized that international action to abandon China's silver standard would alienate the American silver lobby. There was a risk that the yuan might be pegged to sterling rather than the dollar, with Chinese silver sold on the London market, which would reduce its price and provoke the hostility of Pittman and his allies. A compromise was reached. Morgenthau agreed to the purchase of some Chinese silver in return for gold that would be held in New York to stabilize the yuan; and Hull insisted that no loan would be made to the Chinese government, so as not to offend Japan. Internal American politics led to Chinese currency instability at a time of deep uncertainty.[29]

During the Second World War, discussions of international economic government offered the Kuomintang a way of securing legitimacy and support against both Japan and the CCP. Soong was the Chinese representative in Washington during the war as well as Minister of Foreign Affairs, and the Nationalist government was anxious to play a role at Bretton Woods. Roosevelt expected China to be one of the great post-war powers with America, Britain and the Soviets, and it had the fourth-largest quota and share of votes in the International Monetary Fund.[30] But the American policy in the war of 'Europe first' and doubts over the weak, corrupt government of Chiang meant that Mao and the Communist Party triumphed in 1949. China took a different direction with consequences for global economic government that resonate in the twenty-first century with China's emergence as the world's second-largest economy.

INDIA: COMPETING VISIONS FOR ECONOMIC DEVELOPMENT

At the end of the nineteenth century, Indian nationalists developed a powerful critique of imperial rule. British rulers claimed to be agents of economic progress, investing in the infrastructure of railways and irrigation, underwriting loans from British investors, encouraging engagement in the global economy, and overthrowing 'backwardness' by access to western science and technology. India was vital to Britain's global economic position, for it was the only major area of the world with which Britain had a trade surplus, and India's exports to other parts of the world helped cover British deficits. Indian nationalists agreed that India was backward, but because of exploitation by British rule rather than through the intrinsic nature of Indian society. In their view, irrigation and transport schemes integrated India into the world economy at the expense of domestic food supplies and distribution networks, which contributed to destructive famines.[31] Further, Dadabhai Naoroji – a founding member of the Indian National Congress in 1885 – argued that the 'home charges' to pay for British rule and debt service drained wealth from India, a transfer intensified by the decline in the value of the silver-based rupee against the gold-based pound.[32]

Romesh Chunder Dutt – another founding member of the Indian National Congress and author of an economic history of India – noted that at the time of Queen Victoria's diamond jubilee in 1897, 'amidst signs of progress and prosperity from all parts of the Empire, India alone presented a scene of poverty and distress'. The celebrations coincided with famine. 'Increasing wealth, prospering industries, and flourishing agriculture, had not followed the flag of Britain in her greatest dependency.' He argued that Indian manufactures were suppressed to create a market for British goods, and farmers in a poor nation were taxed to send money to the richest, which 'drains the life-blood of India in a continuous ceaseless flow'. Dutt hoped that the problems could be rectified by replacing exploitation by a policy that 'lightened land taxes, revived industries, introduced representation, and ruled India for the good of her people' who could feel 'they were citizens of a great and United Empire'. Dutt advocated *swadeshi* – Sanskrit for 'one's own country' – or the consumption of domestic goods, and reducing the home charges and military expenditure that did not benefit India.[33]

In the late nineteenth and early twentieth centuries, these arguments were employed by nationalists to persuade the colonial state to reform. By the 1930s, they had become powerful arguments against colonial rule. But how exactly should India develop? The contrasting ideas of Jawaharlal Nehru and Mahatma Gandhi were influenced by different strands in British thought. Although Gandhi was a leading opponent of imperial rule, he was influenced by British discourse, especially John Ruskin's cultural critique of industrialization in *Unto This Last*, and Henry Maine's *Village-Communities in the East and West* with its notion of the Indian village as a harmonious society. Gandhi insisted that judging civilization in terms of machines and technological progress would merely lead to 'English rule without the Englishmen'. Instead, he wanted appropriate technology and 'trusteeship' by which the rich would hold their property 'in trust' for the good of society. This 'constructive programme' was based on communal unity between Muslim and Hindu, the removal of 'untouchability', the provision of education, raising the status of women, economic equality and *khadi* – hand-spun and woven cloth that symbolized rural self-employment, in place of imported factory-produced cloth. *Khadi* would lead to a revival of 'ruined village artisans', creating self-contained and prosperous villages. The idea connected with *swadeshi* and self-sufficiency through boycotting British goods and reviving domestic production. Although Gandhi's vision was a spinning wheel in every home, he knew that heavy industry was needed in some sectors, and that villages could not be entirely self-sufficient in all goods. Nevertheless, he believed that mass unemployment meant there should be labour-intensive production rather than mechanization. Industrialization would also concentrate power in a wealthy urban elite, which would undermine the dignity of labour and lead to corruption. He feared that economic growth would entail dependence on foreign markets and hence exploitation and the adoption of western lifestyles. The solution was self-employment in village industries with close relations between workers and owners. He rejected both socialism and capitalism as materialist ideologies that neglected the moral basis of the traditional village.[34]

By contrast, the left wing of the Indian National Congress associated with Nehru and Subhas Chandra Bose argued for large-scale industrialization to escape dependence on advanced countries. They established the National Planning Commission (NPC) in 1938. Nehru commented to Gandhi in 1945 that 'I do not understand why a village should necessarily embody truth and non-violence. A village, normally speaking, is backward intellectually and culturally and no progress can be made from a backward environment. Narrow-minded people are much more likely to be untruthful and violent.' Nehru favoured socialist planning and capital-intensive industry, though he tried to create a modus vivendi with cottage industries by community development programmes. Heavy industry would exist alongside private agriculture and industry producing labour-intensive consumer goods in a self-sufficient Indian economy.[35] Bose went further in rejecting Gandhi and supporting socialist planning and industrialization. In 1938, he was asked whether

> the India of the future is going to revive the philosophy of village life, of the bullock-cart – thereby perpetuating servitude, or is she going to be a modern industrialised nation which, having developed all her natural resources, will solve the problems of poverty, ignorance and defence and will take an honoured place in the comity of nations?

This leading question elicited a forceful response that looked to the Soviet model:

> India is still in the pre-industrial stage of evolution. No industrial advancement is possible until we first pass through the throes of an industrial revolution. Whether we like it or not, we have to reconcile ourselves to the fact that the present epoch is the industrial epoch in modern history. There is no escape from the industrial revolution. We can at best determine whether this revolution ... will be a comparatively gradual one, as in Great

Britain, or a forced march as in Soviet Russia. I am afraid that it has to be a forced march in this country.

Industrialization should 'aim at national autonomy, especially in the field of our principal needs and requirements' and should develop the crucial infrastructure of power, metals, chemicals and transport. During the war, Bose established the Indian National Army to fight alongside Japan.[36]

Nehru was sceptical about the Soviet route to modernity. He pointed out in 1937 that the Soviet five-year plan 'has impressed itself upon the imagination of the world. Everyone talks of "Planning" now ... The Soviets have put magic in the word.' But he disliked the absence of democracy, and his views were closer to British democratic or Fabian socialism. He explained to the NPC in 1940 that

> the very basis of our Planning is a free India, democratically fashioned, where no external authority can interfere or obstruct the nation's work ... Political domination is patent enough, but a far more dangerous and insidious thing is economic domination. While the public can see and feel political domination, and therefore react to it, it is not so conscious of the economic stranglehold which throttles the life of the nation and prevents industrial and other growth.[37]

Planning appealed to the professional middle class of engineers, scientists, academics and politicians who sought national self-respect and an escape from 'backwardness'. The application of science would 'solve these problems of hunger and poverty, of insanitation and illiteracy, of superstition and deadening custom and tradition, of vast resources running to waste, of a rich country inhabited by starving people'. It was a vision of ordered, disciplined progress and nation-building.[38]

The British rulers of India responded to nationalist critiques by establishing inquiries that reflected their assumptions yet allowed Indians to take part and question justifications for British rule. British officials reformulated the idea of 'trusteeship' in a way that implied they would depart as soon as India was ready for self-rule. The Raj was torn over the best policy. George Schuster, Finance Minister in India between 1928 and 1934, argued for active intervention and economic planning, though he assumed that India would remain an agricultural complement to British industry. His successor, James Grigg, took a different approach that emphasized balanced budgets and sound finance, and opposed the use of protection to raise revenue and stimulate industry.[39]

The war made these debates more pressing, for British rule was challenged from outside by Japan, as well as internally. The Congress Party withdrew co-operation after India was brought into the war without consultation. The situation was not helped by Churchill who had opposed the Government of India Act of 1935 that granted India a degree of self-government. He continued to support the rule of the British Raj and adopted a high-handed attitude to India during the war. Leo Amery, Secretary of State for India from 1940 to 1945, supported imperial preference and self-government and was not sympathetic to the tactics of Indian nationalists. Nevertheless, he was critical of Churchill and saw the need to bring Indians into the Viceroy's Council and to respond to the devastating Bengal famine of 1942–43. In 1942, he wrote to the viceroy, Lord Linlithgow, wondering whether the British might

> set ourselves . . . to a complete overhaul of India's national life? . . . Might it not be our duty after the war to put ourselves in the position of a bold, far-sighted and benevolent despot, determined in a few years, in a series of five-year plans, to raise India's millions to a new level of physical well-being and efficiency?

Schuster agreed that a positive programme was needed to secure Indian support for the war. Here was 'a vast opportunity – an opportunity for India to accomplish something like an industrial revolution'.[40]

The Cabinet sent the left-wing politician Stafford Cripps to India in March 1942 in the hope of placating American criticism of British imperialism and to secure Indian co-operation in the war effort. The sincerity of the British government, and particularly Churchill's, was doubtful – and Cripps's conditional offer of independence after the war was predictably rejected. Gandhi opposed war, and the Congress Party, which wanted immediate independence, embarked on its 'Quit India' campaign, whereupon the leaders of the party were imprisoned. In August 1942, the Cabinet agreed that 'urgent attention should be given to the development of a more progressive social and industrial policy in India' to remove grievances that could be exploited by the nationalists. After his failed mission, Cripps went on to recommend 'modern techniques of economic planning' with public corporations and an All-Indian Programme of Industrial Development.[41]

These attempts to develop a more progressive imperial policy were too little, too late. Ramaswami Mudaliar, an Indian lawyer and politician who served as a representative of the Government of India to the British War Cabinet from 1942 to 1945 (and was chairman of the United Nations Economic and Social Council in 1946), informed the viceroy that it 'would be resented as a bribe and as a sign of death-bed repentance'.[42] The suspension of the NPC because of the arrest of leaders of the Congress Party left room for Indian businessmen to produce the Bombay Plan of 1944, a modified version of the NPC that undertook large-scale economic planning in a way that would preserve capitalism. The Government of India's report on reconstruction planning of 1944 shared assumptions with both the NPC and Bombay Plan in a new form of 'constructive imperialism'. All three approaches shared a common discourse of planning and development that was central to both imperial justification and nationalist critiques of British rule.[43]

The new institutions of global government were implicated in debates over empire, with tensions between Washington and London over decolonization. The discourse of development was also present at Bretton Woods, where India was represented both by British officials and Indian representatives, including Ardeshir Darabshaw Shroff, a leading businessman and co-author of the Bombay Plan. He challenged the failure of the agreement to address the desire of India and developing nations for planning and industrialization behind tariff barriers, and the failure to release the huge sterling balances accumulated by India in payments from Britain during the war so that they could be used for economic development. When India gained independence in August 1947, planning and development were crucial to the new state's legitimacy and freedom from foreign control. It was an economic policy that differed from the American commitment to an open global economy and free markets.[44]

Despite America's Good Neighbor policy, there were also tensions with the scheme of import-substituting industrialization in Latin America – the replacement of imported by domestically produced industrial goods through the use of tariffs and state encouragement. The case for protection of local industries by tariffs and quantitative restrictions, for regional preferences and full compensation of the use of national resources, and an increase in the price of primary commodities, challenged the ideology of multilateral trade and open markets.

THE DEPRESSION AND THE PERIPHERY: THE CASE OF LATIN AMERICA

The drop in the price of primary products after 1929 had serious consequences for advanced economies with a large primary sector such as the United States, and even more for major exporters such as Brazil, Argentina, and Australia. These economies were highly dependent on exports of foodstuffs and raw materials to Britain, the United States and continental Europe; they borrowed capital to develop their infrastructure; and they faced difficulties servicing debts and paying for imports as their terms of trade deteriorated and farmers in the United States and Europe demanded protection. Primary producers faced default, balance of payments deficits, and a drive to replace imported manufactures by domestic industry. Secretary of State Hull warned the British ambassador to the United States of the consequences of such economic isolationism:

> The food and raw-material-producing countries would be driven to establish their own crude manufacturing plants to produce their manufactured necessities at double and treble prices. And the industrial countries would be desperately attempting to do their own farming at five to ten times the present cost of production. The world would then find itself in the most uneconomic condition it had been in within two hundred years.[45]

The benefits of comparative advantage would be lost and the standard of living would fall. But in the developing world, comparative advantage seemed an ideological justification for exploitation.

Before the First World War, Latin America depended on export-led growth. Massive inflows of foreign capital led to the development of sectors such as coffee in Brazil and livestock in Argentina. After 1929, the price of exports of commodities fell more than that of manufactured imports, and the decline in purchasing power was serious in countries so dependent on trade. In 1928, exports from Argentina were 22 per cent of GDP, in Chile, 31.3 per cent and in Brazil 14.1 per cent. Governments relied on trade for their revenues: in 1929, 47.1 per cent of tax revenue in Argentina came from import duties and 2.5 per cent from export duties; in Chile the figures were 36.8 and 27.2 per cent, and in Brazil 23.0 and 10.7 per cent. The cost of servicing external debt rose to as much as 70 per cent of government revenue, foreign investment dropped, and many countries defaulted.[46]

The response was to turn from export-led growth to import-substituting industrialization (ISI), with high tariffs imposed on imports and state support for local industries, often complemented by a right for workers to unionize within a corporatist system that represented workers, employers and the state.[47] Nevertheless, traditional exports could not be neglected. They were a large part of the economies of Latin America, and depreciation of local currencies made them more competitive. Of course, the impact of depression differed between countries. Chile's exports were dominated by copper and nitrates, and it was difficult to absorb unemployed miners in an agrarian sector which was based on large estates. By contrast, the export sector in Mexico was smaller and the government's policy of replacing large estates by small family farms provided a buffer against depression.[48] Despite these differences, the example of Brazil indicates some of the main themes, not least because it became the site for a battle between Hull and Schacht, between incorporation into the economic sphere of America or of Germany. Their competition gave the Brazilian government an opportunity to play them off against each other and retain a degree of autonomy.

After an uprising in 1930, Getúlio Vargas became President of Brazil. He was elected constitutional president in 1934 but seized power in 1937 and established the Estado Nuovo, a corporatist authoritarian regime that continued until 1945. The economic situation was alarming. By 1931, the price of coffee – the main export crop – was only a third of the level during the five years before the Great Depression.[49] At the same time, Brazilian politicians such as Oswaldo Aranha felt threatened by stronger powers in a 'new era of colonial ambitions' and of enslavement to international capitalism. An adviser to Vargas warned that 'countries that neglect their industries will play only the role of colonies. That is the spectacle we see today in Africa. Ethiopia was an agrarian country, rich in unexplored mineral resources ... An industrial power absorbed it. Agrarian China is crumbling ... Agrarian Manchuko [Manchuria] and Korea are dependencies of industrial Japan.' Brazil was also surrounded by 'Indo-Spanish' countries – and such concerns meant that industrialization was needed for strategic as well as economic reasons.[50] Imported goods should be replaced by Brazilian products behind high tariff walls, with an economic zone in central Latin America where Brazil exchanged manufactures for raw materials. Exports of primary products were still needed to earn foreign exchange to develop the manufacturing sector, and higher agrarian incomes would allow farmers to buy industrial goods. Vargas therefore supported growers to maintain domestic incomes, and he invested in education and welfare to improve living standards and to encourage economic development.[51] On his visit to Brazil in 1936, Roosevelt flattered Vargas by saying he had launched a 'South American New Deal', which, more realistically, was a form of authoritarian corporatism.[52]

Both Hull and Schacht approached Brazil for, respectively, a most favoured nation agreement and a bilateral deal. Vargas played one off against the other to secure the best outcome for trade, as well as to obtain armaments which the United States would not supply. He also had to deal with divisions within Brazil. Some members of his government supported a deal with Germany on ideological grounds of opposition to Communism, and on economic grounds that German dominance of Europe would create a market for Brazilian goods. Germany was eager to secure Brazilian food and raw materials to replace supplies from the British empire. Others, including Aranha, feared 'German neocolonialization' and preferred closer ties to the United States. Vargas exploited the confusion caused by the

STRATEGIES OF ECONOMIC DEVELOPMENT

ideological battle between George Peek's protectionism and Hull's internationalism to strike both a deal with Berlin and a trade agreement with the United States – a strategy that Aranha denounced as lacking integrity. Economic links with Germany became stronger. In 1933, Germany took 8.1 per cent of Brazilian exports and supplied 12 per cent of imports; by 1938, the figures were 19.1 per cent and 25 per cent. Nevertheless, the United States remained Brazil's largest single market, taking 46.7 per cent of its exports in 1933 and 34.3 per cent in 1938. Vargas realized that Washington wanted good relations with Brazil and was therefore unlikely to impose sanctions for violating the trade agreement, but he also knew that he could not go too far in offending the American administration.[53]

In Washington, radical New Dealers felt that Hull's free trade policies were inadequate. They wished to help fellow victims of New York financiers in Latin America and to raise living standards as the basis for political stability. They rejected the approach of 'money doctors' who recommended a standard programme of balanced budgets, cuts in spending, tight monetary policies and a return to gold.[54] Roosevelt's speech in Buenos Aires in 1936 captured this ambition of spreading New Deal values:

> Through democratic processes we can strive to achieve for the Americas the highest possible standard of living conditions for all our people. Men and women blessed with political freedom, willing to work and able to find work, rich enough to maintain their families and to educate their children, contented with their lot in life and on terms of friendship with their neighbors, will defend themselves to the utmost, but will never consent to take up arms for a war of conquest.[55]

Such an approach built on the Good Neighbor policy and would counter German influence in the western hemisphere. In 1938 Morgenthau argued for a 'financial Monroe doctrine' to counteract German plans in Latin America.[56] In 1939 and 1940, plans were drawn up for an Inter-America Bank – an intergovernmental institution that would take control from Wall Street bankers and promote long-term economic development through public development loans rather than private investment. It was not ratified because of opposition from Wall Street bankers, and from Senator Carter Glass, who feared a lack of congressional control and demands from spendthrift Latin Americans. Nevertheless, it did have an influence, for Harry Dexter White's initial thoughts on a new international monetary system emerged from this initiative.[57] American commitment to internationalism started in Latin America in creating solidarity against German intervention.

Plans to integrate the economies of the Americas continued in 1940.

Emilio Collado – an economist specializing in international monetary and financial affairs at the Treasury and Federal Reserve Bank of New York who joined the State Department in 1938 – proposed an 'economic program for the Americas', and Nelson Rockefeller – the Coordinator of Inter-American Affairs – suggested a plan for 'hemispheric economic defense'. Instead of using military force to demand debt repayment or imposing austerity, debt should be rescheduled. The approach was exemplified by Adolf Berle, who was Assistant Secretary for Latin America from 1938 to 1944. In March 1940, he remarked that public lending for development 'should be the beginning of a system in which finance is the servant of exchange and development ... in direct contrast to the older system, which insisted that the development and the commerce must serve finance.' These ideas were developed in White's economic missions to Cuba in 1941 and 1942 which marked a change from the approach of 'money doctors' such as Edwin Kemmerer to a new concern for development.[58]

Although the United States delegation to the Inter-American Conference on Problems of War and Peace held at Chapultepec in February–March 1945 claimed that it was the culmination of the Good Neighbor policy, in reality this conference, and the conferences of American states held at Rio de Janeiro and Bogota in 1947 and 1948, marked a divergence between Latin American support for import substituting industrialization and American calls for an 'open door', multilateralism and a fair treatment of foreign capital. The divergence had been apparent at Bretton Woods, and even more so in the post-war talks on trade at Havana in 1947–48 and the growing calls for a structural shift in the global economy in favour of primary producers.[59]

The Latin Americans were not alone, for Australia insisted that the agenda should cover both trade and – crucially – employment. Only with the full employment of the resources of the world would it be safe to remove tariff barriers and the freedom to vary exchange rates, without which primary producers such as Australia would be left without any defence against any future depression.

DEPRESSION ON THE PERIPHERY: THE CASE OF AUSTRALIA

India, the Soviet Union and China were large peasant economies with differing approaches to agrarian reform and industrialization. By contrast, Australia was a self-governing Dominion of the British empire with a small population of 6.5 million, predominantly white Europeans, who mainly

lived in large cities. It was heavily dependent on exports of primary products, above all wool and grain, which suffered from a steep fall in prices.
Australian export prices fell by 38 per cent relative to import prices
between 1929 and 1932, which led to a 9 per cent drop in GDP.[60] Although
Australia depended on the London capital market and British export markets, within these constraints it could set its own economic policies which
took a distinctive character in response to the Great Depression and came
to play a surprisingly important role in debates over the post-war order.

The policy of Stanley Melbourne Bruce, Prime Minister from 1923 to
1929, was 'money, men and markets' – borrowing by federal (Commonwealth) and state governments for development would lead to increased
revenues, more immigrants, and the growth of markets. Economic development would mean an increase in the scale of the Australian economy,
especially in the rural sector. Bruce supported wage arbitration to maintain
the standard of living behind tariff barriers, which would prevent competition from countries 'with larger production or lower standards of living and
hence lower costs of production'. Tariffs should be complemented by export
bounties, preferential access to British markets, and improved efficiency. By
these means, rural development would allow the absorption of more people
and require large-scale borrowing for railways, roads and irrigation. He
insisted that '[i]n a new country with a limited population, in a world of
more populous, wealthy and highly developed nations, growth must be
rapid and Governments must of necessity do many things which in older
civilizations might conceivably be left to private enterprise.'[61]

Problems soon arose. Even before prices started to fall, creditors in
London were alarmed that imports exceeded exports and that the cost of
servicing the debt was covered by new borrowing. An economic mission
of leading businessmen and a senior Treasury official was despatched
from London in 1929, which found that the debts could be serviced and
that creditors had no reason for anxiety, but that expenditure had not
always been wise. The government 'mortgaged too deeply that future
prosperity upon which she can reasonably reckon, thus throwing the burden of her borrowings upon future generations who will have their own
needs to meet'. It found that protective duties and wage arbitration had
raised costs to an excessive level, which made exports uncompetitive and
service of the debt problematic. Deflation was required, and future borrowing for development should be reduced and subject to more rigorous
scrutiny. Douglas Copland, an economist at Melbourne University,
summed up the general sentiment: 'Extravagant borrowing, extreme protection, a closely regulated standard of living and chaos in public finance
provide ample ground for the belief that Nemesis is upon a nation that

has worshipped false gods.' Nemesis soon appeared with the sharp fall in prices in 1929, just at the moment that the new Labor government of James Scullin took office.[62]

In 1930, the Bank of England sent Otto Niemeyer to advise (or brow-beat) the Australian Commonwealth government. Niemeyer was in the same mould as the American 'money doctors' – a pillar of fiscal ortho-doxy and a supporter of the gold standard. He had a long record of criticizing Bruce's policies for leading to high costs that made it difficult to sell increased production in foreign markets. As early as 1926, he felt that Australia 'already shows many signs of a country where public works out of loan moneys have been developed too rapidly for economic health'. In 1929, Scullin needed support from the Bank of England to deal with the financial situation – and Neimeyer used the request for short-term assis-tance to demand a major change in domestic policy to cut costs, reduce the standard of living (artificially high thanks to wage arbitration), stop overseas borrowing, and balance the budget. Deflation, managed by the Commonwealth Bank rather than spend-thrift politicians, was the only way to proceed.[63]

Despite the dangers of unemployment and deflation, Niemeyer's approach was adopted in the 'Melbourne agreement' of August 1930 between the premiers of the Australian states. The Commonwealth gov-ernment was under pressure to implement the agreement, both from the Commonwealth Bank, which refused credit to cover the budget deficit, and from the arbitration court which reduced wages by 10 per cent. Defla-tion imposed by a British banker led to hostility to 'Money Power'. In New South Wales, the Labor Party rejected the policies of 'loan mongers and capitalists' and fought the election on a programme of public works. When Labor came to power in the state in October 1930, the new pre-mier, Jack Lang, rejected the Melbourne agreement. The Commonwealth Bank responded by refusing to fund his programme.[64]

A number of economists were concerned at the destructive social and political impact of deflation and argued for a more imaginative approach. In 1931 the commercial banks decided – independently of the government – to force down the value of the Australian pound, which fell by 30 per cent. The policy was instigated by Edward (E. O. G.) Shann, economic adviser to the Bank of New South Wales, who rejected the policy of tariffs and high wages as creating rigidities in the economy and stifling enter-prise. So far, Niemeyer would agree. Their positions then diverged, for Shann rejected the 'fetish' of fixed exchanges, holding that they should be set 'with reference primarily to the economic balance of our whole price-structure so that all industry will get going again in tolerable mutual adjustment'. Shann believed that economic freedom and enterprise rested on stability of prices so that 'debts can be paid and the wheels of production can turn' rather than on trade restriction and fixed exchanges.[65]

The Commonwealth Labor government invited a group of economists to devise an alternative to deflation. Their approach, as Douglas Copland explained, was to steer between 'the fears and doubts of so-called sound financiers, and the vicious enthusiasm of the inflationists'. He thought that neither policy would work. Inflation collided with

> a deep-rooted conviction in many quarters in Australia that real costs were too high, and that government expenditure was on too extravagant a scale. To have attempted to reduce these costs by inflation in a world that was deflating would have quickly sapped confidence in the currency and the financial structure.

Consequently, wages would have to be cut. On the other hand, deflation alone was not enough to resolve economic problems. Copland recommended a middle course that formed the basis of the 'Premiers' plan' of 1931 – a compromise by state premiers between advocates of inflation and deflation. The loss of income caused by the drop in export prices should be shared between all classes by combining the cut in wages recommended by the arbitration court with a cut in interest payments and a tax on fixed incomes to ensure 'equality of sacrifice'. Further, central bank credit should be expanded to finance deficits and maintain public works. Copland argued that

> the success of the Australian plan lay in its neat balance of orthodox and unorthodox measures. The deflationary elements created confidence in the capacity of the governments to make the necessary adjustments. The inflationary elements prevented these deflationary forces from causing further slackening of enterprise, and laid the foundations for financial recovery, which always precedes economic recovery.[66]

These policies were attacked from both ends of the political spectrum. On the left, Lang proposed a default on interest on overseas loans, lower interest on domestic loans, and replacing the gold standard by an inflationary 'goods standard' based on the wealth of Australia. As a result, New South Wales was expelled from the Labor Party, Lang was removed from office by the governor of New South Wales – the representative of the British crown – and the Commonwealth took control of the state's finances. On the right, Robert Menzies, the future prime minister, denounced the Premiers' plan as 'a very clever and well-considered scheme for bilking the public creditor'. The Commonwealth Bank and Senate blocked finances for public works. Labor left office and the new government was dominated by the populist United Australia Party, which did little beyond 'keep Australia steady' while waiting for an increase in world prices. Bruce, who was now the country's High Commissioner in London, renegotiated the terms of Australian loans, and imperial preference gave Australian farmers privileged access to British markets. The government attempted to raise domestic prices which could subsidize exports, and it imposed import duties on manufactures. But the ability of the Commonwealth government to influence the domestic economy was limited by the power of state governments, and by the weakness of the party as a coalition of popular movements without an effective organization.[67]

Despite the inadequacy of the government, Australian economists devised a new approach that had a significant role in the wartime debates on international economic policy. The Australian delegation at the Ottawa conference in 1932, led by Bruce and advised by Shann, rejected Neville Chamberlain's proposal of increasing the price of primary products by restricting their supply. In their opinion, increased production had saved Australia from default, and output restrictions could not raise prices in general. Monetary action was needed that would raise all prices and also reduce interest rates and encourage public investment.[68] Prior to the World Monetary and Economic Conference, the Australians informed Roosevelt that 'much more prominence should be given to an examination of [the] effect of a simultaneous adoption by [a] majority of stronger countries of a vigorous public works policy as a means to an initial fostering of activity and consequent stimulation of private investment'.[69]

The Australian economists' thinking on employment and the full utilization of resources complemented the work on nutrition that was associated with McDougall and Bruce at the League. McDougall moved from advocacy of imperial economic integration or 'sheltered markets' to a nutritionist approach that aimed to restore agricultural prosperity by a redefinition of comparative advantage (see Chapter 3).[70] Above all, during the war Australian economists stressed an international commitment to the full employment of the resources of the world as a prior condition for the American ambition of lower tariffs and multilateralism, which would expose exporters of primary products to the vagaries of the world market. In September 1942, Ben Chifley, the Australian Treasurer, announced radical plans for post-war reconstruction, and he soon took on the additional post of Minister for Post-War Reconstruction. The director general of this new department, H. C. Coombs, became the leading advocate of full employment as the 'primary social purpose'. Coombs saw that 'the very confusion and flexibility of the situation' offered an 'opportunity to move consciously and intelligently towards a new economic and social system'. American multilateralism alone would make Australia and other primary producers susceptible to a collapse of primary product prices and severe depression. International co-operation to create full employment of the resources of the world should therefore precede the removal of trade barriers in order to reduce the dangers of reliance on export markets and an unstable American economy. Higher incomes were more important than lower tariffs.[71]

The British and American proposals for the monetary system were viewed with scepticism. In September 1943, Coombs complained that the result would be 'a serious sacrifice of economic freedom to vary [Australia's] own exchange rate, and to impose exchange controls', and that at the same time 'it offers no assurance that the major economic countries of the world will maintain a high level of employment and incomes and avoid the accumulation of persistent credit balances'. Given the experience of deflation in the 1930s, the Australian government did not intend to surrender its ability to alter exchange rates in response to a decline in world demand for exports. In January 1944, the employment approach became official government policy for the forthcoming conferences of the ILO at Philadelphia and at Bretton Woods.[72]

The different economic approaches set out above were in tension with the ambition of the advanced industrial, capitalist countries to reform the post-war global economy. The history of the Bretton Woods institutions is usually told through the story of the United States and Britain, but other voices were present. The United States had to engage with their neighbours in Central and Latin America and the Caribbean. In 1939–40, Harry Dexter White was negotiating with the Latin American countries for a development bank, and his thinking fed into the plan that led to Bretton Woods. And while the Americans were negotiating the creation of a post-war trade organization, they were also preparing for the conference of American states at Bogota in 1948. Similarly, Britain had to deal with colonies and Dominions that had different ambitions from the metropole. The Australians used their proposals to challenge the financial and monetary schemes at Bretton Woods in the interests of primary producers. Meanwhile, Indian nationalists pressed for policies to help development and release sterling balances. At Bretton Woods, the views of the less developed or primary producing countries were marginalized but they were articulated at the conference on food and agriculture at Hot Springs in 1943, and in the ILO conference in Philadelphia in 1944, and in the discussions for an International Trade Organization in 1947–48. Above all, they would return in the challenges to the post-war global economic order that emerged at the conference of Asian and African countries at Bandung in 1955, where Nehru joined with Kwame Nkrumah of Ghana and Sukarno of Indonesia to press for an end to neo-colonialism; at the Economic Commission of Latin America, where the Argentinian economist Prebisch pressed his views on the need for a change in the structure of the world economy; and in the demands of the G77 of less developed countries that led to the United Nations Conference on Trade and Development in 1964.

In Part Two, we turn to the creation of the international institutions during the Second World War and in the immediate post-war period. The outbreak of war in Europe in September 1939 meant that the British government appealed to Roosevelt for assistance in the provision of armaments and materials. The result was the Lend Lease programme, which gave Cordell Hull a bargaining weapon to press the British to abandon imperial preference and to join in a common battle against the errors of Schacht. The British government was not so sure – and these tensions over Lend Lease and imperial preference meant that talks on trade policy were fractious. Instead, progress was made on the creation of a new international monetary regime at Bretton Woods in 1944, before serious discussion resumed on trade policy after the war which brought the views of the less developed countries back on the table.

PART TWO

The Bretton Woods Era

In the 1930s, tentative steps were taken towards economic co-operation in an alliance of western capitalist democracies. During the Second World War, the process was taken further by the allies of the 'United Nations', including the Soviet Union after its invasion by Germany in June 1941. These efforts culminated in the Bretton Woods conference of July 1944, which created two new international institutions – the International Monetary Fund and the International Bank for Reconstruction and Development – and continued after the war with conferences to create an (abortive) International Trade Organization. The Bretton Woods conference was only part of a wider set of concerns for development and employment; and implementation of the wartime plans on the return to peace was far from straightforward. The global economy was in a state of disarray; the inclusion of the Soviet Union in the new institutions was problematic with the onset of the Cold War; and the European empires faced challenges from nationalists who demanded independence and a more radical approach to the global economy. The 'Bretton Woods era' did not emerge fully formed in 1944, but involved a long process of implementation, contestation and adaptation.

Lend Lease war materials: cases of TNT gunpowder from the USA
stacked in an underground store somewhere in the west of England, 1941–44.

5
'Handling the English'
Lend Lease, Commercial Policy and Sterling Balances

'The matter of handling the English seems to me to require some thought. In the [First] World War we came so into the English camp that we became virtually an adjunct to the British war machine ... This time it seems to me that the thing should be the other way around ... [W]e are the inevitable economic center of the regime which will emerge ... [T]he salvation of the world will be the building of a system more nearly like that which we have on this hemisphere than like anything which the British are likely to produce, with their experience, their habits and their all too justifiable hatreds.'

Adolf Berle, Assistant Secretary of State, 11 October 1940[1]

'It is interesting to see how closely parallel British and American suspicion of each other seems. The Americans, when viewing our Empire, accuse us of economic imperialism; we ... see considerable evidence that the Americans regard Latin America as their preserve, reserved to American exploitation. They think the disorderly inter-war world the result of British failure to accept proper responsibility for its ordering; we are quite sure it was largely due to American refusal to take a hand in its regulation. They think British selfishness will spoil the next peace; we nurse the suspicion that America won't want to cooperate fairly in the work of reconstruction. They fear that we want to use the Empire as a means of balancing growing American importance in world affairs; we fear they want to attract its members into their orbit in order to lessen our world influence.'

F. E. Evans, British Foreign Office, 12 May 1942[2]

In September 1939, Hitler invaded Poland and Britain declared war on Germany. After the fall of France in June 1940, Britain is often portrayed as standing alone against German aggression. In reality, the country had access to the resources of the world's largest empire, which had become more economically cohesive in the 1930s with imperial preference and the consolidation of the sterling area. The story, in the words of the historian David Edgerton, is one of 'plenitude and power rather than scarcity and sacrifice'. The problem was financial: how to pay for the resources obtained from the empire and sterling area? During the war, Britain paid for resources and the stationing of troops in sterling, which was essentially a promise to pay. Sterling balances were 'blocked' and not available for current use or convertible into other currencies. Abundant wartime resources therefore led to a post-war problem of how to release the accumulated sterling balances, which led to tensions with those countries holding the balances (who wished to use the funds for post-war development) and with the United States that worried that sterling would be used to create a trade bloc and avoid the adoption of multilateral trade.[3]

The other major source of goods was the United States, particularly for munitions, warships, planes and industrial products needed for mechanized warfare. The Johnson Act (see Chapter 2) and continued tensions over the debt from the First World War meant that borrowing was impossible. Attempts to reopen the issue were blocked in April 1939, and an American opinion poll found only 21 per cent support for an amendment to the Johnson Act. Representative Dewey Short (R: Missouri) doubted the wisdom of 'forming an alliance with those people who have shown their gratitude and appreciation by pointing at us a finger of scorn and calling us Shylocks when we try to collect'. The British ambassador, Lord Lothian, admitted in June that 'many of the Isolationists in Congress at present are only too glad to keep the debts alive and in default because they provide an argument against American participation in any future war'. In the absence of loans, the only way to secure goods would be through gold and the sale of assets. By the summer of 1939, the British Treasury feared the result would be the 'imminent collapse of the nation's economy'.[4]

The 'cash and carry' provision of the Neutrality Act of 1937 (Chapter 2) expired early in 1939 and opposition from isolationists meant that Roosevelt failed to secure its renewal until November 1939 when the embargo on purchases of armaments was also lifted. Britain could secure resources so long as it had dollars or gold to pay and shipping available to carry them. But both the military and economic situation were soon alarming: British forces were evacuated from Dunkirk and France fell to the Third Reich in May–June 1940. In September the bombing of British cities started. By the end of 1940, the limits of 'cash and carry' were reached, and the difficulties of the Johnson Act remained. When Lothian returned to the United States from London in November 1940, he allegedly announced to waiting newspapermen: 'Well boys, Britain's broke; it's your money we want.'[5] In December 1940, the Treasury's Sir Frederick Phillips was despatched to Washington to find out if Henry Morgenthau would agree to an outright gift, and he was soon joined, in an uneasy relationship, by Keynes.

Roosevelt wished to help, but domestic politics dictated caution. Morgenthau asked for a list and selling price of all British assets in the US and Latin America. Churchill responded with an emotional appeal to Roosevelt that Britain was the first line of defence for the United States, and on 17 December 1940 the president informed his treasury secretary that he wished to 'get away from the dollar sign'. His solution was to lease resources to fight the war. He explained the principle of Lend Lease in folksy terms in one of his 'fireside chats'. If a neighbour's house was on fire, the natural thing was to lend a garden hose without asking for payment. When the fire was extinguished, there would be no payment if the hose were returned intact; if the hose were damaged, it would be paid for or replaced. Similarly, planes and guns should be supplied to the British as the best way of defending America, 'with the understanding that when the show was over, we would get repaid sometime in kind, thereby leaving out the dollar mark in the form of a dollar debt and substituting for it a gentleman's agreement to repay in kind.' The Lend Lease Bill authorized Roosevelt to provide materials that were, in his view, necessary for the defence of the United States. In order to remove doubts that American generosity was being exploited, Morgenthau urged that Britain sell any assets in the United States. Keynes was outraged by this approach, which he complained rested on the assumption that Britain owned the empire 'lock, stock and barrel'. He insisted that Britain should retain 'enough assets to leave us capable of independent action'. Morgenthau, he complained, was dealing with Britain more harshly than 'we have ever ourselves thought it proper to treat the humblest and least responsible Balkan country'. Keynes had little grasp of politics on Capitol Hill and the need to assuage opinion there. In reality, few assets were sold. The Act passed both Houses of Congress, against considerable opposition from isolationist Republicans and with frequent references to the failure to repay debts. It was signed into law on 11 March 1941.[6]

Suspicions remained about British intentions, given its failure to repay loans from the First World War. The precise terms on which goods were supplied to Britain were not laid down in the Lend Lease Act, which provided aid on condition that the United States secured repayment in kind, in property, 'or any other direct or indirect benefit which the President deems satisfactory'.[7] The approach was typical of Roosevelt in offering assurance to sceptics in Congress without any defined commitment from Britain. The attempt to give the words precise meaning led to divisions within the American administration and to mutual suspicion between London and Washington. As a Foreign Office mandarin put it, the American attitude was 'screw the British'. The British perception that it stood alone as a sole guardian of freedom while America prospered looked different in Washington, where the question arose of why the empire did not supply goods to Britain on the same basis as Lend Lease.[8] More generally, there was suspicion of British imperialism, which conjured up images of redcoats and the Boston tea party, of 'taxation without representation' and exploitation. Imperial preference and the sterling area led to a perception that Britain was fighting to preserve its empire.

Attitudes to the empire did shift with the American entry into the war when Allied victory was the priority and India was crucial in the campaign against Japan in the Pacific and South-East Asia. The British government mounted a propaganda campaign in the United States to portray the empire as akin to America's own western frontier, with sturdy white settlers spreading progress; and to reimagine the empire as a benign British Commonwealth. Nevertheless, differences remained. One American sceptic thought that the South-East Asian Command created in 1943 to oversee the Allied war effort in that theatre should be renamed Save England's Asian Colonies. Roosevelt hoped that the war would lead to peaceful decolonization based on 'trusteeship' by a parent state to prepare colonies for independence, with international accountability. His approach built on the mandated territories of the League after the First World War, and the idea of a pan-American trust for the Latin American and Caribbean colonies of Nazi-occupied countries.[9]

These squabbles over imperial preference, the sterling area and the empire more generally provide the context for the shaping of post-war economic policy.

LEND LEASE: DEFINING THE 'CONSIDERATION'

The crucial issue was what 'consideration' – as it soon became known – would be imposed in return for Lend Lease. Here, the Treasury and State Department had different views. The matter was initially left to the

Treasury. Although Morgenthau wanted the sale of Britain's overseas assets and a reduction of its gold and dollar reserves to a bare minimum, his priority was to defeat Hitler and keep Britain in the war. He was driven by hatred of two things: Germany and high finance. His German-Jewish ancestry and loathing of the Nazi regime made him a supporter of Britain as a matter of necessity, though not conviction. Morgenthau viewed the City of London and Wall Street, in the opinion of his biographer, as 'basically hostile, often in common concert, to the spirit and aims of the New Deal, and therefore to the good of the country'. His ambition was to remove the influence of finance over the world economy and to shift power to Washington, where the dollar could be used for wider benefit than the personal gain of bankers. He was therefore ambivalent about assisting Britain if it propped up the power of the City as well as sustaining the empire.[10]

When officials at the Treasury turned to the 'consideration', they viewed it in terms of a contract and balance sheet rather than as a way of reforming post-war economic relations. Here, the Treasury came into conflict with Hull and the State Department. To Hull, the 'consideration' was an opportunity to force Britain to abandon imperial preference and to prepare the way for a post-war global economy based on non-discrimination and multilateral trade. This approach had the danger, as Jacob Viner of the Treasury pointed out, that linking assistance with the end of imperial preference was

> really lowering . . . rather than raising the tone of this by mixing the Lease-Lend with the millennial blueprint . . . You are saying to the English, 'We are doing these things for you. We want compensation. The compensation is that you have to be decent in a decent world after the war', and then inform the English . . . that it is part of a settlement of a debt to us instead of being part of a common upsurge of humanity to reform the world and fix it up on a broad scale.

Viner argued that the British might react more positively to a broader programme that was separate from an obligation which would be resented as an imposition in a time of need. In reality, it would be very difficult to keep the 'consideration' of ending imperial preference distinct from discussion of post-war policy.[11]

The Treasury soon lost the lead to the State Department. Morgenthau told Treasury officials to 'let the damn thing go' – he was not willing to be 'the President's whipping boy on the foreign affairs stuff', for 'every time the President asks me to do something, Mr Hull goes into a sulk and gets mad'. Negotiating the 'consideration' was handed to the State Department, where it became part of the ambition of Hull and Assistant Secretary

Harry Hawkins to reshape the global economy by spreading American economic liberalism by dismantling protectionism and abolishing imperial preference. This ambition was not consistent with Morgenthau's wish to reduce Britain's monetary reserves, which would force the government to impose import duties and maintain imperial preference. Hull realized that Britain needed to build up its reserves if it were to create an open, non-discriminatory trading system. Lend Lease was thus more than a balance sheet between the United States and Britain: it was the venue for a battle over the future shape of the world economy.[12]

In Washington, the lead was taken by Dean Acheson, who returned to the administration in 1941 as Assistant Secretary of State with responsibility for Lend Lease. Acheson was, like Hull and Hawkins, committed to an open, multilateral world economy. Unlike them, he was more realistic about Britain's plight. He was an Anglophile and a member of the Committee to Defend America by Aiding the Allies, and he argued that a stronger Britain would help America create stability in post-war Europe, the Middle East and Asia. He feared that Morgenthau's hard line would mean that the war would end with both enemies and allies prostrate, whether through military defeat or bankruptcy. He saw that Britain needed to be financially strong if it were to adopt a liberal economic policy. In Acheson's view, unless Britain was assisted, it would turn to protectionism, which would harm American trade and security, and delay the emergence of a liberal world economy and politics. He wanted 'an agreement which is sensible, which can be carried out so that we won't come to the end of this war and then have charges of bad faith and all that kind of stuff going on'. Acheson admitted that 'We really don't know what the intention of Congress was. It obviously couldn't have been that these things have to be paid for, because after the experience of the last war, they just know that that can't happen', and unrealistic demands for repayment 'would create more trouble after the war than not to attempt it'. His aim was to impose

> as much of an obligation as it seemed within the realms of fact could exist and also have something which would encourage the British to want to go on instead of being completely sunk by something absolutely overwhelming, and we laid the foundations for an agreement with them for post war reconstruction.[13]

The Foreign Office took the lead on the British side, in theory removing responsibility from the Treasury and Keynes. In reality, Keynes was the main player in the talks in Washington in May–July 1941. Any hopes that he would reach an agreement were soon dashed. He was in a difficult position, caught between 'the lunatic proposals of Mr Hull' and disagreements over trade policy in London. The coalition government was split between the free trade or 'Atlanticist' position of Anthony Eden, the foreign secretary, and supporters of imperial preference such as Leo Amery, Secretary of State for India, and Lord Beaverbrook, the newspaper proprietor and Minister for Aircraft Production and Supply. Others adopted Keynes's pragmatic view that 'control mechanisms' would be needed to deal with the deficit after the war.[14] As a result, the British draft agreement on Lend Lease made no commitment on post-war trade policy. By contrast, the American draft of July 1941 contained Article VII which specified that the 'consideration'

> shall be such as not to burden commerce between the two countries but to promote mutually advantageous economic relations between them and the betterment of world-wide economic relations; they shall provide against discrimination in either the United States of America or the United Kingdom against the importation of any product originating in the other country; and they shall provide for the formulation of measures for the achievement of these ends.[15]

Keynes was suspicious and enquired whether the article raised the issue of imperial preference and other trade controls after the war. It obviously did.[16]

Acheson reassured Keynes that Article VII did not impose unilateral obligations on Britain but required 'the two countries in the final settlement to review all such questions and to work out to the best of their ability provisions which would obviate discriminatory and nationalistic practices and would lead instead to cooperative action in preventing such practices'. Lend Lease had to be 'sold' on Capitol Hill, and Acheson realized that a form of words was needed that would both satisfy Congress and be acceptable to the British. Keynes, however, was furious. The Americans were taking advantage of Britain's plight and failing to appreciate the political situation in London. Britain could not make a unilateral commitment to abandon preferences without calling an imperial conference to consult the Dominions, which was not practical in the midst of war, and at a time when Britain relied on their manpower and resources. He was even more concerned about the wider implications of Article VII, which

> saddled upon the future an ironclad formula from the Nineteenth Century . . . it contemplated the impossible and hopeless task of returning to a gold standard where international trade was controlled by mechanical monetary devices and which had proved completely futile . . . the only hope

of the future was to maintain economies in balance without great excesses
of either exports or imports, and that this could be only through exchange
controls, which Article VII seemed to ban.

Keynes realized that Britain's post-war trade deficit would make Article
VII impossible, and, at the same time, America would have a large trade
surplus. Creditor nations should therefore adjust as well as debtors – and
he soon came up with a plan for a new international monetary policy to
ensure this would happen.[17]

Keynes returned to London without reaching an agreement. He was
caught between the conflicting policies of the US Treasury for a reduction in reserves and the State Department's demand for the end of
preferences, both of which were unacceptable. The situation was confused in London, given divisions over trade policy and resentment at
American attempts to force the government's hand. By instinct, Keynes
was a liberal internationalist. He was also a realist who saw that circumstances might force Britain into bilateralism, and he decided to explore
both Schachtian economic nationalism, in case American support for
post-war deficits was not forthcoming, and the American approach of
liberal economics if it were.[18]

The draft agreement was caught up in the grand strategy of the Atlantic
Charter agreed by Churchill and Roosevelt in August 1941. The United
States was not yet at war and Churchill had so far failed to secure a military
alliance. He was sceptical about ambitious statements on the post-war
world before the war was won, commenting that the would-be peace planners 'should not overlook Mrs Glass's Cookery Book recipe for Jugged
Hare: "First catch your hare".'[19] By contrast, Roosevelt wanted a statement
of principles to counter domestic concerns that America was propping up
imperialism or betraying democracy through Britain's support of the Soviet
war effort since June. The third principle of the Charter pledged the two
countries to 'respect the right of all peoples to choose the form of government under which they will live; and they wish to see sovereign rights and
self-government restored to those who have been forcibly deprived of
them.' This return to Wilsonian self-determination was readily accepted for
the conquered territories of Europe. To Churchill, it did not apply to the
British empire. Roosevelt wanted to include rejection of imperial preference. Churchill refused and Roosevelt agreed to a wording of the fourth
point of the Charter that Britain and the United States 'will endeavor, with
due respect for their existing obligations, to further the enjoyment by all
States, great or small, victor or vanquished, of access, on equal terms, to the
trade and to the raw materials of the world which are needed for their

economic prosperity'. The fifth point went further: 'they desire to bring about the fullest collaboration between all Nations in the economic field with the object of securing, for all, improved labor standards, economic advancement and social security.' These grandiose statements of good intentions drew a sharp distinction with the Axis Powers and held out the prospect of a better world after the sacrifices of war. The latter two points also weakened Article VII of the Lend Lease agreement, for Hull realized that 'endeavoring' was weaker than a commitment to end imperial preference, and that 'due respect' to existing obligations could allow it to survive.[20]

The Atlantic Charter has been both dismissed as 'grand and vacuous phrases' and praised as 'a defining inaugural moment for what we now know as the modern doctrine of human rights'. It led to the UN Charter and was used by opponents of imperial rule such as Gandhi and Nehru – not the expectation of Churchill, an arch-opponent of Indian self-government, let alone independence.[21] More immediately, the Atlantic Charter provided an opportunity for Britain to present a new draft of the Lend Lease agreement in October 1941. In this new version of Article VII, conditions

> shall be such as not to burden commerce between the two countries, but to promote mutually advantageous economic relations between them; they shall provide for joint and agreed action by the United States and United Kingdom, each working within the limits of their governing economic conditions, directed to securing as part of a general plan the progressive attainment of a balanced international economy, the avoidance of harmful discriminations, and generally the economic objectives set forth in the [Atlantic Charter].

The phrases 'mutually advantageous' and 'governing economic conditions' gave leeway to the British and were not acceptable to the American negotiators, to whom the draft was weak and ambiguous.[22]

Hull was adamant that imperial preference should be ended and in December 1941 insisted that nothing more could be done to meet Britain's problems:

> We ask no unilateral commitment from Britain but impose identical obligations on ourselves. Nor do we ask Britain to join with us in seeking the attainment of objectives which would be beneficial to us but harmful to Britain. On the contrary, what is sought is the creation of conditions in the post-war period which would operate not merely to our advantage but to their advantage and that of all peoples. Indeed it might be argued that since the prosperity of Britain depends to an even larger degree on the condition

of international trade than does that of the United States they are even more
vitally concerned in the conditions we are seeking . . . Article VII lays down
a broad program around which all liberal forces in both countries can
gather.[23]

Acheson was more pragmatic and diplomatic. He assured the British
ambassador that it was not possible to ask the British 'to move with us in
the direction of liberal economic relations without recognizing that common action in other directions was required to enable them to do so'. Tariffs
should be incorporated into a wider concern for 'expanding economic
activity in production, employment and the exchange and consumption of
goods', without imposing unrealistic burdens on the British, and permitting
flexibility 'in the light of governing economic conditions'.[24]

By January 1942, Roosevelt felt that the British should accept the Lend
Lease agreement without further time-consuming efforts to refine the language of Article VII.[25] Churchill resisted, for divisions in Cabinet made
concessions on imperial preference problematic. He also calculated that
Roosevelt and Morgenthau were 'indifferent' about preferences and that
only Hull was bothered.[26] The British insisted that 'discrimination' could
not apply to special arrangements between members of the same federation, and that the British Commonwealth was no different from the
United States which gave preferences to the Philippines – indeed, it was
even suggested that the United States itself was really a federation that
allowed 100 per cent preference between its member states. More plausibly, the British insisted that any modification of imperial preference
would require consultation with the Dominions.[27]

Roosevelt informed Churchill on 11 February 1942 that he wanted 'to
make it perfectly clear to you that it is the farthest thing from my mind
that we are attempting in any way to ask you to trade the principle of
imperial preference as a consideration for Lend-Lease' – a statement that
would have surprised Hull. Roosevelt accepted that the Dominions must
be consulted. 'All I am urging,' Roosevelt assured Churchill, 'is an understanding with you that we are going to have a bold, forthright, and
comprehensive discussion.' The matter should remain confidential, and
the two governments should not exchange notes to avoid the impression
that the Allies were divided (and to keep the understanding out of the
reach of Hull). Roosevelt urged the British government to sign the Lend
Lease agreement on the basis of his assurances:

What seems to be bothering the Cabinet is the thought that we want a commitment in advance that Empire preference will be abolished. We are asking
for no such commitment, and I can say that Article 7 does not contain any

such commitment . . . [B]oth of us are going to face in this realistic world adjustments looking forward to your 'free and fertile economic policy for the post-war world', and that things which neither of us now dreams of will be subjects of the most serious consideration in the not too distant future. So nothing should be excluded from the discussions.[28]

It was typical of Roosevelt's approach: a nod and wink in private that a public agreement should not be taken at face value. On the basis of these reassurances, the British signed the Lend Lease agreement on 23 February 1942.[29]

The final text of Article VII laid down that the conditions for aid 'shall be such as not to burden commerce between the two countries, but to promote mutually advantageous relations between them and the betterment of world-wide economic relations'. The United States, and any other country which wished to participate, would take steps for 'the expansion, by appropriate international and domestic measures, of production, employment and the exchange and consumption of goods', as well as eliminating discrimination in commerce and reducing tariffs. Hull was delighted and read Article VII as committing the British to eliminate imperial preferences. It was 'a long step toward the fulfillment, after the war, of the economic principles for which I had been fighting for half a century . . . The foundation was now laid for all our later postwar planning in the economic field.' He overlooked the final sentence that referred to discussions 'in the light of governing economic conditions' – an escape clause that could be exploited by the British.[30]

The Lend Lease agreement, in the opinion of Warren Kimball – the leading historian of Roosevelt's wartime policy – 'found the United States remarkably willing and even eager to destroy what it believed to be a cornerstone of Great Britain's empire . . . [T]he Roosevelt administration . . . saw its proposals as a means of saving Great Britain from herself.' The agreement showed a willingness 'to remake other nations in the American image' and to pursue America's preferred policy for the post-war world.[31] Members of the British government were not convinced, in some cases for ideological and in other cases for pragmatic reasons. The agreement of February 1942 did not resolve the issue, for the terms for Lend Lease and the abolition of imperial preference resurfaced at the end of the war. Meanwhile, the differences between the British and Americans created serious problems in the wider talks on trade policy that started in the summer of 1942. As a result, discussions on post-war trade were overtaken by proposals on international monetary relations that were more technical and less politicized.[32]

COMMERCIAL TALKS: FROM
TRADE AGREEMENTS TO THE
COMMERCIAL UNION

Responsibility for trade policy rested with the Department of State, and in December 1941 Hull's adviser on post-war policy, Leo Pasvolsky, produced a memorandum on 'possibilities of conflict of British and American official views on post-war economic policy'. It could have been retitled 'realities of conflict'. Keynes was scathing about its

> dogmatic statement of the virtues of *laissez-faire* in international trade on the lines familiar forty years ago, much of which is true, but without any attempt to state theoretically or to tackle practically the difficulties which both the theory and the history of the last twenty years has impressed on most modern minds. Mr Pasvolsky *looks* like Rip van Winkle and evidently *is*, in fact, he!

Keynes did not assume that laissez-faire would automatically maximize everyone's trade, and even claimed that bilateralism might create trade. He reasoned that Argentina sold meat to Britain which sold its motor cars in Argentina. American motor cars were cheaper than British, but America had no need for Argentinian meat. In conditions of laissez-faire, Britain could not sell its cars and buy Argentinian meat; hence a bilateral deal would allow Argentina to sell its meat in return for British cars, and both would be better off. A supporter of multilateralism could point to a fatal flaw in Keynes's argument: Britain could sell its manufactures in a third market and earn money to buy meat from Argentina, which could then buy cheaper American cars, and everyone would be better off. Keynes was using whatever argument came to hand to support British interests, with little regard for consistency. It suited him to argue that the State Department's commitment to multilateralism was 'pathological', leading to 'false alignments and dangerous misunderstandings'. He urged a return to discussions rather than proceeding independently 'behind two sets of closed doors'.[33]

Hull was doubtful of the wisdom of 'sitting down and engaging in long-winded conversations and formal conferences about post-war policies and programs, which it is possible could and would never eventuate'. Nevertheless, he agreed to informal, unofficial talks in Washington in August 1942 with Richard Law, a Conservative politician and Foreign Office minister. Hull was wary of moving faster than domestic opinion, for his experience of the First World War showed that internationalism could fall victim to domestic isolationism. Above all, he saw ambitious policies as a distraction from trade agreements and the cautious reduction of trade barriers that had been proceeding since 1934. He preferred to start by creating the foundations for economic stability without which there would be unemployment and distress, leading to dictatorship, war and economic isolationism. Only then should attention turn to creating international organizations.[34]

The talks with Law were ineffectual and the British took a new approach in late 1942: informal discussions on commercial and economic policy with the Dominions and exiled governments in London, attended by observers from China and the Soviet Union.[35] Hull refused to participate, and explained to Eden in March 1943 that he had to proceed carefully to deal with fickle American public opinion.[36] Hull realized that renewal of the Reciprocal Trade Agreements Act meant convincing Congress that trade agreements were vital to post-war reconstruction, and he was wary of any initiative that might suggest that the Act was no longer crucial. The American ambassador in London complained that the British government did not realize that, by limiting congressional interference, the RTAA offered a better prospect of trade liberalization than wider commercial plans that would 'be exposed to the hazards of legislative debate and voting'.[37] In fact, the British government had good reason to prefer an ambitious scheme of international reconstruction to deal with a post-war crisis in its balance of payments. The British recalled America's retreat from international engagement in 1919, and the American embassy in London reported that

> fear of an American withdrawal from its due interest in the building of the new world is the dominant factor in British feeling toward the United States today. Neither the British public nor the British Government dares count too strongly that the changed world and the lessons of the aftermath of 1919 will effectively prevent another American 'back to normalcy' wave with all its power to destroy the spirit of cooperation founded on wartime need.[38]

The wider scheme for international reconstruction rested on James Meade's plans for a Commercial Union. Meade had been part of the 'circus' of brilliant young economists at Cambridge that started to meet in 1930 to discuss Keynes's *Treatise on Money* and helped prepare the ground for the *General Theory*. He was a 'liberal socialist', who combined a belief in the market with egalitarianism and internationalism. He advised Hugh Dalton, a Labour politician and Cambridge-educated economist who played a crucial role in devising the party's economic policy in the 1930s, and took leave from his post at Oxford in 1937 to join the League of Nations. Meade's general approach was to reduce trade barriers; to introduce fixed yet flexible exchange rates; to use exchange controls to limit capital movements; and to pursue domestic policies of full employment. Further, he argued that international regulation of economic affairs required an international organization, with restriction of national action on money and trade to prevent economic depressions and to allow the free movement of goods, capital and labour. In 1940, he returned from the League and joined the Economic Section of the Cabinet. When Dalton became President of the Board of Trade in February 1942, he secured Meade's services to develop plans for a commercial union.[39]

Meade presented his scheme in July 1942. He saw that Britain would have problems with its trade balances after the war due to dependence on imports of necessities and difficulties in increasing exports of goods which other countries could do without. British trade had been multilateral in the past, with exports going to less developed areas (above all, India) and the surplus being used to buy goods from the United States, where Britain had a deficit. 'If ever there was a community which had an interest in the general removal of restrictions to international commerce, it is the United Kingdom,' claimed Meade. This ambition meant reducing high American tariffs and ending Schachtian bilateral trade, with a continued right to discriminate against countries that persisted with high tariffs and to control purchases of non-essential goods so long as a serious balance of payments deficit continued. Meade went beyond Hull's commitment to freer trade by arguing that multilateral trade did not necessarily entail laissez faire and was compatible with state trading. Britain could not, he realized, 'afford *unconditionally* to abandon all protective devices ... so long as we are faced with acute problems of restoring equilibrium to our international balance of payments'. He called for a wider policy of financial and economic expansion to increase purchasing power in export markets. He also saw that solving the currency problem was a precondition for progress on trade, for 'it was only in a general milieu of economic expansion that the pressure on the balances of payments of debtor countries is likely to be sufficiently relieved to make possible a really effective lowering of protective devices.' A monetary agreement should come first, complemented by an International Commercial Union to reduce trade restrictions, and an international commission to adjudicate on disputes.[40]

Dalton accepted that post-war prosperity required the removal of barriers to trade to assist British exports by a more dramatic approach than Hull's reliance on trade agreements. In November 1942, he suggested to Eden that Meade's proposal be considered by a committee on post-war commercial policy, to be chaired by Arnold Overton of the Board of Trade, with Meade as a member. The foreign secretary agreed: 'What we must do is to think up constructive and practical ideas of large scope calculated to catch the imagination and fire enthusiasm both here and in America. Your idea of a possible Commercial Union strikes me as just the sort of thing we ought to consider for this purpose.'[41] Nevertheless, there were sceptics in Whitehall with one Foreign Office official warning that 'It seems to savour rather too much of a League of Nations in the economic field and could so easily be brought into disrepute by evasions of its rules which were difficult to check.'[42] Despite these reservations, the Overton Committee supported the idea of the Commercial Union. By taking the initiative, American demands for an unconditional end of imperial preference could be fore-stalled by a wider scheme that would be in general sympathy with Lend Lease's Article VII and take account of British conditions. The committee went a long way towards American demands for free trade, suggesting a sweeping removal of barriers to trade by multilateral action, a reduction in preferences by half, with tariffs set at a maximum of 25 per cent and any already below that level to be cut by a quarter. Subsidies allowing the export sale of goods below the home price should be banned; and quantitative restrictions should be removed after a transitional period.[43]

The proposed cut in imperial preference was controversial in Britain. Hubert Henderson – a student and friend of Keynes before they parted company over the *General Theory* – became an economic adviser to the Treasury during the war. As a member of the Overton Committee, he adopted an economic nationalist position, fearing an irreversible cut in preferences and acceptance of American conceptions of trade. He thought that the future was more likely to rest on planning and regulation than free trade, and he urged delay until the post-war situation became clear.[44] Henderson was ignoring both the commitment in Article VII to end imperial preference and American hostility to planning. A Foreign Office official was more realistic in pointing out that 'Such co-operation as [the Americans] appear to have in mind is designed rather to create a large frame-work of control within which a great deal of freedom and compe-tition may thrive in almost nineteenth-century conditions.'[45]

Keynes welcomed the Overton report, for it undermined American claims that Britain was blocking freer multilateral trade. Nevertheless, he worried that the report conceded too much to an influential minority of free traders in the State Department. Keynes also feared that protectionist Republicans would see 'a dangerous British plot and just what it would suit the Isolationists to accuse the State Department and ourselves of conspiring to produce'.[46] Although he did not fully support imperial preference, he warned against concessions until Congress committed to multilateralism. He doubted the wisdom of the Overton report's 'excessive prejudice against autarky' and over-reliance on comparative advantage. He worried that a full-scale multilateral proposal would provoke opposition in most other countries, and he was 'fearful of prejudicing our other post-war plans by associating them too closely with something as full of dangerous political dynamite'. He saw that 'we should have shot our bolt, leaving the rest of the world with its ammunition in hand . . . [W]ithout a more robust – if you like, a more selfish – policy, we are sunk.'[47] Keynes failed to appreciate that the Commercial Union was a pre-emptive strike to seize the initiative from the Americans and remove the risk, as a Foreign Office official pointed out, of their 'putting forward a much more theoretical and dangerous scheme, or alternatively making such a demand as the complete abolition of Imperial Preference without any real quid pro quo'. On this view, it made more sense to carry the battle to the Americans by a positive British policy rather than fighting a rear-guard action against demands to end imperial preference.[48]

Meetings resumed with the Americans in September and October 1943. Richard Law, the leader of the British delegation, stressed that deficit countries such as Britain could only remove tariffs and controls if there was an increase in the volume of trade and a flow of capital for development; and that creditor countries like the United States needed confidence that it would not face competitive devaluation of currencies. He emphasized the need to consider policies as a compelling interconnected package rather than a jigsaw puzzle of separate parts, and to move from bilateral Anglo-American talks to wider international discussions as the basis for a lasting peace. Bold and imaginative action was imperative:

> The world today is in the melting-pot. Men's minds are open. Ideas are fluid. We are receptive, because we have been badly scared . . . We have great demands to make upon the intelligence and restraint of mankind. It is a fearful responsibility that rests upon us who have some measure of responsibility for decisions which, made now, will shape the destiny of mankind for a century to come. And not one of these decisions will be easy.

He insisted that action was needed before post-war economic chaos led countries into 'the confusion and anarchy of competing economic nationalism'.[49]

The British strategy was both idealistic and self-serving, in seeking to contain American demands to end imperial preference within a wider scheme. The attempt to widen the debate had some success, for the Anglo-American report of the meetings proposed a multilateral commercial convention.[50] At this point, the British lost the initiative, for Churchill realized that trade and imperial preference would split the coalition government. A Canadian observer noted the government was an

'extraordinary harlequinade' of 'old fashioned Imperialists and old fashioned protectionists, of doctrinaire socialists wedded in principle to
planning and opposed in principle to gold and to international bankers'.
Churchill had been a committed free trader before the First World War but
now stood aside so that officials lacked clear direction on post-war plans.[51]

Hull complained that the British government failed to support 'a
broader and more liberal commercial policy', and he was exasperated
when Law visited Washington in July 1944 to plead for a delay to the discussion of Article VII. The Secretary of State urged Britain to emulate his
efforts in securing the RTAA in 1934 and overturning economic isolationism, and argued that Lend Lease and financial assistance should be
conditional on Britain's adopting policies to revive international trade.
He was concerned that Roosevelt was providing continued support to
the British without such a commitment and without enforcing Article VII.
He saw a danger that post-war policy might be 'based on discriminatory
bilateral agreements. This was the method of Hitler and the totalitarians.
It didn't work for Germany and we know that it won't work for Britain.'[52]
The State Department was alarmed that there might be 'an explosion in
public opinion' if America's assistance was seen as supporting competition
with its exports after the war, and that the empire was providing goods to
Britain at full price and accumulating sterling balances. 'The combination
of all of these things may bring about an uproar which will result in a situation that will make US–UK relations after World War I (and God knows
they were bad then) look like a love feast by comparison.'[53] Equally, the
British complained that Hull was failing to act. The American ambassador
in London shared their exasperation that Hull had not sent representatives
to London to discuss trade, even informally. At the State Department,
however, Acheson was critical of the sterility of the 'Hull–Pasvolsky establishment' which lacked 'insight or prophecy' and failed to rise above 'a
dissertation on the benefits of unhampered international trade and the true
road to it through agreements reducing tariffs'.[54]

The combination of divisions in the British Cabinet, Churchill's hesi-
tancy and lack of direction in the State Department meant that discussions
on commercial policy reached an impasse during the war. Keynes worried
at the delay and pointed out to the Americans that long-term commercial
policies to create multilateral economic relations were urgently needed at
the end of the war to ensure that emergency measures adopted during the
transition to peace did not become permanent.[55] A concern for trade did
revive early in 1945 as the war drew to a close, and Anglo-American talks
resumed. In part, the re-emergence of a trade agenda reflected a change at
the State Department from Hull's cautious approach and obsession with

trade agreements. He resigned as Secretary of State in November 1944 because of ill-health, and was briefly succeeded, until June 1945, by Edward Stettinius, the former chairman of US Steel who participated in the early New Deal at the National Recovery Administration. He joined the War Resources Board and became the administrator of Lend Lease before his appointment as Deputy Secretary of State in 1943 with a mission to reform the chaotic organization of the State Department that had led to a lack of policy co-ordination both internally and with other departments. His new team included Will Clayton who took responsibility for international trade talks; he was a Southern cotton trader who was as insistent as Hull on the need for Britain to abandon imperial preference, and just as committed to free trade.[56]

The Americans now regained the initiative. After monetary agreement was reached at Bretton Woods in July 1944, talks could resume on the general principles of post-war trade. By March 1945, the State Department set out the steps needed to expand international trade through high levels of employment and income sustained by domestic and international measures, as well as action on import duties, quotas, export subsidies, discrimination, exchange controls, and commodity agreements to deal with surpluses, protect consumers and stimulate demand.[57] The approach was more ambitious than Hull's bilateral trade agreements and contained a new commitment to an international organization.

A major problem remained at the end of the war: how to deal with preferences. The British wanted to incorporate them in the trade negotiations as a bargaining weapon to secure cuts in American tariffs. The Americans argued that the issue was off the table, for Article VII already committed the British to abandon imperial preferences.[58] However, talks on trade policy were soon taken in a new direction by the emergence of another issue – the full employment of the resources of the world that was demanded by the Australians as a solution to the difficulties of primary producing countries and as a complement to the removal of tariff barriers, as we will see in Chapter 7. The Australians insisted that full employment of resources was a precondition for the establishment of stable exchange rates, for the Bretton Woods agreement limited their ability to use devaluation in response to the perils of the trade cycle in an open, unstable capitalist economy. Similarly, Latin American countries and India pressed for trade talks to cover development and to address the structural problems of the global economy. As we will see, the post-war trade talks raised wider issues of distributive justice.

STERLING BALANCES

American hostility to imperial preference was related to another issue – the sterling area and the accumulated sterling balances, which were seen as devices to bolster British power. In December 1939, Britain owed sterling balances of £556m. Spending on resources and stationing of troops meant that by mid-1945 the balances were £3,355m, compared with £5,504m for transfers through Lend Lease. Above all, India ended the war with considerable holdings of sterling, over £1,321m: equivalent to seventeen times the annual revenue of the Government of India, and almost 20 per cent of British GNP. In 1938–39, a government committee had recommended that India cover the cost of its own defence and Britain would pay for forces sent abroad. A financial settlement was reached in 1940, when it was expected that the war would be mainly fought in Europe. This changed with the entry of Japan. Funding the campaign against the Japanese in Burma – a colony that had been separated from India in 1937 – and paying for British troops in India fell on Britain, as did the cost of any material supplied from India to British armies in the Middle East. The next largest holder of sterling balances was Egypt – a major base for troops in the Middle East and North Africa – with sterling holdings of about £400m. During the war, the sterling payments were not convertible and were held in 'blocked' accounts, which led to serious problems of how these large sums would be released after the war.[59]

By 1942, Churchill was alarmed at the mounting debt to India, though he agreed with the finance member of the Government of India that arousing suspicion about British intentions towards the sterling balances would play into the hands of the nationalists. In 1942, the Cabinet decided to allow the 1940 settlement to stand, but informed the Government of India that the issue would be raised at the end of the war. Churchill was not happy with the situation: 'are we to incur hundreds of millions of debt for defending India in order to be kicked out by the Indians afterwards? This may be an ill-contrived world but not so ill-contrived as all that.' Leo Amery disagreed: 'When driving to the station to catch a life or death train ... I should hardly think that you ... would tell the cabby man you have no intention of paying when you get there as you mean to raise a counter claim.' Nevertheless, in August 1944 Churchill asserted the right to readjust the settlement to take account of Britain's contribution 'to save India from invasion'. To Amery, the demand that India make a larger contribution 'sounded like a memory from another world. Unfortunately, that other world is the one that Winston still lives in.' Despite Britain's huge liabilities, it was scarcely equitable – nor practical politics – to cancel India's sterling balances. A refusal to pay would renege on the agreement reached at the start of the war, lead to more unrest, and require more troops to maintain order.[60]

The American administration suspected that the sterling area was another example of British duplicity in exploiting its generosity – and the British in turn despaired that 'the sterling area is one of the facts of life that the Americans will not believe in'.[61] In 1946, Cameron Cobbold, deputy governor of the Bank of England, remarked that

> a section of American opinion (led by Harry White and the former US Treasury Staff) have shown an almost superstitious dislike both of exchange control and of our sterling area arrangements as if they were a sort of black magic mainly directed against the USA. We have tried time and again to prove to them that the sterling area is something which has grown up gradually over about a century and ... it is harmful to nobody and is in fact one of the few areas of currency stability and comparative freedom of payment.[62]

British officials complained that American criticism 'seemed to be based on the assumption that the Sterling Area had come into existence by some sort of "social contract" which only had to be terminated to achieve the result which the Americans wanted'. Rather, the sterling area emerged by 'natural evolution' because colonial trade was handled by British merchants and used British banks to remit funds and not from a conscious policy with central direction.[63] Convincing the Americans was an uphill task during the war and in the negotiation of an American loan at the end of the war.

The United States Treasury Department also attacked the 'dollar pool' into which members of the sterling area paid dollars from any trade surplus with America. In January 1943, Roosevelt, with British agreement, set the British gold and dollar reserves at $600m to $1bn; by November, the reserves stood at $1.2bn. Here, it seemed, was a cunning British ploy to create a cohesive sterling area that complemented imperial preference and worked against the United States, and to exploit Lend Lease to build up reserves. Morgenthau complained that Britain was failing to use all its resources, and he urged a cut in non-military assistance and a reduction of reserves. The British insisted that pooling dollars allowed members of the sterling area with a dollar deficit to buy American goods, that the reserve was needed against the large liabilities for financing the war effort in the Middle and Far East, and that the net overseas position was deteriorating. The State Department was more sympathetic, and Acheson accepted the validity of the British argument. His priority was to restore multilateral trade and finance, and he realized that restricting British dollar holdings would create problems in dealing with post-war difficulties and would lead to continued blocking of sterling balances and economic controls. Morgenthau conceded – but misunderstandings continued at the end of the war when the American administration wanted swift action to settle Lend Lease, deal with blocked sterling balances, and remove imperial preference.[64]

Will Clayton doubted it would be possible to convince Congress to make a post-war loan to Britain if larger payments were made to sterling creditors than to the United States. He therefore wanted to ensure that American money was not used to bail out the sterling area. In November 1945, he explained to the British that the widespread assumption in America was that

> the sterling obligations represented to a very large degree debts in respect of supplies and services which had been required for the winning of the war and which ought therefore to have been made available to the UK on a basis analogous to lend lease. In some cases, too, the obligations had been swollen by reason of inflated prices charged for such supplies and services. It was fundamental to the US position that they should be able to assure Congress that the US credit was not being used to redeem such obligations.[65]

A British inquiry found that prices were not inflated, and it was clearly unrealistic and unreasonable to expect famine-stricken India to supply goods to Britain on the same terms as the United States. Nevertheless, the State Department official with responsibility for British Commonwealth affairs saw that 'we will never be able to explain to the taxpayers of the United States why the American people should treat the United Kingdom more generously than the people of other parts of the Commonwealth and Egypt should treat the United Kingdom.' American help should therefore be conditional on dealing with the sterling balances by a combination of writing them off or converting them into funded loans to be repaid in instalments, as well as restoring convertibility.[66] Clayton's insistence that the empire should make a greater contribution to the war effort and that an American loan should have priority over sterling balances was dismissed by the Treasury in London as 'a complete mental muddle'. In its opinion, releasing blocked balances was not a way of 'outsmarting' the Americans, but of creating stable demand for British goods which would help restore international trade.[67] The treatment of sterling balances remained problematic throughout the war, and after.

*

The trade talks stalled during the war. Meanwhile, the treasury departments in London and Washington made progress in devising new monetary institutions for the post-war world, building on their success in the Tripartite Agreement of 1936.[68] In the next chapter, we turn to the negotiations that led to the Bretton Woods agreement of 1944, and the significant breakthrough in establishing the post-war monetary system and creating two international organizations – the International Monetary Fund and the International Bank for Reconstruction and Development. New, rules-based international institutions were constituted a decade after the failure of the World Monetary and Economic Conference, with the hope that the monetary chaos of the interwar period would be replaced by stability that would provide the basis for a return to multilateral trade.

6

'A firm foundation'

Reforming the Monetary System

'The problem was to find a system of international currency relations compatible with the requirements of domestic stability.'
Ragnar Nurkse, *International Currency Experience*, 1944[1]

'All of us have seen the great economic tragedy of our time. We saw the worldwide depression of the 1930s. We saw currency disorders develop and spread from land to land, destroying the basis for international trade and international investment and even international faith. In their wake, we saw unemployment and wretchedness – idle tools, wasted wealth. We saw their victims fall prey, in places, to demagogues and dictators. We saw bewilderment and bitterness become the breeders of fascism, and, finally, of war.'
Opening address by Henry Morgenthau at the
Bretton Woods conference, 1 July 1944[2]

The Tripartite Agreement of 1936 marked an attempt to create stability in the monetary system of the democratic powers of Britain, France and the United States. The economic disorder of the 1930s had contributed to international tensions that led to war in 1939 – and a general scheme for monetary reform could provide a positive programme for a better post-war world. The new conflict now provided an incentive and opportunity to consider wider plans for reform. The timing of the initial plans for monetary reform reflected the course of the war. The occasion for John Maynard Keynes's initial thoughts on post-war monetary reform, in December 1940, arose from a need to respond to Germany's plans for its occupied territories. The Japanese attack on the American fleet at Pearl Harbor on 7 December 1941, and the declaration of war on the United States by Germany on 11 December, were followed days later by Henry

Harry Dexter White, Assistant Secretary, US Treasury (*left*), and John Maynard
Keynes, honorary adviser to the UK Treasury (*right*), at the inaugural
meeting of the International Monetary Fund's Board of Governors in
Savannah, Georgia, 8 March 1946.

Morgenthau's request to Harry Dexter White to draw up American plans for monetary reform.

As we shall see, the two plans initially developed in parallel before talks started between the two countries in 1942. Unlike the public dissension that marred the London monetary and economic conference of 1933, the talks between Britain and the United States were mainly carried out in private by technical experts. The British negotiations were led by Keynes, who was based in the Treasury in London, though he made a number of visits to Washington to discuss Lend Lease, monetary reforms and the financial support needed at the end of the war. Keynes was intellectually brilliant, but his arrogance, rudeness and lack of political sense sometimes led his colleagues to despair. He was surrounded by a formidable group of senior British officials and economists, on both sides of the Atlantic, who tested his ideas, provided technical detail and tried to maintain good relations with their American counterparts. The economists included Lionel Robbins, who had been a leading critic of *The General Theory*; he was now director of the Economic Section of the War Cabinet Office. Despite their intellectual differences, he was in awe of Keynes as 'one of the most remarkable men that have ever lived'.[3] Hubert Henderson, a pupil and formerly a close ally of Keynes, now attacked his plans as unrealistic; Dennis Robertson, a temporary civil servant at the Treasury before he returned to Cambridge as professor of political economy, maintained good relations with his counterparts in Washington; and James Meade, the future Nobel laureate, was the most original thinker after Keynes, though considered by one leading Treasury official 'ridiculously academic and perfectionist'.[4] In Washington, Frederick Phillips acted as Treasury representative from 1940 to his death in 1943; his role was subsequently taken by Frank Lee. Alongside them, Robert Brand, a London merchant banker, was based in Washington from 1941. The British team combined intellectual brilliance and technical knowledge that could not entirely compensate for their status as supplicants for American help. The American negotiations were led by White, a competent academic economist who lacked the originality of Keynes and his colleagues, but who had the resources of the American economy. Much of the technical thinking was undertaken by Edward Bernstein who was Assistant Director of Monetary Research at the Treasury.

Until the final stages in 1944, the negotiations were almost entirely between the United States and Britain. The two countries' ability to set the agenda was understandable, despite the disparity in their power. Britain was in relative economic decline and would emerge from the war with serious problems of debt, blocked sterling balances, and loss of export markets. Nevertheless, sterling was still the world's major reserve currency, and the City of London and Treasury had long experience in international finance. In 1947, 87 per cent of foreign exchange reserves were held in sterling, with the dollar lagging far behind on 10 per cent.[5] Clearly, these reserves were well out of alignment with the strength of the British economy after the war, when the balance of payments deficit and debt would lead to a lack of confidence in the pound. The United States, in contrast, would end the war with a trade surplus and the status of the world's creditor. These two countries had good reason to turn to the reform of the international monetary system, for replacing a reserve currency is a rare occurrence. Many in Britain still wished to retain the role of sterling as the basis for a powerful economic bloc, and it would be difficult to come to terms with a diminished role. Meanwhile, the United States had to accept its responsibilities as the rising economic power. The transition would take time, with potential for misunderstanding and resentment.

The representatives from the two Treasuries worked out a well-developed set of ideas before Bretton Woods. Despite differences between the schemes, which reflected the divergent economic interests of the two countries, they shared sufficient assumptions for the British and American experts to reach a compromise – largely, it must be admitted, on American terms. Only then were other countries brought into the discussions, in a preparatory conference of seventeen countries at Atlantic City in June 1944 and then the full conference of forty-four countries at Bretton Woods in July 1944, which involved other Allies – including the Soviet Union and China, the British Dominions and India – as well as European governments in exile, and countries in Latin America. The role of the conference was largely to publicize and legitimize the deal.[6]

Progress was faster in reaching an agreement on monetary policy than on commercial policy, for it was more technical and less politicized, and monetary reform was insulated from dissent over contentious issues of trade policy or commodities. Morgenthau's opening remarks at Bretton Woods set out his belief that the descent of the world into chaos and warfare started from currency disorders – unlike Hull who believed that the economic problems of the 1930s started from trade. Morgenthau's claim was understandable given the occasion on which he was speaking, but it did make sense to give priority to monetary issues. Shortly before setting out for the Bretton Woods conference, Keynes explained why monetary stability was a prerequisite for reconstructing the world economy:

> Without currency agreements you have no firm ground on which to discuss tariffs. In the same way plans for diminishing the fluctuation of international prices have no domestic meaning to the countries concerned until

we have some firm ground in the value of money. Therefore, whilst the other schemes are not essential as prior proposals to the monetary scheme . . . a monetary scheme gives a firm foundation on which the others can be built. It is very difficult while you have monetary chaos to have order of any kind in other directions.[7]

It therefore made sense to start with monetary stability before turning to commercial policy.

In this chapter, we turn to the genesis of the British and American monetary plans. They shared many assumptions – the need for currency stabilization, the right to control speculative capital flows, and the desirability of a balance between domestic and international considerations that rested on formal rules and institutions that went beyond the gentleman's agreement of 1936. They also differed in the details of how to achieve these ends, which reflected the economic strengths and weaknesses of the two countries. White's scheme represented the interests of a creditor nation and passed the burden of adjustment to deficit countries. Keynes's scheme reflected the needs of a deficit country that wished to ensure that the burden of adjustment also fell on the creditor nation, with an international currency that would provide liquidity apart from the dollar. White was more concerned with extending the New Deal policies of the good neighbour; Keynes with preserving Britain's position in the world. The debate between these two plans and their authors shaped the institutions of the post-war world.

JOHN MAYNARD KEYNES AND THE CLEARING UNION

Soon after the disappointing negotiations in Washington over Lend Lease's Article VII, Keynes turned to the question of the post-war monetary system.[8] In his opinion, the gold standard was not an automatic self-equilibrating mechanism, and its apparent success before 1914 depended on recycling Britain's balance of payments surplus to the world economy through capital exports and on maintaining liquidity for multilateral trade. He also realized from the experience of returning to gold in 1925 that the gold standard would not work when the burdens of maintaining a fixed exchange rate fell on wages and employment. This changing economic and political context was reflected in Keynes's *Treatise on Money* of 1930, where he argued that fluctuations in the supply of gold and the policies of central banks failed to create a stable standard of value, and led to periods of inflation and deflation. The gold standard did not impose discipline on weak countries who would abandon it in a crisis; at the same time, it limited action by more progressive countries. Keynes accepted that an international monetary standard would have to be based on gold in order to attract support, but it need only be 'gold camouflage'. A super-national body should manage the value of gold by the price of a basket of commodities so that domestic money incomes or prices were not forced to adjust to a fixed rate. Gold should become a 'constitutional monarch, wholly subject to the will of a cabinet of Central Banks who would hold the sovereign power'. Ideally, an international bank could issue 'super-national bank money' and lend to central banks. Unlike the rigidly fixed gold standard, individual national currencies could be varied by 2 per cent in either direction to allow a measure of national self-determination. Keynes was seeking a balance between domestic welfare and international stability.[9]

Keynes's return to international monetary issues was triggered by German plans for the economies of Europe proposed in 1940 by Walther Funk, the German minister of economics from 1938 to 1945, president of the Reichsbank from 1939 to 1945, and a member of the Council of Ministers for the Defence of the Reich. Funk had joined the Nazi Party in 1931 and was found guilty at Nuremberg of war crimes and of crimes against peace and humanity; he was sentenced to life imprisonment and released in 1957 on grounds of ill health. Funk's New Order extended Schacht's bilateral exchange of goods. Bilateralism would continue for external trade, but a 'new order' of multilateral clearing within Europe would be run from an office in Berlin that would settle balances between members. Funk assumed that no surplus or deficit would remain after the balances were cleared, for trade would reflect a division of labour that was subordinated to Germany, with any balance to the rest of Europe written off. Consequently, there was no need for a bank to make loans to countries in overall deficit. Rather than 'embedded liberalism', Funk's plan has been defined as 'embedded hierarchy', a racist and nationalist exploitation of other countries for German needs. The British government saw a danger that Funk's New Order could be portrayed in positive terms, and the Ministry of Information asked Keynes to criticize it in a radio broadcast. He refused. Keynes realized that Funk's plan was far from benign, for the 'rational' division of labour meant that Germany would supply industrial goods to countries that were reduced to producing food and raw materials for the Reich in 'an up-to-date version of imperialist exploitation verging on slavery'. In other respects, Funk's plan seemed 'excellent and just what we ourselves ought to be thinking of doing', only 'much better, much more honestly and with much more regard to other people's interests'. A benign version of the New Order was needed as a positive plan for post-war Europe.

Keynes's initial proposal was a clearing union based on a larger sterling area (including some European countries) as a complement to the dollar area. Payments in the sterling area would be cleared in a multilateral way as in Funk's plan, but Keynes accepted that some countries would remain in deficit at the end of the process. Accordingly, a central bank was needed to provide credit. At this stage, the United States had not entered the war, so Keynes assumed bilateral trade between the sterling and dollar areas.[10]

Keynes's ideas became more imaginative over the next months, drawing on James Meade's *The Economic Basis of a Durable Peace*, a book he wrote shortly before leaving the League. Meade developed Keynes's proposals in the *Treatise on Money* and argued that international regulation of economic affairs required an international organization which necessitated members restricting their freedom of action on money and trade in order to prevent economic depressions and to allow the free movement of goods, capital and labour. He proposed an international bank with authority to issue money in support of national monetary policies that should be designed to prevent booms and slumps. Each national currency should be pegged to the international currency but, unlike the rigid gold standard, it could be adjusted to maintain the balance of payments in equilibrium and so avoid deflation and unemployment. Competitive devaluation would be prevented by use of criteria to test whether variations in exchange rates were justified. The bank should have a fund to offset speculative flows of capital and exchange controls to prevent disruptive short-term capital movements; other capital movements should not be controlled.[11] These ideas informed Keynes's more ambitious 'international currency union' of September 1941.

Keynes started from his earlier contention that the gold standard before 1914 rested on the flow of capital from creditor countries to economies that supplied food and raw materials to the developed world and served as a market for their manufactures. As a result, 'the system of international investment pivoting on London transformed the *onus* of adjustment from the debtor to the creditor position.' The situation changed after the First World War, for capital flows shifted to Europe and no longer expanded the supply of resources in new areas of the world economy. In the 1930s, funds sought safety in surplus countries so that the movement of capital became short-term and destabilizing. He concluded that 'nothing is more certain than that the movement of capital funds must be regulated.' He elaborated the point in his next revision in November, where he insisted that 'central control of capital movements, both inward and outward, should be a permanent feature of the post-war system', distinguishing between destructive speculative movements and genuine investment to develop the world's resources and preserve equilibrium. The result would be 'the restoration of international credit for loan purposes' in place of the speculative flight of short-term funds.[12]

Above all, Keynes wanted adjustment in the balance of payments to fall on the creditor nation – the United States – as well as debtors such as Britain. As he explained,

> the social strain of an adjustment downwards is much greater than that of an adjustment upwards. And besides this, the process of adjustment is *compulsory* for the debtor and *voluntary* for the creditor. If the creditor does not choose to make, or allow, his share of the adjustment, he suffers no inconvenience. For whilst a country's reserve cannot fall below zero, there is no ceiling which sets an upper limit ... The object of the new system must be to require the chief initiative from the creditor countries, whilst maintaining enough discipline in the debtor countries to prevent them from exploiting the new ease allowed them in living profligately beyond their means.[13]

The issue remained of how much discipline was possible and appropriate. Could a new international body intervene in the domestic policies of a sovereign country to insist on prudence, or should it accept that domestic policies were beyond its remit?

Keynes extended Funk's clearing union for the settlement of surpluses and deficits in the balance of payments to include super-national money and an international bank that would provide credits to cover deficits. These credits were similar to overdrafts offered by British banks – a facility that allowed customers to draw more money out of their accounts than they had deposited, to a specified limit and for short periods – a facility that did not apply to American banks.[14] Balances would be settled in bank money, with each member having an overdraft facility to cover any deficit. He assured Montagu Norman at the Bank of England that the proposal

> is the extension to the international field of the essential principles of *banking* by which, when one chap wants to leave his resources idle, those resources are not therefore withdrawn from circulation but are made available to another chap who is prepared to use them ... [I]t is only by extending these same principles to the international field that we can cure the manifest evils of the international economy between the two wars.[15]

The clearing bank would issue bank money to which national currencies would be pegged, with flexibility in exchange rates. Gold would be gradually de-monetized through 'one-way convertibility': a member could buy bank money with gold but could not sell bank money to acquire gold. Consequently, over time gold would disappear from national reserves. Keynes was anxious to impose symmetry so that both deficit and surplus countries would be *permitted* to devalue or revalue if their balances rose or fell above a set limit, and *required* to act if a higher limit were reached. Deficit countries would pay interest in order to impose discipline; more surprisingly, surplus countries would also pay interest on their credit balances, with larger sums transferred to the reserve fund of the clearing bank. In this way, the burden of adjustment would fall on creditors, who now had an incentive to reduce their surpluses. The new international clearing bank would be run by a board of eight and a chairman, with one member from Britain, one from the British empire, one from the United States, one from the Soviet Union, one from Latin America, two from Europe, and one other. Keynes envisaged the 'management and the effective voting power as permanently Anglo-American', with a head office in London under an English chairman responsible for banks in the Commonwealth (except Canada, part of the dollar zone), Europe and the Middle East, and a second head office in America for the Americas and the Far East.[16] It was framed to give Britain and its empire the largest voice and to limit the influence of American creditors.

Keynes's plan would obviously not play well in Washington. Nor did it command universal assent in London. At the Treasury, officials worried that the overdraft facility might be misused by a weak or corrupt country to expand credit or allow wages to rise, so that 'lending would only be an opiate which would prevent the temperature of the patient rising and make it more difficult for the doctor to diagnose'. The range of exchange rate variation might be too narrow so that countries wishing to avoid deflation would adopt exchange or import controls. Creditor countries – above all America – might refuse to offer 'compulsory charity' to debtors. Granting the international bank power to recommend 'appropriate changes in the level of wages and costs' would threaten national sovereignty. Debtors might refuse to accept the 'ignominies and restrictions' of supervision by an international bank, and American suspicion of central banks meant it was unlikely to hand over authority. Keynes countered that it was 'no greater surrender ... than is required in any commercial treaty' and was 'entered into voluntarily'. Hubert Henderson rejected this 'Utopian' approach:

> I do not believe that the new wine of internal planning can be put in the old bottle of the gold standard, Free Trade, the most-favoured-nation clause and the open door. I am convinced that a satisfactory international system can only be rebuilt along lines ... of planning and control; and that in such

a system quantitative regulation, exchange control and bilateral agreements
have a legitimate part to play.

Henderson thought that imperial preference and the sterling area were
vital for Britain's post-war survival. Keynes had flirted with Schachtianism out of necessity, but now dismissed it as a 'patched up contrivance'
which might help with the post-war transition without providing a long-
term solution. He knew that members of the sterling area would not
accept an obligation to reduce purchases from the United States and
increase orders from Britain, and they wished to pursue their own policy
goals. Keynes feared that Henderson's approach would create something
like Soviet state trading, and he preferred to start from the American
approach of an open international economy.[17]

Keynes took account of the Treasury's concerns in a new draft in
November 1941. He retreated from the confiscation of credit balances,
which would alienate the Americans, and confined himself to the proposition that 'the creditor should not be allowed to remain passive'. He
argued that weak discipline against persistent debtors was better than
nothing, and that limits on exchange rates were sensible in preventing
competitive devaluation. An automatic register of debtor and creditor
positions would provide a 'danger signal' and allow rules for both appreciation and depreciation of exchange rates. This system would allow
countries to give an undertaking not to use protectionism and discrimination, which would 'enable us to give complete satisfaction to Mr Cordell
Hull, since we should be accepting a non-discriminatory international
system as the normal and desirable state of affairs'. The currency union
would, he insisted, restore 'unfettered multilateral clearing between its
members', for a country only needed to take action when it was out of
balance with the entire system. Although sovereign rights had to be surrendered, membership of the union was voluntary and could be terminated.
Finally, he inserted a proposal from the American economists Alvin
Hansen and Luther Gulick that an International Development Corporation and International Economic Board should advise governments on
domestic policies for full employment, which would create a more stable
world economy and reduce pressure on the clearing scheme.[18]

This idea was stressed by Roy Harrod, an Oxford economist who was
briefly in government service. In his view, the clearing union was 'essentially a palliative' and was less important than a bank or international
investment board that could take on the role played by British overseas
investment prior to 1914 and extend the use of public works advocated in
The General Theory to the international level to prevent unemployment

and to fund development projects. The clearing union was, he insisted, 'quite inadequate *by itself* as a constructive British proposal' and should be part of a wider set of proposals covering international institutions for investments, commodities, nutrition and commerce so that the Americans did not 'think we are only internationally minded in so far as it suits our interests' in an attempt to resolve 'our own tiresome little difficulties'. Keynes was not convinced. Britain was not likely to have resources to help others, and the Americans were unlikely to write-off deficits or accept potentially inflationary schemes to maintain employment by an international agency.[19] He preferred to concentrate on the clearing union without wider ambitions that might prevent progress.

Keynes's new version of December 1941 accordingly stressed liquidity rather than development loans. Super-national bank money now had a new name – Bancor – that brought together the French words for bank and gold. Bancor would be accepted as equivalent to gold; exchange rates would be fixed in gold though not convertible and with some flexibility. Persistent creditors should discuss the situation with the bank and themselves decide whether to expand their domestic economy, appreciate their currency, reduce tariffs, or make loans. Debtors should only act when deficits reached a set limit, at which point they could depreciate their currency rather than deflating the domestic economy or imposing trade restrictions. There was less pressure on debtors and creditors to balance their accounts, and he dropped – with reluctance – the automatic surrender of credits above a certain amount and the payment of interest on credit balances. The system would allow greater discretion rather than the application of automatic rules. Keynes thought his scheme would give 'substantial satisfaction' to Hull in helping remove protection – a shift from his earlier expectation of 'complete' satisfaction.[20] Keynes was building support at the expense of weakening his initial proposals.

The Treasury representative in Washington, Frederick Phillips, foresaw hostility. New Dealers would worry at the influence of central bankers and reject any notion that creditors should raise their exchange rates. Thomas Lamont of J. P. Morgan complained that Britain made the mistake in the 1930s of 'permitting the trade unions ... to impose a rigid wage scale on British industries and subsidising the resulting unemployment by the dole'. Would Britain make its economy more flexible and competitive, or would it again take the easy option of allowing the pound to fall in value? Keynes responded with a provision that the governors of the super-national bank would be appointed by member states and not the central banks, and by dropping the compulsion on creditors to revalue.[21]

Keynes completed the definitive version of his scheme in January 1942. It permitted a deficit country to devalue if its debits reached a set limit and allowed the governing body to request action if debits reached a higher limit; there were no similar provisions for the creditor. A separate commercial treaty would deal with issues of trade, with credit and debit balances offering a guide to exceptions to multilateral trade such as trade barriers or exchange controls. Keynes now felt that Hull might derive 'some' satisfaction.[22] The Treasury submitted the scheme to Cabinet with the ambivalent recommendation that it was the best plan of its type that could be contrived, and soon recommended full endorsement when it heard of the less attractive American scheme. The problem, as Harrod realized, was that ministers 'are bound to be rather at sea in these technical questions'. Ernest Bevin, the minister of labour and former leader of Britain's largest union, had bad memories of the deflationary consequences of the return to gold in 1925 and worried at 'an Anglo-American bankers' conspiracy against the working class'. He was assured that the scheme did not entail the return to the 'contractionist system' of the gold standard, or an Anglo-American conspiracy of bankers, and that it would allow an expansionist policy of managing the domestic economy without unemployment or under-consumption. Keynes inserted an explicit rejection of adjustments by deflation and dear money, and the plan was approved by Cabinet on 7 May 1942 as the basis for discussions with the Americans on Article VII of Lend Lease.[23]

The clearing union was presented to the Americans as a positive measure to remove foreign exchange difficulties that would permit the abolition of barriers to trade. It was a pragmatic response that Harrod and Robertson thought too timid. Harrod continued to argue for an investment board, and Robertson thought too much emphasis was placed on Anglo-American relations and on currency and trade, without a clear statement of ambition. 'Have we really a "political philosophy"? Or are we tinkering with snaffles and curbs and forgetting the "bloody horse"?' The best way of selling the scheme to the Americans was by 'a really thoroughgoing plan of our own domestic New Jerusalem' based on 'Social Security, Family Allowances and a New Model Income Tax, Guaranteed Minimum Wage, 40-hour week, Nationalize the Land, Real Equality in Education, and Planned Control of Industry – that would be my ticket for Anglo-American relations'. This wide-ranging domestic policy might play well in Britain as a promise of a better world. It was, however, likely to reinforce congressional fears that Britain was exploiting the generosity of the American taxpayer instead of creating an efficient and productive economy.[24] Even Keynes's modified proposals faced criticism in Washington as a device to exploit the United States and to preserve Britain's status as an imperial power and finance centre.

HARRY DEXTER WHITE AND THE STABILIZATION FUND

Cordell Hull realized that an open world economy would be blocked by post-war balance of payments imbalances, and in 1941 he asked Adolf Berle for his thoughts on an international financial scheme. Berle assumed that America would maintain economic hegemony in the western hemisphere, and that Latin America would receive capital from the American government for development to preserve economic stability, security and order as part of a co-operative family of nations. In Berle's opinion, no western European country would be able to maintain economic leadership after the war without brute force to hold together a 'rickety combination'. Consequently, 'we are about to assume in economics a position analogous to that of Great Britain in politics in the last century – that is, we are being asked to assume the responsibilities of leadership tantamount to empire.' The outcome would be an 'economic mastodon', with its economic centre in the financial and economic institutions in Washington. Berle felt that the British did not grasp the emergence of this new system in which America would 'have to be the financial and economic pumping station, shock absorber, and general supply station for the whole unit'.[25]

Berle proposed extending the principles of the Federal Reserve system to international finance. Before the creation of the Federal Reserve in 1913, internal trade was periodically paralysed by a shortage of currency and credit, and the same would happen with freer multilateral trade after the war. The solution was for countries to subscribe to an international reserve bank with the power to issue bank notes in the currency of individual countries that would be convertible into gold – an implausible surrender of sovereignty. The aim of the State Department was to stabilize exchange rates and create credit vital for multilateral trade, but Berle saw that it was 'fairly plain that unless the suggestion comes from the Treasury, that Department will object and its *amour propre* would be wounded'. In any case, Berle was no expert in monetary economics. The State Department tended to respond to immediate issues and think in terms of bilateral deals, rather than the global terms of economists dealing with financial issues.[26]

The Treasury Department had its own reasons for devising a plan for financial stability. Morgenthau's ambition was 'to move the financial center of the world from London and Wall Street to the United States Treasury, and to create a new concept between nations in international finance' based on international institutions that would be the 'instrumentalities of sovereign governments and not of private financial interests'.[27] During the New Deal, the power of the Federal Reserve was concentrated in Washington, where the Board of Governors was more under the control of the Treasury and President. The Thomas amendment authorized the president to issue currency if the Fed refused to purchase government securities, and in 1934 the Exchange Equalization Fund was established at the Treasury to manage the dollar.[28] Morgenthau's aim, as he explained at Bretton Woods, was to 'drive only the usurious money lenders from the temple of international finance' – a reference that harked back to Roosevelt's inaugural address.[29] On 14 December 1941, Morgenthau asked Harry White to produce a memorandum on a stabilization fund and international currency.

Keynes and White both wanted to create a multilateral institution for stability and growth, and they were intellectually close. The American's social background was far removed from Keynes's patrician upbringing at Eton, Cambridge and in the Bloomsbury set. White was the son of Jewish immigrants to New York, where he worked in the family hardware business before he served in the war and subsequently studied economics at Columbia University and Harvard. He was not in Keynes's league as an original thinker, whom he 'revered ... as the greatest living economist'. Nevertheless, White was experienced in international monetary affairs, through the Tripartite Agreement of 1936 and missions in Latin America, and he was aware of Keynes's work on money. Colleagues variously described him as 'brash, truculent and ... somewhat unscrupulous', 'the unpleasantest man in Washington', a 'son-of-a-bitch' and an 'intolerable human being'. In the opinion of one colleague,

> You couldn't rely on what he would tell you. You thought he'd agreed to something and a few days later he would deny that he agreed to that ... It was very difficult to do business with him. He was a very competent person, extremely competent and very good to his own people in the Treasury.[30]

Keynes's assessment of White was ambivalent: he was

> over-bearing, a bad colleague, always trying to bounce you, with harsh rasping voice, aesthetically oppressive in mind and manner; he has not the faintest conception of how to behave or observe the rules of civilised intercourse. At the same time, I have a very great respect and even liking for him. In many respects he is the best man here.[31]

The two men were to work together in devising the post-war order in a tempestuous relationship that set Keynes's intellectual arrogance against White's competence and ability to deny access to American resources.

Although White and Berle agreed on the need for planning, they differed in their attitude towards the Soviet Union. Berle was suspicious of the Soviets; by contrast, White believed that America should co-operate in a planned international economy that would guarantee peace. Indeed, it was alleged at the end of 1945 that White passed confidential information on American financial policy to the Soviets. Despite this claim, he was appointed as the American director of the IMF; he resigned in June 1947 and appeared before the House Un-American Activities Committee on 13 August 1948. He suffered a heart attack and died a few days later. Raymond Mikesell, a member of the American technical team at Bretton Woods, defended White on the grounds that Russia was bearing the brunt of the land war against Germany, and that he would not be condemned for passing information to other allies such as Britain and Canada. Mikesell argued that White was anxious to keep the Soviets involved in plans for financial reform, but that he supported capitalism and was 'oblivious' to ideology. Mikesell's plea of mitigation is not convincing, for evidence from decrypted Soviet files show that White was a Soviet agent who used his position to promote and protect Soviet sympathizers. He was pursuing an unstated agenda that had implications for negotiations with Britain. He hoped to create post-war stability based on American–Soviet co-operation rather than a declining Britain with its continuing delusions of empire. He supported a large loan to the Soviets and opposed a generous loan to Britain, which he wished to see displaced as a major power. Nevertheless, he was not, as Benn Steil has implausibly claimed, at 'the heart of foreign policy making', pursuing a masterplan with a 'private army' of experts to control the outcome at Bretton Woods. White was important, but he was not the mastermind behind American foreign policy. Many members of the Treasury, including Morgenthau, had the same ambition of displacing sterling as a vestige of imperial power and a block to American exports. Both Morgenthau and Hull wished to maintain wartime co-operation with the Soviets. Roosevelt hoped to convince Stalin that the United States was not working with Britain against his country, and that the Americans could act as a broker between the other two great powers after the war.[32]

White's draft plan was shaped by his experience in Latin America – something he had in common with Berle. As we saw in Chapter 4, the administration turned from military intervention in support of American creditors to a 'good neighbor' policy to assist fellow victims of Wall Street financiers. White's mission to Cuba in 1941/2 departed from the 'money doctors' in arguing for development and an active monetary policy, rather than balanced budgets and the gold standard. White was able to respond so quickly to Morgenthau's request for a report on international stabilization and a single post-war international currency because he was already working on a plan to present to the Inter-American conference at Rio de Janeiro in January 1942, and he drew on his experience with the Tripartite Agreement and the Inter-America Bank. Morgenthau decided that White should take the lead on international issues: 'I want it in one brain and I want it to be Harry White's brain.' By 30 December 1941, White produced a memorandum on 'Suggestions for Inter-Allied Monetary and Banking Action', proposing an inter-allied stabilization fund and an inter-allied bank. A more detailed plan of January 1942 went through a number of drafts before a definitive version emerged in April 1942.[33]

White's plan is often criticized as being less ambitious than Keynes's proposal. He did not recommend an international currency, as suggested by Morgenthau, and focused on currency convertibility and pegged rates as 'more realistic and just as effective'. Neither did he propose anything like Bancor to create liquidity for international trade. White doubted the feasibility of a single international currency, for the value of one currency in terms of another was 'a consequence of a complex of monetary and economic forces ... The adoption of the same unit of currency no more eliminates foreign exchange problems than would ... general adoption of Esperanto solve international political problems.' He argued that the obstacle to trade came from not the use of different currencies but their variation. He did not follow Keynes in proposing bank money to create international liquidity for expanding trade. Criticism of White's scheme reflects British complaints that their interests as a debtor were ignored. In other respects, White's approach was wider than Keynes's, for he was concerned with development. The influence of Latin America and 'good neighbor' policies was clear in White's early draft, which pointed out that 'the lesson that must be learned is that prosperous neighbors are the best neighbors; that a higher standard of living in one country begets higher standards in others, and that a high level of trade and business is most easily attained when generously and widely shared.' He went beyond Keynes in proposing international development finance, short-term loans to cover balance of payments deficits and to assist with restructuring international debt. His drafts mentioned two issues that were close to the interests of Latin America – stabilization of commodity prices and protection of infant industries – and he made the heretical point (as far as the State Department was concerned) that free trade was 'unreal and unsound'.[34]

White's proposal focused on currency as a tactical decision without abandoning the wider development agenda. In May 1942, Morgenthau informed Roosevelt that White's plan was 'a New Deal in international economics' to eliminate poverty. Roosevelt continued to press the needs of Latin America. Early in 1943, he asked an interdepartmental committee, which included Acheson, Will Clayton, Emilio Collado and Nelson Rockefeller, to produce a memorandum to show the benefits to the United States of assisting others. In June, the president informed Rockefeller that 'I do want to get across the idea . . . that the economy and social welfare of Jesus Fernandez in Brazil does affect the economic and social welfare of Johnny Jones in Terre Haute, Indiana.' In this spirit, as we saw in Chapter 4, Collado and Rockefeller devised plans for Latin America. In the Federal Reserve's mission in Paraguay in 1943 and 1944, Robert Triffin saw that the currency plan could allow capital controls and exchange rate adjustments that would limit external influences on Latin American economies, and permit policy autonomy and state-led development. At the same time, domestic economic stability in Latin America would reduce international instability and facilitate the work of international agencies.[35]

White initially intended to announce his plan at Rio in January 1942, but Morgenthau felt that more work was needed. So White turned to Edward Bernstein, a man described by Keynes as 'a regular little rabbi, a reader out of the Talmud'. Their more precise draft was submitted to Roosevelt in May 1942. It proposed two international institutions with a blurred demarcation – the Stabilization Fund and the Bank for Reconstruction and Development. The Fund would create stable foreign exchange rates by restricting them to a narrow range, unless permission were given for a change; it would encourage the flow of productive capital, liberate blocked balances, help settle international debts, deal with disequilibria in the balance of payments, stabilize price levels, remove foreign exchange controls, end bilateral clearing, promote sound credit and monetary policies, and reduce barriers to trade. It was a formidable list of tasks. Members would subscribe at least $5bn to the Fund in gold, cash and interest-bearing government securities, which might amount to $3,196m from the US, $635m from Britain, and $164m from the Soviet Union. Each member would appoint an executive director whose voting rights would be 'weighted' by a basic allowance of one hundred votes plus one vote for each $1m subscribed, which would give the United States four times as many votes as Britain – and some decisions would be taken by a 'super majority' so that the United States could block any unwelcome decision. White argued that equal votes would be 'palpably unwise' given the membership of many small countries, but that votes entirely by subscription would destroy international legitimacy. The issue of voting rights resurfaced in other international bodies, and the balance between universalism and effectiveness was a difficult one to strike.

Changes in the exchange rate would only be allowed to correct 'fundamental disequilibrium' and with the consent of 80 per cent of the votes. White also set out a procedure to create equilibrium in the balance of payments. If Britain had a balance of payments deficit with the United States, it could cover its deficit by borrowing dollars from the Fund up to its contribution. It could sell sterling to the Fund provided that it took steps to correct its deficit in a reasonable period and implemented measures recommended by the Fund. The scheme was more limited than the clearing union and reflected the deposit banking system of the United States. In Keynes's clearing union, countries could draw out more money than they put in; in White's stabilization fund, they could only draw out the quota they contributed. One concession to Britain was assistance in 'unblocking' accumulated sterling balances to stimulate trade and reduce pressure on exchanges. White proposed that the Fund should purchase sterling so that a country holding blocked sterling balances would be able to secure dollars and remove barriers to trade, without imposing a burden on British reserves. Generally, White started from the position of a creditor nation. There was no requirement on the surplus country to adjust, and the Fund could intervene in the domestic policies of countries in deficit.

White proposed that the Bank for Reconstruction and Development would have a capital of $10bn. A country could subscribe as much capital as it wanted but would have no more than 25 per cent of the vote. The Bank would make loans at a low interest rate on condition that any project was sound and would raise the standard of living of the borrowing country. It could guarantee loans to private investors as well as the state. No loans were to be made to a defaulting country unless terms to renew payment were agreed and 90 per cent of members approved. Further, the Bank could set up a raw material development corporation and a commodity stabilization corporation to increase the supply of raw materials at stable prices.[36]

When Morgenthau presented the scheme to Roosevelt in May 1942, he stressed the wider strategic implications. '[T]he time is right to dramatize our international economic objectives in terms of action which people everywhere will recognize as practical, powerful and inspiring.' He suggested a conference of finance ministers of the United Nations – at this point referring to the Allies rather than the new international organization created at San Francisco in 1945 – to develop an attractive alternative to the 'new orders' of Germany and Japan. Morgenthau argued that there 'could be no more solid demonstration of our confidence that the tide is turning than the announcement of the formulation in concrete terms, and the preparation of specific instrumentalities for what really would be a New Deal in international economics'. Roosevelt insisted on involving the State Department. Although the monetary proposals would complement the trade plans, there were differences over how to proceed. At the State Department, Acheson preferred to start with informal discussions with the British, who 'are very nervous that we will produce a large meeting, have some plan which we will put before that meeting, and that they will not have an opportunity to go over the whole thing with us freely, privately, and frankly before the thing starts'. Morgenthau thought that the British would be obstructive, and that Acheson's proposal was a cover for opposition to the Fund and Bank. Acheson dismissed these concerns and argued that bilateral talks with Britain would be more effective. In his view, the British were

> Tremendously anxious to do almost what we want, but they want a chance to talk the matter over with us before the thing is crystallised ∴.. there is a rather pathetic feeling on the part of the British that we really are going to write the ticket, and all they want is a chance to go over it with us.

In any case, a large meeting would be less likely to succeed. Morgenthau realized that a dispute between the State Department and Treasury would be counterproductive, and he agreed to initial discussions with the British, who were given a revised version of the White plan in July 1942.[37]

The two schemes had emerged in parallel and now needed to be reconciled. The Americans had the upper hand of control over resources, but economic hegemony could not necessarily be translated into political dominance. Would the British be willing to let the Americans write the ticket?

ANGLO-AMERICAN DISCUSSIONS

Keynes was not impressed by White's plan, for it did not adopt the 'banking principle' and was 'not much more than a version of the gold standard, which simply aims at multiplying the effective volume of the gold base'. Unlike Keynes's one-way convertibility, White's scheme allowed gold to be converted both into currency and back into gold, so that it would not be demonetized. Keynes complained that 'the volume of international currency is not adjusted to need but remains as before mainly dependent on the volume of gold mining and the policy of those countries which already have large gold reserves'. He missed the point that the United States had the ability to issue dollars that were accepted as being as good as gold.

Keynes was offended by voting rights that would allow Latin America to outvote Britain and its empire, and the United States to outvote the British and Dutch empires, Russia and China added together. His consolation was that White did not insist on multilateral trade at all costs and offered a solution to blocked balances. Keynes made further revisions of his plan in preparation for divulging his thoughts to the Americans, above all emphasizing the banking principle as a means of turning hoarding into spending and encouraging production. His plan was submitted to Washington at the end of August 1942.[38]

Berle was hostile. Keynes's plan would impose an indefinite liability on the United States, with little control over debtors, inadequate voting rights for creditors, and the risk of inflation by the creation of Bancor. Further, limiting talks to Britain and America would give an impression of collusion, and he urged the involvement of members of the United Nations and, above all, China and the Soviet Union. The British were equally insistent that their document should only be discussed with the Americans. White's compromise was that American and British consideration of the clearing union should run alongside a general discussion of stabilization with other countries. In October 1942, the British agreed that the United States could inform the Soviets and Chinese that general post-war financial arrangements were being considered, without divulging the details of the British and American proposals.[39]

Although White hoped that other proposals would be considered, alternative schemes were not well developed. The Canadian idea of an international exchange union that drew on both the White and Keynes proposals was ignored.[40] Nor was attention devoted to the scheme of Hervé Alphand and André Istel, economic advisers to the French National Committee of Liberation based in London under the leadership of General de Gaulle. Their modest proposal built on the Tripartite Agreement of 1936, in which Alphand had been involved, and continued the Franco-British agreement of December 1939 to stabilize their currencies during the war. They hoped that other countries might follow this example and that monetary authorities would fix parities by buying each other's currencies, with changes to parities only after consultation. The scheme was intended as a first step back to gold – an idea that did not appeal to the United States or Britain, nor did it attract much attention.[41]

The most plausible alternative to the White and Keynes schemes was an 'unofficial' proposal from the American economist John H. Williams, one of the experts who prepared the agenda for the 1933 World Monetary and Economic Conference. He had worked with Viner in opposing Fisher and Warren's programme of dollar devaluation, in drafting the Gold

Stabilization Act of 1934, and in negotiating the Tripartite Agreement. Williams agreed with White on the need for monetary stability and economic co-operation, but stayed closer to the Tripartite Agreement in adopting a flexible approach for a few currencies without adopting formal rules and institutions. In Williams's opinion a single system was unnecessary, for countries needed different kinds of monetary system depending on the extent of their reliance on foreign trade and capital, and hence the impact of exchange rate fluctuations. Relatively self-contained countries like the United States or France could accept a stable exchange rate and rely on internal economic management. By contrast, countries with a heavy reliance on foreign trade or capital, like Australia or Argentina, needed the right to depreciate or appreciate their currencies. Britain fell somewhere between the two and was torn between internal and external monetary stability. Williams's solution was to rely on 'key currencies' – the dollar and sterling. The United States and Britain together were responsible for a large part of the world's economic activity, were the major sources of capital, and the most likely cause of booms and depressions in the world. They should co-operate to maintain their exchange rates and ensure a high level of real income to remove conflict between internal and external monetary stability. In his view, 'stabilization of the leading currencies with reference to each other, combined with cooperation among the countries concerned for the promotion of their own internal stability, would be the best foundation for monetary and economic stability throughout the world.' Once this stable core had been created, other countries could decide what was appropriate for them: 'it seems preferable to have some compromise, or combination of compromise systems, which, while excluding no form of variation which might be serviceable in a constantly changing world, would resort to currency variation only sparingly and when other means had failed.' Like Keynes and White, he was seeking a balance between national interests and international stability. Unlike them, he did not think that international organizations were necessary.[42]

The initial meeting in London in October 1942 ground to a halt and the British decided to take pre-emptive action by starting talks with the Dominions and India to build support for the clearing union. They also opened discussions with allied governments in exile in London in February 1943, in particular to consider the proposal of the exiled Belgian academic, central banker and politician Paul van Zeeland for a commission to study the economic reconstruction of Europe. The Americans agreed to send an observer to these talks but refused to circulate the White plan, on the grounds that discussions should be taking place in Washington with a wider group of countries. At this point, the British postponed the talks in London to remove the risk that wider conversations might weaken their position. Instead, they urged bilateral Anglo-American discussion to make 'real progress towards the formulation of a single and agreed scheme' before a wider meeting of the United Nations. After all, 'the American memorandum and the Clearing Union Plan have a great deal in common and are not so far apart as to preclude the usefulness of trying to conflate them. This is the course which we should much prefer.' The British also hoped to deal with monetary policy in conjunction with other issues so that Article VII could be placed in a wider context. The State Department countered by suggesting that all issues should be discussed with individual governments – an approach that was certain to fail, for a comprehensive agreement with a single government would be impossible without the framework of a general agreement. More realistically, the United States Treasury saw that the only feasible approach was to consider a single topic with a group of countries. Accordingly, the Americans sent a revised draft of White's plan to the British, Chinese and Russians on 1 February 1943 and invited experts from various countries to discuss monetary co-operation on the basis of the White scheme, or 'any other lines they may wish to suggest'.[43]

The White and Keynes schemes were discussed in private between officials in a few countries, and rumours of what was involved led the British government to propose formal publication to inform MPs and the public. When the Americans opposed making their views public, the British decided to publish the clearing union scheme to steal a lead. White's plan was then leaked to the press by one of the allied governments and both schemes were published on 7 April 1943. Matters were now in the open, and preliminary, bilateral discussions started with technical experts in Washington, to be followed by group discussions in June 1943.[44] Meanwhile, talks proceeded between the United States and Britain to produce a joint statement on their two schemes. This step was crucial, for the debates over the strengths and weaknesses of White's and Keynes's plans were now 'a focused negotiation for reaching agreement on a specific plan'.[45] The discussions were technical and held in private between the British and American experts. Once they agreed a joint statement, an international drafting committee, drawn from representatives of Britain, America, Russia and China (and possibly one or two other countries) would meet to settle the proposals for the international conference.[46] A consensus was gradually built by widening the number of participants.

Keynes left for Washington for preliminary, informal and non-committal talks from 15 September to 9 October 1943. His supreme confidence in his intellectual brilliance led, in the words of one British official, to 'provocative insouciance'. Harry Hopkins, who had oversight of Lend Lease and advised Roosevelt on foreign policy, complained that Keynes was 'one of those fellows that just knows all the answers', and White referred to him as 'your Royal Highness'. Keynes's colleagues had similar complaints that his bad manners and rudeness led to difficulties in negotiations. James Meade admitted that dealing with Keynes's 'wit, petulance, rudeness, and quick unscrupulousness in argument' reduced him to tears. Robbins agreed that Keynes was 'not always a good *negotiator* ... But as an *envoy* he was supreme. Not even Mr Churchill could state more magnificently the case for this country than Keynes at his eloquent best.'[47]

The financial power of the American negotiators made the task of Keynes and his colleagues difficult. One issue was the modest size of the stabilization fund. The British persuaded White to increase the size of the fund from $5bn to between $8bn and $10bn, with American liability raised from $2bn to $3bn – still well below Keynes's proposal of $26bn for the clearing union. The British delegation realized that a small fund would require more freedom to devalue and to impose exchange and import controls. This point led to discussion on how to determine exchange rates and their flexibility. White set par values in terms of gold and suggested that the rate could be adjusted by 10 per cent for three years after the war, after which it should only be changed in case of 'fundamental disequilibrium', with the adjustment agreed by three-quarters of votes. Keynes wanted greater freedom for deficit countries, with an objective measurement to prevent a return to competitive devaluation. White argued that giving the Fund discretion would be 'more satisfactory in a matter so full of politics', and the British Treasury also had reservations about formulae that would limit its freedom to vary exchange rates to protect employment. In the end, White accepted that a country could change its rate once by up to 10 per cent, and that the Fund would give permission for any further change within 48 hours. He dropped the requirement of approval by three-quarters of the votes and agreed that domestic policies should not be considered. In effect, countries would have considerable autonomy to change their rates. In practice, this freedom was only likely to be used by deficit countries to devalue; surplus countries had no incentive to revalue so that they were able to avoid the burden of adjustment. Here, White made a concession by inserting a clause on 'scarce currencies': if a currency were in short supply, as anticipated for the dollar after the war, other countries would be allowed to impose import restrictions. Keynes came to see that this concession 'puts the creditor country on the spot so acutely that in the view of us all, the creditor country simply cannot afford to let such a situation arise'. The

State Department probably did not know about this concession – though in practice it did not matter, for the clause was a dead letter. White also withdrew a major concession to Britain that the Fund would buy blocked sterling balances – a change with serious repercussions as Britain struggled to deal with the financial consequences of the war.[48]

These detailed negotiations resulted in an Anglo-American joint statement by experts on the establishment of an International Monetary Fund in April 1944. Although White agreed to the statement, he refused to sign so that only Keynes's name appeared. Keynes complained that White's decision was typical of American behaviour during the negotiations: 'on no single occasion have they answered any communication of mine in writing, or confirmed in writing anything which has passed in conversation.'[49] Nevertheless, it proved easier to secure support for the agreement in Washington than in London. White had the backing of Morgenthau, who was supported by Roosevelt, and the president wanted everything settled before the election in November 1944. This deadline entailed a conference in March/April 1944, with a treaty going to Congress in May.[50] The British now dragged their feet, for opinion in London was divided. At the Board of Trade, Hugh Dalton saw a 'high-powered intrigue' against Keynes by an unlikely alliance of supporters of imperial preference (such as Amery and Beaverbrook), opponents of gold (such as Bevin), and socialists committed to planning. Churchill was not interested and was – not unreasonably – more worried about the imminent invasion of France. The Treasury was split, with Keynes strongly in favour and Henderson strongly against, with others doubting the virtue of precise rules at a time of uncertainty, or unenthusiastically accepting that it was better than nothing. The Bank of England feared that the Fund would by-pass London and lead to the demise of the sterling area. Lord Catto, governor of the Bank, felt that the Fund should focus on 'practical cooperation' after the war, when 'abnormal convulsions' would require improvisation rather than fixed principles. In his opinion, Britain and its empire were still a 'vital force in world economic and financial affairs', and 'we must not go to America on our knees, creating an impression that only their wealth can save us. We can, if need be, save ourselves, but the process will be hard.'[51] Keynes, a director of the Bank, thought that his colleagues were living in a fantasy world. The alternative to American assistance was 'extreme austerity in domestic consumption . . . and the very opposite of an expansionist domestic policy'. He saw no prospect of forming a sterling currency bloc, so the only way that Britain could continue as an international banker was by American assistance within an international scheme.[52]

When the War Cabinet recommended acceptance of the scheme on

9 February 1944, it also set up a Committee on External Economic Policy to consider other aspects of the 'Grand Design' – the whole range of issues from money to investment, trade, buffer stocks and employment that had been talked about in other venues in less developed form. Churchill failed to provide a lead, and Keynes complained of 'complete bedlam' with ministers 'driving one another crazy with their mutual ravings'. Supporters of the monetary scheme realized that if progress were to be made, talks should be kept separate from other elements of the Grand Design, and – above all – apart from disagreements on commercial policy. Keynes saw that the commercial scheme needed the monetary scheme if it were to succeed – but the monetary scheme did not need the commercial scheme. He succeeded in convincing the chancellor that the Fund should 'go it alone'. A confused meeting of Cabinet on 14 April agreed to publish the joint statement without official commitment, with provisos that it would not apply during the transitional period after the war and that additional assistance would be needed for reconstruction. Talks on other elements of the Grand Design were suspended and the proposals were published as a White Paper on 22 April 1944. The timetable had slipped from Morgenthau's and Roosevelt's aim of reaching an agreement by the Democratic Convention in July as a crowning success for the president. But talks could now proceed.[53]

The Keynes and White plans had different motivations and ambitions – the one more concerned with providing an alternative to the German new order and reassurance for Britain as a deficit nation, the other more concerned with 'hemispheric economic defense' and development in Latin America. Keynes had been pushed back on his ideas for international bank money and symmetrical obligations on deficit and creditor nations, but he and White had common ground in a shared understanding of the dangers of currency warfare and unfettered flows of speculative money and of the need for international institutions and rules. Despite the difficulties, monetary issues were more technical and more likely to reach resolution than the intensely political and divisive issue of trade, where the British could not easily accept Hull's panacea of free trade, and where the Cabinet was split between supporters of imperial preference and multilateralism. Unlike the World Monetary and Economic Conference in 1933, progress was possible because issues were segmented rather than inclusive, and because a small group – in particular, Britain and the United States – could agree on the outlines of a plan before it was put to other countries.

Before we turn to the gathering of the United Nations at Bretton Woods in July 1944 to discuss the monetary plan, we should reflect on the other elements of the 'Grand Design' that were being pressed by primary producing and less developed countries, and by advocates in Britain and the United States of the League's approach of 'positive security'. Two conferences were held prior to Bretton Woods – one on food and agriculture at Hot Springs in May–June 1943, the other a gathering of the International Labour Organization in Philadelphia in April–May 1944. Together, they proposed a different approach to the post-war order from the monetary discussions at Bretton Woods – a focus on issues of distributive justice and welfare within countries and in the global economy. Although these alternative approaches had only limited traction at Bretton Woods, they did re-emerge in the post-war debates over plans for an International Trade Organization, and in the challenges of the less developed nations to the Bretton Woods institutions.

7

'An integrated program'

Food, Employment and Commodities

'It was too much to expect that the general public would understand the details of plans covering such subjects as currency arrangements. On the other hand, if the plans made in the various fields were put together as a general policy the broad sweep of this policy could be understood by the people and could catch their imagination and enthusiasm.'

John Maynard Keynes, 21 September 1943[1]

'Perfect harmony will not be reached; but it would, I think, be a mistake to put the monetary proposals into operation in an international economic setting so adverse that the prospects of successful operation were remote. An early breakdown would discredit the whole idea of international collaboration. The monetary plan should be regarded as only one part of an integrated program.'

Louis Rasminsky, 1944[2]

The technical monetary issues that dominated at Bretton Woods were part of a wider debate about the future of the world economy and a just international order. In 1942, Charles Kindleberger and Alvin Hansen, economists who advised the American government and Federal Reserve, explained that 'the larger aims of economic policy' might include: '1, a positive expansionist program designed to achieve and to maintain full employment; 2, a program of development designed to raise productivity throughout the world; and 3, the establishment of higher minimum standards of nutrition, health, education and housing everywhere.' Post-war prosperity needed more than monetary stabilization: Hansen claimed it required 'an expansionist program designed to promote full employment in the industrially advanced countries and to raise the productivity in the economically backward areas, and with institutions designed to minimize

Food stamps were introduced in the United States in 1939 to dispose of surplus commodities, as in this publicity photograph of the same year at a grocery store.

cyclical fluctuations.' Hansen and Kindleberger looked to 'an international public development corporation to promote large-scale projects in industrially backward countries and areas', and schemes to support the prices of food and raw materials. The approach amounted to a 'new deal for the world economy' with international agencies to plan for economic development and full employment, and to control the trade cycle.[3]

Harry Dexter White had started his consideration of the post-war monetary system with a concern for development and had retreated for tactical reasons. The risk was that failure in one element of an integrated programme could prevent an agreement on anything. Keynes concurred. He saw the need for a wider vision and a 'concerted policy over the whole range of international economic relations', but preferred each element to be treated separately – and he was, in any case, less interested in development.[4] When Anglo-American talks on international monetary reform started in September 1943, proposals on commodities, commercial policy, cartels, nutrition, employment and investment were less advanced, and each element was treated as a distinct scheme with different rates of progress and chances of success.

These other issues did not disappear. They were supported by progressive demands both within the United States and by less developed countries and exporters of primary products who wished to restructure the world economy. Indeed, the first international conference was not on money: it was on food and agriculture at Hot Springs, Virginia, in 1943, which posed questions of the relations between industrial and agricultural countries, between the developed and the less developed world.[5] It was followed by a conference of the International Labour Organization held at Philadelphia in 1944. Discussions started before and ran alongside Bretton Woods, and they continued into the post-war period with the creation of the Food and Agriculture Organization and the deliberations of the conference on trade and employment.

HOT SPRINGS: FOOD AND AGRICULTURE

In March 1943, President Roosevelt issued an invitation to forty-three allied nations to attend a conference on food production and trade 'in the light of possibilities of progressively improving in each country the levels of consumption within the framework of an expansion of its general economic activity'. The conference would also consider 'equitable' agricultural prices from the point of view of producers and consumers, and 'the possibilities of international coordination and stimulation of national policies

for the improvement of nutrition'.[6] The conference met at Hot Springs in
May–June 1943. E. F. Penrose – economic adviser to John Winant, the
American ambassador in London – recalled Keynes's sceptical reaction:
'What you are saying is that your President with his great political insight
has decided that the best strategy for post-war reconstruction is to start
with vitamins and then by a circuitous route work round to the international balance of payments!'[7] Lionel Robbins, a British representative
at the conference, thought it pointless:

> It is not difficult to agree that people should have more food, that agricul-
> ture should be widely balanced, that the economy should expand and that
> peace should be assured. It is very easy to be friendly in a luxury hotel with
> all expenses paid and no binding commitments on the agenda. When we did
> touch on bread and butter questions, as in the discussions on buffer stocks,
> opinion was by no means so united.[8]

In fact, the conference was less of a distraction than Keynes and Robbins
believed.

In the eyes of primary producers, less developed economies and nutritional scientists, food and nutrition were more important than reforming
the international monetary system as a strategy to create a prosperous,
socially equitable world economy. It brought together two important considerations. As we have seen in Chapter 4, health and inadequate diet had
become an important theme in the work of the League of Nations and in
national and imperial discourse. A second concern was the economic difficulties faced by agricultural producers because of unstable or low prices.
These two issues were both connected and in tension. Together, they
offered a solution to the problem of economic development by structural
change to the world economy. Better nutrition might increase the demand
for food and so create prosperity for farmers, in turn increasing demand for
industrial goods. There was also tension, for the attempt to stabilize
or increase the price of food might lead to commodity agreements that
benefitted producers and reduced the welfare of consumers in industrial
countries. These questions were fought between countries that were predominantly consumers (such as Britain) and predominantly producers
(such as Australia), and also within countries that were both major producers and consumers – above all the United States. Furthermore, the
issue of food and nutrition connected with the full employment of the
resources of the world.

Roosevelt saw political benefits in calling the conference, for adequate
food was more immediate and personal than abstruse economic policy. It
connected with the commitment of the Atlantic Charter of August 1941

to the 'fair and equitable distribution of essential produce' and 'the fullest collaboration between all nations in the economic field with the object of securing, for all, improved labor standards, economic advancement and social security'. Food offered a way of countering domestic critics who believed that America was too generous to the Allies and that policy was moving in an internationalist direction. Who could be in favour of starvation?[9]

A focus on food also made sense given pressing problems in 1943. Bengal was in the early stages of a famine that resulted in perhaps 3 million deaths.[10] The situation in Europe was also alarming. G. H. Bourne's *Starvation in Europe* reported that 'it is a pathetic story and the desire just to relieve this hideous by-product of war is in itself almost a sufficient war-aim at this moment.'[11] The Oxford Committee for Famine Relief – Oxfam – was set up in 1942 to allow food through the Allied blockade to relieve starvation in Greece.[12] Starvation was integral to the strategy of the Third Reich by clearing the population – both Jewish and Slavic – from eastern Europe in order to secure food supplies for Germany.[13] For its part, Britain relied on imported food. In June 1942, the British and American governments formed the Combined Food Board in Washington to co-ordinate transport and distribution between North America and Europe, complementing the London Food Board that covered the empire. The management of food supplies and entitlements was therefore a central concern during the war, and serious issues were anticipated on the return to peace.[14]

Hot Springs was also concerned with agriculture – a major part of the world economy and source of employment. Britain was an exception among the developed economies, with only 7.6 per cent of its population employed in agriculture in 1930. By contrast, in Germany, 29.9 per cent of the workforce was still employed in agriculture in 1935.[15] In the United States, the farming population was 24.8 per cent of the total population in 1930.[16] Roosevelt could not ignore the agricultural states, for each returned two senators and had a disproportionate influence, and the South was vital to Democratic control of the Senate. Many advanced industrial economies turned to policies of agricultural protection and autarky in the 1930s to support their rural populations, with the result that domestic food prices were often above prices on world markets – which hit both domestic consumers and primary producers abroad who lost their markets.[17]

Major exporters of agricultural commodities with large, efficient export-oriented farms, such as Australia and Argentina, suffered from a collapse in exports, low prices, balance of payments deficits and deep depression. Other parts of the world had a different problem: of subsistence peasants who were barely able to feed themselves, let alone secure sufficient income to buy industrial goods. Paul Rosenstein-Rodan, a leading development economist, argued that five 'vast international depressed areas' contained 80–90 per cent of the world's population, in the Far East (India and China), the colonial empires (above all Africa), the Caribbean, and the Middle East. The economic development of these backward areas with their 'agrarian excess population' and disguised unemployment was, he argued, 'the most important task facing us in the making of the peace'.[18]

These issues had come together at the League of Nations, which sought a new understanding of the links of agriculture and nutrition with welfare and economic stability. The League had been concerned with food and nutrition from its foundation in response to the *Hungerkatastrophe* in central Europe at the end of the First World War. Herbert Hoover, a member of the Supreme Economic Council set up by the Allied governments to handle post-1918 reconstruction, established the American Relief Administration which disposed of surplus American food in central Europe and Russia, so linking policies to help American farmers with assistance for Europe. Hoover stressed that stability meant resolving the problems of hunger and unemployment rather than the 'legalistic processes' of President Wilson.[19] The issue was taken up by Fridtjof Nansen, the League's commissioner for refugees, who pointed out in October 1921 that 'Argentina is burning its grain surplus; America is letting its grain rot in silos; Canada has more than two billion tons of left over grain – and yet, in Russia, millions are dying of hunger.' The League considered utilizing wartime international co-ordination to respond to the coexistence of food and famine, and to prevent price fluctuations and economic instability.[20]

Food security was linked to nutritional science, which redefined the problem as a lack of vitamins rather than a shortage of calories. The analysis of nutrition and deficiency diseases joined domestic welfare with the plight of the imperial population.[21] The most important scientist in terms of impact on public policy was John Boyd Orr, director of a research institute at the University of Aberdeen where his work moved from animal to human nutrition in Britain and the empire. He campaigned for the provision of milk for school children and his report of 1936 on *Food, Health and Income* found that an adequate diet was achieved by only the upper half of incomes in Britain. It was a reproach to the harmful impact of agricultural protectionism and the low level of welfare payments to unemployed families. Boyd Orr called for an adequate diet to be brought within the reach of everyone, with a national food policy to raise the level of health and nutrition in Britain.[22]

These ideas were developed at the League, where Frank McDougall called for a restructuring of agriculture to produce 'protective' foods close to the consumer, with bulky 'energy' foods imported from efficient, large-scale producers (see Chapter 3). The League's initial interest in agrarian reform in central and eastern Europe was frustrated by local political hostility, and it turned its focus to Asia and 'rural hygiene' that brought together poverty, poor nutrition and development. In India, scientists at the Nutrition Research Laboratories at Coonoor argued that deficiency diseases were as serious as endemic and epidemic disease, for 'malnutrition maims its millions, and is the means whereby the soil of the human body is made ready for the rank growth of the pathogenic agents of many of those diseases which afflict the Indian people'.[23] Wallace Aykroyd, a nutrition specialist who became director of the Coonoor institute in 1935, had previously worked at the League on issues such as the impact of mass unemployment on public health, malnutrition in the rural economy of Romania, and a schedule of nutritional standards. At Coonoor, Aykroyd argued that malnutrition halted colonial economic development.[24] This work informed nationalist critiques of British rule in India. It could justify state planning, advocated by Nehru and Bose as a way of overcoming malnutrition by 'systematic crop planning' of 'heavy-yielding, energy-producing and also protective food stuffs'. It was also used by Gandhi to call for a new Indian diet with a social obligation by those who were better off for those who were starving. He drew on the work of nutritionists to argue that the value of food given by the market – such as machine-milled rice – was not the same as its nutritional value. The solution was ethical production and consumption of healthy food in the village community.[25]

In the United States, Henry Wallace at the Department of Agriculture had attempted to combine prosperity for farmers by stabilizing prices and incomes through the 'ever-normal granary', with food stamps to distribute surplus output to unemployed workers and poor consumers. In 1941, Wallace, now Vice-President, pressed for the extension of the ever-normal granary to the world as a means of preventing a repeat of conditions after the First World War when excess production led to lower prices and a lack of purchasing power for manufactures. Producers should be protected against violent fluctuations in income by ensuring that 'prices stabilized at a point to be fair to producers and consumers', allied with a restructuring of agriculture between producers of protective and energy foods. Wallace called for 'an economy of abundance' through full employment, lower trade barriers, productive investment, reduction of inequality of incomes, and the application of technology to undeveloped areas.[26]

The idea for a conference on agriculture and food therefore arose from

a combination of nutritional science in the metropole and colonies, thinking in the League about the links between agriculture and depression, and
the policies of Wallace in the United States. These strands came together
in 1940 and 1941. Boyd Orr was advising the British government on food
policy and urged the creation of a National Food Board, with commodity
boards for individual foodstuffs to ensure that supplies were sufficient for
everyone at a guaranteed price. Still more ambitiously, he called for the
establishment of world government and planning to provide everyone
with an adequate diet for health.[27] Meanwhile, McDougall was in Washington for the International Wheat Conference where he met Wallace. In
1942, Wallace and Sumner Welles of the State Department asked McDougall to convene an informal group of officials from the State and
Agriculture departments, which produced a 'memorandum on a UN programme for freedom from want of food'. The memorandum called for an
expansive economy with full employment, better labour conditions and
social security. Better nutrition was not only an end in itself; it would prevent the resurgence of economic nationalism.[28]

The conference at Hot Springs was the first to be held on the reconstruction of the post-war world. It pulled together discussions of
agriculture in the less developed countries, the plight of primary producing countries, the depression faced by American farmers, concerns over
malnutrition, the development of domestic welfare policies, and the
reshaping of world agricultural production. Marvin Jones, the head of
the American delegation and president of the conference, later recalled
that Roosevelt 'wanted to see if the representatives of the various nations
could work together. This was an experience in their sitting around a
table.' There were lessons to be learned. The venue was a hotel in an isolated location in Virginia that allowed the delegates to concentrate on the
task at hand. Roosevelt decided to exclude the press and representatives
of Congress, which led to criticisms of secrecy that undermined attempts
to win over public opinion to the cause of internationalism. The Republican leader in the House argued that 'This war is a people's war, and the
peace must be a people's peace. The representatives of the Congress represent the people, and they should sit in at these . . . conferences.' Paranoid
members of Congress feared that Roosevelt was becoming autocratic,
and that the conference 'was called primarily to begin the construction of
the world super-state . . . along communist lines'. Jones eventually
relaxed the ban on the press on his own initiative. Walter Lippmann
pointed out that it was impossible 'to have a large mass meeting act as if
it were a small executive committee'. The answer was to have a small
confidential meeting to thrash out a deal prior to a large, open meeting

to secure public consent – exactly what happened with the monetary conference.[29]

The Hot Springs conference considered consumption deficiencies and recommended establishing national nutritional bodies. The achievement of better nutritional standards entailed more than an expansion of output; it required sustainable agriculture, a restructuring of the production of energy and protective foods, and better provision of credit, with co-operatives and changes in land tenure. Furthermore, action was needed to combine national and international policies by expanding international trade, raising the consumption of low-income groups, disposing of surpluses, and creating buffer stocks to ensure equitable prices. Much of the discussion at Hot Springs was idealistic and high-minded. The declaration that emerged from the conference made a link both with Roosevelt's commitment in his State of the Union Address of January 1941 to the 'four freedoms' of speech and worship, and from want and fear, and with the Atlantic Charter. It stressed the need 'to win and maintain freedom from fear and freedom from want' in an 'economy of abundance':

> There must be an expansion of the whole world economy to provide the purchasing power sufficient to maintain an adequate diet for all. With full employment in all countries, enlarged industrial production, the absence of exploitation, an increasing flow of trade within and between countries, an orderly management of domestic and international investment and currencies, and sustained internal and international economic equilibrium, the food which is produced can be made available to all people.

Each nation should take responsibility for the health of its citizens through adequate social security and protective foods at low prices. National action was not enough: it was necessary to have 'concerted action among all like-minded nations to expand and improve production, to increase employment, to raise levels of consumption, and to establish greater freedom in international commerce'. This ambition entailed 'full employment of human and material resources, based on sound social and economic policies' in order to increase production and purchasing power, linked with the 'sound expansion of industry in undeveloped and other areas' which would stimulate purchasing power for agriculture. Barriers to the production, distribution and consumption of food and other commodities should be reduced by removing tariffs and restrictions to trade; controlling fluctuations in exchange rates through 'orderly management of currencies and exchange'; and international commodity arrangement should promote the expansion of an orderly world economy.[30]

The conference agreed to create a permanent body for food and agriculture, though there was disagreement on its character. McDougall wanted a strong organization that would increase production, stabilize prices and ensure full employment of the world's resources. The United States preferred a weak consultative body. The interim commission that emerged was limited to collecting statistics, promoting research and providing technical assistance. Boyd Orr complained that 'the old men had crept back into power determined to resist any economic change which threatened their financial interests.'[31] When the Food and Agriculture Organization was created in 1945, Boyd Orr reluctantly accepted the post of director general where he was joined by other advocates of the nutritionist approach. He saw that the FAO 'looked like a victorious end to the long struggle for international cooperation in a food policy, but it seemed to me to be a sterile victory because the organisation had neither the authority nor the funds to initiate a policy which would achieve the results hoped for.' He did not abandon a more activist policy without a fight. Aykroyd joined the FAO as director of its nutrition division, with McDougall as assistant director and Boyd Orr's prospective successor. Boyd Orr scrapped research projects in favour of policies to deal with longer-term problems of feeding the world's growing population. The FAO calculated that the world's population was increasing by 22 million a year, compared with 7 million in the nineteenth century, and that the world's output of food must double in the next twenty years. The answer was a World Food Board to purchase and stockpile surplus commodities when they were cheap, so helping to stabilize prices and increase production; the goods could then be sold to poorer countries at low prices to ensure that they had an adequate diet. Farmers would have a higher income so they could buy more goods; if people were fed properly, it would end the notion that some races were 'inferior'. The British embassy was not impressed and complained that Boyd Orr was promising an 'Agricultural Paradise' in a 'light-hearted manner verging on frivolity'. A conference was called in Copenhagen in September 1946 to consider the issue.[32]

In the United States, Wallace's radical policies were in retreat. The State Department feared that a World Food Board would raise prices at the expense of consumers, so attracting more capital and labour into agriculture, and increasing the output of inefficient producers. The result would be to accumulate larger stocks, which would be swallowed by 'the bottomless pit of oriental hunger', and to create an unaccountable international agency that would threaten market prices and private trading. Neither did the British government welcome Boyd Orr's plans, which threatened higher prices for food imports and a heavy bill for distributing food to poorer countries. Instead, the new Labour government emphasized the need for full employment in industrial countries to create demand for primary products. Despite these concerns, the Copenhagen conference approved the principle of a World Food Board.[33]

The danger of the FAO, as far as the governments of Britain and the United States were concerned, was that undeveloped countries and exporters of primary products formed a majority. Washington and London blocked the World Food Board, to the fury of Boyd Orr at their 'underhand subversive measures' and self-interest:

> England's wealth had been created by the import of cheap food and raw materials produced by natives with wages so low that they lived in abysmal poverty, and paid for by expensive industrial products. The suggestion of a 'new deal' for the native producers, beginning with a fair price for the food Britain imported, seemed to threaten English economic prosperity.

He resigned from the FAO in April 1948 and left America in despair, melodramatically wiping its dust from the soles of his shoes as he boarded the ship. He complained that America had turned its back on Roosevelt's plans at Hot Springs as surely as it had turned its back on Wilson's plans for the League of Nations.[34] The FAO relocated from Washington to Rome where the new director general – and former US secretary of agriculture – Norris Dodd focused on short-term food aid, technical assistance to farmers, statistical intelligence to stabilize markets, and projects on locust control, fisheries, forests and rice cultivation.[35]

These debates over food and nutrition ran parallel to the more technical reform of the international monetary system. By linking social, economic and political rights, and combining them with a concern for security, the debate offered a more capacious view of international relations than the narrower 'embedded liberalism' of Bretton Woods. As we will see in Chapter 19, the issue returned in the context of debates over the limits to growth and the balance between population and food, and informed demands for a more just global order in the 1960s and 1970s.[36] It also connected with another strand of policy: the need for stable prices to provide security for primary producers.

COMMODITY POLICY

After the First World War, several commodity schemes were established for food and raw materials. They were undermined by the depression, and at the World Monetary and Economic Conference discussion of various commodities proved inconclusive. A number of schemes were proposed in

the 1930s, and by the Second World War international commodity agreements controlled output and prices for tin, wheat, sugar, rubber and tea in
an attempt to create equilibrium between supply and demand.[37] In addition to these formal agreements, cartels of producers regulated output
and competition by voluntary, often secret, agreements between private
companies to set prices and divide up world markets. The League of
Nations identified twenty-two cartels covering commodities such as petrol, copper and wood pulp, and on one estimate cartels covered 42 per
cent of world trade between 1929 and 1937 – a phenomenon that troubled American critics of the 'production-restricting cartels that infest
Europe'.[38] Cartels in the interwar period reflected excess capacity; American critics thought this situation was unlikely to occur after the Second
World War and that the opportunity should be taken to shift to higher
productivity in competitive firms. To their supporters, however, commodity schemes and cartels stabilized the income of hard-hit producers and
prevented destructive competition, helping to plan the economy in an efficient and rational manner.

In 1938, Keynes reflected on the economics of schemes to stabilize the
price of basic commodities. He pointed out that private firms had no
incentive to store surplus stocks to smooth periods of low and high
demand, for the cost was high and it was not clear how long stocks would
need to be held. He suggested that strategic reserves created by the Essential Commodities Reserves Act of 1938 in case of war could be used to
dampen the trade cycle and reduce price fluctuations.[39] He developed this
idea during the war. Trade was disrupted by fighting and blockades so
that some countries had surpluses they could not export; and the British
were anxious to limit German access to strategic raw materials. The British government decided to purchase surplus commodities and gave
responsibility for this to Frederick Leith-Ross at the Treasury, with Keynes
as his adviser. Leith-Ross hoped that Anglo-American co-operation would
provide goods for post-war relief, assist producers whose markets were
disrupted, and regulate output in order to prevent a repeat of the depression of the 1930s. Keynes was in broad agreement, though he was 'rather
frightened by the atmosphere of comprehensive and open-hearted philan-
thropy which seems to prevail' with the assumption that Britain would
buy everything at a price acceptable to the producers.[40]

The Americans also wished to limit German access to raw materials
and food, a concern that was linked to Good Neighbor policies in Latin
America. In September 1939, the Inter-American Financial and Economic
Advisory Committee was created to encourage economic co-operation.
Emilio Collado proposed that the United States should acquire strategic

goods and commodities formerly sold to Europe through a trading corporation on the lines of the Agricultural Adjustment Act. Morgenthau,
Wallace and Welles agreed and urged Roosevelt to supplement America's
'military defense program with effective and decisive action in the field of
economic defense'. The initial idea of an over-arching Inter-American
Trading Corporation gave way to a more limited approach. The Rubber
Reserve Company and the Metal Reserves Company would buy and
stockpile these strategic raw materials, with the Export-Import Bank taking responsibility for American purchases of raw materials in Latin
America. In July 1940, a conference of foreign ministers of the Americas
issued a declaration of reciprocal assistance and co-operation to defend
the collective security of the western hemisphere, partly in response to the
German occupation of European countries with American colonies, and
partly to encourage economic co-operation through commodity agreements and the distribution of surpluses.[41]

In November 1940, Leith-Ross approached the State Department to
discuss wartime co-ordination of British and American policies on commodities, and more generally the 'chronic maladjustment of supply and
demand'. He saw 'an opportunity to set on foot an international cooperative effort of great post-war as well as war-time significance' by storing
surpluses, regulating production and meeting the post-war needs of Europe. He realized that government control schemes might collide with
economic nationalism as each country sought the best deal for its producers, but he hoped that American commitments in Latin America and
British in the empire would provide the basis for progress.

> Our ultimate aim should be a world-wide extension of some of the prin-
> ciples of the AAA schemes applied in the United States ... If we could
> succeed in preventing sharp fluctuations in the prices of the chief primary
> materials, we should have gone a long way towards smoothing out the
> cyclical depressions of trade in manufacturing countries ... [that were]
> the breeding ground of social disturbances and future wars.[42]

Keynes took up the idea of stabilizing the price of internationally traded
raw materials, and even the creation of an international holding cartel
based on the 'ever-normal granary'.[43]

Wallace had a similar idea, and a joint British-American committee
was established to pursue the proposal. The ambition was scaled down to
concentrate on immediate surpluses and food shortages in Europe after
the war, with a focus on specific commodities. Even here, disagreements
soon appeared. Wallace started talks with wheat producers for an international agreement in August 1941 which led Keynes to worry that export

quotas and an agreed floor to prices would limit Britain's ability to buy in the cheapest market.[44] Balancing the interests of consumers and producers would not be easy. Early in 1942, Keynes returned to the issue in a memorandum on international controls of buffer stocks that aimed to achieve 'the internationalisation of Vice-President Wallace's "ever-normal granary".' He pointed to different approaches to commodity policy. Producers hoped to raise prices to improve the terms of trade between primary producers and manufacturers. Clearly, such an approach was not welcome to Britain as a major importer of food. Keynes rejected restrictions on output which would preserve the existing distribution of production, limit the expansion of the most efficient producers, and remove the benefits of competition. Neither did he want higher prices that would depress demand and keep inefficient producers in business. His aim was to stabilize prices and smooth the cycle to avoid the 'adverse effect on trade stability of the truly frightful *price* fluctuations'. Buffer stocks with a 'Control' for each commodity under an over-arching Council for Commodity Controls, or 'Commod Control', would stabilize the price of primary products entering international trade and hold stocks to cover fluctuations in supply and demand. A basic price would be determined by the long-term equilibrium cost of the most efficient producer, so avoiding both artificially high prices caused by restricting output, and the low prices of producers with an inadequate standard of life. The basic price could be adjusted 5 per cent a year so that, over time, it would fall as efficient, profitable producers expanded, and less efficient producers reduced their output. His aim was to combine 'a short-period stabilisation of prices with a long-period price policy which balances supply and demand and allows steady rate of expansion to the cheaper-cost producers'. The result would be a gradual fall in prices rather than changing the terms of trade between producers of primary products and manufactures. The Cabinet accepted Keynes's approach as the basis for discussions with the State Department – though to Roy Harrod, even stabilization was 'mere sentimentalism' that overlooked the fact that Britain's economic recovery in the 1930s was helped by the distress of primary producers.[45]

Discussions with the Americans soon ran into problems. Will Clayton's experience as a Southern cotton merchant led him to doubt that buffer stocks were the solution. In 1929, the price of cotton fell from 20¢ to 5¢, and he questioned how to decide the point at which it should be stabilized. In his view, the main cause of booms and busts was the misuse of credit. Buffer stocks 'underrated the constructive aspect of private trade on the commodity exchanges in regulating market forces, and . . . assumed that a board of a few men would be wiser in its decisions with respect to prices than the impersonal operation of the free market.'[46] On the other hand, the Department of Agriculture favoured regulation of output to support American farmers. Paul Appleby, who had been executive assistant to Wallace at Agriculture from 1933 and became Under-Secretary from 1940 to 1944, argued that the price system was too slow in correcting supply and that the average price of agricultural products needed to be raised to close the income gap between farmers and industry.[47]

These disagreements on commodity policy were apparent at Hot Springs. The British wanted buffer stocks to remove short-term price fluctuations and to allow a gradual shift to more efficient producers with a gradual fall in prices. Efficient, competitive exporters such as Canada agreed. Other primary producers supported commodity agreements to restrict production, increase prices and alter the terms of trade. This discussion of commodity schemes was subsumed into the post-war talks on trade and employment when the American approach now reflected Clayton's support for free markets and free trade rather than the radical ideas of Henry Wallace.[48] Disagreement over the stabilization of prices around a falling trend or a shift in the terms of trade in favour of primary producers continued to divide countries after the war, above all in the campaign of the United Nations Conference on Trade and Development in the 1960s to alter the terms of trade between industrial and primary producers.

EMPLOYMENT

During the First World War, the labour movements of the Allies proposed the creation of an international body to protect the rights of workers in return for their support of the war effort. In February 1919, the International Labour and Socialist Conference met in Berne to formulate their demands. The conference was split between those who wished to make a case at the Versailles peace conference and those – above all Samuel Gompers of the American Federation of Labor (AFL) – who preferred to avoid politics and to rely on strong labour unions. Despite these divergences, the meeting devised a programme for freedom of association, equal pay for equal work, a minimum wage, an eight-hour day, and unemployment insurance. These proposals formed the basis for the Commission on International Labour Legislation that was established during the Versailles conference, thanks to the realization by Wilson, Lloyd George and Clemenceau that the contribution of workers to the war effort should be recognized. The Commission could draw on existing networks such as the International Association for Labour Legislation that was created in 1900, and whose International Labour Office gathered information and organized meetings. The Commission proceeded to draft a legal framework for labour legislation and workers' rights.

More problematic than the general principle of establishing labour standards was the form to be taken by the new International Labour Organization that was approved by the Versailles conference in April 1919. It was accepted that it should have a tripartite structure of labour, employer and government representatives, who would not vote as national delegations. There was disagreement over their relative weight. Wilson chose Gompers as one of the American representatives of the Commission and insisted that he should be the chairman. The AFL did not have a political wing, unlike the British trade unions with the Labour Party, and preferred to rely on private agreements between employers and workers. The result was a divergence between the British, who wanted each government to have two representatives or two votes to one each for labour and business which would ensure that any proposals would be accepted by national legislatures, and Gompers who wished to minimize government involvement. The compromise was to have three representatives, each with one vote as Gompers wished, but the government representatives would have double votes in plenary meetings to agree on conventions, as the British wished. There was also disagreement on the ability of the ILO to make agreements that were binding on national governments. The Italians and French argued for a supranational organization that could vote for binding conventions with a two-thirds majority. The Americans rejected such a delegation of sovereignty – and in any case, labour legislation was a matter for individual states and not the federal government. The compromise was to refer any convention that was agreed by a two-thirds majority to national legislatures for ratification; any proposal accepted by a simple majority would be a recommendation. By this means, it was hoped to strike a balance between maintaining sovereignty and securing international agreement – a constant tension in international organizations.

The International Labour Organization came into existence in October 1919 without, as it transpired, American membership, due to the United States' failure to ratify the Versailles Treaty. The preamble to the ILO's constitution claimed that 'universal and lasting peace can be established only if it is based upon social justice' and that 'conditions of labour exist involving such injustice, hardship and privation to large numbers of people as to produce unrest so great that the peace and harmony of the world are imperilled'. The ILO's ambition was to ensure that 'labour should not be regarded as a commodity or article of commerce', that unemployment should be prevented, that workers have a living wage, that women should be paid equal wages for equal work, that workers should have freedom of association, that goods produced by children under the age of fourteen should not enter international trade, and that working hours should be limited with the provision of days of rest.[49]

In the interwar period, the ILO agreed to a total of sixty-seven conventions ranging from general principles on hours of work and freedom of association to conditions in particular trades. It also criticized monetary policy and called for co-ordinated responses to financial crises, and in the 1930s called for the reflation of the global economy through public works and economic planning.[50] In 1934, the United States joined the ILO on the insistence of Frances Perkins – a social reformer and campaigner for labour rights who worked closely with Roosevelt when he was Governor of New York. She served as Secretary of Labor throughout his presidency and saw the ILO as a way of extending the policies of the New Deal. Indeed, in 1939 the new director general was John Winant – a social-reforming state governor and first head of the Social Security Board in the United States – until his appointment as ambassador to London in 1941.[51] In February 1939, the ILO agreed that in the event of war it should continue its work 'at the highest possible level' and that social policy would be vital to secure the support of workers. In November 1939, the AFL delegate to the ILO remarked that 'organized labor should have a determining voice in fixing the terms of the peace settlement . . . Only by giving labor such a voice can we ensure that the peace settlement, unlike that of 1919, is based upon justice for all people in all nations.' The ILO relocated to Montreal in 1940 and convened a conference in New York in October–November 1941– chaired by Perkins – where it built on the Four Freedoms and the Atlantic Charter to mobilize social and democratic values and internationalism against the threat of fascism, to articulate a programme of social security, and to call for an end to unemployment, a minimum living wage, and public works to develop the world's resources.[52]

Informal Anglo-American discussions in October 1943 concluded that an international agency was needed to overcome the economic nationalism of the 1930s and to ensure that domestic employment policies were co-ordinated.[53] Agreeing that domestic employment was a foundation for multilateral trade was easier than defining what was meant by full employment, and how far it should be the main aim of policy. The issue was still more difficult when primary producers and less developed countries took part, for full employment was not a meaningful concept in countries with reserves of labour and endemic under-employment. Above all, the question arose whether to allow trade to grow in a free enterprise capitalist system or to ensure that everyone had an opportunity of secure and stable employment which might involve planning and government intervention. These issues arose when the ILO met in Philadelphia in April–May 1944 to draw up a new charter.

The meeting provided an opportunity for the Australian government to argue their case that full employment was an essential complement of the monetary proposals which would limit their ability to respond to economic shocks by varying the exchange rate. At a meeting of the Dominions and India in London in February–March 1944, the Australians had presented a draft international employment agreement to create 'a national obligation to its own people and an international obligation to the other signatory governments henceforth to take all measures necessary to provide such opportunities for its people that all who are able and willing to work may do so'. This agreement would entail reporting national data to an annual conference on employment and explaining what measures were taken to combat unemployment; a special conference would be called if any country were in serious breach of its obligations. The British agreed to support a modified version of this proposal and to request that the United States hold an employment conference.[54] The Australians now presented their policy to the ILO conference.

By contrast, the American proposal was more limited, offering the 'opportunity of useful and regular employment' and 'liberation from unreasonable restriction of trade' rather than a commitment to full employment. The Australian delegation realized that the American approach was shaped by a fear of 'antagonizing the strong republican old-time capitalistic group' but nevertheless decided to press its more radical proposal, for 'our whole future is at stake in negotiations such as these'. The Australians were adamant that 'dependent economies cannot be expected to enter into obligations which restrict their freedom of action unless the countries on whom they are dependent are willing to enter into employment obligations'. A compromise was agreed between the Australian and American drafts – only for the State Department to object. The final resolution merely stated that 'each Government recognizes its duty to maintain a high level of employment'.

Even so, the Declaration of Philadelphia of May 1944 contained a commitment to economic growth, full employment and higher standards of living, with 'employment of workers in the occupations in which they can have the satisfaction of giving the fullest measure of their skill and attainments and make their greatest contribution to the common well-being'. It was now stated more bluntly than in 1919 that 'labour is not a commodity', and that 'all human beings, irrespective of race, creed or sex, have the right to pursue both their material well-being and their spiritual development in conditions of freedom and dignity, of equal security and equal opportunity.' The conference pledged to co-operate with other international bodies to secure 'the fuller and broader utilization of the world's productive resources' by 'measures to expand production and consumption, to avoid severe economic fluctuations, to promote the economic and social advancement of the less developed regions of the world, to assure greater stability in world prices of primary products, and to promote a high and steady volume of international trade'. The Declaration stressed that the development of poorer countries would not threaten advanced economies, for higher world income would encourage trade, provide opportunities for investment by countries with abundant savings, and increase demand for capital goods. International organizations could ensure that savings were directed to areas that lacked capital; and developed countries should devise policies to allow them to adapt to competition as poorer countries industrialized. Rather than turning to protection, advanced countries should retrain workers and encourage research and development. At the same time, poor countries should limit population growth, encourage domestic savings and improve social overhead capital.[55]

The conference at Philadelphia marked the high point of the ILO, which was marginalized in the discussion of the post-war international order. In the United States, the influence of the Department of Labor declined with an increase in the voice of private business interests who were doubtful of calls for public works and planning. The Soviet Union was also suspicious of the ILO's commitment to ensuring the dignity of labour. In Marxism, labour was a commodity whose value was expropriated, and the solution was to replace capitalism. The ILO failed to secure responsibility for the wider economic mandate, which was taken by the International Monetary Fund and International Bank for Reconstruction and Development, and the Economic and Social Council of the United States in the new multilateral system – bodies that all relied on governmental representation rather than the tripartite structure of the ILO.[56]

The Australians had not secured everything they wanted at Philadelphia, but they had unanimous agreement for a further conference on employment. They also pressed their point in the preparations for Bretton Woods. They convinced the British to amend the joint statement to ensure that 'the pressure put on a country to correct a maladjustment in its balance of payments will not prevent it from following a policy of expansion intended to maintain a high level of employment.' The Australians thought it 'imprudent' to surrender freedom to vary exchange rates to an international body dominated by 'highly industrialised countries' who were

unsympathetic to primary producers. Cutting wages and reducing government spending was no longer an option as in 1931, for 'workers would not
remain docile and to the economic dislocations would be added grave
social disorders which would greatly intensify the loss of income'. The
Australian delegates therefore urged a change in the purpose of the International Monetary Fund 'to give more emphasis to employment and less
emphasis to exchange stability'. As we will see, they did not get their way
at Bretton Woods, but the conference on employment agreed at Philadelphia would provide a further opportunity to argue that the monetary
agreement should be complemented by a commitment to full employment.[57] The ambition at the ILO conference at Philadelphia for social
justice for all peoples did not disappear; it re-emerged in the post-war conference on trade and employment, and in the demands of the less developed
and formerly colonial countries for a restructuring of the global economy.

8

'The threshold of the future'

The Bretton Woods Agreement

'What we have done here in Bretton Woods is to devise machinery by which men and women everywhere can freely exchange, on a fair and stable basis, the goods which they produce through their labor. And we have taken the initial steps through which the nations of the world will be able to help one another in economic development to their mutual advantage ... Here is a sign blazoned upon the horizon, written large upon the threshold of the future ... a sign that the peoples of the earth are learning how to join hands and work in unity ... None of us has found any incompatibility between devotion to our own countries and joint action. Indeed, we have found on the contrary that the only genuine safeguard for our national interests lies in international cooperation ... [T]he only enlightened form of self-interest lies in international accord.'

Closing address by Henry Morgenthau at the
Bretton Woods conference, 22 July 1944[1]

'Our choice is not whether we will be a "creditor" or "debtor" nation but whether we will be a "creditor" or a "sucker" nation ... I am not in favor of this country being a Santa Claus to the world ... We must undertake measures which will help the world get on its own feet ... rather than establish a relationship of tutelage, support and subsidy by this country ... Any kind of proposal has to be subjected to the test of being essentially in the interests of the United States, but on the basis of far-sighted self interest rather than of a narrow one which is not really in our best interests.'

E. A. Goldenweiser, 'Bretton Woods', 22 November 1944[2]

The United States invited the representatives of forty-three other nations to the Mount Washington Hotel at Bretton Woods, New Hampshire, for

The United Nations Monetary and Financial Conference
at the Mount Washington Hotel in Bretton Woods, 4 July 1944.

the United Nations Monetary and Financial Conference between 1 and 22 July 1944 – the first international meeting to discuss the world's financial arrangements since the abortive conference at London in 1933. It marked the culmination of the Anglo-American discussions on the post-war monetary system that had produced the joint statement. The task now was to secure support from other countries at a crucial time of the war. Obviously, the Axis powers – Germany, Japan, Italy – were not represented, and the governments in exile of occupied countries such as France had limited capacity to contribute to the emerging plans.

The exigencies of the war meant that the United States was eager to involve the Soviet Union and China. In June 1941, Hitler had launched Operation 'Barbarossa', a surprise attack on the Soviet Union, that was finally turned back at Stalingrad by February 1943. The Red Army suffered devastating losses as it counter-attacked, and shortly before the Bretton Woods conference mounted a major offensive in Belorussia, which took it to the borders of Poland by mid-July. Although the Soviets had not played a role in the formulation of the plans, the scale of their sacrifices meant that the United States wished them to be part of the new regime. Meanwhile, Allied forces had landed in Normandy in June 1944, and were engaged in fierce fighting as the conference started, before breaking German resistance and liberating Paris by 25 August. In the Pacific and Asia, the Japanese had been at war with China since 1937 and had followed the attack on Pearl Harbor by invading the Philippines, Indonesia, Malaysia and Burma, which were defeated by May 1942. In March 1944, Japanese forces were threatening India, where nationalists were also campaigning against British rule. The Chinese Nationalist government of Chiang Kai-shek was engaged in the war against Japan, and Roosevelt hoped that China would be one of the 'four policemen' after the war, with the United States, Britain and the Soviet Union.[3] These four countries were involved in the Bretton Woods conference, and the monetary discussions were informed by geopolitical and military considerations to hold together the Allies, and to seize the opportunity to create a post-war order that would allow economic recovery and stability.

Immediately before the conference, the task of building support for the monetary scheme started in the deliberations of a drafting committee of seventeen countries at Atlantic City between 15 and 29 June 1944. A balance had to be struck between the need to build on Anglo-American understanding as the basis for the conference and avoiding the impression that the conference was merely a formality. Keynes reported that

White is anxious that not too many doubts and choices shall be finally settled here at Atlantic City, since it is important for him that there shall be no
appearance of asking the members of the American Delegation who are not
here and the other powers not represented here to rubber-stamp something
already substantially finished.

Nevertheless, White hoped that he and Keynes

should reach as high a degree of agreement behind the scenes as to which
of the alternatives we are ready to drop and which we agree in pressing.
Thus to the largest extent possible White and I will have an agreed text
but on the surface a good many matters may be presented in alternative
versions.[4]

White realized that success was more likely if the scheme could be presented as not just American, so he needed the support of the British – but
he also wished to avoid the impression of Anglo-American collusion.
The aim, as Keynes pointed out, 'has been not to reach formal agreement on any matters, since White is much concerned not to present
Bretton Woods with anything like a *fait accompli*.' The meeting at
Atlantic City took the Anglo-American joint statement as the basis
for discussion and received amendments – many of them merely
clarifications – which were considered by four specialist groups that
reported back to plenary meetings. Anglo-American meetings ran
alongside these discussions. The amendments were mainly left for consideration at Bretton Woods, against Keynes's preference for submitting
a revised Anglo-American text. A number of substantial issues did
remain to be settled. Above all, the British wanted greater flexibility for
nations to amend exchange rates, with a longer transitional period than
three years after the war. There were differences over the allocation of
quotas and votes in the IMF, and whether access to the Fund's reserves
would be automatic or discretionary. Further, it was not clear whether
loans from the International Bank for Reconstruction and Development should be confined to specific projects or for general reconstruction
and recovery. Despite these remaining issues, Keynes was pleased with
the outcome at Atlantic City:

There has not been a single moment of heat or serious dispute, and amiabil-
ity has prevailed. White has proved an altogether admirable chairman. His
kindness to me personally has been extreme. And behind the scenes he has
always been out to find a way of agreement except when his own political
difficulties stood in the way.

Of course, White's emollient approach most likely reflected his realization that he needed British support for a successful outcome at Bretton Woods.[5] On 30 June, the delegates left Atlantic City for Bretton Woods.

THE BRETTON WOODS CONFERENCE

On 1 July 1944, the wider group assembled at the Mount Washington Hotel – a vacation resort that had been closed for two years, whose inadequate services were supplemented by a team of Boy Scouts.[6] Unlike at Hot Springs, the press was in attendance and the American delegation included senior members of Congress such as the chairs of the House and Senate committees on banking and currency, and Edward (Ned) Brown, chairman of the First National Bank of Chicago. Senator Robert Taft (R: Ohio), an arch-conservative opponent of Roosevelt, was kept away, and Morgenthau also wished to exclude Charles Tobey, the senior Republican on the Senate committee. Acheson pointed to the failure to engage Congress after the First World War and argued that Tobey should be invited: Bretton Woods was in his state and he was running for re-election. The gamble succeeded. Tobey gave the 4 July speech at the conference, 'calling down the blessings of God on the Conference and saying that we shall be untrue to Christ if we did not put these plans through'.[7]

Discussions at Bretton Woods were carefully controlled to show sufficient involvement without too much dissension that might prevent settlement. The conference was smaller and more focused than at London in 1933, and concentrated on money, where many delegates lacked expertise (and often linguistic skills) to play a major role. The 'technicians' could control business. Raymond Mikesell, part of the American team, remarked that the committees were 'a facade of democratic procedure' for the outcome was predetermined by the British and Americans, with the backing of Canada.[8] Roy Harrod recalled that Keynes and White would meet each day to agree the business, on which they then took the lead. Nevertheless, the relationship between the two men was not as harmonious as at Atlantic City. In the opinion of Emanuel Goldenweiser, director of research and statistics at the Federal Reserve, Keynes was the 'world's worst chairman' of the sessions dealing with the IBRD. Dean Acheson, the leading American delegate on that committee, complained that Keynes

> knows the thing inside out so that when anybody says Section 15-C he knows what it is. Nobody else in the room knows. So before you have an opportunity to turn to Section 15-C and see what he is talking about, he

says 'I hear no objection to that' and it is passed. Well, everybody is trying to find Section 15-C. He then says, we are now talking about Section 26-D. Then they begin fiddling around with their papers, and before you find that, it is passed.

Morgenthau had to tell Keynes to slow down. Tensions also arose between White and Keynes, whose health was failing and impatience mounting. An eyewitness recalled:

> Occasionally bitterness would creep in. Keynes would take White out of his depth; White would feel, but not admit, his intellectual inferiority; he would say something to remind Keynes that he, not Keynes, represented the stronger party in the negotiations. There would be angry words; papers would be thrown on the floor; one of them would stalk out of the room. The other negotiators would stay to patch up the quarrel. The next day the same procedure would be repeated.[9]

The Soviet Union attended the conference, and the American administration wished to include them in the post-war order by linking money and security. The five largest shareholders in the IMF – the 'four policemen' plus France – were to be the permanent members of the United Nations' security council. There were practical reasons, too, to engage the Soviets at Bretton Woods. The Soviet Union had borne the brunt of the land war against Germany thus far, and Stalin wanted American credit as a recompense for the delay in opening the second, Normandy front until that summer.[10] The Soviet delegation, led by Mikhail Stepanovich Stepanov, the deputy commissar of foreign trade, faced difficulties at the conference, 'struggling between the firing squad on the one hand and the English language on the other. They seemed to be very much afraid of the reactions in their own country, and didn't dare to take a step without consultation by 'phone or cable with their government.' Nevertheless, Keynes saw that the Soviets secured everything they wanted by 'stonewalling tactics'. The Soviet quota was on a par with the British, reflecting military rather than economic considerations. The Soviets also demanded the right to change the value of the rouble on their own authority and they virtually opted out of the exchange rate regime. Keynes thought that the 'American policy to appease the Russians and get them in . . . was wise'. It did not work. The Soviets signed the final act at the conference but they did not join the IMF, which was irrelevant to their controlled economy and state trading.[11]

Despite the careful management of business, other voices were heard at Bretton Woods, though not much heeded. White informed the American delegation that he expected trouble over quotas from China, France, India and, above all, Australia. The French turned out to be a 'pathetic group' who suffered from 'a very bad case of inferiority complex'. The Australians were more effective, and White complained that they were 'participating to an extent far beyond the proper roll [sic] of a country of her size and importance'. The Australians wished to avoid domestic deflation as in the 1930s and worried at losing exchange rate adjustment. Article VII of the Mutual Aid agreement of 3 September 1942 with Australia followed the same lines as the Lend Lease agreement with Britain. The Australians argued that ending imperial preference would only be feasible if all countries adopted a policy of full employment, which should be embedded in the Bretton Woods agreement. They were wary of giving power to international bodies in which they had only a minority voice. Prior to Bretton Woods, the Australians had pressed for stronger obligations by creditors and a greater voice for smaller countries. In 1943, the Australian experts had explained to White that the IMF 'might be in large measure controlled by individuals with traditional attitudes towards international economic adjustment, who would not recognize in all circumstances the propriety of an Australian policy of sustaining employment'. They wanted an explicit declaration that Australia 'is not to be penalized for trying to combat deflationary pressure'.[12] Australian acceptance of the Bretton Woods agreement remained in doubt, with one over-excited minister fearing that the IMF would turn Australia into a vassal state, end the 'white Australia' policy, and create 'a world dictatorship of private finance more complete and terrible than any Hitlerite dream'.[13]

The Chinese Nationalist government had the largest delegation after the Americans. It was led by Kung Hsiang-hsi, brother-in-law of Soong Tse-ven, Sun Yat-sen and Chiang Kai-shek. He was a Christian, educated in the United States, and was a wealthy businessman and politician. He served as Minister of Finance from 1933 to 1944 – a position he used to his own financial benefit. Kung had initially looked for support from Germany, which encouraged trade with and investment in China. On a visit to Berlin in June 1937, Kung assured Hjalmar Schacht that 'China considers Germany its best friend' in developing its raw materials and industries. At the same time, Germany was making a deal with Japan, and claimed to be neutral between the two countries. The strategy in Berlin was to ensure that Japan would offer support in the event of a German attack on Russia, and to counter the threat of Communism in China that might lead it to an alliance with the Soviet Union. Japan's attack on Pearl Harbor and subsequent alliance with Germany ended this strategy and left China dependent on the United States. Kung now argued for international development on

the lines of Sun Yat-sen (Chapter 4), and for American support against the
Japanese. General Joseph Stilwell, Deputy Supreme Allied Commander in
South-East Asia with responsibility for China, had doubts and thought
that the Communists had a clearer grasp of Chinese society than the
corrupt and reactionary regime of 'the peanut', his derogatory term for
Chiang. Bretton Woods was an opportunity for the Nationalists to press
their case, but in September 1944 Stilwell and Roosevelt lost patience
with Chiang, and relations broke down.[14]

The Indian delegation at Bretton Woods was in an ambivalent position.
The subcontinent remained part of the British empire, yet the delegation had
Indian representatives who were looking ahead to independence and urged
the conference to adopt policies for development. Ardeshir Darabshaw
Shroff – one of the authors of the Bombay Plan – argued that 'Our country
is pulsating with hopes and aspirations of large-scale industrial development
to raise the standard of living of 400 million of our population.' He pressed
for action on the blocked holdings of sterling built up during the war, and he
insisted that 'We cannot ... wait indefinitely till the United Kingdom has
reached a stage where sterling would be freely convertible into other currencies.' Keynes thought that Shroff was 'a snake in the grass, trying to catch us
out and filled with suppressed malice'. Of course, the Indian delegation saw
matters differently. They recalled that Britain's debt to India at the end of the
First World War was reduced by manipulating the exchange rate of the
rupee, and that India's reserves were diverted to support the pound between
the wars. They wanted the IMF to liquidate some of the blocked balances,
which White had accepted in an early draft before realizing it would impose
too great a burden. Keynes promised that Britain could be relied on 'without
any delay to settle honourably what was honourably and generously given' –
but on returning to London, he published an article arguing for a revision of
the agreement between Britain and India on the allocation of the costs of the
war. Purshottamdas Thakurdas – a founder of the Indian Currency League
in 1926 that urged a reduction in the exchange rate of the rupee, and a contributor to the Bombay Plan – joined in denouncing Keynes's article as
'cynical and fallacious' and a 'pure and simple repudiation of England's debt
to India'. The Indians wanted a multilateral settlement rather than relying
on the doubtful good intentions of Britain. The Bombay Plan assumed that
10 per cent of the finance for development would come from the sterling
balances, and Theodore Gregory, the economic adviser to the Government
of India, realized that Indian sacrifices in accumulating wartime sterling
balances had a 'high degree of emotional significance' for post-war industrialization. However, nothing was done at Bretton Woods to settle the sterling
balances. The Americans thought that the issue was a distraction, that the

Fund lacked resources, and that their own claims for repayment had precedence over the sterling balances. This failure to deal with sterling balances was, in the opinion of E. F. Penrose, the most important failing at Bretton Woods.[15] In 1946, V. S. Krishna, an Indian economist, spoke for many when he remarked that

> the restrictions laid on the convertibility of these [sterling] balances are in conformity neither with the declarations of the statesmen of the United Nations to help the backward countries to develop their industries nor even with the more limited purpose for which the Fund is to be organised, viz to facilitate the settlement of current transactions.

A leading member of the Indian Communist Party claimed that the failure to deal with the balances added 'another chapter to the history of predatory British finance in India'. Matters did not improve when the Government of India, prior to independence, accepted the Bretton Woods agreement without consulting the Legislative Assembly – a decision that led to complaints of treachery and an Anglo-American conspiracy to give priority to American debts over British obligations in India. India's experience at Bretton Woods left it 'with a foundational ambivalence toward the new liberal international order'.[16]

The Latin American countries had nineteen delegations at Bretton Woods, and they joined India in pressing for an amendment to the IMF's articles to make it more supportive of economic development. Although the final version of the articles did not explicitly mention underdeveloped countries, they did go some way in securing recognition of their demands. The Fund was pledged 'to facilitate the expansion and balanced growth of international trade, and to contribute thereby to the promotion and maintenance of high levels of employment and real income and to the development of the productive resources of all member countries as primary objectives of economic policy'. Carlos Lleras Restrepo of Colombia welcomed the wording, which gave 'the right of new nations whose resources are not sufficiently developed to move forward on the road . . . toward a more complex economy'.[17] Mexico inserted an amendment authorizing the new bank to consider reconstruction and development equally, and the Cuban delegation secured a resolution that called for international commodity agreements, for 'if the prices of staple commodities are not stabilized the purposes of monetary stabilization cannot be attained'.[18] In the event, nothing came of protection of infant industries or commodity agreements. The articles of the Fund contained a commitment to development, but implementation would fall to the International Bank for Reconstruction and Development, which was reduced to a shadow of

White's initial scheme. It was now a more conservative institution with limited lending powers as favoured by Wall Street bankers and the Federal Reserve. The bankers wanted it to be restricted to specific projects rather than wider development programmes. A compromise was reached that 'loans made or guaranteed by the Bank shall, except in special circumstances, be for the purpose of specific projects of reconstruction or development'. Although 'special circumstances' might permit general developmental loans, in practice the emphasis remained on the ability to repay.[19] In December 1947, Diego Luis Molinari – a leading supporter of Juan Perón in Argentina – expressed his disappointment that Bretton Woods was 'typified by the dollar sign, gold at Fort Knox, international cartelism, and a spider-web of Shylocks squeezing out the heart of hungry multitudes'.[20]

The major concern at Bretton Woods was to finalize the stabilization fund. A degree of flexibility to adjust rates for domestic reasons was ensured by the provision that the IMF would accept a change of up to 10 per cent, with larger changes in cases of 'fundamental disequilibrium'. The term was not defined. Gottfried Haberler saw that one possibility was to define the 'true equilibrium rate as one that maintains the balance in equilibrium without the need for mass unemployment at home' but that would be problematic if export industries suffered mass unemployment as a result of world depression. To prevent competitive depreciation to secure markets, he thought devaluation should only be allowed if there was an objective and unambiguous criterion of a balance of payments deficit – but he realized that there would still be discretion in defining how large and how long the deficit needed to be before it was sufficiently 'fundamental' to justify change in the exchange rate. The issue was never resolved. Although the IMF could object to an economic policy that was bound to lead to maladjustment and could refuse a change in the rate, the provision was vague and ignoring the IMF's view counted as a disagreement rather than a violation.[21]

The articles of the IMF were also vague on whether assistance would be given automatically, as Keynes wished, or with discretion and conditions as the United States preferred. Prior to the conference, Keynes complained that the Americans wanted the IMF to have 'wide discretionary and policing powers and should exercise something of the same measure of grandmotherly influence and control over the central banks of the member countries, that these central banks in turn are accustomed to exercise over the other banks within their own countries'. At Bretton Woods, he thought the Americans were

persuaded of the inacceptability of such a scheme of things, of the undesir-
ability of starting off by giving so much authority to an untried institution,
and of the importance of giving the member countries as much certainty as
possible about what they had to expect from the new institution and about
the amount of facilities which would be at their full disposal.

He hoped that the IMF's 'initiative and discretion' had been limited to
clear cases of infringement of rules, and that it would be 'entirely passive in all normal circumstances, the right of initiative being reserved
to the central banks of the member countries'. Keynes was mistaken,
for the United States had not abandoned discretion.[22]

The joint statement of April 1944 specified that 'a member shall be
entitled to buy another member's currency from the Fund' provided that
'the member *represents* that the currency demanded is presently needed'
for payments consistent with the purposes of the Fund. Hence a member
would have an absolute right to currency merely by stating or representing its wish. The United States wanted to amend this statement so that a
member '*may buy*' currency on condition that the country '*needs* the currency requested' to make payments consistent with the purposes of the
Fund. Keynes was suspicious, for it was not clear who decided whether
the request was consistent with the aims of the Fund, unlike in the joint
statement which allowed the members to decide for themselves. The crucial words 'entitled' and 'represents' were in the final text, and Article IV
stated that the IMF 'shall not object to a proposed change because of the
domestic social or political policies of the member proposing the change'.
It seemed that Keynes had won, and that the IMF could not challenge a
member's request or object to its policies. His confidence was misplaced.
In private, White assured the American delegates that the IMF would
retain control, for Article V limited access if money were used 'in a manner contrary to the purposes of the Fund'. He had to maintain a careful
balance. In October 1943, he had taken a relaxed view of conditionality
when he argued that 'no restrictions should be imposed unless misbehav-
iour is flagrant', and he informed the American delegates at Bretton
Woods that 'I don't think the Fund should butt into every country's business and say "We don't like this or that".' On the other hand, he realized
that congressional opposition to unconditional rights to deficit countries
would risk ratification. The result was constructive ambiguity, the press
release at the close of the conference offering comfort to both sides.
Resources could only be used if consistent with the purposes of the Fund,
but 'in international agreements between sovereign States no method of

enforcement can be as important as reliance on the good faith of the participants'. Walter Lippmann saw that 'none of the great powers is willing to sacrifice the freedom of its internal policy' so that there was 'almost unlimited domestic freedom and diversity at the expense of international conformity and stability'. The Fund was 'a consultative pact, an agreement to explain to all the others why each nation, exercising its freedom, does what it does'.[23]

The British were content. In November 1946, George Bolton – a London banker who joined the Bank of England as its leading expert on foreign exchange issues in 1933, and who served as Britain's executive director of the IMF from 1946 – reported: 'For the time being there is no reason to fear a policy of persistent and irresponsible interference in the domestic affairs of members.' The Treasury was similarly confident that the 'battle for "automaticity" may be largely regarded as won'. Camille Gutt, a Belgian industrialist and former finance minister who was the Fund's first managing director from 1946 to 1951, agreed. The Fund lacked capacity and was 'a sort of automatic machine selling foreign exchange to members'. It might warn members and, in exceptional cases, declare them ineligible but it should focus on its role as 'a most important policy-making body, consulted by and advising its members during the critical periods they may pass through'. Nevertheless, the Americans did not abandon their wish to impose conditions. White had to keep an eye on hostility from bankers and Congress, and in seeking ratification claimed that the Fund could refuse a drawing, and that drawings above a certain limit would be referred to the executive board. In May 1947, the executive board decided that what a member 'represents' could be challenged for good reasons, and in 1949 it vetoed loans unless the debtor gave guarantees.[24] The way was prepared for the IMF to impose conditionality in return for assistance, as we will see in Chapter 21.

The transitional period to restore convertibility after the war was extended from three to five years – a concession the Americans reversed in negotiations of a post-war loan for Britain. An amendment to the scheme fixed the dollar to gold and then pegged other currencies to the dollar, which meant that all other currencies could devalue against the dollar whereas the dollar could only devalue against gold. No one in 1944 contemplated a future in which the dollar would be weak and might need to devalue – and equally, they did not contemplate a situation in which other currencies would be strong, so no obligation was laid down for revaluation. These two omissions were to create difficulties by the 1960s when the German Deutschmark and Japanese yen were undervalued against the dollar.

After the demise of the Bretton Woods system of pegged rates in the

1970s, economists wondered why the commitment to stable rates was so strong at the conference. In discussions in the 1930s over the future of monetary policy, few economists had supported floating rates. In 1937, Haberler's report for the League, *Prosperity and Depression*, suggested that floating rates might insulate countries from the transmission of booms and depressions by removing the need for a 'flow of money across borders'. Nevertheless, he was ambivalent and accepted the Bretton Woods consensus in 1945 when he remarked that 'a system of "free exchanges" would lead to extremely undesirable results. It would incite capital flight and violent fluctuations.'[25] Frank Graham and Charles Whittlesey of Princeton were more forceful advocates of freedom to vary exchange rates and saw that fixed rates would entail controls over prices, wages and capital flows. In their view, capital flows were not destabilizing so long as domestic policies were sensible and the economy sound. They argued that misaligned fixed rates were more likely to encourage speculation and trade barriers than floating rates set by the market, and that traders could insure against fluctuations through the use of currency futures.[26] Such views were marginalized in the discourse leading to Bretton Woods.

The dominant position at the League was Ragnar Nurkse's report of 1944, which argued that 'interwar experience has clearly demonstrated ... that paper currency exchanges cannot be left free to fluctuate from day to day under the influence of market supply and demand', for speculation would 'play havoc' with trade and domestic economic stability. The risk of fluctuations would discourage trade, and constant movement of labour and resources between domestic and export markets would create frictional unemployment, speculation and disequilibrating capital flows. In his view, stable exchanges were essential for 'international economic intercourse' and domestic stability. Robbins agreed that 'the fluctuations of the exchanges have an actively disequilibrating tendency' and would lead to 'cumulative financial chaos'. Similarly, Hayek thought that flexible rates would lead to competitive devaluation and mercantilism, and that fixed rates were needed to reduce trade barriers and to encourage foreign investment.[27] Few at the time saw fixed rates as an artificial interference with market forces by necessitating regulation of prices and wages, and blocking capital flows. Even Geneva liberals such as Robbins and Hayek who opposed planning and favoured markets did not advocate floating rates. Milton Friedman, who became the leading critic of fixed rates in the 1950s and 1960s, thought that the case for floating rates was ignored at Bretton Woods both by 'traditionalists', who wanted to return to the gold standard, and by 'reformers' who distrusted the price mechanism. This 'curious coalition of the most unreconstructed believers in the price system, in all its other roles, and its most extreme opponents' meant that floating exchanges were not considered.[28] The consensus was that the ability to alter rates led to monetary chaos and economic malaise as in the 1930s.

The compromise of fixed rates with some flexibility to escape the rigidity of the gold standard was generally accepted. Jacob Viner expressed the consensus that 'exchange stability is desirable per se, provided it can be established without involving helpless submission to undesired inflation or deflation'.[29] In practice the system became less flexible with adjustments in exchange rates an infrequent emergency measure involving a large adjustment after sustained speculative pressure. A few advocates of greater flexibility pointed to the problem. In 1948, James Meade argued that adjusting exchange rates was preferable to the British Labour government's policy of restraints on imports to maintain the rate, provided that surplus countries did not keep their currencies undervalued or retain trade barriers, and that they maintained stable domestic demand to allow deficit countries to recover. In 1949, Frank Graham returned to his criticism of fixed rates as a 'vicious anachronism', and in 1953 Milton Friedman made a forceful case for floating.[30] But they were still outliers as the world struggled to return to convertibility and complete the work of the Bretton Woods conference.

At Bretton Woods, the trade-off in the trilemma was to combine stable exchange rates that had an element of flexibility with domestic monetary policy autonomy, with the aim of balancing the pursuit of international trade with national welfare. It would be an escape both from the rigidity of the gold standard, where the exchange rate had priority, and from the pursuit of economic nationalism that had marred the 1930s. This trade-off entailed capital controls. White and Keynes agreed that short-term capital flows undermined stable exchange rates and provoked protectionism. White had argued in his doctoral thesis on French international accounts before the First World War that 'the orthodox attitude towards unrestricted capital exports is open to criticism; the assumption that capital exports benefit both the lending country and the world at large is not unassailable ... some measure of intelligent control of the volume and direction of foreign investments is desirable.'[31] The draft of White's monetary scheme of March 1942 accepted that countries should block flows of capital that were devices for the rich to evade 'new taxes or burdens of social legislation', though in April he did accept flows of capital to areas where it could be profitably employed.[32]

In 1933, Keynes had argued that 'advisable domestic policies' could be achieved by stopping 'flight of capital':

There may be some financial calculation which shows it to be advantageous that my savings should be invested in whatever quarter of the habitable globe shows the greatest marginal efficiency of capital or the highest rate of interest. But experience is accumulating that remoteness between owner-ship and operation is an evil in the relations among men, likely or certain in the long run to set up strains which will bring to nought the financial calculation.[33]

At this point, Keynes advocated protectionism. During the war, he real-ized that capital controls could sustain a return to open trade – a point made by Bertil Ohlin, the Swedish economist and expert on trade theory, who saw that the movement of goods 'is a prerequisite of prosperity and economic growth' whereas the movement of capital was not.[34] Keynes came to the same view. In April 1942, he rejected the view that capital controls were unnecessary. On the contrary, capital flows should be con-trolled to ensure that they played 'their proper auxiliary role of facilitating trade' and allowing domestic policy autonomy:

Freedom of capital movements is an essential part of the old *laissez-faire* system and assumes that it is right and desirable to have an equalisation of interest rates in all parts of the world ... In my view the whole management of the domestic economy depends upon being free to have the appropriate rate of interest without reference to the rate prevailing elsewhere in the world. Capital control is the corollary to this.

The result, as Keynes pointed out in the House of Lords in May 1944, was that the proposals to be discussed at Bretton Woods 'not merely as a fea-ture of the transition, but as a permanent arrangement ... accords to every member government the explicit right to control all capital move-ments. What used to be a heresy is now endorsed as orthodox.'[35]

Capital transfers were covered by Article VI of the Bretton Woods agreement. Section 1 banned the use of the Fund's resources to cover 'a large or sustained outflow of capital' and authorized it to request mem-bers to use controls to prevent such a call on resources. Section 3 went on to say that 'members may exercise such controls as are necessary to regu-late international capital movements', though not to restrict payments for current transactions – a line that was not always easy to draw.[36] Restraints on speculative money removed the need to use interest rates to sustain stable exchange rates; instead, interest rates could be set to maintain domestic economic activity. In 1946, Arthur Bloomfield of the Federal Reserve Bank of New York remarked that 'It is now highly respectable doctrine, in academic and banking circles alike, that a substantial measure of *direct* control over private capital movements, especially of the so-called "hot money" varieties, will be desirable for most countries not only in the years immediately ahead but also in the long run as well.'[37]

Not all bankers were convinced. Wall Street had benefitted from capital flight from Europe in the 1930s, and worried that controls might be used to support the City of London against competition from New York. The bankers wondered why interest rates should be used to pursue domestic economic policies rather than allowing short-term capital to be attracted by higher rates to cover any external imbalance. In their view, speculative flows arose from mistrust of currencies caused by a government running budget deficits, or failing to control inflation, and could impose discipline on spend-thrift politicians. At most, controls should be confined to the transitional period before the global economic order returned to normality. Capital controls, they argued, were coercive and dictatorial.[38] Their position was backed by Viner, who argued that capital controls were undesirable and 'as an unreconstructed liberal, all of this, quite frankly, rather frightens me'. He worried that attempts to differentiate between current and capital account transactions would require censorship of communications and exchange restrictions, and that evasion would be easy unless all sorts of penalties and rules were imposed. In his view, international capital movements in the nineteenth century were 'one of the many great blessings which cupidity has procured for mankind', and more international capital flows were needed after the war. But even Viner thought that the task of providing capital should involve international agencies and a fund to stabilize employment.[39]

The future of the Bank for International Settlements was questioned at Bretton Woods. Although board meetings were suspended at the outbreak of war, the BIS continued to operate from Switzerland, where it claimed to follow a policy of neutrality under the presidency of the American banker Thomas McKittrick. The wartime activities of McKittrick and the BIS were, in fact, deeply contentious. McKittrick was friendly with Emil Puhl, the vice-president of the Reichsbank and a director of the BIS who visited Basel during the war. Puhl was closely involved with the BIS in recycling Nazi gold that was acquired from occupied countries and from the victims of the Holocaust to buy raw materials and to assist allies of the Third Reich. The Third Reich was granted the holdings of the occupied countries at the BIS, which gave the Axis powers 67.4 per cent of the bank's shares – and about 80 per cent of the BIS's income came from interest on German investments. It is true that McKittrick did supply information gleaned from Puhl to the American intelligence service. Equally, Per Jacobsson visited Puhl at the Reichsbank in 1942 and noted that 'the future of the BIS depends on Puhl's possibilities of holding the fort in Berlin'. Jacobsson returned to Berlin to discuss the Keynes and White plans in May 1943.[40]

The wartime record of the BIS was at the very least questionable. At Bretton Woods, the Norwegian delegation proposed that the BIS be abolished 'at the earliest possible moment'. The resolution was supported by Morgenthau and White in their campaign against international bankers, and White proposed that no country could join the IMF unless its central bank agreed to take steps to liquidate the BIS. Some delegates felt that the issue was not a matter for the conference, but the resolution passed as a compromise between immediate liquidation and continuation – as Keynes saw, 'the earliest possible moment' might be some time off. Indeed, Wall Street bankers and the Federal Reserve Bank of New York doubted the wisdom of abolishing an institution that could support monetary and financial orthodoxy. Similarly, European central bankers welcomed it as a forum for central bank co-operation in the difficult post-war period. Although Hugh Dalton, Chancellor of the Exchequer in the post-war Labour government, thought the BIS 'smells of the Schacht-Norman period' and should be liquidated, the British Treasury was aware of the technical complexities in winding it up and felt there were more pressing issues. In September 1945, Catto at the Bank of England pondered:

> What British interest is served by liquidation? We do not yet know when the Monetary Fund will be in effective operation; and in the meantime questions may easily arise in Europe as an entity which would call for urgent solution. A purged BIS might be very serviceable in that event. It must not be forgotten that the BIS staff have had 15 years' experience on matters in which the Monetary Fund has none ... Europe's problems are by no means all world-wide and it is far from clear that a meeting of European central banks is no longer required.

Pressure for liquidation subsided, and in November 1946 the new president of the BIS – the governor of the National Bank of Belgium – established a working arrangement with the IBRD. Jacobsson's annual report to the BIS explained the need for international financial organizations and claimed that the BIS was the only body to cover the whole of Europe. Attitudes at the US Treasury also shifted. The European central bankers resumed their regular monthly meetings in December 1946, and it became the agent for post-war schemes for European recovery. Astonishingly, in 1947 a report by the Federal Reserve Bank of New York found no evidence of the BIS's conniving with Germany during the war. In 1960, the Federal Reserve rejoined the organization and the BIS played a leading role – arguably more important than the IMF's – in maintaining the international monetary system (see chapters 16, 18 and 21).[41] Despite its morally reprehensible wartime record the BIS was too useful to abolish.

THE INTERNATIONAL BANK FOR RECONSTRUCTION AND DEVELOPMENT

Harry Dexter White's initial plan for the international monetary system drew upon the abortive Inter-America Bank, a multilateral financial institution in support of economic development and Roosevelt's Good Neighbor policy. In the draft of January 1942, he warned that rich countries could ignore their poorer neighbours only at the cost of imperilling their future prosperity. White suggested a Bank for Reconstruction whose task would be 'chiefly to supply the huge volume of capital . . . that will be needed for reconstruction, for relief, and for economic recovery'. In his mind, reconstruction had a wide definition of major changes in society, rather than its later, narrower, sense of post-war recovery. White was concerned with the Latin American reception of his plan, and his early drafts contained measures to assist development there by providing governments with long-term capital to undertake projects, guarantees for private loans, provision for debt restructuring, stabilization of the prices of international commodities, and protection for infant industries. He rejected free trade as 'unreal and unsound'.[42]

In the discussions leading to Bretton Woods, priority was given to resolving the technical details of the proposed Fund, and progress on the Bank was also constrained by domestic politics. White's rejection of free trade and acceptance of protection for infant industries were anathema to Cordell Hull and encroached on the talks on post-war trade. Neither was Morgenthau convinced that the Bank should be involved in debt restructuring, which he feared would lead to 'dollar diplomacy'.[43] American overseas investment after the First World War stood as a warning that ill-considered investment could lead to default, political unrest and intervention by the American military or 'money doctors'. The problem was not only feckless borrowers but also reckless American financiers who received large commissions for wasteful loans with onerous terms. One way of ensuring that overseas investment was beneficial and to avoid default and intervention was to rely on public investment through an international institution, rather than erratic and uncoordinated private investment. In 1943, a State Department task force recommended an inter-governmental investment agency with its own capital to influence the volume and direction of international investment, so stabilizing economic conditions and promoting full employment. A technical committee was set up under White to consider the issue, and this approach fed into his proposals for the post-war order.[44] In a draft of September 1943, White explained that 'large investment sums will be needed to help raise the very low productive level of countries in the Far East, South America, in the Balkans, and the Near East'. Morgenthau agreed and stressed that 'one great contribution that the United Nations can make to sustained peace and world-wide prosperity is to make certain that adequate capital is available on reasonable terms for productive use in capital-poor countries', by encouraging and supplementing private capital.[45] The question was whether this capital should be available for wider programmes or only for specific projects that would deliver a clear return.

The invitation of May 1944 to the Bretton Woods conference referred to formulating 'definite proposals' for the IMF but only 'possibly' for a Bank. White explained to the American delegates that the conference should concentrate on the IMF 'as the thing to get out of the way first; it was more complicated, involved more work, and there were more differences of opinion.'[46] The British opposed large direct loans by the Bank, from which it would not benefit and to which it could not afford to make a contribution. The Americans had to agree that the Bank 'should primarily be concerned with aiding and encouraging the provision of private funds for international investment by means of guarantees' rather than making its own loans.[47] The scale of the Bank's lending would be determined by the ratio of loans to assets. White suggested a generous ratio of 400 to 500 per cent, for 'There is nothing that will serve to drive these countries into some kind of ism – Communism or something else – faster than having inadequate capital to reconstruct their railways, their port facilities, their power development – things which have been destroyed during the war, or things which have deteriorated.' Imperial powers who feared possible interference and conservative financial interests in the United States were more cautious. Keynes was doubtful about ambitious lending plans. In June 1944, he saw the 'primary duty' of the Bank as ensuring that 'investment is not made haphazard, but that the more useful schemes are dealt with first; also to co-ordinate investment ... and in short to see that international lending is a more wisely conceived plan than it was after the last war, and is not the ill-conceived racket that it was on that occasion.'[48] Co-ordination did not require large investment by the Bank, and Ned Brown, a Wall Street banker and American delegate at Bretton Woods, settled for a 100 per cent ratio that suited the British, limited White's ambition and gave a larger role to private finance.[49]

In his opening remarks at Bretton Woods, Keynes remarked that the initial aim of the Bank was to make loans 'in proper cases and with due prudence' to countries suffering from devastation because of war. But he also argued that 'a second primary duty' would become more important over time:

> to develop the resources and productive capacity of the world, with special
> attention to the less developed countries, to raising the standard of life and
> the conditions of labour everywhere, to make the resources of the world
> more fully available to all mankind, and so to order its operations as to pro-
> mote and maintain equilibrium in the international balances of payments of
> all member countries. These two purposes ... are not exclusive or compre-
> hensive. In general, it will be the duty of the Bank, by wise and prudent
> lending, to promote a policy of expansion of the world's economy.[50]

The balance between loans to overcome devastation and encouraging development soon created difficulties, however. The Soviets were initially committed to the Bank, but their preference for loans for reconstructing devastated countries would alienate the Latin Americans, who had not suffered in the war.[51] The solution was to change the wording to say that 'the Bank is established both for the reconstruction and for the development of the member countries, and these two objectives are to be pursued on a footing of equality'.[52]

The question was whether 'development of the member countries' permitted loans that did not produce a direct commercial return. Both Alvin Hansen and Arthur Bloomfield of the Federal Reserve argued that the Bank should provide funds for development projects such as sanitation and the eradication of disease, which would not deliver a commercial return but would raise productivity and make private investment effective. In 1942, Hansen and Kindleberger had urged that '[i]ncreases in the productivity of the Balkan peasant, of the Hindu and Moslem in India, of the Chinese may seem of remote interest to many Americans; but they will contribute in the long run to both the economic and political security of the United States.'[53] The New Deal sentiment of the Good Neighbor remained powerful, but it was not clear that American public opinion and Wall Street would accept the use of American funds for non-productive purposes. The activities of the IBRD were constrained, for only 20 per cent of its initial capital of $10bn was called to provide direct loans, with the remainder available to guarantee private loans. The Bank was instructed to ensure that borrowers could afford to service the loans, with an emphasis on capital for 'productive purposes' which would 'except in special circumstances, be for the purpose of specific projects'. The precise definition of 'special circumstances' and 'productive purposes' was left open at

Bretton Woods so that, as Harrod commented, 'The biggest question at issue was never fully discussed, namely, whether the Bank should be a sound conservative institution on normal lines or depart from orthodox caution in the direction of greater venturesomeness.'[54] The issue would soon be contested in the Bank's initial activities in Latin America – with the outcome that it adopted a 'sound conservative' approach (see Chapter 12).

AFTER BRETTON WOODS

The World Monetary and Economic Conference had tried to deal with many interconnected issues at the same time. By contrast, the Bretton Woods conference dealt with one major issue and reached agreement on a post-war monetary system. Paul Volcker, a leading official in the US Treasury at the time of the collapse of the Bretton Woods regime in 1971, saw that success had been helped by the suspension of normal monetary relations during the war: 'It's hard to conceive of such a detailed agreement, completely reorganizing the world monetary system, being accomplished at any time except when there wasn't any system operating at all and when the enormous burdens of war effectively silenced more parochial concerns.'[55] The Bretton Woods conference was hailed as a huge success by Henry Morgenthau – a sign that the world would emerge from conflict into co-operation, from nationalism to internationalism. In 1953, Penrose was more cautious when he criticized Bretton Woods and the IMF for failing to address deep-seated maladjustments arising from the war, instead dealing with short-term fluctuations that affected the balance of payments. 'Starting on ambitious lines conceived by men of insight and imagination, it was whittled down in successive stages to pass the scrutiny of little men of conventional views and partisan political motives.'[56]

Both men were right. Morgenthau's optimistic assessment was correct to the extent that the creation of new multilateral institutions was a great achievement compared with the failure of 1933. Morgenthau's closing remarks were broadcast live on national radio, addressed to the American public as well as the delegates. 'What we have done here in Bretton Woods is to devise machinery by which men and women everywhere can freely exchange, on a fair and stable basis, the goods which they produce through their labor.' He launched a pre-emptive strike against critics who did not see that international co-operation was 'the wisest and most effective way to protect our national interests . . . Today the only enlightened form of national self-interest lies in international accord.'[57] Nevertheless, Penrose's criticism was also correct. The idea that convertibility and a new multilateral world order could be restored within five years failed to appreciate the depth of post-war economic disruption and the scale of reconstruction needed. Further, international co-operation designed to restore multilateral trade during a period of American economic dominance might be neither equitable nor feasible. European economies were devastated by the war, unable to export goods or to secure sufficient funds to purchase imports desperately needed for reconstruction. To less developed economies or primary producers, international co-operation meant dominance by the interests of advanced industrial countries, and the Bretton Woods agreement had not gone far enough in redressing the structural imbalances of the world economy.

Shortly before the conference, as we saw in Chapter 7, the ILO meeting in Philadelphia had agreed to a further conference on employment that would provide an opportunity to reinsert the demands of primary producers and less developed countries – and of progressive voices in the developed world – for a more radical approach to global economic government. The British government was wary, for a conference organized by the ILO would require representation by employers and workers as well as governments, and it preferred to link discussion of employment with settlement of Article VII of the Lend Lease agreement. The coalition government eventually agreed that the United States should be approached to call a conference. In Australia, meanwhile, Coombs drafted a 'Proposal for an international agreement concerning employment policies' that made some concessions to America on the need to reduce trade barriers, but insisted that multilateralism alone was no solution without high employment and consumption to absorb exports. In January 1945, the Australians pressed the State Department to call an international conference on employment policy, for 'freedom from want . . . can be achieved only by maintaining a high level of employment':

> without high employment in all countries, the world's production and consumption must remain continuously short of levels that are technically practicable, and . . . many wage-earners and others are deprived of the purchasing power to demand the goods and services which they need. The achievement of a high and stable level of employment in all countries is therefore one of the main objectives of international collaboration.[58]

The State Department was uneasy and insisted that high and stable employment must be linked with trade and a reduction of tariffs. The danger, as it saw it, was that action on employment without an international framework for trade and commodities might lead to policies that entailed uneconomic production and barriers to trade. In March 1945,

Edward Stettinius, the new Secretary of State, denied that full employment was a prerequisite for multilateral trade and reversed the causality:

> the employment problem is inextricably linked with problems of exchange and trade ... there can be no sound basis for the stability of productive employment at a high level in the various nations if there is no general international agreement to remove the excessive barriers and prevent the discriminatory practices which have restricted world trade in the past ...
>
> Only through the coordination of employment policy and trade policy will it be possible for each country to achieve the fullest and most economic use of its resources and the high levels of production and consumption which are essential if the general goal of freedom from want is to become a reality.

The American government agreed to a conference on condition that it dealt with multilateral trade as well as the 'international aspects of the problem of maintaining high and stable levels of productive employment [in] all countries'.[59] The Australians welcomed the decision as a 'great triumph'.[60] Of course, the Americans hoped that consideration of employment could be contained more safely in the context of trade talks than in separate discussions at the ILO. Even so, the definition of 'high and stable levels of productive employment' was likely to be contentious.

The post-war conference on trade and employment would pit Australian demands for full employment against the American preference for a multilateral order based on free trade and markets, with a more restrictive definition of full employment. It would provide an opening for Latin America and India to renew their demand for policies to assist economic development. Clearly, it was likely to be a complex affair of competing visions of the post-war economic order that could be less easily managed than the wartime conference at Bretton Woods.

The delegates at Bretton Woods who signed the Final Act of the conference were not committing their governments to implementation. It is one thing for delegates at an international conference to strike a deal; it is quite another to secure domestic political support as part of a two-level game. Above all, Congress in the United States and Parliament in the United Kingdom needed to ratify the agreement if the new institutions were to be established. There were vocal critics on both sides of the Atlantic. In the United States, there were fears of international engagement and the costs of economic reconstruction, and concerns by Wall Street bankers that they were losing control of the financial system. Morgenthau's closing remarks were an opening gambit in the domestic campaign for ratification. Above all, acceptance of the Bretton Woods agreement by the British government involved deeply contentious issues. The issue for the post-war Labour government was whether the benefits of multilateral trade, on which the British economy was so dependent, could be secured without surrendering trade restrictions and abandoning imperial preference at a time of severe economic difficulty, and whether it was possible without a commitment to full employment at home and in the global economy. The conference on trade and employment would involve discussion of unfinished Anglo-American business on Lend Lease and the final determination of the 'consideration', as well as negotiations for a post-war loan to assist Britain in the transition to peace that would allow Washington to withdraw some concessions made at Bretton Woods. The agreement in 1944 was far from a final settlement; implementation was to be a long, drawn-out affair of adaptation in changing circumstances in a post-war economic order that faced greater problems than appreciated in 1944, and in the shifting geopolitical context of the Cold War.

9

'A financial Dunkirk'

The United States, Britain and Germany

'I cannot see how the rest of Europe can expect effective economic reconstruction if Germany is excluded from it and remains a festering mass in their midst; and an economically reconstructed Germany will necessarily resume leadership. This conclusion is inescapable, unless it is our intention to hand the job over to Russia . . . I am assuming . . . that our post-war policy towards Germany will favour her economic reconstruction and will concentrate all our punitive and preventive measures in the political and military settlement.'

Keynes, 'Proposals to counter the German "new order"',
1 December 1940[1]

'Some of us, in the tasks of war and more lately in those of peace, have learnt by experience that our two countries [Britain and the United States] can work together. Yet it would be only too easy for us to walk apart. I beg those who look askance at these plans to ponder deeply and responsibly where it is they think they want to go.'

Keynes, House of Lords, 18 December 1945[2]

At the end of the war, the American administration had to decide how to respond to the plight of the British and European economies and the defeat of the Third Reich. During the war, Roosevelt's aim was the construction of a liberal world order. He had saved capitalism in the United States by the New Deal and had looked for economic stability in Latin America through the Good Neighbor policy; now, he wished to reform the world by spreading American values of free enterprise, personal initiative and responsibility. Such a desirable outcome, he believed, would not be possible so long as Europeans clung to their empires. Britain should abandon imperial preference, prepare its colonies for independence, and return to its pre-1914 commitment to multilateralism and open markets.

Three women help to clear rubble at the Krupps works in Essen, 1946.

Germany had embarked on an imperial venture within Europe, and action was needed to ensure that 'Prussianism' would not lead to war again – a policy that entailed disarmament, breaking up the German Reich, and even root-and-branch de-industrialization.[3]

The American response to both its major European ally and its foe raised serious problems. Germany was the major economy in continental Europe, and Keynes warned of the dangers of repeating the mistake – as he saw it – of Versailles. A realization that punitive treatment of Germany would prevent economic recovery in Europe, with disastrous consequences, meant that British policy diverged from the American approach of destroying Germany's heavy industry. Keynes was also concerned about American attitudes to Britain. Its economy was in a parlous situation at the end of the war, and the government wanted a large grant or gift from the United States. In Washington, the seriousness of the situation in Britain was not fully understood, and there was suspicion that Britain's failure to repay its debts after the First World War would be repeated, exploiting American generosity to remain a colonial power and financial centre, and embarking on socialist policies with the election of the Labour government in July 1945.

The United States administration could use Britain's desperate need for assistance as a lever to force the abandonment of imperial preference and adoption of an open, multilateral economy. The British, in turn, could delay ratifying the Bretton Woods agreement as a bargaining device to secure financial support. Formal acceptance of the Bretton Woods agreement therefore became part of a complex set of negotiations over the final settlement of Lend Lease, the negotiation of a new loan and resumption of talks on trade. Keynes faced his last battle with the Americans as he tried to negotiate financial aid on terms that reflected the fact that Britain 'is immensely exhausted and has made sacrifices so far as encumbering the future goes, far beyond those of the other United Nations'.[4] Until those negotiations were completed, the future of the Bretton Woods agreement hung in the balance. The terms reached in New Hampshire had to be ratified in the United States Congress and British Parliament, which was by no means a foregone conclusion.

RATIFYING BRETTON WOODS: THE UNITED STATES

In the United States, the agreement was to be ratified by legislation which required a simple majority, rather than by a treaty which required a super-majority of two-thirds. In 1945–46, the Democrats had a sizeable majority

of 243 to 190 in the House and of 57 to 38 in the Senate, but opposition
to Bretton Woods and to a loan to Britain meant that success was not certain. The plan was represented by its critics as 'a nefarious plot to rob the
United States of its gold reserves; as an attempt to make Uncle Sam the
milch cow for the rest of the world; as a subtle scheme to restore world
financial supremacy to the United Kingdom'.[5] Senator Robert Taft – a
long-standing opponent of the New Deal and advocate of libertarianism –
saw a violation of sovereignty and argued that 'no international body
should have any jurisdiction over the domestic policies of the United
States', especially one controlled by debtors who were exploiting American
generosity.[6] To counter such complaints, the Bretton Woods agreement –
unlike in Britain – had to be defended as a way of instilling the discipline
of the gold standard that would prevent debtors from taking the easy
option of inflation or devaluation.[7]

The intellectual argument against Bretton Woods drew on the Austrian
School of economics and especially Ludwig von Mises, whose ideas were
popularized by Henry Hazlitt, a founder of the free-market Foundation
for Economic Education in 1946 and of the Mont Pèlerin Society in 1947,
and by Benjamin Anderson, an economist who worked at the Chase
National Bank before joining the University of California. Anderson
claimed that White and Keynes would create 'a super-national Brains
Trust which is to think for the world and plan for the world, and to tell
the government of the world what to do'. In Anderson's opinion, their
plans reflected Keynes's thinking and British interest in lax fiscal and
monetary policy. He urged Congress to reject Bretton Woods on the general principle that '[i]n the direct handling of economic life, governments
are usually clumsy and ineffective. In economic life their main business
should be that of traffic cop, not that of driver, and above all not that of
back seat driver.' He advocated a return to gold that was not 'capricious',
for '[a]ll it requires of men and governments and central banks is that
they . . . create debts only when they can see how these debts can be paid.'
He saw no need to control international capital movements, for speculative flows of money arose from inappropriate government policies, which
would be prevented if budgets were balanced. He was equally hostile to
the IBRD and preferred an American institution working through equity
finance. His wish was for 'free markets, sound money, orthodox money
market policy, and free banking machinery'.[8]

Wall Street shared these concerns. In 1943, Adolf Berle complained
that 'fundamentally, the New York banks really wanted to go back to the
days when Ben Strong and Montagu Norman settled things secretly in the
Federal Reserve Bank of New York'.[9] He had a point. Winthrop Aldrich,

president and chairman of Chase National Bank, believed that the Bretton Woods scheme was 'unrealistic and unnecessarily complex', dealing with symptoms rather than the causes of exchange instability. He recommended a grant to Britain to stabilize the key currencies of the dollar and sterling, followed by stabilization of other currencies – essentially, the approach of John Williams at the Federal Reserve.[10] To Williams, the schemes of White and Keynes were a mirage of 'high sounding words and sentiments', and the 'adoption of the Monetary Fund ... would be premature and would hurt more than it would help the cause of international cooperation'. In his view, the relationship between the dollar, sterling and European currencies could only be settled after restoring 'proper economic health in the leading countries' and resolving the conflict between international and domestic monetary stability. Williams advocated a two-speed approach that started from stable exchange rates between sterling and the dollar, followed by a second stage when other currencies were linked to either sterling or the dollar. The worldwide approach of the IMF, he concluded, was bound to fail, for countries were at different stages of development, with distinctive domestic political ambitions. A gradualist and flexible key currency plan was more likely to succeed. Williams's approach secured the unanimous backing of the Federal Reserve Bank of New York and strong support from the American Bankers' Association (ABA) as an alternative to Morgenthau's transfer of power to the Treasury and international institutions.[11]

The president of the ABA, W. Randolph Burgess, informed Morgenthau that Wall Street bankers 'are distrustful of any program for giving away American gold; they are distrustful of all spending programs, especially when sponsored by Lord Keynes' and his 'philosophy of deficit spending over again – the use of credit as a cure-all'. The ABA accepted that 'we need freedom from fear of war and freedom from hampering trade barriers, subsidies, and other economic weapons', but the solution was not New Deal policies. Rather, '[o]ne of the greatest contributions the United States can render for the world is to make available to other countries the virility and productiveness of our system of private enterprise.' Despite these concerns, Morgenthau believed that he had an assurance from the ABA that it would support the Bretton Woods agreement. He was wrong: on 5 February 1945, the ABA urged Congress to reject it.[12]

The key currency plan had no real chance of success. White realized that it rested on an Anglo-American deal that would not be accepted in Europe – and he wanted to weaken the sterling bloc and give a greater role to China and the Soviet Union.[13] Louis Rasminsky of the Bank of Canada pointed out, reasonably enough, that 'the "key currency" approach is the

monetary counterpart of the Great Power doctrine of international organization'.[14] At the Federal Reserve, Emanuel Goldenweiser castigated the
key currency scheme as 'contrary to democratic ideals', unlike the IMF
which 'is not to be an exclusive club where people have to pass an examination in the Bank of England and the Federal Reserve before they can get
in'. The wider membership of the IMF 'will add a lift to the situation as no
agreement between two great countries could'.[15] Even Walter Lippmann –
a supporter of liberalism against collectivism and socialism – saw that the
alternative to Bretton Woods would be greater government control over
trade through bilateral and regional agreements.[16]

The ratification debate coincided with the peak of support for internationalism. Morgenthau could turn the opposition against itself, for
attacks on Bretton Woods by bankers, big business and conservative
Republicans helped mobilize idealistic supporters of world peace. White
warned the Senate Committee on banking and currency that it was vital
to avoid the mistakes of 1921, when America failed to support the new
League of Nations. Senator Tobey agreed:

> We have a world that is prostrate. If we are going to live in it ourselves we
> have got to make some effort to get it back on its feet. There has to be an
> element of faith, an element of confidence somewhere. That is what we are
> trying to do here. We can afford to take some chances ... The risks are
> small compared to the benefits that will come from this. The world is in
> extremis. We have got to do something.[17]

In 1945, the Treasury, from Morgenthau and White down, toured the
country and hired publicists to counter Taft's opposition to Bretton Woods.

The technical criticisms of bankers had little impact on members of the
public and Mikesell recalled that the case rested on avoiding a repeat of
the chaos after the First World War with an 'orderly regime ... Virtually
every speech touted stable monetary conditions and exchange rates as
defenses against future dictators and World War III. International monetary
cooperation would somehow generate world peace.' The Congress of Industrial Organizations (CIO)'s pamphlet *Bretton Woods Is No Mystery* pointed
out that B and W stood for Bread and Wages; it represented Taft as the puppet of bankers who had led the world to ruin. In the opinion of the CIO, the
agreement was formulated by experts who 'studied the problem not for personal gain but for the good of their own nations and for the good of the
world'. Tobey and Robert Wagner, the Democratic chair of the Senate Banking and Currency Committee, claimed – with little justification – that 'neither
of us heard any politics at all at Bretton Woods'. Morgenthau took the same
technocratic line that the new institutions would be run by financial experts

and would be 'wholly independent of the political connection'. The case was credible thanks to overwhelming support from economists: a poll of members of the American Economic Association found that 90 per cent supported the Bretton Woods agreement. It was decisively adopted by Congress. On 7 June 1945, the House voted 348 to 18 in favour of the agreement, and on 19 July the Senate followed with a vote of 61 to 16. President Truman signed the bill into law on 31 July 1945.[18]

It now remained for Britain to ratify the Bretton Woods agreement. Failure to secure support from the country that had been the partner of the United States in its genesis would be fatal – not least because sterling was still the world's largest reserve currency, and there was a possibility that Britain could turn inwards and create 'two worlds': a sterling and a dollar area.

THE 'CONSIDERATION' AND FINANCIAL ASSISTANCE

At the end of the war, in straitened circumstances, Britain's ability to accept multilateral trade, end imperial preference and allow convertibility of sterling would depend on financial assistance from the United States. Wilfrid Eady, a senior official at the British Treasury, remarked that 'in an ideal world complete convertibility and complete multilateralism probably suited our geographical position and our far-flung interests better than any other system. But this was a real world and multilateralism was only possible for us if it was made possible for us.'[19] The question was whether the Americans would offer assistance, and on what terms. Much would depend on the Americans agreeing that assistance was in their interest. Robert Brand, an astute banker who represented Britain in Washington, explained in 1944 the need

> to bring somehow home to the public and Congress that American interests also are vitally concerned. We want to make them feel that it is highly important to them, if the world is to be the sort of world they want, that we should not be *forced* to abandon cooperation with them for a Brave New World; to go by necessity in a completely opposite direction and to develop a wicked old world in a manner which will be extremely distasteful and injurious to them. We want the fact to sink in that the cards are not all in their hands, but that if we are driven to use our bargaining power, we can no doubt get through but by means that will cut across a policy for the world acceptable to the United States.[20]

The task would not be easy, for the British case could easily be interpreted as special pleading.

In 1944, Keynes was clear that assistance should not be a loan on commercial terms, for

> [t]o commercialise a war debt between Allies which leaves no productive asset behind, as though it were yielding an annual income, would be unreasonable and wrong. Interest, where there is not and in the nature of things could not have been any current income yielded by the loan has been stigmatised in most ages of history ... as an intolerable and immoral imposition.

The risk was to incur 'liabilities greater than we can meet, and then hope by deft management to keep so many of the chickens in the air, that they never come home to roost'.[21] Keynes saw that Britain's interest, as a trading nation, in removing barriers to international trade had to be balanced with an ability to adopt safeguards at the end of the war. Britain therefore needed an intermediate position somewhere between America's complete laissez-faire and the Soviet Union's complete state trading, which would treat 'the system of Imperial Preference as a domestic matter which cannot be regarded as involving a discriminatory treatment of foreigners. To treat the preference system as having some extra measure of original sin is ... to treat the extremes as legitimate and anything in between as illegitimate.'[22]

In May 1945, Keynes set out three options for the War Cabinet. The first option was Austerity or Starvation Corner advocated by the 'Schachtians' – both supporters of imperial preference and left-wing socialists who wanted to plan the economy. Keynes rejected this approach as incompatible with Britain's need for multilateral trade and with American policies. The second option was Temptation: a large commercial loan on easy terms, conditional on full convertibility and an end of preferences. Keynes rejected this approach as debt bondage. He favoured the third option: 'the sweet breath of Justice between partners, in what had been a great and magnanimous enterprise.' Brand doubted that Justice would play well with the American public or Congress, for it assumed that the United States should have joined the war earlier, and that they had not played a full role since they entered – indeed, *their* perception was that American and Dominion forces had played a greater part than Britain in the fighting in North Africa, Italy, Burma and Normandy. As he realized, the Americans might consider that Lend Lease was already an act of Justice, especially given that Britain paid other countries in full. He thought it unwise to seek 'a free grant of money as a sort of restitution. If they were to give it, the Americans would certainly regard it as an act not of Justice, but of generosity.' Keynes ignored his advice and proposed that America should write off $3bn spent by Britain prior to Lend Lease as a moral obligation and provide a credit of $5bn for ten years at a token rate of interest and easy terms of repayment. In return, Britain would make sterling convertible within a year of the return to peace. Meanwhile, a quarter of the sterling balances should be cancelled and half should be funded, so that the sterling area would contribute about $4bn to Britain. At Bretton Woods, he promised to deal 'honourably' with the sterling balances. Now he was more pragmatic. Britain should be retrospectively compensated for its war efforts both by the Americans and by members of the sterling area, so that it could join the post-war liberal world economy.[23]

Keynes continued to develop his thoughts, and on 13 August circulated a paper to ministers as the basis for an appeal to Washington. There were two options. The first solution would be to rely on the sterling area, dollar pool and bilateral trade. Much better would be the second option – 'a liquidation of the financial consequences of the War amongst all those chiefly concerned who have won a common victory by a common effort. Not a complete liquidation – that would be asking too much.' He admitted that Britain would 'accept for themselves and their posterity, as the price of deliverance, a burden of external indebtedness to their Allies which no one else will be expected to carry, not even the defeated enemy.' The wartime sterling area had been crucial to success, '[b]ut it has resulted in the economic and financial affairs of half the world becoming inextricably intertwined with our own. Thus, unless means can be found to bring this burden within the limits of what is practicable, immeasurable and lasting confusion to the world's international economy cannot be avoided.' He now hoped for relief by writing off about $4bn of the sterling balances and an outright grant-in-aid from the United States of $5bn as a means of 'establishing after the war the type of commercial and financial relations between nations which they wish to see established'. Britain had 'held the fort alone'. 'It cannot ... appear to those who have borne the burden of many days that it is a just and seemly conclusion of this sacrifice to be left ... with a burden of future tribute to the rest of the world beyond tolerable bearing.'[24]

An outright gift would not be accepted in Washington, as Brand realized. Will Clayton admitted that Britain's financial problems would be the greatest barrier to multilateral trade, but when he visited London in August he rejected the idea of a gift and proposed a credit of $3bn at a low interest rate and some flexibility in the case of economic difficulties. Financial assistance was used as a lever to prevent bilateralism and to encourage liberal trade and convertibility. The conditions for assistance were to close the dollar pool, fund or write down the sterling balances, end or reduce preferences, and make sterling convertible. Clayton made it clear that the political situation in Washington meant it was 'essential that we discuss both finance and trade simultaneously' and that it was 'necessary for us to come to a broad understanding as to postwar trading methods and policy before we can ask the Congress for any large scale financial aid to British [*sic*]'. Clayton hoped that Britain and the United States would reach an agreement on trade policy before talks started between a nucleus of fifteen leading economies. Keynes countered by urging the continuation of Lend Lease, urgent talks in Washington on Britain's financial position, and a delay to discussions on trade given the time those talks would take and Britain's immediate need for assistance. The alternative, he warned Clayton, was a turn to bilateralism. In Clayton's view, Keynes was 'putting up a very determined front' to compensate for 'a basically very weak financial position'. The lines were drawn for difficult negotiations.[25] The outcome would have wide ramifications, for at the end of the war Britain was still the world's second-biggest economy, with the largest reserve currency and a central role in international trade. The prospect of failure was welcomed by Leo Amery, who hoped that 'sheer necessity will force Attlee and Co onto a policy of Empire trade'.[26] If this happened and Britain did not adopt multilateralism, American policy would have little chance of success. Britain remained finely balanced between those who advocated a 'two-worlds' policy – a sterling area and imperial preference alongside the dollar area – and 'one world' of a multilateral global economy.

Britain's post-war financial position was dire, and it became even worse. Lend Lease would expire at the end of the war with a final settlement of obligations that Keynes feared would be a 'financial Dunkirk'. Five years earlier, a fleet of small boats crossed the English Channel to evacuate the defeated army; now, escape required increasing exports, economizing on overseas expenditure and securing a loan or gift from the United States. The result might be 'a sudden and humiliating withdrawal from our onerous responsibilities with great loss of prestige and an acceptance . . . of the position of a second-class power', with austerity and postponement of the government's plans for post-war reconstruction. The British government hoped there would be a gradual process of running down Lend Lease – but things moved faster than expected. Japan surrendered on 15 August 1945 and on the 17th Truman terminated Lend Lease – a decision he later regretted as the greatest mistake of his presidency. In reality, he had little room for manoeuvre. Concerns about Britain's debt had led to resistance to the renewal of Lend Lease in February 1945, and Truman could not ignore this pressure when he took office after Roosevelt's death on 12 April. Bernard Baruch, an influential adviser to both Roosevelt and Truman, urged the new president not to 'rob Britons of their native self-reliance' by offering hand-outs. On 23 August 1945, senior Whitehall ministers, with Keynes in attendance, met to consider his paper of 13 August in the shock of the sudden end of Lend Lease. They had to decide the terms on which he should seek financial assistance in Washington.[27]

Keynes calculated that $5bn was needed – and he 'thought that he should not be authorised to agree to anything except an out and out grant'. In return, Britain should ask the sterling area to cancel part of the blocked balances; accept Bretton Woods; and agree to a joint invitation to an international trade conference in 1946. On this basis, Keynes secured authority to accept an outright grant, with no discretion to accept anything else without ministerial approval. He also insisted that negotiations with Washington should start on financial aid apart from trade to avoid being forced to accept American views on commercial policy out of financial necessity. Preferences should not be part of the financial settlement but part of a package that would include a reduction in American tariffs. Keynes arrived in Washington in September 1945 to embark on his final negotiations with the Americans – tired, ill, and with a fatally flawed negotiating position.[28]

Keynes ignored the political reality in America. Lord Halifax, the British ambassador, who participated in the talks, pointed out that 'it is quite plain that the Americans would like to help us, but are quite genuinely doubtful about what they can get through Congress.'[29] Nevertheless, Frederic Harmer, a Treasury official in the British delegation, thought Keynes 'more than half-persuaded that we shall find a pretty good atmosphere in Washington: I doubt it.' He pointed out that 'the pro-British line always needs defending in this country; the anti-British one never ... They must always be shown they haven't been outsmarted.'[30] Paul Bareau, the press officer for the British delegation in the United States, realized that 'the United States did not in any way regard assistance to us as a reward for good behaviour in the past but as the means to enable us again to dispense with the protective devices of inconvertibility of sterling, licensing of imports and bilateral payments agreements.' Financial aid could not be separated from trade policy. Bareau reported that an opinion poll in September 1945 found that 60 per cent of Americans opposed and only 27 per cent were in favour of a loan to Britain, with little difference between Republicans and Democrats.[31] The Labour Party's success in winning the general election did not improve sentiment in Washington. The Foreign Office worried that the American administration might assume that Labour's domestic programme of welfare reform, full employment and planning could only be achieved 'by shielding the domestic economy behind currency and commercial controls'. The danger was that

at a time when America was ready and eager to enter into broad international commitments, we were intent on pursuing, what in American eyes,
was a contrary policy ... 'Discrimination', 'Exclusiveness', 'Monopoly',
'Imperialist Economy' – all these unsavoury words will be freely used
against us, and will gain spontaneous, and often unthinking response from
the US public.[32]

Keynes's unrealistic approach soon collided with reality in Washington.
At the end of September, Lionel Robbins noted – as had always been
obvious – that 'a pure grant-in-aid is right out of the picture'. The problem now, as he saw, was that

we shall have great difficulty in dehypnotising London; and I think that
Maynard will have to be told that, having himself made the magic passes
that now hold the King's Treasurers entranced in rapturous contemplation
of ideal 'justice', it will be up to him ... to reverse the process and bring
them back to considering soberly nice questions of more or less day-by-day
convenience and expediency.[33]

Keynes started to 'dehypnotise' the new Chancellor, Hugh Dalton, informing him that there was 'no sign that a naked grant-in-aid for the full
amount will prove practicable'.[34] As Bareau put it, Keynes 'consigned his
earlier concepts of Justice to a limbo amid the ghosts and skeletons of
which only fools and dullards would roam and search'.[35] Assuming that a
grant-in-aid was not possible, Keynes sought authority to negotiate an
interest-free loan of $5bn, repayable over fifty years, with the first pay-
ment delayed for five to ten years and a waiver in case of economic
difficulties, in return for accepting Bretton Woods and reducing sterling
balances. If the Americans refused, he laid out other possibilities ranging
from a grant of $2bn with a further $3bn or $4bn credit that might or
might not pay interest, to a loan at 2 per cent. He warned Dalton that the
alternative would be to reduce domestic consumption in order to save on
imports and boost exports:

It would be a brave man who says we can face this. It would mean that we
should decline for the time being to the position of a second rate power
abroad and we should not only have to postpone for at least five years any
improvement in the standard of living at home but would have to ask the
public to accept greater sacrifices than at any time during the war.[36]

Ministers in London were not easily dehypnotized, and as Dalton
later remarked, 'those who represent us out there and we here at
home have drifted into a condition of mutual incomprehension.'[37] After

a ministerial meeting in London, Dalton instructed Keynes that a loan at 2 per cent interest was not acceptable, and that he should accept a grant of $2bn with a further credit of $3bn to $4bn at 1 per cent, or, failing that, an interest-free loan of $5bn over fifty years, with a right to restrict imports and a waiver of payment in difficulties. On 9 October, Keynes presented the first option to Clayton, hoping that after it was rejected, he would be able to secure the second option. He was wrong. Clayton countered with a proposal for a loan of $5bn at 2 per cent interest, repayable in fifty instalments starting in five years' time, with a waiver in case of difficulty. Keynes thought that the offer was the basis for a settlement, but Dalton rejected Clayton's terms as inequitable and lacking the 'sweet breath of justice' – Keynes's phrase coming back to haunt him.[38]

Rather than pressing London to accept reality and make a clear case for acceptance, Keynes went into detail over the terms of the waiver and continued to think that the Americans were engaged in 'play acting and poker playing', with White working in the background to secure an interest-free loan. It was a misjudgement. Keynes entered into talks on the basis laid down by Dalton, without any success. On 18 October, he requested permission to accept a loan of $5bn at 2 per cent over fifty years. Despite goodwill from the American negotiators, he assured Dalton that the Truman administration lacked leadership and instead followed public and congressional opinion, so that 'we cannot demand what they tell us does not lie within their power to give'. But he still did not give up on the hope of a grant of $2bn with a further interest-paying credit. He failed to give a clear steer to London and had miscalculated – the offer of $5bn was withdrawn. Far from being an ally, White argued that the British could reduce their debt to the sterling area and draw down their reserves. Instead, the Americans offered $3.5bn at 2 per cent. Keynes was trapped by his unrealistic advocacy of a grant and tried to persuade Dalton that a 'grand gesture of unforgetting regard' exceeded Truman's ability to convince Congress. Matters had changed, he remarked, since the days of Roosevelt's 'gay, generous and brilliant spirit'.[39]

The discussion of the loan also raised concerns about the trade talks, for the Labour government realized that the Americans were using the financial talks to impose their commercial policy and even to interfere in domestic politics. Dalton insisted that preferences were only to be considered as part of a tariff settlement involving concessions on American duties. He predicted a 'very violent reaction here if preference issue is formally linked, not with commercial talks, but with financial deal.

Indeed, a financial settlement otherwise acceptable might be wrecked on this issue.' Dalton worried about the consequences in Parliament 'if anyone can represent that a financial pistol has been held to our head on subject of Imperial Preference'.[40] The talks dragged on in confusion and recrimination, with Keynes in failing health and veering between unrealistic optimism and anger. A draft agreement was rejected by Cabinet in November. Dalton found it 'unacceptable, both in form and spirit' with 'the risk of American audit of our affairs' to secure any waiver of interest payments. The loss of the five-year transition to convertibility obtained at Bretton Woods was particularly galling. The view in Washington was that restoration of trade and financial support removed the need for a longer transitional period – a claim that alarmed British officials who feared a loss of options in dealing with the parlous balance of payments. The American demands also risked incensing opponents of the Bretton Woods agreement. Dalton complained that 'legally-minded low grade American officials' failed to understand the issues. Eady was disappointed that 'legions of lawyers' had produced a 'money lenders contract' that marked 'a sorry conclusion to your gallant voyage and would mean that on both sides of the Atlantic the agreement would be regarded with shame-faced dislike.' Attlee's direct approach to Truman did not resolve the difficulty, for he lacked Churchill's charisma and Truman ran a more coherent administration than Roosevelt.[41] British feelings of sacrifice and superiority collided with American feelings of exploitation by a delusional declining power.

Attlee, Dalton and Cripps were adamant that the Bretton Woods agreement was not acceptable on the terms offered for the loan. The Americans countered that Congress would not agree to the loan without acceptance of Bretton Woods. Attlee was in a difficult position, for he saw that

> if we tried to get Bretton Woods through Parliament without the transitional period we should probably fail . . . In every speech advocating Bretton Woods, the five years transitional period has been put forward to justify our acceptance, and by no one more strongly than by Keynes. The abrogation of a solemn under-taking signed at Bretton Woods by forty-four nations would place our Government in an indefensible position.

He had no option. The Anglo-American financial agreement was signed on 6 December 1945 with an outcome that was clear to one British official: humiliation.[42]

The agreement gave Britain a credit line of $3.75bn to buy goods in the United States, meet transitional post-war balance of payments deficits, and assist in the adoption of multilateral trade. A further $650m would cover Lend Lease. Any credit drawn by 1951 would be repaid in fifty annual instalments at 2 per cent interest, with a waiver of interest if reserves fell or the deficit rose. The transitional concessions in the Bretton Woods agreement were surrendered and current sterling earnings would be convertible within a year of the effective date of the agreement (15 July 1946), unless there were exceptional circumstances. Britain agreed to negotiate a settlement with holders of sterling balances on what should be released and convertible, and what should be adjusted 'as a contribution to the settlement of war and post-war indebtedness and in recognition of the benefits which the countries might be expected to gain from such a settlement'. The American loan was not to be 'junior' to the sterling balances. Indeed, there was a feeling that the countries that had accumulated sterling should, like the United States, have provided goods on Lend Lease terms (see Chapter 11).[43]

Robert Brand remarked that 'the British public, and even the British government, was very ill-prepared to face the cold bath of reality'. Their belief that 'they had played for their size and wealth, a longer and greater part in the war than any other country' looked different in the United States. The Americans felt they had also 'done great deeds' and that other countries – not least the Soviet Union – had suffered even more:

> They are willing to put us first, and give us terms that they do not at present intend to give anyone else. But they are not ready to make a single exception for our case as to give us our money free, on terms hopelessly different from that which they intend to demand from others.

The outcome was unsatisfactory, but Brand was right when he remarked that 'I regard the alternative of no agreement and no loan as calamitous, disastrous, or any other adjective you can think of, provided it is stronger. It must have led to unforgiveable results.'[44] As Dalton realized, failure to reach an agreement would mean 'less than an Irish peasant's standard of living' with 'sure defeat at the next election'. In the end, there was no alternative other than to accept the American terms. His summary of the story captured his frustration:

> We retreated, slowly and with a bad grace and with increasing irritation, from a free gift to an interest-free loan, and from this again to a loan bearing interest; from a larger to a smaller total of aid; and from the prospect of loose strings, some of which would be only general declarations of intention, to the most unwilling acceptance of strings so tight that they might strangle our trade and, indeed, our whole economic life.[45]

BRITISH RATIFICATION: BRETTON WOODS, THE LOAN AND TRADE

Little progress had been made on the issue of trade during the war. It now returned to the agenda. Cordell Hull's successors at the State Department wished to create a new body to establish rules for trade just as the Treasury had for international monetary relations, and they looked to establish a new International Trade Organization. The success of Australia at the Philadelphia meeting of the ILO meant trade would be linked with the discussion of employment.

In September 1945, the British government accepted Keynes's advice that talks on financial aid should proceed alongside, rather than form part of, discussions of the principles of commercial policy to separate the two issues and to prevent America imposing its views in return for assistance. An official from the Board of Trade was despatched to Washington to discuss commercial policy. Cripps accepted that

> we should agree that, <u>provided that our position is safeguarded in certain important respects</u>, a multilateral commercial convention, if one can be obtained, may be very much in our interest. The vital objective of a 50 per cent expansion of our exports is not likely to be reached in a world in which the markets of other countries are hedged about by arbitrary and unregulated barriers to trade.

The safeguards were that multilateralism should allow imperial preference and import controls in the interest of economic recovery. All discussions in Washington were to be non-committal, with reference back to London. The British team in Washington was in a weak position and the talks were dominated by the American proposal for an International Trade Organization.[46]

The American 'Proposals for consideration by an international conference of trade and employment' were published on 6 December 1945 – the same day as the Anglo-American financial agreement. They started with a grand statement that collective measures to safeguard peace must be based 'on economic co-operation among nations with the object of preventing and removing economic and social maladjustments, of achieving fairness and equity in economic relations between states, and of raising the level of economic well-being among all peoples'. The basis of such a policy was 'the attainment of approximately full employment by the major industrial and trading nations' which was essential to the expansion of international trade on which the full prosperity of these and other nations depends; to the full realization of the objectives of all liberal international agreements in such fields as commercial policy, commodity problems, restrictive business practices, monetary stabilization, and investment; and, therefore, to the preservation of world peace and security.

The pursuit of full employment meant avoiding national policies that would create unemployment elsewhere or were incompatible with expanding international trade. The American Proposals gave priority to Clayton's view that open trade came first, and that lower trade barriers would 'contribute substantially to the maintenance of productive employment'. Employment was to be the responsibility of the United Nations Economic and Social Council (ECOSOC) rather than the ITO.[47]

Attlee announced the loan agreement and the trade Proposals in the Commons on 6 December 1945. He endorsed the Proposals as the basis for discussion and accepted the objective of a code of conduct for international commerce and its expansion. He also made his doubts clear and gave more weight to domestic policies to create high and stable employment as a condition for trade expansion. He did not pledge Britain to adopt multilateralism and stressed the need to control imports so long as necessary to restore the balance of payments. He agreed to reduce imperial preference, but with the significant condition that 'there is adequate compensation in the form of improvement in trading conditions between Commonwealth and Empire countries and the rest of the world.' Attlee argued that multilateralism could not be a one-way process of Britain surrendering its preferences; the Americans needed to open their own markets.[48] Later in December, the loan, Proposals and Bretton Woods agreement were presented to Parliament for ratification.

Keynes's earlier attacks on the gold standard provided ammunition for critics of Bretton Woods. Joan Robinson, a Cambridge economist who had been a leading member of the 'circus', reported to Keynes the comment of the Conservative MP Robert Boothby that the Commons 'learned from you to hate gold and you can't de-bamboozle them now'. In Washington, the Bretton Woods agreement was presented as being like the gold standard; in London, the opposite applied. Keynes did his best to convince critics that Bretton Woods, unlike the gold standard, would allow flexibility with the exchange rate determined by domestic policies, so that deflation and unemployment would be avoided. It would also preserve sterling and the role of the City of London, for '[w]ith our own resources so greatly impaired and encumbered, it is only if sterling is firmly placed in an international setting that the necessary confidence in it can be sustained.'[49] Keynes also needed to respond to supporters of imperial preferences who suspected that Bretton Woods was part of a wider strategy that would undermine Britain's economic prosperity. Meanwhile, left-wing economists such as Robinson felt that planning of trade was needed to ensure full employment, overcome the balance of payments deficit, and respond to a future American slump.[50] Keynes therefore argued that 'currency multilateralism is quite distinct from commercial multilateralism and . . . the former does not imply or require the latter. Indeed, currency multilateralism has been in the past the normal state of affairs without in fact being accompanied by commercial multilateralism.'[51] The American administration would have been surprised by this claim, for they saw currency and trade multilateralism as mutually dependent. Indeed, Keynes accepted that imperial preference could not survive. He informed Dalton that 'it would be a counsel of madness to organise an economic and financial rupture with the United States and a large part of the rest of the world immediately at the end of hostilities, when we shall be in the weakest position ever to sustain a position of economic isolation and attempted self-sufficiency.' He insisted that

> [t]he idea that there is some bilateral system which would weld the Empire more closely together is a pure delusion. Nothing would be more likely to break up the economic relations within the Empire and destroy the primacy of London in the sterling area system than a wanton rupture with the currency and commercial systems of North America.[52]

It was easier to secure consent to the Bretton Woods agreement in the British parliamentary system, where an executive with a majority in the Commons could impose party discipline, than in the American political system where Congress and the executive were often opposed. Labour secured a large majority in the general election in July 1945, but a vocal minority of Conservative opponents, led by Boothby, and a few dissident Labour MPs opposed the loan as leading to subservience to the United States. Lieutenant-Colonel Sir Thomas Moore informed the Commons that his cleaner told him to 'stand up for Britain and not trail after the Americans and their spam . . . Britain has not fought and won, has not suffered and survived, two world wars to become the poor relative of even the most kindly, the most benevolent but most autocratic of kinsmen.' Boothby agreed: a commercial loan, without conditions, to get through the next few years would be preferable to selling out Britain to the 'free, knock-about Capitalism' of the United States.[53] Necessity was a stronger argument than the outrage of Moore and Boothby, however, and the loan was accepted as part of a general motion that settled Lend Lease, welcomed the proposals on the ITO, and approved the Bretton Woods agreement. The general principles of the Bretton Wood agreement were not discussed in the debate on the loan, for it required separate legislation – and when the bill to accept the agreement came to the Commons, discussion was prevented because it had been accepted as a condition of the loan. The government was exploiting parliamentary procedure to avoid detailed discussion of Bretton Woods. Boothby fulminated that 'We have never been allowed to have a discussion' and that 'we are handing over world economic power, outside the Soviet Union, fully and decisively to the United States.'[54]

Churchill was in a difficult situation. He could hardly recommend opposition to the Bretton Woods agreement that was negotiated when he was Prime Minister, and he realised that Lend Lease must be settled and a loan secured from America. Neither was he willing, as Leader of the Opposition, to vote with the government and he urged Conservative MPs to abstain on the package of measures that 'is only commended to us by the fear of an even darker alternative. It is for the Government and their great majority to bear the burden.' For good measure, he argued that the American administration was taking a tough line because they supported free enterprise against the 'collectivist and totalitarian conceptions' of socialism. The American ambassador castigated this decision to abstain as 'political and weak'. Churchill was certainly shocked by his electoral defeat, but also aware that divisions in the Conservative Party made a 'whipped' vote unwise. Allowing Conservative MPs freedom to vote as they wished would be even worse. The large Labour majority meant the agreement would easily pass in the Commons – but a free vote in the unelected House of Lords with a built-in Conservative majority risked defeat that would postpone acceptance. Abstention was therefore probably the sensible option. Both the loan and the bill to adopt the Bretton Woods agreement passed the Commons with large majorities. By delaying approval of Bretton Woods until he had secured a loan, Attlee had a bargaining weapon with the American administration; and by taking all the measures together in the Commons, he ensured that individual elements could not be rejected.[55]

Keynes made a final appearance in the House of Lords to justify the outcome. He regretted the failure to secure an interest-free loan but argued that everything had been done to prevent a repetition of the debts after the First World War. More positively, he saw 'a great step forward towards the goal of international economic order amidst national diversities of policies'. The Proposals

are calculated to help us regain a full measure of prosperity and prestige
in the world's commerce ... They aim, above all, at the restoration of multilateral trade which is a system upon which British commerce eventually
depends ... The separate economic blocs and all the friction and loss of
friendship they must bring with them are expedients to which one may be
driven in a hostile world ... But it is surely crazy to prefer that. Above all,
this determination to make trade truly international and to avoid the establishment of economic blocs ... is plainly an essential condition of the
world's best hope, an Anglo-American understanding which brings us and
others together in international institutions which may be in the long run
the first step towards something more comprehensive.[56]

The loan needed congressional approval, which would not be straightforward. When Attlee addressed Congress in November 1945, he informed
them – perhaps unwisely – that every country should follow the 'course
decided by the people's will ... We shall be working out a planned economy. You, it may be, will continue in your more individualistic methods.'
Congressional support to build a socialist society was a risky proposition,
and there were doubts that the loan would pass. Senator Vandenberg,
Republican senator for Michigan, confided in his diary that he felt he should
support the loan from a 'nebulous affinity' with Britain and need for 'mutual
self-defense', but that 90 per cent of his constituents would not agree. As
one Congressman put it, the loan would 'promote too damned much Socialism at home and too much damned Imperialism abroad'.[57]

Churchill was in Washington as the issue came to Congress and, despite
his earlier decision to abstain in the vote in the Commons, actively campaigned for the loan. His 'iron curtain' speech at Fulton, Missouri, in March
1946, calling for an Anglo-American alliance against the Soviets, could
have backfired, for at this stage the American administration was supportive of co-operation with the Soviet Union. Further, the argument that the
loan was needed to support Bretton Woods was rejected by Senator Taft,
who recalled White's assurances that Bretton Woods removed the need for
a loan. Vandenberg worried that 'Our prospective debtors are already
beginning to "shylock us" before the papers are signed.' The case that a
loan was essential for multilateralism, given Britain's crucial role in world
trade, and that it would allow swifter action than Bretton Woods in removing imperial preference and exchange controls, was not compelling. Doubts
remained whether the loan would secure congressional approval.[58]

Success became more likely when relations with the Soviet Union deteriorated. Joseph Kennedy, the former ambassador to (and critic of) Britain,
now supported the loan on the grounds that 'the British people and their

way of life form the last barrier in Europe against Communism'. Vandenberg agreed, and his support for the loan ensured the Senate's approval. In the House, the majority leader warned that the Soviets 'are challenging our civilization' and that failure to help Britain would 'leave those countries who look toward Washington with a friendly eye no alternative but to be subjected to the sphere of influence of Moscow'. The *Washington Post* argued that the loan would encourage a more open economy by removing the need for exchange controls and restrictions on trade. 'By giving such aid, we shall be working to arrest rather than to speed up the socialization of Britain's economic system.'[59] The loan bill passed the Senate in May and the House in July 1946. The British embassy believed it was accepted as a counter to Soviet influence, as a device to slow down the Labour government's socialist policies, and in the expectation that it would lead to a removal of British tariffs and preferences.[60]

CREATING THE NEW INSTITUTIONS

Ratification of the Bretton Woods agreement by the United States and Britain was followed by other countries, and the IMF and IBRD came into existence in December 1945. Their status was still a matter of concern. Robert Brand worried that the new international organizations lacked an over-arching body to which they were responsible, and that they might be no more than talking shops. The result was that '[we] are . . . trying to create *executive* world organisations without there being *any* executive world power to which they are responsible. The administrations of these organisations are therefore a law unto themselves, except insofar as they are governed by the charter and regulations under which they work.' He saw a risk that the United States would take an active interest – especially if the organizations were located in Washington. 'It will be a constant struggle to keep them out of US politics.'[61]

The issue arose at the first meeting of the new institutions in Savannah, Georgia, in March 1946. Keynes attended as the British representative of both institutions – a final appearance before his death on 21 April. Achievement in creating the institutions was blighted by his concern that the new multilateral institutions were falling under American control, rather than being run by an international secretariat standing above national politics. During the discussions in Congress, bankers pressed that the American representatives to the IMF and IBRD should report to a committee directly responsible to Congress. The outcome was a compromise: a National Advisory Council on International and Monetary and Financial Problems reporting to Congress once a year, with membership of the secretaries of the Treasury, State and Commerce, and the chairmen of the Federal Reserve and the Export-Import Bank. Keynes initially welcomed the Council as a sign of American engagement with international economic and financial collaboration, but was soon alarmed that an activist Council might monitor the Fund and Bank if they were based in Washington:

> We had not conceived it as possible that either institution would be placed away from New York. In New York they would be in the daily contacts which can be provided by a great centre of international finance; they would be sufficiently removed from the politics of Congress and the nationalistic whispering gallery of the embassies and legations of Washington; and they would probably be sufficiently near to the seat of the UNO [United Nations Organization] to be able to co-operate closely on the economic and statistical side of their work.

He worried that the new bodies might become 'American concerns, run by gigantic American staffs, with the rest of us very much on the side lines':

> The Americans at the top seem to have absolutely no conception of international co-operation; since they are the biggest partners they think they have the right to call the tune on practically every point. If they knew the music that would not matter so much; but unfortunately they don't.[62]

The institutions were indeed based in Washington, with a real risk that they would pursue the interests of the United States.

As we noted in the Introduction, the new institutions have been portrayed by the political scientists John Ruggie as 'embedded liberalism' and by Dani Rodrik as 'shallow multilateralism'. Their argument is that the principles of open, multilateral markets were incorporated into formal institutions and rules to prevent a return to beggar-my-neighbour policies, while ensuring that the pursuit of international trade was combined with a concern for domestic welfare.[63] This account is accurate as far as it goes. The multilateralism was unlike that of the 1930s, when economic nationalism was in the ascendant, and that of the later twentieth century when the pursuit of multilateralism went much further. It is also incomplete. A particular form of liberalism was being embedded. It did not follow the vision of the 'Genevan liberals' of the 1930s such as Hayek and Robbins, who wanted formal rules with federal or supranational bodies that limited the nation state and enabled the market. Instead, the new institutions were intergovernmental and gave more weight to the nation state and domestic welfare.[64] The balance between internationalism and domestic welfare in the new multilateral institutions also prioritized the needs of the leading capitalist economies, and they came to define the 'West'. The institutions excluded the controlled economies of the Soviet Union and, after 1949, China; and they were contested by the less developed countries of Latin America and the newly independent countries of Asia and Africa. To them, what was being embedded was a form of neo-colonialism and a global economy based on the interests of the advanced industrial economies. Indeed, the Swedish economist Gunnar Myrdal went so far as to argue that the welfare state – a central element in embedded liberalism – was a form of nationalism which created vested interests in support of domestic spending and against policies to assist the under-developed world.[65] The pursuit of a particular form of international economy was in the national interest of advanced industrial countries and not what came to be termed the Third World or Global South.

For the Global South, the issue was not restoring a balance of payments equilibrium; it was removing systemic or structural bias against producers of primary goods and victims of colonialism or dependence. They wished to restructure economic power and not just restore multilateral trade. Similarly, the domestic agenda of full employment was more attuned to the interests of industrial economies than to less developed countries that suffered from under-employment and under-development. As we saw in Chapter 8, these demands had been made at Bretton Woods, where they were marginalized. After the war, and particularly with the decline of European imperialism and the emergence of independent nations, starting with India and Pakistan at midnight on 14–15 August 1947, the principles of embedded liberalism were challenged. In the talks on trade between 1946 and 1948, India and Latin American countries demanded the right to subordinate trade to development. In 1955, recently independent countries from Africa and Asia railed against neo-colonial economic dependence at Bandung, which was followed by the creation of the United Nations Conference on Trade and Development in 1964, and the declaration of a New International Economic Order in 1974. The embedded liberalism of the international institutions was challenged.

There was also a marked difference between the expectations that underpinned the Bretton Woods agreement in 1944 and the circumstances in which the new institutions operated in the post-war world. Despite the hopes at Bretton Woods, the Soviet Union did not join the IMF or IBRD; nor did it engage in the post-war talks on trade that led to the General Agreement on Tariffs and Trade in 1947. Matters in Europe also turned out to be more complicated than assumed by the Americans, who expected a short post-war transition to convertible currencies and multilateral trade. In reality, the European economy was in deep crisis in 1947. Although the

Americans did not expect to play a direct and formal role in Europe at the end of the war, European governments invited them to participate, and in the process American plans for a liberal multilateral order were reshaped into support for European welfare states, which was not entirely what the Americans wished. Embedded liberalism was adapted during implementation, and recovery meant long-term reconstruction with direct American assistance that had not been anticipated. In 1947, Marshall Aid offered the outright gift that Keynes had requested in 1945, now available to other European countries. John Williams also turned out to be partially right. The transition to convertible currencies and multilateral trade would take time and occur in stages – though not starting from the dollar and sterling but from a European Payments Union to settle balances between economies with surpluses or deficits.[66] This shift in American policy in Europe also entailed a major reassessment of the place of Germany in the post-war order.

THE GERMAN PROBLEM

In 1940, Keynes had urged that the mistakes of the Versailles Treaty should be avoided. Germany should be de-militarized and should contribute to an international defence fund to preserve world peace, while resuming its economic leadership in central Europe. His approach was endorsed by the British government's Interdepartmental Committee on Reparations and Economic Security in 1943.[67] Washington took a different line. The State Department suggested partitioning Germany and integrating it within a larger European customs and monetary union that was possible because Germany's occupation of much of Europe 'wiped the slate clean' in removing tariff barriers and undermining national currencies. The result could be 'an economic region with reasonably open tariff barriers' and even a common currency. Rather than punitive measures, the solution was controls to prevent preparations for war, and to allow Germany to contribute to European reconstruction within an expanding world economy. The State Department's policy was 'stern peace with reconciliation', converting Germany from self-sufficiency to reliance on world markets.[68] By contrast, Treasury Secretary Henry Morgenthau took a tough line. He was Jewish with German ancestry, and during the war he pressed Roosevelt and the State Department to rescue European Jews. Afterwards, he feared that 'the Germans were going to be treated in a manner so that ... at the end of ten years, they would be prepared to wage a third war'. To prevent such an outcome, Germany should be de-industrialized and turned into a society of agricultural smallholders. When White tried to moderate the plan, Morgenthau exploded: 'The only thing you can sell me . . . is the complete shut-down of the Ruhr . . . Just strip it. I don't care what happens to the population . . . I would take every mine, every mill and factory and wreck it . . . Steel, coal, everything. Just close it down.' He wanted to turn Germany into a 'cabbage patch' with the 'highly humanitarian' aim of preventing a Third World War.[69]

Keynes was horrified. '[W]hilst the hills are being turned into a sheep run, the valleys will be filled for some years to come with a closely packed bread line on a very low level of subsistence at American expense' – though he was also conscious that 'Liberality to us is at the bottom of [Morgenthau's] mind part of his revenge against Germany.'[70] In Washington, Secretary of War Henry Stimson was alarmed by Morgenthau's 'very bitter atmosphere of personal resentment against the entire German people without regard to individual guilt', and feared that 'mass vengeance . . . in the shape of clumsy economic action' might lead to the starvation of 30 million people. He warned that the policy would be catastrophic. Reducing Germany to a subsistence level would 'obscure the guilt of the Nazis and the viciousness of their doctrines and their acts', and would 'be poisoning the springs out of which we hope that the future peace of the world can be maintained'. De-industrialization would lead to 'a great dislocation to the trade upon which Europe has lived . . . I cannot conceive of turning such a gift of nature into a dust heap.' Morgenthau's response was blunt. 'Why the hell should I worry about what happens to their people? . . . We didn't ask for this war; we didn't put millions of people through gas chambers, we didn't do any of these things. They have asked for it.'[71]

Initially, Roosevelt accepted that 'The German people as a whole must have it driven home to them that the whole nation has been engaged in a lawless conspiracy against the decencies of modern civilization.' He invited Morgenthau to a meeting with Churchill in Quebec in September – and he left a furious Cordell Hull behind in Washington. Morgenthau was shaken by Churchill's response to his plan.

> I have never seen him more irascible and vitriolic . . . He turned loose on me the full flood of his rhetoric, sarcasm and violence. He looked on the Treasury Plan, he said, as he would on chaining himself to a dead German . . . I have never had such a verbal lashing in my life.

The plan was, Churchill said, 'un-Christian'. The next day, on the advice of his adviser – 'the Prof' Frederick Lindemann – Churchill performed a volte-face and produced a memorandum that industries that could easily be converted to war use should be dismantled, and Germany turned 'into a country primarily agricultural and pastoral in its character'. Morgenthau believed that Churchill changed his mind because of the prospect of taking over German exports. A more plausible explanation was Churchill's desire to extend Lend Lease until the defeat of Japan, and his realization that he could block Morgenthau's plan because the industrial heartland of the Ruhr was expected to be in the British zone of occupation.[72]

Stimson and Hull thought the understanding reached at Quebec was 'a pretty heavy defeat for everything that we had fought for'. Roosevelt started to waver when the plan was leaked and exploited by Thomas Dewey, the Republican presidential candidate, who made the damaging though dubious claim that it provoked stronger German resistance and cost American lives. More realistically, engineering businesses argued that German industry was crucial to restoring Europe's economy. There was also the strategic question of whether hostility to Germany should be used to maintain an alliance with, or a buffer against, the Soviet Union.[73] Keynes wanted a united Germany to provide a buffer and argued that partition would make each part 'so weak economically that a bourgeois economy on the Western model can scarcely be expected to survive. These weak states will be seed-beds of social revolution in Europe' and they might even be sucked into 'a unitary German USSR'.[74] By contrast, Morgenthau worried that using a strong Germany as a buffer and possible ally would alienate Russia, and he complained that opponents of his policy 'are largely motivated by anti-Russian attitudes'. Morgenthau was hoping for an American–Soviet understanding – an outcome that opponents at the State Department feared would 'replace a German hegemony on the Continent with a Russian one'.[75]

Roosevelt played along with both sides. He assured Hull that 'No one wants to make Germany a wholly agricultural nation again', and that the way to prevent war was by controls rather than eradication of industry. When Stimson pointed out that at Quebec Roosevelt had accepted the proposal to make Germany an agrarian nation, the president 'was frankly staggered by this and said he had no idea how he could have initialed this'. The situation remained unclear and contested. Morgenthau continued to press his plan against State Department protestations that 'sweeping deindustrialization' would threaten security and lead to 'a chaotically unmanageable economic situation'.[76] American policy remained unclear as Roosevelt wavered.

At the Yalta conference in February 1945, Roosevelt, Churchill and Stalin agreed to 'eliminate or control all German industry that could be used for military production', but in March 1945 Roosevelt accepted a more moderate paper from the State Department. The eventual outcome was

JCS 1067, a directive to the commander of the United States forces that was agreed by President Truman in April 1945. The 'principal Allied objective is to prevent Germany from ever again becoming a threat to the peace of the world'. 'Industrial disarmament and demilitarization' would permit only 'the production and maintenance of goods and services required to meet the needs of the occupying forces and displaced persons in Germany, and essential to prevent starvation or such disease or civil unrest as would endanger the occupying forces.' Nothing should be done 'to support basic living standards of Germany on a higher level than that existing in any one of the neighboring United Nations'. Further, 'All economic and financial international transactions . . . shall be controlled with the aim of preventing Germany from developing a war potential.' German heavy industry should not be restored, and other countries should not become dependent on the German economy.[77] At the Potsdam conference of July–August 1945, Truman, Stalin and Attlee, the new Prime Minister, agreed that Germany's war potential should be eliminated by prohibiting 'the production of arms, ammunition, and implements of war as well as all types of aircraft and sea-going ships'. Metals, chemicals, machinery and other items needed for a war economy 'shall be rigidly controlled and restricted to Germany's approved post-war peacetime needs', and 'primary emphasis shall be given to the development of agriculture and peaceful domestic industries'.[78]

Although JCS 1067 moderated the Morgenthau plan, it still blocked any prospect that the German economy would be the powerhouse of European recovery. The economic adviser to the US high commissioner complained that JCS 1067 was the work of 'economic idiots. It makes no sense to forbid the most skilled workers in Europe from producing as much as they can in a continent that is short of everything.'[79] In March 1946 the Allies agreed that Germany's 'level of industry' should be reduced to half of its pre-war amount, with steel reduced to only a quarter, and the price of coal set below the cost of production. This decision would delay recovery in Europe as a whole, a situation exacerbated by mass migration, food shortages, a lack of housing, and the poor state of the infrastructure. In the harsh winter of 1946–47, a repeat of the *Hungerkatastrophe* and social unrest experienced after the First World War was a serious possibility, with the risk that the Soviets would exploit the situation.[80]

White's plan for the international monetary system had started as a more ambitious approach to economic development. The decision to limit discussions to money was pragmatic and sensible but those other issues had not gone away. As we saw in Chapter 7, they had been discussed in other venues during the war. They now came together in a post-war conference to consider not only trade but employment and distributive justice in the world economy. The demands of less developed countries re-emerged and would not be so easily controlled as at Bretton Woods. The difficulties came not only from these countries, for the British government was not entirely committed to the American approach. In January 1946 the American ambassador in London realized the difficulties of creating a new world from the embers of the old:

> Britain has swung decisively from conservative to progressive courses and this change has benefited the forces in US striving for world economic cooperation and freer trade. But the progressive forces in UK look doubtingly at the US because they have little confidence that Congress and the US public will move in a progressive direction in economic matters. They fear that the US public is swinging in opposite direction to UK public and putting its faith in outworn slogans of reliance on private enterprise and *laissez faire*, except when it suits vested interests to have Government intervention of a type that is usually against the interests of other countries . . . Hence at present in economic matters the US has little attraction for the predominant political and intellectual groups in Britain.[81]

In this climate of hope and fear, in February 1946, fifteen core countries were invited to negotiate reductions in trade barriers and to prepare for a conference on trade and employment.[82] The United States submitted its draft Charter for an International Trade Organization to the UN, and preparatory meetings were held in London between 15 October and 26 November 1946, and in Geneva between 10 April and 22 August 1947. These meetings completed the trade negotiations, and twenty-three countries signed the General Agreement on Tariffs and Trade on 30 October 1947. The full conference then convened in Havana between 21 November 1947 and 24 March 1948 to finalize the Charter.

The question was whether the Havana conference would fail, as in London in 1933, or repeat the success of Bretton Woods. The circumstances were unlike those of 1944, when countries met as the war was being fought and the reality of post-war devastation in Europe and the weakness of the British economy had not been fully appreciated in Washington. As delegates gathered to consider trade and the creation of an International Trade Organization, the world had changed. The plight of the British economy and the devastation in Europe were now clear; cooperation with the Soviets was giving way to the Cold War; the countries of the Global South were more assertive.

10

'Happier relations between all countries'

The Failure of the International Trade Organization

> '[The UN Conference on Trade and Employment] is of supreme
> importance and must succeed or there will be so serious a gap in
> the international relations structure as to bring everything down in
> ruins ... Despite the foregoing, it would be better to have no con-
> ference at all than to call one and have it fail. The London Economic
> Conference fiasco in 1933 did vast damage and another failure like
> it now would mean chaos for a generation ... It is essential that
> international commitments be obtained before national policies are
> formed that disregard international considerations.'
>
> Harry Hawkins to Will Clayton, 30 April 1945[1]

Harry Hawkins was the head of the Division of Commercial Policy and
Agreements at the State Department, where William L. Clayton, Assistant
Secretary of State, was committed to multilateral trade. Clayton believed a
permanent institution – an International Trade Organization – was needed
as a forum for negotiations, to implement recommendations, to restrain
self-seeking economic nationalism, and to restore multilateral world trade.[2]
When members of the American delegation assembled for the conference
on trade and employment at Havana in November 1947, he assured them
that they were participating in 'the most important international economic
conference that has ever been held in the history of the world. There is no
question about that.' He followed Hull in claiming that 'international collaboration for world peace can never succeed unless it is accompanied by
international collaboration in the economic field'.[3] The conference at
Havana would offer an escape from the tragedy of the interwar period:

There are only two roads open to us, one leads to multilateral, non-
discriminatory trade with a great increase in the production, distribution
and consumption of goods in the world and happier relationships between

The Havana Charter of the International Trade Organization was signed by fifty-three countries. Will Clayton signed on behalf of the United States, 24 March 1948.

all countries; the other leads to economic nationalism, restrictionism, bilateralism, discriminatory practices, a lowering of the standard of living and bad feeling all around. We must choose now which road we will take.[4]

Such sentiments led Harold Wilson, a rising Labour politician, to find Clayton 'nice and well-intentioned but woolly in his mental processes and dominated by rigid conceptions held in a sort of self-righteous haze', whose contribution to discussions 'often seemed like discourses on points of theological dogma or morality'.[5]

The proposal for the ITO reflected post-war optimism and idealism about a new world before a greater sense of reality emerged in 1947. By the time discussions took place at Geneva and the Charter was signed at Havana in 1948, the ITO was marginalized. The talks between 1946 and 1948 coincided with changes in the context of policy both within the United States, as the New Deal faced challenge, and internationally as the extent of the problems in Europe became clear, relations with the Soviet Union deteriorated with the onset of the Cold War, and the less developed countries mounted a challenge to the agenda of the advanced industrial countries. In these new conditions, the idealistic and unrealistic ambitions of the ITO were replaced by pragmatism and caution.

CHANGING CONTEXT: THE USA

The delay in formulating trade proposals until after the war worried officials in the State Department, who thought that Hull's obsession with reducing trade barriers had distracted attention from the real needs of the post-war world so that the opportune time for innovation had passed.[6] By the time delegates met in Geneva and Havana, changes in the economic and strategic context made fulfilment of Hull's and Clayton's vision of free trade extremely difficult.

President Roosevelt had died on 12 April 1945. Harry S. Truman, a surprise choice as Vice-President who had only been in office for a few months, had a different approach to running the administration. Frederic Eggleston, the Australian minister in Washington, remarked that Roosevelt

surrounded himself with men drawn . . . from outside, and there was a gulf between these advisers and the Department of State and other regular Government agencies. There was a dualism in the conduct of policy. The departments were thinking on one line, the political amateurs were often thinking on other lines and the President often took his own line. Mr Truman is likely to assert his own point of view less, to exercise far less

creative influence in current opinion, to rely far more on the permanent
departments and to be swayed by his party advisers on questions of political expediency.

Eggleston doubted that Truman was powerful enough to overcome
domestic interest groups and secure the monetary, employment and trade
policies pursued by Roosevelt.[7] Wilfrid Eady agreed: Roosevelt's administration made up its mind and then tried to get the policy through Congress;
Truman's administration was 'more likely to start from guessing what
they could get past Congress and then making that their policy'.[8]

Despite these doubts about Truman's ability to enforce his views, in September 1945 he adopted an ambitious domestic programme of improved
unemployment pay, increased minimum wages, maintenance of price controls, legislation for full and fair employment, a housing programme,
expansion of public works and a revision of taxation. His main concern
was to ease the transition from the war economy. Clayton realized that
reducing American tariffs might hit business and labour, so leading to
demands for protectionism in the congressional elections of November
1946.[9] He therefore called on Henry Wallace, now Secretary of Commerce,
to offer 'reasonable assistance to adversely affected groups of citizens':

> In our system of free enterprise, it is not up to the Government to cushion
> every shock that disturbs the economic situation of every individual or
> every group ... However, a good case can be made, in terms of socio-
> economic justice, for the Government providing some special assistance to
> adversely affected persons when it takes rather abrupt and somewhat unex-
> pected action, albeit in the general interest of the country ... If something
> could be done in this field, I believe it would go a long way toward eliminat-
> ing objections to reasonable tariff reductions.[10]

The pursuit of multilateral trade connected with contentious domestic
policies to deal with the transition to peace.

Many Republicans and moderate Democrats viewed Wallace, Roosevelt's
former vice-president, as a dangerous radical who threatened free enterprise. In Sixty Million Jobs (1945), Wallace argued that the 'planlessness' of
the 1920s led to unemployment in the 1930s. Therefore the Department
of Commerce and the Federal Loan Agency should promote 'a maximum
of national employment by private business' – a policy that raised the
spectre of state intervention. Wallace's confirmation as Secretary of Commerce was only accepted on condition that the Federal Loan Agency was
removed from his department.[11] Above all, the case for state action
was fought in the Full Employment Bill of 1945, which reflected Alvin

Hansen's Keynesianism and Wallace's belief that unemployment was a consequence of free enterprise. Senator Robert Wagner, the chair of the Full Employment Committee, explained that a free enterprise economy was liable to 'brief periods of growth and development culminating in peaks of prosperity that gave way to disastrous collapse'. The bill therefore proposed supplementing free enterprise by setting the level of federal 'compensatory finance' to ensure that 'all Americans able to work and seeking to work are entitled to an opportunity for useful, remunerative, regular and full-time employment'. At the start of each session of Congress, the president would submit a budget showing the output needed to generate full employment and would adjust government spending to ensure this target was met.[12] The bill provoked considerable opposition and Republican control of Congress in 1947 led to hostility to Truman's domestic policies and uncertainty over the international conferences. Truman's surprise re-election in 1948, and the return of Democratic control over Congress, allowed him to embark on an ambitious domestic agenda. In his State of the Union address of 5 January 1949, Truman announced that 'Every segment of our population and every individual has a right to expect from our Government a fair deal.' He built on his proposals of 1945 to extend welfare spending, repeal anti-union legislation, implement civil rights measures, provide subsidies to farmers and impose higher taxes. These controversial proposals faced opposition even with Democratic control of Congress.[13]

Attitudes had shifted away from radical New Deal policies to a belief that productivity, efficiency and growth would resolve political and class conflicts over post-war reconstruction between business and labour, between proponents of spending and reduced taxes, and between advocates of planning and free markets. In the war, business elites who had been discredited after 1929 returned to Washington. Edward Stettinius, who had been a vice-president of General Motors and chairman of US Steel, became chair of the War Resources Board and succeeded Cordell Hull as Secretary of State in December 1944. Similarly, the Department of Commerce's Committee for Economic Development was established in 1942 under the chairmanship of Paul Hoffman of the Studebaker Motor Co.; it advocated 'enlightened internationalism' based on a prosperous domestic economy. Although the war machine rested on the public ownership and operation of industrial plant, management of supply chains, and controls on prices and profits, business leaders stressed the contribution of private enterprise. The result was to contain radical policies for full employment, welfare reform and counter-cyclical spending by what the historian Charles Maier terms 'the supposedly apolitical politics of productivity', based on limited planning with the co-operation of business to raise economic output in the service of all classes. As he put it, 'the true dialectic was not one of class against class, but waste versus abundance', with reliance on productive efficiency rather than redistribution. The United States adopted 'commercial' Keynesianism – a reliance on non-discriminatory taxation and the corporate sector – rather than 'social' Keynesianism based on a centrally funded welfare state, deficit finance and redistribution. The Committee for Economic Development and its allies in the National Association of Manufacturers and US Chamber of Commerce accepted a modest role for fiscal and monetary policy in stabilizing the economy, but rejected the approach of the Full Employment Bill. Setting prices and wages, and allocating resources, were matters for the market rather than federal bureaucrats.[14]

This realignment was confirmed in the context of the Cold War. Leon Keyserling, vice-chairman and later chair of Truman's Council of Economic Advisers (CEA), had been committed to full employment and welfare, and had strong ties with the American Federation of Labor (AFL). After the war, Keyserling and George Meaney of the AFL looked to military spending that linked full employment with anti-Communism.[15] American policies in Europe were designed to secure support from labour and centrist – including social democratic – politicians, provided that they accepted the need for growth and productivity. The result was to divide the European labour movement between Communists and Social or Christian Democrats, and to force the United States into a centrist position. The outcome was 'consensual American hegemony' in Europe that was based on productivity and increased output.[16] The Marshall Plan was central to this shift in policy in the context of the need to return Germany to its role at the heart of the European economy and 'containment' of the Soviet Union. Appropriately, the American body that administered Marshall Aid – the Economic Cooperation Administration (ECA) – was run by Paul Hoffman.

CHANGING CONTEXT:
EUROPE AND THE COLD WAR

The international context of American policy was also changing as the conferences proceeded. At Bretton Woods, the adoption of a new monetary regime and the return to convertibility were expected to take five years – a concession from the original proposal of three years that was then shortened as a condition of the loan to Britain so that sterling was to be convertible after an absurdly unrealistic period of one year. When the convertibility of sterling on current account resumed on 15 July 1947, the pound came under speculative pressure, reserves were depleted, and convertibility was suspended little more than a month later.

The economies of Europe were in a dire condition in 1947, the year when the fate of the continent hung in the balance. Food shortages were acute, with the individual average daily intake of calories in Germany falling to 1,050 in early 1947. The winter of 1946–47 was the harshest since 1880 at a time when fuel supplies were already disrupted. Coal output could not keep up with demand, and steel output fell by 40 per cent. In 1947, agricultural and industrial output in Europe was still 17 and 21 per cent, respectively, and exports 41 per cent below pre-war levels. Europe was dependent on American food and industrial goods but had little to sell in return, which led to deficits and payments in hard currency, which was in short supply. Germany did not even have a functioning currency and relied on the black market. The risks were obvious: economic collapse would force countries into self-sufficiency and protectionism; and hardship provided an opportunity for Communist parties. In April 1947, the French Minister of National Economy warned: 'We are threatened with total economic and financial catastrophe.'[17]

In January 1947, Truman asked Herbert Hoover, the former president who had been involved in relief in Europe after the First World War, to consider the food situation. He agreed on condition that he could also report on 'what further immediate steps are possible to increase their exports and thus their ability to become self-supporting; what possibilities there are of payment otherwise; and when charity can be expected to end.' In February, Hoover reported that nutrition was inadequate for health and work, and that the Germans 'have been sunk to the lowest level known in a hundred years of Western history'. His solution was to create a regime that would prevent a return to militarism: 'If Western Civilization is to survive in Europe, it must also survive in Germany. And it must be built into a cooperative member of that civilization.' In March 1947, Hoover argued that

> We desperately need recovery in all of Europe. We need it not only for economic reasons but as the first necessity to peace . . . There is only one path to recovery in Europe. That is production. The whole economy of Europe is interlinked with [the] German economy through the exchange of raw materials and manufactured goods. The productivity of Europe cannot be restored without the restoration of Germany as a contributor to that productivity.

Hoover rejected JCS1067, for Germany could not be reduced to a pastoral state 'unless we exterminate or move 25,000,000 people out of it'. He criticized the 'illusion . . . that Europe as a whole can recover without the economic recovery of Germany'. Europe needed German capital goods, and forcing a conversion from heavy to light industries would hit firms in other countries:

> If her light industries were built to become self-supporting, she would become an economic menace to Europe; if her heavy industries are allowed to function, she has an ability to export and would become an asset in Europe's recovery. To persist in the present policies will create, sooner or later, a cesspool of unemployment or pauper labor in the center of Europe which is bound to infect her neighbors.[18]

At last, a new sense of realism was emerging in Washington as the conference proceeded at Geneva and ahead of the discussions at Havana.

Attitudes to the Soviet Union were also changing. Roosevelt had hoped to co-operate with the Soviets after the war, and he tried to allay Russian fears of an Anglo-American alliance by acting as a mediator between Britain and the Soviets. Morgenthau and White wanted Soviet involvement in the IMF, and Truman still hoped to work with them at the Potsdam conference. The Potsdam agreement of 1 August 1945 assumed that the wartime alliance of the United States, Soviet Union, Britain and France would continue, with a joint Allied Control Council for occupied Germany. The British were sceptical and concerned about Soviet domination of eastern Europe, and possibly of Germany. British concern for the balance of power in Europe, and more generally in the world, meant that its post-war policy was based on creating a coalition to contain the Soviets. Initially, however, it was not possible to abandon a wartime ally and reject Potsdam. Consequently, Ernest Bevin – now Foreign Secretary – and the Foreign Office pursued a dual policy of appearing to co-operate as agreed at Potsdam while also trying to convince Washington of the threat to peace in western Europe and the need for a western alliance against the Soviets. American attitudes started to change with diplomat George Kennan's telegram from Moscow in February 1946, which urged defensive containment of the Soviet Union. James Byrnes – Secretary of State from July 1945 to January 1947 – called for a shift from appeasement to opposition to Soviet aggression. Even so, Truman expressed public doubts about Churchill's 'Iron Curtain' speech in Missouri the month after Kennan had sent his telegram, in part because of domestic support for troop reductions in Europe. Bevin continued his balancing act of both accepting four-power co-operation and encouraging German participation and economic recovery in the British zone of occupation. The prospect of an independent British zone that included the crucial industrial area of the Ruhr led Byrnes to suggest an economic unit of two or more zones. In February 1947, Bevin set out a plan that claimed to continue four-power control with conditions for the economic and political unity of Germany that the Soviets were expected to reject, so that they would take the blame for failure.[19]

American attitudes began to shift. At a joint session of Congress on 12 March 1947, Truman announced: 'I believe that it must be the policy of the United States to support free peoples who are resisting attempted subjugation by armed minorities or by outside pressures.'[20] Co-operation with the Soviets that had been agreed at Potsdam was now rejected, and in 1947 'Bizonia' merged the economies of the British and American occupation zones and established a new German currency. Stalin responded by creating a new currency for the Soviet zone. In 1949, France joined what was now Trizonia and the division of Germany was completed with the creation of the Federal Republic of (West) Germany in May and the (East) German Democratic Republic in October 1949.[21]

The revised American policy towards recovery in Europe and towards the Soviets was confirmed on 5 June 1947 when George Marshall – the army chief of staff during the war and from January 1947 to January 1949 Secretary of State – spoke to the graduating class at Harvard of the urgent need for American financial assistance for European reconstruction. In July 1947, Marshall also replaced JCS1067 with JCS1779, which argued that 'an orderly, prosperous Europe requires the economic contributions of a stable and productive Germany'.[22] As we shall see in Chapter 11, the Marshall Plan divided Europe into Communist and capitalist blocs in the same way as Bizonia had divided Germany.

This change in relations with the Soviets had implications for the conference on trade and employment. It was initially expected that the Soviet Union would participate, and in December 1945, Dean Acheson – Under-Secretary of State – hoped Soviet involvement would allow a framework for international trade covering both private enterprise and state trading.[23] Others were doubtful. In a telegram to Washington, Averell Harriman, the American ambassador in Moscow, pointed out that '[u]nder the Soviet system foreign trade is a monopoly of the State. All foreign trade transactions are controlled according to plan for furtherance of national economic interests and often political objectives. Soviet national monopoly of foreign trade is integral part of Soviet system and cannot be altered.' Discussion of tariffs was pointless, for '[i]n a totalitarian economy such as that of USSR where whole economy and foreign trade included are operated by State according to plan, concept of "protection" has no mean-ing in connection with tariffs.'[24] Kennan agreed.

> Soviet instincts are autarchic. They view international trade for themselves
> as a means of increasing Soviet strategic economic strength and of achieving
> economic independence. They would never admit that there was any prob-lem
> of employment at all in the Soviet Union or that employment problem
> in capitalist countries was susceptible of solution by increasing foreign trade.

The Soviets were invited to the initial meeting in London in 1946 but did not attend. Discussion of state trading was postponed in case the Soviets appeared in Geneva – but they did not attend the conference, nor that in Havana. They portrayed the ITO as a device to avert a crisis of capitalism caused by under-consumption by disposing of surplus American produc-tion, securing a monopoly of world trade, and keeping less developed countries in poverty. The risk for Western powers was that, if the Soviets were involved, they might have sabotaged international cooperation by forming an alliance with the less developed countries – a consideration that led the Soviets to return to the idea of a world trade organization in the 1960s, as we shall see in Chapter 15.[25]

The Marshall Plan was both a complement to Clayton's aim to create a multilateral world economy and a potential source of conflict. The assis-tant secretary realized that progress in restoring multilateral trade and creating the ITO could not succeed without action to restore the Euro-pean economies. On his way to the conference in Geneva, Clayton was 'surprised and in some cases shocked by conditions in the countries of western Europe'. On his return to Washington in May 1947, his plea to the Secretary of State for action to deal with the European crisis was one of the inspirations for the Marshall Plan. His memorandum to Marshall accepted that

> we grossly under-estimated the destruction to the European economy by the
> war. We understood the physical destruction, but we failed to take fully into
> account the effects of economic dislocation on production – nationalization
> of industries, drastic land reform, severance of long-standing commercial
> ties, disappearance of private commercial firms through death or loss of
> capital, etc, etc.

He shifted from confidence that a multilateral economy could be recon-structed to an apocalyptic vision of economic and political collapse, the slow starvation of millions of people, and incipient revolution. Without American assistance, 'economic, social and political disintegration will overwhelm Europe', with 'awful implications . . . for the future peace and security of the world', as well as for America's ability to sell its surplus production. He urged American assistance 'in order to save Europe from starvation and chaos (*not* from the Russians) and, at the same time, to preserve for ourselves and our children the glorious heritage of a free America'. Clayton accepted that 'Europe cannot recover from this war and again become independent if her economy continues to be divided into many small watertight compartments'. He therefore suggested a European economic federation or customs union.[26]

Escaping from Schachtian bilateral deals would not be easy, and there was an attraction in creating 'a strong integrated Europe' in place of 'a highly divided nationalistic and autarchic series of economies'. But was a customs union compatible with multilateralism? In a customs union, a group of countries agree to a common external tariff so that all members apply the same rate on imports and remove tariffs between themselves, unlike in a free trade area where members reduce tariffs between themselves, without a common external tariff and surrender of sovereignty over trade deals. The risk, as an official at the Department of Commerce saw, was that 'we in the US are in a peculiarly inconsistent position. We have favored Customs Unions, but are opposed to Empire Preference.' Clayton denied inconsistency. In his view, the meetings of European countries to discuss Marshall Aid and a free trade area or customs union complemented the discussions in Geneva. Without the Marshall Plan, the world would be 'thrown into economic chaos', and without the ITO there was a risk of a 'return to bilateralism, restrictionism, and economic isolationism'. The ITO's rules were needed to ensure that any European trade zone did not become closed and a constraint on multilateralism.[27]

The French government was supportive of a customs union as a way of securing access to Germany's coal and coke to stimulate economic growth, as well as to contain Germany in an integrated European economy – a strategy that went back to the 1920s. The British government was sceptical. Harold Wilson thought that Clayton 'is far too prone to think that because a customs union has succeeded in the US (where the economic systems of the States are complementary and interdependent) it would work the same way in Western Europe'. Industry in the United States had developed in conditions of free trade, unlike in Europe where national boundaries influenced industry. Of course, the British government was also conscious that a European customs union would create problems with imperial preference: if Britain were inside a common external tariff, it would not be able to offer a preference to, say, Australia. The Foreign Office thought that the American position was confused, with conflict 'between the desire for multilateral trade with no preferential organisation and no discrimination as expressed in the ITO proposals, and the desire for some form of European "integration". Clayton himself does not seem to have fully realised the possibilities of conflict between these two conceptions.'[28] The tension has continued ever since with attempts to insert free trade deals and customs unions within the framework of multilateralism.

NEGOTIATING TRADE: THE GENERAL AGREEMENT ON TARIFFS AND TRADE

The initial phase of the discussion of the Proposals, as set out above, was to negotiate a trade deal at Geneva between April and August 1947 – a process that was complicated by disagreements between Britain and the United States. Although Attlee accepted the Proposals as the basis for discussion, he made his doubts clear in his Commons statement in December 1945. He did not make a pledge to multilateralism and stressed the need to control imports to restore the balance of payments, along with domestic policies for high and stable employment as a precondition for trade expansion. He agreed to act on imperial preference, with the significant condition that 'there is adequate compensation in the form of improvement in trading conditions between Commonwealth and Empire countries and the rest of the world' – that is, the United States should reduce tariffs and open their markets.[29] The situation was difficult. The American trade surplus after the war led to a severe shortage of dollars and global liquidity. The British Treasury feared 'a world economic crisis comparable with that of 1929 to 1932' and insisted that countries should have a right to impose controls until production recovered.[30]

Clayton was not impressed and complained to Stafford Cripps that the terms of the US loan of 1945 had not been fulfilled. Cripps countered that preferences could not be abandoned without the consent of the Dominions and that post-war difficulties could not be solved by free trade dogma. Nor were the British willing to reduce tariffs by the same proportion as the United States. British tariffs were already lower than American ones, so the same percentage cut would not create a level playing field and a liberal world economy. The Board of Trade attempted to convince Clayton that the issue was not, as in the trade agreements of the 1930s, for both sides to offer equivalent reductions. Rather, the 'guiding considerations' should be '(1) how far can the United States go in offering effective tariff reductions, and (2) how little (not how much) must be given in return?' – an approach that Clayton pointed out was contrary to the Reciprocal Trade Agreements Act. The British thought – or hoped – that the State Department had shifted from Hull's 'almost religious convictions'. Cripps's attitude was castigated by the Americans as 'complete indifference bordering on open hostility towards the objectives of the Geneva conference', and he adopted a high-risk strategy of facing down the Americans that threatened progress in negotiating a trade deal.[31] Clair Wilcox, the head of the Office of International Trade Policy at the State Department and a leading member of the American team at Geneva and Havana, complained – with some truth – that Cripps was a '"self-righteous man" who "knows that all his ideas are correct and all his thoughts are just"', and he condemned British officials as 'lacking in the courage necessary to compete in an open market'.[32]

This tension between the United States and Britain threatened to jeopardize the trade talks at Geneva and the creation of a multilateral trade order. Wilcox hoped for a striking headline for domestic newspapers proclaiming 'Empire Preference System Broken at Geneva' to ease renewal of the RTAA, and he foresaw political problems of reducing tariffs without sufficient recompense. 'American opinion regards the Hawley–Smoot tariff and the Ottawa system as related parts of inter-war trade restrictions. We are undertaking the liquidation of the Hawley–Smoot rates. We cannot support this action at home unless we obtain, in the process, the liquidation of the Ottawa system.'[33] Cripps rejected Clayton's offer of delaying the elimination of preferences, and even members of Clayton's delegation had concerns about continued pressure on Britain: 'Even though we are right, we appear to the world as Uncle Shylock' demanding a pound of flesh from Britain. The result would be a propaganda victory for the Soviets, and without an agreement 'we will end a joint effort with our best friends in bitterness and disillusionment'. In the event, the success of tariff negotiations at Geneva allowed the failure on preferences to be overlooked. Winthrop Brown, a leading member of the American delegation, recalled that 'each side found that so much had been accomplished that it could not be lost. This total accomplishment just had to be saved somehow.' Cripps's gamble paid off: the American delegation needed an agreement on trade and tariffs, and reluctantly agreed to proceed without an undertaking to eliminate preferences. The Foreign Office concluded that the terms 'do not represent the end of imperial preferences nor even a damaging inroad into them'.[34]

The trade talks raised a technical but politically important issue of the procedure for negotiating tariff cuts. Before the war, trade agreements were bilateral and proceeded on a product-by-product basis so that individual rates were reduced by differing amounts to create reciprocity of benefits. A bilateral deal was then extended through the unconditional most favoured nation principle, rather than a single multilateral package. This approach could not work at Geneva where a number of countries were engaged in multilateral talks. John Leddy, a trade expert in the State Department, recalled that 'People threw up their hands and were appalled, and said, "How can you do that?" I mean, you can't have ten or fifteen countries all negotiating bilaterally with one another on these long lists of things. I mean this was an impossible thought, it couldn't be done.'[35] The quickest solution would be 'horizontal-multilateral' talks, that is, uniform or 'linear' percentage reductions in tariffs by all participating countries at the same time. This approach would be easier to negotiate, but it was impossible politically, for the same level of reduction by all parties would still leave a discrepancy between countries that started with high or low tariffs. The American negotiators maintained that their tariffs had already been reduced before the war, and that further cuts would take them to the lowest level for a century. The approach would also lead to domestic opposition in Congress, for a linear cut would remove the ability of industries to negotiate special terms – and it would contradict the principle that concessions should be reciprocal.

The State Department's solution was 'multilateral-bilateralism'. Bilateral negotiations would start between pairs of countries for individual commodities in the 'nuclear group' of major trading countries, with deals generalized among themselves. These negotiations followed the 'principal supplier' rule devised by Harry Hawkins in 1934 to overcome the difficulty that unconditional most favoured nation treatment gave countries something for nothing (see Chapter 3). Only the country that was the major supplier of a good to another country could request a cut in the tariff. This procedure meant that trade talks could concentrate on America's allies by extending benefits to a small group of countries that imported goods from each other in an 'exclusive country club' of the United States, Canada, France, Britain and, subsequently, Germany. Meanwhile, other aspects of trade policy – quotas, preferences, subsidies, cartels, commodities – would be handled by multilateral talks among all members of the nuclear group. Once the core, or 'nuclear', talks were concluded, other countries would be invited to take part. This approach was not as straightforward as an across-the-board cut, but it was acceptable to Congress in retaining bilateral trade agreements and was as close to the British position as was feasible under the RTAA.[36]

The 'bilateral-multilateral' negotiations were, as Raymond Street – the spokesman for the Lancashire cotton industry – pointed out, 'a business of unbelievable intricacy and frustration. A dozen nations all engaged in cross negotiations on tariff schedules of appalling complexity.'[37]

It involved haggling over commodities one by one until a deal was struck. It worked. In all, 123 bilateral deals were negotiated covering about 50,000 tariff rates, and these deals were then extended to all members and covered 70 per cent of world trade. The General Agreement on Tariffs and Trade was signed by twenty-three countries on 30 October 1947. It remained to secure support for GATT on Capitol Hill against criticism that the State Department had given away more than it had secured, especially from the British, and that it had sacrificed American interests.[38]

GATT was a considerable achievement at Geneva. The next task was to reach an agreement on a Charter for the International Trade Organization. A draft was produced in Geneva which would be discussed in the larger conference that opened in Havana in November 1947. The American delegation had a poorer hand at the Havana conference than at Bretton Woods. After it ended, Clair Wilcox expressed 'shock and perhaps surprise and some worry' at the attitudes of Britain and other countries in western Europe who were more preoccupied with their immediate economic problems than with liberal trade policy. The only surprise is that he was surprised. Wilcox was also alarmed that many countries had a belief in 'government regimentation of private business'. He accepted that 'we can't go to Mars or Venus or anywhere else' so that concessions were needed to avoid the risk that 'the non-Russian part of the world' would be 'split up into a lot of small units that can be picked off and communized one by one rather than binding it together in a strong combination, the center of which would evidently be the economic strength and power and leadership of the United States'. Further concessions were needed to secure the support of less developed countries. The organizers of the preparatory meeting in London and conferences in Geneva and Havana were less able to shape the agenda and contain critical voices than at Atlantic City and Bretton Woods. The smaller group of countries that prepared for the final conference met resistance from countries who felt that their interests were not represented and accordingly submitted a mass of amendments, in particular the demand to raise their standard of living by industrializing behind tariff walls. As Wilcox admitted, 'I don't know that we are in a very good position to criticize that in view of our own history of policy during our period of industrialization.'[39] Here was the problem for Wilcox and Clayton, who were playing a two-level game. At Havana, they had to build support for the Charter of the ITO by making concessions that went beyond the initial draft produced in Geneva − but success came at the expense of losing on Capitol Hill.

DRAFTING THE ITO CHARTER

The IMF had adopted weighted voting that gave more voice to the United States and Britain, unlike other international organizations that had one member, one vote. When it came to the ITO Charter, the Americans initially wanted to limit voting rights to full members of the United Nations, in contrast to the British who thought that success was more likely by allowing all countries the 'full opportunity to put their point of view *and to press it to a vote*'. Argentina caused particular problems, for it had rejected the Good Neighbor policy, embarked on protectionist policies and failed to support the Allies during the war. The United States broke off diplomatic ties in 1944, but Argentina had close economic ties with Britain, which owned much of its infrastructure and was a major importer of foodstuffs. The British won the argument and every country – whether or not a member of the UN – was allowed to vote. But should the vote be weighted, as in the IMF, which would give the United States a dominant voice?[40]

Various proposals were considered to weight votes by population or trade which would, depending on the precise formula, give the majority to either the British empire or the United States. Clearly, neither option appealed to less developed countries and resolutions passed by the weighted vote of a few countries would not build consent. The Americans accepted that 'one country one vote' was politically expedient and of little practical significance. 'The influence which the US exerts because of its economic, political and military strength is, after all, very great, and in most cases is likely to be a more important factor than any specific voting procedure in ensuring a favorable decision on particular issues.' The United States would still have a veto on issues such as import restrictions to deal with a balance of payments crisis, which needed IMF approval, and industrial countries would be permanent members of the executive board of the ITO. The concession of equal votes was an attempt to secure support for the Charter from under-developed countries by giving them more of a voice, with the result that support in Washington and London was undermined. Harold Wilson, President of the Board of Trade from September 1947, complained that too much was conceded 'but the United States and the others have apparently come to the view that in the present state of the world a comprehensive international trade organization is more important than the securing of a Charter with only limited adherence but which safeguards our and their position more effectively.'[41]

The discussions in Geneva and Havana also raised questions over the compatibility of planning the domestic economy with an open multilateral economy – a particular problem for Britain's Labour government. Raymond Street pointed out that

> multilateralism was inconsistent with too much planning at home. In a multilateral world you could not say beforehand that the cotton industry should be of such and such a size. You had to let the efforts and ingenuities of the exporters determine what size of an export trade was obtainable and that must govern the size of your industry.[42]

Labour's solution was to complement domestic with international planning, which left two problems: that international planning implied a loss of national control over the domestic economy, and that it was incompatible with American definitions of multilateralism. As Attlee admitted in 1946, '[i]n certain specific points of world economic planning, we find the United States in agreement with us, but, generally speaking, they hold a capitalist philosophy which we do not accept.'[43] The concern in London was that the American free-market economy was prone to instability so that multilateral trade would only be safe if it were committed to postwar full employment.[44]

At the Economic Section of the Cabinet, James Meade offered a way to reconcile domestic and international planning within a multilateral framework. In the League's world economic survey of 1939, Meade had argued that 'attempts to secure freedom of trade are intimately connected with the maintenance of buying power'. During the war, the League made the case that freer trade needed countercyclical policies to manage aggregate demand and maintain full employment, with international rules and co-ordination of domestic action.[45] Meade developed this line after the war. He saw that multilateralism should be combined with a national commitment to policies to stimulate domestic employment and maintain worldwide demand. The achievement of full employment could not be left only to national governments. It also needed international buffer stocks to maintain stable demand and prices, and international public works funded by the IBRD to offset fluctuations in employment. Changes in national credit policy should be co-ordinated; exchange rates and duties should be adjusted in response to employment; and international capital flows should be controlled. This approach gave a major role to the IMF, the IBRD and the putative ITO in co-ordinating national policies for international purposes. Meade therefore reconciled two elements of Labour's policy – a commitment to domestic planning and support for multilateral trade – through ITO support for full employment at home and abroad. He offered a way of controlling a destructive, capitalistic American economy, prone to intense booms and slumps that could spill over to the rest of the world.[46]

Meade's scheme differed from the State Department's commitment to free markets. It also had critics in Britain. James Grigg, the first British executive director of the IBRD, pointed out that the new institution had scarcely begun its work and that its lending policies should not be 'determined only by the doctrine of universal full employment – which I personally believe to be chimerical anyhow unless there is a much greater abandonment of national sovereignty than now looks probable'. George Bolton of the Bank of England, who was Britain's executive director at the IMF, feared overburdening the IMF and IBRD at a time when they were handling reconstruction and stabilizing exchanges, with a risk they would become 'pure debating societies' involved in protracted discussions over full employment.[47] But the Labour government was convinced by Meade's approach. R. W. B. ('Otto') Clarke – a financial journalist who had entered the civil service during the war and moved to the Treasury in 1945 – thought that the ITO, in the absence of a commitment to full employment, was 'a series of trade measures which are on the whole creative of unemployment and which certainly greatly hinder individual countries from pursuing an internal full employment policy'. He worried that

> We tie ourselves up to the highly peripatetic US economy – and, what is more, we agree to increase our dependence upon international trade . . . We are, in fact, embarking upon a high import–high export policy with no safeguards at all about the stability in USA and with very limited powers to take protective action in co-operation with like-minded countries to ease the impact of US depression on our economy.[48]

A Treasury colleague agreed. Meade's scheme 'is perhaps a bit on the theoretical and utopian side, but on the whole it seems to me good socialism and good sense'. As he put it, 'countries cannot afford to disarm if the elephant [the US] is going to run amok. Especially if the elephant then says that it is the only sane and virtuous animal in the zoo.'[49] Accordingly, the British delegation stressed the international importance of full employment and that 'a free society can engage in sufficient economic planning to prevent serious economic depressions'.[50] That the American administration would accept the compatibility of good sense and good socialism was deeply implausible.

The British policy was consistent with the coalition government's White Paper on employment of 1944, with its pledge to 'the maintenance of a high and stable level of employment after the war'.[51] By contrast, the United States moved away from Wallace's approach and the Full Employment Bill. Secretary of State Stettinius worried that management of the domestic economy implied economic nationalism that would be 'destructive of international economic collaboration' and lead to 'the stimulation of uneconomic production'. John Leddy recalled that many thought 'an excessive concern with full employment would lead to rigid controls . . . and state planning, and socialist planning, and all the rest of it'.[52] Opponents of the Full Employment Bill argued that some unemployment was inevitable, that business cycles were essential to economic adjustment, and that full employment would lead to inflation and artificial prosperity which would be followed by depression. Southern Democrats, whose votes in Congress were critical after losses of northern Democrats, feared that public works spending by the federal government and direct involvement in the labour market would threaten the racial order.[53] The Employment Act of 1946 dropped the proposed production and employment budget, and had a more modest commitment to 'practicable means . . . calculated to foster and promote free competitive enterprise and the general welfare' that would ensure 'useful employment opportunities . . . for those able, willing, and seeking to work, and to promote maximum employment, production and purchasing power'.[54]

The Australians wished to go further than the British, reflecting domestic politics and the country's position in the world economy. In 1945, the Australian government published a White Paper that insisted that 'full employment is a fundamental aim' and that it could 'be maintained only as long as total expenditure provides a market for all goods and services turned out by Australian men and women, working with available equipment and materials, and fully employed after allowing for the need for leisure'. The government 'should accept the responsibility for stimulating spending on goods and services to the extent necessary to sustain full employment'. This policy would help solve a domestic political difficulty of reconciling a commitment to the re-employment of returning soldiers and a preference for trade unionists. The problem of meeting both commitments disappeared if international resources were fully used and everyone had work.[55]

Above all, the White Paper reflected the Australian approach to the world economy. Multilateral trade, as defined by the Americans, was potentially harmful, given Australia's dependence on exports of food and raw materials which were subject to wide fluctuations in demand and price. The governor of the Commonwealth Bank concluded that Australians were 'justified in claiming a greater degree of protection in safeguarding our balance of payments'. The Australian government proposed that any country could request an investigation of any member of the ITO who failed to maintain high employment and standards of living and, if the charge were upheld, to release the complainant from an obligation to keep markets open. This mistrust of the Americans was borne out during the conference at Geneva when Congress accepted the demands of American wool-growers for protection. Although Truman vetoed the bill, it indicated the fragility of congressional support for multilateralism.[56]

The Australian approach to full employment was directed at the Americans, but it was viewed with suspicion in London, for it would raise the price of raw materials and food. Even more alarming, under-developed countries pressed the argument on employment in ways that were unacceptable to the industrial economies. R. K. Nehru (Jawaharlal's cousin) argued that

> the obligation of countries with undeveloped economies to develop their resources could only be fulfilled by instruments such as developmental tariffs and quantitative controls, and by adequate safeguards. India was wedded to economic planning as opposed to free enterprise ... A developing country was ... likely to cause immediate unemployment in other countries in the industries it was developing ... Developed countries should be obliged to make reasonable adjustments in their own industries.[57]

The British government could not accept that it should help Indian industrialization when it needed to increase its own exports. The Cubans pressed another line. Members of the ITO 'should be obliged to take every action against conditions detrimental to work-people, and towards raising their standard of living'. They should eliminate sweated labour which created 'unfair competition, not through efficiency, but through the exploitation of the working class; the members, therefore, should endeavour to establish a salary regime and general working conditions which would enable the workers to bear a dignified existence.'[58]

The under-developed countries were challenging American assumptions about the ITO and multilateralism. The Cubans complained that the ITO

> would be freezing the actual economic status of the different countries of the world. The agricultural countries would continue to be agricultural. The monopoly countries would continue to be monopolies, and the more developed countries would continue selling typewriters and radios, etc to those nations that were trying to produce the primitive tools.[59]

Carlos Lleras Restrepo of Colombia continued the criticism:

> For the United States, full employment is to be achieved by the expansion of world trade within a system of economic freedom. For us, the words 'full employment' have a special and quite different meaning. What, indeed, can

it mean to us that all our workers are employed, so long as they work in the least productive branches of economic life for wages ten times lower than those of other nations? And how can we ensure stability in this 'full employment' if we are limited to producing a commodity which is exposed, as coffee is, to such violent fluctuations of price and volume of consumption on the international market?

Full employment required reduction in price fluctuations, diversification of production, and an increase in manufacturing. In Restrepo's view, infant industries should be protected and 'a policy of trade freedom should be developed in harmony with the peculiar conditions prevailing in industrially backward countries.' Indeed, Claude Corea of Ceylon (now Sri Lanka) accused the developed world of hypocritically using protection for their own economic development and then imposing rules that would 'preserve the trade of manufacturing countries at the expense of the under-developed countries'.[60]

These claims alarmed developed countries. The British saw that the inclusion of employment and protection of infant industries might become a threat rather than a buffer against the United States.[61] The American delegation was willing to discuss employment to build support for an agreement on trade. But the issue escaped their control, for the sub-committee at the preparatory conference in London in 1946 included Australia, Brazil, Cuba and India as well as Britain and the United States. Its report made a strong case for a commitment to full employment and for the need of surplus countries – the United States – to bear the weight of adjustment.[62]

Drafting the employment clauses of the ITO Charter was therefore fraught with difficulties. The Americans secured the exact words of the Employment Act of 1946 with an emphasis on domestic measures rather than international action. But they did not entirely get their way, for each member agreed to develop its economic resources and raise production; and a country could adopt 'measures appropriate to its political and economic and social conditions'. The Latin Americans secured an obligation of countries to take whatever action was appropriate and feasible to eliminate substandard conditions of labour in production for export. A country should also take corrective action to deal with a fundamental disequilibrium in its balance of payments. The conflicting and inconsistent demands of the various approaches to employment came together in a statement of pious hope with few concrete proposals to manage the international economy.[63]

The debate over employment policies was connected to questions of economic development and distributive justice. In the initial talks in London and Geneva, representatives of the under-developed world demanded protection for infant industries, and quantitative restrictions and preferences between neighbouring states. They did not make much progress at Geneva, and the less developed countries criticized the draft of the Charter as 'heavily weighted in favour of the big commercial countries'. At Havana, more under-developed countries were present and the British delegates noted that '"development" became a rallying cry of the Conference and the justification for all kinds of amendments'.[64] One member of the American delegation was concerned that

> some people believe that the technology and capital of the United States is like a great big stockpile; that we have accumulated this stockpile at the expense and to the detriment of other countries; and that in any event we 'owe' a 'fair share' to other countries who are less developed than the United States; and that we can 'give' this to them by making it easy for them to restrict trade and otherwise damage the interests of other countries ...

On this view, the path to development was not through 'restrictive and nationalistic measures' or public loans by international agencies; it was through private enterprise and incentives to take risks.[65] The less developed world had different ideas.

During the initial discussions in London, Australia took the lead in arguing for measures to raise the volume of world trade by increasing the capacity of countries to buy each other's goods. In Coombs's view, the American proposals would '"fossilise" ... production and trade substantially in patterns which exist in the world at the present time ... [W]e feel there is an underlying assumption that the present distribution of production and therefore of trade is in some way natural and therefore based on the most efficient use of resources.' A more effective use of resources in the under-developed countries would increase world trade, just as happened when Europe and the USA followed Britain on the path of industrialization.[66]

At Geneva, the lead passed to India, which criticized the Proposals as 'too much directed to the preservation of the existing pre-eminence of the USA and UK in world trade. Instead a positive obligation should be placed on the more advanced countries to assist the development of the backward ones.' The Congress Party favoured planned economic development and industrialization with control over imports and exports to expand production and employment. The India Office – the responsible government department in London – doubted India's capacity to organize industrial expansion with complete control over the economy, and worried that economic development based on protected industries would result in high costs and low-quality goods. It therefore recommended opposition to protection of uncompetitive industries. The Indian delegates countered that the British had created an undeveloped and poverty-stricken economy, and it was time for change. Consequently, discussions should 'pay special attention to: (a) the maintenance and stability of incomes of primary producers, (b) the diversification of employment, and (c) industrial and economic development', with a right for countries to take action appropriate to their stage of development and to their social and political institutions.[67]

At Havana, the initiative passed to Latin America as 'the storm center of the conference; the source of many of the most difficult problems ... While we [the United States] were never particularly optimistic regarding probable Latin American behavior at Habana [sic], nonetheless their actual performance was initially shocking and has been continuously disappointing.' The Americans hoped to divide and rule, for the Latin American delegations were split between the extreme views of Argentina, Chile and Uruguay, and the more moderate views of Brazil, which presented itself a mediator with the United States. The Americans gambled that the appointment of Ramón Beteta, the finance minister of Mexico, as chairman of the committee on economic development would allow compromise. They were disappointed. Although the Latin Americans did not coalesce into a well-organized bloc to put forward a single position, they still caused annoyance through their 'preposterous' amendments that were 'long on objective and short, if not nonexistent, on practicability'. Concessions did not help, for they 'resulted in an appetite for more concessions and no bargain would stick if it appeared later to the seller that he could sell the same horse again'.[68]

Above all, the Latin Americans complained that Marshall Aid meant 'the fairy godmother of the North' was deserting them for Europe. The reaction, in the opinion of the Canadian representative at Havana, was their conversion to 'a form of international socialism in which the richer countries were under an obligation to the poorer countries to promote the economic development of these countries and to raise their standard of living up to that of the richer countries'.[69] Latin American industries that grew during the war faced European competition, which led to demands for quantitative restrictions and preferences to encourage economic integration and import-substituting industrialization.[70] The government of Juan Perón in Argentina was particularly problematic. Perón embarked on a five-year plan to increase wages, achieve full employment, improve social welfare, develop industry, reduce dependence on exports, and nationalize foreign-owned assets. To pay for these expensive policies, the Institute for the Promotion of Trade would purchase commodities from the agrarian elite to sell overseas at a large profit. By investing the proceeds in state-sponsored economic development and welfare it was hoped to boost the domestic market. The policy brought Argentina close to economic collapse by 1947.[71] Diego Luis Molinari, the leader of the Argentinian delegation, attended the conference in Havana with the aim of wrecking it. The choice, as he saw it, was between capitalism (represented by the ITO), totalitarianism (as in the Soviet Union), or a socialized economy as in Argentina.[72]

The Latin American approach was captured by the Venezuelan delegation:

> The equality embodied in the Charter must not be of the nineteenth-century type, which actually established disequality by making it impossible ... for Latin American Countries to develop new economies. During that period they had furnished raw materials and had been a dumping ground for finished products. This had now been substituted by the just idea of economic interdependence for the welfare of all.[73]

As one American official commented, 'the real trouble is probably that they (Latinos) are looking for a hand-out and that we are planning to give them only soft-soap. It is my tentative opinion that we should at least change the brand of soap.'[74]

A major issue was the use of quantitative restrictions (QRs) – non-tariff barriers to limit imports and foster economic development. Wilcox feared they were like a powerful drug that produced a 'superficial appearance of animation' when what was needed was a proper diet and exercise.[75] The Americans eventually compromised on QRs and on Latin American demands for new preferences, provided they were within the same economic region and were needed for development. There was an obvious inequity in permitting new preferences that might harm British exports, and at the same time obliging Britain to remove its own preferences. The difficulty was resolved by defining an economic region by integration as well as proximity – so preserving British imperial preferences. Members of free trade areas and customs unions were exempted from extending most favoured nation treatment to other countries – a provision that was needed so that they could offer preferences to each other. The concession was required to cover the possibility of a European customs union, as well as a possible free trade area between the United States and Canada.[76]

Overseas investment led to further difficulties. The less developed countries argued that advanced economies had an obligation to provide capital for development without threatening their sovereignty, and that profits from natural resources should go to the nation concerned and not to foreigners. American businesses feared that their investments would be threatened without adequate compensation. The American delegation saw little point in inserting safeguards which could not be enforced and would make the ITO appear to support imperialistic monopoly capitalism. What made political sense in Havana again appeared as weakness at home in failing to protect American investment.[77]

At Havana, a rift opened between different economic ideologies and modes of governing the global economy. In Wilcox's view, 'Human liberty was dependent upon economic freedom ... We in the US ... do not want to go in for statism. We will fight as long as we can to preserve in the US a free economy.'[78] Despite the Good Neighbor policy, many in Latin America thought that economic freedom meant American exploitation. Many Latin American delegations arrived in Havana 'honestly believing that the Charter is deliberately designed to serve the interests of the United States and to damage the legitimate aspirations of the Latin American countries'. In Mexico City, articles of the Charter were read out to a mass meeting, where the speaker 'demanded of the mob whether Mexico were to be enslaved by such provisions, being reassured, with a great roar, in the negative'.[79] The Mexican Chamber of Manufacturing denounced the Charter as 'a document leading to the perpetuation of a world economic status quo, with colonial and noncolonial imperialist countries. Its significance is that of a document in which colonial countries are compromised by not using these measures which are necessary to break precisely this economic state.'[80] The American delegation at Havana was in a difficult position, for the conference would be followed by the Inter-American Economic Conference at Bogotá where the issues would be reopened. A balance had to be struck between taking a firm stand in Havana and not alienating the Latin Americans before they met at Bogotá.[81] What looked like shrewd tactics in Havana could look like weakness in Washington.

THE SUCCESS OF GATT AND THE FAILURE OF THE ITO

The Charter of the ITO was signed in Havana on 24 March 1948. Will Clayton was delighted. Each signatory

> will surrender some part of its freedom to take action that might prove harmful to others and thus each will gain the assurance that others will not take action harmful to it. This may well prove to be the greatest step in history toward order and justice in economic relations among the members of

the world community and toward a great expansion in the production, distribution, and consumption of goods throughout the world.[82]

He was far too optimistic. The concessions made at Havana to secure an agreement were not acceptable on Capitol Hill – and the international economic and geopolitical context had changed since the Proposals were first issued in December 1945.

The Charter seemed to the British government to be a risky venture – and Wilcox suspected that they were hypocritically paying lip service to multilateral trade while 'seeking to destroy' the ITO. Wilson and Cripps felt that the Havana conference 'has not on the whole gone well for us' as a result 'of a tendency on the part of the United States to appease countries other than ourselves – they had appeased us fairly extensively at an earlier stage – by making concessions contrary to both American and UK interests'.[83] The British reluctantly agreed to the Charter to avoid blame for failure and to prevent a return to isolationism on the part of the United States. In fact, the Havana compromise was more favourable to the British than might have been expected. Britain preserved imperial preferences and accepted that the ITO was

> a focus for energies working in favour of a restoration of multi-lateral trade in a world which increasingly conducts its trade on a principle of bilateral barter. It is important that such a focus should exist, particularly from the point of view of this country which cannot hope to recover viability at a tolerable standard of living without a restoration of the triangular flow of trade.[84]

But before Britain and other countries could ratify the Charter and create the ITO, the United States had to act – and that was not likely to happen.

The American delegation in Havana realized that there was little prospect of ratification in the current session of Congress, where the priority was to renew the RTAA. Wilcox saw political dangers: discussion of the RTAA might lead to consideration of GATT, which would in turn lead to discussion of the Charter, 'without any opportunity for favorable or friendly presentation', by 'the most hostile and violently prejudiced forum in either house of Congress, the Committee on Ways and Means'.[85] Intensification of the Cold War meant it was easier to sell Marshall Aid on Capitol Hill as a response to Communism than to press ahead with the ITO. In London, Otto Clarke saw that attitudes in Washington had changed by early 1948:

> The concept of world economy which lay behind IMF, the Loan Agreement, and ITO now carries increasingly little weight or respect in Washington.

> The new [European Recovery Programme] and pseudo-strategic concepts
> are in the saddle; the Americans who count are now thinking in terms of
> creating stable economic systems in Western Europe and elsewhere rather
> than in terms of non-discrimination theology. The US delegation at Havana
> is a last remnant of the old ideas.

Wilcox's endeavours in Havana had been overtaken by new priorities in
Washington.[86]

The advocates of the ITO did not give up without a fight. Clayton
hoped that Truman's re-election in November 1948 and Democratic control of Congress provided an opportunity. He mounted a campaign to
secure ratification of the Charter, without which 'there will be no restraint
on the unbridled practice of all kinds of nationalistic devices ... [T]he
world will soon become a kind of economic jungle with every fellow for
himself and the devil take the hindmost.'[87] His attempt failed. Few businessmen were willing to join his campaign. Many feared that the Charter
'reflects the economic philosophy of socialistic countries far better than
our own', threatening 'our private, free enterprise system' by 'an international hot bed of state socialism, monopolies, cartels, and free trade
fanaticism', leading to international bureaucracy and planning, and a loss
of sovereignty and prosperity. Rather than open trade, they expected that
the 'full employment dogma' would lead to unsupportable state debt,
inflexible costs, 'socialistic nationalism', and the demise of the free market.
Supporters of the Charter suspected these claims were a cover for protectionism and argued that the Charter was the best that could be achieved in
preserving 'economic liberalism in the international realm, adapted to
present-day conditions', and that failure would be a gift to the Soviets. The
more that supporters of the ITO argued that it was a liberal, capitalistic
measure for domestic consumption, the less appealing it was in many other
parts of the world which favoured planning or socialism.[88]

Truman had not completely abandoned the ITO and he transmitted
the Charter to Congress in April 1949 as a 'practical, realistic method for
progressive action toward the goal of expanding world trade'. Although
it was not ratified on this occasion, the president still presented the Charter in his State of the Union address of January 1950 as a way of preventing
a return to the 'anarchy and irresponsibility in world trade' of the 1930s.[89]
But attitudes had changed, and free trade multilateralism and the ITO no
longer offered peace as promised by Cordell Hull. Instead, Dean Acheson,
Secretary of State from January 1949 to January 1953, linked foreign economic policy with national security. A State Department official recalled
that 'Acheson's main preoccupation in those days was ... not really with

the long-term beautiful world envisaged in the ITO Charter. It was in the immediate world that faced him on getting dough out of the Congress for the Marshall plan, and getting the Marshall plan going, and European recovery, and the Atlantic Alliance.' Acheson's approach to foreign economic policy was 'broader, more comprehensive, and not so exclusively concentrated upon trade as the end-all and be-all of foreign economic policy'.[90] In December 1950, Truman realized that submitting the Charter for ratification would lead to pointless arguments, to the detriment of American foreign policy. He decided not to proceed and a press release from the meeting of GATT in the improbable location of Torquay mentioned, as an aside, that the Charter would not be re-submitted to Congress.[91] It was an anti-climactic end to a project on which so much time and effort had been spent.

The new order was set out in National Security Council paper NSC-68 of April 1950 – a vision of a world that was divided into two blocs with two ambitions. On one side, the United States wished to 'maintain the essential elements of individual freedom' that leads to 'the marvelous diversity, the deep tolerance, the lawfulness of the free society'. On the other side was the Soviet Union, 'animated by a new fanatic faith, antithetical to our own' which 'seeks to impose its absolute authority over the rest of the world' by subverting government and society in the non-Soviet world and replacing them 'by an apparatus and structure subservient to and controlled from the Kremlin'. The task was to create 'a world environment in which the American system can survive and flourish', for '[n]o other value system is so wholly irreconcilable with ours, so implacable in its purpose to destroy ours'. The aim was to combine a 'healthy international community' and containment of Soviet power through superior power with space for negotiation, and without directly challenging Soviet prestige so that they could retreat without a loss of face. Acheson pointed out that 'Wilsonian liberalism and a utopian dream' of 'classical economic goals' were not practical in the circumstances of the Cold War. Consequently, greater importance was given to stimulating European recovery and to the strategic policy of the North Atlantic Treaty Organization (NATO).[92]

More immediately, the tariff cuts negotiated at Geneva in the GATT needed to be accepted and the bargaining authority of the RTAA renewed, which were more important to Truman and the State Department than the ITO Charter. In the United States, GATT and the Charter were caught between two, fundamentally opposed, criticisms. The 'perfectionists' complained that the American delegation had abandoned free trade to the demands of the Europeans and less developed countries. The 'protectionists' believed the opposite, that the Charter had pursued free trade to the

detriment of American farmers and industrialists. The American negotiators realized that their tariff concessions were the minimum that could
achieve agreement from other countries; they were also aware that the
concessions would provoke 'vociferous political protests from many well
organized and powerful special interests'.[93] The result was a backlash
against renewal of the RTAA and acceptance of GATT.

The Republicans controlled the Senate from 1947 to 1949, which gave
more voice to protectionists who were – as one Congressman put it – 'for
America first, last and always'. They resisted the tariff cuts at least until
an investigation by the Tariff Commission. Senior Republicans such as
Senator Vandenberg, chair of the Foreign Relations Committee, and Senator Eugene Millikin of Colorado, the chair of the Finance Committee,
did not agree with a Hull-ite vision of free-trade multilateralism and were
concerned about the impact of lower tariffs on American producers.
Nevertheless, they supported moderate internationalism. In February
1947, they suspended their opposition to GATT on condition that it contained an 'escape clause' allowing the withdrawal of any concession if the
Tariff Commission found it to be harmful to industry. Truman had to
concede for GATT to proceed.[94]

In March 1948, Truman requested an extension of the RTAA for three
years but was only granted one year, with greater power for the Tariff
Commission to review tariffs and to set 'peril points' below which tariffs
could be reduced only in exceptional circumstances. The support of
Southern Democrats was vital for its renewal even in this truncated form.
Lyndon Johnson, a Representative from Texas, rallied Southern Democrats by pointing out that the RTAA was 'not pleasing to rich northern
and eastern industrialists. They wanted to bring back the high tariffs
which keep the South in a state of economic dependency.'[95] Truman could
not veto the bill, as powers under the RTAA would lapse. Instead, he
focused on Marshall Aid and made it clear that he would reject Republican protectionism and strengthen the RTAA if re-elected. In 1949, he
secured renewal of the RTAA for three years and removed the peril
points – only for them to return at the next renewal. Hull-ite free trade
was constrained and the Republicans secured some Democrat support.
Lyndon Johnson now urged caution: 'the time has come to stop, look and
listen before making further concessions because trade barriers in the
countries with which we trade have been growing and growing.' Senator
John F. Kennedy of Massachusetts agreed that free trade was only feasible
if domestic industries were secure.[96]

The RTAA allowed a balance between domestic welfare and internationalism by reducing tariffs, on condition that employment at home

was not threatened. GATT, like the IMF, established rules that prevented free riding and beggar-my-neighbour policies, without pursuing multilateralism at the cost of domestic welfare. The risk, as far as other countries were concerned, was that they were making tariff concessions only for America to revert to protection. A Bank of England official warned that

> The real significance of the Vandenberg–Millikin escape clause is that the Americans have now abandoned the whole concept of a radical adjustment of their economy – which certainly could not be achieved without some industries suffering in the process. Meanwhile, we are in danger of finding ourselves bound to the concessions which were to be the contributions on our side.[97]

The ITO had proved to be a 'grand fantasy' that faded in the harsh light of post-war realities.[98] In retrospect, Winthrop Brown was not sorry. The ITO

> eventually floundered because our Congress wouldn't touch it with a ten-foot pole. And in my opinion, looking back on it, I think that was a hell of a good idea because the ITO would have been a mess. It would have been a futile thing . . . [W]e're a heck of a lot better off with the GATT organization than we would have been with an ITO. The GATT organization is very small and it is very practical, and a good place for resolving disputes and making complaints.[99]

The limited scope of GATT was more palatable to Congress and to business. It did not have an executive board and was only informally connected with the UN and ECOSOC. It was merely an arrangement between contracting parties who would meet to discuss trade on an ad hoc basis, with the aim of reaching agreement by consensus. Its secretariat was small and poorly funded. Its first executive secretary, Eric Wyndham White – a British lawyer who worked in the Ministry of Economic Warfare before joining the United Nations – was a skilled mediator. He had close contact with leading trade officials that helped him build coalitions; and he thrived on breaking deadlocks in negotiations. He was committed to liberal internationalism but was careful not to encroach on national sovereignty or to be subservient to the United States. GATT created a system of rules and norms, without the wider ambitions of the ITO – a limited and practical achievement, though always with the criticism that it was an exclusive body committed to one view of the world order.[100] It complemented NATO and the Organization for European Economic Co-operation that ran the Marshall Plan in consolidating a bloc of non-Communist market economies.

Commercial policy was connected with strategic policy. The Korean

War created a new urgency in enhancing 'the security of the United States as part of a free world' and, in 1950, Truman requested Gordon Gray, the former Secretary of the Army, to report on foreign economic policy. Gray stressed, and Truman endorsed, the 'unity of foreign policy in its economic, political, military, and informational aspects'. Gray pointed out that

> The objective of our foreign economic policy has been and is to encourage among the nations of the free world those economic conditions and relationships essential for the development of stable democratic societies willing and able to defend themselves and raise the living standards of their peoples . . . Neither we nor they can live alone or defend ourselves alone.

In 1952, Truman expressed concern that protectionist views in the United States undermined his attempt to 'build up the military and economic strength of friends and allies throughout the free world'.[101] To Hull, trade policy was a means to prevent war; now, it was part of the strategy of the Cold War, with GATT a means of bolstering capitalist democracies against Communism.

The United States – despite some concern from Britain and France – pressed that the occupied territories of West Germany, Japan and South Korea should join GATT to link them with the Western alliance. In the words of a leading historian of GATT, it was 'redefined as a forum of the western alliance' and became 'a partisan body that worked to defeat communism as an economic doctrine', with trade liberalization 'emphasizing security and survival rather than peace and stability'. GATT was a Western-dominated body for democratic capitalism and markets into which Western allies were admitted and from which Communist powers were excluded. It was not possible to expel Czechoslovakia, which signed GATT in 1947 prior to the Communist Party takeover in 1948, but the United States did revoke its tariff benefits and cut trade links. The Americans also allowed the Nationalists in Taiwan to withdraw China from GATT in 1950 – a decision contested by the Communist regime in Beijing, which nevertheless opted not to send representatives. In the late 1950s, the Communist countries of Poland, Romania, Hungary and Yugoslavia applied to join GATT. Wyndham White was aware of challenges to GATT as a club of rich capitalists and of its failure to deal with relations between market and state trading economies. Wider membership could counter such criticism and potentially weaken the Soviet bloc. The secretariat decided, on its own authority, to grant observer status to Poland and Romania, and Wyndham White even favoured full membership for Poland to foster 'greater independence of the Soviet Union and . . . new ties with the West'. The British and American governments were not convinced. The compromise was to create a new status of 'associate state' that gave access to discussions without commercial privileges – an attempt to balance the competing strategies of containment and engagement. In 1958, the balance shifted to containment when Hungary's application for observer status was rejected. Membership was used as a reward for countries willing to work with the Western alliance or at least to weaken their ties with the Soviet Union.[102]

The talks that dragged on from 1946 to 1948 had not created an International Trade Organization. Nevertheless, they were not a complete failure. GATT was important in creating 'a reference point about the direction in which trade policies should be headed', preventing a drift into higher tariffs and economic nationalism in response to the post-war problems.[103] Tariffs fell from the peak of 1931, with the exception of Britain (see Figure 2). The discussions showed that the American administration was committed to the leadership of the world economy to prevent a return to instability and economic warfare by creating a rules-based global order. Of course, the international institutions and embedded liberalism had limitations. The wider ambitions of the ITO for employment and distributive justice in the world economy were narrowed to GATT's concern for tariffs, to the IMF's concern for exchange rates, and to the IBRD's limited agenda for projects that paid their way. Nevertheless, the larger normative questions did not disappear, for less developed nations started to express their concerns and develop their agenda for the government of the world economy in the context of decolonization and the Cold War.

By 1947, it was also clear that the restoration of convertibility and multilateralism was threatened by economic crisis in Europe. By the time that GATT was agreed, it was apparent that the major issue was not the level of tariffs but the inability of European economies to restore multilateral trade because of their lack of hard currency and severe deficits on their balance of trade. At the same time, the United States had a large trade surplus, which led to a 'dollar gap': other countries had to pay for

Figure 2: Average tariff levels, %

	1925	1931	1952
France	9	38	19
Germany	15	40	16
UK	4	17	17
US	26	35	9

Sources: Douglas Irwin, 'The GATT's contribution to economic recovery in post-war western Europe', NBER Working Paper 4944 (1994), 31. GATT, 'International trade' Geneva (1952), 62.

goods in scarce hard currency, limiting trade and pulling liquidity out of the world economy. American policy now turned away from the unquestioning pursuit of multilateralism and convertibility after an unrealistically short transitional period. By 1947, it was generally accepted in Washington that reducing tariffs and establishing parities for currencies would not be sufficient to restore multilateral trade and permit economic recovery. Rather, American assistance in the form of Marshall Aid was needed for the recovery of European economies. Even more important, the German economy needed to be restored as a driving force in Europe, and financial liquidity was needed to allow a shift from bilateral deals that continued to hamper European trade. The difficulty for the British government was that American support for European economic integration was a potential threat to the sterling area and to Britain's identity as a global power. The British government faced a crisis of economic identity. At the end of the war, sterling was the world's largest reserve currency and a major trading currency. The Labour government had to decide whether it should cling to the sterling area in a 'two-world' system alongside the dollar, throw in its lot with the dollar in a 'one world' system, or participate in the emerging European system of economic co-operation. The shape of the global economy remained in doubt.

There was also a growing realization in Washington that steps were needed to close the 'dollar gap' and deal with America's balance of payments surplus. Dean Acheson feared they were weakening attempts to bolster the free nations against Communism and might lead to 'a substantial shift of power from the democratic to the Soviet sphere'.[104] In 1952, Truman appointed a working group to review economic foreign policy and to reflect on 'what equilibrating forces are expected to operate so as to prevent persistent surpluses and deficits'.[105] His presidential successor, Eisenhower, continued the same line and appointed Clarence B. Randall to chair the Commission on Foreign Economic Policy. In March 1954, Eisenhower's message to Congress accepted Randall's conclusion that the 'dollar gap' forced other countries to impose trade restrictions and that it should be closed not by dollar grants but by 'a higher level of two-way trade' that would create prosperity for American exporters and improve security against Communism. 'Beyond our economic interest, the solidarity of the free world and the capacity of the free world to deal with those who would destroy it are threatened by continued unbalanced trade relationships – the inability of nations to sell as much as they desire to buy.'[106] The restoration of multilateral trade and convertibility was taking much longer than anticipated in 1944 and required different policies.

Secretary of State Dean Acheson (*left*) and Economic Cooperation Administrator
Paul Hoffman (*centre*) present to George Marshall a large bound report on the
operation of the Marshall Plan on its second anniversary, 3 April 1950.

I I

'Convertible currencies in the free world'

Sterling and Europe

'... the creation of the conditions of free multilateral trade and investment and convertible currencies in the free world is a much more difficult task than was supposed immediately after the war. The belief that these conditions would be restored more or less automatically, or by simple agreement among sovereign governments, as soon as production had recovered from the war, is waning. In its place is a growing conviction that we must first help to overcome the problems of those members of the peaceful trading community who cannot now participate in a fully multilateral, convertible system. In Europe the obvious solution is a closer unification of the national economies through the development of supranational institutions and a harmonization of economic policies.'

'Statement on dollar shortage' by staff of the Economic
Cooperation Administration, 9 June 1950[1]

At Bretton Woods, the restoration of convertibility of currencies and a return of multilateral trade were expected after a brief transition. The hope was misplaced, and in 1949 Robert Hall – director of the Economic Section of the Cabinet Office – pointed out that 'we are trying to start from a position which no one expected we would dream of starting from'.[2] The economies of Europe were devastated and had difficulties in purchasing goods needed for survival and recovery. By contrast, the United States had a massive trade surplus. The result was a 'dollar gap': a persistent balance of payments deficit between Europe (including Britain) and the United States, whose surplus meant that it accumulated foreign exchange reserves and reduced global liquidity. The restoration of multilateral trade and escape from bilateralism were constrained. The solution was the Marshall Plan, a restoration of the German economy and its integration into the European economy, and the creation of the European

Payments Union (EPU) – a clearing system between European countries that economized on foreign currency and contributed to the restoration of intra-European trade. These initiatives marked the demise of the impractical approach to the restoration of convertibility at Bretton Woods and of the destructive proposals of the Morgenthau plan to de-industrialize Germany.

Britain had particular difficulties. In 1947, the IMF calculated that the dollar accounted for a little over 10 per cent of foreign exchange reserves; by contrast, sterling accounted for 87 per cent, largely the result of blocked balances for payment for goods accumulated during the war.[3] Despite the large holdings of sterling by other countries, Britain's own reserves were modest so it was vulnerable to external pressure. The relationship between the dollar, the sterling area and the EPU raised questions for the British government about its economic policy and national identity: was it a European, imperial or global power? Not only did the British economy differ from its continental neighbours in the international role of sterling, but also in its trade pattern. In 1922, the two-way trade between Britain and the empire and Dominions was 1.08 times trade with Europe; it rose to 1.32 in 1933 and 2.04 in 1948.[4] The British government faced a real dilemma in deciding how to react to European integration, for its economic interests and problems were different.

The American administration had to devise policies to sustain or manage the decline of one of the world's major international currencies, and it had to abandon its unrealistic assumptions by adopting a more active role in European recovery. The Marshall Plan and the EPU were steps towards European integration that led to the Treaty of Rome in 1957 and the creation of the European Economic Community in 1958, in tandem with the return to convertibility. The risk was that the integration of European economies might lead to an inward-looking economic bloc or rival to the United States, rather than to the restoration of multilateral trade.

BRITAIN AND THE STERLING BALANCES

After the war, Keynes saw two problems: Britain's ability to increase its exports, and 'America's capacity to accept goods and services from the rest of the world on a scale adequate to secure a reasonable equilibrium in her overall balance of payments'. Opinion was divided on both issues. Keynes thought the dollar gap would not continue, for wages in the United States were already two and a half times higher than in Britain and were rising more rapidly. 'The United States is becoming a high-living, high-cost country beyond any previous experience ... they will discover ways of life which, compared with the ways of the less fortunate regions of the world, must tend towards, and not away from, external equilibrium.'[5] But it was not enough to wait for the United States to become a high-cost, high-consumption country with open markets. Britain needed to become more efficient to penetrate American markets, or at least sell goods to the sterling area which had a dollar surplus. Others were sceptical. Thomas Balogh, an Oxford economist, doubted that United States imports would increase in line with income. Rather, its large domestic market and low-cost mass production provided a basis for exports and made it difficult for other countries to move into new areas of production. In his view, 'the dollar "shortage" might well prove to be a recurrent phenomenon involving a continued deterioration of (at least the relative) standard of life of countries other than the US.' Such pessimistic assessments of Britain's ability to compete led many to turn to a 'two-world' system, with the sterling area and Commonwealth providing a market for British goods and a source of raw materials. The limited capacity of the sterling area and colonies to meet these expectations led others to call for a one-world policy in which Britain was part of a competitive, dynamic, multilateral world order.[6]

The treatment of sterling balances had been part of the discussion with the United States on the post-war loan. There were several possible approaches. If sterling became convertible (as required by the American loan), a rush to change pounds into dollars would lead to pressure on the exchange rate and to devaluation. British exports would be more competitive, but imports would cost more and holders of sterling would, in effect, suffer partial default from a loss in the value of their balances. Another possibility was to 'unblock' sterling balances without allowing convertibility into other currencies, so that holders would use their money to buy British goods. The problem was that British exports would shift from markets that provided desperately needed foreign earnings. Another option was to 'fund' the blocked sterling balances by turning them into loans with an annual interest payment and gradual redemption. This approach had a serious shortcoming: holders of sterling wanted to spend the accumulated balances on economic development rather than receive a flow of income over many years. Many Indians, for example, believed that British rule had prevented economic development in the past and they now wished to push ahead with investment in growth. They were even less likely to accept another approach – writing down sterling balances as a tax on wartime profits or a retrospective contribution to the British war effort.[7]

A frequent complaint in Washington was that India should have provided goods on the same footing as Lend Lease. The Government of India did not agree: commodities were sold in good faith on the promise of payment, and, unlike the United States, it was a poor country which suffered hardship and famine during the war. Despite some advocates of a tough line with India, in 1945 the British government saw that

> Our sterling obligations ... are part of our war effort and are owed almost entirely to poor countries. American opinion would have professed high indignation if, for example, we had encumbered the national development of India for years by compelling the Indian Government to finance a much larger part of the war effort against the Germans in Africa and the Japanese by increasing still more their internal indebtedness.[8]

Of course, not everyone in London was sympathetic. In his history of the Second World War, Churchill made the startling claim that 'the peoples of Hindustan ... were carried through the struggle on the shoulders of our small island'.[9] He was not alone. In 1946, one official complained that the colonies were treated as 'favoured children', and that 'we must stand up for the oppressed taxpayer in this country, who has regularly contributed, e.g. to the relief of hurricane damage and similar calamities all over the Colonial Empire as need arose. This time we have had the hurricane.' But it was neither equitable nor practical politics to cancel or reduce sterling balances, which would provoke unrest and require more troops to maintain order.[10]

Nehru suspected that the 'honourable intention' to repay promised at Bretton Woods was being broken, and argued that the sterling balances represented 'the hunger, famine, epidemics, emasculation, weakened resistance, stunted growth, and death by starvation and disease of vast numbers of human beings in India'.[11] As James Meade realized, treatment of the sterling balances was crucial to an orderly retreat from the Raj:

> the political settlement with India was of overriding importance. India's sterling balances were the largest and the crucial test. And would we have got and maintained a political settlement with India if at that very moment we had said to her: 'For years you have been in debt to us and now you have paid up: our political control of you ensured that. Now the wheel of fortune has turned full circle: we are indebted to you. It is true that you are poor and we are rich and that you need our funds for your economic development. But I am afraid that we are not going to pay up'?[12]

In 1949, the Treasury's working party on sterling balances pointed out that 'India suffered privation by way of famine and inflation and the repayment of the sterling balances would not involve more than a relatively small sacrifice on the UK's part, having regard to the disparity in the standard of living of the two countries.'[13] The outcome was debt reduction by stealth – paying lower than market interest, selling gold in India above the market rate, reaching a favourable deal on the pension liabilities of British officials, and, above all, devaluation in 1949. The remaining balances were gradually run down over the next twenty years.[14]

The American administration came to realize that the sterling balances placed Britain in a difficult situation that limited its ability to support American policies for European integration, stability in the Near and Middle East, resistance to Communism in the Far East, and promotion of multilateral trade. Despite criticism of British policies that favoured welfare and controls rather than a free market, there was also a realization that Britain had economic problems and international commitments.[15] The British government hoped to secure support for the gradual reduction of sterling balances in the context of the Cold War by repurposing the sterling area against Communism. At the Colombo conference of Commonwealth foreign ministers in January 1950, Ernest Bevin argued that resistance to Soviet ambitions in western Europe meant that the Communists turned to the east. Rather than a formal pact on the lines of NATO,

> The right policy was for like-minded countries with interests in the East to keep in close contact and to be ready to help each other in resisting any attempt to hinder peaceful development on democratic lines. I stressed the close interdependence of East and West and the great need for the expansion of capital development and food production in less-developed countries, and said I hoped that a policy of financial help without domination could be adopted towards those countries.

The aim was to improve the standard of living of South and South-East Asia to counter 'the menace of Communism'. The United States was unlikely to offer more aid for Britain's domestic economy; aid to Asia might appeal as a way of resisting Communism. Sterling balances were, it was admitted, not entirely coterminous with Communism in South-East Asia, for sterling was held in some countries (such as Egypt) that were outside the sterling area, and some countries in South-East Asia were threatened by Communism without holding sterling (such as Burma and Indonesia). But the two problems coincided in Malaya, which was threatened by a Communist insurgency as well as being the largest dollar earner in the empire.[16]

The American response was not enthusiastic. William Diebold, an economist at the Council on Foreign Relations, was cautiously supportive; he saw that the alternative strategy of repudiating debts would undermine British and American influence, and that funding would prevent the use of sterling balances for development. However, most officials at the State Department were wary of combining the problem of sterling balances with development in South and South-East Asia. The Colombo plan was viewed as a device to avoid effective action on British economic recovery and a means of securing more aid.[17] Nevertheless, the Colombo Plan for Co-operative Economic Development was launched by the Commonwealth in 1951 to show the people of Asia 'that their true interests are best served by continued association with the free world', and to impress on 'the United States Administration and public the urgent necessity for economic assistance to this area'. At the Commonwealth Economic Conference of 1952, the British government pledged 'a special effort to provide additional capital for Commonwealth development by facilitating the financing of schemes in other Commonwealth countries which would contribute to the improvement of the sterling area's balance of payments'. The initial members – Australia, Canada, Ceylon, India, New Zealand, Pakistan and Britain – were soon joined by others and extended beyond the Commonwealth in the belief that improved living standards would create political stability and counter Communism. There was, however, little appetite for British proposals to reinvigorate imperial preference. The Commonwealth was more interested in restoring an open international economy than reliance on British exports of doubtful quality with limited access to capital.[18]

Convertibility of sterling was required by 15 July 1947 as a condition of the American loan, as we have seen in Chapter 9. The government anticipated difficulties as holders of sterling rushed to switch to dollars and urged delay, warning that convertibility would have dire consequences:

Either we are forced into import restrictions on a scale which would make it impossible for us to provide for our people even their present threadbare standards, or we are compelled to abandon the whole concept of multilateral trading and seek to eke out a painful existence on the best terms of bilateral trade which we can secure.

The British government realized that American policies of trade liberalism and convertibility were 'mutually contradictory and ... will remain so as long as the dollar is a scarce currency'. The plea went unheeded, with predictable results. Sterling was converted into dollars, British foreign exchange reserves were exhausted, and convertibility was suspended on 20 August 1947. The Americans had ignored reality with the risk that Britain might reduce its imports, withdraw troops from Germany and retreat from a leading role in the economic integration of Europe. The American ambassador observed that

> if we are to be successful in Western Europe, we cannot afford to permit the British position so to deteriorate that her moral stature will be reduced to a low level. If some relief is feasible, it should not, I think, be of a nature or an amount which will permit Britain to avoid grappling in earnest with some of her problems.

A balance had to be struck between encouraging Britain to stand on its own feet and ensuring that it did not abandon multilateralism and withdraw from military commitments. The wider strategic context meant that 'in interest of overall recovery, we are and will continue to do utmost to keep Britain afloat but it is clear she must stop biting our hand'.[19]

The exchange rate for the pound was clearly out of alignment with the dollar. Both the United States administration and IMF saw that devaluation was needed as part of a general realignment of European currencies and as an indication that Britain was moving from discrimination towards 'the one world conception of trade and finance policies'. This one-world approach was supported by Otto Clarke, considered to be 'the most notoriously temperamental man in the Treasury' and who held ministers and colleagues 'in high disesteem'.[20] He pressed for urgent action after the war 'to mould the economic structure so that it will stand in the post-war world' by competing within a 'one world' economy rather than turning inwards to the sterling area and imperial preference. 'One world' would require the Americans to make a generous deal on Lend Lease, and allow some restrictions to help Britain's balance of payments; it should also reduce its own tariffs and pursue full employment. In return, Britain should make sterling convertible for current transactions as soon as possible, free some of the sterling balances, and end discrimination against the United States. The two countries should therefore work together – and by 1949, his advocacy of a 'one world' policy led him to propose an Atlantic Economic Committee of Ministers to synchronize policy, or even 'complete union between the United States and the British Commonwealth'. To Clarke the 'two-world' approach of a dollar and sterling area would be a 'paupers' alliance'. '[A] "little England" policy in which we abandoned all forms of international leadership ... and cultivated our own garden with the objective of becoming a rather bigger Belgium or Sweden seems to me politically out of the question and economically extremely dubious.'[21]

Supporters of devaluation argued that tough measures to restore

competitiveness would not be politically acceptable to a Labour government committed to creating a welfare state and a more equal society, so
that devaluation was a necessary first step to deal with the crisis. Stafford Cripps, Chancellor of the Exchequer from 1947 to 1950, did not
agree. He was sceptical that the price mechanism would solve Britain's
problems by making exports more competitive, and favoured planning
and direct controls with large cuts in dollar spending. On his view,
devaluation was a short-term solution before wage demands and price
increases eroded any benefit and forced a return to controls – so why
not adopt controls at the outset rather than devalue? He urged a 'two-
worlds' approach of 'international state planning' and discrimination
between the dollar and non-dollar worlds. Devaluation was also rejected
by officials who realized that it might be an easy option that avoided
tough action against inflationary pressures caused by excessive public
spending, over-full employment and lack of incentives. The Cabinet
naturally rejected criticism that the balance of payments problem was
caused by their public spending and maintained that 'more would be
gained by adhering firmly to the political principles to which the Government were committed than by subordinating United Kingdom policy
to American economic theories'. Bevin also rejected devaluation, and
saw the solution as a more constructive approach to European recovery.
For these varied reasons, the Cabinet was reluctant to devalue – a decision that puzzled Robert Hall, who likened it to the decision in the
1920s to maintain fixed rates on gold. Eventually, the worsening deficit
and a realistic assessment of the difficulties of maintaining the rate
meant that the pound was devalued on 18 September 1949 by 30 per
cent, from $4.03 to $2.80.[22]

Britain's failure to consult other European countries – and particularly France – was criticized by Secretary of State Acheson as a setback
to European economic co-operation. It was also clear that realignment
of currencies and convertibility alone would not restore trade and multilateralism. More importantly, it was necessary to stimulate multilateral
trade within Europe by encouraging economic integration and facilitating payments between countries.[23] It was obvious, too, that European
economic recovery was not possible without the restoration of its largest single economy – Germany. This objective entailed a shift in American
policy and in European concerns that the continent might again be dominated by a militaristic economic power that threatened peace and
stability.

GERMAN RECOVERY

The replacement of JCS1067 by JCS1779 in 1947 (see Chapter 10) helped German recovery, but even more important were the currency and financial reforms of 1948. During the war, the Nazi regime did not remove the 'inflationary gap' between spending and available goods, and this inflationary pressure was exacerbated by increased monetary circulation arising from the sale of government bonds to banks. The response was rationing and controls which led to hoarding and black markets. After the war, a decision was needed on how to respond and how to reach an equitable balance between different forms of debt and property, and between rich and poor. Ludwig Erhard, an economist at a research institute for manufacturing industries, had started to think about these issues during the war on the assumption that Germany would be defeated. He sent his ideas to Carl Goerdeler and other opponents of Hitler, and they were also taken up by Otto Ohlendorf, a leading Nazi and perpetrator of the Holocaust, who was appointed to the Economics Ministry in 1943 and started to plan for the post-war economy. He was executed in 1951 for crimes against humanity. After the war, Ludwig Erhard became an adviser to the American military administration in Bavaria, and in 1947 was appointed chairman of the commission to reform the currency and head of the special office for money and credit in the Bizone. His aim was to replace Nazi planning and state control with a free market, and his thinking on economic and financial recovery influenced the Homburg plan, produced by German experts in April 1948. This plan proposed the conversion of existing Reichsmarks into new marks at a ratio of 10 to 1, most of which would be 'blocked' or non-convertible to prevent inflation; and 80 per cent of the Reich debt would be cancelled.

Currency reform was also proposed by the Detroit banker Joseph Dodge and the American economists Gerhard Colm and Raymond Goldsmith, both émigré Germans who had experienced hyperinflation in the Weimar Republic. 'A Plan for the Liquidation of War Finance and the Financial Rehabilitation of Germany' of May 1946 differed from the Homburg plan in proposing that the Reich debt be cancelled in full, as the liability of a criminal regime, and that currency would not be 'blocked', on the grounds that 'constant pressure for deblocking' would create uncertainty and inflation. The Colm–Goldsmith–Dodge Plan aimed to spread burdens in an equitable way by a mortgage of 50 per cent on real assets to create a fund for the equalization of war losses (*Lastenausgleich*), and a capital levy on gains by the largest owners of wealth between 1935 and 1945. Taxation of wealth and the capital levy alarmed the US War Department, and they were left to a decision by a future German government.

The situation in the country was alarming, with hunger, rampant black markets, the continuation of the Nazi wage freeze, grass-root strikes in the British zone, and general anti-capitalist sentiment that found one expression in the Ahlen programme of the Christian Democrats of February 1947. This programme started from the proposition that '[t]he capitalist economic system has served neither the state's nor the German people's vital interests. After the terrible political, economic, and social collapse that resulted from criminal pre-war politics, a new order is required.' The pursuit of capitalistic power and profit should be replaced by a 'socialist economic order' that gave priority to welfare and 'accords with the rights and dignity of the individual, services the intellectual and material development of our nation, and secures peace both at home and abroad'. The programme supported planning by autonomous bodies rather than the state, the break-up of cartels, nationalization of large-scale industry, encouragement of small enterprises, and 'co-determination' that gave workers representation in company management.[24]

The outcome of these debates was the currency reform of 20 June 1948. The Reich's debt held by German citizens was cancelled and Reichsmarks were converted into the new Deutsche Mark at a rate of 10 to 1; half the holdings were blocked and most were soon cancelled, with the result that 100 Reichsmarks became 6.5 Deutsche Marks. This strategy removed inflationary pressure – and it also favoured entrepreneurs. Middle-class savers lost their monetary assets whereas the owners of property and industrial plant retained their real assets and benefitted from writing off debts. Corporations retained 96 per cent of their real assets in contrast to 6.5 per cent for savers – which has been characterized as 'one of the greatest confiscations of wealth in history'.[25]

The other major issue was removing economic controls and escaping from Schacht's bilateral trade system. To Hermann Abs – a leading German banker and director of industrial companies under the Third Reich who remained a central figure in post-war reconstruction – the problem was the weak balance of payments and the risk that liberalizing the economy would lead to increased imports. He therefore resisted international demands both for compensation and for the liberalization of the economy. By contrast, Erhard and Leonhard Miksch – a financial journalist and economist who worked for the British and then Bizonal administrations – stressed the possibility of growth within a liberalized economy. The Colm–Dodge–Goldsmith report proposed ending wartime controls in a gradual manner, in contrast to the British who wanted tighter control. In

June 1948, Miksch drafted a law on price policy that would be adopted after currency reform. Erhard, who became director of economics at the Bizonal Economic Council in April, started to remove price controls and rationing when the new Deutsche Mark was introduced, against the wishes of the Allies and the Social Democrats. The immediate result was chaotic, for it was not clear which goods were regulated and which were not now controlled. Prices rose, wages were frozen, savings had been lost in the currency reform, with the outcome of protests and strikes. Erhard narrowly avoided a vote of no confidence brought by the Social Demo-crats and he made concessions in the *Jedermann Programm*, or Everyman's programme. He regulated the price of basic consumer goods and allo-cated raw materials, so that the transition to a free market was not as rapid as originally intended. This shift to a more bureaucratic policy was concealed by continuing to speak of a free-market economy, and by turn-ing to a 'social market economy'. The CDU moved from the Ahlen programme to the Düsseldorf guidelines of July 1949 that rejected both a command economy – whether by the state or autonomous institutions – and 'the so-called free enterprise economy of liberal hue'. The social market entailed a 'socially anchored law ... according to which the achievements of free and able individuals are integrated into a system that provides the highest level of economic benefit and social justice for all'. This approach entailed 'genuine performance-based competition' by pre-venting monopolies, ensuring fair competition and equal opportunity, and rewarding better performance. These principles provided the basis of the CDU's victory in the election of 1949. Erhard's policy was ultimately suc-cessful, and he went on to serve as Minister of Economics from 1949 to 1963 and Chancellor from 1963 to 1966.[26]

Erhard and Miksch were influenced by Wilhelm Röpke, a German economist who opposed the Nazis' rejection of the individual and their interventionism and idolization of the state. He was dismissed from his university post in 1933 and – as we saw in Chapter 3 – worked at the Graduate Institute at Geneva. Röpke attended the Lippmann Colloquium in 1938 and was a member of the Mont Pèlerin Society– as was Erhard. In Röpke's view, economic dislocation arose from the dissatisfaction of workers, and welfare policies were palliatives that passed costs to other groups and prevented economic progress. The correct solution was to end the 'devitalization' of workers' lives by liberating Germany from 'the degeneracies of monopoly–and–proletariat capitalism, of the growth of the masses, of agrarian and industrial feudalism, of proletarianization, of concentration and over-organization, of the agglomeration of industrial power and the destruction of the individuality of labour'. Free markets entailed '[i]ndividual responsibility and independence in proper balance with the community, neighborly spirit and true civic sense – all of these presuppose that the communities in which we live do not exceed the human scale'. It was a vision of 'a reintegrated society of freely cooperating and *vitally satisfied* men'. Competitive markets were democratic, reflecting 'innumerable, individual economic acts' unlike the autocracy of state planning. To Röpke, the Marshall Plan subsidized a failing economy of controls and delayed the arrival of free markets. 'Without a drastic internal reform of the national economy, to put an end to inflation and socialist controls, foreign credits can have no lasting effects, just as a man cannot be kept alive indefinitely by perpetual blood transfusions if the cause of his hemorrhage is not removed.' Recovery needed a market economy with a sound currency and immediate end of controls. 'Ordo-liberalism' or 'liberal conservatism' limited the state to imposing rules (*Ordnung*) and enforcing competition within a 'social market' that offered dignity of work and individuality in a 'humane economy'.[27] To the German ordo-liberals, the spiritual and social dangers of free markets required a role for the state to make rules, enforce competition and provide social security. Ordo-liberalism continued to have a major role in West Germany through the work of economists such as Alfred Müller-Armack and Franz Böhm and the idea of a co-ordinated market economy that combined free competition with regulation and welfare.[28]

The process of settling debts was completed in 1952 – a complex balancing act between compensation to German migrants, foreign creditors who had lent to Germany before 1933 and since 1945, and to Israel as recompense for the Holocaust. The London debt agreement of 1953 forgave over 50 per cent of foreign debts incurred prior to 1933 and 56 per cent after 1945. The United States reduced Germany's post-1945 debt by 62.5 per cent, which made it difficult for other creditors to demand harsher terms. Abs, who was the German negotiator, argued that a smaller debt reduction would prevent Germany from compensating Israel and contributing to defence, which would only be possible if Germany were politically stable and economically prosperous on the front line of the Cold War. As a result, priority was given to compensation to German refugees and payments for the Allied occupation and defence, rather than to foreign creditors, Israel, or occupied countries and forced, slave labour. In 1952, the *Lastenausgleich* was approved by the Bundestag – a fund from a wealth tax of 50 per cent to be paid over thirty years that would compensate German migrants. It was, as Adam Tooze remarks, 'one of the most dramatic welfare measures in modern history'. The priorities were clear. In 1954, military expenditure, including occupation costs, was

DM16,786m and *Lastenausgleich* DM5,500m; payments to creditors under the London debt agreement were DM734m and to Israel DM354m. Germany did, it is true, still pay considerable 'hidden' reparations through loss of intellectual property, and on some estimates paid more than the Weimar Republic had done.[29]

The contrast with Britain was striking. There, controls, debt and the monetary overhang continued. Britain could not cancel its debts to the United States or its sterling balances in India and Egypt in the same way as West Germany repudiated the Third Reich's debt to domestic bond-holders and rescheduled foreign debts. Otmar Emminger of the Bundesbank realized that only an occupation authority could undertake drastic monetary reform so that other countries had a *Klotz am Bein* – a shackled leg. In 1950, the German public debt was only 19.3 per cent of GDP, compared with 197 per cent in Britain – and the London debt agreement further reduced external debt. As a result, West Germany had capacity for public investment, a lower cost of borrowing, and less inflation.[30]

THE MARSHALL PLAN AND EUROPEAN INTEGRATION

George Marshall's speech of 5 June 1947 did not provide details of how the United States would assist European reconstruction. The Secretary of State was calling on the Europeans to take action. Ernest Bevin and his French foreign minister counterpart, Georges Bidault, reacted favourably to Marshall's initiative and urged Europe to develop a response, with or without Soviet involvement. The Soviets were ambivalent. Nikolai Novikov, the Soviet ambassador in Washington, had warned in September 1946 that American foreign policy had changed from Roosevelt's desire to continue the three-power coalition against Hitler to a more hostile policy under Truman, with a coalition of 'reactionary Southern Democrats and the old guard of the Republicans'. In his view, the foreign policy of the United States reflected 'the imperialistic tendency of American monopoly capital' and its 'desire for world domination'. On this interpretation, the Marshall Plan – or European Recovery Programme as it was officially known – was a continuation of the Truman Doctrine to create an American-led western European bloc.[31] However, the Soviet position was still fluid and Stalin had not yet opted for confrontation. After the war, the Soviet Union had more security from outside challenge than at any time since 1917, and it could accept economic relations with the West that could aid recovery, even though its rhetoric emphasized conflict with capitalism. Stalin reasoned that old imperial rivalries were more powerful than conflicts between socialism and capitalism, and that capitalism had changed, with a greater commitment to planning. Confrontation might threaten the consolidation of Soviet power, and Stalin initially favoured peaceful co-existence, which the Marshall Plan might facilitate. Vyacheslav Molotov, the Soviet minister of foreign affairs, therefore joined Bevin and Bidault in Paris in June–July 1947 to consider their response to Marshall.[32]

The Western powers had not expected the Soviets to be interested. In May 1947, George Kennan had argued that aid to Europe should be formulated in such a way that 'the Russian satellite countries would either exclude themselves by unwillingness to accept the proposed conditions or agree to abandon the exclusive orientation of their economies'. When Bevin and Bidault met Molotov, their intention was to exclude the Soviets unless they gave up control over eastern Europe. They hoped the Soviets would refuse to co-operate and 'in any event they will be prepared to go ahead full steam even if the Soviets refuse to do so'. When Molotov withdrew from the meeting, Bevin whispered to his principal private secretary that 'This really is the birth of the Western bloc' – as it turned out to be. Bevin was pleased with the outcome, and informed Cabinet that

> from a practical point of view, it is far better to have them definitely out than half-heartedly in ... Any other tactics might have enabled the Soviets to play the Trojan horse and wreck Europe's prospects of availing themselves of American assistance ... [A]t least the gloves are off, and we know where we stand.

The Bizone had divided Germany; now, the Marshall Plan divided Europe.[33]

In July 1947, Britain and France called a conference of European Economic Co-operation in Paris, to which the Soviets were invited. The Soviet Union declined, though initially Moscow encouraged eastern and central European countries to attend. The Polish and Czechoslovakian governments accepted the invitation, but subsequently pulled out of what was viewed as an anti-Soviet bloc. To Bevin, the issue went beyond economic recovery. Economic security was vital for democracy, but more than that: 'We must also organise and consolidate the ethical and spiritual forces inherent in this Western civilisation of which we are the chief protagonist.' To Bevin, Britain was the moral leader of the West against Soviet ideology.[34]

Molotov was convinced that Novikov had been right. He rejected the

Marshall Plan as a device for the French and British governments to create (and dominate) a new organization that would interfere in the internal affairs of European states and divide Europe into two blocs. American aid would require 'an obedient attitude' which 'might lead to a denial of their economic independence . . . incompatible with national sovereignty'. He also complained that Marshall Aid gave priority to the recovery of the German economy rather than reparations, and that the country was being federalized in the western occupation zones, rather than creating a united Germany. Hence American aid would be a way of

> separating themselves from the other European states and thus dividing Europe into two groups of states and creating new difficulties in the relations between them. In that case American credits would serve not to facilitate the economic rehabilitation of Europe but to make use of some European countries against other European countries in whatever way certain strong powers seeking to establish their domination should find it profitable to do so.[35]

To the United States, the Marshall Plan was a defensive measure to prevent economic collapse in western Europe, and to counter internal threats from Communism and external threats from Soviet expansion. To the Soviets, the Marshall Plan was a hostile act. Stalin concluded that 'using the pretext of credits the Great Powers are attempting to form a Western bloc and isolate the Soviet Union', and capitalism remained prone to instability. Both sides had started with defensive steps to sustain an unstable status quo which were interpreted by the other side as aggression. In September 1947, Communist parties from nine countries met in Poland and formed a new international organization – the Cominform – as a response to the Marshall Plan, and Molotov launched the 'Brother Plan', a system of bilateral trade deals between members. The economies of the Soviet bloc would be integrated through the Council for Mutual Economic Assistance (COMECON) established in 1949, with subsidies from Moscow and trade through agreements to exchange goods over three to five years – a far cry from American multilateralism. The political situation deteriorated with the installation of a Communist regime in Czechoslovakia in February 1948, the blockade of Berlin from June 1948 to May 1949, the detonation of a Soviet atomic bomb on 29 August 1949, and the outbreak of the Korean War in 1950.[36]

Kennan was not impressed by the outcome of the conference in Paris between July and September 1947. He had denounced the Soviets as aggressive; now, he castigated the Europeans as weak. They were uncertain how to deal with German integration into the European economy, and in general the 'gingerly approach' to Marshall aid 'reflects ... all the weakness, the escapism, the paralysis of a region caught by war in the midst of serious problems of long-term adjustment, and sadly torn by hardship, confusion and outside pressure'. Above all, he was scathing about Britain, whose 'position today is tragic to a point that challenges description'. Grave difficulties required an energetic response but 'as a body politic Britain is seriously sick. She is incapable of viewing her own situation realistically and dealing with it effectively.' The Labour government would only adopt the policies needed for economic recovery under the pressure of necessity, with the risk that catastrophe might hit before readjustment. Kennan saw that a careful assessment was needed of how far 'cruel pressure' would force the British government to accept realism – and even then, the government 'will be unrealistic, erratic, slap-happy'. The British government, he concluded, should not be treated as responsible or rational.

> If we choose to hold the British government fully responsible, as a rational body, and to treat it accordingly, we may have to despair of it – and of European recovery. If we chose to treat it as a sick man, then perhaps, by a judicious admixture of patience and pressure, we can string things out to a better state of affairs.[37]

In fact, the conference was more successful than Kennan assumed, and the Committee of European Economic Co-operation, as it became, developed a plan. The initial estimate was that $29bn was needed, which was modified to $19.3bn – a sum that was still too large for Truman to request from Congress. The plan encountered opposition from Hoover and above all Senator Robert Taft, who feared that America was being drawn into European politics, risking a high price for American taxpayers, a threat to European self-reliance and a subsidy for socialism. Even so, Hoover realized that assistance would create 'a dam against Russian aggression'. Truman stressed American support for freedom and democracy, and a world order based on law, against the Soviet Union that 'has not only refused to cooperate in the establishment of a just and honourable peace, but – even worse – has actively sought to prevent it'. He welcomed the 'encouraging signs that the free nations of Europe are drawing together for their economic well-being and for the common defense of their liberties'. The withdrawal of the Soviets from the meeting in Paris and the Communist takeover of Czechoslovakia convinced Congress to accept the Marshall Plan, and the Economic Cooperation Act was signed in April 1948 that granted $5bn of aid. It established an Economic Cooperation Administration (ECA) under the direction of Paul Hoffman, to run the European Recovery Program in association with the Organization for European Economic Co-operation (OEEC) – a new, permanent body that evolved into the Organization for Economic Co-operation and Development in 1961. Over the next four years a total of around $13bn of American aid – there is no definitive figure – was allocated to rebuild infrastructure, reduce trade barriers, restore industry and agriculture, as well as to contain Communism. The United Kingdom received the largest amount – on one estimate, 24 per cent – followed by France (20.4 per cent); West Germany, with 10.5 per cent, was more cautious, for it was expected to repay the money until a settlement was reached on its pre-war debts in 1953.[38]

A major question was the relationship between economic and political integration. Hoffman and the ECA looked to political integration; the State Department was not sure that the loss of national sovereignty would be accepted. The British government was in a particularly difficult position. Clayton assumed that Congress would only support economic co-operation if Britain were treated as part of Europe, and Marshall hoped '[s]he will be able to play the role which only Britain can play in integrating the economic program for Europe'. The Cabinet was not entirely convinced that Britain should play a leading role, for integration and a customs union that surrendered national control over tariffs had implications for 'our internal freedom of action and the future of Imperial Preference'. In March 1948, the government's economic policy committee realized that a balance had to be struck between economic security and national sovereignty:

> If the Governments of Western Europe failed to take this opportunity, they would face economic disaster which would gravely threaten their political independence. But it was important that the full economic and political implications of this project should be clearly understood. If European economic co-operation was to achieve its objectives, each of the participating countries must be prepared to surrender, in the interests of Western Europe as a whole, some part of its national sovereignty in economic affairs.[39]

The question was whether a partial loss of sovereignty within Europe was an acceptable price to pay for economic recovery and geopolitical security.

In June 1947, officials at the British Treasury countered Clayton's view that Britain was part of Europe. 'Our position was different from that of the Continental European countries. We had world-wide commitments' – and schemes for European integration would not provide the necessary resources. Otto Clarke pointed out that

The US like the idea of a Customs Union for Western Europe. This is completely out of the picture as far as we are concerned because it would mean breaking the Empire relationship. A Customs Union including the Empire and the participating countries would take a decade to negotiate. It is not at all clear in any case whether it would be in our interests because the European countries are, on the whole, competitive with us and not complementary. In the modern world also Customs Unions imply going much further into economic and political union.[40]

Others felt that economic co-operation with Europe was desirable. Above all, Bevin thought that British involvement in Europe was crucial to restoring leadership, securing financial assistance from the United States, and resisting the threat of Communism. To Bevin, it was not a case of Europe or the empire, but of Europe and the empire, by joining the British and French empires against the Soviets and as a balance to the United States. As he explained to Bidault, their task was 'to save Western civilisation' and its 'ethical and spiritual forces' by 'some sort of federation in Western Europe'. It might be necessary to accept American aid, but

> the countries of Western Europe which despise the spiritual values of America will look to us for political and moral guidance and for assistance in building up a counter attraction to the baleful tenets of communism ... We have the material resources in the Colonial Empire ... and by giving a spiritual lead now we should be able to carry out our task [in] a way which will show clearly that we are not subservient to the United States of America or to the Soviet Union.

Any European union should therefore be imperial to ensure independence from the United States by exploiting the resources of Africa in conjunction with France and possibly Portugal – the idea of 'Eurafrica'. This notion arose in the late nineteenth century when competition from the United States led to proposals in Germany and France to replicate American success by reorganizing European economies so that the resources of an African hinterland would complement metropolitan, industrial Europe, just as the resources of the frontier regions supported the industrial heartlands of America. This strategy could be linked with proposals to fully integrate European economies, as in the United States. As Gladwyn Jebb at the Foreign Office argued in 1948, going beyond a customs union to a political union would avoid a 'dismal choice between becoming a satellite state or the poor dependent of an American plutocracy'. In March 1948, the Cabinet agreed that Bevin should proceed to explore a western

European union in association with both the Commonwealth and United States.[41]

Talks soon ran into difficulties over the constitutional form of European integration. Bevin 'hoped it would not be necessary to have formal constitutions' and was suspicious of the plans of Robert Schuman, the new French foreign minister, for a federal Europe and European Assembly. Bevin pointed out that Britain was 'at the centre of a Commonwealth of 400 million inhabitants, which did not seek to consolidate its bonds by means of a constitution but formed a voluntary association of nations provided with a spirit of co-operation'. Britain's unwritten constitution rested on the premise that 'whatever the monarch enacts in parliament is law': the sovereignty of Parliament was absolute, with no superior power within Britain or, by extension, outside. Bevin worried that a European Assembly might clash with a democratically elected sovereign parliament and, at most, he would accept a Council for Europe – an intergovernmental body where ministers met to discuss issues. His position changed from supporting the empire and Europe as a third force against the United States and the Soviet Union, to advocating closer links with the United States 'not only for the purpose of standing up to Soviet aggression but also in the interests of Commonwealth solidarity and of European unity'. The solution was a western alliance rather than a European bloc.[42]

These issues were crucial in the British response to the Schuman plan of May 1950, which aimed to move from the OEEC as a forum for discussion to a European Coal and Steel Community (ECSC) that would pool resources in 'a truly joint planning operation' under a High Authority. The idea was suggested by Jean Monnet, who had worked on Allied economic co-operation during the First World War and proposed a new economic order of European co-operation at Versailles, before moving to the League and subsequently working on schemes of currency stability, above all in China. On the outbreak of the Second World War, Monnet moved to London, where he co-ordinated French and British war industries, and subsequently to Washington to purchase war supplies. In 1943, he joined de Gaulle's government in exile where he developed his proposals for European integration: 'There will be no peace in Europe if the states are reconstituted on the basis of national sovereignty . . . The countries of Europe are too small to guarantee their people the necessary prosperity and social development. The European states must constitute themselves into a federation.' The ECSC was less a scheme to contain Germany than to secure access to coal and coke from the Ruhr, on which the expansion of France's steel industry – and the competitiveness of French industry – depended. In 1952, Monnet became the first head of the

High Authority of the ECSC which brought together the resources of France, Germany, Italy, Belgium, the Netherlands and Luxembourg. It did not include Britain. Monnet looked to a Franco-German alliance rather than Anglo-French co-operation, and the announcement of the Schuman plan was made after consulting the German chancellor, without informing London.[43]

The Labour government was not attracted to the Schuman plan and the ECSC. It had already nationalized the coal industry and was about to nationalize steel, and it had no interest in pooling resources under a High Authority that would threaten economic planning and parliamentary sovereignty. Officials reported to the Cabinet meeting of 2 June 1950 that 'It is not merely pooling of resources, but also ... the conception of fusion or surrender of sovereignty in a European system which the French are asking us to accept in principle.' As they explained, 'in view of our world position and interests, we should not commit ourselves irrevocably to Europe either in the political or the economic sphere unless we could measure the extent and effects of the commitment.' Although the Cabinet welcomed the Schuman plan as a new start on Franco-German relations, it was 'impossible in view of [its] responsibility to Parliament and people to associate [itself] with the negotiations on the terms proposed by the French Government'. The Labour Party's national executive agreed: Britain was 'not just a small crowded island off the Western coast of Continental Europe', for its Commonwealth and empire covered all continents. 'In every respect, we in Britain are closer to our kinsmen in Australia and New Zealand on the far side of the world, than we are to Europe. We are closer in language and origins, in social habits and institutions, in political outlook and in economic interest.' Neither was economic and political union compatible with socialism:

> No Socialist Party with the prospect of forming a government could accept a system by which important fields of national policy were surrendered to a supranational European representative authority, since such an authority would have a permanent anti-Socialist majority and would arouse the hostility of European workers.

Attlee explained to the Commons in July 1950 that 'we could not accept in advance of discussion the principle that the most vital economic forces of this country should be handed over to an authority which is not responsible to Governments'. By contrast, many Conservatives supported membership of the ECSC, or at least entering discussions to prevent the French taking the lead with Germany and to remove supranationality.

The Commons voted 309 to 289 against joining the ECSC, largely on party lines.[44]

In August 1951, Roger Makins at the Foreign Office captured the ambivalence of Britain's position. He argued for cohesion in the Commonwealth, empire and sterling area, partnership with the United States, and promoting the integration of western Europe without entering 'an organic relationship' – all while maintaining the economic independence of Britain. In his view, Britain was *in* but not *of* Europe, and should resist both pressure from the United States and the pull from Europe to participate:

> We want Europe to be strong, but if we are classed as just a European Power and bound in an organic relationship to a predominantly Latin and Catholic grouping, we should soon lose our world position and a great deal of our liberty of action without strengthening either Europe or ourselves.[45]

Such sentiments meant that Britain was not involved in the discussions that led to the Treaty of Rome in 1957 and the creation of the European Economic Community (EEC). Britain did however join the European Payments Union, albeit reluctantly and with serious worries about the position of sterling.

THE EUROPEAN PAYMENTS UNION

At the end of 1949, the Economic Cooperation Administration suggested that the OEEC devise a system of payments for the multilateral settlement of trade in western Europe that would allow the reduction of tariffs and ensure that it did not become a discriminatory trade area. The outcome was a clearing union: country A would no longer need to pay its deficit to countries B and C in full, while receiving payment of a surplus from country D; it would need only make a single payment of its net balance to the EPU, and the same applied to countries B, C and D. Trade would no longer be hindered by a lack of liquidity and the European economy could return to multilateralism. Each member would start with a credit in the EPU, with payment only needed when it was exhausted. Payment would be partly in gold, which would impose discipline on the deficit country – and the management board of the EPU could force corrective measures to restore equilibrium in the balance of payments.[46] The EPU had similarities with Walther Funk's 'New Order' multilateral clearing plan of 1940 (discussed in Chapter 6), for both accepted the logic of a clearing union to handle payments within Europe. There were also major differences. The EPU relied on negotiations between equal sovereign states and central banks, and administration through an inter-governmental body, with the aim of stimulating multilateral trade in western Europe as part of an open world economy. Funk's plan rested on domination by Berlin and the Reichsbank, with burdens falling on the occupied territories and with separation from the world economy. Rather than giving special privileges to Germany, the EPU would embed, and so tame, a prosperous Germany in a wider economic area.[47]

The EPU had implications for the sterling area, imperial preference and Britain's identity as a major imperial power. The question was whether Britain should join this new European venture or maintain its separate identity. Oliver Franks had been head of the British delegation to discuss Marshall Aid, and became first chair of the OEEC before his appointment as British ambassador to Washington in 1948. He hoped the Americans would realize that assisting the sterling area would help European recovery. The issue, as Franks pointed out, was 'whether the sterling area was to be subordinate to the European Payments Union, superior to the European Payments Union, or co-equal with it'.[48] Averell Harriman, America's special representative in Europe, thought that Britain should provide leadership for European integration rather than cling to the sterling area, which should, at most, be prevented from collapsing and causing economic disturbance. The Labour government was in a dilemma. European economic integration might undermine independent economic policies and sovereignty, and it believed that sterling was vital for trade and convertibility given that it accounted for around half of all international payments. But if Britain did not join the EPU, the Americans would be unsympathetic. This balance of considerations meant that British membership should be on terms that allowed the survival of the sterling area, with sterling a large element in European reserves. The government also wished to preserve imperial preference, to ensure freedom from interference in domestic economic policies by the management board of the EPU, and to avoid discipline by the settlement of deficits in gold. These uncertainties over British membership and its terms posed risks for the entire enterprise.[49] Paul Hoffman believed that the EPU required more authority to review the economic and financial policies of members, and feared that unless the British 'forego their extreme nationalistic policies, the discussions of the mechanism of the Clearing Union will be futile'.[50]

In March 1950, the governor of the National Bank of Belgium, with justice, criticized the British attitude as 'access to the Payments Union when a settlement through that channel is better, without its having to assume any commitments under the Union or share any of the risk involved in setting it up'.[51] The ECA complained that 'Britain is in fact seeking to avoid having its national economic policies limited, influenced or altered in any way by external conditions'. Its insistence

> on the right arbitrarily to reimpose bilateral [quantitative restrictions] without prior consultation is in effect insistence on the right to cut the British Isles off from the continent to the extent necessary to prevent continental economic conditions from influencing the economic program of the British government ... The issue is not the desire of the United Kingdom to preserve its legitimate sovereign rights or conduct an independent economic policy ... [I]t is whether the United Kingdom will insist, at the one extreme, on economic isolation and autarchy or, at the other extreme, on the right to coerce other countries to accept economic policies of benefit mainly to Britain.[52]

American patience was wearing thin. The British, it seemed, failed to see that they had 'lost their old position of power and would have to face up to a changed status in the world', and that they needed to choose between being 'a European country with overseas commitments and an empire with European connections'. Although the Commonwealth might counter Communism in the Far East, there was also a risk that Britain's imperial delusion might mean that 'if they will drift away from the Continent, they will drift into opposition to it'.[53] The State Department complained that 'the belief that state economic management is necessary to achieve social and economic welfare leads to the practice of trying to protect the economy against adverse economic developments in the outside world'. Such attitudes meant limiting 'competitive economic forces' and undermining 'the ability of the British economy to adapt itself to changing world conditions'. Instead of allocating resources by market signals, 'the British government has deliberately chosen to let the impact of strains fall on the reserves and exchange rates as the lesser of two evils.' The State Department realized that the Labour government was unlikely to change its approach, for

> independence of action and maneuverability is of great importance to them, particularly at a time when their internal economy is kept going at its present level only through detailed manipulation of price and wage controls, subsidies and other forms of government direction of the economy. Any proposal which would transfer to a European grouping the power to make executive decisions with regard to the British economy would appear to them to be placing their destinies in the hands of foreign countries whose

abilities they doubt and in many cases whose economic philosophies they disagree with.[54]

The result was mutual incomprehension between American complaints that the British economy was too controlled and the Labour government, which believed that the American economy was unstable.[55]

Eventually, the British government opted to join the EPU, in part because of difficulties in discussions with America and Canada after the pound was devalued in 1949. The British were reluctant to deflate the economy and cut expenditure on social welfare to make goods more competitive, strengthen the balance of payments, and prepare for convertibility. Instead, they wanted the Americans to open their markets and fund the sterling balances, or accept that convertibility would require restrictions on American imports. The Americans refused and the British government realized that the European negotiations might offer more room for manoeuvre.[56] The British dropped their impracticable ambition that sterling be central to European reserves; and other countries came to share British concerns over a strong management board. A compromise was reached, and the Americans accepted that sterling had special needs. The wider strategic context was that British ministers saw that membership of the EPU would help secure American support for NATO and make a greater contribution to the defence of Europe.[57]

The American administration shifted its attitude to the sterling area, for – as the historian Alan Milward remarked – 'its real interests were more affected by the world-wide ramifications of British and sterling area trade than by Britain's role in Europe'. A member of the American embassy in London pointed out that the sterling area was the largest trading zone outside the United States and that its break-up 'would be as disruptive to the Western world as if the United States were divided into half a dozen or more separate nations'. A managed retreat from sterling as a major reserve currency was needed to ensure that Britain did not withdraw into the sterling area and a 'two-world' system. The result, as Charles Maier remarked, was that 'Americans learned that they had to prop up sterling even as they partially displaced it, since it remained such an extensive international means of payment'. Meanwhile, growing British acceptance that the pound could not maintain its dominant role created room for compromise. The outcome was pragmatic support for managed decline to ease the shift from one core currency (sterling) to another (the dollar) that was not completed for another fifteen or twenty years.[58]

The EPU was part of a political trade-off between capital and labour. Workers agreed to wage moderation and savers accepted their losses; in

return, industrialists agreed to reinvest profits to create higher productivity and longer-term gains. This pact was underwritten by state provision
of welfare and by tax policies to encourage investment. The EPU was an
important component of this settlement, for it encouraged exports without recourse to devaluation, which would entail higher import prices and
threaten living standards. It brought the balance of payments into equilibrium by limiting purchases of non-European goods and encouraging
intra-European trade, with a gradual reduction of trade barriers, a restoration of multilateral trade within Europe, and an eventual return to
currency convertibility in 1958.[59] The outcome was not a dash to convertibility but gradualism as trade and production recovered.[60]

The EPU locked Germany into a European institution and integrated
the country into the European economy, removing concerns that it might
again be tempted to war. Together, the EPU and growth of the German
economy were more important than the Marshall Plan in the recovery of
Europe. There was also a striking absence. The IMF was established to
manage exchange rates, yet it played no role in the restoration of convertibility. Raymond Mikesell pointed out that 'the Fund remained largely
irrelevant for the first fifteen years of its existence'. Indeed, a British Treasury official thought European bodies such as the OEEC, EPU and Bank
for International Settlements worked better than the IMF, which was
dominated by the United States, treated with suspicion by its members,
burdened by an impossible management structure, and suffered from procedures that were 'excessively heavy-handed and indecisive'. As a result,
he predicted that it was in danger of being forgotten apart from some
'timid' interventions in Latin America.[61] He exaggerated, yet it was clear
that the Bretton Woods institutions were not as significant as had been
anticipated. The task of recreating multilateral trade and currency convertibility meant adaptation of the plans discussed at Bretton Woods in
1944 and Havana in 1947–48.

FLOATING THE POUND?

In 1951, the Conservatives returned to power in Britain with the aim of
abandoning Labour's austerity and economic controls. Leroy Stinebower
of the US State Department welcomed the prospect. In his view, the use of
controls to suppress inflation caused inflexibilities that resulted in balance
of payments crises – and inflationary pressure was exacerbated by 'cheap
money' and budget deficits to maintain full employment and social spending. At the same time, a strong domestic market diverted resources from

exports and led to import controls that reduced competitiveness. Stine-bower castigated British policy as 'weak and opportunistic', and he advocated removing controls and subsidies, cutting taxes and encouraging competition to make the economy more flexible. In the absence of such change, the State Department was reluctant to offer further help that would 'accustom that country to a standard of living which depends on the continuation of US assistance and in a sense tends to postpone the necessity for becoming competitive and earning its own way'.[62] It remained to be seen whether Churchill's government could succeed in creating a more competitive free-market economy.

Floating exchange rates – or, more accurately, flexibility within wider margins – were central to the proposed shift in economic policy. They had been mooted at the Treasury in 1948 and 1949 as an alternative to devaluation. The case rested on allowing the pound to find its level in the market without the need to defend a fixed exchange rate, which would ease the resumption of convertibility and removal of exchange controls. Otto Clarke saw 'many attractions in the idea of letting the rate find its equilibrium level' but he also realized it 'would only be possible if it were part of a pretty general return to a free economy. Clearly the true equilibrium could not be reached if demand were still in part restricted by rationing and in part stimulated by subsidies.'[63] He recognized that floating would only work if the economy could respond to market forces – which was not possible given Labour's commitment to planning and controlled prices. Political realism prevailed, not least because floating would repudiate the agreement at Bretton Woods and alienate the United States.[64]

The Conservatives' aim of ending controls and restoring convertibility meant that floating became more attractive. Oliver Lyttelton, a business-man and member of the wartime government, hoped that '[u]nder convertibility we can resume the financial leadership of the sterling area, and occupy a place just second to the United States in world finances.' A floating rate offered a means to this end.[65] At the Bank of England, George Bolton argued that a fixed exchange rate was only possible by adopting exchange controls, which had worked during the war when most trade was in the hands of the government. They were less likely to succeed with the restoration of private trade and foreign transactions in sterling. There was already 'leakage' from the sterling area by non-residents who exploited loopholes to exchange sterling at a 15 per cent discount – and imposing additional controls would only weaken sterling's status as an international currency. In his view, the choice was clear: sterling would cease to be an international currency unless non-resident sterling was convertible.[66] Bolton's concern was predominantly with maintaining the City of London as a major financial centre, but floating could also help restore a freer market economy. Here Bolton worked with Otto Clarke and Leslie Rowan, an official in the Treasury's overseas finance division. Their names were combined to name Operation 'Robot' (ROwanBOltonOTto) – with the suggestion of an automatic, effective solution to the difficulties facing the British economy.

Operation Robot aimed to make the pound convertible for current earnings outside the sterling area only, not for current earnings by residents of Britain and the sterling area, and not for capital accounts. At the same time, 80 per cent of accumulated sterling balances would be funded by conversion into government bonds. Sterling would find its own level in a wide band around a parity of $2.80, and ensuring it did not fall too much would mean 'determined internal measures' to contain inflation and improve the balance of payments by cutting government spending, imposing tight money policies, providing incentives, increasing production and releasing capacity for exports – in other words, by replacing Labour's economic controls by free markets.[67] Operation Robot aimed to combine the preservation of sterling as an international currency with a shift in domestic policy to create competitiveness and flexibility. Changes in the exchange rate would – so the advocates of the scheme argued – create 'equilibrating pressures on the economy'. If the rate fell, import prices would rise and reduce consumption, exports would be more competitive, and '[t]he whole economy feels these movements, and adjusts itself to them'. By contrast, supporters of Operation Robot argued that retaining a fixed exchange rate would lead to an outflow of Britain's reserves 'without anybody noticing it at all – and no adjustment until the Government decrees it; and then it is the Government's fault, imposing artificial restrictions, and the real conditions of life go on as before.' Clarke admitted

> that a floating rate makes for instability both in internal and external trade (it is terrible for planners). But of course when the pattern of prices, production, consumption, imports and exports is not the correct one for solvency, we can't afford to have it stable; we must have some forces at work which will set up incentives which tend to right it.

Clarke reassured sceptics that floating would allow full employment 'if the structure and incentives are of a character which make the economy viable ... [O]ur economy must always be flexible ... in order to be able to adapt itself quickly.'[68]

Opponents of Operation Robot saw political and economic risks. To Robert Hall, it was a 'leap in the dark' that would destroy the post-war social pact. There was no certainty that exports would increase in response to a fall in the pound so that import controls would still be needed. The price of imports would definitely rise, triggering wage demands which would be held down by tight credit or unemployment. Consequently, the post-war trade-off between international trade and domestic full employment would be overturned. Other countries might follow, with 'a downward spiral of the level of world trade as each country which is short of dollars tries to earn dollars by cutting its imports from non-dollar countries'. The result might be a return to the beggar-my-neighbour policies of the 1930s, high levels of unemployment and declining trade. 'We would in fact be serving notice to our own people and to the rest of the world that we had been forced to abandon full employment and a high level of trade as immediate objectives.' Meanwhile, Operation Robot would threaten the EPU and economic recovery in Europe.[69] Lionel Robbins went further: Robot was 'not in fact strictly honourable' for it would undermine Britain's reputation for looking after other people's money and would violate international agreements.[70]

The opponents of Operation Robot denied that it would create incentives, for international competitiveness could be maintained by the easy option 'to "take on the rate" the consequences of our inability to put things right'. By allowing the pound to float – or, rather, sink in value – there would be less need to improve productivity or maintain domestic discipline. Supporters of Robot accepted that floating could only work if it was combined with sweeping changes in 'the whole field of internal policy – budget economy, tight monetary conditions, savings, incentive, harder work, more production, and the release of productive capacity for export – and also emergency cuts in dollar and other overseas expenditure'. To critics, such an outcome was both implausible and politically dangerous. 'Convertibility cannot make a weak currency strong or restore confidence . . . If we haven't got the resolution to get ourselves out of our present difficulties, why suppose that we should have more resolution when convertible? Surely we would simply choose the slippery slope of depreciation.' They doubted that a sweeping change in domestic policy would be electorally acceptable, and that 'a deliberate return for its own sake to the price mechanism, with its effect on employment, as the sole regulator of the economic system' might have 'terrible consequences to the Government and to the political party of which it is formed'.[71] Nevertheless, Richard ('Rab') Butler – the new Conservative Chancellor of the Exchequer – told a horrified Hall that 'he fully appreciated all that this means, that it would end the Conservative Party, but that it had to be done' to save the country.[72]

Otto Clarke believed that Operation Robot offered a one-world alternative to the two-world reliance on the sterling area. Advocates of Robot thought that reliance on 'soft trade' areas had gone too far and that 'Two Worlds is an illusion. We have neither the political nor economic strength to drive the thing through, and to collect the waverers and back-sliders.'[73] On the other hand, the one-world strategy might fail if Britain did not break into the largely self-sufficient American market or compete with its exports. Hall therefore rejected 'too violent a plunge towards one world' and continued to support two worlds. Edwin Plowden, head of the economic planning staff, saw that the only way 'one world' could succeed was by co-operating with the United States – but that acting unilaterally would alienate the Americans and lead back to a two-world policy.[74] He was right. Robot was developed without consulting the Americans, the Commonwealth, Europe, or the IMF, and the scheme was incompatible with membership of the EPU. Even Clarke admitted that the proposal was so far-reaching that 'the imagination boggles at rushing it through'.[75]

Operation Robot appealed to some Conservative ministers as a way of restoring free markets and breaking with Labour's controls and planning. In retrospect, Nigel Lawson – Chancellor of the Exchequer in Mrs Thatcher's government – thought Robot was the moment when a free-market ideology could have been adopted and twenty years of failed economic policy avoided.[76] He was guilty of ahistorical wishful thinking, for the risks were too great in 1952. The ambition of restoring free markets was certainly present, and it was noted in February 1952 that '[t]here was something to be said, politically, for moving towards the system by which individuals were influenced, by the operation of the price mechanism, to make their own adjustments to changing economic circumstances.' When Butler presented the scheme to Cabinet, Churchill was initially attracted before retreating when his confidant and adviser Frederick Lindemann – now Lord Cherwell – warned him that Robot would be a 'terrible mistake', for 'monetary tricks' would not solve the underlying economic problem that the sterling area spent more than it earned. He warned Churchill that '[t]o rely frankly on high prices and unemployment to reduce imports would certainly put the Conservative Party out for a generation.' Cabinet discussions pointed out that '[u]nder democratic government with universal suffrage such violent reversals of policy are hardly practicable'. Anthony Eden, the foreign secretary, was particularly concerned about the impact on the proposed European Defence Community – the plan for a European army. The dangers seemed too great, and the Cabinet rejected Operation Robot in February and again in June 1952, preferring to maintain the post-war social contract of the welfare state and full employment.[77]

Floating re-emerged in the form of the 'collective approach' which aimed to involve the Commonwealth, Europe and the United States. European currencies and non-resident sterling would all become convertible at the same time to prevent speculation, and the United States would provide a jointly managed support fund and adopt 'good creditor' policies by reducing tariffs and dealing with its persistent surplus. Convertibility would, so Butler hoped, restore sterling 'as a strong world currency' at a floating rate and allow the removal of import restrictions – though imperial preferences should continue. The scheme was presented to the American administration in February 1953 as a means towards 'economic expansion and consolidation of the free world' and ensuring that 'the restrictive policies which were inevitable for dealing with the initial post-war problems' were not 'permanently embedded in the world economy'. It would also help the 'struggle against Soviet communism' for 'economic instability breeds political instability'.[78]

Butler borrowed Bismarck's dictum that politics is the art of the possible for the title of his memoirs. The principle did not apply to the collective approach. Cherwell was more realistic: there was no point in pressing an 'unwanted plan on an unwilling world'. The sterling area was sceptical, for fluctuations in sterling would impact on the value of holdings in the reserves of countries such as India and Pakistan.[79] Neither were the Americans supportive, for they now preferred more gradual progress to convertibility through the EPU and European integration. Clarence Randall, the chairman of President Eisenhower's Commission on Foreign Economic Policy, argued that convertibility should rest on 'a strong internal economy willing and able to control its money supply and its budget as safeguards against inflation, sufficiently mobile to make the best use of its resources, and able and willing to save in order to increase its productivity and improve its competitive position in world markets'. Clearly, he did not think that Britain met these conditions. The Europeans were also alarmed, for – as Hall pointed out – 'they are extremely nervous of early convertibility, desperately afraid that we will break up EPU, and most jealous that we want to talk about their affairs to the US over their heads.' The collective approach came to nothing and illustrated the continued lack of realism about Britain's ability to shape the world economy. Britain failed to make a firm commitment to Europe, mistook its influence in Washington, and was caught in a sterling area whose members were increasingly suspicious of British policies.[80]

By 1956, doubts were already raised about the viability of the sterling area and whether the costs were worthwhile. Sterling was a declining proportion of reserves, and the City of London saw a new future as a market for offshore dollars.[81] Consequently, British politicians and officials were less concerned to maintain the status of sterling at the cost of domestic deflation and reduced government spending on hospitals and schools. There were doubts 'about the desire of the British people to "be great" and run a world banking and financial system with all the burdens that this involves. They are too tired and want to lay down the white man's burden.' Peter Thorneycroft, Chancellor of the Exchequer in 1957–58, thought that the sterling area should be retained only because 'we have not the means to wind it up' – scarcely a ringing endorsement.[82]

The history of post-war reconstruction and the delayed return to convertibility meant that the monetary regime agreed at Bretton Woods in 1944 was not adopted for a considerable time, and only after a fundamental change in policy. The rigidity of American policy towards Britain at the end of the war, the forced convertibility of sterling in 1947, the expectation of continued co-operation with the Soviets and the draconian treatment of Germany were abandoned. Instead, Europe was assisted with Marshall Aid, West Germany was integrated into the European economy, and the EPU was adopted to restore multilateral clearing. The institutional architecture also changed with the re-emergence of the BIS and the creation of the OEEC alongside the IMF. The Cold War provided the context for the greater sense of reality about the state of Europe after the war. The outcome was a slow return to convertibility. By 1958, the British government was willing to take the risk: the dollar gap had closed, inflation was under control, its reserves had increased, and convertibility was expected to lead to an expansion of world trade.[83] The transition had taken longer than anticipated – and tensions soon emerged in the modified Bretton Woods system, which only survived by a series of short-term fixes.

David Lilienthal, director of the Tennessee Valley Authority, stands in front of the Wilson Dam in Colbert County, Alabama, 1934.

12

'Damn it, we're a bank'
Contesting Development

'... prosperity has no fixed limits. It is not a finite substance to be diminished by division. On the contrary, the more of it that other nations enjoy, the more each nation will have for itself. There is a tragic fallacy in the notion that any country is liable to lose its customers by promoting greater production and higher living standards among them. Good customers are prosperous customers ... Prosperity, like peace, is indivisible. We cannot afford to have it scattered here or there among the fortunate or to enjoy it at the expense of others. Poverty, wherever it exists, is menacing to us all and undermines the well-being of each of us. It can no more be localized than war, but spreads and saps the economic strength of all the more favored areas of the earth. We know now that the thread of economic life in every nation is inseparably woven into a fabric of world economy. Let any thread become frayed and the entire fabric is weakened.'

Henry Morgenthau, opening remarks at the United Nations
Monetary and Finance Conference, Bretton Woods, 1944[1]

When the International Bank for Reconstruction and Development started work, its initial and primary role was the reconstruction of areas devastated by war. It was slow to act. The first loan of $250m to France was not made until May 1947, and by the end of 1948 only $497m had been provided for reconstruction. The Bank's first, short-tenure president, from June to December 1946, the Wall Street investment banker Eugene Meyer, remarked that he was not running a relief agency. He and his successor, John McCloy – a corporate lawyer with close links with Wall Street and German industry, who served to June 1949 when he became US High Commissioner in Germany – were adamant that the IBRD's loans must be self-financing. McCloy argued that accepting additional funding from the United States to assist Europe would mean that the Bank would 'lose our character as an international organization and ... the chance of accomplishing what we were formed for, as an international banking agency'. Above all, he wanted to ensure that the IBRD pursued market discipline.[2] As a result the IBRD was over-shadowed in war-torn Europe by assistance derived through the United Nations Relief and Rehabilitation Administration (UNRRA) and Marshall Aid. This inactivity of the IBRD in funding European reconstruction meant that it conserved its capital and could offer loans to less developed countries – above all, in Latin America, for at the end of the war the European imperial powers looked to reassert their control over their colonies in Africa and Asia and to embark on their own 'development' programmes.

The fine words of Morgenthau at Bretton Woods had to be translated into practical policies, and the new Bank grappled with what sort of economic development it should sponsor – progressive New Deal policies on a world stage or the more cautious views of Wall Street bankers. Just what was meant by 'development' and how to deliver it were deeply contested within the Bank. The debates at Hot Springs, Philadelphia, and Havana over the nature of distributive justice in the global economy continued within the IBRD and in other United Nations agencies such as the Food and Agriculture Organization, World Health Organization, and Economic and Social Council where developing countries could express their views, as well as in American foundations that formulated their own development strategies.

INVESTING IN DEVELOPMENT: THE INTERNATIONAL BANK FOR RECONSTRUCTION AND DEVELOPMENT

In 1946, an application from Chile for a loan of $40m triggered a conflict between Meyer and Emilio Collado, the first American executive director at the Bank, who wanted a more expansive role. Conservative investors feared Collado would make the Bank a political agency, with scant regard for economics. John McCloy insisted on his removal and demanded that power be concentrated in the hands of the Bank's staff rather than the executive directors appointed by member governments. Collado was replaced by Eugene Black, a banker at the Chase National Bank, who became President of the IBRD from 1949 to 1963. The triumph of fiscal conservatism was complete when Robert Garner – formerly of the Guaranty Trust and General Foods – was appointed Vice-President. These changes of personnel sent a clear message to Wall Street that the Bank would be a sound institution and would not make 'political' loans that were, in McCloy's words, 'inconsistent with American foreign policy' – a comment that exposed the Bank to the charge of partisanship. Chile secured a loan with conditions imposed on its monetary and fiscal policies, balance of payments, relations with foreign companies, and an agreement on earlier defaulted bonds. Although the Bank was starting to help under-developed countries to a greater extent than originally expected, loans were based on the 'sound and productive' nature of specific projects and the ability to repay.[3] This 'Wall Street' approach differed from the wider ambitions of investment in programmes for public health or education that did not produce an immediate return. There was a deep division in the IBRD.

The reduction in the power of executive directors meant that decisions on lending shifted from governments to a 'denationalized professional staff'. Officials were not seconded from national governments and formed an international civil service with loyalty to the Bank. Black commented that 'We do not think of a man as a Dane, a Cuban or an Indian, but as an economist, a lawyer or an accountant. Our intramural differences are professional, not national.' In his view, the Bank was immune 'to the many competing and conflicting pressures – political and commercial – which must affect *national* financial institutions'. Consequently, it could 'apply objective yardsticks' and avoid issues of sovereignty, so insulating both lender and borrower 'from the frictions and tensions that inevitably attend a foreign lending program'. Black remained hostile to loans made by national governments for political purposes, for '[a] single country offering aid . . . wants to be loved so it agrees to finance the plans which, justifiable or not, are dear to the recipient government's heart. An international organization has no need to erect monuments to its generosity.' Black's stress on the apolitical nature of the Bank and self-financing loans was crucial, for most of its funds came from issuing bonds on the New York money market rather than from government grants. The result was a double bind: the Bank had to consider the attitudes of the financial market; and the presidents were chosen to gain the support of Wall Street and to show that the Bank was not a tool of New Deal idealism. The executive directors complained that officials were not independent and that they were subordinated to American leadership. To Latin Americans, the IBRD was the bill collector for Wall Street. The 'objective' measures used by Black were partisan, following a vision of freedom based on 'sound' development within a liberal internationalist economy that rang hollow when the Bank was lending to dictators in Nicaragua or the Philippines, to repressive colonial regimes

in Portugal, or to apartheid South Africa. In his own eyes, Black was a
custodian of freedom; to others, he was a hypocritical peddler of double
standards, whose 'objective' economic standards excluded policies that
might create freedom by a fairer distribution of the world's resources.[4]

The debate over the role of the IBRD related to the place of private
foreign investment and capital flows in the world economy, and their role
in creating or disrupting stability and economic development. Many
economists saw international capital movements in the interwar period as
destabilizing.[5] The articles of the IMF embodied suspicion about short-
term capital flows, but the criticism was less applicable to long-term
investment. Britain's foreign investment before 1914 helped stabilize the
world economy by returning its balance of payments surplus to the world
economy and was countercyclical. When the British economy was booming, its open market provided an outlet for goods from borrowing
countries and generated income to service loans; when Britain was in
recession, it invested overseas and helped to stabilize the international
economy.[6] By analogy, America should invest overseas after 1945 to
return its surplus to the world economy and to overcome the dollar shortage. This reading of economic history meant that international investment
for recovery and long-run development was desirable, whereas speculative and disruptive movements of funds were not. The question was
how to draw a distinction between the two types of capital movement to
secure the benefits and avoid the pitfalls, and whether the task should be
left to the private sector or to international co-ordination.

Ragnar Nurkse, the League economist who had moved to Columbia
University in 1945, argued that the world could not return to Britain's
pattern of overseas capital investment. He pointed out that capital exports
before 1914 were mainly government loans or investments that aided
development and took the form of fixed interest bonds. He claimed that
such investment was not of a colonial nature for it went overwhelmingly
into overhead capital and, particularly, into railways in temperate zones
of recent settlement – such as Argentina and Canada – which benefitted
both the domestic economy and Britain as the recipient of food and raw
materials. Although capital flows after the Second World War avoided the
speculative dangers of the 1920s and 1930s, Nurkse felt they had not
returned to the beneficial pattern that existed prior to 1914. In his opinion, the export of private American capital was not a solution to the
problem of the dollar gap or the supply of funds for economic development. Such capital arose from the reserves of businesses and would
produce a few basic commodities at low prices for the industrial world.
Furthermore, most capital exports before 1914 were associated with

migration of labour to areas of recent settlement. After the Second World War, direct ownership of capital by American firms meant that American technology was combined with low-waged local labour in an export-oriented sector that had limited connection with the rest of the domestic economy. The result was a colonial type of investment.[7]

This analysis of capital investment before 1914 and after 1945 led to the conclusion that direct investment by business corporations was inadequate for economic development. The need was large-scale investment in social overhead capital with a more beneficial impact on the domestic economy. Above all, Hans Singer – a German-Jewish émigré who had studied with Keynes in Cambridge – pushed for a radical change in the structure of the world economy. In 1947, he joined the UN economic affairs department where he was, in Black's opinion, 'one of the wild men of the UN'. He argued for the stabilization of commodity prices and 'soft' – that is, non-performing – loans to developing countries. He identified a dual economy in which the export sector was separate from the internal economy, and most of the benefits of investment went to the country providing capital. The result was dependence on foreign demand for a few commodities, low levels of internal demand, and economic instability. Foreign investment should change rather than reinforce the existing division between advanced and primary producing countries. 'A flow of international investment into the undeveloped countries will contribute to their economic development only if it is absorbed into their economic system; i.e., if a good deal of complementary domestic investment is generated and the requisite domestic resources are found.' This outcome needed intervention by governments or international institutions such as the IBRD – a conclusion that was contested.[8]

During and immediately after the Second World War, discussions took place within the American administration about whether private foreign investment should be controlled to ensure that it did not, as in the 1920s, lead to resentment against American exploitation of resources and to political interference to protect creditors. In 1946, a working group recommended registration and administrative controls over foreign loans. The State Department was doubtful that regulation was desirable or feasible. The Committee on Foreign Investment Policy went further in rejecting the recommendation on the grounds that 'properly conceived foreign investment' – a vague and undefined term – would lead to more trade and production, to prosperity, employment, and higher standards of living. 'This country's desire to see established a world trading system on a liberal, multilateral, and non-discriminatory basis cannot easily be achieved if American capital is not available to foreign countries in adequate amounts for economically desirable purposes.' The committee argued that capital should be provided by private rather than government loans, the latter only being used when private capital was unavailable or when schemes were very large and public in nature.[9]

These issues resurfaced at the Havana conference where American business interests proposed an addition to the Charter of the ITO to stimulate investment in 'economically desirable purposes' as a way of assisting recovery and dealing with America's trade surplus by injecting funds into the world economy. Business argued that the Charter of the ITO should provide security for investment, which was risky because many countries pursued policies that created 'hazards of debt repudiation, property confiscation, foreign exchange blockages, and discriminatory practices'. Without security, American overseas investment would come to a halt and the costs of stimulating recovery would fall on the American taxpayer. The Charter should therefore create confidence for private (largely American) investment. The less developed countries countered with amendments to the Charter to allow the expropriation of foreign investment with compensation – and American business in turn criticized the ITO as a device for socialistic planning rather than 'the revival of abundant and sustained private foreign investments, which are indispensable for promoting economic advance throughout the world'.[10]

Debates between wider programmes for economic development and narrower, financially viable, project loans continued within the IBRD. The economist Paul Rosenstein-Rodan joined the IBRD in 1947 and argued for 'balanced growth' to resolve the problem of 'agrarian excess population' by bringing machinery and capital to labour through large-scale international investment and integration into the world economy. In his view, international investment could no longer be self-liquidating, as in the nineteenth century, by exchanging agricultural and manufactured goods. Investment in individual firms would not lead to industrialization of a whole area, and investment in fixed capital and overheads for industrialization was risky. State supervision and guarantees were therefore needed. Further, returns to private international investors did not take account of social returns and externalities which could be captured by planning industry as a complementary system.[11] Nurkse came to a similar view that it was vital to escape the constraints of the domestic market, which discouraged private firms, and to embark on 'a wave of capital investments in a number of different industries' so that 'people working with more and better tools in a number of complementary projects become each other's customers'. He called for 'a front attack' by capital investment in different industries. By contrast, he argued that investment by the IBRD in a specific project was less beneficial: it might be a marginal project that would not have proceeded without the loan, and it might even allow the government to divert its own money for a less valuable purpose. As Rosenstein-Rodan remarked, 'the Bank thought it financed an electric power station, but in fact financed a brothel.' The development of a group of complementary industries rather than a single project required a coherent plan for domestic economic growth. Singer took a somewhat different approach, though it still required a wider programme than a narrow assessment of the ability of individual projects to pay their way. He favoured 'judiciously unbalanced growth' or 'guerrilla tactics' by selecting particular sectors for investment and accepting that economic growth could come from exports as well as the domestic market.[12]

These programmatic solutions were anathema to the 'banker's approach' of the IBRD, which preferred self-financing, productive project loans such as the construction of a hydro-electric scheme or railway.[13] At Bretton Woods, the precise meaning of the phrase 'productive purposes' in the articles of the IBRD had not been defined. It was quickly resolved in favour of 'sound conservative' views, in part from ideological hostility to the New Deal. To Garner, Roosevelt was 'a man completely without principle' who 'did more harm to this country than anyone else in history'.[14] The Bank also justified its caution by the argument that programmatic loans would interfere with domestic policies and national sovereignty, and that normative issues of the distribution of wealth and poverty were matters for national governments. In Garner's view, '[t]he Bank should concentrate its efforts on projects which will yield the greatest and quickest increase in output and productivity' – criteria that would not be met by investment in social overheads even where the benefits were considerable. The Bank should support 'directly productive projects' that led to economic growth and enabled the recipients of loans 'to provide out of their own resources better municipal services, better housing, better health and education – in fact, all of the fruits of greater economic productivity'. This cautious, commercial approach was captured by the Bank's comment that the 'clothing and feeding of most Chinese and Hindus could only be justified on the basis of charity, and the world cannot afford this at the present moment'. Not surprisingly, the American ambassador to Chile reported that 'our enemies are . . . charging that the International Bank is under the domination of Wall Street and that we are back to Dollar Diplomacy with the Good Neighbor Policy scrapped.'[15]

The choice between investment in wider programmes or in specific projects was fought out in the IBRD's first general mission, to Colombia in 1949. The head of the mission was Lauchlin Currie, a Canadian economist who had studied at the LSE before moving to Harvard for his PhD and joining the Treasury and Federal Reserve, and then, in 1939, becoming an economic adviser to Roosevelt. Like his friend Harry Dexter White, he appeared before the House Un-American Activities Committee in August 1948 and was accused of being a Soviet agent. He survived, though justified suspicions remained. He joined the IBRD, where he continued to urge New Deal policies. Above all, Currie argued for broad, balanced growth by moving labour from the land into a block of industries that would help create a market, provide incentives to invest, and deliver a 'big push' into self-sustaining economic growth. Rather than 'piecemeal and sporadic efforts', he proposed a 'generalized attack' on 'the vicious circle of poverty, ignorance, ill-health and low productivity'. This approach required programme loans, an integrated development plan and investment in social overhead capital to escape from a low equilibrium of poverty, limited savings and inadequate investment. Tensions soon appeared over Currie's proposals. Garner put the matter pithily in 1951: 'Damn it, Lauch, we can't go messing around with education and health. We're a *bank*!' As Garner later commented, 'the Bank was not the place for the development of broad economic policies.'[16]

The IBRD turned to Albert Hirschman, a German émigré who joined the Federal Reserve after the war, where he reported on the dire situation in France and Italy. His stress on the need to stimulate regional trade and create a payments system made him one of the 'invisible men' of the Marshall Plan. His post at the Fed was not renewed and he moved to the IBRD. In his view, the problem facing undeveloped countries was not scarcity of resources but the lack of motivation to mobilize existing resources that were 'hidden, scattered or badly utilized'. He criticized 'balanced growth' for imposing a new self-contained modern sector on a stagnant and self-contained traditional sector. Instead, he saw opportunities within the traditional sector, and doubted that domestic capital, skills and institutions could sustain a 'big push'. He called for smaller steps to stimulate investment, starting from the 'micro-foundations' of social agents who responded to local difficulties according to local conditions, rather than programmatic aid which might benefit some social groups and harm others with the risk of domestic political conflict. He turned from a 'propensity to plan' based on suspect theory and statistics to a 'propensity to experiment and to improvise', so that balanced growth would eventually appear as entrepreneurs rose to the challenges of the market. His approach was 'possibilist' – groping for change in conditions of uncertainty in which small-scale interventions were preferable to grand schemes. It was closer to Latin American economists such as

Celso Furtado, Roberto Campos and Alexandre Kafka than to American economists who built sweeping models of development without close engagement with local conditions. Despite their disagreements, Hirschman and Currie had a common concern for practical advice based on local circumstances, and both men supported a wider approach than the IBRD's emphasis on specific, self-liquidating loans.[17]

Between 1946 and 1949, 81 per cent of the IBRD's modest loans of $220m went to Europe, compared with 19 per cent to Latin America, and 76 per cent of the loans were for programmes with only 2 per cent for specific investments. Between 1950 and 1959, the volume was larger ($390m) and the geographic spread was wider, with 15 per cent of loans going to Africa, 38 per cent to Asia, 20 per cent to Europe, 22 per cent to Latin America and 5 per cent to the Middle East and North Africa. Loans for programmes dropped to 21 per cent, and the proportion for specific projects rose to 53 per cent. Infrastructure (especially transport, irrigation and power generation) took the bulk of IBRD loans; education and health were neglected. Between 1948 and 1961, 83 per cent of funds to less developed countries went to power and transport projects.[18]

Although the wider, more inclusive approach of development and poverty reduction was marginalized in Washington, the IBRD's missions in the field were more supportive. Between 1949 and 1953, the IBRD organized eleven missions to less developed countries which, like the report on Colombia, were concerned both with the top management's stress on productivity and with the alleviation of extreme poverty. One staff member thought it 'ridiculous' that loans could be given for irrigation projects and not for urban water supplies on the grounds that they were not 'productive'. Neither should the division between conservative bankers and progressive development economists be exaggerated. Many officials, economic advisers and politicians in less developed economies also believed that development meant industrialization and urbanization, an end to traditional beliefs, and an increase in capital investment, largely from outside because of the limits imposed on domestic savings by poverty. They accepted the transformative capacity of large-scale capital projects such as those of the Tennessee Valley Authority or the great dams and irrigation projects of the Soviet Union. W. A. Lewis, for example, remarked in 1955 that

> The little man can improve his own house, or his small farm, or invest in a
> shop or a lorry, but this is less than half of the investment required for eco-
> nomic growth. The biggest lump of investment has to be in public works
> and public utilities, and . . . there is need for vast expenditures by public and
> public utility agencies on roads, railways, harbours, electric power, and

other big projects which are far beyond the capacity of the little man adjusting himself to his environment.[19]

Pressure on the IBRD's conservative approach emerged as newly independent countries joined the United Nations and urged a shift in policies. However, at the end of the war, the European imperial powers – Britain, France, the Netherlands and Belgium – still hoped that 'developing' their colonies in Africa and Asia offered a way of overcoming the 'dollar gap'.

IMPERIAL DEVELOPMENT

At the end of the Second World War, the European imperial powers had the challenge of reconstructing empires that had lost territory in North Africa and Asia to Italy, Germany and Japan – the latter a defeat by non-Europeans that could inspire nationalists, some of whom had an understanding with the Japanese. After the defeat of Japan, Sukarno in the Dutch East Indies and Ho Chi Minh in French Indo-China laid claim to territory that had to be recolonized – something that led to continued warfare and often failure by the European powers, who tried to find ways to make empire legitimate (at least in their eyes) at a time when their economic weakness made colonial production even more important.[20]

The independence of India was a foregone conclusion. The military costs of maintaining the Raj were too high and the resources of Britain too stretched – and India was no longer a net contributor to the balance of payments. In the past, India had a surplus with the United States and a deficit with Britain, so that its dollar earnings helped cover Britain's deficit with the United States.[21] The British retreat from India and the French from Indo-China meant that both countries turned to Africa, as we noted in Chapter 11. In 1946, an official at the British Colonial Office remarked that 'Africa is now the core of our colonial position; the only continental space from which we can still hope to draw reserves of economic and military strength.'[22] The solution, it seemed to Stafford Cripps in 1947, was to 'increase out of all recognition the tempo of African economic development' and to produce anything that 'will save dollars or will sell in a dollar market'. In his view, 'the whole future of the sterling area and its ability to survive depends . . . upon a quick and extensive development of our African resources.' Bevin went further: 'If only we pushed on and developed Africa we could have US dependent on us, and eating out of our hand in four or five years.' Africa was seen as a market for British goods and a source of raw materials. There were some successes, such as copper from Rhodesia which provided supplies to Britain and earned dollars from the United States, and cocoa from Ghana. In many cases, the colonial authorities took over marketing and distribution through marketing boards that bought raw materials and controlled prices and exports, such as the Cocoa Marketing Board in Ghana. There were also failures, most notoriously the East African Groundnuts scheme that aimed to grow peanuts to reduce shortages of cooking oil. The ambition for large-sale mechanized production outran any consideration of feasibility.[23] Malaya was particularly significant, for its rubber and tin were important resources for Britain and major earners of dollars, which encouraged both reconstruction after the defeat of Japan, and the military campaign against the Communist Party after 1948.[24]

Similar strategies were pursued by other imperial powers. The Dutch attempted to restore their colonies in Asia after the Japanese occupation – a difficult task given the resistance from nationalists.[25] In France, an attempt was made to hold on to colonies in Indo-China and, as in Britain, to develop Africa. In January and February 1944, the provisional Free French government had met in Brazzaville to consider the future of the French empire in Africa in response both to Roosevelt's opposition to colonies and to African nationalism. 'The object of our colonial policy', so it was claimed, was 'the development of the productive potential of the overseas territories and the growth of their wealth as to assure the Africans of a better life by raising their purchasing power and improving their standards of living.' After the war, Jean Monnet's plan for the French empire gave less weight to the conditions of colonial people and more to supplying raw materials to France, reducing imports from other countries, and selling more commodities to earn dollars. Monnet even hoped that the industrialization of Indo-China would lead to opportunities for French business in Asia after the collapse of Japan. However, the crisis of the French empire in the region meant that Africa became more important, with an expansion of agricultural production through schemes for irrigation and mechanization, such as cotton-growing in Sudan, which was scarcely more successful than the groundnuts scheme, and increasingly mining for bauxite, manganese and phosphates, and oil in Algeria. A franc zone was established on similar lines to the sterling area, with the CFA – Colonies françaises d'Afrique – franc pegged to the French franc. All foreign earnings were to be paid into a common fund, from which hard currency would be allocated to the colonies to cover their imports. Although the intention was to assist French firms and the metropolitan economy, most former colonies retained the CFA franc on independence, which offered the advantage of a stable currency, unlike some of their neighbours.[26]

These programmes of colonial economic development required action by the state. In Britain, unrest in the West Indies and central Africa led to interventions in 1940 that were extended in the Colonial Development and Welfare Act of 1945. The aim was to show that economic development could be linked with welfare in an ethical colonial policy based on trusteeship. Many colonial officials thought they were doing good: previous generations had helped the working class to respectability at home, and now they were helping Africans. Colonies were to devise ten-year development plans, and in 1948 the Colonial Development Corporation was established, with borrowing powers to encourage colonial production. Similarly, in France the Fonds d'Investissement pour le Développement Économique et Social des Territoires d'Outre Mer was created in 1946. This overturned the prohibition on supporting colonies from the French budget; now, the French state took the leading role, with 1,340bn francs of public investment between 1949 and 1955, compared with 100bn francs from private investors between 1947 and 1955. Colonies were to draw up development plans, with most of the investment going into infrastructure which benefitted French firms, both in securing construction contracts and in handling commodity trade.[27]

Alongside these economic plans, both Britain and France attempted to create a new colonial political identity. The British offered a subsidiary form of Commonwealth citizenship in the Nationalities Act of 1948, and embarked on the Africanization of local government with a promise of eventual independence in the Commonwealth. The result was to create demands for participation in the legislature and executive of the colony, and for better wages and fairer prices – with repression when they went too far. France went further. In 1946, the empire became a French Union in which the colonies were *territoires d'outre mer*. Colonial subjects became citizens without the need to submit to French civil law, with representation in Paris, an end to forced labour, and abolition of the system of separate justice (*indigénat*). Michel Debré, a leading French politician, claimed in 1953 that 'France is not only a European territory, she is not only a European nation; she is also an African nation, a musulman power, and her citizens embrace not only many religions but many races. The French Union forms a whole, a single legal conception.' It was a policy of integration that was combined with harsh treatment of any group that posed a threat, and it was challenged by doubts that Africa was really compatible with being French. The aim, in the words of Nicholas White, was 'to rejuvenate colonialism by making colonial peoples partners in their own economic exploitation'. It could also provide an opening for nationalists such as Léopold Sédar Senghor of Senegal, who was a member of the National Assembly in Paris. Rather than Eurafrica as a combination of African raw materials and European industry, he argued that Africa should participate in European institutions, and have the same rights as other members. To Senghor, the implication of Debré's claim that Africans were part of the French people was that they had a right to take part in any European initiatives, with both 'vertical' solidarity with Europe and 'horizontal' solidarity within Africa. This claim divided opinion in France. On the one hand, including French Africa would make France the largest member of any European grouping, as well as providing access to raw materials. On the other hand, Africans might ally with other European countries against France, with other members securing access to African raw materials and leaving France with the costs. This question of whether to integrate Africa into Europe was a major source of debate leading to the Treaty of Rome, as we will see in Chapter 14.[28]

American policy shifted from Roosevelt's anti-colonialism, in part because the Europeans presented themselves as embarking on development, and in part because Washington was concerned with economic recovery and political stability in Europe and the colonies.[29] In the short term, the British colonies helped with the dollar deficit, unlike in France where the colonies continued to have a dollar deficit and their subsidized production increased the costs of French firms. Development contributed to rising political tensions in the colonies because of shortages and inflation, with major strikes in British and French Africa at the time when production was vital to the empires. Colonial officials tried to incorporate trade unions into a settled urban workforce living in male breadwinner households, separated from backward rural villages. This ambition was far from the reality of life in cities with their continued links with the countryside and patterns of family life that were unlike Eurocentric assumptions. The unions' social networks could be used by nationalist leaders such as Senghor to oppose colonial rule. Development projects and regulations to protect forests or limit grazing of livestock disrupted local agriculture and alienated farmers. At the Colonial Office, the head of the economic division was clear: 'African systems of land tenure and the cultural routines associated with them, if maintained to the full in their traditional forms, would effectively prevent any rapid technical change, possibly any change at all.' Similarly, the French saw Africans as 'frozen in anachronistic and archaic concepts' and who 'do not see the necessity to participate in a voluntary and reasoned effort in the progress of their country'. Such attempts to make Africans into 'modern' farmers against their will created support in the countryside for nationalist leaders such as Jomo Kenyatta in Kenya and Kwame Nkrumah in Ghana. Both the French extension of citizenship to the colonies and the British creation of local African government had the opposite effect from what was intended – they gave space to more radical activists.

There were also tensions in London and Paris between those who looked to development to increase welfare and those who stressed the need for revenue. The lack of coherence in policy alienated imperial business interests who saw little reason to sustain the empire. Frank Samuel, an executive at Unilever, epitomized the shift in attitude. He suggested the disastrous groundnuts scheme in 1946; by 1951, he rejected 'wishful thinking ... that Tropical Africa is an El Dorado of wealth sorely neglected in the past and capable of being developed rapidly on a grand scale'. The future would not be European-led development but working with Africans, which required companies to devise strategies to operate in the new environment by seizing the business opportunities of aid, turning to a discourse of development to legitimize their presence, and making connections with political elites.[30]

THE UNITED NATIONS, EMPLOYMENT AND DEVELOPMENT

Debates over employment continued after the Havana conference, above all at the United Nations and its Economic and Social Council, which gave more voice to less developed countries. The Soviets and Czechoslovakians were members of the Council and they could act as 'Machiavellian self-styled protectors of the under-privileged'. The adviser to the US delegation to the UN realized that the less developed countries could exploit the Cold War, for 'there is always in the background the implication that unless the richer nations, particularly the United States, can provide adequate material assistance the underdeveloped countries must resort to communism and totalitarian means in an effort to lift themselves by their own boot straps'. ECOSOC allowed the less developed countries to express their views – and the best response by the West might be to counter with an 'affirmative economic policy'.[31]

When full employment was discussed at ECOSOC in 1949, the American economy was facing a downturn and a group of experts was appointed to report on 'national and international measures to achieve and maintain full employment' and to ensure non-discrimination in trade. The United States was attracted by the reference to trade, and under-developed countries by the promise to consider 'a high and stable level of international investment, particularly in under-developed areas of the world'. India, Pakistan and China wished to go further and add under-employment and development to the agenda. In November 1949, ECOSOC agreed to a wider remit and resolved that 'action is needed to overcome unemployment and under-employment such as that arising, particularly in under-developed countries, among large numbers of people engaged in agricultural pursuits; and that, to this end, it is necessary inter alia to stimulate the economic development of under-developed countries.' Full employment in advanced economies was therefore complemented by a concern for under-employment in less developed countries.[32]

The ensuing report on 'National and International Measures for Full Employment' was largely the work of Nicholas Kaldor, a left-wing Cambridge economist. It recommended Keynesian measures to create domestic full employment. Each country would announce its full employment target and the 'automatic counter-measures' of fiscal and monetary policies, investment and production planning, wages and prices policies to deal with unemployment or inflation. In addition, international measures were needed to prevent fluctuations spreading around the world. Any country that allowed its imports to fall below a level consistent with full employment would be obliged to deposit at the IMF an amount equivalent to its deflationary impact on the world, for use by countries whose exports were affected – a reaffirmation of Keynes's attempt to make creditor nations share the burdens of adjustment. The report argued that 'without the restoration of over-all equilibrium in balance of payment, it will be impossible to achieve the kind of stable international framework within which full employment policies can succeed'. Stable exchange rates and free trade could not restore equilibrium in a world of dollar scarcities, and the report therefore recommended that ECOSOC call a conference on world trade adjustment. It also argued that full employment needed economic development based on planned and stable capital movements between governments, organized by the IBRD through programmatic rather than project loans.[33]

When the report was discussed at ECOSOC in 1950, some British officials saw virtue in the scheme. Robert Hall pointed out that Britain already had full employment so that it had nothing to lose and much to gain from adoption of the report. The chances of that happening were remote, however. The IMF and IBRD argued that multilateral trade was the priority, and that the currency deposit scheme would delay adjustment. Jacob Viner was scathing. He saw a threat of socialism as well as technical problems of implementation. In his view, the report treated the economy as 'simple and mechanical and completely responsive to political regulation', with decisions reached by 'unified and sovereign authorities and of their subsequent execution or enforcement by government officials' – an approach that was far from the messy reality of political life.

Rather, mass unemployment should be prevented 'by means which serve to strengthen rather than to undermine the foundations of what remains of a free market, free trade, free enterprise world'. Henry Wallich, a member of President Eisenhower's Council of Economic Advisers and former head of the Federal Reserve Bank of New York's foreign research division, complained that the emphasis on full employment was the extreme opposite of the gold standard. It assumed complete internal rather than external stability and would subject the economy to 'the dictates of the fully employed instead of the golden calf'. The outcome would be inflation, on which the report was silent – and as a German émigré with experience of hyperinflation, Wallich had reason to believe that 'like burglary, inflation is an extra-legal form of redistribution'.[34]

The report ended discussion of full employment in international organizations. To Charles Kindleberger, its 'fairly extreme Keynesian solution' was the 'high-water mark of academic naivety' at the UN. Interest in policies to stimulate full employment was ebbing both in industrial countries, where unemployment was at a low level, and in under-developed countries which were more concerned with economic development. The immediate response of ECOSOC was to appoint a second group of economists to recommend ways of dealing with international recessions. Their report on 'Measures for International Economic Stability' proposed international commodity agreements; an increase in the capital of the IBRD; and larger reserves and greater flexibility for the IMF. The IMF and IBRD rejected the recommendations on the grounds that 'primary reliance for the avoidance and cure of depressions must be placed upon appropriate measures at the national level, especially in industrial countries'. Nor were the less developed countries convinced. At the ECOSOC meeting in 1950, Brazil, Chile, India, Pakistan and Peru argued that the real issue was under-employment. As a result, an expert panel was established, including W. Arthur Lewis, who provided much of the intellectual agenda for 'Measures for the Economic Development of Under-Developed Countries' of 1951.[35]

This report foresaw, and even welcomed, 'painful adjustments' to allow economic progress: 'Ancient philosophies have to be scrapped; old social institutions have to disintegrate; bonds of caste, creed and race have to burst; and large numbers of persons who cannot keep up with progress have to have their expectations of a comfortable life frustrated.' It rested on Lewis's assumption that undeveloped economies had a dual structure of traditional and capitalistic sectors, and that labour should move from the first to the second. In Lewis's model, labour was available at a low cost as a result of under-employment in agriculture, where its marginal productivity was low or even negative – that is, the marginal worker might eat more than he or she produced. Labour could therefore be moved from agri-culture without any loss of production and at a low wage. The under-developed countries could utilize the technology of advanced countries and employ workers in industry at a stable, real wage which would allow industrializa-tion, exports and a high return on capital, which could be reinvested. When the pool of surplus labour in the country was eventually depleted, wages and employment would assume the character of those of developed economies. Hence economic development meant industrialization and long-term struc-tural change, with an increase in the level of savings from 5 to 20 per cent of GNP. It also needed a political elite committed to a development strategy, and the creation of appropriate social, economic, political and legal institu-tions. Lewis's approach moved beyond Keynesian demand management and a concern for the transmission of recessions. He ignored agrarian reform, for he assumed that agriculture was stagnant and divorced from the capitalist sector, with no role for agricultural improvement or the release of incentives in peasant agriculture as ways of stimulating economic growth. Despite their differences, the discourse of development at the IBRD and among its critics shared a vision of modernity.[36]

'FUZZY' LOANS

In 1952, the United Nations General Assembly instructed ECOSOC to consider a Special Fund to make grants and low-interest long-term loans to under-developed countries 'to finance non-self-liquidating projects which are basic to their economic development' – a direct challenge to the bankers' view at the IBRD. Although the United States saw the risk of a split between developed and under-developed countries, participation made more sense than opposition. The American strategy was to attempt to pass responsibility for any loans to the IBRD and to private capital flows rather than to a new international agency that gave voice to under-developed countries.[37]

When the plan for the Special UN Fund for Economic Development – SUNFED – came to ECOSOC in 1953, American attitudes shifted, for political reasons. President Eisenhower stressed that the arms race with the Soviet Union had diverted resources from dealing with poverty and fostering prosperity. The death of Stalin that spring provided an oppor-tunity to replace spending on armaments by 'the dedication of the energies, the resources, and the imaginations of all peaceful nations to a new kind of war. This would be a declared total war, not upon any human enemy but upon the brute force of poverty and need.' Savings from disarmament should be applied to a 'fund for world aid and reconstruction ... to help other peoples to develop the undeveloped areas of the world, to stimulate profitable and fair world trade, to assist all peoples to know the blessings of productive freedom'. Eisenhower was offering a 'golden age of freedom and peace' to take the initiative at a vital point of the Cold War.[38] Despite Eisenhower's rhetoric, Congress refused to grant funds for the UN's technical assistance programme, a decision that was criticized by Arthur Bloomfield of the Federal Reserve as an 'act of self-mutilation' that might 'cost us very dearly in the scales of the cold war'.[39]

The American administration was suspicious of schemes that required the developed world to provide large capital funds to assist developing countries without adequate oversight and control. At the same time, it recognized that the IBRD's insistence on 'performing' loans was too narrow. The Bureau of Economic Affairs' report to the State Department insisted that a more active foreign economic policy was needed to maintain 'leadership of the free world'. NATO alone was not enough, for

> an alliance without economic underpinnings would be inadequate and unreliable ... Our efforts in the international field to promote a freer system of trade and payments and a freer flow of capital are aimed fundamentally at achieving a more efficient international use of resources and thereby maximizing the economic and military strength of the free world.

The IMF and GATT were appropriated to this Cold War project: 'These are the instruments through which we try jointly with other countries to establish a world trading system that will provide the real basis for high standards of living and a maximum contribution to military security.' The threat came not only from war but from internal subversion in underdeveloped countries, which meant responding with 'policies conducive to local investment and initiative and the establishment of a rational system of priorities in development programs'. American leadership should also entail high domestic activity to remove the 'pathological' fear of an American depression. In general,

> The US should assert an affirmative interest in the economic well-being of the free world as something which is good in itself and not merely as a defense against Communism. This is both good policy and good propaganda ... The worst mistake we can make ... would be to link our constructive economic programs so directly and obviously to our military objectives as to raise doubts in the minds of free world countries as to whether we are really interested in economic welfare as something which is good in itself.

Poverty and hopelessness in under-developed areas led to subversion that could only be overcome by 'steady economic improvement and the creation of a sense of hope for the future'. Action was needed to deal with distortions in the world economy and to encourage economic development on lines approved by the American administration. The Bureau was clear what this meant. 'A major task for US foreign economic policy is to get across to other countries an understanding of our conception of the role of government in economic affairs.' The approach, as Clarence Randall, chair of the Commission on Foreign Economic Policy, explained to Eisenhower in December 1954, was 'the release of normal forces within the framework of free enterprise and competitive markets, and is the antithesis of global spending'. The adviser to the American delegation to the UN admitted that American assistance could be viewed as an ideological, self-interested response to Communism at a time when 'many of the newly sovereign underdeveloped countries consider foreign private capital as a form of colonialism while many of the long independent underdeveloped countries consider it a means of exploitation'. Nevertheless, an attempt should be made at 'a really affirmative' policy to counter Soviet influence.[40]

The challenge was taken up by John Foster Dulles, Secretary of State from 1953 to 1959. Dulles realized the dangers of the IBRD's adherence to self-financing loans: 'It might be good banking to put South America through the wringer, but it will come out red.' He saw that the Communist East and capitalist West were engaged in a battle for development and that defeat 'could be as disastrous as defeat in the arms race'. The president of the Bank, Eugene Black, did not agree. He continued to insist on strict financial terms for loans and opposed '"fuzzy" transactions' that confused loans and grants, and would 'impair the integrity of all international credit operations':

> Diplomatists and military strategists [who] offer economic aid in exchange
> for a military alliance or a diplomatic concession ... are certainly not serv-
> ing the interest of orderly economic development; in fact they may well be
> abetting and perpetuating conditions which in a short time will render their
> military alliances and diplomatic concessions quite hollow victories.[41]

Despite these doubts, Black had to make concessions.

The ECOSOC proposed an International Finance Corporation (IFC) to provide equity finance to developing countries. The State Department was doubtful, for profitable firms could already secure private finance. When the IFC started operating in 1956, it provided debenture and not equity capital, and was run by the IBRD to encourage free enterprise and private capital in under-developed countries.[42] In 1958, the General Assembly agreed to establish SUNFED as a 'transient compromise' between two approaches. On the one side, a group of developing countries from Latin America and Asia, together with the Netherlands, Greece and Yugoslavia, proposed a fund to finance infrastructure such as roads, schools, hospitals and housing. On the other side, the Americans preferred to give money to the UN's Expanded Programme of Technical Assistance. The compromise was a Special Fund to draw on savings from world disarmament complemented by technical assistance to assess programmes and ensure that money was not wasted. The developing countries secured half of the seats on the governing body of SUNFED, but its managing director – Paul Hoffman once more – ensured that most funding went on surveys, training and research institutes rather than on capital development, so that its modest funds were used in a more conservative manner than the developing countries wished.[43] The risk, in the opinion of many in the developed world, was that 'fuzzy loans' from SUNFED and the IFC would blur the line between grants and prudent 'hard' loans. The risk of opposing the less developed countries, however, was that the UN might create an agency that would be hostile to America. The Eisenhower administration shifted from delaying tactics to reluctant acceptance of 'fuzzy' loans to avoid a loss of influence by taking a 'perpetual negative position'. Meanwhile, at the IBRD, Eugene Black agreed to the establishment of regional development banks, starting with the Inter-American Development Bank in 1959, and in 1960 to an International Development Association to offer soft loans or 'credits' for wider programmes of poverty alleviation. Rosenstein-Rodan welcomed the Bank's acceptance of 'fuzzy loans' as a sign of 'intellectual progress'. In reality, it was a pragmatic response to Cold War politics and the IBRD continued its cautious use of project loans.[44]

MALTHUSIAN VISIONS

The new institutions dealing with issues of development after the war included the Food and Agriculture Organization and the World Health Organization. Both had links to initiatives of the League and the Rockefeller Foundation in the 1930s, and their concern for hunger, nutrition and public health went beyond the 'bankers' approach' of the IBRD. They became part of debates over the ability of the resources of the world to sustain a growing global population that reopened Thomas Malthus's fear that a geometric increase in population would outstrip an arithmetic increase in the output of food until a new balance was struck by the preventative check of reduced birth rates or the positive check of disease, famine and war. Escape from this Malthusian trap might be possible by scientific interventions in agriculture to increase output, or by limiting population growth through birth control, or by raising prosperity and changing social attitudes so that families looked to a higher standard of living and greater opportunities rather than having more children.

In 1948, the FAO's director general, John Boyd Orr, remarked that 'those who have never known hunger are rightly interested in political freedom. The ill-fed masses are rightly interested in the freedom from want.'[45] After the war, he saw an immediate problem of low food production and rapid population increase that could only be resolved by a higher standard of living and education in developing countries that would reduce birth rates without a need for population control. In the interim, the World Food Plan, overseen by ECOSOC and the IBRD, would ensure adequate nutrition. To Boyd Orr's chagrin, the FAO was confined to collecting data, offering technical assistance to farmers, and researching issues such as rice cultivation and locust control. But he continued to believe that science could resolve the problem of the world's food supply through plant genetics, pesticides, fertilizers, animal breeding and investment in dams and irrigation schemes, complemented by better distribution of resources through international action. In his view, hunger was a way that rich, developed countries maintained the power they had obtained over two-thirds of the world's population during centuries of conflict. What was now needed was an end to over-consumption in the West and over-population in the Third World by creating a world of plenty and fair distribution that would end the economic dependency of less developed countries and create the conditions for a fall in the birth rate.[46]

The director general of the FAO from 1956 to 1967, Binay Ranjan Sen, tried to revive this more radical approach. He had been a relief commissioner during the Bengal famine and India's director of food from 1943 to 1946. In 1959, the FAO approved the Freedom from Hunger Campaign, which would lead to a World Food Congress to celebrate the twentieth anniversary of the Hot Springs conference. In preparation, Sen called a UN Special Assembly on Man's Right to Freedom from Hunger which he claimed was 'the biggest human problem of the century', and that solving it would raise the 'moral and intellectual stature' of humanity more than putting men on the moon. He called for a new ideology of development for the 'fullest and most effective use of all human and natural resources'. He supported training and incentivizing local people, the adoption of genetically improved crops, and population control, without which he feared 'uncontrolled famines'.[47]

A scientific approach to food was supported by American philanthropic foundations, especially by Raymond Fosdick at the Rockefeller Foundation which provided a link with the internationalist ambitions at the end of the First World War. Fosdick had been an assistant secretary general of the League before the United States failed to join, and he continued to be active in the League of Nations Association. Above all, he worked closely with John D. Rockefeller as his lawyer and as trustee of the Foundation, before he became its president from 1936 to 1948. The Foundation had been involved in questions of health since its inception in 1913 and ran programmes such as developing a vaccine against yellow fever and taking measures to control malaria. This concern for public health in the 'backward' agricultural areas of the American South, Europe, Latin America, South Asia and China was complemented by an interest in food supply. In 1924, Fosdick pressed the need to 'take stock of our planetary resources . . . to develop the method by which the population of the globe can best be sustained'. Unlike Malthus, he did not fear that population would outstrip food supply, for science had the solution. In 1943, the Foundation invested in plant breeding at the Mexican Agricultural Program, where Norman Borlaug ran a research programme on wheat and became a leading figure in the 'green revolution' of the 1960s that was hoped would end hunger and starvation. The Foundation's focus was above all on the supply side of Malthus's equation – and its interventions in public health could increase population pressure by reducing deaths.[48]

The Rockefeller Foundation provided between 30 and 40 per cent of the budget of the World Health Organization, which grew out of the League's Health Organization. In 1946, its constitution claimed that 'the right to health is one of the fundamental rights to which every human being, without distinction of race, sex, language or religion is entitled'. The new institution had fifty-five member countries, including colonies with associate status, each with one vote. They met in the World Health Assembly, which was conceived as a global health parliament where national representatives would decide policy. The WHO's operations were run by medically qualified staff in Geneva, with a high level of delegation to six regional offices which pursued a technological, scientific campaign against individual diseases – above all by spraying insecticides from planes in the hope of eradicating malaria and by developing vaccines against smallpox and tuberculosis. This technocratic approach avoided the need for the WHO to intervene in local culture; it also failed to escape from colonial assumptions about the ignorance of native populations.

These activities were supported by the American government to gain influence in the Cold War, as well as by the Rockefeller Foundation. But it was not only a Cold War project. When the Soviets re-joined the WHO in

1956 (having withdrawn from the body in 1949), they offered backing for the smallpox programme, and many countries in Latin America and Asia welcomed the programmes as part of their development strategy. The WHO's medical experts were drawn from Latin America and Asia to a greater extent than in other international organizations. In particular, India was the centre of a network in South-East Asia with an ambivalent relationship to the legacy of the colonial state.

There were some successes. The programme to eradicate malaria started in 1955, building on the work of the Rockefeller Foundation. At first it went well, with 8,704 anti-malaria teams in India by 1958; recorded cases fell from 75 million in 1951 to 50,000 in 1961. Before long, however, mosquitoes developed resistance, and the harmful human and ecological effects of spraying insecticides became apparent. More successfully, the programme to eradicate smallpox was launched in 1959 and completed the task by 1979. The approach of the WHO rested on combining modest funding with effective – often draconian – scientific interventions. This technocratic approach encountered opposition, whether in the form of the practical issues of delivery in difficult conditions or hostility to control over people's bodies. What was not feasible was a more democratic approach to public health through primary health care and tackling the more general respiratory or gastrointestinal diseases caused by poverty and nutritional deficiencies. The 'magic bullet' of tackling specific diseases had priority over social medicine.[49]

The development of scientific agriculture was linked with land reform. In the late 1930s, large estates in Mexico were broken up and land distributed to *ejidos* or communes of small farms which would provide schools, clinics and credit. Nelson Rockefeller welcomed this approach, for 'under the ejidal system, profits, though less, stayed in and were spent in Mexico. The financial structure is considered an important experiment in exploring solutions for the world-wide agrarian problem.' This policy might reconcile peasants with urban elites, and it seemed to many in the United States to be preferable to either a right-wing agrarian state or left-wing revolution. The combination of land reform and agricultural technology offered an alternative to Soviet collectivization by creating small, competitive farmers whose attitudes were expected to be transformed by the profit motive and education. The approach had its critics, such as George Messersmith, the American ambassador to Mexico, who complained in 1942 that the *ejido* could be a block to efficiency. Indeed, the Rockefeller Foundation's programme in Mexico shifted from a strategy of modernizing peasant holdings to large-scale farms that could better use Borlaug's improved crops and agricultural techniques.[50]

After the war, land reform was advocated by the United States government for political rather than economic reasons – to create stable, democratic societies as in a Jeffersonian American republic of yeomen farmers. At the Department of Agriculture, Wolf Ladejinsky, the son of a Ukrainian landowner whose property had been confiscated by the Soviets, argued that small holdings could democratize Asia and create a bulwark of independent yeomen against the threat of Communism. In 1945, he joined the staff of the Supreme Commander of the Allied Forces in Tokyo, where he carried out a programme of land reform to break up great estates whose owners were thought to be feudal relics and militarists, and to transfer the land to tenants.[51] The policy was also adopted in Korea and Taiwan.

In North Korea, the Communists confiscated the property of large landowners. In South Korea, the American occupation forces needed both to secure support from conservative landed elites and to make a concession to peasants to prevent their backing the Communists. In 1948, both aims were achieved by distributing land owned by the defeated Japanese imperial government, companies and individuals – a step that contributed to successful democratic elections. The new government then embarked on a wider programme of land redistribution as part of a project to build a modern, anti-Communist state. In Taiwan, the Nationalist Kuomintang government withdrew from mainland China after its defeat in 1949. They had few links with the local landed elite, which gave them more freedom, and they could – as in South Korea – redistribute land from the Japanese who had taken control of the island in 1895. In Japan, the socialist minister of agriculture wanted to solve the problem of rural poverty by land reform, which was feasible because military defeat and American intervention broke vested interests. The policy was politically successful but less so economically, for small farms and agricultural protection slowed down the release of labour.[52]

Land reform played a role in the transformation of Japan, South Korea and Taiwan but it was not pursued with the same vigour or success in other parts of Asia. In North Vietnam, the Communists embarked on land reform by confiscating land from large landowners and rich peasants and distributing it to small peasant farmers organized into co-operatives. They were able to apply this policy in parts of South Vietnam, too, as a strategy for securing support for the Vietcong. In 1954, the American government urged the government of Ngo Dinh Diem to undertake land reform in South Vietnam but the programme was modest. In 1967, Roy Prosterman – an American lawyer – argued that impoverished Vietnamese peasants' support for the Vietcong could be weakened by 'land to the tiller' – that is, all land should be owned by those who farmed it, with landowners fully compensated by the United States government. The programme commenced in 1970 as one element in the 'Vietnamization' of the war. By then, it was too late to reshape society and the war was soon lost. The policy of land reform was less successful here than in South Korea because there was less capacity to redistribute land from Japanese imperialists, and the ruling elite lacked interest. In other countries such as the Philippines or India, political conditions were not conducive to reform, and there was a powerful counter view that prioritized large-scale mechanization or better crops and fertilizers rather than land redistribution.[53]

In the absence of land reform, other policies were developed to transform the social world of the peasant. The Ford Foundation and American aid looked to 'Community Development' in India, Indonesia and the Philippines to improve sanitation, education, animal husbandry and crops, by raising expectations and encouraging a 'modern' work ethic. The experience of China showed that the villages of Asia were a 'breeding ground for violent revolution'. Paul Hoffman, President of the Ford Foundation from 1950 to 1953, warned that the threat of a Communist takeover in India required 'economic areas of strength' to complement America's military power in Japan and the Philippines. Community Development was not a success and was abandoned by the Ford Foundation, though it had an afterlife in the creation of fortified strategic hamlets in Vietnam in the hope of gaining support from the 'apathetic rural population' that was vulnerable to Communism.[54]

Community development and land reform focused on human relations. By contrast, the engineers of the great dams viewed poverty as the result of constraints on resources. The Tennessee Valley Authority (TVA) offered 'democracy on the march' – a model for liberal development as an alternative to state control in the Soviet Union. David Lilienthal of the TVA stressed private–public co-operation that linked large-scale planned and socially transformative development with local control and participation in a public corporation. Engineering expertise would harness natural resources for development by providing hydro-electric power, controlling floods and bringing land into cultivation through irrigation. By tapping natural resources, regional economic and social development would be encouraged, and prosperity extended to deprived regions. The TVA and its imitators were more than capital projects; they were expected to provoke social and cultural change, transforming lives and views of the world. From the 1930s, these ideas were projected internationally by Lilienthal and Eugene Staley, an economist at Tufts University who called for a global system hospitable to American liberal values through international co-operation and systematic intervention in poorer parts of the world. These ideas were picked up by Nationalist China's grandiose scheme for a Yangtze Valley Authority as a response to the threat of Communism. In 1949 the historian Arthur Schlesinger linked the democratic and inclusive model of the TVA with the 'politics of freedom' that would harness the technological dynamism of the United States to counter Soviet political ideology: 'Our engineers can transform arid plains or poverty-stricken river valleys into wonderlands of vegetation and power . . . The Tennessee Valley Authority is a weapon which, if properly employed, might outbid all the social ruthlessness of the Communists for the support of the peoples of Asia.'[55]

This vision was integral to President Truman's inaugural address in January 1949, when he set out a 'program for peace and freedom' to strengthen the United Nations, support world economic recovery, and strengthen freedom-living nations from aggression. In Point Four, he urged

> a bold new program for making the benefits of our scientific advances and industrial progress available for the improvement and growth of under-developed areas . . . For the first time in history, humanity possesses the knowledge and skill to relieve the suffering of these people. The United States is pre-eminent among nations in the development of industrial and scientific techniques . . . We should make available to peace-loving peoples the benefits of our store of technical knowledge in order to help them realize their aspirations for a better life . . . The old imperialism – exploitation for foreign profit – has no place in our plans. What we envisage is a program of development based on the concepts of democratic fair-dealing . . . Greater production is the key to prosperity and peace. And the key to greater production is a wider and more vigorous application of modern scientific and technical knowledge.[56]

Truman's speech reflected the assumptions of Lilienthal and Staley – and of the Rockefeller Foundation's medical programmes – that technology would stimulate politically acceptable social and economic change by linking state planning with non-governmental groups and international institutions. It would create stability and prevent Asia sliding into Communism. In 1954, Staley argued that the future of under-developed countries involved a choice between two competing systems – Communist totalitarianism or liberal, democratic capitalism. As Staley remarked, 'we can have a TVA . . . without nationalizing all the enterprises along Main Street.'[57]

Liberal development failed in the Yangtze valley when the Communists took power in 1949, but the ideas were transferred to other parts of the world. Lilienthal set up a consulting firm to advise countries from

Colombia to Iran and Vietnam on liberal development as a means of transforming attitudes:

> If a great dam . . . inspires people in a country with a feeling that this is theirs, and that it provides an opportunity, a leverage by which they and their young people can look to the future with hopefulness in specific ways, then that great dam as an inspiration will produce more than electricity and irrigation . . . It will produce a change in spirit, a release of energies and self-confidence which are the indispensable factors in the future of that country.[58]

The approach was adopted around the world, from the Helmand Valley Authority in Afghanistan to the Damodar Valley in India (see Chapter 13), the Akosombo Dam in Ghana, and the Aswan Dam in Egypt – often with limited success, both economically and politically. This rhetoric of modernization could be used just as well by the Communist Soviet Union, which embarked on massive infrastructural schemes under direct state control, as well as funding projects in other countries in competition with the United States.

In their different ways, Boyd Orr and Lilienthal were confident that science and technology could avoid a Malthusian crisis. Others were less sure. In 1954, American businessman and government adviser Hugh Moore warned of a 'population bomb', and asked: 'Is homo sapiens destined to consume his food supplies and perish as many other species have done in history?' Such Malthusian fears led some to think it prudent to act on population as well as resources. At the start of the war, the League's demographic committee had moved from Geneva to Princeton, where Frank Notestein, who ran the Princeton Office of Population Research, shared their wider interests in food security, health and reproduction. He became director of the UN Division of Population, which had less freedom to advocate birth control because of the large number of Catholic members. In 1952 an attempt to add family planning to the responsibilities of the World Health Organization was blocked by a combination of Roman Catholic and Communist countries.[59]

Julian Huxley, an evolutionary biologist and first director of the UN Educational, Scientific and Cultural Organization (UNESCO), was less constrained. In 1950, the UNESCO statement on 'The Race Question' argued that 'the unity of mankind from both the biological and social viewpoint is the main thing'. In Huxley's view, eugenics should remove undesirable variations in the genetic pool of all ethnic groups and classes, and eliminate impediments to ability by ensuring that the poor had good nutrition and education. Talent could only be identified after removing social and economic inequality in a 'single equalized environment'. At that point, biological inequality could be identified, and human reproduction regulated by controlling the quality of the population through social and economic planning, birth control and voluntary sterilization of the small number who were defective. 'No-one doubts the wisdom of managing the germ-plasm of agricultural stocks, so why not apply the same concept to human stocks?'[60] Huxley accepted that food supplies would increase and also that population control was needed.

UNESCO turned to the relationship between food and population. One of the leading contributors to the discussion was Kingsley Davis – an American sociologist and demographer – who saw a dangerous demographic transition. In an influential article of 1945, he argued that a society started from high death and birth rates with little or no growth of population. Medical intervention then reduced death rates, high birth rates continued, and population grew rapidly. Davis feared that public health policies that reduced the death rate of poor countries would lead to a Malthusian crisis of overpopulation, famine and epidemics: 'in the long-run perspective, the growth of the earth's population has been like a long, thin powder fuse that burns slowly and haltingly until it finally reaches the charge and then explodes.' In time, industrialization and modernization would lead to a modern demographic regime of low death and birth rates, but there was the immediate pressure of rapid population growth and migration from Asia to less densely settled areas of the world occupied by Europeans. His solution was a positive policy to encourage lower birth rates. In 1959, Huxley agreed: 'Death control can get out of control. To this there is only one desirable answer – birth control.' Similarly, John D. Rockefeller III, who was somewhat marginalized in the Rockefeller Foundation, worried that its work on public health contributed to population growth and undermined its projects to improve human welfare. In 1952, he convened a group of experts that led to the Population Council, whose work on fertility control ran alongside the Foundation's concern for public health and agriculture.[61]

The debate over food and population connected with debates over global ecology and the environment that viewed the planet as a single ecological system – from bacteria in the soil to humans. In 1948, Boyd Orr warned of the collapse of the cycle from soil to plants, animals and mankind and back to the soil: 'wanton waste of the fertility of the earth, which nature has taken many thousands of years to create, is going on to a greater or lesser extent in all continents'. Fairfield Osborn's *Our Plundered Planet* (1948) and *The Limits of the Earth* (1953), and William Vogt's *Road to Survival* (1948) were bestsellers that called for action to protect the earth from a surge in population growth that resulted in soil erosion, dustbowls, depleted rivers and deforestation that would threaten the future of food supplies. Osborn's concern was geopolitical as much as environmental. For the first time, the world lacked new land and 'one of the principal causes of the aggressive attitudes of individual nations and of much of the present discord among groups of nations is traceable to diminishing productive lands and to increasing population pressures.' Vogt suggested halting measures to reduce the death rates in undeveloped areas so that 'natural' death control could return. He also felt that conservation was pointless without birth control. He was director of the Planned Parenthood Foundation of America and president of the Family Planning Association, not from a concern for the right of women to control their fertility or for economic security so much as from his commitment to nature. Birth control remained politically difficult, and Hugh Moore's and Vogt's apocalyptic visions were not accepted by advocates of science and technology. At the Rockefeller Foundation, Warren Weaver, the director of natural sciences from 1932 to 1955, continued with a non-Malthusian argument. He accepted that the earth was a closed system but argued that the constraint was neither crops nor the land – it was energy, which was potentially inexhaustible from solar, tidal and nuclear power.[62] These competing visions of Malthusian disaster or technological abundance continued to divide opinion in the coming decades.

New initiatives and concerns over development changed the dynamic of global government. At the same time, the Cold War and decolonization changed the dynamic of international debate. The IBRD's limited approach of project loans was challenged within the organization and, even more, from outside. The American administration recognized that the IBRD's commercial approach did not provide an adequate response to the Cold War, and that economic aid was closely allied to strategic need. The IBRD was also challenged by independent bodies such as the Rockefeller and Ford foundations, and by other international agencies such as the FAO, WHO and UNESCO, which viewed global governance in terms of the balance of resources and population rather than the international monetary system or multilateral trade. These anxieties over population and hunger were mainly concerned with the less developed countries and led to an interplay between fears in the Global North of mass migration and instability and demands in the Global South for a fairer distribution of the world's resources.

A common element in the approach of international organizations, philanthropic foundations and national governments to less developed countries is that they needed to modernize and become more like the developed world. Experts enquired into their economic and social conditions and defined the problems of population growth, lack of technology and capital, inefficient agriculture, illiteracy and cultural attitudes. The rhetoric of development was permeated by cultural and racial attitudes that saw other countries as child-like and in need of guidance by experts. The focus was on cash crops, industrialization and the application of capital and science, rather than domestic food crops and the use of intermediate technology – and the discourse largely ignored the role of women as producers. Although development was linked with anti-Communism, the Soviet Union – and indeed many newly independent countries – shared assumptions about the need for modernization and economic development to create a new society that broke with tradition.[63]

The discourse of development defined the under-developed world and its problems in a particular way. Could an alternative discourse challenge the Global North and redefine the agenda? ECOSOC gave space for the Soviets 'to criticise and to propagandise' and 'a sounding board for arguments for and against policies which it has no part in making'. It proved to be a disappointment and was little more than a talking shop. Manuel Pérez-Guerrero, a Venezuelan official who became the president of ECOSOC, remarked that over time it 'was divested of its own tasks and functions, because it did not work'.[64] As a result, in the 1950s less developed countries – many of them newly independent – looked elsewhere to formulate an approach to employment and development that sought radical changes in the world economy by altering the terms of trade in favour of primary producers. Politicians in undeveloped countries denied that the world economy was organized fairly between industrial and non-industrial countries, and they proposed measures to raise, as well as stabilize, the prices of primary products. In their view, international trade did not offer the benefits of comparative advantage to all participants. Rather, it supplied cheap raw materials to manufacturing countries, leading to exploitation and dependence. Hence the system had to be changed and international organizations needed to give more voice to developing countries.

The process of articulating an alternative approach started at the Bandung conference in April 1955 – a meeting co-sponsored by India, Indonesia, Burma, Pakistan and Ceylon that brought together representatives of a further twenty-four nations from Africa, Asia and the Middle East. It was a diverse group that included Japan, the People's Republic of China, North and South Vietnam, Saudi Arabia, Egypt, Iran and Iraq. Their alternative agenda eventually led to a new body – the United Nations Conference on Trade and Development (UNCTAD) – with a vision of the international economy that challenged the IMF, IBRD and GATT.

13

'A common detestation of colonialism'

Development, Nationalism and the Cold War

'We are united ... by a common detestation of colonialism in whatever form it appears ... We are often told "Colonialism is dead." Let us not be deceived or even soothed by that. I say to you, colonialism is not yet dead. How can we say it is dead, so long as vast areas of Asia and Africa are unfree. And I beg of you do not think of colonialism only in the classic form ... Colonialism has also its modern dress, in the form of economic control, intellectual control, actual physical control by a small but alien community within a nation. It is a skillful and determined enemy, and it appears in many guises. It does not give up its loot easily.'

President Sukarno, speech at the opening
of the Bandung conference, 18 April 1955[1]

'The wealth of the imperial countries is our wealth too ... From all these continents, under whose eyes Europe today raises up her tower of opulence, there has flowed out for centuries towards that same Europe diamonds and oil, silk and cotton, wood and exotic products. Europe is literally the creation of the Third World.'

Frantz Fanon, *The Wretched of the Earth*, 1963[2]

After Japan surrendered in August 1945, war in Asia continued as a nationalist struggle against the reimposition of western imperial rule by the Dutch, French and British. Before the war, Sukarno had been a nationalist leader against the Dutch; during the war, he collaborated with the Japanese in exchange for support in spreading nationalist ideas. When Japan surrendered, he declared himself President of Indonesia, and secured formal recognition of his country's independence in 1949. The British offered support in restoring their French and Dutch colonial counterparts and faced their own difficulties in returning to Burma and Malaya.[3] The

Leaders of five non-aligned countries met in New York in September 1960:
(*left* to *right*) Prime Minister Pandit Jawaharlal Nehru of India, President Kwame
Nkrumah of Ghana, President Gamal Abdel Nasser of the United Arab Republic,
President Sukarno of Indonesia and President Josip Broz Tito of Yugoslavia.

costs were high, and Britain retreated from the Indian subcontinent in 1947 with the creation of newly independent states in Pakistan and India. The western imperial powers continued to look to colonies in Africa as a source of prosperity, but by the 1960s Britain, France, Belgium and, eventually, Portugal were in retreat. The decline of formal empire intersected with the Cold War as the Americans, Russians and Chinese competed for influence in the newly independent countries of Africa and Asia, which could play these rivals off against each other. Formal independence was only part of the story. In Latin America, political independence from Spain and Portugal since the 1820s had not created economic independence; the 'informal imperialism' of British and American capital investment and their reliance on exports of primary products to the advanced industrial economies kept Latin America in a subordinate position. Sukarno was adamant that the newly independent countries should not succumb to such neo-colonial economic dependence.

The views of recently colonized or primary producing countries were articulated at Havana and at the United Nations where, for different reasons, the Americans, Soviets and Chinese were anti-imperialist. The British position was complicated, for different parts of the empire had diverging views. The initial work on the creation of a permanent United Nations organization was undertaken by Leo Pasvolsky at the State Department and was designed to preserve the wartime alliance against the Axis powers. However, the preamble of the UN Charter was largely drafted by Jan Smuts, the leader of the Boers against Britain in the second Boer War of 1899 to 1902. After defeat in 1902, Smuts worked with Britain to create a united South Africa. He was both a proponent of white supremacy and an 'imperial internationalist' who played a major role in the creation of the League of Nations. Now, the preamble to the Charter reaffirmed 'faith in fundamental human rights, in the dignity and worth of the human person, in the equal rights of men and women . . . and to promote social progress and better standards of life in larger freedom'.[4] Mark Mazower, the historian of world government, points out that some of those attending the founding conference in San Francisco saw this 'universalizing rhetoric of freedom and rights as all too partial – a veil masking the consolidation of a great power directorate that was not as different from the Axis powers, in its imperious attitude to how the world's weak and poor should be governed, as it should have been.' To Mazower, both the League and UN Charter were less an expression of Woodrow Wilson's idealistic internationalism – itself permeated by racism – than of British imperial thought. Smuts hoped the UN would prolong white rule through international co-operation, so that South Africa could incorporate the mandated territories it had held from the League since the end of the First World War.[5]

Smuts' style of 'imperialist internationalism' and white supremacy was challenged. The UN gave voice to African opinion and refused Smuts' request for South Africa to take over the mandated territories, despite backing from London. Above all, India – still part of the British empire – took a crucial role in opposing South African ambitions. The status of Indians living in South Africa had been raised by Gandhi before the First World War. In 1946, Nehru responded to growing discrimination by taking the issue to the UN General Assembly rather than to London which had no intention of taking sides. White supremacy in South Africa could not be insulated from the rest of the Commonwealth and the UN was not, as the British had hoped, a supporter of the empire. The Indian complaint against South Africa was upheld by the UN, which determined that discrimination against Indians was incompatible with the Charter. At the same time, Nehru insisted that the Indian delegation should remain neutral between the rival power blocs, and that they were making not just an Indian but 'a world cause' for Asians and Africans in demanding 'equality of opportunity for all races and against the Nazi doctrine of racialism'. These arguments had implications for the Dutch in Indonesia and the French in Indo-China. Smuts' hopes for the UN were dashed. Rather than supporting imperial internationalism, it might challenge European rule and white supremacy. To Smuts, it was the end of European civilization.[6]

During the 1950s and 1960s, more countries in Asia and Africa secured independence and took seats in the UN; by 1960, the Afro-Asian bloc had forty-six votes out of ninety-nine.[7] At Bandung in 1955, they embarked on a process of articulating a 'third way'. One way was American liberal capitalism, with its emphasis on free markets and multilateral trade; another was Soviet state-directed transformation through the collectivization of agriculture and forced industrialization. The third way was non-alignment between the Americans and Soviets. The result was a challenge to the international institutions' identification with the advanced industrial economies of the West, and the emergence of new national economic models that had long-term implications for the reordering of global government.

THE BANDUNG CONFERENCE: DEVELOPMENT IN ASIA AND AFRICA

The Bandung conference of 1955 arose from the complex politics of Indonesian insurgency and independence, followed by continued political tensions and Communist challenge. It was in this context that President Sukarno presided over the conference held in his country, with its call to defeat colonialism. He urged the peoples of Africa and Asia – half the population of the world – to unite and show that 'we, the majority, are for peace, not for war'.[8]

At Bandung, Jawaharlal Nehru – the prime minister of the world's largest democracy – set out the basis for non-alignment between the advanced Western economies and Communism that would offer self-sufficiency and freedom in a world divided by the Cold War:

> So far as I am concerned, it does not matter what war takes place; we will not take part in it unless we have to defend ourselves. If I join any of these big groups I lose my identity ... If all the world were to be divided up between these two big blocs what would be the result? The inevitable result would be war. Therefore every step that takes place in reducing that area in the world which may be called the *unaligned area* is a dangerous step and leads to war. It reduces that objective, that balance, that outlook which other countries without military might can perhaps exercise.[9]

His approach went back to India's strategy at the UN in 1946 and the Inter-Asian Relations Conference of 1947 that looked to India's return to Asia, from which it had been separated by British rule. Despite his fine words at Bandung, Nehru realized that hopes for Asian solidarity were already lost because of internal divisions during the Cold War.[10]

The leading African representative at Bandung was Kwame Nkrumah, who had created a mass nationalist party in the British colony of the Gold Coast (Ghana), which secured partial self-government in 1951 and full independence in 1957. Nkrumah's policy was non-aligned Marxism. As he explained in *Neo-colonialism: The Last Stage of Imperialism* (1965), '[t]he essence of neo-colonialism is that the State which is subject to it is, in theory, independent and has all the outward trappings of international sovereignty. In reality, its economic system and thus its political policy is directed from outside.'[11] Hence his policies were designed to lessen Ghana's dependence on foreign capital and to industrialize. To these leaders of the 'third world', capitalism was associated with colonialism and subordination, and Soviet Communism was too European and too rigid. Both sides in the Cold War were considered colonialists who wished to impose political control and economic development based on their own system. The countries attending Bandung had a common hostility to past imperialism and current neo-colonialism. Their aim was to secure political and economic sovereignty, to construct solidarity between the former colonies, and to press for a peaceful resolution of conflict.[12]

The final communiqué at Bandung confidently reported participants' 'general desire for economic co-operation ... on the basis of mutual interest and respect for national sovereignty'. The Bandung Declaration called on countries to diversify their export trade; to establish national and regional banks; and to develop peaceful nuclear power. It denounced colonialism in all its forms, and urged independence for Tunisia, Algeria and Morocco, and support for Palestine. Despite these shared commitments, politically and economically, the countries that met at Bandung were highly diverse. Japan had been a colonial power and was already industrialized – and Iran and Iraq were major oil producers with large revenues. These countries were hostile to the anti-American rhetoric of other participants. Asian countries were peasant societies with huge labour surpluses; Africa, by contrast, had abundant land with a need for different development strategies. Some countries faced Communist insurrections, yet the Communists were represented at the conference by Zhou Enlai of China, at that time still an ally of the Soviet Union and distrusted by other participants. The non-aligned countries could exploit the competing interests of America and the Soviet Union to secure assistance without formally committing to one side or the other. However, the chances of holding together such a diverse group of countries were slim – indeed, India and China went to war in 1962, and India and Pakistan in 1965.[13]

Before long, Indonesia faced ethnic conflicts, Islamic extremism, Communist insurgents, and demands from the military. In 1957, Sukarno declared martial law and embarked on economic nationalism by taking over Dutch companies. When the Americans provided aid to the rebels, Sukarno turned to China and the Soviet Union for military assistance – so provoking Eisenhower and Kennedy to increase aid. Sukarno was playing the West off against the Communist powers, accusing both of spreading neo-colonialism and imperialism. In 1959, he replaced party-based democracy with 'guided democracy' and mobilized the mass base of the Communists against the army. In 1961, he launched the Non-Aligned Movement with Gamal Abdel Nasser of Egypt, Josip Broz Tito of Yugoslavia, Nkrumah and Nehru. In practice, Sukarno was moving into an alliance with the Communists of China, North Korea, North Vietnam and Cambodia. In 1963, he opposed Britain's creation of the Federation of Malaysia and supported Communist guerrillas there. He nationalized British firms in Indonesia and increased anti-American rhetoric, which led to the removal of foreign aid. The export economy collapsed, loans could not be serviced, and monetary expansion to finance the military led to hyperinflation. The army, nationalists and Islamists became increasingly concerned about Sukarno's growing reliance on the Communists, and in 1967 he was removed from power.[14]

Despite these internal tensions, the Non-Aligned Movement alarmed the United States as a challenge to its model of liberal capitalism and multilateralism, and by the drift of former colonies towards Communism. In 1956, President Nasser drew on the rhetoric of Bandung to proclaim Arab unity in 'a single national front against imperialism and foreign intervention' and to nationalize the Suez Canal, owned by Britain and France. Eisenhower refused to condone the subsequent invasion of the Canal Zone by France, Britain and Israel, but American prevarication about offering aid for Egyptian economic development provided an opening for the Soviet Union. For their part, the Soviets were equally worried that a third way between capitalism and Communism would threaten the 'correct' path of replacing capitalism. In addition, China's relationship with Moscow deteriorated between 1958 and 1962: the Soviet Union was viewed as a European power that lacked China's experience as a victim of colonialism – including at the hands of Tsarist Russia.[15] The ideology of anti-colonialism had powerful expression in books such as Frantz Fanon's *The Wretched of the Earth*, with its analysis of the dehumanizing effect of colonialism on the mental health of individuals and nations, and in the Pan-Africanism of George Padmore and his circle.[16] Such thinking informed demands by less developed countries in the 1960s and 1970s as they challenged the agenda of the postwar international organizations and American liberal capitalism.

VISIONS OF THE FUTURE: GANDHI, NEHRU AND INDIAN ECONOMIC DEVELOPMENT

After independence in 1947, the government of India was dominated by the Congress Party, whose members ranged from socialists who called for an end to private property to advocates of a freer market and private enterprise. At independence, the outcome was a compromise. Although Congress's Economic Programme Committee recommended large-scale nationalization in 1948, public ownership was limited to three sectors, with permission given for the government to start enterprises alongside private firms in a further six sectors. In other sectors, private business operated within a system of permits. The result was what Chakravarti Rajagopalachari, a leading Congress politician, termed the 'licence Raj': extensive controls over import competition, the entry of domestic firms, product diversification, expansion of capacity, allocation of imported inputs, and investment. Planning for development was crucial to Congress's quest for legitimacy. It relied on import-substituting industrialization, high tariffs and import licences to protect local firms, an inconvertible currency, and hostility to foreign investment.[17]

After independence, P. C. Mahalanobis – who studied physics and mathematics in Kolkata and Cambridge and founded the Indian Statistical Institute in 1931 – played a major role in developing five-year plans for the Indian economy.[18] The first five-year plan of 1952 concentrated on investment in infrastructure and agriculture rather than industry. The aim was not just the efficient production of goods; it was a society based on equality of opportunity, social justice, the right to work with an adequate wage, and social security for all citizens. Nehru explained that planning was a 'mighty cooperative effort of all the people of India' that required 'the spirit of a missionary for a cause' and would stop Indians from going 'astray in the crooked paths of provincialism, communalism, casteism and all the other disintegrating tendencies'. As he said, 'to solve the problems of poverty and unemployment in a democratic way is something that has not been done anywhere.' He aimed to succeed. Democratic planning would involve sacrifices that would, unlike Soviet totalitarian planning, be voluntary and based on general acceptance of its aims. The plan rested on the Directive Principles of State Policy set out in the constitution, that the state should 'endeavour to organise agriculture and animal husbandry on modern and scientific lines and to promote cottage industries on individual or cooperative lines' – a hedging of bets between Nehru and Gandhi.[19]

The second five-year plan was more ambitious, aiming to sweep away 'backwardness'. Nehru consolidated his hold over Congress and the country, and he and Mahalanobis were frustrated by the gradual nature of change. The second plan was based on rapid import-substituting industrialization in heavy industry, capital goods and large-scale hydro-electric schemes 'to strengthen the foundations of economic independence'. The plan assumed an almost closed economy with strict currency controls, far removed from the American vision of the world economy. Mahalanobis's objective was 'to attain a rapid growth of the national economy by increasing the scope and importance of the public sector and in this way to advance to a socialistic pattern of society'. In the words of the second plan,

the most important single factor in promoting economic development is the community's readiness to develop and apply modern technology to processes of production ... Underdevelopment is essentially a consequence of insufficient technological progress ... The search for new resources and for new techniques and the readaptation of the available labour force to the new tasks which development connotes are indeed, the foundation of development.

The key issue in Indian development was taken to be a shortage of capital in relation to abundant labour, an approach that relied on W. A. Lewis's analysis. The aim was to raise the proportion of investment from 5 per cent of national income in 1950–51 to 20 per cent in 1968–69. The argument ran as follows. Development was limited by a low capacity to save, and a shortage of capital prevented the use of more efficient technology; agriculture suffered from diminishing returns whereas industry would use under-employed workers from agriculture at increasing returns to scale; reliance on the market would lead to over-consumption by the upper classes and under-investment in sectors needed for development. Mahalanobis rejected the collectivization of agriculture on Soviet lines and instead looked to land reform to protect farmers from rapacious landowners, with high export prices as compensation for low domestic prices, complemented by the growth of cottage industries.[20]

A major element in Congress's strategy was large-scale capital investment to break traditional values. In 1954, Nehru celebrated the initial phase of the Bhakra-Nangal Dam, which, like the Damodar Valley project, adopted the approach of the Tennessee Valley Authority to generate electricity and irrigate land to industrialize and raise food production. He hailed the scheme as a temple of the new age: 'these days the biggest temple and mosque and gurdwara is the place where man works for the good of mankind . . . Where can be a greater and holier place than this?' Work for a large number of people and investment were needed to increase production. More than that, the scheme threw off colonialism and superstition, and brought together nationalism and modern science. Of course, it was one thing to adopt the engineering designs and approaches of the TVA, and to repeat the rhetoric of modernity and liberal development; it was another matter to insert the Damodar Valley Corporation into the realities of local politics.[21]

Although the second five-year plan emphasized industrialization, the Planning Commission realized that the expansion of industry would require more food and raw materials to be produced, with a risk of inflation. The success – as it appeared – of China suggested that mobilizing under-employed rural labour would provide food and produce a surplus for capital formation. Nehru saw China as disciplined, unified and hard-working compared with India, and he assumed that if China could get an extra 30 per cent from its surplus rural labour, India could achieve 15 per cent. Nevertheless, Nehru did not entirely reject Gandhi. Community projects and National Extension Service schemes were adopted to develop agriculture and cottage industries in villages by providing roads, water tanks, wells and schools to remove villages from 'the rut of passivity and stagnation'. In 1952, on Gandhi's birthday, the government announced a plan to remake rural India by building over 15,000 model villages, funded by the Ford Foundation and the Point Four programme of the United States. Nehru hoped it would create a rural revolution by peaceful means rather than violence.[22]

Community development was more than a Gandhian vision. As noted in Chapter 12, it was also part of an American strategy of counterinsurgency across Asia by ensuring that disruption to traditional society, and weak ties between government and the rural population, did not allow Communist subversion. Community development was intended to create links between the government and peasantry. Chester Bowles, the American ambassador to India, thought it was 'the key to the future of India and Asia', offering 'an administrative framework through which modern scientific knowledge could be put to work for the benefit of hundreds of millions of people who have long lived in poverty'. Village life could be improved by specialist knowledge and by motivating peasants through better sanitation, animal husbandry, crops and education. The aim was to overturn low expectations and to create a modern work ethic and rationality that would foster a new dynamism and allow development by the peasants' own initiative. Community development proved to be a disappointment, however, and it was soon dropped by Nehru.[23]

Nehru's middle course was criticized by Marxists, for not nationalizing enough, and by Gandhians who preferred better environmental management to constructing dams. Neither did it convince Milton Friedman. When he visited India in 1955, he criticized the plans as obsessed with capital-output ratios rather than human capital. In his view, mathematicians – such as Mahalanobis – who turned to economics were dangerous, for 'they produce specific and detailed plans in which they have confidence, without perhaps realizing that economic planning is not the absolute science that mathematics is'. He criticized the plans for concentrating on two extremes: large factories using too little labour and cottage industries using too much. His recommendation was to create the 'basic requisites' of

> a steady and moderately expansionary monetary framework, greatly widened opportunities for education and training, improved facilities for transportation and communication to promote the mobility not only of goods but even more important of people, and an environment that gives maximum scope to the initiative and energy of farmers, businessmen, and traders.[24]

India had freed itself from British chains in 1947, only to find – in the words of the historian Sugata Bose – that it had 'unwittingly tied up its development potential in a tangled web of self-imposed constraints'.

Planning focused on means – such as raising the rate of savings – rather than the ends of eradicating poverty, illiteracy and high mortality.[25] Despite Friedman's scepticism, many Americans felt that Nehru offered a more acceptable approach to economic development in populous countries than Mao's model of growth in China.

CHINA: THE 'GREAT LEAP FORWARD'

In 1949, China fell to the Communists. Economic development on the lines advocated by Sun Yat-sen or the liberal development agenda of the Yangtze Valley Authority was replaced by a different path of economic transformation that had implications for China's emergence as the world's second-largest economy in the early twenty-first century. Under Mao, China experienced the triple disasters of the Great Leap Forward, the Great Famine and the Cultural Revolution, which meant that a rigid economic system on Soviet lines did not emerge – with the unintended consequence of creating space for the reformist agenda of the next generation of leaders after Mao's death in 1976.

Mao's approach to transforming the economy was unlike the Soviet Union's. Where Marx and Lenin despised peasants as 'potatoes in a sack' and looked to the revolutionary potential of the urban proletariat, Mao thought that 'several hundred million peasants ... will rise like a fierce wind or tempest, a force so swift and violent that no power, however great, will be able to suppress it'. His power rested on the countryside, and he believed that wisdom resided in the correct ideas of the rural masses, and in the experience of heroism and sacrifice in the People's Army. Intellectuals and urban residents were sent for 're-education' in the countryside – though the rural population was also treated with cruelty to impose discipline and expose errors.[26] Mao did not follow the Soviet policy of rapid growth of heavy industry, with large, capital-intensive plant operated by expert technicians. Instead, he looked to small-scale, labour-intensive enterprises, often located in the countryside.

In 1955, Mao launched a 'Socialist high tide' to press ahead with farm collectivization and increased output, which led to famine and shortages. In 1956, Premier Zhou Enlai warned against rushing ahead and suggested that 'if the leader becomes too hot-headed, a splash of cold water might clear his head'. The result was a purge of 'right-deviating conservatism', implemented in part by Deng Xiaoping, who returns in Chapter 23 as one of the major forces for economic reform after Mao's death. Mao decided to press ahead. When he visited Moscow in November 1957, he assured his hosts that 'the forces of socialism have become overwhelmingly superior to the forces of capitalism'. He set out an ambitious target for economic growth. Khrushchev aimed to overtake American production in fifteen years; Mao announced that China would overtake Britain – still the world's second-largest economy – in the same timescale. Back in Beijing, Mao presented his programme at the Communist Party conference in March 1958. 'In comparing the two methods, one a Marxist "rash advance" and one a non-Marxist opposition to rash advance, which should we adopt? I believe we should adopt the rash advance.' Even if targets were unrealistic, 'there's no great harm in it, and it doesn't call for a hard spanking. This is not the time to dash cold water on the proceedings.' He launched the Great Leap Forward, and a repentant Zhou became its main administrator.[27]

In some ways, Mao followed the same approach as Nehru in the Damodar Valley or the Soviet Union's 'virgin lands' programme, with massive irrigation schemes such as the Three Gates Gorge on the Yellow River between 1957 and 1959, and the diversion of water from tropical areas in the south to arid regions in the north. The Chinese schemes differed in that they relied on abundant labour, diverting thousands of villagers to move earth in hand carts, with little regard for engineering expertise. Predictably, the result was often failure at the cost of great suffering.[28] Similarly, industrial development rested on the exploitation of traditional techniques and the wisdom of peasants. 'The humblest are the cleverest,' Mao asserted, 'the privileged are the dumbest.' Just as the construction of dams and irrigation schemes did not need geological measurements and engineering calculations, so industry relied on backyard workshops rather than large-scale plant. Farmers were diverted to produce steel in inefficient furnaces, scrambling to find fuel and ore, and commandeering any scrap metal they could find, including household pots and farm tools. Even when the target was met, much of the output was unusable and expensive.[29]

Agriculture was no more successful. The state had taken control of grain supplies and created collective farms in the early 1950s. The Great Leap Forward went further in merging collective farms into communes of up to 20,000 households that were run on military lines, using labour-intensive methods. One East German visitor referred to *Kasernenkommunismus* – a Communism of the barracks – in which all food was assigned to communal kitchens, with home stoves, utensils and firewood handed to the commune. The diversion of farmers into building irrigation schemes and industry meant that the agricultural labour force consisted of inexperienced women, directed by inexperienced cadres who pursued inappropriate policies to raise output, such as deep ploughing that destroyed the topsoil. Output did not meet unrealistic targets, yet the state continued to requisition food on the basis of inflated figures. Across the country, teams and villages competed with each other in an 'exaggeration frenzy' to offer the largest target which was passed to the county, region and province, with an additional exaggeration at each stage. When these inflated projections of agricultural output reached Li Fuchun, the head of the state planning commission, he increased them rather than expressing concern about their implausibility. These figures provided the basis for unrealistic procurements to feed the cities, and failure to meet the unrealistic targets was then interpreted as an indication of 'rightist conservatism' and of hiding grain. Tan Zhenlin, the vice premier in charge of agriculture, urged leaders in South China that 'you need to fight against the peasants ... There is something ideologically wrong with you if you are afraid of coercion.'[30]

The Great Leap Forward was expected to produce a world of plenty, and in August 1959 the Chinese Academy of Sciences met to discuss what to do with all the extra food. The reality was famine, but Mao insisted that the Great Leap Forward was a military campaign in which there would be casualties before achieving victory. In March 1959, Mao had announced that a ruthless approach was needed in any war: 'When there is not enough to eat people starve to death. It is better to let half of the people die so that the other half can eat their fill.' He purged opponents who expressed concern and pressed ahead.[31] The result was famine and death on a massive scale: estimates of additional deaths between 1958 and 1962 are difficult to calculate and have been put at somewhere between 30 and 60 million.[32] When teams were despatched to report on the situation, the extent of the disaster became clear. Liu Shaoqi, President of the People's Republic from 1956 and a potential rival to Mao, had been doubtful of the scheme from the start, and was shocked by what he found in the regions. In May 1961, he blamed the party and, above all, the central leadership. But could the blame be placed on Mao? Li Fuchun admitted the problems of the Great Leap Forward yet accepted that 'Chairman Mao's directives are entirely correct' and that the fault lay with 'mistakes in executing them'. Zhou accepted blame to deflect criticism of Mao.[33]

Mao feared his legacy was in danger from Liu Shaoqi and Secretary General Deng, who were proposing to return land to the peasantry and production to individual households. Mao responded in August 1966 with the 'Great Proletarian Cultural Revolution' to remove 'a bunch of counter-revolutionary revisionists' who threatened to turn the dictatorship of the proletariat into a dictatorship of the bourgeoisie. Mao's target was the upper level of the party and the bureaucrats. He needed them to carry out his wishes, yet also believed their private and family interests led to materialism and privilege in opposition to the masses. Both in 1958 and during the Cultural Revolution, Mao departed from the Soviet model by shifting power from central ministries to lower levels and using populist messages to encourage conflict between officials and the masses. The result was massive social upheaval as Mao and the Red Guards attacked the established party leadership and the educated elite. Liu disappeared from public life and was denounced as a 'renegade, traitor and scab hiding in the party and a running dog of imperialism, modern revisionism and the nationalist reactionaries who has committed innumerable crimes'. He was beaten, cruelly mistreated in prison and died in 1969. Deng Xiaoping was also purged as the supposed leader of the 'capitalist roaders'. Mao used 'nationwide chaos' to 'attain greater order throughout the land'. His tactic was 'roasting the bureaucrats for a while without scorching them', but the process escaped from his control and China toppled into chaos as different groups fought over revolutionary purity. The army was drawn into the turmoil, deciding whom to support and whom to repress. China became a 'garrison state', in which Mao could impose his will on so-called traitors and renegades – including the Red Guards, who had been carrying out his wishes. Around 4 million people were despatched to the countryside for 're-education' by peasants through manual labour. Deaths in the Cultural Revolution possibly reached 1.5–2 million people from persecution, torture and suicide.[34]

The triple tragedy of the Great Leap Forward, famine and Cultural Revolution had consequences for economic reform after Mao's death and the removal of the 'Gang of Four' who attempted to carry on his legacy. Deng was rehabilitated in 1977, and as we will see in Chapter 23, China underwent remarkable economic growth under his leadership. There was a marked difference from the Soviet Union, where Stalin's policies in the 1930s led to large, capital-intensive plants within a controlled economy and to collective farms. By contrast, Mao did not create large industrial enterprises, and China's industrial economy was dominated by small-scale concerns. A larger proportion of the population still lived in the countryside than was the case in the Soviet Union – and there, the Great Leap Forward and famine had the unintended consequence of empowering peasant households and undermining the planned economy. Frank Dikötter points out that a 'silent revolution' by millions of villagers was 'one of the most enduring legacies of a decade of chaos and entrenched fear ... [C]adres in the countryside were defenceless against myriad daily acts of quiet defiance and endless subterfuge, as people tried to sap the economic dominance of the state and replace it with their own initiative and ingenuity.' Moreover, the experience of the famine and Cultural Revolution had led to a crisis of trust in the system. The solution of Deng and his colleagues was to focus on economic development and modernization, with tight party control under the guidance of a restored bureaucratic elite and their families whom Mao had sought to destroy in the Cultural Revolution.[35] The ensuing transformation of the Chinese economy was to have far-reaching consequences for the global economy and economic governance.

The human misery and suffering inflicted by Mao did not prevent the export of Maoism overseas, and competition with the Soviet Union for influence in the Third World. As relations with Moscow deteriorated, China turned to western Europe to replace imports of industrial machinery, which meant it had to pay by exporting agricultural commodities, often of very poor quality. Yet at the same time, Mao was competing with the Soviets by donating grain and rice to Africa, Vietnam and Cuba, even as people in China starved.[36] Mao also embarked on support for insurrection and guerrilla warfare to overthrow colonial or national governments. In April 1960, on the 90th anniversary of Lenin's birth, the CCP's *Long Live Leninism!* asserted that socialism could not be achieved by peaceful means. In Paris, Jean-Paul Sartre welcomed Maoist revolutionary violence as 'profoundly moral', and student radicals in 1968 brandished Mao's Little Red Book. In the Third World, attitudes were ambivalent. Maoism had adherents in revolutionary movements but had little appeal to nationalist leaders when in office. When it came to a choice between Maoist rhetoric with limited aid or Soviet assistance, they were more likely to opt for the Soviets – or to use Soviet aid as leverage to secure more American assistance.[37]

INFLUENCING THE THIRD WORLD

By the end of the 1950s, relations between China and the Soviet Union were increasingly strained, with Khrushchev supporting India in its border dispute with China in 1958 and withdrawing Soviet aid in 1960. The two Communist regimes became competitors for influence in the developing world and adopted distinctive approaches that reflected their different experiences of colonialism and strategies of economic development.

The ideology of the Soviet Communist Party rested on a critique of capitalism and domestic opposition to the Tsarist regime, rather than a concern for subjection to an imperial power. Tsarist Russia had not been colonized and had expanded into neighbouring territories such as Ukraine and central Asia. After the Revolution, the new regime – the Union of Soviet Socialist Republics – lacked a defined geographic or national identity. It was a collection of republics such as Kazakhstan and Uzbekistan that were identified with a 'titular' nationality, with national minorities that sometimes had their own autonomous territories within the republic. The Soviet Union could therefore present itself as a multinational state and not a Russian empire – though the experience of Ukraine showed the limits of claims to national identity that had to be contained within rather than challenge Soviet identity. Although the capital of the USSR was in Russia and Russian was the common language for Soviet institutions, in theory it was only another republic with its own autonomous regions for minorities such as the Chechens and Tatars. Russian nationalism was discouraged in favour of loyalty to the party and the Soviet state. The emphasis did, it is true, shift. Stalin was more inclined to see the Russians as the 'elder brothers' and for Khrushchev to celebrate national culture – but it was always possible, within limits, to be both a nationalist and a patriotic socialist, Soviet citizen. The process of nation-building was not just an external imposition. It had predated the Revolution, and the Tsarist empire could be presented in terms of voluntary annexation rather than conquest; as a way of saving central Asia from British imperialism and creating progress. Under the Soviet Union elites in central Asia often welcomed secular modernization, with most of the leading officials drawn from local people.[38]

This view of the Soviet state as multinational and multicultural had implications for its approach to decolonization in the 1950s and 1960s. Stalin had shown little interest in anti-colonialism, but Khrushchev defined the Soviet Union as Eurasian and Islamic, and presented the central Asian republics as successful models for overcoming feudal rule in the developing world. When he visited India and Afghanistan in 1955, he pointed out that the Soviet delegation included representatives from Uzbekistan and Tajikistan, with their large Muslim populations. 'All the peoples of our country are worthy members of the great Soviet Union and make a united family of the peoples of our country.' The Soviet claim that it had solved the national question and offered equality to former Russian colonies informed its self-presentation to newly independent countries. Khrushchev offered aid to developing countries such as India, and in 1956 announced that the day had arrived 'when peoples of the East take an active part in settling the destinies of the whole world . . . They now have no need to go begging to their former oppressors for modern equipment. They can obtain such equipment in the socialist countries.'[39]

The Soviet Union's approach reflected its internal development through large-scale industrialization and infrastructure projects. Khrushchev offered aid for big projects such as the Aswan Dam in Egypt as a response to American and IBRD loans for liberal development. Like the United States, the Soviets focused on large-scale infrastructure and industry, though by public rather than private enterprise and with a requirement to purchase Soviet equipment, often on barter terms that avoided the need for hard currency. The terms – usually repayment over twelve years at 2.5 per cent interest – were less generous than western aid, and the sums available were modest: from 1945 to its collapse, the Soviet Union provided $41bn of economic aid, which was no more than the United States paid to Israel. The Soviet Union promoted state-controlled industrialization based on economic planning, large heavy industries and nationalization, in alliance with 'bourgeois nationalists' who played a leading role in the struggles for independence and should complete the task by following a non-capitalist form of economic development.[40]

The 'national bourgeoisie' did not fulfil the role expected by the Soviets. In Guinea, for example, the French withdrew all aid on independence in 1958 and destroyed existing facilities. The new president, Ahmed Sékou Touré, accepted Soviet aid, though he doubted that Marxism was applicable in Africa. Meanwhile, the Americans played a game of 'wait and see'. They did not wish to alienate France, expected the Soviets to prove a disappointment, and anticipated that Touré would decide that he was not a Soviet puppet. They turned out to be correct. Touré made overtures to both the United States and the Soviet Union, especially for aid for the construction of a major dam to generate electricity to use the country's reserves of bauxite to produce aluminium. At the end of 1961, Touré's complaint that Guinea was treated in a paternalistic manner by the Soviets led him to expel their ambassador. The Soviets could not retaliate from fear of undermining their position elsewhere in Africa. Touré was also disappointed by the West and turned instead to Arab oil-producing states. His approach rested on 'flexibility, pragmatism and balanced neutrality' rather than subservience.[41]

Much the same applied in Ghana during the government of Kwame Nkrumah. He aimed to use income from Ghana's main cash crop – cocoa – to diversify the economy. In 1947, the British colonial government had created a Cocoa Marketing Board under the control of British firms to stabilize cocoa prices. In the early 1960s, prices were rising and Nkrumah and his economic adviser, W. A. Lewis, opted to tax the farmers' profits on the grounds that they would waste the money on luxuries and stimulate inflation. Instead, the proceeds from higher cocoa prices should go to the government for development projects and economic diversification. The cocoa farmers protested that they were being exploited to fulfil unrealistic government schemes and to transfer money to parts of the country that supported Nkrumah. In practice, much of the revenue went on current spending rather than long-term development, and the economic situation was parlous when cocoa prices started to fall. The Soviets turned to Nkrumah as a 'bourgeois nationalist' who could undermine feudal elites and imperialism. They denounced western companies and the Marketing Board as predators and adopted a system of bilateral exchange between Ghanaian cocoa and Soviet technology in order to modernize agriculture in collectives and to develop industry through import substitution. This strategy – in Ghana and elsewhere – allowed the Soviets to save on hard currency for the purchase of raw materials, and linked trade with industrial aid. However, the Soviets could not absorb the entire cocoa crop and they fell behind in payments so the Marketing Board and western firms continued to be important. Nkrumah played one side off against the other. American business corporations, the IBRD, and the British and American governments funded the Akosombo hydro-electric dam on the Volta river to provide energy to the aluminium industry. At the same time, Nkrumah assisted the Soviets in the Congo in the expectation that the Americans would counter with more assistance.

Averell Harriman characterized Nkrumah's approach as a combination of co-operation with the Soviets on 'socialism and anti-imperialism' with 'economic, cultural, intellectual, and moral ties with the West which the Communists do not share'. Nkrumah urged both the socialists and capitalists to adopt the principle of 'no interference in our internal politics, no transmission of cultural ideas which we find degrading, no economic ties which limit our independence'. He, and other African leaders, took advantage of confrontations in the Cold War to seek support from the Soviets to deal with the imperialist threat, while at the same time keeping their distance from Soviet ideology. Nkrumah's main aim was African unification and prosperity, and in the end he turned to the Soviets when his ambitions for leadership in Africa were blocked by neo-colonialism. He had a degree of political autonomy, but only a degree, and he was playing a dangerous game. The Soviets doubted the commitment of bourgeois nationalists and the Americans were frustrated by Nkrumah's turn to autocracy. Nkrumah's calculation turned out to be mistaken, and he was removed in a CIA-backed coup in 1966.[42]

The Chinese were more interested in revolutionary movements and support for guerrillas against colonialism than in providing aid for economic development, which would impose a strain on the Chinese economy. It could not afford Soviet state-led heavy industrialization which, in any case, it did not follow in the Great Leap Forward. Rather, it looked to encourage the domestic market through light industry, allied with a militant ideology of anti-colonialism and attacks on racism. Unlike the Soviet Union's self-presentation as multinational, Mao portrayed China as a fellow victim of imperialism and racism from Western and Japanese aggression – a representation that ran counter to Chinese intolerance of multinationalism and emphasis on a single state based on Han China. China annexed Tibet in 1951 and adopted repressive policies in Muslim Xinjiang province, yet successfully portrayed itself as a victim of imperialism in providing revolutionary leadership in Asia, Africa and parts of Latin America. As at home, Mao looked to disorder and chaos against the 'paper tiger' of imperialism through military violence and support for the peasantry. The Chinese Communist Party rested on the countryside and Maoism, and as Julia Lovell remarks, 'styled itself as a rural religion that represents and fights for toiling farmers'. Mao criticized Khrushchev as a bourgeois appeaser of capitalism and focused on militant anti-imperialism and continuous revolution at home and abroad. Peaceful transition by a reformist national bourgeoisie was 'preposterous'. Instead, the Cultural Revolution was exported in a 'culture of insurgency'.[43]

Khrushchev was wary of competing with China by adopting a militant policy of anti-colonialism that would undermine detente with the West. At the second Afro-Asian Peoples' Solidarity Organization Conference in Guinea in April 1960, the Soviets rejected Chinese calls for armed struggle in favour of peaceful coexistence so that money would be available for aid.[44] The Soviets were also constrained by commercial pragmatism and an assessment of the costs and benefits of aid that led to wariness towards worldwide armed struggle. The Soviet Union was not as autarchic as often assumed, for foreign trade comprised about 12 per cent of national income in 1960 – and became more important as western Europe imported oil to reduce dependence on American companies. As a result, the Soviet Union was earning dollars which it placed on the London Eurodollar market, as we will see in Chapter 21. The Soviets were also interested in securing commodities – such as cocoa from Ghana – rather than armed struggle.[45] Nevertheless, Khrushchev had to show some support for national liberation movements, which he linked with the productive possibilities of socialism. If developing countries were no longer 'subordinated to the mercenary interests of foreign monopolies', they would be 'in a position to make ample use of their rich natural resources and to proceed with their industrialization, and ... a better life [would have] begun for their peoples'. All the same, China had changed the terms of debate. The Soviet Union had more resources than China, but to win support from nationalist leaders such as Ahmed Ben Bella in Algeria, the Soviets had to show commitment to national liberation movements by adopting more radical anti-imperialist rhetoric and policy, without threatening war with the West.[46]

The chaos of the Cultural Revolution undermined support for China by leaders of newly independent countries who were less interested in violent struggle than practical aid for economic development and nation building. China's standing in the Third World fell, and pledges of loyalty to Mao usually had ulterior motives of leveraging aid from the Soviets. China's war with India in 1962, and Mao's view that India was a colonial construct rather than a real state, alienated opinion in Asia.[47] Nevertheless, the ideology of Maoism continued to cause disruption in the developing world. After the removal from power of Khrushchev in 1964, Leonid Brezhnev and Alexei Kosygin co-opted elements of China's anti-imperialist rhetoric with the danger that it would provoke a collapse of detente. The solution to this tension was to establish more control over the Soviet Union's allies in the later 1960s by turning from reliance on the national bourgeoisie to ideological indoctrination based on a Leninist party structure. The Cultural Revolution had shown the dangers of instability in post-colonial agrarian societies, and a strong Marxist–Leninist party might contain the threat of Maoism and avoid the military coups that had overthrown Soviet allies such as Ben Bella in Algeria. At the same time, political and strategic control from Moscow would permit greater flexibility and pragmatism in economic policy.[48]

Maoism lived on as an ideology distinct from the direct influence of Beijing. In Indonesia, the Communists turned to Maoism in the early 1960s, which provoked the army's brutal destruction of the party in 1965–66. In other cases, Maoism drew support from disaffected rural communities with guerrilla warfare and violence. The Communist Party of India split after a peasant revolt in Naxalbari in 1967, with the Maoist 'Naxalites' turning to violence. Most notoriously, the Khmer Rouge took power in Cambodia by 1975, expelled city dwellers to the countryside, and killed up to 2 million people by starvation, disease, overwork and execution in the most extreme example of global Maoism. In Peru, the Shining Path branch of the Communist Party launched guerrilla warfare in 1980 to overturn the state, and in Nepal, the Maoists embarked on armed insurrection in the countryside in 1996. By 2008 the Maoists had the largest number of seats in Nepal's parliament, though Maoist insurrection was not easily converted into stable institutions of government.[49]

The Cold War was not a straight conflict between the Soviets and the United States. Different views of modernity were on offer – American liberal capitalism, Soviet state socialism, and Chinese anti-colonialism. The policies of both the Soviets and Chinese rested on inadequate knowledge of local conditions, and on competing assumptions derived from Marxism–Leninism – and American policies were equally shaped by normative assumptions. National leaders were able to exploit the situation, playing China against the Soviets and both against the Americans and international organizations. At the same time, the less developed countries articulated their own vision through the United Nations Conference on Trade and Development and the New International Economic Order, which brought together ideas from recently decolonized countries of Asia and Africa with Latin America.

CHANGING THE TERMS OF TRADE

A central claim of Latin American economists was that the terms of trade between primary producers and advanced industrial countries were skewed against the former and in favour of the latter. The contention was not entirely novel, for Charles Kindleberger remarked in 1943 that 'inexorably . . . the terms of trade move against agricultural and raw material countries as the world's standard of living increases' so that a lower proportion of income was spent on food and its price fell compared with a rising demand for industrial goods.[50] Similarly, W. A. Lewis blamed the persistence of the Great Depression on the collapse of primary product prices and the inability of producers to buy manufactured goods, so that industrial countries in turn bought fewer primary products in a downward spiral.[51] But the significance of terms of trade was stressed, above all, by Hans Singer and Raúl Prebisch.

In 1947, the UN appointed a subcommission on economic development for which Singer produced a report on the relative price of exports and imports of under-developed countries. He found that the price of capital goods had increased relative to primary products since the war, so causing problems for development. Singer decided to analyse longer-term trends and found that the terms of trade of under-developed countries declined by a third from the 1870s to 1938, with some improvement between 1938 and 1946–48. He concluded that the 'dice were loaded' against primary producers. Disparities in market power and technology meant that trade led to 'unequalizing growth' so that under-developed countries helped to increase the standard of living of the developed countries without an equivalent benefit. He explained in December 1948 that 'Marxist analysis, in which rising standards of living for given groups and sections are somehow held to be compatible with general deterioration and impoverishment, is much truer for the international scene than it is for the domestic.' Positive discrimination was therefore needed to change comparative advantage by investment in the domestic economy and diversifying exports into manufactures.[52]

The argument was developed by the Argentinian economist Raúl

Prebisch. His views were shaped by the experience of a country that prospered before 1914 on the basis of exporting beef and wheat to Britain and
importing capital to build its infrastructure. His early work in the 1920s
analysed the cycle of boom and bust from 1810 to the First World War,
stressing Argentina's vulnerability compared with Canada or the United
States, which had a more balanced pattern of development. He carried
out studies for the Argentine Rural Society and the National Statistical
Office on grain markets, before joining the Argentinian National Bank
and Finance Ministry. He attended the preparatory meeting of the World
Monetary and Economic Conference in Geneva in 1932, and on his return
to Buenos Aires produced a recovery plan. Argentina suffered from a
serious drop in exports as a result of European tariffs and depression, and
the price of exports fell more than the price of imports, which made debt
service difficult. Prebisch proposed debt rescheduling, devaluation and
management of the exchange rate, protective tariffs, and the creation of a
board to manage wheat. He also played a major role in the creation of the
Central Bank of Argentina in 1935, where he became chief executive. In
common with other Latin American countries, Argentina had turned to
greater self-sufficiency and import-substituting industrialization.[53]

In 1943, Prebisch lost his official positions because of a military coup.
By the end of the 1940s, his position in Argentina was untenable and he
was invited to join the IMF. His appointment was blocked both by the
United States (now building bridges with Argentina's new leader, Perón)
and by Brazil, which was suspicious of its rival in Latin America. Instead,
Prebisch joined the Economic Commission for Latin America that was
founded in 1948 on the initiative of Hernán Santa Cruz, the Chilean delegate to the UN, who felt that Latin America was being neglected by the
great powers because it had escaped wartime devastation.[54]

Prebisch's report, *The Economic Development of Latin America and
Its Principal Problems*, was published by the United Nations in 1950 and
drew on his earlier studies on Argentina and on Singer. Both men argued
that trade benefitted exporters of manufactured goods at the expense of
primary producers, and that per capita income between the two groups of
countries widened as trade grew. In this report, Prebisch concluded that
the international division of labour was an 'out-dated schema' and 'industrialization is the only means by which the Latin-American countries may
fully obtain the advantages of technical progress'. His policy rested on the
import-substituting industrialization and regional integration that had
been pursued in Latin America since the depression of the 1930s, but with
a new emphasis on the long-term deterioration in the price of primary
products compared with industrial goods and a need for structural change

in the world economy. Disequilibrium between agricultural and industrial economies was embedded in the global economy and unequal power needed to be rectified by political intervention.

Prebisch explained the deterioration in the terms of trade by a division between core and periphery. Costs were sticky in core industrialized countries because of the power of unions, and labour was better able to secure gains from technical improvements. Hence the 'core' countries kept the benefit of technical progress. He also stressed that the trade cycle was the 'characteristic form of growth of the capitalist economy'. The price of primary products rose faster than did industrial prices in booms, whereas in a slump they fell more because workers in the core countries resisted wage cuts. By contrast, workers in primary producing countries could not increase wages so much in the boom or maintain them in the slump. The result was 'to divert cyclical pressure to the periphery (causing a greater reduction of incomes of the latter than in that of the centres)' so that 'income at the centres persistently tends to rise more than in the countries of the periphery'. Like Perón, he saw that primary producing countries were dependent on advanced industrial centres, and that the relationship needed to be changed. His solution differed. Perón looked to internal domestic policies such as nationalization of assets and seizing the profits of large exporters of agricultural commodities. By contrast, Prebisch and the ECLA wanted international action to change the terms of trade. Multilateral trade advocated by the Americans was not fair unless linked with an increase in the price of primary products. Nor was it sufficient to stabilize primary product prices. What was needed was a secular increase in their relative prices. If the productivity of agriculture could be increased by technical progress, and real wages raised by industrialization and social legislation, 'the disequilibrium between incomes at the centres and the periphery can gradually be corrected'. By the late 1950s, as we will see in the next chapter, Prebisch shifted from advocating import-substituting industrialization, which led to inefficiency in too many small markets, to export-led growth in a wider Latin American market. His aim was not to reject a multilateral world order; it was to reshape it in the interests of less developed primary producers.[55]

The Prebisch–Singer interpretation did not convince economists in the developed world. Jacob Viner argued that data did not show a secular decline in the terms of trade. It was an illusory measurement, for the nature of primary products remained constant, unlike manufactured goods whose price did not reflect improvements in quality or the emergence of entirely new goods. Hence motor cars did not exist in the nineteenth century – and when they were produced in large numbers, their price remained constant in real terms despite the addition of heaters or automatic gear boxes. Further, a large part of the reduction in the price of primary products was the result of lower transport costs, which were less significant for low-bulk high-value manufactures. The discovery of a long-term movement of the terms of trade against the primary producers also depended on the choice of the base year, and there might be a long cycle rather than a secular trend. It might even be that less developed countries with surplus labour and low levels of labour organization might be able to compete with the developed world, where wages were inflexible because of full employment, welfare benefits and unionization. The general view of supporters of free markets was summed up by Gottfried Haberler in 1959, who concluded that the Prebisch–Singer theory was 'based on grossly insufficient empirical data' and 'misinterpreted the facts on which it is based'. Consequently, it was 'irresponsible' to base policy on these uncertain extrapolations of trends in the terms of trade.[56] To many in the less developed countries, Viner and Haberler were apologists for neo-colonial exploitation of the periphery countries.

EXPORT-LED GROWTH

The shift from import-substituting industrialization had started earlier and went much further in Asia, where countries embarked on industrialization and modernization by planning and export-led growth. Japan had industrialized after the Meiji Restoration of 1868 as a strategy to avoid colonization, and soon embarked on imperial ventures in Korea, which became a Japanese protectorate in 1905 and part of the Japanese empire in 1910. Korea industrialized under Japanese rule, especially in the north, with an emphasis on heavy industries and the exploitation of coal and iron ore to serve the Japanese army for its invasion of Manchuria, alongside investment in the infrastructure of railways, utilities and schools. The Japanese owned most large enterprises, accounting for 92 per cent of firms employing over two hundred people in 1939. Most Koreans remained engaged in subsistence agriculture where pressure to supply rice to Japan led to a fall in domestic consumption. Korea was subordinated to making Japan self-sufficient in pursuit of its military ambitions, with the modern sector an enclave that did not lead to wider economic development. Even more than in Japan after the Meiji Restoration, the Korean economy was dominated by the state and the army.[57]

Both South Korea and Japan were occupied by the American military after the war, with policies determined by the Supreme Commander of the Allied Powers (SCAP) and by missions despatched from Washington. In

Japan, two missions vied for influence. Carl Shoup, an economist from Columbia University, aimed to create a wide tax base and a democratic system of engagement with the state. His mission was adamant that taxation should not be used to promote capital investment in ways that might be inefficient and would reduce the fiscal capacity of the state. He wanted to create a sense of equity and neutrality that would legitimize taxation, avoid the need for government debt, and provide revenue for the state. The second mission, that of the Detroit banker Joseph Dodge, preferred to retain tax breaks for savings in banks that would invest in private business, as well as making sure that inflation was controlled by a programme of austerity or *taibo seikatsu* ('bear a hard life') – policies that would help export-led growth by providing finance and holding down domestic consumption. The Japanese were able to exploit the differences between the American advisers to shape the fiscal system and economic policy on the lines that had been pursued since the Meiji Restoration. Rather than removing tax breaks on savings and creating a broad-based tax system, the government cut personal income taxes to secure popular support and offered tax breaks to savings which gave the government access to funds on cheap terms. The result was a high level of investment in public works, often for electoral purposes, and a high level of debt – precisely what Shoup had hoped to avoid.[58]

Lower levels of personal taxation meant that the government was reliant on corporate taxation, which was made possible by the structure of Japanese business. After the war, SCAP wished to break up the *zaibatsu*, combines that were seen as undemocratic monopolies. The attempt was soon abandoned as attention turned to rebuilding the Japanese economy as a bulwark against Communism. The *zaibatsu* were succeeded by *keiretsu* – groups of businesses with large cross-holdings, linked to a major bank that provided finance and oversight. Japanese corporations were less reliant on equity capital, so dividends were low, and inter-corporate payments were exempt from tax. Their ability to pay corporation tax was further eased by abundant savings encouraged by tax breaks which meant that banks could make loans on favourable terms. Large corporations also used small and medium enterprises as a cushion to deal with the trade cycle. The Japanese policy of investment from domestic savings had, as its corollary, a low level of inward foreign direct investment. The Foreign Investment Law of 1950 prevented inflows of foreign capital so that major American firms such as Ford and General Motors could not buy Japanese motor manufacturers. Further, access to the Japanese market was limited by high tariffs and import controls, and the shape of the economy was planned by government agencies, above all the Ministry of

International Trade and Industry that was formed in 1949 as the central element of a capitalist developmental state.[59]

After the war, Korea was divided between the Communist north and American-occupied south, where reform of the economy was vital. Arthur Bloomfield of the Federal Reserve Bank of New York visited South Korea with proposals to reform the banking system by creating an independent central bank that could focus on long-term investment and the restoration of domestic stability.[60] The Americans were also eager to overcome what they saw as the country's technological and cultural backwardness. The occupiers viewed the Koreans as the Irish of the Orient, fond of fun and drinking and with an inferiority complex due to domination by the Japanese. Consequently, Korea – in their view – was prone to instability and mob psychology. In 1947, the American army embarked on a programme of reforming transport and utilities, agriculture and education. The task was soon transferred to the Economic Cooperation Administration whose director, Paul Hoffman, realized that the fall of China to Communism made it imperative to show that western economic ideas could work. In 1948, South Korea regained self-rule under its first president, Rhee Syngman, an anti-Communist authoritarian. Despite concern in Washington about the cost, the Communist threat meant that economic assistance continued, and the North's invasion of the South in 1950 soon confirmed the need for action. A new body was created in 1950 – the American-dominated United Nations Korean Reconstruction Agency (UNKRA).[61]

Until the Second World War, South Korea had provided agricultural goods within the Japanese empire. Rhee turned to import-substituting industrialization, with about three-quarters of investment provided by aid from the United States. After the ceasefire of 1953, attention shifted to the task of modernization. In 1954, a report commissioned by UNKRA explained that Japanese rule 'hardly provided a foundation for a prosperous, well-knit, knowledgeable and vigorous government and economy'. Koreans suffered from Japanese discrimination that limited their participation in managing the economy, so that the '[t]ransformation of Korea into a self-sustaining, independent economy will require a concentrated effort in developing new abilities in overcoming the harmful effects of war suffering and in adapting ancient traditions to new requirements.' The report concluded that

> To the free world, Korean reconstruction affords an opportunity to constructively participate in a great endeavour – an endeavour to build a progressive and dynamic economy in a part of the world where millions are unable to eke out a bare subsistence, where competing systems of

government and economics threaten freedom and peace. They have an opportunity to help in a practical demonstration of the immeasurable benefits of a free economy and a democratic way of life.[62]

Lack of progress by the South Korean government meant that Washington looked to liberal modernization under American leadership. The assistant secretary of state for Far Eastern affairs complained in August 1960 that

> there has not been a leader or group in Korea with the imagination, vision and energy to give the nation the definite and believable national ideals, goals and programs which are essential to give meaning to this democratic framework, to end the Korean spiritual and social confusion . . . and to give the country a sense of unity, direction, and destiny . . . Until adequate native leadership emerges, it is incumbent upon us to do what we can to encourage the development of the Republic of Korea in the face of social inertia and ignorance until it can ultimately go it alone as a self-sustaining member of the Free World . . . If we cannot do this ourselves, our Communist competitors will be given an opportunity to try it their way.[63]

Korean leadership was about to come – though not on the lines of American liberal free-market capitalism.

In 1961, Park Chung-hee took power as the head of a military junta. Park trained as an officer in the Japanese army during the war, served in Manchuria and took a Japanese name. After the war, he joined the South Korean army but was sentenced to death on suspicion of supporting Communism. The sentence was commuted, and he resumed his military career during the Korean War. He was elected President in 1963 and served until his assassination in 1979. Park pursued a 'development dictatorship' that gave a greater role to technocrats, who introduced institutional reform and improved planning, shaped by the policies of the Japanese army during the colonial period and the Japanese government after the war. His time in power saw the 'Miracle on the Han River' – the transformation of South Korea into a major industrial power on the basis of export-led industrialization.

Successful industrialization depended on the state's playing an entrepreneurial role to shape the industrial structure through industrial development zones, subsidies, price controls, international flows of finance, direct investment and protection of the domestic market. The state provided guidance through an Economic Planning Board and the Ministry of Trade, and, above all, worked with a few diversified business groups or *chaebol* such as Hyundai that dominated the economy and spread risk across a wide range of industries. Sales by the largest ten *chaebol* increased from 15 per cent of GNP in 1974 to 67 per cent in 1984, with many internal transactions shaped by managerial decisions rather than the market. The *chaebol* were rewarded with cheap loans, tax cuts and subsidies if they met their targets, and they formed intimate connections with the state and leading politicians. The state played a major role. It owned enterprises such as a major steel producer that supplied material to successful shipbuilders and engineers; it channelled finance from nationalized banks and provided a guarantee for foreign borrowing by private firms; it rewarded groups that did well, above all in exports, and punished those that were less successful. The aim was to shift the industrial structure to more capital intensive, high value-added and technologically advanced sectors – a strategy that needed state support given the long time-horizons and low initial profits. In South Korea, as in Japan, the efficient use of labour and technology, with high levels of technical education, was vital in overcoming the lack of natural resources. The successful industrialization of South Korea therefore rested on an alliance between the state and businesses in a 'governed market' of private enterprises that co-operated and competed under state supervision.[64] As we will see, the economic system of South Korea was criticized by the IMF in the Asian financial crisis of 1998 as 'crony capitalism' – but it succeeded in turning the country into a prosperous industrial economy.

One of the major complaints about the Bretton Woods institutions was that they were dominated by a particular view of economics that ignored alternative paths of development. This chapter shows that alternative models – some more successful than others – were available, from the controlled economy of the Soviet Union to import-substituting industrialization in Latin America, and export-led development in East Asia. These approaches were under-represented in the institutions of global government that were dominated by the developed industrial economies. To critics in the Third World, these institutions were a form of neo-colonialism that maintained existing inequalities in the global economy and its governance. In the 'development decade' of the 1960s, the newly decolonized countries of Asia and Africa, and the primary producers of Latin America, demanded fundamental change in both international organizations and economic relations within the global economy in order to rebalance the relationships between the metropolitan core and the periphery. These demands intersected with the deterioration in the United States balance of payments and closing of the dollar gap, and growing concerns in Washington that European economic integration was posing a threat to multilateral trade.

14

'Competitive cooperation'
The Kennedy Round, the United States and the Common Market

'In initiating the current trade negotiations the participants have embarked on two major ventures. The first is the launching of a negotiation designed to secure a degree of liberalization of the present barriers to international trade which is both deeper and more comprehensive in coverage than has been secured in previous negotiations, covering all classes of products ... The second is a series of activities to meet the urgent trade and economic development problems of less-developed countries. Special responsibilities rest on the shoulders of the more highly developed countries.'

Eric Wyndham White, Director General of GATT,
3 January 1966[1]

'We started on the road to expanding trade about 30 years ago, under the policies of a great Secretary of State and President. Its advances, I think, are pretty evident to us all. Now, to retreat from it would, I think, set a chain reaction of counter-protection and retaliation that would put in jeopardy our ability to work together and to prosper together. What captain of industry or what union leader in this country really yearns and is eager to return to the days of Smoot–Hawley? ... So, this day of declining trade barriers in a world of unprecedented prosperity and growth is something we want to continue. We must and we will, I hope, keep it that way.'

President Lyndon Johnson, on signing the Kennedy Round,
16 December 1967[2]

Presidential inaugural addresses are occasions to make ambitious declarations about the future. John F. Kennedy's was no exception. On 20 January 1961, he offered America's allies help in meeting challenges; he promised newcomers to the 'ranks of the free' that in escaping from colonial control

President John F. Kennedy meets with the president of the Commission of the European Economic Community Dr Walter Hallstein. Under-Secretary of State George Ball sits at far left. Oval Office, White House, 12 April 1962.

they would not succumb to 'a far more iron tyranny'. They would, he hoped, always support their own freedom, and 'remember that, in the past, those who foolishly sought power by riding the back of the tiger ended up inside'. The Cold War context became clearer as his speech continued:

> To those peoples in the huts and villages of half the globe struggling to break the bonds of mass misery, we pledge our best efforts to help them help themselves, for whatever period is required – not because the communists may be doing it, not because we seek their votes, but because it is right. If a free society cannot help the many who are poor, it cannot save the few who are rich.

He made a 'special pledge' to Latin America to create 'a new alliance for progress – to assist free men and free governments in casting off the chains of poverty' and 'to oppose aggression or subversion anywhere in the Americas'. He renewed a pledge to the United Nations 'to prevent it from becoming merely a forum for invective – to strengthen its shield of the new and the weak – and to enlarge the area in which its writ may run'.[3] His claim to altruism coincided with an acute phase of the Cold War, with the threat of Soviet missiles in Cuba and conflict in Vietnam. Decolonization was proceeding in Asia and Africa, with newly independent countries pressing international agencies to pay more attention to less developed economies. These demands intersected with the Cold War and the challenge of Communism, and led to his call for a 'development decade' that is the subject of the next chapter. Kennedy was also facing tensions within the West, for the United States economy was no longer as dominant as it had been after the war, with the recovery of Europe and the emergence of the European Economic Community (EEC) in 1958. The dollar came under pressure as other currencies – above all the Deutsche Mark – became stronger. The result, as we will see in Part Three, was tension in the Bretton Woods monetary settlement. More immediately, Kennedy faced the problem of how to improve the American balance of payments, and how to ensure that the EEC did not become a closed trade bloc that threatened the post-war ambitions of multilateralism.

CHANGING CONTEXTS

By the time Kennedy came to office, the post-war 'dollar gap' had disappeared. The European Payments Union had resolved the liquidity problem in Europe and had helped restore trade and convertibility. The United States continued to have a surplus on commodity trade, and to receive investment income from abroad, but the balance of payments on its current account moved slightly into deficit in 1958, and seriously so in 1959. There had been deficits during the Korean War, but the situation during peace raised concerns about American economic malaise. In the presidential election of 1960, Kennedy seized on the deficit to castigate the Republicans for inertia and to present himself as the saviour of the American economy. Kennedy's rhetoric of decline was political – a way of attacking the Eisenhower administration and a rallying call to create a 'great society'. A current account surplus reappeared in 1960 and continued until 1968, when deficits contributed to the demise of the Bretton Woods system of pegged exchange rates. Even so, Kennedy and Lyndon Johnson remained troubled by what they saw as a deterioration in America's external position, with the costs of troops in Europe and war in Vietnam, and an outflow of long-term capital. Reserve assets fell from a peak of $26.024bn in 1949 to $19.359bn in 1960 and $12.167bn in 1971. The post-war dollar gap was replaced by a dollar glut as the United States provided more liquidity to the global economy at the risk of speculation against the dollar, which was considered to be overvalued.[4]

A month after his rousing inaugural address, Kennedy warned Congress of serious difficulties. America's trade surplus

has not been large enough to cover our expenditures for United States military establishments abroad, for capital invested abroad by private American businesses and for government economic assistance and loan programs.

Figure 3: US balance of payments, 1946–1973

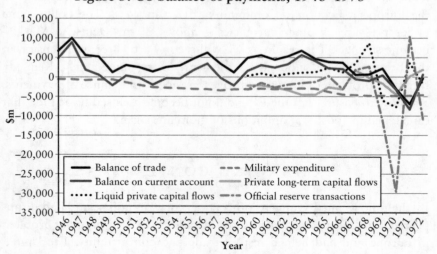

Source: *Economic Report of the President, Transmitted to Congress (February 1974), Together with the Annual Report of the Council of Economic Advisers* (Washington, 1974), Table C88.

All of these outlays are essential. Our military establishments in foreign countries protect the national security. Private investment promotes world economic growth and trade and, through the return of profits to our country, will strengthen our balance of payments in future years. Our economic assistance programs, much the smallest of these three items in its effect on payments balance, is vital in the continuing struggle against tyranny and oppression, and the poverty on which they feed.

The president realized that a deficit provided liquidity for the world economy and allowed other countries to earn dollars. He also feared that the deficit might become unsustainable, with America no longer able to afford its international commitments and resistance to Communism. The continued outflow of dollars might be good for trade but would also undermine confidence in the dollar and threaten the entire international monetary system.[5] The dollar was fixed against gold at $35 an ounce and could not easily be devalued, and other countries with balance of payments surpluses had no obligation to revalue.

These concerns about the American balance of payments pitched different solutions against each other. Should there be a turn to protection or a pursuit of international markets? A restriction on financial flows or encouragement of open markets? A reduction in defence spending and international commitments or escalation of war in Vietnam and troop deployments in Germany? The Kennedy administration was reluctant to tackle the balance of payments through domestic deflation, which would undermine economic growth and the 'vigor and vitality of a free economy'.[6] Similarly, reducing the deficit through cuts in defence expenditure would harm America's international standing at a critical time in the Cold War. Imposing controls on capital outflows by American corporations and Wall Street bankers would alienate important business interests. The best solution was therefore to restore the American balance of payments by reinvigorating the domestic economy and encouraging trade liberalization to open overseas markets to American goods.

American action was prompted by the Treaty of Rome of March 1957 that established the EEC on 1 January 1958. The United States had encouraged European economic integration to restore multilateral trade and remove external trade barriers, and was now alarmed at the prospect of an inward-looking trade bloc with barriers against American exports.[7] The Common Agricultural Policy (CAP) offered support to European farmers and would potentially harm American food exports. GATT negotiations had, to this point, only covered industrial goods; now there was a need to cover agriculture. The EEC was also removing tariffs between members and creating a customs union. In a free trade area, countries reduce tariffs between members and retain control of tariffs with non-members. In a customs union, tariffs are removed between members with a common external tariff set by the group as a whole, so removing the ability of a member to negotiate a trade deal. Although a common external tariff would not necessarily increase protection against the outside world, it could still harm non-members. Customs unions are trade creating: a larger internal market leads to economies of scale which stimulate demand and encourage trade, including with non-members. They are also trade diverting. A German domestic appliance with tariff-free access to the Italian or French markets might replace an American refrigerator or washing machine which was still liable to import duty. The American aim was to maximize trade creation so that European economic growth would lead to more world trade, thus outweighing trade diversion.[8]

In addition, there was a risk that the EEC was creating regional discrimination and preferential agreements with former colonies. In 1956, Guy Mollet, the French prime minister, proposed an imperial customs union between the French union and British empire as an alternative to a common market with West Germany. The idea was never likely to succeed and was rejected by the British government, which feared the impact on relations with the United States and preferred there to be a free trade area in Europe. In 1957, Mollet argued that France's overseas territories should be part of the EEC, in particular to resolve difficulties in Algeria by offering the country integration into a larger economic zone that was not merely French – a strategy that could provide a justification for repression. Other Europeans were not convinced, above all Germany, which had no wish to be involved in the war in Algeria. African politicians were also sceptical. Léopold Sédar Senghor saw that the EEC's focus on economics meant there would be few political gains, and that Africans would have only a marginal voice. His emphasis therefore shifted to nation building in Africa. France had to back down on including Africa (with the partial exception of Algeria) in the EEC. Instead, the overseas territories became associate members, with access to a European development fund, some protection for their industries, and preferences for their commodities.[9]

The failure of Mollet's initial strategy led him to turn to the Treaty of Rome to solve France's economic problem by competition within a larger European market. In 1958, this strategy was completed by the plan of Jacques Rueff for a 17.5 per cent devaluation of the franc, with cuts in spending and higher taxes, which contributed to the growth of the French economy and to the success of the EEC.[10] France's imperial strategy came to an end but the former colonies of France, the Netherlands and Belgium were associated with the EEC to promote trade and economic development. The search for French global influence turned to a formal agreement between the Association of African States in the Yaoundé Convention of 1963 that gave access to the EEC while allowing the African countries to impose non-discriminatory duties on goods from the EEC. It was essentially a French scheme that was imposed on other members of the EEC to maintain France's role in francophone Africa and potentially as a partner of the non-aligned nations – an ambition that was to cause friction with the United States.[11]

America's continued support for European integration made sense for strategic reasons as a counter to the Soviet bloc. The problem was the prospect of domestic political opposition. The CAP and common external tariff were vital to European integration; they were resented by American farmers who wanted access to the EEC and by industrialists and workers who feared trade diversion. The Kennedy administration therefore had to ensure that European integration did not lead to a backlash against the multilateral system of open markets. Kennedy's concern for trade was also a response to demands of less developed countries for policies to redress their position in the global economy, with potential support from the Soviet Union. Kennedy recognized that all elements of external policy – economic, strategic and military – had to be integrated, and that economic development and 'modernization' were needed to deal with the threat of Communist insurrection. International economic policy in the Kennedy and Johnson administrations rested on the complementary initiatives of the Kennedy Round of GATT trade negotiations and the Development Decade of the 1960s.

Trade negotiations were carried out through GATT, the supposedly interim body that survived the failure to ratify the Charter of the ITO. The review of GATT chaired by Dana Wilgress of Canada in 1954–55 suggested that it should become a more powerful Organization for Trade Co-operation to avoid the possibility of 'anarchy in trade'. Wyndham White agreed, though he realized that the proposal could rally opponents of multilateralism in the United States. In 1955, President Eisenhower submitted the proposal for an Organization of Trade Co-operation to Congress as a way of consolidating GATT and open trade, and as a complement to NATO in building an alliance of the free world against Communism. It was not accepted on Capitol Hill, however, and without American support it could never reach the threshold needed for ratification. Winthrop Brown – like Wilgress, an old hand of the ITO talks – thought that the failure of the United States to ratify the organization would destroy GATT. He was wrong and had learned little from Havana. GATT survived precisely because it was institutionally weak and did not threaten national sovereignty.[12]

Wyndham White worried that GATT and multilateralism would be threatened by the Treaty of Rome's regionalism and discrimination – a tension that had been apparent in the discussions at the time of the Marshall Plan and post-war European recovery (see Chapter 11). When the European Coal and Steel Community applied to GATT for a waiver for breaching the most favoured nation principle, Wyndham White realized it was 'an important test . . . of the possibility of harmonizing the universal and regional approaches to trade liberalization'. Despite the concern of the secretariat and members of GATT at the potential threat to open trade, the Americans agreed 'for reasons of broad political and military policy'. To critics of the decision, the waiver subverted GATT rules for the sake of European integration, and this tension continued with the negotiations leading to the Treaty of Rome.[13] Wyndham White wanted an investigation prior to ratification of a treaty that would give 'an impetus to . . . regional arrangements with a strong bias towards discrimination and autarchy', which could 'spread like the plague'. Many members of GATT shared this concern, but the prospective members of the EEC were adamant that the Treaty should be considered as a whole and only after ratification. The United States was in a dilemma, for it wished to support both GATT and the EEC. The French suspected that GATT was the proponent of Anglo-Saxon values, and made it clear that they would not ratify the Treaty if the Americans criticized it. Washington gave in and the Treaty of Rome was ratified without prior consideration of its compatibility with GATT. Once signed, it was difficult to challenge individual elements. GATT could do little to contain the threat to multilateralism posed by the CAP and the common external tariff, and action was limited both by the EEC's threat of leaving GATT and the United States' support for European economic integration – not to mention its own waiver on agriculture in 1955.[14]

Despite the potential threat to America's trade, the administration in Washington was willing to support European economic integration for wider geopolitical reasons. A related question was whether countries in the Soviet bloc should be allowed to send observers – or even become members of GATT – as a means of weakening the Soviet bloc's COMECON organization. The process started with Yugoslavia, which was moving away from Moscow: it sent observers before becoming a full GATT member in 1966. Poland also applied to join, in 1963, and both Wyndham White and the United States were supportive as a way of aligning the country with the West and stimulating internal economic reforms. Poland became a full member in 1967, and other countries in the Soviet bloc were soon granted observer status. A line was drawn with the Soviet Union and China, which remained outside GATT.[15]

Membership of GATT was also increasing as a result of decolonization. The number of countries at GATT conferences rose from twenty-three at Geneva in 1947 to sixty-two in the Kennedy Round. In 1963, a British official complained that 'GATT has become a most unwieldy body, the voices of the major trading countries being drowned by the clamour of the under-developed, which raises the question whether any meeting held on such a vast scale is capable of taking sensible decisions on trade policies and practice.' However, the alternative was 'an even more awful prospect' – a world organization with Soviet participation.[16] Newly independent and under-developed countries complained that their interests were still ignored. K. B. Lall, an Indian diplomat, criticized GATT in March 1965:

> The developing countries of course had had no bargaining power, politically or economically. The rule of reciprocity has required them to give a matching concession, but clearly they are not in a position to give any. While over the last fifteen years, tariffs on industrial products of interest to industrial nations have been gradually brought down, those on products of interest to developing countries have remained at a high level.[17]

The GATT secretariat shared this concern that the trade of developed countries was expanding at a faster rate than that of the less developed countries. In 1957, an expert committee chaired by Gottfried Haberler was appointed to consider trends in international trade; its members included former League economists and future Nobel Prize winners James Meade and Jan Tinbergen, as well as the Brazilian Roberto Campos, an economic adviser to the governments of Getúlio Vargas and Juscelino Kubitschek. The Haberler report of 1958 found that fluctuations in the value of world trade in primary products were mainly the result of changes in prices rather than volume, and that prices were influenced by fluctuations in economic activity in the industrial countries. Since 1955, slower growth in North America and western Europe had led to a decline of 5 per cent in the price of primary products; at the same time, the price of manufactures rose by 6 per cent. Although the terms of trade had moved in favour of non-industrial countries since the war, they had only returned to the level of 1928, with little prospect of improvement. It followed that industrial countries should avoid business cycles and maintain steady growth to stabilize the market for primary commodities. Further, national and international buffer stocks should be established where practicable, with a reduction of agricultural protection and subsidies in North

America and western Europe. The report warned that the EEC might lead to protectionism and trade diversion, and that preferences to the associated territories would 'give rise to discrimination against other countries in Africa and elsewhere'. The report concluded that '[w]e think that there is some substance in the feeling of disquiet among primary producing countries that the present rules and conventions about commercial policies are relatively unfavourable to them.' Furthermore, Haberler was suspicious of the EEC as a protectionist threat to worldwide integration and wanted GATT to act as a counterweight. The report marked a shift in the policy of GATT, which agreed, in November 1958, on a programme to expand international trade, including unilateral reductions in trade barriers against the exports of less developed countries.[18]

This initiative raised the expectations of less developed countries. The Haberler report was used by countries such as Ghana, Indonesia and Brazil to counter the EEC's discriminatory preferences for France's former colonies, and they called for an end to subsidies, price support schemes and quotas. They also turned to a more radical approach to rectify past inequities by preferential treatment for their commodities, price support, and assistance in dealing with balance of payments deficits. Their campaign challenged the legitimacy and effectiveness of GATT.[19]

THE TRADE EXPANSION ACT AND AMERICAN TRADE POLICY

An American initiative to ensure that the EEC remained an open economy within a multilateral trade system resulted in the Trade Expansion Act (TEA) of 1962, the most important delegation of power to the president since the Reciprocal Trade Agreements Act of 1934 and a major legislative achievement in reconciling global co-operation with domestic legitimacy. The reduction of tariff barriers had stalled since the GATT round at Geneva in 1947, with little progress in the trade rounds at Annecy in 1949, Torquay in 1951, Geneva in 1956, or the Dillon Round of 1960, named after Douglas Dillon, the under-secretary of state. Truman had used most of the authority granted by the renewal of the RTAA in 1945; Eisenhower had only limited powers in the Trade Agreements Extension Acts of 1955 and 1958 to cut tariffs by, respectively, 15 and 20 per cent, hedged around with protectionist concessions of 'peril points' and 'escape clauses' that allowed the withdrawal of any concession that the Tariff Commission believed would damage an industry.[20]

The limited powers of the Reciprocal Trade Act of 1958 were about to

Figure 4: GATT trade rounds, 1947–1993

Round/scope	Date	Members	value of trade	average tariff cut %	average tariff after cut %
Geneva Industrial tariffs	1947	23	$10bn	35	na
Annecy Industrial tariffs	1949	33	na	35	na
Torquay Industrial tariffs	1950/51	34	na	35	na
Geneva Industrial tariffs	1955–56	22	$2.5bn	35	na
Dillon Industrial tariffs	1960–62	45	$4.9bn	35	na
Kennedy Industrial and agricultural tariffs, anti-dumping	1964–67	48	$40bn	35	8.7
Tokyo Industrial and agricultural tariffs	1973–79	99	$155bn	34	6.3
Uruguay Industrial and agricultural tariffs, non-tariff barriers, customs procedures, services, intellectual property	1986–93	120+	$3.7tn	38	3.9

Source: John H. Jackson, *The World Trading System: Law and Policy of International Economic Relations* (Cambridge, MA, 1997), 74.

expire at the time of the presidential election. Kennedy had voted for peril points and escape clauses as a senator for Massachusetts, whose textile industry faced competition from low-wage producers. He denied that he was a protectionist and argued that his aim was to prevent the collapse of entire industries by offering 'adjustment assistance' to compensate or retrain workers, and to support areas affected by imports. This policy would allow 'constantly increasing international trade so essential to the economic health of the United States without jeopardizing the welfare of affected industries and their employees' – a balance between domestic welfare and internationalism to create electoral and congressional support. He was not a doctrinaire free trader so much as a 'fair trader' who realized that liberal trade was crucial to counter Communism in less developed countries, by offering access to markets and showing that democracy would lead to prosperity. During the presidential campaign, Kennedy argued that the 'best protection' against imports was positive action to boost American economic growth and competitiveness. America had become 'overly fat and a little self-satisfied' in the complacent years of the Eisenhower administration, so it was vital to modernize to compete with the 'lean, thin and hungry' EEC. Renewal of the Reciprocal Trade Act would, he claimed, 'encourage our domestic industry to produce for foreign markets'. Commitment to liberal trade was combined with support of domestic interests affected by imports.[21]

Kennedy won the election and looked to a wide-ranging policy on trade and security. He took an active personal role together with George Ball, the under-secretary of state for economic affairs and a committed free trader. Ball and the Task Force on Foreign Economic Policy devised a new trade policy based on 'competitive cooperation' with Europe. Ball realized that America was now the 'strongest of the strong' rather than the single dominant power that it had been after the war, and could not expect an 'unquestioning response to our demands for a common policy'. The Reciprocal Trade Act should be strengthened to allow the United States to compete with the EEC and prevent the Atlantic alliance from disintegrating into trade blocs. At the same time, the costs of defence and aid should be shared more equitably. Ball was also concerned by the poor economic performance of less developed countries and proposed removing duties and quotas on their raw material exports, without requiring reciprocal concessions. Preferential arrangements offered by Britain and the EEC to their former colonies should also be removed on the grounds that they penalized Latin America. To facilitate negotiations, he proposed a change in the process of negotiation by replacing item-by-item cuts with 'linear' cuts of 50 per cent across the board – an approach that had not been politically feasible in the 1947 Geneva Round discussed in Chapter 10.[22]

The president turned to the difficult task of securing authority. In messages to Congress in February 1961, he insisted that the balance of payments could only be strengthened if the American economy produced competitively priced goods and if the rate of economic growth were increased 'to reverse the downtrend in our economy, to narrow the gap of unused potential, to abate the waste and misery of unemployment, and at the same time to maintain reasonable stability of the price level'. He set out an ambitious domestic programme to use the full capacity of the American economy through improved welfare, encouragement of investment and assistance to distressed areas. He then turned to measures to strengthen the dollar so that it remained the principal reserve currency of the free world, and to improve the 'commerce of the free nations'. He stressed the need to deal with the loss of reserves and to strengthen the balance of payments which affected confidence in the dollar. He ruled out both raising the price of gold, which would devalue the dollar, and imposing controls on trade and investments. Instead, he opted for policies to make exports more competitive. 'A return to protectionism is not a solution. Such a course would provoke retaliation; and the balance of trade, which is now substantially in our favor, could be turned against us with disastrous effects to the dollar.' Furthermore, '[t]he flow of resources from the industrialized countries to the developing countries must be increased ... we cannot strengthen our balance of payments at the expense of the developing countries without incurring even greater dangers to our national security.'[23]

Congressional agreement would not be easy. Kennedy appointed a special task force that was chaired by a Republican banker, Howard Petersen, to create non-partisan support. Petersen was a free trader and, like Ball, believed that authority was needed to cut tariffs by 50 per cent. They disagreed over tactics. Petersen feared congressional opposition and suggested minimal authority. Ball preferred a more radical alternative to this 'hypercaution and negativism', based on a wide authority to reduce tariffs without peril points and with adjustment assistance for any industry that suffered. Kennedy was convinced that delay would lead to a loss of momentum, and that protectionism could be more easily contained once negotiations started.[24] William Clayton wished to go further, by creating a common market that could cover all free nations as 'an effective instrument which the West could use in fighting the war of production and trade which Khrushchev has declared against us'. In November 1961, he joined the former Republican Secretary of State Christian Herter in submitting a report to Congress that called for an extension of the RTAA and a trade agreement with an enlarged EEC as part of the strategy of winning the Cold War.[25] Kennedy saw the difficulty that an agreement with the EEC would create a large discriminatory trade bloc in defiance of GATT rules, and he realized that it should be part of a wider programme of trade liberalization. In November 1961, he announced that he would seek new powers to liberalize trade and, above all, to negotiate with the EEC: 'One-third of our trade generally is in Western Europe, and if the United States should be denied that market, we will either find a flight of capital from this country to construct factories within that wall, or we will find ourselves in serious economic trouble.'[26]

Kennedy set out his strategy to the National Association of Manufacturers, an organization sceptical about free trade. He explained that America needed to seize the initiative in the battle with Communism by strengthening the balance of payments – a policy that demanded an extension of the RTAA as 'a new and bold instrument of American trade policy'. America had supported 'greater European unity' since the war and the EEC would soon be twice as populous as the United States, with double the rate of economic growth:

> It could be – it should be – our most reliable and profitable customer ... If, however, the United States is to enjoy this opportunity, it must have the means to persuade the Common Market to reduce external tariffs to a level which permits our products to enter on a truly competitive basis.
>
> That is why a trade policy adequate to deal with a large number of small states is no longer adequate ... [T]his is no longer a matter of local economic interest but of high national policy. We can no longer haggle over item-by-item reductions with our principal trading partners, but must adjust our trading tools to keep pace with world trading patterns – and the EEC cannot bargain effectively on an item-by-item basis.

A new American trade initiative would 'make it possible for the economic potential of these two great markets to be harnessed together in a team capable of pulling the full weight of our common military, economic and political aspirations'. Capitalism was on trial – so Kennedy argued – and needed to justify its claims about free competitive enterprise.[27]

By linking the RTAA to the survival of capitalism and the free world, Kennedy aimed to wrench trade policy from the narrow self-interest of individual sectors. In his State of the Union Address in January 1962, he warned that failure 'could well affect the unity of the West, the course of the Cold War, and the economic growth of our Nation for a generation to come'. By contrast, decisive action would encourage exports to growing markets, help the balance of payments, and create 'across the Atlantic a trading partnership with vast resources for freedom'. The risk of 'deference to local economic pressures' was that industry and capital would move to the EEC:

> Millions of American workers – whose jobs depend on the sale or the transportation or the distribution of exports or imports, or whose jobs will be endangered by the movement of our capital to Europe, or whose jobs can be maintained only in an expanding economy – these millions of workers in your home States and mine will see their real interests sacrificed.[28]

Trade was not a zero-sum game of putting America first; domestic welfare could benefit from an international trade deal.

Kennedy's strategy was to limit the discriminatory threat of the EEC by creating an Atlantic alliance as a low tariff area of economic interdependence. The EEC would be embedded in a multilateral world economy and in the political solidarity of the free world, and should make a larger contribution to the costs of defence. On Independence Day 1962, in

Independence Hall in Philadelphia, Kennedy issued a Declaration of Interdependence – 'a concrete Atlantic partnership, a mutually beneficial partnership between the new union now emerging in Europe and the old American Union founded here 175 years ago'.[29] The president was seeking to provide leadership of the West that reflected America's diminished role as the European economies recovered. This connection between trade negotiations and anti-Communism played better in the United States than in Europe. Why should Europe share the burdens of defence, admit American goods and still accept American leadership? And would American support for European integration entail an Atlantic partnership based on the American ideals of capitalism and free trade? Both German ordo-liberals and French planners were suspicious of American capitalism – and in France President de Gaulle doubted the wisdom of accepting British membership of the EEC, given its Atlantic-oriented or 'Anglo-Saxon' assumptions. The EEC did not wish to embark on sweeping liberalization in an Atlantic free trade area, preferring to create a regional economic bloc based on a common external tariff and CAP.[30]

Kennedy sent the Trade Expansion Bill to Congress on 25 January 1962. The change of name was a marker of intent. The bill proposed general authority to cut tariffs by 50 per cent, based on reciprocity and the most favoured nation principle. American interests would be protected by escape clauses and peril points that would be less stringent: it was necessary to show that the main cause of an industry's problems was direct harm from imports, and the Tariff Commission could only make recommendations to the president. Trade adjustment assistance would be available to those suffering from increased imports 'to afford time for American initiative, American adaptability and American resilience to assert themselves'. In negotiations with the EEC, tariffs could be cut or removed where the US and EEC were the 'dominant supplier' with 80 per cent of world trade – a threshold that would only be met for many commodities if Britain were an EEC member. This incentive for the British to join and create an Atlantic free-trade zone was central to Kennedy's strategy.[31] He threw down a challenge to Congress. Its decision

will either mark the beginning of a new chapter in the alliance of free nations – or a threat to the growth of Western unity. The two great Atlantic markets will either grow together or they will grow apart. The meaning and range of free economic choice will either be widened for the benefit of free men everywhere – or confused and constricted by new barriers and delays ... This bill, by enabling us to strike a bargain with the Common Market, will 'strike a blow' for freedom.[32]

Success was not guaranteed, for a protectionist group in Congress worried at the weakening of the escape clauses and peril points that threatened, in the opinion of Senator Prescott Bush (R: Connecticut), the 'reckless destruction of jobs'. The issue was especially acute in textiles, and Kennedy accepted the need to protect domestic producers. GATT allowed a country suffering 'market disruption' to ask the exporter to reduce volumes or, failing agreement, to request authority to control imports – a concession that was resented by exporting countries but was crucial for American domestic politics. Similarly, the chemical industry wished to retain the American Selling Price (ASP), which set the tariff as a percentage of the American price rather than the lower price of imports: hence a 50 per cent tariff on a commodity sold at $50 in America and supplied for $40 by a German firm would incur a tariff of $25 rather than $20.[33]

American agriculture was more dependent on export markets than was industry. Agricultural exports accounted for 14 per cent of farm income in 1962 – and the EEC took almost 30 per cent of American exports. Consequently, support for the bill in the agricultural states would depend on increased access to European markets. The difficulties were exposed by the 'chicken war'. Exports were vital to American poultry producers, but the EEC imposed controls just as the Trade Expansion Bill was about to be discussed. American farmers demanded better access to European markets yet wished to retain their subsidies and domestic market protection. It would be difficult to negotiate a package covering both industry and agriculture that would satisfy the United States and EEC.[34]

Despite these domestic problems, the bill passed the House by 298 votes to 125 in June 1962, and the Senate by 78 to 8 in September. The concessions to the textile and other industrial groups undercut the protectionist lobby, and there was support from agricultural exporting states that hoped to gain access to European markets. Wilbur Mills, the powerful chairman of the House Ways and Means Committee, played a crucial role in securing the passage of the bill. He proposed that advisers from labour, industry and agriculture should attend trade negotiations in return for weakening peril points. George Ball agreed, on condition that they represented national interests rather than specific commodities and sectors. Section 232 also allowed the president, on the recommendation of the secretary of commerce, to impose duties on any good that might 'threaten or impair national security'. Mills realized that congressional acceptance of the bill would be eased by limiting the role of the State Department, which was concerned with international issues more than with domestic interests. The solution was the establishment of the Office of the Special Representative for Trade Negotiations, reporting directly to the president and with authority to negotiate tariff reductions for five years, expiring on 30 June 1967. The majority needed to override the president on escape clauses was reduced from two-thirds to a simple majority; and two members of the House and two senators were to attend the negotiations. Crucially, the Trade Expansion Act gave the president freedom to negotiate tariff reductions in any way he wished. Senator Eugene McCarthy (D: Minnesota) described the Act as 'in reality a "fair trade" bill' that combined the right of American businessmen to compete around the world with protection of American workers and firms from unfair competition, and with assistance for economic adjustment.[35] The TEA attempted to balance internationalism and domestic welfare in the United States. Success would depend on the willingness of the EEC to accept a compromise between integration of its national economies and multilateralism on American lines. And would the voice of the less developed countries be heard in the negotiations between these two major economic areas?

THE NEGOTIATING TEAMS

Kennedy's first task was to appoint a Special Representative for Trade Negotiations. George Ball recognized that the appointee should command the respect of the business community, to 'give them confidence that they are not being sold down the river by State Department'. Robert McNamara, Secretary of Defense and former president of the Ford Motor Co., recommended William Gossett, a Republican lawyer from New York who had been the company's general counsel. Ball was sympathetic but also realized the need to have someone who would look beyond tariffs: 'The main thing is to have a man who will resist domestic pressure and who has a big vision of what this thing is about because this could make or break putting the Western world together.' Christian Herter fitted the specification. He was born in Paris where his parents were expatriate artists; he married a wealthy Standard Oil heiress and entered politics as a moderate Republican. His interest in international politics went back to his time as secretary to the American delegation at Versailles, and he was Secretary of State from 1959 to 1961. Ball was delighted: 'He will carry more weight and prestige in dealing with the Europeans. This is not just a trade job – it is putting the whole Atlantic Partnership together and is something Herter is very much suited for.' Gossett was appointed deputy to provide a 'guy with business training'.[36]

Herter's main role was to support the negotiators with a direct line to the president. Negotiations in Geneva were largely undertaken by Michael

Blumenthal, an official of the State Department, who was, in Ball's estimation, 'a brilliant negotiator'. His family had fled from Germany to Shanghai in 1939. He moved to the United States in 1947, where he studied economics and embarked on a business career before joining the State Department in 1961.[37] Ball argued that negotiations should be co-ordinated by the State Department, which had overall responsibility for military, monetary, economic and political relations with Europe. Kennedy agreed, and Ball took personal responsibility for co-ordinating policy.[38]

Problems soon emerged, for the choice of personnel reflected political considerations rather than expertise. Ball criticized Gossett as

> a very small-minded rather petty man, who thinks his experience negotiating things with Ford Motor Company gives him all the answers to a very complicated and sensitive international negotiation. He called me aside and said 'Now, you don't understand this problem, because when the President appointed me he said "Be tough" ... I said 'I'm not so much interested in being tough as getting an adequate result.'[39]

Meanwhile, Herter's failing health and disorganization caused problems. He died in December 1966 and was replaced in March 1967 by William Roth, a Democrat shipowner from California with limited experience of trade policy. Matters were not helped by Blumenthal. He did not get on well with the leading Europeans – nor with many American colleagues, who found him abrupt, abrasive and, contrary to Ball, 'an inept negotiator'. A British official worried that 'the negotiations are going to be difficult enough intrinsically and, with so much national and personal *amour propre* involved, there may be serious risk in the US being represented by an aggressive and tactless "whizz-kid" like Mr Blumenthal.'[40]

By contrast, the British negotiators were experienced career civil servants who operated within a formal structure. The British were able to act as intermediaries with the EEC and played a significant role at some stages of the negotiations. The British government was ambivalent about the political project of the EEC and had opted for membership of the European Free Trade Area, a grouping of countries established in 1960 for industrial goods, without a common external tariff or ambitions for political integration. The free trade area allowed members to negotiate their own tariffs with third parties, with less loss of sovereignty. Nevertheless, in July 1961, Prime Minister Harold Macmillan announced that Britain would seek membership of the EEC. The American administration welcomed the application, for the British favoured liberal trade policies – precisely what de Gaulle feared. He suspected the British would support the American strategy of an Atlantic partnership, and informed

Chancellor Erhard that 'the Americans were aiming by means of the Kennedy Round to establish their position in Europe, with a view to making Europe a satellite. The British would play the role of their Trojan horse.'[41] De Gaulle vetoed Britain's application in 1963:

> The Treaty of Rome was concluded between six continental States, States which are, economically speaking ... of the same nature ... England in effect is insular, she is maritime, she is linked through her exchanges, her markets, her supply lines to the most diverse and often the most distant countries; she pursues essentially industrial and commercial activities, and only slight agricultural ones. She has in all her doings very marked and very original habits and traditions.[42]

De Gaulle's veto weakened America's ability to use the 'dominant supplier' provision to create an Atlantic free trade area.[43]

The institutional structure of the EEC created difficulties in reaching an agreed position and provided de Gaulle with an opportunity for disruption. The Commission consisted of officials acting in the general interests of the EEC who proposed policy to the Council of Ministers, comprising politicians who represented individual states. Once the Council agreed a position, the Commission was responsible for day-to-day negotiations, but its ability to conclude a deal was limited by the need to refer concessions back to the Council. National interests remained important so that deciding on a mandate for negotiations was time-consuming and complicated. All six members needed to agree, which allowed one dissident to block progress. The machinery of the EEC was too cumbersome for rapidly changing international negotiations and the time spent on internal debates between six capitals meant it was seldom able to take the initiative.[44]

Jean Rey, the European Commissioner for external relations, argued that the Commission had a mandate to carry out negotiations. De Gaulle had a different view. He insisted on the primacy of the Council in a *Europe des Patries* and opposed any increase in the authority of the supranational Commission. De Gaulle was suspicious of both liberal internationalism and European supranationalism, and was strongly opposed to the view of Walter Hallstein, the first president of the European Commission from 1958 to 1967, that national sovereignty was a 'doctrine of yesteryear' and that he was 'a kind of Prime Minister of Europe'. To Hallstein the dangers of the nation state had been apparent in Nazi Germany, and he supported a federal solution for Europe, on the lines of post-war West Germany. De Gaulle disagreed. To him, nations were the source of historical legitimacy by linking people through their 'own soul, their own history, their own language, their

own misfortunes, glories and ambitions'. He saw France's destiny as
seeking 'grandeur', which meant a strong state to overcome internal
divisions. He disliked supranational organizations as artificial bodies
that lacked loyalty and legitimacy, and preferred intergovernmentalism
and a veto power to preserve national sovereignty. He was strongly
hostile to Hallstein, who was 'ardently wedded to the thesis of the super-
State, and bent all his skilful efforts towards giving the Community the
character and appearance of one. He had made Brussels . . . into a sort
of capital. There he sat, surrounded with all the trappings of sovereignty.' Disagreement over funding the CAP by increasing the EEC's
budget, and the prospective shift to majority voting on 1 January 1966,
were too much for the French president. In July 1965, he triggered the
'empty chair' crisis by recalling France's permanent representative and
announced that the country would not take its seat in the Council of
Ministers.[45]

In London, the Foreign Office concluded that de Gaulle's central aim
was 'to make Europe separate from the United States economically,
which he regards as a necessary condition for it being separate politically', and that he viewed the Kennedy Round as 'part of the American
grand design for an Atlantic free trade area run by the United States'. In
the opinion of the Foreign Office, de Gaulle had two aims: to create a
Common Agricultural Policy that would allow France to sell its agricultural surpluses to Germany and reduce American food imports; and 'to
ensure that the Kennedy Round either fails altogether or produces only
the most meagre results'. Hence 'the optimum from his point of view
would be 100% success with the common agricultural policy and the
100% failure of the Kennedy Round.'[46] George Ball and the State Department saw de Gaulle's ambition as a larger European market for its
agricultural produce, help for its former colonies in Africa, and in general
to recover France's status as a great power. These aims should be achieved
without

> any alienation of French sovereignty. His concept of united Europe is
> apparently that of an intimate alliance of sovereign states led by France,
> the one world power among them. This grouping, based on a special
> Franco-German bond, would then deal with the United States on equal
> terms within the Atlantic alliance and, when Soviet policy has evolved suf-
> ficiently, would be in a position to negotiate with the USSR on European
> problems.

The French tactic was to play on American fears that they would wreck
the Kennedy Round and GATT.[47]

DEALING WITH THE AMERICAN
BALANCE OF PAYMENTS

The international strategy of improving the American balance of payments by increasing export earnings in an expanding world economy was complemented by policies to stimulate the domestic economy through 'increased investment and modernization for greater productivity and profits, continued cost and price stability and full employment and faster growth'. These policies would take time, with the risk that weakness in the balance of payments would lead to a loss of confidence in the dollar and undermine American strategic ambitions. A number of other options were therefore explored, which pitted different parts of the administration against each other.[48] J. K. Galbraith, an economic adviser to Kennedy, saw that not all departmental interests could be satisfied and 'someone's ox must be gored'.[49] But which one?

James Tobin, a Yale economist who served on the Council of Economic Advisers, proposed devaluation. Galbraith disagreed, for other countries would follow and 'promptly restore the previous exchange and trading relationships'. Walt Rostow of the State Department proposed another monetary solution: reducing the 'gold cover' for dollars so that more notes could be issued. This increase in the money supply was expected to reduce interest rates and stimulate the economy. Rostow realized that without domestic full employment, it would be difficult to cut tariffs, and without a strong balance of payments it would not be possible to afford military commitments in Europe.[50] Douglas Dillon – a Republican who was appointed Secretary of the Treasury – recognized that the problem with Rostow's proposal was that it would provoke 'intense and emotional conservative opposition' without a long-term solution to the underlying causes of the balance of payments difficulties.[51] Equally, Rostow rejected Galbraith's proposal of cutting overseas military spending. In Galbraith's opinion, America's position as leader of the Western alliance was already threatened by its weak balance of payments, and it 'would be in far better shape with fewer American troops and a strong American payments balance than a large American soldiery in Europe for which we have to beg from the French or the Germans'. Secretary of State Dean Rusk disagreed: troop withdrawals would undermine the 'real and unequivocal commitment of the US to involvement in any future aggression in Europe' and weaken 'the immense American political influence over a delicate and vitally important complex'. Even more worryingly, troop withdrawals would 'force us to accept what is essentially a nuclear trip-wire posture in Europe'.[52]

Galbraith favoured a further possibility: capital controls would improve the balance of payments, allow savings to flow into domestic investment, and keep interest rates low.[53] Ball agreed that capital flows were 'draining off our capital simply to provide financing for the competitors ... What we're doing now is serving as the capital market for the world because they won't organize their own.' Controls would be less of a threat to American leadership and political objectives than either deflation or troop deployments. He accepted that 'it'll make New York banks mad' – but argued that the problem of whether the government or money markets directed the economy had been experienced by all Democratic presidents since Andrew Jackson – including Roosevelt, as referred to in his inaugural address of 1933.[54]

Naturally, Wall Street and multinational corporations opposed capital controls and they had support from Dillon, a former Wall Street financier, who insisted that savings from capital controls would be small. William McChesney Martin of the Federal Reserve agreed, pointing to

> the evanescent character of business confidence. We were facing the real possibility of a crisis ... Liberal policies in trade and in investment matters have been our tradition. We should have the strength and the courage to follow them. If that tradition were impaired, we would start undermining the entire fabric of our liberal policy ... We should not show the white feather unless we are against the wall.[55]

The lines were being drawn over whether to continue the trade-off agreed at Bretton Woods of stable exchange rates and capital controls with an independent domestic monetary policy.

Kennedy was sympathetic to restricting capital flows. In 1963, he remarked that 'it was really not sensible for Henry Ford to be able to lay hands on $300 million of America's gold reserve by a single private decision' – that is, a decision to invest in a car plant in another country would lead to a reduction in reserves. Rather than direct controls, Kennedy suggested raising interest rates to encourage money to remain in the United States.[56] Kennedy followed the lead of his Democratic predecessors in striking a blow against bankers and Wall Street by reducing capital outflows. His strategy had its origins in Operation 'Twist' of 1961 – a device to attract funds to New York by raising short-term interest rates while holding down long-term rates to stimulate the domestic economy. The Interest Equalization Tax (IET) of 1963 achieved the same result by imposing a tax on new issues of foreign securities and equities sold in the United States, so discouraging borrowing by foreigners without increasing interest rates for domestic investment. The IET avoided direct controls, which

Robert Roosa – a former official of the Federal Reserve Bank of New York and Under-Secretary of the Treasury for Monetary Affairs from 1961 to 1964 – thought would 'literally congeal the bloodstream of American capitalism'. Instead, the IET used market incentives by adjusting the relative price of capital at home and abroad. When Japan complained, Dillon offered reassurance that

> Our markets remain completely open and free. The only difference is an additional element of borrowing cost that will deter some borrowers but not all ... [W]e will not be required to choose among countries nor among borrowers. The tax method will assert its effects through the market process, with an increase in the comparative cost of borrowing here acting to reduce the amount that will be borrowed.

Roosa also aimed to attract foreign money by issuing United States government bonds in European currencies between 1962 and 1971, which would help support the dollar.[57]

These measures did not affect direct foreign investment by American corporations. Galbraith wished to go further and had made the implausible suggestion of closing capital markets under the Trading with the Enemy Act of 1917. More realistically, the largest American corporations could be asked to defer direct investment and to notify the Treasury of existing commitments – with the possibility of stronger steps if they ignored the request.[58] In 1965, a voluntary capital control programme discouraged American corporate investment and spending abroad, and constrained foreign access to American capital markets. Alongside the IET, the Federal Reserve and Treasury requested banks to limit lending overseas, and the Department of Commerce and Treasury urged business leaders to limit direct investment abroad, deposits in foreign banks and holdings of foreign financial assets.[59] In 1967, President Johnson moved from exhortation to greater controls by a tax on direct American foreign investment, which the Europeans were expected to welcome as constraining takeovers and stimulating European capital markets. 'The Economic Report of the President' justified controls on the grounds that free markets did not always lead to an optimal use of capital. The outcome was to subordinate finance to domestic and strategic objectives, with controls preferred to deflation and cuts in military spending.[60] These interventions had the unintended consequences of encouraging offshore capital markets and reviving the City of London as an international financial centre, as we will see in Chapter 21.

Galbraith urged postponement of trade negotiations with the EEC which would make matters worse at a time when the elimination of internal European tariffs was harming American exports:

The hard truth is that traditional trade policy is now at odds with the balance of payments problem ... The existing policy was born in reaction to the incongruity of high tariffs in a creditor which had no unilateral transfers abroad. It accommodated the need of foreign countries to make large payments to the United States. The policy remains; the situation has been reversed. If we are going ahead with the Kennedy round we must expect it to worsen the payments balance.[61]

The danger of this approach was that it would undermine an open multilateral trade system. Kennedy could not agree, and the Round opened on 4 May 1964.

THE KENNEDY ROUND

Powers under the Trade Expansion Act expired at midnight on 30 June 1967 and success was in doubt until the last minute. Indeed, a deal was only concluded by the expedient of stopping the clock. The stakes were high. In the words of the Foreign Office, the Kennedy Round marked 'a new stage in the battle between the outward-looking and the protectionist concepts of Europe' whose outcome would shape 'the future evolution of Europe: whether, economically as well as politically, it is to be pro-American, open and outward looking; or whether, alternatively, it is to settle down into the kind of protected fortress which General de Gaulle would like.'[62] The British government was in an ambivalent position. At the start of negotiations, Britain was outside the EEC and its bargaining position was weaker than that of either the EEC or the United States and, as a Treasury official remarked, 'demonstrated very clearly the difficulties of negotiating outside any major economic grouping'. Britain's interest outside the EEC would be to secure as many concessions as possible on the common external tariff in alliance with the United States. However, in November 1966, Harold Wilson, the prime minister in the Labour government, started to explore a second membership application, and in May 1967, talks resumed. If the application succeeded, Britain would be inside the common external tariff and would therefore gain from a tough stance against the United States.[63] The outcome was a second veto by de Gaulle of British membership in November 1967 after the Kennedy Round concluded.

The greatest difficulty came from France. The American ambassador to Paris realized that the French attitude to the Trade Expansion Act was 'very unenthusiastic', and that the common external tariff was considered important in promoting the EEC's cohesion and 'essentially European character'.

The French attitude to tariff reductions was also influenced by concern about competition from American firms 'organized on a scale so vast and with resources so great that French enterprises could not compete'. A reduction in tariffs should therefore be delayed until European enterprises could merge and compete with American ones.[64] The issue of agriculture was crucial for France, and de Gaulle did not want the Kennedy Round to start until the Common Agricultural Policy was finalized. The British embassy in Paris reported that '[t]here is no "give" whatever in the French official position: it is rigidly opposed to any concession in terms of guaranteeing the volume of imports of agricultural produce into the Common Market.'[65] The French government insisted that the other five members of the EEC accept its position on CAP; the Americans hoped that the five would only make concessions to France if there were progress in the Kennedy Round.[66] The Americans lacked direct leverage over France and therefore had to rely on the other members of the EEC. The stakes were high, and Herter worried whether the EEC could survive, with the risk of 'a return to nationalistic protectionism both here and in Europe, tending to stifle the opportunities for expansion of our foreign trade and our economy'.[67] In 1965, he complained that 'It is becoming clearer every day that French agricultural policy and the curious foibles of Le Grande Charles make it more and more doubtful as to whether any meaningful Kennedy Round can be achieved prior to the expiration of the Trade Expansion Act.'[68]

In Europe, the Americans were suspected of not negotiating in good faith. Both Britain and France accused the United States of hypocrisy in offering to reduce tariffs and, at the same time, retaining protective devices such as the Buy American Act, American Selling Price, tied aid and anti-dumping measures.[69] Above all, the EEC was critical of 'linear reductions'. The EEC's common external tariff averaged the national tariffs of members, which removed the highest rates, and a linear percentage cut would not eliminate disparities with higher American tariffs. The EEC wished to consider industrial tariffs by écrêtement, that is capping or harmonization on an item-by-item basis. The American negotiators were reluctant to agree, for Congress might reject a deal that cut any tariff by more than 50 per cent or departed from reciprocity. In May 1964, the British brokered a compromise. Negotiations would proceed on the basis of a linear cut of up to 50 per cent, with a list of exceptions to remove disparities, provided that the overall bargain resulted in 'adequate' reciprocity.[70]

The negotiations coincided with the creation of the Common Agricultural Policy, which, Washington accepted, was necessary for European integration, provided that the EEC did not adopt a more autarchic position. In December 1963 Europe indeed seemed to be turning towards autarchy when the Council of Ministers adopted the 'Mansholt 2' plan, named after Sicco Mansholt, a Dutch farmer and politician who was Commissioner for Agriculture between 1958 and 1972. The plan replaced fixed tariffs by the *montant de soutien* ('support amount') – a guaranteed support price for agricultural goods with a variable import levy to prevent imports undercutting domestic production. Michael Blumenthal realized that this policy 'provides much greater freedom of action for increasing protection than does a fixed tariff', and the chief agricultural negotiator saw that the EEC was 'insulating domestic agricultural production of importing countries almost entirely from foreign competition' and potentially setting prices at a level that encouraged production and surpluses.[71] The American negotiations were in a bind: the CAP was both central to the European project and unacceptable to American farmers. Furthermore, the EEC had a stronger bargaining position on agriculture, for American farmers were more reliant on EEC markets than EEC farmers were on American markets. The chance of a deal that would satisfy American farmers was low unless the American bargaining power could be increased by combining industry and agriculture in a single bargain. Cuts in industrial tariffs could then be used as a bargaining chip to increase access for American agricultural goods in Europe and to ensure overall reciprocity.[72]

The Americans could exploit internal divisions in the EEC, though these disagreements also created problems in reaching a common European position. The German chancellor, Ludwig Erhard, was an Atlanticist who supported liberal trade based on industrial exports. He realized that Germany needed both American markets and defence against the Soviets, and he wished to reduce industrial tariffs and expand export markets. He was also ambivalent on the CAP, for Germany imported food and protected its inefficient farmers. The French were reluctant to cut industrial tariffs, which had already been reduced by the common external tariff. On the other hand, they stood to gain from CAP and increased access to German markets.[73] The Americans encouraged Erhard to reach a compromise so that France would accept trade liberalization in return for German support for CAP. It was a risky strategy that threatened the stability of Europe, for '[w]e should not give Erhard indiscriminate support against De Gaulle or publicly take sides in this internal EEC problem. In these circumstances, we must take care to give De Gaulle no additional pretext for carrying out his threat to break up the Common Market.' For its part, the German government was constrained by memories of the war and 'could simply not afford to take the aggressive stance within Europe which the French have taken . . . The Germans do not dare to play the role of "bad boy" in international negotiations.'[74]

These difficulties in formulating a European position and agreeing on the list of 'exceptions' for agriculture meant that the Kennedy Round was soon close to collapse. Wyndham White thought that negotiations should be delayed and that America's 'continual pressure . . . amounted to harassment'. Blumenthal disagreed, for the EEC was 'on a hook and we should be careful before we left them off it'. The question was how to proceed. Should the United States table an offer on agriculture as well as industry, which might lead to delays as the Europeans formulated their agricultural offer, or should the link be abandoned and 'exceptions' be tabled only for industry? Eventually, the Americans tabled only their industrial exceptions on 16 November 1964, in the absence of a European offer on agriculture. Industrial negotiations could proceed. However, the decision to drop agriculture created political difficulties in the United States, for industrial concessions could not be used as a bargaining weapon to gain access to European agricultural markets. Progress in reaching European agreement on agriculture was then stymied by the 'empty chair' crisis of July 1965 to February 1966. Mansholt informed the American ambassador that 'the present crisis is one which has been created by the French with malice aforethought.'[75]

The American negotiators were in difficulties, for their authority was time limited and failure would have serious consequences, not least in increasing French influence in Europe. For the United States, the result would be 'an immediate decrease in our influence in Europe coupled with a corresponding increase at home in pressure for go-it-alone approaches to political and economic problems. In a word, more narrow-centered nationalism in Europe, less cohesion between Europe and America.'[76] Dean Acheson warned that American priorities were wrong:

> We have been so dazzled by the commercial negotiations that we . . . have lost all sight of our foreign policy goals. The Kennedy Round is a political struggle for power; it is one of the forces that will shape the future of European unification and of our Atlantic relations. What we do will bear on whether de Gaulle and nationalism are to prevail.[77]

How to break the deadlock was far from clear. The risk of pressing ahead with negotiations with the other members of the EEC was that they might opt to support France rather than 'run the risk of pushing de Gaulle into a position where he would have no graceful avenue of retreat and thus leave him no option other than to destroy the Communities'. The imminent expiry of the TEA might strengthen the American negotiating position by creating a sense of urgency – or lead the Europeans to calculate that the Americans would have to accept modest concessions.[78]

The Europeans failed to make their offer on agriculture by the deadline of 16 September 1965, which left the American negotiators in a dilemma. They could table their own agricultural offer to show that they were not 'throwing in the towel on agriculture without a real try', with the hope of using industrial concessions to secure a better deal on agriculture. The risk, as the Department of Agriculture realized, was revealing the American negotiating position before the Europeans decided on their offer. The outcome was to table an agriculture offer.[79] Progress was at last possible when the empty chair crisis began to be resolved in January 1966 by a compromise brokered by Pierre Werner, the prime minister of Luxembourg and president of the Council of Ministers. When a country felt that its vital interests were affected, talks would continue until a compromise was reached – though it was not clear how vital interests were defined, or what to do if a compromise proved impossible. The EEC could now agree on its agricultural offer and negotiations could start on both industry and agriculture.[80]

The final stages of negotiation were not helped by Blumenthal's aggressive approach of responding to every European claim with a new demand or threat of withdrawal. The American ambassador to the EEC, Robert Schaetzel, saw

> this approach rests on a false premise ... that the Europeans are as interested in a successful Kennedy Round as we are. I think that this is true of the Commission. But this never has been true of the Member States. Even the Germans, who among the Six have the most to gain from a successful Kennedy Round, do not have as much at stake as we do.

The result of Blumenthal's tactics would be to alienate supporters in Europe and to create dangers at home, for the approach of claiming that the agreement was 'monstrously unbalanced' would make it 'exceedingly difficult to retreat when we want to justify the ultimate result'.[81] Wiser heads at the State Department urged abandonment of 'the blunderbuss approach' for greater reality, and thinking 'in terms of what would be the elements of the largest achievable partial success'.[82]

Matters came to a head between April and June 1967. Failure would have serious consequences, and Secretary of State Rusk feared the impact on the Atlantic relationship and a resurgence of protectionism. The British embassy in Washington prophesied that '[t]he internationalists and liberal traders in the administration, and their allies in Congress and in the country at large, would be confused and demoralised, and in no state to resist the pressures upon them.'[83] The administration saw that a more coherent approach was needed. Francis Bator, Deputy National Security

Adviser, urged President Johnson that only a 'handpicked top-level group, under direct Presidential discipline, can both keep on top of a fast moving situation involving enormous amounts of technical detail, and make certain that your options will be protected'.[84] A small inter-agency command group was created in the White House under Bator's direction to explain critical issues that required presidential decisions, and to offer suggestions to the negotiators in Geneva.

The final stages of negotiation between April and June 1967 turned on three issues. The industrial negotiations were dominated by the EEC's insistence on the abolition of the American Selling Price. Roth hoped this demand gave him 'a high card in the negotiations. Because the Europeans have made so much of it, there is a good chance that we can buy with it much more than it's really worth.' He recommended replacing the ASP with a normal customs valuation that would still provide sufficient protection. However, the TEA did not give authority to eliminate the ASP, which was therefore a separate deal with a risk that Congress would refuse this.[85]

The second issue was agriculture, and particularly the minimum trading price of grain. The EEC and major exporters such as Canada and Australia wanted high prices, in contrast to the United States' preference for competitive prices for its efficient farmers, combined with food aid to dispose of surpluses. The American approach had its origins in the Agricultural Trade Development and Assistance Act of 1954 that diverted surplus American produce to countries with food deficits; it was extended by the Food for Peace Act of 1966. Orville Freeman, Secretary for Agriculture, warned that the growing gap between the Global North and South would lead to social unrest and political instability, and that global security rested on the provision of food and technical assistance – a plea for altruism that was in the interest of American farmers and national security. The EEC developed an alternative approach based on a 'self-sufficiency ratio', that is the proportion of total consumption in each country that was met by domestic production compared with imports. Production above this level would create an obligation to provide food aid in kind or in cash. In the end, the grain agreement was modest, merely raising the minimum trading price with a vague commitment to food aid and without a scheme to adjust production.[86]

The third issue was the balance of concessions in agriculture and industry. The Commission needed to show it could strike a hard bargain, for an American official realized it was

with only slight exaggeration, on 'trial for its life' in the Kennedy Round negotiations. It must prove itself as the stalwart defender of Community

interests. Insofar as it hopes to exercise a liberalizing influence on latent
EEC protectionism, the Commission doubtlessly figures that it can make
concessions only after a demonstration of both toughness toward and
reasonableness from the other negotiators in Geneva.[87]

Roth and Blumenthal had to convince the EEC that the Americans could
make no further concessions, and the command group therefore recommended that Roth announce he would leave Geneva on 9 May and that
the Kennedy Round had failed, though with a willingness to attend a final
ministerial meeting.[88]

This risky strategy was justified by the high political and economic
stakes. Failure of the Kennedy Round would, in the opinion of a State
Department official, be a failure of American leadership of the free world.
He worried, in apocalyptic terms, that the outcome would be a return to
Smoot–Hawley, a weakening of the Atlantic partnership, an increase in
Gaullist nationalism, a division between developed and less developed
countries, a challenge to the role of GATT, and 'an eventual return to the
economic nationalism and autarchism of the Depression years'.[89] Bator
agreed: 'international trade would become jungle warfare, commodity
by commodity, and country by country. I think that the failure of the
Kennedy Round would risk just that kind of deterioration into spiraling
protectionism.' The result might be 'to make the EEC into an isolationist,
anti-US bloc, while at the same time further alienating the poor countries'.[90] Deadlock was overcome at the last minute and a settlement was
reached as a result of the tactics of Roth and Bator, and the mediation of
GATT's Eric Wyndham White.[91]

The Kennedy Round was the largest multilateral tariff reduction since
the formation of GATT. Considerable progress was made in reducing
industrial tariffs, which were cut by 35 per cent on average. The results in
agriculture were disappointing, however. In the end, the American government was not willing to jeopardize the Kennedy Round in industrial
goods to secure more access for agriculture in European markets. Roth
presented the deal as 'a balanced and mutually beneficial reduction of
trade barriers opening vast new commercial opportunities for all the free
world community', with equitable concessions between the United States
and other developed countries, and modest gains for less developed countries. President Johnson celebrated the continuation of post-war success
in expanding trade and stopping destructive trade wars. He pointed to
two 'fundamental standards': reciprocity that benefitted consumers and
exporters; and safeguarding of domestic industries so that multilateralism
was combined with domestic legitimacy. The president proclaimed that

the Kennedy Round was 'the most successful multilateral agreement on tariff reduction ever negotiated'.[92] For their part, British officials were relieved that the deal avoided 'the most unfortunate economic and political repercussions, particularly on American/European relations' and hoped that 'the Round may carry its own momentum forward in the sense that, at their eventually reduced levels, many remaining tariffs will be found to have little or no value either as protection or as bargaining counters, and many of them, therefore, may well "wither away".'[93]

Despite these claims of success, the Round had major shortcomings. Developing countries were disappointed. The tariff cuts were mainly on finished goods traded between industrial countries, rather than commodities imported from less developed countries. Although forty-one developing countries refused to participate, seventeen negotiated under special terms that did not require them to offer reciprocal concessions. As we will see in the next chapter, the results of the Kennedy Round disappointed the less developed countries, who turned instead to UNCTAD, the UN Conference on Trade and Development.[94] There was little progress on non-tariff barriers to trade, which the Round had aimed to tackle, other than a stronger rule on anti-dumping; the issue was taken up in the next, Tokyo, Round. Congress also refused to implement the deal on the ASP. Even the industrial deal lacked reciprocity. Japan, for example, benefitted from many concessions without opening its domestic market. Alexander Trowbridge, the secretary of commerce, remarked that the 'American domestic market – the greatest and most lucrative market in the world – is no longer the private preserve of the American businessman'. The result was increased domestic hostility to trade liberalization, with ninety-seven of the one hundred senators at one time or another backing a protectionist measure. In 1968, the attempt to extend the TEA for another two years and to remove the ASP failed.[95] By 2000, some politicians were blaming the Kennedy Round for the travails of the American economy. Jack Metcalf, a Republican member of the House of Representatives, attacked the Kennedy Round as the beginning of 'the slow decline in Americans' living standards' and complained that multilateral agreements 'may mesmerize and motivate Washington policymakers, but in the American heartland those institutions translate as further efforts to promote international order at the expense of existing American jobs'.[96]

Of course, the Kennedy Round was not just about trade. Economic policy was always influenced by geopolitics. The president's main interest had been political, to sustain the Atlantic alliance. As Blumenthal remarked, the Kennedy Round 'occurred during the depths of the Cold War. The US–European relationship, the strengthening of Europe, the frontier in the

Cold War, was of great importance to the United States.' He pointed out that market access for chickens from Arkansas did not change the course of history – the collapse of the EEC would. The successful completion of complex trade negotiations without too much damage to relations with Europe was, in his view, 'a political accomplishment in the broadest terms'. The outcome was to turn American attitudes towards the EEC and European integration into what one scholar has called 'hostile support'.[97]

The completion of the Kennedy Round also had implications for GATT. Tariffs on industrial goods were reduced to about 9 per cent and GATT needed to find a new role if it were not to become 'a back-water commercial policy debating society or a second-class imitator of the UNCTAD'. The balance of power at GATT shifted. The United States was less able to shape international economic policy, and when it did take a lead at GATT it was criticized for pursuing self-interest. The EEC was a major player but was less supportive and on occasions highly critical of GATT. Wyndham White thought that GATT had survived the challenge of the EEC. John Jackson, GATT's general counsel, was not so sure and felt that it survived by 'ignoring or bending rules'. Wyndham White also worried that 'the rules of the GATT will become diluted by a host of special arrangements for the [less developed countries] condoned or connived in by the developed countries.' In particular, he was concerned that preferences and bilateral deals came at the expense of the most favoured nation principle. The solution, he argued, was to increase the involvement of less developed countries in GATT:

> A large place will have to be found in the future programme of GATT – in partnership with other international organizations – for a determined and concerted attack on the formidable obstacles which lie in the path of the less-developed countries in their struggle for the economic development of their peoples.[98]

Despite protectionist sentiment in Congress, the Johnson administration remained committed to a multilateral agenda. Even before the completion of the Kennedy Round, George Ball and Dean Rusk looked to a new trade strategy to contain regional blocs, above all in Europe, and to respond to the less developed countries.[99] In 1966, Roth called for an international conference of developed countries to produce a world economic plan to mark the twentieth anniversary of the Marshall Plan that would offer generous aid, international monetary reform, full employment and price stability. He rightly admitted that 'this plan is grandiose'.[100] More realistically, Rusk looked to new authority for trade negotiations, with tariff cuts for poor countries, rejection of regional preferences by rich countries, and more liberal adjustment assistance for American industry to ensure that internationalism was combined with domestic legitimacy. In line with these recommendations, at the meeting of American heads of state at Punta del Este in April 1967, Johnson offered 'Generalized Preferences' to all developing countries (see Chapter 15).[101] He was responding to complaints of less developed countries that the Kennedy Round had made little progress with distributive justice in the world economy.

The Kennedy Round marked a change in the leadership role of the United States. Even after the Second World War, its hegemony had been constrained. Now, it faced a powerful and rapidly growing EEC whose ambitions were at odds with those of America. The geopolitics of the Cold War meant that presidents Kennedy and Johnson wished to hold together an Atlantic alliance that was not welcome in Paris. Talks over trade were complicated by political differences between Washington and the European capitals, with the British government caught uneasily in the middle without the bargaining power of a major trade bloc. The weakening American balance of payments also had implications for international monetary relations. The dollar glut provided liquidity, but with a potential risk of speculative pressure on the dollar which would have serious implications for the survival of the Bretton Woods regime of exchange rates pegged to the dollar. In Part Three, we turn to this crisis.

The Kennedy Round also reflected the limited voice of less developed countries, which had only had a modest role. They were a major concern of another aspect of Kennedy's international economic policy. In 1961, he launched an Alliance for Progress with Latin America and called for a UN Development Decade, in response to the Cold War and the challenge of Communism, and to respond to the demands of newly independent countries. To the less developed countries, GATT and the IMF were clubs of rich countries, and they articulated an alternative agenda for distributive justice in the global economy that aimed to overcome past exploitation.

President Lyndon B. Johnson and Walter Rostow during the announcement
of a halt of bombing in North Vietnam, October 1968.

15

'Progress towards self-sustaining growth'

The Development Decade

'The International Monetary Fund is the watchdog of the dollar in the capitalist camp; the International Bank for Reconstruction and Development is the instrument for the penetration of US capital into the underdeveloped world; and the Inter-American Development Bank performs the same sorry function in Latin America. All these organizations are governed by rules and principles that are represented as safeguards of fairness and reciprocity in international economic relations. In reality, however, they are merely fetishes behind which hide the most subtle instruments for the perpetuation of backwardness and exploitation.'

Che Guevara at the first meeting of the United Nations
Conference on Trade and Development, 25 March 1964[1]

'The moral climate of the world has changed since President Roosevelt issued his famous call for freedom from want, and President Truman announced his Point Four Program. Through one of the mysterious leaps of the human spirit, mankind in our generation has resolved to abolish conditions of poverty and ignorance which have been accepted for millennia as the order of nature. New and persistent hopes have seized the mind of man. Those hopes have become aspirations, and then programs. The theory of economic growth is as old as economic history. What is new . . . is man's determination to accelerate the pace of economic progress in the developing world. We have determined to make long-run economic growth a task for the short-run.'

Eugene V. Rostow, Under-Secretary of State,
United Nations Conference on Trade and
Development, New Delhi, 5 February 1968[2]

At Bandung, newly independent countries of Asia and Africa had articulated their ambitions for economic development; and in Latin America, ECLA, the Economic Commission for Latin America, had set out policies to tackle core–periphery relations. Independence also gave underdeveloped countries a voice in the United Nations, where membership had more than doubled by the early 1960s and less developed countries were close to the two-thirds majority needed to pass resolutions. The result was the emergence of the United Nations Conference on Trade and Development (UNCTAD) that provided a venue to criticize the IMF, IBRD and GATT as agencies of the developed countries that were indifferent to poor countries. The approach of ECLA and UNCTAD did, it is true, share assumptions with the dominant discourse on development – the need to escape from low productivity through industrialization and higher levels of capital formation, and a change in cultural attitudes – but they also demanded a change in the structure of the world economy and in patterns of global government.[3]

The newly independent nations were often the battleground – both literally and metaphorically – between the West and Communism. The Korean War resulted in the country's partition and a stand-off between North and South. After Cuba fell to Communism in 1959, Fidel Castro supported armed struggle in Angola and insurgencies in Latin America. In Vietnam, the war against the Viet Cong and Communist North increasingly involved the Americans and conflict spilled over into Laos and Cambodia. More generally, Odd Arne Westad, a historian of the Cold War, points out that the United States and the Soviet Union were 'locked in conflict over the very concept of European modernity – to which both states regarded themselves as successors', and intervened in the Third World

> to prove the universal applicability of their ideologies ... By helping to expand the domains of freedom or of social justice, both powers saw themselves as assisting natural trends in world history and as defending their own security at the same time. Both saw a specific mission in and for the Third World that only their own state could carry out and which without their involvement would flounder in local hands.[4]

A discourse of liberty, progress and citizenship shaped America's involvement in less developed countries and was linked to the extension of civil rights to African Americans at home. On the right, politicians stressed the need to contain Communism and to reduce the role of the state. On the left, politicians emphasized the need for aid. Both agreed on the power of technology and the adoption of the American market model. By contrast, the Soviet vision of modernity rested on collectivism, equality

and justice to overcome backwardness within its own borders and overseas. Both visions assumed a march of history towards a world of the
future that would be like present-day America or the Soviet Union. Both
could be viewed as a further stage in European domination, but the Americans and Soviets saw a difference from earlier imperialism. Rather than
exploitation and subjection, they claimed to identify with the people who
were to be assisted. Naturally, the leaders of the less developed countries
were not convinced and played one side against the other in pursuit of
their own agendas. In the 1960s, these ideologies of economic development were in conflict in a battle for minds that spilled over into brutal
warfare in the name of a greater good.[5]

MODERNIZATION THEORY AND ECONOMIC DEVELOPMENT

In the United States, modernization theory combined confidence that
nations would undergo the transition from tradition to modernity with a
realization that this fundamental change posed dangers. Traditional society was characterized as inert and inflexible, introverted and superstitious,
wary of change, dominated by agrarian elites, lacking a powerful middle
class and relying on a simple economy with limited technology, subservience to nature and a general sense of fatalism. A modern society was
characterized as similar to that of America: flexible and adaptable, welcoming change, secular and outward looking, with a complex economy
based on division of labour and a willingness to subjugate the physical
world. In *Becoming Modern: Individual Change in Six Developing Countries* (1974), Alex Inkeles and David Smith devised an 'overall modernity
scale' from 1 to 100. A single pattern was found in all countries: modernization was a universal phenomenon leading to new citizens who were
'independent and autonomous', 'open-minded and cognitively flexible'.[6]
It was a crude view of history that was no more than a tautology: engagement with sectors that were defined as modern (cities, factories) made
people modern. In reality, neither tradition nor modernity were uniform,
and they coexisted with radically different outcomes. Albert Hirschman
recognized its shortcomings, but the simplicity of modernization theory
was more easily understood than his complex understanding of differences,[7] and it shaped American economic and foreign policy in the 1960s.
President Kennedy was influenced by the thinking of the Center for
International Studies (CIS) at the Massachusetts Institute of Technology.
Its director, the economist Max Millikan, had been Assistant Director of

the CIA which contributed to its funding. Walt Rostow – an economic historian at MIT and a member of CIS – denied CIA influence on the findings of the Center, which he claimed always met the high academic standards of MIT. His denial was disingenuous. The CIA did not need to influence the CIS for they shared the same assumptions, and both Walt and his brother Eugene held political appointments in the Kennedy and Johnson administrations. Academia and politics were intertwined.[8]

Walt Rostow, with Millikan and Paul Rosenstein-Rodan, devised the economic and strategic analyses of the CIS. He had worked for the UN's Economic Commission for Europe before joining MIT in 1950, and wrote on British economic history as well as producing studies of the Soviet Union, China and Asia. Rostow was involved in Kennedy's presidential campaign and joined the administration to deal with issues of economic development. He became Deputy Special Assistant for National Security Affairs, and in 1961 was chair of the Policy Planning Staff at the State Department with a remit for long-term strategy. In 1966, he was appointed Special Assistant on National Security Affairs to President Johnson, where he argued that the Vietnam War could be won. His 'hawkish' stance on the war was closely linked with his approach to economics.[9]

Rostow developed his approach to economic development in two books – *The Process of Economic Growth* in 1952 and, above all, in *The Stages of Economic Growth: A Non-Communist Manifesto* in 1960 where he offered a capitalist alternative to Marx and the Soviet path to modernity. He warned that '[t]here may not be much civilization left to save unless we of the democratic north face and deal with the challenge implicit in the stages-of-growth, as they now stand in the world, at the full stretch of our moral commitment, our energy, and our resources.' Rostow believed that non-economic factors or 'propensities' could set off economic development, such as the propensity to develop fundamental science and apply it to the economy, or the propensity to seek material advance and to consume. Such 'propensities' meant that traditional societies acquired the 'preconditions' for the 'take-off into self-sustained growth' that was first experienced by Britain at the turn of the eighteenth and nineteenth centuries. Like a jet gathering speed on a runway, its economy was powered into self-sustained growth by a rise in the level of capital formation and a leading sector – the cotton industry – which stimulated activity in the rest of the economy. Tradition was overturned and modernity triumphed, and this was followed by the 'drive to maturity' and, eventually, high mass consumption. Specialists in British economic history were sceptical, but his interpretation appealed to politicians and shaped economic and geopolitical strategy.[10]

In Rostow's account, the dangerous stage of economic development came at the point when traditional society was breaking down and before the benefits of self-sustained growth delivered a high living standard. It was precisely at this point in Britain's history that Marx and Engels had developed the argument in *The Communist Manifesto* in 1848 that capitalism would collapse. The traumas of transition from tradition to modernity created 'dangers of instability inherent in the awakening of formerly static peoples' and provided an opportunity for the Communists. The transition was particularly dangerous in societies that were emerging from colonialism. European empires had destroyed the cohesion of traditional societies without making them fully modern and, even worse, led to suspicion of modernity as a colonial imposition. Exploitative colonialism should therefore be rejected in favour of benign American modernization. Rostow believed that the result would be 'a new post-colonial relationship between the northern and southern halves of the Free World . . . As the colonial ties are liquidated, new and most constructive relationships can be built . . . a new partnership among free men – rich and poor alike.'[11] Millikan argued that a more ambitious programme of economic development

> can and should be one of the most important elements in a program of expanding the dynamism and stability of the Free World and increasing its resistance to the appeals of Communism. The best counter to Communist appeals is a demonstration that these same [development] problems are capable of solution by other means than those the Communists propose.[12]

In Rostow's view, Communism was 'not the wave of the future; it is a disease of the transitional process which well-trained, well-organized cadres seek to impose on societies at the early stages of modernization'. The Communists were 'relying heavily on the possibility of exploiting the internal turbulence which inevitably comes with the drive toward modernization to seize power from within'. He was confident that

> as momentum takes hold in an underdeveloped area – and the fundamental social problems inherited from traditional society are solved – their chances to seize power decline. It is on the weakest nations, facing their most difficult transitional moments, that the Communists concentrate their attention. They are the scavengers of the modernization process.

The crucial point was therefore to complete the take-off into self-sustained growth as quickly as possible. In Rostow's non-Communist manifesto, the outcome would not be the collapse of capitalism, as predicted by

Marx; it would be abundance, and the end of ideology and class conflict as societies moved to the age of high mass consumption.[13]

In 1954, Rostow and Millikan rejected the concern of Allen Dulles, the head of the CIA, that Communist China was more successful in achieving growth by cruel and autocratic methods than were democracies such as India. Rather, China's methods hindered modernization by destroying the village gentry and creating a 'smouldering, unproductive peasantry'. They argued that India's democratic and non-coercive approach would be more successful in the longer run, and assured Dulles that 'free world success in seeing the underdeveloped countries through their difficult transition to self-sustaining growth would deny to Moscow and Peking their dangerous mystique that only Communism can transform underdeveloped countries'.[14] On this view, 'the attractions of totalitarian forms of government will be much reduced' if standards of living could be raised in a democratic system – but the threat during the transitional phase meant that 'in the short run communism must be contained militarily' before economic development delivered benefits. Hence Rostow's hawkish stance in the Vietnam War. Economic aid and military assistance were interconnected in 'a mission to see the principles of national independence and human liberty extended on the world scene'.[15]

These ideas informed National Security Action Memorandum 182 of 1962 on 'indirect aggression through the use of subversion and insurgency against Free World institutions'. The Communists could use violence because of the 'stresses and strains of the developmental process brought about by the revolutionary break with the traditional past and uneven progress towards new and more modern forms of political, social and economic organization':

Social patterns and institutions in most under-developed nations are extremely malleable. They are often a legacy of shapeless, frequently illogical political units which are derived, in part, from a colonial past. The disturbance of man's mind and environment caused by the last World War still lingers on in the Cold War . . . Intensifying and exaggerating these factors, and sweeping on with a momentum of its own, a social and economic revolution of great force has been spreading throughout much of the world. Purposefully or otherwise societies are gearing themselves to higher levels of economic and social activity. The necessary substructures inevitably cut into traditions and habits fostered by rural isolation . . . [T]he revolution of modernization can disturb, uproot, and daze a traditional society. While the institutions required for modernization are in process of being created, this revolution contributes to arousing pressures, anxieties, and hopes which seem to justify violent action.

Hence the most dangerous phase for a modernizing state was 'the interim, between the shattering of the old mold and its consolidation into a viable modern state of popularly accepted and supported institutional strength'.[16]

A more ambitious plan was needed than Eisenhower's concern for short-term instability. Rostow complained that there was no 'defined forward objective nor the fresh capital to move towards it. We begin with a program that is almost wholly defensive in character and one which commands neither the resources, the administration, nor the criteria designed to move the underdeveloped countries towards sustained economic growth.' Furthermore, development assistance was too diffuse in supporting individual projects rather than 'developing whole nations'. He urged a major shift from

> a defensive effort to shore-up weak economies and to buy short-run political and military advantage, to a coordinated Free World effort with enough resources to move forward those nations prepared to mobilize their own resources for development purposes. The goal is to help other countries learn how to grow. Aid ends when self-sustained growth is achieved and borrowing can proceed in normal commercial ways.[17]

The implication was that aid should be offered to all non-Communist countries, without imposing political obligations and 'unlinked' from military conditions, provided their economies had 'absorptive capacity' and could create incentives for a shift from economic stagnation into self-sustaining growth. By stimulating an economic 'take-off' and becoming more modern, Rostow thought that societies would be able to increase their military strength and have a direct interest in opposing Communism as their interests became more aligned with those of the United States.[18]

The new aid criteria set out by the Policy Planning Council in 1961 were based on 'self-help and long-range planning' which 'holds out the promise of more prudent and effective use of our aid funds. No less important it aligns the US with the forces for economic and social progress in the less developed countries.'[19] David E. Bell, the administrator of the United States Agency for International Development (USAID), pointed out that '[w]ith respect to developing countries that are ready to sacrifice and work hard, the best and cheapest aid policy ... is to give them maximum help, which will lead to economic independence, and the end of the need for aid.'[20] It entailed changing the attitudes of the local population, for Secretary of State Dean Rusk believed that capital and training would not lead to sustained economic growth without action on the 'basic conditions which dull the desire, sap the will, and destroy the capacity of most of the world's people to better their lives'.[21] Discussion of the allocation of aid concluded that thirty countries capable of both self-help and self-sustaining growth should receive long-term assistance. Another twelve to fifteen countries, such as Brazil, had potential, if only they had competent leadership. They could receive assistance on a provisional basis. Other countries had the right ideas on paper, but they were not being implemented. Aid should be offered when they 'bestirred themselves'. Yet others, especially in Latin America, 'though they have the capability, have no great sympathy or understanding for self-help since it strikes at the heart of entrenched interests with which existing regimes are identified.' Still others, above all in tropical Africa, lacked capacity for self-help and the role of America in these cases should be to develop technical competence. The final group of countries needed help because of strategic interests or political problems, such as Korea, Vietnam, Thailand and Laos.[22] In reality, military concerns became more important as the Cold War entered a new phase.

The new approach was supported by Rusk, who informed Kennedy in March 1961 that

> we have come to an important crossroads. In all likelihood, a fresh, positive aid program, scaled to the requirements, and presented with persistence and boldness, has a much better chance of Congressional approval and popular acclaim . . . We are facing a period much like 1940, when Lend Lease would never have been thought politically possible by ordinary politicians, but when farsighted leadership and Presidential initiative achieved a breakthrough. This is also a time like 1947, when neither the Congress nor the country was supposed to be ready for the Marshall Plan, but when a similar energy and influence provided the national momentum we needed.[23]

The president could not resist this plea to make his mark on history – and his mind turned to Latin America, which was so politically important for the United States.

THE ALLIANCE FOR PROGRESS AND THE DEVELOPMENT DECADE

President Eisenhower had preferred to leave development to private enterprise and to seek stability by supporting dictators or autocrats, such as Fulgencio Batista in Cuba. When the president of Brazil, Juscelino

Kubitschek, proposed Operation 'Pan-America' in 1958 to counter Communism by removing poverty through a major development programme, Raúl Prebisch saw an opportunity to position himself as an ally of America against Communism in Latin America. The overthrow of the Batista government in 1959 and Fidel Castro's subsequent allegiance to Communism demanded a new policy to prevent other countries going the same way.[24]

Prebisch had returned to Argentina on the fall of Perón in 1955, where his proposals for economic reform met resistance and were criticized as a tool of the oligarchy and central bankers under the influence of Britain. His position weakened both in Buenos Aires and Washington, as well as in the ECLA, where he returned for a final five-year term as Director in 1956. His economic policies were shifting. He accepted that industrialization was necessary to improve the standard of living, but that protectionism constrained productivity and the private sector by encouraging a large, inefficient state. What was needed was limited, focused intervention to support the private sector. He accepted that private enterprise had 'tremendous possibilities', but that '[i]t is unrealistic to wait for the free inter-play of economic forces alone to provide a solution' to the challenge of Communism. The free market 'cannot spontaneously generate the far-reaching changes that will have to take place in the patterns of production and the structure of the Latin American economy, or create the conditions and incentives that private enterprise requires if it is to enact its primary role in economic development'. The survival of private enterprise required higher standards of living and social mobility achieved through 'a large-scale international transfer of capital and technique', with the state providing financial assistance to domestic private enterprise. He urged the United States to 'envisage as a basic objective the intensive development of the Latin American economies through the region's private enterprise, with the consequent relegation of United States investment to a secondary plane'. He called for a third way between foreign domination and nationalism, based on co-operation through state development programmes, reform of land tenure, encouragement of more dynamic groups in society, and the pursuit of distributive justice. Communism could not be countered by 'obsolete nineteenth-century concepts of economic development' but only by America taking bold and imaginative action to support a more progressive form of capitalism.[25] His approach both incorporated elements of the dominant discourse of development and modernization and challenged the existing structure of the world economy and global governance.

Prebisch now argued that the 'water-tight compartments' of import-substituting national economies were too small to achieve the economies of scale required to produce advanced industrial goods. 'Rational' and 'orderly' protection for new industries should be combined with an open market. Above all, a Latin American common market was needed to allow greater regional specialization and diversification of exports. This strategy should not mean that 'we are going to exchange the twenty autarchic markets of Latin America with one large autarchic zone *vis à vis* the rest of the world'. Rather, 'Latin America has to export more and more ... there is a perfect compatibility between the idea of a progressive integration of our economies and the equally meritorious idea of the most intense export thrust.'[26] The American response to Prebisch's proposal for a common market was guarded, for it might divert trade and create a closed system that would lead to monopoly and protectionism. Thomas Mann, an American official specializing in Latin America, thought that 'It would be wrong to create an artificial or uneconomic industry in automobiles or any other product that could never compete', and that it was better to rely on foreign investment and American multinationals in an open market. At GATT, Eric Wyndham White rejected the scheme – and Brazil saw a threat to its sovereignty. The outcome was a more modest free trade area, established by the Treaty of Montevideo of 1960.[27] A Southern Common Market – Mercosur – was eventually established in 1991 as a free trade area that removed barriers between members without imposing a common external tariff; it became an imperfect customs union in 1995 in which individual members could still make bilateral treaties with other countries.[28]

On his election, Kennedy set up a Latin American task force, which concluded that reliance on private enterprise alone would not prevent Communists exploiting the social conditions of the region. He worried that the United States had 'no clear philosophy of its own, and has no effective machinery to disseminate such a philosophy'. The task force seized on Walt Rostow's analysis. The 'preconditions' were already present in much of Latin America 'in sharp contrast to most of Africa, which still lacked the preconditions for take-off, and South and Southeast Asia, which would have to overcome the ancient cultural obstacles' of 'Oriental fatalism, sacred cows, or caste systems'. In Latin America, the obstacles of a semi-feudal agrarian economic structure could be removed by land reform, social welfare and support for democracy to create a middle-class revolution and a modern technical society. In March 1961, Rostow urged Kennedy to announce an 'economic development decade' for the 1960s, when many countries – above all in Latin America – would experience take-off into self-sustained growth, ceasing to be dependent on international aid or prone to Communism.[29]

On 13 March 1961, the president announced the Alliance for Progress. He declared that Latin America was at a point of 'maximum opportunity' that would allow it to fulfil the ambitions of Simón Bolívar, the leader of independence from Spain in the early nineteenth century, and strike off the 'bonds of poverty and ignorance'. Latin America was also at a point of danger from 'alien forces which once again seek to impose the despotisms of the Old World on the people of the New'. The countries of Latin America, he argued, were allies of the United States, shaped by a shared history of struggle against colonialism and encounter with the frontier, with 'a common heritage, the quest for the dignity and the freedom of man'. Even Kennedy admitted that linking Thomas Paine in North America and Simón Bolívar in Latin America in a single struggle for freedom was questionable, and he accepted that the United States had not always pursued a common mission – but governments in Latin America were also guilty of failing to raise their people from poverty and ignorance. It was therefore time to turn from past errors to a new future in 'a vast cooperative effort, unparalleled in magnitude and nobility of purpose, to satisfy the basic needs of the American people for homes, work and land, health and schools.' He proposed a 'vast new Ten-Year Plan for the Americas' in a 'historical decade of democratic progress' to raise living standards, provide education for all, and remove the need for external assistance. As a result, 'most nations will have entered a period of self-sustaining growth'. The United States would provide financial and technical assistance, take steps to stabilize commodity prices, and defend any country whose independence was threatened. It was also vital for Latin America to take initiatives: 'Each Latin nation must formulate long-range plans for its own development, plans which establish targets and priorities, ensure monetary stability, establish the machinery for vital social change, stimulate private activity and initiative, and provide for a maximum national effort.' It meant social change to create opportunity so that everyone could share in prosperity through a fairer distribution of income. Above all, 'political freedom must accompany material progress ... we call for social change by free men – change in the spirit of Washington and Jefferson, of Bolivar and San Martin – not change which seeks to impose on men tyrannies which we cast out a century and a half ago.' Kennedy was calling for an American revolution of democracy, liberty and progress against a Communist revolution of tyranny – not least in response to Castro's success in Cuba and support for guerrillas in other Latin American countries and in Africa.[30]

The Alliance for Progress was modernization theory in action, a Monroe Doctrine for the era of the Cold War that provided a vision of liberal

capitalism to guide Latin America safely through the transitional stresses
of take-off. The failed invasion of Cuba at the Bay of Pigs in April 1961
and Soviet installation of missiles made the success of the Alliance all the
more imperative to challenge a model that others might follow. As Adolf
Berle pointed out, the Cold War could not be won but could be lost in
Latin America. The programme of the Alliance for Progress was formally
agreed by the Organization of American States at Punta del Este in August
1961.[31] Prebisch seized on the Alliance as an opportunity for ECLA to
work with the OAS, and Kennedy initially welcomed Prebisch's support.
The Argentinian soon met opposition in Washington where he was seen
as hostile to business, in favour of planning, and in conflict with the IMF
and IBRD.[32]

The Alliance for Progress potentially implied that the United States was
creating a trade bloc with Latin America that would threaten multilateralism. Kennedy therefore needed to combine containment of Communism
in Latin America with support for multilateral trade and a concern for
other continents. Consequently, he looked to India as a democratic alternative to China's Great Leap Forward. In February 1959, when Kennedy
was still a member of the Senate, he remarked that 'to nations in a hurry
to emerge from the rut of underdevelopment, Communist China offers a
potential model', in contrast to India, which was facing difficulties in
financing loans and meeting its need for food. He proposed a resolution
that the United States and 'friendly and democratic nations' should assist
India in fulfilling its second five-year plan:

> the continued vitality and success of the Republic of India is a matter of
> common free world interest, politically because of her four hundred million
> people and vast land area; strategically because of her commanding
> geographic location; economically because of her organized national devel-
> opment effort; and morally because of her heartening commitment to the
> goals, values, and institutions of democracy.[33]

He built on this commitment as President.

American assistance for India went back to food aid that had started in
December 1950. The newly independent government of India had aimed
for self-sufficiency in food by 1952, but the situation deteriorated and led
to requests for assistance. The State Department saw that food shortages
and famine created opportunities for Communist subversion and that a
refusal of aid would be exploited as a sign of American 'greed and cold
bloodedness'. In 1954, the Agricultural Trade Development and Assistance Act devised a general programme to sell American surpluses to
friendly nations, and to donate commodities as humanitarian assistance

during famine and shortages. The programme would help American farmers without interfering in regular markets or provoking a drop in world prices, and would also ensure that the recipients were independent of the Soviet Union. The aim was captured in the title of the agency set up in 1958 to run the programme: the Office for Food and Peace. Kennedy applauded the scheme in his presidential campaign: 'Food is strength, and food is peace, and food is freedom, and food is a helping hand to people around the world whose good will and friendship we want.' As President, he hoped that Indian modernization would show that democracy could work more effectively than Soviet and Chinese autocracy in overcoming rural poverty. In Lippmann's words, India could show that 'a very big and very poor country' could 'take off from the ancient stagnant poverty of Asia toward a progressive, independent modern economy'. Kennedy's expectations were disappointed, for Nehru played the Soviets off against the United States and used American aid under the Food for Peace Program to cover shortages caused by the diversion of resources to industry; by 1963, Kennedy had dropped India as a main beneficiary of American aid in Asia.[34]

Kennedy adopted a more general approach. A week after announcing the Alliance for Progress, he proposed foreign aid to the 'whole southern half of the world' in Latin America, Africa, the Middle East and Asia. On 22 March 1961, he sent a special message to Congress that followed Rostow in stressing encouragement of 'self-sustained growth' as a way of stopping the spread of totalitarianism and ensuring that 'an enlarged community of free, stable and self-reliant nations can reduce world tensions and insecurity'. He called for 'a historical demonstration that in the twentieth century, as in the nineteenth – in the southern half of the globe as in the north – economic growth and political democracy can develop hand in hand.' The task demanded 'a truly united and major effort by the free industrialized nations to assist the less-developed nations on a long-term basis', allowing them to attain 'sufficient economic, social and political strength and self-sustained growth to stand permanently on their own feet'.[35]

In September 1961, the Act for International Development marked a shift to a strategy of supporting military and political security by a commitment to long-term economic development to 'make a historic demonstration that economic growth and political democracy can go hand in hand to the end that an enlarged community of free, stable, and self-reliant countries can reduce world tensions and insecurity'. Military considerations should have primacy only in a few cases, such as in Laos and Vietnam. A Development Loan Fund would promote long-term economic development, informed by the soundness of the activity, whether funds were available from other sources, and whether the recipient was encouraging self-help and free enterprise. It authorized the creation of an agency for economic aid, and Kennedy brought existing institutions together in USAID within the Department of State.[36] In 1963, he explained the rationale for USAID and the Alliance for Progress:

> Had the needs of the people of Cuba been met in the pre-Castro period – their need for food, for housing, for education, for jobs, above all, for a democratic responsibility in the fulfillment of their own hopes – there would have been no Castro, no missiles in Cuba, and no need for Cuba's neighbors to incur the immense risks of resistance to threatened aggression from that island.

The answer was to create hope for a better future 'not through obeying the inhumane commands of an alien and cynical ideology, but through personal self-expression, individual judgment, and the acts of responsible citizenship'.[37] What applied to Latin America would apply elsewhere as part of a wider international response.

On 25 September 1961, Kennedy turned to a global approach and called for a United Nations Decade of Development as 'a cooperative and not a competitive enterprise – to enable all nations, however diverse in their systems and beliefs, to become in fact as well as in law free and equal nations.' He pledged American support for national self-determination, in contrast to the Communist empire imposed by foreign troops.[38] In December 1961, the UN's General Assembly agreed to designate the 1960s as the UN Development Decade

> in which Member States and their peoples will intensify their efforts to mobilise and to sustain support for the measures required on the part of both developed and developing countries to accelerate progress towards self-sustaining growth of the economy of the individual nations and their social advancement so as to attain in each under-developed country a substantial increase in the rate of growth . . . taking as the objective a minimum annual rate of growth of aggregate national income of 5 per cent at the end of the Decade.

The resolution called for policies to create stable, remunerative prices for less developed countries so that they could finance their economic development from export earnings and domestic savings. The UN was invited to consider policies to secure 'sound self-sustaining economic development' in the less developed countries through industrialization, diversification and productive agriculture.[39]

Although the proposals reflected American ideas for the Development
Decade, wider representation at the UN meant that resolutions might go
further and potentially subvert American policy. The United States delegation decided to be sympathetic in the hope of moderating radical demands,
but two issues caused concern. Iraq proposed that commodity producing
countries should have an increasing share of profits from the exploitation
of natural resources by foreign capital. The outcome was a resolution that
urged members of the UN 'to pursue policies designed to ensure to the
developing countries an equitable share of earnings from the extraction
and marketing of their natural resources by foreign capital, in accordance
with the generally accepted reasonable earnings on invested capital'. The
definitions of 'equitable' and 'reasonable' were ambiguous but the intention was clear – to justify action against western multinationals. The
second area of concern was the Soviet proposal that the UN Economic
and Social Council (ECOSOC) consider the principles of international
economic co-operation for the improvement of world economic relations.
This intervention followed Soviet proposals in 1955 and 1956 to create a
world trade organization, and in 1958 to hold a second UN conference
on trade and employment. It was a strategy designed to provoke criticism
of western dominance of the global economy.[40]

The Americans resisted Soviet demands for a world trade organization
and preferred to continue with GATT, which did not need congressional
approval. Richard Gardner, the deputy assistant secretary of state for international affairs, explained that '[t]he United States, though not prepared to
marry the lady it had been living with since 1947, settled down to a comfortable common law alliance, encouraging the formation of the GATT
Council and the enlargement of the GATT Secretariat.' He admitted that
GATT lacked the comprehensive coverage proposed by the ITO Charter
for areas such as commodity agreements and foreign investment. Consequently, 'the less developed countries became convinced that their interests
required the creation of a forum for the comprehensive review of trade and
development policy' and 'considered the preoccupation of GATT with the
reduction of trade barriers and the elimination of discrimination as largely
irrelevant to – or even inconsistent with – their interests in development'.[41]
Less developed countries had good reason to be critical of GATT. It operated on the principle of reciprocity: one country would make a 'concession'
provided that the other side 'paid' with a more-or-less equivalent concession. Reciprocity benefitted countries with the highest tariffs who had the
most to offer and it assumed a 'commercial' transaction that excluded distributive justice. The developing countries took an alternative view. Rather
than removing historical tariffs, trade talks should take positive action to

change the structure of the world economy by adding 'special and differ-ential treatment' to GATT's discourse of reciprocity.[42]

Wyndham White had been concerned for some time that developing countries would lose confidence in GATT, and had a difficult balanc-ing act in retaining support of the developing economies without alienating the developed world. He tried to convince developing countries that they would benefit from GATT rules, with greater flexibility in the use of quantitative restrictions (QRs) on trade, provided they had prior approval and an annual review. This compromise was disliked by both sides. Developing countries resented prior approval and wanted the right to impose QR both for balance of payments reasons (as did other mem-bers) and also to overcome past centuries of exploitation. Opinion in the developed economies was divided. The French supported the less devel-oped countries as part of an attempt to maintain sovereignty against GATT's rules; the Americans wanted to ban QRs other than in excep-tional cases; and other developed countries feared that their own QRs would be more strictly controlled. The Indian representative, L. K. Jha, resolved the conflict: QRs could be adopted for balance of payments reasons without prior approval, which was a defeat for the United States; and developing countries could use QRs for development purposes, pro-vided GATT was informed and that countries that were adversely affected could take compensatory action. Winthrop Brown thought that Jha was wise, reasonable, well informed and 'thought like a Westerner'.[43]

In 1957, Wyndham White asked Gottfried Haberler, along with James Meade, Jan Tinbergen and Roberto de Oliveira Campos, a Brazilian economist and politician, to report on trends in international trade. As noted earlier, the Haberler report found that exports of developing coun-tries were lagging behind world trade, yet their imports were growing. In response, GATT established a committee to consider trade in commodi-ties exported by developing countries, which pointed to restraints in their export markets by the use of high tariffs, state monopolies and QRs. Little progress was made and in November 1960, the developing coun-tries protested at the failure to take action.[44] The number of developing countries in GATT was growing as a result of decolonization, yet little had been done to consider development. On the contrary, the 'long-term arrangement on international trade in cotton textiles' of 1963 allowed developed countries to impose restrictions on imports that threatened domestic markets, and the United States proceeded to limit imports from seventeen countries. GATT was easily, and justifiably, castigated as a rich man's club that failed to take positive action and permitted harmful mea-sures.[45] Despite the growth in membership of less developed countries and the principle of one member one vote, they continued to have less voice than the United States and the EEC, for GATT relied on compromise rather than voting, and new members sought acceptance by playing by the existing rules.[46] Margaret Potter Leddy, an official in the State Department who dealt with GATT and subsequently joined its secretariat, later commented that too many developing countries joined too early and that UNCTAD had a 'very bad effect' in getting Wyndham White into development and adding new articles, which 'was a very bad business'. Her remarks serve to confirm criticism of GATT as a club of developed countries into which less developed countries were admitted on sufferance.[47]

In countering Communist criticism of liberal capitalism, Kennedy's proposal for a Development Decade offered an opening for critics of the GATT's inaction and of American and Soviet models of development. The IMF came in for similar criticism, for little had been done to act on Article 1 that set the objective of 'the development of the productive resources of all members'. Instead, the IMF focused on short-term stabilization rather than long-term balance of payments deficits caused by structural problems. In 1961, *The Economist* – hardly a radical voice – remarked that the IMF's programmes in Latin America were so harsh that Per Jacobsson, the managing director, was 'Mr Khrushchev's secret weapon' and that 'Latin American economists see strict orthodoxy of the Fund's tenets as a challenge to them to find ways of outwitting the lawgiver'. Dissatisfaction with GATT and the IMF led the less developed countries to press for a more sympathetic institution that could urge reform of both international trade and monetary relations.[48]

UNCTAD AND THE DEVELOPING WORLD

In 1961, the first summit of the non-aligned nations at Belgrade called for a greater voice for the Third World in the UN and for action to remedy less developed countries' economic subjection. Soon afterwards, two resolutions were presented to the General Assembly of the UN – from six Latin American countries, and from sixteen African countries and Indonesia. Both groups called for action on international trade, though the latter went further in demanding an international conference. The outcome was a resolution on 'International trade as the primary instrument for economic development' that would allow a country to use its productive resources and increase its foreign exchange income by expanding the value and volume of exports. It urged developed countries to consider the interests of less developed countries: trade deals should not require reciprocity;

developed countries should not protect their markets or discriminate against the commodities of less developed countries; disposal of surplus food should not harm the markets of developing countries; regional economic groupings should not hamper external trade; action should be taken on fluctuations in commodity prices and on the declining terms of trade of primary products; and industrialization should be encouraged. It welcomed action by the IMF to help less developed countries deal with seasonal and cyclical fluctuations in export earnings, and action by the Food and Agriculture Organization and other bodies to prevent disposal of surpluses in a way that harmed commodity exporters. The secretary general of the UN was asked to consult governments on whether a conference was desirable, and what its agenda should be. A total of sixty-six countries replied, with forty-five socialist and developing countries in favour, and with the advanced industrial countries opposed or doubtful.[49]

The Soviets saw an opportunity. In 1961, they denounced 'closed Western economic groupings' as damaging economic development, and in May 1962 Khrushchev attacked the Common Market as a form of neocolonialism. He pointed out that subordinating 'the young sovereign states of Africa to the Common Market' would continue their colonial status as suppliers of food and raw materials to the metropole. He called for an international trade conference and an increase in the average price of raw materials.[50] Then in July 1962, thirty-six countries gathered in Cairo for a conference on Problems of Developing Countries – the first time that African, Asian and Latin American countries had come together, with Prebisch attending as the representative of the secretary general of the UN. The resulting Cairo Declaration called for an international economic conference under the auspices of the UN to consider 'all vital questions relating to international trade, primary commodity trade and economic relations between developing and developed countries'. The idea was backed by ECOSOC in August 1962, which put the United States in a difficult position. Hostility would confirm Soviet criticism, and given that the conference could not be stopped, it was better to engage in an attempt to influence the agenda. The proposal for a conference was endorsed by the UN General Assembly in December 1962.[51]

In 1963, the preparatory committee met to consider the expansion of international trade, international commodity problems, trade in manufactures and semi-manufactures, the invisible trade of developing countries, regional economic groupings, and the financing of international trade. The ensuing United Nations Conference on Trade and Development met in Geneva between March and June 1964. Alfonso Patiño of Colombia expressed the hopes of the less developed countries that UNCTAD will show whether the developed countries are capable of discharging the obligations imposed on them by their wealth. It will also require them to renounce their traditional policy of passively accepting the supremacy of market forces. Against blind respect for those forces and against the trade restrictions imposed by the strongest against the weakest ranges the new ideology which inspired the convening of the conference. That ideology . . . will constitute a new phase in the age-old struggle for the liberation of peoples and respect for human dignity.[52]

Sidney Dell of the UN was more doubtful, and pointed out that '[a]lthough the underdeveloped countries are pressing for this conference, and have persuaded the West to go along with it, they are so drastically divided amongst themselves that they seem incapable of coming to any significant degree of agreement on conference objectives.'[53] Prebisch was appointed Secretary General of the conference as a result of lobbying by the Latin Americans. The British were alarmed. They admitted his 'intellectual suitability' but were 'doubtful of his impartiality' and would have preferred Jha. The Indians could not oppose a Latin American with strong support, however, so it fell to Prebisch to articulate a consistent view of the less developed countries against the 'alien and old-fashioned' free-trade views of the UN Secretariat in New York.[54]

The ambition of the developing countries was set out in a Joint Declaration to the General Assembly in November 1963. It expressed the hope that '[i]nternational trade could become a more powerful instrument and vehicle of economic development', both by increasing the traditional exports of less developed countries and 'also through the development of markets for their new products and a general increase in their share of world exports under improved terms of trade. For this purpose, a new international division of labour, with new patterns of production and trade, is necessary.' It meant overturning the existing organization of trade that had failed to increase their purchasing power, and to secure 'fair and remunerative' prices for their commodities, with capital on favourable terms. To succeed, 'a dynamic international trade policy is required' that offered 'special assistance and protection for the less developed parts of the world economy' that went beyond tariff cuts and the most favoured nation principle. 'More positive measures aimed at achieving a new international division of labour are essential to bring about the necessary increase in productivity and diversification of economic activity in the developing countries.' The Joint Declaration called for an ambitious set of policies: reduced barriers to the exports of developing countries without reciprocal concessions; stabilization of the price of primary products at fair and remunerative levels; larger markets for manufactures and semi-manufactured goods from developing countries; financial support on favourable terms for capital goods needed for economic development; better co-ordination of trade and aid policies; and a reduction of debt charges. The Joint Declaration hoped that UNCTAD would shift the institutional balance in favour of less developed countries:

> The developing countries are looking to more stable and healthy international economic relations in which they can increasingly find from their own resources the means required for self-sustaining growth. The developing countries are confident that the United Nations Conference on Trade and Development will not only be able to contribute to the acceleration of their economic development, but will also be an important instrument for promoting stability and security in the world.

The less developed countries were adopting elements of the development discourse of modernization based on expanded international trade and 'self-sustaining growth', with a more radical edge of 'collective economic security' for newly independent countries.[55]

Prebisch presented his agenda for UNCTAD in February 1964. It rejected free-trade orthodoxy and the multilateral institutions' inappropriate application of standard rules to fundamentally different situations. Systematic biases reduced the benefit of trade to under-developed economies: exports of a few primary products distorted national institutions and economic structures and left them defenceless against First-World monopolistic capitalism. The solution was to reverse the long-run decline in the terms of trade of primary producers and to abandon import-substituting industrialization, which led to excessive industrialization and harmed welfare. Prebisch returned to his proposal for a Latin American common market in place of small national markets and protective tariffs, which 'generally insulated national markets from external competition, weakening and even destroying the incentive necessary for improving the quality of output and lowering costs under the private-enterprise system. It thus tended to stifle the initiative of enterprises as regards both the internal market and exports.' Import-substituting industrialization reduced welfare unless regional integration created larger markets, and unless industrialization was planned to prevent the emergence of uneconomical industries. He was shifting towards 'outward-looking' industrialization based on import substitution and industrial exports, which required developed countries to open their markets on preferential terms.[56]

UNCTAD was a challenge to the dominance of multilateral institutions by the advanced industrial economies. It questioned the IMF's concern for stable exchange rates and short-term adjustment to the balance of payments rather than the provision of compensatory finance for fluctuations in export earnings arising from long-term structural inequalities in the global economy. Further, the IBRD emphasized self-financing loans for specific projects rather than the wider aims of the Special UN Fund for Economic Development. GATT was most directly affected. Wyndham White realized that UNCTAD was a response to GATT's failure to consider the needs of developing countries and the limited chance that the Kennedy Round would deliver benefits to them. He therefore attempted to give a higher profile to development and to the voice of developing countries. In 1963, a GATT committee on the trade of developing countries proposed encouraging exports by removing quantitative restrictions that limited their exports and by reducing tariffs. Little was achieved, with the only positive outcome being the creation of an International Trade Centre in 1964 to assist developing countries in trade negotiations. A study group was also established to consider whether preferential tariffs for goods from developing countries would encourage exports. The idea was opposed by the United States as a breach of liberal trade, and developing countries were divided, for preferences might threaten the trade of some at the expense of others. In 1966, GATT did agree to add a new section on development to its mission – a statement of good intention rather than practical action. The institutional relationship between GATT and UNCTAD was also problematic. One solution was a new international trade organization, as proposed by the Soviets. Another was the French proposal that GATT should be replaced by two bodies – UNCTAD and the Organization for Economic Co-operation and Development (OECD) of developed countries. This suggestion would merely entrench the two blocs and was not feasible.[57]

One outcome was for the two bodies – GATT and UNCTAD – to continue side-by-side. Periodic meetings of the UN Conference on Trade and Development would be held, with a standing committee and secretariat. The intention was to co-ordinate the activities of other organizations dealing with trade and development – the FAO, GATT, IMF and ECLA – without threatening their autonomy and 'without the need for setting up a separate specialized agency which may raise the same sort of political, institutional and constitutional problems which were faced by earlier proposals for setting up an ITO'. Prebisch accepted that GATT had led to orderly trade and that it had been considering development since the Haberler Report. It should therefore continue, provided that it did not assume that liberalized trade led to the efficient use of the world's resources. He suggested periodic conferences with a standing committee and 'an intellectually independent secretariat with the authority and ability to submit proposals to Governments within the framework of the United Nations'. Such an approach would be a partial step in the direction of the ITO without the risk of rejection by Congress. Wyndham White countered that the past failings of GATT would be rectified in the Kennedy Round, and that it was no longer a rich man's club now that developing countries had two-thirds of the membership. He insisted on the benefits of GATT as an inclusive organization and denied the need for UNCTAD to represent the developing countries. Nevertheless, in June 1964, the conference decided that GATT should be complemented by periodic conferences with a standing committee – the Trade and Development Board. Relations remained uneasy between the two bodies, with Prebisch pressing for UNCTAD to be the 'central organ on all matters of trade in relation to development. This fact should be fully recognised within the United Nations family so that GATT may not present itself as an equal or more competent partner.'[58]

The developing countries dominated UNCTAD with ninety members, compared with thirty developed countries. Each member had one vote. The Americans were alarmed and tried – and failed – to secure dual voting, which would require a majority of both developed and developing countries. The developed countries also wanted equal representation on the Trade and Development Board and a strict limit to the authority of the conference. There was no chance that they could win. The fifty-five members of the Trade and Development Board were chosen by four lists of countries. Group A comprised Africa and Asia, plus Yugoslavia (twenty-two); B covered western Europe, the US, Canada, Japan, Australia, New Zealand and Cyprus (eighteen); C represented Latin America and the Caribbean (nine); and D consisted of the socialist countries (six). Diego Cordovez, the chief of staff to Prebisch at UNCTAD, welcomed these groups on the grounds that they would allow members to reach a common position before discussions at the general meeting. In fact, the system guaranteed failure, for formalized bargaining coalitions prevented cross-group concessions and alliances. Developing countries put forward excessive, rhetorically satisfying, demands for justice, which created cohesion but were not realistic in solving problems. The developed countries responded with damage limitation that resulted in stalemate.[59] One of Prebisch's staff despaired: there were too many ill-prepared, long meetings; there was a failure to establish priorities that reflected a lack of co-ordination with other organizations, or consultation with national delegations. The result was confusion that played into the hands of the developed countries.[60]

UNCTAD was to have a 'full time secretariat within the United Nations Secretariat'. The lower case 's' was important, for the developed countries were anxious that it should not become an autonomous body. In practice, the secretariat did become independent, for it was based in Geneva rather than at the UN in New York. Prebisch and his colleagues were widely seen as partisan in presenting the controversial views of the less developed countries and shaping the agenda of the conferences. A group of developing countries – the G75, soon the G77 – emerged at the conference to agree a common position, and the secretariat participated in its meetings and helped to formulate demands. A delegate from a developed country reputedly remarked that 'This is not a secretariat – it's a sectariat!' Prebisch accepted that he had to be impartial, yet he also commented that 'as for neutrality, we are not more neutral to develop-ment than [the World Health Organization] is neutral to malaria'. He claimed that the 'concept of a neutral secretariat' assumed 'the automa-tism of economic phenomena' with policy dictated by the need to remove 'obstacles standing in the way of a smooth and automatic functioning of those economic forces'. In his view, responding to under-development demanded an active role for the secretariat – an assertion that was not accepted by the developed countries.[61]

Prebisch's approach undermined acceptance of UNCTAD in Washing-ton. George Ball realized it

> would come to be regarded as automatically unacceptable in US Congress if it were clear Secretariat was serving not as impartial servant of both developing and developed countries, trying to increase relevance of dia-logue between them, but was helping developing countries in efforts [to] seek changes in trade policies of US and other developed countries.

In Ball's opinion, the less developed countries were 'the victims of a high-class confidence game conducted in elegant economic jargon', and that 'UNCTAD may provide a forum in which some well-intentioned people – encouraged by others less benign – can do considerable mischief'. His concern was that 'the Kremlin has seen possible pay-dirt in an effort that might create discomfort for the West'. Ball admitted that GATT was viewed as 'an institution run by and for the benefit of the great trading nations' and that a body was needed to counter the 'orthodox ideal of a multi-lateral, non-discriminatory trading world'. The American adminis-tration needed to manage the situation so that 'the breakage could be minimized and a degree of useful education achieved'. Although criticism of America was inevitable, Ball hoped that the conference could end 'with a whimper and not a bang' by striking a balance between concessions to less developed countries without inflaming protectionist Republicans. Ball's tactic was to use a 'Socratic method' of drawing out other countries.

'We can be reasonably confident that chaos will result since the interests and views reported will be many and diverse. At the end we should try to pick up the shards and put together all that is good and salvageable.' He expected the less developed countries to see through Prebisch's 'gimmickry' and to realize that 'we have held out no false hopes and that, from the beginning, we have told them the truth'. At this point, the United States would offer 'a constructive set of proposals that will be both economically sensible and politically feasible'.[62]

The less developed countries focused on a number of issues. The UN had previously considered an international commodity agreement with no practical outcome as a result of disagreements between developed and undeveloped countries over fair and equitable prices. Now, the less developed countries demanded commodity agreements to increase world prices to provide funds for development.[63] They also pressed for non-reciprocal, preferential treatment for manufactures from less developed countries – the Generalized System of Preferences (GSP). In Ball's view, GSP was 'ingenious but really quite silly', for industrial growth in developing countries

> must be of a kind that will make use of that country's natural advantages. For most developing countries the sole natural advantage consists of an ample supply of low-cost labor. In most cases this should be adequate to assure markets for labor-intensive goods – provided only that the advanced countries would eliminate restrictive and discriminatory measures.

He saw no need to grant preferences that would provoke a backlash in Washington against imports produced by cheap Asian labour.[64]

A further demand was compensatory finance for shortfalls in export earnings. In 1963, the IMF proposed a Comprehensive Financing Facility to make short-term loans to countries that experienced a decline in export earnings. UNCTAD countered that export prices could fall for long periods and undermine development plans, and pressed for finance to cover persistent falls in export earnings. The proposal soon unravelled over concerns about the imposition of conditions for assistance and monitoring performance.[65] During the debates over international monetary reform in the 1960s, the less developed countries complained that their interests were neglected and that attention focused on the developed countries' concern for liquidity for world trade and stabilization of exchange rates.

Success was limited. The first meeting of UNCTAD in Geneva in 1964 was the largest trade conference ever called, with 2,000 delegates from 119 countries.[66] It was chaotic and its subsequent meetings were no better. The less developed countries lacked administrative support and the G77 formulated demands with little concern for practical outcomes. The secretariat was identified with the G77 and avoided issues that might split the group, and it did not broker agreement with the industrial countries. Unrealistic declarations led to the marginalization of UNCTAD rather than to its playing a central role in relationships between North and South. A State Department official dismissed UNCTAD as a forum for posturing: a developing country would make an impassioned speech of solidarity and report home that 'I really told those developed guys to go to hell today', before taking a more emollient line at GATT.[67] More optimistically, John Leddy, the chairman of the American delegation, thought that the conference

> may have laid the basis over the long term for a new, constructive relationship between the industrialized and developed countries of the North and the relatively underdeveloped, often desperately poor countries of the South, a relationship which is an increasingly vital problem in the evolution of the world under conditions of political freedom.

He looked ahead to mutual understanding with leadership of the less developing countries passing from the radicals to moderates. In retrospect, the first meeting of UNCTAD was judged to have given the United States a 'black eye' for voting against proposals that it found unacceptable, unlike other countries that abstained to secure short-term popularity or even, like the French, came up with 'fine sounding', though vacuous, proposals. The main purpose of UNCTAD, in the American assessment, was 'putting pressure on the conscience of the rich'.[68]

In October 1967, the G77 met at Algiers to review the situation. They claimed that more than a billion people in the developing world faced deteriorating conditions, with a slower rate of growth and a widening disparity with the affluent world. Their list of complaints was formidable. Developing countries' share of total world exports declined from 27 per cent in 1963 to 19.3 per cent in 1966, and the purchasing power of exports from developing countries declined by 10 per cent in the mid-1960s so that indebtedness mounted. Modern technology that required capital and skill did not benefit developing countries, and the slower increase in food production compared with the growth of population resulted in undernourishment. No new commodity agreement had been signed for primary products, and developed countries had increased protection of many of their agricultural products. In response, the G77 set out an ambitious programme of buffer stocks and diversification of output to increase export earnings of primary producers and to improve their terms of trade. Developed countries should remove barriers against primary products and guarantee a share of markets for the products of developing countries.

A Generalized System of Preferences should encourage exports of manufactures, and each developed country should commit to 1 per cent of GNP for aid. The IBRD should become a development bank; private investments should ensure that the host country had a permanent benefit; and debt should be consolidated into long-term obligations at low rates. Supplementary finance to cover long-term balance of payments deficits should be provided without imposing conditions that would compromise sovereignty, and the provision of any new international liquidity should be linked to development finance.[69] These demands were a wide-ranging challenge to the existing policies of multilateral institutions.

The American administration had to decide on its stance. One possibility was to support proposals that made sense to the United States, agree to study proposals about which there was uncertainty, and reject those that were harmful – 'in short, to make clear by tone and substance that we take UNCTAD seriously but will not be stampeded into unwise actions.' The US trade representative, Michael Blumenthal, suggested a more activist approach. He called for a 'Johnson Plan', an ambitious policy for international economic relations with less developed countries within the GATT framework of multilateral trade.[70] Another possibility was regional free trade areas among developing countries to create larger internal markets for efficient modern industry – a major break with American policy. Ball was sceptical of the wisdom of creating 'a series of North–South closed trading systems. Our advocacy of an open and non-discriminatory approach has seemed to me the only position appropriate for the leader of the Free World.'[71] Alternatively, tariffs could be cut by the most favoured nation principle, complemented by increased aid and improved access for imports of 'less sophisticated manufactures'.[72] American policy had to adjust in some way to the demands of the less developed countries.

The GSP was considered during the Kennedy Round and agreement was reached in 1965 that tariffs on industrial exports from developing countries could be reduced without reciprocity. Developed countries would not increase tariffs on their exports, except where there were compelling reasons, and they would consider reducing tariffs on processed goods more than on raw materials so that producers would be able to capture some of the value added. It was far from what the less developed countries wanted.[73] The concession was of little use in the absence of a binding commitment by GATT to a GSP. The EEC was sympathetic. Maurice Brasseur, the Belgian trade minister, proposed that tariff preferences could be linked to a policy of stabilizing commodity prices and compensatory finance within a more controlled system of trade with less developed countries. The Americans thought this proposal was 'grand-standing' and incompatible with GATT by consolidating preferences for the European Community's Associated Overseas Countries. They also realized that growing European support meant that a limited form of GSP would have to be accepted. The American position was that GSP should only apply to less developed countries that did not participate in discriminatory preferences with developed countries and should not prejudice the most favoured nation principle and non-discrimination. The decision was pragmatic, for 'the move toward preferences for the [less developed countries] is rapidly gaining strength and . . . the present US position of total opposition is rendering US influence progressively weaker'. The United States 'should be able to play an active and influential role in shaping any scheme of generalized preferences' and should prevent the European Community making concessions to the associated territories with the danger of 'contending blocs on North–South axes, with neo-colonialist overtones'.[74]

In April 1967, President Johnson informed the heads of state of Latin America at Punta del Este that '[w]e recognize that comparable tariff treatment may not always permit developing countries to advance as rapidly as desired. Temporary tariff advantages for all developing countries by all industrialized countries would be one way to deal with this.'[75] The important word was 'all', to avoid preferences being offered by some developed countries to selected developing economies. Less developed countries that fell outside such agreements urged a more open trading system with the abolition of quotas and subsidies by the developed countries. The outcome was that developed countries continued to grant subsidies to their farmers and to impose restrictions on manufactures from less developed countries; generalized preferences were some compensation. GATT's rules-based system was not creating an open global economy so much as permitting constraints on trade in response to the political need to support particular interests in the developed economies, and to make concessions to less developed countries.[76]

At its second session in New Delhi in January–March 1968, UNCTAD agreed to the principle of GSP, which went to GATT for approval. Washington was divided. The State Department was supportive on foreign policy grounds, for a refusal to support GSP would undermine American influence in the Third World. The departments of Commerce and Labor were concerned about the domestic political risk of competition from cheap imports and argued for exemptions. Progress was slow and Congress only approved GSP in 1976. Industrial trade preferences for developing countries were finally embodied in GATT in 1979 – the one, belated, success of Prebisch's policy.[77]

*

As the Development Decade closed, modernization theory was failing in South-East Asia as the United States faced defeat in Vietnam. The approach to economic development had to be rethought both by the American administration and the IBRD. At the same time, the IMF was struggling to deal with the tensions within the Bretton Woods regime. The post-war order was unravelling with the demise of the regime of pegged exchange rates, calls for a New International Economic Order, and the success of the Organization of the Petroleum Exporting Countries (OPEC) in the oil shock of 1973. The system of global government that had been painstakingly constructed in the 1940s was facing a crisis of legitimacy.

PART THREE

Washington Consensus

On 15 August 1971, President Richard Nixon announced the suspension of the dollar's convertibility into gold. The Bretton Woods regime faced a crisis of legitimacy. Although suspension was intended to be a temporary step before exchange rates were realigned and the Bretton Woods system of pegged exchange rates was restored, the task proved to be impossible. By 1973, the world had moved to floating rates set by the market and managed by central banks and finance ministries – with the European Economic Community turning to a zone of monetary stability to complement its common external tariff. Meanwhile, in the United States the removal of discipline provided by fixed rates allowed monetary expansion and inflation. This change in the international monetary regime coincided with growing demands from less developed countries for a New International Economic Order that was symbolized by the 'oil shock' of 1973. The result was stagflation – a combination of rapid inflation and economic stagnation – before a new global order emerged. Inflation was tackled by stricter monetarist policies; financial liberalization was encouraged; the challenge of the Third World was contained; the Soviet Union collapsed; and Communist China was transformed. The 'shallow multilateralism' of Bretton Woods gave way to a new global order, that is often – and contentiously – characterized as hyper-global and neo-liberal and dubbed the 'Washington consensus'. In Part Three, we explore why these changes occurred.

Robert Triffin of Yale University lecturing on the international monetary system
in the late 1960s: the board refers to gold at $35 an ounce and
to Special Drawing Rights (SDRs).

16

'Trying to live with an anomaly'

The Limits of Bretton Woods

'the notion of "fundamental disequilibrium" was more than a technical concept; it was a moral concept in that it distinguished between proper and improper behavior and pointed directly to those nations which were failing to adhere to the rules of the game. In the Bretton Woods concept no nation was to be permitted to follow beggar-my-neighbor policies. In this concept, use of an undervalued exchange rate to enhance domestic employment and production at the expense of others was clearly proscribed.'

James Schlesinger, Assistant Director of the Office of Management and Budget, to Peter Peterson, the President's Assistant for International Economic Affairs, 20 July 1971[1]

'We as a nation and the world as a whole were too slow to realize that basic structural and competitive changes were occurring; as a result, international policies and practices were too slow in responding ... The international institutions created after World War II were simply not equipped to deal with these changes, and governments were either disinclined or thought themselves unable to cope effectively with the rapidly changing realities ... We have been trying to live with what in many ways is an anomaly – a system presuming that in a world of increasingly rapid economic change, exchange rates should not change.'

Peter Peterson, 27 December 1971[2]

The restoration of current account convertibility in 1958 marked the end of a long period of adaptation and implementation of the Bretton Woods agreement. Any thought that it would work in a way that ensured stability was soon proved to be false. The dollar, against which all other currencies were pegged, came under pressure as the American balance of payments deteriorated and the economies of the EEC recovered. There was mutual misunderstanding. Washington complained that the Europeans were not taking an active role in providing a reserve currency, and that Germany was failing to revalue the Deutsche Mark. For their part, the Europeans – above all the French – complained that the United States was failing to pursue domestic economic policies that were necessary to maintain confidence in the dollar. Meanwhile, sterling – still the world's second-largest reserve currency – was in decline, falling from over 80 per cent of globally disclosed foreign exchange reserves to about 10 per cent by 1970, and Britain's frequent balance of payments crises undermined confidence in the pound.[3] The Bretton Woods system as it emerged in 1958 had to be kept afloat by a series of expedients, so that global government did not follow the rules devised in 1944. The IMF failed to provide leadership and flexibility in changed circumstances, or to reach a clear view on reform of the monetary system. The initiative passed to other bodies – to central bankers at the BIS who managed currencies, or to smaller, exclusive clubs of the advanced industrial economies in the G10 and OECD, which gave more voice to Europeans than to the United States. These bodies largely excluded the less developed economies, which felt that their demands for supplementary finance to cope with deficits caused by fluctuations in commodity prices and for structural reform of the global economy were ignored. Further, economists – above all Milton Friedman – insisted that the Bretton Woods system of pegged exchange rates had been a mistake that resulted in unnecessary controls over the economy in pursuit of the secondary objective of stable exchange rates. The operation of the Bretton Woods system between 1958 and its existential crisis in 1971 therefore raised serious questions about who could show leadership; whether the rules were appropriate and whether they were obeyed; how the system could adapt to changes in economic fundamentals; and how economic analysis and understanding shifted.

TENSIONS IN BRETTON WOODS

Paul Volcker, a dominant figure in American monetary policy as a Treasury official and chair of the Federal Reserve in the 1980s, remarked in 1992 that the Bretton Woods regime had been seen as 'a kind of wonderful totem, representing stability of exchange rates, freedom of payments, and less tangibly, a spirit of international cooperation', and that it was difficult 'to recapture the strength of the emotional and intellectual commitment to the international stability of the dollar and the fixed gold price'. The system was indeed accepted as the natural order and as the basis for post-war growth yet concerns about its sustainability arose almost as soon as it became operational.[4] The Bretton Woods system was designed to resolve the problems of the 1930s, not the circumstances after the war or the period of rapid recovery of the European economies in the 1950s and 1960s.

The Bretton Woods regime assumed fixed exchange rates with an element of flexibility. In practice, there was more emphasis on fixity. Peter Peterson, President Nixon's Assistant for International Economic Affairs, pointed out in 1971 that '[c]hanges in exchange rates were seen as painful evidence of the failure of political and economic policies. Exchange rate changes were postponed. As a result, the realignments needed became larger, more disruptive internally, and therefore postponed even longer.' Exchange rates were kept at values that were out of line with economic fundamentals, which led to speculation that unrealistic parities could not survive. Devaluation was then made reluctantly and with a large adjustment in a situation of crisis that Charles Coombs of the Federal Reserve Bank of New York compared to 'major surgery on a human patient'.[5] In the absence of devaluation, the only means of correcting a balance of payments deficit was to deflate the domestic economy – a politically unpopular option that governments avoided – or a retreat into protectionism and controls that would threaten the multilateral world economy.[6] Rather than underpinning multilateral trade, as assumed at Bretton Woods, clinging to pegged exchange rates could be counterproductive.

The Bretton Woods system was also asymmetrical, which led to difficulties in rectifying disequilibria in the world economy. Countries had differing rates of growth and inflation, and adopted divergent economic and social policies with different choices between domestic and international priorities. The result was wide variation in their balances of payments. Countries with a deficit could devalue a weak currency (such as sterling), but surplus countries had no obligation to revalue their currency (such as the Deutsche Mark) and were naturally reluctant to take action that would reduce export competitiveness. Peterson saw that 'the ghost of 17th century mercantilism, which held the accumulation of gold to be the principal purpose of trade, rose again . . . in the policies of the stronger countries.'[7]

The system's dependence on the dollar created further problems. The 'dollar gap' removed liquidity from the world economy after the war. The situation changed to a 'dollar glut' from the late 1950s as the United States increased its imports, lost its international competitiveness, and paid for overseas military commitments (Figure 3, page 368). The weakening of the American balance of payments created the potential for a crisis of confidence in the dollar and, by extension, in the international monetary system. In 1959, the economist Robert Triffin warned the Joint Economic Committee of Congress of the dangers posed by the restoration of convertibility. International liquidity created by American deficits injected dollars into the world economy and fostered the liberalization of exchanges and trade. If the United States did not allow deficits, the world's dollar reserves would be too low for the expanding global economy. Here was the 'Triffin dilemma': global liquidity relied on the weakness of the American economy. He saw that dollars might be created too fast, with an over-expansion of credit and a loss of confidence in the dollar, with a risk of something like the 1931 financial crisis.[8] Triffin's solution was the creation of new reserve units other than gold or the dollar, so that the United States could reduce its balance of payments deficit without removing liquidity from the global economy – a return to something like Keynes's Bancor. James Tobin, an economist at Yale who served on the Council of Economic Advisers, pointed out in 1961 that 'we must remember that in the long run if we [the United States] get back in balance and the UK does also, and if we haven't a new reserve currency, we have the question of the mechanism for supplying liquidity thereafter.'[9]

A revival of capital mobility created tensions in the Bretton Woods' trade-off in the 'trilemma'. In 1944, fixed exchange rates were combined with an active domestic economic policy by allowing controls on the movement of capital. Jacques de Larosière, managing director of the IMF from 1978 to 1987, later reflected that 'Bretton Woods was based on a simple notion. You have to free the current payments, but you are not obliged to free capital movements when they create disturbances and tensions on the fixed exchange rate system.'[10] At Bretton Woods, two mechanisms were proposed to deal with capital flight. The first was the use of offsetting finance from the IMF, which was constrained by its lack of funds and willingness to act. The alternative was co-operative capital controls. However, immediately after the war, Wall Street bankers gained influence and pressed for a swift return to convertibility and open capital markets. This turned out to be a disaster. When capital fled from political and economic instability in Europe to New York, Wall Street bankers refused to block inflows that provided them with profitable business. Instead, they pressed European countries to deflate. The result was to undermine the credibility of their policy of open capital markets, and to sacrifice Wall Street's programme of financial liberalization in favour of stimulating European recovery by the Marshall Plan and European Payments Union that would remove the risk of capital flight.[11] In 1956, the executive board of the IMF reaffirmed the use of capital controls reached at Bretton Woods when it ruled that 'members are free to adopt a policy of regulating capital movements for any reasons ... [and] they may, for that purpose, exercise such controls as are necessary ... without approval of the Fund'.[12] The Kennedy and Johnston administrations restricted capital flows, as we saw in Chapter 14, as did many European states.

The task of controlling capital flows became more difficult in the 1960s when convertibility and growth of the international economy led to greater capital movements. Although most countries retained capital account exchange controls after 1958, it was difficult to prevent 'leakages' through centres such as Hong Kong with a free market in foreign currencies, or through capital movements disguised as current account transactions.[13] Foreign assets had been around 7 per cent of world GDP in 1870 and rose to 19 per cent in 1900; the level fell to 8 per cent in 1930 and 5 per cent in 1945. The recovery after the war was modest and was still only 6 per cent in 1960; the level only later grew rapidly to 25 per cent in 1980.[14] However, the problem was less the revival of direct foreign investment, which both Keynes and Harry Dexter White had valued, than the resurgence of short-term capital flows. In 1967, Robert Roosa – now a partner in a Wall Street financial firm and a trustee of the Rockefeller Foundation – thought that occasional problems caused by interest-rate differentials were acceptable side-effects of rational global financial markets, with only temporary interventions needed in response to occasional excesses.[15] Despite his confidence, flows of speculative money destabilized the fixed-rate regime. The problem, as the US Treasury realized, was that 'in a world where short-term capital can move freely between money-market centers, an independent monetary policy becomes difficult to achieve: an attempt by the monetary authorities to restrict the expansion of credit is frustrated as banks and non-bank firms increase their borrowing abroad.'[16] Above all, John Connally, Treasury Secretary from 1971 to 1972, pointed to the problem of 'enormous short-term money flows' that grew 'out of the success in achieving broad, fluid, and integrated international capital and money markets throughout the free world. But now ... the child of success is threatening the mother that nurtured it – the system of fixed exchange rates and freely convertible currencies.'[17]

The resumption of global financial flows contributed to the demise of the Bretton Woods regime. In 1968, American interest rates rose to contain inflation and an overheated economy, so attracting short-term funds from western Europe. The American balance of payments returned to surplus, but it was not to last: the United States interest rate fell in 1970 and short-term funds moved to Europe and, particularly, West Germany, to earn higher interest and to avoid the risk of a devaluation of the dollar.

Figure 5: US interest rates and short-term financial flows, 1960–1972

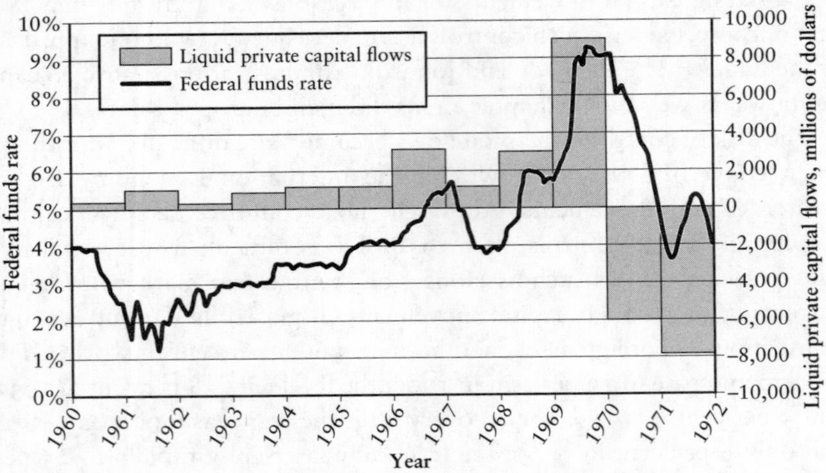

Sources: IMF, International Financial Statistics; and White House, *Economic Report of the President* (1974).

The American balance of payments moved into serious deficit (see figures 3 and 5). The IMF realized that dollars held outside the United States, above all in London, had become 'the key swing factor' in the American balance of payments. The movement of short-term funds that the Bretton Woods regime aimed to control contributed to its downfall.[18] In retrospect, Kit McMahon of the Bank of England saw that maintaining the Bretton Woods system 'would have been impossible because we could not have controlled capital flows enough'.[19]

Survival of the Bretton Woods regime rested on an assessment of benefits and costs. The White House, Federal Reserve and Congress were all reluctant to subordinate domestic policy to the balance of payments as the competitive position of the United States weakened and the dollar became overvalued. It was difficult for the American government to adjust its exchange rate by changing the gold price of the dollar, for it was the foundation of the system. In any case, other countries were pegged to the dollar and their currencies would therefore maintain their relative value. The alternative of restoring the balance of payments by deflation would threaten the prosperous domestic economy needed to deliver Johnson's 'Great Society' or Nixon's attempt to win support from traditional Democrat voters. As we saw in Chapter 14, the response was to turn to devices such as Operation 'Twist', Roosa bonds and the Interest Equalization Tax. These measures, backed by American threats to cut defence spending in

Europe, could work only as long as foreign central banks and governments were committed to preserving the Bretton Woods regime and supporting the dollar as the source of liquidity needed by the growing global economy. This commitment was contingent on an assessment of the benefits of preserving the regime against the dangers of an inflow of speculative funds. The United States was disinclined to raise interest rates to support the dollar, and – at some point – other countries would abandon their efforts to keep the system afloat.[20]

The faults of the Bretton Woods regime were clear, but fixing them would not be easy. The IMF might seem the obvious body to reform the international monetary system, but it was cumbersome and unimaginative, and pursued technical expedients rather than fundamental reform. In 1944, agreement on creating a new monetary regime was possible when exchange markets were strictly regulated. Major reform was more difficult when the markets were open. The IMF was legalistic and rules-based with a focus on removing short-term market imperfections by technical solutions rather than an appreciation of the wider politics informing economic decisions. It was trapped by 'path dependency', so that rules drawn up in response to the problems of the 1930s were not appropriate in the new conditions. In 1961, the Council of Economic Advisers complained that '[t]he goal of serious reform is poorly served by the timidity with which these issues have been approached so far in discussions in the IMF. Disproportionate attention has been devoted to ways of accommodating all proposed reforms to the traditional modes of operation of the Fund.' Harold Macmillan, the British prime minister, went further and complained that Per Jacobsson, the managing director of the IMF from 1956 to 1963, 'threatens to turn out to be the reincarnation of Montagu Norman' – a jibe justified by Jacobsson's orthodox support for gold and balanced budgets at the BIS in the 1930s. Further, the executive directors of the IMF lacked discretion to take decisions without referring back to their home governments, and they represented national interests rather than wider concerns.[21] Despite the IMF's wide membership, it was criticized both by less developed countries as the voice of the advanced economies, and by Europeans as an institution dominated by the deficit countries of the United States and Britain.

The OECD offered an alternative forum that brought together the leading Atlantic economies. Its Working Party 3 on Policies for the Promotion of Better International Payments Equilibrium was established in 1961 as a technical advisory group with members from France, Germany, Britain, Italy, the Netherlands, Belgium, Sweden, Denmark, Switzerland, Canada, the United States and, from 1964, Japan. The initiative reflected the

American preference for a smaller group that could facilitate 'frequent confrontation and consultation on alternative approaches to policies still in the making', rather than 'infrequent and therefore more widely publicised' meetings. It marked a shift in approach in bringing together leading officials from finance ministries and central banks, including Roosa of the US Treasury, Tobin of the Council of Economic Advisers, Otmar Emminger of the Bundesbank and Rinaldo Ossola of the Banca d'Italia, to discuss the balance of payments of leading deficit and surplus countries. WP3 overlapped in membership with the G10 group of leading economies created in 1962 to oversee the General Arrangements to Borrow (see below) – Belgium, Canada, France, Germany, Italy, Japan, the Netherlands, Sweden, Britain and the United States, with Switzerland joining in 1964. The agenda of the G10 – the relationship between balance of payments adjustments and international liquidity – also overlapped with that of WP3, and together they provided a different approach to the highly formal, rules-based IMF. In the words of Kazuhiko Yago, the historian of the WP3, it was 'a "soft" and more informal forum that existed within the "hard" and more formal structure of the OECD', with the G10 a still more informal grouping. WP3 and the G10 lacked the authority to enforce rules, provide credit or create liquidity, unlike the IMF. What they did offer was a forum for discussion of issues such as the role of capital flows and exchange rate adjustments to resolve balance of payments imbalances, with the possibility that each country would set its balance of payments aims and use objective indicators to show when action was needed. However, there were disagreements between the United States and Europeans over the desirability of regulating capital flows and the need for action on the American deficit.[22] The high level of representation of EEC members in both the WP3 and the G10 led to apprehension in Washington. Indeed, many Europeans – above all President de Gaulle – preferred the G10 as a body dominated by creditors who could control the feckless British and American governments. On this view, the IMF was 'too much an Anglo-Saxon institution in which they do not have sufficient say'. Equally, Harold Wilson, the British prime minister after October 1964, complained that France believed it 'had all Anglo-Saxons by the throat. Although the pound and the dollar financed three-quarters of the world's trade between them, on the question of liquidity France had a veto.'[23]

In 1963, Robert Roosa chaired a G10 study group – with input from the BIS – on gold and currency markets, which led to multilateral surveillance or an 'early warning system' for prospective difficulties. Rather than systemic reform, the solution was better information and co-ordination.[24] This task was largely left to the BIS, which was gaining influence. Every month for fifteen years central bankers met in Basel and engaged in what Charles Coombs called a 'major cooperative effort to keep the world financial system functioning effectively in the face of threatening disintegration'. Coombs believed that central bankers were 'fully cognizant of the social pressures straining the delicate fabric of democratic government'. They would not support 'futile defense of the prestige value of an overvalued currency' and could advise whether the problem could be solved 'by restoring the health of the domestic economy or instead called for drastic surgery in the form of a currency devaluation'. The problem, of course, was that central bankers could warn of incipient problems without the authority to compel governments to change their domestic economic policies – which might entail deflation. Nevertheless, Coombs believed that central bank intervention would protect the market from itself by dealing with the 'inherent instability' of the foreign exchange market, which was 'a nervous, high risk, ultra-sensitive mechanism, primarily geared to short-run development'. In pursuit of this ambition, he helped establish 'swap networks' at the BIS that allowed central banks to exchange currencies to maintain stable markets. These swaps would, he argued, offer 'a fair chance of converting the capriciously harsh discipline of the Bretton Woods system into more sophisticated machinery capable of controlling speculation'.[25] Coombs, like Roosa, was committed to the Bretton Woods system of fixed rates, which he felt could survive through careful management by central bankers at the BIS.

Uncertainty over the most appropriate forum was linked to disagreement over the cause of the problem. The Americans blamed undervaluation, initially of the Deutsche Mark and subsequently the yen, which should be resolved by revaluation. These surplus countries were not keen to revalue, given the political difficulties involved of harming exporters and exposing domestic industry to competition.[26] Instead, they blamed the United States for abusing the Bretton Woods system by the right of 'seigniorage' which allowed them to print dollars to fund 'greenback imperialism'. In February 1965, President de Gaulle attacked the Bretton Woods system as 'abusive and dangerous', and complained of what came to be called the 'exorbitant privilege' of the dollar:

> The fact that many States in principle accept dollars on the same basis as gold so as to offset, if need be, the deficits in their favor in the American balance of payments, leads the United States to indebt itself abroad at no cost ... This unilateral facility which is granted to America is serving to cloud the idea that the dollar is an important and international medium of exchange, when it is a means of credit belonging to one State.[27]

He was right, though we will see that his solution was perverse.

In 1965, West Germany complained that the Americans were exporting inflation through monetary expansion. Otmar Emminger, a member of the board of the Bundesbank, worried that '[c]ost and price developments in the US economy, the world's largest producer and consumer, determine largely whether the world economy, in the longer run, moves in the direction of inflation, deflation or stability.' Instability in the United States would have serious consequences for other countries, and 'pinning the European currencies to the Dollar through a fixed par value means pinning it to an anchor which may itself be carried off by a high tide of inflation'.[28] The dominant European view was that the Americans should tackle their lack of competitiveness and lax monetary policies. At the IMF annual meeting in 1970, Valéry Giscard d'Estaing, the French minister of economy and finance, stressed that

> Nations whose currency is widely used in the world thereby have increased responsibilities, a natural counterpart to the advantages they derive from the dissemination of their currency ... A currency that aims to play an international role as an accounting unit must obviously be of a highly fixed nature, since the other currencies cannot be permanently determined in relation to a standard that is no longer fixed but variable. None of you would agree to set his watch by a clock that was out of order ... [T]he restoration of the US payments position is the most urgent task still to be accomplished in the sphere of international payments.[29]

The European perception, according to the US Treasury, was that America 'should devalue, because we have sinned and should expiate'; and surplus countries should not be forced to revalue as a result of American obduracy, 'particularly since these surplus countries have followed virtuous anti-inflation policies and kept their balances of payments in order'.[30] The American perception was that the surplus countries with undervalued currencies were engaging in unfair competition.

The situation was inherently unstable. In 1962, George Ball realized that this sense of American weakness 'undermines our international prestige, our foreign policy, our domestic economic program', for the dollar survived

> only by the sufferance and forbearance of two groups of people: (1) European treasury officials and central bankers, and (2) private bankers, traders, investors, and speculators here and abroad. Their patience and confidence, we are repeatedly told, may run out at any moment ... confining us in a constantly shrinking and more uncomfortable box. We are insistently told

that unless we tailor our foreign and domestic policies to the tastes of Zurich and New York bankers, 'the dollar' and our gold stock will be threatened. The result is that every currency speculator in Europe regards himself as a self-appointed financial adviser to the United States Government . . . This is no way to run the government of any nation – much less to exercise the leadership of the Free World.

He called for a shift from narrow discussion of the IMF's 'special body of arcane rules to satisfy a special priesthood' to a greater concern for

political problems that exist among the Free World powers . . . [W]e must raise the negotiations to a political level . . . by cooperation with those leaders of the major Atlantic powers who have <u>political</u> responsibility for the maintenance of effective Free World relations and who – unlike central bankers – regard our exertions for Free World strength and security not as reckless and imprudent conduct but as vital to the survival of their own countries.

Ball drew an uncomfortable conclusion:

What we must tell our European allies is . . . clear enough. If we are to continue to carry our heavy share of the Free World burdens we can do so only under conditions where our exertions in the common cause do not imperil the dollar and, in fact, the whole international payments system. To create those conditions is the first and most urgent task for the Atlantic partnership.[31]

His rationale was unlikely to appeal to Europeans who would at some point conclude that it was not a 'common task'.

LIQUIDITY AND WORLD TRADE: PRESERVING BRETTON WOODS

Already by 1962, Ball worried that the limits of the existing international monetary system had been reached. Finance ministers and central bankers had been too conservative in responding to the liquidity needs of an expanding world economy, and Ball called on them to think in terms of 'a new world in which the volume of trade is three times more than it used to be and the gold supply is substantially the same'. He complained that 'the whole burden of being a reserve currency rests on the dollar. In the meantime, Europe has more or less gone into the de-colonization process, and it is getting strong. The United States is carrying burdens around the world.' He had a point. Sterling had declined to around 30 per cent of globally disclosed foreign exchange reserves by 1962, with the dollar accounting for just under 70 per cent (Figure 6). Ball wondered whether Europe should now

> carry some of the burden of the currency ... They see the maintenance of the dollar as a reserve currency, rather than being prepared to examine the question as to whether there shouldn't be some new arrangement within the payments system which inject something else – perhaps an international currency ... Or are we going to try to find that solution simply by trying to maintain the dollar and piecing it out by some holdings on our part and other currencies ... Or are we going to move toward some adventurous solution.

His solution, in the absence of a European contribution, was 'some kind of internationalism of the reserve holdings'.[32]

The French preferred to maintain gold as the basis for monetary stability and a counter to the 'exorbitant privilege' of the dollar. The main advocate of gold was Jacques Rueff, who had a long-standing concern for price stability as the basis for both economic stability and civil and political liberty. He had played a leading role in the deflationary policies of France in 1935, and when de Gaulle returned to power in 1958, he was appointed head of the committee for financial stabilization and author of the scheme to restore the franc (see page 370). Rueff feared that basing liquidity on the dollar might lead to a repeat of the crash of 1929. The Americans had found the

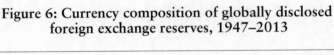

Figure 6: Currency composition of globally disclosed foreign exchange reserves, 1947–2013

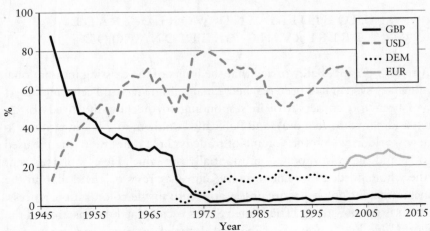

Source: Eichengreen, Mehl and Chiţu, *How Global Currencies Work*, 119.

'marvellous secret of a deficit without tears' and were creating an 'artificial pyramid of credit' that would collapse if foreign creditors asked for payment in gold. Rueff's solution was to return to the gold standard. An American balance of payments deficit would then lead to an outflow of gold, reduce its domestic purchasing power, and restore equilibrium to the world economy. Dollars and sterling could be replaced, and liquidity provided by the simple expedient of doubling the price of gold.[33]

Rueff's obsession with gold was not universally accepted even in France. Raymond Aron, a leading conservative-liberal public intellectual, thought gold was old-fashioned 'like sailing ships and oil lamps'. Supporters of planning and modernization thought that Rueff's plea for price stability and gold favoured an old France of peasants and rentiers. Rueff – a member of the Mont Pèlerin Society – in turn rejected postwar planning and Keynesianism as threats to social equilibrium and liberty. He admired American free enterprise and saw the role of the state as establishing free markets, which required monetary stability based on gold. De Gaulle took up Rueff's argument for a different reason: the preservation of national sovereignty. Shortly before a press conference on 4 February 1965, de Gaulle converted some of France's dollar holdings into gold and made a symbolic gesture of sending an Air France plane to collect the bullion in New York and transfer it to Paris. At the press conference, he argued that gold did not need supranational management and 'does not bear the mark of any individual country'. Returning to gold was a way of limiting American global power by dethroning the dollar.[34] In 1968, Michel Debré, a leading Gaullist politician, argued that

> We shall only build the Europe and the West of tomorrow if we respect national independence – an independence which is perfectly compatible with solidarity between countries. To demonetise gold in the interests of a single national currency would, on the contrary, amount to subjecting the policies of other countries to that of a single nation, the one whose currency was adopted as a standard for all the others.[35]

The French obsession with gold caused puzzlement in other capitals. David Ormsby-Gore, the British ambassador in Washington, wondered whether there was

> any rational or moral sense in tying the speed of our advance directly or indirectly to the amount of gold in the world? Is it not really rather ludicrous that if a large hoard of gold was discovered in the United States and transported to Fort Knox the Americans could safely adopt a more

expansionist policy, in spite of the fact that the discovery of the gold added
nothing useful to the welfare of the human race?[36]

The French proposal of increasing the price of gold was not a solution to
the creation of liquidity, for it would be an abrupt 'one-shot increase' that
would create a sudden, inflationary rise in the money supply rather than
a steady, long-term provision of liquidity. It would be a temporary stop-
gap with unfortunate distributional consequences. Countries holding
dollars – above all Germany – would lose from what would be seen as 'a
wanton and irresponsible decision' of the United States. The beneficiaries
would be gold producers (above all South Africa and the Soviet Union)
whose policies were not compatible with civil rights at home or security
abroad, and France, which was using its gold against the United States.[37]
In February 1961, President Kennedy rejected changing the gold price of
the dollar as inflationary and immoral. In any case, the Act of 1934
required congressional approval for such a change, which could not be
guaranteed and would lead to speculation and uncertainty.[38]

Maintaining the gold price of the dollar at $35 an ounce required the
United States to reduce pressure on the exchange rate by resolving its
balance of payments difficulties. It was also possible to manage the gold
market through international co-operation. Gold was bought and sold on
the open market in London, where its price rose to $40 by the end of 1960.
Banks could convert their dollar holdings into gold at the official price of
$35 for sale on the private market at a higher price. The Council of Eco-
nomic Advisers saw that the increase in the market price of gold was a
'symptom of the weakness of an international monetary structure that is
simply not adjusted to present-day realities'.[39] In 1964–65, the Federal
Reserve sold gold in an attempt to stabilize its price, and central banks
created a 'gold pool' to keep the price at $35. Between 1961 and 1964,
Treasury Secretary Douglas Dillon and Under-Secretary Roosa worked
with William McChesney Martin, chairman of the Federal Reserve, and
Coombs at the Federal Reserve Bank of New York to phase out gold, which
they realized would not continue as the basis of the monetary system. They
returned to the idea of John Williams that key currencies should be stabilized by less formal methods than the global approach of the IMF. The
official price of gold could be maintained by 'swaps' and mutual credit
arrangements between central bankers, and gold should 'sink to the bottom of the reserve barrel'. At this point, the gold pledge could be withdrawn
in an orderly manner. The United States would be rescued from 'the entirely
passive role of banker for the world financial system it had chosen for itself
under the Bretton Woods agreements'. Coombs and Roosa thought that

central bank co-operation through the BIS converted the 'capriciously harsh discipline' of the Bretton Woods system into 'more sophisticated machinery capable of controlling speculation'.[40] Despite the intention at Bretton Woods, global governance of the monetary system had moved to central bankers at the BIS.

The London gold market and the possible devaluation of sterling were, in Coombs's opinion, 'two time-bombs embedded in the Bretton Woods system and an explosion of either one would probably set off the other, and destroy confidence in the gold parity of the dollar'.[41] The bombs exploded in November 1967 when devaluation of sterling and conflict in the Middle East sparked a flight to gold as a safe haven. The crisis continued into March 1968 and raised doubts whether the international monetary system could survive. An official at the European Commission noted that

> The French were in the middle trying to stir up more trouble in an already difficult situation . . . If the United States balance of payments were strong, then the French could do absolutely nothing and we could laugh off any of their attempts to stir up a gold crisis or weaken the position of the dollar. However, in the present context, with speculative fever high, the French were able to play with considerable effectiveness a very dangerous game.[42]

The Federal Reserve's Open Market Committee was alarmed that a run on sterling meant that 'the international financial system was moving toward a crisis more dangerous than any since 1931'. On 15 March 1968, the United States requested the closure of the London gold market, and the gold pool was replaced by a two-tier gold market that separated monetary transactions from the private market. Emminger pointed out that this two-tier market was 'a landmark in the process of gradually diminishing the role of gold' in the international monetary system.[43] In effect, the world was now on a dollar standard.

In the early 1960s, Robert Triffin had suggested a solution to his dilemma. Countries should deposit reserves other than gold with the IMF, which would create international credit like any bank that accepted deposits.[44] The British government welcomed an approach that would take pressure off sterling, and the prime minister, Harold Macmillan, wished 'to start a movement to bring some rational system of international credit into being'.[45] In 1962, Reginald Maudling, a minister in the Colonial Office and later Chancellor of the Exchequer, proposed a 'mutual currency account' which would spread reserves from the dollar and sterling to the G10. Maudling saw

an ever-growing case for really imaginative measures to increase the volume
of world liquidity. I know that these are likely to enable the bad boys to
continue unjustified inflation at the expense of the rest of the world . . . But
this seems to me to be a relatively small price to pay for eliminating a
system which at present imposes upon the good boys a policy of deflation
at times when it is justified by the needs neither of their own economies nor
the world as a whole.[46]

Jacobsson thought the scheme was 'half-baked' and that Macmillan was
'a New Dealer masquerading as a conservative'.[47] He opposed lax monetary policies and assumed that the existing system could withstand any
shock. Neither was Maudling's idea well received by Dillon at the US
Treasury, who realized that it arose from a lack of confidence in America's
ability to improve its balance of payments.[48]

In 1962, the IMF's modest innovation of the General Arrangements to
Borrow (GAB) was designed to supplement its resources and use existing
reserves more efficiently. The scheme had its origins in a proposal of
Edward Bernstein, a leading figure at Bretton Woods who had been director of research at the IMF from 1946 to 1958 before setting up an
economic consultancy. Bernstein proposed that the IMF should borrow
from countries with large reserves and lend to those in deficit, so dealing
with the problem of imbalances and contributing to the stability of currency reserves. His proposal would not increase liquidity and the system
would continue to be based on gold and reserve currencies. Essentially, it
formalized the 'swap' networks run by the BIS. The attraction, as Jacobsson argued, was that 'borrowing could not really be improvised in a crisis:
some advance arrangements had to be made'. The countries of the G10
provided $6bn to the IMF to increase its resources, above all to sustain
the pound and dollar. The European concern that GAB could be abused
by the Americans and British led to a 'double-lock' to impose discipline.
The managing director of the IMF had to agree to the request, and then
obtain the consent of participants. Understandably, less developed countries complained that GAB – like other proposals for reform of the
international monetary system – ignored their need for compensatory
finance to deal with imbalances caused by the low price of primary products and structural inequities in the global economy.[49]

In 1963, Bernstein went further and proposed that the members of the
G10, plus Switzerland, should create a Composite Reserve Unit of their
currencies. The IMF opposed this scheme that covered only a small number of countries, and America and Britain were isolated in wishing to create
a new reserve unit.[50] Indeed, in 1964 the G10 and the IMF concluded that

there was no immediate liquidity shortage, though they admitted that additional reserve units would be needed at some point. The G10 appointed a study group of experts led by Ossola of the Banca d'Italia, with members from the G10, the IMF, the OECD and the BIS, which reported in May 1965. It set out various proposals for liquidity creation and posed several questions, without agreement on the answers. A fundamental issue was the role of gold, which the French insisted was needed to impose discipline. If reserves were created to supplement gold and dollars, should the scheme cover all IMF members or a small group of industrial countries? If the IMF had the power to create new reserve units, would that undermine its role in imposing monetary discipline, or did it have the experience to carry out both functions? Who should have power – the IMF dominated by Britain and the United States, or the G10 dominated by Europe? And should decisions be unanimous (as in the G10) or by weighted voting, as in the IMF? Ossola pointed out that creating new reserve units 'substantially implies the reciprocal surrender of rights on real resources. It therefore implies choices of a political character.' It entailed a loss of autonomy in economic policy and granting an automatic right for others to draw on a country's resources. The Ossola Report avoided the issues and merely looked to the evolution of the existing system of exchange rates pegged to the dollar and gold, complemented by new reserve units with co-operation by the IMF, OECD, G10 and BIS.[51] The report also failed to explain how complementarity and co-operation would be achieved.

Discussions in 1964 and 1965 exposed a wide divergence. The EEC 'saw excess liquidity in the world which should be curtailed or, at any rate, regulated closely if the resultant inflation was to be avoided'. On the other hand, '[t]he "Anglo-Saxon" group (ie the USA, UK, Canada and Sweden, plus Japan) had more expansionary ideas about the future needs for world liquidity.'[52] The Americans were moving towards the acceptance of a new form of liquidity to supplement gold and reserve currencies that would take pressure off the dollar and sterling, and replace the informal co-operation of central bankers at the BIS with a formal system of liquidity creation.[53] In 1965, a congressional subcommittee and the administration's Committee on Long-Run International Payments concluded that gold, dollars and sterling were no longer sufficient and that an alternative, supplementary reserve was needed.[54] The French had a different idea: a collective reserve unit of G10 currencies linked to gold at a higher price as the 'essential basis of the world payments system', and with strict institutional control. Their aim was to prevent the United States from abusing the system and creating inflation.[55]

At this point, the American administration decided to take the initiative by suggesting a new international monetary conference to consider 'what steps we might jointly take to secure substantial improvements in international monetary arrangements'. But the situation was different from Bretton Woods when the foreign exchange markets were tightly controlled, and Britain and the United States could shape the agenda. Now, a conference would create market uncertainty and there were more voices demanding to be heard. Central bankers at the BIS were appalled by the suggestion, and the Europeans wanted discussions to be limited to the G10. The American intervention did at least provoke the IMF to convene a joint meeting between its executive board and the G10, and to prepare plans for a new form of liquidity.[56]

During these discussions, the French mounted a rear-guard action to limit the creation of reserve units and to insist that America remove its deficit. The European Community demanded an increase from 80 to 85 per cent in the majority needed for important decisions at the IMF – so ensuring that their 16 per cent of votes would give them a veto. Treasury Secretary Henry Fowler resisted European demands to take action on the American deficit on the grounds that the United States had 'special responsibilities' for defence, aid and capital. He warned Karl Schiller, the German minister for economic affairs, that action on the deficit might have 'savage repercussions on the economic circumstances of the rest of the world and on the stability of the international monetary system'. The outcome would be a shortage of reserves, protectionism, restrictions on capital exports, and 'excessive, "beggar thy neighbor" deflationary measures at home. Competition to attract or retain reserves would tend to force interest rates higher and higher ... The lessons of the late '20s and '30s are salutary ... A significant and forward-looking plan for reserve creation is needed to provide insurance.'[57]

A new form of reserve asset – the Special Drawing Right (SDR) – was eventually agreed at the IMF's annual meeting in September 1967.[58] The IMF allocated SDRs to member states as a supplement to official reserves. If a member wished to use its SDRs, it had to find another country willing to purchase and convert the SDRs into currency; there was no other market. Members did not need to participate and the obligation to accept SDRs was limited. The result was disappointing, and the SDR made only a modest contribution to liquidity. The exact status of the SDR was ambiguous. It was not a currency issued by the IMF but a claim on reserves and a line of credit. Volcker recognized that 'financial markets viewed it as something of a synthetic creation that was not really as good as gold or the dollar'. Nevertheless, he welcomed SDRs as a sign that the major financial countries could work together to strengthen the system.

Similarly, Coombs remained confident that swaps and SDRs would absorb shocks and provide resources and the co-operation that were 'needed to protect the world financial system against the risk of a national currency crisis escalating into a world-wide financial explosion'.[59] They were overly optimistic. SDRs were just another sticking plaster on a patient in need of major surgery. By the time SDRs were finally introduced in 1970, they were too little and too late to deal with the crisis. The time and effort spent in devising the scheme were out of all proportion to its practical importance.

These proposals to create liquidity would not rectify another problem: the limited flexibility of the Bretton Woods system that meant rate changes occurred only after extended pressure and in large, sudden steps. The radical solution was to abandon fixed exchanges for floating rates or, more modestly, to increase the margin of variation around par from plus or minus 1 per cent so that markets would have a larger role. Floating had been supported by a few economists in the early 1950s who saw that fixed exchange rates were incompatible with convertibility and multilateralism. In 1952, James Meade saw a 'fundamental intellectual muddle' arising from the 'failure to realise that in the modern world it is impossible to restore free convertibility of currencies except in a system of variable exchange rates', and that it is 'impossible to get rid of import restrictions or to make sterling convertible in any real sense except in conditions in which variations in exchange rates have become a principal instrument of equilibration'. Fixed exchange rates meant that a country facing a balance of payments deficit would have to deflate, but an increase in unemployment was unthinkable so that deflation was soon abandoned in favour of direct controls on imports. 'Free trade and fixed exchange rates are incompatible in the modern world; and all modern free traders should be in favour of variable exchange rates.' Meade rejected the assumption at Bretton Woods that stable rates were needed to prevent beggar-my-neighbour policies. Times had changed from the Great Depression of the 1930s when politicians had turned to competitive devaluation to boost employment by reducing imports and stimulating exports. At a time of full employment in the 1950s, competitive devaluation was no longer needed to stimulate employment so that the rationale for fixed exchange rates had disappeared.[60]

Milton Friedman came to a similar, more aggressively free market conclusion. In 1950, he was attached to the Economic Cooperation Administration, where he produced a paper that formed the basis of an article in 1953 advocating floating rates. They were 'absolutely essential for the fulfillment of our basic economic objective: the achievement and maintenance of a free and prosperous world community engaging in unrestricted multilateral trade.' Although multilateral trade was the main aim of policy, there had been little success in removing trade barriers because of the commitment to 'an essentially minor goal' of rigid exchange rates. A country could potentially respond to changes in its balance of payments in one of four ways. It could adjust reserves, which was not possible given their low level after the war. It could alter internal prices and incomes, as happened after the First World War when Britain tried to force down wages and costs. Friedman accepted that such an approach was no longer politically feasible because of the commitment to domestic stability. The third – and in his view the best – approach was flexible exchange rates so that any move in the balance of payments immediately affected the exchange rate, and at once prompted corrective action. Friedman expected that even though rates would be free to vary, in reality they would be highly stable for 'instability of exchange rates is a symptom of instability in the underlying economic structure'. The fourth, and in Friedman's view worst, option had been chosen: fixed rates, which meant that correction was by administrative controls on capital flows or prices rather than automatic market forces. As a result, the economy was 'frozen'.[61]

Friedman's argument had little support in the early 1950s. He returned to the case in the 1960s. By this time, he had established a formidable reputation as a leading figure in the 'Chicago School' of economics, with its rejection of Keynesianism and support for monetarism and free markets. In his *Capitalism and Freedom* in 1962, and during a debate with Roosa in 1967, Friedman set out his case for floating rates. In his view, instability in exchange rates arose from instability in the underlying economy that would not be rectified by rules to stabilize exchange rates. Pursuit of the minor goal of rigid exchange rates, allied with the desire to preserve internal stability, led to controls to limit trade deficits, and produced a 'frantic scurrying of high government officials from capital to capital' – a jibe at Coombs and Roosa. His solution was to remove rigidities so that the economy could adjust to market forces. Exchange controls were 'congealing the blood of capitalism' and should be removed, along with import quotas and tariffs, by adopting floating rates. 'Fix prices – and the problems will multiply; let prices find their own level in free markets – and the problem will disappear.' To Friedman, it was absurd to force the 95 per cent of the American economy based on domestic markets to adjust in pursuit of a fixed rate, which affected only the remaining 5 per cent that depended on foreign trade. 'Why not have one price [the exchange rate] – and that a potentially highly flexible one – do the adjusting rather than require the myriads of domestic prices to vary, with all their stickiness and all the side effects? Why not have the dog wag the tail, instead of the tail wag the dog?' The 'discipline' of fixed rates forced the United States to deflate and Germany to inflate, or it meant foreign exchange controls as in Britain. 'There is one and only one satisfactory solution: abolish governmental price fixing. Let exchange rates become free market prices determined primarily by private dealings. Let the government simply stay out of the picture.' Floating exchange rates would immediately solve the liquidity problem, for 'private individuals will provide the reserves needed – just as they do in commodities that trade in a free market'. There was no reason for floating rates to be unstable, provided that internal stability was maintained – and even if rates did vary, the risk could be hedged on the market for currency futures. Friedman rejected the dominant view that the problems of the 1930s arose from competitive devaluation: rather, economies recovered when they abandoned fixed rates; and the existence of full employment now removed the temptation to embark on 'beggar my neighbour' policies. Pegged rates were, he claimed, only maintained because of 'the tyranny of the status quo'.[62]

The case rested on an ideology of free markets. Whether it was practical politics was another matter. As we saw in Chapter 11, floating rates, or greater flexibility at least, had supporters in Britain at the time of Operation 'Robot'. In 1962, Reginald Maudling returned to the issue when he claimed that '[w]e have built too much rigidity into our economic system', and that maintaining fixed parities with full employment and a rigid wage system left the government 'only the weapon of general deflation to deal with the fluctuations that inevitably affect any economy'.[63] The Bank of England and Treasury were wary, and rejected floating as a threat to the Bretton Woods regime that would create uncertainty, which is 'most destructive of economic expansion and international economic (and political) relations generally'. The solution was the 'proper management of the domestic economy' by 'strenuous efforts to avoid over-full employment, and to bring our wage levels more closely under control'.[64]

The question was whether it was politically feasible to control wages so that British exports were competitive, with a balance of payments surplus that could maintain the fixed exchange rate. The British economy faced a cycle of 'stop–go'. Domestic full employment led to high domestic demand, an increase in imports and a squeeze on exports. The balance of payments moved into deficit and led to speculation against the pound, which triggered domestic deflation and unemployment, which, in turn, created pressure to reflate the economy in time for the next election. When the Labour Party came to office in 1964, it faced a serious balance of payments crisis. The chancellor's economic adviser, Nicholas Kaldor, favoured floating the pound to restore competitiveness.[65] The government rejected this, and also tried to avoid devaluation that would lead to higher prices for imports and undermine wage restraint. Instead, it adopted an idea that had been devised by the Conservatives – a temporary import surcharge, which contravened GATT rules, intensified the run on the pound and resulted in higher interest rates. The governor of the Bank of England – Rowland Baring, the earl of Cromer – informed the chancellor that the crisis 'stemmed from a basic lack of confidence overseas in the policies of the Government' to solve long-term problems. He opposed devaluation, for '[i]f it were resorted to now in preference to restraint at home it would be regarded as an act of extreme irresponsibility'. The Labour government preferred a third option to either devaluation or deflation. Its aim was to modernize the British economy by an ambitious five-year plan, which Cromer thought was 'blurred and insufficiently concretised'. The strategy of encouraging exports without deep cuts in domestic demand was difficult to achieve, and in the end the ambition of transforming the British economy was overwhelmed by the need to satisfy creditors. The government borrowed from both the IMF and central banks and resorted to deflation and austerity. After a losing battle, Labour devalued by 14 per cent, to $2.40, in November 1967, so detonating the second of Coombs's time bombs. The decision reflected not just the weakness of the British economy but also the difficulty of stabilizing currencies by government action when large private financial balances could move swiftly in response to crises at home and overseas. The government rejected import controls and a siege economy and turned instead to austerity and devaluation.[66]

When Richard Nixon won the US presidential election in 1968, Friedman saw an opportunity to adopt floating rates. His reputation as a leading free-market economist with close ties to the Republican Party, and a public profile as a columnist in *Newsweek*, allowed him to press for a change in policy. He admitted that floating was 'most likely to be adopted . . . as a result of a widespread international liquidity crisis which leaves that as the only alternative open to the authorities'. Nevertheless, he saw a chance for change immediately after Nixon assumed office and before the administration was trapped into defending the status quo. Friedman presented the president-elect with a 'proposal for resolving the United States balance of payments problem' to end the endemic crisis in the monetary system, and to ensure Nixon's re-election in 1972. He drew a comparison with West Germany: 'On one Sunday afternoon in 1948, Ludwig Erhard abolished price controls, setting the mark free . . . He thereby unleashed the German economic miracle and assured the Christian Democratic Party unquestioned dominance for several decades.' The reality, as we saw in Chapter 11, was different: the end of controls led to unrest and a shift in policy.

Friedman was accepting Erhard's rhetoric rather than reality. He warned that the unattractive alternative was to be like Harold Wilson, whose failure to float in 1964 'forced on him one unpopular expedient after another' without, in the end, avoiding devaluation. Friedman believed floating would solve the balance of payments problem at once, and he dismissed fears of a long-lasting trade war. He assured Nixon that floating would contribute 'simultaneously to greater freedom of US citizens from government control, increased economic prosperity, liberalization of international trade, and the freedom of maneuver of the US government in foreign affairs'. He even offered Nixon a draft speech to be delivered within days of his inauguration in which he would abandon Bretton Woods. Nixon's administration should 'put its faith in . . . its free enterprise system, not in a growing network of bureaucratic controls', and he rejected Kennedy's and Johnson's belief that devaluation was a defeat. To Friedman, greatness was not synonymous with the rigidity of Bretton Woods:

> We are a great nation. The dollar is the leading currency in the world. We should behave like a great nation, not engage in demeaning and niggling negotiations to get other countries to agree to 'let' us depreciate by x per cent vis à vis this currency, by y per cent vis à vis that currency.

It was a clever appeal to Nixon's sense of destiny.[67]

Nixon, however, was not particularly interested; his main concerns were foreign policy and ensuring that the domestic economy would create favourable conditions for his re-election. Friedman's main ally was George Shultz, Secretary of Labor and later Director of the Office of Management of the Budget and Treasury Secretary. The two men had been colleagues in the economics department at Chicago and remained close. But even Shultz was aware that he could not press the argument, and the defenders of the status quo remained powerful. Arthur Burns, an economist at Columbia University and the National Bureau of Economic Research, who was the economic counsellor to the president and, from 1970, chair of the Federal Reserve, urged Nixon that 'whatever else we may do, let us not develop any romantic ideas about a floating exchange rate: there is too much history that tells us that a fluctuating exchange rate, besides causing a serious shrinkage of trade, is also apt to give rise to international political turmoil.'[68] Robert Roosa agreed: the existing system of fixed rates was 'fully adequate to the range of tasks confronting it', and there was 'no monetary escape route from the elements of economic discipline – neither within nor among countries'. Floating would lead to speculation and destabilization, for governments would intervene to prevent currency appreciation from harming exports or would succumb to the temptation of competitive devaluation to avoid domestic adjustments. Fixed rates forced countries to assume responsibility for their own economy and to take corrective action on their competitiveness so that they 'will have been unambiguously spurred to greater productivity, greater promotion, greater effort'. By contrast, flexible rates would allow a country to avoid adjustments to the domestic economy, for 'with no norms to defend, and with no pressure from reserve losses or from needed borrowing to reinforce the policy-maker's resolve, the likelihood of any corrective reaction pattern is a little hard to predict'. He foresaw a return to 'the kind of chaos experienced in the thirties that the Bretton Woods system was specifically designed to avoid'. Fixed rates were an 'armed truce'. By contrast, floating rates offered 'a continuous invitation to economic warfare as countries maneuvered their rates against each other'. To Roosa, fixed rates were the 'most hospitable environment for encouraging market-oriented adjustment within and among nations'. They provided 'an established scale of measurement, easily translatable from one country to another, which enables merchants, investors, and bankers of any one country to do business with others on known terms'. Flexible rates offered only a 'rubbery unreality' and would increase the costs of international business to cover the possibility that exchange rates might change. He denied that banks could use currency futures, which would involve 'an unknown array of unknowables'. He feared that

> the sheer wear and tear of trying to do business with a rubber yardstick for a measure, would . . . contribute to a greater economic isolationism. A wall of currency uncertainty would be built around every country . . . dampening influences on the long-run expansion of multilateralized world trade that would come with a flexible-rate system.[69]

Roosa's position continued to attract support from Treasury officials and central bankers who grew up with the Bretton Woods system and associated it with the post-war recovery of the world economy.

A more modest option than floating rates was wider margins than 1 per cent above and below par or frequent small adjustments in the rate. When Richard Kahn, a Cambridge economist and protégé of Keynes, reported in February 1968 to the British government on the position of sterling, he argued that '[t]he feeling of the exchange rate as something sacrosanct must not be allowed to revive. In future exchange-rate policy must be one of the normally accepted methods of influencing the economy.' He ruled out floating, and suggested increased flexibility through

> more frequent, though smaller, movements in the major exchange rates, with much less drama accompanying a change . . . One of the major evils of

the present system is the huge speculative movements which build up when one or another authority is trying to prevent a change (either way) which the financial world believe to be on the way. A system in which small and frequent movements occur would not be free from speculative pressure, but it could work successfully if the authorities succeed in making movements somewhat unpredictable so that speculation is made risky.[70]

In 1965, John Williamson, a British economist, proposed a variant: a 'crawling peg' with par adjusted in small steps over time in a continuous process.[71]

The problem with greater flexibility was its impact on European economic integration on the grounds that the internal market and setting of prices for the Common Agricultural Policy required stable currencies.[72] Most European central bankers also believed that corrections to the domestic economy should be made through budgetary and monetary policies rather than exchange rate adjustment. Hubert Ansiaux, governor of the Belgian central bank from 1957 to 1971, warned McChesney Martin that a crawling peg would

> throw doubt on the will of the US authorities to go on with their present policy – aimed at improving the balance of payments – and would give the impression that the United States intended to improve its position by forcing other countries to revalue their currencies, which would amount to the same thing as devaluing the US dollar without modifying the price of gold.[73]

Nevertheless, greater flexibility had some support in West Germany. The obligation of the Bundesbank to enforce price stability was made difficult by an inflow of dollars. Purchasing the dollars to prevent appreciation of the Deutsche Mark led to an inflationary increase in the money supply which was opposed by savers. The alternatives were either to impose controls on inflows of dollars and on exchange markets, or to allow adjustments to exchange rates, which would reduce the need to buy dollars and so moderate inflationary pressure – though with harmful consequences for exporters as the Deutsche Mark appreciated. This choice of policy set different interests against each other and led to conflicts within and between the Bundesbank and the West German government.[74]

In 1970, the IMF's Research Department set out the possibilities of wider margins, of small and more frequent changes in parity, or the suspension of margins to allow particular currencies to float. The report prevaricated. It worried whether the rule that permitted devaluation in response to 'fundamental disequilibrium' could allow correction by small changes over a period of time. It pondered whether a crawling peg needed 'presumptive criteria' – an automatic formula to determine whether exchange rates should rise or fall – to prevent the manipulation of rates, or whether such an innovation would threaten national autonomy. When the IMF's executive board considered the issue, it excluded wider margins and the crawling peg, and complacently concluded that the problem had been solved by changes in the parities of the pound, franc and Deutsche Mark in 1967 and 1969, and by the introduction of SDRs. Pierre-Paul Schweitzer, the managing director of the IMF from 1968 to 1973, lacked dynamism, and the British Treasury complained that he looked and sounded bored, ignoring fundamental issues. As the product of the French Treasury and Banque de France, he was unsympathetic to greater flexibility. Certainly, he was in a difficult position given divisions within the IMF. William Dale, the American executive director of the Fund, saw that interest was 'flagging' and that both developed and developing countries were reluctant to consider change. He could only hope that inconclusive discussions 'served some purpose in softening overly rigid attitudes and thus, almost insidiously, laying the psychological groundwork for more flexible attitudes' and a gradual 'loosening of inhibitions'. Could the Americans have done more, given that they were the largest shareholders in the IMF? Lisle Widman, a Treasury official, felt that 'we must either exercise some forceful leadership or throw in the sponge', but reform would be seen as a self-interested substitute for domestic action and an admission of inability to control inflation. Dale pointed out that '[a]lthough virtually all of the major initiatives in the international financial and economic fields since World War II have heavily involved US leadership, exchange rate flexibility represents an area in which aggressive US leadership presents peculiar difficulties.' He recommended that the United States 'keep the discussions continuing in an educational and productive manner'. Advocacy of exchange rate flexibility, it seemed to the US Treasury, 'would best be carried on persistently but in a low key'.[75]

The debates over the future of Bretton Woods, as one historian comments, were exhausting, time-consuming and largely pointless, merely patching up the system and keeping it alive 'by a series of extraordinary measures that made little long-term macro-economic sense'.[76] Discussion dragged on for a decade, producing ad hoc solutions to particular crises rather than systemic reform. In 1968, Walt Rostow reported to President Johnson that the attitude on Capitol Hill was 'one of almost anarchistic willingness to pull down the temple around their ears on the grounds that our budgetary expenditures are out of control'. Rostow felt that the issue 'goes to the heart of our nation's capacity to carry out its external commitments; maintain the world trade and monetary system; and avoid a serious domestic breakdown in our economy'. Europeans had the same concern that the executive and Congress were 'incapable of generating a tax–expenditure policy that would keep us in reasonable order'. Frustration at American failure to reform the system or address domestic economic problems led to a European response that risked creating separate, possibly competing, economic blocs.[77] As Hendrik Houthakker of the Council of Economic Advisers complained, the US Treasury 'could not see the Bretton Woods for the trees' – a comment that equally applied to the IMF.[78] It was becoming clear by 1968–69 that the Bretton Woods regime could not survive as tensions mounted, above all with pressure on the weak pound and franc, and the continued strength of the Deutsche Mark.

STERLING, THE FRANC AND THE DEUTSCHE MARK

Sterling faced renewed problems soon after its devaluation in 1967. The governor of the Bank of England, Leslie O'Brien, saw that 'positive confidence in sterling remains non-existent' and that 'in the atmosphere of distrust of currencies generally, the weakest and most extended naturally suffers most'.[79] Members of the sterling area had lost from devaluation and were not confident that the new rate would hold. They therefore continued to sell sterling, which provoked worries that it might float and jeopardize the Bretton Woods regime. In 1968, the British government prepared contingency plans that included blocking sterling balances and imposing exchange, capital and import controls in an attempt to hold the rate, with floating as an alternative. These plans would all have unfortunate side-effects. Blocking balances or floating would undermine confidence in sterling, encourage the disposal of sterling balances, and place further pressure on the rate. Floating would increase the price of imports, so stimulating inflation and wage demands that were already causing alarm. The only positive point was that the pound's weakness and threat of floating could be a bargaining weapon to secure support from the United States, IMF and BIS to prevent speculation from spilling over to the dollar and disrupting the international monetary system. This support might then allow the British government to avoid domestic deflation to support the pound.

Co-operation was needed to ensure that running down the reserve role of sterling did not lead to disorderly flight and contagion. During the 1960s, the IMF offered Britain credits and stand-by grants which were supplemented by assistance from the BIS. In 1966 and 1968, the BIS and the British government negotiated the 'Basel arrangements', which created joint responsibility for a managed decline of sterling. The British government provided a guarantee that official sterling balances would retain 90 per cent of their dollar value, underwritten by the right to draw on the BIS in Basel; in return, the overseas sterling area agreed to hold part of its reserves in sterling and would surrender the dollar guarantee if they fell below the limit. The Basel agreement turned a voluntary choice on how a country held its reserves into a contractual commitment. The agreement posed a problem for the IMF. Should it support a scheme that dealt only with countries linked with sterling, and on terms that might not be in their best interests? Its response was guarded: it welcomed a measure that would create stability but only if negotiations with holders of sterling reached acceptable terms. The British government soon found that it was easier to strike an agreement with central bankers from developed countries in Basel than it was to reach deals with former colonies who had reason to feel betrayed. The official line in London was that the Basel agreement did not involve winding up the sterling area:

> What we are proposing now is a strengthening of the sterling area system and another step in its evolution. It is most important from the point of view of the United Kingdom, the holders of sterling and the whole world monetary system that sterling should be able to continue to play an important part.

The sterling area, so it was claimed, would 'achieve a measure of stabilisation, in the interests of the members of the sterling area themselves and of the smooth functioning of the international monetary system generally'. The reality was that the Basel agreement confirmed the end of sterling's role as a major reserve currency. The aim was to ensure that the process was gradual and orderly.[80]

The decline of the sterling area had implications for Britain's application to join the EEC. During the first, abortive, application of 1961, the government assumed that membership would not undermine sterling and so threaten the international monetary system at a time when the dollar was under pressure. Indeed, the Bank of England hoped that sterling would be used for settlements within and outside Europe, and that the City of London would be the EEC's financial centre. The expectation was that the EEC would support sterling. But opinion was divided in European capital cities. De Gaulle, in particular, saw a risk that a deterioration in Britain's balance of payments would require sterling to be supported, and that the sterling area had a global rather than European commitment. In 1967, the Labour government renewed the application to join the EEC, at the same time working with the United States on multilateral solutions to ensure that the decline of sterling did not undermine the international monetary system. The British government had to reconcile, as far as possible, its relations with the United States, members of the sterling area and the EEC. Despite the public rhetoric of maintaining the global role of sterling, the British government accepted that sterling was a drain rather than an asset. The strategy was to ensure that retiring sterling as a reserve currency did not reduce global liquidity before creating a new reserve asset by multilateral action.

It is often alleged that the British government supported the international use of sterling against domestic interests. On the contrary, it imposed exchange controls in the 1950s and 1960s that undermined its international role. In the City of London, the assumption that sterling was vital to restoring its status as a major financial centre was replaced by a realization that the market in offshore dollars was a better prospect. The Bank of England and Treasury had even less reason to defend the international role of sterling at the expense of domestic policies. The difficulty was that managing the decline of sterling and a commitment to multilateral solutions led to French concerns that Britain was tied to the United States. In November 1967, de Gaulle rejected Britain's second application to join the EEC, for 'the state of sterling would not allow it at present to become part of the solid, interdependent, and assured society in which the franc, the mark, the lira, the Belgian franc and the guilder are joined.'[81]

In fact, the franc was also under pressure. Strikes and student protests in France in May 1968 led to expansionary fiscal and monetary policies that resulted in a flight from the franc. In June 1968, the Americans provided a rescue package and in November monetary and fiscal policies were tightened to prevent devaluation. Speculative pressure then moved to West Germany with an inflow of funds in anticipation of revaluation, which provoked controversy over the best response. German savers were obsessed with controlling inflation, for they had lost both in the hyperinflation of the 1920s and from currency reforms in 1948. The alternative to the Bundesbank's purchase of dollar inflows and consequent increase in the money supply was revaluation or floating the Deutsche Mark, which would harm German exporters and European economic integration. Initially, the West German coalition government refused to revalue and opted to restrict capital inflows and impose temporary border taxes.[82] The crisis resumed in 1969 when the IMF provided a stand-by credit to support sterling and France devalued by 11.1 per cent. The influx of money into Germany led Schiller, a member of the Social Democratic Party, to break with other parties in the coalition. He did not think that capital flows could be controlled by bureaucratic means which were too reminiscent of both Nazi currency controls and French *dirigisme*. Instead, he opted to float the Deutsche Mark to contain imported inflation; it appreciated by 10 per cent prior to its revaluation by 9.3 per cent in September 1969.[83]

These pressures on exchange rates and the failure to reach consensus on reform meant that the Bretton Woods system was heading for a terminal crisis. The IMF was not providing leadership, which had passed to the BIS and G10. The rules laid down in 1944 were not fit for purpose and were under pressure from economic imbalances and shifting ideas about global economic government. In 1971, the fragile edifice of the Bretton Woods system, which had only operated since 1958, collapsed and attempts to put it back together were unsuccessful.

17
'Benign neglect'
Closing the Gold Window

'*Can it make good sense to blow the present system apart in order to paste it together again in a basically-unaltered form? If exchange rates need to be changed and if such changes cannot be successfully brought about within the context of the present system, there is a strong presumption that the present system does not deserve re-incarnation.*'

Volcker Working Group papers, 3 March 1969[1]

'*. . . an international monetary system which to a large extent is based on a particular key currency is unlikely to perform well unless the key currency in question is kept reasonably stable and commands sufficient confidence: <u>The key to the functioning of the key currency system is the stability of the dollar.</u> In this context, the idea of setting up a <u>common European currency</u> is, of course, of particular interest because it might one day provide an alternative to the dollar, both as a reserve asset and as an intervention currency.*'

Otmar Emminger of the Bundesbank, 19 May 1970[2]

NIXON'S POLITICAL STRATEGY

When President Nixon took office in January 1969, the American balance of payments was in deficit because of military spending in Vietnam, overseas investment, and a deterioration in trade. The new president was more concerned with national power than with international co-operation on monetary issues and had other priorities as the crisis in international monetary issues reached its denouement in August 1971. During the presidential campaign, he had suggested that relations with China should be put on a new footing. Henry Kissinger – the president's national security adviser – embarked on a secret mission to Beijing in July 1971, and on 15

President Richard Nixon and Treasury Secretary John Connally
at Camp David, 15 August 1971.

July Nixon announced that he would visit China in 1972. Nixon and Kissinger were attempting to move from the Cold War between the United States and Soviet Union to 'triangular diplomacy' that would exploit suspicion between Moscow and Beijing to the advantage of Washington. The normalization of US relations with China would put pressure on the Soviet Union and encourage both Communist powers to reduce their aid to North Vietnam, thus persuading Hanoi to negotiate an end to the war.[3]

By contrast with these major geopolitical initiatives, Nixon had little interest in international monetary affairs. A month after taking office, he told Treasury officials that '[n]ow is the time to examine our international monetary system to see where its strengths are, and then to supply the leadership which is responsible, not dictatorial leadership that looks to the good judgment and good advice that we can get from our friends abroad.'[4] In reality, he provided little leadership. In March 1970, Nixon told his chief of staff that 'I do not want to be bothered with international monetary matters ... I will not need to see the reports on international monetary matters in the future.' The chairman of the Council of Economic Advisers concluded that Nixon 'may even have had an almost psychological block about economics' which he viewed 'somewhat like a little boy doing required lessons'.[5]

Nixon left economics to a so-called 'Troika' for whom he had little regard. Treasury Secretary David Kennedy was a Chicago banker who was out of his depth; the director of the Office of Management and Budget, Robert Mayo, was weak and disliked by Nixon; and the chairman of the CEA, Paul McCracken, was dismissed as boring. On occasions, the Troika became the 'Quadriad' with the addition of the long-serving chairman of the Federal Reserve, William McChesney Martin. Nixon disliked Martin as 'a stereotypical tennis-playing Eastern Ivy League banker who considered himself wholly independent of the administration' – a cultural clash compounded by Nixon's conviction that Martin had lost him the presidential election in 1960 when he refused to ease monetary policy to avoid an economic downturn. Nixon wished to replace him as chairman of the Federal Reserve by Arthur Burns, who rejected management of the economy both by Keynesian adjustments to spending and by Friedman's advocacy of monetary policy. Burns regarded both methods as unrealistic, for '[i]t's an argument about how well this or that group of economists can forecast the future. They cannot do so.' He was more concerned with the business cycle and the role of confidence, and he was willing to use direct controls. The attraction to Nixon was that he might be a more amenable chairman, for in 1960 Burns had recommended an easing of monetary policy. When Martin refused to resign, Burns became

economic counsellor to the president. Nixon's view on the economy was
clear: it should not imperil control of Congress or his re-election in 1972.
The scene was set for a conflict on monetary policy. Martin thought that
'inflation is the primary economic problem facing the nation', whereas
Nixon thought that the electorate was more concerned about unemployment. Above all, his aim was to create a New Majority by winning over
blue-collar Democrats and small businessmen who were hostile to the
east coast elite. Tight monetary policy and deflation would threaten success. As Nixon remarked in March 1971, 'We just can't have the American
domestic economy constantly hostage to the manipulation of the international monetary interest.'[6]

Nixon's domestic electoral concerns and geopolitical strategy had
priority and led to fatalistic impotence in reforming the international
monetary system. In 1969, the 'Nixon Doctrine' promised that the United
States would give assistance to its allies without fighting their wars, and
would provide a nuclear shield if they were threatened by another nuclear
power. Otherwise, the allies had to take responsibility for themselves –
and what applied to geopolitics applied to international monetary and
financial policy. The administration adopted a policy of 'benign neglect', a
pragmatic view that reform might only be possible after a crisis. Coombs
defined the approach as 'aggrieved acceptance of whatever the future held
in store'.[7]

The policy of benign neglect had its origins in the task force on the balance of payments chaired by Gottfried Haberler, who largely wrote the
report submitted before Nixon's inauguration. The premise was that balance of payments controls 'should be rapidly eliminated because they are
wasteful and inefficient, undermine our free enterprise system, and thus
reduce the rate of growth in the economy'. Instead, negotiations should
begin in the G10 with a one-off readjustment of currencies, followed by
wider bands of up to 2 or 3 per cent either side of par, and automatic adjustment of rates by small amounts when persistently at the upper or lower end
through 'self-adjusting pegs'. This approach would create greater flexibility
and ensure that surplus countries would bear some responsibility for adjusting imbalances. The scheme would work, provided there was no rush to
convert dollars into gold. In this eventuality, the report proposed suspending convertibility and then negotiating increased flexibility. The report was
pragmatic in suggesting limited exchange rate flexibility rather than Friedman's recommendation of floating rates.[8] The idea was to adopt a passive
approach, allowing the situation to deteriorate until an opportunity arose
for reform. The State Department's European bureau saw a danger. 'The
dilemma of full acceptance of the "benign neglect" concept is that if carried

to its extreme it seems to leave little room for international cooperation.'[9] Coombs later criticized benign neglect as 'an intellectual rationale for all the accumulated frustrations of the Nixon administration in the trade policy area ... [B]enign neglect had a corrosive and generally demoralizing influence on the will of the Nixon administration to take any decisive action to protect the dollar in the exchange markets.' In his view, the policy led to speculation against the dollar in the expectation that the United States would adopt 'shock tactics' that would leave other countries with a choice between monetary disorder or 'yielding under duress to our demands for a general revaluation of foreign currencies'.[10]

In the new administration, Kissinger proposed a working group on international monetary issues with membership drawn from his office, the CEA, State Department, Treasury and Federal Reserve. His incursion into Treasury territory arose from the strategic implications of monetary issues, but he soon lost interest and left the working group to produce a stream of technical reports on the administration's response to the incipient crisis. The working group was chaired by Paul Volcker, a protégé of Roosa who had secured his appointment as Deputy Under-Secretary of the Treasury in 1962 with the technical task of managing the gold pool. Volcker departed for Wall Street in 1965 and returned to the Treasury in 1969 in Roosa's old position of Under-Secretary for Monetary Affairs. Like Roosa, Volcker was committed to preserving the Bretton Woods regime. In retrospect, he wondered if he had been mistaken and that the system was too flawed to maintain – but in 1969 he 'was not prepared to accept passively that the breakdown would be inevitable within a single generation'. Volcker denied that he supported benign neglect, but the Europeans understandably saw little difference between that and his policy of muddling through until the recovery of the American economy allowed Bretton Woods to continue.[11]

Not everyone agreed with the policy and worried at the potential harm to multilateral trade. In September 1968, Lisle Widman at the Treasury worried that 'the world is moving rapidly toward the center of a swamp of sophisticated restrictionism' with 'much broader and much more severe import restrictions'. A one-off realignment of exchange rates would not be enough, for the new parities would soon depart from economic fundamentals, with renewed demands for protection. Consequently, the attempt to maintain the Bretton Woods regime threatened the multilateral system of trade and capital flows with 'the grave possibility of a trade war, splitting the world into discriminatory trade and payments blocs which will in turn strain the political and military partnership between the US and Europe'.[12] Soon after taking office, Nixon offered reassurance that he would maintain freer trade rather than turn to protectionism in response to the overvaluation of the dollar.[13] In reality, domestic considerations were pushing him towards protection, particularly for steel and textiles to win over labour to the New Majority. After his first trip to Europe, Nixon 'pointed out the great pressures we are under here for quotas on imports and I told them this is not the time for new breakthroughs in trade procedures. There will not be a new Kennedy Round – that's not on the cards – it's time to digest what we already have on the plate.'[14] The misalignment of currencies was a potential threat to freer trade.

Kennedy and Johnson had balanced internationalism with support for domestic industries within GATT rules. The politics of trade were now changing, with growing concern at the loss of jobs in textiles. Nixon imposed quotas on textile imports as part of his campaign to win over the South, where textiles were a significant share of industrial employment, especially in South Carolina. In 1969, he struck a deal with the prime minister of Japan to end the American occupation of Okinawa in return for restraint on textile exports, though the agreement collapsed because of opposition in Japan. Wilbur Mills, the Democratic chair of the House Ways and Means Committee, countered with a bill proposing import restrictions that would violate GATT rules. Mills was a free trader but he had ambitions of becoming the Democratic presidential candidate and gambled that the bill would force Japan to adopt 'voluntary' quotas, which would secure support from the South. His strategy failed: the Japanese did not respond, and the Republican Nixon supported the bill. In July 1970, the Ways and Means Committee then added a provision to the bill to impose quotas on any imported good whose share of the American market exceeded 15 per cent. Even Nixon thought the risk of a trade war was too great, and he threatened to veto the bill. Although Congress adjourned before the bill went to the Senate, there was a real threat of protectionism.[15]

Both Kennedy and Johnson had regulated capital outflows to improve the balance of payments. In his election campaign, Nixon promised to restore free movement of capital. In office, however, he reconsidered this as the balance of payments deteriorated. Kissinger cautioned that restoring overseas investment would have implications for foreign policy, for it would create pressure on the balance of payments which could be improved by troop withdrawals, demands for West Germany to cover defence costs, reduction of aid, or trade measures in breach of GATT rules. Fred Bergsten, the assistant for international economic affairs at the National Security Council, warned that savings from troop withdrawals would be modest and would signal to the Soviets that 'the US had become so pitifully weak on the economic and financial front that we could no longer make any pretense of maintaining our defense position around the world'.[16] Kissinger argued that capital controls were less damaging and were accepted as legitimate by most European governments. Nevertheless, Treasury Secretary Kennedy relaxed capital controls in 1969 to show 'a firm intent to reject "creeping restrictionism" as an answer to our problems' and to show a commitment to a 'philosophy of achieving solutions consistent with market forces'.[17] In 1971, George Shultz, now the director of the Office of Management and Budget, pressed for further liberalization on the grounds that capital controls imposed costs on businesses and financial institutions, and led to an inefficient allocation of resources with little evidence of improvement in the balance of payments.[18] Volcker was sympathetic to removing capital controls but cautioned against immediate action:

> It seems to me unavoidable that removing the controls at this time would be interpreted abroad as 'malign neglect' of our responsibilities as a key currency country for the stability of our currency and the monetary system and as an overt affront to other countries dealing with what they consider to be highly excessive dollar inflows ... [A]ction could not only trigger loss of confidence in the dollar and a major international financial crisis, but, in the eyes of much of the world, cast us in the role of initiating villain.[19]

Consequently, some capital controls continued as a way of supporting pegged rates. The Bretton Woods trade-off in the trilemma was under pressure, but survived.

Realignment of parities offered a solution to the American balance of payments deficit by removing 'unfair' competition from undervalued currencies, without the use of trade and capital restrictions. The problem, as Bergsten realized, was that countries with undervalued currencies would resist, and other countries facing unfair competition might impose trade restrictions and 'disruptive nationalistic policies'. In February 1969, he struggled to find a solution and explained to the Volcker working group that the choice was essentially political:

> For <u>domestic</u> reasons, countries are unwilling to rest their destinies on either the impersonal forces of the market or a supranational management. As a result of this reality our practical objective must be to foster a system which will maximize the political and economic benefits of international economic intercourse with a minimum of invasion of national sovereignties.

He agreed with Kissinger that using the 'financial deterrent' of suspending convertibility would be 'a massive display of US power and rupture all of our efforts to forge a new partnership with Europe on the basis of greater equality'. Suspending convertibility, like using the nuclear deterrent, would indicate failure and could only be used once, so that 'it may be better retained as a fallback if all else fails and a lever for seeking more constructive changes'. He ruled out deflation as a response to the balance of payments deficit as 'politically infeasible as well as economically undesirable'. He also rejected an increase in the price of gold to create liquidity. The choice therefore came down to a dollar area run by the United States – with the risk of competing economic blocs – or evolutionary change of the Bretton Woods system to improve liquidity and adjustment through SDRs, exchange rate flexibility and co-ordination of domestic policies, with the possibility of 'eventual supranational management at some far distant point in time'. Bergsten saw the task for the Volcker group:

> The US must decide which type of world it wishes to seek ... It may be impossible to achieve the desired outcome, and we must also decide what kind of world would be acceptable as a fallback. We must make these choices not only to guide any possible initiatives we might wish to take, but to provide a framework for any crises responses which might be required. Given the timing considerations ... the choices need to be made rapidly.[20]

Bergsten's reflections showed how difficult it would be to come to a clear solution which involved geopolitics as well as technical monetary considerations.

By June 1969, Volcker was ready to present his group's thinking at a high-level meeting with the president, the treasury secretary, national security adviser, chairman of the Federal Reserve, and Arthur Burns. The meeting took place at a time of uncertainty, with speculation that the franc and sterling might devalue and that the Deutsche Mark revalue. Volcker set out the 'basic options'. He ruled out a higher price of gold to increase liquidity as a temporary solution that would not resolve the underlying issues. It was deemed inconsistent with the evolution of 'a more smoothly-functioning, multilaterally-managed international monetary system'. Volcker's preferred option was 'substantial but evolutionary change' to restore 'a pivotal role for the US dollar as the leading reserve and vehicle currency'. It meant a 'negotiated multilateral solution' that would activate SDRs, realign undervalued currencies and secure greater exchange rate flexibility in the hope of long-term equilibrium. Volcker hoped that Bretton Woods would survive if the United States cured its deficit and followed West Germany in giving 'extremely high priority' to resisting inflation by using monetary policy in a regime of fixed exchanges and capital controls. Of course, evolutionary change might fail: the Europeans might reject realignment and flexibility as a threat to economic integration, and it might not be rapid enough to deal with the immediate crisis. This left the final option – the 'financial deterrent' of 'unilateral flaunting of US power' by suspending gold convertibility and forcing other countries to accept greater flexibility of exchange rates. Volcker aimed to convince the Europeans that realignment of currencies was preferable, which meant that the threat of suspending convertibility had to be credible. It was a risky venture. The shock to the financial system and resulting hostility to the United States for suspending convertibility could only be justified if it led to major changes in the system – but it might fail, with other countries refusing to realign and resorting to controls.[21]

Kissinger agreed that unilateral action would antagonize other countries and that a 'negotiated multilateral option is most consistent with our overall foreign policy'. Indeed, '[s]uccess in this effort could mark a major milestone in building a truly cooperative Atlantic Community and represent a major foreign policy achievement.' He recommended pressing West Germany and other countries to achieve a multilateral solution, which would require considerable efforts in negotiations, including Nixon's personal involvement. Kissinger foresaw difficulties, however. Unilateral suspension of convertibility might force Europe to make difficult choices and lead to a multilateral solution – but might also alienate countries that held dollars and threaten European integration if some countries linked their currencies to the dollar and others did not. The short-term political costs of forcing the Europeans to make hard choices would be high; the long-term benefits of reforming the monetary system might be higher. West Germany's opposition to revaluation meant it was unlikely to co-operate, and if it did take the lead it would create resentment from other members of the EEC. Hence the French would have to provide leadership – which would take time to achieve, even with de Gaulle's replacement as President in 1969 by the more pragmatic Georges Pompidou, a former Rothschild banker. Kissinger wrote off Britain as 'financially prostrate', and Japan 'simply does not play a role commensurate with its economic power'. He saw that 'political realities . . . suggest that it will be extremely difficult to reach a negotiated multilateral agreement on a sufficient scale within a relevant time period unless the alternative were clearly perceived as worse by the key Europeans.' Kissinger therefore supported Volcker's strategy, while emphasizing that agreement must not entail tighter controls over the American economy or concessions on foreign policy. Gold convertibility should be suspended if multilateral negotiations failed or if a crisis forced immediate action.[22]

Nixon's policy in response to the crisis of August 1971 was therefore already in place. The default option was the 'financial deterrent' of suspending convertibility as the 'only leverage we have to get foreign countries to take the needed action'. In November 1969, Widman suggested that

> we should quietly pursue a very thorough study of the tactics, timing and techniques of proceeding with this action [suspension of convertibility]. We could move quickly before the crisis breaks or we could wait and suspend in response to crisis. We could move formally and publicly or ask countries to renounce conversion 'voluntarily'. We could simply turn down a request or two. We could meet with key countries bilaterally and inform them of our intent. We could call a meeting of key Finance Ministers . . . The threat of suspension could be used next spring to speed up agreement on a crawling peg system and suspension might accompany the new technique.[23]

In the meantime, multilateral negotiations were unlikely to succeed. Nixon did not give them priority and other countries were suspicious. In September 1969, David Kennedy reported that the G10 was reluctant to make changes which would be a defeatist reaction to America's domestic economic problems.[24] Both in Europe and Japan, it seemed that the Americans were blaming others for failing to put their own economy on a sound basis to compete in world markets.

EUROPEAN AND JAPANESE REACTIONS

The creation of the European Economic Community and reform of the international monetary system were closely linked, above all in the proposals of Robert Triffin. He joined the IMF in 1946 and in 1948 became head of its office in Europe, before joining the Paris office of the Economic Cooperation Administration where he was involved in the Marshall Plan and the EPU. In 1951, he became professor of economics at Yale while retaining close links with Jean Monnet as the monetary expert of his Action Committee for the United States of Europe, and with Robert Marjolin, the first secretary general of the OEEC in 1948 and, from 1958 to 1967, European Commissioner for Economic and Financial Affairs. As we saw in Chapter 16, Triffin looked to the internationalization of foreign exchange reserves to resolve the dilemma of relying on a weak dollar to provide global liquidity. He also realized that global action would be difficult. Progress was more likely 'on the regional scale within smaller and more homogeneous groups of highly interdependent countries, keenly conscious of their interdependence, and better prepared by a common geographical and historical background to understand one another's problems and policies'. Worldwide action should therefore be 'supported and supplemented by regional agreements'. The EPU provided a model for reform of the international monetary system on the basis of regional monetary integration, with Europe as one of the pillars. Triffin adopted a 'monetarist' position – that is, monetary union should come first, prior to economic convergence. In 1957, he remarked that

> monetary unification would not require ... a full unification of national levels of prices, costs, wages, productivity or living standards. Neither does monetary unification require a uniformization of the budgetary, economic, or social policies of the member countries ... The problem of monetary unification is therefore a political rather than an economic problem.

In 1958, Triffin proposed that the EPU should evolve into a European Reserve Fund into which member states should deposit part of their reserves; the Fund could handle balance of payments difficulties and speculative movements of money, and so avoid the need for exchange rate adjustments or controls. A single currency was 'highly hypothetical' and would be taken 'only as the ultimate step of a monetary integration process'. His caution arose from a realization that exchange rate stability could be revoked, unlike a currency merger that 'would be very nearly irrevocable and irreversible in practice. This irreversibility constitutes a strong argument against a premature merger.' He proposed gradual evolution. The EPU unit of account could be a parallel currency, extended to international and even national capital transactions in the EEC; national currencies could be fixed against this unit and accepted for payment across the Community; the final stage would be to transfer central bank assets and liabilities to a European Monetary Authority, and to create a single currency. The European Monetary Authority could help countries with balance of payments difficulties, support growth and respond to financial crises. Such a system could replace assistance from the IMF, provided that the EEC as a whole had a balance of payments surplus. 'Monetary unification must be conceived ... as the crowning step of the six countries' integration policies.'[25]

The proposal for a European Reserve Fund was put forward by Monnet's Action Committee, and the Commission agreed in principle in 1958. Circumstances then changed. France's restoration of convertibility by devaluation removed the need for the Fund, and central bankers on the EEC monetary committee were sceptical about handing over their reserves. Above all, the West German government adopted an 'economist' approach: economic convergence of wages, prices, growth and productivity should precede monetary integration. Robert Marjolin initially supported Triffin's approach, before moving to a more balanced approach to harmonize monetary and economic policies, complemented by indicative planning at the level of the Community, more on the lines of the post-war planning that he had adopted as a minister for the reconstruction of France. He still hoped to achieve monetary union by gradual steps, for he believed that fixed exchange rates were crucial to planning and for common prices for the CAP. In 1965, Marjolin proposed shared reserves and a gradual process of monetary union, though without success.[26]

Disillusionment with American monetary policy meant that support grew for a stable European monetary zone in the later 1960s. Raymond Barre, a centre-right French politician, succeeded Marjolin as Commissioner for Economic and Financial Affairs from 1967 to 1973. Like most French economists and politicians, he supported stable exchange rates. Unlike them, he opposed protection and supported capital account liberalization – and exposure to German thinking at the Commission made him more favourably disposed to the market. He looked to a compromise between the French and German positions, and at the end of 1968 produced a plan for a common monetary policy that went beyond a customs union. He moved the Commission away from Triffin's renewed proposal for a European Reserve Fund and supported parallel action on monetary union and economic convergence, with low inflation and exchange rate targets to discipline domestic policy. The Commission looked ahead to

> common economic policies designed to transform the customs territory into an economically organized continent . . . [W]e must gradually replace the old national policies with Community policies, changing the European area into an organized European society, with a general economic policy thought out and built up to the scale of the continent . . . A political Europe . . . must be built up in the same way as our large countries, Germany, France and Italy, were gradually unified by major political decisions. Europe must have institutions enabling it to become a politically organized continent.

Barre believed that a customs union without co-ordination of economic and monetary policies could not deal with monetary crises, handle balance of payments disequilibria, or encourage convergence in growth and prices. The monetary committee and central bank governors were instructed to examine his proposal, and they reported in 1969 that '[o]nly those ignorant of the true nature of modern economics can believe that a multinational community could be organized solely on the basis of a customs union for manufactures, a common agricultural policy, and some measures of harmonization.' The case was supported by the French finance minister, who thought a common monetary policy was needed to prevent isolationist measures. Giscard d'Estaing also argued that Europe needed a common position on reform of the international monetary system in which a European monetary agency and unit of account replaced the dollar for settlements between members. 'This practice is extraordinary for a zone that has larger reserves than the United States and whose objectives include that of ending the dollar's supremacy.'[27]

In December 1969, the European Council of heads of government met at The Hague with the aim of 'confirming the irreversible nature of the work' of the EEC and 'paving the way for a united Europe capable of assuming its responsibilities in the world of tomorrow'. They expressed determination to create economic and monetary union based on the harmonization of economic policies and a European reserve fund.[28] In March 1970, the Council appointed a committee chaired by Pierre Werner, the prime minister and finance minister of Luxembourg, to develop such a programme. The choice of Werner reflected his reputation as a consensus builder, though his concern for the interests of Luxembourg inclined him to the monetarist position. He wished to make the country an international financial centre that would attract foreign banks and issue bonds denominated in European units of account. Luxembourg did not have its own central bank or national currency, and Werner was supportive of a currency union. Initially, the committee was wary of proceeding with monetary union ahead of economic convergence, and Werner looked for a compromise. He pointed out that 'a powerful lever is needed' for the Community to have 'a successful commercial and economic policy', and that 'monetary unification is a very effective way, even a brutal way, of promoting economic integration. Its ultimate effect is to force the economy into a new mould, at the cost of very serious tensions and pressures.' His support for monetary union was therefore tempered by a realization that the process should be gradual and be complemented by economic integration. He argued for a 'fundamentally dual approach' that combined monetary union and economic convergence, and stated that 'we need to encourage the economic and financial fields to interact with each other . . . [W]e need to tackle the problem from both ends and develop parallel initiatives.' The Werner Report accordingly 'tried to draw a line midway between the view that monetary union is the crowning glory of European integration and the view that would turn it into the virtually all-powerful engine driving integration'.[29]

The Werner Report appeared in October 1970 and proposed 'falling forward' by parallel movements in economic convergence and monetary union, with a transfer of power to the supranational level. The first stage was to reduce margins between members' currencies to ensure closer integration. Narrower margins implied convergence between national economic policies and would therefore require guidelines for national economic policy. The second stage was to integrate financial and banking markets, so allowing the free movement of capital, eliminating exchange rate fluctuations, and co-ordinating short-term economic policies. In a third stage, exchange rates between national currencies would be fixed, with convergence of economic policies and a Community system of central banks. The result would be a major shift in the relative power of the Community and individual nation states, for '[e]conomic and monetary union means that the principal decisions of economic policy will be taken at the Community level ... These transfers of responsibility and the creation of the corresponding Community institutions represent a process of fundamental political significance which entails the progressive development of political cooperation.' Economic and monetary union would lead to political union and to 'the total and irreversible convertibility of currencies, the elimination of margins of fluctuation in rates of exchange, the irrevocable fixing of parity ratios and the total liberation of movements of capital.' The report assumed that countries could both retain sovereignty over taxes and achieve monetary union and a single currency – a flawed view that was to cause problems in the future, as we will see in Chapter 24. In March 1971, the Council agreed to implement the proposals for economic and monetary union within ten years.[30]

The Werner Report coincided with the crisis of the international monetary system, without explicitly considering this wider context. The implications were clear in Washington. The European initiative would affect the role of the dollar as a reserve currency and would impact on the world monetary system. The outcome might be a two-bloc system based on the dollar and European currencies (or even a single currency), with exchange rates more-or-less fixed in each bloc and free to vary between them. The Werner plan might have the undesirable consequence – as far as Washington was concerned – of making the EEC

> more inward looking and adopt European rather than wider solutions to international economic problems. In order to avoid disturbing its own efforts in forming an economic and monetary union, the EEC may stall efforts to improve the international monetary system until the Community is well advanced in its process of unification.[31]

Widman was pessimistic, for the Europeans 'don't have the unity to act together and the French will not let them act separately'. The United States should proceed 'on the assumption that <u>no significant changes in the monetary system can be brought about in the next ten years except through unilateral action by the United States</u>'. Use of the 'financial deterrent' was becoming more likely:

we can ride along with the situation until the Europeans complain severely ... When that time comes, however, we should take unilateral action to suspend convertibility into gold. Perhaps the pressure could be forestalled or delayed considerably if it became obvious to the European officials that this would be the US response. We may have to become increasingly frank in acknowledging the existence of our intractable disequilibrium, reminding the Europeans and the Japanese that they are the ones who set the exchange rates in relation to the dollar.[32]

The European Community's concern for internal integration meant that it did not give priority to evolutionary multilateral reform, and intimidation by the United States would not lead to a co-operative solution.

Neither was co-operation with Japan likely. After the war, Japan imposed strict controls on domestic and international financial markets in pursuit of a development agenda.[33] Economic development was helped by the exchange rate, which was fixed at 360 yen to the dollar in 1949 rather than at the American occupation forces' suggestion of 300 to 330 yen. The lower rate meant that Japan's exports were competitive, which contributed to its economic recovery in the 1950s and 1960s. By 1968, Japan had a large surplus on its current account that provoked the United States to call for revaluation. In 1970, Philip Trezise, the assistant secretary of state for economic affairs, complained, 'I seek in vain for the dramatic and sweeping acts which will represent to the world and to the United States full Japanese recognition of its own economic strength, of the importance of the international system, and its willingness to act to support it.'[34]

The Japanese government felt that such complaints were unreasonable. The country had suffered from trade deficits and a collapse in the standard of living after the war, and the government was reluctant to threaten the progress that had been made. In 1970, Tadashi Sasaki, the governor of the Bank of Japan, argued that the balance of payments surplus was not yet deep-seated so that revaluation was premature. Indeed, the rate of 360 yen was viewed as sacrosanct as the basis of an economic recovery that rested on sacrifices made by Japanese workers and consumers who were overworked and underpaid by European and American standards. Why should they forego the benefits of their endeavours to help inefficient Americans who were incapable of resolving their economic problems? Japanese industrialists claimed that labour-intensive production meant they were less able to cope with a change in the exchange rate than their West German counterparts. Furthermore, virtually all export deals were made in dollars, so that Japanese companies held large sums in deferred payments and would lose if the yen were devalued. Business demands for compensation would then place strain on the national budget.

A few dissenters did favour revaluation. Taizo Hayashi of the Ministry of Finance and Bunji Kure of the Bank of Japan were both in Germany when the Deutsche Mark was revalued in 1961, and when Germany again revalued in 1969, they thought the yen could do the same. Discussion was closed down by Yusuke Kashiwagi, the leading official at the Ministry of Finance, who argued for a reduction of import barriers and regulations rather than revaluation. In March 1971, the finance minister, Takeo Fukuda, explained to the Upper House Budget Committee:

> If we revalue the yen, it would mean a huge national loss ... In terms of foreign trade, it would decrease our ability to export. Our country has built up our current position on certain efforts, but weaker countries are asking us to diminish it. I rather believe that we should insist on foreign countries setting their affairs straight by themselves ... Right now, domestic prices are in an unstable condition. The revaluation of the Deutsche Mark did not stabilise wages or consumer prices. If anything, it brought confusion to the German economy.

In June 1971 an eight-point programme was announced to liberalize the Japanese economy as an alternative to revaluation. It was modest and even these tentative steps led to fears that the 'black ships' were returning – a reference to Commodore Perry's arrival in 1853 to force Japan to trade with the west. Japanese resistance both to revaluation and to the opening of markets was more than a matter of economic calculation: it involved deeper concerns about nationalism and identity.[35]

CLOSING THE GOLD WINDOW

Nixon's relegation of international monetary policy behind domestic politics and national security priorities meant that little progress was made with multilateral, evolutionary negotiation.[36] A crisis of confidence in the dollar was clearly possible at any time and funds moved into foreign currencies – especially the Deutsche Mark. A new exchange rate structure would be extraordinarily difficult to negotiate without recourse to the 'financial deterrent' of suspending convertibility of the dollar into gold.

The problem was taken more seriously in January 1971 when Nixon set up a Council on International Economic Policy (CIEP), chaired by himself or the Secretary of State, to ensure that domestic and foreign economic policies were consistent. The executive director was Peter Peterson, the president's assistant for international economic affairs, an advertising businessman and chief executive officer at Bell and Howell, a manufacturer of cameras and projectors. After his time in the White House, he became chair and chief executive of Lehman Brothers and founder of the Peterson Institute for International Economics that continues to support open international markets. He acted as a counter to Kissinger, who, in Nixon's opinion, 'doesn't know a damn thing about economics. What's worse, he doesn't know that he doesn't know.' Peterson saw the competitive decline of the American economy as a result of low growth, stagnant productivity, reliance on income from foreign investments, and excessive imports. His gloomy conclusions supported Nixon's belief that the global economy was one of conflict in which other countries – Japan, Europe and even China and the Soviet Union – were challenging the United States. As Nixon put it, '[u]nless we're number one economically, we can't be number one politically'. Peterson argued that devaluation was not sufficient: it was vital to oppose unfair practices of other countries and to make American business more dynamic. A main task of the CIEP was therefore to put pressure on the inward-looking economic protectionism of the EEC by creating a North Atlantic Free Trade Area, or a Multilateral Free Trade Area that might include Japan, Australia and New Zealand.[37]

The CIEP failed to create a coherent American policy, for it cut across the authority of the Treasury and Volcker's working group. In June 1971, Nixon agreed that it was 'too large a group with too many people who talk a lot about subjects they know little about'. He decided to hand authority to John Connally, the former Democratic governor of Texas, who was appointed Treasury Secretary in December 1970 as part of Nixon's strategy of winning support from conservative Southern Democrats. Nixon decided that 'the Connally 1-man responsibility route is the best. This is an area in which he should be the lead man.' Kissinger was not convinced and later remarked that 'Connally's swaggering self-assurance was Nixon's Walter Mitty image of himself. He was one person whom Nixon never denigrated behind his back.'[38] Connally's approach to the international monetary system was summed up in his blunt words: 'My basic approach is the foreigners are out to screw us. Our job is to screw them first.' He assured a European banker that '[w]e're sick and tired of all these countries like Holland, the Netherlands [sic] and Switzerland telling us how to run our business ... and contribute nothing to the cause of freedom.'[39] Arthur Burns, now chair of the Federal Reserve, was at first impressed by Nixon's 'brilliant discovery' of Connally before doubts set in. Connally might be 'able, clever, and enchanting', but Burns worried that 'this power-hungry and most charming man ... will not be the kind of leader that the nation so badly needs'.[40]

Meanwhile, domestic monetary policy was contentious. Soon after Nixon took office, William McChesney Martin informed the Joint Economic Committee of the House and Senate that the Federal Reserve's wish to stop inflation meant that monetary restraint should not be abandoned 'at the first sign of a cloud on the horizon'.[41] In the final months of his chairmanship, Martin was anxious to show the Fed's credibility in controlling inflation, but political resistance prevented restrictions from being maintained long enough to change inflationary psychology. In May 1969, he remarked that 'I am disturbed by the defeatist attitude that inflation cannot be brought under control or the cynical conviction that the Government will not see the anti-inflation measures through.' The next month, he claimed that '[i]t is more important to settle the problem of inflation than to settle the war in Vietnam' and that 'even sterner restraints' such as forced savings and tax increases might be needed. He raised interest rates and tightened credit to squeeze inflation from the economy by removing expectations of continued price rises. Martin was turning to a tighter monetary policy than Nixon desired, the president being willing to accept gradual measures to cool down the economy and contain inflation, without causing a recession or pushing unemployment above a politically acceptable level.[42]

Friedman thought that gradualism was working and that a tighter policy would lead to recession. In May 1969, he remarked that '[i]t would be a major blunder for the Fed to step still harder on the monetary brakes. This would risk turning orderly restraint into a severe economic contraction.' Martin also faced opposition at the Fed, where one member of the Board felt that 'attempts to influence psychology and spending directly by Federal Reserve action is an incorrect policy objective'. Nevertheless, Martin persisted with his tighter policy on the grounds that inflation was a greater danger than recession, and that monetary restraint should not be removed for political reasons as soon as it started to have an impact. He warned of a 'surge of inflation' before the 1970 elections, urging that 'we shouldn't relax the pressure prematurely. The risk of underkill is worse than overkill. I personally discount the risk of recession.'[43] The result was both inflation and recession.

The appointment of Burns as chair of the Federal Reserve gave Nixon hope for a looser policy. He interpreted applause at Burns' swearing in on 31 January 1970 as 'a standing vote of appreciation in advance for low interest rates and more money'. The president expressed support for the independence of the Federal Reserve, before remarking that 'I hope that independently he [Burns] will consider that my views are the ones that should be followed.'[44] The relationship between the Federal Reserve and the executive had been a matter of controversy since its foundation. In the New Deal, power had shifted from the Fed to the Treasury; after the war, the pendulum swung back towards independence. Congress supported the Federal Reserve for reasons that differed between parties. The Democrats wished to give the Fed responsibility for ensuring employment under the Employment Act of 1946; the Republicans wanted to give it authority to control inflation and to make life difficult for the president. During the Truman administration, the Treasury wished to ease government finance by using the Federal Reserve to purchase government bonds – a suggestion that Marriner Eccles, the chairman of the Fed, resisted on the grounds that it would become 'an engine of inflation'. In January 1950, a bipartisan panel appointed by Congress's Joint Economic Committee recommended that the Fed should have 'primary power and responsibility' for money and credit, and that both the Treasury and Fed should pursue policies for employment, production and prices. The report emboldened the Fed in its battle with the Treasury. The outcome was the Accord of 1951 that gave the Fed greater independence from the Treasury.[45] In 1970, the question was whether Burns would succumb to presidential pressure and threaten the Fed's independence.

The new chairman had a close relationship with the president. Burns confided to his diary that Nixon's friendship was one of the three that mattered most to him, and that 'there was never the slightest conflict between my doing what was right for the economy and my doing what served the political interest of RN'. He remarked that 'if a conflict ever arose between these objectives, I would not lose a minute in informing RN and seeking a solution together'.[46] Burns persuaded the Fed to raise the money target from zero to 4 per cent – a return to gradualism rather than a radical easing of monetary policy. Friedman welcomed the move, which he hoped would produce stable prices and growth, though he warned that 'it will require continued determination and political courage'.[47] The risk, as George Shultz realized, was that failure to control inflation might increase support for the Democrat's incomes policy, which would distort markets and weaken fiscal and monetary discipline. In August 1970, the Democrats inserted presidential authority to impose controls on wages and prices into a bill – a power that Nixon might be tempted to use if gradualism failed to contain inflation.[48]

The economic situation deteriorated, and when the Pennsylvania Central Railway filed for bankruptcy in June 1970, Burns responded by increasing the money supply. Shultz at the Office of Management and

Budget urged a continuation of gradualism and a 5 per cent increase in the money supply; the CEA and McCracken argued for 7 to 8 per cent to reduce unemployment.[49] Nixon was sympathetic to a looser policy that would boost the economy and appeal to blue-collar workers who were crucial to the Republicans winning control of the Senate. As Vice-President Spiro Agnew explained, 'the time has come for someone ... to represent workingmen of this country, the forgotten men of American politics' who were 'written off by the old elite' and 'radical liberals' in the Senate. The outcome was disappointing, for recession and unemployment meant that Nixon took only two seats in the Senate in November 1970 rather than the seven he needed to win control. He was adamant that he 'doesn't want to take any chance on screwing up 1972' when standing for re-election.[50] Early in 1971, Burns changed tack. The Fed had made a mistake in 1931 in saving the dollar rather than the domestic economy. He decided not to make the same mistake and gave priority to the domestic economy by reducing interest rates and adopting an easy money policy.[51] Despite this change, relations between Nixon and Burns had deteriorated as a result of the president's demands. Although Burns assured Nixon that 'I have always been your true friend, and I am that now and expect to remain so', he was more honest in his diary: 'I knew that I would be accepted in the future only if I suppressed my will and yielded completely – even though it was wrong at law and morally – to his authority.'[52]

Lower American interest rates, the easing of capital controls and loss of confidence in the dollar led to a massive outflow of dollars to West Germany in anticipation of the devaluation of the dollar and revaluation of the Deutsche Mark. The result, as Emminger complained, was imported inflation that created difficulties for the Bundesbank's constitutional responsibility for stability. In 1970, Germany urged the United States to change its lax monetary policies, without success. Inflows amounted to $800m in February 1971 and, despite a cut in German interest rates in March 1970, continued at $900m in both March and April. Most members of the board of the Bundesbank wished to retain fixed parities by using capital and exchange controls, with the notable exception of Emminger. He argued that floating would provide greater autonomy for the Bundesbank, which would not need to purchase dollars to maintain a fixed rate and would therefore avoid an increase in the money supply. This approach was supported by the Organization of German Savings Banks (with its 30 million savers) and by five leading economic research institutes. Schiller, the minister for economic affairs, accepted that capital flows could not be controlled by bureaucratic means, and he now proposed a joint float of the Deutsche Mark with other European currencies to allow 'inward stability, outward elasticity'. Willy Brandt, the West German Chancellor from 1969 to 1974, agreed to the strategy as 'a decisive step on the path toward European monetary union' – though Germany would float unilaterally if the proposal were rejected.[53]

The French rejected Schiller's plan and opposed wider margins and free markets in favour of fixed rates, exchange rate control and a higher price for gold. The result was a massive speculative inflow into Germany on 3–5 May 1971. On 4 May, Nixon and the Quadriad met to consider options. Volcker turned to the fall-back position he had proposed in 1969: suspension of gold convertibility and floating the dollar to force a re-adjustment of rates. Burns urged the retention of fixed rates and an increase in the price of gold. Nixon admitted that 'I don't follow ... this on a blow-by-blow or hour-by-hour basis ... it's [an] extremely complex, difficult, tangled sort of issue.' Indeed it was – and no decision was taken. Nixon made his position clear the next day: he would not increase interest rates to defend the dollar. 'To hell with it! We've got to do what's necessary to keep this economy moving up ... There's no crisis of the dollar.' In public, Connally insisted that the price of gold and the exchange rate of the dollar would remain unchanged, and he claimed that the United States was controlling inflation. When Germany announced on 6 May that it would float the Deutsche Mark, Nixon was unmoved. 'The dollar is firm, we're going to stand by it. Hell, if the Germans float, then we'll export a little more.' Germany's action divided the EEC's monetary committee, which eventually agreed to a temporary float of the Deutsche Mark until the governors of the European central banks were able to prevent large inflows of speculative funds. In retrospect, Emminger saw that Bretton Woods 'broke down because the limit of tolerance for the inflationary effect of such currency inflows had been reached'. The United States' failure to deflate or limit inflationary wage settlements led to a flight of dollars to surplus countries, with an outcome that Emminger felt was 'the most inflationary mixture imaginable. It has helped to pervert fixed parities from being an instrument of discipline on deficit countries to one forcing monetary debauchery on surplus countries.'[54]

The crisis in Europe coincided with Britain's third application to join the EEC, which would have implications for sterling and its possible participation in any economic and monetary union. The French demanded that sterling should be phased out as a reserve currency as a condition for entry. In London, the preferred solution was to reform the international monetary system rather than a separate European initiative. A vague and ambiguous approach was agreed: the matter would be settled after accession rather than by a firm commitment to end the reserve role of sterling prior to joining the EEC; and an international solution should be found, given the lack of sufficient resources in Europe and the need for the overseas sterling area to co-operate. The EEC accepted the need for global support for sterling, and the French extracted a commitment to run down its reserve role, which was, in any case, now only 7 per cent of world reserves. In April 1971, Anthony Barber, the Chancellor of the Exchequer, announced that he would end sterling's reserve role 'provided that means could be found which avoided an unacceptable burden on the UK, promoted the healthy development of the international monetary system, and protected the interests of sterling holders'.[55]

As negotiations proceeded with the EEC, the British government became increasingly impatient with Washington. Prime Minister Edward Heath was outraged when Connally announced to the American Bankers' Association international conference in Munich in May 1971 that other countries needed to take action to resolve the American deficit. Heath felt that 'we need to treat this seriously and work out our position. The United States cannot be allowed to get away with this.'[56] In 1970, Lord Cromer – the former governor of the Bank of England – had accepted that Britain should take the lead in a new European monetary initiative

> to bring about the creation of a European Monetary System in which the sovereignty, which we have effectively lost due to our chronic Short Term Indebtedness, would be at least equated with that of the other European Powers and build a System of materially greater stability for all those who form part of it.

The Treasury and Bank of England were more cautious and argued that there was no advantage in taking the initiative when the members of the European Community were still engaged in their deliberations; at most, the British government should express interest without taking a position. However, the imminent prospect of America's closing the gold window and suspending convertibility of the dollar into gold and other currencies, and of Britain's joining the Community, made a choice between a dollar or a European currency bloc imperative. The case for British membership of the dollar bloc was that revaluation of other currencies against the dollar would offer competitive advantage without the need 'to make some more fundamental effort to deal with wages and prices'. On the other hand, 'adherence to the EEC bloc would almost certainly be demanded as evidence of our fitness and readiness to join Europe'. Cromer, who became Britain's ambassador in Washington in 1971, assured Connally that British involvement in a European bloc might prevent its being used against America. On 13 August 1971, the Bank of England took the view that if the United States were to close the gold window, the preference would be to reopen it as quickly as possible to preserve the Bretton Woods system; the next option would be to have dollar and Community currency blocs floating against each other; the worst course was 'completely generalised floating . . . possibly leading to widespread restrictions on trade and payments'. To avoid such a disastrous outcome, Britain should join the Community bloc and '[i]t might even be desirable for us to take a lead in getting the bloc established despite our private doubts'.[57]

Connally's line of blaming foreigners for the problems of the dollar led to stalemate. In May, he informed the American Bankers' Association that

> no longer can considerations of friendship, or need, or capacity justify the United States carrying so heavy a share of the common burdens . . . [N]o longer will the American people permit their government to engage in international actions in which the true long-term interests of the United States are not just as clearly recognized as those of the nations with which we deal.

The United States, he claimed, was acting responsibly and was 'dedicated to assuring the integrity and maintaining the strength of the dollar'. There was no need to devalue or change the price of gold, for '[w]e are controlling our inflation. We are also stimulating economic growth at a pace which will not begin new inflation.' He rejected the 'monetary magic' of tighter monetary policy to rescue the dollar, which would harm the domestic economy without increasing efficiency or opening foreign markets to American goods. Rather, the solution was to use trade policy to secure greater access to European and Japanese markets, and a fairer sharing of defence burdens. Connally complained that American benevolence was being exploited by other nations who 'have grown accustomed to our being relaxed, fairly generous, always forgiving, always easy in our dealings with them'. (This line attracted Nixon, who saw that trade could be used in a nationalistic policy to create jobs and so win votes for the New Majority.)[58] The thinking was captured by Connally's comment during hearings in the Senate: 'Senator, that's the theory of comparative advantage. In the first place, the reason I do not understand it is that I am not an economist. But if I were an economist, I would not want to understand it because I do not believe it is going to work.' To Connally, the solution to the American deficit was not reforming the international monetary system but controls on capital and trade, with the risk of protectionism and trade wars. He proposed a 10 per cent border tax, which would be politically popular and would force other countries to make concessions.[59]

Despite Connally's commitment to maintain the value of the dollar, Paul Volcker realized that realignment of rates was likely and that the real question was when, and by how much. In June 1971, Volcker started to plan for the suspension of convertibility and to put pressure on other countries to change their rates. Friedman went further. George Shultz arranged for him to meet Nixon to urge floating rates. The monetary crisis was, Friedman assured Nixon, 'the best thing that could happen. It's a fine thing ... they all float their rates. It eliminates this problem of the large capital movements ... let rates vary. Then it costs them something to speculate.' McCracken did not go so far. He warned Nixon of the risk that direct controls would be used to support fixed exchange rates, with growing protectionism and a threat to an open world economy. Rather than floating, he favoured an international agreement to allow greater flexibility and the adaptation of Bretton Woods to 'contemporary needs'. Connally took 'vigorous personal exception' to McCracken's analysis. Rather than 'muddling through', Connally believed he had successfully held back domestic controls, calmed international markets and increased the role of the IMF's surveillance over exchange rate policy. Connally assured Nixon that he had maintained co-operation and that

> Changes in our present international economic and financial position must be achieved without – and this is the key – undermining confidence in the dollar and the general stability of the monetary system. Should we fail, forces of economic nationalism and isolation in one country after the other – including the United States – could become unmanageable.[60]

For all his protestations, what Connally took to be co-operation seemed to many Europeans, and to some in Washington, to be an aggressive policy of economic nationalism.

Nixon was exasperated by the disagreements and wanted a bold policy. 'Now, as I understand it in the Treasury ... there are people, ideologues, who just, you know, they grew up with Bretton Wood and all that business and just don't want anything to change ... Why be bound by all that stuff? It's back to the China policy ... Now is the time to do something dramatic.' Despite his liking for bold action, Nixon was also concerned at the political costs of closing the gold window and floating. At the end of July he hesitated, and informed Connally that '[o]ur primary concern has to be the domestic political effect. The international crisis ... is going to be with us till hell freezes over, and we can't let that tail wag the dog.' He thought that the 'international monetary crowd' were alarmist, and he wanted to downplay any change in policy. Nixon asked Connally to consult with Shultz, McCracken, Burns and Petersen to develop a plan – essentially, a revision of Volcker's earlier proposals.[61]

On 2 August 1971, Connally presented his plan to Nixon. It combined both domestic and international policies. At home, Connally suggested restoring the investment tax credit that had been introduced by Kennedy to stimulate investment; cutting the budget to show fiscal responsibility; and imposing controls on wages and prices for ninety days. Internationally, he proposed closing the gold window and floating the dollar so that it fell in value against the Deutsche Mark and yen, at which point it would be possible to look to new parities and a return to fixed rates with wider margins. American leverage would be increased by imposing a surtax on imports until the new rates were agreed. Connally presented the domestic and international proposals as a single package. Devaluation and the import surcharge would raise prices, which would be contained by price and wage controls; devaluation and the investment tax credit would encourage economic growth and competitiveness. 'Whatever we do in the international field, ought to be coupled . . . with action on the domestic front, so that they tend to shield each other.' Nixon would be taking the initiative rather than reacting to events, making a dramatic intervention with something to please everyone. Connally assured the president that this package would 'be as big as your China thing'. Nixon was not convinced and preferred to keep the domestic and international policies apart, starting with the domestic policies and 'as a last resort doing the international thing . . . Closing the gold window sounds as if the dollar's going to hell.'[62]

Nixon continued to hesitate and thought that action should be delayed until September when Congress reconvened, for some elements of the plan might need approval. Further, the annual meeting of governors of the IMF that month offered an opportunity for action. William Dale, the American executive director at the IMF, saw a chance to secure a multilateral settlement by closing exchanges and suspending convertibility of the dollar into gold in the week before the meeting and then negotiating a realignment of rates.[63] Events took over and forced action, however. A crisis of confidence in the dollar was triggered by the publication on 6 August of a report on 'Action now to strengthen the dollar' from the Congressional Subcommittee on International Exchange and Payments chaired by Henry Reuss. He wished to preserve the Bretton Woods regime of fixed rates with 'cooperative monetary policy tools for managing Eurodollar flows' that would 'discourage or neutralize massive international transfers of liquid assets'. However, Reuss's report weakened confidence in the dollar. He pointed out that overvaluation might lead to an international crisis that would destroy the Bretton Woods system, and he suggested the suspension of convertibility and the abandonment of gold to force reform. His warning of crisis became a self-fulfilling prophecy that was reinforced by the announcement of a large balance of payments deficit. Heavy selling of dollars on 12 August led Connally to press for action, but Nixon still worried that closing the gold window and floating would be electorally harmful. Connally and Shultz argued that, on the contrary, a bold domestic policy would provide cover for international action. On 12 August, Nixon conceded, and the main lines of policy were in place. The following weekend, an emergency meeting was held at Camp David – a gathering that Herbert Stein of the CEA claimed was the most important weekend in economics since Roosevelt's inauguration.[64]

Nixon later claimed in his memoirs that he had never seen so many intelligent experts disagree so much as at Camp David. In reality, the main lines of policy had already been agreed with Connally and the task at Camp David was to build support among members of the economic team, and to devise the best way of presenting the policy to the public. Despite the obvious impact of the decision on international relations, neither the Secretary of State nor Kissinger were present or consulted. Connally pressed an aggressive line of closing the gold window, freezing prices and wages, imposing an import tax of 10–15 per cent and offering tax cuts on investment. He appealed to Nixon's pride and sense of destiny: such a programme would show that he could make big decisions and exhibit courage and statesmanship. Reuss's report reduced the domestic political risk and Connally dismissed foreign criticism. 'So, the other countries don't like it. So what? ... Why do we have to be "reasonable"?' How acceptable would his approach be to the other participants?

Burns continued to press for negotiating new exchange rates with the gold window open. In May, he had argued that gold convertibility should only be suspended under duress: 'We want to portray suspension as a last resort and to present a public image of cool-headed government responding to ill-conceived, self-defeating actions of others.' The government would weaken its bargaining position by taking the initiative and allowing foreign governments to 'claim that the US Government had been eager to throw down the gauntlet and had done so with insufficient excuse'. The United States would be blamed for the ensuing chaos, which would make it harder to secure exchange rate flexibility or a sharing of defence burdens. He took the same line at Camp David: suspension of gold convertibility would lead to retaliation, destroy the mystique of gold, reduce trade and undermine international liquidity. He preferred a border tax, cuts in spending, and controls on wages and prices without suspending gold convertibility:

> These major actions will electrify the world. The gold outflow will cease. If I'm wrong, you can close the window later. The risk is if you do it now, you will get the blame for the demonetization of gold and the devaluation of

the dollar. There is a certain mystique about gold. It is a symbol of strength and stability. I could write the editorial in *Pravda*: 'The Disintegration of Capitalism' ... Once the dollar floats, the basis for trade will change. It will be constricted because the risk will be greater. Most trade is based on narrow profit margins – I would fear this. I would fear retaliation by other countries.

In the meantime, Volcker should start to negotiate a realignment of currencies.

Nixon had strongly opposed the use of wage and price controls but he now accepted that they were necessary – and the Democratic Congress had provided him with the authority to act. What remained unclear was how long the controls would last and how they would be administered. Nixon's main worry was that controls on wages and prices would put 'the economy in a strait jacket under the control of a bunch of damn bureaucrats'. Shultz reassured him that '[i]t will stop when labor blows it up with a strike. Don't worry about getting rid of it – labor will do that for you.' The president's change of mind on controls was welcome to Burns, though he continued to oppose closing the gold window. Volcker thought closure was necessary, provided that the United States encouraged other governments to negotiate new rates at once. Shultz went further and proposed that the dollar should float, though he realized it was politically impossible at this stage. He was therefore willing to accept the package proposed by Connally and to play a longer game in the aftermath of suspension. Volcker opposed an import surcharge, though Shultz – a supporter of freer trade – accepted that it would be a useful bargaining lever with other countries to force a realignment of rates. What remained unclear was how long it would last, and what concessions would be needed from other countries before it was removed. Nixon came to see political advantage in the overall package. Labour would not be concerned by closing the gold window, but 'they will sure as hell understand the border tax, the price freeze and the other actions that would stimulate employment'. The president welcomed the opportunity to present the policy in a way that would be 'concise, strong, confident. Not a lot of stuff whining around that we are in a hell of a shape. If a speech rambles around it doesn't look confident.'[65]

To Volcker's chagrin, neither long-term reform of the monetary system nor working with other countries were discussed at Camp David. Nixon's speech writer Bill Safire commented that

Volcker was undergoing an especially searing experience. He was schooled in the international monetary system, almost bred to defend it; the Bretton Woods Agreement was sacrosanct to him; all the men he grew up with and

dealt with throughout the world trusted each other in crisis to respect the
rules and cling to the few constants like the convertibility of gold. Yet here
he was participating in the overthrow of all he held permanent; it was not
a happy weekend for him.[66]

Burns was also distraught at the decision to close the gold window. 'We
now have a government that seems incapable, not only of constructive
leadership, but of any action at all. What a tragedy for mankind!' His
reading of the situation was that Nixon made a political calculation that
leaving the window open would only lead to a small adjustment of rates
with another crisis before the election. It was therefore better to take
action at once and face immediate criticism with the hope of later
approval. Burns' worry was that 'postponement of serious efforts to
rebuild international monetary order would probably lead to a wave of
protectionism and restrictions of all kinds, and that he [Nixon] was taking a chance of ushering in an era of growing restrictionism, trade wars,
currency wars, and the like'. Nixon, he complained, 'was governed mainly,
if not entirely, by a political motive' – to win the election in 1972.[67]

On the evening of Sunday 15 August 1971, Nixon went on prime-time
television to announce the closure of the gold window and the suspension
of convertibility of the dollar into gold at $35 an ounce. The price of gold
was not changed – something that would require congressional approval –
so that it was left to other countries to revalue against the dollar and adjust
rates. He set out his New Economic Policy. The war in Vietnam had ended,
he informed the viewers, and it was time to rise to a new challenge of prosperity. The speech was about success and opportunity rather than failure, a
cleverly crafted piece of rhetoric that focused on three issues. The first theme
was to create more jobs and full employment. Jobs were needed for returning soldiers and to convert production from war to peace. He announced
tax cuts and credits, with a Job Development Act as an incentive for investment. These measures would boost consumer spending, and the Federal
budget would be cut to offset the loss of tax revenue. The second theme was
to deal with inflation that had been stimulated by war. It would be contained by a ninety-day freeze on pay and wages, and a call on corporations
to extend the freeze to dividends. The freeze on pay and wages could be
enforced by government sanctions, though Nixon hoped to rely on voluntary co-operation rather than a 'huge price control bureaucracy'. He also
established a Cost of Living Council to extend the freeze after ninety days.

Nixon's third theme was an attack on international currency speculators who took advantage of crises and were now waging war on the dollar,
which rested on the strongest economy in the world. Nixon proceeded to

reassure Americans that they had nothing to fear from the 'bugaboo of what is called devaluation', which would not affect the overwhelming majority of people who bought American products in America. He would, with the IMF and others, create a new international monetary system that would never again leave the dollar hostage to international speculators. He announced a temporary 10 per cent import tax, which would be removed when unfair competition stopped – an indeterminate period. His speech presented the United States as a generous benefactor exploited by malign international speculators and unfair competition. After the war, the United States had invested in the recovery of other countries; now they should take some of the burdens of defence, with fair exchange rates and competition on equal terms. The speech was a call to action by the American people to create a still better country – to become competitive rather than 'build a protective wall around ourselves, to crawl into a shell as the rest of the world moves ahead'.[68]

The speech played well at home. Volcker saw that Nixon had turned the suspension of gold from a defeat into 'a bold new initiative' and had used the international crisis as 'a plausible rationale for what otherwise might have been criticized as an abrupt and embarrassing change in domestic policy'. The stock market rose after the announcement, and an opinion poll found that 75 per cent backed the New Economic Policy. The pollster had 'never seen anything this unanimous' in his career, except possibly the reaction to Pearl Harbor. It was a remarkable change from July 1971 when an opinion poll found 73 per cent were critical of the government's handling of the economy. Even the *New York Times* – normally hostile to Nixon – remarked that '[w]e unhesitatingly applaud the boldness with which the President has moved on all economic fronts'. Controls did, it is true, attract criticism. Nixon had long opposed them and thought in the long run 'there was an unquestionably high price for tampering with the orthodox economic mechanisms'. Nevertheless, they were 'politically necessary and immensely popular in the short run'. Friedman, as might be expected, was horrified even in the short term. He pointed out that all attempts to impose a wage–price freeze had failed since the times of Emperor Diocletian, and that the result would be suppressed inflation. He was joined by organized labour, which resented the wage freeze without action on profits and interest. In the opinion of George Meaney of the American Federation of Labor–Congress of Industrial Organizations (AFL–CIO), the New Economic Policy was 'Robin Hood in reverse, robbing the poor to pay the rich'. Matters only worsened when previously agreed wage increases were blocked. Later in the year, as a price for continuing the freeze beyond the initial ninety days, Nixon reached an understanding with Meaney. A new Price Commission would represent the public interest, with a Pay Board representing labour as well as business and the public, with effective independence from the Cost of Living Council. Nixon also agreed to a government committee to monitor dividends. Before long, the policy started to unravel, with competing demands from labour for higher wages and industry for higher prices, and bureaucratic complexities. In the short term, the policy was welcomed as a blow against excessive demands for higher wages and prices by organized labour and business, and it worked in reducing the rate of inflation.[69]

The reaction outside the United States was hostile. Connally invited the managing director of the IMF, Pierre-Paul Schweitzer, to his office to watch Nixon's speech on television – the first he knew of the plan. To add insult to injury, both Connally and Volcker were called away at the end of the broadcast. In Europe, stock markets fell and foreign exchange markets were closed. To one leading German newspaper, the New Economic Policy marked 'a relapse of the world's strongest economic power into nationalism and protectionism'.[70] Cromer realized that the timing of the closure of the gold window was 'largely fortuitous' but that the lack of consultation showed that

> the Americans no longer consider it necessary to consult with the UK as an imperial or World power ... [T]he old concept that the dollar and Sterling should stand together as the two major world trading currencies is now obsolete. Sterling is not of the importance that it used to be; the dollar alone really matters. With the dissolution of the Sterling Area, the power and the influence which went with being the centre of it has disappeared.

What was needed, in Cromer's view, was 'a European monetary bloc of a scale that signifies'. He warned Connally 'that it would not be in the US interest if a European monetary bloc came into being in a spirit of retaliation to the US. The present American attitude seems quite likely to result in exactly that.'[71]

Nixon's policy reflected, as the historian Daniel Sargent remarks,

> an array of competing outlooks and agendas. These included Nixon's preoccupation with national vigor, Connally's boisterous nationalism, Kissinger's Atlanticism, Shultz's urbane neoliberalism, and the engrained commitment to international consultation that officials from Arthur Burns to Paul Volcker shared. No single analytical framework – whether economic nationalism or ideological neoliberalism – can explain the complexities of policy development during these tumultuous years.[72]

The question now was whether the legitimacy crisis of the Bretton Woods regime and Nixon's unilateral action could be used to reform the system or whether it would collapse. A clear programme for reform was unlikely to come from the IMF, which had failed to take the lead before the crisis and was, in the words of *The Economist*, 'sheepishly sorry for itself, pushed on to the sidelines and quite impotent'.[73] In Washington, the Treasury was aware that closing the gold window 'exposed world economic and political relationships to grave risks. Yet it also created an opportunity to achieve a quantum-jump improvement in international monetary arrangements whose importance can scarcely be exaggerated.'[74] Whether the opportunity would be used was another matter and would require a clear position in the ensuing negotiations. The danger was that Nixon would again give priority to domestic politics over reform of the international monetary system, with the risk that the world would slide into restrictionism and recession. It was not clear how long the suspension of convertibility would last, when the import surcharge would be removed, how much other currencies would need to adjust, whether the United States would change the price of gold, whether rates would remain fixed or by how much margins would change. Robert Triffin hoped that 'the world has been forced to look the problem in the face, instead of trying to patch up the system.'[75] But had it? The strategy set out in June 1969 assumed that the United States would have proposals for reforming the system after the suspension of convertibility, yet there was no clear position. There was a risk of patching up the Bretton Woods system and returning to the expedients that failed before 15 August 1971, rather than embarking on fundamental reform.

Paul Volcker (*left*), Under-Secretary of the Treasury for International Monetary Affairs; George Shultz (*centre*), Secretary of the Treasury; and Arthur Burns (*right*), chair of the Federal Reserve, at a meeting in Paris, 16 March 1973.

18

'Music without any Middle C'

The Floating World

'A resolution of the current period of uncertainty in international financial markets ... depends critically on strong leadership from the US Government. A prerequisite for strong leadership on our part is a clear conception of our own preferred outcome. How do we want the script to read for Act III? I believe it is a matter of great urgency for the Administration to develop a well-thought out answer to this question, and to do so quickly. As far as I can tell from my limited perspective, we have not yet done so.'

Ralph Bryant to Arthur Burns, 'Checklist of issues to be resolved in coming weeks', 17 August 1971[1]

'This new system must be characterized by shared leadership, shared responsibility and shared burdens, to which at least all the free world's strongest nations commit themselves. It will be a system which fully recognizes, and is solidly rooted in, the growing reality of a genuinely interdependent and increasingly competitive world economy whose goal is mutual, shared prosperity – not artificial, temporary advantage.

Such is the perspective which the President's actions of August 15 have opened for us and for the world.'

Peter Peterson, 'A foreign economic perspective', 27 December 1971[2]

'We have lost the one constant around which relative movement could be measured and hence a distrust in relative and indigenous money values ... It is like trying to write down music without any Middle C so that you cannot relate the staves or trying to navigate with the standard meridian of longitude moving about indeterminately.'

Lord Cromer to Edward Heath, 18 February 1973[3]

When the gold window was closed on 15 August 1971, the Nixon administration had yet to decide how to deal with the risks of 'spreading antagonism, protectionism, and retaliation'. One option was to 'sit on our hands and let other countries take the initiative' – but leaving other countries to adjust 'would unquestionably be viewed by the outside world as a turn toward economic nationalism and isolationism'. If the United States were to take the lead, should the preferred outcome be explained at the outset, or kept in reserve to strengthen its bargaining position? Should 'evolutionary continuity' be actively sought through multilateral reform of the existing system, or should a passive approach be adopted that might lead to floating rates and the demise of 'one world'? The preferred plan, so far as one existed, was evolutionary reform: other countries should realign their currencies, followed by greater flexibility of exchange rates and the use of Special Drawing Rights to increase liquidity. But rather than putting forward a clear set of proposals, the initial American stance was indeed to sit on their hands.[4]

The day after Nixon closed the gold window, Paul Volcker met representatives of Britain, Japan, Italy, Germany and France in London and assured them that the absence of a plan allowed open-minded consultation:

> the Administration had no specific programme or blue-print for reform in mind. Rather they had an objective which was that the United States must now be put back into a strong balance of payments position, enabling them to increase reserves and buy back dollars from the large holders. This must be done in a lasting way. The step of ending gold convertibility had been taken with reluctance but in some sense 'to free the world's hands' for new approaches.

He gave no indication of what the new approaches might be, beyond insisting that a change in the dollar price of gold was unacceptable to Congress. He handed over responsibility: 'it was basically now for the other main countries to consider what programme of measures, including parity changes, would bring about the necessary strengthening of the American payments position.'[5]

Volcker's announcement was greeted with understandable surprise that the United States was abdicating responsibility for its economic problems and reform of the international monetary system. Treasury Secretary Connally did nothing to address European and Japanese concerns. His bargaining strategy of intimidation and complaints about others' failure to revalue was encapsulated in his notorious remark to the G10 finance ministers that the 'dollar may be our currency but it's your problem'. Nixon went along with Connally's aggressive approach on the assumption that 'this country wants to kick foreigners in the ass.' He calculated that if 'we are going to be good neighbors, and we are going to grin and bear it, believe me the American people are going to say what the hell, we thought we had a president who was going to stand up for us.' The import surcharge was popular at home, and '[i]f the American people had their way, they'd build a wall around themselves today'. To avoid a lurch to protectionism, Nixon realized that he had to take a tough stance in the international monetary negotiations that might lead to confrontation with other countries. The dangers of Connally's negotiating style were apparent to some members of the Nixon administration who feared the demise of 'a stronger, orderly multilateral system'. As they realized, Europe 'is capable of "going it alone". Left to themselves, they are likely to do so in a divisive manner, arguing, rightly or wrongly, we cast the first stone.' Indeed, Mario Ferrari Aggradi, the Italian minister of finance, saw that 'the American move calls for a European initiative for an international monetary system based on conditions of equality . . . This is the moment for Europe to take an initiative: if Europe really exists, this is the time for it to present itself as a united community.' The worry in Washington was that the outcome would, at best, be 'benign regionalism' with open trade between blocs; at worst, the world economy could 'degenerate into uncooperative, protectionist blocs'.[6] In August 1971, the post-war multilateral system faced a crisis of legitimacy and a new system gradually emerged in the 1970s with a shift in the policies of national governments and international institutions.

FROM CLOSING THE GOLD WINDOW TO THE SMITHSONIAN AGREEMENT

A month after the gold window was closed, Peter Peterson pointed out that

> [s]o far, we have left it to others to adjust to the situation we have created. But soon we will have to clarify what we want multilaterally and what we want bilaterally from key countries. Most feel that having taken the essential but shock-producing moves of August 15, we should be prepared to propose some positive initiatives in the reasonably near future.

He pointed to a lack of clarity on how long the surcharge would continue; whether the dollar should be devalued against gold or realignment left to other countries; on what concessions would be needed on money, trade and defence; whether the monetary system would return to fixed rates or adopt floating; and what might be the foreign policy implications.[7]

Progress would not be easy. The EEC was divided on monetary policy, and there was a risk that Japan's reluctance to open its markets would prevent the removal of the surcharge and so lead to protectionism in the EEC. Robert Hormats of the National Security Council saw a need for clarity on what other countries were expected to do to allow monetary reform, removal of the American surcharge and prevention of retaliatory countermeasures. He worried that Nixon was not being presented with the full range of options and suggested that Kissinger inform the president that floating would be better than restoring a fixed rate with continued problems of divergence from market rates, overvaluation and instability. George Shultz also continued to press the case for floating, and Nixon informed Connally in October that 'knowing as little about it as I do, I lean to the proposition which is basically the Shultz, the Friedman and all that bunch ... which is to float ... I do not believe we should go back to a fixed parity system under any circumstances.' Since August, Nixon had come to see that devaluation was not a political liability. On the other hand, Burns at the Fed and Volcker at the Treasury preferred to renew Bretton Woods, multilateralism and free trade. Although Nixon's views were shifting, he did not provide a clear lead. He had other concerns at that time: Vietnam, rapprochement with China, winning the presidential election, and then dealing with the Watergate scandal that arose from attempts to cover up the White House's involvement in a break-in at the Democratic headquarters in June 1972 that eventually led to his resignation in August 1974.[8]

The American position remained uncertain, with divisions in the administration over floating or a return to fixed rates, a lack of clarity over what concessions were needed from other countries and growing concern that Connally was ignoring the geopolitical implications. In November, Kissinger warned Nixon that

> We're uniting all of these countries against us by not telling them what we want. My feeling is that we ought to say what we want ... [If] we screw everybody in this free world, and force them to surrender, we are going to give them an incentive to organize ... [W]e will then undermine the whole structure of free world cooperation ... The danger is that at the precise moment that a new generation is coming to power in Europe, we are putting it to them in such an abrupt way ... Texans hate foreigners ... and ... think that the way to make a deal is to get the other guy by the balls and squeeze them.

In his memoirs, Kissinger recalled that his 'major concern was to end the confrontation when it had served its purpose and to prevent economic issues from overwhelming all considerations of foreign policy'.[9]

Connally took the lead in negotiations. He calculated that America's bargaining position was strong, for it was less dependent on international trade than other countries and he could therefore use the import surcharge to force a realignment of rates. At a press conference on 16 August 1971, he reassured his domestic audience that closing the gold window would create more jobs, control inflation and increase productivity. He insisted that the gold value of the dollar would not change 'one iota' from $35 and that other countries should realign their currencies with the dollar to restore America's balance of payments surplus. Connally informed the G10 on 15 September that 'We have not come here with any precise plans or details worked out'; other countries should embark on 'considerable negotiations' between themselves.[10]

Volcker came to value Connally as a 'master tactician' whose 'tough talk produced results because he had the political clout to back it up'. Burns was sceptical, for while Connally was tough in expressing American views, failure to understand other countries' positions undermined negotiations. Volcker's emollient style was a complement, though Burns thought that he was indecisive. It was not a winning combination.[11] In November 1971, Peterson informed Nixon that Connally was creating European resentment by his 'saber rattling' and 'don't give a damn attitude'. Lyndon Johnson – for whom Connally had worked as campaign manager in Texas – reportedly remarked that he 'could leave more dead bodies in the field with less remorse than any politician I ever knew'.[12] British officials saw Connally as 'a tough Texan who thinks like a shrewd poker player and not a sophisticated exponent of diplomacy'.[13] The danger, as Ambassador Cromer reported to London, was that Connally's nationalistic approach

> put on foreigners the onus of helping the US solve its economic problems . . . Connally might find the domestic political impact of his present external stance so seductive that he might be reluctant to settle on terms which other G10 members and even others in the administration would regard as reasonable.

In Cromer's assessment, there was 'a general feeling of impotence and frustration' in Washington, for closing the gold window had not produced results and Connally's tactics blocked any new initiative. He worried that Connally might turn to a trade and currency war:

> The facade that Connally has adopted that the United States can sit back and wait for results could drop, and drop abruptly. In the present mood of feeling towards the foreigner in the United States at the present time, more

aggressive tactics would in terms of domestic American politics be highly popular.[14]

In November 1971, Burns at the Federal Reserve was similarly frustrated by the lack of coherence. In his jaundiced opinion, Shultz was a 'woefully ignorant ideologist' and 'confused amateur economist'; Kissinger was 'a brilliant political analyst, but admittedly ignorant of economics'; and Connally 'a thoroughly confused politician, suppressing his desire to punish foreigners in view of the President's moving away from narrow domestic political considerations'. Burns admitted his own lack of expertise on some international issues. 'What a way to reach decisions!'[15]

At the meeting in London on 16 August Volcker had ruled out a full meeting of the IMF. Like most European governments, the IMF's managing director Schweitzer thought that a new pattern of exchange rates meant devaluation of the dollar by raising the price of gold – a rejection of Connally's insistence that the dollar rate would not change. The IMF research department's 'multilateral exchange rate model' indicated that the gold value of the dollar should be $37.50. Jacques Polak, the Dutch economist who ran the research department, took the view that

> a satisfactory new pattern of exchange rates could not be found by letting all currencies float for a certain period. Quite apart from the profound uncertainty that such a situation would create, a regime of many floating currencies cannot even in theory be expected to lead to a viable system of rates.

Schweitzer agreed: rather than market forces, realignment of rates 'needs, with the guidance and participation of the Fund, an international negotiation'.[16]

Confidence in the IMF was low. Cromer was highly critical of the IMF's 'feeble leadership' and lack of 'collective creative ambition' which meant that it turned to 'esoterics' and failed to take a wider view of the international monetary system. The permanent staff were defensive and unimaginative, taking a legalistic view that aimed to preserve the status quo rather than considering major reform. Furthermore, the Board of Governors was too large, with one representative from each member, and the executive board of twenty directors with responsibility for day-to-day operations was appointed by member countries without direct engagement with national policymaking. Volcker saw that effective international institutions needed direct involvement with national decision makers, which was difficult given that some executive directors represented a group of countries with divergent views. The Americans held the bulk of the votes in the IMF, but the managing director was always a European with different assumptions. Connally was barely on speaking terms with Schweitzer. A British official noted the treasury secretary's 'passionate dislike of the Fund and all it stands for ... Not merely do the Fund decline to act as a US Agency but their chief official is a foreigner with notably un-Texan habits such as kissing ladies' hands.' Further, the Americans felt that the less developed countries were over-represented, with nine executive directors – and for their part, the less developed countries complained of American dominance. The question was whether an alternative forum could be found that was small enough to be manageable and large enough to be representative.[17]

The result was a 'furor over fora'. As an official pointed out to Volcker, 'G10 is a negotiating body; WP-3 is a discussion group; the IMF is a regulatory body designed to administer the Bretton Woods agreement', and none was fit for the task of reform. Washington preferred a ministerial meeting of the G10 to the IMF, but without enthusiasm, given that the EEC had six members. When Giscard d'Estaing and Volcker met on 16 August 1971, they admitted that the G10 would not be able to arrive at a common position. They were right: the G10 ministerial meeting in London on 15–16 September failed to reach an agreement when Connally refused to change the gold value of the dollar as part of a realignment of currencies, or to remove the surcharge, which was a bargaining weapon against other countries and a sop to domestic politics.[18]

Nixon's unilateral decision to close the gold window led to discussion of a joint European approach. Reaching an agreement would not be easy. Otmar Emminger's solution was to rehabilitate the dollar and so end volatile flows of capital and the transmission of inflation to Germany. Capital controls could be used to block inflows, but Emminger doubted their effectiveness and thought greater exchange rate flexibility would be needed. Schiller continued to support floating as a way of limiting inflationary pressure – though German industry and unions feared the impact on exports and employment as the Deutsche Mark appreciated. Pompidou and Giscard d'Estaing were more inclined to adopt capital and exchange controls and to end the 'exorbitant privilege' of the dollar. They also feared that the Deutsche Mark would dominate any European monetary system and lead to an appreciation of the franc that would threaten the competitiveness of French industry.[19]

Connally calculated that the Deutsche Mark and yen would appreciate, and that the surcharge and inconvertibility should be retained until the dollar depreciated by 15 per cent.[20] His strategy was criticized by Coombs, who believed that allowing the market to set appropriate exchange rates was 'an appalling miscalculation of the role and functioning of the foreign exchange markets, which are an indispensable guide but a very poor master of national policy. By its very nature, the foreign exchange market is a nervous, high risk, ultra-sensitive mechanism, primarily geared to short term developments.'[21] To Connally's critics in Washington, his combination of bullying and lack of clarity would lead to disaster.[22] Connally's hard-line tactic could only force other countries to realign their currencies; it would not produce agreement on reform. Nevertheless, there were signs that a more considered approach was emerging in Washington. After the collapse of the G10 talks, Nixon set up a group to co-ordinate a new foreign economic policy, chaired by Peterson and including Volcker as well as representatives from the CEA, State Department, Federal Reserve and National Security Council. Its remit was to define priorities and determine a negotiating strategy, and Volcker's group was – at last – instructed to start 'intense dialogue and work' on what kind of reformed monetary system should be adopted. Opinion in Washington coalesced on flexibility by prompt rate adjustments, the orderly creation of reserves to reduce dependence on gold and key currencies, followed by talks on long-term trade liberalization, a more equitable sharing of the burdens of defence, and the restoration of capital flows.[23]

The G10 ministerial meeting in Washington on 26 September again failed to reach agreement. The American strategy remained to allow the crisis to continue, with other countries making concessions on trade and permitting their currencies to find their market rate without changing the gold price of the dollar, at which point parities would be fixed and the surcharge removed. Cromer observed that 'each inconclusive G10 meeting . . . is bound to diminish progressively confidence in financial markets', with a failure to bridge the gulf between Europe and America. 'Without being alarmist I do feel that the all too obvious vacuum that exists is potentially dangerous . . . There are disturbing likenesses in monetary and trade fields to the early 1930s.'[24] The BIS thought the Americans were irresponsible, for 'the US, which had declared its currency to be in fundamental disequilibrium, was evading its responsibility under the IMF rules by being unwilling to devalue . . . It was unlikely that adequate exchange rate adjustments could be brought about if countries in fundamental disequilibrium refused to adjust.'[25] Such complaints led Peterson to warn Nixon that

> you will soon have to decide whether you want the US to adopt a more positive stance on the international economic negotiations . . . [B]eginning a serious negotiating process does not mean . . . 'caving in' and certainly does not mean accepting a 'bad deal'. It does mean, however, conveying to the US

public and foreign countries that it is in our mutual interest to take positive steps to <u>try</u> to resolve the situation constructively.[26]

There were signs that a compromise was emerging.

Appreciation of the Deutsche Mark hit German exports, and the German government wished both to end the American import surcharge and to avoid retaliation by the EEC. The German government therefore supported French demands that the dollar be devalued against gold, on condition that the French agreed to wider margins, more frequent changes of rate, and the use of SDRs.[27] The finance ministers of the European Community met on 4 November and agreed to realign parities, including devaluation of the dollar, with wider margins and a narrower band within the Community. Connally started to modify his position. Above all, Nixon did not want conflict over monetary issues to frustrate progress in talks with heads of states concerning his negotiations with Moscow and Beijing. Connally pointed out that a deal at the G10 meeting in Rome on 29 November would require devaluation of the dollar against gold, and handling trade and defence costs at a later date. Nixon agreed: 'Make a deal on monetary things. Say the trade deal will come later.'[28]

Volcker presented a package to the G10 deputies to remove the import surcharge in return for concessions on agriculture, and an agreement to negotiate on trade and defence costs, with an appreciation of other OECD currencies against the dollar of at least 11 per cent, and a margin of +/-3 per cent, without a change in the dollar price of gold. On 1 December, Connally was in the chair and invited Volcker to make an offer on the price of gold: he suggested an increase in the price by 10 to 15 per cent. This sudden change caused surprise, not least given that the Europeans were only looking for an increase of 5 per cent. Schiller was willing to accept up to 12 per cent but the French did not have authority to negotiate. There was also the issue of whether removing the import surcharge would require trade concessions and a sharing of defence burdens. The Americans wanted the EEC to agree to take part in trade talks to secure congressional approval for changing the price of gold, but French opposition meant the Commission could not make a commitment. Despite progress, the agreement collapsed. The G10 ministerial meeting was scheduled to resume in Washington on 17–18 December.[29]

When Pompidou and Brandt met on 3–4 December, differences still remained. The French gave priority to European monetary integration with a more *dirigiste* approach to the economy and less concern for inflation. The Germans stressed economic integration, free markets and stability.[30] Nevertheless, there was sufficient common ground for a deal

with the United States. Nixon realized that he would need to make a concession to France by changing the gold price of the dollar as part of a
general realignment of rates. As Kissinger remarked, '[t]he political dimen-
sion has been put in. Everyone understands basics now.'[31] The crucial
breakthrough came at a meeting between Nixon and Pompidou (in effect
representing the EEC) on the Azores on 13–14 December 1971. Kissinger
later commented that 'the extraordinary aspect of the encounter was that
France and the United States should have taken it upon themselves to work
out the exchange rate for every one of the world's important currencies' –
not least because '[i]f given a truth serum, [Nixon] would no doubt have
revealed that he could not care less where in the new scale the various
currencies were to be pegged'. By contrast, the French president 'fancies
himself as something of a monetary expert'. Connally did not want to
change the gold price without concessions on trade and would have
been happy for the talks to fail. Between Nixon's lack of interest and
Connally's intransigence, Kissinger played a major role. The agreement
was designed to settle 'immediate problems of the international monetary
system' by a 'prompt realignment of exchange rates', including devaluation of the dollar by raising the price of gold from $35 to $38. This
realignment would be accompanied by wider margins. Pompidou secured
a reduction of the band from +/–3 per cent to +/–2.25 per cent, inserted
gold convertibility as a future topic of discussion, and secured a commitment to fixed rates rather than the weaker American proposal of
'established' rates. To Volcker, closing the gold window was a temporary
measure to force a realignment; to Nixon 'the convertibility thing is dead',
and he vowed after the Azores summit never to discuss the issue of restoring the right to convert dollars into gold. The one-way convertibility
between dollars and gold that had been agreed at Bretton Woods was
effectively over. The Americans agreed to 'assist in the stability of the system and the defense of the newly fixed structure of exchange rates in
particular by vigorous implementation of its efforts to restore price stability and productivity'. The French obtained – so they thought – discipline
over the Americans in return for agreeing to trade negotiations which
would help Nixon convince Congress to accept devaluation. Meanwhile,
discussion over burden-sharing was handed to NATO and dropped as a
bargaining weapon for currency realignment.[32]

    The Azores deal formed the basis of discussions at the G10 meeting at
the Smithsonian Institute in Washington on 17 December 1971. Germany
agreed to revalue the Deutsche Mark by 13.57 per cent. Japan was more
reluctant, and the Americans realized that 'revaluation is undoubtedly
seen as a <u>traumatic</u> possibility with effects on Japanese exports and trade

balances that are likely to be both <u>large</u> and <u>uncertain</u>'. Yusuke Kashiwagi had kept markets open until 27 August at the existing exchange rate of 360 yen to the dollar, and during this interlude the Ministry of Finance and Bank of Japan bought dollar credits from businesses. This tactic reduced the potential damage to Japanese industry from revaluation so that Finance Minister Mizuta and Governor Sasaki could allow a gradual appreciation of the yen by 9 per cent. At the Smithsonian, the Japanese agreed to revalue by 16.9 per cent.[33] Overall, the dollar was devalued against other G10 currencies by 10 per cent, with a widening of the band to create more flexibility. At the same time, the import surcharge was removed. Connally's tough tactics seemed to have worked, and the *New York Times* reflected that 'his threats and pressures did produce a realignment of exchange rates more advantageous . . . than had been anticipated'. Nixon welcomed the Smithsonian agreement as 'the most significant monetary agreement in the history of the world. I know that may seem to be an over-statement, but when we compare this agreement with Bretton Woods, which . . . was the last very significant agreement of this kind, we can see how important this achievement has been.' Volcker was more realistic when he remarked that 'I hope it lasts three months.'[34]

Volcker was right: the Smithsonian agreement did not last. It had been agreed by bullying tactics and was an uneasy compromise between two principles for setting exchange rates. In theory, rates were fixed by agreements between governments; in practice, market pressures drove the realignment. As Shultz recognized, 'US officials had formed an alliance with the market itself to force a change in the behavior of foreign officials' – a Faustian pact, for the market could not always be relied on to support official action.[35] Coombs was scathing. Instead of regular meetings at the BIS of experienced central bankers (like himself), the task was left to inexperienced finance ministers in a 'dialogue of the deaf'. He realized that the United States was not committed to defending the new parities and 'one-sided agreements reached under duress generally turn out to be bad bargains for all concerned'.[36] A British official rightly saw that the agreement merely bought time:

> The importance of the Washington settlement lies not in what it did but in what it may make possible for the future. The patient has suffered a severe fever. The doctors have found a way to bring his temperature back to 'normal'. They have not found a cure for the complaint which caused the fever. But they now have time to do so while the patient is off the danger list. They can operate if they can agree what needs to be done. But unless they do operate, the next attack of fever will probably prove fatal. From the

international standpoint it will only be possible to pass judgement upon the Washington settlement when it can be seen whether it paved the way for the reform of the international monetary system or whether it merely served to delay it still further.[37]

The patient was not cured and suffered from a long, lingering illness before the death of the Bretton Woods system.

THE ROAD TO FLOATING

Debates continued after the Smithsonian agreement. In February 1972, Volcker thought '[t]he time has probably come when we should undertake more determined efforts to reach agreement on proposals for US positions in future discussions of international monetary reform'. A member of the Volcker group saw that the Smithsonian agreement could not survive without 'more fundamental international monetary reform'. At Bretton Woods, the main concern had been to prevent competitive devaluation. Now, the issues were inflation, liquidity, adjustment to the balance of payments, and avoidance of disruption caused by capital flows. The Smithsonian agreement patched up a system designed for different purposes. Removing the shortcomings of the existing system was not enough: it was necessary to respond to changes caused by a decline in the relative power of the United States, by the weakness of the IMF in finding a solution, and by larger capital movements.[38] Volcker later reflected that

> the most important lesson of the Smithsonian agreement, and of the traumatic events leading up to it, was an almost subconscious one: The world didn't come apart ... While there were inevitable distortions and uncertainties, neither the world economy nor its trading system seemed so sensitive to monetary disturbances as had been feared by those of us raised in the Bretton Woods system and dedicated to protect it.[39]

Nixon did not deflate the American economy to defend the new rates, and in February 1972 Pompidou complained to him of 'uneasiness with regard to the evolution of the international monetary situation'. He pointed to 'shortcomings which risk weakening the correct implementation of our agreements as well as to my preoccupation over steps taken or of positions envisaged by your administration and which, at first glance, do not seem to me to be consistent with what we agreed.' Specifically, 'the combination of a large budgetary deficit and of a policy of systematically low interest rates' was weakening confidence in the dollar. Pompidou was surprised that Nixon was turning to greater flexibility in exchange rates.[40] Nixon was unrepentant and claimed that he would defend the new rate by 'vigorous efforts to restore price stability and productivity to the United States economy . . . I assure you that these fundamental objectives remain the basis of our domestic policies. We shall break the back of inflation in the United States. We shall seek new breakthroughs in productivity growth.'[41] The reassurances were empty, for Nixon's priority was re-election. The European response was to create a zone of currency stability. The wider bands of the Smithsonian agreement were a threat to the integration of European markets, and in April 1972, the governors of the European central banks met in Basel and agreed to narrower fluctuations of +/−1.125 per cent (the 'snake') that wriggled within the wider Smithsonian 'tunnel' of +/−2.25 per cent.[42]

In May 1972, Connally resigned and was replaced by George Shultz as Treasury Secretary. The new secretary's experience as a conciliator in labour negotiations meant that he did not need Volcker as an emollient counterpart. He did need Volcker's expertise, however, whom he asked to devise a plan that would attract support at the next meeting of the IMF – a marked change from Connally's belief that a precise scheme was premature and impracticable.[43] Events soon intruded. On 22 June 1972, Volcker explained to the House Banking and Currency Committee that reform would take two years and that Britain would not devalue – only for the pound to float the next day. Volcker later remarked that the British decision to float was 'the first formal break in the Smithsonian central rates'. When Nixon was informed, he merely commented 'I don't care. Nothing we can do about it', and when he was told that the lira would be next in line, his response was blunt: 'I don't give a shit about the lira.'[44]

The British decision to float entailed an assessment of national interest prior to becoming a member of the European Community on 1 January 1973. Even before the closing of the gold window, the Treasury accepted that as a member of the EEC it should co-operate with other members, and that '[i]f it is felt . . . that the reserve role of sterling is not compatible with the economic and monetary development of the Community, we have no objection in principle to an orderly rundown.'[45] When Pompidou visited London in February and March 1972, the Treasury looked to 'a more nearly symmetrical system in which the US dollar is just one more currency, and indeed the world will have proper control of the supply of international liquidity instead of being at the mercy of US policies'.

[The] eventual objective for Europe is to gain a proper measure of control of monetary affairs and get away from the dollar standard . . . [A] radical reform of the world monetary system and a progressive movement towards European economic and monetary integration should be pursued urgently as complementary, not conflicting, means to this end.

The aim should be to secure French support for world and European monetary reform that would displace the dollar.[46] Accordingly, on 1 May 1972 sterling joined the 'snake' as a sign of commitment to the EEC.

Tension soon arose between domestic and European policies, for the obligation to keep exchange rates within narrow bands constrained policies to reduce unemployment and encourage growth. Chancellor of the Exchequer Anthony Barber made his priorities clear in March 1972 when he proposed a 'dash for growth' to reduce unemployment and increase investment, with higher public spending and cuts in personal taxes. To Barber,

> it is neither necessary nor desirable to distort domestic economies to an unacceptable extent in order to retain unrealistic exchange rates . . . I do not believe that there is any need for this country, or any other, to be frustrated on this score in its determination to sustain economic growth and to reduce unemployment.[47]

Peter Jay, the economics editor of *The Times*, claimed that these were 'the most important words to be spoken by any Chancellor for a decade'. He supported floating and realized that Barber's announcement meant that when sterling came under pressure – as it surely would – the exchange rate would not be held within the narrow bands of the European currency agreement.[48]

Britain's balance of payments deficit, high level of price and wage inflation, and prospect of serious labour disputes soon led to speculation against the pound. Barber's attempt to protect the rate failed and the pound fell to the lower limit of the 'snake'. Holding a new fixed rate would be difficult. Devaluation was therefore rejected and on 23 June 1972, sterling floated – a decision welcomed by Friedman as a blow to the Smithsonian agreement. By contrast, Pompidou expressed his disquiet to Prime Minister Heath:

> I am convinced that a regime of fixed rates of exchange, in addition to the fact that it will favour the development of trade and investment, also constitutes one of the indispensable conditions for the proper functioning of the Common Market, which [Great Britain] is to join on 1 January 1973. Such a regime also seems to me to constitute the foundation of all progress in European monetary cooperation and all developments in the reform of the international monetary system whose necessity, as you yourself have observed, has been demonstrated by recent events.[49]

Funds shifted from London to Europe – especially Germany – which led to the closure of European currency markets on 26 June. Schiller favoured floating and opposed capital controls, but further appreciation of the Deutsche Mark would hit exports and jobs. He resigned, and the new finance minister – Helmut Schmidt – was willing to use controls to stem the inflow of funds.[50] Speculation then moved against the dollar. Although Shultz's preference was to float, he realized that taking an 'entirely passive role' might lead to a 'defensive wall of controls' in Europe and 'a poor launching pad for a constructive trans-Atlantic dialogue on long-term reform'. He therefore suggested limited intervention in exchange markets to support the dollar so that there would be 'a more favorable atmosphere for the longer-term negotiations'. The attempt was soon abandoned, for confidence in the Smithsonian rates was not easily achieved.[51]

Rather than creating a stable, free-market, flexible economy, as promised by Friedman, floating the pound removed monetary discipline. The balance of payments deficit could now be rectified by a lower exchange rate with less need to maintain competitiveness by limiting wage demands. Floating led to instability and inflation, with a recourse to price and wage controls. Although the pound's float was intended to be temporary, the Treasury saw that high inflation and a large balance of payments deficit meant sterling would again drop to the bottom of the snake, with suspicion that the pound would float. The reason to re-join was political: to impose external discipline on wage demands and to show a commitment to the EEC. The problem was that re-joining the snake would threaten deflation and higher interest rates that would undermine the government's policies for growth and employment. Membership of the snake would only be practical if trade unions moderated their wage demands – not a likely outcome as labour relations worsened during Heath's premiership.[52]

The 'furor over fora' resumed. The realignment of rates in December 1971 had been implemented by the G10, which over-represented the EEC. The IMF represented more countries but was not an ideal forum, for it was too cumbersome, limited itself to monetary issues – and Schweitzer openly opposed the war in Vietnam. Connally had complained that international organizations 'are not always coordinated and tend to impede the solution of problems. In a fast-moving age, when problems arise we cannot afford to be bogged down by hide-bound institutional arrangements.' His preferred forum was the OECD – a different model of global government by the advanced economies. It had been instrumental in the emergence of economic growth as the central aim of industrialized countries, captured by a standardized measure of GDP. Unlike the IMF or GATT, its contribution to global economic government was not based on rules or the provision of finance, but on the supposedly objective data that embodied a common value system articulated by officials in member countries. The problem was that the OECD was also dominated by Europe, and monetary reform was not a core element of its mandate. The less developed countries were excluded and had a different paradigm of development rather than economic growth. The IMF proposed a way forward: a new advisory committee drawn from the twenty countries or groups of countries that elected an executive director to the Fund. It would comprise finance ministers and their deputies with direct links to national governments that would allow a more strategic approach to reform. Although the committee was wider than the G10, it still marginalized less developed countries, and it would remain an advisory body with decisions made by the Board of Governors of the IMF. In July 1972, the outcome was the Committee of Twenty – the C20 – answerable to the Board of Governors. It could consult the OECD, which would consider other areas of international economic relations. The Americans feared that the C20 would be dominated by the IMF's legalistic approach – and it was not a success.[53]

Each member of the C20 was entitled to send nine representatives to meetings of ministers and deputies. Alexandre Kafka, the Brazilian executive director for a group of Latin American countries and vice-chair of the C20 deputies, complained that the result was 'a large itinerant international monetary conference having about two hundred participants at each level, with sixty entitled to speak at each level'.[54] At Bretton Woods, agreement was reached on the basis of drafts that were 'elaborated in considerable detail in self-consistent form by the experts of a major country'. By contrast, few countries in the C20 had a coherent position, and reform was considered without a dominant voice or consensus. Marcus Fleming, deputy director of the IMF's research department, remarked that the C20 adopted a 'Socratic procedure'. After general discussion, the bureau of C20 tried 'to elicit points of agreement and clarify points of difference on all the manifold and interrelated issues, and to resubmit the results for further general discussion'. The process was 'extremely demanding on the time and energies of all concerned' and it made little or no progress.[55] In retrospect, Jeremy Morse – a London banker and director of the Bank of England who was the first chair of C20 – saw that '[i]t was the end of the post-war idea that everything could and should be managed', and that the alternative to reform would be to hand control to markets.[56]

Meanwhile, Volcker responded to Shultz's request for a scheme for reform with Plan X, a compromise between floating and fixed rates. Countries should declare a 'central value' for their currency, defined in SDRs, with a margin of +/-3 or 4 per cent; they were expected to intervene to maintain the central rate and to alter it should reserves rise or fall above various thresholds. Rather than a free float, the central rate would be adjusted automatically by an objective indicator. A country should have the option of floating, either as a transitional step to a new central value or indefinitely on condition that it abandoned the use of controls on capital and trade to correct the balance of payments, adopted stricter reserve criteria and was placed under surveillance. Further, reform of the monetary system should be linked with reform of multilateral institutions. GATT should work with the IMF, which should appoint ministers as executive directors to make stronger links with domestic politics.[57] At Bretton Woods, the Americans had opposed Keynes's plea for creditors to take some responsibility for adjustments; now they proposed 'to make the monetary system more symmetrical by placing almost automatic adjustment obligations on surplus countries'.[58] Burns welcomed a symmetrical, rules-based system:

> Right now, when a country has a deficit, it is an international sin. With a surplus, it is practising an international virtue. We should do away with morality in our thinking. Apply rules that surplus countries have the obligation to reduce and eliminate surpluses and deficit countries have a similar obligation to reduce their deficits. We should establish rules to achieve this.[59]

When Shultz presented Plan X to the IMF meeting in September 1972, his willingness to compromise came as a relief after Connolly's bullying tactics. 'The world,' he pointed out, 'needs a new balance between flexibility and stability in its basic approach to doing business. The world needs a new balance between a unity of purpose and a diversity of execution that will permit nations to cooperate closely without losing their individuality or sovereignty.' His starting point was freer trade in goods and services, with a 'flow of capital to the places where it can contribute most to economic growth' – a reversal of the Bretton Woods acceptance of capital controls to protect fixed exchange rates. Open trade required a shift from 'an ancient and recurring fallacy' that surpluses were 'a symbol of success and of good management'. Instead, he called for 'a common code of conduct to protect and strengthen the fabric of a free and open international economic order' through 'clear disciplines and standards of behavior to guide the international adjustment process' by obliging surplus as well as deficit countries to adjust. Adjustment could not be left to the discretion of national authorities; neither would they accept firm rules or orders from an international institution. The answer was 'a kind of compromise which involved a presumptive indicator which was intended to put the burden of proof on the national authority to show why it should not take some adjustment action.' The level of reserves would indicate to deficit and surplus countries that adjustment was needed, and in the absence of action would allow the imposition of international sanctions or discriminatory surcharges on goods from countries that failed to adjust. The historian Daniel Sargent remarks that Shultz was offering 'an evolutionary roadmap to a radical destination'. Countries that wished to retain a fixed rate could do so, provided they revalued when building up surpluses, or they could float and let the market decide.[60] The proposals marked a shift from the Smithsonian agreement without abandoning a fixed gold price for the dollar – though Shultz's end destination was clear.

Coombs was not convinced and preferred to maintain rates by central bank co-operation. Even Volcker was sceptical about Shultz's ultimate destination of floating. Neither was the plan for indicators popular with other countries. The Japanese realized that the use of indicators was directed against them and preferred the Bretton Woods system, which allowed them to build up large surpluses and dollar reserves. Claude Pierre-Brossolette of the French Treasury thought that the American proposal merely reflected 'the continuing bias of the United States that surplus countries should be the ones to make the adjustment when international payments get out of balance'. Giscard d'Estaing favoured 'few rather than frequent parity changes ... the main technique of adjustment should be internal policies rather than exchange rates.' The proposal also created a political problem of defining the balance between national discretion and international surveillance, between 'the apparent "freedom" of the looser exchange rate regime, while keeping the advantages of a strong international consensus as to certain basic rules of good behavior.'[61]

Good behaviour was not a defining feature of Nixon's approach and he pressed Burns to loosen monetary policy to deliver a boom that would help secure re-election. In January 1972, Nixon pointed out that

> Bankers, as a group, thrive on high interest rates and they really don't give a damn what happens to the economy provided they make profits ... We cannot accept this kind of obstructionist attitude ... You have given me an absolute assurance that the money supply will move adequately to fuel an expanding economy in 1972 ... We come down to the fundamental point that if the Fed is not able to move the money supply up vigorously and aggressively in the first quarter of this year, the Fed in general and you as its leader will inevitably get a major share of the blame.[62]

Burns did not reply to this 'outrageous' threat but did ease monetary policy as a result of error rather than political calculation. Nixon's economic team assumed that boosting demand would use idle capacity without creating inflation. In reality, there was no idle capacity and Herbert Stein, the chairman of the CEA, later commented that 'We misinterpreted.' Nixon was unwilling to take action to support the balance of payments and exchange rate, for deflation would affect his chances of re-election.[63] He then started his second term by removing controls on prices and wages which led to inflationary pressure that was not contained by tighter domestic monetary policy.[64]

Helmut Schmidt complained of American 'passivity' and doubted the United States' commitment to the Smithsonian agreement. In February 1973, Chancellor Brandt urged Nixon to defend the dollar's exchange rate with the Deutsche Mark. Continued monetary instability was, he insisted, an existential threat to the West. Volcker responded by suggesting another realignment by devaluing the dollar against gold by 10 per cent and revaluing the yen by 10 per cent, with other countries standing still. Nixon agreed and Volcker departed on a 'secret' world tour. He first met the Japanese minister of finance, Kiichi Aichi, who was shocked by the proposal to revalue the yen by 20 per cent against the dollar. He agreed to a temporary float to allow the yen to find its own level, but was not willing to commit to a revaluation until he knew what Germany would do. The yen appreciated by 17 per cent – a move that was less contentious than the revaluation in 1971, for Japanese business was now confident that it could compete. Volcker then flew to Germany, where he met Schmidt and suggested a common float of European currencies against the dollar. He continued to London, Paris and Rome, and the day after he returned to Washington, Shultz devalued the dollar against gold by 10 per cent.[65]

The Smithsonian realignment was re-negotiated after only fourteen months. It was no more likely to last. Volcker's frantic activity merely demonstrated that periodic readjustments by economic diplomacy and arm-twisting were not a solution. Indeed, he undermined the realignment with a public comment that the American balance of payments deficit would worsen before devaluation had any impact. His accurate, though ill-judged, remark triggered speculation against the dollar. The new rates did not last, and the continued inflow of dollars into Europe – above all Germany – and Japan threatened inflation. Early in March 1973, the Bundesbank and other central banks started to close foreign exchange markets. What was at stake was less a question of floating versus fixed rates than a clash between European and international solutions. Brandt informed President Pompidou that the choice was 'further integration, or the danger of a collapse of the community into a mere customs union'.

The implication was that, in the absence of a collective European float, Germany would float unilaterally. Giscard d'Estaing invited Shultz, Burns and Volcker to an emergency meeting in Paris on 9 March with representatives from the EEC. Schmidt had tried to use capital controls earlier in the year with little success; now, he proposed a joint float of European currencies against the dollar, which was agreed on 12 March 1973, except by Britain and Italy, which had left the 'snake' in 1972 and 1973 respectively. The German government welcomed the outcome. France had agreed to joint action; there was no need to support weak currencies that remained outside the collective float; and the Deutsche Mark was insulated from speculative inflows, which helped the Bundesbank control inflation.[66]

Milton Friedman welcomed the renewed problems in the international monetary system as 'another nail in the coffin of the obsolete system of fixed exchange rates that has produced such crises repeatedly in the past few years'.[67] The American administration had to formulate its position before the next meeting of the G10 in Paris on 13–16 March. Shultz recognized that pressure would build up against currencies with pegged rates, and he needed to decide whether to intervene to support the dollar or to accept that another crisis would ensue. Nixon complained that 'the goddamn crises come one year, two years, so forth', but he had doubts about floating and wondered whether intervention would provide an opportunity to create a more stable system. Nixon did not want 'the American domestic economy constantly hostage to the manipulations of international monetary situation', yet he also wanted to show international leadership and create a more stable system. 'In other words,' he reflected, 'might there be a need for a new – what do you call it? Bretton Woods?'[68]

Opinions in Washington were divided. Burns preferred to intervene and deal with speculators before approaching other heads of states to create a new system – a strategy Nixon characterized as 'to give them a shock. And that'll get 'em off their butts so that they work with us.' The question was whether the shock was best delivered by floating or intervention, and whether America could show leadership. Stein thought that floating would allow the transition to a more stable system, and Shultz agreed that fixed rates were only possible when the United States had been the dominant economic power. 'I don't see how we have the muscle to so dominate the situation to make a real fixed rate system of the kind we had in the post-war period.' He therefore recommended a gradual move to a flexible system with some commitment to par values rather than an immediate free float.[69]

Nixon, as always more interested in geopolitics than economics, assured Shultz that

> you can't think of this, basically, as an economist. The whole European rela-
> tionship is in a state of ... very profound change at this point. And to the
> extent we can, we should use our economic and monetary stroke to try to
> affect that change in a way that will ... serve our interests. I don't know.
> Maybe, it may.

He worried that Europe might react by turning inwards, with a threat of internal socialism and Soviet domination. Although Nixon accepted Shultz's advice on economics, he turned to Kissinger – Secretary of State since February 1973 – to make the decision in terms of international politics and, above all, 'as a means to keep the Europeans closer to us, rather than having them push away'. Kissinger's line was that the Europeans must be part of an Atlantic partnership and not adopt a common position without consulting Washington – and the United States should not accept 'soppy palaver' about European integration. He urged Nixon to 'show the Japanese and the Europeans that we're not in a passive position. I mean, just to sit there while the Europeans devalue us again and put in a few hookers and get pap like this, that isn't very strong.' Nixon hesitated. Would a 'positive leadership role through possible intervention' serve American 'interests in keeping the Europeans apart; keeping them from developing a united policy against us', or might they just go their own way?[70]

Nixon's views soon crystallized: Connally had been right. 'The way the Europeans are talking today, European unity will not be in our interest ... [W]e have to recognize the stark fact that a united Europe will be led primarily by Left-leaning or Socialist heads of government' who were more likely to confront the United States than combine against the Soviets. The solution was to build a bloc of the United States, Japan and under-developed countries. '[P]olitical considerations must completely override economic considerations in monetary and trade talks. This is going to be a bitter pill for Shultz to swallow but he must swallow it.' Although Kissinger accepted that 'we couldn't bust the Common float without getting into a hell of a political fight', it was possible to create conditions in which it would not work. In Kissinger's view, it was not a technical economic issue: 'from now on we have to throw our weight around to help ourselves. And then they'll start paying attention to us again.'[71]

The meeting of the G10 deputies in Paris in March 1973 marked the effective end of the Smithsonian agreement and the Bretton Woods system of pegged exchange rates. Kissinger's logic meant that the Americans refused to intervene to support the exchange rate, and Shultz's preference for monetary flexibility meant he did little to defend Volcker's new parities. The G10 could only agree that intervention 'may be useful at appropriate times, to facilitate the maintenance of orderly conditions'. The decision was left to individual countries 'when necessary and desirable, acting in a flexible manner in the light of market conditions and in close consultation with the authorities of the nation whose currency may be bought or sold'. Kissinger would have preferred individual national floats against the dollar rather than a collective float that consolidated the EEC, but he hoped it would collapse as a result of Shultz's refusal to intervene. Shultz was delighted by the emergence of a 'market-based system' that was 'a great improvement over the inflexible gold-based system that preceded Camp David.' Volcker was less sure and continued to prefer fixed rates that were more suited to international consultation and rule-making.[72]

At the end of the G10 meeting, Shultz, Volcker and Burns faced the press. When Shultz was asked to explain the implications of the collective float for domestic monetary policy, he deferred to the autonomy of the Federal Reserve. He turned to Burns, who responded that 'American monetary policy is not made in Paris; it is made in Washington.' His answer had serious implications. At a time when America was experiencing inflation and the international monetary system was under threat, domestic needs were given priority. By defending the autonomy of the Federal Reserve, Burns gave the impression that he did not support the international role of the dollar – a fatal mistake. Volcker later remarked that '[w]e were ignoring our responsibility as custodian of the international medium of exchange, a responsibility that coincided with our obligation domestically to control money and credit.' He saw that

> [w]e were at one of those points in economic history when Burns's sensitivity (and many others') about the legitimacy of international considerations in conducting what is thought of as merely domestic monetary policy was misplaced. In the particular circumstances early in 1973, price increases were already beginning to accelerate in the United States. Within only a few weeks, monetary policy *was* tightened and the discount rate *was* raised. But it was all too late; too late to save the dollar exchange rate, and far too late to head off an incipient inflation.

Although Volcker sympathized with Burns' scepticism that the market offered an 'infallible indication' of the correct rate, he also realized that defending fixed rates required a tighter domestic money supply than Burns was willing or able to pursue. Burns' comment paved the way for floating the dollar.[73]

Nixon had relaxed capital controls in April 1969 and now that the Fed did not need to defend the dollar, Shultz proceeded to their abolition in January 1974. Attitudes to financial liberalization were shifting from an acceptance that capital controls might be necessary to defend exchange rates. In January 1973, the annual report of the Council of Economic Advisers had pointed out that

> restrictions have a distorting influence whether they are focused on trade in commodities, in services, or in assets (the capital account), and ... this parallelism should be recognized in the rules governing the reformed international monetary system. In contrast, the provisions of the earlier system made a sharp distinction between controls on trade and other current transactions and controls on capital transactions.[74]

This shift in attitude was supported by multinational corporations that wanted greater freedom and by Wall Street bankers who looked overseas to escape from regulated domestic markets. In April 1974, Nixon welcomed 'maximum reliance on market forces to direct world trade and investment' and a new trade-off in the trilemma was established. The expansion of international finance had put pressure on the Bretton Woods regime of pegged rates. When that regime was abandoned, capital controls were no longer needed to maintain the exchange rate and larger flows were possible. Financial markets were too large and powerful for central bankers and governments to continue to manage exchange rates as Coombs had hoped. As we will see in Chapter 21, commercial banks had a major role in recycling petrodollars after the oil shock of 1973. The change in policy was not the result of explicit campaigning by bankers – rather, they learned to benefit from changes that were occurring as a result of political responses to the pressure of events and of structural change in the world economy.[75]

Britain had fallen out of the 'snake' in 1972, and in 1973 faced the decision of whether it should re-join the collective float of European currencies. The Treasury's working party had doubts. Floating independently 'implied a higher priority for employment and growth than for our commitments to fixed parity and European monetary arrangements; conversely a decision to refix implies a reversal of these priorities.' The Treasury feared that the collective float would require a reduction in demand, and warned that

> If the unions felt that we were deflating solely in order to be able to join the collective float (ie that we were sacrificing growth in order to conform to Community ideas about the merits of a fixed parity) their reaction might be very damaging to the prospects for the counter-inflation policy.

The collective float could only work if inflation were under control so that the pound remained within the narrow band. The Treasury saw that 'there is no way in which the time of our joining the Community float can be advanced by deliberately making the pay side of the counter-inflation policy more severe, and little prospect of finding ways of further moderating impending price increases' which 'could be the last straw as far as the unions were concerned'. The economic case against joining the collective float therefore rested on the weakness of the government's counter-inflationary policies, the threat of labour unrest which would make defending the exchange rate difficult, and a desire to retain control over monetary policy.[76] The difficulties were brutally exposed in late 1973 when coal miners demanded a large wage increase and embarked on industrial action that led to the imposition of a three-day working week from 1 January to 7 March 1974.

This looming economic crisis made a mockery of Heath's wish to join the collective float. He argued that

> we did not join the Community in order to behave like little Englanders. Monetary cooperation is an area in which the Community sees an opportunity of making progress. So long as we are detached from that progress, our ability to influence Community policies and the willingness of other members to accommodate Community policies to our needs will be diminished.

The government realized that the collective float 'would need to be vigorously presented to domestic political and public opinion, in order to counter charges of a surrender of sovereignty' – a choice that Heath was willing to make to replace formal, largely theoretical, sovereignty by practical sovereignty that was pooled within the Community as a whole.[77]

Heath's assessment reflected a realization that the reserve status of sterling and the sterling area were harmful rather than a source of independence and status. The Basel agreement (Chapter 16) was due to expire in September 1973, and holders of sterling balances faced losses as the pound depreciated. Former colonies were aggrieved, with Malaysia accusing the British government of 'deliberate duplicity'. To steady markets, the British government announced a short-term extension of the sterling agreement at a rate of $2.42, and the BIS negotiated a final Arrangement in 1976–77 on condition that the British government accepted the terms of an IMF loan. The shift was striking. In December 1968, sterling had made up over 50 per cent of the reserves of twenty-three countries; by September 1976, no country had over 50 per cent of their reserves in sterling, and half the countries held 10 per cent or less.[78] The sterling area finally expired.

Britain did not join the collective float, which had its own problems. The 'tunnel' of the Smithsonian regime collapsed so that currencies of the European 'snake' floated together in a 'lake' of currencies that were not pegged to each other. The 'snake in the lake' faced problems thanks to divergent responses to the 1973 oil shock. Germany maintained a tight monetary policy and refused to accommodate the rise in oil prices; it had low inflation and a large balance of payments surplus. By contrast, France – like Britain – expanded its economy to prevent higher unemployment, which resulted in inflation and balance of payments deficits. This divergence made stable exchange rates impossible. Britain had left the snake in 1972, Italy in 1973, and France departed in 1974. Although France re-joined in 1975, it left again in March 1976. Giscard d'Estaing later commented that '[t]he experiment had shown conclusively that we could never make a European monetary system work as long as the weakest currencies had to bear the full brunt of responsibility for maintaining the fixed differential while the strong currencies continued to forge ahead.' In effect, the 'snake' became a Deutsche Mark zone that covered Germany, Belgium, Luxembourg, the Netherlands and Denmark. Rather than converging, the economies of the EEC were diverging, and the Werner plan was on hold.[79]

In retrospect, it was astonishing that so much effort had been devoted to preserving the regime of fixed though variable rates. The outcome was not a 'clean' float in which markets set the rate but a hybrid system with wider fluctuations in rates than under the Bretton Woods regime (see Figure 7). The IMF registered 129 currency areas, of which 97 pegged their currencies. Out of fourteen industrial countries, thirteen floated – though some maintained a par value system between themselves, mainly in the European monetary system. By 1975, countries accounting for 46 per cent of the trade of IMF members floated independently with varying degrees of intervention; 14 per cent of trade was pegged to a single currency (usually the dollar); and 23 per cent of trade was in a joint float (principally in Europe). Floating was not a conscious policy decision. It arose from the pressure of circumstances and political calculation and was, in the words of Gottfried Haberler, a 'nonsystem'. In 1971, most officials and politicians had still assumed that a realignment of rates was needed; they only changed their minds when the Smithsonian rates could not hold, and the domestic political costs of defending exchange rates by deflation, unemployment and recession were not acceptable. In June 1972, Arthur Laffer (the chief economist to the Office of Management and Budget) informed the IMF that floating rates were not the preferred option but 'might not be such a bad alternative'.[80] The alternative seemed to work. The IMF reported in 1975 that 'exchange rate flexibility appears to have enabled the world economy to surmount a succession of disturbing events, and to accommodate diverse trends in costs and prices in national economies with less disruption of trade and payments than a system of par values would have been able to do'.[81] Raymond Mikesell – a veteran of Bretton Woods – agreed that 'the experience with relatively free floating rates ... has shown that a general system of floating rates does not mean world financial chaos, and since then the idea of a more or less permanent system of floating rates has gained respectability, at least as a second-best alternative.'[82]

Coombs hoped that the result would be a return of informal co-operation by central bankers. They had ensured that the Bretton Woods system worked in the 1960s. He now looked to them to create an orderly market. He saw that 'managed rather than free floating of the key exchange rates has now become the order of the day ... [S]uch managed floating will probably gradually evolve into a reasonably stable system of *de facto* adjustable parities linking up the dollar with other key currencies.'[83] Of course, there was a risk that governments would try to manage the float to secure an advantage in trade which could provoke retaliation by other countries, as in the 1930s. Attention therefore turned both to finding a mechanism to prevent a return to currency warfare that the Bretton Woods agreement had been designed to prevent, and to a new round of trade talks to prevent a lurch to protectionism and retaliation.

Figure 7: Currency fluctuations after the end of pegged rates: yen and DM/euro against the dollar, 1950–2019

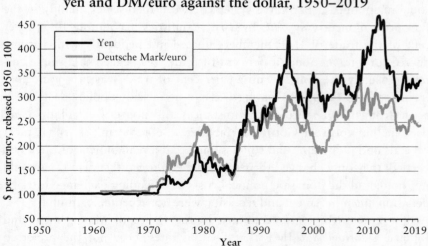

Source: IMF, International Financial Statistics.

MANAGING THE FLOAT

Discussions initially took place outside any formal structure, in private meetings between leading countries. On 25 March 1973, Shultz convened a meeting of finance ministers of the United States, France, Germany and Britain at the White House library which, Helmut Schmidt pointed out, was 'hidden from the public and from the authority of the IMF'. This 'library group' was joined by Japan in September 1973. Denis Healey, the British Chancellor of the Exchequer from 1974 to 1979, later remarked that '[a]s Finance Ministers, we often disagreed with one another both in theory and practice. But, belonging as we did to the most depressed and unpopular caste in the political life of all our countries, as untouchables we developed a friendly freemasonry which transcended our economic differences.' These informal gatherings proved more effective than the larger meetings of the C20 or IMF. The nature of global governance was changing.[84]

Desultory discussions at the C20 produced an 'Outline of Reform' paper in June 1974. Despite the collapse of fixed rates and the adoption of floating, the C20 did not discuss the future exchange rate regime in any detail. It looked to 'stable but adjustable' par values and thought that 'floating rates could provide a useful technique in particular situations'. It left the solution open – not surprisingly, given the split between members who preferred floating and those who wanted to return to fixed rates.[85] The executive board of the IMF subsequently adopted 'Guidelines for the management of floating' that encouraged members to 'prevent or moderate' disruptive fluctuations in rates by intervening in exchange markets, and urged them to avoid manipulating rates over the longer term by capital controls, interest rates, or fiscal intervention. The guidelines were ineffective, for countries were reluctant to give the IMF authority over exchange rates, or to consult it before opting for a pegged or floating rate.[86]

Discussions between a smaller group of advanced industrialized economies were more feasible than a comprehensive, multilateral agreement, provided that the positions of the United States and France could be reconciled. Shultz resigned as Treasury Secretary in May 1974 in opposition to continued controls on wages and prices, and was succeeded by William Simon, a Wall Street banker at Salomon Brothers who believed that 'there is only one social system that reflects the sovereignty of the individual: the free-market or capitalism system.' In September 1975, Simon informed the IMF that 'the right to float must be clear and unencumbered'. The American position rested on flexibility, removal of capital controls and adjustment by countries in surplus. By contrast, the French supported fixed rates, capital controls and action by deficit countries. In 1975 Ed Yeo, Under-Secretary of the Treasury for monetary affairs, and Jacques de Larosière of the French Ministry of Finance (and later managing director of the IMF) sought a compromise – 'a stable system of exchange rates' rather than (as the French preferred) 'a system of stable exchange rates'. The IMF would exercise 'surveillance' over floating rates by encouraging countries to adopt domestic economic policies that would ensure 'orderly underlying economic and financial conditions' and so maintain international stability. Larosière secured the insertion of the word 'firm' before surveillance, and insisted that a return to pegged rates should not be ruled out.[87]

This compromise was agreed at the Rambouillet summit of November 1975 that was convened by Giscard d'Estaing. The summit aimed to bring five heads of government – those of the United States, Britain, West Germany, France and Japan – together in a 'house-party atmosphere' in the chateau at Rambouillet, on the lines of the 'library group'. The desire to keep the meeting small collided with pressure from other states to be included. Italy was allowed to attend at Rambouillet, and Canada joined the group in 1976, so becoming the G7, which has met regularly ever since (for a time becoming the G8 when Russia was a member). In the opinion of the British ambassador, Giscard d'Estaing hoped that the summit would allow 'a conversation in depth among the main principals about the main principles, a major reckoning or *prise de conscience* of the leaders of the West about the need to put their economic and monetary house in order'. Robert Hormats of the National Security Council was more sceptical and worried that Western leaders would either make 'boldly confident statements' about problems that they did not understand or express their frustrations, which would undermine confidence. Indeed, the Americans suspected that the meeting at Rambouillet was a French ploy to return to a fixed rate regime and to call for an economic stimulus. The US Treasury took a different line, that 'interference by governments in the operation of an open world market system is counterproductive'. In the opinion of one official, the American approach at Rambouillet should be to 'emphasize what we are trying to do structurally to revitalize the private sector, through deregulation etc. Stimulation is not the whole answer.' Nevertheless, Kissinger welcomed the summit as a means 'to confirm and consolidate allied cooperation' and restore American leadership. The result was the Rambouillet Declaration that accepted a compromise between France (which dropped an insistence on fixed par values) and America (which dropped full legalization of floating). The British ambassador noted that 'the prolonged doctrinal argument on the virtues of floating rates as against fixed parities has been set aside'.[88]

The next stage was to revise the IMF's Articles of Agreement to reflect this new reality. In October 1974, the 'Interim Committee' of the Board of Governors of the IMF was established in place of the C20, until a Council of Governors could be created with decision-making powers – a proposal that was never implemented due to disagreement over its status. The Interim Committee therefore continued to provide advice to the Board of Governors, and carried forward the C20's proposals for the gradual evolution of the monetary system. In January 1976, the committee met in Kingston, Jamaica, and proposed reform on the basis of the Rambouillet settlement. In the words of Simon, it was the

> first sweeping revision of our international monetary arrangements since the Bretton Woods Conference in 1944. As a result, we will now have a flexible monetary system which can adapt to changing international circumstances, avoiding the strains and stresses of the 60s which resulted in an uncompetitive US economy and eventually a breakdown of the system in August 1971.[89]

The Jamaica Accord proposed amending the IMF's articles to eliminate rigidity, and countries were given freedom to choose their exchange system with a stress on economic stability rather than fixed exchange rates. The right to change the dollar into gold had effectively been abandoned in 1971. Now, the official price of gold was abandoned too; it no longer provided the peg for the value of the dollar. Nevertheless, gold remained an important reserve asset. In return, the French made concessions on flexible exchange rates. The articles still allowed a par system based on wider margins and flexibility, with no expectation that it would be restored, for a majority of 85 per cent was needed, which gave the United States a veto. No country would be forced to adopt a par value; and any country which did adopt a par system could abandon it unless 85 per cent objected. The IMF was to promote a 'stable system of exchange rates' and the new regime was simply described as 'the one in force at January 1, 1976'. The Fund was to 'oversee the international monetary system in order to ensure its effective operation' and was to 'exercise firm surveillance over the exchange rate policies of members, and shall adopt specific principles for the guidance of all members with respect to those policies'. The IMF was to 'respect the domestic social and political policies of members', who should provide the IMF with information needed for surveillance and, if requested, consult with the Fund on exchange rate policies. Members were to 'avoid manipulating exchange rates or the international monetary system in order to prevent effective balance of payments adjustments or to gain an unfair competitive advantage'.

Despite these provisions, the role of the IMF was minimal. The only surprise, as Alexandre Kafka pointed out, was that it took so long to come to
this 'not very sensational agreement'. One commentator remarked that it
was a 'non-reform' – a view captured by the comment by Simon as the
Jamaica meeting concluded: 'All is well that ends.' The Jamaica Accord
allowed the existing system (or non-system) to continue, with the rules-
based approach of the IMF replaced by collaboration between the major
economic powers. The Articles of Agreement of the IMF were formally
revised by the Board of Governors on 30 April 1976 and took effect from
1 April 1978.[90]

Less developed countries were not represented at informal meetings
between a few advanced industrial economies. In 1973, Manmohan
Singh, the chief economic adviser to the Indian Ministry of Finance,
remarked at the C20 that 'a built-in mechanism for an adequate transfer
of real resources to developing countries must be an essential element of the
reformed monetary system'. Exchange rate flexibility left less developed
countries vulnerable to unstable primary product prices and to the costs
of servicing debts, but their concerns were largely overlooked. The less
developed countries took no part in the discussions at Rambouillet, and
the IMF ratified an agreement reached by a few advanced economies with
only a modest concession of a more generous Compensatory Financing
Facility to offset fluctuations in the export earnings of less developed
countries. These countries complained that the continued use of gold as a
reserve would 'greatly reduce the chance of further allocations of SDRs,
thereby detracting from the agreed objective of making the SDR the principal reserve asset'. They wished to finance development by linking the
creation of additional liquidity with the provision of aid.[91] As we will see
in the next chapter, the less developed countries challenged their exclusion
by demanding the construction of a New International Economic Order.

A 'second Rambouillet' was held at Puerto Rico in 1976 with the aim
of averting rather than reacting to crises and of showing American leadership. Simon welcomed the informality and frankness of discussions, and
Alan Greenspan – chair of the CEA – saw 'a real intellectual grappling
with major philosophical issues . . . We may have developed a new form
of international institution. We have broken down the formality and
protocol of summit meetings so that true dialogue can take place.' Kissinger agreed: 'not since the early '50s has there been such a spirit of
cooperation among the allies.' In reality, tensions were apparent. President Ford blamed global inflation on the over-commitment of governments
to policies to reduce inequalities. Schmidt shared this concern for inflation, but the British prime minister, James Callaghan, argued for the

addition of economic stimulus and employment. The summit at least allowed dialogue, even if the outcome was minimal.[92]

Little was done to give the IMF effective powers or even to apply the guidelines for floating currencies. The Fund was caught between the Europeans (who wanted it to take a broader role) and the Americans and British (who preferred to follow market forces and limit the Fund to preventing exchange rate manipulation). Surveillance of exchange rates to ensure that countries adjusted and did not gain competitive advantage was a matter of consultation rather than regulation, based on pragmatic acceptance that members were not only concerned with exchange rates but also with 'sustained sound economic growth and reasonable levels of employment'. The IMF's policy shifted to encouraging liberal financial policies that gave a greater role to markets, both internationally and domestically. It now welcomed capital mobility – both short- and long-term – without surveillance of the international financial system and only stepped in after things went wrong, to rescue bankers from their mistakes and to impose conditions on borrowers.[93]

Robert Triffin was disappointed with the outcome and complained that twelve years of official debates and negotiations had achieved minimal results. The IMF merely legalized the existing system without imposing any commitments to deal with destabilizing capital flows, establish symmetrical adjustment, or assist the less developed countries. 'Are all these problems really solved – as some would maintain – by the simple abolition of the par-value system? Were they all the mere by-products of a gigantic mistake – Bretton Woods?' He hoped that habits of multilateral consultation would survive and so avoid beggar-my-neighbour policies:

> Unable to negotiate the fundamental reforms that would make the international monetary system less prone to crises, our officials have nevertheless demonstrated repeatedly an uncanny ability to mount, nearly overnight, the rescue operations needed to minimize their deflationary – if not their inflationary – impact upon the world economy.[94]

This modest outcome reflected a belief, as Kafka commented, that 'no compelling need was felt for anything more' and that closing the gold window had not led to a 'disastrous rise in internationally antisocial behaviour'.[95] The multilateral IMF was marginalized in the new world of managed floating rates, and international oversight moved to the regular meetings of G7 and of central bankers at the BIS, who co-operated in exchange market interventions that avoided 'aggressively competitive or predatory behaviour'. The new order meant that the IMF had lost its role as the custodian of international monetary arrangements and needed to redefine its purpose.[96]

TRADE POLICY: NIXON AND THE TOKYO ROUND

The shift in the monetary regime had consequences for trade policy. The assumption at Bretton Woods was that multilateral trade required an end to currency warfare and competitive devaluation. In reality, pegged rates led to the prospect that surplus countries could maintain undervalued rates that gave them a competitive advantage and might lead to a protectionist response. In the United States, a backlash had started soon after the Kennedy Round. Fred Bergsten – assistant to Henry Kissinger for international economic affairs at the National Security Council – pointed out in October 1970 that 'it is becoming increasingly clear that our major trade problems with the [European Economic] Community are not politically susceptible to resolution satisfactory to the United States, and I envisage increasing difficulty in overall US–European relations as a result'.[97] Meanwhile, the Europeans complained that American tariffs remained high and that the American Selling Price continued in force, despite the promises in the Kennedy Round. To make matters worse, Nixon imposed an import surcharge when the gold window closed in August 1971, with the possibility of European retaliation. The oil shock and slump of 1973 further intensified protectionist pressures in the United States and threatened American leadership in multilateral negotiations. The emergence of floating rates also created the prospect of currency manipulation that might lead to retaliation in trade policy. The crisis in the international monetary regime therefore had potentially serious consequences for trade.

Nixon and, after his resignation, Gerald Ford aimed to balance growing congressional and public support for protectionism with a commitment to open markets and multilateralism, above all for wider geopolitical reasons. When Nixon assumed office, he had to decide whether to adopt a 'grand design' to counter protectionism in Congress, or to pursue a cautious approach that would avoid reopening trade policy. Lyndon Johnson's attempt to renew the Trade Expansion Act had failed to secure congressional support and Nixon initially opted for a cautious approach. In November 1969, he presented a Trade Bill to Congress which did not seek additional authority to reduce tariffs and only requested the renewal of unused powers and the repeal of the American Selling Price, with more generous adjustment assistance and escape clauses for affected industries. He also hoped that the appointment of a presidential commission on the expansion of world trade would signal commitment to a liberal trade regime and to a long-term consideration of policy.[98]

This politically pragmatic policy encountered difficulties when Congress imposed restrictions on textile imports and refused to repeal the American Selling Price. Protectionist sentiment was increasing, and in 1970 Wilbur Mills, the chair of the House Ways and Means Committee, reported that 20 of the 25 members of the committee, and 299 members of the House, supported legislation to impose quotas.[99] Kissinger feared the impact of protectionism, not only for the international trading system but also for foreign policy: 'the rest of the world would regard such a step as the most concrete possible sign of US isolationism, replicating our policies of the 1930s. Its impact on our overall foreign policy would be devastating – in Europe, Japan and the less developed world.'[100] The American embassy in Bonn warned that the emergence of antagonistic trade blocs on both sides of the Atlantic 'threatens to lead the West into a serious crisis in trade relations and thus poses grave dangers for our political and economic objectives in Europe and elsewhere in the world'. The embassy thought the solution was a 'Nixon Round' to contain protectionism and make a strong commitment to GATT.[101] Kissinger was sympathetic, but progress was stymied by fear of provoking protectionists in Congress. The report of the presidential Commission on International Trade and Investment Policy did not help, for it attempted to combine a general commitment to liberal trade with an assertion of American power that breached GATT rules.[102]

Deteriorating economic relations with Europe and Japan had wider political and strategic ramifications. Bergsten pointed out that 'all of our great "economic" initiatives (IMF-IBRD, Marshall Plan, Kennedy Round, SDRs, etc) have been undertaken for essentially foreign policy reasons, and foreign policy considerations have dictated the U.S. position on virtually all issues of foreign economic policy.' He urged the continuation of this approach and warned against making foreign policy subordinate to international economic policy. Indeed, the general view in the White House was that multilateral foreign economic policy was best sustained by linking it to wider strategic ambitions. This approach complemented a second theme – that authority for trade negotiations should rest on 'progress toward free and fair trade' that would remove 'inequities for US producers'. The use of the term 'fair trade' was crucial, for it went beyond cutting tariffs on industrial goods to a concern for agriculture – especially the impact of the EEC's Common Agricultural Policy – and for non-tariff

barriers (NTBs). These NTBs included a wide range of techniques: regulations on sanitary standards could restrict imports on the grounds of
consumer protection; rules on public procurement and local content
could keep foreign firms out of markets; subsidies and bailouts for domestic producers could be used to deal with competitive imports; or the
simple expedient of bureaucratic delays at the border could frustrate
importers. These barriers were increasingly significant in limiting access
to foreign markets as tariffs fell from their high post-war levels,[103] and in
1972 the OECD posed the question of how best 'to limit distortions in
international competition and to preclude non-tariff barriers in trade,
erected in the name of a nation's health, clean living, or safety. How, in
effect, to prevent environmental protection from becoming another
form of protectionism?'[104]

Before the election in 1972, Nixon ruled out a comprehensive liberal
trade programme with new negotiating authority, for nationalist and protectionist sentiments were strong both in the labour movement and parts
of business. 'Let there be no doubt that our position before the election is
one of protectionism. We should not indicate that we are preparing any
concession not in the interest of the US.' Nevertheless, he realized that
'more is involved here than just questions of "horse-trading" between
soybeans and cheese. The question is what Europe wants its position to be
vis-à-vis the US and the Soviet Union.' Hostility over trade could encourage demands in Congress to remove American troops from Germany and
so threaten NATO. Nixon gave priority to geopolitical strategy:

> If NATO comes apart, they [Europe] will be an economic giant but a mili-
> tary and political pigmy. The USSR will encroach on them ... European
> leaders are terrified at that prospect. European leaders want to "screw" us
> and we want to "screw" them in the economic area. But political relation-
> ships should be overriding for us and for them. What will matter in trade is
> its relationship to the total problem ... We should examine what price we
> might have to pay on the trade side for this political relationship, and they
> should do so as well. We should not allow the umbilical cord between the
> US and Europe to be cut and Europe to be nibbled away by the Soviets. We
> need to strengthen the bonds of trade, monetary relations, exchanges, etc.

These considerations led Nixon to argue that 'we cannot turn isolationist
in the broader context'. The United States should be 'as tough as we can
without going over the line where anti-US sentiment will cause them to
turn against us and break with us'. He could present himself to the Europeans as battling with isolationist sentiments at home, 'not because our
economic survival is at stake but rather because we have a major interest

in our overall relations with them, which we value highly, and in the interest of world peace'. He opted for a middle ground of 'modified confrontation' – a carefully calibrated approach that used domestic protectionism to frighten the Europeans and made sufficient concessions to sentiment at home without provoking a breakdown of relations with Europe. The difficulties of selling trade liberalization to the public and to Congress meant that action would be delayed until after the election of November 1972, which would allow time to develop a stronger case based on the wider strategic issues.[105]

After his re-election, Nixon had to decide whether to take the risk of seeking fast-track authority for tariff reduction, which might be rejected by Congress. The alternative was a less definite commitment, by a congressional resolution setting out the objective of reducing tariffs and NTBs, with more generous escape clauses and adjustment assistance. But Europe and Japan were unlikely to start talks in the absence of fast-track executive authority, for all aspects of a deal would be open to congressional challenge without it.[106] Peter Flanigan, Special Trade Representative, argued for an ambitious approach: 'the true choice before Congress will not be a narrow one concerning trade policy, but a basic issue of national direction for the United States. The task for the Administration is to cast trade legislation in the broad context of the President's foreign policy.' He saw that the situation would be favourable in 1973 when Nixon had a clear mandate, and protectionists had less influence at a time of economic recovery, lower inflation, improved trade and peace in Vietnam. He stressed that

> We are at a major crossroad in international economic relations. We can move toward a more open and interdependent world, or we can drift into a world of controls and new trade barriers. What we can negotiate over the next few years can easily determine the system under which the international economy will function for the rest of this century or beyond.[107]

He was overly optimistic, for Nixon's position was weakened by Watergate and protectionist sentiments were still strong in Congress.

Senator Vance Hartke (D: Indiana) and Representative James Burke (D: Massachusetts), with the backing of the AFL–CIO, had already introduced a protectionist Foreign Trade and Investment Bill that would impose quotas to protect jobs and discourage American corporations from relocating production overseas by taxing foreign earnings and regulating the outflow of capital and technology. As Treasury Secretary, George Shultz felt that such measures were not needed, for devaluation had made American goods more competitive. Instead, he looked to 'lay the legislative groundwork for broad and outward-looking trade negotiations' based on 'freer and fairer trade'. Otherwise, 'pressures to retreat inward will be intense. We must avoid that risk, for it is the road to international recrimination, isolation and autarky.' The outcome was a two-track approach that combined a 'more open and more equitable trading system' with domestic safeguards. Flanigan assured Nixon that '[t]he possibility of attack by both free traders and protectionists confirms me in my belief that it is a balanced bill'. Striking the exact balance was difficult, for a weak bill might not block protectionism and a strong bill would 'feed "red meat" to the protectionists'. The administration turned to the ambitious option of a comprehensive trade bill to provide fast-track authority to raise or lower tariffs without limit for five years; to allow negotiations on NTBs, subject to a veto by Congress; and with power to retaliate against unfair restrictions on American exports and to safeguard domestic workers and industries.[108]

Securing these powers was not easy. Senator Russell Long (D: Louisiana) spoke for the protectionists when he protested that the United States was 'the least favored nation in a world full of discrimination'.[109] The bill also raised a strategic problem. The United States–Soviet trade deal of 1972 proposed to extend 'most favoured nation' treatment to the Soviet Union. The Jackson–Vanik amendment sought to block this concession as a response to restrictions on Jewish emigration from the Soviet Union. Nixon wanted detente with the Soviets and threatened to use his veto against the amendment. Kissinger preferred to go further and delay the trade bill, with priority given to 'making our international economic policies responsive to your overall foreign policy requirements'.[110] Nixon pressed ahead but the Act was emasculated. In December 1973, Congress rejected Nixon's request for fast-track authority.[111]

The lack of authority had serious implications for trade policy and the attempt to launch a new trade round at a time when the international monetary system was in flux. The proposal for a round had its origins at the G10 finance ministers' meeting in Rome in December 1971 and a call by the governments of Japan and the United States for GATT to undertake a comprehensive review of international economic relations and to start multilateral negotiations in 1973. The round was launched at the GATT ministerial meeting in Tokyo in September 1973, which declared that

[t]he policy of liberalizing world trade cannot be carried out successfully in the absence of parallel efforts to set up a monetary system which shields the world economy from the shocks and imbalances which have previously

occurred. The Ministers will not lose sight of the fact that the efforts which are to be made in the trade field imply continuing effort to maintain orderly conditions and to establish a durable and equitable monetary system.

The meeting looked to monetary reform as a complement to trade liberalization and made a commitment 'to solve in an equitable way the problems of all participating countries, taking into account the specific trade problems of the developing countries'. Discussion of a new trade round therefore coincided with both the demise of the Bretton Woods exchange rate system and the growing demands of developing countries for a New International Economic Order.[112] To more pessimistic observers, the world was on the brink of trade and currency warfare unless firm action was taken – and effective talks could not start until the president secured fast-track authority.

President Ford broke the impasse over negotiating authority by securing the Trade Reform Act of 1974 that balanced liberalization and protectionism. On the one hand, it gave the president fast-track authority for five years to negotiate tariffs. Congress could not amend the proposed trade agreement and would take a straight 'up-or-down' vote. It retained a veto on NTBs and granted a direct role for trade groups in the negotiations. On the other hand, the Act strengthened adjustment assistance and escape clauses, anti-dumping and countervailing duties, and gave new authority to respond to unfair foreign trade practices. It incorporated the Jackson–Vanik amendment. Above all, Section 301 gave authority to retaliate against 'unjustifiable' and 'unreasonable' barriers – vague terms that allowed the United States to act unilaterally as both judge and jury. Senator Long was reassured that the Act had 'literally hundreds of provisions which provide protection in one respect or another for various segments of American labor and industry'. America's post-war pursuit of free trade based on non-discrimination gave way to 'fair trade' based on 'aggressive unilateralism' in assessing the policies of other countries. Other countries feared that the United States was moving to protectionism. To the American administration, however, it was a way of containing protectionism, for 'a more responsive domestic process for considering and for acting upon domestic grievances . . . is essential to maintain broad public support for an open US trade policy'. The Act provided a credible basis for negotiations at the Tokyo Round of trade talks.[113]

Negotiations stalled because of the oil shock, high unemployment, inflation, monetary instability and a threat of renewed protectionism. In 1975, Kissinger saw that the Trade Reform Act was 'increasingly being perceived not as a device for trade liberalization but rather as a mechanism for advancing protectionism. It seems that almost every country I deal with is raising complaints along these lines.'[114] Despite the president's fast-track authority, other countries worried that a protectionist Congress might reject the entire package. Problems also arose because the United States wished to combine industrial and agricultural concessions and to make linear cuts in tariffs; the EEC aimed to keep agriculture and industry separate with larger cuts to high American tariffs. Negotiations reached stalemate during the Ford administration.[115]

When President Carter took office in 1977, he compromised on a modest deal before the expiry of the Trade Reform Act's authority. Duties were cut, with larger reductions in the highest tariffs, which meant some harmonization of rates. Although a modest start was made on NTBs, concessions were confined to a few, mainly industrial, countries as informal codes rather than binding rules. The greatest failure was on agriculture, where American demands for liberalization collided with the European Community's and Japanese preferences for stable prices. The main innovation was a new emphasis on procedural issues for the settlement of disputes and surveillance of trade policy, though as yet without legal power.[116] To secure support for this deal on Capitol Hill, 'offensive' liberalization had to be complemented with a 'comprehensive and aggressive defensive package' for fair trade, based on a stronger mechanism to settle disputes and the provision of safeguards and adjustment assistance. The Special Representative for Trade Negotiations noted that the 'steady chilling in the atmosphere on Capitol Hill . . . created an atmosphere which is the worst imaginable in which to seek approval'. Consequently, the Round would pass 'only after a bruising and costly fight. It will pit the relatively small and disorganized, though highly respected constituency which supports liberal trade against a formidable coalition of labor and management from numerous industries.' Despite various 'sweeteners', Congress refused to make concessions on textiles that were desired by developing countries, nor on countervailing duties. The result was a stand-off with the European Community.[117]

The developing countries were disappointed with the Tokyo Round. In their view, GATT benefitted economically advanced countries, and they pressed for a shift to distributive fairness based on non-reciprocal deals and preferences to overturn past injustices, with a greater concern for development. The advanced industrial countries were more concerned to ensure that GATT survived at a time when other elements of 'embedded liberalism' were challenged by the demise of the Bretton Woods regime. Negotiations were mainly bilateral between dominant suppliers, so that any gains for developing countries came through the most favoured nation principle – a process that the Peruvian delegation complained gave them only 'marginal and residual advantages'. Developing countries did secure some modest gains. They were offered differential treatment that exempted them from reciprocity and non-discrimination and the Generalized System of Preferences was incorporated into GATT. However, these provisions made it difficult for the developing countries to object when developed countries used temporary import restrictions and 'safeguards'. The developing countries complained of their lack of voice and claimed that the concessions were so modest that they boycotted the signing of the Tokyo agreement.[118]

The Development Decade of the 1960s and UNCTAD had not met the demands of the less developed countries for a restructuring of the world economy. The crisis of the early 1970s potentially gave them more chance of success. The economic government of the world was in flux, with a challenge to the embedded liberalism of the post-war order in the ending of pegged exchange rates and the potential threat to the multilateral trade system. The major advanced economies were experiencing economic difficulties of slower growth and rapid inflation, and the developing countries were more assertive in their ambition for a New International Economic Order.

Norman Borlaug and trainees in the fields of the International Center for Maize and Wheat Improvement, Sonora, Mexico, April 1962.

19

'A trade union of the poor'

The New International Economic Order and the Limits to Growth

'The ultimate objective of development must be to bring about sustained improvement in the well-being of the individual and bestow benefits on all. If undue privileges, extremes of wealth and social injustices persist, then development fails in its essential purpose. This calls for a global development strategy based on joint and concentrated action by developing and developed countries in all spheres of economic and social life: in industry and agriculture, in trade and finance, in employment and education, in health and housing, in science and technology.'

Resolution adopted by the UN General Assembly, 2626 (XXV).
International Development Strategy for the Second United
Nations Development Decade, 24 October 1970

Although the UN Conference on Trade and Development failed to deliver a significant rebalancing of the global economy during the Development Decade of the 1960s, hopes were rising in the 1970s. The Global North was weakened by the crisis in the international monetary system, by American withdrawal from Vietnam in 1975, and by internal tensions: domestic terrorism in Germany and Italy, anti-war and civil rights protests in the United States, and labour unrest in Britain. Protest movements were sympathetic to Third World liberation and there were calls (not easily reconciled) for improved welfare in the West and wealth redistribution to the developing countries.[1] Above all, in 1973 the Organization of the Petroleum Exporting Countries (OPEC) succeeded in increasing the price of oil, a development that might lead to solidarity between primary producers and change the balance of power with industrial countries.

The result, as the historian Nils Gilman points out, was 'a narrow and specific window of geopolitical opportunity' in the early to mid-1970s during which 'political and economic leaders throughout both the postcolonial

world and the industrial core of the global economy took seriously the possibility . . . that they might be witnessing the downfall of the centuries-long
hegemony of what was coming to be known simply as "the north".'[2] To
Gottfried Haberler, now at the right-wing American Enterprise Institute,
the call for a New International Economic Order (NIEO) was a greater
threat than either Communism or western protectionism. Opponents of the
NIEO could, in the words of the development economist Hollis Chenery,
imagine that 'the Saracens were at the pass of Roncesvalles, the Golden
Horde at the Vistula, and Suleiman the Magnificent just outside Vienna,
such was the enormity of the danger to Western civilization posed by the
NIEO'. Such fears had a racist edge. A correspondent of Wilhelm Röpke
worried that the demands for distributive justice by the Global South and
for civil rights at home threatened an 'unholy combination of the Africa
Negro question with US Negroes'. Röpke agreed: non-whites should be
controlled to prevent the emergence of world government in which 'non-
Europeans would hold an overwhelming majority'. Although few followed
him into explicit support for apartheid and white supremacism, there was
alarm at the perceived threat to the culture of the West and to free markets.
The challenge from the Global South meant that the Global North needed
a new strategy of containment, whether by co-operation or confrontation.[3]

DEPENDENCY AND DEVELOPMENT

In October 1970, the General Assembly of the UN proclaimed a new
Development Decade to 'create a more just and rational world economic
and social order' and to raise the rate of growth in the developing countries to at least 6 per cent, on the assumption that population growth could
be reduced to 2.5 per cent. The programme would include domestic policies for greater equality, social justice, efficiency, security, education,
health, nutrition and social welfare. Internationally, action was needed on
commodities, on assistance for diversification, and on the implementation
of generalized, non-discriminatory, non-reciprocal preferences for the exports
of developing countries. Developing countries should encourage regional
integration and trade expansion between themselves, take responsibility
for financing their own development, adopt sound fiscal and monetary
policies, and reform their institutions. At the same time, advanced countries should provide aid amounting to at least 1 per cent of GNP. Both
developing and developed countries should encourage the effective use of
private foreign capital, the IBRD should provide supplementary finance to
deal with adverse movements in export earnings, and developing countries

should have 'full exercise ... of permanent sovereignty over their natural resources'.[4]

At its third meeting in Lusaka in 1970, the Non-Aligned Movement went still further in stressing the continued impact of neo-colonialism, the need for restitution to compensate past victims, and the imperative to reform the world's economy to reduce the power of exploiters. Julius Nyerere – Prime Minister and later President of Tanganyika/Tanzania from 1961 to 1985 – announced that 'the real and urgent threat to the independence of almost all non-aligned states ... comes not from the military, but from the economic power of the big states'. The Lusaka declaration on peace, independence, development and the democratization of international relations called for 'the fundamental right of all peoples to self-determination'. It noted widening disparities between rich and poor countries and called for structural change in the world economy:

> the poverty of developing nations and their economic dependence on those in affluent circumstances constitutes a structural weakness in the present economic order ... The persistence of an inequitable world economic system inherited from the colonial past and continued through present neo-colonialism poses insurmountable difficulties in breaking the bondage of poverty and shackles of economic dependence.[5]

These demands were taken up by UNCTAD. Manuel Peréz-Guerrero of Venezuela became its secretary general in 1969. He had long experience of working for international organizations, having been at the League of Nations in the 1930s, attending both the San Francisco conference to establish the UN and the inter-American conference at Chapultepec in 1945, and in 1967 becoming the president of ECOSOC.[6] In 1972, on the suggestion of Luis Echeverría of Mexico, UNCTAD appointed a working group to draft a Charter of Economic Rights and Duties of States.[7] This initiative was taken further at the fourth meeting of non-aligned nations at Algiers in 1973, which called for a new international economic order to restructure the international economic system and end dependency.

The Algiers Declaration stated that imperialism was 'still the greatest obstacle to the emancipation and progress of the developing countries', and that the non-aligned nations should take an 'aggressive attitude towards those who oppose its plans, trying to impose upon them political, social and economic structures which encourage alien domination, dependence and neo-colonialism'. Although the form of imperialism changed, its aim remained to undermine sovereignty and economic development. Imperialism created 'ever-increasing disparity between the industrialised countries and the under-developed world'; and it maintained a 'stranglehold on the resources of the developing countries to ensure all kinds of privileges and reliable outlets for their manufactured products and services'. The Algiers Declaration urged remedial action through non-reciprocity, preferential treatment, an extension of the Generalized System of Preferences, and reform of the international monetary system. Above all, it stressed 'the vital necessity' of non-aligned nations 'making every possible effort to consolidate their national independence and reinforce their fighting front by challenging imperialist and neo-colonial exploitation structures and by organising cooperation and solidarity with one another in intercontinental and regional organizations.' The Declaration went on to 'reaffirm each country's inalienable right to the full exercise of national sovereignty over its natural resources and all domestic economic activities'. Each state had the right to nationalize their resources on whatever terms it wished, and to free itself from transnational corporations that infringed the sovereignty of developing countries.[8] It was a radical call for distributive justice in the global economy.

The intellectual case rested on dependency theory, which viewed under-development as the corollary of the development of advanced industrial economies. Paul Baran, an American Marxist economist, argued in *The Political Economy of Growth* (1957) that the surplus produced in developing countries was taken as profit by international corporations rather than invested productively in the economy. This critique was developed in the 1960s by the Brazilian sociologist (later President, from 1995 to 2002) Fernando Cardoso and the economist Celso Furtado, and by the French-Egyptian economist Samir Amin's analysis of under-development in West Africa. In the Caribbean, Walter Rodney's *How Europe Underdeveloped Africa* (1972) drew on dependency theory to argue that Africa's poverty was a direct consequence of colonial rule, and above all the slave trade. His claim rested on Eric Williams' argument that the British industrial revolution relied on the profits of slavery – a thought that did not inform Walt Rostow's account of the take-off into self-sustained growth. The title of Andre Gunder Frank's influential book encapsulated this radical critique – *The Development of Underdevelopment*. These books were influential in western universities and contributed to radical support for civil rights at home and abroad.[9]

The demand for an NIEO also appealed to China, which wished to restore its standing after the chaos of the Cultural Revolution. In 1974, Deng Xiaoping articulated the theory of the three worlds at the sixth special session of the UN General Assembly, which was elaborated by Mao.

The first world comprised two hegemonic powers – the imperialistic United States and the social imperialist Soviet Union:

> They have become the biggest international exploiters, oppressors and aggressors and the common enemies of the people of the world, and the rivalry between them is bound to lead to a new world war. The contention for world supremacy between the two hegemonist powers, the menace they pose to the people of all lands and the latter's resistance to them – this has become the central problem in present-day world politics.

The less powerful developed economies – Europe, Japan and Canada – of the second world 'oppress and exploit the oppressed nations and are at the same time controlled and bullied by the superpowers'. The third world of Asia, Africa and Latin America were 'the worst exploited and oppressed' and 'the main force in the world-wide struggle against imperialism and hegemonism'. China supported the NIEO as a weapon against both the United States and the Soviet Union as white industrial powers plundering the developing world.[10]

Even more importantly, the changing political economy of oil seemed to shift the balance of power between industrialized and primary producing economies. At the end of the Second World War, Venezuela was the major oil exporter, and in 1948 Juan Pablo Pérez Alfonzo, the minister of development, negotiated a deal with American oil companies for a 50:50 split in profits. In the Middle East, imperial powers and oil companies imposed more stringent terms on sovereign landlords, but the 50:50 split was also adopted there as production increased. The states had no say in the price of oil, for the companies set a 'posted price' for purchases from the oil states, which could only increase revenues by raising output. In 1958, Alfonzo returned to Venezuela from political exile and was appointed Minister of Mines and Hydrocarbons. The next year, Venezuela proposed a new international body to regulate oil prices, coinciding with a meeting of Arab oil producers in Cairo. Alfonzo attended and entered into discussions with Abdullah Tariki of Saudi Arabia and Mohammad Salman of Iraq to increase the states' share of revenue, for a say in setting the 'posted price', for a greater role in all stages of the industry, for national oil companies, and for regulation of prices and production. In 1960, representatives of Iran, Iraq, Kuwait, Saudi Arabia and Venezuela met in Baghdad and formed the Organization of the Petroleum Exporting Countries, which other countries soon joined. OPEC was not a cartel, for the members did not control prices or output; it was a grouping of sovereign states who were divided by political regimes and allegiances. It countered the cartel of oil companies by questioning the 50:50 deal, claiming a larger share of revenues, and demanding a voice in management. In the 1960s, the oil companies fought back and exploited the divisions in the oil producers between those who wanted higher production and those who favoured high prices to increase revenues. Matters changed in the later 1960s. Algeria joined OPEC in 1969, and new regimes came to power in Iraq, in 1968 and Libya in 1969. OPEC took a more aggressive line in demanding 'participation' and 'best practices' to conserve their natural resources, and from 1970 individual members, starting with Libya, attacked the oil companies. By 1971, most petrol states agreed that more direct control was needed, whether that was by nationalization, as in Algeria and Iraq, or by participation as in Iran.[11]

In October 1973, Egypt attacked Israel and, in retaliation for western support for Israel, the Arab producers imposed an embargo on oil exports. On 16 October, OPEC raised the price of oil from $3.02 to $5.12 a barrel and in December to $11.60 – the first unilateral increases by producers (see Figure 8). In the 1970s, OPEC members pushed ahead with control over production and turned the oil companies into junior partners. The less developed countries hailed a victory over the advanced economies. In the eyes of the less developed countries, the achievement of OPEC stood in stark contrast to the limited success of UNCTAD. At the UN in 1974, the delegate from Guinea praised OPEC's 'brilliant victories in bringing about a just and more harmonious equilibrium in international economic relations'. Members of OPEC emphasized their status as 'developing countries, which believe that their first and foremost duty is to raise the standards of living of their peoples in all spheres, in order that they may keep pace with world progress . . . and make an effective contribution to international development in general'. Development funds such as the Saudi Development Fund and the Iraqi External Development Fund amounted to 2.9 per cent of the members' GDP in the late 1970s – well ahead of the aid given by OECD countries. This strategy reflected an ideological commitment by countries such as Algeria and a more pragmatic strategy by Saudi Arabia and the Gulf states of building an alliance against the OECD and protecting the elites of the petro-states from attacks by oil-importing developing countries who might work with domestic critics or threaten regional stability. Despite the impact of high prices, oil-importing developing countries maintained a common front in demanding an NIEO. In the words of Nyerere,

> within the existing structures of economic interaction we must remain poor, and get relatively poorer, whatever we do . . . The demand for a New

International Economic Order is a way of saying that the poor nations must be enabled to develop themselves according to their own interests, and to benefit from the efforts they make.[12]

The industrial countries were hit by high oil prices that slowed economic growth (which had already fallen from the high levels of the 1950s and 1960s) and raised the level of inflation. They feared producers of other commodities would follow the same tactic as OPEC. In response, the EEC embarked on greater integration in Europe and less co-operation with the United States on monetary reform, combined with a search for alliances with developing countries that would maintain ties with former metropoles. Above all, the French saw a chance to mediate between Arab oil producers and western consumers, and in January 1974 proposed an international energy conference. President Houari Boumédiène of Algeria, chairman of the Non-Aligned Movement, thought it 'could be of value if, instead of being restricted to the problem of energy alone, it covered all the questions relating to all types of raw materials'. He requested a special session of the General Assembly on raw materials and development, which would meet between 9 April and 2 May 1974. The United States was uneasy and called a conference of the major oil-consuming nations in Washington in February 1974.[13] Dependency theory was countered by the idea of interdependence.

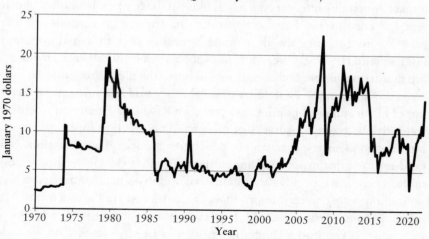

Figure 8: Real crude oil price (West Texas Intermediate), 1970–2022 (January 1970 = 100)

Source: IMF staff calculations at https://www.imf.org/wp-content/uploads/2022/05/oil-intensity-chart-cotw.jpg.

INTERDEPENDENCE

Henry Kissinger responded to Algeria's 'lousy idea' of a special session of the UN by arguing that 'we should be in the rear guard of those who are joining in', and that the best approach was to indicate problems without adopting a 'blocking position'. He therefore suggested making a major statement to the special session as a damage limitation exercise.[14] He drew on the notion of economic interdependence in a growing world economy rather than conflict between the Global North and South – an idea that had currency across the political spectrum. In 1973, the future president Jimmy Carter, Zbigniew Brzezinski (who served as Carter's National Security Adviser) and David Rockefeller set up the Trilateral Commission to enhance co-operation between the industrial democracies of Japan, western Europe and North America, and to move towards 'a more just global community'. Rockefeller had been chair of the Council of Foreign Relations since 1970 where he argued that the post-war settlement was collapsing because of 'the emergence of strong non-governmental but transnational forces'. These concerns resonated in the national security community. Elmo Zumwalt, the chief of naval operations, saw that the energy crisis led to vulnerability, and in 1974 he convened a meeting with leading figures such as George Shultz and Defense Secretary James Schlesinger to consider 'economic interdependence and the nation's future'. In Zumwalt's opinion, the strategic obsession with South-East Asia had missed the major change in the world economy, and 'the time has come to take a look at the growing economic interdependence of nations and the impact which this interdependence is likely to have upon US policy'. Such was the context for Kissinger's 'southern strategy' in response to the NIEO – to convince the developing countries that they had common interest with the North in a dynamic global economy rather than engaging in distributional conflict that would harm the global economy.[15]

At the Washington conference that February, and at a subsequent meeting of five leading economies in September, Kissinger attempted to create solidarity between consumers of oil, including less developed countries. He rejected 'a never-never land in which tiny, poor and weak nations can hold up for ransom some of the industrialized world'. Why should 800 million people in the advanced industrial countries be 'mesmerized while 50 million people in certain producer countries control the situation'? He urged oil consumers in the OECD to take robust action against producers by paying $15bn into a Common Trust to assist any member hit by high oil prices, and to fund research on reducing dependence on oil. 'Project

Interdependence' aimed to create consumer solidarity under American leadership. Detente with the Soviets should be complemented by inter-dependence within the West. The Europeans were sceptical. Denis Healey, the British chancellor, preferred to 'use existing institutions as much as possible' and proposed that OPEC deposit funds at the IMF for distribu-tion to countries in need. The German government similarly preferred an IMF initiative, and Giscard d'Estaing saw an opportunity for France to act as an intermediary between producers and consumers by supporting the NIEO in return for OPEC's agreeing to negotiate the price of oil.[16]

Kissinger's speech on 'the challenge of interdependence' to the sixth special session of the General Assembly pursued interdependence and called for co-operation within an open economy. He urged that the

> great issues of development can no longer realistically be perceived in terms of confrontation between the haves and have nots or as a struggle over the distribution of static wealth. Whatever our ideological belief or social struc-ture, we are part of a single international economic system on which all of our national economic objectives depend ... We are all engaged in a com-mon enterprise. No nation or group of nations can gain by pushing its claims beyond the limits that sustain world economic growth. No one bene-fits from basing progress on tests of strength.

He made a plea for 'developed and developing nations alike to perceive and pursue their national interests by contributing to the global interest'. The developing nations needed 'an open expanding world economy' for their exports and access to capital; and Kissinger pledged the United States to support development that would overcome 'brutal inequality' and foster 'the peace of cooperation, not the illusory tranquillity of con-dominium'. He called for co-operative action in an interdependent economy that would expand energy supplies and allow an escape from a cycle of surpluses and shortages of raw materials so that poor and rich countries were not opposed. A recession in the industrial economies reduced demand for raw materials so that producers and consumers should work together to create the highest real income over the longest period. Food production and consumption should be balanced by build-ing up reserves and encouraging productivity. Finally, Kissinger stressed that the oil shock, inflation, protectionism and shifts in financial flows were the greatest challenge to the world since the 1930s. He urged coun-tries to avoid restrictions on trade and payments, and promised that the United States would keep its capital markets open and allow imports from developing economies. 'Development requires above all a spirit of cooperation, a belief that with all our differences we are part of a larger community in which wealth is an obligation, resources are a trust, and joint action is a necessity.'[17]

Kissinger saw the need for a geopolitical strategy that would divide the less developed countries and unite the West. It went too far for some members of the administration, who feared concessions to the Global South. Arthur Burns worried that Kissinger was conceding too much, 'and I kept wondering about the role that private enterprise is expected to play'. To these critics, it was wrong to imply – as Kissinger had – that the solution was more international economic management by the UN. Such a strategy might entail a 'high degree of market intervention by governments' that would produce 'primitive forms of social management whose end result will be slower economic and social progress for poor countries as well as rich nations'. They saw a threat to 'the traditional US objective of an open economy with free trade and freedom of movement for capital'. As an official at the National Security Council pointed out, the developing countries that coped best with higher oil prices, such as South Korea, adopted policies to 'set loose the productive forces'. Those who suffered, such as India, showed a 'continued unwillingness or inability of their governments to adopt policies which will set loose the productive forces in their societies'. These countries were deferring action by blaming others, so that 'the right response to [less developed country] attempts to externalize their internal pressures is to ignore it politely while we concentrate in the development institutions such as the IBRD and in our bilateral relations on solving their real problems'.[18] As we will see, the challenge of the Global South did lead to a shift in the development policies of the IBRD.

THE NEW INTERNATIONAL ECONOMIC ORDER

On 1 May 1974 the General Assembly agreed, without a vote, to establish a New International Economic Order. Despite reservations, the United States and other developed countries went along with the proposal, for opposition would be counterproductive. The Declaration on the NIEO called for

> equity, sovereign equality, interdependence, common interest and cooperation among all States, irrespective of their economic and social systems which shall correct inequalities and redress existing injustices, make it possible to eliminate the widening gap between the developed and the developing countries.

Developing countries wanted 'active, full and equal participation ... in the formulation and application of all decisions that concern the international community'. The prosperity of developed and developing countries were interrelated, with a need for 'cooperation between all the members of the international community on the basis of sovereign equality and the removal of the disequilibrium that exists between them'. Radical redistribution would benefit everyone in an interdependent global economy.

Several principles followed. All states had the right to adopt whatever social and economic system they wished, and they should co-operate on the basis of equality in the 'accelerated development of all the developing countries'. Each state was to have

> full permanent sovereignty ... over its natural resources and all economic activities. In order to safeguard these resources, each State is entitled to exercise effective control over them and their exploitation with means suitable to its own situation, including the right to nationalization or transfer of ownership to its nationals, this right being an expression of the full permanent sovereignty of the State.

Further, the less developed countries demanded full compensation for the exploitation of their resources by colonial powers and regulation of transnational corporations. There should be 'a just and equitable relationship' between the price of developing countries' imports and exports 'with the aim of bringing about sustained improvement in their unsatisfactory terms of trade and the expansion of the world economy'.[19]

In December 1974, the UN adopted the Charter of Economic Rights and Duties of States. It reiterated the Algiers Declaration and went further, in claiming that compensation for the nationalization of foreign property 'shall be settled under the domestic law of the nationalizing State', and that states must not use economic and political measures against organizations of primary producers. In effect, less developed countries had a right to form cartels against the interests of the developed countries who had a duty to do nothing about it. Further, developed countries should extend general, non-reciprocal and non-discriminatory preferences to developing countries; and developing countries had a right to extend preferences to each other. The Charter picked up on environmental ideas that were, as we will see later in this chapter, becoming important, by stating that 'the protection, preservation and enhancement of the environment for the present and future generations is the responsibility of all States'. This strategy of preventing the wasteful use of cheap oil helped improve the image of OPEC in the West. Alfonzo became a fierce critic of increased production and over-consumption of cheap oil, and he called for a shift to higher value uses with care of the environment and a fairer redistribution of oil revenues and energy within and between countries. Members of OPEC saw that too much oil had been sold too cheaply and believed that reserves would run out. OPEC's demand for higher prices was therefore presented both as an act of distributive justice and a solution to the problems of environmental degradation. What the Charter did not accept was population control, as advocated by the North. A child in North America or Europe consumed far more than a child in India or Africa, and the onus of adjustment should not fall on the Global South.[20]

The NIEO, as Gilman remarks, was 'a political brand holding together a set of loosely compatible agendas, which together formed something less than a coherent strategy'. The NIEO drew together earlier thinking from the ITO, ECLA and UNCTAD. Gamani Corea, a Sri Lankan diplomat and politician who became Secretary General of UNCTAD in 1974, pointed out that while specific policies were little different,

> What was new in the NIEO was rather its general flavour and its particular emphasis on structural change in the world economy on the one hand, and on collective self reliance on the part of the developing countries on the other. The language of the NIEO reflected ... the sense of the developing countries of having, for the first time, a 'presence' on the world economic scene.[21]

The NIEO was not explicitly hostile to trade or globalization so much as demanding interdependence in a global economy based on equality between North and South. The NIEO would, as Nyerere put it, form 'a trade union of the poor'. It would allow freedom in the internal organization of national economies and sovereign equality alongside international co-operation between states in the management of markets. Such a strategy demanded a change in international law and in the rules of GATT and the IMF so that they no longer reflected the interests of the leading economic powers prior to decolonization. Mohammed Bedjaoui, an Algerian lawyer, argued that post-colonial states need not accept obligations made by colonial states, and that international law should be reshaped so that authority was given to the UN General Assembly, in which developing countries had a majority. The problem was that global economic co-operation and supranational rules were in tension with national sovereignty. If the Global South could break a legal agreement for national reasons, what was to stop the Global North doing the same? Despite the claim to a common identity based on resistance to colonialism, there were also differences within the developing countries. Boumédiène adopted a radical stance of confrontation between 'domination and plundering' and 'emancipation and recovery' and warned of 'uncontrollable conflagration' if the North refused to surrender control of resources. Others looked to mutually beneficial co-operation.[22]

Success in raising the price of oil was not easily replicated, for it was fundamental to the world economy in a way that was not true of, say, tea or coffee. Neither was output so easily organized in metals such as copper and tin. Nevertheless, an attempt was made to extend OPEC's achievement by Corea's 'Outline of an overall integrated programme' for commodities. Instead of international agreements for individual commodities, he proposed a new international agency that would own stocks and manage commodity prices, supported by a central or common fund that would be financed, in part, by oil producers. Prices should be 'remunerative to producers and equitable to consumers'.[23] The developed economies were alarmed by this threat, and by the expropriation of foreign enterprises that affected fifty-seven American firms in 1972–73 alone. The NIEO coincided with high-profile cases such as the nationalization of western oil interests in Libya and Iraq, and of mining companies in Chile and Zambia. As yet, foreign assets were not effectively protected by bilateral investment treaties (see Chapter 21).[24] The stakes would be high at the seventh special session of the General Assembly that was scheduled to meet from 1–16 September 1975 to settle the details of the NIEO.

In the United States, there was cross-party support for a firm stance. Daniel Patrick Moynihan, a Democrat who worked on Kennedy's 'war on poverty' before joining the Nixon administration to advise on social policy, was the United States ambassador to the UN, where he felt besieged by socialists and Third World radicals. Irving Kristol, a leading neo-conservative, called for a stand in a new cold war against the 'mau-mauing' of the North. The Economic Policy Board – a Cabinet-level body established by President Ford to co-ordinate advice – similarly favoured a tough position, for 'a socialist economic order outside the United States would require us to either (a) become socialist or quasi-socialist or (b) become economically isolationist.' It was therefore essential to fight for 'the basic principles of free enterprise and free markets'. Treasury Secretary William Simon agreed on the need to defend free markets. 'There are many in the world who support the Socialist principles of the world economic order, but there are many who look to us for defense of the system.' At the National Security Council, Robert Hormats denied that income and wealth differentials arose from imperialism and capitalist exploitation. The solution was neither reparations nor replacement of the market by intergovernmental agreements. In his view, the main impact of higher prices of food and raw materials fell on resource-poor developing countries. Furthermore, the terms of trade fluctuated rather than moving constantly against primary producers; and reduced demand in developed countries would harm the developing countries. Rather than a direct attack on the rhetoric of the developing countries, he proposed to 'take the high road – asserting that, correctly conceived, collaborative actions by the governments of producing and consuming countries could be achieved for mutual benefit. A strengthening of the *present* international economic system can provide for growth from which every country can benefit.'[25]

Kissinger admitted that 'I am not reliable on economic matters', but he thought the issue was primarily political – the need to 'project an image of the US which is progressive'. In preparation for the seventh special session, he saw that 'we have to avoid an international dispute where Americans say the existing system is great and the [less developed countries] call for a new economic order. This is a losing wicket.' He drew on European diplomatic history to point out that 'it is suicide to defend the existing system. We would be like the Austrians in the 19th century.' His approach was to 'fuzz it up' – to make supportive noises about a just system and to proceed on specific issues rather than matters of general principle. As he said, 'we can't accept the new economic order, but I would like to pull its teeth and divide these countries up, not solidify them'. In pursuit of this strategy, he was 'willing to give them something on rhetoric':

> We should not accept the proposition of the new economic order; on the other hand we must not go to the barricades. We will be totally alone if we do ... My position is that we should not debate whether it is a new order or an old order but fight on technical issues. If we get into a fight, a theological fight, between free market and regulated market we will be beaten back.

The risk of a 'theological position' was that '[t]he [less developed countries] will unite and the developed countries will split up. We are much better off doing this on a concrete basis in which there are some who have something to gain. We should appear forthcoming so that we are not outside of the process.' Ford agreed: there was 'no reason to talk theory when we can in a practical way just screw up the negotiations'. Hence Kissinger urged Moynihan not to argue the virtues of a market economy:

> Our basic strategy must be to hold the industrialized powers behind us and to split the Third World. We can only do that if we start with a lofty tone and a forthcoming stance ... Bloc formation in the Third World can be inhibited only if we focus attention on practical measures in which they have a tangible stake.

His tactic was to show that 'their disruptive actions could stop discussions on commodities or that they will pay a price in terms of cooperation, or military exports'. Support of free enterprise should be linked with pragmatism on specific issues, so defending the existing system without creating a new order.[26]

The seventh special session of the UN announced its determination 'to eliminate injustice and inequality' and to accelerate development by expanding and diversifying trade, improving productivity and export earnings, and shifting the terms of trade 'in order to eliminate the economic imbalance between developed and developing countries'. The fourth session of UNCTAD, to be held in Nairobi in May 1976, should adopt policies to secure 'stable, remunerative and equitable prices' for raw materials and export commodities, to provide compensatory finance for fluctuations in export earnings, to encourage the processing of raw materials in order to capture more value, and to expand the Generalized System of Preferences. Developed countries should renew their commitment in the second Development Decade to provide aid of 0.7 per cent of GDP. The IMF should use Special Drawing Rights for development assistance as well as liquidity, and provide more resources for the World Bank – the overarching name for the IBRD and its new agencies such as the International Finance Corporation and International Development Association – and regional development banks. UNCTAD should also convene a conference of creditor and debtor countries to reduce the burden of debt; and developing countries should have better access to the capital markets of the developed countries. The special session called for 'adequate international financing facilities' for stockpiles and marketing of export commodities, without going so far as endorsing Corea's common fund. Instead, Corea was asked to consider options to preserve the purchasing power of developing countries and to analyse the relationship between the prices of exports from the developing world and the final consumer price. These findings would be presented to the next meeting of UNCTAD.[27]

The French preferred an understanding with the less developed countries rather than 'divide and rule'. They aimed to continue earlier debates over Eurafrica and the 1963 Yaoundé agreement with francophone Africa, which had been extended to East Africa in 1969. The EEC also started negotiations with Egypt, Israel and Lebanon, and this regional strategy led to worries in Latin America and Asia that they were being excluded. The response was a global initiative. In 1974, the EEC created a fund to help countries hit by the oil shock, and in 1975 the Lomé Convention, signed with countries in Africa, the Caribbean and the Pacific, granted preferential access to the customs union. These regional and global initiatives meant that the EEC was both proceeding with internal European integration and becoming an international actor. Giscard d'Estaing pursued this strategy at the Rambouillet summit in November 1975, alongside discussions of monetary reform. Opinions were divided. The British prime minister, Harold Wilson, called for a Marshall Plan for poorer countries and global economic recovery. Helmut Schmidt followed Kissinger and argued that 'we must find a way to break up the unholy alliance between the [less developed countries] and OPEC', and educate developing countries 'to understand, think, and operate in market economy terms'. Nevertheless, the Rambouillet summit committed the participants to closer co-operation with less developed countries to overcome high unemployment, inflation and energy problems. Multilateral negotiations should restore growth in world trade; reform the international monetary system to create economic and financial stability; stabilize the export earnings of developed countries; and assist in financing their deficits. The Rambouillet Declaration stressed that '[a] co-operative relationship and improved understanding between the developing nations and the industrial world is fundamental to the prosperity of each.'[28]

To the NIEO, a shift in the distribution of wealth would create prosperity for the Global North and South. To the United States, redistribution would threaten an interdependent global economy; the answer was to consolidate the Global North. At the summit in Puerto Rico in 1976, President Ford welcomed the discussions, which created 'interdependence among the industrial powers' and confirmed the United States' leadership in a new international system of informal talks. Kissinger was delighted. As he remarked in 1976,

> the solidarity of the Western democracies is the best guarantee of peace. The industrial democracies have 60 per cent of the world GNP . . . Not since the early 50s has there been such a spirit of cooperation among the allies. All this talk about the Soviet bloc being on the offensive and the democracies on the decline just isn't true. These leaders are dynamic and the West under this sort of coordinated action can handle all the problems before us easily.

His ambition was to unite the western industrial nations in the G7 and to end conflict between the Global North and South over finite resources by reconciling their needs in a growing world economy.[29]

Of course, less developed countries suspected self-interest on the part of the developed world. The fourth session of UNCTAD was scheduled to meet in Nairobi in May 1976 and it was likely to be confrontational and to strengthen the alliance between less developed countries and OPEC. The preparatory meeting of the G77 countries in Manila in

January–February 1976 dropped the integrated programme for commodities in favour of individual agreements on specific commodities. President Marcos announced that the Philippines would contribute $50m to a common fund to support this modified scheme; other countries, and particularly the oil producers, did not follow. When UNCTAD met, for the first time the Secretary of State attended. Kissinger recalled that 'I chose to speak on behalf of the United States in order to symbolize the political importance we attached to the need for new cooperative international arrangements.' His approach was, again, to offer pragmatic solutions and to separate moderate developing countries from the G77. He was prepared to consider buffer stocks on a commodity-by-commodity basis, and to review IMF lending to poorer countries in response to short-term price fluctuations and long-term declines in commodity earnings. Above all, he proposed an International Resources Bank with a capital of $1bn to provide funds for the development of resources on 'sound' principles through multilateral guarantees for investment based on equity, stabilization of commodity markets and earnings, and promotion of technological transfers. The plan failed because the Soviets saw 'an industrialized nation plot to continue the exploitation of the poor', and because African nations resented their exclusion from the negotiating group by the leadership of the G77.[30]

The Nairobi conference did agree to improve the terms of trade of developing countries, diversify their trade and production, improve their productivity, and increase export earnings. Commodity trade should be stabilized at prices that were 'remunerative and just to producers and equitable to consumers' and 'promote equilibrium between supply and demand within expanding world commodity trade'. The meeting agreed to a common fund to finance stockpiles, manage the supply of commodities, and to establish price ranges to stabilize export earnings around a rising trend. The UK's trade secretary pointed out that 'the developing countries saw [the common fund] as a political symbol – an independent institution with financial power – and there was no hope at all that they could be disunited from their commitment to it'. It was only a symbol, however, for most commodity agreements had collapsed by the time the common fund was ratified in 1988. There were few commodities other than oil that could disrupt the global economy – and countries disagreed over the allocation of quotas between new and existing producers, such as established tea growers in Sri Lanka and new producers in Kenya. Only one new agreement was created – for rubber in 1979 – and a policy that went back to Henry Wallace's ever-normal granary and the World Food Board faded away.[31]

The North–South dialogue continued in the Conference on International Economic Cooperation between 1975 and 1977, a French initiative following from the Rambouillet summit that brought together twenty-seven developed and developing countries to discuss energy, commodities, development and finance. It agreed to increase aid, but it had little impact. The discussions concluded with an 'uncommonly bland' report that reflected a lack of agreement. The United States was not impressed by 'the ever-escalating series of demands made by the [less developed country] group. These are varied but usually boil down to a one-sided demand for transfer of wealth and resources from richer to poorer countries.' The United States complained that an increasingly radicalized Third World was demanding a major change in the world economic order with 'broad-brush, politically-based' demands such as automatic triggers for debt moratoria and indexation of commodity prices, as well as guarantees that OPEC's investments would not be affected by devaluation. The Americans were unsympathetic. Automatic rescheduling of debt was not allowed by American law and would increase borrowing costs for prudent countries; and anyone investing overseas should calculate the exchange risk. The American administration hoped to secure the support of moderate developing countries whose greater realism would break the link between OPEC and less developed countries and create an alliance of oil importers. At the same time, the OPEC countries' huge dollar earnings led to their integration into the western financial system, as we will see in Chapter 21.[32]

The election of Jimmy Carter in November 1976 marked a potential change in the direction of American policy. During his presidential campaign, Carter proposed a 'world development budget' and a thorough review of American aid. The United States, it appeared to Carter's advisers, was 'the most hard-nosed of the industrial countries in resisting the demands of the developing countries for a "new international economic order"', and he might 'soften its rhetoric and explore the more moderate proposals sympathetically' by shared responsibility in a just world economy. Such a strategy would entail a shift from President Ford's linking of military aid with bilateral economic assistance in pursuit of foreign policy interests. Instead, multilateral aid should be used, and international institutions could 'insist on tough self-help conditions without being accused of US "imperialism"'. 'Putting US influence squarely behind multilateral aid, which is politically disinterested, would be convincing evidence that the US objective is to improve the welfare of poor countries, not to influence their politics. This would be effective foreign policy for North–South relations.'[33]

Thinking in the Carter administration favoured an open multilateral system and worried that 'stringent challenges by the poorer countries to the economic system's equity and legitimacy could undermine the world economy, global political stability and the potential to cope successfully with the new "global order".' It was not a rejection of Kissinger's approach so much as a shift in emphasis. Rather than breaking the bloc of developing countries by 'ostensibly positive proposals' whose 'insincerity was clearly perceived', the United States should 'negotiate seriously. When the [less developed countries] begin to realize we have an end-picture in mind, they will get into the details of a proposal and differing interests will divide countries.' At the Conference on International Economic Cooperation and General Assembly, different issues were combined; discussion of specific issues should move to the IMF and World Bank, which should be reformed to encourage the participation of those developing countries who were 'regional influentials'. The United States could then take the initiative from the G77 and provide 'leadership in moral and humane values' complemented by programmes to deal with specific problems. Above all, it meant self-sustaining growth and a search for equity and 'basic human needs' to 'increase the capabilities of the poor people of all countries to participate more fully in the social and economic lives of their nations. The purpose of reforming global institutions is to increase the participation of developing countries and thus the responsiveness of the institutions to their needs.' Such an approach complemented Kissinger's policy of 'divide and rule' with a more idealistic approach to the poor of the world.[34]

At UNCTAD's fifth meeting in Manila in 1979, the Americans were pleased that it was non-confrontational and that it dropped sweeping demands to restructure the world economy. Nevertheless, divisions remained between the pragmatic approach of Latin America and the more radical demands of Africa, as well as between oil producers and importers. The Americans hoped to proceed with programmes on energy, food, technology, trade and finance which would win support from developing countries for concrete economic and development policies.[35] Meanwhile, the North–South dialogue resumed. This initiative had its origins in the Club of Rome – a gathering of businesspeople, scientists, officials and politicians that was founded in 1968 by Aurelio Peccei, a leading Italian businessman, and Alexander King, the director of scientific affairs at the OECD. It defined a 'problematique' of interconnected issues on a global scale that could not be analysed in isolation – the environment, health, poverty and economics. In 1974, the club commissioned a report that was co-ordinated by the Dutch socialist economist Jan Tinbergen on reform of the international economic system. When the report appeared in 1976, it called for wider representation in international institutions and criticized the World Bank for its limited approach to the broad issues. The report looked beyond the Washington institutions to international aid on socialist lines. Robert McNamara, the president of the World Bank, responded by establishing an independent commission under the chairmanship of Willy Brandt to follow up the Conference on International Economic Coopera- tion. The commission drew together senior politicians and experts from across the world and the political spectrum – social democrats such as Brandt and Olof Palme, the former premier of Sweden, as well as Edward Heath from the centre-right and the free marketeer Peter Peterson. Brandt's rejection of interdependence in favour of support for the sovereignty of developing countries soon alarmed McNamara. Brandt was advocating global social democracy and making a moral case for wealthy nations to accept additional responsibilities to alleviate poverty in the poorer devel- oping countries – a policy that was self-interested given the dangers of war, poverty and famine. By the time the report, *North–South: A Programme for Survival*, appeared in 1980, the context had changed, and the North– South summit at Cancún in October 1981 marked the closing of the 'window of geopolitical opportunity'.[36]

DEVELOPMENT AND THE LIMITS TO GROWTH

Discussion of the NIEO and OPEC ran alongside a related concern that the pursuit of growth had reached its limits, with the prospect of environ- mental disaster and a Malthusian crisis. The result was debate about population growth and policies to limit the birth rate; attempts to pro- duce a wider definition of the quality of life than Gross Domestic Product; a reconsideration of narrow project loans by the World Bank; schemes to increase the food supply by a green revolution; and the revival of pro- grammes for food, nutrition and health that looked back to the 1930s. The idea that the carrying capacity of the world had been reached was countered by techno-optimists who felt that scientific progress could pro- duce a world of plenty; and worries in the Global North that the environment was degraded by growth was challenged by the Global South as hypocritical and neo-imperialistic.

At the World Bank, the challenge of the NIEO and Club of Rome led to a reconsideration of policy. Large-scale technological programmes to bring natural resources under control had failed to deliver the expected benefits. By the early 1960s, the Bank started to move from judging the success of projects by their direct return to a wider view based on cost–benefit analyses that took account of indirect benefits. This approach was laid out in the OECD's 'Manual of Industrial Project Analysis in Developing Countries' of 1968, and the United Nations Industrial Development Organization's 'Guidelines for Project Appraisal' of 1972. Albert Hirschman expressed doubts about the apparent precision of cost–benefit analysis and favoured a historical, qualitative approach with a stress on uncertainty. The difficulty with his approach, however, was that it did not provide an operational tool for the IBRD to decide where to invest. Cost–benefit analysis did at least allow the Bank to move beyond the narrow question of whether a loan could be repaid to a wider analysis of its impact. It allowed unsubstantiated claims about the transformative impact of large technical schemes to be scrutinized, and it might permit programmes that had previously been rejected. More generally, the Bank embarked on a critique of ideas of development.[37]

George Woods, an investment banker who was president of the World Bank from 1963 to 1968, saw that it was losing its role and influence. He turned to a wider concern for development and the reasons for under-development, looking to reduce disparities of wealth, action on the terms of trade and burden of debt, reform of agriculture, better provision of education and health, and an increase in financial assistance through the International Development Association, as well as encouraging private investment and reducing risk through the creation of the International Centre for Settlement of Investment Disputes in 1966. Woods saw that a new initiative was needed after the disappointment of the first Development Decade, and in October 1967 he announced a 'grand assize' to recommend the next steps. The challenge was taken up by his successor, Robert McNamara, who moved from his post as Secretary of Defense to become president of the Bank from 1968 to 1981. He appointed a Commission on International Development under the chairmanship of Lester Pearson, the former premier of Canada. In November 1969, the Pearson report gave legitimacy to a new approach by the World Bank and set an aid target of 0.7 per cent of GNP – an idea taken up in the second Development Decade. The Pearson report was only one of several initiatives at this time. In 1967, ECOSOC appointed a Committee on Development Planning under the chairmanship of Jan Tinbergen that reported in March 1970. The UN launched a study of the capacity of the UN Development System in July 1968 which reported in January 1970, and Raúl Prebisch's report for the Inter-American Development Bank appeared in April 1970. Alongside these international initiatives, President Nixon appointed a task force on development that reported in March 1970.[38] Development was being scrutinized around 1970, and this was reflected in a change in the World Bank's policy.

During McNamara's presidency, the World Bank moved from a concern with capital accumulation and large-scale projects which assumed that poverty reduction was a by-product of industrialization, a higher savings ratio and a reduction of the non-wage sector of the economy. Instead, poverty reduction became a primary concern. McNamara combined two approaches: integrated rural development and 'basic needs' of health, nutrition, shelter, water, sanitation and education. He was influenced by the experience of the Vietnam War where he was a 'hawk', but he was also an internationalist who believed that rich countries had a moral duty to help the poor, thus making them safer by removing rural poverty that provided a motivation for insurrection. During his time as Secretary of Defense, he pointed out that the 'wealthy and secure nations of the world . . . cannot possibly remain either wealthy or secure if they continue to close their eyes to the pestilence of poverty that covers the whole southern half of the globe'. He aimed to make the Bank more effective by changing its culture from 'leisurely perfectionism' and by hiring a new breed of economists such as Hollis Chenery of Harvard and Mahbub ul Haq, the chief economist of the Planning Commission of Pakistan, who became head of Policy, Planning and Program Review in 1970.[39]

In the late 1960s, approaches to development were changing. In 1968, Gunnar Myrdal's *Asian Drama: An Inquiry into the Poverty of Nations* argued for an institutional approach and a focus on agriculture. The first director of the Institute of Development Studies at the University of Sussex, from 1966 to 1972, was Dudley Seers, who collaborated with Chenery and recruited Hans Singer. To Seers, the 1960s were 'the decade of disillusion' in which development based on government investment programmes 'proved of limited use as guides to policy decisions'. He came to understand that 'what holds up development is not only, or even primarily, lack of capital but systems of education or land tenure, politicians unwilling or unable to change the social structure, administrative systems which are archaic or nepotic'. The Institute focused on the stagnation of the welfare of most of the population at a time of economic growth, and the need to reduce poverty, above all in rural areas. Its concern was population, land holding, nutrition, agrarian structure, resource allocation and administration, and its methodology was the close study of villages as the basic unit in which most people lived. Villages were highly diverse, according to whether they relied on rain or irrigation, grew wheat or rice, and experienced in- or out-migration. This was a more nuanced historical and sociological approach than the simplicities of modernization theory or grand technological schemes.[40]

In 1974, a joint report by the Institute and the World Bank, *Redistribution with Growth*, pointed out that 'the fact of poverty is not new ... What *is* new is the suspicion that economic growth by itself may not be able to solve or even alleviate the problem within any "reasonable" time period.' Chenery and his co-authors pointed out that an aggregate measure of GNP was misleading: an investment that benefitted the better-off 40 per cent of the population who held 75 per cent of the GNP in a typical developing country would produce a large overall gain; a policy that helped the bottom 40 per cent who typically held 12 per cent of GNP would have less impact. The solution was to weight income growth in proportion to incomes, so that an increase of $10 in a family income of $1,000 would be given equal value to an increase of $1 in a family income of $100. The report called for policies to stimulate employment and redistribute income.[41]

Here was the intellectual basis for McNamara's approach. Absolute poverty led to life 'so degraded by disease, illiteracy, malnutrition, and squalor as to deny its victims basic human necessities'. McNamara looked to expand exports by dismantling discriminatory tariffs against agriculture, and to increase development assistance, which had reached only half the target of 0.7 per cent of GDP. Although there was a self-interested motive in increasing trade and stability, McNamara emphasized the moral obligation of the rich and powerful to act from a sense of community to help the poor and weak. 'Are not we who tolerate such poverty, when it is within our power to reduce the number afflicted by it, failing to fulfil the fundamental obligations accepted by civilized men since the beginning of time?' He pointed to a glaring disparity between the United States' share of the world's population (6 per cent), its consumption of 35 per cent of the world's resources, and its lamentable record as fourteenth out of sixteen developed countries in the level of assistance provided to the developing world. He doubled the amount of aid provided by the Bank in his first five years as president and directed it towards improving living conditions. McNamara also worried that 'overly rapid population growth ... simply erodes and dissipates development gains in every sector: savings evaporate, scarcities multiply, resources are stretched so thin that in the end they cannot cover the most essential needs'. He thought that 'population planning must have high priority in most of the developing countries – even in those countries where the symptoms of overpopulation are not yet fully evident'. Although he welcomed the adoption of population planning policies in a number of countries, he realized that the impact would be slow. He created a Population Projects

Department to provide technical advice, and in 1972 the World Bank embarked on projects in two highly populated countries – India and Indonesia – to support their population planning programmes.[42]

Above all, the main focus of the Bank from 1970 was rural development aid. Most people lived in the countryside, and McNamara criticized policies that concentrated on investment in the cities and support of domestic industries that squeezed the income of farmers. The Bank aimed to help small subsistence farmers by providing better roads to reach markets, improved seeds, training, the creation of smallholder associations or co-operatives, stimulation of self-reliance, reform of land tenure, better access to credit, and provision of technical and public services. Such policies would reach the poor, absorb the Bank's funds and utilize the skills of its professional staff. McNamara's concern was the 'critical relationship of social equity to economic growth' and the 'need to design development strategies that would bring greater benefit to the poorest groups in the developing countries – particularly to the approximately 40% of their populations who are neither contributing significantly to economic growth nor sharing equitably in economic progress'. McNamara called for an ambitious programme to respond to the malnutrition that contributed to high infant mortality and impaired human capacities, and to remove underemployment – all of which required a focus on agricultural and rural development. His aim was to reverse the trend to inequality and to reduce the absolute poverty of those 'living at levels of deprivation that simply cannot be reconciled with any rational definition of human decency'. Absolute poverty was a denial of basic human needs that led to 'a condition of life so limited as to prevent realization of the potential of the genes with which one is born; a condition of life so degrading as to insult human dignity.'

McNamara turned from growth to distribution. In the long run, they were mutually supportive; in the short term, growth in modern sectors did not help subsistence farmers who needed policies for 'greater social equity'. The choice was 'between the political costs of reform and the political risks of rebellion'. Although the policy choice was a matter for individual countries, the World Bank could advise on better data on income distribution, targets for income growth in the bottom 40 per cent, policies to absorb surplus labour, institutional reform of land, tax and finance to redistribute economic power, shifts in public expenditure away from the privileged, and measures to ensure that credit and resources were available to the poor as well as the wealthy. McNamara's focus was on rural development, yet he also accepted the need for industrialization – not by import substitution but by export-led growth to escape from the limits of the domestic market, which entailed improved access for labour-intensive exports to the developed world.[43]

The shift is clear in the record of Bank lending. Rural development loans rose from 2.9 per cent in 1969 to 11 per cent in 1974; infrastructure projects fell from 55 per cent in 1967 to 30 per cent in 1977. A higher proportion of funds went to the poorest countries where GNP per capita was below $150: the share rose from 22.5 per cent in 1964–68 to 38.2 per cent in 1969–74. The effectiveness of the Bank's new priorities was much more difficult to measure than for loans which were meant to pay their way. Measuring GDP per capita did not capture all elements of 'basic needs', or the impact on the poorer 40 per cent of the population. In the 1960s and 1970s, the Bank therefore attempted to utilize a wider range of social indicators. International organizations collected data – the WHO on health, ILO on employment, UNESCO on education – which were difficult to combine into a single measure that could rival GDP or GNP. In the mid-1970s, an attempt was made to combine literacy rates, life expectancy and the infant death rate in a summative Physical Quality of Life Index. The results purported to show that some countries with low growth, such as Cuba, had a higher Index measure than others with higher growth, such as Brazil. It was open to criticism: why these three measures and why were they given equal weight? An alternative, and simpler, measure was adopted in the Bank's report, *The Assault on World Poverty*, of 1975, which advocated rural development to reduce poverty, improve nutrition, health and education and at the same time improve productivity. The report set a monetary level for absolute poverty at $50, with relative poverty defined as an income above $50 but less than a third of the national average. Progress could be measured by a shift in the proportion of the population below these two thresholds. Monetizing poverty still defined the problem in terms of increasing GDP, but the idea of an absolute global standard and a concern for the needs of the very poorest in society were significant changes at the Bank.[44]

Alongside these debates over development and growth, there was a concern for ecology and the environment, the Malthusian balance between population and available resources of food and energy, and the notion of sustainability. To some commentators, a Malthusian crisis was a real possibility. In the late 1950s, Binay Ranjan Sen at the UN's Food and Agriculture Organization was concerned that population growth would lead to famine. Although the influence of the Roman Catholic Church meant he could not actively promote birth control, he did convene conferences on population and rural development, and offered assistance to governments in developing countries if requested.[45] Above all, the balance between population and resources was a major concern of the Club of Rome from its formation in 1968. The Club was critical of short-term thinking in international affairs and turned to the consequences of the unlimited consumption of the world's resources resulting from rising population and economic growth. Its report, *The Limits to Growth* (1972), was funded by the Volkswagen Foundation and written by a group of systems scientists from MIT who produced computer simulations based on cybernetics (the science of control and feedback loops in large systems). The Club of Rome used this approach to understand the world economy as 'spaceship earth' with finite resources. It considered five variables – population, industrialization, pollution, food production and resource depletion – and their interrelationships in a feedback loop. Economic growth was no longer the solution, given its impact on the environment in a global ecosystem. The computer simulation produced several scenarios. If exponential economic and population growth continued, the result would be worldwide collapse within a century, for 'the behavior mode of the system . . . is clearly that of overshoot and collapse'. Technological change would not solve the problem, so the answer was a 'state of global equilibrium' by a deliberate reduction of population and capital with limits on individual freedom to have children and consume resources. By concentrating on activities that did not consume large amounts of resources – education, art, music – limits on growth could still lead to human improvement. 'Without such a goal and a commitment to it, short-term concerns will generate the exponential growth that drives the world system towards the limits of the earth and ultimate collapse.' If controls were adopted, the world's population and wealth would remain constant, and disaster could be averted.[46]

The Club of Rome report reflected, in the words of the historian Matthias Schmelzer, 'an ideological crisis of the growth paradigm' that went beyond social scientists and reflected the worries of student radicals, churches and environmentalists about the consequences of materialism and the exploitation of the natural environment and Third World. Rachel Carson's *Silent Spring* (1962) had pointed to the impact of pesticides on the environment and human health – claims that provoked the chemical industry to predict famine and disease if their use were restricted. In 1970, Alvin Toffler's best-selling *Future Shock* warned that rapid change was leading to 'shattering stress and disorientation' as a result of disposable goods and a general 'lack of permanence'. The Club of Rome had close links with the OECD through its science directorate and, above all, its head Alexander King. In many ways, the link was surprising, for the OECD had been a main advocate of growth since its formation. In 1961,

THE NEW INTERNATIONAL ECONOMIC ORDER

it set a growth target of 50 per cent by 1970, which was exceeded. Further growth of 65 to 70 per cent was expected in the 1970s. The definition of the problem now changed. Emiel van Lennep, the secretary general of OECD, wondered '[t]o what uses should this growth be put? If increased growth does not create improved conditions of life, will not growth become an illusion? What is the point of more unless more also means better?' GNP was, he thought, a 'conventional concept of limited scope'. In this spirit, the OECD launched an inquiry into 'the problems of modern society' and the need for alternative indicators, with the aim of finding the optimum level of growth consistent with social well-being. The shift in emphasis was captured in 1972 when the OECD's working group on 'the promotion of economic growth' changed its name to 'the problems concerning economic growth and the allocation of national resources'. It went on to point out that the major policy issue was how to use the wealth created by growth 'to meet social needs, to improve the quality of life, and to mitigate the unwanted, undesirable and potentially dangerous side effects of the growth process'.[47]

The Limits to Growth was hotly debated and widely read, with sales of about 12 million copies worldwide. It appealed to a technocratic belief in global planning, which led Edward Heath's government chief scientist to acclaim the report as 'the most important development of its kind since Keynes's General Theory'. It also appealed to ecologists and conservative cultural critics of growth. In the 1960s, biologist Julian Huxley worried that decolonization would undermine imperial protection of Africa's flora and fauna, and that economic development assumed that nature was a static entity that could be exploited. He called for environmental protection to preserve the natural world – and since national governments would not undertake the task, global organizations such as the World Wildlife Fund were needed. Developed countries called for international agreements; developing countries accused them of neo-imperialism and demanded financial compensation. Environmentalists and conservationists such as Friends of the Earth were sympathetic to the Club's report. By contrast, developing countries were critical, for limiting growth would harm the poor and block redistributive justice. The methodology of the report was also criticized for its 'computer fetishism' and heavy dependence on a few questionable assumptions. Wilfred Beckerman, a British economist who had worked at the OECD before resuming an academic career, thought it 'a brazen, impudent piece of nonsense' that ignored the ability of the price mechanism to remove bottlenecks in a market economy. Similarly, Henry Wallich rejected it as 'irresponsible nonsense' and worried that stopping growth would remove the ability of technology to deal with problems and so consign billions of people to poverty.[48]

In the late 1960s, the notion of 'sustainable development' emerged as a way of reconciling or integrating growth and environmental protection. Environmental non-governmental organizations pressed international agencies to shift from capital-intensive large-scale projects to small-scale 'appropriate' technologies; to include the environment and ecology in reviews of lending and development policy; and to encourage inter-national co-operation on the environment. To critics in the developing countries, the demands by NGOs and the involvement of developed countries threatened national sovereignty and growth – and they coun-tered with demands for a transfer of resources to cover the costs of environmental protection. The issues were debated at the UN Conference on the Human Environment in Stockholm in 1972. The preliminary report for the conference was mainly written by Mahbub ul Haq, who was a key influence in the World Bank's shift to poverty reduction. This report argued that the 'narrowly conceived objective of economic growth as measured by the rise in gross national product' should give way to 'attainment of social and cultural goals as part of the development pro-cess'. Environmental issues that troubled the rich nations should be linked with poverty reduction. Such thinking was encapsulated by Barbara Ward and René Dubos – an economist and a microbiologist respectively – in *Only One Earth: The Care and Maintenance of a Small Planet* that set the agenda for Stockholm. Their aim was to 'establish a conceptual frame of reference [to] consider fully environmental problems rooted in poverty as well as those rooted in industrialized societies' and to provide 'the concep-tual basis for synthesizing concerns for economic development with concerns for environmental quality which are so often and so mistakenly assumed to be in conflict'.[49]

This strategy was challenged by the oil shock and resulting stagflation that gave renewed emphasis to growth and energy security. The OECD retreated from its enthusiasm for environmentalism – or, more accurately, the economists defeated King and the scientific department in an internal struggle for influence. The search for a wider measure than GDP to cap-ture environmental and social costs was delegated to special working groups, which left the Economics Department to continue the older, nar-rower approach. Economists at the OECD continued to argue that high levels of growth would deliver welfare so that it should support 'the high-est possible growth of production as an end in itself'. In 1973, the OECD shifted its position to argue that 'maintaining or promoting an acceptable human environment must now be developed in the framework of policies for economic growth'. In 1975, it launched a new programme on 'Inter-futures' that denied physical limits to growth and claimed that the 'main objective must be to preserve the mechanisms of the market economy'. When its report appeared in 1979, even Jim MacNeill, the OECD's director of environment, accepted that 'slower growth, with a slower replacement of capital, can reduce the rate at which newer, less polluting processes find their way into the system'.[50]

The Club of Rome's subsequent report on *Reshaping the International Order* (1976) was more sympathetic to the agenda of the NIEO. Its co-ordinator, Jan Tinbergen, brought together experts from developing and developed countries and, unlike *The Limits to Growth*, stressed redistri-bution, development and improved welfare that would require continued growth within a reformed, democratized international order.[51] A similar line was taken by a report commissioned by President Carter in 1977 that aimed to predict the state of the world in 2000. Its computer models of the relationship between population, economic growth and resources reached the gloomy conclusion that

> if present trends continue, the world in 2000 will be more crowded, more polluted, less stable ecologically, and more vulnerable to disruption than the world we live in now. Serious stresses involving population, resources, and environment are clearly visible ahead. Despite greater material output, the world's people will be poorer in many ways than they are today.

The report claimed that the earth was close to its capacity to provide a decent life yet saw ground for optimism if national and international pol-icies were changed. The problem was less a lack of resources than a failure of co-ordination, and the United States should provide leadership to reduce poverty and hunger, stabilize the world's population, and increase economic and environmental productivity.[52]

How to redress the balance between population and resources had been debated over the previous couple of decades, with some commenta-tors aiming to reduce population growth and others looking to technical solutions to increase the amount of food and energy by the application of science and technology. In 1952, Warren Weaver of the Rockefeller Foun-dation believed that talk of a Malthusian crisis was exaggerated and could be overcome by research on plant genetics and, above all, by the unlimited supply of solar, tidal and nuclear energy. Although many of Weaver's ideas were utopian and impractical, yet agronomists and plant scientists developed new strains of rice at the International Rice Research Institute in the Philippines, and Norman Borlaug did the same with wheat at the International Maize and Wheat Improvement Center in Mexico. Both programmes were supported by the Rockefeller Foundation. Weaver hoped that raising the yields of crops would provide food and, at the same time, lead to a drop in the birth rate by breaking traditional habits and creating new incentives for smaller families.[53]

These efforts were hailed as a great success. In 1968, William Gaud of the United States Agency for International Development (USAID) announced the defeat of 'violent Red Revolution' by a 'green revolution' that could be 'as significant and as beneficial to mankind as the industrial revolution'. The results were impressive in terms of yield. India moved from food shortages in 1966–67 to self-sufficiency by 1974. The green revolution was expected to create abundance and lead to a cultural shift by creating incentives to be entrepreneurial and improving health, with consequent gains in productivity and incomes. When agricultural experts met in Oxford in 1969, their concern was no longer starvation but that surpluses might lead to falling prices and depression, as in the United States in the 1920s. An FAO official commented that '[w]e have been forced to redefine the population problem; now we worry more about idle arms than hungry mouths.'[54]

The green revolution also attracted criticism. Rising yields were a mixed blessing, for they could bring unemployment as surplus labour left the countryside and intensified urban problems. New crops and fertilizers meant an increase in inputs with the danger that small farmers would fall into debt, the benefits accruing to large farmers. The new crops could disrupt the social cohesion of villages and replace varied crops with high-yield strains that delivered low-quality carbohydrates with deficiencies in vitamins, minerals and amino acids. Environmentalists worried that pesticides and herbicides harmed biodiversity, with health risks for rural populations. Borlaug was scathing:

> Some of the environmental lobbyists of the Western nations are the salt of the earth, but many of them are elitists. They've never experienced the physical sensation of hunger. They do their lobbying from comfortable office suites in Washington or Brussels. If they lived just one month amid the misery of the developing world, as I have for fifty years, they'd be crying out for tractors and fertilizer and irrigation canals and be outraged that fashionable elitists back home were trying to deny them these things.

His sentiments were understandable, yet critics had a point that the green revolution bought time without offering a solution. The oil shock of 1973 drove up the cost of artificial fertilizers; yields could only increase up to a point; and, in some cases, crops encountered new diseases. In Sri Lanka, the green revolution failed and the government was defeated. In other cases, such as Indonesia and the Philippines, the green revolution survived because of government repression. As the development economist Amartya Sen pointed out, famine is rarely the result of absolute shortages so much as the political issue of entitlements, and technical fixes are never the entire answer to complex social questions.[55]

An attempt was made to incorporate the work of plant geneticists into a holistic view of the social and economic system of food that extended from crops, farming systems and rural development to nutrition, consumption and health, and integrated the work of scientists and medical experts with economists and planners. In a sense, it was a return to the ambitions of Boyd Orr and McDougall in the 1930s and 1940s. In 1971, the International Conference on Nutrition, National Development and Planning at MIT drew on the work of the FAO, USAID, WHO and the Rockefeller Foundation, and the next year it announced a comprehensive programme of Food and Nutrition Policy and Planning. The policy was implemented in Latin America and Asia by the World Bank, WHO and FAO, working in association with national governments. By the mid-1980s, however, most of these ambitious schemes had failed, as a result of a lack of capacity and over-reach.[56]

The other side of the equation was population growth, which some commentators thought would overwhelm the green revolution. Kingsley Davis, an American sociologist, had warned in 1952 that an increase of 1 per cent a year in the world's population 'will eventually take all of the planet's energy no matter what', so that action was needed on population.[57] As we saw in Chapter 12, there were concerns about overpopulation in the writings of Fairfield Osborn and William Vogt which returned in 1968 with Paul Ehrlich's *The Population Bomb: Population Control or Race to Oblivion*. He picked up on Davis's warnings. 'The battle to feed all of humanity is over. In the 1970s hundreds of millions of people will starve to death despite any crash programs embarked upon now. At this late date nothing can prevent a substantial increase in the world death rate.' He saw the choice as being between population control and oblivion. These warnings informed both the Club of Rome's *Limits to Growth* and Garrett Hardin's 'tragedy of the commons'. Hardin was an evolutionary biologist and ecologist who saw that individual self-interest in exploiting a common good could lead to over-stocking of common pasture, to polluting rivers and the air, and to population rising above a natural 'set point' which would produce famine and fighting. He turned to cybernetics. In some cases, systems were self-regulating; in others, over-use of the commons could be resolved by private ownership or by the imposition of laws and regulations. As far as population was concerned, Hardin argued that individuals should stop breeding to prevent an over-exploitation of global resources. He appealed to evolutionary theory and eugenics. Individual conscience was not enough, for couples with a sense of responsibility already had fewer children, and the welfare state meant imprudent people survived so that future generations would be less responsible. His chilling solution was mutual coercion, for '[t]he only way we can preserve and nurture other and more precious freedoms is by relinquishing the freedom to breed, and that very soon.'[58]

There were different reactions to this concern for population. In 1968, the same year as Hardin's intervention, the WHO included birth control in its primary health programme, without his turn to coercion (while Pope Paul VI issued a declaration against birth control). The governments of India and China, in particular, acted on the warnings of population growth. In India, voluntary sterilization, usually of men, was adopted from the early 1950s to reduce population growth. In Madras and Kerala, men who already had three children and were unable to support more could have a free vasectomy and a cash payment – an approach that was taken further in the late 1960s, and particularly in the 'emergency period' of 1975–77 when it came close to compulsion.[59] In Communist China, population growth had initially been considered beneficial and the population rose from about 540 million in 1949 to 940 million in 1976. By the end of the 1970s, population growth was reconceptualized as causing economic backwardness and environmental disaster. *The Limits to Growth* inspired a group of Chinese scientists with expertise in mathematics and control theory to argue that an optimal population of 700 million could be attained by a 'one child' policy that was adopted in 1979. Expertise in demography had virtually ended under Mao, and social scientists had been marginalized. The one-child policy was devised by a privileged group of scientists based in the defence sector with access to computers and data, with little understanding of the longer-term social consequences for family life and care of the elderly. The policy became a central element in the programme of socialistic modernization and was enforced by financial penalties, by fitting women with intrauterine devices after the birth of the first child, and by sterilization after the birth of a second child.[60]

The late 1960s and early 1970s marked a turning point in the economic government of the world. The 'embedded liberalism' of Bretton Woods faced a crisis as pegged rates gave way to floating and controls on capital movements were criticized by the advocates of financial liberalization. Economic growth in the advanced industrial countries slowed down after the rapid recovery of the 1950s and 1960s; inflation started to rise; and the social contract between capital and labour broke down. Meanwhile, the developing or primary producing economies challenged the post-war order. In the early 1980s, a new economic order did emerge in place of embedded liberalism – one epitomized by Margaret Thatcher and Ronald Reagan and based on neo-liberalism and the Washington consensus. Inflation was contained by tighter monetary policies and deflation associated with Paul Volcker, the chairman of the Federal Reserve from 1979 to 1987. The NIEO became, in Gilman's words, 'the figment of a now all but lost political imaginary'. Oil prices dropped from their peak and OPEC's petrodollars were recycled by the City of London and Wall Street, above all to Latin America. The financialization of the world economy, and the emergence of integrated supply chains, led to 'hyper-globalization', a shift in the policy of international institutions, and a changed relationship between national and international economics.

President Ronald Reagan gives a televised Address to the Nation from
the Oval Office on tax reduction legislation, 27 July 1981.

20

'Expansion of economic freedom'

The Rise of Market Liberalism

'... we should vigorously pursue the idea of suggesting a policy of a truly new international economic order – one based on the expansion of economic freedom, rather than a further diffusion of outmoded socialist economics. In other words, let's export the "Reagan economics revolution" abroad.'

Martin Anderson, Cancún summit, 11 August 1981[1]

The Great Depression of the 1930s marked a crisis of capitalism. It was resolved by the impact of the Second World War, the creation of a new institutional structure for the world economy, and growth in the major developed economies from the late 1940s to early 1970s. By the time of the oil shock, growth in OECD economies was higher than it had been before the Second World War. In the United Kingdom and United States, growth in GDP per man year between 1951 and 1973 was, respectively, 2.4 and 2.3 per cent, compared with 1.0 and 1.4 per cent between 1924 and 1937. In other countries, growth was even higher in the post-war Golden Age. In France, growth in GDP per man year rose from 1.4 per cent in 1924–37 to 4.4 per cent in 1951–73; in Germany from 3.0 to 4.8 per cent; and in Japan from −1.3 to 7.9 per cent.[2] In all countries, faster growth arose from high levels of capital investment encouraged by low interest rates and wage moderation, by the application of improved technology and work practices, recovery from wartime disruption, the restoration of multilateral trade and high levels of domestic demand that rested on a commitment to full employment. In western Europe (other than Britain) and Japan, the still higher growth rates arose from structural changes, with a shift of labour from low productivity agriculture into industry. In 1950, 24.3 per cent of the workforce of West Germany was still employed in agriculture, compared with 5.1 per cent in the UK and 11.0 per cent in the United States. By 1990, agricultural employment in

West Germany had fallen to 3.4 per cent, when the level in the UK was down to 2.0 per cent and in the US 2.5 per cent. European integration and lower trade barriers provided a further boost to economic growth that entailed convergence with Britain's higher levels of per capita GDP and productivity. In 1950, labour productivity in West Germany was only 74.4 per cent of the level in the UK; by 1973, it was 114 per cent.[3]

After the Second World War, a new social bargain was struck in OECD countries between labour, capital and the state. Although it took different forms, in general the 'politics of productivity' – to use Charles Maier's term – replaced conflicts over wealth distribution in a common commitment to growth and fairer distribution of the proceeds of increased production. It rested on workers limiting themselves to moderate wage demands, complemented by higher levels of social spending on welfare. Capital was able to secure decent profits that could be ploughed back into investment, so raising productivity. The result was a combination of steady employment, increasing though not excessive rises in wages, and low levels of inflation. Workers were trading lower current consumption for higher living standards in the future, based on the belief that industrialists would reinvest profits and that the state would provide better schools, health care and social support. Governments underwrote the deal by tax breaks on condition that firms made investments, by schemes for industrial support, and by welfare provision. The result, as Barry Eichengreen points out, was a 'web of interlocking agreements' that increased the cost of breaking the post-war settlement. Underlying this social bargain was Fordist mass production that offered steady and secure employment at a decent wage to workers who often lacked formal qualifications and acquired skills through their employment in engineering workshops, car plants or steel mills (see Chapter 25).[4]

By the early 1970s, however, confidence that economic growth would continue gave way to concern that capitalism was facing a crisis of stagflation – slower growth and rising inflation – that challenged the post-war settlement. The web of interlocking agreements started to unravel in a process that led to serious tensions. In western Europe – including the UK – GDP growth fell from an average of 4.8 per cent a year between 1950 and 1973, to 2.1 per cent between 1973 and 1994.[5] The rapid transfer of labour from agriculture meant that gains from structural change were exhausted. Clearly, the oil shock of 1973 caused serious problems, for cheap energy had been a major source of growth in the OECD countries in the post-war period. Higher oil prices now led to increased costs of production and hit non-energy consumption by private households. But it was not the only cause of the fall in growth rates, for the social contract and economic structures that underpinned post-war performance had already started to change before 1973.

From the late 1960s, low levels of unemployment allowed workers to demand higher wages that exceeded gains in productivity. Labour unrest and militancy started to appear, most obviously with the combination of student protests and workers' demands in France in 1968. The experience of France – and the radical anti-war and civil rights protests in the United States – indicated a shift in social attitudes that went beyond purely economic demands. Members of the immediate post-war baby-boom generation were moving into adulthood and rejecting their parents' self-restraint during the war and post-war recovery, and in many cases were questioning their wartime actions (and post-war forgetting). Greater affluence was complemented by a desire for self-expression and individuality in matters of sexuality and cultural identity, with demands for the legalization of homosexuality and abortion, for action on race and environmentalism. The personal became political in a way that cut across left and right. The criticism of bureaucratic welfarism came not only from the right but also from social activists who argued for a localized welfare system, who rejected grand urban schemes and criticized corporatist solutions to labour relations.[6] This cultural shift went beyond student radicals and built support for Thatcher and Reagan, despite their social conservatism. From the later 1960s, there was a general growth of what one historian of Thatcherism terms 'popular individualism'. The rise of consumerism, home ownership and the spread of secondary and higher education led to a decline in social deference and to blurred class identities. De-industrialization and the decline in Fordist mass production also helped to weaken workplace identities, leading both to resistance to competition from foreign competitors and to the remaking of workers as consumers. These cultural shifts played into youth culture and feminism, into protests against war and environmental degradation, and into the right to choose in the marketplace. Arthur Seldon, the editorial director of the right-wing Institute of Economic Affairs, pointed out in 1966 that people who had freedom to choose their clothes and furniture, and were 'treated like lords and ladies . . . on the plane to their fortnight in Spain', were less likely to 'tolerate much longer being treated as servile, cap-in-hand supplicants in the local state school, the doctor's surgery, the hospital'.[7]

By the turn of the decade, workers in most countries in the OECD were demanding a greater share in their states' prosperity, and their demands became particularly urgent when trade unions came to realize that inflation would continue. The end of the Bretton Woods regime removed external discipline over wage demands, for competitiveness could now be maintained by allowing the exchange rate to drop when costs and inflation rose ahead of other countries. By around 1970, fewer opportunities for continued productivity growth by the application of new technology, and demands for higher wages, meant that profits were being squeezed. In Britain, the economists Andrew Glyn and Bob Sutcliffe found the rate of profit on net assets in industrial and commercial companies had already fallen from 13.7 per cent before tax in 1964 to 9.7 per cent in 1970; after tax, the fall was from 7.1 per cent to 4.1 per cent.[8] The data in Figure 9 show that the profit squeeze continued in other countries in the 1970s and contributed to the breakdown in the social contract between labour, capital and the state. Lower profits led to a decline in investment, which in turn exacerbated the drop in productivity. Attempts to limit inflationary pressure by wage and price controls soon failed – and uncertainty about exchange rates led to speculative flows of capital. One possible response was to turn to protectionism and capital controls, as advocated by some in Britain in 1976 and in the United States in 1979–80. This approach was rejected and instead inflation was removed from the economy through tighter monetary policy and higher unemployment, allied to a pursuit of deeper globalization.[9]

This economic crisis led to a search for new policies both for the economic government of the world and domestic management. On the left as much as the right, there was a need to fill a policy vacuum in response to the onset of stagflation. John Hicks – an economist closely associated with Keynes – pointed out in April 1973 that the *General Theory* was devised

Figure 9: Gross rates of return for all business and manufacturing for selected OECD countries, %

		1960	1973	1982
United States	all business	16.2	14.5	10.9
	manufacturing	18.9	18.5	10.6
United Kingdom	all business	13.3	11.0	10.1
	manufacturing	16.4	9.5	5.5
Germany	all business	24.3	17.2	14.5
	manufacturing	26.2	16.5	11.7
Japan	all business	– no data	– no data	– no data
	manufacturing	33.3	32.4	20.7

Source: James H. Chan-Lee and Helen Sutch, 'Profits and rates of return in OECD countries', OECD Economics Department Working Papers 20 (May 1985) 22.

deal with deflation and offered no solution to the problems of rising
lation. Hicks hoped for a 'reformulated Keynes' that would be closer to
n than to 'cruder forms of neo-classical doctrine'.[10] Others were not so
re. Ideas for an alternative approach had been evolving in a network of
ink tanks and pressure groups, and now had their chance. In the words
Daniel Stedman Jones, 'just as in 1932 or 1945, the 1970s were a rare
oment when the pieces of the political and economic jigsaw were strewn
l over the place, in need of painstaking rearrangement'. The result was
ot the adoption of a single, coherent neo-liberal position. As we have
een, Hayek and his colleagues at Geneva in the 1930s rejected the use of
tatistics and remained wary of the state's use of macroeconomic policy
and monetarism, given the unknowable nature of the market. Hayek
explained to Arthur Seldon in 1985 that he regarded 'the abandonment of
the whole macroeconomics nonsense as very important' – and expressed
regret that he had not followed his criticism of Keynes with an attack on
Milton Friedman, for they were both macroeconomists. Hayek's preference was to contain state power within global economic institutions that
would prevent nationalists from threatening private property and disrupting market exchange. By contrast, Friedman used statistical analysis of
the money supply and unemployment to manage the economy. In other
respects, Friedman and the Chicago School retreated from management of
the economy. Once barriers to entry by new firms had been removed by
deregulation, there would be no need for anti-trust measures. Monopolies
were less harmful than the attempts of state bureaucracies to break them
up; if monopolies were inefficient, the market would correct. This belief
that monopolies did not threaten democracy was not shared by ordo-
liberals. Wilhelm Röpke stressed the crucial role of the state in preventing
monopoly power that could be so powerful that it blocked the emergence
of competitors. Neo-liberalism therefore had different strands – so much
so that some historians and political scientists warn against using the term
as unhelpful and imprecise.[11]

Certainly, we need to avoid giving too much explanatory power to the
independent role of ideas. These different strands of thought were drawn
on by politicians to justify policies that were adopted for pragmatic or
electoral reasons. As Leader of the Opposition, Mrs Thatcher is reputed
to have brought Hayek's *Constitution of Liberty* to a meeting and
announced: 'This is what we believe.' If she did say it, her claim was only
partially true, for she derived her belief in rules from her legal training,
and she was shaped by her desire for moral rejuvenation and self-reliance
even more than by economics. Above all, she was a politician concerned
with what was feasible and electorally desirable.[12]

Many of the changes in policy arose from non-ideological cause such as the emergence of popular individualism, de-industrialization the demise of the Bretton Woods regime, or the need to recycle petro-dollars after the oil shock. Nevertheless, the concept of neo-liberalism is useful. Neo-liberals had internal differences but also common enemies: the power of trade unions and state bureaucracies; planned economies, especially in the Soviet bloc but also at home; and post-colonial demands for redistributive justice in the world economy. Above all, they looked – in different ways – to the liberation of markets. If we were to use a different term, the best alternative would be 'market liberalism' – the idea that human relations are based on buying and selling, and that individual self-interest maximizes collective welfare. The award of the Nobel Prize in economics to Hayek in 1974 and to Friedman in 1976 indicated that attitudes were shifting. The driving force was largely changes in economic structures and conditions, in popular attitudes, and in political and electoral calculations – but the theoretical writing of economists offered intellectual credibility and authority. Above all, economists now dominated the discourse in a way that they had not done so previously. Notions derived from public choice and game theory such as the prisoner's dilemma and free rider problem moved from economics departments into law and social sciences, and out into the wider public arena. Friedman's address to the American Economic Association on 'the role of monetary policy' gave priority to monetary stability over reducing the rate of unemployment and provided politicians with a new language to justify their actions. Politically, the adoption of monetarism was useful, for it allowed politicians to escape from negotiating wages with trade unions. Social and economic changes were interpreted through a particular set of assumptions that created a narrative to hold together coalitions of support. Economic interests and understandings of social change do not exist apart from the rhetoric by which they are defined, so that ideas were crucial in how the crisis of stagflation and its possible solutions were defined. Above all, there was a belief that markets were more efficient and effective than planning, that private property rights were more appropriate than collective ownership, that growth and incentives were more important than questions of distribution and economic security, that the power of capital and finance were superior to labour, and that the pursuit of cosmopolitan capitalism had priority over national capitalism.

In the late 1970s, both in the United States and Britain, steps were taken to break the cycle of stagflation and to create a new economic order at home and in global government.

THE VOLCKER SHOCK AND
THE RISE OF MONETARISM

In 1978, Robert Triffin characterized the international monetary system as an international monetary scandal. Floating removed the need to defend a fixed exchange rate, weakened resistance to inflationary policies and led to a rapid increase in liquidity in the world economy. Rather than creating stable exchange rates as Friedman had assumed, Triffin saw that floating 'tended ... to amplify anticipatory capital movements: *overcorrecting* exchange rates well beyond what would be needed' (see Figure 7, page 518).[13]

One response was for central banks to use monetary targets to replace the discipline of fixed exchanges. The Federal Reserve experimented with this as early as 1970, and the Bank of England adopted (unpublished) broad money supply targets in 1972. The task was technically difficult, and targets were often missed, but central banks hoped they at least provided some guidance. The greatest success was in West Germany where the politically independent Bundesbank was committed to stability by using monetary targeting to establish expectations for inflation. Many Germans had lost their savings in the hyperinflation of the 1920s and again in the currency reform of 1948. Stability became politically and culturally entrenched, with the Bundesbank constructing a historical narrative/myth that it had taken a responsible position against Hitler before the war. The Bundesbank Act of 1957 imposed an obligation to defend the currency, and in 1974 the Bundesbank adopted a formal quantitative monetary target to control inflation and guide the expectations of those setting wages and prices. The Bundesbank did not promise to hit the monetary target precisely, but the exercise disciplined policymakers and forced them to explain their actions. Such 'pragmatic monetarism' was more difficult in Britain and the United States where deflation was politically unacceptable. The Bundesbank's reputation for sound money meant that it was trusted to adjust – or miss – targets when needed for technical reasons; in Britain and the United States, targets lacked credibility and pragmatic adjustment was not feasible. Consequently, monetary policy was less effective in controlling inflation and maintaining the exchange rate.[14]

In the United States, monetary policy was loose under presidents Ford and Carter. At the Federal Reserve, Arthur Burns was aware of the problem but his attempt to tighten monetary policy in 1975 faced opposition in Congress. The House and Senate, and from January 1977 the presidency, were controlled by Democrats who had a greater commitment to employment than to containing inflation. The Federal Reserve Act of 1977 made the Fed more accountable to Congress by introducing a dual mandate 'to promote effectively the goals of maximum employment, stable prices, and moderate long-term interest rates'. Some Democrats wished to go further by adding the right to a job, and a veto on the pursuit of price stability over full employment. The Full Employment and Balanced Growth Act of 1978 amended the Full Employment Act of 1946 by requiring that unemployment should not exceed 3 per cent for those aged over twenty, and that inflation should be 3 per cent or less provided that cutting the rate did not impact on the employment target. Although Republicans and conservative Democrats urged prioritizing inflation, supporters of full employment were in the ascendant in Congress.[15]

Not surprisingly, Burns talked of the 'anguish of central banking' – a recognition of the dangers of inflation and the inability to act decisively.[16] He had to tread warily in balancing inflation, employment and growth, and negotiating the Federal Reserve's relationship with the executive and Congress. Nixon had tried to browbeat both William McChesney Martin and Burns into changing monetary policy for political reasons, and the issue returned in November 1977 when Senator Hubert Humphrey (D: Minnesota) – a leading promoter of the Full Employment and Balanced Growth Act – urged President Carter not to reappoint Burns. 'If the Federal Reserve tightens up on credit and raises interest rates whenever purchasing power expands, it can frustrate any attempt by the President and Congress to stimulate economic growth and reduce unemployment.'[17] The Fed's independence was constrained and Burns realized that pursuing a tight monetary policy 'would be frustrating the will of Congress to which it is responsible – a Congress that was intent on providing additional services to the electorate and on assuring that jobs and incomes were maintained, particularly in the short run'. More generally, the political and cultural environment meant that '[f]ear of immediate unemployment – rather than fear of current or eventual inflation – . . . came to dominate economic policymaking.' Burns lacked political support to act and was resigned to the fact that the Federal Reserve was fighting a losing battle against increased government spending and generous wage settlements.[18]

In May 1975, Paul Volcker became president of the Federal Reserve Bank of New York. He had anticipated that floating would lead to serious problems of inflation, volatile exchange rates, and higher interest rates, and he now felt that Burns was admitting that the Fed was impotent. Volcker had explained in 1969 that '[p]rice stability belongs in the social contract. We give government the right to print money because we trust our elected officials not to abuse that right, not to debase the currency by inflating.' Accordingly, as a member of the Federal Open Market Committee (FOMC), he urged a firmer line. By 1979, Carter's economic policy was failing. He had adopted the 'locomotive strategy' proposed by the OECD in 1976 – that the United States, Germany and Japan should adopt fiscal and monetary expansion to pull the world out of recession in the expectation that it would utilize spare capacity without provoking inflation. It did not work. The United States experienced inflation, mounting deficits and lower growth; Germany and Japan had lower inflation, faster recoveries and surpluses, and were reluctant to abandon their tighter policies to boost the world economy. Gottfried Harbeler warned that encouraging faster growth in countries with surpluses was 'tantamount to an attempt to eliminate the inflation differential by inflating the low-inflation countries rather than disinflating the high-inflation countries'. Carter's attempt to control inflation by budget restraints and voluntary controls over prices and wages lost credibility, leading to the impression that 'our policy is one of drift and mere appeals for altruistic individual behavior'.[19] In March 1979, Volcker remarked that 'we are at a critical point in the inflation program, with the tide against us. If we don't show any response at all, we are giving an unfortunate signal.' The failure to control inflation was, he warned, 'likely to give us the most problems and create the biggest recession'. In July 1979, President Carter nominated Volcker as chairman of the Federal Reserve who argued at his Senate confirmation hearings that inflation must be controlled through monetary restraint. The new chairman soon embarked on a major policy shift: tight domestic money and high interest rates to stabilize the dollar and squeeze inflation out of the American economy, at the cost of a severe recession and high unemployment.[20]

The new approach came into effect on 6 October 1979 when the FOMC accepted higher short-term interest rates to provide 'assurance that the money supply and bank credit expansion would be kept under firm control'. The *New York Times* saw the decision as Volcker's Verdun:

> By forcing interest rates to shoot up like a signal flare, Mr Volcker, like France's Marshal Petain at Verdun, seeks to assure his own forces that the enemy 'shall not pass'. Marshal Petain did hold the fort – at the cost of 350,000 casualties. No lives are directly at stake in slamming the gate on credit but the risks are nonetheless substantial.

Volcker was unrepentant. He explained to the Joint Economic Committee of the House and Senate that he wished to break inflationary expectations:

> An entire generation of young adults has grown up since the mid-1960s knowing only inflation ... it is hardly surprising that many citizens have begun to wonder whether it is realistic to anticipate a return to general price stability, and have begun to change their behavior accordingly. Inflation feeds in part on itself. So part of the job of returning to a more stable and more productive economy must be to break the grip of inflationary expectations.

His aim was to end 'the uncertainties and distortions inherent in inflation' and 'to restore a solid base for sustained growth and stability ... Above all, the new measures should make abundantly clear our unwillingness to finance a continuing inflationary process.' In his view, fear of recession must not lead to an economic stimulus that would reinforce inflationary expectations. In the past, efforts to control inflation had been 'prematurely truncated' so that 'markets had developed a high degree of cynicism' about the Federal Reserve's willingness to stand firm. Volcker argued 'that may be all fine and prudent when the prices and expectations are relatively stable. But in the midst of accelerating inflation, what the Fed might think of as prudent probing looked to the rest of the world like ineffectual baby steps.' Volcker took a giant step to show that the Fed meant business in bringing inflation under control that 'would have a chance of affecting ordinary people's behavior'.[21]

Unsurprisingly, Volcker's policy encountered hostility. Ray Moore, a Democratic state senator from Washington, complained to the president that high interest rates were not the solution, and that '[t]he sooner you realize that having Mr Volcker as Chairman of the Federal Reserve Board is like having Dracula in charge of your local blood bank, the better off we all will be!'[22] Carter shared concern about Volcker's strategy. He accepted that the Fed was independent but

> that doesn't mean I have to sit mute. My own judgment is that the strictly monetary approach to the Fed's decision on the discount rate and other banking policies is ill-advised ... [T]he Fed ought to look at the adverse consequences of increased interest rates on the general economy as a major factor in making their own judgments ... [T]hey put too much of their eggs in the money supply basket and are not adequately assessing the other factors.[23]

Members of the administration worried that 'the Fed has made us all prisoners of its own rhetoric' and that short-term fluctuations in monetary indicators were taking precedence over the real economy. Volcker responded by proposing a 'social compact' of tax cuts in return for wage moderation and some relaxation of monetary policy, on condition that expenditure was brought under control.[24]

Unlike Martin and Burns, Volcker was able to persist with his tight monetary policy. The political situation had changed. In November 1980, the Democrats lost control of the Senate and of the presidency with the election of Ronald Reagan. Inflation was hitting creditors, savers and anyone on a fixed income, and it now took priority. The change was captured by Roger Guffey of the Federal Reserve Bank of Kansas City at the FOMC in July 1981:

> Historically, the Federal Reserve has always come up to the hitching post and then backed off simply because the Administration and the Congress have thrown bricks at us or have not been supportive of a policy of restraint . . . I think we have an opportunity this time to carry forward what we should have done before because for the first time ever we do have . . . the support of the Administration at least.

George Shultz later reflected that 'to do something difficult, even if you are the independent Federal Reserve, it makes a huge difference if the president is on your side and is strong and understands the problem, and when things get tough he doesn't go the other way and denounce you.'[25] Reagan was on the side of the Fed, which could persist with the 'Volcker shock'. Inflation fell from 13.5 per cent in 1981 to 3.2 per cent in 1983, at the cost of a deep recession and high unemployment (see Figure 10).

The difficult economic conditions of the 1970s allowed Reagan to sell the idea of the market as a solution to the perceived failure of the post-war order. The oil shock contributed to a sense that the government could

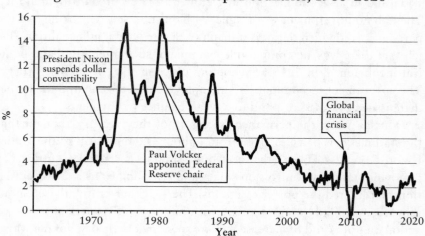

Figure 10: Inflation in developed countries, 1960–2020

Source: OECD.Stat.

not resolve problems. Project Interdependence had failed to achieve self-sufficiency either by increased production or by conservation and federally funded alternatives. Democrats were divided between New Deal liberals, who wanted fairer access to affordable energy, and environmentalists who wished to reduce consumption. By contrast, conservatives argued that there would not be a crisis if the market were allowed to function – indeed, Reagan claimed that the Federal government created the crisis.[26] He presented a more optimistic future to a weary electorate. The new ideas offered an approach in which growth and prosperity were possible through 'populist market optimism' expressed in the major tax cuts of 1981. These ideas were popularized in two best-selling books in the United States. Jude Wanniski's *The Way the World Works: How Economies Fail – and Succeed* (1978) propounded a supply-side approach, arguing that taxation interrupted trade between producer and consumer; if it could be reduced, the economy would flourish. The Democrats had offered spending to help the poor. Rather than opposing spending, the Republicans promised tax cuts which would (so they claimed) recreate full employment, reduce public spending and shrink the public sector. The second book was George Gilder's *Wealth and Poverty* (1981), which presented an optimistic account of economic growth once the entrepreneur had been released from the fetters of taxation. Reagan made sure that the members of his Cabinet were given copies.[27]

A similar situation arose in Britain where serious economic problems, strikes and the three-day week led Edward Heath to call a general election on the issue of who controlled Britain – to which the answer was 'not the Conservatives'. A minority Labour government took office in March 1974 and in a second election in October 1974 secured a tiny majority. The Labour government was fragile, with one minister remarking that the party was 'so divided that it is difficult even to regard it as a coalition'. He felt that there was 'no comparable example of such intellectual and political incoherence' in any party holding office in the twentieth century.[28] The government faced inflation, unemployment, recession and the immediate issue of how to respond to a weak balance of payments.

Douglas Wass, the permanent secretary of the Treasury, thought that the sterling crisis of 1976 arose from Labour's commitment to the Trades Union Congress (TUC) that it would support a 'Social Contract' by removing statutory controls on wages and repealing Conservative legislation that limited the power of unions. The TUC agreed to advise unions that wages should only rise in line with prices; the government promised action on prices and to increase welfare spending. In theory, linking wages to price increases would allow any gains in productivity to squeeze inflation out of the economy. In practice, wages continued to rise ahead of prices.[29] Joel Barnett, the chief secretary of the Treasury, remarked that the Social Contract rested on give and take between the government and unions: the government gave and the unions took.[30] Chancellor of the Exchequer Denis Healey was not in favour of the easy option of depreciating sterling to restore competitiveness but was defeated in Cabinet when he proposed the alternative of cutting public spending. When Harold Wilson unexpectedly resigned as Prime Minister in April 1976, his successor, James Callaghan, inherited a difficult situation.

Confusion over policy and demands for higher wages led to a loss of confidence in sterling and an outflow of capital. The managing director of the IMF, Johannes Witteveen, urged Healey to tighten monetary policy and reduce public spending. The Dutchman was not sympathetic to Labour, for he had been a politician in the People's Party for Freedom and Democracy in the Netherlands which combined social liberalism with support for free markets, private enterprise and a reduced role for government. The demand for the government to cut spending and restrain wages was politically sensitive. A special meeting of the TUC was to be held in June 1976 and it might reject the Social Contract and provoke inflationary wage demands. Healey had to steer between domestic politics and pressure from the IMF, which he might use as a threat to encourage wage restraint. He secured some breathing space by a 'swap' arrangement with the Federal Reserve and a 'safety net' from G20 central banks to allow speculative pressure to subside and, more controversially, to take action on inflation and government spending.[31]

The crisis continued to deepen. On 28 September 1976, Callaghan warned the Labour Party Conference that 'Britain has lived too long on borrowed time, borrowed money, borrowed ideas', and that it had postponed 'facing up to fundamental choices and fundamental changes in our society and in our economy':

> The cosy world which we were told would go on for ever, where full employment would be guaranteed by a stroke of the Chancellor's pen, cutting taxes, deficit spending, that cosy world is gone ... [Unemployment] is caused by paying ourselves more than the value of what we produce ... We used to think that you could spend your way out of a recession, and increase employment by cutting taxes and boosting Government spending. I tell you in all candour that that option no longer exists, and that in so far as it ever did exist, it only worked ... by injecting a bigger dose of inflation into the economy, followed by a higher level of unemployment as the next step.

Callaghan accepted the need for the Social Contract and for socialism, but also stressed that industry must make a profit if it were to invest and create wealth before it was distributed. He warned that domestic production was growing by 2 per cent a year, compared with public expenditure which was growing by 18 per cent. 'It is by a healthy and expanding manufacturing industry that we shall be able, in due course, to resume the growth and improvement of our social services and also create the jobs that are necessary if we are to reach ... our full employment targets.'[32] The next day, the chancellor reinforced the message when he informed conference that he would apply for a loan from the IMF and continue the pay policy and 'the very painful cuts in public expenditure'. Any increases in output should go to exports and investment rather than public spending or private consumption.[33]

The Cabinet was divided. As in the United States in 1979–80, two views of the economy were at stake: to retain or regain national policy autonomy by controlling international finance; or to adopt deflationary policies and maintain an open economy.[34] The left rejected Healey's deflationary policies as a sop to the IMF and argued for an Alternative Economic Strategy (AES) – an approach that had been adopted by the Labour Party Conference. It was particularly associated with Tony Benn, the Secretary of State for energy, who warned of the consequences of depreciation, tight fiscal and monetary policy, and cuts to public spending. In his view, depreciation would lead to high inflation; and austerity and higher interest rates would reduce industrial investment. So far, his economic logic was consistent with the Keynesian approach of members of the Cabinet who opposed cuts at a time of high unemployment and spare capacity for exports. Benn then took a line that the Keynesians could not accept: Britain's relative economic decline was linked with trade liberalization that left domestic markets open to foreign competition, and it could not compete as a result of old capital equipment, a high burden of debt, and the cost of rearmament. By contrast, Germany had rebuilt its industry with modern equipment after the war, and Japan had developed new industries behind protective barriers. Britain needed to increase its industrial capacity, modernize factories and raise the amount of capital per worker by turning from trade liberalization to protection. Industry could then invest without fear of deflation or the loss of domestic markets. In his view, protectionism meant a siege economy that brought the trade unions rather than international bankers within the citadel. The AES marked a fundamental rejection of multilateralism and the EEC in favour of economic autarchy – a policy of protectionism and capital controls rather than globalization and financialization.[35]

The choice between Benn's economic nationalism and Healey's deflation divided the Cabinet. As an adviser to Callaghan put it, the decision was 'between the suicidal extremism of the Treasury and the protectionist extremism of Mr Benn'.[36] Callaghan warned President Carter that, if carried too far, deflation would be 'catastrophic ... If we were to undertake further significant deflation, the economy would be on an unacceptable downward ratchet, with revenues down, unemployment up, and production hardly moving', with a danger of protectionism and a strain on social cohesion.[37] Callaghan was equally unsympathetic to the AES's vision of a siege economy.[38] Healey was in a difficult situation, for the Americans were critical of Labour's management of the economy. Treasury Secretary William Simon thought that the Labour government had lost control of the budget, money supply and inflation, and he doubted 'whether we are going to continue to be a party to this unsatisfactory approach'. Simon reflected that

> [i]f that same time and energy had been devoted to creating the political basis for the policies that ultimately must come, the outlook would be different ... In concrete terms this means supporting the IMF's efforts to negotiate a sound stabilization program which will combine foreign financial support with UK policy changes, and avoid any commitment of even larger amounts of money.[39]

Healey worried that the continued depreciation of sterling would allow foreigners to buy British assets on the cheap, and he foresaw 'continuous and probably accelerating depreciation, leading to South American-style inflation, with higher import prices feeding through to wages and vice versa'.[40] In this nightmare vision, IMF support was crucial to prevent an 'uncontrollable slide' in the value of sterling. Critics of the AES argued that the strategy was not feasible, for import controls were not permitted in the EEC and might lead to retaliation under GATT rules, leaving Britain economically protectionist and politically isolated. Rather than facing up to competition and creating a more dynamic economy, a siege economy would allow British industry to remain inefficient and uncompetitive. The Keynesians sided with Healey and Callaghan, and in December 1976 Britain secured a loan of $3.96bn from the IMF, the largest since its creation. The chancellor and prime minister followed the advice of the Fund, which was largely consistent with their own position.[41]

Callaghan's speech in 1976 is often seen as the end of Keynesianism and the emergence of monetarism to discipline the domestic economy. Nigel Lawson, a leading member of the Thatcher government, was doubtful, for he thought that Labour still followed a 'bastard form of Keynesianism'. He was largely right. Although Callaghan saw that existing policies were not working, he and Healey were still committed to redistributive taxation, public spending and ownership, and to working with the trade unions. Labour hoped that inflation could be contained by a successful incomes policy that would lead to a lower rate of monetary growth. The Social Contract continued until the strikes in the 'winter of discontent' of 1978/9. The decision of 1976 meant that the Labour government rejected the AES and controls on capital that would have turned back financial liberalization and globalization. Nevertheless, it did not positively encourage financial liberalization, and the left remained powerful in the party. Ideological conversion was not complete: in 1980, Denis Healey lost to a left-wing opponent in the contest to succeed Callaghan as party leader. The Conservative government of 1979 went beyond Callaghan in adopting a major shift of policy. The Conservative chancellor, Geoffrey Howe, abolished the remaining exchange controls in 1979, and in 1980 he adopted a 'medium-term financial strategy' to set firm limits to the money supply, and reduced the public sector borrowing requirement that was thought to be the 'main determinant of money growth'. In Britain, as in the United States, inflation was brought under control at the cost of a serious recession. Over the next few years, the power of trade unions to demand large wage increases was weakened by high levels of unemployment and changes in their legal position; the tax regime was recast to provide incentives for enterprise and personal responsibility; state assets were privatized; the City of London was deregulated to encourage the financial service sector; capital and wealth were prioritized over labour and equality; and globalization was privileged over the national economy. The tentative steps taken by Labour in 1976 now amounted to a major transformation of economic policy.[42]

Of course, politicians were aware of the electoral risks of controlling inflation at the expense of recession and unemployment. Capital liberalization led to reductions in corporate taxation to attract capital, but not to a race to the bottom in welfare spending. Politicians saw that social safety-nets were needed for those who lost from the change of policy and from de-industrialization and globalization – which does not mean, as some historians have suggested, that neo-liberalism is an inappropriate term. In many cases, welfare policies worked to support neo-liberalism. Minimum wages or in-work benefits replaced trade union bargaining power and offered some compensation for widening inequalities and job precariousness. Indeed, Friedman had been advocating a 'negative income tax' – the payment of benefits to support incomes below a certain threshold and of taxes by those above it – since 1947 as a way of tackling poverty. He had assured the Mont Pèlerin Society that breaking up unions meant they would need to 'combat the evils which unions were designed to counteract', and that welfare support was necessary in a democratic society. A minimum income would allow everyone to behave as a consumer in the market. Fellow members of the Society dissented on the grounds that it would create dependency and discourage work, but political expediency meant that cash transfers became an important and growing complement to a market-based society with increasing levels of inequality that privileged capital and profits over labour.[43]

The response differed between countries, for considerable national autonomy remained in the allocation of social benefits, shaped by existing national welfare systems and by electoral bargains. In general, capital market liberalization in developed countries mainly affected macroeconomic policy, above all in the priority given to controlling inflation, with a rise in social spending in response to market liberalization by offering compensation for the weakened commitment to full employment, the loss of trade union rights, and higher profits. In developing countries, the impact of capital liberalization was wider. Borrowers had a greater need for external finance and lenders were concerned about a wider range of macro- and microeconomic policies. Welfare spending was more likely to focus on education (which helped create a competitive global economy) rather than on social security, welfare and health (which would be costly for the middle and upper classes, and without perceived benefits for competition in the global economy).[44]

THE END OF THE NIEO

In October 1981, the North–South summit – the International Meeting on Cooperation and Development – met at Cancún. François Mitterrand had won the French presidential election for the socialists in May and pushed ahead with negotiations with the Global South. At Cancún, he welcomed Willy Brandt's report, *North–South: A Programme for Survival*, as a continuation of France's policy of mediation. It was also supported by the premier of China as a way of criticizing both the Soviet Union and the United States. But circumstances were not auspicious for co-operation and dialogue. In the OECD countries, inflation and unemployment were still high. In OPEC, many countries had drawn down their surpluses by increasing imports and exporting capital, and they were facing domestic demands for improved welfare and political participation. Meanwhile, oil-importing developing countries were facing economic difficulties. The solidarity of the Global South could not be sustained in the face of the growing divergence between the successful industrializing countries in

East Asia and countries in large parts of Africa where there were falling growth rates, or even decline. The global situation was also deteriorating. In 1979, the Iranian Shah was overthrown and a new Islamic republic was created, followed in 1980 by the start of a long war with Iraq. On 24 December 1979, the Soviets invaded Afghanistan, ending detente and reviving the Cold War.[45] The meeting at Cancún was therefore marginalized by wider geopolitical concerns and by the lack of sympathy for the NIEO shown by both Margaret Thatcher and Ronald Reagan.

In 1981, Reagan announced that at Cancún, 'we will promote a revolutionary idea born more than 200 years ago ... It is called freedom and it works. It is still the most exciting, progressive and successful idea the world has ever known.' At the conference, he accepted that government might have a role 'in helping develop a country's economic foundation' by encouraging private investment, providing incentives and opening markets rather than 'a reef of misguided policies that restrain and interfere with the international market-place or foster inflation'. Most importantly, it was necessary 'to help the developing countries to help themselves. It is here that trade and private finance is of such importance.' Thatcher agreed. In her memoirs, she explained her rationale for attending the meeting at Cancún:

> I felt that, whatever our misgivings about the occasion, we should be present, both to argue for our positions and to forestall criticism that we were uninterested in the developing world. The whole concept of 'North–South' dialogue, which the Brandt Commission had made the fashionable talk of the international community, was in my view wrong-headed.

She was adamant that 'there was no way that I was going to put British deposits into a bank which was totally run by those on overdrafts'.[46]

North–South dialogue ended in disillusion and disappointment, and the challenges of the NIEO and OPEC were contained. From 1981, oil prices started to fall, from nearly $40 a barrel to under $10 by 1986. In western Europe, petroleum fell from 62 per cent of energy consumption in 1973 to 45 per cent in 1985 as a result of replacement by coal, gas and nuclear energy. At the same time, oil production increased outside the OPEC in areas such as the North Sea and Alaska. OPEC attempted to hold up prices by cutting production, without success (see Figure 8, page 539). The balance of power shifted from OPEC and more generally from the NIEO.[47] China turned to internal economic development and abandoned competition with Moscow for leadership of the less developed world. The Soviets attempted to reassert their leadership and sacrificed peaceful coexistence with the United States in favour of anti-imperialism, armed struggle and a restructuring of the international economic order.

However, this strategy was undermined by the heavy economic costs of the resurgence of the Cold War that led to the crisis of 1989.[48]

The NIEO failed, though for a time it had challenged the post-war multilateral system and the dominance of the advanced industrial powers. It was a brief moment that caused alarm in the North and hope in the South, before the political solidarity of the developing world fractured and the Global North regained its economic and political power.[49] The NIEO's demand for economic rights based on the state was defeated by an emphasis on free markets and mistrust of the state that led to changes in the policies of the IMF and World Bank away from state-led development to market liberalization, as we will see in the next chapter.[50] The demise of the NIEO also led to changes in the architecture of global governance. Negotiation by 'groups' at GATT had reached the end of the road, for they could not maintain an agreed position on all issues. The members of the G77 – actually 125 in all – could not be held together by solidarity based on high-minded generalities, for divisions emerged when negotiations moved to specific issues. A well-informed observer saw that

> What worked well as operating procedures for discussions leading to the definition of general principles have become counterproductive for negotiating the details of binding international agreements. For the latter, technical expertise and subtle calculations of national interest for a specific problem area are required, not political finesse and knee-jerk reactions of support or rejection.[51]

Divisions were more apparent than unity. Oil producers such as Saudi Arabia recycled their petrodollars through banks in London and New York to indebted countries in Latin America and Asia, which encouraged the financialization of the world economy, and they also used their new wealth to entrench autocratic elites. At the same time, the 'Asian tigers' were experiencing rapid economic growth through export-led industrialization, and African countries were looking to special deals with the EEC. The general principles of the NIEO in opposition to the developed world gave way to pragmatic negotiations on individual issues and to a search for greater say within GATT.[52]

The NIEO led 'Genevan liberals' at GATT to reconsider global economic government. Ernst-Ulrich Petersmann and Frieder Roessler of its legal department – both students of Hayek – and Jan Tumlir, the director of economic research, viewed the world economy as constantly shifting in response to market signals, with an unknowable future. They agreed with Hayek that the world economy operated beyond reason and that seeking a 'mirage of social justice' in the international economy through state action would block the transmission of market signals and be 'the destroyer of a civilization which no brain has designed but which has grown from the free efforts of millions of individuals'. To Tumlir, the 'order' of the NIEO meant refusal to adjust. Consequently, GATT should look to a Hayekian system of rules and law that would bind nation states, facilitate market signals, and constrain both protectionism in the North and distributive justice in the South. Tumlir put the matter succinctly in 1983: 'international rules protect the world market against governments.' At the same time, national governments should be protected from imprudent electors and short-sighted politicians who offered voters what they wanted, without concern for the long-term consequences. International rules could protect the world economy from states and insulate states from internal interests. In the 1930s, Hayek and Robbins had looked to federal authority to guard against the threats of democracy and nationalism. The Geneva liberals now looked to stronger enforcement of rules.[53]

At a conference on the NIEO convened by Haberler at the American Enterprise Institute in 1977, Tumlir argued that unlimited national sovereignty was dangerous. In an interdependent global economy, 'legitimate national objectives . . . have to be sacrificed to the discipline of the international order'. The solution was multilevel governance on the lines of the EEC, where European law and the European Court of Justice (ECJ) stood above national law. The Genevan liberals had been divided on the EEC. To Röpke and Haberler, it was another form of national autarky on a larger scale that needed to be controlled by GATT. A younger generation, such as the leading German lawyer and member of the Mont Pèlerin Society Ernst-Joachim Mestmäcker, looked to a European court and laws above the nation. This was the outcome in 1963 when the ECJ ruled that national legislation must comply with Community regulations, and in 1964 that citizens could appeal to it against their state. The result, as the political scientist Luuk van Middelaar has put it, was 'a remarkable judicial coup' that went beyond the wording of the Treaty of Rome. In the same way, the Genevan liberals at GATT believed that a more powerful court was needed to enforce rules on recalcitrant national governments. The transformation of GATT into the World Trade Organization on 1 January 1995 reflected the political contingencies of the 1990s, as we will see in Chapter 22, but its intellectual origins went back to the 1930s and to the threat – as the Geneva liberals saw it – posed by the NIEO's demands for justice to an unknowable world of market signals. This notion that legal rules in the European Union and World Trade Organization would create a neutral economic space has been both castigated as a threat to national sovereignty and welcomed as a protection of the market

from national self-interest. This debate over legal norms in global governance became a contentious issue that divides both left and right.[54]

In the next chapters, we turn to this and other ways in which the economic government of the world changed with the demise of the NIEO
and the emergence of neo-liberalism. The approach to the economic government of the world was in flux. In 1980, the OECD's working party
that pursued Keynesian growth policies and long-term planning was
merged with a working party that focused on 'policy-analytic aspects of
macro economic and structural problems', with a concern for supply-side
economics and limiting public spending. The costs of the welfare state
were seen as a barrier to growth, which would be encouraged by lower
spending, labour market flexibility (a euphemism for precarity), greater
incentives to enterprise, and liberalized capital movements. Matthias
Schmelzer, the historian of the OECD, claims that under Jean-Claude
Paye, the secretary general from 1984 to 1996, it became 'a market-liberal
think tank promoting the liberalization of global markets for products,
services, investment and capital – all justified in the name of trying to
increase the now precarious growth rates'.[55]

Similar changes were also apparent in the international institutions in
Washington. The World Bank shifted to emphasize market reforms during
the presidency of Alden W. ('Tom') Clausen from 1981 to 1986. He had
been president of the Bank of America and returned there after his World
Bank term ended. In 1982, he appointed Anne Krueger as chief economist
who was best known for the notion of rent-seeking behaviour – that is,
higher profits or rents could be achieved by lobbying governments for
tariffs, subsidies and barriers to entry of new firms than by investing in
new technology. She argued that the result was a vicious circle, for new
firms could only succeed by engaging in the same process, with political
implications of casting doubt on the fairness of the market system. The
perception was that such government intervention led to abnormal profits
for those who benefitted from distortions of the market. The state was
seen as creating rents rather than using anti-trust laws to control monopolistic firms and remove rent-seeking.[56] Both the World Bank and IMF
pursued structural adjustment lending that imposed conditions of market
liberalization and financialization on its recipients. Meanwhile, GATT
and the WTO pressed ahead with proposals that went beyond trade in
physical commodities to services and intellectual property that were now
of greater interest to the advanced economies as they de-industrialized.

One of the most striking economic trends from the 1970s (and especially
the 1980s) was the financialization of both national and the global

economies. Particularly in Britain and the United States, the decline of industrial employment and widening income disparities led households to a greater reliance on credit to maintain a desired standard of living that was often sustained by rising house prices. This process went much further than in West Germany or Japan where household savings remained high. The difference reflected cultural assumptions that were shaped by government policies and by the response of households to changing circumstances.

A comparison between Japan and the United States illustrates the point. After the war, the Japanese government's National Salvation savings campaigns encouraged a high savings rate. Deferring consumption was a patriotic duty, and women were advised to monitor spending in detail by keeping account books. Consumption was culturally devalued. By 1960, as the economy grew, the government accepted the virtue of consumption, and in 1988 it went further in removing tax exemptions on savings. Although savings did fall, they still remained higher than in the United States. The old attitudes survived and households dealt with stagnant income by continuing to limit consumption without turning to credit. What applied to Japan was also true of Germany (see Figure 11).

By contrast, in the United States savings fell from the 1980s, with consumption maintained by credit. In the United States – as in Britain – the ownership of goods purchased on instalments remained with the retailer until the last payment, which reduced the risk of selling on credit. Higher levels of home ownership with expectations of rising values encouraged households to put their wealth into housing rather than savings. In the United States, tax deduction of interest was ended for instalment purchases and credit cards in 1986, but it remained on home equity loans or second mortgages. The promoters of this measure hoped it would encourage 'good' credit based on releasing equity for home improvements, education and health. But banks aggressively sold second mortgages for holidays and consumer goods so that houses became giant credit cards that incurred lower interest. Why save when it was possible to buy with easy money? And credit cards became more profitable for banks with changes in the regulation of interest rates in the 1980s. The proportion of American households with a credit card grew from 16 per cent in 1971 to 73 per cent in 2001, and aggressive promotion of credit cards fuelled debt-funded spending. What applied to the United States also applied to Britain. In both countries, low savings and high levels of debt-fuelled consumption were a response to stagnant household incomes, growing inequality and economic precarity, and the power of financial interests to change legislation. As we will see in Chapter 25, this reliance on debt-fuelled consumption by households was a major reason for the financial crisis of 2008.[57]

Figure 11: Net household saving rate: % of disposable household income

	1985	2005
US	8.5	1.5
UK	6.9	−1.2
Japan	16.5	3.9
Germany	12.1	10.5

Source: Sheldon Garon, *Beyond Our Means: Why America Spends While the World Saves* (Princeton, NJ, 2012), 4.

During this same period, the power of international finance increased, especially through the influence of Wall Street and the City of London which were closely connected in the emergence of a less regulated global financial system based on recycling petrodollars and offshore Eurodollars. The New Deal regulation of domestic banking, as well as the attempts of presidents Kennedy and Johnson to control flows of American capital, had led to the growth of offshore Eurodollars that allowed the City of London to restore its status as sterling declined. The flow of petrodollars and their recycling in Latin America led to a rise in the influence of commercial bankers and a changed relationship with the IMF. At Bretton Woods, governments wished to control bankers and capital flows; now, the IMF started to encourage financial liberalization and to bail out bankers when creditors were unable to service their debts. The question is how this change came about – whether by the power of finance to shape government policy, or through economic changes that led to a greater role for finance, which subsequently captured the state. Some members of the European Union – above all Germany – were more cautious about these offshore capital markets, and the Bundesbank wanted more regulation – a battle it lost. Where the British did agree with the other EU members was over the need for a single market for goods – a project strongly supported by Mrs Thatcher. She parted company with Brussels, however, over the creation of a single currency that marked the culmination of Pierre Werner's 1970 report.

The adoption of neo-liberalism by the Thatcher and Reagan governments was complicated by political considerations, and the same applies to global economic government. There was tension within the international institutions, for the World Bank did not always pursue the more extreme forms of market liberalism advocated by Krueger's research department. The operational staff still saw a role for the state and did not always impose the conditions contained in formal agreements with client states. Further, the rising number of people in absolute poverty led to renewed concern for poverty alleviation. The World Development Report of 1990 urged steps to increase the productivity of the poor and to provide basic social services of primary health care, nutrition and primary education. A new global poverty line was set at $1 a day and Mahbub ul Haq at the UN Development Programme devised a Human Development Index that combined life expectancy, education and per capita income into a single measure that would 'shift the focus of development economics from national income accounting to people-centered policies'.[58] At the WTO, criticism from activists in the West as well as the developing world led to a new development agenda, as we will see in Chapter 22.

Despite the rise of neo-liberalism, a concern for the environment and its relationship with growth did not disappear. A commitment to 'sustainable development' continued in *Our Common Future* (1986), the report of the World Commission on Environment and Development chaired by Gro Harlem Brundtland, the former prime minister of Norway, with Jim MacNeill as Secretary General. The report linked social and ecological issues to global inequalities, and to the need for redistribution. It defined sustainable development as 'development that meets the needs of the present without compromising the ability of future generations to meet their own needs'. This definition of sustainable development was soon narrowed, and in 1989 the OECD ministerial meeting claimed that economic growth and protecting the environment would be reconciled by technology. This view was criticized at the UN Conference on Environment and Development – the Rio Earth Summit of 1992 – which urged developed countries to abandon their 'unsustainable patterns of production and consumption'. But resolving the tensions between growth and the environment was not easy. The dominant view was that technology and efficient markets could increase production while reducing the environmental impact. Some economists, such as Wilfred Beckerman, even rejected sustainable development as a flawed concept. He accepted that the present generation should not squander resources and leave nothing for the future, but it did not make sense to ascribe enforceable rights to those who do not yet exist and to impose controls on the current use of scarce resources. To many developing countries, growth could solve current poverty, and sustainable development was a threat to their sovereignty and a device used by the developed world to maintain power. They questioned why the developed world should escape responsibility for its past pollution, block growth in developing countries and fail to address global inequalities.[59]

At the United Nations, a new synthesis emerged that combined the poverty alleviation schemes of the 1970s and market liberalization of the 1980s in the Millennium Development Goals set by the UN in 2000. Instead of a single composite figure, there were eight goals with twenty-one targets and sixty indicators: to eradicate extreme poverty by reducing the proportion of people living on less than $1.25 a day by half; to achieve universal primary education; to end gender inequality in education; to reduce child mortality by two-thirds and maternal mortality by three-quarters; to halt and reverse the spread of HIV and malaria; to integrate sustainable development into country policies and halve the proportion of people without safe water and sanitation; and to create a global partnership for a non-discriminatory trade and finance system that could provide for less developed countries and deal with debt. These goals were well meaning and desirable, but were they to be achieved by international aid that might lead to dependency and support state corruption? Was a focus on technical assistance preferable, or would private investment and globalization bring more people out of poverty? The targets and measures of success, however, were at least clear – which is more than could be said for the Sustainable Development Goals introduced by the UN in 2015. They were imprecise, idealistic and impracticable, with 17 goals, 169 targets and 230 indicators. The first goal, for example, was to end poverty in all its forms everywhere. One target was to reduce poverty in all its dimensions by half by 2030; another was to build the resilience of the poor and reduce exposure and vulnerability to climate-related extreme events and other economic, social and environmental shocks. These desirable aspirations lack precise measurements to assess the effectiveness of policies.[60]

These initiatives provided a counter to the neo-liberalism of the Washington institutions, without challenging the overarching direction of policy. Nevertheless, the IMF, World Bank and WTO did not always succeed in imposing their wishes on recipients of aid, as we will see in the following chapters. In Latin America, for example, ECLAC – the former UN Economic Commission for Latin America which, since 1984, had incorporated the Caribbean too – reflected on its lack of success compared with export-led growth in East Asia and combined neo-liberalism with an attack on poverty and social inequality. This approach was adopted in Chile. The governments of Argentina and Brazil also devised alternative strategies to deal with hyperinflation in the mid-1980s that did not entirely follow the IMF's solution of fiscal and monetary retrenchment. Indeed, the IMF could be captured by local elites with whom it formed close links, as in Mexico. The IMF's intervention in South Korea after the East Asian debt crisis of 1997 is often castigated for failing to understand policies and institutions that had led to rapid economic growth – though it was also the case that local officials used the IMF's intervention to secure reforms that had been blocked by domestic politics. Neo-liberalism was therefore negotiated both within the international institutions and with client states – and nowhere was this more true than in the former Soviet bloc and China. In some cases, as in Poland, the international institutions worked with the government in a sudden transition to a market economy after the fall of Communism. In other cases, most obviously in Russia, this 'shock therapy' failed, in part because the IMF lacked trustworthy allies in Moscow. The contrast with China was striking. Shock therapy was avoided there, and the Communist Party drew on a wide range of economic ideas while maintaining control over the process of market liberalization. The rise of China, more than any action on the part of global institutions, brought a large part of the world population out of poverty – and at the same time fundamentally altered the balance of power in the world economy.

From around 1980, the world embarked on market liberalization and hyper-globalization that seemed to have reached the end of the road in the financial crisis of 2008. The next chapters explore this period of fundamental change with the collapse of the Soviet Union, the emergence of China as a powerful economy, the creation of the Eurozone, the rise of finance power, and the transformation of global institutions.

21

'Market fundamentalism'

The Washington Consensus and Financial Liberalization

'It is time to add a new chapter to the Bretton Woods agreement. Private capital flows have become much more important to the international monetary system, and an increasingly open and liberal system has proved to be highly beneficial to the world economy. By facilitating the flow of savings to their most productive uses, capital movements increase investment, growth and prosperity.'
Statement of Interim Committee of IMF to annual meeting of IMF and World Bank, Hong Kong, 21 September 1997[1]

'... markets are an expression of the deepest truths about human nature and ... as a result they will ultimately be correct.'
Alan Greenspan, chairman of the Federal Reserve, February 1999[2]

'... we are once again in danger of drawing the wrong conclusions from the lessons of history. This time the danger comes not from communism but from market fundamentalism. Communism abolished the market mechanism and imposed collective control over all economic activities. Market fundamentalism seeks to abolish collective decision making and to impose the supremacy of market values over all political and social values. Both extremes are wrong. What we need is a correct balance between politics and markets, between rule making and playing by the rules.'
George Soros, *The Crisis of Global Capitalism*[3]

The 1970s marked a moment of transformation in the IMF as it moved to 'market liberalism' and deregulation, which it sought to impose through conditions it laid down in return for assistance, with little regard for local circumstances or national policy preferences, or for the

A member of staff of Seoulbank protests against the intervention
of the IMF, 2 December 1997.

success of alternative approaches. It shifted from doubts about financial liberalization to acceptance and, eventually, encouragement. One of the most striking features of the last quarter of the twentieth century was the return of foreign capital investment to a level last seen at the height of globalization before the First World War: gross foreign assets rose from a modest 6 per cent of world GDP in 1960 to 25 per cent in 1980, 49 per cent in 1990 and 92 per cent in 2000.[4] Short-term flows of money grew in search of a better return or expectation of currency movements; large flows of funds threatened to subordinate governments to global financial markets; and large banks became more important than officials and politicians.[5] Both national and global economies were increasingly financialized.

The shift in approach reflected structural changes in the global economy with the expansion of multinational corporations, the growth of integrated global supply chains, changes in information technology that allowed the rapid movement of funds in response to small differentials in prices, and the existence of economies with excess funds looking for profitable outlets. But the belief that markets are efficient and reach the 'correct' decision was also a political and ideological choice. Markets do not exist apart from political, social and cultural preferences that give priority to some interests and marginalize others. The Bretton Woods agreement was designed to contain the power of financial capital, and its reassertion in the last quarter of the century was politically contingent. The process started before the collapse of Bretton Woods and the emergence of neo-liberalism, with the development of the offshore Eurodollar market in the City of London from the late 1950s. The City of London re-emerged as a major financial centre as it replaced sterling transactions with new business that arose, in part, from American bankers and multinational corporations holding dollars offshore to avoid domestic regulations. These developments put pressure on the Bretton Woods regime of pegged rates – and once floating was adopted, there was less need to control financial flows, and competition between London and New York undermined such regulations. There was also a need to recycle the earnings of petrostates after the oil shock, which increased the role of commercial bankers. At the same time, domestic economies, especially those of Britain and the United States, were becoming increasingly financialized, with a growing reliance on mortgage finance and credit. As the power of financial interests grew, so the political balance moved to their advantage, with consequences that became apparent in the global financial crisis of 2007/8.

CONDITIONALITY AND THE
WASHINGTON CONSENSUS

At Bretton Woods, Keynes thought he had secured 'automaticity' in access to the resources of the IMF, as we saw in Chapter 8. In the 1950s, the argument was lost. The executive board adopted conditionality in February 1952: the IMF would provide a 'stand-by agreement' that gave access to the resources of the Fund if the member could show the problem was temporary and that the policy response was appropriate. The aim was usually to stop unsustainable expansion of demand caused by excessive public spending, and the IMF needed an indicator that could be applied to both developing and developed countries. In 1957 Jacques Polak – an economist who worked at the League, represented the Netherlands at Bretton Woods, and in 1947 joined the statistical division of the IMF – devised Domestic Credit Expansion for this purpose. The indicator arose from his experience in Mexico in 1948, where he realized that devaluation was an inadequate response. The balance of payments deficit there arose from consumption and investment exceeding domestic output, so that the solution was to cut government spending, increase taxes and reduce domestic credit creation. Since developing countries lacked reliable national income statistics, Polak used available data on money and the balance of payments to produce a single number – the expansion of domestic credit plus the deficit or surplus on the balance of payments current account. His approach provided a straightforward target for governments, though it had a serious shortcoming. The balance of payments deficit was treated as a short-term domestic problem with the expectation that rapid recovery would follow from corrective action through fiscal austerity.[6] The under-developed countries were more inclined to stress long-term structural factors arising from commodity cycles or the terms of trade. They were also aggrieved that the rule was applied to them with greater rigour than to developed countries. Hence IMF loans to Britain in the early 1960s did not refer to Domestic Credit Expansion, and when the IMF attempted to use the measure in 1965 and 1966, the British government protested that the IMF was exceeding its constitutional powers. Domestic Credit Expansion was reluctantly accepted by the British government as a price for IMF support in 1969, but the terms were not published to avoid the impression that the Labour government had surrendered its policy autonomy.[7]

The IMF articles were amended in 1969 to give legal status to conditionality 'that will establish adequate safeguards for the temporary use of the general resources of the Fund'. As yet, the change was limited, and the

IMF's economists remained committed to full employment, demand management, and incomes policy. Change went much further in the 1980s as conditionality shifted from the Bretton Woods principle that members should make their own social and political choices to the imposition of a particular set of policies.[8] The use of stricter conditions was facilitated by a change in the IMF's pattern of lending. From the late 1970s, it stopped lending to advanced economies, which created a clear division between lenders in the developed world who wished to impose strict conditions, and borrowers in the less developed countries who preferred fewer constraints. The developed countries had more voice and the rules increasingly reflected market liberalism rather than less developed countries' concern about structural imbalances in the global economy. The IMF now focused on rigidities in the domestic economy as the cause of balance of payments problems and shifted from 'stand-by' agreements that usually lasted for a year to the Extended Fund Facility, introduced in 1974. The aim was to reform the domestic economy and remove cost and price distortions, with drawings phased against performance criteria. The IMF was still anxious that aggregate demand was not excessive, but Polak complained that it was giving Domestic Credit Expansion an ideological slant by dividing credit between the private sector (to be encouraged) and the government sector (to be discouraged). The IMF gave more weight to supply-side reforms to ensure the efficient use of resources by market incentives and the price mechanism, and believed the solution to debt and balance of payments difficulties was faster growth. In 1990, Michel Camdessus – managing director of the Fund from 1987 to 2000 – commented that '[o]ur prime objective is growth. In my view, there is no longer any ambiguity about this. It is toward growth that our programs and their conditionality are aimed. It is with a view toward growth that we carry out our special responsibility of helping to correct balance of payments disequilibria.'[9] The IMF's annual report of 1990 did point to a 'need to identify more closely the poor, assess the impact on them of policy reforms, and improve the policy mix in programs'. In practice, there was little interest in removing the underlying causes of poverty or dealing with politically sensitive issues such as income distribution.[10] Growth would be achieved by market liberalization, privatization, a reduced role for the state, and monetary stability, regardless of the economic, social and political context.

Structural performance criteria became more intrusive, increasing from an average of 2 in each programme in 1987 to 6 in 1990, 12 in 1995 and 16 in 1997, with as many as 94 in South Korea and 140 in Indonesia in the Asian financial crisis of 1997.[11] Manuel Guitián, a Chicago-trained economist at the IMF, defended the approach as designed 'to attain over the medium term, a viable payments position in a context of reasonable price and exchange rate stability, a sustainable level and growth rate of economic activity, and a liberal system of multilateral payments'. Not everyone felt that the outcome was benign. In 1983, a former IMF official pointed out that the institution had

> not been established to give guidance on social and political priorities, nor has its voting system been designed to give it the moral authority to oversee priorities of a non-economic nature. Its functions have to be kept narrowly technical if it is to be effective in the exercise of its role as a partner of the adjustment process. For this purpose, the Fund has to accept that the author- ities of a country are the sole judges of its social and political priorities.[12]

Similarly, Joseph Gold, the director of the IMF's legal department, saw an unwarranted abandonment of the founding mission of responding to the balance of payments and foreign exchanges. In his view, 'in neither logic nor law is it defensible to transform [the Fund's] purpose into jurisdiction over economic growth'. Joseph Stiglitz – a Nobel Prize-winning econo- mist who was chair of the Council of Economic Advisers between 1993 and 1997 and then chief economist at the World Bank to 2000 – criticized the IMF for pursuing an ideological agenda that assumed prices and the market were the route to growth rather than an active role for the state and planning.[13] After all, Japan and the 'tiger economies' of Asia grew by adopting state-led policies rather than the market liberalism advocated by the IMF, and growth in Britain and the United States was lower than these countries. Neither did the IMF consider the impact of the structure of the world economy on the balance of payments of developing coun- tries. In March 1979, the developing country members of the IMF complained that 'in determining the volume and conditionality governing balance of payments assistance, a clearer distinction needs to be made between the causal factors attributable to the domestic policies of the developing countries and the external elements beyond their control'.[14]

The concern of the IMF for growth led to a blurring of the boundary between the Fund and the World Bank. In December 1966, the two institu- tions had drawn up a memorandum to clarify their relationship, with the Bank responsible for development programmes and project evaluation, and the Fund for exchange rates and temporary balance of payments disequilib- ria. They agreed to inform each other of their views but not to consider matters that lay within the competence of the other, nor to seek tighter co- ordination. This demarcation became less clear as the IMF moved from the oversight of exchange rates to a concern for growth and structural adjust- ment, and both the World Bank and IMF imposed conditions for assistance.

A possible solution was 'cross conditionality' – that is, one institution would impose a veto if the terms laid down by the other were broken. The prospect that the outcome would be a merger of the two institutions led to a compromise on informal cross-conditionality so that loans were consistent within an agreed policy framework. In 1986, the former Mexican finance minister David Ibarra worried that 'we have conditionality by the IMF, conditionality by the World Bank, and the process goes on ... So after a while you end up with so many rules of conditionality and cross-conditionality that you give the government no leeway to decide a proper adjustment policy well adapted to their internal needs.'[15]

The policies pursued by the Fund and Bank have been termed 'the Washington consensus', a phrase coined in 1990 by John Williamson to describe 'the lowest common denominator of policy advice being addressed by the Washington-based institutions [the IMF, the World Bank and the US Treasury] to Latin American countries as of 1989'. Williamson did not claim that the reforms were *imposed* by the Washington-based institutions. Rather, he thought that the Washington consensus emerged from sensible, pragmatic policies over the previous twenty years with intellectual convergence on free-market economics and a shift in attitudes towards the role of the state. The consensus was defined by fiscal discipline; redirection of public expenditure to areas offering high economic returns and improved income distribution, such as primary health care, education and infrastructure; tax reform to reduce marginal rates and broaden the tax base; financial liberalization; the use of competitive exchange rates; trade liberalization; free inflows of foreign direct investment; privatization; deregulation of business in order to remove barriers to entry and exit; and secure property rights.[16] James Boughton, the official historian of the IMF, pointed out that the problem was that the Washington consensus became 'a synonym for a narrow-minded and excessive zeal for laissez-faire economics' – or what George Soros termed 'market fundamentalism'. Williamson distanced himself from this use of the term and regarded himself as 'slightly left of center' rather than a 'neoliberal reactionary'. He pointed to his dislike of Reagan and Thatcher, to the exclusion of capital account liberalization from his definition, and to his view that the policies were recommendations appropriate to some countries rather than requirements that applied to all. He came to regret the term as a 'damaged brand name'. His protestations are not entirely convincing. Although he was not a fundamentalist, he was closely involved with the Institute for International Economics founded in 1981 by Peter Peterson, an advocate of open markets in the Nixon administration who became head of Lehman Brothers, a founder of the Blackstone hedge fund as well as chair of the New York Fed and the Council on Foreign Relations. To Peterson, internationalism meant the global spread of American free-market ideals and rolling back the state in opposition to social democratic values. Williamson shared the same assumptions and was a senior fellow at the Institute from its foundation until 2012.[17]

Williamson was right that policies in Latin America changed in the 1980s, and not just through external imposition. The change arose in part from internal dynamics, and the prescriptions of the Washington institutions were contested and adapted. In Chile, the socialist government of Salvador Allende was overthrown in 1973 with the involvement of the CIA and American corporations and replaced by the repressive and autocratic government of General Augusto Pinochet. Opponents 'disappeared' in large numbers, unions were suspended, inequality soared and corruption was rife. The 'Chicago boys' who followed the free-market ideology of Milton Friedman provided economic advice, but policies changed as much for internal reasons. The Chilean economy was soon hailed as the most successful in Latin America, with inflation brought under control, assets returned to their private, often foreign, owners, and a return to foreign loans and investment. To the right-wing Hoover Institution, Pinochet, rather than Thatcher or Reagan, was the first 'to make that momentous break with the past – away from socialism and extreme state capitalism towards more market-oriented structures and policies'.[18]

Economic policy in Latin America was in flux. ECLAC was based in Chile and underwent a marked ideological change in the mid-1980s as it moved from import-substituting industrialization and a concern for the terms of trade to emphasize international competitiveness and reform of domestic production, in part as a response to the greater success of economies in East Asia. There were some similarities with Pinochet's advocacy of market liberalism, but ECLAC also realized that controlling inflation and increasing exports came at a cost of falling real wages, rising unemployment and growing inequality. ECLAC combined competitiveness and a more open market with an attack on poverty and social inequality, stressing that 'the prime common task' was 'the transformation of the productive structures of the region in a context of growing social equity'. Changes in production should be linked with redistribution by supporting microentrepreneurs and peasants, developing social services for the poorest members of society, and using fiscal policy and public expenditure. These 'economic strategies and policies must be applied within a democratic, pluralistic and participatory context' that reflected majority opinion and 'concerted strategies' of agreements between the state and the main political and social actors. The role of the state was to create agreement on long-term aims, and to ensure that the public sector had a 'positive impact on the efficiency and effectiveness of the economic system as a whole'. This 'integrated approach' gave a larger role to the state in industrial, technological and educational policy than did the 'Chicago boys', and it encouraged links between the private sector and state intervention. ECLAC's combination of neo-liberalism with attacks on poverty was taken up by Patricio Aylwin, a Christian Democrat who succeeded Pinochet in 1990. He combined free-market policies with increased social spending and tax increases to deal with poverty and inequality.[19] Changes in economic policy in Latin America therefore did not come entirely from outside and were influenced by local developments. Moreover, the policy prescriptions of the IMF were not simply imposed, as we will see later in the chapter when we consider the Mexican debt crisis of 1982, and in Chapter 23 when we turn to its intervention in Russia.

We should also be careful not to assume that the change in the policy of the IMF reflected only neo-liberal economics of either the Austrian or Chicago schools. The intellectual composition of the IMF's staff was certainly changing as senior staff who joined in the late 1940s and early 1950s retired by the 1980s. They had been shaped by Keynesian ideas that financial flows were destabilizing and that equilibrium was temporary rather than the natural state of affairs. They were replaced in senior positions by staff recruited during the 1960s and early 1970s, predominantly from leading American graduate schools – Harvard, MIT, Chicago, Yale, Princeton, Stanford, Berkeley. Many of them were influenced by the 'new Keynesianism' or 'new neoclassical' economics. Economists such as Paul Krugman, Joseph Stiglitz, Janet Yellen, Ben Bernanke and Larry Summers who advised the Washington institutions and worked at the US Treasury and Federal Reserve pointed to market imperfections and the difficulty of achieving equilibrium in the economy so that macroeconomic stabilization could lead to a more effective outcome. Even so, they agreed with 'market fundamentalists' that households and firms have rational expectations and analyse information to predict the future level of prices, and that self-interested choices by individuals determine the course of the economy as a whole. Economists from other intellectual traditions were under-represented, and a shared, narrow methodology reduced difficult problems to basic propositions about individual rational expectations with little comprehension of the messy realities of social institutions or values, and little space for experiment.[20] Rather than adopting Albert Hirschman's approach of understanding the economic, social and political structures and aims of their clients, economists usually accepted a priori that states are inefficient compared with the perfect markets of the theoretical constructs. They failed to ask whether collective action and socialized provision might be more effective, and ignored the ways that in America successful companies relied on long-term state investments in new technology.[21]

The IMF was a hierarchical, centralized bureaucracy that created conformity, without external input from political scientists, sociologists or historians who had a deeper understanding of the societies in which it was intervening. There was a 'one size fits all' approach. In 1994, the IMF's Interim Committee – the 1974 successor to the Committee of Twenty that advised the Board of Governors – presented its Madrid declaration on 'cooperation and strengthening the global economy', which noted that 'the recent success of many developing countries illustrates ... the validity of a strategy based on steadfast implementation of strong programs of macro-economic adjustment and structural reform. The Committee urges other countries to follow a similar bold strategy.'[22] It did not ask whether other policies were more successful. In 1997, Jeffrey Sachs – a leading economist who advised on the transition of the Soviet bloc and on global economic development – complained that 'it defies logic to believe that the small group of 1,000 economists on 19th Street in Washington should dictate the economic conditions of life to 75 developing countries with around 1.4 billion people.' He had a point, for half the economists were engaged on surveillance, management and research, or were concerned with advanced economies, which left an average of seven economists for each developing country. Resources were inadequate to grasp what was happening, especially when economists were guided by prior assumptions, as in 1997 when 'the IMF threw together a Draconian program for Korea in just a few days, without deep knowledge of the country's financial system and without any subtlety as to how to approach the problems'.[23] (This criticism could be turned against Sachs' own advice to Poland and Russia in their transition to market economics, as we will see in Chapter 23.)

The IMF neglected alternative approaches and failed to understand or appreciate the institutional structures and policies of many countries with impressive records of growth, including Japan, Taiwan, South Korea and China. At UNCTAD, Charles Gore suggested a 'Southern consensus' that combined East Asian state-led development with ECLAC's structural approach – an alternative based on capital accumulation through domestic savings, investment, exports and 'strategic integration' into the world economy rather than rapid opening across the board. The 'Southern consensus', he argued, combined action to reduce inflation and deficits with steps to bring productive capacity into use through policies directed to technology, human resources, physical infrastructure and industrial organization. Such an approach entailed co-operation between business and government in a developmental state.[24] The Washington consensus also rejected social democracy with its assumption that collective provision of welfare often costs less and is more effective than the market, as shown by the better outcomes of socialized health care in Europe compared with the privatized system of the United States. Further, buying labour as if it is another commodity, with 'flexible' (i.e., precarious) employment, is socially unjust when obligations such as mortgage payments, pensions or education are long-term commitments that are difficult to reconcile with short-term, fluctuating employment. The result was double standards: intervention was permitted to control inflation and rescue banks but not to ensure secure and dignified employment.[25]

Nevertheless, the relationship between the IMF and its clients was more complex than a simple imposition of policies. In some cases, the IMF provoked political hostility and social unrest against externally mandated policies that threatened national sovereignty. On the other hand, the IMF's conditionality could be used in internal debates as different groups vied for control over policy, or it could be a scapegoat for unpopular policies that the government wished to adopt. Mike Blumenthal, Treasury Secretary in the Carter administration, saw that

the IMF has for years served as a kind of whipping boy. Countries facing severe economic difficulties and the need for strong corrective measures often need an external source to blame. The IMF is an ideal candidate and is accustomed to being in that position. If we didn't have the IMF, we would have to invent another institution to perform this function.

He pointed out that in most countries, there was 'a division between those who support needed actions and those who want to ignore the economic facts of life ... The IMF would not be doing a borrowing country any favor by coming down on the wrong side.'[26] The question was whether the IMF could or should decide on the 'right' side when it was a matter for domestic politics.

The implementation of conditionality depended on an interplay within the client state between proponents of different policies, the power of interest groups, and their links with the IMF. If policies were to be sustained, the IMF needed dependable allies – which was feasible where a political elite that supported market liberalism was in the ascendant and new officials changed the preferences of the bureaucracy. In Mexico, the debt crisis of the 1980s discredited older statist policies and allowed the IMF to work with a centralized executive and bureaucratic elite. The risk was that the IMF could be complicit in internal political debates and become too trusting of seemingly dependable allies so that

warning signs were missed.[27] In other cases, the IMF lacked allies able
to retain power for long enough to implement policies. This was the case
above all in Russia, where reformers lost out in the complex power
struggles of post-Soviet politics. Although the IMF was wary about giving more assistance to an unreliable partner, it was under pressure from
the US State Department which was anxious to assist Russia for geopolitical reasons and used the Fund to circumvent the need for congressional
approval for assistance.[28]

From the early 1990s, the IMF and the World Bank responded to the
failure of many of their interventions by turning to 'good governance' to
encourage political accountability and to ensure that policies were followed
through. The aim was to move from the external imposition of conditionality to 'ownership' that would make programmes more successful through
greater involvement in decision-making and implementation – with the
hope that the IMF would no longer bear the blame for unpopular policies.
In 1993, Camdessus pointed out that '[f]or a program to have its chance, it
has to be seen as really the program of the country, elaborated by the country.' In reality, 'good governance' had cultural and ideological overtones.
This approach was often well intentioned, for budgets and taxation should
be fair and based on sound information and audit; the rule of law should
be observed; and banks should be properly regulated. But good governance
came with normative assumptions. The IMF's report on good governance in 1997 stressed institutional reforms to maintain private sector
confidence; to liberalize exchange, trade and price systems; and to stop direct credit allocation. Good governance was defined as allowing the private
sector to work effectively rather than creating administrative and institutional capacity for planning. The laudable ambition of removing corruption,
rent-seeking and preferential treatment for individuals or organizations
imperceptibly slid into policy choices. The IMF claimed that its concern
was governance rather than politics, and that its 'judgements should not be
influenced by the nature of the political regime of a country ... Nevertheless, the IMF needs to take a view on whether the member is able to
formulate and implement appropriate policies.' What was 'appropriate'
was political and ideological, as shown by its intervention in Asia in 1997,
which is considered in detail later in the chapter.[29]

By the turn of the century, the IMF was concerned with the need for
legitimate governments that could carry out painful adjustments. The
Fund therefore now began to consider the political situation within member countries, such as the level of military spending (as in Pakistan), the
incidence of corruption (as in Indonesia), the extent of democracy (as in
Russia), or the existence of 'crony capitalism' (as in Malaysia). It led to a

new reluctance to carry out reform in alliance with authoritarian govern-ments, as had occurred in Chile under Pinochet.[30] The IMF's 'Guidelines on Conditionality' of 2002 focused on 'sound economic and financial pol-icies' that were 'owned' by the government to improve implementation. The basic principle was that a member had primary responsibility for selecting, designing and implementing economic and social policies, and that domestic support of these policies should be broadened and deep-ened. This approach seemed more responsive to the needs of member states, though in practice the IMF confined resources to policies that were 'sound' according to its definition. The Guidelines referred to prerequi-sites in core areas (macroeconomic stabilization, monetary, fiscal and exchange rate policies, financial markets) and laid down specific actions and outcomes.[31] To critics, the IMF continued to impose Western values on societies with different norms. What the IMF denounced as 'crony capitalism' might be a successful way of organizing the relations between the state and business – and little attention was paid to cronyism by rent-seeking and exploitation of political power by large private corporations in the United States.

'Ownership' was a pious aspiration rather than a practical reality. The IMF's contacts were with a small group of policymakers in central banks and finance ministries, and attempts to involve business, labour and non-governmental agencies in drafting 'policy framework documents' were a matter of form rather than substance.[32] In 1994, two officials at the World Bank pointed out that

> Participation has often been equated with explaining the project to key stakeholders (individuals and groups who stand to gain or lose from the project) instead of involving them in decision-making. Borrowers are not committed to project goals. Their 'ownership' has been sought by making them responsible for preparation and implementation, instead of ensuring that the impetus for the project is local and that the process provides ex-plicit opportunities for consensus building.[33]

Moreover, the IMF urged others to adopt 'good governance' without imposing democratic accountability and transparency on its own opera-tions. Its Board met behind closed doors with no formal record of its decisions, and the United States was suspected of imposing its definition of good governance and what policies should be 'owned'. The IMF con-tinued to be dominated by OECD countries, and voting did not give voice to developing and transitional economies.[34] Paul Volcker captured the problem when he reported the comment of the finance minister from a developing country: 'When the Fund consults with a poor and weak country, the country gets in line. When it consults with a big and strong country, the Fund gets in line. When the big countries are in conflict, the Fund gets out of the line of fire.'[35]

One response to the IMF's policies was reduced demand for its funds. Countries in East Asia vowed not to use the IMF again after its disastrous intervention in 1997, and they paid off loans and accumulated reserves. In 2006, three of the four largest borrowers – Argentina, Indonesia and Brazil – announced they would repay early and avoid borrowing from the IMF in future. The result was a decline in outstanding loans, from $107bn at the end of 2003 to $35bn in mid-2006 (see Figure 12). The IMF relied on interest payments and fees to cover its costs, so the drop in loans led to a budgetary crisis. The Fund also depended on financial support from the United States and needed to persuade Congress that public money was not being wasted or substituted for private finance. In 2005, the G7 agreed that Highly Indebted Poor Countries should have their liabilities to the IMF and other multilateral bodies written off – a policy that appealed both to progressive opponents of the Washington consensus and to right-wing American critics who pointed to the encouragement of reckless lending and 'moral hazard'. The aim was to force the IMF to absorb the costs and so constrain any future imprudent activity.[36] The Fund was rescued by the global financial crisis.

Figure 12: IMF lending during economic crises, 1952–2013

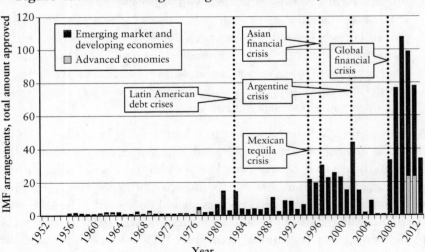

Source: IMF, Monitoring of Fund Arrangements database.
Note: Amount is in billions of dollars from 1952 to 1971 and in billions of SDRs from 1972 to 2013.

CAPITAL MOBILITY AND EURODOLLARS

Intellectual changes played a part in the shifting approach of the IMF but were not the only reason for this reassessment. The global economy was altering too, with the growth of financial markets after the restoration of convertibility in 1958, the flow of speculative funds in anticipation of currency realignments, and the emergence of the Eurodollar market. Financiers responded to these opportunities with alacrity; within the City of London such opportunities allowed a recovery from the decline in sterling, and for the City to build upon its long tradition of self-regulation. American banks turned to London to escape from New Deal regulations and the Kennedy and Johnson administrations' controls on financial markets, which led to competitive pressure to reduce regulatory controls in both the City and Wall Street.

International rules on movement of capital started to change soon after the resumption of convertibility in 1958. In December 1961, the OECD's Code of Liberalization of Capital Movements looked to 'progressively abolish' restrictions on capital movements 'to the extent necessary for effective economic cooperation'. It still accepted that controls should be permitted for security or to deal with a severe balance of payments deficit, and that they were 'often considered necessary to buttress domestic monetary policy'. At this stage, liberalization was voluntary, and only applied to flows of productive capital rather than to short-term flows of 'hot money'.[37] The position of the IMF was also changing. At Bretton Woods, Article 6.1 stated that resources could not be used to finance deficits arising from capital flows, and most economists accepted that the IMF lacked sufficient resources to contain speculation. Per Jacobsson disagreed. He favoured financial liberalization, argued that speculative flows were 'a normal element in the convertible system', and claimed that 'even speculators have not got unlimited funds at their disposal' so that disruption could be contained. In 1961, the Fund revised its interpretation of Article 6.1 to permit its funds to offset speculative flows – a substantive change that was disguised as a procedural adjustment. As yet, these initiatives were designed to ensure that speculative flows did not lead to exchange controls or protectionism, though Louis Rasminsky – an executive director of the IMF from 1946 to 1962 and governor of the Bank of Canada from 1961 – realized that a further step might be taken to promote capital mobility and financial liberalization. This suspicion led France to oppose the reinterpretation of Article 6.1 as 'a trick of the Anglo-Saxon nations'.[38]

The resurgence of capital mobility pre-dated the rise of neo-liberalism and in part reflected structural changes in the global economy during the golden age of economic growth. The rise of multinational corporations and the recovery of international trade, as well as changes in communication technology, encouraged greater flows of finance. Above all, the emergence of the Eurodollar market from around 1960 was central to the growth of a more liberal international financial market. It was shaped by political choices – whether to impose or relax capital controls, reduce or remove taxes on financial transactions, accept or reject offshore financial markets, or adopt weak or strong regulation of financial intermediaries.

Communist countries were reluctant to place their dollar earnings in New York where they might be 'frozen', as happened after the Soviet invasion of Hungary in 1956. They also saw that they could use their dollar holdings to create friendly relations with Europe. George Bolton – erstwhile director of the Bank of England and proponent of Operation 'Robot' to restore the status of sterling, now chairman of the Bank of London and South America and a pioneer in the Eurodollar market – welcomed Soviet involvement as a way of creating interdependence and reducing tension between the West and the Communist bloc.[39] Others were not so sure. The financial journalist Paul Einzig worried that the Soviets might order all Communist bloc banks to call in their Eurodollar deposits, for '[m]ajor decisions of policy are made in the Kremlin and these bankers will have no choice but comply'. Despite these concerns, the Bank of England accepted that the Moscow Narodny Bank – a central player in the Eurodollar market – had been registered as a British company since 1919 and its customers included local authorities within Britain. The City of London was a transnational space that transcended the Cold War.[40]

Above all, bankers in both the City of London and Wall Street saw the Eurodollar market as a way of overcoming constraints on their operations. In Britain, the banking industry had long been run by a cartel that limited the ability of individual banks to compete for domestic retail deposits and so meet the demand for loans. Offshore dollars offered greater freedom to circumvent restrictions on their activities – an innovation that started with the Midland Bank in 1955.[41] The City emerged as an offshore tax haven for Eurodollar loans, starting in 1963 with the bond issued by the Italian *autostrade* construction company and expanding from such public borrowers to American corporations and British companies that used the market to circumvent the Labour government's limits on foreign direct investment.[42]

Similarly, in the United States, the Eurodollar market was a way around New Deal regulations such as the Federal Reserve's Regulation Q of 1933.

Before the banking crisis of the early 1930s, competition between American banks for deposits forced them to reduce the margin between the rate offered to lenders and that charged to borrowers, which led to greater risk-taking to maintain profits. To create greater stability, Regulation Q both prohibited payment of interest on deposits that could be paid on demand and imposed limits on interest paid on time and saving deposits. The aim was to restore bank profits and replace risky activities with sound business loans. Regulation Q was not a problem so long as the market rate was below the permitted limit. In 1966, mortgage finance was squeezed by the demand for business loans. The Fed responded by imposing a ceiling on interest rates paid by savings and loans associations that provided mortgage finance and by cutting the interest rate for deposits in commercial banks, with the aim of increasing funds available for house purchases. The interest rate ceiling for commercial bank deposits was now below the market rate, and savers responded by moving to money-market funds in search of a higher return, while commercial banks looked to the Eurodollar market in the City of London where profits were not constrained and they could avoid New Deal regulations.[43] The attempts by the Kennedy and Johnson administrations to limit outflows of dollars (see Chapter 14) offered a further incentive to hold dollars offshore. American bankers' preference for dealing with the balance of payments deficit by deflation and reduced spending on the military was not acceptable politically because of the administrations' commitment both to the domestic welfare policies of the Great Society and pursuit of their geopolitical ambitions. American corporations and bankers responded to controls on financial flows by keeping dollars in the City of London. As a financial commentator remarked in 1969, '[t]he empire may have disintegrated and the UK may now be a third-rate military power, but the City of London has staged a comeback which would be the envy of any child movie star reaching maturity.'[44]

The City had a long tradition of self-regulation by bankers who specialized in international finance, with leading members sitting on the Court of the Bank of England which oversaw financial markets with limited involvement by the state. The revival of the City drew on this club-like institutional pattern of its heyday before the First World War, though with the major difference that its renewed status no longer rested on sterling but on the Eurodollar market. The Bank of England saw an opportunity for the City to recover from the loss of status after the Great Depression, the limits of the Bretton Woods regime on financial flows, and government restrictions on capital exports. Imposing tougher rules on Eurodollar loans was not feasible, for they could not easily be distinguished from other business. The Bank adopted a minimalist approach of a 'gentlemen's agreement' between a few leading banks to keep their positions liquid in a world of informal supervision and moral suasion. The Treasury took a relaxed attitude, for capital inflows and 'invisible' earnings from financial services helped the balance of payments. The City of London presented itself as a solution to Britain's economic difficulties, arguing that Britain's comparative advantage was never in manufacturing, and that its service sector was always the most successful. This narrative of British economic history – and the obvious de-industrialization of the British economy – helped convince the Treasury and politicians that the City should exploit the new opportunities. The British state did not play an active role in the emergence of the Eurodollar market as a conscious economic policy but did not stand in the way.[45]

After the City regained its status, the state became a major supporter of the financial sector. Geoffrey Howe, Chancellor of the Exchequer in the early Thatcher governments, gave little role to international organizations, for it was 'probably the market and the influences of the marketplace which are, on the whole, dominant and beneficent'. His confidence in markets led him to abolish exchange controls on capital transactions in October 1979. Exchange controls were no longer needed, for revenue from North Sea oil removed pressure on sterling, and Howe saw a chance to abolish controls to 'further our aim of freeing the market economy to operate efficiently'. Thatcher was more cautious, for she realized that abolishing exchange controls might weaken government influence over the money supply and that the City would benefit at the expense of industry, which was suffering from a lack of investment and a high exchange rate. She preferred to wait for the government's market philosophy to work, but Howe won the argument with the backing of the Treasury and Bank of England.[46] Howe and his successor, Nigel Lawson, went on to encourage financial liberalization in the 'Big Bang' reforms of 1986, which ended the separation between traders in shares and advisers to clients, abolished fixed minimum commissions, and allowed foreign firms to own British brokers. In 1998, taxation of international bond interest was abolished, and in 2001 the new Financial Services Authority established a still-looser regulatory framework. In speeches in 2000 and 2006, Gordon Brown – Chancellor of the Exchequer in the then Labour government – praised the City as a model for the country of the need to 'think globally' and to emulate its creativity, enterprise, openness to the world, and even – without irony – its 'belief in duty and fair play'.[47]

The US Treasury and Fed were initially ambivalent about the relocation of American banks to London and the growth of the Eurodollar market. The Eurodollar market had the advantage of allowing American bankers to maintain their role in international finance, helping multinational corporations, and assisting the administration by making dollar holdings more attractive.[48] On the other hand, the Fed's control of domestic liquidity would be undermined if money returned home, and there was a risk of international monetary instability from lending long and borrowing short. In 1963, the Treasury's Robert Roosa captured the dilemma that the Eurodollar market 'was politically a vehicle for instability but also an important part of liquidity'. His response was merely to ask American banks to consider whether they were serving the national interest.[49] Similarly, Dewey Daane of the Federal Reserve only asked a few large corporations why and how they used the market, without imposing restraints. The Fed, much like the Bank of England, realized it had little capacity to regulate the market and that any attempt would lead to avoidance and still greater risks. By 1969, worries that dollars might return to the United States and undermine domestic monetary policy led to more serious consideration of imposing a liquidity requirement on banks, but the idea was rejected on the grounds that it would not resolve the deeper problem of vulnerability to short-term capital flows. The National Advisory Committee on International Monetary Affairs realized that the Eurodollar market was a symptom, rather than a cause, of instability and decided against controls on American banks and corporations. Indeed, access to the Eurodollar market reduced demands to remove capital controls, which would be damaging to the balance of payments.[50] Thus in the United States, as in Britain, the emergence of the Eurodollar market in the 1960s was not, as some scholars have argued, actively encouraged by the state as a way of using an open financial system to gain 'structural power' in place of declining influence within the Bretton Woods system. Rather, it offered a way around New Deal regulations and attempts to control international flows of finance. Positive state support came after finance had emerged as a more powerful economic interest.[51]

From the 1960s, the City of London and Wall Street interacted in what the political scientist Jeremy Green calls a 'transatlantic regulatory feedback loop'. The loose regulation of the City encouraged American banks to open branches in this offshore financial market, which led to pressure on both sides of the Atlantic to maintain competitive advantage. The incursion of American banks challenged the existing regulatory framework of the City, and in the United States, financiers on Wall Street pressed the Federal Reserve and Treasury to liberalize the New Deal regulations, remove limits on international finance and mimic the offshore status of London. In 1981, the Federal Reserve allowed New York banks to operate as if offshore, free of tax and regulation, and Regulation Q was phased out.[52] The emergence of the offshore Eurodollar market in the 1960s contributed to the demise of the Bretton Woods regime – and the removal of the need to maintain pegged rates then reduced the need for controls on international finance.

Once these two centres had liberalized their financial markets, it was difficult to stop the process. An open market for goods required an agreement between many countries to reduce tariff barriers or controls – unlike in finance, where Britain and the United States could open their financial markets and block collective action on co-operative controls.[53] Liberalization of finance created fewer political problems than liberalization of trade. It is true that capital account liberalization benefitted Wall Street and the City, and owners of mobile financial capital and multinational corporations, rather than owners of immobile capital who were confined to a particular location. But these distributional consequences were not immediately obvious.[54] The implications of financial liberalization were far-reaching but did not provoke as much popular political attention as trade policy. Financialization did not produce immediate losers or hit defined areas in the same way as changes in trade policy: even when a private equity firm closed a local factory, the blame could be laid at the door of foreign competition. Financialization came to permeate society through a wider range of interests, from consumer credit, the ability to buy shares in privatized assets, or the encouragement of tax-efficient investment in the stock market and pensions – and, above all, in mortgages for house purchases which created a 'property windfall economy' based on the expectation of continual increases in values.[55] The result was a radical shift from the approach at Bretton Woods, when finance was subordinated to nation states, to the freedom of financial capitalism. Holdings of offshore dollars were beyond the control of a single state and, despite the wish of some European central bankers, were not subject to regulation. The Eurodollar market opened a space for financial liberalization that, as Vanessa Ogle remarks, 'allowed free-market capitalism to flourish on the side-lines of a world increasingly dominated by larger and more interventionist nation-states'.[56]

Anglo-American financial globalization was not universally welcomed. In 1962, the BIS pondered whether central bankers should 'leave the Eurocurrency markets without supervision or management'. The answer was that international controls would conflict with national sovereignty and would encourage offshore centres that were less reliable than London. In December 1963, most central bankers felt that, despite their concerns, the market was no different from other short-term capital movements.[57] Attitudes changed when the crisis of the Bretton Woods regime led to large sums moving in response to speculation that the Deutsche Mark would be revalued and the dollar devalued. In 1971, Treasury Secretary John Connally thought that the 'enormous short-term money flows' in the Eurodollar market posed a 'clear and present danger to our monetary system' and should be controlled.[58] Arthur Burns urged central bankers at the BIS not to transfer dollars from New York to the Eurodollar market, and they agreed to stop this 'mischievous exercise in finance'. Many European finance ministers and central bankers were worried at the threat to stability, and the BIS set up a Standing Committee on the Euro-Currency Market to consider regulations. At the Smithsonian Agreement meeting in December 1971, the Europeans ensured that 'attention should be directed ... to measures dealing with movements of liquid capital'.[59]

Opinion was divided. Otmar Emminger of the Bundesbank argued that the Eurodollar market aggravated inflation and created dis-equilibrating capital flows so that international controls were needed. On the other side, the Bank of England argued that the Eurodollar market was effective in providing international liquidity for trade and finance for investment.[60] In the United States, Burns' wish to control speculative flows was constrained by the commitment of George Shultz to market efficiency and free moment of money. Above all, the oil shock of 1973 weakened support for regulation and strengthened the case for open markets. As a result, Western Europe and Japan failed to secure regulation in the face of British and American commitment to open financial markets.[61]

The collapse of the Bretton Woods system reduced the need to limit capital flows, and international finance markets were also encouraged by the need to recycle petrodollars. Oil prices were rising from 1971 and producers looked for outlets for their earnings. In populous countries such as Algeria or Iran, funds could be used for development; Saudi Arabia and other Gulf states, with small populations, needed foreign outlets. In March 1973, the head of the Saudi Arabian central bank remarked that he was 'sinking under a sea of billions of dollars'. The issue became urgent in October 1973 when OPEC increased the price of oil. The risk – so it seemed in the west – was that oil producers might disrupt the monetary system as a deliberate political act or, more likely, through inadvertence. Petrodollars needed to be recycled to ensure stability.[62]

The Europeans favoured a multilateral solution and the managing director of the IMF, Johannes Witteveen, proposed an 'oil facility' that would use money provided by the oil producers to assist countries whose reserves were hit by higher oil prices, with minimal conditionality. The IMF's oil facility was adopted in June 1974 and in August 1977, fourteen countries, including seven oil producers, agreed to provide $10bn to assist oil importers.[63] By contrast, the Americans favoured a market-based solution. Treasury Secretary William Simon was, in the opinion of Denis Healey, 'far to the right of Genghis Khan and was totally devoted to the freedom of the financial markets'. Simon argued that the private market 'performed marvelously. Commercial banks and the Euro markets have been able to absorb the inflows.' In his view, '[t]here is only one social system that reflects the sovereignty of the individual; the free market, or capitalist system.'[64] By 1974, American policy favoured capital flows and 'an international investment environment or system in which government actions affecting investment flows would be as neutral as possible', with investment capital 'free to move to its most productive use in response to market forces and motivations, with the minimum possible distortion resulting from national policies or practices governing investment'.[65]

The IMF proved less important than commercial banks in recycling petrodollars. A British Treasury official realized that the Arab oil producers had 'little alternative but to keep their money in the Western system. Money cannot just lie about: it has to be invested . . . and the main facilities for investment are in the West.' Charles Goodhart, an economist and adviser to the Bank of England, noted that official attitudes to the Eurodollar market shifted from worries that it was a source of instability to a concern that it would not be large enough to recycle petrodollars and ensure the growth of the global economy. Such considerations help explain the revision of Article 4.1 of the IMF's charter in 1976 to include a statement that 'the essential purpose of the international monetary system is to provide a framework that facilitates the exchange of goods, services and capital among countries.' Article 6.3 still gave the right to control capital movements, but the direction of travel was clear.[66]

In January 1977, an IMF discussion paper pointed out that '[r]ecognizing the scale and difficulty of the recycling process, it is considered unwise to seek any sharp reduction in the scale of commercial bank operations. Rather, the broad aim should be to encourage a role by the commercial banks which would constructively assist in the adjustment process.' The IMF was confident that bankers could draw on local knowledge to assess the credit of borrowers. In reality, American bankers were not prudent in seeking markets to replace the drop in lending to corporate clients, and to compensate for narrow margins in domestic markets. The banks earned large fees from risky long-term lending of the oil producers' short-term deposits, with loans used to cover balance of payments and budget deficits rather than self-funding projects. Commercial bankers and the IMF were working together and, in the opinion of one critic, the tacit agree-ment that banks would be bailed out in return for recycling funds was 'moral hazard on a quite immoral scale'.[67]

Advocates of regulation staged a comeback in the late 1970s, until the second oil shock of 1979 led to renewed pressure for recycling petrodol-lars. A Bank of England memorandum of June 1980 borrowed the title of Francis Ford Coppola's recent film about Vietnam, *Apocalypse Now*, to warn of default. Nevertheless, the Bank still rejected regulation. Gordon Richardson, the governor of the Bank, realized that recycling would be impossible without international bankers and that 'the primary responsi-bility for the prudent conduct of their business must be left with the banks'. The Fed worried that the Eurodollar market and international bankers could threaten the pursuit of tight domestic monetary policy, but nothing came of suggestions that the BIS should impose a reserve require-ment. It was opposed by the Bank of England, and Congress also rejected the proposal for a Eurocurrency Market Control Act. Rather than regula-tion, tax havens and offshore markets were brought onshore and the governments in Britain and the United States started to provide active encouragement to their financial sectors.[68]

The BIS played a central role in the new financial system. The Bretton Woods agreement had been designed to support individual states experi-encing balance of payments deficits and pressure on exchange rates, with little attention paid to the need for a lender of last resort or prudential regulation. Although its constitution did not include acting as a regulator, the BIS stepped into the gap; soon it took the lead in this new world of finance. When two American banks with large foreign exchange commitments – the Herstatt and Franklin – collapsed and threatened the financial system in 1974, the Federal Reserve worked with the BIS. The Bank of England suggested that the BIS should consider how to deal with any future banking crisis, and in 1974 the Basel Committee on Banking Supervision of the Central Banks of the G10 was established. In 1975, it agreed to the Basel Concordat on regulatory and supervisory rules in international banking.[69] In December 1987, it specified that banks super-vised by central bank members of the BIS should adopt a capital-to-asset ratio of 8 per cent by the end of 1992. Although the IMF adopted surveil-lance of 'unsustainable flows of private capital' in 1995, in practice it paid little attention to surveillance and more to liberalization and integration of capital markets.[70] The G7 commissioned Hans Tietmeyer of the Bundesbank to recommend steps to secure better co-operation between national and international supervisory bodies, which led in 1999 to the Financial Stability Forum to co-ordinate the supervision and surveillance of financial institutions, with its secretariat based at the BIS.[71] It was little more than a talking shop. In 2004, the minimum capital requirements of the Basel Committee on Banking Supervision were revised, though the global financial crisis soon revealed the limitations of 'Basel II'.[72]

The BIS's role was not surprising. Ivar Rooth, the managing director of the IMF from 1951 to 1956, and his successor Per Jacobsson had been deeply involved with the BIS from its origins. Both men were advocates of the morality of sound money and balanced budgets and opposed redistributive policies and welfare states. In 1942, Jacobsson confided in his diary that deficit funding 'diverts attention from the real problems to be solved. It provides, so to say, an easy way out, palatable to the politicians; it is the duty of the economist to emphasize the sterner measures which have to be taken to attain full employment.' He warned that generous welfare systems might impede economic progress and that '[i]mproved standards for the many can be obtained in a wide field by the operation of the market system ... without direct intervention by the government'. Rooth and Jacobsson also argued that central banks should be independent.[73] On this view, regular meetings at the BIS in Basel were a counterweight to the IMF and allowed central bankers to monitor the financial system. As Paul Volcker commented in 1992, central bankers 'are almost uniquely able to deal with each other on a basis of close understanding and frankness' because of their shared 'experience, training and tenure'.[74] The IMF effectively ceded supervision to the BIS.

The Fund saw its role as assisting commercial banks and thought that excessive regulation would hinder their efficiency. In 1980, Jacques de Larosière, the managing director of the IMF, assured the German bankers' association that

> The banking system has proven to be an efficient vehicle for the transfer of financial savings internationally and it is extremely important that this process be allowed to operate smoothly and effectively. Prudential regulations must keep pace with market developments, but without causing disruptions in the process of international intermediation ... I believe that the market mechanism is basically sound and that banks should be playing a major role in the current phase of recycling, without facing undue strain. Bankers have a wealth of experience in judging the merits of investment, the quality of management, and the risks involved.

In May 1982, de Larosière pointed to a major change in the international financial system. 'Twenty years ago – and perhaps even as recently as ten years ago – the international monetary system was dominated by governments and official institutions. Today, the private commercial banks play

a key role in the running of that system.' At the IMF, one of the few dissenters was Alexandre Kafka, the executive director for a number of Latin
American countries, who had more grasp of reality. The dangers of de
Larosière's approach became clear as the terms of trade deteriorated,
interest rates rose and borrowers had difficulty servicing their debts. The
crisis started in Mexico in 1982, and by early 1983 more than twenty-five
countries had rescheduled their debts.[75]

DEBT AND FINANCIAL CRISES

The international debt crisis of 1982 marked a turning point in the IMF's
response to financial crises. In earlier episodes – support to France, Britain
and Egypt after the nationalization of the Suez Canal and military intervention, the sterling crisis of 1967, the oil shock of 1973 – the IMF
supported countries in temporary difficulties and was not directly involved
in managing or resolving the crises. The response to the 1982 crisis
marked a change to a more systematic approach of imposing conditions
and co-ordinating concessions from creditors.[76] The IMF did not take
steps to prevent a crisis by regulating commercial bankers or ensuring
that loans were prudent. Instead, it stepped in afterwards to help negotiate agreements between debtors and creditors, imposing austerity and a
free-market economy as a condition of assistance.

Latin America had been at the core of the IMF's activities for some time.
Much of Africa remained under colonial rule into the 1960s and American
assistance to Asia was shaped by the Cold War. As a result, Latin America
accounted for 65 per cent of all stand-by agreements between 1952 and
1960. Governments in Latin America also borrowed from private financial
institutions, which replaced aid and direct investment by multinationals.
From 1961 to 1965, 59.8 per cent of the net flow of foreign resources to
Latin America was public, 25.1 per cent direct investment, 7.3 per cent
from banks and bonds, and 7.8 per cent from other sources. Between 1976
and 1982, the share of public funds in a much larger total dropped to 14.7
per cent, direct investment declined to 20.6 per cent, and banks and bonds
surged to 62.7 per cent, with just 2 per cent from other sources. Foreign
indirect investment from international bankers was vital to government-led
'indebted industrialization'.[77]

In Mexico, most lending was either to or guaranteed by the public sector under the auspices of the Partido Revolucionario Institucional (PRI),
which controlled the government from 1929. Inefficient domestic industries created by import-substituting industrialization, as well as pressure

of population growth on agricultural exports, led to a balance of payments deficit in the 1970s. The government responded by public investment funded by bank loans. The number of state-owned corporations rose from 86 in 1970 to 740 in 1976, with a major role for the Nacional Financiera, a state body that obtained about two-thirds of its investment from abroad. The government secured funds through it to assist industry and shape the economy, avoiding nationalist criticism of direct investment by foreign multinational corporations.[78]

In 1976, the Mexican debt crisis had led to domestic political tensions. On one side were the economic nationalists at the Ministry of National Patrimony and Industrial Development who advocated import substitution and economic nationalism. On the other side were technocrats at the budget ministry, including the future presidents Miguel de la Madrid and Carlos Salinas de Gortari, who were in favour of liberalization. The nationalists were initially in the ascendant and in September 1982, the outgoing president, José López Portillo, attacked the 'financing plague' that 'is wreaking greater and greater havoc throughout the world ... The remedy of the witch doctors is to deprive the patient of food and subject him to compulsory rest.' Portillo imposed exchange controls and proposed nationalizing the banks. The outcome was capital flight and panic. His successor Madrid announced that he would change these policies when he took office, and he was supported by bankers, business leaders and officials who doubted their ability to enforce exchange controls along the border with the United States. Portillo backed down and negotiated with the IMF, and Madrid dropped exchange controls when he took office. He and his successor, Salinas, supported the bankers, corporations and officials who favoured open markets.[79]

By the early 1980s, the international financial system was in difficulties as commercial banks' recycling of funds led to mounting problems of debt service. Until this point, the IMF dealt with national governments and had an arms-length relationship with private banks. When crisis hit Mexico, it took an active role in co-ordinating a collective response by commercial banks and governments. Creditor banks and debtor governments had a common interest in avoiding default, but they differed in their preferred solution. The banks wanted to ensure that debt was serviced, even if it meant domestic austerity, unemployment and economic contraction. The debtor governments preferred banks to reschedule the debt and resume lending to avoid domestic problems. The IMF brokered a compromise between these views. When Mexico approached the IMF for assistance in November 1982, de Larosière realized that the banks and the IMF had a common interest in the international financial system. The IMF made loans to Mexico conditional on an agreement between the banks and government to reschedule, with a contribution of $5bn by the banks. The banks agreed, on condition that Mexico accepted an IMF adjustment programme and agreed to service the debt. The outcome of this 'concerted action' was to protect the large commercial banks. Prudential regulation continued to be lax; the debtor country maintained payment; financial markets were reassured that conditionality would restore credibility; and banks did not suddenly withdraw.[80]

After the crisis, the IMF developed relations with sympathetic technocrats in Mexico, especially liberalizers in the finance and budget ministries and central bank. This alliance involved an internal political conflict between the liberalizers and economic nationalists, as well as radicals who wanted Latin America to unite against creditors. In 1984, Latin American debtors met at Cartagena in Colombia and argued that repaying debt was less important than development, and that debt servicing should in future be tied to the level of export earnings. Differences in the timing of crises in the countries of Latin America made collective action impossible, though the threat could be useful as a bargaining weapon with the IMF. The liberalizers won the policy debate in Mexico and pressed ahead with foreign investment and open access to world markets. Officials sympathetic to the IMF consolidated their position – and the IMF's confidence that the right people were in charge led it to overlook emerging problems.[81]

In reality, the relationship between the IMF and Mexico was fragile. Commercial bank lending did not recover, reform was inadequate, and Mexico did not grow out of debt. In 1989, US Treasury Secretary Nicholas Brady – a Wall Street investment banker – turned to the IMF to assist in restructuring the debt. Camdessus, the new managing director of the Fund, agreed to a flexible interpretation of the Fund's rules so that it could act as a crisis manager and avoid instability in the international financial markets. The commercial banks accepted a supposedly voluntary reduction of Mexico's debt that was encouraged by a threat of taxation if they did not comply. The banks exchanged existing bonds for 30-year debt reduction or 'Brady bonds' that were issued at a discount of 35 per cent or at par with interest below market rates. Existing debt was reduced, and new loans could then be issued at market rates.[82]

Relief was short-lived and crisis returned in December 1994. The IMF loaned $17.8bn to Mexico early in 1995, and Camdessus justified this 'unprecedented package' by arguing that the IMF had responsibility to support Mexico's reform programme and 'to respond to the systemic implications of the Mexican crisis and to give confidence to the international financial system ... [T]he crisis of confidence in Mexico could have raised doubts about the situation in other countries as well – doubts not warranted by fundamentals.' The rescue package created political problems in Mexico as a result of cuts in real wages and consumption, a reduction in imports and an increase in exports, and higher taxation combined with lower public spending. It became more difficult for the technocratic liberalizers to work with the IMF, whose influence rested on Mexico's need for finance and the ability of officials to pursue reforms in a single-party regime with a powerful president, executive and government bureaucracy. After 1994, opposition mounted to the PRI, which initially sought populist support by nationalizing the banks and imposing capital controls. It soon backtracked and in 1996 lost its majority in Congress.[83]

The IMF had entered a Faustian pact. It lacked sufficient funds to replace commercial lenders and offered an implicit guarantee that allowed more lending – mainly for real estate rather than investment in productive assets. The beneficiaries were corrupt elites and holders of existing assets whose value rose; the losers were workers whose income and quality of life suffered.[84] The IMF was criticized by supporters of free markets who complained that rescuing imprudent bankers led to moral hazard. Allan Meltzer – a leading free-market economist and member of the Mont Pèlerin Society – likened the Brady plan to selling fire insurance at bargain rates to a town where half the inhabitants were arsonists. In his view, 'capitalism without failure is like religion without sin. It doesn't work well.' The result was to destroy 'the dynamic process that makes stockholders responsible for losses and disciplines managers who make mistakes.'[85] Meltzer wanted free markets rather than the alternative approach of limiting or regulating financial liberalization more strictly. The IMF accepted that 'concerted action' marked

> a new relationship between the Fund and private creditors. The success of Fund-supported programs now depended, more than ever before, on the reactions of the banks. While the banks needed the Fund's expertise and its ability to obtain credible policy commitment from the member, the Fund needed the banks to contribute resources to cover financing gaps, and assurance that potential Fund lending would not just lead to a commensurate reduction in bank exposures.[86]

Crisis also hit the rapidly growing economies of Asia in 1997, largely a result of the 'carry trade' (the practice of borrowing at low rates to invest in higher-yielding assets). Asian countries pegged their currencies to the dollar to remove exchange rate risk; American investors borrowed at home at a low interest rate and obtained higher returns in Asia without fear of changes in the exchange rate. Problems arose when the peg came under pressure and lenders converted local currencies into dollars to pre-empt the risk of devaluation. In 1997, the Thai and Malaysian currencies collapsed, and the crisis spread to South Korea. The IMF intervened and blamed the financial crisis on Asia's weak financial institutions and lack of transparency in corporate governance that led to corruption and 'crony capitalism'. The solution was clear to supporters of the Washington consensus: a shift from planned or state-led capitalism to free-market American capitalism.[87]

In 1997, South Korea had neither a large current account deficit nor a high level of foreign debt, and the problem was temporary illiquidity. The IMF's approach was not to maintain lending and restructure short-term debts but to put together a large loan with onerous conditions in association with the World Bank, Japan and the United States. Banks were closed and minimum capital standards laid down, with tight domestic credit, higher interest rates and fiscal contraction. The result was panic, a collapse of domestic lending and the sale of sovereign debt, which was reduced to junk-bond status. The government was forced to introduce major structural changes that would open markets to foreign involvement, reform the corporate structure of *chaebols* (family-run conglomerates) and create more flexible labour laws. Banks were urged to abandon developmental lending with an implicit government guarantee and to adopt Western forms of credit evaluation, with the Bank of Korea making a commitment to price stability. These macroeconomic policies reduced growth and increased unemployment, and high interest rates caused problems for companies that relied on high levels of debt. This external pressure did, it is true, allow South Korean reformers to carry out changes that had been blocked by domestic politics, but sovereignty was undermined on sensitive political issues such as labour law, corporate governance and the role of the state. The IMF ignored the principle laid down at Bretton Woods that countries should have the freedom to make their own choice of economic system.[88]

Critics of the IMF argued that inappropriate intervention intensified the crisis. The IMF failed to understand the Korean economic system on its own terms and was blinded by its lack of detailed knowledge and its commitment to market liberalism. Martin Feldstein – an economist at Harvard, former chair of the Council of Economic Advisers under Ronald Reagan, and president of the National Bureau of Economic Research – pointed out that a member state applying for assistance was the IMF's client or patient, but not its ward. The legitimate political institutions of the country should determine the nation's economic structure and the nature of its institutions. A nation's desperate need for short-term financial help does not give the IMF the moral right to substitute its technical judgments for the outcomes of the nation's political process.

Feldstein rightly pointed to double standards. European countries had rigid labour laws and Japan had similar corporate ownership and bank structures to South Korea. Moreover, South Korea had a record of rapid growth, low inflation and high employment – so why was it necessary or desirable to make it more like the United States? Feldstein's damning judgement was that the IMF was interfering in the affairs of other people, that it should be less ambitious and arrogant, and that it should focus on measures to prevent future crises rather than imposing its own culturally loaded and ideological views.[89]

The IMF was also criticized by Milton Friedman. In 1998, he argued that the Mexican bailout had helped create the East Asian crisis, for '[i]t encouraged individuals and financial institutions to lend to and invest in the East Asian countries ... reassured about currency risk by the belief that the IMF would bail them out if the unexpected happened and exchange pegs broke.' Congress reacted by establishing the International Financial Institution Advisory Commission in 1998 under the chairmanship of Meltzer. Its report was critical of financing long-term development with short-term capital flows that benefitted favoured individuals and interests, of the moral hazard arising from banks securing a premium for risk and then relying on IMF guarantees, and of the administration for using the Fund to circumvent congressional doubts about aid for Russia. The Meltzer report recommended that the IMF should focus on preventing crises and, if a crisis did emerge, ensuring it did not spread. It did not need to bail out lenders or impose the Washington consensus: structural reform should be left to capital markets and regional development banks.[90]

The handling of the East Asian crisis did considerable harm to the IMF's reputation. Debtor countries drew a lesson that reliance on short-term debt through the securities market was risky, for the supply could dry up; and the cost of servicing debt denominated in foreign currency could fluctuate. The lesson was to use capital controls, to encourage local markets for long-term debt, and to build up currency reserves to ensure they did not need IMF help in future – a strategy that meant they were largely unaffected by the financial crisis of 2008.[91] Despite evidence of the harmful consequences of the IMF's intervention, Camdessus claimed success. He pointed to 'the sheer magnitude of the structural reforms that had to be initiated from the outset' to restore confidence in the financial and corporate systems. He insisted that countries in Asia needed to be more like America in dealing with 'fundamental weaknesses in the corporate sector, especially the excessively close relationship between banks, corporations and the state'. The next stage was 'liberalizing domestic markets, lowering trade barriers, privatization, easing restrictions on entry by foreign investors, and strengthening bankruptcy laws and procedures'. He rejected the successful model of economic development of Japan and the 'Asian tiger' economies:

> The approach of 'managed development' underlying economic policy, characterized by mechanisms that interfered with market allocation of resources, has become increasingly out of tune with the rigorous demands of our globalized economy. Basic changes in the approach to policymaking, allowing market forces to operate more freely, will be essential.

There was only one true path – free-market capitalism. His assessment was blinkered. The most successful economy in the globalized world – China – did not rely on market allocation of resources, and development in Japan, South Korea and Taiwan was state-led; moreover, the United States had its own version of 'crony capitalism' with the close relations between the state and Wall Street.[92]

The debt crises of Latin America in the later twentieth century differed from the experience of the late nineteenth and early twentieth centuries when countries frequently defaulted; now, the solution was austerity, repayment and co-ordinated rescheduling. In 2016, only 0.2 per cent of world public debt was in default, despite an increase in outstanding sovereign debt from 20 per cent of world GDP in 1980 to 80 per cent. The change reflected the role of the IMF in co-ordinating commercial bank creditors and sovereign debtors, but also changes in the political economy of lending. Before 1914, most international capital movement involved long-term investment in bonds issued by utility companies and public bodies. The bonds were held by a wide and diffuse group of retail investors and allowed diversification of portfolios in creditor countries. When capital flows returned in the 1970s, loans to developing countries were mainly from private banks and institutional investors who were more easily organized than the diffuse bondholders, with greater leverage through withholding credit on which states, firms and households relied. Powerful firms, financial elites and technocrats in the debtor countries aligned with foreign creditors, creating close links between bankers and authoritarian regimes, especially in Latin America where they were viewed as technocratic bulwarks against Communism. When officials from Barclays Bank – one of the largest lenders – visited Argentina in 1970 they praised the military dictatorship and, astonishingly, reported that there was 'tolerance, no racial problems, and an air of liberty, even though there are no free elections and the military govern'. This change in the nature of loans gave banks more power, and they also benefitted from the IMF's willingness to bail out distressed borrowers with conditional loans that kept debtor countries solvent and released resources to service foreign debt.[93]

Procedures were also established to adjudicate disputes between private investors and both private and state debtors that might include nationalization of assets or breach of contract. An extra-national system of arbitration started with the London Chamber of Arbitration (established in 1892) and the International Chamber of Commerce's international court (created in 1923). The League's protocol on arbitration clauses left approval of private arbitration to judges in national courts where the arbitration took place, but in 1925, the US Chamber of Commerce secured legislation that made private arbitration legally binding. The outcome was the creation of the American Arbitration Association in 1926, and from 1939 its decisions would apply where an American party was involved, leaving other cases to the International Chamber. In most countries, private arbitration was still not legally binding and there were limited powers of enforcement, with no authority over sovereign debtors. The International Chamber called for greater oversight, and in 1958 the UN responded with the Convention on the Recognition and Enforcement of Foreign Arbitral Awards that committed the signatories to enforce cross-border arbitrations. In 1965, the Convention on the Settlement of Investment Disputes between States and Nationals of Other States was agreed by members of the World Bank, and in 1966 the International Centre for Settlement of Investment Disputes was established as an agency of the Bank to arbitrate in disputes between investors and sovereign states.[94]

In addition, bilateral investment treaties or treaties of friendship and commerce made vague promises to offer 'fair and equitable treatment', to provide compensation for direct or indirect expropriation, and to ensure the repatriation of profits and capital, with the use of extra-territorial settlement of disputes. Borrowers assumed the treaties were no more than a 'diplomatic token of goodwill' that would encourage foreign investment, with the result that – as the political scientist Lauge Poulsen found – developing countries 'signed up to one of the most potent international legal regimes underwriting economic globalization without even realizing it'. These treaties dealt with disputes between private investors and sovereign states. Relationships between sovereign creditors and sovereign debtors were handled by the 'Paris Club'. The first meeting was held in Paris in 1956 to negotiate Argentina's settlement with public creditors, and regular meetings continued with a secretariat and chair from the French Ministry of Finance, and observers from the IMF, World Bank, UNCTAD, the European Commission and regional development banks. Members of the Paris Club aimed to reach consensus on the conditions to be imposed, including implementing an IMF programme of reform. Similarly, the 'London Club' brought together commercial banks to reach agreement with debtors, meeting for the first time in 1976. These clubs did not have formal charters or memberships, and were not international organizations. To supporters, they were pragmatic and flexible; to opponents, they lacked transparency and accountability. Global governance was changing with agreements outside the remit of international organizations, both in the arbitration of investment disputes and in a proliferation of codes for the standardization of goods and food safety. Public and private international law came together and fed back into national law.[95]

SLIPPING INTO OBSCURITY: THE IMF'S ROLE

In 2006, Mervyn King, governor of the Bank of England, wondered whether the IMF might 'slip into obscurity'.[96] There was no doubt that it had changed and abandoned some of its founding purpose. When the IMF was created in 1944, it had a clear aim: to manage the system of pegged exchange rates by providing short-term assistance to countries with balance of payments difficulties. It failed to provide much guidance on the reform of the Bretton Woods system in the 1960s or on the emergence of the floating regime in the 1970s. The task was left to more informal discussions between governments, such as in 1985, when appreciation of the dollar hit American exports, encouraged imports and threatened a protectionist backlash in Congress. In September 1985, representatives from the United States, Britain, France, Germany and Japan met at the Plaza Hotel in New York and agreed to manage floating rates by adopting policies that would resist protectionism, control inflation, liberalize financial markets, reduce taxation and cut public expenditure – a clear commitment to market liberalism. The Plaza Accord also made a commitment that exchange rates should 'better reflect fundamental economic conditions' and would adjust external imbalances. Paul Volcker later remarked that '[t]he whole episode represented the most aggressive and persistent effort to guide exchange rates on both a transatlantic and transpacific scale since floating had begun more than a decade earlier.' In reality, the Plaza agreement lacked credibility, for central bankers were wary of firm commitments and finance ministers were reluctant to surrender control. Volcker admitted that 'no budget, trade or structural policy was changed as a result of the Plaza', and it 'was fated to be just one more episode in the saga of reacting to exchange market emergencies'. Co-ordination was accepted in response to an immediate and serious threat; as soon as the crisis passed, co-operative intervention was abandoned and national policies had priority.[97] This pattern was repeated in the Louvre Accord of 1987. Members of the G7, with the exception of Italy, agreed that currencies should be 'broadly consistent with underlying economic fundamentals' and that they should co-operate to create stability based on target rates or 'reference zones'. Toyoo Gyohten, a Japanese representative, recalled that discussion of the rates 'took place over dinner, while all the participants were quite busy cutting their meat and sipping their wine. No effort was made to formalize the agreement and obtain firm commitments to the figures from the finance ministers. That left a rather ambiguous, blurred agreement.' As Gyohten remarked, there were no 'tangible, clear results'.[98]

The IMF was not taking the lead in these efforts to manage exchange rates. From 1987, meetings of the G7 became more formalized, with gatherings of finance ministers up to four times a year, an annual summit of heads of government, and public reports of decisions. The managing director of the IMF was invited to provide an overview of the world economy but usually left before any decisions were reached. Volcker pointed out that representatives of each country explained their policies and circumstances, and the meetings avoided reconciling inconsistencies of analysis and policies, with 'nothing to force a decision or a conclusion, barring, of course, a crisis on the doorstep'.[99] The G7 – or G8 as it became with Russian membership between 2002 and 2014 – was the major forum for discussion of the world economy. The formal multilateral institution of the IMF was replaced by intergovernmental discussions in smaller, more informal meetings of the G7 which permitted a freer exchange of views than a larger, bureaucratic and rules-based organization. The problem was that these discussions excluded most countries and failed to impose rules or provide enforcement mechanisms if a country manipulated its currency.[100]

At the start of the new century, currency warfare seemed to have returned. The United States accused China of currency manipulation, and China blamed the weak fiscal policy of the United States for the deprecation of the dollar. The IMF was powerless to change the domestic policies of two major players. In 2006, a senior American Treasury official complained that 'the perception that the IMF is asleep at the wheel in its most fundamental responsibility – exchange rate surveillance – is very unhealthy for the institution and the international monetary system.' In June 2007, the IMF responded with a new approach, defining external stability as a balance of payments on current account that was 'broadly in line with its equilibrium' and a capital account that was not vulnerable to sudden shifts in capital flows. Members were recommended to 'avoid exchange rate policies that result in external instability' and to permit IMF review in case of 'fundamental exchange rate misalignment'.[101] The proposal was clearly targeted at China and led to deadlock.

The IMF had abandoned its role in managing exchange rates, and the corollary of floating rates was that it could drop capital controls that were accepted at Bretton Woods as a device to maintain pegged rates. The IMF had started to change its policy even before the crisis of the Bretton Woods regime, and it soon moved from scepticism to enthusiasm for capital account liberalization. The main disagreement was over speed. From the late 1980s, gradualists, who argued that controls should remain until market distortions were removed, lost influence to supporters of rapid liberalization who stressed the costs of control and benefits of liberalization. Guitián urged an amendment of rules, on the grounds that controls were ineffective, gradual phasing was pointless, and market discipline was better than prudential regulation. The experience of the Mexican debt crisis of 1994, however, led to a revival of gradualism. In 1995, Camdessus accepted that temporary controls might be needed 'until domestic financial markets and institutions become well established and resilient'. Nevertheless, he remained committed to liberalization, for '[i]t would be a mistake to try to avoid such crises by reverting to closed economic systems with exchange controls and less open markets: to do so would be to run the clock back and forgo the benefits of globalization.' In April 1997, the IMF's Interim Committee proposed that the articles be amended to 'make the promotion of capital account liberalization a specific purpose of the Fund and give it jurisdiction over capital movements'. To Camdessus, this mandate would add 'a chapter to the uncompleted work of Bretton Woods' – a misinterpretation of thinking in 1944. In September 1997, the Interim Committee called for 'a new chapter to the Bretton Woods agreement' to encourage capital flows, provided they were backed by adequate national policies and multilateral surveillance. These provisos were largely forgotten. Despite the financial turmoil in East Asia, the executive board pressed for liberalization of capital flows to be an explicit purpose of the IMF. Camdessus admitted the risks:

> But let us not forget that markets also provide tremendous opportunities to accelerate growth and development ... Freedom has its risks. But are they greater than those of complex administrative rules and capricious changes in their design? Freedom has its risks. But is there any more fertile field for development and prosperity? Freedom has its risks! Let us go then for an orderly liberalization of capital movements.[102]

In 1998, Jacques Polak – now retired from the IMF – questioned this enthusiasm for financial liberalization. He pointed out that 'the promotion of the worldwide flow of capital is not listed among the purposes of the Fund' and that the explicit commitment to liberalization was a radical change. He accepted that 'stale' provisions permitting controls could be removed and that the IMF could promote orderly liberalization of capital movements; he stopped short of active encouragement. The Asian crisis reopened criticism of financial liberalization, but Camdessus was unrepentant. In his view,

> The lesson to be drawn from recent developments is not about the risks of globalization – and still less about demonizing the markets – but rather about the importance of exercising good citizenship when tapping them. Indeed, countries cannot compete for the blessing of global capital markets and refuse their disciplines.

Larry Summers – successively Deputy, Under and Secretary of the Treasury in the Clinton administrations between 1993 and 2001 – argued that the problems in Asia were largely the result of domestic mistakes in channelling 'excess inflows of private capital ... into unproductive investments'. At the Fed, Alan Greenspan went still further in claiming that '[a] well-functioning international financial system will seek out anomalies in policy alignments and exchange rates and set them right ... We used to describe capital flight as "hot money". But we soon recognized that it was not the money that was "hot", but the place it was running from.' The critics did at least block a revision of the IMF's articles. The Treasury backed down as a result of Democrat opposition to increasing the IMF's quota if the amendments were adopted. Revision of the articles was suspended. The IMF shifted from rapid liberalization to concern for 'sequencing' by working with sympathetic domestic policymakers to ensure an institutional framework was in place. The result was greater caution rather than a loss of faith in the benefits of financial liberalization.[103]

In 1998, the economist Dani Rodrik criticized the IMF's commitment to liberalization of capital accounts as 'genuinely odd':

One wonders which of the ills of international capital markets the proposed medicine will cure. Will the African countries get the foreign capital they need if they remove capital controls? Will 'emerging markets' be less at risk of being flooded with foreign capital when such flows conflict with the domestic goals of controlling inflation or of maintaining a competitive exchange rate? Will sudden reversals in flows become less likely than before? Will contagion across countries become less severe? Will more of the inflows take the form of long-term physical investments rather than short-term financial flows?

The implied answer to all the questions was 'no': controls did not harm economic performance or hamper the efficient global allocation of capital, and there was no reason to encourage capital flows which increased systemic risk. He warned that

canonizing capital-account convertibility ... would leave economic policy in the typical 'emerging market' hostage to the whims and fancies of two dozen or so thirty-something country analysts in London, Frankfurt and New York. A finance minister whose top priority is to keep foreign investors happy will pay less attention to developmental goals. We would have to have blind faith in the efficiency and rationality of international capital markets to believe that the goals of foreign investors and of economic development will regularly coincide.[104]

At Bretton Woods, Henry Morgenthau had hoped to expel usurious money lenders from the temple of finance. During the 1970s and 1980s, the IMF had invited them back with little concern for effective surveillance or prudential regulation which was left – to a modest extent – to the BIS. Rather than adopting policies that might prevent crises from arising, the IMF brokered deals between sovereign states and imprudent commercial banks after the event.[105] To supporters of free markets such as Meltzer, this intervention created moral hazard and banks should have been left to pay the price of their imprudence. To critics such as Rodrik, the IMF was guilty of encouraging financialization without considering the risks, turning from 'shallow multilateralism' that balanced domestic welfare and internationalism to 'hyper-globalization' based on trade liberalization, privatization, open capital markets and flexible labour markets.

Worries started to emerge even within the IMF. Rodrigo de Rato, the managing director from 2004 to 2007, suggested that more attention should be paid to the interconnection of macroeconomic and financial markets.[106] His worry reflected the analysis of Raghuram Rajan, chief economist at the IMF and future head of the Indian central bank, who expressed concerns in 2005 at an event to honour Alan Greenspan, the chairman of the Federal Reserve since 1986. Rajan welcomed changes in financial markets but warned that excesses usually developed when things seemed to be going well. In particular, he pointed to the ability of investment managers to gain from high returns without losing when they did less well. The result was to incentivize risk – and by 'herding' in their choices of investments, asset prices departed from economic fundamentals. The high level of risk was concealed from investors, and banks' balance sheets were less secure given the need to hedge their complicated products. This prescient analysis led Rajan to the conclusion that 'even though there are far more participants today able to absorb risk, the financial risks that are being created by the system are indeed greater', with 'a greater (albeit still small) probability of a catastrophic meltdown'. He saw that '[w]hile the techniques and instruments to absorb fluctuations have improved, there is uncertainty about how they will perform in a serious downturn. Even as financial markets evolve, it is our duty to constantly rethink the ways they are regulated.' He made one mistake: the probability was large. Rather than heeding his warning, Larry Summers thought Rajan's 'slightly Luddite, premise ... to be largely misguided'. Summers claimed that traffic accidents became larger as horses were replaced by trains, and so did financial crises. It would therefore be wrong to stop global banks and financial innovations. His analogy was mistaken. Railways were designed by engineers and overseen by regulators with the aim of minimizing crashes. Meanwhile, at the Fed, the new chairman Ben Bernanke celebrated the 'great moderation' of reduced volatility. What could possibly go wrong?[107]

Rajan left the IMF at the end of 2006, and the IMF remained confident that 'core commercial and investment banks are in a sound financial position, and systemic risks appear low'. The assessment was deeply misguided – and not only with hindsight. In 2007, the BIS expressed concern at the over-extension of private credit and adoption of 'securities of growing complexity and opacity', and worried that 'tail events affecting the global economy might at some point have much higher costs than is commonly supposed'.[108] The dangers of financialization were soon apparent with the global financial crisis of 2007/8 – the worst economic crisis since the Great Depression. The IMF had done nothing to prevent the crisis, but it now had a new role in brokering deals between creditors and debtors, above all in the Eurozone.

22

'Rules-based system'

Creating the World Trade Organization

'Poverty does not make poor people into terrorists and murderers. Yet poverty, weak institutions, and corruption can make weak states vulnerable to terrorist networks and drug cartels within their borders. The United States will stand beside any nation determined to build a better future by seeking the rewards of liberty for its people. Free trade and free markets have proven their ability to lift whole societies out of poverty – so the United States will work with individual nations, entire regions, and the entire global trading community to build a world that trades in freedom and therefore grows in prosperity.'

US National Security Strategy, September 2002[1]

When the Tokyo Round of trade talks concluded in 1977, the NIEO was still challenging GATT as a club of rich countries and pressing for distributive justice in the world economy. The developing countries boycotted the signing of the agreement and at UNCTAD in 1979 complained of their lack of voice. Not only was the representativeness of GATT questioned, but also its agenda. The developing countries were still demanding preferential treatment for their exports, while the advanced economies had moved on from their concern for industrial tariffs that had dominated earlier rounds of talks. By the end of the Tokyo Round, tariffs on goods had been reduced to low levels and were no longer central to the creation of a multilateral global economy. Now, the greater concern of business corporations was non-tariff barriers that were used to restrict trade through environmental standards or product specifications; the need to defend intellectual property rights in new technology or the branding of commodities; and to secure open trade in services – not least in finance. These issues were much less relevant to emerging economies, which suspected – with considerable

Demonstrators blocking the city streets on the opening day
of the WTO conference, Seattle, 1999.

justice – that GATT reflected the needs of the developed world. There was also a growing sense that GATT should be more concerned with the enforcement of rules to ensure that countries did not adopt measures in restraint of open markets. The result was the transformation of GATT into a new body – the World Trade Organization – which attempted to combine the demands of the developing economies with the new issues of the developed world, and to create a more formalized system of rule enforcement.

After the completion of the Tokyo Round, it seemed that progress on trade liberalization had stalled, and politicians at the end of the decade were naturally more concerned about inflationary pressures and low growth. If progress were to be made, it was more likely to come from regional deals than time-consuming and complex multilateral negotiations. An agreement with a few neighbours on a more defined agenda was easier to achieve than with all the members of GATT and might sustain trade liberalization by creating an incentive for recalcitrant members to negotiate and so avoid exclusion from the benefits. Equally, there was a risk that regional agreements might divide the world into trade blocs by diverting rather than creating trade. Article 24 of GATT allowed free trade areas and customs unions to encourage freedom of trade and close integration, though they were not permitted to create barriers against other countries by imposing higher duties or stricter regulations. The most obvious regional agreement was the European Economic Community, which had caused some difficulties for GATT at the time of its creation. In the 1980s, interest in regional associations revived. Within the EEC, from 1988 Mrs Thatcher strongly supported the creation of a single market that went beyond a customs union by removing barriers to the free movement of goods; it was adopted in 1993. In 1991, a number of countries in Latin America agreed to create a southern common market, Mercosur; and the Abuja Treaty set out stages for the creation of an African Economic Community. In 1992, the Association of South-East Asian Nations (ASEAN) agreed to create a free trade area; and in 1993, the United States, Canada and Mexico ratified the North American Free Trade Agreement (NAFTA). Growing regionalism was in tension with multilateralism and created problems for global economic government.[2]

REGIONALISM VERSUS MULTILATERALISM

In the United States protectionist pressure in Congress was creating problems regarding the renewal of presidential authority to make trade agreements. The Trade Agreements Act of 1979 only passed by accepting tighter rules on imports of subsidized or dumped goods, a more generous definition of injury, and a shift of authority from the Treasury to the more protectionist Department of Commerce.[3] President Reagan continued the pragmatic policy of his predecessors in balancing multilateralism with rules to protect domestic interests. Bills were introduced to restrict imports of copper, steel and shoes, and in 1982 a bill passed the House to impose rules on domestic content in the production of automobiles. In response to such protectionist sentiment, former presidents Ford and Carter called for support of liberal trade to sustain geopolitical alliances and economic growth. The balance was difficult to establish. The Trade and Tariff Act of 1984 adopted measures to support domestic industries, ensure reciprocity and permit retaliatory tariffs, without accepting the stronger protectionist demands.[4]

To critics at home and abroad, the Act seemed a shift towards American unilateralism and a violation of the most favoured nation principle. A generous interpretation is that the Reagan administration was preempting more protectionist measures in Congress. In September 1985, Reagan assured business leaders that

> free trade is, by definition, fair trade. When domestic markets are closed to the exports of others, it is no longer free trade. When governments subsidize their manufacturers and farmers so that they can dump goods in other markets, it is no longer free trade. When governments permit counterfeiting or copying of American products, it is stealing our future, and it is no longer free trade. When governments assist their exporters in ways that violate international laws, then the playing field is no longer level, and there is no longer free trade. When governments subsidize industries for commercial advantage and underwrite costs, placing an unfair burden on competitors, that is not free trade.[5]

Nevertheless, the administration refused to accept all protectionist measures proposed. In December 1985, Reagan vetoed a bill to protect textiles and footwear, and during 1986 and 1987 the White House opposed protectionist devices that would violate GATT obligations.[6]

CREATING THE WORLD TRADE ORGANIZATION   635

As already said, the difficulties in negotiating multilateral deals led to bilateral or regional free trade agreements. During his presidential campaign, Reagan talked of a North American free trade zone covering the United States, Canada and Mexico that together possessed 'the assets to make it the strongest, most prosperous and self-sufficient area on Earth'. He believed that by co-operating in the use of resources, land, food and technology, they could achieve more than they could alone. 'In fact, the key to our own future security may lie in both Mexico and Canada becoming much stronger countries than they are today.'[7]

John Crosbie, the Canadian trade minister, agreed that a US–Canada free trade area might encourage multilateral trade liberalization. At the 'Shamrock summit' in Quebec in March 1985, Reagan and the Canadian prime minister Brian Mulroney – both of whom claimed Irish ancestry – agreed to explore a free trade agreement.[8] Despite protectionist views on Capitol Hill, Reagan pushed ahead. In 1987, he assured the Canadian parliament that

> We can look forward to the day when the free flow of trade, from the southern reaches of Tierra del Fuego to the northern outposts of the Arctic Circle, unites the people of the Western Hemisphere in a bond of mutually beneficial exchange, when all borders become what the U.S.–Canadian border so long has been: a meeting place, rather than a dividing line.[9]

A deal would bring the two countries together economically and politically, and would sustain open markets, for 'as strains in world commerce create protectionist pressures, a successful [free trade agreement] with Canada will serve as a model for the future'.[10] Canada and the United States signed a free trade agreement in 1988. The Mexican debt crisis and ensuing recession led President Salinas to approach the new American president, George H. W. Bush, for a similar deal. In June 1990, Bush's 'Enterprise for the Americas' made 'a comprehensive free trade zone for the Americas our long-term goal', and in 1992 the three heads of government agreed terms. Legislative approval was not easy. In Washington, opponents of NAFTA feared a loss of jobs and an undermining of environmental and consumer standards because of competition from Mexico. Renewal of fast-track presidential authority had been difficult in 1991, and in the elections of 1992, members of Congress pledged opposition to NAFTA in return for support from labour. Bill Clinton, the Democratic presidential candidate, only backed a deal on condition that side agreements were made to protect the environment and labour rights. After his election, he strongly supported NAFTA, however, which was ratified by Congress in November 1993.[11]

Although Canada and the United States were careful to argue that the agreement was compatible with GATT, the turn to regionalism was causing concern. In 1994, 61 per cent of world trade was covered by regional free trade agreements, with the Asia-Pacific Economic Cooperation (an intergovernmental group of countries on the Pacific rim, formed in 1989), accounting for 23.7 per cent of world trade, the EEC for 22.8 per cent, NAFTA for 7.9 per cent, and a number of other smaller deals for 6.6 per cent. One view was that regional free trade agreements were engines for growth – and Paul Volcker thought that, even if they led to some trade diversion, they were 'relatively benign'. The 'bicycle theory' held that regional deals could keep the system moving and prevent a return to protectionism – like riding a bicycle, forward momentum was essential. As Fred Bergsten pointed out, 'failure to move steadily forward towards liberalization condemns the trading system to tip over or fall backward in the face of protectionist pressure'. GATT concluded that NAFTA would be trade creating rather than diverting and did not offer a view on whether it was compatible with its rules – a politically wise position. Nevertheless, the GATT secretariat worried that the growth of regional trade blocs could threaten multilateralism and claimed a right to assess regional agreements – a formality that at least tried to maintain some sense of accountability. The trade economist Jagdish Bhagwati thought that GATT had become a General Agreement to Talk and Talk, and to do little. Certainly, the involvement of the United States in a regional deal made it more difficult to ensure that all agreements were trade creating.[12]

THE URUGUAY ROUND

One attraction of a new GATT round was that it might reduce the need for regional deals. The task would not be easy. GATT's special and differential treatment for developing countries without reciprocity seemed unfair to developed countries, which faced growing competition from East Asia; and developing countries wanted action on developed countries' protection of declining industrial sectors. Resentments continued over agricultural subsidies and the EEC's Common Agricultural Policy. In 1982, the GATT ministerial meeting failed to launch a new round of talks, though the head of the American delegation felt that the meeting at least achieved 'the avoidance of tragedy and limited movement in the right direction'. In December 1983, Arthur Dunkel – a product of the Graduate Institute in Geneva who was director general of GATT from 1980 to 1993 – established a group of experts which reported on the erosion of GATT rules and recommended a new round to strengthen the organization and prevent a drift to regionalism. In April 1985, the US followed suit with a call for a new round to counter growing domestic protectionism and to create rules for free and fair trade. GATT agreed to prepare an agenda for negotiations that would be presented to the ministerial meeting at Punta del Este in Uruguay in September 1986.[13]

Dunkel was aware of the threat to GATT from increasing protectionism, but there was tension between the American wish to widen the agenda and suspicion from developing countries. In the United States, tariffs and non-tariff barriers were of less concern to business than new issues relating to services (the General Agreement on Trade in Services, or GATS), trade-related investment measures (TRIMS), and trade-related intellectual property rights (TRIPS). The service sector took a larger share of employment and trade in the developed world – in the United States, employment in manufacturing fell by 4.4 per cent between 1989 and 1999, compared with an increase of 45 per cent in services. In 1980, services accounted for 17.5 per cent of American exports; in 1990, for 27.6 per cent. The intangible capital of intellectual property, from brands to Hollywood movies and technical innovations, was increasingly important.[14] Developing countries suspected an attempt to shift the agenda away from their concerns and to limit the policies pursued by successful East Asian economies to encourage their industries.[15]

Prior to the meeting at Punta del Este, draft declarations set out different positions. Developing countries in the G10, led by Brazil and India, attempted to block the inclusion of services, intellectual property and investment. By contrast, the 'café au lait' group led by Colombia (coffee) and Switzerland (milk) saw the possibility of trade-offs, and this position was supported by developed countries such as the United States, the European Community and Japan. Rather than a demand for distributive justice, the café au lait strategy was based on an integrative approach and reciprocity. In return for accepting new issues, the developing countries could seek trade-offs on agriculture and textiles in a single undertaking or 'grand bargain'. Instead of a general coalition of developing countries based on general principles, a pragmatic pursuit of specific issues could bring together developed and developing countries. This shift was reflected in the Cairns group that emerged from a meeting of agricultural exporters convened by the Australian government in 1986. It included New Zealand, Canada, Argentina, Brazil, Indonesia and Malaysia in opposition to American and European subsidies. The café au lait declaration formed the basis of discussions at Punta del Este.[16]

The Punta del Este Declaration of 20 September 1986 announced a new round of multilateral trade talks to reverse protectionism, remove trade distortions, preserve the principles of GATT and develop a multilateral trading system that would promote growth and development. It set out fourteen 'subjects for negotiation', including tariff and non-tariff barriers, tropical products, import quotas for textiles and clothing, agriculture, subsidies and countervailing practices, a reduction in safeguards, as well as consideration of the rules and procedures of GATT. The 'new subjects' included TRIPS and TRIMS as well as services. The Declaration met widespread scepticism that was reflected in the *Financial Times*'s comment that '[s]etting an agenda is one thing: repairing that worn fabric of the GATT by rewriting the rules and negotiating mutual concessions that would liberalize trade is another.'[17] Despite these doubts, the Round was welcomed by developing countries that hoped to benefit from liberalized trade – a sentiment that was not confined to countries such as Taiwan and South Korea with export-led growth. In 1990, Bangladesh was also hopeful that 'success in the Uruguay round is the surest insurance for us all to sail on the boat of multilateralism to a safe and predictable voyage of liberalizing the global trading system and thus make interdependence of nations truly meaningful'.[18] Such sentiments were a major change from the demands for distributive justice in the NIEO that had foundered on the opposition of Reagan and Thatcher in 1981.

The Uruguay Round entailed over eight years of tortuous negotiations on issues that had proved difficult in previous rounds as well as on new, complex issues.[19] Congress made its intentions clear in the Trade and Competitiveness Act of 1988, which renewed authority for trade negotiations on even stricter conditions, and it would not easily accept a deal without a stronger dispute settlement mechanism within GATT and progress on TRIPS and TRIMS.[20] The ministerial meeting in December 1988 made little progress before talks broke down because of disagreement between the United States and Europe over agricultural protection. Michael Duffy, the Australian trade minister, described the warring US and EEC factions as 'a pair of rippers', adding that 'I think we're staring down the barrel of an all-out farm trade war.'[21] The American and EEC delegations proposed that agriculture be left to a further round so that progress on other areas could be consolidated. The idea was rejected by Latin American members of the Cairns group and developing countries who were sceptical about proposals on intellectual property rights. A separate deal would undermine their strategy of securing trade-offs in a 'grand bargain'.[22]

Dunkel suspended talks and embarked on consultations to bring the sides together before the meeting resumed in April 1989. A package was agreed to freeze support prices in agriculture and make progressive reductions to them; to phase out textile quotas (without a fixed schedule); to create a framework for trade in services; to start work on sanitary and phytosanitary regulations; and to accept that a deal was needed on trade-related intellectual property. No progress was made on safeguards or anti-dumping provisions. The need for a reformed dispute settlement system was accepted and a Trade Policy Review Mechanism was established in 1989 to carry out periodic surveillance of members' policies, and to require governments to 'explain and defend their overall trade policies'. The package was largely an agreement on what needed to be agreed, with a commitment to be virtuous – but not yet.[23]

Negotiations limped forward. Dunkel asked negotiating groups to submit clear issue 'profiles', with decisions to be made by senior officials – leaving only the most difficult questions for ministers to resolve when they met at the end of 1990. His attempt to facilitate negotiations was hit by the crisis engendered by the collapse of the Soviet Union, the reunification of Germany, Iraq's invasion of Kuwait, and ambitions for deeper European integration in the single market. Meanwhile, bilateral or regional trade agreements were proliferating. In this context, the ministerial meeting aimed to settle difficult issues with final negotiations early in 1991, before US fast-track authority expired on 31 May. The GATT secretariat produced a draft comprehensive agreement only for negotiations to collapse on the issue of agriculture, largely because the French were reluctant to allow the European Commission to have negotiating flexibility. Dunkel had the unenviable task of again consulting to resolve the differences.[24]

In May 1991, the renewal of fast-track authority for two years to complete the North American Free Trade Agreement removed the need for urgency that had brought earlier trade rounds to a close. Although Dunkel's consultations with governments and meetings of negotiating groups led to modest progress in the spring and summer of 1991, agriculture remained deadlocked and demonstrations by farmers in Europe and Asia showed the sensitivity of the issue. French obduracy led to the resignation of the European agriculture commissioner, Ray MacSharry, in November 1992. The breakthrough came when George Bush was defeated by Bill Clinton in the presidential election of November 1992. He had nothing to lose before his term expired and he retaliated when the Europeans imposed a tariff on oilseed. The French backed down and MacSharry was reinstated as commissioner with a new mandate. In the Blair House Accord of 20 November 1992, the United States and European Community agreed a compromise on agriculture that allowed completion of the round. Clinton secured a one-year extension of fast-track authority and the new US trade representative, Mickey Kantor, was able to work with Leon Brittan, the new trade commissioner, who was a former trade minister in the Thatcher government and strongly committed to liberal trade. Peter Sutherland, an Irish politician and former European commissioner for competition policy who helped complete the internal market, was director general of GATT from 1993 to 1995 and pushed matters forward with the 'Quad' – the informal group of the European Community, Japan, Canada and the United States that provided leadership in GATT talks – before agreement was reached on 15 December 1993, the evening before the deadline.[25]

'Can it be true?' asked *The Economist*, capturing the sense of relief (and disbelief) that the Uruguay Round had been completed. Tariffs for industrial goods were reduced by 40 per cent in industrialized and 20 per cent in developing countries. Non-tariff barriers in agriculture were converted to tariffs and reduced by 36 per cent for industrialized and 24 per cent for developing countries. Industrialized countries agreed to reduce export subsidies by 36 per cent in value and 21 per cent in quantity, and to phase out textile and clothing import quotas over ten years. Rules were introduced on sanitary and phytosanitary measures, an agreement was reached on TRIPS and TRIMS, and a General Agreement on Trade in Services provided a 'framework of rules and principles for trade in services, including most-favoured-nation treatment, safeguards, transparency, dispute settlement, and the free flow of payments and transfers'. A Dispute Settlement Understanding was created that allowed experts to decide if policies were in accord with GATT rules and to permit sanctions if not. Government trade policies were to be subject to a Trade Policy Review Mechanism.[26]

The agreement was signed at Marrakesh on 14 April 1994 by 123 'contracting parties'. One partisan view was that it was 'the most important and successful of all the eight GATT rounds of multilateral negotiations'.[27] A more realistic view was that it was little more than 'a grubby set of global guidelines drawn up at the behest of the powerful for the benefit of the powerful'. This 'GATTastrophe' was criticized as an undemocratic challenge to domestic policies on the environment, health and safety by giving priority to trade. In particular, the 'new subjects' of the service sector, intellectual property and investment were criticized as self-serving responses by developed countries to their changing comparative advantage. The G77 claimed that the new measures shifted revenue to the developed countries. The Global North agreed to cut tariffs, phased in concessions on access for textiles over a considerable period, and only partially fulfilled promises on barriers to agricultural trade. In return, the South accepted controls over intellectual property and services, and faced large costs in implementing commitments. The deal was one-sided. A World Bank report pointed out that the concessions made by the North benefitted the North as well as the South; by contrast, the concessions made by the South benefitted the North and often imposed a cost on the South. The North's concessions on merchandise trade were less than the South's, and in the new issues the gains for the North were not balanced by benefits to the South. Critics of the deal complained that '[t]his is the politics of imperialism, of extracting from a less powerful party'. The political scientist Sylvia Ostry concluded that the grand bargain was a 'Bum Deal'.[28]

The developing countries had moved, with only limited success, from wide coalitions that demanded distributive justice to pragmatic, issue-based coalitions within a framework of reciprocity. Nevertheless, a return to a general coalition of developing countries would be difficult. The South was not a monolithic bloc. Brazil was more concerned with agricultural exports and India with food security; developing countries in East Asia were more interested in trade liberalization for industrial exports; others wished to preserve domestic markets. The disappointment of the Uruguay Round did not lead to a return to the NIEO's call for distributive justice. It did, however, lead to a search for a new way of dealing with developed countries through institutional reform that would give more voice to developing nations and lead to greater procedural fairness.[29]

THE WORLD TRADE ORGANIZATION

The agenda for the Uruguay Round included a better dispute settlement mechanism to enforce trade rules and strengthen compliance. At GATT, the Genevan liberals argued that rules were needed to contain the destructive potential of the nation state and the demands of the NIEO.[30] Similarly, back in 1978 Julian Jackson of the University of Michigan Law School worried that GATT lacked legal certainty, for it consisted of about 180 different agreements, codes and 'understandings' with varying purposes and membership, often incompatible with each other or the guiding principles of GATT. During the Uruguay Round, he proposed the creation of a World Trade Organization and in October 1989 discussion started in the Quad on the initiative of John Crosbie. The idea was taken up by the European Community as a response to the United States' unilateral use of sanctions. In GATT, all members had to agree to the findings of a dispute panel, which gave the offending party an effective veto. A stronger dispute settlement mechanism would oblige the errant member to comply, and in June 1990 the European Community proposed the creation of a new 'Multilateral Trade Organization'.

The motivation for the WTO was therefore in large part legalistic, to codify rules and embed them in a stronger dispute settlement mechanism. However, the transformation of GATT into the WTO did not entirely follow the precepts of the Genevan liberals, for it was also an expression of national power. The United States administration understood that institutional reform was intended to limit its unilateral policies and that the proposal raised issues of sovereignty that would be a focal point for congressional hostility. In contrast, rather than seeing a threat to their demands, the developing countries welcomed the proposal in the hope that a rules-based system could enforce greater equity. At Marrakesh, the Indonesian delegation looked to the WTO as 'the guardian of a rules-based, predictable and non-discriminating multilateral trading system and the guarantor of the rights of the weaker trading partners against arbitrary and unilateral actions of the strong'.[31]

The establishment of the WTO in January 1991 raised the issue of how decisions should be made. In theory, GATT had a one-country-one-vote system and differed from the weighted voting in the IMF. In practice, GATT operated by consensus. The Americans wished to continue with consensus in the WTO. Others wanted to give more voice to countries that had been marginalized. The compromise was that most decisions would be consensual with votes as a fallback. In practice, consensus continued to dominate, which created a risk of deadlock. Completing another trade round would be difficult if a country or group held out, for nothing was agreed until everything was agreed. Consensus did not entail equality in decision-making for it was often reached by meetings in the 'green room' that were by invitation only and excluded developing countries, with a lack of transparency. The result, in the words of one political scientist, was 'organized hypocrisy': the United States and Europe supported consensus on the principle of sovereign equality, but then proceeded to use their power to set the agenda and produce an unequal outcome.

Another issue was the relationship of trade in services and intellectual property with existing trade agreements. It was agreed that membership of the WTO would be a 'single undertaking' with membership on an 'all-or-nothing' basis to prevent 'free riders' choosing only those elements from which they gained. The disadvantage was that partial agreements could not be made on specific issues. Furthermore, cross-retaliation was permitted, which meant that trade sanctions could be used against a country violating intellectual property rights – a measure of greater interest to developed countries eager to protect their patents and new technology.[32]

The outcome was a compromise between developing countries, which

wanted more influence in a stronger multilateral organization, and industrialized countries which wanted developing countries to accept the
Uruguay package as the price for WTO membership. The United States
was, at best, ambivalent, for the creation of a stronger dispute settlement
process and appellate review body raised questions of national sovereignty.
The American negotiators opposed the WTO until the very last day and
thought it would be rejected by Congress, which only agreed when the
Republican Senate majority leader, Robert Dole, proposed a panel of
retired federal judges to monitor decisions by WTO dispute panels, with a
congressional vote on withdrawal from the WTO if the judges disagreed
with the panels on three occasions in five years. American acceptance of
the WTO was thus not wholehearted, and doubts remained whether the
new body could be effective. To the extent that the WTO ceased to be a
'rich man's club' and reduced the informal leadership of the Quad, greater
inclusivity would weaken its decision-making capabilities. The collapse of
the Soviet bloc had removed the binding power of an ideological opponent
and encouraged a triumphalist narrative of market liberalism. The result,
as the *Atlantic* magazine pointed out, was that the outcome of the Uruguay
Round 'was utopian. It called for nothing short of a common framework
of global international law – a major delegation of national sovereignty.'
Hostility emerged in the developed countries from both the progressive left
and populist right, and developing countries saw a danger that the new
agenda marginalized their concerns. GATT had been an interim solution
to the 1948 congressional failure to ratify the agreed International Trade
Organization, and was remarkably successful in negotiating a series of
trade rounds that reduced trade barriers. By contrast, the WTO did not
manage to complete its first – and only – round.[33]

The WTO sounded like a return to the ambitious agenda of the ITO
which had a wide concern not only for trade but also for employment,
commodities and development. The WTO's agenda was, initially, more
concerned with intellectual property and investments but soon expanded to
give more voice to less-developed and emerging economies, and to respond
to radical demands in the Global North to include development.[34] The outcome, as with the ITO, was too wide a remit that prevented a decision on
specific items given the need for agreement on a single package. In Geneva,
the preparation for ministerial meetings was inadequate, and increasingly
complex issues could not be resolved in meetings of ministers for a brief
period every two years. The result was to put pressure on the timetable and
to encourage grandstanding by politicians looking to domestic audiences
who were affected by 'behind the border' issues of labour or environmental
standards that were matters of national politics.[35] The chances of

successfully completing a round were slight, and the credibility of the WTO was undermined by the repeated failure of ministerial meetings.

The legal system of the WTO changed the dynamics of negotiations by removing flexibility. GATT handled disputes through 'diplomats' jurisprudence', i.e., trade negotiators reached a mutually acceptable solution that tolerated escape clauses and countervailing duties as a pragmatic price to pay for balancing demands for protection with a commitment to liberalization. They often conceded more than they could deliver in the knowledge that enforcement was weak. The WTO's 'lawyers' jurisprudence' meant that a country could be brought before a panel and forced to comply, which made negotiators more wary of making concessions.[36] GATT was a relatively informal organization that depended on the personal skills of the secretary. Wyndham White was effective in bringing the Kennedy Round to a conclusion, and Dunkel played a similar role in the Uruguay Round in drafting the ministerial declaration in 1985 and facilitating the relaunch of the round after it was suspended. His successor, and the first director general of the WTO, Peter Sutherland was crucial in bringing the Uruguay Round to a conclusion and was looking ahead to the next round, before he left the WTO in 1995 to become chairman of Goldman Sachs and British Petroleum – a career path that led to understandable suspicions that the organization was closely aligned with the Global North. The choice of the director general of the WTO – a more formal position than at GATT – soon became a matter of controversy.[37]

At the best of times, free trade is difficult to achieve in a democratic system. The case for free trade and comparative advantage rests on the aggregate benefits to society as a whole, and there are always winners and losers. Groups that suffer are usually concentrated in particular regions and sectors, such as textile workers in South Carolina or steel workers in Pennsylvania, who are more easily organized or better able to express their views in elections. By contrast, those who stand to gain – consumers buying cheaper clothes or businesses benefitting from cheaper imported steel – are more diffuse and difficult to organize or mobilize. In 1997 and 1998, President Clinton failed to obtain fast-track authority, in part because labour was demanding protection. Alan Reuther of the United Auto Workers remarked that 'we're not saying that every country has to have our minimum wage today. But we don't want to see a race to the bottom, a competition based on who can have the lowest wages or worst health and environment standards.' At Geneva in November 1998, Clinton picked up this theme and argued that 'we should be levelling up, not levelling down. Without such a strategy, we cannot build the necessary public support for continued expansion of trade. Working people will only assume the risks of a free international market if they have the confidence that the system will work for them.' Workers in the developed world naturally feared their standard of living was threatened by 'outsourcing' to countries with lower wage costs – a trend arising from integrated global supply chains that were encouraged by the containerization of maritime transport, information technology, and the changing structure of multinational corporations. Even a radical shift in trade policy was unlikely to restore lost jobs that reflected a wider process of de-industrialization and technological change – but demands for protection offered an easy answer to a complicated question.[38]

Clinton's rhetoric played well with American workers, but representatives of emerging markets saw a threat. Veerendra Kumar, the Indian minister for labour, insisted that the 'rising spectre of neo-protectionism in the name of labour standards . . . need[s] to be recognized, viewed with concern and combated with all force'.[39] Despite American and European attempts to include labour standards in the next round of talks, they were ruled out at the Singapore ministerial meeting in 1996 on the grounds that they might be used for protectionist purposes and should be left to the International Labour Organization. At Singapore, the agenda was shifting away from trade liberalization, which was of little concern to the Global North, to intellectual property and services, which were of less concern to the Global South. The Singapore ministerial meeting called for action on investment, government procurement, and trade facilitation by easing customs regulations. The main supporter of this new agenda was Leon Brittan. By contrast, the Clinton administration was ambivalent, torn between concerns that NAFTA and Uruguay Round were losing electoral support for the Democrats and a desire to press ahead with the new issues. Charlene Barshefsky, US Trade Representative, doubted the wisdom of a new round given opposition in developing countries. Furthermore, agricultural exporters wished to open up markets and end subsidies, which would not be acceptable in Europe or Japan.[40]

A WTO ministerial meeting to launch a new round of trade negotiations was scheduled for Seattle in November 1999, to be chaired by Barshefsky. The prospects were not good, for the appointment of a new director general was contested. The procedure was more formal than in GATT, with the term limited to four years with the possibility of renewal for one term. The United States backed Mike Moore, a former New Zealand trade minister (and briefly prime minister), whose concerns were for labour, the environment and reduced farm subsidies. The developing countries backed Supachai Panitchpakdi, the former minister of commerce of Thailand, who was more interested in development and supporting farmers. The compromise was that each would serve for three years, starting with Moore – and he was barely in post before the Seattle meeting. Divisions over the priorities of the next director general and lack of time led to difficulties for the secretariat in formulating an agreed agenda that might bridge the differences.[41]

The difficulties were not only within the WTO. When ministers convened at Seattle, they met protests. 'Market fundamentalism', so the critics alleged, viewed the environment, labour rights and development from the perspective of business and non-interference. Attitudes towards free trade were changing. To Cordell Hull, free trade was the basis for social justice, fairness, peace and prosperity; protection was about self-interest, perversion of the democratic process and corruption. Now, radical progressives such as Lori Wallach and Michelle Sforza saw free trade as a self-interested pursuit of corporate greed. They complained that the WTO 'favors huge multinational companies and the wealthiest few in developed and developing countries ... [G]lobal commerce takes precedence over everything – democracy, public health, equity, the environment, food safety and more.' The WTO was, in their view, responsible for a 'slow motion coup d'état' that created a new global economic system to increase corporate profits with little regard for social and ecological consequences. In 1995, Wallach created Global Trade Watch to monitor the WTO and oppose fast-track authority. It was affiliated to Public Citizen, a campaigning body founded in 1971 by consumer advocate and environmentalist Ralph Nader to counter corporate power on issues such as campaign finance and vehicle safety. Some American protest groups were linked to Direct Action Network, a loose affiliation of anti-corporate, anti-authoritarian bodies that emerged from People's Global Action, an anti-globalization movement that was created in opposition to the WTO ministerial meeting in Geneva in February 1998. In turn, People's Global Action drew on bodies such as the Brazilian Landless Workers Movement, which occupied unused land, the Karnataka State Farmers Union, which opposed genetically modified crops, and Mexican opposition to NAFTA. There was no central control or clear leadership but rather a network of shifting groups that opposed globalization and capitalism, rejected trade agreements, and favoured direct action in preference to lobbying.[42]

Less radical were demands for ethical consumption by bodies such as the Rainforest Alliance, founded in 1987, and the Fairtrade groups that came together in an international body in 1997. Unlike Nixon's and Reagan's definition of fair trade, this movement certified producers who met defined standards and paid them a price that covered the average costs of sustainable development, with an additional premium for producers' or workers' co-operatives to invest in improving the quality of lives. The schemes covered commodities such as tea, coffee and cocoa produced by small farmers, as well as plantation crops such as bananas, and depended on the willingness of consumers to pay a higher price from a sense of social justice. It appealed to Western students, church groups and affluent, socially conscious members of the middle class. Critics complained that well-meaning action could lock farmers into small-scale rural production, and would not help extractive industries such as copper that needed a shift in the structure of the global economy. Nevertheless, Fairtrade did produce benefits. One case study of coffee producers in Costa Rica found that Fairtrade increased the income of coffee farmers (though not of unskilled labour), shifted profits from middlemen, which reduced inequality, and aided the construction of schools.[43] These social movements reflected a wider criticism of the pursuit of free trade and globalization.

The demonstrations in Seattle brought together trade unionists, environmentalists, critics of global capitalism and anarchists who blocked streets, disrupted the meeting, and targeted the offices and shops of businesses judged guilty of corporate crime. The Seattle police lost control and the opening ceremony was cancelled. When the ministers met, their discussions were confused and inconclusive. Barshefsky's scepticism had been overruled by the State Department which wished to press ahead. The UN Human Development Report of July 1999 had called for the protection of labour and the environment and asserted that 'an essential aspect of global governance is responsibility to people – to equity, to justice, to enlarging the choices of all'. Clinton was playing to a domestic audience in his response that November in committing the United States to reviewing the impact of trade agreements on the environment and sustainable development.[44] Developing countries saw the risk of disguised protectionism and were uneasy that the rich countries were running the meeting behind the scenes in the 'green room'. The developing countries demanded greater equity in the WTO's decision-making process to overcome the limits of the Uruguay Round. African trade ministers, for example, protested that 'there is no transparency in the proceedings and African countries are being marginalised and generally excluded on issues of vital importance for our people and their future . . . We reject the approach that is being employed.' Similarly, Latin American and Caribbean countries announced that 'as long as conditions of transparency, openness and participation . . . do not exist, we will not join the consensus required to meet the objectives of this ministerial conference.' Protests outside and dissension within the meeting were an inauspicious start to the WTO's efforts.[45]

The WTO could not afford another setback at the next ministerial meeting at Doha, in November 2001. At the venue in the Qatar capital, protests were not possible, though critics could still make their case in briefing papers – such as Oxfam's complaint that the WTO neglected the world's poor and reinforced global inequality by unfair protectionist policies, agricultural subsidies, and rules on investment and intellectual property.[46] In October 2001, Mike Moore stressed that the stakes were high: 'Ministers are resolute. They do not want a repeat of the failure of Seattle ... Failure to get consensus on a forward work programme will lead many to question the value of the institution. It could condemn us to a period of hibernation.' He urged

> [m]inisters to reinvigorate our processes, boost global economic confidence and strengthen the multilateral trading system. It is a chance to affirm the importance of the rules-based system governing trade amongst nations. It is a chance for all Members to participate in a process that is win–win and promises benefits for all.[47]

Moore was speaking not long after 11 September and the destruction of the World Trade Center in New York – a terror attack on a symbol of the liberal trade order. The new round, it seemed to Moore, must respond to major questions facing the world, above all how to rescue 1.2 billion people who lived on less than a dollar a day and another 1.6 billion who lived on less than $2. Trade was redefined as the engine of growth to improve the conditions of the poor in the hope of appealing to the left (which complained that the organization neglected developing countries) and the right (which wished to replace aid with a focus on economic growth stimulated by open trade in agriculture, manufactures and ser- vices). Moore recognized that trade liberalization should be complemented by good governance, debt reduction, and the creation of domestic capacity to benefit from open trade. But there was a final reason for a new round that was 'more fundamental, more profound and more immediate ... This meeting is a chance for the international community to reaffirm its com- mitment to common values of openness, sharing, peaceful exchange and rule of law rather than rule of the jungle.' Moore quoted Robert Zoellick, US Trade Representative from 2001 to 2005, who remarked soon after 9/11 that '[e]recting new barriers and closing old borders will not help the impoverished. It will not feed hundreds of millions struggling for subsis- tence. It will not liberate the persecuted. It will not improve the environment in developing countries or reverse the spread of AIDS.' Zoellick argued that protectionism would not help orphans in India or union members in Latin America – nor, in a telling comment, would it help Indonesians 'try- ing to build a functioning, tolerant democracy in the largest Muslim nation in the world'. The Doha ministerial meeting and new trade round were influenced by the 'war on terror'. Pierre Pettigrew, the Canadian trade minister, set the tone of the meeting. 'Terrorism and hatred grow their strongest roots in poor soil ... Economic and social development in the world's poorest nations will help to erode the hopelessness that can breed hate.'[48]

THE DOHA DEVELOPMENT AGENDA

The ministerial meeting at Doha succumbed to the temptation of unrealistic ambitions. The Doha Development Agenda sought to place the interests of developing countries

> at the heart of the Work Programme adopted in this Declaration ... We recognize the particular vulnerability of the least-developed countries and the special structural difficulties they face in the global economy. We are committed to addressing the marginalization of least-developed countries in international trade and to improving their effective participation in the multilateral trading system.

Negotiations were to be completed by 1 January 2005 – an ambitious target given that the more limited Uruguay Round took longer.[49]

The Doha Development Agenda's attempt to secure support after the protests at Seattle led to new problems. Critics such as Dani Rodrik complained, with justice, that the WTO confused raising living standards with maximizing trade which 'has become the lens through which development is perceived, rather than the other way around'. In his view, 'development' was a rhetorical move to seize the moral high ground from the protesters at Seattle while prioritizing market integration as the source of growth. In Rodrik's opinion, the WTO took a wrong turn in pursuing a normative view of the global economy, rather than permitting developing countries to formulate their own development policies or allowing advanced economies to protect their labour and environmental standards. He was right. The WTO was part of a wider trend of thought. At the OECD, the secretary general in 2000 thought that that organization should become 'a champion of more open flows of goods, services and capital as a vehicle for increasing world economic growth and welfare'. Such claims were justified by the escape from poverty of millions of people in the developing world, but also fuelled criticism of globalization dominated by corporate and financial interests. The benefits of hyperglobalization were not spread equally, with many people in the Global North experiencing a loss of work and growing inequality, even as many in the Global South escaped from poverty. In any case, the success of many emerging economies did not rely on the neo-liberal agenda of the international institutions so much as state-led development.[50]

Negotiating an agreement in a member-driven organization based on consensus would be difficult. Moore complained that

> we have 144 handbrakes and one accelerator. Sometimes it feels more like one of those old Laurel and Hardy movies, with the car out of control and the steering wheel coming off in your hands. It's like trying to run a parliament with no parties, no whip, no speaker, no speaking limits and no majority voting system. It is consensus by exhaustion.[51]

In a sense, there were 'parties' of coalitions based on regional or sectoral interests that made compromise even more difficult. In GATT, coalitions such as the G77 were ideological and usually fragmented when different material interests led countries to make side deals in the final stages of negotiation. In the WTO, coalitions were based on issues and regions, and they had formal recognition. In March 2019, the WTO listed nineteen coalitions on its website. Five were regional, ranging from the institutionally powerful European Union (EU) to weaker organizations such as Mercosur, and loose groups such as ACP (countries in Africa, the Caribbean and the Pacific). The remainder had common interests that ranged from the wider G90 of African, ACP and less developed countries, to the Cairns group of agricultural exporters, the NAMA (Non-Agricultural Market Access) 11 developing countries, which wanted open markets for their industrial goods, and the Cotton 4 of African producers who opposed subsidies for American cotton growers.[52] These groupings contributed to deadlock by creating a collective agenda that potentially offered members greater gains than individual deals. In response, Pascal Lamy, the former European trade commissioner who was director general of the WTO from 2005 to 2013, adopted a strategy of 'concentric circles', i.e., consulting coalitions that reported back to their members. His rationale was that the large membership of the WTO made discussions cumbersome; by reducing the number of negotiating parties and concentrating on issue-specific deliberations by a smaller group, he would allow more voices to be heard on topics that mattered to them. These smaller groups would report to a larger group or the wider membership to reach a consensus decision. This approach would, he hoped, increase legitimacy by reducing the power of the Quad. It was well-meaning but with the unfortunate effect that groupings became more rigid, resulting in greater difficulty in reaching compromise. In effect, informal discussions in the 'green room' continued, which damaged the WTO's credibility.[53]

The Doha Round aimed to cover trade in services which was of interest to developed countries. Reaching an agreement on services would be difficult. Tariffs of trade in goods were relatively easy to adjust, but services involved licences and professional qualifications, regulation of the financial sector, or long-standing institutional barriers as in telecommunications. These issues went 'behind the border' into domestic politics and were hard to resolve. Similarly, developing countries feared that measures to defend intellectual property in medicine and new technology would work to the advantage of advanced economies and impose costs on poor countries.[54] Even negotiations over manufactures (now renamed Non-Agricultural Market Access) were problematic. Some countries wished to adopt a formula to cut high tariffs more than low tariffs; others preferred the time-consuming 'request–offer' system, where each country set out what it would cut and what offers it would expect in return which would be generalized by the most favoured nation principle. Agreement was more complex with more countries involved and more varied interests. China pointed to the heavy burden of accession to the WTO; India opposed opening its markets; Kenya needed revenue from tariffs; and so on. In November 2002, Zoellick proposed that all tariffs on consumer and industrial goods be removed by 2015, which would give the United States access to the markets of the developing world. The result, he argued, would not only benefit the United States. It would raise people in the developing world from poverty and so create peace and prosperity. The EU thought the idea unrealistic, and developing countries with low tariffs, such as South Korea and Mexico, preferred a middle course of increased access for their industrial exports. The problems were compounded by negotiations on agriculture, which meant that concessions on one could be held hostage by the other, and by the attempt to reduce non-tariff barriers which opened up complicated issues about the relationship between economic growth and environmental standards.[55] The range of issues and competing interests made a single understanding virtually impossible.

The situation was not helped by problems in Washington, where President George W. Bush had difficulties in securing fast-track authority to complete the round. Although the Republicans had a majority of twelve in the House, around fifty opposed granting the authority and Bush had to buy support by offering protection to the steel industry and subsidies to farmers. Meanwhile, the Democrats wanted to include labour and environmental standards to protect workers from a 'race to the bottom'. Bush and Zoellick appealed to Congress for support in the context of the war on terror. In Zoellick's view, economic strength was the foundation of America's hard and soft power. Earlier enemies learned that America is the arsenal of democracy; today's enemies will learn that America is the economic engine for freedom, opportunity and development … Trade is about more than economic efficiency. It promotes the values at the heart of this protracted struggle.

Bush insisted that '[t]rade creates the habits of freedom' by fostering consumers and entrepreneurs in a free society. 'Societies that are open to commerce across their borders are more open to democracy within their borders. And for those of us who care about values and believe in values – not just American values but universal values that promote human dignity – trade is a good way to do that.' In 2001, fast-track authority passed the House by a single vote, with most Democrats opposed and Republicans in support. It imposed a strict limit on the trade negotiators, who were denied flexibility and were required to undertake detailed consultation with Congress.[56]

The next ministerial meeting, at Cancún in September 2003, needed to resolve three issues if the round were to be completed by 2005: a deal on agricultural support and export subsidies; market access or tariffs; and the inclusion of the 'Singapore issues' of investment, government procurement, trade facilitation and competition. The ministers agreed that an 'explicit consensus' was needed, rather than the earlier practice of assuming consensus unless it was opposed by a member. As a result, every member had a veto and there was no consensus that the Singapore issues should be included. The EU was initially in favour of their inclusion but agreed to drop – or 'de-link' – investment and competition to make progress on procurement and trade facilitation. Japan and South Korea wanted to keep all the Singapore issues, and developing countries refused to consider any. The Cancún ministerial meeting collapsed in mutual recrimination. The EU was blamed for not 'de-linking' issues earlier and then failing to secure support for its position; the developing countries were accused of inflexibility to secure their aims on agriculture and market access. More generally, the fault lay with the intrinsic difficulty of securing a multilateral agreement between all members in a single undertaking on an expanded agenda that affected domestic political autonomy.[57] It was an object lesson in how not to negotiate.

Failure to reach a multilateral deal led to more bilateral or regional trade agreements. The WTO was aware of about 250 by the end of 2002 and they continued to proliferate. The Asian Free Trade Area, for example, expanded its membership and made separate deals between 2008 and 2010 with Japan, Australia, New Zealand, India and South Korea. The situation was complicated by other initiatives. Japan looked to a Comprehensive Economic Partnership for East Asia, and ASEAN turned to an East Asian Free Trade Agreement with China, Japan and South Korea. In 2006, the Asia-Pacific Economic Cooperation proposed a free trade area for the Asia-Pacific region in response to the failure of the Doha Round and the tangled 'noodle bowl' of around sixty free trade agreements in the area.[58]

Zoellick thought these regional deals were essential: 'I'm a believer in the multilateral system and worldwide free markets. But I also understand how to use national power. Bilaterals have been a very useful means of exerting influence. They also have benefits in their own right.' His strategy was to work with 'can do' countries rather than to be blocked by 'won't do' countries. Above all, he invoked the success of the NAFTA and assured the House Committee on Ways and Means that it

> will be crucial in our quest to build a prosperous and secure hemisphere. Free trade offers the first and best hope of creating the economic growth necessary to alleviate endemic poverty and raise living standards through the Americas ... NAFTA has been a case study in globalization along a 2,000-mile border; it demonstrates how free trade between developed and developing countries can boost prosperity, economic stability, productive integration, and the development of civil society.

Trade agreements, he believed, would link the United States to other people and encourage reforms essential for long-term development through the rule of law, private property rights, competition, sectoral reform and regional integration.[59]

Nevertheless, Zoellick remained committed to multilateralism and he tried a new approach when talks resumed in July 2004. He aimed to replace the old Quad with the Five Interested Parties (the US, EU, Brazil, India and Australia) meeting at the American mission. In July 2004, the Five Interested Parties produced a package that Supachai Panitchpakdi welcomed as a 'truly historic' achievement. This 'framework agreement' was approved as an agenda for discussions: it proposed to abolish agricultural export subsidies and reduce trade-distorting domestic support; to take action on the Singapore issue of trade and customs procedures; and to open trade in manufactures, especially to help developing countries. Supachai saw an end to deadlock and looked to progress. He was disappointed, for an agenda is not the same as a deal. Not even the Five Interested Parties were of a similar opinion. Kamal Nath, the Indian minister of commerce and industry, demanded 'livelihood security' for farmers – an economically dubious policy that would hit consumers, but with a compelling electoral argument of winning support from small farmers. Agriculture remained an intractable issue that went beyond comparative advantage and economic efficiency to questions of electoral influence and national identity.[60] Deadlock returned, and the deadline of 1 January 2005 passed.

By July 2006, Lamy was in despair: 'There's no beating around the bush. We're in dire straits.'[61] In the United States, presidential fast-track authority expired on 30 June 2007, with little chance of renewal in the face of protectionism and the lack of confidence in the Doha Round. In the European Union, commercial policy was in principle covered by majority voting, but unanimity was needed on a deal that would prejudice the responsibility of member states for social, educational and health services. Neither was there much chance that the emerging powers would offer concessions that would be sufficient to buy off domestic opposition in the United States and Europe.[62] Hopes briefly revived when the New Zealand representative, Crawford Falconer, put forward proposals on agriculture, only for the glimmer of hope to disappear early in 2008 when higher food prices and unrest led some countries to impose export controls or taxes to retain food for domestic consumers. Lamy devised a package on agriculture and non-agricultural market access in July 2008, but negotiations again broke down. Brazil was a major exporter, supported multilateralism, and was willing to accept the package. India, with its large population of small farmers, took a different stance, for Nath realized that agreement would be interpreted as selling out India's farmers. Brazil eventually sided with India to maintain unity, and their foreign and trade ministers were delighted: 'One thing we can celebrate is that rules here are no longer made by the rich countries. They have to take us into account.'[63]

The global financial crisis that broke in 2008 made the Doha Round an irrelevance when there were more pressing problems. A single package covering all issues for all countries was impossible, and the WTO did not complete the round. In Congress, opposition to the WTO was growing, with eighty-six members of the House of Representatives voting to withdraw from it in 2005. Protectionist groups were better organized and demanded anti-dumping measures or countervailing duties, and to limit fast-track authority. There was no United States Trade Representative for the first fifteen months of the Obama administration, for Senator Jim Bunning of Kentucky blocked nominees in protest against a Canadian anti-smoking law that would harm tobacco farmers. 'Buy American' provisions were inserted into the stimulus package of February 2009, and subsidized loans given to General Motors and Chrysler.[64] When the WTO met at Geneva in the aftermath of the global financial crisis, in December 2009, the *Financial Times* reported that the 'Doha round of trade negotiations is so deadlocked that it is not even on the formal agenda – the rough equivalent of holding the 1919 Versailles conference without talking about the war.' Talks dragged on without success.[65] The Doha Round was not formally abandoned – it just faded away. It confirmed the experience of Bretton Woods and the ITO: success can be achieved by focusing on one issue rather than an ever-growing set of issues. A more viable solution than a 'single undertaking' with its doomed requirement that 'nothing is agreed until everything is agreed' was to be less ambitious and utopian in considering defined topics or geographic regions, to move from bilateral deal to 'plurilateral plus' agreements, in the hope of extending the benefits to all members of the WTO.[66]

Despite the failure of the Doha Round, the WTO could claim that past successes were locked in by a rules-based system and the dispute resolution mechanism when the global financial crisis hit. Even so, there were problems. The WTO's secretariat remained small, with only 621 staff in 2008/9 compared with 10,000 at the World Bank and 2,478 at the IMF. The secretariat was responsible for regular reviews of members' trade policies that were intended to create greater transparency and prevent free riding. In principle, a regular cycle of country reviews was established, with the largest four traders covered every two years, the next sixteen countries every four years and the remainder every six years, with an annual report to encourage a shared commitment to liberalization. The secretariat was too small and too stretched by the Doha negotiations to make this cycle practicable, and the reports had little visibility or impact on domestic policy.[67]

A main responsibility of the secretariat was the operation of a legalistic dispute settlement mechanism that was more formal than that of GATT. It was a victory for lawyers in codifying rules that had evolved by custom. In the event of failure to resolve a dispute, the secretariat – or (if one party objected) the director general – would appoint a panel of three members. The contesting parties could appeal to an appellate body, with three members drawn from a panel of seven judges who served for a maximum term of four years with one renewal. Members could less easily break treaty obligations and impose protectionist measures, but there was also a risk that the WTO was giving power to an independent judiciary that could make law through judicial interpretation and threaten national sovereignty. To limit this risk, the panels and appellate body reported to the Dispute Settlement Board on which all members were represented. Many problems remained. Should a country found to be in breach of the rules be obliged to comply with the ruling, or could it continue in breach either by paying compensation or accepting retaliation – and how was the appropriate level of compensation or retaliation to be determined? Could the panels and appellate body refer to non-WTO law where it might be relevant, and could they consider the social concerns of countries that imposed trade restrictions on grounds of environmental, health or labour standards?[68]

The panels and appellate body had great difficulty deciding where to draw the line between legitimate regulations and illegitimate devices to restrict trade. Decisions involved a range of complex issues such as public morals, health, or protection of the environment and natural resources. One example was the 'shrimp–turtle' case. The United States banned the importation of shrimps from India, Pakistan, Thailand and Malaysia because their fishing practices did not protect turtles. The appellate body found the United States' action was justified on the grounds that a member could impose restrictions that protected public morals, human, animal or plant life and health, and that it did not lead to arbitrary or unjustifiable discrimination between countries. The appellate body could also rule whether commodities were 'like' or directly competitive. Japan taxed vodka, gin and whisky at a higher rate than locally produced *shochu*. The court ruled they were like and directly competitive so that the differential tax was not legitimate. A related rule forbade differential treatment of products based on their method of production as opposed to their properties for consumption. When the United States banned both imported and domestic tuna that led to excessive killing of dolphins, the panel ruled that it could not unilaterally impose its own environmental standards on the exporting country: tuna is tuna regardless of how it is caught and must be treated the same. This decision does not appear consistent with the outcome in the shrimp–turtle dispute.

The same complications arose over social rights. The panel accepted that public morals vary in time and space, and that members should have some freedom of definition. The result was tension between the WTO's support for liberalization to create competition and acceptance of divergence in regulatory practice to allow for different values. The most contentious area was food safety. Countries were bound to adopt harmonized international sanitary and phytosanitary standards unless they could provide scientific evidence to support a still stricter standard that would limit trade. In 1997, the United States brought a case against the European Community, which had banned hormone-injected beef. The panel commissioned scientists to report whether the use of hormones was a health hazard within the limits of the international standard set by the Codex Alimentarius Commission, a joint FAO–WTO body that first met in 1963 to produce a published body of standards and codes of practice.

All but one of the scientists reported that there was no risk. The panel therefore found in favour of the United States, which could impose retaliatory tariffs. The Community appealed and the appellate body ruled that the panel should not have commissioned its own experts and should have assessed the Community's evidence that hormones were abused. The outcome was a mixed ruling, in that Europe could continue its ban and the US could continue to retaliate.[69] Environmental and health issues such as genetically modified crops or the use of hormones were more easily grasped in public debates than arcane trade negotiations.

Potentially, less developed countries could use the dispute resolution mechanism to further their interests within the WTO rather than in opposition to the multilateral system. In 2004, for example, Brazil, with the support of Benin and Chad, brought a case against the United States' cotton subsidies and won a preliminary ruling. The problem was that a developing country that won a legal case against the United States or EU might not secure an adequate remedy. The use of trade retaliation was one-sided, for the developing country was unlikely to inflict meaningful damage on the developed country unless they could secure collective retaliation or monetary compensation for harm – both proposals being resisted by developed countries.[70]

The WTO's dispute mechanism raised major questions about the relationship between trade liberalization and democratic national regulations. Should the panel and appellate body oblige national legislatures to comply with international law or should priority be given to democratically determined policies that reflected differing cultural norms? International regulatory standards such as the Codex Alimentarius lacked transparency and democratic legitimacy to deal with highly contentious issues such as genetically modified crops. How were the panels to decide when regulations were a hidden form of protectionism that benefitted special interests or justifiable aspirations for animal welfare or the environment? To critics, the dispute panels and appellate body were exceeding their authority by, in effect, legislating through the interpretation of rules.[71]

By the time of the global financial crisis, merchandise trade had reached a record level as a share of GDP (see Figure 13). The trade rounds played a part in reducing barriers, though the expansion of trade had more to do with the integration of global supply chains and outsourcing to lower-wage economies. These developments, encouraged by a reduction in the cost of transport and improvements in information technology, allowed 'just in time' delivery and changes in the structure of business corporations that not only co-ordinated production across the globe but also moved profits. The global economy had changed in fundamental ways since the creation of GATT in 1947 when trade was mainly the sale of raw materials and food to the industrial countries who exported finished goods. GATT and the WTO, in the eyes of their critics, were associated with facilitating these trends rather than mitigating their impact. Defenders of the WTO could point to the undoubted gains for many people in the Global South, and to the way it locked in trade liberalization and prevented the resurgence of trade wars. Nevertheless, it was widely seen as a failing organization. No round had been completed since 1993, and there was no prospect that one would be feasible in future. Even the dispute resolution system was threatened when President Trump refused to nominate new members of the appellate board so that it was no longer quorate by the end of 2019, and from 2018 he embarked on a trade war with China. The WTO faced an existential crisis. As we will see in the next chapter, the transition of China to become one of the powerhouses of the global economy – and the breakup of the Soviet Union – created a new economic order that has led to serious tension in the economic government of the world.

Figure 13: Global merchandise exports as a % of GDP, 1830–2014

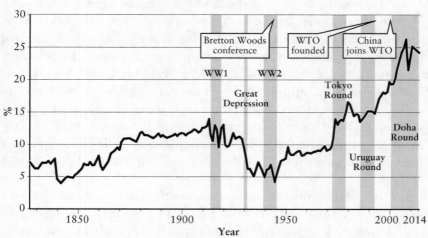

Source: Our World in Data at https://ourworldindata.org/grapher/merchandise-exports-gdp-cepii?country=~OWID_WRL

23

'Setting the bird free'

Economies in Transition

'*One cannot hold a bird tightly in one's hand without killing it. It must be allowed to fly, but only within its cage. Without a cage, it would fly away and become lost. Of course, the cage must be of appropriate dimensions; it must have the necessary room ... [R]egulation of economic activity by the market must not entail abandonment of the orientation provided by the plan.*'

Chen Yun, quoted in Richard Baum, *Burying Mao: Chinese Politics in the Age of Deng Xiaoping*[1]

'*[T]here wasn't much choice: it was either constantly increasing chaos or, with no preparation whatsoever, an immediate start-up of the free market mechanism – with the understanding that the parts required for it to function normally would be built in later, as we went along.*'

Yegor Gaidar, *Days of Defeat and Victory*[2]

On 4 June 1989, protests in Beijing's Tiananmen Square were brutally suppressed and the authority of the Chinese Communist Party reaffirmed. On 9 November 1989, the fall of the Berlin Wall marked the beginning of the end of the Soviet bloc in eastern and central Europe. In December, President George H. W. Bush and General Secretary Mikhail Gorbachev met in Malta and announced the end of the Cold War that had shaped the post-war multilateral order. The following year, the Soviet Communist Party ended single-party rule, and in 1991 the Soviet Union dissolved.

The crisis of the 1970s in the West led to the survival of capitalism in a new form of market liberalism and financialization. In the Soviet Union and its satellites, it led to failure as controlled economies collapsed under the strain of supporting large armies and competing in the arms race with the United States, while attempting to legitimate the regimes through

Deng Xiaoping greets Mikhail Gorbachev in the Great Hall of the People
in Beijing, May 1989.

investing to secure higher growth and consumption, which led Poland, East Germany and Hungary to rely on Western loans.[3] The economies of the former Soviet Union and its satellites embarked on a transition from command to a market economy through what came to be called 'shock therapy'. The aim was to replace centrally controlled economies in a 'big bang' by a new market economy based on price liberalization, privatization, opening of trade, and stabilization of the economy through strict fiscal and monetary policies. The IMF played an important role in the transition, which reflected confidence in the superiority of markets – though the outcome was to create a class of oligarchs who exploited opportunities for personal gain. The outcome was different in China. Although there were some advocates – both internal and external – of shock therapy, it was rejected in favour of a dual-track policy that combined continued state control with the market – a process of 'growing out of the plan' and into the market. Here, the IMF had no role and the World Bank contributed to an eclectic mix of ideas that remained under the control of the Communist Party.

The two approaches had strikingly different outcomes. In 1970, the United States' GDP per adult was about sixteen times that of China. By 2010, the difference was only fivefold. By contrast, in Russia GDP per adult collapsed in the 1990s and then only grew modestly so that it had not returned to its previous peak by 2010. These different transitions from command to market economies shaped the world in which we now live. During the Cold War, the Soviet Union had not been a member of the international institutions or integral to the global economy to anything like the same extent as China, which has become the world's second largest economy, deeply integrated into the global economy while retaining Communist rule. It operates on fundamentally different principles from the United States, which poses serious difficulties for the economic government of the world. At the same time, the demise of the Soviet Union left Russia as a resentful and weakened economic power with continued geopolitical ambitions.

India provides a third experience of transition – a democratic postcolonial state with an economy largely in the hands of private firms within a framework of planning and controls. At first sight, it should have been possible to undergo a smoother transition to a liberalized market economy with faster growth than either Russia or China. In reality, the outcome was disappointing. In 1960, India's GDP per adult was slightly below China's – by 2010, it was under half (see Figure 14). Understanding the relative economic performances, and political choices, of the Soviet Union, China and India at the end of the twentieth century sets the scene

Figure 14: Purchasing power parity by GDP per adult at constant 2021 Euro, 1960–2020

Year	USA	Russian Federation	India	China
1960	23,876		1,515	1,768
1970	31,545	16,301	1,885	2,002
1980	35,446	21,232	1,975	2,393
1990	42,853	22,918	2,668	3,302
2000	53,197	14,396	3,614	5,389
2010	56,239	22,243	5,535	11,172
2020	61,443	25,856	7,974	19,729

Source: World Inequality Database at https://wid.world/data/.

for the global economic order of the present day, and the problems facing global economic government.[4]

CHINA: TRANSITION IN AN AUTHORITARIAN REGIME

In 1973, Deng Xiaoping returned from disgrace after the chaos of the Cultural Revolution as first vice-premier and Zhou Enlai's preferred successor. He faced opposition from the 'Gang of Four' – the hard-line leftists led by Mao's wife – who mounted a campaign to 'Criticize Deng and Oppose the Rehabilitation of Right-leaning Elements'. Deng was not chosen as premier when Zhou died in January 1976 and was removed from all leadership positions. Mao died in September 1976, the Gang of Four was displaced, and Deng was rehabilitated in 1977. Although Deng was never head of government or General Secretary of the CCP, he was the dominant figure in the country by 1978 when he embarked on the liberalization of the Chinese economy under the slogan of 'socialism with Chinese characteristics'. He was careful not to challenge Mao's status as the founder of the Chinese state whom he judged 'seven parts good and three parts bad'. The excesses of the Cultural Revolution were blamed on the Gang of Four, and the power of the Communist Party was not in doubt.[5]

Deng initially tried to restore the planned economy, but soon realized that the Cultural Revolution had weakened the state's dominance of the countryside. As he said in March 1979, '[p]honey, ultra-left socialism' had resulted in 'factionalism and anarchism' with considerable damage to scientific and technological progress. His aim was 'socialist modernization' based on the 'four cardinal principles' of keeping to the socialist road, upholding the dictatorship of the proletariat, maintaining the leadership of the party, and returning to the correct path of Marxism–Leninism and Maoist thought. In Deng's opinion, China lagged behind other countries not because socialism was inferior to capitalism, but because of imperialism and feudalism. The solution was to use capitalist methods of profits, incentives, markets and advanced technology to create the material base for a socialist society, without adopting a capitalist system or creating a 'bourgeoisie or any other exploiting class ... who engage in corruption, embezzlement, speculation and profiteering'. Socialism remained vital, for it

> is designed to meet the material and cultural needs of the people to the maximum extent possible – not to exploit them. These characteristics of the socialist system make it possible for the people of our country to share common political, economic and social ideals and moral standards. All this can never happen in a capitalist society. There is no way by which capitalism can ever eliminate the extraction of super-profits by its millionaires or ever get rid of exploitation, plundering and economic crises. It can never generate common ideals and moral standards or free itself from appalling crimes, moral degradation and despair.

The dictatorship of the proletariat must continue, based on links between the masses and 'correct and effective leadership' by the Communist Party. Although Deng admitted that the party had made errors, 'each time the errors were corrected by relying on the Party organization, not by discarding it'. What was needed was

> socialist democracy, people's democracy, and not bourgeois democracy, individualist democracy ... We practise democratic centralism, which is the integration of centralism based on democracy with democracy under the guidance of centralism ... Under this system, personal interests must be subordinated to collective ones, the interests of the part to those of the whole, and immediate to long-term interests ... Our advocacy and practice of these principles in no way means that we can ignore personal, local or immediate interests. In the final analysis, under the socialist system there is a unity of personal interests and collective interests, of the interests of the part and those of the whole, and of immediate and long-term interests.[6]

Deng was not alone in advocating reform. Zhao Ziyang was equally important, though he has been written out of the Communist Party's official account. Like Deng, he was disgraced in the Cultural Revolution. He was rehabilitated in 1971 and by 1975 was the party secretary in Sichuan where he adopted an economic policy based on greater freedom for household production, which he extended on a national level when he was called to Beijing.[7] These two men were 'builders' or 'marketers' who were willing to contemplate rapid liberalization and, in 1986 and 1988, even policies that were close to 'shock therapy'. In the event, shock therapy was blocked by reformers associated with Chen Yun, a leading political figure who was from 1979 the head of a new Economic and Finance Commission. These 'balancers' or 'adjusters' gave a greater role to the containment of markets within a framework of central planning and controls. Both groups agreed that marketization was needed; they differed over the speed. In Chen's formulation, the bird of the free market should be free to fly within the cage of planning with steady progress rather than a 'headlong rush'. In 1980, he insisted that the approach should be 'to start with experiments at selected points and to draw lessons from experience at the right times'. He likened this policy to 'groping for stones to cross the river. In the beginning, steps must be small, walking slowly.' Chen favoured pragmatic experiment and a dual-track approach of maintaining price controls and planning alongside a liberalized market sector that handled excess production by state enterprises and the un-controlled sector. As a result, the economy could 'grow out of the plan' or – given that the planned sector remained much the same size – grow into the market.[8] The influence of these two approaches shifted over time, with the marketers pointing to contradictions between the controlled and market sector, and the balancers fearing inflation and social unrest – not least the uprising in Tiananmen Square.

Growing into the market was possible because of the nature of the Chinese economy. In the late 1970s, around 80 per cent of China's popu-lation lived in the country and around 70 per cent on peasant farms. Only around 20 per cent lived in cities, and the same proportion worked in state enterprises. As a result, there was greater capacity for change in the countryside, and the urban industrial economy was less rigid than in the Soviet Union, where state-owned enterprises employed over 90 per cent of workers and there was an emphasis on heavy industry in a tightly controlled planned economy. In China, growth in the market sector was possible without disrupting the controlled sector.[9] Reform was also facili-tated by the Cultural Revolution, which had the unintended consequence of empowering peasant households and undermining the planned economy. Frank Dikötter points out that a 'silent revolution' by millions of villagers was 'one of the most enduring legacies of a decade of chaos and entrenched fear . . . [C]adres in the countryside were defenceless against myriad daily acts of quiet defiance and endless subterfuge, as people tried to sap the economic dominance of the state and replace it with their own initiative and ingenuity.'[10] After the disaster of the great famine, Zhao and other reformers aimed to replace the inefficient communal system with individual household responsibility. The dissolution of the communes started in the late 1970s, and in 1980 the party leadership allowed 'household responsibility' on a voluntary basis. The change was encouraged by the cadres so that virtually all peasant households came under the new regime within three years. Land remained in collective ownership, but it was farmed by individual households that contributed part of their output to cover taxes and a sales quota and retained any surplus for their own use or sale. As a result, individual farmers had incentives to increase yields and provide more food to the towns. The motivation of the party leaders was pragmatic – to resolve the problem of grain production and improve food supplies. The removal of food shortages could then facilitate reform in the urban-industrial sector.[11]

In 1982, communes were abolished, and communal workshops became town and village enterprises (TVEs) that were allowed to compete in national and global markets. Deng's aim was to release the dynamism of the countryside. As he said in 1985, 'if you want to bring the initiative of the peasants into play, you should give them the power to make money.' The 'balancers' worried that these new enterprises were harming state enterprises, which lacked flexibility and incurred the higher welfare costs of the 'iron rice bowl', and conservatives worried that free enterprise was subverting socialism. Deng responded that Marx referred in *Das Kapital* to employers of eight people exploiting the workers; it followed that a household head with seven workers was not an exploitative capitalist. Even this limit was soon breached, and in 1987 household enterprises were officially allowed to employ more than seven workers.[12]

The TVEs were central to the economic transformation of China. In 1985, 12.2 million TVEs employed 69.8 million people. The largest group comprised 1.57 million collective enterprises employing 41.5 million people; there were 0.53 million private concerns employing 4.75 million; and 10.1 million household enterprises employing 23.5 million. Growth was largely in the second and third categories. By 1996, 23.4 million TVEs employed 135.1 million workers. The collective enterprises remained relatively stable with 1.55 million collectives employing 59.5 million workers, so that their share of total employment in TVEs fell from 59.5 to 44 per cent. By contrast, private concerns expanded to 2.26 million employing 24.6 million workers, and household enterprises to 19.6 million employing 50.9 million.[13] The TVEs were complemented by special economic zones (SEZs) on the coast, starting in Guangdong and Fujian provinces in 1979, and extending to fourteen coastal cities in 1984. The SEZs allowed new forms of enterprise that drew on foreign direct investment and technological transfer through joint ventures that limited the power of foreign capital. The result of these developments was a shift from economic self-reliance to export-led growth, with foreign trade growing from 7 per cent of GNP in 1978 to 40 per cent in the early 1990s.[14]

In China, unlike in the Soviet Union, local experimentation sifted success (that could be adopted elsewhere) from failure (which could be denounced as deviation). Experimentation was possible both because the economy was less rigid and because China's 'regionally decentralized authoritarian system' allowed provincial and municipal governments to experiment, so long as they did not blatantly violate Communist ideology and central authority. Local leaders had an incentive to improve their economies and to maintain social peace – and the party rewarded those who succeeded and punished those who failed. The result was a combination of discretion exercised by semi-independent local leaders within a centralized single-party state. There were also risks, for local authorities could pursue development policies that rested on high levels of debt from state banks, with inefficiencies and self-interest on the part of local elites.[15] Experiment and reform remained under the control of the Communist Party – a point on which the 'builders' and 'balancers' agreed. They had no intention of surrendering the party's monopoly of power or allowing greater political freedom that risked challenging Communist rule, as happened with the Solidarity movement in Poland. There was certainly no intention of surrendering single-party rule as Gorbachev did in the Soviet Union. The 'bird' of political debate had to be contained within the 'cage' of the party whether by force, repression, or economic policies that served to sustain the regime.[16]

Although the structure of the Chinese economy made gradualism and a dual approach more feasible than in the Soviet bloc, the transition was still problematic. The transformation within the countryside created social problems, for the state's one-child policy collided with the incentive for peasants to have more children to farm their land and provide security in the absence of collective welfare. The abolition of production brigades meant that the collective infrastructure of dams and reservoirs deteriorated, and local government did not have the capacity to take over. The allocation of communal tools and animals to households gave rural cadres opportunities for favouritism and corruption. Migration from the countryside to towns caused difficulties. The system of *hukou* or household registration determined access to goods and services such as health care, pensions, housing, schools and access to loans. Individuals were classified as either city dwellers or peasants, with their status inherited from their mother. Migrants could not easily change their registration, which led to a disadvantaged group lacking the entitlement of other urban residents, and local officials were reluctant to change a system that would increase their costs. In theory, migrants could be sent back to the countryside to reduce pressure on the urban food supply or in response to a recession, and this threat meant that migrant workers had limited bargaining power. The absence of a comprehensive social security system encouraged high levels of household savings, and the absence of a buoyant domestic market led to a high reliance on exports for economic growth.[17] Moreover, loosening price controls led to inflation and social unrest. The co-existence of two price systems meant market dislocations and opportunities for corruption by allowing state enterprises to buy at controlled prices and sell on the market at a higher price. The main beneficiaries were the families of high officials who exploited opportunities for private gain, with a blurred line between criminal activity and socialist entrepreneurship. This situation posed a dilemma for the authorities: draconian action against corruption might harm initiative, but failure to respond would undermine the reputation of the party. Further, tackling inflationary pressure by imposing fiscal or monetary restraint could lead to political and social tensions.[18]

The result was continued debate between the 'builders' and 'balancers' which drew on experience from other countries. Unlike in the Soviet Union, tight party control allowed consideration of a range of options from an eclectic mix of experts. One model was the 'rationalizing reform' of eastern Europe, and especially Hungary, that aimed to make the command economy work more efficiently by a shift from output targets to sales and profits, with investment from funds retained by productive units. This approach aimed to use market-like elements to improve planning rather than to shift to a market economy. Mandatory planning would be replaced by indicative planning, administrative controls by economic incentives, with decentralization and new forms of ownership so that managers could behave like profit-seeking businessmen within the state plan. In this approach, the market remained a tool of central planners and prices were set to steer the economy rather than to balance supply and demand or distribute resources. Many economists from the Soviet bloc came to see such rationalizing reform as a dead end that preserved state socialism without real change in the economy. They turned to radical 'shock therapy' to break the old system. In China, some economists similarly started to argue for sudden price liberalization to overcome the difficulties of dual pricing. Others continued to support gradualism, for the system of controls was less entrenched and inflexible than in the Soviet bloc. Chinese reformers also looked to the capitalist West, with visiting

delegations of both free marketeers such as Milton Friedman and Keynesians. The approach was pragmatic and eclectic, allowing the Chinese
leadership to develop its own thinking in dialogue with a wide range of
views without being subordinated to any one approach, and with the
party remaining in control.[19]

The influence of 'builders' and 'balancers' shifted over time. In 1982,
with inflation under control, Deng and Zhao pressed ahead faster than
Chen felt wise given the economic risks and the dangers of 'spiritual pollution' as economic freedom threatened socialist cultural norms.[20] Zhao
and Deng emphasized a 'planned commodity economy' – a formulation
that allowed some market forces and the sale of goods outside the system
of state planning. In September 1984, Zhao provided a deliberately
ambiguous explanation of his approach to the politburo standing committee. China was not a market economy, and 'blind and spontaneous'
market forces would only apply in a few sectors. He then remarked that
planning meant guidance rather than compulsion and should use the 'law
of value' or prices, for it was no longer the case that 'planning is number
one, and the law of value number two'. The implication was that prices
would be determined by supply and demand. This ambiguity allowed him
to overcome opposition, and his approach was ratified by the party in
October 1984. Reform would follow a dual-track approach, removing
some price controls, delegating others to subsidiary bodies, and ensuring
that market prices did not fluctuate too much by the involvement of state
agencies.[21]

The programme started by reforming state-owned enterprises to make
them self-managing and responsible for their workforce and prices, with
more freedom to engage in markets within the general parameters of the
state plan. The aim was to end 'eating out of a common pot' and to 'smash
the iron rice bowl' – the system by which state enterprises received operating funds and returned revenues to the state, with life-time employment
and standardized salaries. Rather than handing profits to the state, enterprises could retain profits to create incentives, to invest and to pay bonuses
to workers.[22] Zhao looked to a gradual reduction in the role of state
prices and an increase in the role of market prices, a dual-track approach
that combined two co-ordination mechanisms – a planned sector with
controlled prices and payment for a fixed output alongside a market
sector and prices for additional production that allowed state firms to
acclimatize to new incentives. The planned sector with a fixed output
would gradually shrink in relative terms as state enterprises responded to
incentives and increased output at market prices. Zhao pushed ahead
more rapidly than his ambiguous formulation implied. Not only did the

bird of the market have more freedom to fly within the cage of planning, as Chen accepted, but Zhao also permitted the bird to fly outside the cage.[23]

The economy started to overheat. Chen and the Economic and Financial Commission urged caution with tighter macroeconomic management to prevent inflation. On the other hand, a number of Chinese economists pushed for rapid change that came close to shock therapy. In their view, dual pricing created difficulties where goods in the controlled sector could enter the market sector, which led to economic distortions and large profits gained by those who could exploit the system. In their view, the solution was rapid price reform and the abandonment of state ownership to allow economic performance to be measured by the return on assets. In May 1985, Zhao thought these ideas were worth exploring. The ensuing report was cautious, but the idea of rapid change was under consideration.[24]

China had replaced Taiwan as a member of the World Bank in 1980, and the Bank's head of mission in Beijing, Edwin Lim, was sensitive to local conditions and eager to work in partnership with the government. The Bank started to provide finance and technical assistance for projects, and in 1980 embarked on a detailed analysis of the Chinese economy. In 1982, it brought eastern European economists to China to discuss their disappointing experience with gradual reform and to observe China's greater success. Despite ideological differences, the relationship between the Bank and China's ruling Communist Party was, according to a Bank economist, 'a marriage made in heaven'. Both were professional bureaucratic organizations, and relations were co-operative but at arm's length.[25] The Chinese government was engaging both with the World Bank and with economists from the Soviet bloc who were experimenting with market reform.

In September 1985, discussions continued in a conference organized in conjunction with the World Bank. Visiting economic experts boarded the *Bashan* for a cruise on the Yangtze River where they could explore different views on market reform. They represented a range of opinions. Alec Cairncross had been an adviser to the post-war British government when it was committed to planning and price controls. He was more cautious than Otmar Emminger, who argued for the dismantling of controls as adopted in Germany by Ludwig Erhard (though the reality was more nuanced than he implied, as we saw in Chapter 11). The leading voices at the conference were János Kornai from Hungary and James Tobin from the United States. Kornai was closely involved with experiments with market reform in Hungary. He argued that a planned economy suffered from chronic shortages and 'investment hunger'. State enterprises had direct input and output directives with a 'soft' budget constraint that meant they were not concerned about failure. The result was chronic shortages and excess demand for a limited output. In Hungary, the reform strategy was to combine 'vertical' or top-down input and output decisions with 'horizontal' market-like forces. Kornai was frustrated by the slow pace of change and argued for market co-ordination and a 'hard budget' constraint. Enterprises could escape from the vertical relations of the command economy and respond to horizontal market forces, supplemented by macroeconomic policies to contain inflation and allow price responsiveness. His approach complemented Tobin's emphasis on macro-economic policy to balance aggregate demand and supply, contain inflation and prevent overheating of the economy. The cruise gave an impetus to a more ambitious agenda for reform in China.[26]

In 1986, Zhao and Deng contemplated a radical programme of rapid price liberalization. Preparations were made for a 'big step', which was blocked by the gradualists. The real problem, it seemed to the gradualists, was disequilibrium caused by scarcities of particular commodities. Price liberalization would not offer a solution and would merely lead to inflation and social unrest that would threaten the gradual transition to a market economy. Zhao was not willing to use repression to deal with potential unrest and backed down.[27] Nevertheless, the case for rapid liberalization did not disappear. In 1987 Zhao made a Marxist case for reform. He explained that the central task during the 'primary stage of socialism' was economic development, and '[w]hatever is conducive to the growth [of the productive forces] is in keeping with the fundamental interests of the people and is therefore needed by socialism and allowed to exist. Whatever is detrimental to this growth goes against scientific socialism and is therefore not allowed to exist.' Zhao came close to saying that anything that led to production and growth was socialist. He argued that 'because our socialism has emerged from the womb of a semi-colonial, semi-feudal society, with the productive forces lagging far behind those of the developed capitalist countries, we are destined to go through a very long primary stage' during which all means should be used to catch up. Only then would it be possible to move to mature socialism. Zhao gave a larger role to the market in allocating resources according to the 'law of value'. He accepted that market reform should be combined with control by the Communist Party but acknowledged that political reform was needed through the delegation of power to lower levels, reforming the bureaucracy and cadre system, allowing consultation between the party and people, and creating representative assemblies. He was advocating a form of authoritarianism combined with capitalism that looked to the experience of Taiwan, South Korea and Singapore – an enlightened autocratic state in which a leader with a clear vision worked with technocrats to overcome barriers to reform.[28]

Chen walked out of Zhao's speech. He was uneasy about the definition of socialism as economic modernization and preferred to maintain the cage of planning. His doubts were confirmed later in 1987 when inflation, profiteering and corruption led to social unrest and student protests. Deng pressed for the removal of price controls and an end to dual pricing to prevent exploitation of discrepancies between controlled and uncontrolled prices, and in the expectation that an increase in the standard of living would secure public support. His proposal was supported by some economists who pressed for the rapid adoption of market prices. It was opposed by others who argued that the main problem was shortages of raw materials and industrial goods, which would be resolved by state action rather than the market. Zhao's reaction was to support price liberalization without reducing aggregate consumption to contain inflation, which arose, in his view, from shortages of agricultural goods and high levels of spending by local government. Inflation should be tackled by dealing with these issues and by continued growth, above all of export industries on the coast. The Asian tigers, he pointed out, had adopted such a strategy at a time of high inflation. Chen was not convinced and foresaw an increase in raw material imports and a trade deficit. He called for austerity to contain inflationary pressures.

Zhao's strategy of growth and reform was caught between Deng's support for price liberalization and Chen's demands for austerity. He opted to back Deng and, if necessary, to use force to push through liberalization. The result was high inflation and mounting unrest, which led to the abandonment of rapid liberalization and the reimposition of price controls later in 1988. This sudden shift in policy caused serious social tensions, alienating both those who suffered from inflation and those who lost from the sudden reimposition of controls. Alongside this economic debate, there was wider intellectual discussion and greater openness. These strands came together in the demonstrations in Tiananmen Square in 1989 that were sparked by inflation, attacks on corruption, and demands for more political freedom. Zhao was blamed both for the instability and then for seeking dialogue with the protestors. The hardliners in the party declared martial law and on 3–4 June 1989, the army suppressed the demonstrations. Anyone suspected of 'bourgeois liberalization' was purged, and Zhao was placed under house arrest and subsequently written out of official party history – as, indeed, was the entire episode.[29]

After Tiananmen Square, Chen argued for a cautious expansion of the bird cage, linked with party control, cultural nationalism, and a revival of Confucian values to limit individual self-expression and representation. Deng was alarmed. Failure of economic reform had led to disaster in other Communist countries, and early in 1992 he embarked on a tour of south China where he called for market reform which 'must not be like a woman with bound feet'; it must 'stride boldly forward'. He argued that market economies were not necessarily capitalistic and planning not necessarily the same as socialism, for both '[p]lans and markets are simply economic stepping-stones . . . to universal prosperity and richness'. Deng combined pragmatic economic reform with hard-line political Leninism and authoritarianism to carry through that reform. He had made his view clear in January 1986 in response to student unrest then: 'Kill a few, produce a shock . . . Be ruthless for two years.' He calculated that economic reform would reduce demand for political change, and he insisted that the Communist Party remain the only source of authority.[30]

The reformist agenda survived as a 'socialist market economy with Chinese characteristics'. Prices were liberalized in 1992 and 1993, though not as rapidly as proposed in 1986 and 1988. By now, the market was much larger so that the shift was less disruptive. Isabella Weber, a historian of Chinese economic reform, points out that '[t]he combination of deep and gradual marketization that had preceded liberalization, as well as the assertion of state power in 1989, ensured that the "small bang" was constrained enough to preserve core economic institutions.' Policy shifted from rural experiments to a more technocratic, urban and state-led approach with massive infrastructure investment. Collective TVEs acquired the assets of successful private concerns (whose property rights were not respected), and decisions over loans became more centralized at the expense of the rural private sector. State-owned enterprises were encouraged to grow in scale. In 1991, the state selected fifty-five state-owned enterprises which were given debt and tax relief and import licences, and in 1994 it specified four 'pillar industries' in electronics, car-making, petrochemicals and construction, where state enterprises dominated. State enterprises had initially been liberalized rather than privatized, and the 'iron rice bowl' continued. In 1997, however, the policy changed to 'grasping the large and letting go of the small', that is, privatizing smaller – and often unprofitable – state-owned enterprises. The 'iron rice bowl' was abandoned for millions of workers, who were laid off. Meanwhile, larger, profitable concerns remained in state ownership, with increased investment.[31]

Unlike most developing countries, China did not rely on foreign savings to raise investment. Gains in productivity did not lead to an equivalent rise in wages, which were held down by large reserves of labour, the absence of unionization, and the precarious position of rural migrants under the *hukou* system. Although household incomes rose at around 7 per cent a year, they fell as a share of GDP. A large proportion of the higher incomes went into savings to provide security, so household consumption was low as a percentage of GDP. In China, consumption by households and non-profit institutions serving households fell from 50 per cent of GDP in 1990 to 34 per cent in 2010 (see Figure 15). Interest rates were below the level of inflation and this 'financial repression' meant that savers lost and borrowers in business and government gained. China's exceptional investment rate allowed it to avoid dependence on foreign capital and achieve rapid economic growth. Insufficient household income to consume the goods it produced led to a reliance on exports and a huge external trade surplus, which was used to purchase US Treasury bonds as a safe and secure asset. In May 2000, Chinese holdings of such bonds were $73bn, rising to $478bn in December 2007 and a peak of $1,315bn in July 2011 (see Figure 16). The flow of funds from China covered American trade deficits and permitted consumption of Chinese exports. In 1985, for the first time, the United States had a small deficit of $6m on trade in goods with China; it reached $258bn in 2007 (Figure 17). Household and non-profit institutions serving households' consumption in the United States was much higher, rising from 64 per cent of GDP in 1990 to 68 per cent in 2010. China's successful development strategy therefore led to an imbalance in the world economy. It also could potentially lead to instability at home, for loans made by state-run banks to state enterprises and infrastructure schemes lacked transparency and could be unsound. The problem was apparent to Premier Wen Jiabao in 2007 who called for a shift to domestic consumption. Change was difficult, for economic growth in regions such as Hubei – one of the powerhouses of development – created powerful interests that opposed change. In any case, households would not switch from savings to consumption without reform of the *hukou* system, which remained a major problem.[32]

Growing reliance on the global economy meant that China sought readmission to GATT in 1986 – it had been a founder member before the Communist takeover. China had already secured observer status, but readmission raised a major question: was the Chinese system compatible with GATT's free-market criteria? Zhao assured the director general of GATT that it was. Others were not convinced. The United States defined China as a non-market economy and the Jackson–Vanik amendment to the Trade Act of 1974 had removed most favoured nation rights from any country that denied its people freedom to emigrate. In 1980, the president used his authority to grant an annual waiver, which encountered opposition from an alliance of economic nationalists and advocates of human rights. Nevertheless, by 1986 Chinese membership of GATT had considerable support as a way of bringing its economy within the multilateral

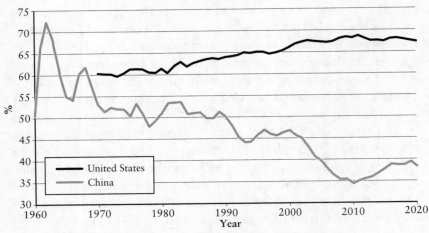

Figure 15: Households and non-profit institutions serving households final consumption expenditure, % of GDP, 1960–2020

Source: World Bank at https://data.worldbank.org/indicator/NE.CONPRVT.ZS?locations=CN-US.

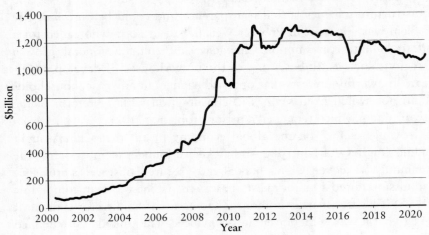

Figure 16: US Treasuries owned by China, in USD billions, 2000–2021

Source: US Department of the Treasury.

system and extending trade liberalization. Accession was not straightforward. China demanded the status of a low-income developing country, which would give it special treatment. GATT's scrutiny of the Chinese economy also raised serious doubts as to whether its prices, subsidies and

Figure 17: US trade deficit in goods with China, in USD millions, 1985–2020

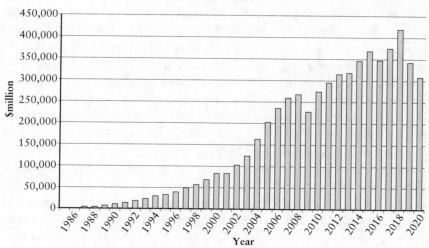

Source: United States Census Bureau: trade in goods with China at https://www.census.gov/foreign-trade/balance/c5700.html.

import controls were compatible with membership. Tiananmen Square halted these discussions.

The Clinton administration of the mid-1990s was willing to consider Chinese membership as a way of bolstering the multilateral trade system and encouraging convergence between the political systems of China and the United States. In Clinton's view, '[b]y joining the WTO, China is not simply agreeing to import more of our products; it is agreeing to import more of democracy's most cherished values: economic freedom.' He admitted that joining the WTO was not 'in and of itself a human rights policy. But still, it is likely to have a profound impact on human rights and political liberty.' In 1998, most favoured nation status was redefined as 'permanent normal trade relations' and Congress agreed to grant it to China in 2000, on condition that it accepted international agreements on workers' and human rights. The way was cleared for China's accession to the WTO in December 2001. Robert Zoellick hoped that China would become a 'responsible stakeholder' in the global system. Similarly, at the WTO Mike Moore welcomed China's membership as a 'defining moment in the history of the multilateral trading system', allowing it to 'take a major step towards becoming a truly world organization. The near-universal acceptance of its rules-based system will serve a pivotal role in underpinning global economic cooperation.' In return for membership, China agreed to offer all foreign individuals and enterprises the same rights to trade as Chinese enterprises; to end dual pricing and differential treatment of goods produced for domestic and export markets; to abolish price controls that protected domestic industry and services; to grant the right to import and export all goods within the customs territory within three years; to remove export subsidies for agricultural commodities; and to adopt the agreement on Trade-Related Intellectual Property Rights. State monopolies were retained in some goods – cereals, tobacco, fuel and minerals – but most restrictions on foreign companies would be removed during the transitional period. Further, a Transitional Safeguard Mechanism would operate for twelve years to cover cases where imports of Chinese goods might cause market disruption for producers in other WTO countries. Many commentators looked ahead to political and economic benefits from accession. The American market was already open to Chinese goods and it was expected that American firms would now be able to export to Chinese markets. Fred Bergsten even calculated that exports would increase by $3.1bn – and a New York human rights group predicted that membership might 'increase pressure for greater openness, more press freedom, enhanced rights for workers, and an independent judiciary'.[33]

By the early twenty-first century, however, China's economic transformation was causing concern in the United States. The renminbi, it was argued, was deliberately undervalued to gain an advantage in export markets. China's purchase of American Treasury bonds limited the ability of the United States to retaliate, given the risk that China would sell off the bonds and undermine American public finances. The Chinese countered that the problem was the imprudent behaviour of American consumers who relied on debt to purchase Chinese imports. To many commentators, the imbalance between China and the United States posed a major risk to the global economy. Neither did it seem that China had obeyed the terms of admission to the WTO, which gave it an unfair advantage in trade, and was 'stealing' intellectual property. To critics the American negotiations at the time of China's accession had either been naive in believing that China would converge with the Western system, or incompetent in being out-manoeuvred. The criticism is not entirely fair. Both the Clinton and George W. Bush administrations imposed strict terms for accession; the real problem was the difficulty in enforcing the terms of membership. It was not easy to disentangle all the forms of state support offered to Chinese exports that ranged from tax exemptions to subsidized land deals, cheap credit and low energy prices, all of which were deniable and difficult to quantify. Another criticism of the negotiators, both from the progressive left and the economic nationalist right, was that they served the narrow interests of American businesses in search of outsourced labour and export markets. Accession was, it is true, supported by bodies such as the National Association of Manufacturers and the US Chamber of Commerce, against union opposition. But American consumers were also happy to buy cheaper Chinese goods.[34]

The emergence of China as a major trading power and the world's second-largest economy by 2010 marked a fundamental transformation in the global economy. It was a huge success in rescuing millions of people from extreme poverty. It also posed a major challenge to global economic government. American and European firms gained from low-cost assembly which benefitted their profits and consumers and held down inflation. It also triggered populist resentment and threats of a trade war. The macroeconomic imbalance between China's low domestic consumption and high exports, and the United States' trade deficit and high consumption became a source of instability before the global financial crisis of 2008.

THE SOVIET UNION: THE FAILURE OF TRANSITION

Unlike the Soviet Union, China had flexibility to 'grow out of the plan'. The Chinese Communist Party had only come to power in 1949, and during Mao's era experienced the turmoil of the Great Leap Forward, famine and the Cultural Revolution. The resulting immense suffering and chaos also meant that China did not have the rigidity of Stalin's commitment to collective farms and heavy industrialization. Large, capital-intensive collective farms in the Soviet Union offered little chance of individual economic initiative. Industry was dominated by state-owned enterprises in a centrally planned regime and the 'iron wheat bowl' applied to virtually the entire workforce. In China, the central government had less control over industry through state-owned enterprises, and regional governments and local communities had more freedom to experiment in a way that led to competition. For the Soviet bloc, growing out of the plan and shifting the sclerotic Soviet economy would be more difficult. As a result, many economists at the international institutions – as well as reformers within the system – believed that a sudden transition or 'shock therapy' was needed to break the existing structure. This approach assumed that all elements of the command economy were so intertwined that it had to be completely destroyed, with a rapid shift to market prices and currency convertibility to bring domestic and international prices into line. The adoption of market prices would be complemented by the privatization of state enterprises and reforming taxation, banking and law.

As a result, the command economy – so it was anticipated – would be replaced by a competitive market economy, albeit with short-term hardship as a result of tight monetary and fiscal policies that were needed to contain inflation.[35]

This strategy of an immediate transition was pursued in Poland. On 4 June 1989, the same day as the suppression of the demonstrations in Tiananmen Square, the first free elections resulted in Solidarity's winning all the seats contested in the lower house and all but one of the seats in the Senate. The economists Jeffrey Sachs and David Lipton advised Solidarity to make a swift move from the Soviet bloc of controlled economies to a market economy that looked to Europe. They argued for 'a dramatic, quick transformation to a market economy – a leap across the institutional chasm'. Their view was influenced by János Kornai's frustration at gradualism in Hungary. Rapid transition would entail market-based trade, an inflow of companies, capital and goods, and the adoption of European laws and institutions. This transition required external assistance to deal with hyperinflation and the unsustainable level of foreign debt. Both were achieved. The United States agreed to support a stabilization fund to devalue the Polish currency and peg it to a new rate, and the German chancellor, Helmut Kohl, accepted that Soviet-era debt should be rescheduled. These reforms created confidence in the currency and in the country's ability to repay loans so that foreign investment picked up and European companies entered the Polish market. Sachs and Lipton started by decontrolling prices to make state enterprises respond to market signals before handing them to private owners. In their view, partial decontrol of prices would not work, for it would be 'the rough equivalent of the British shifting from right-hand to left-hand driving by just switching over the trucks at first'. The attempt to maintain two incompatible systems would allow goods with controlled prices to be resold at market prices, with opportunities for officials to make private profit. On 1 January 1990, devaluation and abolition of most price controls led to a sudden increase in prices – though Sachs pointed out that comparison with black market prices told a different story. He anticipated that the emergence of a market economy would soon lead to more goods in shops – but there were serious problems for large state-owned enterprises that were linked to the Soviet planned economy and dependent on cheap Soviet energy. Many of these heavy industrial enterprises laid off workers, and Sachs accepted that a social safety net was needed to cope with the disruption.[36]

The next stage was privatization. Sachs rejected attempts by Communist regimes to give state enterprises greater freedom. As Kornai said, in Hungary 'the basic idea of market socialism simply fizzled out'. A 'big bang' was therefore needed to sweep aside officials whose only experience was with bureaucratic planning. In Sachs' view, the lack of proper ownership caused inefficiency, and workers and managers distorted enterprises for their own benefit. He was scathing: 'the Communist reformers failed to understand the basic flaw of socialism, whether of a "market" variety or not: when there are no capitalists, there is nobody to represent the interests of capital.' In the absence of a market, privatization could not be implemented by using the approach pioneered in Britain – public offerings of shares. Instead, Sachs and Lipton recommended transferring shares at zero or low cost to workers and households, and handing large blocks of shares to private banks. Sachs observed that 'as soon as economic and political liberties were established, new enterprises surged forward with energy, determination and capacity'. Looking back in 1993, he claimed that 'events have disproved the idea of a "Homo sovieticus" spoiled by decades of communism'. Instead, change was accepted and society 'is ready to slough off the brutality and artificiality of the communist system ... markets spring up as soon as the central planning bureaucrats vacate the field'.[37]

Poland was reasonably successful in making the transition to a market economy and integrating with the capitalist economies of western Europe. It applied to join the EEC in 1994 and on 1 May 2004 became a member of what had become the European Union. Poland's transition was eased by its proximity to Germany, by its earlier experience as a market economy, by its educated workforce, and by hostility to Soviet occupation after the war.[38] Nevertheless, Sachs took too optimistic a view of the transition. Sudden privatization allowed the old political elite or foreign investors to capture much of the benefit. The pain of transition was greater than he admitted, and was eased by migration to Germany and Britain – a safety valve that was not possible in the Soviet Union. Joseph Stiglitz was more sceptical. In his view, privatization exaggerated the benefits of property rights in providing incentives for profit-maximizing behaviour, and minimized the costs of rent-seeking through the acquisition of existing enterprises. The solution, in his opinion, was neither state enterprises nor the shock therapy of privatization, but a 'third way' of state encouragement of competition and small enterprises on the lines of China – a recommendation that ignored the circumstances that allowed China to 'grow out of the plan'. Certainly, such an approach would be difficult to implement in the Soviet Union.[39]

The Soviet economy had recovered after the war, despite economic institutions that were, if anything, more rigid. The Soviet economy was more militarized after 1945, and competing with the United States in the Cold War meant that defence industries formed a large proportion of

Soviet production. Wartime planning led to tighter centralized control of the economy and a growing use of forced labour. After the war, defence production and research institutes were located in closed, secretive towns. This military economy was unusually large and, in contrast to the civilian sector, relatively successful. Economic recovery was possible because of unexploited potential after earlier disasters, and because of Stalin's changed approach to the use of terror. In the 1930s, he had relied on indiscriminate terror against large numbers of people to capture those whom he suspected of being disloyal. During the war, improved information allowed Stalin to pinpoint his enemies without recourse to mass terror. Political authority was also vital to the functioning of the command economy, and if it were weakened, even the limited efficiency of the system would be difficult to maintain.[40]

In practice, the command economy did not operate as expected. In principle, Stalinist production was highly centralized, with managers and workers obediently fulfilling plans that presupposed accurate information in a system that was, in theory, more efficient than the market in meeting consumers' wishes in a rational, orderly manner. In reality, it was grossly inefficient and wasteful. Planners and managers did not know the preferences of consumers, with the exception of the military that had access to political power to ensure that equipment was reasonably efficient. Consequently, while the Soviet Union won the space race and built missile systems, it was not able to produce basic consumer products in sufficient quantity or quality. State control of resources and lack of political accountability resulted in higher levels of spending on warfare than on welfare or household consumption, which led to chronic shortages. Repression and restriction of the lives of workers, and the priority given to accumulation at the expense of consumption, reduced motivation. Managers had little incentive to be efficient, for they did not depend on making a profit and their monopoly position made them indifferent to quality and consumer satisfaction. Their task was to meet targets set by superiors whose own careers depended on survival within the party apparatus rather than on the judgement of electors or consumers. Targets were liable to change over the year so that managers stockpiled materials and employed more workers than necessary to ensure they had capacity to 'storm' in a final push at the end of the planning period. The result was collusion between workers, who depended on the enterprise for housing, health care and access to scarce goods, and managers, who ignored their absenteeism, alcoholism and poor quality of work. In the cynical joke, the workers pretended to work and the managers pretended to pay them.[41]

The failures of the official economy were offset by illegal sales on the black market, ranging from a few goods pilfered by workers to large-scale activities by corrupt officials. Above all, the planned economy could only function through a 'grey' semi-legal market. State enterprises employed agents to swap goods outside the planning regime, and individuals exchanged goods and favours such as preferential access to university or medical care. This system of *blat* depended on trust and reciprocity that were unlike commercial transactions in the market.[42] A Russian economist explained in 1991 that

> What Russia had was not a command economy, but a system of understandings, a complex bureaucratic market built on trade and exchange by both official state agencies and individuals. Unlike the usual money-based market of goods and services, the bureaucratic model traded in not only (and perhaps not primarily) material goods ... but in power and rank, rules and exceptions, social position – basically, in anything that had any value at all.

In China, officials and managers could show initiative in TVEs. In the Soviet Union, they gamed the system. Yegor Gaidar, a leading reformer after the demise of the Communist regime, realized that the system was deeply flawed, for 'the faster the bureaucratic market grew, the faster the traders on that market began to consider themselves an independent social force with its own interests to defend'.[43]

The system was on the brink of crisis when Mikhail Gorbachev became General Secretary of the Communist Party in 1985. He embarked on reform or *perestroika*. State enterprises received lower subsidies and were expected to finance their own activities by setting production plans and marketing any surplus beyond their commitment to the state. The problem was that managers had no experience in deciding what to produce, in what quantities, and at what price; in ensuring that workers turned up and maintained quality; or in selling enough to remain solvent. Neither was there a functioning market to provide information and guide decisions. Although private enterprises were legalized, they were often linked to state enterprises and their stockpiles of materials. The result was disastrous. Established ways of life were undermined, with shortages of consumer goods, inflation and discontent. In 1986, Gorbachev responded with wage reform to overturn the informal bargain between workers and managers. Payment for over-fulfilling targets was cut, workers were moved to lower grades, wage differentials were increased, and alcoholism was attacked. In return, workers were promised a higher standard of living, political liberalization, and participation in the enterprise.

The reforms failed. A higher standard of living would take time to achieve, and in the short term existing deals between managers and workers were disrupted, and economic interest groups resisted reforms that threatened systems of patronage. Furthermore, state finances were stretched by the fall in oil revenues on which the Soviet Union had become dependent for foreign currency. The economy was strained by high defence expenditure with the war in Afghanistan between 1979 and 1989, the renewed arms race with the United States, as well as the costs of the disaster at the Chernobyl nuclear plant in 1986. The Soviet Union borrowed heavily to cover the loss of foreign earnings and to pay for modernization and faced difficulties in servicing loans. In 1985, earnings from oil were $22bn and net debt $18bn; in 1989, oil earnings were down to $13bn and net debt rose to $44bn. The outcome was discontent, demands for higher wages, higher consumption of illicit alcohol, and a collapse of state finances. Co-ordination between enterprises collapsed, monopolistic producers responded to shortages of materials by cutting their output and raising prices, and consumers hoarded whatever was left in the shops, which led to still more shortages. The old system of planning and favours was disrupted without creating a new market economy.[44]

The command economy worked, as far as it did, because of strong political authority. This was now lost. Gorbachev undermined the role of the party, overturned the planning system, and attacked the middle levels of the state and party bureaucracy. There was nothing like the technical and intellectual debate in China about the best way of reforming the economic system, and Gorbachev made a decision that Deng thought disastrous. In 1988, Gorbachev gambled on the creation of the Congress of People's Deputies – with a third of the seats reserved for the Communist Party and the others open to contest. In Gorbachev's view, the bourgeoisie had disappeared, which left non-antagonistic classes of workers and peasants with a layer of intelligentsia, all able to live by Soviet ideals. Consequently, democratization and *glasnost* (openness) – so he hoped – would create popular support for reform that would overcome the hostility of senior officials. The first elections in March 1989 did not have the outcome he expected. He was criticized both by Communists, who remained powerful in Congress, and by liberal reformers. Gorbachev was in a bind: he needed democratization to encourage reform but it weakened his power to make changes. Hardships created by economic reform led to discontent and *glasnost* allowed discussion of the contentious issues of collectivization, famine, terror and the Gulag. In February 1990, large-scale demonstrations in Moscow demanded 'peaceful revolution' and decried Soviet history with banners that proclaimed 'Seventy-two years on the road to nowhere'. The Soviet ideals that Gorbachev assumed were embedded in society were challenged – much to the alarm of Communist Party leaders and officials.[45]

As we saw in Chapter 13, the Soviet Union accepted that its fifteen constituent republics could develop a national identity alongside Soviet patriotism. The elections to the Congress of People's Deputies in each republic of the Soviet Union now gave voice to nationalist movements in these fifteen republics. The opposition took control in the Baltic republics, Armenia and Georgia – and in elections to the Congress of the Russian Republic the 'Democratic Russia bloc' won a majority and elected Boris Yeltsin as President. The dangers were clear when nationalist demonstrations were suppressed in Georgia in April. Gorbachev opposed the use of violence, not least after the massacre at Tiananmen Square. Meanwhile, Communist rule collapsed in central and eastern Europe. The Soviet Union was no longer able to bear the costs of supporting its satellites and Gorbachev was not willing to use military suppression, as in East Germany in 1953 or Hungary in 1956. He needed detente with the West to divert resources from the arms race to boost welfare and consumption. By the middle of 1990, the satellite countries were democracies and within the Soviet Union the Baltic republics had declared their independence. In response, Gorbachev turned to a new strategy to hold the Soviet Union together – a referendum on a new federation of sovereign states. Six states boycotted the referendum, Ukraine proposed a looser confederation, and the central Asian republics voted to preserve the Soviet Union. In Washington, the administration of George H. W. Bush was alarmed that the fragmentation of the Soviet Union would threaten geopolitical stability. Bush urged Ukraine to remain in the new union and announced that the United States 'will not support those who seek independence in order to replace a far-off tyranny with a local despotism' or 'aid those who promote a suicidal nationalism based upon ethnic hatred'.[46]

As the economic and political position deteriorated, the old guard in the Kremlin attempted a coup in August 1991 to block the new union treaty. Gorbachev was placed under house arrest at his holiday house in Crimea, and the State Committee on the State of Emergency announced that it had taken control. The attempted coup exposed the incompetence of an ageing regime, for the plotters failed to arrest Yeltsin or mobilize the KGB, and the army stood aside. Yeltsin took charge and Gorbachev returned to Moscow. The end of the Soviet Union was close. In August 1991, Ukraine declared its independence, and in December 1991 Yeltsin met leaders from Ukraine and Belarus to dissolve the Soviet Union and replace it with a loose commonwealth of independent states.[47] Yeltsin now had to carry through economic reforms in the Russian Republic that had started so disastrously under Gorbachev.

To Russian nationalists, America was pursuing a strategy to weaken Russia by expanding NATO to its borders and allowing former members of the Soviet bloc to join the European Community. In reality, the Western strategy was not to weaken Russia; it was to create a stable partner by encouraging consumers and businesses in a market economy to build support for democratic reform. The failure was in under-estimating the scale of the task in a naive belief that a 'big bang' would create a market economy and lead to prosperity and democracy. Direct American assistance was ruled out and the Bush administration turned to the IMF and World Bank which could – so it was hoped – offer assistance that was less of a threat to Russian sovereignty. The IMF welcomed its new role, for its influence had declined after the Latin American debt crisis, and Yeltsin wanted to become a member. In 1990 Managing Director Michel Camdessus visited Moscow and proposed reform based on spending cuts, tax increases, price liberalization and privatization. The programme was not imposed from outside, for Yeltsin's advisers made similar recommendations. In October 1991, Yeltsin embarked on a course of privatization, liberalization and stabilization to create a full market economy, with external assistance from the IMF, World Bank and the European Bank for Reconstruction and Development. He secured authority to rule by decree for a year and he appointed Gaidar as Minister of Finance, and subsequently Deputy Prime Minister in charge of economic reform. Their commitment to the IMF's approach meant that Russia secured associate membership of the organization in October 1991, with access to technical advice, followed by full membership and access to funds in June 1992.[48]

Gaidar accepted 'shock therapy' for internal political reasons. He was concerned that the parlous state of the economy might allow the old guard to return to power, and his solution was 'to force the issue, to put the game on a fast track' towards a free market. He realized the collapse of the Soviet Union had undermined non-market economic relations that linked plants across newly independent republics that could now ignore orders from Moscow. His response to this 'catastrophic rupture' was 'a spontaneous economy of natural exchange'.[49] Gaidar believed that the collapse of the command economy and absence of a market meant that price liberalization had to be adopted at once, without an intermediate system of dual prices which would create price distortions and shortages, and deepen the economic crisis. Privatization was considered to be a prior condition for a market economy, with the danger of conflicts between groups with a stake in state-owned concerns. Workers had an interest in the collective enterprise; managers viewed the plants as their own; local government saw enterprises as sources of revenue; and citizens as a whole had a claim to ownership. Gaidar realized that these groups had to be reconciled. In the absence of a private sector for the sale of state assets through flotations on the stock market, he offered 'vouchers' to all citizens, with the aim of creating widespread ownership that would overcome opposition.[50]

Poland offered a precedent, yet the situation was different. Early in 1990, Gorbachev had sent Grigory Yavlinsky, a leading economist in the Soviet system who had proposed reforms ten years earlier, to report on the economic reforms in Poland. In mid-1990, he proposed a 500-Day Programme for a swift transition to a market economy, with large-scale privatization that would require large-scale financial assistance from the United States and Europe. Initially, Yeltsin and Gorbachev were both committed to the plan, but Gorbachev backed away – to the chagrin of Yeltsin, who resented Russian subordination to the Soviet Union. Jeffrey Sachs also became an adviser to the Russian government and realized that price and market liberalizations alone could not solve the problem. He saw that, as in Poland, international assistance would be needed for debt reduction, currency stabilization and the provision of a social safety net. In this case, such assistance was not forthcoming. The IMF did not support debt rescheduling and, to make matters worse, it opposed the creation of separate currencies for the new republics and insisted on the preservation of the rouble as a common, shared currency – a politically naive decision that lacked credibility. Sachs admitted that scaling-up the experience of Poland to Russia was doomed. Germany and the United States had been willing to assist Poland, which formed the boundary of the Western Alliance. Now, the European Union was more concerned with the costs of German reunification, and Dick Cheney and Paul Wolfowitz, Secretary and Under-Secretary of Defense respectively, opted to contain Russia through military superiority and pre-emptive strikes against potential enemies. In November 1991, Gaidar had no help from the G7 finance ministers either, who insisted that successor states repay Soviet-era debts, unlike Germany in 1953 or Poland in 1991. Assistance came in the form of short-term loans at market rates.[51]

Gaidar was trapped. He could not impose monetary discipline thanks to the continued use of the rouble in other republics and the lack of a separate Russian national currency. Nor could he postpone price liberalization given the collapse of the command economy. There was a risk of hyperinflation and he thought that gradualism was bound to fail. At the end of 1991, he gambled on a strategy of radical change that he admitted was risky. He decided to liberalize prices, press ahead with structural reforms and market mechanisms, and to float the rouble. At the same time, he cut food subsidies, defence spending, capital investment and social services, and introduced a value added tax and balanced budget. Nothing was done to provide a social safety net for workers who were losing both their jobs and the welfare support provided by state enterprises.[52] The Supreme Soviet of Russia – the legislature elected by the Congress of Deputies – did insist that 51 per cent of the shares of privatized enterprises should go to employees at a discount. Privatization cheques, or vouchers that could be used to buy shares in companies, were distributed equally to all Russians. These vouchers were tradable, and most holders lacked financial experience, which allowed unscrupulous entrepreneurs to buy up vouchers and take control of former state assets. Furthermore, auctions for the sale of state assets were not transparent, so people with experience in making deals in the old economy benefitted from insider dealing and corruption. Managers of state oil and metal companies secured massive profits, for they could sell commodities at low prices to private trading firms who then exported them at world prices. Managers of state enterprises, government officials, politicians and traders made huge gains that laid the basis for a rent-seeking economy, and they formed a powerful block against further reform. Meanwhile, ordinary citizens suffered low incomes and insecurity.[53]

Gaidar and the reformers lost ground in 1992. Failure to stabilize the rouble and continued shortages of goods led to inflation that reached 1,354 per cent by the end of the year. Yeltsin's response was to replace Gaidar – who had become acting Prime Minister in June 1992 – and bolster his political position by turning to industrialists. The new prime minister, Viktor Chernomyrdin, was chairman of Gazprom, a company created in 1989 with majority state ownership that now received tax exemptions and monopoly rights. When the government pressed the IMF and World Bank to remove strict conditionality and to allow a moratorium on debt service, the Fund's opposition was overruled by the Bush administration on strategic grounds. The Bank and IMF were in a difficult situation. They lacked a consistent relationship with officials in Russia and imposing economic discipline led to growing support for Communists and nationalists. Although the international institutions were disinclined to make new loans until existing conditions were met, presidents Bush and Clinton urged them to lend with weak conditionality to bolster Yeltsin's position.[54] Yeltsin needed business support to finance the election in 1996 and more revenue to fund the deficit, which led him to further privatization through 'loans for shares'. At the end of 1995, the right to lend money to the state was auctioned with collateral provided by the state's share in enterprises. If the loans were not repaid by September 1996, the creditors could sell state assets and keep 30 per cent of the profit. The loan auctions were run by banks controlled by oligarchs and rigged so that assets passed to a few financial-industrial groups who wished to secure the re-election of Yeltsin rather than Communists who would roll back privatization. The result was not a democratic capitalist order with an efficient, dynamic market economy as hoped by Gaidar: it was a 'kleptocracy' of rent-seeking oligarchs. The state lost huge sums through the plundering of assets that might have been used to restructure the economy and provide a social safety net to mitigate the impact of the transition. Gaidar realized that members of the Soviet *nomenklatura* had profited from their own demise by converting state property into their private possessions.[55]

The IMF's and Bank's role in this sorry tale of greed and corruption was criticized both by nationalists, who saw a deliberate plot to undermine Russian sovereignty, and by western critics who complained that their ideological commitment to neo-liberalism failed to understand local conditions. The first charge is not credible. The IMF's attempt to impose strict conditions was undermined by American strategic concerns to bolster Yeltsin, and its policies were supported within Russia, above all in Gaidar's belief that shock therapy was the only feasible response to the collapse of the command economy. The IMF's ability to shape policy was limited by the lack of consistent allies, and the oligarchs' exploitation of state assets was not part of its economic model. Nevertheless, the IMF was guilty of serious failings. Gaidar justifiably criticized the IMF for insisting on the preservation of the rouble zone rather than allowing a Russian national currency which would have made it easier to control inflation. The IMF must also bear some responsibility for failing to warn of the consequences of what was happening. It was trapped by its narrow intellectual focus that assumed that privatization and markets were desirable, and lacked a wider grasp of Russian history, politics and culture. The Fund blamed internal politics for the failings of Russian privatization, which is certainly correct – the scheme emerged from internal politics rather than being imposed from outside. But it did not oppose loans for shares or sufficiently consider the risk of capture, and even – astonishingly – hailed the success of privatization. The reality was that the lack of rules for the distribution of assets from privatization led to a 'capture economy' dominated by oligarchs who gained at the expense of the rest of the population.[56]

Russia's GDP declined by a third in the early 1990s, unemployment rose to 22 per cent by 1998 and around 40 per cent of the population was in poverty. Male life expectancy declined from sixty-four in 1991 to fifty-seven in 1994, with deaths concentrated among young men of working age as a result of alcohol poisoning, suicide, homicide and injury caused by stress and anxiety as factories closed. In the Soviet Union, the funding of public health and social services relied on state-owned enterprises so that privatization meant a loss of both work and welfare that was particularly stark in towns based on a single industry. Data from twenty-five post-Communist countries between 1989 and 2002 showed that rapid, mass privatization led to an increase in mortality that was around double the increase in countries with a more gradual process, in large part reflecting the impact on male unemployment. In Russia, rapid privatization with economic dislocation and cuts to social welfare had a more detrimental effect than in countries where reform was slower and welfare systems were maintained.[57]

By April 1997, Camdessus belatedly realized the dangers of 'the exceedingly close relationship between the government and a number of large enterprises, which allows many to benefit from explicit or implicit tax exemptions'. The Fund and Bank turned to 'good governance' by more transparent and less corrupt institutions – an unrealistic ambition now that the oligarchs were entrenched. The IMF continued to press for further liberalization, with an end to capital controls in 1998. It even congratulated itself that 'the most important battles in securing macro-economic stabilization and creating a market economy have been won'. The reality was different from this astonishingly complacent view. An inflow of capital removed the budget restraint without a need for politically sensitive tax reform, and higher interest rates after the Asian crisis then led to difficulties in servicing the debt. Crisis hit in August 1998. The rouble collapsed, banks closed and failed, the government defaulted on domestic debt and Russians lost their savings. In Congress, the IMF was criticized for mishandling the situation, and there is considerable justice in the complaint that it failed both in the immediate aim of stabilizing the Russian economy and in the longer-term aim of creating the conditions for reform. Congress (and the Europeans) were also to blame for refusing assistance at an early stage of the transition – though funding the huge sums that were needed was scarcely in the realms of political possibility.[58]

In 2000, President Yeltsin resigned and appointed Vladimir Putin as his successor. Initially, the prospects seemed good, and Putin was welcomed as more competent than Yeltsin's chaotic administration. Russia had started to attend meetings of the G7 in 1998, except for meetings between finance ministers; it became a full member in 2002 of what now became the G8. Clinton hoped that Russian membership would offer recompense for NATO's eastwards expansion in 1997 and indicate support for Putin's reforms after the crisis of 1998. Meanwhile, the long process of joining GATT continued. In 1983 and 1984, the Soviet Union had been denied observer status – not surprising given the Cold War and its earlier denunciation of GATT as the 'reincarnation of capitalism'. In 1986, the aim of diversifying trade from oil and gas led to an application for membership, with a commitment to the most favoured nation principle, non-discrimination and open trade. The request was denied. Observer status was granted in 1990, though doubts about full membership remained. Finally, in December 2011 Russia was admitted as a member of the WTO, taking effect in August 2012.[59] Confidence had grown that Russia had overcome its difficulties and was joining a liberal global order. The Russian economy grew to 2008, with a buoyant private sector and a strong commitment to macroeconomic stability through fiscal reform and a stabilization fund for the rouble. Matters were to deteriorate after the global financial crisis.

The contrast with China was stark. In 1989, the Communist regimes faced two challenges: the massacre in Tiananmen Square in June and the fall of the Berlin Wall in November. Chinese Communism survived and the Soviet regime collapsed. The difference reflected the solidarity of the party elite and army in China which allowed the reassertion of party discipline. The difference was not only effective repression. Opposition was limited by the absence of well-established institutions of civil society, by splits in the student movement, and by the students' failure to form an alliance with workers.[60] In the Soviet Union, the collapse of oil earnings and a large external debt led to serious economic problems. Attempts to reform state-owned enterprises undermined public revenues and limited the ability to mitigate the loss of work and benefits. Nor did the collective system of agriculture deliver an increase in food production. Economic disruption and social malaise, a sense of loss of status as a great power that was humbled by a triumphalist West, created resentful hostility. Both the success of China and the failure of Russia would create problems for the economic government of the world after the global financial crisis.

Unlike both China and Russia, India had had a democratic political system since independence in 1947. Its industrial economy rested on planning and controls rather than the extreme form of command economy found in the Soviet Union; and it had a large class of peasant farmers who had not been dragooned into collective farms or communes. Would it be able to make a transition to a liberalized market economy with rapid growth?

INDIA

In 1954, Ardeshir Darabshaw Shroff – an author of the Bombay Plan and a representative at Bretton Woods – launched a Forum of Free Enterprise as a counter to the Planning Commission's 'indifference, if not discouragement' towards business. A leading figure in the Forum was Minoo Masani, who had created a socialist group in Congress in 1934 and subsequently supported democratic socialism and a mixed economy. Masani portrayed the Forum as non-partisan and non-political with the aim of educating the public on the benefits of free enterprise and its contribution to economic development and democracy. In reality, the Forum was anti-Congress. Masani worried that the Nagpur resolution of 1959 committed the Congress government to village co-operatives, with land pooled for joint cultivation – a proposal Masani saw as a step from private property to collectivization and Communism. He wanted a clear, non-Communist alternative to Congress, and he made common cause with Chakravarti Rajagopalachari, the influential critic of the 'licence Raj' who founded the Swatantra Party in 1959. Rajagopalachari called for 'a strong and articulate Right' to counter Congress and to reject licences, bureaucratic delays and corruption. The new party represented itself as a guardian of private property and small farmers against the Nagpur resolution, although without supporting free-market capitalism that would lead to economic exploitation of the poor. Although Rajagopalachri wanted an alternative to the government Planning Commission, he gave a role to the state in starting new, heavy industries and protecting labour against high prices and profits. 'Free Enterprise . . . is not advocated today in terms of the outmoded doctrine of *laissez faire*', which was 'as dead as the dodo and can make no contribution to the industrial, social and economic advancement we seek'. Masani hoped that the new party would offer 'effective opposition to the State Capitalist policies of the present government' through a coalition of peasants and the urban middle class in 'defence of their rights and property. If they do not hang together, they will assuredly hang separately.' He trod a careful line between seeking independence from large business corporations and portraying them as hapless victims of the licence Raj.[61]

Nehru died in 1964 and his successors – Lal Bahadur Shastri and then, in 1966, Nehru's daughter Indira Gandhi – slightly reduced the role of the Planning Commission. This trend was soon reversed. In 1967, Swatantra – now the largest opposition party – pressed for a more liberalized economy and Gandhi responded by taking Congress to the left with a policy of nationalization and control. In 1969, banks were nationalized and larger commercial enterprises were banned from expansion or diversification. In 1970, industrial licences were strengthened, and nationalization was extended to more sectors. In 1974, the maximum limit on foreign equity in Indian firms was reduced from 51 per cent to 40 per cent.[62] At the same time, the political situation deteriorated with mounting inflation, unemployment and shortages.

In 1974, Jayaprakash Narayan, who had been an important figure in the socialist wing of Congress, re-emerged as the leader of protests in Bihar which led to a new organization, 'Citizens for Democracy'. Narayan complained that '[a]fter 27 years of freedom, people of this country are wracked by hunger, rising prices, and corruption ... oppressed by every kind of injustice ... It is a Total Revolution we want, nothing less!' This call for Total Revolution gained support from students and opposition parties, with huge rallies protesting against the undemocratic policies and corruption of Congress. When Indira Gandhi was convicted of electoral malpractice, Narayan called for her to resign and for the police and army to ignore unconstitutional orders. On 25 June 1975, Gandhi responded by declaring a state of emergency, suspending free speech and assembly, censoring the press, limiting the power of the judiciary, and arresting Narayan and other opposition leaders. The Emergency marked a break with democratic politics and, potentially, with the economy of planning. One sign of the shift was the attempt of Gandhi's son Sanjay to produce a small 'people's car', the Maruti, to replace controlled, planned and protected production, and to free the economy for consumer capitalism. In reality, his project was an example of crony capitalism that soon failed. Sanjay went on to use the Emergency to embark on modernization through state coercion, above all by so-called voluntary sterilization to reduce the birth rate.[63]

In 1977, Gandhi and the Congress Party were defeated by Janata – a grouping of opposition parties including both socialists and Swatantra.[64] Demands were growing for a shift from import-substituting industrialization and for the removal of controls and licences. In 1979, a report by Vadilal Dagli stressed the harmful effect of delays and corruption on the economy, and, in 1981, J. R. D. Tata, the head of India's largest industrial group, pointed to the success of South Korea, Taiwan and Singapore, where governments had supported private enterprise. When Gandhi returned to power in 1980, she looked to the IMF for assistance. The result was to delay liberalization and structural reform, for the resources of the IMF were used to support the public sector and improve the balance of payments. In 1984, Mrs Gandhi was assassinated and her elder son, Rajiv, became Prime Minister. He showed a willingness to reform the sclerotic economic system and to embark on liberalization, but modest reforms in 1985 were opposed by a combination of protected industries, workers accustomed to sheltered markets, and bureaucrats and politicians benefitting from kickbacks.[65]

The breakthrough came with a foreign exchange crisis in 1991 triggered by a balance of payments deficit and borrowing from abroad. It provided an incentive to move from import-substituting industrialization sustained by tariffs, import controls, overvalued exchange rates and licences. P. V. Narasimha Rao, the prime minister from 1991 to 1996, and Manmohan Singh, now the finance minister, were committed to liberalization. Singh's doctoral dissertation had proposed opening Indian trade, and his experience as governor of the Reserve Bank of India and head of the Planning Commission made him aware of the failings of the licence Raj – low productivity and growth, difficulties in improving welfare, and a fiscal crisis caused by subsidies. Singh embarked on a programme of reform to end the licence Raj. In his first budget in July 1991, he explained that

> The origins of the problem are directly traceable to large and persistent macro-economic imbalances and the low productivity of investments, in particular the poor rates of return on past investment ... Budgetary subsidies, with questionable social and economic impact, have been allowed to grow to an alarming extent ... The public sector has not been managed in a manner so as to generate large investible surpluses. The excessive and often indiscriminate protection provided to industry has weakened the incentive to develop a vibrant export sector ... The increasing difference between the income and expenditure of the Government has led to a widening of the gap between the income and expenditure of the economy as a whole.[66]

In 1991, Rao turned to the IMF, which reinforced the government's policies and offered legitimacy that secured support from the Federation of Indian Chambers of Commerce and Industry and the Confederation of Indian Industry. The rupee was devalued, controls removed, licences abolished, tariffs and taxes cut, foreign direct investment welcomed, public monopolies ended, competition encouraged and the fiscal deficit reduced. The import-weighted tariff fell from 87 per cent in 1991 to 27 per cent in 1996. These changes threatened established industries with foreign competition, but also encouraged newer sectors such as software engineering, pharmaceuticals and call centres that benefitted from the widespread use of English and high-quality education in the Indian Institutes of Technology. India's poor physical infrastructure hampered trade in physical goods – a striking contrast with the huge levels of investment in China. However, the new growth sectors only needed a satellite dish to contact the rest of the world. Growth rose from 3.5 per cent a year during

1972–82 to 6 per cent in 1992–2002, but there was still a long way to go. The powerful and inefficient bureaucracy meant that it took longer to start a business than in other Asian countries, and permission was still needed to close an unprofitable plant.[67]

Interest in economic reform was mainly limited to English-speaking, educated and urban elites, with mass politics dominated by ethnic, religious and caste issues. A survey in April–July 1996 found that only 19 per cent of electors were aware of the economic reforms, varying from between 14 per cent in the countryside to 32 per cent in cities and from 66 per cent of graduates to 7 per cent of the poor. By contrast, 80 per cent of electors had views on marriage codes and 87 per cent on affirmative action for castes. Reform of trade, investment and finance had less impact on electors and was therefore easier to introduce. Deep divisions on religious and social issues also helped Rao and Singh by creating an alliance with other parties that disliked Hindu nationalism and communal violence more than they disliked economic reform.[68]

Of course, Hindu nationalists exploited communal divisions, as happened in 1998 when the Bharatiya Janata Party (BJP) came to power as part of a coalition that rejected both planning and market reform in favour of *swadeshi* or home-grown consumption. The BJP transformed the concept from Mahatma Gandhi's stress on the consumption of local goods and boycotts of British commodities to refer to an integrated, organic national economy and society based on Hindu cultural values. The Sanskrit word can be translated as 'of one's own country', which the BJP defined as ensuring 'local resources and talents have the full scope for development in the national interest and the benefits therefrom should primarily flow to the people. Integration into a global economy should not mean obliteration of national identity and predominant sway of powerful economic forces from the outside.' Liberalization and the creation of a modern economy should be used to build 'a strong, prosperous and confident nation, occupying her rightful place in the international community'. Economic reform was linked to Hindu nationalism. State control over the economy was rejected as corrupt, inefficient and centralized, and the BJP looked to 'a liberal economic regime in which the full creative genius of the Indian people could flower'. The process should start with internal liberalization so that Indian firms would be able to compete when markets were opened to foreign firms; and foreign direct investment should encourage exports rather than compete with domestic businesses. The BJP stressed the interdependence of agriculture and industry to 'reverse the process of economic, social and political marginalization of India's rural population and effectively fight the elitist, anti-*kisan* [farmer] Congress mind-set'. It argued that *swadeshi* was compatible with globalization provided that it strengthened the national economy and ensured that 'India shall be built by Indians'. In the words of the finance minister, *swadeshi* 'will make India great. And India can be great only when we become an economic superpower.' Hence '*swadeshi*, globalizer and liberalizer are not contradictions in terms . . . Globalization is the best way of being *swadeshi*.'[69]

In 2004, Congress returned to office and Singh, who was now Prime Minister, embarked on liberalization by opening India to foreign direct investment, breaking monopolies, and encouraging competition. Growth was faster but problems of low agricultural productivity, endemic corruption, continued bureaucratic inertia and high levels of poverty remained. Despite signs of progress and the emergence of a more prosperous middle class, India was lagging behind China. There was still a failure to invest in the basic infrastructure of sanitation and water, and to raise standards of education for the bulk of the population. After the global financial crisis, the BJP returned to power in 2014 and renewed its toxic mix of Hindu nationalism and economic reform.

Economic growth in China, and to a lesser extent India, as well as the success of the 'tiger' economies of Asia, meant that a large part of the world's population escaped from absolute poverty. The transformation in the global economy is captured in Branko Milanović's graph (Figure 18), which can be likened to an elephant. In the twenty years before the financial crisis of 2008, there were two sets of winners: at the head of the elephant were the 'emerging global middle class' around the median point of the income distribution, above all in China, India, Thailand, Vietnam and Indonesia; at the tip of the elephant's uplifted trunk were the 'global plutocracy' of the top 1 per cent, predominantly in the United States and western Europe. At the dip of the trunk were the losers: the middle or lower middle class in the 'old rich' countries of the United States, western Europe and Japan, at around the 80th percentile of the global income distribution. They were still well-off in global terms but were losing in relative terms. These shifts in global inequality had major consequences for attitudes in the West towards globalization and international economic policy.[70]

By the time the global financial crisis hit in 2008, China was the world's second-largest economy, and for the first time it played a critical role alongside the United States. The shift in the global economic order in the last quarter of the twentieth century was of world-historical significance. The policy choices in the Soviet Union/Russia and China had fundamental consequences, and as Isabella Weber, a leading historian of China's

Figure 18: Real income growth at various percentiles of global income distribution, 1988–2008 (in 2005 $)

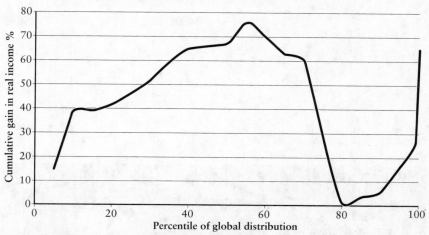

Source: Branko Milanović, *Global Inequality: A New Approach for the Age of Globalization* (Cambridge, MA, and London 2016), 11.

transition, remarks, '[i]t is hard to imagine what global capitalism would look like today if China had gone down Russia's path.'[71] After the collapse of the Soviet Union, many in the West hoped for an end to great power conflict and that the IMF's and World Bank's support of free markets and financial liberalization would lead to convergence with American democratic capitalism. Similarly, there were high hopes that Chinese integration into global supply chains and membership of the IMF, World Bank and WTO would result in political convergence and co-operation with the West. Both expectations were disappointed as Russia slid into authoritarianism and economic stagnation, and China asserted the power of the Communist Party. The economic government of the world was facing difficulties at a time of existential threat arising from the interconnected issues of climate change, global public health emergencies, migration, geopolitical tensions, and economic imbalances.

Valéry Giscard d'Estaing, President of France, and Helmut Schmidt, Chancellor of the Federal Republic of Germany, at a European summit in Brussels, December 1977.

24

'Eurofantasies'

From Economic and Monetary Union to the Euro

'Monetary union is like marriage between partners of very unequal assets. Prenuptial arrangements are naturally the rule and must be followed closely. But when the passion is gone, the agreements endure.'

Rudiger Dornbusch, 'Euro fantasies', 1996[1]

'I think the euro is in a honeymoon phase. I hope it succeeds, but I have very low expectations for it. I think that differences are going to accumulate among the various countries and that non-synchronous shocks are going to affect them.'

Milton Friedman, 2000[2]

'A full decade after Europe's leaders took the decision to launch the euro, we have good reason to be proud of our single currency. The Economic and Monetary Union and the euro are a major success. For its member countries, EMU has anchored macroeconomic stability, and increased cross border trade, financial integration and investment. For the EU as a whole, the euro is a keystone of further economic integration and a potent symbol of our growing political unity. And for the world, the euro is a major new pillar in the international monetary system and a pole of stability for the global economy.'

Joaquín Almunia, Commissioner for
Economic and Monetary Affairs, 2008[3]

The initial task of the European Economic Community had been to create a customs union, but Walter Hallstein, the first president of the European Commission, thought it would not stop there. In his view, 'a customs union pure and simple, a union which is a customs union and no more, would not be realistic in a modern economy.' In 1957, the Treaty of Rome had already looked to a common monetary policy, and a monetary committee was created 'to promote co-ordination of the policies of Member States in monetary matters to the full extent necessary for the functioning of the Common Market'. By 1962, the European Commission's 'action programme' anticipated co-ordination of monetary policy and fixed exchange rates between members' currencies. It recommended a committee of central bank governors, which started to meet in 1964.[4] At this stage, the main concern was to ensure that the payments system was compatible with opening trade between member states, and a more ambitious European monetary policy was not needed so long as the Bretton Woods regime was working and exchange rates were stable.

Earlier chapters explored the debates over European monetary union up to the closing of the gold window. In this chapter, we pick up the story with the adoption of wider exchange rate bands at the Smithsonian G10 meeting in 1971. Larger variations in intra-European exchange rates seemed to threaten progress towards an integrated European market and to affect payments for the Common Agricultural Policy.[5] The result was a search for currency stability within Europe that culminated on 1 January 1999 when most member states of the European Union (as the EEC had become) decided to introduce a single currency – the euro – rather than continue with managed rates between national currencies, which allowed governments some scope for an independent monetary policy. In 1996, Rudiger Dornbusch, a leading expert on international monetary economics, thought that 'experimenting with a new money is a bad idea' and warned of 'eurofantasies'.[6] The Italian scholar Giandomenico Majone thought that the motivation was political – to raise the profile of the EU and to secure prestige – rather than economic.[7] As we will see in Chapter 25, the impact of the eurozone crisis of 2010 raised serious doubts about whether the decision made either political or economic sense. The honeymoon was over – the puzzle is why the wedding ever seemed a good idea.

ECONOMISTS VERSUS MONETARISTS

The crisis of the Bretton Woods system encouraged discussion of a European monetary arrangement to reduce the potential threat to the customs union from currency fluctuations, and to fulfil the ambitions of the Treaty of Rome. 'Monetarists' and 'economists' disagreed over such an arrangement's sequencing and timing. The dispute is often viewed as a clash between France and Germany, though in reality most commentators were on a continuum rather than at two polar opposites, and there were differences within as well as between each country.[8] Nevertheless, the distinction captures the issues that were at stake.

The 'economists' favoured incremental steps towards convergence between the economies of Europe. In their view, harmonization of economic policies on the bases of debt reduction and fiscal rectitude, and convergence of wages, prices, growth, productivity trends and business cycles, were prerequisites for monetary integration, which should come after the creation of Community-wide decision-making and political cooperation. Monetary union would mark the completion of the project as a 'coronation'. This position was most closely associated with Germany and owed something to the experience of unification in the nineteenth century. Economic integration started in 1834 with the creation of a customs union – the *Zollverein* – before the political unification of the Reich from thirty-nine states in 1871. Monetary union followed, with a gold-backed Reichsmark in 1873 and a central Reichsbank in 1875. On this reading of history, monetary union came after economic and political union, and tensions continued over taxing powers between the states and Reich – which only secured an income tax in 1913. After the Second World War, the federal system of West Germany needed formal legal codes to ensure that monetary and fiscal policies did not benefit one region at the expense of others, or that the centre did not spend too much compared with individual states. Furthermore, the central Bundesbank was independent of political control, reflecting the experience of hyperinflation in the 1920s and a pervasive *Stabilitätskultur* that monetary stability was vital for welfare and social peace. The presidents of the Bundesbank between 1957 and 1969 had served at the Reichsbank and created a self-justificatory myth that they (and Hjalmar Schacht) had stood up to Hitler in 1939 as guardians of sound money and central bank independence. The Bundesbank's policy was complemented by the system of labour relations and company structure in the country. German trade unions adopted a collaborative approach in the social market economy, and many businesses were small and medium enterprises. The Bundesbank's monetary targets set expectations for employers and workers by making regular announcements of its policy stance and projections of monetary growth; it explained the principles for its decisions and the circumstances for any deviation. This approach allowed co-operation between labour, capital and the government by reducing uncertainty and limiting expectations, but with flexibility in response to unexpected changes. Debt and fiscal profligacy were to be avoided, with priority given to price stability. Growth would be achieved by structural reforms rather than spending, and restraint in the present would lead to long-term benefits. The 'economists' felt that other countries in the EEC should adopt the German policies of low inflation and balanced budgets.[9]

By contrast, the 'monetarists', above all in France, argued that monetary union, with fixed parities or a single currency, should come first. Their approach rested on a 'big leap forward' or 'rushing at fences'. The experience of keeping currencies in alignment and developing common policies would – so they believed – lead to economic convergence in productivity, costs and income. The French also favoured discretion in monetary policy rather than rules. The French state was unitary, with an all-important central budget that did not require rules to determine transfers that were needed in a federal system. Further, the Banque de France was more susceptible to political control and its autonomy was not enshrined in the constitution. In general, rules were secondary to politics, and constraints on a government's action were considered undemocratic. The government did not assume, as did their German counterparts, that present pain would lead to future benefits – the result might simply be lower growth. The French approach rested on discretion and adaptability in response to economic difficulties, with greater concern for liquidity, which could be tackled by new lending or bailouts.[10] There were exceptions, such as Raymond Barre, who was sympathetic to the 'economists'. He thought that exchange rate targets and tighter monetary policy could reinforce labour market reform, remove price controls, constrain public spending, encourage domestic competition and reduce protection. He hoped that a stronger currency would force France to follow Germany in becoming more competitive by rationalizing older industries and encouraging a shift to higher technology exports that were less price sensitive. Nevertheless, the broad distinction between the German and French approaches remains.[11]

British governments – both Conservative and Labour – were more sympathetic to the 'economists' and generally agreed that monetary union should not be created before economic convergence, though monetary union was sometimes seen as a useful means of disciplining domestic policy. In other respects, Britain differed from Germany. The Bank of England was less concerned with maintaining stability and more with preserving the international position of the City of London, unlike the Bundesbank which discouraged an international role for the Deutsche Mark. British attitudes to monetary union were ambivalent during negotiations to join the EEC. On the one hand, the Treasury saw that monetary union

will arouse strong feelings about 'sovereignty' and provoke vigorous discussions of its implications for future policy in such fields as demand management and the exchange rate . . . At the ultimate stage economic sovereignty would to all intents and purposes disappear at the national level and the Community would itself be the master of overall economic policy. The degree of freedom which would then be vested in national Governments might indeed be somewhat less than the autonomy enjoyed by the constituent States of the USA.

On the other hand, Lord Cromer – offering advice as a former Bank of England governor – assured Heath that the decline of the pound meant 'the advantage lies in throwing in our weight towards the creation of a European Monetary System using our diplomatic skills in a manner to re-establish our independence and influence in international affairs'. A joint Treasury and Foreign Office paper realized that membership of a 'functional' rather than 'federal' economic and monetary union would be acceptable, for there was little chance of avoiding a decline in financial power outside the Community. However, the conclusion of the Bank and Treasury was to wait and see: the Community was divided and taking sides would not be helpful in negotiations for membership. To the City, of course, the best way to regain its status was increasingly seen as the Eurodollar market, rather than in preserving sterling as a reserve currency within a European system.[12]

These differences between 'economists' and 'monetarists' ran through the extended discussions that led from economic and monetary union to the euro, which was a triumph of the monetarist position in combination with elements of Germany's commitment to central bank independence and fiscal prudence. The outcome was politically contingent rather than economically rational and led to a flawed system.

FROM THE MARJOLIN REPORT TO THE EUROPEAN MONETARY SYSTEM

In January 1974, the Commission invited Robert Marjolin to chair a group of experts to report on economic and monetary union. They convened at a time of uncertainty in international monetary policy and divisions in Europe. In June 1974, President Giscard d'Estaing and Chancellor Helmut Schmidt agreed that action was needed 'to call a halt to the ongoing process of weakening' European economic integration. Although they were converging on stability and an 'economist' approach, agreement would not be easy. The German and British governments wished to work with the United States on international monetary reform; the French preferred to 'affirm the existence of a European monetary personality and to bring the most efficient contribution possible to the sorting-out of the international monetary system'. One possibility had been favoured by Willy Brandt: a 'two-speed' Europe, with some countries integrating sooner than others. Another approach was a 'parallel currency' to operate alongside national currencies. In September 1974, François-Xavier Ortoli, a former finance minister of France who was President of the Commission from 1973 to 1977, suggested that the European Unit of Account (used for internal Community payments) should evolve into a 'new monetary unit, which we could call the ECU', a term that he hoped would appeal in France as the name of its pre-Revolution currency and that 'the Anglo-Saxons would be happy to see the English initials of the "European Common Unit" for the common European currency'. The ecu could form the basis of a parallel currency for intra-European trade, circulating alongside and gradually replacing national currencies.[13]

By the time Marjolin's report appeared in March 1975, progress to economic and monetary union had stalled because of divergence between economies after the oil shock. The report was committed to European unity and regretted the retreat into national policies and lack of a joint political response to unexpected external factors. The report also criticized the decision at The Hague in 1969 to create economic and monetary union without serious consideration of the conditions that needed to be met, 'in the naïve belief that it was sufficient to decree the formation of an EMU [Economic and Monetary Union] for this to come about'. The report rightly pointed to the difference between a customs union, which only involved a modest surrender of sovereignty over tariffs, and monetary union, which required a transfer of significant powers. The Marjolin group denied that economic and monetary union could come about 'in an almost imperceptible way' and insisted that the 'Europe of small steps' had not worked. Instead, the 'grave dangers' of inflation, balance of payments deficits and unemployment might demand 'a radical and almost instantaneous transformation' based on economic and monetary union as 'the manifestation of a political will' so that 'grand designs ... might once again seem conceivable'. The report set out a wide-ranging programme of support for investment to assist industrial restructuring; a regional policy to reduce disparities; participation by unions, employers and local authorities in shaping policy; and an exchange stabilization fund to support external and internal monetary policies. Such steps would encourage economic convergence and create the conditions for economic and monetary union. The report stressed that monetary union would only be possible by creating a sense of belonging to a wider political entity which would allow central decision-making. It looked to a single central bank and currency, to free movement of people, goods and capital, to a federal budget on the scale of Germany's (13 per cent of GNP) or Canada's (16–19 per cent), and to centralized fiscal and social security systems.[14]

The Marjolin report was a compromise between German 'economists' and French 'monetarists', though it was more sympathetic to the 'economists' in stressing prior economic convergence, which would entail ambitious economic policies with supranational political authority. In retrospect, Marjolin saw a 'fundamental error' in expecting governments 'to relinquish authority simply because an "inner logic" – the reality of which is moreover debatable – left it no alternative'. He came to realize that the central objective of the Community, that of securing European peace, had been achieved, and that pressing for further integration and ignoring the 'strength and vitality of the nation state' might be counter-productive and provoke nationalism.[15] He identified the tension in ambitions for economic and monetary union: that continued concern for national sovereignty blocked a sizeable federal budget or social security system proposed by his report. His diagnosis of the problem was astute but was ignored in the genesis of the single currency.

Alongside the earlier Werner report and the Marjolin report, technical discussions on European monetary management took place among monetary experts and central bankers at the Monetary Committee of the Commission and the Committee of Governors of central banks that had been meeting at Basel since 1964. In 1973, a European Monetary Co-operation Fund was created, followed in 1974 by a group that considered the 'harmonisation of monetary policy instruments'. These bodies brought together academics, administrators, bankers and politicians and led to a common understanding of technical detail – a slow process of reaching a new consensus without explaining the implications of deeper economic integration to electors.[16] In July 1976, interest in economic and monetary union resumed when Wim Duisenberg, the finance minister of the Netherlands, proposed co-ordinating medium-term economic policies to encourage convergence and to set 'target zones' for currencies to restore stability.[17]

A further push came when Roy Jenkins became President of the Commission in January 1977. As Chancellor of the Exchequer in the Labour government between 1967 and 1970, he had experience of sterling crises, the decline of the Bretton Woods regime, and the difficulties caused by Germany's economic strength. He was convinced that European economic integration was vital for Britain. By July 1977, he saw an opportunity for a 'decisive policy' to rescue monetary union, which had become 'immobilised in scepticism'. Jenkins became a committed supporter of economic and monetary union, for '[e]conomic welfare in Europe would be improved substantially if macro-economic policy was not subject to present exchange rate and external financial risks'. Economic and monetary union, in his opinion, would end inflation by removing the risks of floating exchange rates; allow greater rationalization of industry and commerce; solve the problem of unemployment by economic policies favouring expansion; and create a new international currency comparable to the dollar and with less dependence on America. 'The Community is the right size of unit for monetary policy in the particular setting of our highly interdependent, closely packed, advanced industrialised societies', and would align the Community with the 'ineluctable internationalisation of western economic life'. This 'decisive policy' would both deepen and widen the EEC by admitting Greece, Spain and Portugal, which were at a critical point of transition to democracy. Jenkins favoured a single authority with 'a transfer of power bigger than the whole of the Community's existing competences put together'. He rejected Germany's opposition to fiscal transfers and insistence on control of inflation and economic convergence. In his view, the 'largely discredited doctrine' that gradual convergence would lead to monetary union 'by osmosis' should be replaced by 'a bigger and politically more attractive proposition' which 'would take Europe over a political threshold'. The United States had a single currency despite regional inequalities that had long been wider than those in the Community. Why delay monetary union?

> The bull has to be taken by the horns. The big step changes – creating a common monetary authority, vastly expanding the regional and redistributive fiscal powers of the Community – will have to be imminent or actually taken before the unconstrained behaviour of national governments, their businesses and trade unions, is to be seriously changed in the ways that would become necessary in a monetary union.

The balance of payments would cease to be a national issue tackled by adjustments in the exchange rate or monetary policy; it would become a regional issue resolved by fiscal transfers or regional policy, as in federal systems. 'The weak regions of the Community must have a convincing insurance against the fear that monetary union would aggravate their economic difficulties. The strong regions must for their part have a counterpart in terms of more stable, secure, and prosperous markets.' Despite his realization that monetary union needed 'powerful fiscal mechanisms', Jenkins still did not envisage a large budget. The report of a study group of independent experts established by the Commission and chaired by Donald

MacDougall, the chief economic adviser to the Confederation of British Industries, concluded that Community spending only needed to rise from 1 per cent of GNP to 2–2.5 per cent to achieve 'pre-federal integration', and to 5–7 per cent for monetary union – a modest level compared with most federal systems, and far below Marjolin's proposal.[18]

Even a French commentator thought Jenkins's *hyper monétariste* approach was unrealistic. Ortoli – now Vice President of the Commission for economic and monetary affairs – preferred to complete the single market and economic convergence before monetary unification, and the Commission's proposals of November 1977 owed more to him and an 'economist' position than to Jenkins. The Commission reaffirmed a commitment to economic and monetary union and claimed (implausibly though diplomatically) that the 'monetarist' and 'economist' approaches were complementary. The outcome was not Jenkins's 'major act of political will' and leap forward but a non-committal agreement to embark on further studies, and to ensure that economic growth was combined with progress towards EMU. Jenkins's scheme had been given 'a first-class burial', remarked a German MEP. The Banca d'Italia hoped that the mistake of assuming that 'the establishment of monetary constraints in the states of the Community would suffice, by itself, to obtain an effective coordination of economic policies' would not be repeated. Jenkins's achievement was to inject enthusiasm into debates over monetary union that had become stale and technical, and to move the debate from central bankers and finance ministers at the EEC Monetary Committee to the European Council, where Helmut Schmidt and Giscard d'Estaing could take the lead.[19]

It was President Carter's failure to take action to support the dollar that revived interest in economic and monetary union. Jenkins informed Margaret Thatcher – the leader of the opposition at this time – that 'one of the many reasons for wishing to move to a common European currency was the disarray of the present world monetary system and the declining fortunes of the dollar.' In February 1978, Schmidt confided to Barre, now Prime Minister of France, that the Americans did not know what they were doing.[20] The German leader suggested a new European initiative with Giscard d'Estaing, who was in search of a different approach after France had twice left the currency 'snake' established in 1972. Schmidt proposed pooling half the reserves of each country, which would be managed by finance ministers. When the band between the strongest and weakest currencies widened, central banks would intervene so that adjustment was not confined to the country with the weak currency. Schmidt's aim was to protect the Deutsche Mark against inflation caused by American indiscipline. The American economy, he argued, was 'too large and uncontrollable: the captain was not in charge, even though he was well meaning.' Schmidt's and Giscard d'Estaing's approach formed the basis of discussion when the Council of Ministers met in Copenhagen in April 1978. Jenkins proposed that the 'snake' should be dissolved, and that the European unit of account should be used for internal settlements, with joint intervention against other currencies, and the possibility that it might become a parallel currency.[21]

At Bremen in July 1978, the Council agreed to draw up proposals for closer monetary co-operation in a 'zone of monetary stability'. Germany, Denmark and the Benelux countries would retain a band of +/-2.25 per cent, other countries would be allowed to have wider margins, and any change in the central rate would be by mutual consent. By confining currencies within a narrower band, the impact of high pay settlements would be clear and national governments would need to be more disciplined. A new unit of account – the European Currency Unit or ecu would be based on a daily calculation of a weighted basket of members' currencies, and would be used by central banks' settlements in exchange markets. The European Monetary Co-operation Fund would intervene against the dollar and other currencies and would marginalize the role of the dollar and the influence of international financial institutions.[22]

Schmidt urged Britain to join but James Callaghan, the Labour prime minister, was in a difficult position. Membership was opposed both by the anti-European left of the Labour Party and by the City, which realized that sterling would fluctuate with oil prices as production from the North Sea expanded. Callaghan preferred to work with the IMF on reform of the international monetary system and an Atlanticist policy based on the dollar and pound. The Treasury was also suspicious of German motives, for '[i]f other EEC countries stick with the mark more and more and with the dollar less, that helps intra-EEC German trade and also helps Germany in competition with its EEC partners in other markets.'[23] In October 1978, Gordon Richardson, the governor of the Bank of England, thought that higher inflation and lower growth in Britain meant that membership of the European Monetary System (EMS) was economically unwise. Nevertheless, he took a pragmatic view that involvement was politically important:

> It is only from the inside that we can influence developments ... We should be able to play an important part in ensuring that the developing EMS is outward- rather than inward-looking; that it is complementary rather than hostile to the US and the dollar; and that it supports rather than competes with the IMF.[24]

Some Conservative politicians agreed. They saw that maintaining the exchange rate of the pound within the EMS would impose external discipline by removing the easy option of depreciation and so encourage resistance to wage claims. Against the case for membership, the EMS was criticized as a device to hold down the value of the Deutsche Mark and benefit German exports at the expense of deflation, unemployment and reduced competitiveness in other countries. The outcome was that the Labour Cabinet, and party generally, opposed joining the EMS and Britain remained outside.[25]

The agreement at Bremen reflected a convergence between French and German views. Chancellor Schmidt felt that stable exchange rates would be helpful, for half of Germany's exports went to the EEC. He accepted a monetary agreement in return for a French commitment to reduce inflation, to create monetary stability, and to promote trade, growth and economic convergence. The Bundesbank was not convinced. An obligation to protect the exchange rate might threaten its commitment to price stability. Schmidt assured the Bundesbank that the currency basket was designed 'to cover up the fact that the French are joining for a third time a European currency association that they twice left', and that the Bundesbank would not be obliged to support other currencies. The European Monetary System was, he claimed, a political rather than a monetary decision and 'the independent position of the German central bank stands outside any discussion'. The EMS would save the Common Market by creating an alliance with France, by forcing the United States to sort out its problems, and by providing cover for German success. He explained to the Bundesbank council in November 1978 that

> The more successful we are in the areas of foreign policy, economic policy, socioeconomic matters, and military matters, the longer it will be until Auschwitz sinks into history . . . It is all the more necessary for us to clothe ourselves in this European mantle. We need this mantle not only to cover our foreign policy nakedness . . . but we need it also to cover these ever-increasing relative strengths, economic, political, military, of the German Federal Republic within the West.

Schmidt later reflected that 'progress made in European integration . . . corresponds to Germany's vital, long-term strategic interest in ensuring peace if our country wishes to avoid a third anti-German coalition . . . Compared with this essential goal, all the nit-picking about the technical details of monetary union . . . is of secondary importance.'[26]

At the Ministerial Council meeting in Brussels in December 1978, Giscard d'Estaing and Schmidt reached a compromise between monetarists and economists that offered an appearance of unity that would show that the EEC could respond to the problems facing the international monetary system. The EMS came into existence in March 1979. The 'snake' became a 'rattlesnake' – a parity grid that imposed stability, with a 'divergence indicator' that would rattle and warn if a currency was out of line, though with no obligation to intervene. Rather than supranational pooling of reserves, the system relied on swaps between central banks, and the ecu was similar to the existing unit of account. In technical terms little was new, but politically the EMS replaced the Common Agricultural Policy as central to the identity of the EEC. Otmar Emminger of the Bundesbank was astonished, rightly observing that 'it is quite remarkable that exchange rate policy is the chosen instrument for a political demonstration of European unity and stability'.[27] Harmony was short-lived. The French came to see the EMS as a German victory that would lead to dominance by the Deutsche Mark, assist German competitiveness and constrain European economic growth. Nigel Lawson, Chancellor of the Exchequer in Mrs Thatcher's government from 1983 to 1989, thought that Karl-Otto Pöhl, the president of the Bundesbank from 1980, 'openly revelled in his role, via the EMS, of the ruler of Europe's monetary affairs and arbiter of its destiny'.[28] The EMS remained vulnerable in the absence of economic convergence and of co-ordination between members' economic policies, not least in the second oil shock of 1979 when Germany adopted a tight money policy and other countries expansionary ones.[29]

DELORS TO THE EURO

The next step to Economic and Monetary Union came in June 1988 when the Council established a committee of governors of central banks and the director general of the BIS, chaired by Jacques Delors, the president of the Commission from 1985 to 1995. Delors' politics had been formed by the Catholic trade union movement in France; he joined the Socialist Party and served as Finance Minister. His vision was a 'social Europe' in which progress towards a single market and monetary union would facilitate social solidarity across Europe. The Delors report followed Werner's in suggesting progress to economic and monetary union in stages, with parallel development of economic convergence and monetary union, and irrevocable fixed exchange rates between European currencies leading to a single currency. By removing exchange costs and risks, economic and monetary union would – so the report claimed – facilitate the movement of people, trade and capital, and encourage investment and growth. The single market required regional policies; monetary union would also require harmonization of fiscal and budgetary policies. The report set out a timetable. The first stage of economic and monetary union was to complete the single market, co-ordinate economic policies, co-operate in monetary matters, and participate in the exchange rate mechanism. This stage could be achieved with existing institutions and would significantly increase the level of integration and economic convergence. Preparation for a treaty on economic and monetary union would lead to a second stage, with new federal institutions and a major transfer of sovereignty. The process would be completed in a third stage, when economic authority would pass to European institutions, with fixed exchange-rate parities and, if possible, a single currency. The report insisted that 'the decision to enter upon the first stage should be a decision to embark on the entire process'. It admitted that exchange rates would no longer be used to correct economic imbalances, and that differences in costs and national policies would be in tension with greater integration. Nevertheless, the report concluded that these imbalances could be mitigated by co-ordinating national economic policies. Moreover, '[w]age flexibility and labour mobility are necessary to eliminate differences in competitiveness in different regions and countries of the Community. Otherwise, there might be relatively large declines in output and employment in areas with lower productivity.'[30]

Although Delors had long supported EMU, he was vague about its purpose, reluctant to align with any one position, and uneasy about federalism and centralization of power. His pragmatic approach allowed him to compromise, but with the disadvantage that crucial issues about the economic implications of the single currency were ignored. Delors realized the need for cross-border financial supervision of banks but without pursuing the point. He opposed binding fiscal rules on the grounds that financial markets would impose discipline, and argued for a larger – though modest – Community budget of 3 per cent to allow fiscal stabilization. The final report dropped these ideas in favour of regional policy to reduce disparities.[31] The report did not adequately address the difficulties of a single currency that were apparent to many. In January 1988, Giuliano Amato, the Italian finance minister, warned that the European Monetary System lacked an 'engine of growth' because of low domestic demand in Germany.[32] For its part, the Bundesbank feared convergence with higher levels of inflation in other countries, and worried that a loss of central bank independence might compromise monetary stability. It urged that 'money and credit policy in an economically unified Europe are not less oriented towards stability than they are today in the Federal Republic'.

At meetings of the Delors Committee, Pöhl tried to 'stop all this talk by people like Helmut Schmidt and Giscard', and opposed their 'utopian' vision of a hard currency union.[33] Similarly, Alexandre Lamfalussy – a leading figure at the BIS and a member of the Delors Committee – warned that 'the interest premium to be paid by a high-deficit member country would be unlikely to be very large, since market participants would tend to act on the assumption that the EMU solidarity would prevent the "bankruptcy" of the deficit country.' Consequently, financial markets would not impose fiscal discipline and countries would persist with deficits and borrowing. He saw a clear risk of 'moral hazard' and financial crises, and called for 'a Community-wide macroeconomic fiscal policy which would be the natural complement to the common monetary policy of the Community'.[34] A fiscal union was both economically vital as a complement to monetary union, and politically impossible as a threat to national sovereignty.

The Delors report was presented to the meeting of the European Council in Madrid in June 1989, which decided to launch the first stage of economic and monetary union on 1 July 1990. Mrs Thatcher was alarmed. In her view, economic and monetary union was not necessary for the single market that she strongly supported as a means of stimulating competition. She had urged Robin Leigh-Pemberton, governor of the Bank of England and a member of the Delors Committee, to make this clear. To her annoyance, Leigh-Pemberton's dissenting memorandum was 'something of a mouse' and the Delors report confirmed her worst fears. She accepted that the first stage complemented the single market, free movement of capital and the end of exchange controls – all areas where Britain took a lead. Her concern was that the report assumed that the next two stages would follow without considering alternative views. She rejected automatic progression to stages two and three that 'involve a massive transfer of sovereignty', the creation of a federal Europe, centralization of power and loss of political accountability. She informed the House of Commons that

> It was just an attempt to coerce us, and we would have nothing of it . . .
> Major derogations of national sovereignty of the kind in the Delors report,
> in which we give up fundamental functions . . . to a group of central bank
> governors who are not democratically accountable, would not be accept-
> able to this House or to me in any way.

John Major, Chancellor of the Exchequer from October 1989 until he became Prime Minister a year later, argued that Delors' approach was 'quite simply the wrong way for the future development of Europe'. In his view, the process should start from 'real changes in economic behaviour in the market place' through a partnership of nation states, with competitive free markets, price stability, and national control over economic policymaking. The result should be interchangeable currencies with the possibility of fixed rates – but there was no need to make an immediate decision, implement major constitutional changes, or move to a federal Europe.[35] Thatcher's opposition was intensified when Delors assured the annual conference of the Trades Union Congress in September 1988 that the Commission would require national governments to protect workers. Labour became less sceptical that the EEC was a capitalist organization and saw that it could offer protection of workers' rights against the Thatcher government.

Thatcher responded with a speech in Bruges. Europe, she informed her audience, was not the creation of the Treaty of Rome, and Britons had had a long engagement with Europe apart from the Community. She urged 'willing and active cooperation between independent sovereign states' rather than centralized power in Brussels. In her view, the Treaty of Rome was 'a Charter for Economic Liberty', a 'Europe open to enterprise' in a single market based on choice and deregulation. Brussels threatened her domestic achievements: 'we have not successfully rolled back the frontiers of the state in Britain, only to see them reimposed at a European level.' The Bruges speech became central to Conservative scepticism about the European Union and marked the Conservative Party's shift away from a predominantly pro-European stance. Thatcher had no intention of accepting 'costly, Delorsian socialism on a continental scale'.[36]

Nigel Lawson feared that Delors was turning the Community from a free, competitive single market into a 'fortress Europe' that substituted 'supranational regulation, not so much one where barriers are broken down, but one where restrictions and controls are levelled up'. He saw 'two rival visions of Europe'. He rejected

> an over-regulated, bureaucratic, protectionist Europe, where uniform standards are enforced by new directives and new regulations from Brussels, where outsiders are excluded, and where competition is seen as a threat, rather than a challenge to greater efficiency, a Europe in which 'regulate and protect' might be the motto.

He praised 'the vision of a deregulated, free-market, open Europe, one where competition is seen as the key to improved economic performance; one driven by consumer choice, by transferring sovereignty not to Brussels but to the people.' British success in removing 'the dead hand of corporatism' should be pursued in Europe by 'hacking away at regulations and bureaucracy' and allowing markets to work. Supply-side reforms were needed rather than an '"easy" interventionist, protectionist, state-subsidy route out of the problems posed by heightened international competition'.[37] Where Lawson departed from Mrs Thatcher was in accepting that the exchange rate mechanism could control inflation by linking Britain to a low inflation country. In March 1987, he decided to 'shadow' the Deutsche Mark, without informing the prime minister. The result was conflict with Thatcher's economic adviser Alan Walters, and the experiment was abandoned in March 1988.[38] Lawson resigned in October 1989 after continued tension with Walters. Despite Thatcher's opposition, John Major also believed that the exchange rate mechanism could help reduce inflation and sterling joined the ERM in October 1990. Mrs Thatcher was uneasy and, shortly before leaving office, assured the Commons that she rejected a

> European central bank accountable to no one, least of all national Parliaments. The point of that kind of Europe with a central bank is no democracy, taking powers away from every single Parliament, and having a single currency, a monetary policy and interest rates which take all political power away from us . . . a single currency is about the politics of Europe, it is about a federal Europe by the back door.[39]

The politics of monetary union were different in France. President Mitterrand wanted a single currency to avoid dominance by the Deutsche Mark and Bundesbank, and Delors – who had been the French minister of finance from 1981 to 1984 – agreed. As Lawson realized, the French were prepared 'to sacrifice their own national independence in order to see the Bundesbank abolished'. France's bargaining position was enhanced by the fall of the Berlin Wall in November 1989. The ultimate victory of French 'monetarists' over German 'economists' reflected political contingencies with the intersection of debates over economic and monetary union with concern about German reunification. Integrating Germany into Europe was a condition of accepting reunification, and Mitterrand insisted that the price for German reunification was replacing the Deutsche Mark. Chancellor Helmut Kohl saw that he had to abandon Germany's long-standing view that economic convergence should come before the 'coronation' of monetary union. The progress to currency union had been encouraged by the failures of the Bretton Woods regime and now concluded as a response to German reunification. In November 1989, the intergovernmental conference that Delors had proposed to implement his plan now had the attraction of embedding a reunified Germany within a European monetary union. Kohl and Mitterrand turned the vague timetable of the Delors report into reality. Kohl accepted the 'monetarist' approach and Mitterrand agreed to German terms in respect to rules and a commitment to the Bundesbank's emphasis on stability rather than the more discretionary, political approach of the Banque de France. The French won on phasing, Germany won on rules, and Britain opted out. Many commentators fell into the fallacy of *post hoc ergo propter hoc* in assuming that the euro was a German device because it made German exports more competitive and meant that other countries suffered from a higher exchange rate than would have been possible with their own national currencies. The outcome was indeed beneficial to Germany, but the euro was not designed with that intention. It was adopted against Germany's doubts about the timetable and as a means of limiting its power.[40]

In 1990, the Commission explained the rationale for a single currency in *One Market, One Money*, a supposedly objective assessment that was, in reality, straightforward advocacy for the policy. It stressed the benefits of complementing a single market, creating macroeconomic stability, encouraging investment, reducing unemployment, and allowing the least favoured regions a 'real opportunity for rapid catch up'. The benefits of ending transaction costs and uncertainties in currency conversion were unsubstantiated and small, and in any case could easily be hedged. Martin Feldstein of Harvard rightly dismissed the claim that a single market needed a single currency as having 'no basis in either theory or experience'. Similarly, the claim that reducing the risk premium for investment by even 0.5 per cent would increase the Community's GDP by 5–10 per cent lacked credibility.[41] The assumed benefits of a single currency could have been secured by fixing rates between national currencies without surrendering the ability of nation states to vary the rate in a crisis. Indeed, joining a single currency without any exit was even more rigid than the 'contingent rule' of the gold standard, which allowed a country to suspend membership when the costs of deflation and unemployment were too high.[42] The warnings about the weakness of the economic case were ignored and stage two was timetabled to start on 1 January 1994 with preparations for stage three within a further three years.

The Council met at Maastricht in December 1991 to draft a new treaty that was signed on 7 February 1992 and came into force in November 1993, when the EEC became the European Union. The treaty promised 'a new stage in the process of creating an ever-closer union among the peoples of Europe', with 'balanced and sustainable' economic and social progress 'in particular through the creation of an area without internal frontiers, through the strengthening of economic and social cohesion and through the establishment of economic and monetary union, ultimately including a single currency'. The Maastricht Treaty set out convergence criteria for the third stage. To join the single currency, a country needed an inflation rate of no more than 1.5 percentage points above the average rates of the three lowest-inflation countries in the EU; interest rates of no more than 2 per cent above the average of the same three countries; an annual government deficit of no more than 3 per cent of GDP or a commitment to reach that level; and a government debt of no more than 60 per cent of GDP or progress towards that level. Price stability would lead to financial stability; fiscal discipline was a prerequisite for monetary union; an independent European Central Bank, free of political control, would prevent the monetization of debt; and there would be no bailout of debtors. The British (and Danish) governments secured an opt-out from the obligation to join a single currency.[43]

The German view dominated, that a bailout or fiscal stimulus would shift costs to others, leading to moral hazard and preventing structural reforms in response to a crisis. There was no fiscal stabilization mechanism as suggested by both Marjolin and Jenkins to provide compensation for the loss of exchange rate adjustment; the cohesion funds to help poorer regions of Europe did not deliver the commitment to social solidarity that Delors hoped to secure from the single market and monetary union. There was no lack of warnings about the shortcomings of the scheme. In 1992, the economic historian Barry Eichengreen drew on his knowledge of financial history to suggest that 'the restraints on national fiscal and monetary policies that will come with EMU may leave member states without adequate options for dealing with national macroeconomic problems'.[44] Indeed, the convergence criteria might even increase divergence: obliging a country to reduce its deficit might lead to a deeper recession. A report by the Federal Reserve Bank of San Francisco pointed out that monetary unions do not usually have fiscal rules – and that the Maastricht criteria were rigid even by the standards of those that did. Charles Bean, an economist at the LSE and Bank of England, thought that constraints on fiscal policies were a 'major error' and a price too high for the limited benefits of monetary union. Nor did the discussions at Maastricht consider the need for supervision of the financial system or how to deal with a financial crisis. The monetary union was not complemented by a banking union; the European Central Bank (ECB) did not have a mandate to act as lender of last resort; and financial supervision remained a national matter. The outcome reflected the experience of Germany, where low levels of securitization and dominance by large universal banks with high levels of reserves and collateralized securities meant that financial instability was not considered a major issue. The focus was on controlling the imprudence of public bodies through deficit and debt limits rather than regulating the destructive behaviour of banks.[45]

The Maastricht Treaty required referenda in Denmark, Ireland and France before it could be ratified, which provided the first opportunity for citizens to express their views. The results were a shock. While Ireland accepted by a clear majority, Denmark narrowly rejected the treaty by 50.7 per cent until concessions were obtained; France approved by a narrow majority of 50.8 per cent.[46] Britain did not have a referendum on the issue, and Vernon Bogdanor, a leading constitutional authority, predicted difficulties. Ratification of the treaty by Parliament was perfectly legal, but he argued that it lacked legitimacy and consent, which was 'likely to have fundamental consequences both for British politics and for Britain's relationship with the European community'.[47] The doubts of the Eurosceptics were intensified by 'Black Wednesday' (16 September 1992) when interest rates rose to 15 per cent in a doomed attempt to stop the pound from falling below the lower margin in the exchange rate mechanism. Managing the exchange rate proved inconsistent with domestic political needs and intensified doubts over future membership of the single currency.[48] Despite the lack of enthusiasm, and warnings about the flawed design, the project continued towards stage three.

The Maastricht Treaty established the European Central Bank (ECB), which started operations in 1998. Eichengreen warned of potential difficulties. When the Federal Reserve system was created in the United States in 1913, there were problems mediating between the regional Federal Reserve banks. Power was only concentrated in the Board of Governors and the Open Market Committee in Washington in 1935. The ECB similarly needed ways of mediating between national central banks, determining the level of autonomy, and deciding on the priority to be given to price stability over other considerations.[49] These issues were scarcely considered in establishing the ECB. Pöhl ensured that the ECB followed the Bundesbank's commitment to price stability, unlike the Federal Reserve which had a dual mandate also to consider employment. The Maastricht Treaty laid down that the 'primary objective of the European System of Central Banks should be to maintain price stability' and that support of the general economic objective of 'economic and social progress which is balanced and sustainable' was 'without prejudice to the objective of price stability'. Pöhl did not want the ECB to be an institution of the Community, for 'success in pursuing a monetary policy in accordance with the primary objectives hinges critically on having safeguards against political pressures. Even more than in some of our countries this is likely to be true in a large Community, given the different traditions and experiences with inflation.' The outcome was a ban on monetary funding of budget deficits, and on either the Community or individual states taking responsibility for the debts of any state. The ECB was the Bundesbank in a new guise – politically independent, committed to a tight money policy to control inflation, and the guardian of fiscal rectitude. Rather than the ECB controlling Pöhl, the Bundesbank's approach dominated – though Britain and the Bank of England were exempted from the European central banking system.[50]

Tommaso Padoa-Schioppa, an Italian banker who served on the executive board of the ECB, pointed out that it had 'the challenge of not being an expression of a political union. This is indeed a challenge, because normally the soundness of a currency does not rest exclusively on the central bank.' He also saw that an independent central bank had the virtue of establishing rules that limited the disruptive power of individual nation states and their self-interested electors.[51] However, delegation of monetary policy to a central bank was more controversial in the European Union than in an individual nation state where the decision was made by a democratically elected national government and could be revoked. The ECB was responsible for the entire eurozone and imposed an inflation target that could not be appropriate for both Germany and Greece, for example. As a result, domestic social bargains were overridden.[52] Milton Friedman was rightly sceptical, for '[n]ever in history . . . has there been a similar case in which you have a single central bank controlling politically independent countries.'[53]

Tensions immediately arose. When the cost of German unification led to a budget deficit and inflationary pressure in 1992, the Bundesbank tightened monetary policy and raised interest rates, and other countries had to follow to maintain parities.[54] Jacques de Larosière, now governor of the Banque de France, criticized Germany for destabilizing French monetary policy and argued that the anchor currency – the Deutsche Mark – needed a commitment to the system as a whole. Despite these problems, in December 1995 the Council of Ministers agreed that stage three would start on 1 January 1999. An attempt was made in 1997 to combine German and French priorities in a Stability and Growth Pact that committed members to a medium-term budgetary objective of balance or surplus, and to corrective action on deficits above 3 per cent. The Commission was charged with 'strict, timely and effective' operation of the Pact – a compromise between the Germans, who wanted automatic fines and central bank oversight, and the French who preferred political discretion by the Council. In 1998, measures were adopted to strengthen the surveillance of national budgets, for 'sound and sustainable public finances are prior conditions for growth and higher employment. The Stability and Growth Pact provides the means for securing this objective and for increasing the scope in national budgets to deal with future challenges.'[55] Nevertheless, the first president of the ECB – Wim Duisenberg – insisted in 1999 that the priority was price stability, which relied on the Bank's independence, and that unemployment could not be removed by an expansionary monetary policy. The solution, in his view, was structural reform within responsive markets and a reduction in government deficits – which he admitted would be 'politically difficult, since they may be painful in the short term and only bear fruit over a longer time scale'. The Stability and Growth Pact proved to be unenforceable. Both France and Germany broke its terms in November 2003 and the Council agreed not to act – a decision that the European Court of Justice later ruled illegal.[56]

Convergence criteria for entry to the euro were not applied with rigour. An open letter from German economists worried that the lack of a shared stability culture would endanger integration, and the BIS expressed concern that political considerations would take precedence, with little attention given to wide disparities of prices and wages.[57] The warnings were justified. Membership was allowed if the deficit was exceptional and close to 3 per cent, or was declining 'substantially and continuously'. Similarly, the debt-to-GDP ratio could exceed 60 per cent if it was 'sufficiently diminishing' at a 'satisfactory rate'. These vague terms allowed countries to join the monetary union without pursuing politically risky deflationary policies. On a strict definition, only three countries out of eleven met the debt test. Italy had a debt ratio above 120 per cent, which was said to be falling at an acceptable rate. (If Italy were denied membership and retained the lira, Italian goods would be able to compete with Germany's.) The deficit criterion was also interpreted in a flexible manner by making optimistic assumptions about the growth of GDP or by creative accounting. Italy reduced its budget deficit by levying a 'euro tax' which was to be repaid after the country joined; the French state assumed responsibility for the occupational pensions of France Telecom in return for a lump-sum payment which reduced the deficit and created future liabilities; in Greece, one-off adjustments and creative accounting raised the size of the country's GDP.[58] Although Greece did not meet any of the convergence criteria, the Commission decided in 2000 that it had made considerable progress and was therefore allowed to join.[59] In reality, budget deficits continued and membership of the eurozone allowed it to borrow on generous terms.

In 1997, Chancellor Kohl assured the Bundestag that 'we need the joint European currency. It is a basic precondition for peace and freedom and building the European House.' Such rhetoric was useful in securing political support. It was bad history, however, for it was not clear how a joint currency created peace. Tony Judt, a leading historian of post-war Europe, was rightly sceptical:

> Melding the economies of countries as different as Austria and Britain, France and Portugal, Sweden and Greece (not to mention Poland or Hungary) is both impossible and unwise: contrasting social and economic practices are born of longstanding political and cultural differences that cannot be obliterated with the wave of a magic monetary wand.[60]

Martin Feldstein went further. In 1997, he worried that monetary union might create conflict rather than peace. The ECB would set a single rate determined by stable prices with no concern for national differences and little ability to use national fiscal policy in compensation. He foresaw disagreement over expectations for the euro: the French wished to contain Germany and the Germans wanted to assert their policies. The result was 'a strange mixture of pro-European internationalism and the pursuit of narrowly defined national self-interest'. And there was no obvious way to leave 'a marriage made in heaven that must last for ever'. In apocalyptic vein, he remarked that 'the American experience with the secession of the South may contain some lessons about the danger of a treaty or constitution that has no exits.'[61]

In Britain, Tony Blair's Labour government, which came to power in 1997, had to decide whether to join the euro. Opinion was divided. Peter Shore, a left-wing former Cabinet minister, feared that policies designed to maintain a fixed rate would have 'a massive deflationary effect . . . we shall suffer ever-increased unemployment and a massive disruption of our industrial relations, as British firms are compelled to cut back the real incomes of their workforce.' He warned that the impact would be as bad as returning to gold in 1925, without the ability to leave as in 1931. In his view, economic and monetary union had the political motive of weakening national governments, strengthening European institutions, and imposing the Bundesbank's commitment to stable prices.[62] He had a point. Ed Balls, a leader writer on the *Financial Times*, had argued in 1992 that

> If countries are affected differently by an economic event – such as an oil shock or German unification – then the desired policy response will not be the same. Tying countries together under these circumstances means large

and persistent regional problems – slow growth and high unemployment in different European countries, precisely what has occurred in Europe since German unification.

In his view, monetary union was 'economically and politically misconceived' in imposing the same monetary policy without fiscal stabilizers, and he worried that it would provoke right-wing nationalism.[63] Balls became an adviser to Gordon Brown, the shadow chancellor, in 1994, and in 1997 became his chief economic adviser at the Treasury and, after election to Parliament, economic secretary.

Brown and Balls devised five economic tests to be met before Britain joined any single currency: sustainable convergence with the economies of the single currency; sufficient flexibility to cope with economic change; the effect on investment; the impact on financial services; and whether it would be good for employment. These tests allowed Britain to opt out without rejecting the possibility of membership. Brown argued that 'to give ourselves a genuine choice in the future, it is essential that Government and business prepare intensively during this Parliament so that Britain will be in a position to join a single currency, should we wish to, early in the next Parliament'. Accordingly, the government prepared a 'National Changeover Plan'. Blair had initially been wary of joining the euro, a move which would have provoked Conservative accusations that he was surrendering sovereignty. His views evolved to cautious support for joining on the grounds that finance and business were increasingly integrated across Europe, that a single currency might be good for British jobs and industry, and that it might enhance British influence and power. 'For the very reason of the sensitivity of these arguments, we have also said clearly that the Government can recommend, but the people will decide in a referendum.' As Blair became more committed to membership, Gordon Brown became more hostile. In April 2003, the Treasury's assessment of the five tests was negative and in June the government decided not to join in the life of the current Parliament. When Brown became Prime Minister in 2007, he ruled out membership for the foreseeable future.[64] His decision was vindicated by the eurozone crisis – though it did create a curious situation that the second-largest economy in the EU and a major contributor to its budget had limited engagement with resolving the problem.[65] The relationship between the wider EU and the eurozone was muddled. Monetary union had become the EU's main political project, yet Denmark and Britain opted out; Sweden voted against joining in a referendum; and some new members who were committed to join did not satisfy the criteria. The result was ambiguity. Could the EU budget that belonged to the whole Union be used in response to problems in the eurozone?

On 1 January 1999, the new currency came into existence. Supporters of the euro anticipated that it would encourage European integration and allow businesses to reap the benefits of a single market. More immediately, it led to disputes between proponents of tight money policy and high interest rates to contain inflation and supporters of looser money and low interest rates to stimulate growth and employment. There were disagreements about whether a weak euro should stimulate exports, or if a strong euro should rival the dollar. The differences were sectoral as well as national, for some groups favoured tight money and stable prices and others looser money and rising prices. Even before the euro came into operation, Harvard's Jeffry Frieden noted that 'the pulling and hauling among different sectors is multiplied many times by the great diversity of Europe's economies and by the even greater diversity of European political and social organizations and institutions.'[66] The euro created political tensions that exposed the weakness of the EU's institutional and democratic structure – and it was economically misguided.

THE EUROZONE: A SUBOPTIMAL CURRENCY AREA

The monetary union was criticized, and not only with the benefit of hindsight. Many economists at the time pointed out that the eurozone was not an 'optimum currency area', i.e. a grouping of regions or states that was affected symmetrically by economic cycles, and between which labour and capital could flow freely. The concept was devised to understand whether a group of countries would benefit from fixed or flexible rates. Fixed rates or a single currency in a monetary union would reduce transaction costs for trade and investment, but loss of control over the exchange rate and domestic monetary policy might lead to unemployment in regions with a balance of payments deficit.[67]

Prior to the adoption of the single currency, economists warned that variations in the impact of economic shocks were greater in Europe than in the United States. Further, labour and capital mobility were weaker than in the United States thanks to the influence of language, culture, and the long history of states with distinctive national narratives and policies. As a result, the response to asymmetrical shocks in Europe was slow. The victory of the 'monetarist' position meant that the euro was adopted at a time when economies still had large differences in productivity and costs, depths of capital markets, levels of education and structures of employment. They had institutional variations so that – to take one example – mortgages in some countries were fixed and less sensitive to changes in interest rates; in others, mortgages were variable and immediately affected by monetary policy. They also differed in openness to trade and their concern for currency stability. It was not obvious that a modest reduction in transaction costs was sufficient to compensate for the inability to use exchange and interest rates in response to recessions, or to justify going beyond a single market with fixed but adjustable rates.[68]

The asymmetric shocks experienced by different countries and the abandonment of exchange rates as a policy option could be compensated by fiscal redistribution from regions or countries which gained to those that lost. Even in a single state or federal system, fiscal transfers could cause political problems – say, in diverting tax revenues from Lombardy to Sicily – but they were much easier than transfers within the European Union where nation states were so powerful. The issue had been recognized in the debates leading to monetary union. In 1970, the *Financial Times* columnist Samuel Brittan thought the Werner plan was heading for the 'worst of all worlds' in removing the ability to change exchange rates without 'a common budget, political union, and some form of European Government'. Nicholas Kaldor agreed: a monetary union needed economically stronger countries to support weaker economies, which required a democratically legitimate political union; he warned that in its absence, a single currency could set countries against each other.[69] Marjolin was more realistic in suggesting a larger budget – but in the end, it was below even the modest proposal of Donald MacDougall. In most federal systems, the federal budget was around 20 or 25 per cent of GDP. In the European Union, the budget was modest, and most spending remained with member states. The EU did not have independent taxing powers and secured its revenues from payments by individual states. In 1973, EEC spending was 0.5 per cent of its Gross National Income and had only reached a little over 1 per cent in 2014, at a time when public spending in the entire EU was 48.2 per cent of GDP. The decision to avoid fiscal union was politically rational, and proponents of retrenchment positively welcomed the constraint on spendthrift governments.[70]

The lack of a fiscal shock absorber was in stark contrast with other federal systems. The ability to offset a decline in personal income by paying less to the federal government and receiving transfers was radically different. In the United States in 1991, a shock to regional income of $1 would reduce federal tax payments by 34 cents, with transfers of 6 cents, so reducing the shock by 40 per cent. In the European Community, the reduction in taxation was only 0.5 cents and transfers were smaller.[71] Further, in the United States regional shocks were offset by labour mobility, It is true that the Maastricht Treaty guaranteed free movement of labour as one of the four foundations of the European Union – the free movement of goods, capital, services and persons – and there were flows of workers from less prosperous regions, above all to Britain and Germany. The result was hostility to the welfare cost (often perceived rather than actual) in the host country and resentment at downward pressure on wages, as well as cultural alarm. Labour mobility was both lower than in most federal systems and more contentious.[72]

The Maastricht Treaty aimed to deal with the differential impact of a common currency by a regional fund or – as the German government and Bundesbank hoped – by structural reform. The compromise between France and Germany led to the worst possible outcome: a single currency before economic convergence was achieved, without a fiscal union or joint responsibility for debt. The wide variations in economic structure and the absence of fiscal transfers meant that gains from increased trade – which were grossly exaggerated – would not outweigh the loss of control over national monetary policies and the ability to devalue the currency. The defeat of the economists' priority for convergence at the same time as the victory of the Bundesbank on budget rules and price stability formed a dangerous combination. Nevertheless, the euro allowed countries in southern Europe to borrow on more favourable terms, on the mistaken assumption that other members provided an implied guarantee, despite the ban on mutualization of debt. Countries also diverged in their balance of payments, without the ability to respond by altering exchange rates. In 2007, Spain had a deficit of 10 per cent of GDP and Germany a surplus of 7.5 per cent, and a change in exchange rates would have helped adjustment. Instead, low spending and excess savings in Germany funded excess spending and investment in Spain and contributed to instability. In a true economic and monetary union such as in the United States, individual states have no reason to measure their balance of payments so that the problem does not arise. Furthermore, a country with its own currency can devalue to reduce the sovereign debt owed to other countries.[73]

Supporters of the euro objected that the critics missed the point that optimum currency area theory is static and ahistorical. On this view, it is misleading to compare Europe at the start of monetary union with the United States at the end of a process that took about 150 years. It is indeed bad history to compare different stages of a long period of change. However, it is not history but prophecy to claim that Europe would follow the same trajectory. The federal system in the United States was created in 1789 and built on a pre-existing customs union in the British empire. It expanded across the continent with new states joining an existing federal system, unlike the eurozone which brought together long-established nation states. Consequently, the creation of a federal system in Europe would be more problematic. Even in the United States, the establishment of a central bank and federal taxing powers remained controversial. A central bank was twice rejected, in 1811 and 1836, and regional differences in economic structure and responses to economic cycles led to divergent views on banking and money. What worked for the agrarian South would not work for the industrial north-east. The situation changed with the creation of the Federal Reserve system and federal income tax in 1913, and the introduction of social insurance and higher federal taxes in the New Deal so that fiscal and banking unions were at last created. An optimal currency union took time to achieve in the United States, and it did not follow that the same process would occur in Europe. Essentially, the euro was a political leap of faith rather than a rational economic decision.[74]

Despite these flaws, the prospects for the euro initially seemed good and some economists thought it might rival the dollar. Fred Bergsten expected the euro to become a real competitor of the dollar, for the EU's economy was as large as that of the United States with a similar level of trade; the EU's commitment to stability was welcomed by financial markets; and it had a stronger external position than the United States. Bergsten anticipated a transition to a currency regime based on the dollar and euro.[75] Even Eichengreen, who had warned about the failure to meet the criteria of an optimum currency area, was hopeful that economic and monetary union and the single market 'can constitute a virtuous and self-reinforcing circle'. In 1998, he was optimistic: exchange rates had stabilized with little desire for greater monetary autonomy and little opposition to the monetary policy of the ECB. He was confident that business cycles would converge and that the ability of national fiscal policies to respond to a recession would remove the need for an independent monetary policy. By 2007, he thought that 'for the first time in living memory, there exists another currency, the euro, with a deep and liquid market issued by an economy as large as the United States'. The change in global reserves was striking. In 1973, the dollar comprised 84.5 per cent of currencies held in foreign exchange reserves, followed by 6.7 per cent in the Deutsche Mark and 5.9 per cent in sterling. By 2004, the dollar had fallen to 65.9 per cent and the euro had risen to 24.9 per cent, followed by the yen with 3.9 per cent and sterling with 3.3 per cent. The euro, so it seemed, had the potential to become a reserve currency alongside the dollar.[76]

On the tenth anniversary of the euro, the Commission was confident that it was a success. In 2009, Jean-Claude Trichet, the president of the ECB, claimed that the euro had 'proven its stability, its resistance to shocks and its resilience in the face of financial and economic turmoil'. His confidence was boundless:

> The financial crisis is demonstrating that in turbulent financial waters it is better to be on a large, solid and steady ship rather than on a small vessel. Would Europe have been able to act as swiftly, decisively and coherently if we did not have the single currency uniting us? Would we have been able to protect many separate national currencies from the fallout of the financial crisis?[77]

The financial historian Harold James observed that 'both Europe's technocrats and its political leaders [were] overconfident about the stability of the order they were creating'.[78] He was right, and the eurozone soon faced an existential crisis that exposed the serious flaws of a system adopted for political reasons with little concern for economic viability.

The European project took a further step just as the global financial crisis broke. The Lisbon Treaty of December 2007 amended the treaties of Rome and Maastricht by replacing unanimity by qualified majority voting in the Council of Ministers, creating a long-term President of the Council, increasing the power of the European Parliament, and ending the pretension of the president of the Commission to executive authority. The aim was to improve democratic legitimacy and to reassert the primacy of the nation state and intergovernmentalism – but the changes also led to concern that a European super-state was in prospect. The treaty was expected to come into force on 1 January 2009 but delays in securing approval in Ireland meant it did not come into force until December. The EU was experiencing major constitutional change just as the global financial crisis hit the eurozone, and the Lisbon Treaty did not accept that debt could be mutualized across the Union. The euro became a source of bitterness and discord rather than prosperity and harmony.[79]

Although the European Monetary System and euro were among the most important changes in the international monetary system since Bretton Woods, the IMF showed little interest. It took no action as the exchange rate mechanism collapsed in 1992, in part because the European Community was anxious to keep it at arm's length, and in part because of internal divisions in the IMF. Despite doubts by some members of the executive board that the euro would be in Europe's best interests, the European executive directors were reluctant to expose these disagreements. The United States raised no objections, and the IMF supported the euro on the spurious grounds that 'no matter how difficult the process turned out to be, its successful conclusion was critically important for Europe, and for the rest of the world'. Michel Camdessus, the Fund's managing director from 1997 to 2000, accepted the dubious case that the euro would reduce transaction costs and exchange risk, and would deepen financial markets and deliver prosperity. In his view, it was 'an essential building block in Europe's growing political unity'.[80] He was hardly a dispassionate observer; before he became managing director of the IMF he had been the governor of the Banque de France.

In their intellectual history of the euro, Kenneth Dyson and Ivo Maes remarked that the euro was without historical precedent – 'a monetary union without a state'. Members surrendered monetary sovereignty to the single currency and the ECB and lost their ability to use exchange and interest rates for domestic economic adjustment. They maintained their sovereignty in economic, fiscal and banking policies, however, which prevented a coherent, co-operative approach to asymmetrical shocks. At Bretton Woods, countries agreed to maintain exchange rates within narrow bands but retained the ability to change the rate in response to 'fundamental disequilibrium'. Similarly, the 'snake' of the European Monetary System allowed flexibility. It was surrendered in the euro. Exchange rates were fixed once and for all at the level at which the national currency joined, and without any realistic prospect of exit. The euro was more rigid than the gold standard that allowed a member to break the link with gold when the economic and political costs became too high, and to re-join when circumstances changed. The danger, as Michael Bordo and Harold James pointed out in 2013, was that the euro 'has more deeply embedded institutions that should foster cooperation and looks stronger; and this makes it possible for strains to build up much longer before the system cracks. When the cracks appear, the damage is deeper.'[81]

Since the 1970s, the global economy had changed in many ways. Financialization and market liberalism in Britain and the United States led to risks, just as Raghuram Rajan predicted. Profits had recovered from their low levels but did not lead to greater investment and productivity. Instead, capital gained at the expense of labour, whose share of income was squeezed by a loss of bargaining power as a result of policy changes and de-industrialization. Meanwhile, China became the world's second-largest economy with a high dependence on exports to the United States and Europe, in part a response to its high level of savings and low domestic consumption. In Europe, high levels of saving and surpluses in Germany allowed southern Europe to borrow. These changes in the global economy created problems that erupted in 2007/8. Could the institutions of global government respond, and might the neo-liberal agenda be challenged?

PART FOUR

Beyond Neo-Liberalism

Financialization led to growing risks to the global economy. Since the 1980s, profits had recovered in the developed economies, the inflationary spiral had been broken by deflation and unemployment, and labour had lost its bargaining power as a result of changes in labour legislation, de-industrialization and the growth of precarious employment in the service sector. Workers became more dependent on credit to maintain their standard of living, and especially on mortgage finance for home ownership. In the eurozone, Ireland and countries in southern Europe borrowed large sums on the (false) assumption that the risk was low, and Germany built up large trade surpluses and maintained fiscal control. Meanwhile, the saving rate in China reached an exceptionally high level. The result was imbalance in the world economy, with China depending on export markets – above all in the United States – that were supported by debt. The global financial crisis started within the United States due to the weak regulation of the financial sector and its dependence on complicated and poorly understood financial products, before spreading to Europe. This final Part explores how this global financial crisis developed, what solutions were adopted and rejected, and what role was played by multilateral institutions. Potentially, the global financial crisis could have marked a turning point, away from neo-liberalism and financialization, with a redistribution from capital to labour as happened after the Great Depression and in the post-war Bretton Woods regime. Instead, the outcome was a survival of the existing system, with growing disparities in the developed world and tensions with China, which emerged as the world's second-largest economy.

The global financial crisis did not overturn neo-liberalism, although the new crises of Covid-19, war in Ukraine, and a return to levels of inflation not experienced since the 1970s might achieve what the financial crisis did not: a turn from financialization and to greater inclusivity. The economic government of the world stands at a critical point – of failure as in 1933, with a slide into economic and military warfare, or of a reassessment of national and global policies to create a more stable and just world.

Leaders of the G20 at the start of the summit chaired by
Gordon Brown in London, 2 April 2009.

25

'Behaving badly'

The Global Financial Crisis

'... at the core the problem was bad behavior on the part of the financial system. But financial systems almost always behave badly, so that is not a surprise. The problem was that the banks and others in the financial sector were not stopped from behaving badly by the regulators ... We prided ourselves on how large our financial system was. We should have realized that it was a symptom that something was wrong. You cannot eat, wear, or enjoy finance; it is a means to an end – to make the economy more productive. But it wasn't making our economy more productive ... [T]he financial sector figured out how to steal as much money as it could from the poorest Americans, to lend to them beyond their ability to repay ...'

Joseph Stiglitz, 'Lessons from the global financial crisis of 2008'[1]

'Whatever role the markets may have played in catalysing the sovereign debt crisis in the eurozone, it is an undisputable fact that excessive state spending has led to unsustainable levels of debt and deficits that now threaten our economic welfare. Piling on more debt now will stunt rather than stimulate growth in the long run ... The recipe is as simple as it is hard to implement in practice: western democracies and other countries faced with high levels of debt and deficits need to cut expenditures, increase revenues and remove the structural hindrances in their economies, however politically painful.'

Wolfgang Schäuble, German Federal Minister of Finance, 'Why austerity is only cure for the eurozone'[2]

The story that dominated as the new century opened was one of the 'great moderation' – the belief that inflation was under control with economic growth and stability.[3] The danger did not seem to come from within the

United States but from the economic imbalance between China and the United States. American purchases of Chinese goods were funded by debt and led to large trade deficits; China had a large trade surplus and bought American Treasury bonds. In 2004, Larry Summers – at this time the president of Harvard University – saw that '[t]here is something odd about the world's greatest power being the world's greatest debtor. In order to finance prevailing levels of consumption, must the United States be as dependent as it is on the discretionary acts of what are inevitably political entities in other countries?' He realized that China was unlikely to dump Treasury bills, but he warned that 'it surely cannot be prudent for us as a country to rely on a kind of balance of financial terror'. The Americans complained that China manipulated the renminbi to secure export markets but feared that action against China would lead to a retaliatory sale of Treasuries; the Chinese complained of America's deficits but needed its markets. Summers thought that the United States should save more and cut consumption to reduce its balance of payments deficit, a policy that carried with it the corresponding danger that ending America's import-led growth would hit global demand and threaten export-led growth in other countries.[4] The diagnosis of global imbalances was certainly correct and does need to be addressed, as we will see in the final chapter. But the assumption that the imbalance would lead to a crisis through a collapse of the dollar proved to be incorrect. The global financial crisis started in the United States' market for sub-prime mortgages.[5] On 15 September 2008, the failure of Lehman Brothers – one of the oldest and most prestigious financial companies on Wall Street – marked the start of the crisis.

In 2005, Raghuram Rajan at the IMF had warned that the financial system in the United States incentivized risk: executives received large bonuses if they performed well, without suffering if they did less well or made a loss. The new financial derivatives were complex and lacked transparency so that even market participants were not entirely aware of the risks. Rather than directing investment to the most efficient and productive uses that would improve the physical infrastructure, raise productivity, provide good jobs and respond to climate change, funds were channelled into mortgages, often for a high proportion or even the full value of the property and to people who would have difficulty in maintaining payments. These sub-prime mortgages were bundled with other loans into collateralized debt obligations, which masked the reliance on high-risk loans. In the United States, mortgages are non-recourse loans where failure to pay results in the surrender of the house without recourse to the borrower's other assets. This system worked so long as house prices rose, as they did in the property bubble that peaked in 2006; when values started to drop below the level of the mortgage, or if payments could not be maintained because of loss of employment or financial hardship, the property would be handed over to the bank. This house of cards started to collapse when Lehman Brothers filed for bankruptcy. The immediate reaction of the George W. Bush administration was to stand aside and allow Lehman to fail as a warning to others. The ensuing crisis in the financial markets meant that government policy shifted to bailing out the banks.[6]

This global financial crisis of 2008 differed from any other since 1945, for its origins were not in Latin America or Asia but in the United States and its sub-prime mortgage market, before spreading across the Atlantic to European banks that were also heavily involved in this business, borrowing dollars to participate in the American mortgage market. In many ways it was a North Atlantic financial crisis that did not affect countries in East Asia, whose governments had built up reserves after 1997 that allowed them to ride out the financial turmoil.[7] There was Schadenfreude in many parts of the world that the United States was now experiencing financial disaster that had previously troubled many countries in Latin America and Asia. At the United Nations in September 2008, President Cristina Fernández de Kirchner of Argentina pointed to the United States which had so often blamed others for imprudence. Now the state was coming to the rescue of American banks and abandoning the Washington consensus.[8] Similarly, Joseph Stiglitz informed his audience in Seoul in 2010 that advisers who urged South Korea to adopt American corporate governance should have looked to reform their own flawed system.[9]

When the G20 met in London in 2009, the worry was that globalization would once more go into reverse as it had after the golden age of the late nineteenth century, with a return to bilateral trade and economic nationalism. Economists were divided on how things would develop. The danger was that the financial crisis could become another Great Depression, when a banking crisis was followed in the next few years by a collapse of production, trade and employment that took a decade (including a world war) to restore. In March 2009, Paul Krugman – a Nobel Prize-winning economist and New York Times columnist – claimed that the fall from the peak of US industrial production in mid-2007 was milder than the fall from the peak of mid-1929, so that there was only 'half a Great Depression'.[10] But the United States is not the world, and two leading economic historians – Barry Eichengreen and Kevin O'Rourke – found that the fall in world industrial production by April

2009 was at least as severe in the nine months after the peak of April 2008 as in the same period after the peak of June 1929. Even more seriously, world trade was falling faster. They concluded that 'the "Great Recession" label may turn out to be too optimistic. This is a Depression-sized event.' The world economy continued to fall for three years after 1929 and Eichengreen and O'Rourke warned policymakers that their action or inaction would determine whether the fall would again continue so long. Their comparison with 1929 was a warning of what might happen if the 'wrong' decisions were taken. In February 2010 they reported partial success. The world economy had stopped its slide into the abyss and both world industrial production and trade started to recover after a year (Figure 19).[11]

This chapter explores how this partial success was achieved and how a collapse of the global economy on the scale of the 1930s was prevented. The outcome was not a resolution of fundamental problems of imbalance in the global economy, and the continuing inequality in national economies and the harmful impact of austerity were exposed by the pandemic in 2020. Larry Summers, who had rebuked Rajan in 2007 for his Luddite tendencies, was director of the US National Economic Council from January 2009 with responsibility for advising President Obama on how to respond. He claimed to have repented and now admitted his mistake, quoting the reputed remark of Keynes that 'when circumstances change, I change my opinion. What do you do?'[12] Nevertheless, there was not a fundamental change as with the New Deal. Finance still remained powerful, with a rentier capitalism that rewarded profits at the expense of labour. The policy response to the global financial crisis prevented a second Great Depression at the cost of continued inequality, stagnant real wages and austerity as others benefitted from rising asset values. President Trump's brand of populism and economic nationalism had strong appeal to voters with genuine grievances of being 'left behind'. The global financial crisis was a point when the legitimacy of the neo-liberal order was challenged – but a new order did not yet emerge. On previous occasions, the threat to the legitimacy of the existing order led to a decade of debate before the emergence of embedded liberalism in the 1940s and market liberalism in the 1970s. On this third occasion, the cycle has not been completed and the nature of a post-neoliberal order is not clear. In this chapter, we will explore why governments made the choices they did after 2008 and avoided the worst outcome without a fundamental change, before looking ahead in the final chapter to what a new order might look like after Covid-19.

Figure 19

a) World industrial production, months after the peaks of June 1929 and April 2008

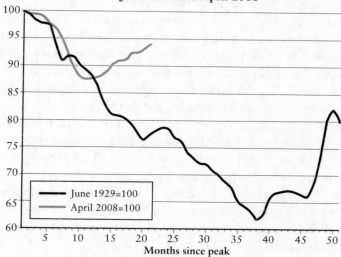

b) Volume of world trade, months after the peaks of June 1929 and April 2008

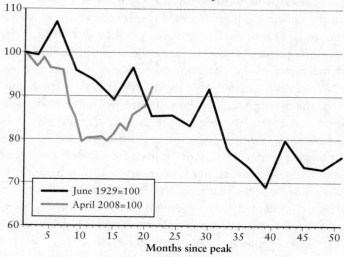

Source: Barry Eichengreen and Kevin O'Rourke, 'A tale of two depressions' (8 March 2010) at
https://voxeu.org/article/tale-two-depressions-what-do-new-data-tell-us-february-2010-update.

THE DEFEAT OF FISCAL STIMULUS

The G20 meeting in London in 2009 marked a brief revival of Keynesianism, with Gordon Brown and Obama proposing to reject balanced budgets and use deficits to boost demand. Eichengreen and O'Rourke pointed out that deficit finance had worked in the few cases where it had been tried in the Great Depression, and suggested that governments should now take advantage of low interest rates to borrow and increase public spending.[13] For a time, the policy seemed feasible. In November 2008, the G20 announced that it would 'use fiscal measures to stimulate domestic demand to rapid effect' and it again supported fiscal stimulus at the London summit in April 2009.[14] At the end of the summit, Brown proclaimed that 'this is the day that the world came together to fight recession not with words but with a plan for global recovery and reform'. The German government was not sympathetic. Peer Steinbrück, the German finance minister, had criticized Brown's 'crass Keynesianism' for 'tossing around billions' that would burden future generations. Chancellor Merkel and President Sarkozy of France saw the solution not in fiscal stimulus but in controlling global financial markets and tax havens – an implied criticism of Brown's deregulating the London markets as Chancellor of the Exchequer.[15]

Brown's approach was also rejected by Mervyn King, governor of the Bank of England, who worried that a fiscal stimulus would increase the size of the deficit. He had informed the Treasury Select Committee of the Commons in February that 'monetary policy should bear the brunt of dealing with the ups and downs of the economy'. His intervention exceeded the remit of the Bank for controlling inflation and was condemned by one over-excited MP as 'a very British coup d'état'. King insisted that short-term fiscal measures to deal with immediate symptoms would only perpetuate the bigger problem of an imbalance between spending now and saving for the future. A fiscal stimulus would boost consumption and hinder the long-term need for the British and American economies to save and invest, to reduce household and bank debt, and to resolve the trade deficit by shifting from domestic spending to exports. King's critics complained that his commitment to reducing public debt intensified the recession, and that fiscal stimulus would allow more investment in infrastructure and would maintain demand.[16]

The return to Keynes was more talked about than implemented. In the United States, the Economic Stimulus Act of February 2008 offered tax rebates to stimulate consumption, and the American Recovery and Reinvestment Act (ARRA) of 2009 boosted public spending. These initiatives were partisan: no Republican voted for the ARRA in the House and only three in the Senate. Although the stimulus increased employment and economic activity, with the result that the government's share of economic activity fell, opponents of fiscal stimulus attacked the policy as a high road to debt. When Christina Romer, the chair of the Council of Economic Advisers, argued for a larger stimulus, Summers feared a loss of credibility. Political caution took precedence over spending.[17]

Fiscal stimulus was soon replaced by what was euphemistically called 'expansionary fiscal contraction' – a belief that growth would return through cuts in public spending to restore balanced budgets, and that the reduction in demand would be outweighed by gains in confidence. The economist Alberto Alesina and his colleagues argued that an increase in taxes would be 'deeply recessionary', and that cuts in spending were more successful in reducing deficits, removing uncertainty, restoring confidence, encouraging investment, and avoiding an unfair redistribution between present and future generations. Indeed, they believed that cuts in spending might lead to increased output where gains to private consumption and investment were larger than cuts in government spending. This analysis had a serious flaw: it ignored the distributional consequences of tax increases versus spending. Robert Lucas, a Nobel Prize-winning economist, had claimed in 2004 that 'of the tendencies that are harmful to sound economics, the most seductive, and in my opinion the most poisonous, is to focus on questions of distribution' – all that mattered was rising production. Such an exclusion of distribution ignored the ways policies benefitted the rich at the expense of the poor. Alesina and colleagues explicitly excluded the consequences of lower public spending, and at no point asked why the priority was to cut debt, and what the political and economic consequences of austerity might be in provoking discontent, harming the prospects of the young, increasing mortality for the elderly, or encouraging economic nationalism. On the contrary, fiscal stimulus might have assisted recovery by bringing forward investment at a time of weak demand and idle resources, so compensating for cuts in private spending and stimulating growth that would increase tax revenues and reduce the ratio of debt to GDP. Instead, cuts in spending led to recession and an increase in the debt-to-GDP ratio. In 2010, the IMF's *World Economic Outlook* was critical of Alesina, finding that 'the idea that fiscal austerity triggers faster growth in the short-term finds little support in the data', and that it had 'contractionary short-term effects on economic activity, with lower output and higher unemployment'.[18] Still greater austerity and a deeper recession were only avoided by non-discretionary government spending on welfare, which led to continued budget deficits.

On the right, austerity was portrayed as essential: the state was inefficient and drove out private investment; public debt was a curse and could not be sustained. Fiscal conservatives in America feared (or hoped) that bondholders would revolt. It did not happen, for Summers rightly calculated that the 'confidence fairies' were wrong and that US Treasury bonds were a safe haven in a dangerous world. Nevertheless, the fiscal stimulus was abandoned in the United States in 2010 in favour of tax cuts which benefitted the rich. Similarly, the coalition government in Britain enthusiastically embarked on austerity, and Merkel and Wolfgang Schäuble – Minister of Finance from October 2009 – pressed the need to control spending as the eurozone stagnated.[19] Schäuble insisted that countries with excessive debt needed to solve their structural problems – which would not be achieved by relying on money from other people. Rather, stricter discipline and fiscal rules were needed, alongside improved competitiveness.[20]

Debt sustainability became the priority, a choice justified by the so-called '90 per cent' rule of Carmen Reinhart and Ken Rogoff. They claimed that historical data showed that a debt-to-GDP ratio above 90 per cent led to a fall in the median growth rate by 1 per cent and more in the average rate; and that an *external* debt above 60 per cent in emerging markets reduced growth by 2 per cent. Politicians on the right seized on the argument.[21] In February 2010, shortly before he became Chancellor of the Exchequer in the Conservative–Liberal Democrat coalition, George Osborne claimed that the study of Reinhart and Rogoff was 'perhaps the most significant contribution to our understanding of the origins of the crisis'. It was not: the crisis arose from sub-prime mortgages and not public debt. The study offered him intellectual justification for his ideological belief in a smaller state.[22] Paul Ryan, the Republican chairman of the House Committee on the Budget, drew a stark choice between two futures: a path to prosperity, with debt completely paid off by the 2050s; or a path to economic disaster as debt rose to almost 900 per cent of GDP by 2080. In his view, the obvious source of this 'crushing burden of debt' was social security, Medicare and Medicaid.[23] Reinhart and Rogoff were more nuanced, for they proposed that debt could also be reduced by restructuring sovereign debt or reducing real interest rates.[24]

Critics pointed to flaws in Reinhart and Rogoff's data. More significantly, their methodology lumped together many countries and periods regardless of circumstances. Debt could sometimes be associated with low growth, as in Britain after the First World War when it arose from the collapse of the global economy and overvaluation of sterling. By contrast, a similar level of debt in the Second World War coincided with rapid economic growth. The impact of debt also depended on policy choices. The experience of Britain after the two world wars was a case in point. After 1918, interest rates were high to prepare for a return to the gold standard and prices fell so that the real value of debt rose; after 1945, interest rates were low and prices rose, so that the real value of debt fell. Where debt was serviced by high tax levels on productive wealth and income, it might harm growth. On the other hand, where debt was serviced by taxation that shifted income to poorer members of society and increased consumption, it might encourage growth. Lower public spending to balance the budget might lead to growth where debt, interest rates and taxation were high (as in Italy in the 1980s and 1990s), but not necessarily in other circumstances.[25] The right was preoccupied with public debt, rather than the extraordinary levels of private debt, and the costs of bailing out the banks. The message that debt was bad and that the crisis arose from the improvident behaviour of the state was easy to explain to electors. Mark Blyth, a leading critic of austerity, explained that the politics of debt became a morality play that shifted the blame from the banks to (in the perception of the right) an overly large and inefficient public sector and generous welfare. 'Austerity is the penance – the virtuous pain after the immoral party – except it is not going to be a diet of pain that we shall all share. Few of us were invited to the party but we are all being asked to pay the bill.'[26]

Fiscal stimulus was in retreat in 2010. In February 2010, the G7 embraced austerity and in June the G20 announced a commitment to '"growth-friendly" fiscal consolidation'. Although the G20 communiqué accepted that '[t]here is a risk that synchronized fiscal adjustment across several major economies could adversely impact the recovery', it gave more weight to the 'risk that failure to implement consolidation where necessary would undermine confidence and hamper growth. Reflecting this balance, advanced economies have committed to fiscal plans that will at least halve deficits by 2013 and stabilize or reduce government debt-to-GDP ratios by 2016.'[27] Even Keynesians admitted that action was needed on the structural deficit that had existed when the economy was booming. What was not justified was the ideological commitment to cuts in government spending. In 2013, David Cameron, the British prime minister, warned that

> There are some people who think we don't have to take all these tough decisions to deal with our debts. They say that our focus on deficit reduction is damaging growth. And what we need to do is to spend more and borrow more. It's as if they think there's some magic money tree. Well let me tell you a plain truth: there isn't.[28]

Such sentiments led a number of countries to adopt fiscal rules to control spending that ranged from a moderate requirement that the return on new debt should be higher than the cost of service, to a rigid rule that the budget must balance over the cycle or even (as in Germany) annually. In Germany, a fiscal rule was adopted as a constitutional amendment in 2009: a 'debt brake' or *Schuldenbremse* limited the federal deficit to no more than 0.35 per cent of GDP. The German demand for a balanced budget was in part a response to internal fiscal transfers after reunification, and taxpayers were not inclined to do for southern Europe what they had already done for East Germany. Apart from electoral considerations, the policy also reflected Angela Merkel's concern that the German – and European – population was ageing. She thought that boosting domestic demand would undermine competitiveness and pass the burden to future generations, and that the solution was to export and accumulate a surplus.[29] Although the United States did not adopt a formal fiscal rule, it had the conservative Tea Party movement. Paul Krugman complained that officials seemed to be 'getting their talking points from the collected speeches of Herbert Hoover', and that the rejection of fiscal stimulus was 'the victory of an orthodoxy that has little to do with rational analysis, whose main tenet is that imposing suffering on other people is how you show leadership in tough times.'[30]

The rejection of fiscal stimulus and turn to austerity reflected an ideological project to limit the role of the state. At a time when interest rates were low and the economy was in serious difficulties, it would have been possible to make investments that would help recovery and make the economy more resilient to climate change. As it was, the level of fixed investment in the United States and Britain was at a low level. The IMF was uneasy about a rigid commitment to austerity and adopted a policy of 'not too far, not too fast' towards fiscal consolidation, especially in countries with 'fiscal space' – room for spending without endangering debt sustainability. It realized that if all countries adopted austerity, the result would be to limit global growth, and leading economists at the Fund supported investment in infrastructure, demand and reduced inequality. The approach of the IMF under Dominique Strauss-Kahn (managing director from 2007 to 2011) and Olivier Blanchard (chief economist from 2008 to 2015) has been characterized by the political scientist Ben Clift as 'reflexive and pragmatic processes of "bricolage"' – that is, combining various things in a creative way.

Of course, the staff had to be aware of the political constraints imposed by members of the IMF and of the need to appear consistent. In 2010, Blanchard's 'ten commandments for fiscal adjustment' accepted the need for fiscal sustainability in the medium term with a long-term decline in the ratio of public debt to GDP. The commandments called for 'a non-trivial first instalment' of cuts, followed by reform of unsustainable pensions and health care. So far, the commandments sounded austere, but they also accepted that 'too much adjustment could also hamper growth'. Fiscal consolidation should encourage growth, should not be front-loaded, and should be equitable by supporting the vulnerable and attacking tax evasion. In time, Blanchard and his colleagues became more critical of short-term fiscal consolidation and more convinced of the need to act on inequality. Jonathan Ostry, the IMF's deputy head of research, and colleagues argued that inequality led to fragile growth by reducing investment, undermining social consensus that was needed to respond to shocks, and harming progress on health and education. They found that lower inequality was strongly correlated with 'faster and more durable growth' and that 'redistribution appears generally benign in terms of its impact on growth'. They supported the position of Rajan and Stiglitz that inequality makes crises more likely by giving power to the rich who allow financial excess and make the poor dependent on credit.[31]

The Fund tried to convince governments with fiscal space to reduce the pace of fiscal consolidation. The attempt did not always succeed. Osborne was committed to the view that the crisis was one of debt to be cured by austerity. To the IMF, the crisis was one of growth and the need to invest. In 2013, Blanchard warned the coalition government that they were 'playing with fire' by ignoring the impact on distribution and the fiscal multiplier of public spending, with little effect. Indeed, Blanchard and his colleagues found that the short-term fiscal multiplier was larger than expected: a reduction in spending of one euro would reduce GDP by almost €2 rather than €0.5 as had been previously estimated. Austerity therefore reduced GDP and increased the burden of debt, and spending might have been a sensible option. Olli Rehn, a Finnish politician who served as the European Commissioner for Economic and Monetary Affairs from 2010 to 2014, did not agree and rejected the IMF's argument as eroding 'the confidence that we have painstakingly built up over the past years in numerous late-night meetings'.[32] He failed to ask whether the result of the meetings in Brussels was to undermine the legitimacy of the EU, threaten national policy autonomy, and damage the welfare of citizens.

By contrast, fiscal policy played a major role in China and helped prevent the global financial crisis from turning into another Great Depression. Unlike Germany, it did boost global consumption. In November 2008, the Chinese government announced a spending package that was 'Keynesianism with Chinese characteristics'. Local and regional governments vied with each other in ambitious infrastructure projects which boosted the economy, although with the potential risk of distorting investment in sectors with excess capacity, leading to unnecessary infrastructure projects and creating unsustainable long-term corporate debt. Domestic consumption was also encouraged in December 2008 by subsidies to rural households to purchase large domestic appliances. The Chinese intervention was the largest single stimulus to the world economy. Adam Tooze, the leading historian of the global financial crisis, saw a fundamental change of 'world historic proportions, dramatically accelerating the shift in the global balance of economic activity towards East Asia ... In 2009, for the first time in the modern era, it was the movement of the Chinese economy that carried the entire world economy.'[33]

MONETARY INTERVENTION: QUANTITATIVE EASING AND SWAPS

The weak fiscal response to the global financial crisis in the United States and Europe meant that reliance was placed on monetary policy. Ben Bernanke, the chairman of the Federal Reserve, was a self-confessed 'Great Depression buff' who followed Milton Friedman's view that monetary policy should be actively used in recessions to restore employment and 'normal levels of inflation'. The Federal Reserve had reduced money supply in the early 1930s, prices and wages fell, borrowers were less able to keep up payments, and purchases were postponed. Although Bernanke supported Bush's fiscal stimulus of 2008 and Obama's of 2009, he thought that an active monetary policy was needed to avoid the mistakes of his predecessors. On 18 March 2009, the Fed embarked on Quantitative Easing (QE), a policy interpreted in the public mind as 'printing money'. In reality, the Federal Reserve bought mortgage-backed securities and Treasury bonds from banks. Bonds were therefore in shorter supply, their price rose and yield fell so that interest rates dropped. The purchase of bonds meant that banks had more cash which (in theory) created easier credit.[34] QE prevented a collapse of the financial system but the outcome was inequitable. Wall Street was saved, and low interest rates meant money moved into equities, which appreciated in value and benefitted those with assets. At the same time, austerity harmed welfare recipients and homeowners who faced foreclosure and negative equity. The Bank of England adopted a similar approach, unlike most European central banks. At the ECB, Trichet followed the Bundesbank's concern that QE would be inflationary. As a result, the Fed stepped in to support European banks that were heavily dependent on the American sub-prime mortgage market: 52 per cent of mortgage-backed securities purchased by the Fed came from Europe. The response of the Fed meant that global money supply continued to grow after 2008, unlike in the early 1930s.[35]

Although QE helped avoid depression, it contributed to new problems. The economist Brad DeLong remarked that Bernanke and the Fed focused on not making the same mistakes as in 1929 because 'they want to make their own, original mistakes'.[36] QE was criticized from both ends of the political spectrum. Opponents on the right argued that it would lead to inflation and currency debasement, and they looked back to Paul Volcker's imposition of tight money to end inflation.[37] In 2012, Congressman Ron Paul, a candidate for the Republican presidential nomination, called for a return to gold to impose discipline, remove 'moral hazard' and limit the role of the Fed. The American right drew on the contention of the Austrian School that gold was free of political manipulation and that combating depression by credit expansion was merely, as Hayek remarked, an attempt 'to cure the evil by the very means which brought it about'. These arguments were recycled by right-wing and libertarian organizations such as the Mises Institute (of which Paul was a member) and the Liberty Fund.[38] Although Obama saved the financial system and rescued bankers, Republicans played to conservative hostility to the state. In 2009, Paul called for the abolition of the Fed 'because it is immoral, unconstitutional, impractical, promotes bad economics, and undermines liberty', and Mitt Romney, the Republican presidential candidate in 2012, asserted that the slowness of recovery was caused by its policies.[39] In reality, the Fed was one of the few effective parts of the American state.

Other failings were pointed out from the opposite end of the political spectrum. Fiscal expansion was often criticized on the grounds that it passed the cost of servicing debt to future generations – but Stiglitz was right to point out that they might benefit from better education and infrastructure, and that loose monetary policy had harmful intergenerational effects in encouraging debt-based consumption. Bailing out the banks and maintaining the supply of money increased bank reserves and gave taxpayers' money to those who least needed relief and were less likely to consume. The state did not use cheap money to invest in the infrastructure; instead, cheap money allowed inefficient firms to survive and boosted corporate profits. The owners of equities also gained from rising values. Meanwhile, workers suffered from reduced or stagnant real wages. In Britain, for example, the average real wage only returned to the level of March 2008 at the start of 2020, and in the United States the median real wage of white men without a four-year degree fell by 13 per cent between 1979 and 2017.[40] In the United States, the fall in house prices hit the main asset of poorer households and wealth was transferred to lenders who retained a claim on the full value of the property. Borrowers reduced consumption to service the debt; the fall in consumption led to unemployment; falling real wages increased the real burden of debt and led to a further cut in consumption.[41]

QE attracted public attention. By contrast, 'swap' networks were largely hidden and were only mentioned in passing by Bernanke in his reflections on the crisis. As we saw in Chapter 16, central bankers sustained the Bretton Woods system in the 1960s with 'swaps' co-ordinated by the BIS. They were again important when European banks were exposed to the collapse of mortgage debt in the United States. In 2007, the three largest banks in the world were European – the Royal Bank of Scotland, Deutsche Bank and BNP Paribas – and they were heavily leveraged by short-term borrowing of dollars on the wholesale money market for lending to the housing market in the United States and to the European periphery. These banks lacked adequate reserves when funds dried up in 2008. The Fed feared they might cut lending in the United States, sell off their dollar portfolios, and so create problems for the American financial system. Supporting the large European banks exceeded the capacity of their central banks and states, and the IMF lacked sufficient resources – and was in any case not designed to handle crises in private banks. In the absence of other actors, the Fed responded swiftly by providing trillions of dollars to central banks through swap lines, as the liquidity provider of last resort to the global banking system – what Tooze calls a 'truly spectacular innovation' (Figure 20). By working through central banks, the Fed avoided direct assistance to private banks and kept its intervention out of the public eye, avoiding scrutiny from Capitol Hill – an understandable decision given libertarian Republicans' criticism of the Fed. The Federal Reserve identified 'Systematically Important Financial Institutions' – a small group of global banks and financial firms – and rescued them, their shareholders, and executives. This decision was understandable, but it meant that large financial institutions became even more dominant after the global financial crisis.[42]

Leading politicians in Europe either missed what was happening or misinterpreted it for public consumption. In 2008, President Sarkozy celebrated the downfall of the dollar, 'which after the Second World War under Bretton Woods was the only currency in the world. What was true in 1945 cannot be true today.' A European central banker was closer to the truth when he commented that Europe was now the thirteenth district of the Federal Reserve system. In October 2013, the Fed, ECB and the central banks of England, Japan, Canada and Switzerland decided – without public discussion or congressional approval – to turn the swap networks

Figure 20: Central bank dollar swaps net outstanding, December 2007–December 2009

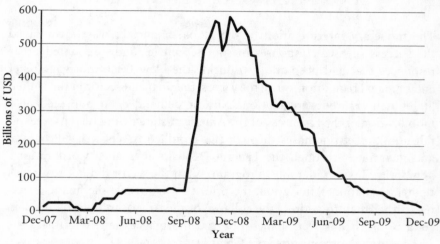

Source: Federal Reserve Board, H.4.1 Release Factors Affecting Reserve Balances and US Treasury Report on US International Reserve Position

into a permanent agreement that underpinned the dollar as the global currency. It was a technical solution that returned to the world of the BIS and central bank co-operation that Morgenthau had rejected at Bretton Woods. Far from declining, the financial crisis reasserted the role of the dollar, for only the Federal Reserve had the scale to act as the global lender of last resort.[43] The result was not the end of American dominance, because only the American state had the capacity to respond by creating more dollars and providing liquidity to the world economy. By contrast, the European response was slow and inadequate, leading to unemployment and depression in what Tooze calls 'one of the worst self-inflicted economic disasters on record'.[44]

The political dangers of supporting large financial corporations at a time when mortgagees were suffering foreclosure were obvious. Saving banks from their own folly required major public intervention that ran counter to the dominant ethos of market liberalization: it had to be kept out of the political limelight and be done quickly.[45] Liquidity delivered by the Federal Reserve and China's fiscal and financial stimulus meant that the global financial crisis of 2008 did not turn into a second Great Depression. These responses in Washington and Beijing were not co-ordinated and arose from a coincidence of self-interest – the United States' desire to rescue the western financial system and China's need to protect itself from the fallout.

THE POLITICS OF MORTGAGE RELIEF
AND FINANCIAL REGULATION

The monetary interpretation of the global financial crisis downplayed the success of fiscal responses in some countries and discounted other responses that had been adopted during the New Deal: mortgage relief and financial regulation. Since the 1970s, the financial sector in the United States had secured deregulation. Now it demanded an unprecedented mobilization of the resources of the American state through loans, recapitalization, asset purchases through the Troubled Assets Relief Program, and guarantees through the Federal Deposits Insurance Corporation's Temporary Loans Guarantee Program. What the sector did not want was tighter regulation. After 2008, the priority was to save the financial system rather than to address the collapse of the American housing market. As a result, banks were bailed out and mortgagees left to suffer – the reverse of the outcome after the Great Depression.[46]

House prices in the United States fell by about a third from peak to trough after both the Great Depression and the global financial crisis. In 1933, borrowers were helped by the Home Owners' Loan Corporation, which removed bad loans from bank balance sheets in exchange for bonds at a lower rate guaranteed by the government. After the global financial crisis, around 9.3 million Americans lost their homes to foreclosure, forced sales or surrender, but forgiveness of mortgage debt was not politically feasible. Bernanke realized that recessions are worse when businesses and households are in debt, and that ideally QE should have been complemented by direct help to indebted homeowners. He saw merit in mortgage debt relief, but the proposal led to a rant by the television presenter Rick Santelli on the floor of the Chicago Mercantile Exchange in February 2009 that is credited as an inspiration for the Tea Party. Federal intervention in the economy was widely perceived to be the problem rather than the cure. Powerful voices from the right argued that the problem lay with irresponsible borrowers and that intervention would affect private property rights. Summers and Treasury Secretary Tim Geithner wanted to show that they were sound managers of the economy, and they took the politically expedient view that the cost of mortgage debt relief would be too high and that resources were better spent elsewhere. Less was done to deal with mortgage finance than after the Great Depression, with only modest interventions by the Affordable Refinancing and Home Affordable Modification Programs to help homeowners switch to cheaper mortgages.[47]

Geithner ruefully remarked in March 2010 that 'we saved the economy, but we kind of lost the public doing it'. He, Summers and Hillary Clinton, Secretary of State in the Obama administration, were viewed (unfairly) on the right as destroying prudent monetary and fiscal policy and by progressives (with some justice) as allies of Wall Street. The left-wing Occupy Movement attacked Wall Street and urged action, but resentment was more effectively directed against the state by the Tea Party and the right of the Republican Party. The explanation was in part the capture of the state by a powerful financial elite, and also a structural change since the 1930s – what Jeffrey Chwieroth and Andrew Walter call 'the wealth effect'. Until the Great Depression, banks were allowed to fail; in the 1930s, policy shifted to regulation in order to avoid banking crises. From the 1970s, the political calculation again changed. More people were bound up in the financial sector through pensions or the purchase of services in health and education. The result was a larger 'bailout constituency' of middle-class voters aligned with the financial elites to protect their assets and access to credit. Of course, younger and poorer voters without pensions or housing wealth had different perceptions, leading to resentment at the cost of the bailout and government support for accumulated wealth – discontent that was turned against the state rather than Wall Street.[48]

Both the Great Depression and the global financial crisis arose in part from weak regulation that allowed an unsustainable boom. In the 1920s, banks took deposits from ordinary Americans, and made short-term loans to securities firms who speculated with the funds. When the bubble burst, many commercial banks failed. In 1933, the Glass–Steagall Act separated commercial and investment banking and imposed stricter regulation to prevent the recurrence of the crisis. In 1999, Glass–Steagall was repealed as part of a cross-party consensus on deregulation, with the support of Summers, the then Treasury Secretary, who had informed a Senate committee in 1998 that the '[t]he dramatic growth of the market in recent years is testament not merely to the dynamism of modern financial markets, but to the benefits that derivatives provide for American businesses.' Regulation would limit the use of financial devices that, so he claimed, acted to reduce risk and to direct investment to its most profitable use; and it would undermine the competitive position of Wall Street which would harm the broader economy by limiting investment. In any case, 'the parties to these kinds of contract are largely sophisticated financial institutions that would appear to be eminently capable of protecting themselves ... proponents of such regulation must bear the burden of demonstrating that need.'[49]

The attitude to financial regulation was well expressed by Howard Davies, the chair of the British Financial Services Authority (FSA) from 1997 to 2003. He alluded to the phrase used at the time when homosexuality was

decriminalized in England and Wales: 'Consenting adults in private? That's
their problem.' Private markets were generally assumed to be self-correcting
with risks reduced by financial intermediation. The economics profession,
with few exceptions, saw the world through the lens of rational expectations
and efficient markets, with crises arising from external shocks. Consequently,
there was little need for regulation or international co-operation. In 2004, the
Basel Committee on Banking Supervision's revised rules were influenced by
the Institute of International Finance that had been established by leading
banks in 1983 in response to the Latin American debt crisis and subsequently
expanded to represent the leading global players in financial services. Basel II
set minimum capital requirements and attempted to ensure consistent regulation between countries to ensure competitive equality between international
banks. In reality, the banks regulated themselves with little oversight and the
global financial crisis soon revealed the limitations. Davies's analogy reflected
the general sentiment of the time. It was mistaken. What individuals do in
their private life is their own business provided they do not cause harm to
others; what large banks do in private has devastating consequences for inno-
cent people.[50]

The main concern of central banks was inflation targeting rather than
financial fragility. Earlier in his career, Alan Greenspan, the chairman of
the Fed from 1987 to 2006, advocated the use of monetary policy in
response to asset bubbles and financial fragility. He then shifted to the use
of monetary policy to contain inflation. He claimed, with little evidence,
that the result would be an incentive to increase productivity: businesses
would not be able to raise prices and would therefore need to be more
efficient. Steady prices would, so he believed, provide a clearer measure of
firms' efficiency and profitability, and help to stabilize financial markets.
He opposed regulation of new financial instruments on the grounds that
markets could manage their own risks, and bankers would learn from
their mistakes to be more prudent in future. Even if a bubble did occur, he
did not believe that it would harm the real economy, and asset prices were
mainly viewed in terms of the impact on inflation. Greenspan had been a
disciple of Ayn Rand, a dogmatic opponent of altruism and collectivism
who argued that regulation meant that the United States never had free-
market capitalism. 'Selfishness,' she argued, 'is a magnificent force.'
Greenspan did depart from her extreme position as he moved into the
political structures of Washington, and as support for free markets became
part of the mainstream. Greenspan's views on inflation were supported by
Bernanke's academic work, and he ignored warnings by other economists
that low inflation might encourage risk. Greenspan did muse about
'irrational exuberance' and ponder whether asset prices and financial

stability should be considered by the Fed, but he did not act as sub-prime mortgages expanded. The focus on inflation had allowed financial fragility to grow unchecked. Although it would have been difficult to change the Fed's policy given the wider political context of deregulation and prioritization of inflation, Greenspan was guilty of taking the easy option.[51]

Martin Wolf of the *Financial Times* rightly pointed out that 'the view that stabilizing inflation was a sufficient condition for economic stability has been proved grotesquely wrong'.[52] Greenspan and Bernanke failed to oversee the financial system which was assumed to be able to look after itself. Bernanke claimed in 2006 that '[t]he management of market risk and credit risk has become increasingly sophisticated ... Banking organizations of all sizes have made substantial strides over the past two decades in their ability to measure and manage risks.' In June 2007, he still took the view that 'the troubles in the subprime sector seem unlikely to seriously spill over to the broader economy or the financial system'.[53] He was spectacularly wrong. Such misplaced confidence had led to deregulation and allowed financial institutions to take on ever larger risks. Alternative views were largely ignored. Hyman Minsky was one of the few economists who saw that a crisis could emerge from within the system rather than from an external shock. He realized that financial markets are inherently unstable and that speculative bubbles are internal to the economy. In a period of economic prosperity, perception of risk drops and the longer the period of prosperity, the more risks are taken by borrowers. Even a slight fall in the value of assets creates a cash-flow crisis, lenders call in loans, banks tighten credit, and the economy enters recession. In Minsky's view, the crucial variable was not sovereign debt but non-government debt, a point overlooked in economists' models.[54] Similarly, Joseph Stiglitz complained that the Clinton administration gave in to financial interests, and that the policies of the World Bank and IMF helped financiers rather than the poor of the world. In his view, the boom in the United States in the 1990s was artificially fuelled by excessive deregulation and perverse incentives given to the chief executives of banks. In 2003, he argued that it was time to accept that what was good for Wall Street was not good for the entire country, and he hoped that the scandals of the 1990s had discredited free-market capitalism. They had not, and his call for greater regulation was ignored in favour of Bernanke's 'complacent, indeed vainglorious' celebration of the 'great moderation'. As Wolf pointed out, the 'crisis happened partly *because* the economic models of the mainstream rendered that outcome ostensibly so unlikely in theory that it made it more likely in practice ... Naïve economics helps cause unstable economies.'[55]

After the crisis, the new chair of the FSA, Adair Turner, learned the lesson. He criticized the assumptions that markets are efficient and rational, and that 'financial markets innovation delivers benefits to customers and the economy'. He understood that individual rationality is not the same as collective rationality, and that general acceptance of a faulty risk model made the entire system more dangerous than anyone realized. Turner argued for stricter regulation.[56] However, the shift to regulation was weaker than after the Great Depression. In May 2009, Simon Johnson, chief economist at the IMF in 2007–8, saw that a 'quiet coup' by leading banks had been entrenched by the policy responses to the global financial crisis. He had been involved with the IMF in Russia, South Korea and Thailand, where business oligarchs formed a close relationship with governments. Johnson saw similarities in the United States, where

> elite business interests – financiers, in the case of the US – played a central role in creating the crisis, making ever larger gambles, with the implicit backing of the government, until the inevitable collapse. More alarming, they are now using their influence to prevent precisely the sorts of reforms that are needed, and fast, to pull the economy out of its nosedive. The government seems helpless, or unwilling, to act against them.

Johnson claimed that the United States had the world's most advanced oligarchy. Rather than bribes and corruption, he saw a more insidious process: 'the American financial industry gained political power by amassing a kind of cultural capital – a belief system . . . It benefited from the fact that Washington insiders already believed that large financial institutions and free-flowing capital markets were crucial to America's position in the world.' Before the financial crisis, regulators placed their faith in banks' ability to control risk. Regulatory capture rested on lobbying and political influence, with confidence that deregulation made the financial sector more competitive. Wall Street and Washington were intertwined, with a circular flow of personnel between the Treasury, the Federal Reserve and financial institutions – above all Goldman Sachs. Johnson saw that 'a whole generation of policy makers has been mesmerized by Wall Street' and unregulated financial markets so that the response to the crisis was characterized by 'delay, lack of transparency, and an unwillingness to upset the financial sector . . . or to question the basic outlines of the system that got us here'.[57] The outcome was not minor corruption where rules were broken for personal gain; it was grand corruption of the system with rules written by organized, influential and wealthy interests that undermined the public interest.[58]

The Obama administration supported banks after the global financial crisis and asked for little in return. The regulatory response was weak, with divergent views on how to respond: to protect consumers from predatory lenders; to break up banks and put a cap on bankers' bonuses; to require higher capital and liquidity levels; to make derivative trading more transparent and to stop extended mortgage chains; to separate commercial and investment banks; to deal with the failures of rating agencies; or to limit the powers of the Federal Reserve? These different views were debated by the Financial Crisis Inquiry Commission established by Congress in May 2009 with the aim of reporting by December 2010. The Treasury could not wait and in June 2009 it made its own proposals. Discussions started in a mood of public anger, lobbying by vested interests, and disagreement over reform so that the outcome lacked coherence. The different regulatory agencies were consolidated with the Fed and Treasury into the Financial Stability Oversight Council (FSOC), and Senator Elizabeth Warren secured a separate Consumer Financial Protection Bureau. Treasury Secretary Geithner feared that the FSOC was too cumbersome and that blocking further bailouts would be dangerous populism. Nevertheless, he realized that widespread criticism of bank rescues required a compromise if he were to secure any legal authority. The outcome was the Dodd–Frank Act, or the Wall Street Reform and Consumer Protection Act, of 2010, a sprawling compromise of badly drafted rules that would be difficult to interpret and implement. The Glass–Steagall Act was a mere 37 pages, compared with 848 pages of the Dodd–Frank Act and a further 8,843 pages of rules that covered only one-third of its provisions. One banker complained that he needed a psychiatrist as well as a lawyer. The FSOC allowed the Treasury and Fed to institutionalize stress testing and 'macroprudential regulation' of capital, debt and liquidity. It also meant that banks that were 'too big to fail' were not broken up, and the new regulatory regime ensured that they could survive another crisis. The result was that banks judged to be safe and systemically important had an implicit guarantee of assistance, and they become more dominant with a closer relationship with the government.[59]

Macroprudential regulation would make American banks less competitive unless similar measures were adopted in other countries. In March 2008, the Financial Stability Forum (the body established in 1999 to coordinate supervision of financial institutions) and the BIS met in Rome to consider the financial crisis, and they suggested that the G8 finance ministers should improve the resilience of financial markets and institutions. As a result, in November 2008, the heads of government of the G8 agreed to widen membership of the Financial Stability Forum to emerging countries such as China and, at the G20 summit in London in 2009, the Forum was replaced by the Financial Stability Board to cover all G20 members. In June 2012, the G20 agreed to convert the Board into a formal institution, a Swiss not-for-profit association based in Basel that comprised central banks, finance ministers and regulators from twenty-four countries and the European Union, as well as the IMF, World Bank, OECD and BIS. Its role was to identify vulnerabilities in the financial system and devise macro-prudential standards on a voluntary basis, providing guidance rather than rules.[60] Responsibility for international regulation was largely left to the BIS. A third set of Basel rules was agreed in 2010–11 for implementation between 2013 and 2018, with the aim of strengthening the capital requirements of banks and improving liquidity. The proposal was scaled back because of pressure from both the Institute of International Finance, on the grounds that it would lead to lower lending, slower growth and lower profits, and from European banks that had not recapitalized to the same extent as those in the United States. The response to the financial crisis was the preservation of the existing system rather than fundamental reform.[61]

In 2013, concern about the redistributive consequences of QE and austerity led Summers to worry that a small elite was prospering at a time when most Americans saw no improvement in their lives. He now called for large-scale investment in the country's infrastructure. In January 2014, Robert Reich, who had been Secretary of Labor under President Clinton, went further and urged action against inequality in a new Progressive movement.[62] The New Deal had, after all, led to an attack on the power of monopolies and finance, and to a redistribution of income and wealth. The challenge of a more progressive approach was taken up by Senator Bernie Sanders (Ind.: Vermont), a contender for the Democratic presidential nomination in the primaries in 2015–16. He supported the reinstatement of Glass–Steagall: 'Let's not forget: President Franklin Roosevelt signed this bill into law precisely to prevent Wall Street speculators from causing another Great Depression. And it worked for more than five decades.' Hillary Clinton, his successful rival for the Democratic nomination, and Summers denied that the decision to repeal Glass–Steagall had led to the global financial crisis. They pointed out that the risks did not arise from the big banks but AIG (an insurance company) and Lehman Brothers (an investment bank). They were only partly correct, for these non-banks secured funding from big banks that underwrote gambling in securities. In 2016, any slim prospect for a new Progressive era was defeated by the 'pluto-populism' of Donald Trump. In February 2017, soon after his inauguration, President Trump announced a review of the Dodd–Frank Act on the grounds that too much regulation strangled business – a decision that Warren and Sanders denounced as another favour to Wall Street and a threat to financial stability.[63]

THE EUROZONE

When the crisis hit the United States, many European politicians thought that they were safe. They were wrong, for their banks were deeply involved in the American sub-prime market and in property loans in southern Europe and Ireland. The euro allowed countries to borrow on favourable terms by removing the risk of devaluation and from the mistaken assumption that stronger countries would bail out debtors, despite the prohibition in the Maastricht and Lisbon treaties on either the Union or any member accepting responsibility for the commitments of any central, regional, local or public authority.[64] The risk premium on sovereign debt of members of the eurozone fell, with the curious outcome that in July 2007 the interest rate on 10-year Irish sovereign bonds was *lower* than on German debt. This situation was untenable and risk premiums started to rise. Borrowers had little room for manoeuvre, for they could not devalue their currencies and lenders refused to reschedule or mutualize debt by issuing Eurobonds held by the Union. The situation in Ireland was alarming. Its banks were exposed to a property bubble which broke in 2008 and in September the government guaranteed the deposits and loans of the largest six banks. The Anglo-Irish Bank was the most seriously affected and it was nationalized in January 2009, with further injections of funds in 2009 and 2010. The costs were crippling, and the banking crisis spilled over into alarm about the public finances. The risk premium on sovereign bonds rose to 300 basis points when the Anglo-Irish Bank was nationalized and reached a peak of over 1,000 basis points. Similarly, the Greek government was unable to borrow in 2010, and the sovereign debt crisis spilled over to Spain, Portugal and Italy. The result was a vicious downward spiral. The high cost of bailing out banks led to deflation to reduce budget deficits; worries about sovereign debt led to a loss of confidence in banks which held government bonds; the costs of rescuing banks hit public finances; and austerity weakened economies and made it harder to deal with the deficit. A crisis caused by excessive bank lending was redefined as a crisis of public borrowing, to be corrected by austerity that would force reform and – so it was believed – stimulate growth. The policy led to immense social hardship that protected private holders of debt and undermined democratic politics.[65]

Adam Tooze characterized the approach in Europe as 'extend and pretend' – that is, a refusal to take swift action to restructure debt, with a long-drawn-out period of denial and lack of initiative characterized by austerity, an inadequate monetary response, and a failure to recapitalize European banks. The ECB did not have authority to purchase public debt and Jean-Claude Trichet was adamant in rejecting quantitative easing. Although Schäuble saw the need for a European Monetary Fund to restructure debts, which would allow the imposition of discipline, Chancellor Merkel had no wish to reopen the compromise reached in the Lisbon Treaty in favour of intergovernmentalism – the acceptance by each state of its obligations. Instead, she turned to the IMF, to the annoyance of Schäuble and Sarkozy, who remarked that '[t]he IMF is not for Europe, it's for Africa, it's for Burkina Faso.'[66] The German government saw benefit in involving the IMF, which would be less susceptible to political pressure and more able to impose discipline and conditionality than a European institution. It would also divert hostility from Germany. On the other hand, Sarkozy was wary of giving power to Dominique Strauss-Kahn, the managing director of the IMF who was potentially the Socialist Party candidate for the French presidency. At first, the IMF was cautious about becoming involved in view of disagreements in Europe, the ECB's opposition to debt restructuring, and doubts over Greek 'ownership' of reform. The outcome was the 'troika' – the IMF, European Union and ECB – which negotiated a rescue package for Greece in 2010. The IMF was in a difficult position. It accepted that Greece – unlike Britain – lacked fiscal space so that fiscal consolidation and reform were needed. It also accepted the need for rescheduling debt, which was part of its rescue packages in Latin America, but in Greece, as in Ireland and Portugal, it had to give way to its partners in the troika who argued for austerity without debt rescheduling. The ECB and Trichet persisted with a hardline policy of tight money and rejection of QE. Refusal to reduce the cost of servicing debt led to cuts in social welfare, higher unemployment, political unrest and a loss of confidence.[67]

Milton Friedman had warned in 1997 that the euro would not create political unity and that divergent shocks would create political tensions.[68] His prognosis was coming true. Germany and other northern countries believed that southern Europe borrowed recklessly because of lower interest rates in the eurozone, and had failed to reform their tax systems, control public spending or curb clientelism. In the south, the imposition of austerity led to criticism of the euro for undermining national autonomy and benefitting German exporters, because the exchange rate of the euro was below what it would have been if the Deutsche Mark had continued and appreciated.

In May 2010, the threat of the Greek debt led the European Union to establish the European Financial Stabilization Facility, with power to borrow €440bn and provide temporary financial support to members of the eurozone. This innovation led to a debate about whether it was desirable to break the 'no bail out' rule and the ban on assuming liability for the debt of a member state. The French wanted to share liability between members; Germany insisted that each member should be separately responsible. The outcome was that the European Council took a pragmatic approach: that the Lisbon Treaty permitted financial assistance if a member faced severe difficulties because of exceptional circumstances beyond its control. However, debt was not mutualized and members of the eurozone made individual contributions without a shared intergovernmental commitment.[69] In October 2010, the crisis in Ireland led Merkel and Sarkozy to propose a German-style debt brake and accept that creditors should take a hit. Trichet was appalled and insisted that Ireland should be treated in the same way as Greece. When Ireland applied for a rescue deal a month later, the finance ministers of the European Union agreed to a joint package with the IMF of €8bn over three years, with strict conditions on reducing the budget deficit. The Irish government was to pay interest on the loan and debt was not rescheduled: rather than bondholders taking a hit, the burden fell on the less well-off. The *Irish Times* pointed out that Ireland had fought for independence from Britain, only to lose control to the troika – and that the crisis in Ireland was not caused by public debt as in Greece but rather by the state bailing out irresponsible bankers.[70]

'Extend and pretend' led to mounting political unrest against the demands of bankers and the troika. The approach was clearly failing, and Merkel and Schäuble finally accepted the need to restructure debt. Trichet remained hostile and the ECB, in a deeply misguided decision, increased its interest rate to force governments to take responsibility for their debts. The attempt of Strauss-Kahn to resolve the stand-off failed when he was arrested in New York in May 2011 on charges of sexual assault. In Washington, the IMF and the White House feared a serious European banking crisis. Angela Merkel resisted a more ambitious programme to recapitalize banks and mutualize bonds, in part because her coalition partners would reject the proposal and trigger an election. In December 2011, the outcome was a compromise with Sarkozy: an intergovernmental agreement on fiscal rules or a 'debt brake' for a balanced or surplus budget and no shared liability for European debts, with debt restructuring limited to standards set by the IMF.[71] It was too late and too little.

The crisis in the eurozone was not resolved and the IMF feared that the imposition of austerity might lead to global recession. As the Spanish finance minister explained, when the *Titanic* sank even those in first class drowned. In June 2012, the finance ministers of the eurozone finally agreed to fund the recapitalization of banks, and the European Council accepted that a banking union was needed to deal with the dangerous intersection of the sovereign and banking crises. Merkel conceded an extension of European powers, and a single supervisory mechanism came into force in November 2014. At last, the eurozone started to come into line with other federal systems where banks were under federal jurisdiction – but it was only a start. The eurozone was still far from the situation in the United States, where a failed bank was a federal responsibility and would not undermine the finances of an individual state. The suggestion of Herman Van Rompuy, the Council president, in June 2012 that banks be directly recapitalized by the European Stability Mechanism was rejected by Germany and the Netherlands, so that individual states retained responsibility.[72]

Debtor countries gambled that refusal to comply with the demands of creditors would not lead to expulsion from the euro. In 2010, Schäuble and Merkel threatened expulsion from the euro of any country that could not resolve its financial problems, despite the lack of provision in the Maastricht Treaty for an exit. Even with such provision, exit would be practically impossible. All Greek contracts, for example, were written in euros, and if the government reintroduced the drachma and converted payments into a depreciated currency, creditors would turn to the courts. Greek courts might accept the change, but creditors could still appeal to the ECJ or to bilateral investment treaties and the International Centre for Settlement of Investment Disputes. Merkel soon backed down and accepted that a rescue package was necessary for the survival of the euro. The pattern was repeated in 2012 when the left-wing Syriza Party adopted an anti-austerity platform in the Greek elections and calculated that creditors would not expel the country. Schäuble repeated his threat and argued that removing the weakest member would strengthen the euro and bring other countries to their senses. Syriza lost in 2012. But it came to power in January 2015 and conflict soon arose with Germany. When the Syriza government rejected the rescue package as too harsh, Merkel initially favoured Greece's temporary exit from the euro before backing down under pressure from France and Italy. The Greek government miscalculated. German creditors were reluctant to offer better terms, and other countries that had suffered austerity and reduced their debts were unsympathetic. In July 2015, Syriza had to accept worse terms than it had rejected earlier in the year.[73]

At last, the ECB changed its stance. In July 2012, the new head of the Bank, Mario Draghi – an American-trained economist who had worked at the World Bank, Goldman Sachs and the Italian Treasury before becoming governor of the Banca d'Italia and chair of the Financial Stability Board – promised that 'within our mandate, the ECB is ready to do whatever it takes to preserve the euro'. His bold claim was supported in Washington and opposed in Berlin, where the government preferred austerity to force structural reform. Merkel and Schäuble had to admit defeat, however, when Wen Jiabao, the Chinese premier, announced that his country would not buy more European bonds until action was taken. Crucially, Merkel overruled the Bundesbank's opposition to Draghi's plan. The ECB slowly took a more active role, which meant finding ways of reinterpreting its mandate. In September 2012, the ECB adopted 'Outright Monetary Transactions' (OMTs) to support the euro by buying bonds from countries facing difficulties and acting as lender of last resort. This innovation was opposed by Jens Weidmann, president of the Bundesbank, who argued that keeping the monetary union together was the responsibility of sovereign states and not the ECB. A number of German academics and politicians thought that Draghi was exceeding the ECB's authority, which was limited to monetary policy and excluded the pursuit of an independent economic policy. Draghi was one of the few people who were willing to act in a sad story of inflexibility and inaction that reflected badly on the leadership of the European Union.[74]

In February 2014, the German constitutional court sought clarification from the ECJ on whether OMTs were in breach of the Lisbon Treaty and Germany's basic law. In June 2015, the ECJ ruled in favour of the ECB and the German constitutional court reluctantly accepted that OMTs did not currently impair the Bundestag's overall budgetary responsibility or 'manifestly' exceed the powers of the ECB. Although OMTs were not used, their existence stabilized markets until they were replaced by QE in January 2015, against the wishes of the Bundesbank and Germany. Even then, QE was confined to individual governments buying their own debts rather than pooling them in Eurobonds. The crisis was forcing the ECB to become somewhat closer to the Fed and Bank of England, against continued opposition from the Bundesbank.[75]

The European response had been woeful. It failed to produce coordinated action and relied on national action which turned a banking crisis into fiscal crises. The inadequacies of the Maastricht and Lisbon treaties forced the ECJ into legal contortions to circumvent the 'no bail-out' clause and the limitation to monetary policy.[76] To many in northern Europe – and above all Germany – the blame lay with lazy, feckless and corrupt countries in southern Europe who had failed to control their budget deficits, borrowed recklessly and failed to carry out structural reform. Both fiscal union and rescheduling or mutualizing debt were resisted. Jeroen

Dijsselbloem, the Dutch president of the European finance ministers, tactlessly remarked that the north had shown solidarity with the south, but 'you also have obligations. You cannot spend all the money on drinks and women and then ask for help.'[77] Criticism of the Greek government had some justice but was not the entire picture. Much of its debt pre-dated the euro and was incurred to create support for democracy after military rule – and much of the money lent to Greece came from a glut of savings in Germany. An improvident borrower needs a reckless lender, and in other episodes – from late-nineteenth-century Greece to Mexico in the 1980s – the burden was shared by rescheduling debt. In Europe, the response was less generous than in Latin America. Ashoka Mody, assistant director of the IMF's European department, criticized the failure to apply the lesson of Argentina's default in December 2001 – that debt should have been rescheduled earlier – or to admit the general principle that rescheduling helped stimulate recovery.[78] Germany was reluctant to help its fellow eurozone members, whether by mutualizing bonds or increasing its own consumption and reducing its surplus. Merkel feared both the domestic electoral consequences and the removal of pressure on debtors to reform. The consequences were serious for southern Europe. The combination of fiscal retrenchment, the sudden end of capital flows and pressure on private consumption led to a deep recession, high levels of youth unemployment, a collapse of welfare, and resentment against the EU and Germany.[79]

In January 2014, the president of the European Commission, José Manuel Barroso, announced that the existential crisis of the euro was over.[80] Certainly, the immediate crisis had passed but the euro remained flawed. Rather than the high growth and economic convergence promised by its advocates, the euro led to slow growth in southern Europe and economic divergence. In 2007, Germany's GDP was 10.4 times that of Greece; in 2015, it was 15 times. Stiglitz castigated the euro as the product of leaders out of touch with their electorates, serving financial interests rather than citizens. The 'economists' had been right: the economies of member states were too far apart, and states surrendered policy options that might have mitigated austerity. A more sensible approach would have been a flexible exchange rate mechanism rather than an inflexible and poorly designed single currency. Far from producing 'ever closer union', deficit countries' resentment of Germany, and that of surplus countries against debtors, created fissures within the European Union. The euro was a mistake from which escape seemed impossible: exit was not an option and neither was 'ever closer union'. In the words of one German official, 'we have invented a machine from hell that we cannot turn off.'[81]

RUSSIA, INDIA AND CHINA

The global financial crisis marked the emergence of China as a key player in the management of the global economy, and the growth of its economy raised many of the world's poor to a higher standard of living. By contrast, Russia's economy stagnated after the crisis. One response was a turn to state capitalism, starting with the Yukos Oil Company, a major private concern that was broken up and taken over by state companies thanks to criminal proceedings for tax evasion – a process that was widely seen as a politically motivated attack on the oligarchs who did well from privatization after the disintegration of the USSR. The large state companies – Gazprom (gas), Rosneft (oil), Vnesheconombank (banking) and Rostec (armaments) – allowed President Putin to appropriate rents to his personal benefit and to individuals who were answerable to him. These state enterprises could ignore competition and a need for investment and efficiency; their main requirement was loyalty to Putin, plus personal enrichment, political control and geopolitical influence. The Russian economy and state finances became heavily dependent on oil and gas revenues, which accounted for 47.3 per cent of federal revenues in 2008 and 51.3 per cent in 2014.[82] The result was to constrain diversification of the economy and to expose it to the risk of lower energy prices – though equally, Europe (and above all Germany) was becoming dependent on Russian gas. Putin also learned the lessons from the rouble crisis of 1998 and the global financial crisis that macroeconomic stability was needed. The liberal economists had lost the battle for reform of the market and corporate governance; they did succeed with macroeconomic policies to contain inflation, maintain reserves through floating exchange rates, and balance budgets by cuts in education, health care and pensions.

The result was a toxic mixture of a state dominated by a 'kleptocracy' answerable to Putin and relying on authoritarianism for survival, with low growth and declining standards of living. Putin's regime could not rely on economic prosperity to secure its legitimacy and he turned instead to anti-democratic Russian nationalism and a succession of small wars, as well as cyberattacks and disruption of American and European elections. Gorbachev had realized that high levels of military spending harmed the civilian economy. Under Putin, spending on an inefficient and corrupt military rose at the expense of investment in education and health care. After Russia's invasion of Crimea in 2014, the Hague Declaration suspended meetings of the G8 'until Russia changes course'. Members of the G7 were divided over the best response. The British and American governments wished to isolate Russia, and the US Deputy National Security Adviser, Antony Blinken, argued that 'as long as Russia is flagrantly violating international law ... there is no need for the G7 to engage with Russia'. By contrast, the German foreign minister argued that 'the format of the G8 is the only one in which we in the west can speak directly with Russia. Shall we really give up this unique format?'[83]

The collapse of the Soviet Union and the humbling of a great power led to resentment in Russia at the emergence of new states, the expansion of NATO, the policies of the IMF, and claims that western capitalism had triumphed. The result was not a turn to democracy and free markets but a mixture of corruption, nationalism, declining welfare and the risk of military conflict. The risk became all too real with the invasion of Ukraine early in 2022. Sanctions against the Russian economy and individual oligarchs entailed a drop in European oil and gas imports from Russia, triggering inflation in Europe without seriously hitting Russian exports. Production of oil was only down 3 per cent in July 2022 from the level before the invasion, with supplies diverted to China and India at a discount that was offset by a general increase in oil prices.[84] The threat to the global economy potentially exceeds the impact of both the global financial crisis and Covid – with the risk of something even worse if there were a disaster in a Ukrainian nuclear plant or an escalation of war.

In India, the Congress government of Manmohan Singh embarked on liberalization after taking office in 2004. Growth accelerated, alongside continued problems of poverty, corruption and bureaucratic inertia. In 2014, the BJP regained power. The prime minister, Narendra Modi, had been Chief Minister in Gujarat between 2001 and 2014 where he pursued development based on *Hindutva*, the association of Indian identity and cultural values with Hinduism. He targeted dissent as cosmopolitanism and minorities as anti-nationalist. Modi also encouraged collaboration between the state and private corporations, which resulted in growth combined with increased inequality as a result of low wages, tax breaks and modest levels of spending on education and health. The losers in Gujarat were mainly the minorities – Muslims, Dalits and Adivasis (indigenous Scheduled Tribes) – who formed around 30 per cent of the population of the state. The winners were the middle class and migrants to the towns who gave Modi sufficient support to win three elections.[85] After 2014, he pursued similar policies as Prime Minister of India. He abolished the Planning Commission and replaced it with the National Institution for Transforming India under his chairmanship, with membership of the chief ministers of the states and leading academics. The finance minister explained that the new approach rested on regional devolution: 'India is a diversified country and its states are in various phases of economic development ... In this context, a "one size fits all" approach to economic planning is obsolete. It cannot make India competitive in today's global economy.' The new institution looked to development through 'cooperative federalism', starting from the village level, with the government as an 'enabler' rather than 'provider of first and last resort'.[86]

The approach had some virtues given the wide regional disparities within the country. There were also serious problems, for the BJP was encouraging nationalism and fundamentalism that provoked communal tensions and threatened India's secular democracy. Economic reform ran alongside attacks on Muslims and repression to clamp down on opposition. In 2019, Modi won a resounding victory over the Congress Party, led by Mrs Gandhi's lacklustre grandson Rahul, who was no match for Modi's presidential campaign and image as a strongman. Despite serious difficulties of rising unemployment, the chaotic 'de-monetization' of the economy to tackle undeclared wealth, and a complex sales tax, economic problems proved less important than Modi's combination of religious polarization and nationalism with promises of welfare for the poor and a robust attitude to national security. Congress lost its dominance, with its vision of India as a secular state in which members of different religions and cultures had equality as citizens. During the campaign, Modi had little to say about economic reform. Growth slowed, with a mounting fiscal deficit, problems with 'shadow' banks and the state-dominated banking system, and low levels of private investment. India still needed to invest in the physical infrastructure of road and rail, in decent water supplies, sanitation and basic education, as well as putting its finances on a sound basis. Indian economic growth did not reach the levels of China – and Amartya Sen pointed to serious flaws in liberalization. The East Asian model of export-led growth needed a literate workforce, health care, land reform and gender equality, but half the population of India, and two-thirds of women, were illiterate; credit for the rural poor was limited; and land reform was not implemented. Sen understood that liberalizing markets and reducing tariffs would not be enough and that more action was needed to deal with basic capabilities in health and education, where India lagged behind China. He rightly worried that half of India would end up like California and half like sub-Saharan Africa with poor basic services of clean water, sanitation and education, continued bureaucratic inertia, and corruption in the disposal of land and sale of state assets.[87] The situation is certainly worrying. Vijay Joshi, an economist with long experience at the Reserve Bank of India, the Ministry of Finance and in international institutions, realized that liberalization was needed but that private business was hampered both by its own crony capitalism and by the failure of the state to fulfil its core functions, making India 'one of the worst places in the world to do business'.[88]

In Russia, economic growth was low and standards of living stagnated as the circle around Putin exploited state enterprises for personal gain. The country was economically weak – yet it retained immense military power and geopolitical importance. India grew faster, but nowhere near the rate of China, with democracy and political stability threatened by Hindu nationalism and Modi's authoritarianism. However, the BJP – unlike the Chinese Communist Party and, increasingly, Putin – is still challenged by other parties, which might allow greater adaptability in the long run. The difficulty is that India has been less successful in dealing with shortcomings of weak infrastructure, health and literacy. In China, President Xi's authoritarianism might lead to decisive economic action and the pursuit of long-term policies without the fear of electoral repercussions – yet there are risks of failing to admit mistakes, of increased reliance on state enterprises that are less efficient, and on loans that lack transparency and a clear economic rationale. Deng Xiaoping combined economic reform with the authority of the CCP and the need to ensure that the party did not again succumb to a single dominant leader. The presidency was limited to two terms with a system of collective leadership. These reforms were overturned by Xi, who removed the limit on his presidential term, weakened collective leadership and imposed strict surveillance. Xu Zhangrun, formerly a professor of law at Tsinghua University, accused Xi of turning to tyranny that

> ultimately corrupts the structure of governance as a whole and it is undermining a technocratic system that has taken decades to build. A party-state system that has no checks and balances . . . invariably gives rise to a clique of trusted lieutenants. Hence we have seen the equivalent of a court emerge and the political behaviour endemic to a court.[89]

Power struggles have occurred in the CCP in the past and might do so again, especially if the economy falters or the benefits are not widely distributed. The consequences will be serious far beyond China now that it is the world's major trading power with growing military and geopolitical ambitions. The country's financial system is also weak, with a property bubble and investments that lack transparency. The mass movement of population from the countryside to cities and industrial employment allowed the growth of the Chinese economy and fuelled a massive property boom based on debt. In 2021, the housing market experienced a downturn; developers failed to complete construction on property sold off-plan to investors, who refused to pay their mortgages. The difficulties of Evergrande, one of the largest Chinese property companies, in servicing its debt in 2021 was potentially China's 'Lehman moment'. Further, provincial and local governments rely on revenues from land sales; they responded to the loss of income by borrowing at high rates. The global financial crisis started in the United States – the next financial crisis might start in China unless its growth model can be changed from reliance on investment in property and infrastructure. The outcome will be vital not only for China but for the global economy.[90]

BACKLASH: WINNERS AND LOSERS

In 1999, Kevin O'Rourke and Jeffrey Williamson pointed to the collapse of globalization in the early twentieth century as a result of hostility in the Americas to the inflow of migrants that depressed wages, and in Europe from landowners and farmers whose rents or livelihood were squeezed by competition from imports of foodstuffs. They concluded that the collapse of globalization at that time was the result of

> a political backlash developed in response to the actual or perceived distributional effects of globalization . . . Far from being destroyed by unforeseen and exogenous political events, globalization, at least in part, destroyed itself . . . The record suggests that unless politicians worry about who gains and who loses, they may be forced by the electorate to stop efforts to strengthen global economy [sic] links, and perhaps even to dismantle them.[91]

Before the First World War, the impact of globalization was mitigated by the growth of the nation state which provided welfare, controlled migration, and adopted protection – with the possibility that it could turn to economic nationalism. In 2001, Harold James did not see any immediate prospect that globalization might again be challenged. He took a benign view of globalization, arguing that unskilled jobs were not disappearing as a result of competition from low-income countries; trade was not dominated by cheap imports from low-income countries; and there was no sign that markets would be saturated. Rather, '[w]e have just become more efficient at producing . . . [T]echnical changes and efficiencies of scale . . . have made purely national markets relatively inefficient, and created pressures on business to rationalize by spreading across borders.' In his view, the forces opposed to globalization were weaker than in the past, with a 'remarkable consensus' around the virtues of trade and capital liberalization, budgetary orthodoxy, privatization and financial deregulation, enforced by international agreements and institutions, and by 'sustained reflection about appropriate policy'. Unlike in the 1930s, he saw no ideology such as fascism and Communism to focus anger against globalization. 'There is no coherent intellectual package that links the resentment. It is incoherent and allusive – in short, postmodern.' James accepted that the pendulum might swing against globalization, but that it would be slow.[92] A decade or so later, the global financial crisis and the policy response had the potential to accelerate the backlash as a result of growing inequality within high-income countries – particularly the United States and Britain. Globalization again faced threats from financial instability, from growing nationalist or identity politics, and from resentment at a loss of secure employment.

As we saw in Chapter 23, the major beneficiaries of the global economy were the growing middle class and workers in emerging economies in the middle of the global income distribution – as well as the top 1 per cent in the western economies. By contrast, the working class and lower-middle class in the developed world, around the 80th percentile of global income, were relative losers. After the global financial crisis, the same trend continued, with an acceleration in the growth of the global middle class, especially in China, and stagnation of incomes further up the income scale in the developed world (see Figure 21). From a global perspective, large numbers of people in emerging markets escaped from poverty and aspired to join the middle class. From a political point of view, inequalities within countries are more visible and electorally significant. The economist Branko Milanović pointed out that

> Politicians in the West who pushed for greater reliance on markets in their own economies and the world after the Reagan–Thatcher revolution could hardly have expected that the much-vaunted globalization would fail to deliver palpable benefits to the majority of their citizens – that is, precisely to those whom they were trying to convince of the advantages of neoliberal policies compared with more protectionist welfare regimes.[93]

The policies adopted in response to the global financial crisis did not assist losers from de-industrialization and globalization, with the danger that economic nationalism could break the link between global capitalism and liberal democracy.

The calculations of Thomas Piketty and Emmanuel Saez of the share of wage income taken by percentiles 90–95, 95–99 and the top 1 per cent in the United States between 1913 and 1998 (see Figure 22) show that the top 1 per cent of incomes fell from a peak before the First World War to a trough after the Second World War.[94] Piketty explained the fall in inequality by the shock of the First World War and the effects of the

Great Depression, when the government expanded welfare support, offered relief to mortgage borrowers, regulated banks and introduced more redistributive taxation. Roosevelt's redistributive agenda was a central element of the second New Deal. Inequality also fell as workers moved from the countryside into towns and industrial employment, and increased schooling reduced the premium on education. The maintenance of equality after 1945 reflected the need for social cohesion in the Cold War, and the trade-off between capital and labour in the politics of productivity.

In the later twentieth century, the trend to equality was reversed and earlier levels of inequality returned. Piketty explains the shift by the ability of capital to secure a return in excess of growth so that owners of wealth gained; and by the way that remuneration committees awarded high incomes to corporate executives in a process of mutual self-interest.[95] This explanation is not the entire story. Greater inequality reflected a political choice against redistributive taxation and social cohesion in favour of incentives to encourage enterprise.[96] The choice was not made in all countries, for income distribution in Japan and France did not return to previous levels of inequality. Furthermore, the policy choice of QE in the United States and Britain meant rising asset prices for the better-off as austerity squeezed wages. Changes in economic structure also had a role.

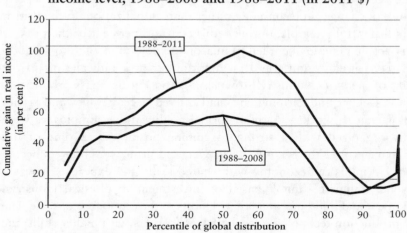

Figure 21: Relative gain in real per capita income by global income level, 1988–2008 and 1988–2011 (in 2011 $)

Source: Milanović, *Global Inequality*, 31.

Figure 22: Income shares of percentiles 90–95, 95–99 and the top 1 per cent in the United States, 1913–1998

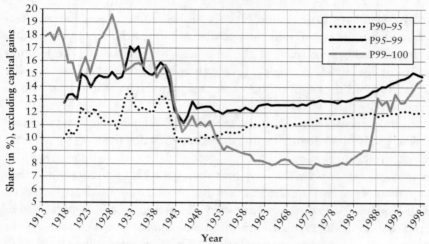

Source: F., Alvaredo, A. Atkinson, T. Piketty, and E. Saez. 'The top 1 percent in international and historical perspective'. *Journal of Economic Perspectives* 27 (2013), 6.

Globalization led to competition from cheaper suppliers, with outsourcing of both industrial and service jobs, migration, and the addition of large numbers of workers in emerging markets to the global workforce. Above all, the loss of jobs and widening disparities of wealth and income were caused by de-industrialization and technological change.

In the United Kingdom, the proportion of workers in industry fell from 48 per cent of the workforce in 1957 to 15 per cent in 2016, largely because of changes in technology rather than globalization. In the British car industry, for example, output returned to 90 per cent of the peak of the 1970s, but employment fell from around 500,000 in 1972 to 140,000 by 2017. Globalization was less important than a radical shift in the nature of the work. Industrial towns based on Fordist mass production, such as Detroit and Birmingham, had offered decent wages and secure employment to workers without formal qualifications. Employees were highly organized with a strong bargaining position at a time of full employment after the Second World War, and firms were interconnected in a local industrial economy with shared skills and expertise. It was a world of 'tangible capital' based on investment in physical industrial equipment and buildings that created limits to the economies of scale. The new production technology needed fewer workers with higher skills: the proportion of workers in British manufacturing with no qualifications fell from 26 per cent in 1993 to 8 per cent in 2013. The polarization between well paid, highly qualified workers and low paid, unqualified workers in insecure jobs was even more striking in the expanding service sector. In Britain, between 1979 and 1999, employment of care assistants expanded by 419.5 per cent and of supermarket shelf fillers by 95.5 per cent. By contrast, workers in information technology or legal and financial services needed formal credentials and were paid high salaries.

The new sectors often relied on 'intangible capital', which had few limits to economies of scale. Microsoft, for example, sells licences to its software and, unlike a car manufacturer, does not need investment in fixed capital to the same extent. The leading entrepreneurs in these sectors made huge fortunes and salaried employees received large incomes. Further, weaker anti-trust policies led to market dominance by a few firms with higher profit margins, and barriers to entry in many sectors of the economy delivered high incomes for professionals and entrepreneurs. At the same time, de-industrialization and erosion of union power weakened the bargaining position of labour. The crucial issue here was not the globalization of trade and offshoring, but the polarization of the labour market by de-industrialization and skill-based technological change. The loss of jobs in the United States between 2001 and 2007 from offshoring was 69,000, out of a total loss of 1.2 million production jobs.[97]

Material inequality went with a political system that gave excessive power to the richest members of society.[98] The result was a sense of disempowerment, especially as solidarity in trade unions and occupational identity fragmented. One outcome was progressive attacks on finance and austerity and calls for a socially just form of capitalism. In France, the Association pour la taxation des transactions financières et pour l'action citoyenne (ATTAC) emerged in 1998 as a single-issue movement to demand a tax on financial transactions, before turning to a wider critique of globalization and a call for a sustainable and socially just global economy.[99] Such sentiments inspired protests in London at the time of the G20 summit of 2009 organized by Put People First, a body supported by NGOs including CAFOD (Catholic Agency for Overseas Development), Oxfam, Christian Aid, Friends of the Earth, the World Wildlife Fund, major trade unions and the Bretton Woods Project that criticized the IMF and World Bank. Put People First claimed that it was not against globalization but that democratic financial institutions were needed to deliver secure jobs and public services, with an end to global poverty and inequality and the creation of a green economy.[100] In 2011, the Occupy Wall Street movement took up the issue of 'we are the 99 per cent' – a reference to Piketty's graph. Piketty campaigned for progressive taxation of income, wealth, carbon emissions and bequests, which would fund capital endowments for young adults and a minimum basic income for all.[101]

Rather than this progressive demand for fairer capitalism, the mood of the electorate in declining industrial towns was captured by populist, nationalist voices of 'identity conservatives'. The economic changes had cultural consequences as ways of life and identity were threatened. The winners were well educated, with a cosmopolitan world view that was at ease with multiculturalism, open global markets and immigration. The losers were more likely to lack formal qualifications, to be tied to declining industrial towns with fewer prospects, uneasy with multiculturalism, and adopting a nativist view. Similarly, the 'squeezed' middle class with formerly secure and well-paid white-collar jobs suffered from computerization, greater job precarity and loss of pension rights which led to nostalgia for a socially conservative past. By contrast, City and Wall Street financial firms, major law firms and tech companies were global in reach, with multinational staff. The result, as one commentator put it in a reductive way, was a divide between the 'somewheres' and the 'anywheres', or between university-educated 'conviction liberals' who valued diversity and 'identity conservatives' who were normally older, without a university education and committed to ethno-centric attitudes. The older class-based divisions of left and right, labour and capital, were giving way to cultural or identity politics.[102]

Globalization was a useful scapegoat that led to President Trump's turn to protectionism and rejection of the post-war multilateral order. In his inauguration address in January 2017, Trump announced that 'we must protect our borders from the ravages of other countries making our products, stealing our companies and destroying our jobs. Protection will lead to great prosperity and strength.'[103] In reality, his 'plutocratic populism' offered false hope to the 'left behinds' and benefitted the rich. In Britain, the scapegoat was the EU. Many supporters of Brexit – British departure from the European Union – embraced globalization as a return to a dynamic global Britain outside the confines of the customs union; a vision that appealed to nostalgia for Britain as the world's greatest industrial and trading power. Opponents have characterized this thinking as 'Empire 2.0'; more accurately, it was not just an atavistic return to the empire, but a de-regulated, neo-liberal, free-market 'Anglosphere'.[104]

Although imbalances within the global economy had not been the trigger for the global financial crisis, they were a continued threat. The growing disparities of income and wealth within countries also contributed to trade wars between countries. The 2020 analysis by Matthew Klein and Michael Pettis had similarities with the argument of J. A.

Hobson in Edwardian Britain, that international free trade should be combined with a 'fair' distribution of income and wealth at home to end under-consumption. In Germany in the early 2000s, domestic consumption was low as a result of reduced welfare benefits in the 'Hartz reforms', opposition to public spending, and high levels of saving. German companies overcame the stagnant home market by selling their goods to other European countries and securing higher profits thanks to static wages. Germany did not, however, reciprocate by buying imports – and the trade deficit of other countries was covered by debt (often financed by German banks). In China, household consumption was an unusually low proportion of output and workers saved a high proportion of their additional income to compensate for poor welfare provision, support in old age, and to purchase housing priced at a very high multiple of annual income. Business and local government benefitted from high profits and cheap loans, but the absence of domestic markets meant reliance on export markets. In both Germany and China, these macroeconomic imbalances led to rising exports, current account surpluses and capital outflows. The United States similarly had a 'savings glut' generated by rich households who saved more and spent less of their incomes. By contrast, workers suffered from stagnant or declining incomes and turned to debt. The United States circumvented under-consumption and continued to buy imports because of its 'exorbitant privilege' – or, more accurately, 'exorbitant burden' – of global demand for dollars as a safe haven. The inflow of funds increased American purchasing power, led to low borrowing costs and lending standards, and held up the value of the dollar. As Klein and Pettis show, trade wars are created by the maldistribution of income and wealth within countries. The global economy had reached the limits of its ability to deal with rising income inequality. The solution should be a return to a redistributive strategy as pursued in the New Deal and after the Second World War, which underpinned the post-war order and global economic government – combined with greater equity between countries.[105]

A decade after the global financial crisis, the economic government of the world faced serious challenges. QE and austerity, as well as changes in the occupational structure, had led to growing inequalities in Britain and the United States. Finance remained powerful and there was a high reliance on consumer credit. The flaws of the euro had not been resolved and China still had an extraordinarily low level of household consumption with problems of how best to use its savings in an effective manner. Then the world was hit by the Covid pandemic in 2020 and Russia's invasion of Ukraine in 2022.

A second Great Depression was avoided in 2008 by the Federal Reserve's use of QE and swap networks and by fiscal stimulus in China – initiatives that were not co-ordinated. The situation now is worse and the ability of both national governments and global institutions to respond is limited. The political system in the United States is increasingly polarized in a way that blocks policy initiatives – and China is increasingly autocratic, with the possibility of crises both in domestic finance and in debt arising from its Belt and Road Initiative. It is not likely that either country could embark on interventions of the same scale as after 2008, which arose from mutual self-interest.

China needs to move away from its model of investment in property and infrastructure to a more balanced economic model before it experiences a serious financial crisis. It is turning to more assertive nationalist geopolitics in the South China Sea and Taiwan with the risk of serious tensions with the United States. After the invasion of Ukraine, Russian oil could be redirected to China – but Russia is a tiny market for Chinese goods, which relies on exports to Europe and America. Despite the close connection between the Chinese, European and American markets, co-operation on issues of finance and trade, and on climate change and public health, will be difficult. The dangers facing the world are greater than at any time since 1945. Multilateral institutions were created during and after the Second World War to deal with the conflicts of the 1930s, and to bring together liberal democratic capitalist societies. Now, liberal capitalism needs to deal with internal divisions and find a fairer social and economic order, and to work with state-led authoritarian capitalism to rebalance the global economy and deal with the challenge of climate change and pandemics.[106] The existing institutions of global government failed to prevent the global financial crisis: a new architecture of global economic government is needed to prevent another financial crisis and to respond to climate change.

26
'Messy multilateralism'
Nationalism versus Globalism

'... there is a deep flaw in our system of global economic governance. According to democratic principles those who are deeply
affected by a policy should have a say in their formulation, and
those who are responsible for massive failures and injury should be
held accountable. Our present system of global economic governance does not meet either of these fundamental tests of democratic
governance.'

Miguel d'Escoto Brockmann, President of the 63rd Session
of the United Nations General Assembly, 2009[1]

'... America will always choose independence and cooperation over
global governance, control, and domination ... The United States
will not be taken advantage of any longer. For decades, the United
States opened its economy – the largest, by far, on Earth – with few
conditions ... Yet, other countries did not grant us fair and reciprocal access to their markets in return. Even worse, some countries
abused their openness [sic] to dump their products, subsidize their
goods, target our industries, and manipulate their currencies to gain
unfair advantage over our country ... We will not allow our workers
to be victimized, our companies to be cheated, and our wealth to be
plundered and transferred ... America will always act in our national
interest ... America is governed by Americans. We reject the ideology
of globalism, and we embrace the doctrine of patriotism.'

President Donald Trump's remarks to the
UN General Assembly, 25 September 2018[2]

In the aftermath of the financial crisis, some American political scientists
were confident that the 'system worked' and the multilateral institutions
had contained national self-interest and beggar-my-neighbour policies.

A figure depicting German Chancellor Angela Merkel ignites a bomb
that reads 'TTIP' on a float outside the Bundestag during a rally
against TTIP, Berlin, 10 October 2015.

The WTO was confident that protectionism had been avoided: new trade restrictions imposed between October 2008 and October 2010 amounted to only 1.8 per cent of G20 imports, and 1.4 per cent of total world imports, so that trade remained more open than it had ever been.[3] In 2011, the political scientist John Ikenberry believed that 'the deeper logic of open and loosely rule-based international order remains widely embraced' and he anticipated 'the renewal and reorganization of liberal order – not its overturning'. He saw an end to great power conflict, a growth of liberal democracies, an expansion of economic interdependence, the incorporation of Russia and China into the rule-based order, and a willingness of other countries to allow the United States, with other liberal democracies, to operate as a 'liberal leviathan', supporting 'practical and consensual functioning global rules and institutions' in a world order of liberal internationalism.[4] He was not alone in such optimism. Another political scientist, Daniel Drezner, argued that the institutions of global governance, for all their faults, provided principles and procedures around which countries could converge to constrain domestic protectionism. In his view, effective international action was possible because economic power was highly concentrated and, despite their differences, the leading economies of the world – the US, EU and China – remained committed to an open international economy. The Great Depression had been different, for a weakened Britain could no longer provide leadership; the United States lacked the will; Nazi Germany acted as a 'spoiler'; and the Soviet Union was outside the world economy. By contrast, he believed that no major power acted as a 'spoiler' in the global financial crisis, and the economic ideas underpinning an open global economy were not, as in the 1930s, discredited by alternative ideologies of Communism, fascism or economic nationalism. He was confident that 'a strong post-crisis consensus among economists constrained the search for alternative paradigms'.[5] Paul Kennedy, a leading historian of international relations, agreed that the situation was unlike 1933, for 'I don't think anyone is busy with revengeful, pre-war militaristic feelings. Certainly not any in the G20.'[6]

Ten years later, such confidence was misplaced, with the Russian invasion of Crimea in 2014 and of Ukraine in 2022, tensions with China over trade and geopolitics, the election of Trump in November 2016 and the return of economic nationalism. Far from expanding, liberal democracies were in retreat, with a turn to autocracy in Russia and China, to authoritarianism in India, and right-wing populism in Hungary and Poland. Although Trump was defeated in 2020, the intense polarization of American politics and shortcomings of its political system damaged the ability of the United States to provide leadership as a 'liberal leviathan' – something that was wishful thinking even in 2011. The continued commitment to market liberalism and financialization after the global financial crisis resulted in gains accruing to the higher income and wealth levels in the developed world and to precarity to those at the bottom, with the prospect of a populist backlash. If the system had worked, it was for some members of society and not others.

The global financial crisis did not turn into a second Great Depression, as we saw in the previous chapter, largely because of national action by the Federal Reserve's quantitative easing and swap networks and China's fiscal stimulus. The global economy was rescued from disaster by the actions of two leading economies, acting largely from self-interest and without co-ordination. The multilateral institutions did not have a major role in rescuing the global economy, and – as Barry Eichengreen pointed out – the avoidance of a worse economic disaster 'weakened the argument for radical action. It took the wind out of reformers' sails. And it allowed the petty disagreements among politicians to slow the reform effort. Success thus became the mother of failure.'[7] Before the financial crisis, the multilateral institutions were widely criticized. Mervyn King, the governor of the Bank of England, wondered whether the IMF was 'slipping into obscurity', and Eichengreen thought it a 'rudderless ship adrift in a sea of liquidity'.[8] Meanwhile, the Doha Round of the WTO failed and it too seemed to be drifting into irrelevance. Mark Mazower, a historian of the idea of world government, was more realistic than Ikenberry and Drezner when he remarked in 2012 that 'the basic trajectory is real enough. We have moved from an era that had faith in the idea of international institutions to one that has lost it.'[9]

THE IMF AND THE GLOBAL FINANCIAL CRISIS

Prior to the crisis, the IMF had lost much of its role. Its rationale in 1944 was to manage the system of pegged exchange rates that no longer applied in a world of floating rates and large capital flows. It had turned to co-ordinating debt re-scheduling in the crises in Latin America and East Asia – an experience that led countries in these regions to avoid recourse to the Fund by building up their reserves. This strategy could divert resources from public investment, but the price seemed worthwhile to maintain sovereignty. One Asian finance minister remarked that 'most Asian countries would rather be dead than turn to the IMF'. Neither had it played much of a role in the supervision of the international financial system which was left to the BIS and Financial Stability Forum. The financial crisis revived the fortunes of the IMF, starting with its first intervention in Hungary in November 2008 and continuing with its participation in the troika during the eurozone crisis. It went on to provide loans to Argentina, Turkey and Pakistan. In April 2009, the G20 agreed to double the IMF's resources and, in the words of one commentator, the IMF was a 'phoenix rising' from the fires of the crisis in the eurozone, where it played a major role with the ECB and European Union.

Although the IMF took a more nuanced view of austerity in countries with fiscal space, many recipients of its assistance at this time thought it was more like a vulture that imposed hardship and austerity, which did little for the institution's long-term credibility. After the crisis, there were renewed calls for changes in the Fund's governance structure by adjusting the voting system and quotas and increasing its financial resources. The initiative came not only from emerging economies that wanted a greater voice but also from the United States, which wished to reduce the number of European executive directors. David McCormick, Under-Secretary for International Affairs at the Treasury Department, wanted the IMF to take on the 'fundamental responsibility' of surveillance of exchange rates – above all the renminbi, which the Americans thought was deliberately under-valued. He also called for the IMF to carry out stress testing of financial systems, but progress was slow and largely left to other bodies. The resources of the IMF were modest compared with private funds, and the IMF's reputation was tarnished by its imposition of financial orthodoxy and continued dominance by developed countries. In 2009, the United States had 16.8 per cent of votes in the IMF, which was, admittedly, less than its share of world GDP at 20.5 per cent. The EU had 32.1 per cent of the votes, far ahead of its 21.3 per cent of GDP. By contrast, the emerging markets of Brazil, Russia, India and China – the so-called BRICs – had a mere 9.6 per cent of votes despite comprising 23.5 per cent of GDP.[10]

The IMF claimed to have changed in the aftermath of the global financial crisis, away from a dogmatic pursuit of the Washington consensus. Its pursuit of financial liberalization and capital flows was now questioned. In November 2009, Dominique Strauss-Kahn – the managing director of the Fund – pointed out that capital controls were 'not something that come from hell' and that 'there is no reason to believe that no kind of control is always the best kind of situation', though he did not recommend controls as a standard response.[11] In 2010, an IMF report pondered whether capital flows in response to short-term interest differentials might undermine export competitiveness by raising exchange rates and creating asset bubbles and financial fragility. In November 2012, the IMF accepted that there was 'no presumption that full liberalization is an appropriate goal for all countries at all times', and it accepted that capital controls might be a sensible policy, provided they did not replace tighter fiscal policy or adjustment to the exchange rate, and did not harm the global economy or limit financial integration. In 2016, members of the IMF's research department suggested that neo-liberalism had been oversold, and that austerity and capital account liberalization led to inequality that damaged growth. Several emerging economies did adopt controls in response to large inflows of capital seeking higher returns in response to the low interest rates created by quantitative easing. Paulo Nogueira Batista of Brazil, the Latin American representative on the IMF executive board, nevertheless thought the IMF was still too cautious and had not realized 'the extent of the damage that large and volatile capital flows can cause to recipient countries'.[12]

In 2017, Gita Gopinath – prior to her appointment as the Fund's chief economist – agreed that capital account liberalization had been a 'mixed blessing ... associated with excess volatility tied to abrupt surges and reversals in capital flows, and consequently there can be prudent limits to capital account liberalization'. She argued for greater surveillance of *gross* rather than net flows. After all, European bank borrowing in the United States to invest in the American sub-prime market did not show up in net cross-border flows, yet it played a significant role in the financial crisis. Disruptive flows of capital into emerging markets in search of yield meant that 'international finance ... turns out to be far less benign than previously thought ... There are sound arguments for intervening in capital markets, including the use of capital controls and macro prudential regulation.'[13] Paul Volcker took a similar line that clear indicators, such as a large swing in exchange rates or reserves, were needed in order to mitigate the risk of cross-border financial transactions.[14] In 2020, the IMF's Integrated Policy Framework accepted that cross-border capital flows could produce shocks as well as benefits, and that reliance on flexible exchange rates might not be the best way to respond. The IMF noted that policymakers drew on an eclectic mix of tools that varied over time and between countries, and it offered a framework to help them decide on the best solution – a turn from dogmatism to pragmatism.[15]

As we have seen, senior economists at the Fund inserted a wider range of ideas about the need for growth, action on inequality, and greater public spending where there was fiscal space. These ideas were articulated more openly by Christine Lagarde, the French minister of finance from 2007 to 2011 before her term as managing director of the IMF from 2011 to 2019. At Davos in 2013, she quoted Roosevelt's comment that '[t]he test of our progress is not whether we add more to the abundance of those who have much; it is whether we provide enough for those who have too little.' She looked to universal access to education, robust social safety nets, access to credit, gender inclusion, solidarity across generations, and 'job-rich', sustainable green growth. She called for greater accountability for states to prevent corruption, for private enterprise to move beyond a search for profit, and for the financial sector to stop hiding 'activity in murky and dark corners' and putting short-term gain ahead of supporting the real economy. In 2014, she argued that the IMF was a reformed institute: 'Structural adjustments? That was before my time. I have no idea what it is. We don't do that any more. No, seriously, you have to realise that we have changed the way in which we offer our financial support.' In 2015 the Fund did call for debt relief in Greece and in 2016 declined to take part in further funding in the absence of measures to reduce the country's debt burden. The IMF started to take a wider view of its responsibilities on issues such as taxation of multinational corporations, corruption, carbon pricing, and a concern for the impact of financial flows across borders. It could be a 'neutral assessor' providing objective analyses of economic and financial spillovers between countries, and co-ordination measures that might help avoid a future crisis.[16] Cynics doubted whether the IMF had really reformed, and found that, in practice, it still imposed conditions that included austerity. What did change was that the IMF faced competition, above all from Chinese loans, as we will see in the next chapter.[17]

THE WTO: REGIONALISM VERSUS MULTILATERALISM

Despite the lack of progress in the Doha Round of trade talks, the WTO was initially confident that its rules-based regime locked in past successes. Pascal Lamy, the director general of the WTO from 2005 to 2013, hoped that the financial crisis would strengthen global economic government. He regretted the adoption of the narrower agenda of GATT in 1947 and called for a return to the ambitions for the ITO at Havana, with its commitment to the full employment of human resources, development, social progress, a stable monetary system, open trade and environmental sustainability. He misread history. The wider agenda of the ITO had been a failure, the focused agenda of GATT had succeeded, and the Doha agenda had made little progress. He also misread current politics, for states were unlikely, as he hoped, to renounce what he saw as illusionary sovereignty for the reality of shared sovereignty. Lamy looked to a 'triangle of coherence' between the leadership of the G20, the legitimization of the UN, and the expertise of specialized institutions, alongside regional governance on the European model where supra-nationality started from shared values and a common goal. He hoped that common international values and objectives would emerge from action on social inequality and a search for global public goods, with a new declaration of global rights and responsibilities in which the WTO took the lead in protecting consumers, the environment and health. Lamy was indulging in an unrealistic fantasy at a time when European supra-nationality was challenged by the eurozone crisis, and international agencies by nationalistic populism.[18]

The real question was whether the WTO could survive. Before the Bali ministerial meeting in 2013, Roberto Azevêdo, the new director general of the organization, warned that

> The multilateral trading system remains the best defence against protectionism and the strongest force for growth, recovery and development. Yet, as I take on this role, it is clear that the system is in trouble . . . People only see us as as good as our progress on Doha. That is the reality. And the perception in the world is that we have forgotten how to negotiate. The perception is ineffectiveness. The perception is paralysis.[19]

Jagdish Bhagwati likened the WTO to a three-legged stool which needed all its legs to stand up – negotiating, adjudicating and monitoring.[20] The first leg was broken and might threaten its other functions. The WTO was in need of reform. It had given more weight to rising powers and development goals without increasing its effectiveness, and reliance on decision-making by consensus in a single undertaking meant that failure on one issue led to deadlock on the entire package. Bhagwati had been a member of the consultative committee chaired by Peter Sutherland, the former director general of the WTO, which had recommended in 2004 increasing the role of the secretariat and director general at the expense of a member-driven approach. It did not find favour with critics, who complained that the WTO was committed to a free-market ideology and threatened national interests – and Sutherland's career at Goldman Sachs gave credence to their perception. Similarly, a shift from consensus to weighted or majority voting, or an executive board as in the IMF, would reinforce criticism of bias in favour of larger developed economies. Any gains in efficiency would come at the expense of legitimacy.[21]

Azevêdo's solution was to change the negotiating process. Instead of a small group reaching an agreement which other countries had to accept or reject, everyone with an interest in an issue would be included and their proposal would be presented to an open meeting. At Bali, the outcome was a modest deal to improve the administration of customs barriers, reduce subsidies on agricultural goods and improve access for less developed countries. It led the European trade commissioner, Karel De Gucht, to announce that 'today we have saved the WTO', and for Azevêdo to claim that 'we have put the "world" back in the World Trade Organization'. This was wishful thinking. Bali effectively marked the end of the wider Doha Development Agenda. Azevêdo was given twelve months to produce a timetable to conclude the remaining issues but the attempt at resuscitation failed. The next ministerial meeting in Nairobi in December 2015 made modest progress on agriculture, cotton subsidies and treatment of less developed countries, without achieving the wider goals of the Doha Round. The *Financial Times* captured the sense of futility: 'After a death-scene so drawn-out it would have done credit to a Victorian melodrama, the curtain has finally come down on one of the longest running farces in global policymaking.' Doha failed because of divisions between developing countries that were net importers or exporters of agricultural goods; the emergence of China as a major exporter that still claimed the status and privileges of a developing country; and difficulties dealing with American farmers who wanted unrealistic market access in return for cuts in their subsidies.[22]

The initiative had already moved to bilateral or plurilateral deals that could maintain momentum, with the danger, as Bhagwati saw, that they were 'termites in the trade system' that would undermine the most favoured nation principle. In 2013, Robert Zoellick warned that '[i]f the WTO does not create opportunities to conclude new liberalising deals within its framework, the action – and the creation of new rules for new issues – will move elsewhere.' The risk was that '[i]f multilateralism fails, unilateralism may prevail'. The solution might be 'plurilateral' deals under the umbrella of the WTO, and to focus on elements of the Doha agenda that could be rescued.[23] President Obama turned to new plurilateral deals. In February 2013, he suggested a free trade agreement with the EU – the Transatlantic Trade and Investment Partnership (TTIP). Negotiations soon followed for a Trans-Pacific Partnership (TPP) with countries on the Pacific Rim which excluded China in a policy of containment. The marginalization of the WTO was clear at the Bali ministerial meeting. The United States Trade Representative arrived from and departed to meetings with partners in the TPP and returned to Washington to discuss TTIP. This shift from 'grand multilateralism' after the war to 'mega-regionalism' led to diverging interpretations; it was either a sign that multilateralism was dying, or an attempt to preserve a liberal, rules-based international order. To Lamy, plurilateral deals could be 'stepping stones' rather than 'stumbling blocks', though he warned that regional regulatory standards could undermine global 'regulatory coherence'. In February 2013, a joint report of experts to the European Commission and White House looked to 'enhanced cooperation for the development of rules and principles on global issues of common concern and also for the achievement of shared global economic goals' which would, the *Financial Times* remarked, 'establish the US and EU as the pre-eminent standard setter for the rest of the world'. Others were doubtful and feared the initiative would weaken the WTO and make it difficult to retain a level playing field across different bilateral or plurilateral deals.[24]

Supporters of TTIP argued it would lead to increased trade and employment. Critics saw a threat to European standards and culture. François Hollande, the Socialist president of France, wanted to exclude audio-visual services to protect French culture, and Lamy – a fellow French Socialist – defended France's *exception culturelle* in subsidizing French films against competition from Hollywood. At the European Commission, José Manuel Barroso criticized these views as 'culturally extremely reactionary', but he was in a weak position in defending TTIP. The negotiations lacked transparency and were widely perceived as threats to sovereignty and to regulatory standards in food safety and the environment. This suspicion was confirmed by TTIP's backing by business groups such as the Transatlantic Business Dialogue and the Transatlantic Economic Council, and in the light of disputes over hormone-injected beef and genetically modified crops. In Britain, some suspected TTIP was a device to allow private American health-care providers to 'McDonaldize' the NHS. In Germany, the economist Max Otte warned that TTIP would force European workers to compete with low-paid Mexican workers who were part of NAFTA and that the European social model would be undermined. Such concerns resulted in 3.2 million signatures for a European Citizens' Initiative – a scheme that allowed voters in the European Union to petition for changes in the law – that called on the European Commission to reconsider TTIP.[25]

TTIP and TPP were attacked from both ends of the political spectrum, in equally apocalyptic terms. On the left, the progressive activist movement AVAAZ – a transliteration of a Sanskrit word for 'voice' – denounced TTIP as 'a horrifying power grab' to hand 'our hard-won democracies to greedy corporations ... It's described as a trade agreement, but TTIP is about so much more – it could let business lobbyists crawl all over our laws before citizens even hear about them, and flood our countries with bee-killing pesticides, gas guzzling cars and GM foods.' Similarly, AVAAZ launched an attack on TPP as 'a top-secret, global corporate power grab of breath-taking scope that attacks everything from a free Internet to health and environmental regulations ... Big business is getting ready to uncloak a giant Death Star on our democracies.'[26] On the right, the libertarian John Birch Society denounced 'the globalists' trade agenda to establish a UN world government', a plot by 'Deep State globalists' to use free trade agreements to create 'a truly global authority'.[27] Radical economic populism overlapped with President Trump's populist economic nationalism. Soon after he entered the White House, Trump abandoned TTIP. In June 2017, he also announced that the United States would withdraw from the Paris agreement on climate change. The European Union was committed to negotiate trade agreements only with parties to that agreement, and in April 2019 decided that the directives for negotiating TTIP were 'obsolete and no longer relevant'.[28] Similar problems arose with TPP. Although Hillary Clinton had supported TPP as Secretary of State in the Obama administration, she retreated from it during the 2016 presidential campaign and Trump withdrew from the partnership on his first day in office. In the absence of the United States, negotiations continued to create a Comprehensive and Progressive Agreement for a Trans-Pacific Partnership. China exploited the withdrawal of the United States by calling a meeting in Beijing in 2019 that led to the Regional Comprehensive Economic Partnership – the largest-ever trade deal with a combined GDP that exceeded the Comprehensive Agreement, European Union and NAFTA taken together.[29]

Trump did not merely pull out of new bilateral or plurilateral deals. He also blamed NAFTA for the loss of American jobs. His inclination was to abandon NAFTA, but his counterparts in Mexico and Canada persuaded him to renegotiate the agreement, and talks started in August 2017. The negotiations were difficult, for Trump made extreme demands, including the possibility that NAFTA would expire in five years unless explicitly renewed; he tried to 'divide and rule' through separate bilateral talks with Mexico and Canada; and he embarked on protectionist measures which led to threats of retaliation. Despite his bluster, a deal was struck in September 2018 for a new United States–Mexico–Canada Agreement that came into effect in July 2020 – in reality, an adjustment rather than a major change.[30]

GROUPS AND NETWORKS

At the UN General Assembly in September 2008, President Luiz Inácio Lula da Silva of Brazil called for urgent action:

International economic institutions today have neither the authority nor the workable instruments they need to inhibit the anarchy of speculation. We must rebuild them on entirely new foundations . . . The global nature of this crisis means that the solutions we adopt must also be global, and decided upon within legitimate, trusted multilateral fora, with no impositions. The United Nations, as the world's largest multilateral arena, must issue a call for a vigorous response to the weighty threats we all face.[31]

The proper venue for discussion, it seemed to the president of the General Assembly, Miguel d'Escoto Brockmann of Nicaragua, was the G192 of the United Nations. Normally, the president takes a passive role as chair; Brockmann, a Catholic priest and admirer of the left-wing revolutionary politicians Daniel Ortego and Hugo Chávez, had different ideas. He appointed a Commission of Experts on Reform of the International and Monetary System under the chairmanship of Joseph Stiglitz. Brockmann and his Commission argued that the G20 was better than G8, but that the proper venue was the G192, given that the crisis was caused by the advanced countries' irresponsible deregulation, risk-taking and debt-fuelled consumption which had consequences for developing countries. On this view, the response should be stimulus to low-income countries, debt standstill, social protection, food security and human development, with reform of the international institutions to allow equitable representation.[32]

President Bush was initially sceptical about convening a meeting of leaders of the world's major economies, but he realized such a gathering could marginalize the UN's inquiry into the financial crisis that offered a platform to critics of America. In November 2008, he convened a 'summit on financial markets and the world economy' in Washington – the first time that the leaders of the G20 economies met. It issued a declaration to strengthen transparency, enhance regulation, promote financial integrity, reinforce international co-operation and reform international financial institutions – and it agreed to meet again. There were hopes that the G20 offered a more inclusive forum than the G8 and that it offered flexibility in co-ordinating a response to the crisis. Fred Bergsten thought it 'an effective steering committee for the world economy'. The shortcoming was that it was a self-selecting body. It included some emerging powers, such as Argentina, Brazil, China, India and Indonesia, with international institutions represented by the managing director of the IMF, president of the World Bank, director general of the WTO, secretary general of the UN, and chair of the Financial Stability Forum. In 2021, it covered about 60 per cent of the world's population and 80 per cent of its GDP. The G20 had a role in responding to the financial crisis, but it had serious flaws. It was sufficiently wide that a common approach was difficult to achieve, yet it excluded much of Africa, poorer countries in Latin America, and central Asia. Rather than turning to the G192 to secure legitimacy, the desire for efficiency led to a greater role for the G8 or G7 in managing the crisis.[33]

Between 2009 and 2011, the G20 was troubled by 'currency manipulation' that some observers feared would lead to competitive devaluation. In September 2010, Guido Mantegna, the Brazilian finance minister, referred to an 'international currency war' – a view that was exaggerated, though there were certainly tensions between China and the United States.[34] The United States claimed that the renminbi was deliberately under-valued to achieve a large trade surplus and build up reserves. The Chinese countered that the dollar was depreciating because of America's lack of discipline. In March 2009, the governor of the People's Bank of China proposed a super-sovereign reserve currency 'that is disconnected from individual nations and is able to remain stable in the long run, thus removing the inherent deficiencies caused by using credit-based national currencies'. He specifically referred to Keynes's proposal for Bancor. Nothing came of the idea.[35] At the G20 meeting in Seoul in 2010, Tim Geithner turned to another of Keynes's suggestions, that the adjustment of global imbalances should fall on creditor as well as debtor countries. At Bretton Woods, America was a creditor and Keynes's proposal was rejected. Now, the United States had a deficit and Geithner argued that creditor countries with a surplus or deficit on their current account of more than 4 per cent of GDP should act. The United States had a trade deficit under 4 per cent of GDP; China had a surplus of just over (and Germany one considerably over) 4 per cent of GDP, so the renminbi should appreciate and domestic consumption be raised. Although the People's Bank of China was amenable to revaluation, fear of unemployment and loss of export markets meant that China ruled out the proposal. Rainer Brüderle, the German economics minister, was also sceptical and the outcome was only a promise to be virtuous at some point in the future.[36]

The *Financial Times* thought the G20 was 'drifting into irrelevance' at Seoul. It was divided between surplus and deficit countries, between currency manipulators and their victims, between democracies and autocracies, between industrial and emerging economies over who was responsible for carbon emissions, and between interventionists and voluntarists on global regulation. The meeting ended with the so-called Seoul consensus of 'resilient growth' and partnership between rich and poor countries. The focus was on improved physical infrastructure, financial inclusion, social protection, good governance and food security – all excellent ideas that did not address the global financial crisis. To critics, it was a move from the Washington consensus without embracing policies that had led to success. Brazil opted not to attend and took unilateral action to raise taxes on foreign bond purchases – and South Korea took steps to curb capital inflows. The outcome was more in the nature of a general statement of good intent than real progress on rebalancing the global economy or tightening regulation of the financial system – with a ritual commitment to complete the moribund Doha Round. 'Seoul searching' had little to show.[37]

In 2012, Brent Scowcroft, the former US National Security Adviser, contrasted the situation after the global financial crisis unfavourably with the 1940s when the IMF, World Bank and GATT provided clear rules. Now, a worldwide financial system lacked a single global response, and he dismissed the G20 as 'a pale reflection of that once-brilliant institutional building'.[38] To Ian Bremmer and Nouriel Roubini, leading political and economic consultants, G20 was G zero, a 'cacophony of competing voices' undermining global economic co-operation and with no country willing to set an international agenda.[39] Some commentators hoped that a G2 of the United States and China – what the historian Niall Ferguson termed 'Chimerica' – could co-operate and make the IMF and WTO work by prior agreements. Robert Zoellick and Justin Yifu Lin, the president and chief economist of the World Bank respectively, agreed that 'without a strong G2, the G20 will disappoint'.[40] In reality it was difficult for two radically different economic and political systems to work together as they drifted into mutual recriminations and threats of trade war – and it was not plausible that other countries would acquiesce. Other economists turned to 'hegemonic stability' and worried about the absence of a single powerful player with 'the power to help countries cooperate with one another for the maintenance and, when needed, the restoration of prosperity. When no country can or will act as a hegemon, a world crisis erupts.'[41] This claim exaggerates the hegemony of the United States after 1945, and the new reality was a multipolar world, with the United States, European Union, China and, potentially, India and Brazil. China was restored as a major player for the first time in over two hundred years, with a fundamentally different political and economic system. The economies of China and America are interconnected but politically opposed – a situation that will cause problems in any future crisis.[42]

Robert Zoellick was more realistic in 2008 in suggesting that a 'New Multilateral Network for a New Global Economy' could replace the Bretton Woods institutions with a flexible network that respected state sovereignty and accepted that the challenges of finance, trade, development, climate change, energy and stabilizing failed states cut across borders. He proposed that the G7 and G20 should be replaced by regular, flexible meetings where views could be exchanged and mutual interests located. 'We need a Facebook for multilateral economic diplomacy' – a touching faith in the ability of social media to create harmony.[43] Similar approaches were proposed by other perceptive commentators. Eric Helleiner, a leading historian of Bretton Woods, thought that the network of the G20, Financial Stability Board, IMF and WTO was deeper and denser than the League of Nations in the 1930s, and success was more likely by building coalitions between countries willing to act than by attempting global agreement that would inevitably fail.[44] In 2010, Richard Haass of the US Council on Foreign Relations made a plea for 'messy multilateralism' – decentralized networks and discussions rather than a formalized system, with the ability of countries to pursue their preferences while respecting an open global economy. Potentially, the G20 would be the central element on the grounds that it had a 'track record of success notwithstanding its awkwardness and incompleteness'.[45]

Tharman Shanmugaratnam, the deputy prime minister of Singapore and chair of the G20 Eminent Persons Group on Global Finance Governance, saw the way ahead as the pursuit of different initiatives through a range of venues. In 2018, he called for a

> new co-operative international order for a world that has changed irreversibly: one that is more multipolar, more decentralised in decision-making, and yet more interconnected . . . There is no going back to the old multilateralism. There is no single conductor. There are already many more orchestras in play. We need a new harmony.

Rather than defending existing institutions, collaboration should be sought in different fora in response to specific problems. The Eminent Persons Group suggested starting from national policies to deal with divisions between winners and losers that threatened 'longstanding social compacts' which were crucial for an open world order. Rather than imposing policies, international organizations should draw attention to the consequences of failing to act, of the need to deal with spillovers from national initiatives, and to avoid a return to beggar-my-neighbour policies. On this view, a new multilateralism should respond to a decentralized and multipolar world by building on 'the strengths of the multilateral anchors, regional and multilateral institutions, and other key stakeholders that make up the system, and build trust and transparency amongst these different players'. Rather than defending the bureaucratic institutions of Bretton Woods, the priority should be networks that deal with specific challenges.[46] In a world where powerful states fail to agree, and where consensus is not possible, 'messy multilateralism' is the best hope. The world has changed from Bretton Woods in 1944, when two countries could develop a clear set of proposals at a time when the world's financial system was in suspense. After 2008, there was no small inner group with a clear set of proposals – and issues relating to climate change and poverty are intrinsically more difficult to negotiate.[47] The Doha Development Agenda showed the futility of seeking consensus on a wide range of issues: flexibility and coalitions of the willing are needed.

TRUMP AND TRADE

The global financial crisis avoided becoming a second Great Depression – yet it was still a huge shock to the global economy and to the prospects of many citizens in the Global North. A decade later, populism and economic nationalism had the potential to undermine international co-operation and to promote a return to the world of trade wars and beggar-my-neighbour policies. President Trump proclaimed that trade wars were easy to win, that economic nationalism was preferable to co-operation, and that bilateral balances with other countries were more important than the multilateral balance of payments. Of course, a balance between every pair of countries would reduce trade as a whole: cutting a deficit with one country would hit that country's earnings and force it to reduce its imports. A persistent overall deficit on trade – as arose in the United States – was problematic, but a recourse to tariffs that damaged both parties was not the obvious solution. An import duty on Chinese steel or aluminium would have less benefit for American producers than the harm caused to other industries that used those metals as an input and to American consumers of the final products.[48] In any case, the loss of American manufacturing jobs was more the result of technological change and de-industrialization than import dumping.

In 2018, Trump embarked on a trade war, above all with China but also with the European Union, and with Canada and Mexico as part of the renegotiation of NAFTA. He imposed or threatened safeguard tariffs on solar panels and washing machines from China; on steel and aluminium imports as threats to national security, including from Canada, Mexico and the EU; on unfair trade practices in technology and intellectual property; on imports of motor cars and parts; on Mexican goods to force tighter controls on illegal migration; and to safeguard American supremacy in semi-conductors. Other countries announced retaliatory measures.[49] There was growing concern that trade restrictions were returning. In November 2012, Azevêdo was alarmed: 'this is the worst crisis not for the WTO but for the whole multilateral trading system since the GATT in 1947. This is the moment when some very basic principles of the organisation, principles of cooperation, principles of non-discrimination are being changed and put into question.'[50] By June 2019, he worried that '[t]he stable trend that we saw for almost a decade since the financial crisis has been replaced with a steep increase in the size and scale of trade-restrictive measures over the last year.' In the six months from May to October 2018, new trade restrictions covered 3.53 per cent of the G20 and 2.73 per cent of world imports, and in the six months from October 2018 to May 2019 a further 2.47 per cent and 1.93 per cent respectively were imposed.[51] At the G20 summit in November 2018, Trump insisted that the ritual pledge to fight protectionism should be removed. In June 2019, the trade ministers of the G20 decided to expose differences rather than to build consensus and stated that both American unilateralism and Chinese state capitalism were causes of concern. Ministers retreated from the pledge made at the G20 in London in 2009 that it would 'not repeat the historical mistakes of protectionism' and would 'refrain from raising new barriers to investment or to trade in goods and services'. Instead, the G20 should 'strive to realise a free, fair, non-discriminatory, transparent, predictable and stable trade and investment environment, to keep our markets open'.[52] In August 2019, the US Treasury labelled China a 'currency manipulator', adjusting the exchange rate to compensate for the imposition of tariffs, which allowed it to be referred to the IMF. The People's Bank of China contended that it adjusted the rate of the renminbi to ensure stability and the IMF agreed that it was in line with economic fundamentals. Trump responded by imposing still higher tariffs.[53] Confidence that open trade would continue gave way to concern that trade wars had returned and that global supply chains would 'decouple'.

Trump rejected multilateral institutions. In January 2018, Robert Lighthizer, the US trade representative, complained of China's refusal to deliver on its promises to dismantle state policies that were 'incompatible with an international trading system ... rooted in the principles of non-discrimination, market access, reciprocity, fairness and transparency'. He concluded that 'the United States erred in supporting China's entry into the WTO on terms that have proven to be ineffective in securing China's embrace of an open, market-oriented trade regime.' In 2019, he returned to the charge that 'China's continued embrace of a state-led, mercantilist approach' imposed costs on others and harmed American companies and workers, even as China benefitted from membership of the WTO. The list of complaints was long: a failure to deal with forced technology transfer; to allow electronic payments; to remove subsidies and restrictions; or to create a transparent regulatory system. China was accused of moving from open, market-oriented reforms to state-led development. The complaints were justified and had wide support across the political spectrum, and there was also concern about gross abuses of human rights and threats to Hong Kong and Taiwan. The question was how to respond.[54] Trump acted unilaterally, rather than working with other countries through the WTO that had similar concerns. Instead, he picked fights with potential allies and saw the WTO as part of the problem.

China was indeed guilty of failing to meet the conditions for WTO membership, and President Obama had attempted to enforce rules by working with other countries and using the dispute system of the WTO. The United States won more cases against China than it lost. Between 2002 and 2019, the WTO determined twenty complaints brought by the United States against China: in eleven, the ruling favoured the United States, nine were settled, and none was lost. By contrast, the WTO determined nine cases brought by China against the United States: China won four, with one settlement, one loss and three split decisions.[55] Nevertheless, the Trump administration rejected the WTO's complaints procedure on the grounds that the organization was not designed to deal with state capitalism and that dispute resolution took too long.[56] Trump refused to appoint new members of the WTO's appellate body, which eventually lacked a quorum. To Secretary of State Mike Pompeo, disruption of the multilateral order was beneficial: 'nations matter. No international body can stand up for our people like a nation can.' Trump's rejection of multilateralism was criticized by Germany's Chancellor Merkel, who pointed out that 'We should understand our national interest in a way that we think about the interests of others, and from that create win–win situations that are the precondition for multilateralism.'[57]

Trump lost the presidential election in November 2020 and Joe Biden took office at a time of great economic difficulties arising from the pandemic. On 1 July 2021, fast-track authority for trade deals would expire, and renewal was not a priority for the Biden administration. The last renewal in 2015 had been difficult, with many Democrats opposed to the measure as a result of trade unions' concern about a loss of jobs, and environmentalists' concern that trade negotiations did not consider greenhouse gas emissions. Another battle on Capitol Hill was not welcome at a time when other issues were more important, such as climate change, health care and a package of measures on jobs and infrastructure. Trade Representative Katherine Tai focused on enforcing the labour provisions of the trade agreement with Mexico and Canada, resolving the trade war with Europe over subsidies for passenger planes, and reviewing the trade negotiations started by Trump. Fast-track authority now seemed out-dated, for it excluded consideration of climate change caused by greenhouse gases embodied in trade, and weakened environmental and labour standards that could potentially be defined as non-tariff barriers. In April 2021, Tai commented that

> For too long, we believed that trade liberalization would lead to a gradual improvement in environmental protection as countries grew wealthier from increased trade flows. But the reality is that the system itself creates an incentive to compete by maintaining lower standards. Or worse yet, by lowering those standards even further.[58]

The future is uncertain, with war in Europe, tensions over Taiwan, an energy crisis and inflation, Republican control of the House of Representatives after the mid-term elections in November 2022, and a return of Trump as a presidential candidate. Survival of the post-war multilateral order is in jeopardy, with differences that rival those revealed at the World Monetary and Economic Conference in London in 1933. In 2018, Christine Lagarde, the managing director of the IMF, warned that 'history shows that, while it is tempting to sail alone, countries must resist the siren calls of self-sufficiency – because as the Greek legend tells us, that leads to shipwreck.'[59] She was alluding to the songs of sirens whose beautiful voices lured sailors to their deaths. The siren voices still need to be resisted and new policies formulated to avoid disaster. The task will not be easy, for multilateral institutions need stable and functioning states and cannot solve the considerable problem of failing states that are a major cause of global poverty. David Miliband of the International Rescue Committee pointed out in 2019 that about 40 per cent of the extreme poor live in conflict zones and in fragile or failed states.[60] Building capacity in Syria, Yemen, Somalia, Libya, or Afghanistan is an issue well beyond the provision of technical advice by the WTO, World Bank, or IMF – and beyond the capacity of the UN.

The Covid-19 pandemic exacerbated divisions between those with precarious jobs and low incomes, and those who gained from new technology and increasing asset values. The pandemic is only one element of a crisis of ecological breakdown linked to climate change that is leading to war, famine, further pandemics and mass migration. The question is whether these existential risks can recast economic policies in a way that the global financial crisis did not achieve. Might we now be at an inflection point as happened with the emergence of embedded liberalism in the 1940s and market liberalism in the 1970s – a new economic order based on a challenge to financialization, a shift from rent-seeking capitalism to better, secure employment, and an effective response to the challenges of climate change and pandemics? Failure to create a new and better democratic capitalism will lead to disaster.

International Monetary Fund director Christine Lagarde (*left*) speaks with Nigeria's minister of finance Ngozi Okonjo-Iweala (*right*) who became director general of the WTO in 2021, during a conference in Lagos, 20 December 2011.

27

Fair Capitalism and Globalization
The Way Ahead

'The decadent international but individualistic capitalism in the hands of which we found ourselves after the [First World] war, is not a success. It is not intelligent, it is not beautiful, it is not just, it is not virtuous – and it doesn't deliver the goods. In short, we dislike it and we are beginning to despise it. But when we wonder what to put in its place, we are extremely perplexed.'
John Maynard Keynes, 'National self-sufficiency', 1933[1]

This book started with the World Monetary and Economic Conference of 1933 when the world was in deep depression and geopolitical tension. It ends in 2023 at another time of great economic difficulty, in the aftermath of a pandemic and during the most serious geopolitical crisis in Europe since the Second World War. The immediate economic impact of the pandemic exceeded that of the global financial crisis, with the world's GDP falling by around 20 per cent between January and April 2020, and around 80 per cent of the world's workforce under restriction. In response, governments embarked on massive spending programmes to support businesses and workers, incurring levels of debt that were not considered feasible during the global financial crisis. In March 2020, investors not only sold shares; unusually they also sold United States Treasury bonds, the safe assets that provide the basis of credit, which was one reason that the financial crisis was potentially more serious than in 2008. The Fed stepped in and bought debt issued by the Treasury, which 'monetized' debt and allowed the government to run a deficit without raising interest rates. Despite their assertion that they were acting to preserve the financial system, the Federal Reserve and other central banks were using 'fiscal QE' to fund governments.[2]

The pandemic exposed the dangers of precarious employment and economic inequality that existed during the era of neo-liberalism, and widened pre-existing health inequalities. Between March and December

2020, the number of years of life lost attributable to the pandemic varied from 916 per 100,000 people in the most affluent areas of England and Wales to 1,645 years in the most deprived areas.[3] Similarly, in the United States in 2020, the number of years of life lost in the most affluent quintile of counties was 0.99 million and in the least affluent 1.38 million.[4] At the same time, asset prices rose above pre-Covid levels as a result of quantitative easing so that those with property and investments gained. There were also striking discrepancies between countries as a result of levels of deprivation and health care, and the provision of vaccines. The pandemic showed the dangers of an interconnected world in which pressures on the environment and ecological stress led to the rapid spread of a disease that needed – though did not receive – a global response. It intensified calls for a new social contract based on greater equality and recognizing the worth of essential workers, for a green new deal, and for a greater appreciation of the risks of globalization. The pandemic showed the need for collective action, and many progressive commentators hoped it would achieve what the global financial crisis failed to deliver: a turn from neo-liberalism and financialization. Might Covid be an inflection point comparable to the emergence of embedded liberalism during the Second World War and neo-liberalism in the 1970s?

Peter Hennessy, a leading historian of modern Britain, hoped that the pandemic had revived the social solidarity that led to the wartime Beveridge Report and the post-war welfare state.[5] Similarly, Adam Tooze thought 'a turning point had been reached. Was this, finally, the death of the orthodoxy that had prevailed in economic policy since the 1980s? Was this the death knell of neoliberalism?' Despite these hopes for a new direction, the pandemic – and then the energy crisis after the Russian invasion of Ukraine – might instead lead to the survival of the status quo. It led to vaccine nationalism, a failure to co-ordinate assistance to low-income countries, and potentially a backlash against the costs of the pandemic with a return to austerity. During the pandemic, presidents Macron and Biden, Angela Merkel and Boris Johnson – all centrists in different ways – drew on the ideas of a green transition, fiscal and monetary interventions, investment in the infrastructure, and 'levelling up' of deprived areas to counter socialist or populist alternatives. They were responding to the problems caused by the pursuit of neo-liberalism that were exposed by the pandemic, but without a radical change in direction. In practice, as Tooze points out, neo-liberalism was 'radically pragmatic' in using the state to stabilize the financial system both in 2008 and 2020, with the result that the responses to the pandemic were 'framed by neoliberalism's legacies, in the form of hyper-globalization, fragile and attenuated welfare states, profound social and economic inequality, and the overweening size and influence of private finance'.[6] These legacies of financialization and inequality threaten political and social stability within countries and contribute to international economic disequilibrium.

The outcome of the pandemic was still uncertain when Russia invaded Ukraine in February 2022. The subsequent crisis in the cost of energy led to inflation at levels last seen in the 1970s, and the threat of recession. After the global financial crisis, politicians and commentators looked to the Great Depression for analogies and lessons. In 2022, talk was of a return to the stagflation of the 1970s, with an oil shock, economic stagnation and inflation. The analogy is understandable but misses fundamental differences. Monetary policy is not likely to end inflation now as it did in the Volcker shock. The issue in the 1970s was the squeeze on profits and investment; now, it is a squeeze on labour combined with higher profits. New solutions are needed, above all to reverse the trend to inequality and economic precariousness in leading developed economies and to reduce capital's share of income. Whether these desirable changes can be achieved remains uncertain. Sadly, the short-lived government of Liz Truss that took office in Britain in September 2022 rejected redistribution and returned to long-discredited 'trickle down' economics and unfunded tax cuts, which provoked market turmoil and a rebuke from the IMF. The government of Rishi Sunak adopted a more fiscally prudent policy with austerity and a failure to redistribute. In the United States, the mid-term elections of November 2022 gave some hope to the Democrats and much will depend on the presidential election of November 2024.

We are, like Keynes, perplexed. 'International but individualistic capitalism' of the era of neo-liberalism has failed, but what can be put in its place is not clear. In 1933, Keynes recommended a turn to self-sufficiency and protectionism; in the war, he turned to plans for a new balance between internationalism and nationalism. We are at a similar point of uncertainty and perplexity about the outcome. The problems facing the global economy are reasonably clear and arise in large part from two interconnected disequilibria. Inequality within countries threatens domestic political, economic and social stability, and in turn contributes to international economic imbalance. As we saw in Chapter 25, the low level of domestic consumption in China led to reliance on export markets, and savings were directed to housing and infrastructure which expose the economy to a risk of financial instability. The low level of savings in the United States led to dependence on debt and deficits in the budget and balance of payments that were covered by the Chinese purchase of Treasury bills and the 'exorbitant privilege' of the dollar. Resolution of global imbalances therefore needs national policies to remove the inequality that fuels populism and reliance on debt in the United States, and to reform China's social welfare system and labour markets to increase the level of domestic consumption. Neither will be easily achieved.

A multipolar world creates the potential for instability, the emergence of economic blocs, and economic and military conflict. At the same time, the existential threat of climate change requires a solution to the ultimate 'tragedy of the commons' to prevent each nation's pursuit of self-interest leading to mutual destruction. The IMF, World Bank and WTO were designed to deal with finance, development and trade. They now face doubts about their relevance and effectiveness in handling different, pressing, problems. Despite their failings, they remain more powerful than other agencies of the post-war order – the World Health Organization and Food and Agriculture Organization – which are more relevant to the threats to the planet from climate change, food insecurity, and the challenge of future pandemics. This chapter aims to set out an agenda to replace neo-liberalism, avoid populist nationalism, and create a fairer and just economy. Whether it will succeed rests on the political choices we make in the next few years.

MULTILATERAL INSTITUTIONS AND RESPONSIBLE NATIONALISM

At the General Assembly of the United Nations in September 2019, António Guterres, the secretary general, called for collective action on climate change. President Jair Bolsonaro of Brazil did not agree. He denounced criticism of deforestation of the Amazon as a conspiracy of deceit that 'questioned that which is most sacred to us: our sovereignty!' He was followed by Donald Trump who claimed that 'The future does not belong to globalists. The future belongs to patriots. The future belongs to sovereign and independent nations who protect their citizens, respect their neighbors and honor the differences that make each country special and unique.' 'Patriots' became a group with privileged access to the national interest, able to 'see a nation and its destiny in ways no one else can. Liberty is only preserved, sovereignty is only secure, democracy is only sustained, greatness is only realized by the will and devotion of patriots.' In his view, 'Wise leaders always put the good of their own people and their own country first.' Criticism of national self-interest and support of the global common good became treachery.[7] The pursuit of hyper-globalization and the growth of inequality and precarity had provoked a turn to populism, identity politics and nationalism at a time when collective action was needed, not least when the pandemic arrived in early 2020.

Although Trump lost the presidential election in November 2020, the crisis of multilateral institutions did not end. Joe Biden dropped aggressive attacks on the WTO and WHO, yet a return to American leadership of the liberal international order remains unlikely, and there is no plausible successor for that leadership. Covid, the greatest threat to global health since the flu pandemic at the end of the First World War, showed that the WHO was ill-equipped to rise to the challenge. Its budget was equivalent to a single large city hospital's and was cobbled together from a variety of sources – national governments, the World Bank, pharmaceutical companies, and charities such as the Gates Foundation. Despite success in eradicating smallpox and polio, it had been criticized for urging travel restrictions in response to SARS in 2003 and for pushing expensive vaccines after swine flu in 2009. When Covid arrived, the WHO was slow to respond, and was accused of being reluctant to criticize China where the first outbreaks occurred.[8] Pharmaceutical companies produced effective vaccines in a surprisingly short time, but the roll out to the poorest and most vulnerable countries was slow. The global initiatives of the Access to Covid-19 Tools Accelerator (ACT) and Covid-19 Vaccines Global Access (COVAX) were inadequate and poorly funded, with a glaring mismatch between modest costs and massive benefits. The WHO's co-ordinator for ACT estimated that the necessary funding would be paid for in thirty-six hours. The result, as Tooze commented, was 'a staggering demonstration of the collective inability of the global elite to grasp what it would actually mean to govern the deeply globalized and interconnected world they have created'.[9] A more effective and powerful WHO is needed before another, potentially more serious, pandemic arrives, and action is needed on climate change and environmental degradation that create the conditions for disease and food insecurity.

The post-war multilateral institutions were limited in their global reach. The IMF and World Bank were initially an alliance of the 'united nations' against Germany before they expanded during the Cold War. They created a coalition of capitalistic economies against Communism, with a limited voice for less developed countries. Truly global economic government has never existed. Realistically, something more pragmatic and limited is needed that turns from the overly ambitious plans of the Doha Round or the IMF's pursuit of financial liberalization to a more modest provision of rules for national action and co-operation, and a more decentralized system that deals with specific challenges. A balance between democracy and multilateralism would be made easier by abandoning an uncritical pursuit of open markets and financialization, and returning to 'shallow multilateralism' that balances internationalism with flexibility that allows nation states to defend domestic welfare. The alternative to 'reflex internationalism' is not the populist nationalism of Trump and Bolsonaro. It is, as Larry Summers pointed out,

> responsible nationalism – an approach where it is understood that countries are expected to pursue their citizens' economic welfare as a primary objective but where their ability to harm the interests of citizens elsewhere is circumscribed. International agreements would be judged not by how much is harmonised or by how many barriers are torn down but whether citizens are empowered.

Similarly, Dani Rodrik urged a 'sane, sensible balance between national and global governance' by shifting from 'globalization-enhancing deals' of financial and market liberalization that have dominated the IMF and WTO. He called for 'democracy-enhancing global agreements' that return to GATT's 'global governance light', which gave flexibility in the use of escape clauses and opt-outs based on clear rules. Global governance should build on the preferences of powerful states and accept that countries have the right to protect their own choices in areas such as labour markets or environmental policies. States should not 'go it alone' as Trump wished, and there are clearly areas where the 'global commons' matter and a collective solution is needed. The aim, in Rodrik's words, should be to 'retain much of the benefits of economic globalization while endowing national democracies with the space they need to address domestic objectives'. As he says, the role of international institutions should be to create 'traffic rules' for the interface between national institutions rather than to impose the normative views of some members. 'A thin layer of international rules that leaves substantial room for maneuver by national governments is a *better* globalization.'[10]

International institutions are certainly flawed and lack legitimacy, but their reform will not be sufficient. The starting point is to remove forces that provoke a backlash against co-operative solutions: stagnation of real wages, de-industrialization, growing inequality and austerity. The Bretton Woods institutions and a liberal international order emerged when the benefits of capitalism were widely shared in advanced economies through rising wages, productivity gains and declining inequality. By contrast, the economic system before and after the global financial crisis rested on growing inequality within countries, stagnant or declining wages for many, and growing precarity – though also gains for many in emerging economies. These domestic problems need to be addressed to provide the basis for a fair and more inclusive economic system, and to create resilience in response to new crises. In 2008 and 2020, central banks, and above all the Fed, intervened to prevent a collapse of what Tooze calls 'the fragile and inegalitarian dynamic of debt-fueled economic growth'. The result of their intervention was to maintain a 'dangerous status quo' based on repeated cycles of credit expansion and glaring inequalities. We should now go further. Rather than relying on central banks to resolve a future crisis, we should act to remove the fundamental problems of inequality and financialization that cause crises.[11]

In Chapter 26, I argued that multilateral institutions should work within networks to build international co-operation incrementally, rather than pursuing grand projects and overarching agreements such as the abortive Doha Round. Smaller groups of willing participants can agree rules on particular topics, which the WTO can oversee to ensure that benefits are extended – an approach adopted in 2019 when the WTO worked with seventy-six countries on rules for e-commerce.[12] In the case of climate change, the WTO could provide reassurance that countries do not free ride on the global commons or reduce carbon emissions by importing carbon-intensive goods. The carbon component of trade could be included in WTO rules so that a country that introduces a domestic carbon tax or emissions trading system can impose a carbon border tax against countries that do not reduce their emissions.[13] In 2021, for the first time the director general of the WTO, Ngozi Okonjo-Iweala, came from Africa. She looked to a new agenda in response to the related threats of climate change and pandemics: action on restrictions in supply chains in medical goods; steps against vaccine nationalism and in support of co-operation in new treatments; and a concern for the interconnection between trade and climate change. However, the meeting of the WTO in June 2022 had few tangible outcomes, with little engagement from the United States and disruption by India. The main achievement, according to the *Financial Times*, was keeping the WTO alive.[14] The IMF has also claimed to have changed from its dogmatic pursuit of the Washington consensus, and has argued for action on inequality, global taxation and carbon pricing, but with little to show so far. Its main role remains to handle debt crises, which are likely to be serious in the near future. But it is doubtful that the debt crisis of, say, Pakistan can be resolved without tackling climate change that has led to devastating floods and economic disaster in that country. Priorities need to change, and a starting point would be a reassessment of economic thinking.

REFORMING ECONOMICS

Unlike the 1930s and the 1970s, the global financial crash of 2008 did not lead to an intellectual revolution in economics, though many well-informed commentators thought that was vital. In some universities, students demanded a change in the curriculum to supplement highly mathematical approaches with a greater appreciation of economic history, politics, and a wider range of economic ideas.[15] The dominant view of economists before the crisis was that shocks were external rather than an intrinsic part of the system; that markets were self-correcting with the economy normally in equilibrium; and that decisions were made by rational, individual *Homines economici* who sought to maximize utility. This way of thinking meant that even economists who accepted that markets are inefficient, and that information is imperfect, still assumed that decisions are made by utility-maximizing individuals. These ideas meant that a market economy became a market society in which transactions were commercialized and given a price.

The failure to remake economics reflected the way that academic appointments and promotion were determined by publication in a small number of mainstream journals that prioritized highly technical, mathematical approaches. John Kay, a leading British economist, complained that 'University economists, of the sort gathered at Bretton Woods, are now under relentless pressure to conform to a narrow, established paradigm. Inexplicably, most supporters of that paradigm also feel that the crisis confirmed its validity.'[16] In 2009, Willem Buiter, a former professor of economics at Cambridge and at one time a member of the Bank of England's Monetary Policy Committee, agreed:

> Most mainstream macroeconomic theoretical innovations since the 1970s . . . have turned out to be self-referential, inward-looking distractions at best. Research tended to be motivated by the internal logic, intellectual sunk capital and aesthetic puzzles of established research programmes rather than by a powerful desire to understand how the economy works – let alone how the economy works during times of stress and financial instability.[17]

Mervyn King, governor of the Bank during the crisis, thought that 'economics has encouraged ways of thinking that made crises more probable', and called for an 'intellectual revolution'.[18]

Some economists accept that macroeconomic theory needs to reject rational expectations for a more realistic depiction of human behaviour that accepts morality and co-operation, under conditions of radical uncertainty. John Kay, Mervyn King and Paul Collier argue that economic actors do not have the information to maximize utility or to know if they have succeeded, for they 'make choices in a radically uncertain world, in which probabilities cannot meaningfully be attached to alternative futures'. Most people take incremental decisions that are designed to make their household or community a better place to live, unlike the individualist and selfish precepts of economics. On this view, it is vital to move from an individualism that had its roots not only in economics and right-wing ideology but also in the shift in left-wing and progressive thought from collective solidarity to a pursuit of individual rights. The new approach to economics needs to displace confidence about decision-making in a world of probabilities measured by statistical regularities and to turn to a realization that we live under conditions of radical uncertainty and mutual obligations within communities. The philosopher Michael Sandel refers to 'contributive justice' – the idea that 'we are most fully human when we contribute to the common good and earn the esteem of our fellow citizens for the contributions we make'.[19]

The economic paradigm advocated by Stiglitz and others rejects the assumption that an economy fluctuates around a single equilibrium with policies designed to take the economy back to a natural equilibrium. Rather, there are many possible outcomes and the task is to decide which equilibrium from many is preferred. The choice becomes political or cultural, shaped by what Robert Shiller calls 'economic narratives'. To historians, this approach is self-evident: we deal with how policy choices in the past were shaped by stories that politicians and reformers tell, whether it be Hull on free trade, Rostow on modernization, or neo-liberals on the inefficiency of the state. These stories do not simply express the self-interest of pre-existing social and economic groups, for identities are influenced by rhetorical devices. Political choices are shaped by narratives that convince the electorate where their interests lie.[20]

The dominant economic narratives after the global financial crisis stressed austerity to restrain the state and economic nationalism to protect jobs. An alternative economic narrative can be devised that is based on the notion of 'rent' and 'rentier capitalism'. 'Rentier' can apply simply to people living off income from land or the income from *rentes*, the French term for government securities. It also had a wider definition that goes back to David Ricardo in early nineteenth-century Britain when population growth resulted in pressure on food supplies and rising prices. Cultivation moved to marginal land where farmers could just cover their costs. Meanwhile, established farmers on more fertile land secured a higher return or unearned increment above what they needed to produce food and make a living. This idea was generalized from land to any income or profit where a return was secured above the level needed to bring assets into use, by exploiting monopolies or limited access, as a result of licences to exploit natural resources or operate a bank, and intellectual property rights through patents or trademarks. The extraction of rent applies not only to dominant firms in social media, information technology, or 'big pharma'. Anne Case and the Nobel laureate Angus Deaton point out that controls over entry to professions such as lawyers and doctors, especially in the privatized health-care system of the United States, allow providers to charge high fees that are covered by insurance companies. Rent-seeking behaviour is often dependent on regulations imposed by the state, as well as the ability of dominant firms to exclude newcomers. The result is to deliver high profits that contribute to inequality and remove incentives to invest in better productivity.[21]

We need to move from 'rentier capitalism' to a fairer and more inclusive capitalism. It will entail shifting from the currently dominant ideology of individualism, a belief that all wealth and property are personal, and that inequality is necessary to provide incentives. It will entail a stronger competition policy, changes in the tax regime to remove tax breaks and to ensure that the excess or unearned profits are captured, and redefining the purpose of corporations to benefit the community rather than managers and shareholders.[22] These changes could be achieved in a number of ways that involve changes in national policies and a shift in the remit of international institutions.

COMPETITION AND CORPORATIONS

During the Progressive era and New Deal, corporate power was viewed as a threat to American democracy and economic dynamism. By the 1970s, however, the dominant view was that large firms benefitted the consumer through lower prices and that corporate success was best measured by shareholder value. In 1970, Milton Friedman asserted that:

> In a free enterprise, private-property system, a corporate executive is an employee of the owners of the business. He has a direct responsibility to his employers. That responsibility is to conduct the business in accordance with their desires, which generally will be to make as much money as possible while conforming to the basic rules of society.

In 2004, Justice Antonin Scalia, the leading conservative member of the US Supreme Court, claimed that 'the mere possession of monopoly power, and the concomitant charging of monopoly prices, is not only not unlawful; it is an important element of the free-market system . . . It induces risk taking that produces innovation and economic growth.'[23] Justice Scalia's economic credentials were unclear. More plausibly, monopoly is a perversion of the free-market system and leads to what Stiglitz calls 'ersatz capitalism' – a decline in free markets and the domination of a few large oligopolistic players, with a growing earnings differential between top executives and the average worker, with managers taking gains when things go well and passing losses to shareholders when things go badly. In 1965, chief executives in the largest corporations in the United States, if realized stock options are included, earned 20 times that of the typical worker; by 1989, the difference was 58 times, and in 2017, 312 times (see Figure 23).[24]

The emergence of dominant firms was not necessarily the result of superior productivity by successful companies. As we have noted, licences and intellectual property could limit entry, and 'intangible capital' escaped from the constraints of economies of scale. Even here, policy choices matter, for corporate concentration rose in the United States and remained stable in Europe. In the United States, competition policy was weaker because of lobbying and legislators' reliance on campaign finance from wealthy business interests. In the European Union, regulation of competition was tougher and largely independent of member states, with the European Commission less susceptible to lobbying than Congress. In the

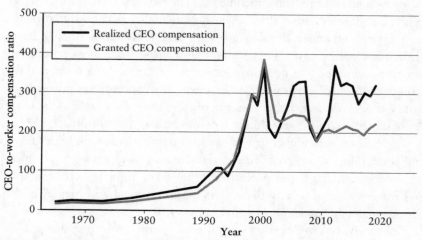

Figure 23: CEO-to-worker compensation ratio
in top 350 US firms, 1965–2019

Source: Lawrence Mishel and Jori Kandra, Economic Policy Institute, 18 August 2020 at epi.org.204515.

United States, the decline in domestic competition resulted in higher prices, profits and payments to shareholders. By contrast, labour power was weakened, with a decline in unionization and a shift from steady industrial work to precarious employment.[25]

Although the shift in favour of capital was most striking in the United States, it was not confined to that country. In April 2019, the IMF's World Economic Outlook Report found that the increased market power of firms in advanced economies led to a rise in the mark-up of prices over marginal costs of 8 percentage points between 2000 and 2015. The report worried that further increases in market power would reduce the incentive for investment and productivity growth, cut the share of labour income, and lead to greater inequality.[26] Similarly, a report for UNCTAD claimed that the rise in profits of the largest transnational corporations at the expense of labour income had created predatory rent-seeking behaviour or 'crocodile capitalism' – the opening jaw between labour and capital (see Figure 24). The Peterson Institute for International Economics pointed out that during the Bretton Woods era (1948–73), real median family incomes in the United States rose by 3.0 per cent a year, with a 96 per cent chance that the next generation would be better off than the previous one. Since 1973, the median family income has grown by only 0.4 per cent a year and 28 per cent of children have lower incomes than their parents.[27] In the 1970s a major concern was the erosion of profit margins, which led to policies in the United States and Britain to limit the power of labour. In the 2020s, the major concern should be the erosion of labour's share of earnings and the growth of profits which reduce the need to invest in higher productivity. Growth will not be achieved by reducing corporation tax or high levels of personal income tax. The IMF's staff discussion papers in 2014 and 2015 found that 'lower net inequality is robustly correlated with faster and more durable growth', and redistribution only harms growth in extreme cases. They found that a rising share of income for the top 20 per cent led to a decline in growth over the medium term, and that growth did not trickle down. Rather, inequality concentrates power in the hands of a few in a way that shapes policy in their interests and facilitates financial crises. An increase in the income share of the bottom 20 per cent was associated with higher growth and productivity through better health and education. What is needed is a reduction in inequality and economic precariousness, and better protection of workers' rights, to create a fairer and more inclusive society that offers better physical and mental health, educational achievement and social mobility.[28]

The survival of free-market capitalism requires a response that is more positive and creative than the empty promises of populism or a belief that

Figure 24: Top 2,000 transnational corporations' profit and the global labour income share, 1995–2015

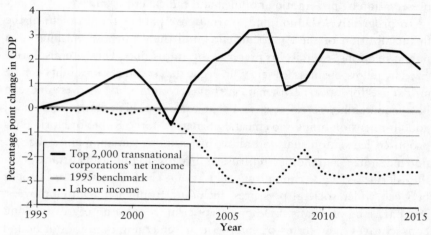

Source: Kevin P. Gallagher and Richard Kozul-Wright, *A New Multilateralism for Shared Prosperity: Geneva Principles for a Global Green New Deal* (Boston, MA, 2019), 12.

gains to the rich will trickle down to the poor. Restoring corporate competition will not be enough. It is also necessary to transform corporate behaviour from a rigid focus on shareholder value to a wider social purpose. In 2018, Senator Elizabeth Warren claimed that she was a capitalist and believed in markets – 'What I don't believe in is theft.' She urged big companies be broken up and a wealth tax imposed on the largest fortunes. In 2020, she challenged the Business Roundtable, a group of 181 leading American corporations, to deliver on the promise of their 'Statement on the Purpose of a Corporation'. It supported free-market capitalism as the best way of creating good jobs, a sustainable economy, a healthy environment and wider opportunities, but argued that companies needed to look beyond their corporate purposes.[29] Seth Klarman, the founder of a Boston hedge fund, joined Jamie Dimon, the chairman and chief executive officer of JP Morgan Chase, in calling for action to restore faith in politics and capitalism by replacing short-term gain and maximizing the share price as corporate *raisons d'être* with long-term benefits, including action on climate change and inequality. Dimon used his annual letter to shareholders to reflect on the need to tackle the 'fraying' of the American dream and to resolve social problems by spending on education and infrastructure, even if taxes were increased on the wealthy. Ray Dalio, founder of Bridgewater Associates, the world's largest hedge fund, made a similar point that capitalism must 'evolve or die'. In 2019, he warned that inequality would lead to social conflict; the previous year, his remuneration was $2 billion. These major capitalists have not been converted to socialism but to self-preservation by pre-empting populist and radical criticism.[30]

To progressives, Dimon and Klarman are part of the problem of the financialization of the American elite, and their 'purpose washing' is a public relations' exercise to preserve the status quo. They are also criticized by fellow business leaders who argue that social responsibility can be an excuse for poor performance, that accountability to everyone can be accountability to no one, and that earning a high return is a social good for pension funds and charities. Senator Marco Rubio of Florida has proposed legislation that will allow investors to sue companies that do not maximize shareholder returns, and many Republicans attack what they deride as 'woke capitalism'. As a result, chief executives are caught between wider societal pressures, including from their own employees, and partisan politicians.[31] Despite scepticism from both progressives and conservatives, new forms of enterprise are emerging that are not bound by the need to maximize profits, and that extend stakeholders to include employees, customers, suppliers locked into supply chains, and the public interest. In the United States, thirty-six states allow public-benefit corporations, and in France a new corporate law in 2019 allowed boards to adopt a *raison d'être* other than profit. Governments can set new legal obligations and incentives to encourage a shift from narrow shareholder value to stakeholder and wider societal values linked with social welfare and the survival of the planet. This approach has links with Catholic social teaching and with the German social market.[32]

Turning back concentration of ownership and the short-termism of focusing solely on shareholder value could reduce rent-seeking behaviour and inequality – and should be complemented by changes in the tax regime.

TAX REGIMES

Rent-seeking behaviour can be limited by competition policy that removes the conditions that allow it to flourish. Case and Deaton argue that the 'the right way to stop thieves is to stop them stealing, not to raise their taxes'. On this view, once competition policy eliminates rent-seeking, the fortunes of Bill Gates at Microsoft, Jeff Bezos at Amazon or Tim Cook at Apple become justifiable rewards for providing better services and goods.[33] In reality, the line between rent-seeking and reward for innovation is difficult to draw, and many of these firms avoid taxation by channelling profits through Luxembourg (Amazon) or Ireland (Apple).[34]

In any case, extreme inequality is harmful, regardless of how it is created. As Stiglitz remarked, 'Widely unequal societies do not function efficiently, and their economies are neither stable nor sustainable in the long term. When one interest group holds too much power, it succeeds in getting policies that benefit itself, rather than policies that would benefit society as a whole.' At the macroeconomic level, inequality leads to a savings glut by the rich and under-consumption or reliance on debt by poorer members of society, and disequilibrium in the domestic economy leads to global imbalance. Case and Deaton argue for public goods – health and social care, education, parks – from which most people benefit and that contribute to higher productivity as well as happiness.[35] Unless they are to be paid for by user charges that typify a market society, these public goods need a just tax regime that fosters a sense of societal fairness, which is a matter of the structure of taxation as much as its level.

Although there was much talk of rolling back the state, taxation and welfare spending have not fallen as a proportion of GDP, as we saw in Chapter 26. Rather, since the 1980s there has been a change in the ways that tax is levied, with a shift from a progressive income tax to sales taxes, with higher taxation of earned income than of capital and business. A 'race to the bottom' is most apparent in corporate taxes, where the global average rate fell from 40 per cent in 1990 to around 25 per cent in 2017.[36] Further, multinational corporations avoid tax by 'profit-shifting' to low tax regimes. Apple routes its European sales through Ireland because the corporate tax rate was cut to 12.5 per cent and the government offered 'sweetheart' deals that avoided tax to other members of the EU. Trump reduced the American corporation tax rate to 21 per cent with the aim of removing the incentive to 'offshore' and to encourage companies 'to stay in America, grow in America, spend in America, and hire in America'. American companies were still allowed to pay a 'global minimum' rate of 10.5 per cent so that profit shifting to low-tax regimes remained attractive. Indeed, more than half the overseas profits of American corporations are reported in low-tax jurisdictions.[37] 'Base erosion' and 'profit shifting' – to use the technical terms – limit government revenues and undermine a sense of fairness.

The rules governing the taxation of multinational corporations were defined at the League of Nations in the interwar period, when it was assumed that each national branch of a multinational corporation tried to maximize its profits and dealt with each other at arm's length as if they were unrelated firms. That might have been true at the time, but the arm's length principle was increasingly implausible with integrated supply chains across national boundaries and with the growth of digital business without a clear geographic location or physical asset. Global companies can reduce profits in high-tax countries by charging for services or loans which are booked as profits in countries with lower rates. The practice became a political issue. Responsibility for rules on international taxation lies with the OECD, and in 2013 it embarked on an inquiry into base erosion and profit shifting in association with the G20 and developing countries. The European Commission challenged Ireland's relationship with Apple, and in 2019 France imposed a tax on digital companies with the result that Trump threatened retaliatory duties on French wine. Although it does not have responsibility for setting the rules, the IMF embarked on a study of options for taxing transactions within large and complex corporate structures, and its executive board accepts the need for a global and equitable solution.[38]

A change in the tax regime requires co-ordination between countries, given the role of tax havens, profit shifting, digital taxes and carbon taxes. The OECD's 'concerted approach' on profit shifting appealed in the straitened financial circumstances after Covid, and there was some movement in 2021. Soon after coming to office, the Biden administration proposed an increase in corporation tax to 28 per cent and a global minimum of 21 per cent to discourage relocation to low-tax regimes. European countries insisted that the United States should also agree to a tax on the global profits of technology firms, and at the meeting of G20 finance ministers in February 2021, Treasury Secretary Janet Yellen indicated she would drop resistance to this. Vítor Gaspar, the head of fiscal affairs at the IMF, was hopeful that the shift in the American position would end the 'race to the bottom' in global corporation tax. In October 2021, a deal was reached by 136 countries to reform corporate taxation, with a minimum rate of 15 per cent and a shift of some taxation from the place of residence of the company to the point of sale. Agreement by the EU was initially blocked by Poland and Hungary, but was agreed in December 2022. It remains for the United States to implement the agreement, which was blocked by opposition to being the first country to impose the minimum rate.[39]

Tackling tax base erosion and profit shifting, and setting a global threshold for corporation tax, are more important as political gestures than as a solution to public finances. Revenue from corporate taxation did not fall as much as implied by the cut in the UK headline rate, from 52 per cent in the 1970s to 19 per cent in 2019, for profits rose over the period and the government removed some exemptions. Neither were corporate taxes a large proportion of total revenue.[40] More important will be reversing the shift away from progressive taxes and rebalancing the taxation of earned income from employment compared with income from capital, which currently pays a lower rate. In the neo-liberal era, the tax system became less progressive in many countries. In 1970, the richest Americans paid about 50 per cent of their income in taxes to federal, state and local governments, or about twice the rate of a member of the working class; by 2018, they paid 23 per cent, the same as people with modest incomes. This was one contribution to growing inequality. Wealthy individuals saved more of their income and accumulated more assets which in turn generated more income. The process was not checked by progressive taxation as it had been during the New Deal. In June 1935, President Roosevelt had called for an end to great fortunes that passed from generation to generation as 'not consistent with the ideal and sentiments of the American People'. He raised inheritance tax to 70 per cent and made income tax more progressive. A backlash started in 1976. In 2001, George W. Bush secured legislation to phase out inheritance taxes by 2010 (though the ambition was never realized, see Figure 25). His policy was criticized by wealthy individuals such as Warren Buffett and George Soros who argued that an aristocracy of wealth would stunt enterprise. Similarly, the Institute of Fiscal Studies in Britain pointed to 'a large, unjustified and problematic bias against employment and labour incomes and in favour of business ownership and capital incomes'. These choices are political rather than an inevitable outcome of globalization or de-industrialization and can be reversed, as happened between the two world wars.[41]

Covid had a similar effect to the global financial crisis, with a rise in asset prices for the better-off compared with deprived communities that

Figure 25: Inheritance tax rates, 1900–2020

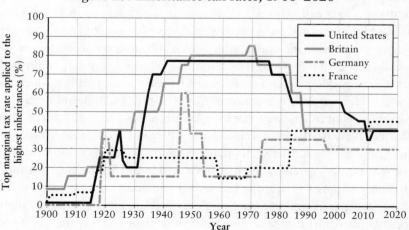

Source: http://piketty.pse.ens.fr/files/equality/pdf/F21.pdf.

suffered from austerity, de-industrialization, and 'lousy' jobs. At first, there were signs that the pandemic might provoke a change in social attitudes and policies. In April 2021, the IMF called for an increase in spending and taxation of wealthy households to maintain public support for government policy and to avoid a potential threat to social and economic stability. It warned that the pandemic could lead to

> rising polarization, erosion of trust in government, or social unrest. These factors complicate sound economic policy making and pose risks to macroeconomic stability and the functioning of society ... The pandemic has confirmed the merits of equal access to basic services – health care, quality education, and digital infrastructure – and of inclusive labor markets and effective social safety nets. Better performance in these areas has enhanced resilience to the pandemic and is key for the economic recovery to benefit all and to strengthen trust in government.

The IMF suggested a temporary 'solidarity tax' paid by high earners and companies that did well in the pandemic, to reduce social inequalities and help those who lost.[42] Such arguments built on calls, even before the pandemic, for more progressive and fairer taxation. In 2019, Thomas Piketty rightly remarked that 'the economic and social success of the capitalist countries in the twentieth century depended on ambitious and largely successful programs to reduce inequality, and in particular on steeply progressive taxes.' As he pointed out, failure to deal with extreme inequality is dangerous, and 'societies need institutions capable of periodically redefining and redistributing property rights. The refusal to do so in as transparent and peaceful a manner as possible only increases the likelihood of more violent but less effective remedies.'[43] In the United States, Emmanuel Saez called for a combination of a progressive wealth tax, taxation of multinational corporations, collective funding of health care, and a more progressive income tax. He looked for a return to the redistributive agenda of the New Deal and funding of education that could make Americans productive and prosperous. At least some wealthy Americans saw the force of Piketty's concern. The Patriotic Millionaires argued for higher levels of inheritance tax to break up passive wealth. Morris Pearl, a former BlackRock director and chair of Patriotic Millionaires, remarked that 'given the choice between pitchforks and taxes, I'm choosing taxes'.[44] The inflation triggered by the Russian invasion of Ukraine and disruption of energy supplies to Europe has led to demands for a windfall tax on energy companies and financial support for those most affected by higher energy bills. Unfortunately, some governments – such as the short-lived government of Liz Truss in Britain – argue for lower taxes (which will most benefit the better off), reject a windfall tax (though high profits are created in part by the regulatory regime), and deny the need for redistribution. This ideological approach returns to the belief of the 1980s that lower taxes rather than greater equality will lead to greater productivity and growth, and it is a serious threat to political and social stability.

Reform will not be easy. In the United States, President Biden and Democrats in the Senate failed in their modest bid in 2021 to tax the wealthiest households earning more than $100 million a year or holding assets of $1 billion. The mid-term elections in November 2022 maintained Democratic control of the Senate, but Republican control of the House of Representatives will create problems.[45] In Britain, the Johnson government's approach to the long-standing problem of the funding of social care was to increase the national insurance payments of workers and employers – a regressive tax that did not tap income from capital assets – and to impose a cap on individual contributions for care that will protect the wealthy compared with those with few assets. Martin Wolf of the *Financial Times* denounced the policy as 'an utter scandal' and many Conservative MPs from deprived areas of the country worried about the electoral consequences. Their complaints were initially unsuccessful.[46] In September 2022, the additional National Insurance contribution was dropped without tackling the wider issue of equalizing taxation of income from earnings and from capital, which pays a lower rate. Higher levels of public debt after the pandemic and energy crisis will be used to justify a new campaign of austerity to avoid burdening future generations. Of course, increased debt will lead to a loss of market confidence if not properly funded. What is needed is a fair and equitable tax system and spending that is justified as a way of stimulating growth. Business corporations routinely borrow to fund investment, and the same point applies to the public sector. The economist Tony Atkinson pointed to the fallacy of considering the debt-to-GDP ratio without also considering the other side of the balance sheet – the net worth of public assets. In 1979, the net worth of public assets in the United Kingdom was 76 per cent of GDP, falling to −20 per cent in 2012. Reducing debt is only one way to return to positive net worth. As Atkinson said, 'The other side is the accumulation of state assets. By holding capital and by sharing in the fruits of technological developments, the state can use the resulting revenue to promote a less unequal society.' It does not mean a return to monolithic state corporations, and could involve sovereign wealth funds, partial state ownership and strategic investments. Investment in better education and training, in health and infrastructure, is needed to produce higher and more sustainable growth, and to regenerate failing communities.[47]

Domestic and international tax reform is therefore a high priority – and resolving the issue of inequality would also help redress the macroeconomic imbalance between countries. Reforming trade rules and dispute resolution at the WTO, or tightening surveillance of capital flows, are second-order issues behind tackling the conditions that create trade imbalances and destabilizing global capital flows. A repeat of austerity and a failure to rectify gross inequalities would be a tragedy.

LOUSY JOBS AND LEVELLING UP

The widening gap between labour and capital reflects structural changes in the economy, and there is a need to change the nature of employment to reduce precarity and offer dignity at work. As we saw in Chapter 25, de-industrialization in the Rust Belt of the United States and in Britain meant a loss of jobs that paid a decent wage without formal qualifications and a growth of precarious or low-paid service employment, as well as well-paid employment for those with formal qualifications. Action is needed to stimulate economic growth that regenerates 'left behind' communities and responds to genuine grievances that create support for economic national-ism and populism. Although welfare policies are needed to deal with immediate economic and social problems, tax transfers cannot regenerate declining towns or create satisfying work. Neither does protectionism help. Even if industry did recover, new technology means it would not cre-ate as many jobs and the outcome would be higher costs for other sectors of the economy. The solution is to revitalize declining cities by place-based policies that can stimulate self-reliant growth and break the spiral of decay.

Raghuram Rajan, the former chief economist at the IMF and governor of the Reserve Bank of India, has called for 'inclusive localism' to strengthen left-behind communities. These areas lack skilled workers to attract new businesses and jobs, and the resources for good schools. Any-one with better education is likely to migrate, so leaving people with lower skills or family commitments to struggle in poorly paid jobs. The pandemic might help, for families in search of more space to work from home might move to towns with lower property prices, and the internet permits small enterprises to serve a wider market. Paul Collier, a former director of development research at the World Bank who grew up in the declining steel town of Sheffield, has suggested a two-track approach. The first strand is to extract rents from booming cities with high incomes and rising property values created by agglomeration rather than by personal effort. This is intellectually plausible but not feasible politically, though it could in part be achieved by reforms of taxation mentioned earlier. The second strand is regeneration, which is vital. An individual firm is unlikely to relocate to a decaying city in the absence of a wider cluster of enterprises and physical and social infrastructure. Government action is therefore needed to assist early arrivals through development banks, business zones and investment promotion agencies, with provision of good childhood education and retraining, improved transport, and links with local universities to invest in human capital and stimulate economic activity. Robert Putnam, a leading American political scientist, grew up in another declining industrial town – Port Clinton, Ohio – and charts the loss of opportunity since his youth. He focuses on support for poor families, childcare, and better education that links school and community. Both approaches require powerful local government and devolution to the locality so that it can respond to the challenges of regeneration, complemented by labour market and regional policies to provide training and support for sectors with the capacity to generate local employment – above all in digital and climate initiatives.[48]

Many residents of declining areas blamed their malaise on migrants, who were seen as competitors for jobs and houses and as putting pressure on schools and health-care systems. These claims were exaggerated, for most migrants were young, active members of the workforce who were net contributors to public finances. Migration was not the main reason for stagnating real wages, which were caused by weaker labour organization, casualized precarious jobs, the increasing power of capital, and outsourcing to low-wage countries. Anti-migrant sentiment was useful political rhetoric for populists and right-wing nativists to mobilize the disaffected. A better strategy would be to negotiate a new social contract that combines flexible labour markets with protection of workers through benefits and a floor to income. The balance of power between labour and capital should be adjusted – and that entails de-financialization.[49]

DE-FINANCIALIZATION

In the late twentieth and early twenty-first centuries, the global economy was 'financialized'. In 2015, even the BIS worried that 'the level of financial development is good only up to a point, after which it becomes a drag on growth', creating credit and money that fuelled its own activities and producing massive 'rents'.[50] Incomes in the financial sector in the United States were, on average, the same as in the rest of the economy until the 1980s when they soared with deregulation and corporate financial activity. Despite the adoption of information technology, the cost of intermediation remained stable over the twentieth century. Innovation was used to trade faster on information rather than to contribute to overall efficiency. There was a shift to high-fee asset managers, and incumbents could impose barriers to entry because of restrictions on banking licences, with the result that remuneration rose with a large element of 'rent' that was not 'earned' by individual ability.[51]

The IMF failed to contain the risks of financial liberalization. During the global financial crisis, the taxpayers of individual states rescued banks with global interests, so that systemically important banks became even larger and intensified the 'too big to fail' dilemma.[52] In 2019, Gita Gopinath, the chief economist of the IMF, saw a mismatch between global finance and national regulation:

> Countries can engage in a race to the bottom with lax regulations so as to win the favor of the financial services industry, while imposing large costs on the rest of the world. The lessons of the financial crisis if anything should highlight the costs of weak financial regulation and the virtues of international coordination of regulatory standards.[53]

One solution is to reduce the financialization of the economy by changes in policy. In Britain and the United States, mortgages were offered with low deposits and larger multiples of income, with the expectation of continued capital appreciation. In the United States, interest on home equity loans or second mortgages was tax-deductible, with the expectation that it would allow 'good' credit for home improvements, education and health. In fact, banks aggressively sold second mortgages for holidays and consumer goods so that houses became giant credit cards with lower interest. At the same time, deregulation of credit cards meant they were more profitable and were aggressively marketed. In the United States, subprime mortgages and the financial crisis left many homeowners in negative equity. Although this did not happen in Britain, households with large mortgages are now at risk from higher interest rates. Credit was used to maintain household consumption and to produce profit for financial firms, leading to greater inequality by redistribution from indebted households to financial firms and managers. This outcome reflected the nature of financial institutions rather than the level of debt. In Britain and the United States, financial firms pursued profits to maximize shareholder value, unlike some other countries with equally high debt where mortgages were provided by non-profit, stakeholder financial institutions.[54]

The task, as Raghuram Rajan argues, is to ensure that finance serves more than a knowledgeable few and is widely available for those who wish to start a new business or to allow households to spread their spending over time. Such an ambition entails removing the economic conditions that lead to over-reliance on credit to cope with low incomes. It also means adopting policies that will minimize risk-taking by financial institutions, by allowing competition that will reduce rent-seeking and provide better services, removing implicit state guarantees, altering the incentives of managers, and preventing institutions from becoming too big to fail. Rajan went on to be governor of the Reserve Bank of India from 2013 to 2016.[55] Another central banker – Mervyn King – also suggests changes in the regulation of finance, and not by imposing costly rules that block new entrants and allow rent-seeking. His solution is for central banks to move away from being lenders of last resort, which creates moral hazard and passes the cost of any bailout to the taxpayer. Instead, King's proposal is to make central banks into 'pawnbrokers for all seasons'. Banks should finance themselves with more equity and hold sufficient collateral – even in risky or illiquid assets – for the central bank to provide finance in an emergency, just as a distressed individual might pledge a watch or piece of jewellery to a pawnbroker. The costs would not fall on the taxpayer but on the banks, and the danger of moral hazard would be removed. The Bank of England did start to move in this direction during King's governorship. Whether it will be feasible for the global financial system is another matter, given the power of vested interests, the weakness of the IMF and the challenge of cryptocurrency. King admitted that reform might take decades, but the important thing is to identify the problem and to see that financialization can be turned back. Given the political influence of the financial sector, this will require enormous determination and strong leadership.[56]

CAPITAL FLOWS

Financialization entailed large flows of capital across national borders. Speculative or hot money has often been criticized but even foreign direct investment is problematic. It reflected tax avoidance as a result of merger activity or 'special purpose' entities that hold intellectual property or receive intra-company payments to take profits in low-tax jurisdictions. This activity created a conspicuous sense of unfairness between mobile and less mobile capital, between companies that can shift profits (such as Amazon) and those that cannot (a high street trader).[57]

As we saw in Chapter 26, the IMF came to accept capital controls as part of the policy mix after the global financial crisis and admitted that capital flows across borders could be destabilizing. In 2021, Maurice

Obstfeld, a leading expert on capital movements and a member of the Peterson Institute, agreed that capital account liberalization had passed the point of delivering the greatest net social benefit. Despite the protests of 'Occupy Wall Street', and the success of books such as Michael Lewis's *The Big Short*, Obstfeld was puzzled that global finance had not provoked more backlash. A possible reason is the contrast between, on the one hand, a highly concentrated, powerful financial sector with considerable political influence and widespread participation in financial markets from credit cards to pension funds, and on the other hand, the more dispersed nature of those who lost from financialization. Nevertheless, Obstfeld suggests that finance might suffer in future 'if national governments fail to enhance multilateral cooperation to manage the financial commons', and he called for intergovernmental co-operation complemented by national regulation that would permit more freedom for domestic policy without losing the benefits of financial integration.[58]

The IMF's role has been to intervene as an honest broker between creditors and debtors after a crisis of sovereign debt rather than to monitor debt before the crisis arose. Even this role has become more difficult. Until recently, most loans were issued by syndicates of banks with provision for repayment of the principal as well as interest. Now, many loans are refinanced, often by hedge funds that are less visible and less open to scrutiny, and more inclined to hold out for better terms than to restructure debt – as with Fidelity and BlackRock in Argentina in 2020.[59] The task is further complicated by China.

At the end of 2015, China created the Asian Infrastructure Investment Bank (AIIB), a development bank based in Beijing that invests in infrastructure in Asia and beyond. It caused alarm in Washington and Tokyo as a potential rival to the World Bank. The American and Japanese governments refused to join, but most European countries ignored American pleas to boycott the new bank. In 2021, China held 26.6 per cent of the votes, followed by India with 7.6 per cent, Russia with 6 per cent, Germany with 4.2 per cent and Britain with 2.9 per cent. The head of the AIIB implausibly denied that it was controlled by China or that it was designed to fund the Belt and Road Initiative. In fact, China had a veto because major decisions require 75 per cent of votes. By 2013, China had become the largest official lender to the developing world (see Figure 26), without joining the 'Paris Club' of creditors that works with the IMF to co-ordinate debt restructuring. Countries borrowing from China avoid the IMF's conditionality requirements, though there are other threats to their national autonomy. Chinese investment is often secured by a charge over assets and revenue so that it is senior to holders of government bonds, and debt can be used to gain control of strategic assets when loans are not repaid, as happened with the Hambantota International Port in Sri Lanka in 2017. Difficulties were apparent in Pakistan in 2019. In 2017–18, the government had borrowed $5bn to develop the China–Pakistan Economic Corridor as part of the Belt and Road Initiative. When Pakistan faced a balance of payments crisis, servicing the loan became difficult. The American government saw the Chinese loans as a strategic incursion and insisted on greater transparency and less dependence on China as a condition for IMF support for Pakistan. In the end, Pakistan secured assistance from China, the IMF and the Saudi Arabian-backed Islamic Development Bank. Many of the countries that borrow from China are financially insecure, and there is little information on the maturity and cost of loans, and doubts whether China will co-operate when things go wrong. The World Bank fears 'a perfect storm' that could produce a debt crisis on the scale of the 1980s.[60]

Lower income as a result of the pandemic forced indebted countries to borrow. The dangers were clear to Carmen Reinhart, the chief economist of the World Bank, but little has been done in response to her call for debt restructuring. The G20 launched a Debt Service Suspension Initiative (DSSI) in April 2020 that only covered the poorest countries, with a short-term moratorium on debt payments that were to be made good over the longer term. Private loans were only covered if the creditors joined

Figure 26: Aggregate external public debt owed by developing and emerging market economies to official creditors, 2000–2017

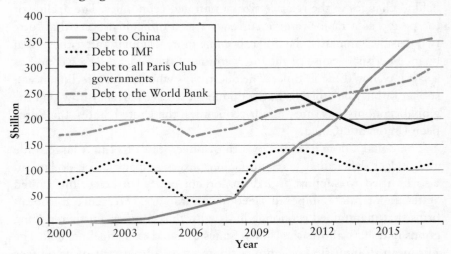

Source: Sebastian Horn, Carmen Reinhart and Christophre Trebesch, 'China's overseas lending', *Journal of International Economics* 133 (2021), fig. 9.

voluntarily under the oversight of the Institute of International Finance – a body that reflected the interests of hedge-fund managers and institutional investors. No private lenders joined the scheme. Uncertainty over China's intentions made other countries reluctant to forgive payments that might allow borrowers to service their debt to China instead. The World Bank did not take part, on the flimsy grounds that it was raising new loans and feared a loss of its triple-A rating. The DSSI was, as Tooze remarks, a 'mockery'. Further, the IMF's and World Bank's proposal for collective action provisions to overrule creditors who were holding out failed as a result of opposition from the Trump administration.[61]

China's lending to emerging markets is leading to a crisis of debt, and as we will see later in the chapter there is also a risk of a collapse of the domestic property market, which is heavily dependent on loans. As a result, the next financial crisis could have its origins in China, unless the Communist Party can resolve the problems. The emergence of China as the world's second-largest economy – with the prospect that it will soon overtake the United States – also leads many to pose another question: will the dollar be replaced as the world's leading reserve currency?

THE FUTURE OF INTERNATIONAL CURRENCIES

The replacement of one global currency by another is a rare event that, as we saw with sterling and the dollar after the Second World War, lags behind changes in the relative size of national economies. The decline of the pound as a major reserve currency was a difficult process that took two decades. Similarly, the dollar became more dominant after the global financial crisis because of the intervention of the Federal Reserve, and as a safe haven in difficult times. The question is whether, like sterling, it will sooner or later be replaced as the dominant reserve currency now that the global economy has three major economies: the United States, the European Union, and China.

The dollar's dominance allows the United States to run a large trade and budget deficit that takes up China's excess capacity. The dollar can also be used to support American foreign policy. In 2018, the United States unilaterally reimposed sanctions on Iran and threatened European firms that maintained economic links with that country. Further, pricing goods in dollars allows the United States to avoid exchange rate risk. The European Commission began questioning why 80 per cent of its oil was billed in dollars, even though only 2 per cent came from the United States;

and why Airbus planes made in the EU and bought by European companies were priced in dollars. In January 2021, the Commission talked about boosting the international role of the euro, but irritation with the role of the dollar is not likely to overcome doubts about the structure of the eurozone.[62] The imposition of sanctions on Russia and its exclusion from international payments might encourage some countries to hold reserves other than in dollars. Equally, the dollar is attractive at times of economic instability, and holding renminbi merely replaces the power of the United States with that of China.

In 2018, the renminbi bloc accounted for 28 per cent of global GDP, compared with 36 per cent for the dollar, but the potential emergence of the renminbi as a reserve currency is limited by controls on international flows of money. In October 2020, the renminbi's share of global payments was only 1.7 per cent, far behind the dollar (37.6 per cent) and euro (37.8), and even the pound (6.9) and yen (3.4). The renminbi only accounted for 2.5 per cent of non-Chinese reserves in 2018, compared with 62 per cent for the dollar and 20.5 per cent for the euro. The renminbi's share of global reserves divided by its share of global output was 0.07 in 2017, compared with 4.1 for the United States and 2.15 for the eurozone. In 2019, Gita Gopinath of the IMF doubted that replacement of the dollar would be swift: 'You are hearing more noise right now for other currencies to become truly global currencies. But the data do not show a more forceful dynamic in this direction and it would take a lot more than what we're seeing now for there to be a switch.'[63]

The solution is unlikely to be the emergence of international money as had been proposed by Keynes. In 2013, Justin Yifu Lin, a Chinese economist who was chief economist of the World Bank from 2008 to 2012, feared that a multicurrency system would lead to speculative flows and instability, and he argued for a single supranational currency on the lines of Keynes's Bancor to balance national and global interests.[64] This was not feasible in 1944, and is even less likely now. Even the modest proposal for a new allocation of Special Drawing Rights in response to the pandemic was problematic. In 2020, a group of African and European countries called for an issue of SDRs to give poorer countries collateral for dollar borrowings. The United States still had the largest voice in the IMF and the Trump administration refused on the grounds that SDRs would hand more money to Venezuela and Iran. After President Biden assumed office, Janet Yellen, the new treasury secretary, returned to the proposal that SDRs should be issued to help countries hit by Covid, and the idea was taken up by the G20. The IMF finally issued new SDRs in August 2021, which offered a respite during the pandemic but they will not become a global currency – any more than in the 1960s.[65]

Another possibility is cryptocurrencies – a form of money above both the nation state and international organizations. Supporters of cryptocurrencies argue that the dollar could lose its value because of mounting debt and loose monetary policy, so that they are safe havens against inflation. Cryptocurrencies have appealed to tech billionaires Elon Musk and Mark Zuckerberg as less susceptible to political intervention and more appropriate to the multipolar world in which markets are global rather than national. To sceptics, the danger of cryptocurrencies is precisely their existence above the state and beyond democratic control and accountability, and both the Chinese and American authorities have taken action to control and regulate them, respectively.[66] The collapse of cryptocurrencies in 2022 showed that they are not as stable as their advocates hoped.

The outcome is likely to be a multipolar world where several currencies – the dollar, euro and renminbi – coexist and reduce the 'exorbitant privilege' of the dollar. The leading analysts of global currencies point out that several international currencies have coexisted in the past and this could happen again, with a wider distribution of the benefits of liquidity and seigniorage. Against this optimism, there is a risk that financial and economic sanctions might lead to a pre-emptive search for self-reliance and a retreat into currency blocs.[67]

GREEN NEW DEAL

The discussions at Bretton Woods focused on international monetary relations and the need for stable exchange rates for post-war recovery. As we saw in Chapter 7, there were also discussions over food security, nutrition and agriculture which led to the creation of the Food and Agriculture Organization. Debates over population and the resources of the planet continued in the Club of Rome. During most of the period covered by this book, these concerns took a secondary place to discussion of international trade and finance by GATT, the WTO and IMF. Now, climate change and the existential threat to life on the planet demands solutions to a truly global tragedy of the commons. What Brazil does with the Amazon or China with emissions of carbon have consequences far beyond their own boundaries – and they might claim that Europe and the United States are hypocritically stopping others from following their own path to prosperity. The collective action problem in dealing with climate change is now the fundamental problem of global economic government.

The transition to a new energy regime is already underway and forms part of the stimulus package in the United States, Britain and the EU. Although the energy crisis in 2022 has led to a short-term return to fossil fuels, in the longer term it will encourage a switch to renewables, which were already becoming competitive. What remains at stake is the urgency of the climate crisis. Some die-hard opponents, with the backing of fossil fuel interests, still deny climate change or at least the need for a rapid move to net zero carbon emissions. The issue has led social movements such as 'Extinction Rebellion' to call for mobilization on the same scale as in the Second World War, and more generally has led to a change in popular sentiment. Where advocates of decarbonization and the green transition disagree is how to encourage the transition.

In 2018, George Shultz (Treasury Secretary in the Nixon administration and Secretary of State under Ronald Reagan) and James Baker (Secretary of State under George H. W. Bush) proposed a carbon tax with 'dividends' returned to the public. The idea was supported by the Climate Leadership Council with backing from Janet Yellen, then a former chair of the Federal Reserve, as well as large companies such as BP, ExxonMobil and General Motors. An alternative to a carbon tax is an emissions trading system such as adopted by the European Union in 2005: a cap is set on emissions, and businesses buy and sell allowances depending on whether they are above or below the cap, with the price of carbon set by an auction market for allowances. The aim in both cases is to use price signals to reduce emissions. The IMF supported carbon pricing and in 2019 a paper suggested a carbon tax rising to $75 a ton by 2030, with revenue used to assist low-income households and displaced workers, and to invest in clean energy. Carbon taxes or permits could be complemented by a border tax on the carbon content of imports, as agreed by the EU in late 2022.[68]

This approach goes back to the 'polluter must pay' principle of the OECD in the early 1970s, a market-based solution that was adopted in the Rio Declaration of 1992. Such 'liberal environmentalism' was not welcome on the left, which saw a neo-liberal project that relies on price signals rather than social justice and imposes a regressive burden on poor households that spend more of their income on fuel. In 2019, over six hundred groups that support a green new deal urged Congress not to accept a market-based solution that puts corporate profits above the community. Carbon pricing, so they argued, was more than a matter of tweaking the price mechanism. Radical change was needed in the nature of capitalism and growth. Their preference was disinvestment in fossil fuels, blocking fracking and coal mines, or individual action by forgoing meat and air travel. This rejection of carbon taxes or tradable emission permits as 'neo-liberal' plays into the hands of climate-change sceptics. Taxes and permits limit the ability of polluters to dump emissions in the atmosphere without cost; and the tax can be progressive to compensate poor households and countries. Thomas Piketty, who is far from neo-liberal, proposes a progressive carbon tax with an exemption for households emitting less than the global average, increasing to $100 a ton for those above the global average, to $500 above 2.3 times and $1,000 above 9.1 times. Rather than rejecting carbon pricing outright, we need to challenge William Nordhaus's flawed analysis that underestimates the long-term damage of climate change and sets too low a price. By contrast, the report of Nicholas Stern for the British government sets a more realistic present cost of damage to the planet's future.[69]

Carbon pricing provides one lever to force emitters to pay the real price for their activities, without losing sight of more fundamental changes in attitudes to growth. Partha Dasgupta, a Cambridge economist who produced a report on biodiversity for the British government, rightly points to a flaw in the pursuit of GDP growth as a principal aim of economics. GDP measures the flow of output each year rather than the social worth of the economy's entire stock of assets. GDP does not include depreciation of assets, including the degradation of the natural environment and climate change. He points out that 'An economy could record a high rate of growth of GDP by depreciating its assets, but one would not know that from national statistics ... in recent decades eroding natural capital has been precisely the means the world economy has deployed for enjoying what is routinely celebrated as "economic growth".'[70] The challenge is whether green growth can be decoupled from the environmental record of capitalism or whether – as some argue – we need 'degrowth'. The ecological economist Tim Jackson puts this position starkly: 'Endless growth – green or not – can only end up leading to no growth at all. There is no growth on a dead planet.' Such arguments entail managed shrinkage of the economy with redistribution to avoid disaster for poorer members of society. Both green growthers and degrowthers agree on the need to shift to public transport, recycle old products, adopt a more plant-based diet, turn to renewable energy and construct more efficient buildings. Degrowthers go further in looking for a reduction in economic activity, changes in property relations by common ownership or use, and reparations to the victims of colonialism. Such changes will require reduced consumption in the Global North through planning as well as national and international redistribution – though who will have the political power to implement such radical policies is not obvious, and more likely to lead to resistance than progress.[71]

A green 'new deal' and green growth will require considerable effort in linking action on climate change with 'green jobs' and growth that can help recovery in decaying cities of the developed world and stimulate growth in Africa, which has both the potential for solar energy and produces rare minerals needed for battery technology. The challenge is to ensure that the benefits of the 'green revolution' are shared equitably and that destructive policies such as the deforestation of the Amazon or building coal-powered generating stations are halted. A group of economists and politicians associated with Piketty argues for a European policy that will offer 'fair and lasting social development' by restoring solidarity and taxing multinationals, wealth, high incomes and carbon emissions to finance research and training, to invest in transforming the economy, and to integrate migrants.[72] In September 2017, President Macron called for an ecological transition supported by a fair carbon price and a border carbon tax, with support for sectors and areas with outmoded production.[73] Piketty and Macron link action on climate change, financialization and taxation of the digital economy with socially equitable policies that offer an alternative to the populist right. Of course, securing support across the EU will be difficult, and the situation is now complicated by the energy crisis arising from dependence on Russian oil and gas, which both creates hostility to the costs of the green transition and encourages renewables to achieve energy security.

In the United States, radical Democrats made a similar case for a green new deal, with support from the 'Sunrise Movement' of young people and established figures such as Joseph Stiglitz, Al Gore, and senators Bernie Sanders, Elizabeth Warren and Edward Markey. In January 2019, 625 organizations wrote to Congress expressing concern about climate change, and the next month Representative Alexandria Ocasio-Cortez's and Senator Markey's draft House motion set out a plan both for a green new deal, and for a family wage, high-quality health care and education, adequate housing, and economic security. President Trump's sarcastic response was that 'I think it is very important for the Democrats to press forward with their Green New Deal. It would be great for the so-called "Carbon Footprint" to permanently eliminate all Planes, Cows, Cars, Gas and the Military – even if no other country would do the same. Brilliant!'[74] In September 2019, he failed to join other leaders at the UN to discuss action on climate change and removed the United States from any leadership role. In 2021, President Biden embarked on promoting investment in clean energy and in 2022, he achieved some success in this in the Inflation Reduction Act.

Climate change is a global common problem that does not respect national boundaries. The question is whether nations can agree on joint action. The World Bank is, in the opinion of Al Gore, the former vice-president and environmental campaigner, 'missing in action' on climate change, and one Bank researcher commented that its president, David Malpass – a Trump nominee – 'has neither the vision nor credibility to make the World Bank a climate leader'. In September 2022, his failure to agree that climate change is man-made led to calls for his resignation, with the US Treasury urging the Bank to act as a global leader. The WTO also lacks a firm commitment to policies to deal with climate change.[75] The main forum has been the annual UN Climate Change Conferences or Conferences of the Parties. At COP21 in Paris in 2015, 196 countries agreed to limit global warming to 2°C above pre-industrial levels, with many committing to 'nationally determined contributions' to cut emissions and to reach net zero by 2050, and to make contributions to poorer countries. Trump pulled out of the subsequent Paris agreement, and progress was difficult even after Biden rejoined. At COP26 in Glasgow in November 2021, the suggestion that countries should 'accelerate the phasing out of coal and subsidies for fossil fuels' was opposed by China and India and diluted to a commitment to 'phasedown of unabated coal power and phase-out of inefficient fossil fuel'. There was some progress, with an agreement to a 'rapid, deep and sustained reduction in global greenhouse emissions', but major issues remained.[76]

At the UN General Assembly in September 2022, a number of developing countries called for reform of the Bretton Woods institutions. Mia Mottley, the prime minister of Barbados, proposed a 'new internationalism' to help poorer countries tackle the consequences of climate change. The Bretton Woods institutions, she argued, 'no longer serve the purpose in the twenty-first century that they served in the twentieth century'. She suggested a distribution of SDRs and funds for climate resilience. The demand for action was supported by Gore, by the UN secretary general, who suggested a windfall tax on global fuel markets, and by Kristalina Georgieva of the IMF. At COP26, developed countries did not agree to a proposal to help poorer countries deal with climate change – and some countries, above all Brazil during the presidency of Bolsonaro, rejected assistance as neo-colonialism. In November 2022, COP27 agreed to 'loss and damage' funding for vulnerable countries affected by climate change – a modest start on redistribution from historic polluters. Malpass's resignation in February 2023 also signals a shift in World Bank policy.[77]

The Bretton Woods institutions should do more to manage the global commons, but top-down initiatives provoke hostility. In 2019, the Australian prime minister Scott Morrison railed against an 'unaccountable internationalist bureaucracy' that 'seeks to elevate global institutions above the authority of nation states to direct national policies'. In his view, 'only a national government, especially one accountable through the ballot box and the rule of law can define its national interests.' There are alternative views within Australia, such as in New South Wales, where the premier had ambitions to become a 'renewable superpower' with the cheapest prices in the OECD – and Morrison was defeated in the election of 2022. The solution is to build up local or national programmes, with international involvement focused on ensuring that national policies, such as border taxes on the carbon content of imports, are not used for protectionist purposes, and to oversee the system of carbon trades and offsets.[78]

Starting at the global level will not generate sufficient trust or compliance from citizens or businesses, and it makes more sense to address collective action problems at various levels – local, regional and national – that will create more support from different stakeholders, better enforcement, and permit adaptation to different ecosystems. Elinor Ostrom, the leading theorist on collective action, argued that such an incremental or 'polycentric' approach – a reliance on networks and a variety of fora – is more likely to succeed than an international agreement. As she points out, climate change is the largest collective action problem ever: all benefit from action to reduce emissions, whether or not they contribute to the costs. There is a huge incentive to be a free rider on climate change mitigation by other countries, and a disinclination to comply with international agreements if we cannot trust that others on the far side of the world are doing the same. As she says, people do not want to be taken as 'suckers' in taking costly actions when others do not. Relying on a single global government is too complex, with too many actors and interests, and global solutions – such as policies to protect forests – do not work unless backed by national action and the creation of local institutions. Although the impact is global, actions generating emissions occur at all levels – by households, by businesses – and it follows that mitigating action should be as close as possible to those actors by creating co-operation at diverse levels. She argues that co-operative action is possible where there is agreement on the need for change, and individuals see themselves as jointly sharing responsibility. The task is to create trust so that people are willing to accept their own short-term costs because of long-term benefits, and that they see others complying – something that is easier at the local than global level.[79] The danger is that the experience of the early 1970s will be repeated, when concerns for the environment were marginalized in response to the oil shock and 'stagflation'. If the same happens in response to the costs of the pandemic and energy crisis, the consequences will be disastrous.

Disequilibrium within the world's three major economies – the United States, the European Union and China – needs to be addressed before co-operative solutions become possible. Inequality and economic precariousness, excess savings or debt lead to macroeconomic imbalances between countries. Changes in domestic policies are needed as a condition for improved relationships between countries in a multipolar world of mounting geopolitical tensions. In 1933, the main participants at the World Monetary and Economic Conference had different understandings of the problems of the world economy and their resolution. In 1944, Britain and the United States – for all their disagreements – had a common wish to create a stable international monetary order. In 2023, finding common ground will not be easy given internal tensions and divergent political systems.

THE UNITED STATES: DYSFUNCTIONAL POLITICS

The United States, the world's greatest military and financial power, faces growing political polarization through a failure to reach consensus, the nature of campaign finance, dominance by powerful vested interests, and with concerns about foreign interference in elections including through social media.[80] Under Trump, the Republican Party turned to white nativism and identity politics, refused to deal with an expensive and inefficient health-care system, failed to deliver on the promise of major infrastructural projects, and undermined multilateral institutions from the WTO to the WHO. The electoral college, voter suppression and gerrymandering of electoral districts, the over-representation of rural interests in the Senate, the nature of campaign finance, and the composition of the Supreme Court gave a disproportionate voice to conservative anti-statism that makes it difficult to tackle inequality and the power of financial interests. The political scientists Steven Levitsky and Daniel Ziblatt have warned of the death of democracy, whose survival relies not only on constitutions and institutions, but on 'unwritten democratic norms' of toleration, acceptance that competing parties are legitimate rivals, and politicians' restraint in maximizing advantage that have been weakened by 'extreme partisan polarization'.[81]

Recently, the one effective part of the American state has been the Federal Reserve which responded quickly to the financial crisis to ensure that the dollar-based financial system did not collapse. After Covid, it again stepped in to fund the fiscal response that exceeded the scale of that of the global financial crisis. In March 2020, the Coronavirus Aid, Relief and Economic Security Act (CARES) increased spending by about 10 per cent of GDP, including a $600 supplement to unemployment benefit, stimulus cheques, and support for business. This massive intervention was needed to deal with the weak welfare system and inequality, with the aim of preserving the existing social and economic order. Support for unemployed workers expired in August 2020 and renewal was blocked by a combination of Democrats who did not wish Trump to claim credit during the election campaign, and Republicans who feared a conservative backlash. In the presidential election, Joe Biden promised a large stimulus, reflecting his concern that rising inequality created political discontent and 'allows demagogues to step in'. Fiscal stimulus seemed unlikely in the polarized American political system but was achieved by an unusual set of contingencies. In December 2020, a group of centrists proposed a spending plan and the Republican leadership in the Senate dropped its opposition in the hope of winning the disputed elections in Georgia. A deal was agreed in December 2020 that provided the second-largest fiscal stimulus after CARES.[82]

When President Biden assumed office in January 2021, Democrat success in the run-off elections in Georgia gave him a window of opportunity to embark on spending plans that far exceeded Barack Obama's response to the global financial crisis. The American Rescue Plan, unlike CARES, focused on the middle class and those with lower incomes, and on small rather than large businesses. This short-term stimulus was supplemented by two longer-term schemes – the American Jobs Plan to invest in infrastructure, including green energy, and the American Families Plan to support education, health and childcare 'to rebuild the middle class and invest in America's future'. Many economists, including Larry Summers, thought the stimulus was too large but the Federal Reserve accepted the programme. Jerome Powell, the chair of the Fed, even remarked in January 2021 that 'we welcome slightly higher inflation ... The kind of troubling inflation that people like me grew up with seems ... unlikely in both domestic and global context that we've been in for some time.' His confidence in low inflation arose from the weakness of organized labour and the expansion of global supply in countries with low wages. Even at the time, sceptics thought that easy money meant that the economy might overheat and that central bankers should have acted sooner. The surge in energy prices in 2022 then exacerbated the problem. Inflation had not disappeared, and the Fed and other central banks are responding by raising interest rates. Higher levels of both private and public debt than in the 1970s mean that higher interest rates threaten a recession and debt crises. Tight fiscal policy and loose monetary policy after the global financial crisis are giving way to loose fiscal policy to deal with the energy crisis and tight monetary policy to deal with inflation.[83]

These spending plans did not provoke the same virulent opposition as after the global financial crisis and the *Financial Times* even anticipated a shift in cultural attitudes as in the original New Deal – an implausible prediction given Republican hostility to Biden's plans. In August 2022, the Inflation Reduction Act – a much-reduced version of Biden's plan to Build Back Better – was passed by the Senate on the casting vote of the vice-president. It adopted a 15 per cent minimum threshold for corporation tax (although on less stringent terms than the proposed international agreement), imposed a levy on share buy-backs, reduced payments to pharmaceutical companies, offered more support for medical costs, reduced the deficit, and took action on the climate. Elements of the original programme were surrendered to conservative Democrats and to Republicans, but it was still a considerable achievement. Of course, it would have been easier to invest when interest rates had been lower, which Trump failed to do. Better late than never, Biden aimed to fund clean energy that will create jobs – though the EU complains that subsidies confined to American products is protectionist and continues Trump's policy of economic patriotism. The mid-term elections in November 2022 unexpectedly maintained Democratic control of the Senate, though not of the House, which is likely to block progress. It remains to be seen whether the presidential election in November 2024 will allow continued progress or a reversion to failed policies.[84]

Roosevelt made changes in the New Deal and Lyndon Johnson in the Great Society. The hope for America is that Biden will have the same success, despite the broken American political system. A return to austerity, and a failure to address the serious problems of those who are 'left behind' and another 'pluto-populist' president will be devastating for social and political stability in the United States and for the rest of the world. The prospects are not good when many Americans falsely consider that elections are stolen and that political violence is legitimate. America's ability to resolve its internal difficulties, and to engage in international solutions, is at a low ebb. Success will depend on the willingness of the Republican Party to return to the 'unwritten democratic norms' and to escape from extreme polarization – something that currently seems unlikely.

THE EUROZONE

The eurozone survived the crisis that started in 2009 but its design flaws remained with the potential for future difficulties. Exit was essentially impossible, which left the alternative of reform by 'ever closer union'. In 2017, President Macron in a wide-ranging speech at the Sorbonne presented a grand vision of recreating European solidarity around security and control of borders, allied to helping the development of countries sending migrants to Europe, and responding to new challenges of the environment and the digital age. He called for a European budget based on a digital or environmental tax and a harmonized corporation tax, with a European finance minister.[85] These ideas were politically unrealistic. Ashoka Mody, an economist who had been assistant director of the IMF's European Fund, saw that weak accountability and lack of tangible benefits had undermined popular support for shared sovereignty and fiscal union.[86] Macron soon faced opposition, both at home from the *gilets jaunes*, who feared higher fuel costs and liberalization of labour markets, and from the right-wing party of Marine Le Pen, and from within the EU.

The pandemic posed the risk of another eurozone crisis triggered by the parlous state of Italian finances. There was a wide disparity between high levels of debt in Italy and lower levels in Germany, though the debts of the EU as a whole were below those of the United States and Britain. The pandemic again exposed the structural flaws of the eurozone. In March 2020, Christine Lagarde announced that the ECB would buy a modest €120 billion of a total €10 trillion sovereign debt, and implied that the Bank would not assist Italy. The spread between Italian and German bonds predictably widened and she changed direction, more closely echoing Mario Draghi's commitment in 2012 to do 'whatever it takes'. The ECB launched the Pandemic Emergency Purchase Programme. Germany was initially hostile. In May 2020, the German constitutional court rejected the European Court of Justice's judgment that found in favour of the ECB's bond-buying programme. The German decision might have been legally sound, but it was economically perverse and potentially a devastating blow to the ECB's response to the pandemic.[87]

Even before the pandemic, there were signs of change by Germany's finance minister (and Merkel's successor as Chancellor in 2021) Olaf Scholz, and his chief economist Jakob von Weizsäcker. Covid pushed Scholz to accept a fiscal stimulus by suspending the debt brake and agreeing to a eurozone package. Merkel changed her position under pressure from France and her coalition partners. This change of approach encountered resistance. In February 2020, the 'frugal four' of Austria, Denmark, Sweden and the Netherlands had aimed to limit the EU budget to 1 per cent of GDP, a ratio of 40 or 50 to 1 between national and EU revenues. In July 2020, a compromise was reached on the NextGen recovery fund that was linked with a green transition. The German constitutional court's ruling was ignored and the ECB pushed ahead. To Scholz, it was a 'Hamiltonian moment'. In 1790 Alexander Hamilton, the first Secretary of the Treasury of the United States, mutualized the debt of the individual states, while raising revenues from the federal customs' service. But the EU did not mutualize debt and allowed joint issuance only as an emergency measure; nor did it have tax-raising powers or a single finance minister. The most that can be said of the 'Hamiltonian moment' was that it was a sign of learning and a first step, with little prospect of a common fiscal policy that would involve a loss of national sovereignty.[88]

Although the EU did more than in 2008, it was still less than the United States, and divisions continued between north and south, and with the right-wing governments of Poland and Hungary. The outcome was a continuation of 'extend and pretend', muddling through until the next crisis hit. This came with the Russian invasion of Ukraine, which created problems for Germany's Faustian pact with Russia for cheap energy to sustain its industrial economy.[89] The EU has shown leadership over carbon border taxes, a minimum corporation tax, and regulation of 'big tech'.

CHINA

China played a major role in the response to the global financial crisis and continued to contribute a major part of the world's economic growth: in 2019, it was responsible for 27 per cent of global growth and, in 2020, it was the only major economy that was still growing. The naive expectation that China would converge with the West and co-operate with the United States in managing the global economy was not fulfilled, however, and its authoritarian political capitalism stood in contrast to liberal democratic capitalism. In 2011, President Obama had responded to the rise of China with a 'pivot to Asia', and in December 2017 the US National Security Strategy identified the Indo-Pacific region as an arena of great power competition. In May 2020, the Trump administration went further with the 'United States Strategic Approach to the People's Republic of China'. It did not simply seek concessions on trade; it took action against Huawei – a Chinese global technology company – and China's strategy of developing high technology. To Trump, American firms working with China were traitors. Biden was more temperate but, of course, was still committed to ensuring that the United States remained the world's largest economy. In March 2021, the American Jobs Plan aimed to 'unify and mobilize the country to meet the great challenges of our time: the climate crisis and the ambitions of an autocratic China'. The dilemma was that, unlike during the Cold War with the Soviet Union, American business invested in China, and its economy was integral to global supply chains.[90]

The EU took a different approach. The EU–China Comprehensive Agreement on Investment treated China as both a competitor and a partner – a balance that will be difficult to maintain. The claims of the chief executive of Volkswagen that he was unaware of detention camps in Xinjiang province, where the firm has had a plant since 2013, was strongly criticized in June 2022 by two powerful members of its supervisory board – the president of Lower Saxony, which is a major shareholder, and the head of the largest trade union. The German coalition's Green Party foreign minister is critical of China, and the economics minister has rejected investment guarantees for the company. Increasingly, China is criticized for its repression of ethnic minorities, digital surveillance of its population and threats to Hong Kong and Taiwan, which limit its ability to co-operate in governing the world economy.[91]

Although Xi Jinping made a commitment to globalization and open markets at Davos in January 2017, his attachment to autocracy made others wary. He was returning to Maoism to restore the links between the Chinese Communist Party and the people and moving from market-oriented reform to state-led growth. His strategy was to combine the Belt and Road Initiative with leadership in advanced technologies set out in 'Made in China 2025'. It was risky, for state enterprises are not as profitable as private firms, and loss-making state enterprises borrowed to service debt, and relied on subsidies and overpriced contracts. Much of the growth in credit came from banks owned and controlled by local government that forced them to lend to under-performing companies to sustain employment, social stability and fiscal revenues. Local authority-controlled companies with fewer profitable infrastructure projects were less able to stimulate growth. The CCP accepted the financial risk of debt and lower profitability in state enterprises as a price for political control and maintenance of employment – but how sustainable was this combination of political repression and economic growth? Indeed, the Chinese economy is facing difficulties. By the end of 2022, Xi's zero-toleration approach to Covid, with continued lockdowns and restrictions, provoked unrest and economic disruption. The sudden change in policy in December to remove restrictions on a poorly vaccinated population threatened a public health crisis, further economic dislocation and, potentially, a loss of credibility for Xi. The result might be temporary disruption; more significantly, China's difficulties come at a time when its recent strategy for growth is in doubt.[92]

China's growth has relied on a combination of exports and investment in property and related infrastructure. The extraordinary level of household savings led to low domestic consumption and high dependence on exports, in particular to the United States, which were funded by flows of money from China, and by America's ability to issue more dollars. Much of Chinese savings went into property, which accounts for between 20 and 30 per cent of GDP, 70 per cent of household wealth, 60 per cent of local government revenue, and 40 per cent of bank lending. As we noted in Chapter 25, a downturn in the property sector has led both to popular unrest and mortgage strikes in response to the failure to complete housing units bought 'off-plan' before construction, and to pressure on local government finance that relies on rising land values. Not surprisingly, the state stepped in to prevent the collapse of Evergrande, one of the largest property companies, and cut interest rates in an attempt to help property developers. The attempt is unlikely to work given the low level of demand for new loans and the risk of creating moral hazard. There is a real possibility that the next financial crisis will be home-grown because of the collapse in the property market, the fragility of the banking system, the high level of non-performing loans, the difficulties of local government in finding worthwhile new infrastructure projects, and heavy investment in risky overseas projects.[93]

The solution to the global macroeconomic imbalance and China's reliance on the property sector would be to move to higher levels of domestic consumption. Chinese economists are aware of the problem, but a solution would require Beijing to tackle powerful local elites, to increase the share of output taken by labour, and to remove the need for high levels of household savings to provide a social safety net. It is unlikely that the CCP will allow free trade unions and collective bargaining to increase wages, so change is more likely to arise from a reform of the household registration (hukou) system by improving conditions for rural migrants and increasing welfare benefits, which would reduce the need for households to save. This will be a major task which might be overtaken by a serious financial crisis.[94]

Resolution of the global macroeconomic imbalances requires a restructuring of both the Chinese and American economies to reduce under-consumption, inequality and reliance on the 'exorbitant privilege' of the dollar to cover deficits. The experience of the 1930s shows that global co-operation is not easy when there are domestic economic difficulties, and that resolving trade disputes does not remove geopolitical tensions. The rivalry between China and the United States is, of course, not only over trade and intellectual property. Xi Jinping aims to overcome the loss of status experienced by China in the nineteenth century and to reassert its place in the world. The Belt and Road Initiative, strategic involvement in the South China Seas, threats to the status of Hong Kong, assertiveness over Taiwan, and human rights violations against the Uighur minority go beyond trade disputes. Reform of international economic institutions would be desirable but will not resolve this Great Power confrontation. The tension between geopolitical hostility and economic interdependence will not be easily resolved. There is a risk that the world might 'decouple' and form competing economic blocs or even embark on military conflict. The best outcome will be peaceful coexistence. The United States will need to work collaboratively with other powers, such as Japan and the EU, to exert pressure on China to abide by the rules of the WTO, and to press for agreement on human rights violations and global issues of climate change. China will also need to resolve the dilemma of offering support to Russia after the invasion of Ukraine and its reliance on markets in the United States and Europe – a tension that was apparent at the meeting of the Shanghai Cooperation Organization in Samarkand in September 2022. The future of the world depends on the way these tensions are resolved, with a weakened and resentful Russia and rising and autocratic China, with European Union reliance on Russian energy and the United States on Chinese supply chains.

GLOBALIZATION AND DEGLOBALIZATION

For global economic government to have a chance, it is necessary to redistribute income and wealth within countries to create a more inclusive form of democratic capitalism, and for China to shift towards a more balanced economy with less dependence on exports and property investment. It means redressing the balance between the Global North and South, not least over issues of climate change and reparations for past colonialism. Successful global economic government is more likely in the context of distributive justice within as well as between nations. None of this will be easy – but failure will be devastating.[95]

There was talk of economic nationalism, trade wars, a decoupling of supply chains and de-globalization even before the Russian invasion of Ukraine, when European and American sanctions against Russia then led to increased exports of commodities to China and India at a discount. The world is more interconnected than ever, which encourages the use of economic sanctions as a form of proxy warfare – but their use intensifies tensions within globalization.[96] There are attempts to limit Chinese access to advanced technology and to create security in the supply of

components, and some signs of on-shoring or 'friend-shoring'. Meanwhile, the Biden administration continues to encourage 'Buy American'.
The economist Bradford DeLong goes so far as to call the United States
'an anti-globalization outlier'. Nevertheless, it is unlikely that globalization will give way to self-contained blocs on the same scale as in the
1930s. After all, China still depends on European and American markets
for its manufactures which Russia cannot absorb.[97]

Economic nationalism is certainly more powerful, but a retreat of globalization is not likely. It will change. Since the financial crisis, world trade
in goods has been stable or even falling relative to output, though mainly –
until recent events – because of a decline in the price of commodities
rather than trade volumes. So far, the uncoupling of supply chains is
mainly a result of China's shifting from assembling imported components
to producing them itself. Globalization is now increasingly in services
rather than trade, in areas such as copy-editing, graphic design or IT support (see Figure 27).[98] These changes will both hit the middle class in
developed economies and contribute to removing poverty in other parts
of the world. What is needed is a move from hyper-globalization to a better balance between responsible nationalism and internationalism.
Securing the continued benefits of such globalization will mean changes
within the developed world to create a greater sense of inclusion, and
replacing the unrealistic pursuit of global solutions with a polycentric or

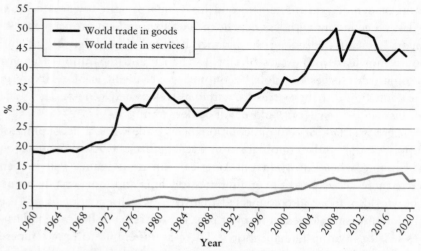

**Figure 27: World trade in goods and services as % of GDP,
1960–2020**

Source: Richard Baldwin, https://cepr.org/voxeu/columns/peak-globalisation-myth-part-4-services-trade-did-not-peak.

messy approach that proceeds by incremental steps where agreement is possible.

We are again at the stage of uncertainty and contestation over the global political economy and the nature of the new order. In the early twenty-first century, multilateral institutions were in danger of losing credibility. Like Keynes, we are perplexed about what to do. The chances of failure are high, as they were before 1914 and in the 1930s. Now, failure to deal with macroeconomic imbalances could result in another financial crisis or trade war, with existential threats of ecological disaster from disease and climate change that contribute to international tensions. The WTO, IMF and World Bank have a role to play by widening their agenda, and by monitoring a polycentric system based on multiple currencies and regional trade blocs, with a need to negotiate between debtors and creditors, rich and poor countries. But a commitment to global cooperation can only be achieved by weakening the appeal of economic nationalism. The task will not be easy; failure will be disastrous.

I opened this book in 1933 at a time of serious geopolitical tension as the world headed for war – and quoted Paul Kennedy's optimistic assumption that in 2009 no one in the G20 was 'busy with revengeful, pre-war militaristic feelings'. Alas, the same cannot be said in 2023, when divisions over the war in Ukraine have weakened G20's ability to resolve global economic issues. As far as global economic government is concerned, the hope is that neo-liberalism and hyper-globalization can be replaced by 'shallow multilateralism' and avoid a turn to populism and economic nationalism. New ideas and approaches are being debated just as in the 1930s and 1970s. The status quo might survive, as it largely did after the global financial crisis, with a repeat of economic instability and inequality that will lead to further political and social unrest. Far better would be a fundamental change in our 'international but individualistic capitalism' to rectify serious economic and social problems, and to create a new inclusive capitalism and more pragmatic global economic government. Destructive conflict must be avoided at a time when cooperation is needed to deal with the global commons of disease, environment and climate change. A better outcome would be engagement through a robust application of rules backed by sanctions. There is one prediction that can safely be made. In the next half century, the balance of power will shift to Asia in general and China in particular, and the future of the world will be decided in Beijing as well as Washington and Brussels. What that world will look like is a matter of radical uncertainty.

List of Illustrations

1. Governor Franklin D. Roosevelt during his presidential campaign trip to West Virginia, October 1932. Photograph: Bettmann/Getty Images.
2. Ramsay MacDonald addresses the World Monetary and Economic Conference, 12 June 1933. Photograph: Sueddeutsche Zeitung Photo/Alamy.
3. Hjalmar Schacht, president of the Reichsbank, with Adolf Hitler, 5 May 1934. Photograph: Deutsches Historisches Museum, Berlin.
4. Russian peasants who were to work on new collective farms, Soviet Union, January 1930. Photograph: Paul Popper/Popperfoto/Getty Images.
5. Lend Lease war materials, 1941–44. Photograph: Everett Collection Inc./Alamy.
6. Harry Dexter White and John Maynard Keynes at the inaugural meeting of the International Monetary Fund's Board of Governors in Savannah, Georgia, 8 March 1946. Photograph: Wikimedia Commons.
7. Food stamps publicity photograph. Photograph: Franklin Delano Roosevelt Library Public Domain Photographs/Wikimedia Commons.
8. The United Nations Monetary and Financial Conference in Bretton Woods, 4 July 1944. Photograph: Bettmann/Getty Images.
9. Three women help to clear rubble at the Krupps works in Essen, 1946. Photograph: Popperfoto/Getty Images.
10. Will Clayton signing the Havana Charter of the International Trade Organization, 24 March 1948. Photograph: United Nations Photo Library.
11. Dean Acheson and Paul Hoffman present to George Marshall a large bound report on the operation of the Marshall Plan on its second anniversary, 3 April 1950. Photograph: Everett Collection Historical/Alamy.

12. David Lilienthal stands in front of the Wilson Dam in Colbert County, Alabama, 1934. Photograph: Alabama Department of Archives and History.

13. Prime Minister Pandit Jawaharlal Nehru of India, President Kwame Nkrumah of Ghana, President Gamal Abdel Nasser of the United Arab Republic, President Sukarno of Indonesia and President Josip Broz Tito of Yugoslavia, New York, September 1960. Photograph: Bettmann/Getty Images.

14. President John F. Kennedy meets with the president of the Commission of the European Economic Community Dr Walter Hallstein, Oval Office, White House, 12 April 1962. Photograph: Gibson Moss/ Alamy.

15. President Lyndon B. Johnson and Walter Rostow during the announcement of a halt of bombing in North Vietnam, October 1968. Photograph: Bettmann/Getty Images.

16. Robert Triffin of Yale University lecturing on the international monetary system in the late 1960s. Photograph: Wikimedia Commons.

17. President Richard Nixon and Treasury Secretary John Connally at Camp David, 15 August 1971. Photograph: Richard Nixon Presidential Library and Museum.

18. Paul Volcker, George Shultz and Arthur Burns, Paris, 16 March 1973. Photograph: Keystone Press/Alamy.

19. Norman Borlaug and trainees in the fields of the International Center for Maize and Wheat Improvement, Sonora, Mexico, April 1962. Photograph: CIMMYT.

20. President Ronald Reagan gives a televised Address to the Nation from the Oval Office on tax reduction legislation, 27 July 1981. Photograph: Ronald Reagan Presidential Library.

21. A member of staff of Seoulbank protests against the intervention of the IMF, 2 December 1997. Photograph: Choo Youn-Kong/AFP/ Getty Images.

22. Demonstrators blocking the city streets on the opening day of the WTO conference, Seattle, 1999. Photograph: Robert Sorbo/Sygma/ Getty Images.

23. Deng Xiaoping greets Mikhail Gorbachev in the Great Hall of the People in Beijing, May 1989. Photograph: Edward Nachtrieb/Alamy.

24. Valéry Giscard d'Estaing and Helmut Schmidt at a European summit in Brussels, December 1977. Photograph: Bernard Charlon/Gamma-Rapho/Getty.

25. Leaders of the G20 at the start of the summit chaired by Gordon Brown in London, 2 April 2009. Photograph: Crown Flickr.

26. A rally against TTIP, Berlin, 10 October 2015. Photograph: EPA Joerg Carstensen.

27. International Monetary Fund director Christine Lagarde speaks with Nigeria's minister of finance Ngozi Okonjo-Iweala, Lagos, 20 December 2011. Photograph: Reuters/Akintunde Akinleye/Alamy.

Notes

INTRODUCTION

1. *Daily Telegraph*, 30 Jan. 2009; Simon Robinson and Catherine Meyer, 'Gordon Brown: sometimes a crisis forces change', *Time*, 25 March 2009.   2. Andrew Ward, 'Can Obama make the difference?', *Financial Times*, 2 April 2009.   3. Steve Le Vine, 'Obama and the G20: is it 1933 all over again?', Bloomberg Businessweek, 30 March 2009.   4. Philip Stephens, 'Summit success reflects a different global landscape', *Financial Times*, 3 April 2009.   5. Eric Helleiner, 'A Bretton Woods moment? The 2007–2008 crisis and the future of global governance', *International Affairs* 86 (2010), 620.   6. John Maynard Keynes, *The Economic Consequences of the Peace* (London, 1919), 9–10.   7. This is the Mundell–Fleming model: Robert A. Mundell, 'The monetary dynamics of international adjustments under fixed and flexible exchange rates', *Quarterly Journal of Economics* 74 (1960), *idem*, 'Capital mobility and stabilization policy under fixed and flexible exchange rates', *Canadian Journal of Economic and Political Science* 29 (1963) and J. Marcus Fleming, 'Domestic financial policies under fixed and floating exchange rates', IMF Staff Papers 9, 1962; M. Obstfeld and A. M. Taylor, *Global Capital Markets: Integration, Crisis and Growth* (Cambridge, 2004), 29–33; Maurice Obstfeld, Jay Shambaugh and Alan Taylor, 'The trilemma in history: trade-offs among currency exchange rates, monetary policies, and capital mobility', *Review of Economics and Statistics* 87 (2005), 423–38; Michael Klein and Jay Shambaugh, 'Rounding the corners of the policy trilemma: source of monetary policy autonomy', NBER Working Paper 19461, Sept. 2013.   8. Martin Daunton, *Royal Mail: The Post Office since 1840* (London, 1985), 149–50; Francis Lyall, *International Communications: The International Telecommunication Union and the Universal Postal Union* (Farnham, 2011).   9. Kevin O'Rourke and Jeffrey Williamson, *Globalization and History: The Evolution of the Nineteenth-Century Atlantic Economy* (Cambridge, MA, 1999), 14–15, 93–4, 119–20, 145, 165–6, 286–7.   10. Donald Sassoon, *The Anxious Triumph: A Global History of Capitalism, 1860–1914* (London, 2019); Harold James, *The End of Globalization: Lessons from the Great Depression* (Cambridge, MA, and London, 2001), 4–5, 13.   11. Patricia Clavin, *Securing the World Economy: The Reinvention of the League of Nations, 1920–1946* (Oxford, 2013); Jamie Martin, *The Meddlers: Sovereignty, Empire and the Birth of Global Economic Governance* (Cambridge, MA, 2022); Madeleine Lynch Dungy, *Order and Rivalry: Rewriting the Rules of International Trade After the First World War* (Cambridge, 2023).   12. See Dungy, *Order and Rivalry*, for a discussion of regionalism.   13. Dani Rodrik, *The Globalization Paradox: Democracy and the Future of the World Economy* (New York, 2011), xvi–xvii; John G. Ruggie, 'International regimes, transactions and change: embedded liberalism in the postwar economic order', *International Organization* 36 (1982).   14. Arturo Escobar, *Encountering Development: The Making and Unmaking of the Third World* (Princeton, NJ, 1995), 155, 171–2, 180.   15. Rodrik, *Globalization Paradox*, xvii–xviii.   16. Garrett Hardin, 'The tragedy of the commons', *Science* 162 (1968), 1243–8; Elinor Ostrom, *Governing the Commons: The Evolution of Institutions for Collective Action* (Cambridge, 1990).   17. WTO, *World Trade Report 2009: Trade Policy Commitments and Contingency Measures*, 19–45.   18. Rodrik, *The Globalization Paradox*, xviii–xix.   19. Robert D. Putnam, 'Diplomacy and

domestic politics: the logic of two-level games', *International Organization* 42 (1988), 427–60. 20. Charles Kindleberger, *The World in Depression, 1829–1939* (London, 1973); *idem*, 'Dominance and leadership in the international economy: exploitation, public goods and free-riders', *International Studies Quarterly* 25 (1981), 247–8, 251–3. 21. Barry Eichengreen, 'Hegemonic stability theories of the international monetary system', in Richard N. Cooper, Barry Eichengreen, C. Randall Henning, Gerald Holtham and Robert D. Putnam, eds., *Can Nations Agree? Issues in International Economic Cooperation* (Washington, DC, 1989); Robert Keohane, 'The theory of hegemonic stability and changes in international economic regimes, 1967–77', in Ole R. Holsti, Randolph M. Siverson and Alexander L. George, eds., *Changes in the International System* (Boulder, CO, 1980); Robert Keohane, *After Hegemony: Cooperation and Discord in the World Political Economy* (Princeton, NJ, 1984); G. John Ikenberry, 'Rethinking the origins of American hegemony', *Political Science Quarterly* 104 (1989), 376. 22. Mark Mazower, *Governing the World: The History of an Idea* (London, 2012), xiii–xvii. 23. Amrita Narlikar, 'Introduction', in Amrita Narlikar, ed., *Deadlocks in Multilateral Negotiations: Causes and Solutions* (Cambridge, 2010), 7–11.

1. 'THE ESTABLISHMENT OF A SOUND NATIONAL ECONOMY'

1. Historical Statistics of the United States, Millennial Edition Online, Da7192, Da757. 2. Brian Mitchell and Phyllis Deane, *Abstract of British Historical Statistics* (Cambridge, 1962), 496. 3. Historical Statistics of the US, Dd494; Brian Mitchell, *European Historical Statistics* (Cambridge, 1979), 68–9, 181; Stanley Lebergott, *Manpower in Economic Growth* (New York, 1964), 512. 4. Tobias Straumann, *1931: Debt, Crisis, and the Rise of Hitler* (Oxford, 2019), v–vi. 5. Richard Overy, *Blood and Ruins: The Great Imperial War, 1931–45* (London, 2021), 32–3; Paul Jankowski, *All Against All: The Long Winter of 1933 and the Origins of the Second World War* (London, 2020). 6. 'Inaugural Address', 4 March 1933, online in Gerhard Peters and John T. Woolley, *The American Presidency Project*. 7. Adam Tooze, *The Deluge: The Great War, America and the Remaking of the Global Order, 1916–31* (London, 2014), 4–5, 9, 10, 15–16, 20–21, 26–7, 28–9, 334, 349–50; Marc-William Palen, The 'Conspiracy of Free Trade': The Anglo-American Struggle over Empire and Economic Globalization, 1846–96* (Cambridge, 2016), xxix–xxxi, xxxv–xxxvi, 268–71, 274. 8. Warren F. Kimball, *The Juggler: Franklin Roosevelt as Wartime Leader* (Princeton, NJ, 1991), 187. 9. Republican platform of 1932, Peters and Woolley, *American Presidency Project*. 10. David Burner, 'Smith, Alfred E.', *American National Biography*; Francis Bowes Sayre, *The Way Forward; The American Trade Agreements Program* (New York, 1939), 1, 37–9. 11. Platform adopted by the Democratic National Convention, 27 June 1932, Peters and Woolley, *American Presidency Project*. 12. Rexford G. Tugwell, *The Brains Trust* (New York, 1968), 194–7, 378–99, 411, 475–6; Raymond A. Moley, *After Seven Years* (New York and London, 1939), 112, 196. 13. *The Diary of Rexford G. Tugwell: The New Deal, 1932–35*, ed. Michael Vincent Namorato (New York, 1992), 296. 14. Tugwell, *Brains Trust*, 49, 76; Jankowski, *All Against All*, 112–13. 15. Robert Skidelsky, *John Maynard Keynes: Fighting for Britain, 1937–46* (London, 2000), 101; see also Robert L. Beisner, *Dean Acheson: A Life in the Cold War* (Oxford, 2006), 15. 16. Richard Hofstadter, *The American Political Tradition and the Men Who Made It* (New York, 1948), 311. 17. Kimball, *Juggler*, 4, 7. 18. Democratic platform, 1932. 19. 'The forgotten man', 7 April 1932, Peters and Woolley, *American Presidency Project*; Moley, *After Seven Years*, 23–4; Tugwell, *Diary*, 291–2; see also Tugwell's *Industry's Coming of Age* (New York, 1927) and his *The Industrial Discipline and the Governmental Arts* (New York, 1929). 20. Eric Rauchway, *The Money Makers: How Roosevelt and Keynes Ended the Depression, Defeated Fascism and Secured a Prosperous Peace* (New York, 2015), 31. 21. Ira Katznelson, *Fear Itself: The New Deal and the Origins of Our Time* (New York, 2013), 30, 37–8, 48, 54, 117, 118–19, 121, 123–4. 22. Sayre, *The Way Forward*, 42–4; World Trade Organization, *The WTO Agreements* (Cambridge, 2017), 19–20. 23. Harry S. Truman Library and Museum, Oral History Interview with John M. Leddy, at http://trumanlibrary

.gov/oralhist/leddyj.htm; Harry C. Hawkins, *Commercial Treaties and Agreements: Principles and Practice* (New York, 1951), 61–8, 97–107; Patricia Clavin and Madeleine Dungy, 'Trade, law and the global order of 1919', *Diplomatic History* 44 (2020), 554–79. **24.** Peter T. Marsh, *Bargaining on Europe: Britain and the First Common Market, 1860–1892* (New Haven, CT, and London, 1999). **25.** E. H. H. Green, *The Crisis of Conservatism: The Politics, Economics and Ideology of the British Conservative Party, 1880–1914* (London, 1995). **26.** Frank Trentmann, *Free Trade Nation: Commerce, Consumption, and Civil Society in Modern Britain* (Oxford, 2008), 1–2, 14–17; *idem*, 'Civil society, commerce and the "citizen-consumer": popular meanings of free trade in late nineteenth and early twentieth century Britain', in Trentmann, ed., *Paradoxes of Civil Society* (New York, 2000), 306. **27.** Martin Daunton, *Trusting Leviathan: The Politics of Taxation in Britain, 1799–1914* (Cambridge, 2001), chs. 4 and 11; Frank Trentmann, 'The resurrection and decomposition of Cobden in Britain and the West: an essay in the politics of reputation', in Anthony Howe, ed., *Rethinking Nineteenth-Century Liberalism: Richard Cobden Bicentenary Essays* (Aldershot, 2006), 264–68. **28.** Trentmann, *Free Trade Nation*, 241–84, 298–300; J. A. Hobson, *Wealth and Life: A Study in Values* (London, 1930), 401; Jamie Martin, *The Meddlers: Sovereignty, Empire, and the Birth of Global Economic Governance* (Cambridge, MA, 2022), ch. 1. **29.** Martin, *Meddlers*, 44–62; Jean Monnet, *Memoirs*, English edn (New York, 1978), 54–5, 62–8, 71–5, 78–9; Frederic Fransen, *The Supranational Politics of Jean Monnet: Ideas and Origins of the European Community* (Westport, CT, 2011); Margaret Macmillan, *Peacemakers: The Paris Peace Conference of 1919 and its Attempt to End War* (London, 2001), 194; Nicholas Mulder, *The Economic Weapon: The Rise of Sanctions as a Tool of Modern War* (New Haven, CT, and London, 2022), 27–108. **30.** Madeleine Lynch Dungy, *Order and Rivalry: Rewriting the Rules of International Trade After the First World War* (Cambridge, 2023) for a detailed discussion; Conan Fischer, *A Vision of Europe: Franco-German Relations during the Great Depression* (Oxford, 2017), 56–84. **31.** Patricia Clavin, *Securing the World Economy: The Reinvention of the League of Nations, 1920–46* (Oxford, 2013), 42–4; Tooze, *The Deluge*, 274; Madeleine Lynch Dungy, 'Writing multilateral trade rules in the League of Nations', *Contemporary European History* 70 (2021); W. Leslie Runciman, 'The world economic conference at Geneva', *Economic Journal* 37 (1927), 465–72. **32.** Anne Orde, 'The origins of the German–Austrian customs union affair of 1931', *Central European History* 13 (1980), 36–7, 39–40, 46–8, 57–8; Robert Boyce, *The Great Interwar Crisis and the Collapse of Globalization* (Basingstoke, 2009), 286–292, 293; Madeleine Dungy, 'Writing multilateral trade rules in the League of Nations', *Contemporary European History* 30 (2021), 60–75; Madeleine Dungy and Patricia Clavin, 'Trade, law and the global order of 1919', *Diplomatic History*, 444 (2020), 554–79; Straumann, *1931*, 128–9, 199. **33.** Douglas A. Irwin, *Peddling Protectionism: Smoot–Hawley and the Great Depression* (Princeton, NJ, 2011), 2, 4, 186. **34.** Chad Brown and Eva Zhang, 'Trump's 2019 protection could push China back to Smoot–Hawley tariff levels', Peterson Institute of International Economics, 14 May 2019; Robert J. Samuelson, 'The ghost of Smoot–Hawley seems to haunt Trump', *Washington Post*, 27 June 2018. **35.** For example, Herbert Hoover, *The Future of Our Foreign Trade* (Washington, DC, 1926); Republican party platform of 1928, Peters and Woolley, *American Presidency Project*; Frank W. Fetter, 'Congressional tariff theory', *American Economic Review* 23 (1933), 415. **36.** Fetter, 'Congressional tariff theory', 424. **37.** Douglas A. Irwin and Randall S. Kroszner, 'Log-rolling and economic interests in the passage of the Smoot–Hawley tariff', *Carnegie-Rochester Conference Series on Public Policy* 45 (1996), 175, 180, 192–3; Patrick J. Maney, *'Young Bob' La Follette: A Biography of Robert M. La Follette Jr., 1895–1953* (Columbia, MS, 1978), 75; Colleen M. Callahan, Judith A. McDonald and Anthony Patrick O'Brien, 'Who voted for Smoot–Hawley?', *Journal of Economic History* 54 (1994); Barry Eichengreen, 'The political economy of the Smoot–Hawley tariff', *Research in Economic History* 12 (1989); E. E. Schattschneider, *Politics, Pressures and the Tariff: A Study of Free Private Enterprise in Pressure Politics, as shown in the 1929–30 Revisions of the Tariff* (New York, 1935). **38.** Herbert Hoover, *The Memoirs of Herbert Hoover: The Cabinet and the Presidency, 1920–1933* (New York, 1952), 292–3; Irwin, *Peddling Protectionism*, 40–41. **39.** Irwin, *Peddling Protectionism*, 142. **40.** Cordell Hull, *The Memoirs of Cordell Hull*, vol. I

(New York, 1948), 81.   **41.** Ibid., 840; Michael A. Butler, *Cautious Visionary: Cordell Hull and Trade Reform, 1933–37* (Kent, OH, 1998), 2, 48–50, 58–61, 70–71.   **42.** J. Morton Blum, *From the Morgenthau Diaries: I, Years of Crisis, 1923–1938* (Boston, MA, 1959), 452–3; see also H. L. Ickes, *The Secret Diary of Harold L. Ickes, III: The Lowering Clouds, 1939–1941* (New York, 1954), 218–19.   **43.** Hull, *Memoirs*, I, 364.   **44.** Herbert Feis, *1933: Characters and Crisis* (Boston, MA, 1966), 99; Hull, *Memoirs*, I, 364.   **45.** Tooze, *The Deluge*, 324–6; Katznelson, *Fear Itself*, 9, 15–16, 18, 21, 23, 24, 25, 95, 127–9, 143, 145–6, 150–55, 161–4, 172–7, 182, 191–4, 233, 261, 265, 274, 280–81, 287–91, 370–72.   **46.** Joseph M. Jones, *Tariff Retaliation: Repercussions of the Hawley–Smoot Bill* (Philadelphia, PA, 1934); Frank Trentmann, 'The transformation of fiscal reform: reciprocity, modernization, and the fiscal debate within the business community in early twentieth-century Britain', *Historical Journal* 39 (1996), 1042–4; Forrest Capie, *Depression and Protectionism: Britain Between the Wars* (London, 1983), 55, 71–4.   **47.** Robert Skidelsky, *John Maynard Keynes: Economist as Saviour 1920–37* (London, 1992), 370–72, 374–6, 476–8.   **48.** Barry Eichengreen and Douglas A. Irwin, 'Trade blocs, currency blocs and the disintegration of world trade in the 1930s', NBER Working Paper 4445 (1993), 17, 23–5.   **49.** *Foreign Relations of the United States (FRUS): Diplomatic Papers, 1933, General*, vol. I (Washington, DC, 1950), doc. 426.   **50.** Chris Meissner, 'A new world order: explaining the international diffusion of the gold standard, 1870–1913', *Journal of International Economics* 66 (2005), 385–406; J. E. Lopez-Cordova and Chris Meissner, 'Exchange rate regimes and international trade: evidence from the classical gold standard era', *American Economic Review* 93 (2003), 344–53; Michael Bordo and Hugh Rockoff, 'The gold standard as a "Good Housekeeping Seal of Approval"', *Journal of Economic History* 56 (1996), 389–428.   **51.** P. J. Grigg, *Prejudice and Judgement* (London, 1948), 183; Martin Daunton, 'Britain and globalisation since 1850: I, Creating a global order, 1850–1914', *Transactions of the Royal Historical Society*, 6th ser., 16 (2006), 13–14.   **52.** Barry Eichengreen, *Golden Fetters: The Gold Standard and the Great Depression, 1919–1939* (New York and Oxford, 1992), xi, 5–12; Marc Flandreau, 'Central bank cooperation in historical perspective: a sceptical view', *Economic History Review* 50 (1997), 735–63.   **53.** Daunton, 'Britain and globalisation: Creating a global order', 26–7; Gretchen Ritter, *Goldbugs and Greenbacks: The Antimonopoly Tradition and the Politics of Finance in America, 1865–1896* (Cambridge, 1997); Lawrence Goodwyn, *Democratic Promise: The Populist Moment in America* (Oxford, 1976).   **54.** M. D. Bordo and A. J. Schwartz, 'The operation of the specie standard: evidence for core and periphery countries, 1880–1910', in J. B. de Macedo, B. Eichengreen and J. Reiss, eds., *Currency Convertibility: The Gold Standard and Beyond* (London, 1996), 12.   **55.** Skidelsky, *Keynes: Economist as Saviour*, 193, 200; Donald Moggridge, *British Monetary Policy, 1924–32: The Norman Conquest of $4.86* (Cambridge, 1972); Philip Williamson, *National Crisis and National Government: British Politics, the Economy and Empire, 1926–32* (Cambridge, 1992), 74.   **56.** Skidelsky, *Keynes: Economist as Saviour*, 202–6.   **57.** Martin Daunton, 'Britain and globalisation since 1850: II, The rise of insular capitalism, 1914–39', *Transactions of the Royal Historical Society*, 6th ser., 17 (2007), 10–11, 22–9.   **58.** Sidney Pollard, *Britain's Prime and Britain's Decline: The British Economy, 1870–1914* (London, 1989), 61.   **59.** Avner Offer, 'Empire and social reform: British overseas investment and domestic politics, 1908–1914', *Historical Journal* 26 (1983), 119–38; J. A. Hobson, *Imperialism: A Study* (London, 1902), 134, 147–8.   **60.** Daunton, 'Britain and globalisation: Insular capitalism', 14–18.   **61.** Philip Williamson, 'A bankers' ramp? Financiers and the British political crisis of August 1931', *English Historical Review* 99 (1984), 770–806.   **62.** E. Nevin, *The Mechanism of Cheap Money: A Study of British Monetary Policy 1931–39* (Cardiff, 1955); Stephen N. Broadberry, 'Cheap money and the housing boom in interwar Britain', *Manchester School of Economic and Social Studies* 55 (1987), 383; S. Bowden, 'The consumer durables revolution in England 1932–38', *Explorations in Economic History* 25 (1988), 52.   **63.** Barry Eichengreen and Jeffrey Sachs, 'Exchange rates and economic recovery in the 1930s', *Journal of Economic History* 45 (1985), 928, 939, 946; Kenneth Mouré, *The Gold Standard Illusion: France, the Bank of France, and the International Gold Standard, 1914–1939* (Oxford, 2002), 10, 69, 70–71, 102–3, 105, 129, 181, 260–62.   **64.** Clavin, *Securing the World Economy*, 16–24.   **65.** Ibid., 51–71; P. Clavin and

J.-W. Wessels, 'Another golden idol? The League of Nations' Gold Delegation and the Great Depression, 1929–1932', *International History Review* 26 (2004); Douglas A. Irwin, 'Anticipating the Great Depression? Gustav Cassel's analysis of the interwar gold standard', NBER Working Paper 1759 (2011). 66. Clavin, *Securing the World Economy*, 51–78. 67. Rauchway, *The Money Makers*, 10–16; Robert Skidelsky, *John Maynard Keynes: Hopes Betrayed, 1883–1920* (London, 1983), 374–5, 378. 68. J. M. Keynes, *The Economic Consequences of the Peace* (London, 1919), 11, 14, 211, 264; Skidelsky, *Keynes: Hopes Betrayed*, 376–400; Skidelsky, *Keynes: Economist as Saviour*, 20–21, 31–4. 69. Bernard Baruch, *The Making of the Reparation and Economic Sectors of the Treaty* (New York, 1920); Skidelsky, *Keynes: Hopes Betrayed*, 395. 70. Skidelsky, *Keynes: Hopes Betrayed*, 396–400 and *Economist as Saviour*, 31–4; Étienne Mantoux, *The Carthaginian Peace: Or, the Economic Consequences of Mr Keynes* (Oxford, 1946); Tooze, *The Deluge*, ch. 15. 71. Tooze, *The Deluge*, 302. 72. Clavin, *Securing the World Economy*, 78–81; Straumann, *1931*, v–vi, xxi–xxiv, 9, 10, 30–34, 52, 127, 135, 161, 195, 196; Harold James, 'The causes of the German banking crisis of 1931', *Économic History Review* 37 (1994), 68–87. 73. Clavin, *Securing the World Economy*, 82–3, 99.

2. 'BARREN HARVEST'

1. Patricia Clavin, *Securing the World Economy: The Reinvention of the League of Nations, 1920–46* (Oxford, 2013), 34, 64, 75. 2. Ibid., 84–6, 93, 96; Gianni Toniolo, *Central Bank Cooperation at the Bank for International Settlements, 1930–1973* (Cambridge, 2005), ch. 5. 3. Clavin, *Securing the World Economy*, 89–90; idem, *The Failure of Economic Diplomacy: Britain, Germany, France and the United States, 1931–36* (Basingstoke, 1996), 196; *Foreign Relations of the United States (FRUS): Diplomatic Papers, 1933, General*, vol. I (Washington, DC, 1950), doc. 336. 4. Clavin, *Securing the World Economy*, 91–2; dimes .rockarch.org/agents/KA3hUipgg556JTjVaHMKBi; Stephen V. O. Clarke, 'John Henry Williams 1887–1980', *The New Palgrave: A Dictionary of Economics*, ed. John Eatwell, Murray Milgate and Peter Newman, 1987 online edition. 5. Toniolo, *Central Bank Cooperation*, 137, 139; Kenneth Mouré, *The Gold Standard Illusion: France, the Bank of France, and the International Gold Standard, 1914–1939* (Oxford, 2002), 180–220; Barry Eichengreen and Marc Uzan, 'The 1933 World Economic Conference as an instance of failed economic cooperation', Department of Economics, University of California, Berkeley, 1990. 6. Avner Offer and Gabriel Söderberg, *The Nobel Factor: The Prize in Economics, Social Democracy and the Market Turn* (Princeton, NJ, 2017), 84–7; Erin E. Jacobsson, *A Life for Sound Money: Per Jacobsson – His Biography* (Oxford, 1979), 40–41, 221; Toniolo, *Central Bank Cooperation*, 138–9, 141–2. 7. *FRUS 1933*, I, doc. 342; The National Archives (TNA), CAB24/237, CP18(33), Report on the second meeting of the preparatory committee for the World Economic Conference, F. W. Leith-Ross and F. Phillips, 23 Jan 1933; *The Monetary and Economic Conference (London 1933): An Account of the Preparatory Work for the Conference and An Outline of the Previous Activities of the Economic and Financial Organisation of the League of Nations* (Geneva, 1933). 8. Clavin, *Securing the World Economy*, 99; Toniolo, *Central Bank Cooperation*, 140–44. 9. Sebastian Edwards, *American Default: The Untold Story of FDR, the Supreme Court, and the Battle over Gold* (Princeton, NJ, 2018), ix–xi, 39, 42, 53, 58–9; Eric Rauchway, *The Money Makers: How Roosevelt and Keynes Ended the Depression, Defeated Fascism and Secured a Prosperous Peace* (New York, 2015), 35–8, 63. 10. Alan Brinkley, 'Coughlin, Charles Edward', *American National Biography*; Ronald H. Carpenter, *Father Charles E. Coughlin: Surrogate Spokesman for the Disaffected* (Westport, CT, 1998), 39. 11. Edwards, *American Default*, 47, 49, 51; Walter Lippmann, *Interpretations, 1933–1935* (New York, 1936), 55; Rauchway, *The Money Makers*, 55. 12. Thomas Clarkin, 'Thomas, Elmer', *American National Biography*; Edwards, *American Default*, 52–3, 57, 60; Liaquat Ahamed, *Lords of Finance: The Bankers Who Broke the World* (New York, 2009), 461–2; Allan H. Meltzer, *A History of the Federal Reserve vol. I, 1913–1951* (Chicago, 2001), 428. 13. Raymond A. Moley, *After Seven Years* (New York and London,

1939), 135. 14. Rauchway, *The Money Makers*, 64–6. 15. William J. Barber, *From New Era to New Deal: Herbert Hoover, the Economists, and American Economic Policy, 1921–1933* (Cambridge, 1985), 55–8; Alan H. Gleason, 'Foster and Catchings: a reappraisal', *Journal of Political Economy* 67 (1959); Elspeth Allgoewer, 'Under-consumptionist theories and Keynesian economics: interpretations of the Great Depression', University of St Gallen Discussion Paper 2002-14, May 2002, 20–27; Rauchway, *The Money Makers*, xx–xxiii. 16. Barber, *From New Era to New Deal*, 58–60, 160–62; Irving Fisher, *Booms and Depressions: Some First Principles* (New York, 1932); *idem*, 'The debt-deflation theory of great depressions', *Econometrica* 1 (1933), 337–57. 17. George F. Warren and Frank A. Pearson, *Wholesale Prices for 213 Years, 1720–1932* (Ithaca, NY, 1932); *idem*, *Gold and Prices* (New York, 1935); Rauchway, *The Money Makers*, 20–21, 27–8. 18. Rauchway, *The Money Makers*, 29, 51. 19. Jeannette P. Nichols, 'Roosevelt's monetary diplomacy in 1933', *American Historical Review* 56 (1951), 300–302. 20. Clavin, *Failure of Economic Diplomacy*, 105–9. 21. *The Diary of Rexford G. Tugwell: The New Deal, 1932–35*, ed. Michael Vincent Namorato (New York, 1992), 352, 379; Moley, *After Seven Years*, 115–16, 217–19; Michael A. Butler, *Cautious Visionary: Cordell Hull and Trade Reform, 1933–37* (Kent, OH, 1998), 30–31, 33–41, 43–5, 69; Herbert Feis, *1933: Characters and Crisis* (Boston, MA, 1966), 173–4; Rauchway, *The Money Makers*, 68; Ahamed, *Lords of Finance*, 467–8. 22. H. G. Wells, *The Shape of Things to Come: The Ultimate Revolution* (London, 1933), 129–31. 23. Moley, *After Seven Years*, 217. 24. Paul Jankowski, *All Against All: The Long Winter of 1933 and the Origins of the Second World War* (London, 2020), 333–4. 25. Tugwell, *Diary*, 352. 26. Butler, *Cautious Visionary*, 31, 69. 27. Feis, *1933*, 99, 101. 28. Butler, *Cautious Visionary*, 43; Moley, *After Seven Years*, 224–9; Tugwell, *Diary*, 86. 29. 'Foreign news: London economic conference', *Time*, 29 June 1933; Nichols, 'Roosevelt's monetary diplomacy', 312. 30. *FRUS 1933*, I, docs. 343, 361. 31. Tugwell, *Diary*, 336; Adam Tooze, *The Deluge: The Great War, America and the Remaking of the Global Order, 1916–31* (London, 2014), 506–7. 32. *FRUS 1933*, I, doc. 426. 33. Rauchway, *The Money Makers*, 69; *The Times*, 13, 14, 15 June 1933; Clavin, *Securing the World Economy*, 117; Tooze, *The Deluge*, 506; Philip Scranton, 'How the US scuttled the 1933 World Economic Conference', Bloomberg View, 17 June 2013. 34. *FRUS 1933*, I, docs. 343, 361; *The Times*, 15 June 1933. 35. *The Times*, 15 June 1933; Wells, *Shape of Things*, 131. 36. Feis, *1933*, 181. 37. Ibid., 178. 38. Tugwell, *Diary*, 301. 39. Feis, *1933*, 102. 40. Moley, *After Seven Years*, 238–41. 41. Raymond Moley, *The First New Deal* (New York, 1966), 467–8. 42. Cordell Hull, *The Memoirs of Cordell Hull*, vol. I (New York, 1948), 257. 43. *The Times*, 14 June 1933; Jankowski, *All Against All*, 337, 343, 347; Tooze, *The Deluge*, 506; Clavin, *Failure of Economic Diplomacy*, 101–3, 121–3, 138–41, 196–7; Eichengreen and Uzan, '1933 World Economic Conference'. 44. Moley, *After Seven Years*, 215–17, 228–32, 235–6, 249, 255–6; Toniolo, *Central Bank Cooperation*, 145–6; Clavin, *Securing the World Economy*, 118–19; Tugwell, *Diary*, 373–5; Rauchway, *The Money Makers*, 71; Nichols, 'Roosevelt's monetary diplomacy', 312–15; Ahamed, *Lords of Finance*, 469–70; *FRUS 1933*, I, doc. 473. 45. *FRUS 1933*, I, doc. 498; F. D. Roosevelt, wireless to the London conference, 3 July 1933, online in Gerhard Peters and John T. Woolley, *The American Presidency Project*; J. Morton Blum, *From the Morgenthau Diaries: I, Years of Crisis, 1923–1938* (Boston, MA, 1959), 64–5; Moley, *After Seven Years*, 259–63. 46. *FRUS 1933*, I, doc. 517. 47. Ahamed, *Lords of Finance*, 471; Rauchway, *The Money Makers*, 71; *The Collected Writings of John Maynard Keynes, Vol. 21, Activities 1932–39*, ed. D. Moggridge (Cambridge, 1982), 273–7; Robert Skidelsky, *John Maynard Keynes: Economist as Saviour 1920–37* (London, 1992), 480. 48. Moley, *After Seven Years*, 263. 49. Moley, *First New Deal*, 474. 50. *FRUS 1933*, I, doc. 563. 51. Barry Eichengreen and Douglas A. Irwin, 'Trade blocs, currency blocs and the disintegration of world trade in the 1930s', NBER Working Paper 4445 (1993), 17, 23–5; Toniolo, *Central Bank Cooperation*, 146–7; Clavin, *Failure of Economic Diplomacy*, 135. 52. Tooze, *The Deluge*, 506–7; David James Gill, *The Long Shadow of Default: Britain's Unpaid War Debts to the United States* (New Haven, CT, 2022), 74, 99–125; Office of the Historian, 'Milestones in the history of US foreign relations: the Neutrality Acts, 1930s'. 53. Elliot A. Rosen, 'Moley, Raymond', *American National Biography*; Moley, *After*

Seven Years, 267–8, 270–77; Moley, *First New Deal*, xiii, 499–507.   54. Andrew R. Heinze, 'Warburg, James Paul', *American National Biography*; James Warburg, *The Money Muddle: An Essay* (New York, 1934), 226; *idem*, *It's Up to Us* (New York, 1934); *idem*, *Still Hell Bent* (New York, 1936), 1; Rauchway, *The Money Makers*, 115–16.   55. Barber, *From New Era to New Deal*, 157–60.   56. Rauchway, *The Money Makers*, 80; Feis, *1933*, 280.   57. Executive Order 6261, Relating to the sale and export of gold recovered from natural deposits, 29 Aug. 1933; F. D. Roosevelt, fireside chat, 22 Oct. 1933, Peters and Woolley, *American Presidency Project*; Edwards, *American Default*, 102, 106, 107.   58. Feis, *1933*, 281; Rauchway, *The Money Makers*, 74–5, 80–89; Edwards, *American Default*, 107–11; J. Butkiewicz, 'The Reconstruction Finance Corporation, the gold standard and the banking panic of 1933', *Southern Economic Journal* 66 (1999), 271–93; *idem*, 'Reconstruction Finance Corporation', EH.net .Encyclopedia; Blum, *From the Morgenthau Diaries: Years of Crisis*, 66–8, 72–3.   59. Blum, *From the Morgenthau Diaries: Years of Crisis*, 70; Ahamed, *Lords of Finance*, 471–3.   60. Edwards, *American Default*, 112–15; Michele Alacevich, Pier Francesco Asso and Sebastiano Nerozzi, 'Harvard meets the crisis: the monetary theory and policy of Lauchlin B. Currie, Jacob Viner, John H. Williams and Harry D. White', *Journal of the History of Economic Thought* 37 (2015), 391; Sebastiano Nerozzi, 'From the Great Depression to Bretton Woods: Jacob Viner and international monetary stabilization, 1930–45', *European Journal of the History of Economic Thought* 18 (2011), 67.   61. Edwards, *American Default*, 64, 67, 70.   62. Ibid., 72, 75, 117, 126, 168–9.   63. Ibid., 136–46, 150–52, 172, 173, 175, 177, 178, 180, 182, 187; Blum, *From the Morgenthau Diaries: Years of Crisis*, 123–31; Gary Richardson, Alejandro Komai and Michael Gou, 'Gold Reserve Act of 1934', www.federalreservehistory .org/essays/gold-reserve-act.   64. Edwards, *American Default*, 115.   65. Rauchway, *The Money Makers*, 70–72, 92, 96, 269 n.72.   66. Ibid., 101–8.   67. Van L. Perkins, *Crisis in Agriculture: The Agricultural Adjustment Administration and the New Deal, 1933* (Berkeley, CA, 1969); Christiana M. Campbell, *The Farm Bureau and the New Deal: A Study in the Making of National Farm Policy 1933–40* (Urbana, IL, 1962); Richard S. Kirkendall, 'Commentary on the thought of Henry A. Wallace', *Agricultural History* 41 (1967), 139–42; *idem*, *Social Scientists and Farm Politics in the Age of Roosevelt* (Columbia, MO, 1966).   68. Lizabeth Cohen, *A Consumers' Republic: The Politics of Mass Consumption in Postwar America* (New York, 2003), 18–19, 24, 28–32, 34–5, 41; Meg Jacobs, *Pocketbook Politics: Economic Citizens in Twentieth-Century America* (Princeton, NJ, 2005), 3–10, 95–6, 104–15, 121–3, 128–30, 135; Kirkendall, 'Commentary', 140–41.   69. Jacobs, *Pocketbook Politics*, 99–104.   70. Jens Beckert, *Inherited Wealth* (Princeton, NJ, 2008), 188–92; Cohen, *A Consumers' Republic*, 54–6; Jacobs, *Pocketbook Politics*, 102, 135–7, 145, 147, 150, 169, 172.   71. Wells, *Shape of Things*, 132, 135.   72. Robert Self, ed., *The Neville Chamberlain Diary Letters*, vol. III: *The Heir Apparent, 1928–33* (Aldershot, 2002), 398.   73. 'Barren harvest', *The Economist*, 29 July 1933, 215.   74. *Collected Writings of Keynes*, 21, 281.   75. E. O. G. Shann, *Quotas or Stable Money: Three Essays on the Ottawa and London Conferences, 1932–33* (Sydney, 1933), 61–4.   76. Stephen Haggard, 'The institutional foundations of hegemony: explaining the Reciprocal Trade Agreements Act of 1934', *International Organisation* 42 (1988), 110.

3. 'BEGGAR MY NEIGHBOUR'

1. Adam Smith, *An Inquiry into the Nature and Causes of the Wealth of Nations*, ed. R. H. Campbell and A. S. Skinner, vol. 1 (Oxford, 1976), bk IV, ch. III, pt II, 493.   2. Eli Heckscher, *Mercantilism*, 2 vols., English trans. (London, 1935, 1936); *The Collected Writings of John Maynard Keynes, Vol. VII: The General Theory of Employment, Interest and Money* (Cambridge, 1973), 333–51.   3. Warren F. Kimball, *The Juggler: Franklin Roosevelt as Wartime Leader* (Princeton, NJ, 1991), 10, 13, 17–18, 187–9.   4. Cordell Hull, *The Memoirs of Cordell Hull*, vol. I (New York, 1948), chs. 23–25.   5. Walter LaFeber, *The American Age: United States Foreign Policy at Home and Abroad, Vol. II: Since 1896*, 2nd edn (New York, 1994), 376; Charles I. Bevans, ed., *Treaties and Other International Agreements of the United States*

of America, 1776–1949, vol. 6 (Washington, DC, 1971), 'Relations with Cuba', 22 May 1903, 1116–19; ibid., vol. 3 (Washington, DC, 1969), 'Inter-American conciliation' [Montevideo convention], 26 Dec. 1933, 161–2.   **6.** L. A. Perez, *Cuba under the Platt Amendment, 1902–1934* (Pittsburgh, PA, 1986); Jules R. Benjamin, 'The *Machadato* and Cuban nationalism, 1928–32', *Hispanic American Historical Review* 55 (1975), 69–91; T. F. O'Brien, *The Revolutionary Mission: American Enterprise in Latin America, 1900–1945* (New York, 1996); B. Wood, *The Making of the Good Neighbor Policy* (New York, 1961); Michael R. Anderson, 'The Shoup Missions to Cuba', in W. Elliot Brownlee, Eisaku Ide and Yasunori Fukagai, eds., *The Political Economy of Transnational Tax Reform* (New York, 2013), 86–109; Noel Maurer, *The Empire Trap: The Rise and Fall of US Intervention to Protect American Property Overseas, 1893–2013* (Princeton, NJ, 2013), 12–13, 22, 23, 55, 245–97; Kimball, *Juggler*, 123–4, 190; Roosevelt Inaugural Address, 4 March 1933, online in Gerhard Peters and John T. Woolley, *The American Presidency Project*.   **7.** Madeleine Lynch Dungy, *Order and Rivalry: Rewriting the Rules of International Trade After the First World War* (Cambridge, 2023), ch. 4 and conclusion.   **8.** Leo Pasvolsky, 'Most-favored-nation principle in the trade agreements program', *World Affairs* 98 (1935), 76–7.   **9.** Kimball, *Juggler*, 4; Hull, *Memoirs*, I, 370.   **10.** Stephen Haggard, 'The institutional foundations of hegemony: explaining the Reciprocal Trade Agreements Act of 1934', *International Organization* 42 (1988), 114–15.   **11.** Herbert Feis, *1933: Characters and Crisis* (Boston, MA, 1966), 264.   **12.** Karen E. Schnietz, 'The institutional foundation of US trade policy: revising explanations for the 1934 Reciprocal Trade Agreements Act', *Journal of Public Policy History* 12 (2000), 419; Haggard, 'Institutional foundations of hegemony', 101.   **13.** Schnietz, 'Institutional foundation', 417.   **14.** Douglas A. Irwin, *Peddling Protectionism: Smoot–Hawley and the Great Depression* (Princeton, NJ, 2011), 197.   **15.** Schnietz, 'Institutional foundation', 419–20; Haggard, 'Institutional foundations of hegemony', 111.   **16.** Ira Katznelson, *Fear Itself: The New Deal and the Origins of Our Time* (New York, 2013), 261, 264.   **17.** Schnietz, 'Institutional foundation', 422, 433.   **18.** Ibid., 429–37; Judith Goldstein, *Ideas, Interests and American Trade Policy* (Ithaca, NY, 1993), 137–54; Harry S. Truman Library and Museum, Oral History Interview with John M. Leddy, at http://trumanlibrary.gov/oralhist/leddyj.htm; Harry C. Hawkins, *Commercial Treaties and Agreements: Principles and Practice* (New York, 1951), 81–2.   **19.** Allen Treadway at https://history.house.gov/HistoricalHighlight /Detail/36918; Schnietz, 'Institutional foundation', 435; Haggard, 'Institutional foundations of hegemony', 117–19; Michael Gilligan, *Empowering Exporters: Reciprocity, Delegation and Collective Action in American Trade Policy* (Ann Arbor, MI, 1997), 135, 138; Karen E. Schnietz, 'The reaction of private interests to the 1934 Reciprocal Trade Agreements Act', *International Organization* 57 (2003), 213–33; Susanne Lohmann and Sharyn O'Halloran, 'Divided government and US trade policy: theory and evidence', *International Organization* 48 (1994), 595–632; Table 1.1.10, FRED economic data, Federal Reserve Bank of St Louis at www.Fred.stlouisfed.org.   **20.** Hull, *Memoirs*, I, 746–8.   **21.** Douglas A. Irwin and Randall S. Kroszner, 'Interests, institutions and ideology in securing policy change: the Republican conversion to trade liberalization after Smoot–Hawley', *Journal of Law and Economics* 42 (1999), 650, 665–6; Irwin, *Peddling Protectionism*, 201–2; Goldstein, *Ideas*, 163–7; Michael A. Bailey, Judith Goldstein and Barry R. Weingast, 'The institutional roots of American trade policy: politics, coalitions, and international trade', *World Politics* 49 (1997), 309–38.   **22.** Adam Tooze, *The Wages of Destruction: The Making and Breaking of the Nazi Economy* (London, 2006), 23; Amos E. Simpson, *Hjalmar Schacht in Perspective* (The Hague and Paris, 1969), 30–32, 179–81; Neil Forbes, *Doing Business with the Nazis: Britain's Economic and Financial Relations with Germany, 1931–1939* (London, 2000), 117.   **23.** Tooze, *Wages of Destruction*, chs. 2–3 for the general situation.   **24.** Ibid., 21–2, 41, 51, 76, 113–14.   **25.** Ibid., 69–70, 75, 78–84.   **26.** Ibid., 70–71, 80–85; Forbes, *Doing Business*, 86–91.   **27.** Tooze, *Wages of Destruction*, 106.   **28.** Ibid., 86–96.   **29.** Ibid., 108, 215–19; Gerhard Ritter, *The German Resistance: Carl Goerdeler's Struggle Against Tyranny* (New York, 1970), 25, 31–2; Peter Hoffmann, *Carl Goerdeler and the Jewish Question, 1933–1942* (Cambridge, 2011).   **30.** Tooze, *Wages of Destruction*, 219–24; Barry Eichengreen and Douglas A. Irwin, 'Trade blocs, currency blocs and the disintegration of world trade in the 1930s', NBER

Working Paper 4445 (1993). **31.** Tooze, *Wages of Destruction*, 217; Ritter, *German Resistance*, 35–6, 80–87, 131, 170–89, 203–5, 208–11, 215–17, 221–6, 237–45, 284–313. **32.** Tooze, *Wages of Destruction*, 217, 230–34; Simon Mee, *Central Bank Independence and the Legacy of the German Past* (Cambridge, 2019), 20, 33–5, 54–76, 82–8; Simpson, *Hjalmar Schacht*, 79; for Schacht's attempt at self-justification, see Hjalmar Schacht, *The Magic of Money*, English edn (London, 1967), 50, 58–60, 100–102, 106–8, 117–20. **33.** Michael A. Butler, *Cautious Visionary: Cordell Hull and Trade Reform, 1933–37* (Kent, OH, 1998), 105–8, 115–20. **34.** Arnold A. Offner, *American Appeasement: United States Foreign Policy and Germany, 1933–1938* (Cambridge, MA, 1969), 98–103. **35.** Forbes, *Doing Business*, 4, 11–12, 72, 81–2, 97–128, 137–8, 167–8, 207–9, 226–7; TNA, CAB 24/248, CP104(34), The future of Germany, 7 April 1934; George C. Peden, *British Rearmament and the Treasury, 1932–1939* (Edinburgh, 1979). **36.** *Foreign Relations of the United States (FRUS): Diplomatic Papers, 1936, General, The British Commonwealth*, vol. I (Washington, 1953), doc. 549; Hull, *Memoirs*, I, 522–3. **37.** *FRUS 1936*, I, docs. 513, 522. **38.** Martin Pugh, 'Runciman, Walter, first Viscount Runciman of Doxford (1870–1949)', *Oxford Dictionary of National Biography*; Arthur W. Schatz, 'The Anglo-American trade agreement and Cordell Hull's search for peace, 1934–1938', *Journal of American History* 57 (1970), 92–3. **39.** Hull, *Memoirs*, I, 524–6; Schatz, 'Anglo-American trade agreement', 95–7. **40.** Schatz, 'Anglo-American trade agreement', 97–8, 100–101. **41.** Sebastiano Nerozzi, 'From the Great Depression to Bretton Woods: Jacob Viner and international monetary stabilization, 1930–45', *European Journal of the History of Economic Thought* 18 (2011), 67–9. **42.** J. Morton Blum, *From the Morgenthau Diaries: I, Years of Crisis, 1923–1938* (Boston, MA, 1959), 131–3, 140–44; Stephen V. O. Clarke, 'Exchange rate stabilization in the mid-1930s: negotiating the Tripartite Agreement', *Princeton Studies in International Finance* 41 (1977), v, 5, 11–12. **43.** Blum, *Morgenthau Diaries: Years of Crisis*, 133; Clarke, 'Exchange rate stabilization', 15. **44.** Clarke, 'Exchange rate stabilization', 18–19. **45.** Ibid., 17–18. **46.** Blum, *Morgenthau Diaries: Years of Crisis*, 139–40; Clarke, 'Exchange rate stabilization', 15. **47.** Clarke, 'Exchange rate stabilization', 8, 20–21; Blum, *Morgenthau Diaries: Years of Crisis*, 134–8; Patricia Clavin, *Securing the World Economy: The Reinvention of the League of Nations, 1920–46* (Oxford, 2013), 155–8. **48.** *FRUS 1936*, I, doc. 369; Clavin, *Securing the World Economy*, 128–52. **49.** Eric Rauchway, *The Money Makers: How Roosevelt and Keynes Ended the Depression, Defeated Fascism and Secured a Prosperous Peace* (New York, 2015), 122–3; Gianni Toniolo, *Central Bank Cooperation at the Bank for International Settlements, 1930–1973* (Cambridge, 2005), 175–82; Kenneth Mouré, *The Gold Standard Illusion: France, the Bank of France, and the International Gold Standard, 1914–1939* (Oxford, 2002), 181, 209, 219–22, 226. **50.** Blum, *Morgenthau Diaries: Years of Crisis*, 145. **51.** Ibid., 140–44; Clarke, 'Exchange rate stabilization', 23. **52.** Clarke, 'Exchange rate stabilization', 24–5. **53.** *FRUS 1936*, I, docs. 440, 442; Blum, *Morgenthau Diaries: Years of Crisis*, 138, 147, 156–7; Clarke, 'Exchange rate stabilization', 25–31. **54.** *FRUS 1936*, I, docs. 443, 444, 446, 447, 448, 449, 450, 451, 452, 453; Blum, *Morgenthau Diaries: Years of Crisis*, 161–4, 166–8; Clarke, 'Exchange rate stabilization', 27–31, 37–9; Mouré, *Gold Standard Illusion*, 228; Max Harris, *Monetary War and Peace: London, Washington, Paris, and the Tripartite Agreement of 1936* (Cambridge, 2021), 6, 261; TNA, T160/685/2 Devaluation of the French franc, September 1936; T177/31, Devaluation of the French franc; T188/116, Exchange stabilization; T188/146, French devaluation: three power currency declaration; T168/211, French devaluation: international currency situation. **55.** Blum, *Morgenthau Diaries: Years of Crisis*, 166–7, 171. **56.** Rauchway, *The Money Makers*, 122–3. **57.** Harris, *Monetary War and Peace*, 233–8. **58.** *FRUS 1936*, I, docs. 454, 455; Blum, *Morgenthau Diaries: Years of Crisis*, 178–81; M. D. Bordo, D. Smail and E. White, 'France and the Bretton Woods international monetary system 1960–1968', NBER Working Paper 4642 (1994), 3–6; Clarke, 'Exchange rate stabilization', 44–7, 55–8; Mouré, *Gold Standard Illusion*, 229–30; Harris, *Monetary War and Peace*, 6–7, 9, 13–14. **59.** *FRUS 1936*, I, docs. 378, 380, 388, 390; Clavin, *Securing the World Economy*, 165–72; Harris, *Monetary War and Peace*, 7, 155–8. **60.** Clavin, *Securing the World Economy*, ch. 1; Patricia Clavin, 'The Austrian hunger crisis and the genesis of international organization after the First

World War', *International Affairs* 90 (2014); Stephen A. Schuker, 'Money doctors between the wars: the competition between central banks, private financial advisers, and multilateral agencies', in M. Flandreau, ed., *Money Doctors: The Experience of International Financial Advising, 1850–2000* (London, 2003); Jamie Martin, *The Meddlers: Sovereignty, Empire, and the Birth of Global Economic Governance* (Cambridge, MA, 2022), ch. 2. **61.** Patricia Clavin, '"Money talks": competition and cooperation with the League of Nations, 1929–1940', in Flandreau, ed., *Money Doctors*, 219–39. **62.** Clavin, *Securing the World Economy*, 36–7; *idem*, '"Money talks"', 239–41. **63.** Clavin, *Securing the World Economy*, 74–6, 127, 160–61, 162–5, 200–228; Neil de Marchi, 'League of Nations economists and the ideal of peaceful change in the decade of the 'thirties', in Crauford D. Goodwin, ed., *Economics and National Security: A History of Their Interaction (A Supplement to History of Political Economy): 23 (History of Political Economy Annual Supplement)* (Durham, NC, 1991), 172–3; Warren F. Kuehl and Lynne K. Dunn, *Keeping the Covenant: American Internationalists and the League of Nations, 1920–1939* (Kent, OH, 1997), 22, 83–7, 144–5, 158, 168, 175. **64.** Alexander Zevin, 'Every penny a vote', *London Review of Books*, 15 August 2019, 27; Quinn Slobodian, *Globalists: The End of Empire and the Birth of Neoliberalism* (Cambridge, MA, 2018), 31, 45–7, 50–53. **65.** Slobodian, *Globalists*, 20–21, 57–8, 69–76, 94; William Rappard, *The Crisis of Democracy* (Chicago, IL, 1938); *idem*, *The Quest for Peace since the World War* (Cambridge, MA, 1940). **66.** Clavin, *Securing the World Economy*, 198–230; Slobodian, *Globalists*, ch. 2. **67.** I. M. Cumpston, *Lord Bruce of Melbourne* (Melbourne, 1989), 40–42; Clavin, *Securing the World Economy*, 165–72, 176–93; Sean Turnell, 'F. L. McDougall: éminence grise of Australia economic diplomacy', *Australian Economic History Review* 40 (2000), 51–70; John B. O'Brien, 'F. L. McDougall and the origins of the FAO', *Australian Journal of Politics and History* 46 (2000), 165–6, 169–70; W. R. Aykroyd and Étienne Burnet, 'Nutrition and public health', League of Nations, *Quarterly Bulletin of the Health Organisation* 4 (1935), 326–474; League of Nations, Health Organisation, *Report on the Physiological Bases of Nutrition by the Technical Commission Appointed by the Health Committee* (Geneva, 1935), 170; speech by S. M. Bruce to the Assembly of the League of Nations, 11 September 1935, reprinted in *The McDougall Memoranda: Some Documents Relating to the Origins of the Food and Agriculture Organisation and the Contribution Made by Frank L McDougall* (Rome, 1956), 18–24; F. L. McDougall, 'The agricultural and the health problem', in *McDougall Memoranda*, 2–17; Amalia Ribi Forclaz, 'A new target for international social reform: the International Labour Organisation and working and living conditions in agriculture in the interwar years', *Contemporary European History* 20, special issue 3 (2011), 324–6. **68.** League of Nations, *The Problem of Nutrition: Volume II. Report on the Physiological Bases of Nutrition* (Geneva, 1936); League of Nations, *Nutrition: Final Report of the Mixed Committee of the League of Nations on the Relation of Nutrition to Health, Agriculture and Economic Policy* (Geneva, 1937), 34; League of Nations Official Journal, 98th and 99th Council Sessions, Dec. 1937, Annex 1681, 'Economic appeasement', Memo by F. L. McDougall, 1222–9; F. L. McDougall, *Food and Welfare: League of Nations' Studies of Nutrition and National Economic Policy* (Geneva, 1938). **69.** De Marchi, 'League of Nations economists', 173; Ruth Jachertz and Alexander Nützenadel, 'Coping with hunger? Views of a global food system, 1930–1960', *Journal of Global History* 6 (2011), 105. **70.** Luciano Tosi, 'The League of Nations, the International Institute of Agriculture and the food question', in Marta Petricioli and Donatella Cherubini, eds., *For Peace in Europe: Institutions and Civil Society between the World Wars* (Brussels, 2007), 117–38; Clavin, *Securing the World Economy*, 85, 167–8; Ribi Forclaz, 'A new target', 319, 321. **71.** M. Zanasi, 'Exporting development: the League of Nations and Republican China', *Comparative Studies in Society and History* 49 (2007), 143–69; J. Osterhammel, 'Technical cooperation between the League of Nations and China', *Modern Asian Studies* 13 (1979), 661–80. **72.** F. Hayek, *Individualism and Economic Order* (Chicago, 1948), 54; *idem*, *The Road to Serfdom* (London, 1944); G. Haberler, *Prosperity and Depression: A Theoretical Analysis of Cyclical Movements* (Geneva, 1937); Ludwig von Mises, *Omnipotent Government* (New Haven, CT, 1944); Patricia Clavin and Jens-Wilhelm Wessels, 'Transnationalism and the League of Nations: understanding the work of its Economic and Financial Organisation', *Contemporary*

European History 14 (2005), 465–92; Mauro Boianovsky and Hans-Michel Trautwein, 'Haberler, the League of Nations, and the quest for consensus in business cycle theory in the 1930s', *History of Political Economy* 38 (2006), 45–89; Louis W. Pauly, 'The League of Nations and the foreshadowing of the International Monetary Fund', Essays in International Finance No. 201, Department of Economics, Princeton, 1996; Slobodian, *Globalists*, 4–21, 50–53, 58–87, 89, 114, 271–2; Zevin, 'Every penny', 28.   73. Slobodian, *Globalists*, 15, 86, 94–5, 97, 99–120; Lionel Robbins, *Economic Planning and International Order* (London, 1937); F. A. Hayek, 'Economic conditions of inter-state federalism', *New Commonwealth Quarterly* 5 (1939).

4. 'ESCAPING FROM BACKWARDNESS'

1. W. Arthur Lewis, *Economic Survey, 1919–39* (London, 1949), 196.   2. Ibid.; Robert L. Tignor, *W. Arthur Lewis and the Birth of Development Economics* (Princeton, NJ, 2006).   3. Warren F. Kimball, *The Juggler: Franklin Roosevelt as Wartime Leader* (Princeton, NJ, 1991), 85. This account of the industrialization of the Soviet economy relies on R. W. Davies, *The Industrialisation of Soviet Russia 1: The Socialist Offensive: The Collectivisation of Soviet Agriculture, 1929–30* (London and Basingstoke, 1980); *idem, The Industrialisation of Soviet Russia 2: The Soviet Collective Farm, 1929–30* (London and Basingstoke, 1980); *idem, The Industrialisation of Soviet Russia 3: Soviet Economy in Turmoil, 1929–30* (Basingstoke, 1989); *idem, The Industrialisation of Soviet Russia 4: Crisis and Progress in the Soviet Economy, 1931–33* (Basingstoke, 1996); R. W. Davies and S. G. Wheatcroft, *The Industrialisation of Soviet Russia 5: The Years of Hunger: Soviet Agriculture, 1932–33* (Basingstoke, 2004); R. W. Davies with Oleg V. Khlevnyuk and S. G. Wheatcroft, *The Industrialisation of Soviet Russia 6: The Years of Progress: The Soviet Economy, 1934–36* (Basingstoke, 2014).   4. Karl Marx, *Capital*, vol. I, ch. 26, 'The secret of primitive accumulation', ch. 27, 'The expropriation of the agricultural population from the land', ch. 29, 'Genesis of the capitalist farmer', ch. 30, 'Results of the agricultural revolution'.   5. Davies, *Industrialisation 1: Socialist Offensive*, 31–4; A. Chayanov, *The Theory of Peasant Economy*, English edn (Homewood, IL, 1966).   6. Davies, *Industrialisation 1: Socialist Offensive*, 33–5; E. Preobrazhensky, *The New Economics*, English edn (Oxford, 1965).   7. Sheila Fitzpatrick, Alexander Rabinowitch and Richard Stites, eds., *Russia in the Era of the NEP: Explorations in Soviet Culture and Society* (Bloomington, IN, 1991); R. W. Davies, ed., *From Tsarism to the New Economic Policy: Continuity and Change in the Economy of the USSR* (Ithaca, NY, 1991).   8. Davies, *Industrialisation 1: Socialist Offensive*, xv–xvi, 28–31, 36–8, 41, 82, 89, 109, 137, 397–400; Davies, *Industrialisation 3: Turmoil*, 42–8, 60–3, 67–87; James Hughes, *Stalin, Siberia and the Crisis of the New Economic Policy* (Cambridge, 1991), 209–10; Robert Service, *Stalin: A Biography* (London, 2010), chs. 22 and 23.   9. Davies, *Industrialisation 3: Turmoil*, 95–7, 110, 139–40, 160, 162–78, 233, 238, 333, 377–9, 478; Davies, *Industrialisation 4: Crisis and Progress*, 15–17, 319–21, 330.   10. Davies, *Industrialisation 1: Socialist Offensive*, 203, 382, 392, 397–400, 403–5.   11. Ibid., 197; Davies, *Industrialisation 2: Soviet Collective Farm*, 171–3; Davies, *Industrialisation 3: Turmoil*, 399–411; Davies and Wheatcroft, *Industrialisation 5: Years of Hunger*, 431–9.   12. Davies, *Industrialisation 1: Socialist Offensive*, 269, 311, 330–34; Davies, *Industrialisation 2: Soviet Collective Farm*, 173–8.   13. Davies, *Industrialisation 3: Turmoil*, 310–14, 320–28.   14. Ibid., 481.   15. Davies, *Industrialisation 4: Crisis and Progress*, 15–17, 40–64, 76, 201–28; Davies, *Industrialisation 3: Turmoil*, 481–6.   16. Davies, *Industrialisation 4: Crisis and Progress*, 176–92, 229–41.   17. Ibid., 242–56.   18. Ibid., 362, 380–81; Robert Conquest, *The Harvest of Sorrow: Soviet Collectivization and the Terror-Famine* (New York, 1986); Davies and Wheatcroft, *Industrialisation 5: Years of Hunger*, 401, 441; Anne Applebaum, *Red Famine: Stalin's War on Ukraine* (London, 2017), xxiv–xxv, 7, 209–11, 217, 226, 245, 296–8, 300–301; Sheila Fitzpatrick, *Stalin's Peasants: Resistance and Survival in the Russian Village after Collectivization* (Oxford, 1994).   19. Davies, *Industrialisation 4: Crisis and Progress*, xiv–xvi, 318–22, 330, 390–91, 407, 457; Davies, Khlevnyuk and Wheatcroft, *Industrialisation 6: Years of Progress*, xiv–xv.   20.

Figures from *Narodnoe khoziaistvo SSSR 1922–1972* (Moscow, 1972), 240 as cited in Wikipedia entry on collectivization in the Soviet Union.   **21.** Rana Mitter, *A Bitter Revolution: China's Struggle with the Modern World* (Oxford, 2004), 21–2, 32–3, 38, 139.   **22.** Eric Helleiner, *Forgotten Foundations of Bretton Woods: International Development and the Making of the Postwar Order* (Ithaca, NY, 2014), 17, 78, 187–9; Mitter, *Bitter Revolution*, 141–2; Sun Yat-sen, *International Development of China* (1918; English edn 1922).   **23.** Mitter, *Bitter Revolution*, 31, 129–30; J. Osterhammel, 'Technical cooperation between the League of Nations and China', *Modern Asian Studies* 13 (1979), 664–5, 675–6; Felix Boecking, *No Great Wall: Trade, Tariffs and Nationalism in Republican China, 1927–45* (Cambridge, MA, 2017), 2, 33–4, 62–3, 66–9, 84.   **24.** Mitter, *Bitter Revolution*, 38–9, 143–6; Rana Mitter, *China's War with Japan, 1937–1945: The Struggle for Survival* (London, 2013).   **25.** Boecking, *No Great Wall*, 62, 65, 84, 193.   **26.** Margherita Zanasi, *Saving the Nation: Economic Modernity in Republican China* (Chicago, IL, 2006), 2–5; Osterhammel, 'Technical cooperation', 670, 672.   **27.** Helleiner, *Forgotten Foundations*, 190; Margherita Zanasi, 'Exporting development: the League of Nations and Republican China', *Comparative Studies in Society and History* 49 (2007), 143–69; Zanasi, *Saving the Nation*, 12–13; Osterhammel, 'Technical cooperation', 668–80; Jamie Martin, *The Meddlers: Sovereignty, Empire and the Birth of Global Economic Governance* (Cambridge, MA, 2022), 156–75.   **28.** Zanasi, *Saving the Nation*, 5–7, 229; Boecking, *No Great Wall*, 192, 199–208.   **29.** J. Morton Blum, *From the Morgenthau Diaries: I, Years of Crisis, 1923–1938* (Boston, MA, 1959), 187, 190–91, 193, 198–9, 204–28, 508; Boecking, *No Great Wall*, 114–16.   **30.** Helleiner, *Forgotten Foundations*, 14, 19, 26–7, 190–200.   **31.** Benjamin Zachariah, *Developing India: An Intellectual and Social History c. 1930–1950* (New Delhi, 2005), 4–8, 16, 58; S. B. Saul, *Studies in British Overseas Trade, 1870–1914* (Liverpool, 1960), 62–3.   **32.** David Lewis Jones, 'Naoroji, Dadabhai (1825–1917)', *Oxford Dictionary of National Biography*; Dadabhai Naoroji, *Poverty and Un-British Rule* (London, 1901).   **33.** Romesh Dutt, *The Economic History of India in the Victorian Age from the Accession of Queen Victoria in 1837 to the Commencement of the Twentieth Century*, vol. 2 (London, 1904), v–xix; Tapan Raychaudhuri, 'Dutt, Romesh Chunder [Rameschchandra Data] (1848–1909)', *Oxford Dictionary of National Biography*; Sugata Bose, 'Instruments and idioms of colonial and national development: India's historical experience in comparative perspective', in Frederick Cooper and Randall Packard, eds., *International Development and the Social Sciences: Essays on the History and Politics of Knowledge* (Berkeley, CA, 1997), 47.   **34.** M. K. Gandhi, *Hind Swaraj or Indian Home Rule* (Phoenix, Natal, 1910), online at www.mkgandhi.org; *The Collected Works of Mahatma Gandhi*, vol. 79, e-book (New Delhi, 1999), 'Implications of constructive programme', 13 Aug. 1940, 111–14 and 'Equal distribution', 19 Aug. 1940, 132–5; on Gandhi and Ruskin, see M. K. Gandhi, *An Autobiography* (1927; London, 2001), 273–4; Zachariah, *Developing India*, 156–65, 170–71, 173–4, 179–87; Ajit Dasgupta, *Gandhi's Economic Thought* (London, 1996).   **35.** J. Nehru, *A Bunch of Old Letters* (New York, 1960), 508; Sukhamoy Chakravarty, *Development Planning: The Indian Experience* (Oxford, 1987), 15–16.   **36.** 'Science and politics' in *Crossroads: Works of Subhas Chandra Bose 1938–40* (Calcutta, 1962), 51–3; Bose, 'Instruments and idioms', 49–50; Sugata Bose, *His Majesty's Opponent: Subhas Chandra Bose and India's Struggle Against Empire* (Cambridge, MA, 2011), 145.   **37.** B. Chakrabarty, 'Jawaharlal Nehru and planning 1938–1941: India at the crossroads', *Modern Asian Studies* 26 (1992), 277–8; Zachariah, *Developing India*, 216.   **38.** Zachariah, *Developing India*, 235–42.   **39.** Ibid., 88–96.   **40.** Ibid., 100–104, 106.   **41.** Ibid., 102, 104–8; Peter Clarke, *The Cripps Version: The Life of Sir Stafford Cripps* (London, 2002), 276–322.   **42.** Zachariah, *Developing India*, 102.   **43.** Ibid., 216, 220–26; Ramachandra Guha, *India After Gandhi* (London, 2007), 205; Frederick Cooper and Randall Packard, eds., *International Development and the Social Sciences: Essays on the History and Politics of Knowledge* (Berkeley, CA, 1997), 'Introduction', 11; Bose, 'Instruments and idioms', 48.   **44.** Aditya Balasubramanian and Srinath Raghavan, 'Present at the creation: India, and global economy and the Bretton Woods conference', *Journal of World History* 29 (2018), 65–94.   **45.** Cordell Hull, *The Memoirs of Cordell Hull*, vol. I (New York, 1948), 523.   **46.** Rosemary Thorp, 'A reappraisal of the origins of import-substituting industrialisation, 1930–1950', *Journal of Latin American Studies* 24 (1992),

181–95; Carlos F. Diaz Alejandro, 'Latin America in the 1930s', in Rosemary Thorp, ed., *Latin America in the 1930s: The Role of the Periphery in World Crisis* (London, 1984), 17–49; Paulo Drinot and Alan Knight, eds., *The Great Depression in Latin America* (Durham, NC, 2014), especially Alan Knight, 'The Great Depression in Latin America: an overview'. **47.** Knight, 'Great Depression in Latin America', 309. **48.** Ibid., 285; Alan Knight, 'The character and consequences of the Great Depression in Mexico', in Drinot and Knight, eds., *Great Depression*, 213–45; Paulo Drinot, 'Introduction', in Drinot and Knight, eds., *Great Depression*, 5. **49.** J. Wolfe, 'Change with continuity: Brazil from 1930 to 1945', in Drinot and Knight, eds., *Great Depression*, 84; Stanley E. Hilton, *Brazil and the Great Powers, 1930–1939: The Politics of Trade Rivalry* (Austin, TX, 1975), 4. **50.** Hilton, *Brazil and the Great Powers*, 11, 14, 16. **51.** Wolfe, 'Change with continuity', 84, 87. **52.** Helleiner, *Forgotten Foundations*, 32. **53.** Hilton, *Brazil and the Great Powers*, table 1, p. 137 for data; negotiations with Berlin and Washington in chs. 2, 3, 5. **54.** P. W. Drake, *The Money Doctor in the Andes: The Kemmerer Missions, 1923–33* (Durham, NC, 1989); B. Eichengreen, 'House calls of the money doctor: the Kemmerer missions in Latin America, 1917–31', in P. W. Drake, ed., *Money Doctors, Foreign Debts and Economic Reforms in Latin America from the 1890s to the Present* (Washington, DC, 1994), 110–132; R. N. Seidel, 'American reformers abroad: the Kemmerer missions in South America, 1927–31', *Journal of Economic History* 32 (1972), 520–45. **55.** Address before the Inter-American Conference for the Maintenance of Peace, 1 Dec. 1936, online in Gerhard Peters and John T. Woolley, *The American Presidency Project.* **56.** Hilton, *Brazil and the Great Powers*, 193, 208. **57.** Helleiner, *Forgotten Foundations*, 10, 24–5, 50–79. **58.** Ibid., 46, 50, 80–81; on Rockefeller's activities, Gisela Cranmer and Ursula Prutsch, 'Nelson A. Rockefeller's Office of Inter-American Affairs (1940–46) and Record Group 226', *Hispanic American Historical Review* 86 (2006), 785–806. **59.** Knight, 'Great Depression in Latin American', 286–7, 302; Arturo Escobar, *Encountering Development: The Making and Unmaking of the Third World* (Princeton, NJ, 1995), 29; *Foreign Relations of the United States (FRUS): Diplomatic Papers, 1945, The American Republics*, vol. IX (Washington, DC, 1969), docs. 92, 93. **60.** R. G. Gregory, 'Overview', in R. G. Gregory and N. G. Butlin, eds., *Recovery from the Depression: Australia and the World Economy in the 1930s* (Cambridge, 1988), 9–10. **61.** W. H. Richmond, 'S. M. Bruce and Australian economic policy 1923–29', *Australian Economic History Review* 23 (1983), 238–57, quotes at 241, 248; I. M. Cumpston, *Lord Bruce of Melbourne* (Melbourne, 1989), 51–3, 63–7, 79–81; W. J. Hudson and Wendy Way, eds., *Letters from a 'Secret Service Agent': F. L. McDougall to S. M. Bruce, 1924–29* (Canberra, 1986), 443. **62.** Alex Millmow, 'Niemeyer, Scullin and the Australian economists', *Australian Economic History Review* 44 (2004), 143, 145, 148–9; D. O. Malcolm, 'Australian loan policy: British economic mission', *Australian Quarterly* 1 (1929), 14; L. G. Melville, 'Report of the British economic mission', *Australian Quarterly* 1 (1929), 93–101; D. P. Copland, 'The Australian problem', *Economic Journal* 40 (1930), 638, 638. **63.** Susan Howson, 'Niemeyer, Sir Otto Ernst, 1883–1971', *Oxford Dictionary of National Biography*; Bernard Attard, 'The Bank of England and the origins of the Niemeyer mission, 1921–1930', *Australian Economic History Review* 32 (1992), 66–83, quote at 69; Millmow, 'Niemeyer, Scullin', 151; Stuart Macintyre, *The Oxford History of Australia: vol. 4, 1901–42: The Succeeding Age* (Melbourne, 1986), 256–9. **64.** Macintyre, *Oxford History of Australia, 4, Succeeding Age*, 259–64. **65.** G. D. Snooks, 'Shann, Edward Owen Giblin (1884–1935)', *Australian Dictionary of Biography*; E. O. G. Shann, *The Boom of 1890 – and Now: A Call to Australia to Put Her House in Order Lest Drought and Falling Prices for Wool and Wheat Overtake Us Again* (Sydney, 1927); idem, *An Economic History of Australia* (Cambridge, 1930); idem, *Quotas or Stable Money? Three Essays on the Ottawa and London Conferences, 1932–33* (Sydney, 1933), 52–3. **66.** Sean Turnell, 'Monetary reformers, amateur idealists and Keynesian crusaders: Australian economists' international advocacy, 1925–50', Ph.D. thesis, Macquarie University, 1999, ch. 2; Millmow, 'Niemeyer, Scullin', 153; E. O. G. Shann and D. B. Copland, eds., *The Crisis in Australian Finance 1929–1931: Documents on Budgetary and Economic Policy* (Sydney, 1931); D. B. Copland, 'Financial and currency proposals', *Australian Quarterly* 3 (1931), 17, 21; idem, 'The Premiers' Plan in Australia: an experiment in economic adjustment', *International Affairs* 13

(1934), 79–92; *idem*, 'Reflections on Australian currency policy', *Australian Quarterly* 4 (1932), 113–21; Neville Cain, 'Recovery policy in Australia, 1930–3: certain native wisdom', *Australian Economic History Review* 23 (1983), 193.   67. Macintyre, *Oxford History of Australia, 4, Succeeding Age*, 264, 271, 273, 290, 299–304.   68. Turnell, 'Monetary reformers', ch. 2, quote at 60.   69. Ibid., ch. 3.   70. F. L. McDougall, *Sheltered Markets: A Study in the Value of Empire Trade* (London, 1925); Turnell, 'Monetary reformers', 77–83.   71. Turnell, 'Monetary reformers', 101–4, 109, 112, 117–18, 129, 130–33; Stuart Macintyre, *Australia's Boldest Experiment: War and Reconstruction in the 1940s* (Sydney, 2015), 6, 59, 62, 110, 117, 120, 133; Tim Rowse, *Nugget Coombs: A Reforming Life* (Cambridge, 2002), 118–21.   72. Turnell, 'Monetary reformers', 136–47; Sean Turnell, 'Australia's "employment approach" to international postwar reconstruction: calling the bluff of multilateralism', *History of Economics Review* 36 (2002), 112–13, 115–17; Rowse, *Nugget Coombs*, 125–40; Marriner S. Eccles Document Collection, available at https://fraser.stlouisfed.org/archival-collection/marriner-s-eccles-papers-1343, Box 36, folder 11, item 2, E. A. Goldenweiser, 'Issues at Bretton Woods', 29 July 1944; Box 36, folder 11, item 3, E. A. Goldenweiser, Federal Reserve, 'Bretton Woods', Director of Research and Statistics, Board of Governors of the Federal Reserve System, Remarks made at joint meeting of directors of Federal Reserve Bank of Cleveland and branches, 22 Nov. 1944.

5. 'HANDLING THE ENGLISH'

1. FDR Presidential Library, Berle papers, Box 212, diary, 11 Oct. 1940.   2. The National Archives (TNA), FO371/30655, F. E. Evans, 12 May 1942.   3. David Edgerton, *Britain's War Machine: Weapons, Resources and Exports in the Second World War* (London, 2011), 2, 281.   4. David James Gill, *The Long Shadow of Default: Britain's Unpaid War Debts to the United States* (New Haven, CT, 2022), 141–4.   5. Robert Skidelsky, *John Maynard Keynes: Fighting for Britain, 1937–46* (London, 2000), 96; Gill, *The Long Shadow*, 145, 148–54.   6. David Reynolds, *The Creation of the Anglo-American Alliance, 1937–1941: A Study in Competitive Cooperation* (London, 1981); Gill, *The Long Shadow*, 154–63; Warren F. Kimball, *The Juggler: Franklin Roosevelt as Wartime Leader* (Princeton, NJ, 1991), 48; Skidelsky, *Keynes: Fighting for Britain*, 102–3; F. D. Roosevelt, Press conference, 17 Dec. 1940 and Fireside chat, 29 Dec. 1940, online in Gerhard Peters and John T. Woolley, *The American Presidency Project*; G. McJimsey, ed., *Documentary History of the Franklin Delano Roosevelt Presidency, vol. 2, The Lend-Lease Act, December 1940–April 1941* (Bethesda, MD, 2001), docs. 28, 37, 41, 42, 75, 76, 117.   7. Lend Lease Act, 1941, Sec 3, 5(b).   8. TNA, FO371/30655, N. Butler, 18 May 1942.   9. Susan Brewer, *To Win the Peace: British Propaganda in the United States during World War II* (Ithaca, NY, 1997), 126–7, 162–5, 197–8; Kimball, *Juggler*, 127–32; on mandated territories, Susan Pedersen, *The Guardians: The League of Nations and the Crisis of Empire* (Oxford, 2015).   10. J. Morton Blum, *From the Morgenthau Diaries: 3, Years of War, 1941–45* (Boston, MA, 1967), 123; Skidelsky, *Keynes: Fighting for Britain*, 98–9; Kimball, *Juggler*, 49.   11. FDR Presidential Library, Morgenthau Papers, Box 908, Book 404, re. Aid to Britain, 4 June 1941.   12. Skidelsky, *Keynes: Fighting for Britain*, 126; Blum, *Morgenthau Diaries: Years of War*, 123–4; Kimball, *Juggler*, 50–53.   13. Robert L. Beisner, *Dean Acheson: A Life in the Cold War* (Oxford, 2006), 13–19, 20–22; FDR Presidential Library, Morgenthau Papers, Box 908, Book 404, re. Aid to Britain, 4 June 1941; Skidelsky, *Keynes: Fighting for Britain*, 127.   14. Skidelsky *Keynes: Fighting for Britain*, 179; *Foreign Relations of the United States (FRUS): Diplomatic Papers, 1941, The British Commonwealth: The Near East and Africa*, vol. III (Washington, DC, 1959), doc. 9; *FRUS: Diplomatic Papers, 1942, General, The British Commonwealth, The Far East*, vol. I (Washington, DC, 1960), docs. 453, 454, 455, 457; Richard Toye, 'Churchill and Britain's "financial Dunkirk"', *Twentieth Century British History* 15 (2004), 331–3.   15. *FRUS 1941*, III, doc. 9 Annex.   16. *FRUS 1941*, III, docs. 9, 11; Skidelsky, *Keynes: Fighting for Britain*, 130.   17. *FRUS 1941*, III, docs. 9, 13.   18. Toye, 'Churchill and Britain's "financial Dunkirk"', 332; Skidelsky, *Keynes: Fighting for Britain*, 201–2; *The Collected Writings of John Maynard Keynes, Vol. 25, Activities 1940–1944*, ed. D. Moggridge (Cambridge, 1978),

draft of 8 Sept. 1941, 23-4. **19.** Reynolds, *Anglo-American Alliance*, 254-5, 363. **20.** Statement on the Atlantic Charter meeting with Prime Minister Churchill, 14 Aug. 1941 in Peters and Woolley, *American Presidency Project*; T. A. Wilson, *The First Summit: Roosevelt and Churchill at Placentia Bay, 1941*, rev. edn (Lawrence, KS, 1991); *FRUS 1941*, III, doc. 30; Cordell Hull, *The Memoirs of Cordell Hull*, vol. II (New York, 1948), 975-6, 1151; Kimball, *Juggler*, 54. **21.** Reynolds, *Anglo-American Alliance*, 213; Elizabeth Borgwardt, *A New Deal for the World: America's Vision for Human Rights* (Cambridge, MA, and London, 2005), 4-5, 8-9, 29. **22.** *FRUS 1941*, III, doc. 32 annex; Kimball, *Juggler*, 56. **23.** *FRUS 1941*, III, doc. 36. **24.** Kimball, *Juggler*, 56-7; *FRUS 1941*, III, doc. 33. **25.** *FRUS 1942*, I, doc. 451. **26.** *FRUS 1942*, I, doc. 452; Kimball, *Juggler*, 59. **27.** *FRUS 1942*, I, 454; S. Howson and D. Moggridge, eds., *The Wartime Diaries of Lionel Robbins and James Meade* (Basingstoke, 1990), entry for 13 Oct. 1943, 136-7. **28.** *FRUS 1942*, I, doc. 458. **29.** FDR Presidential Library, Morgenthau papers, Box 909, Book 498, Acheson to Morgenthau, 18 Feb. 1942 and FDR to Churchill, 11 Feb. 1942. **30.** The text is at http://avalon.law.yale .edu/20th_century/decade04.asp; Hull, *Memoirs*, II, 1153. **31.** Kimball, *Juggler*, 59-60; Brewer, *To Win the Peace*, 200, 205-6. **32.** G. John Ikenberry, 'A world economy restored: expert consensus and the Anglo-American postwar settlement', *International Organization* 46 (1992), 291, 292, 314, 316, 319. **33.** A. Williams, 'Leo Pasvolsky and an open world economy', in M. Cochran and C. Navari, eds., *Progressivism and US Foreign Policy between the World Wars*, The Palgrave Macmillan History of International Thought (New York, 2017); *The Collected Writings of John Maynard Keynes, Vol. 26, Activities 1941-1946*, ed. D. Moggridge (Cambridge, 1980), Notes on Mr Pasvolsky's memo, 5 Jan. 1942, 239-41; ibid., Keynes to Opie, nd, 243. **34.** *FRUS 1942*, I, docs. 156, 157, 159. **35.** *FRUS 1942*, I, docs. 165, 166, 167, 171; *FRUS: Diplomatic Papers, 1943, General*, vol. I (Washington, DC, 1963), doc. 933. **36.** *FRUS: Diplomatic Papers, 1943, The British Commonwealth, Eastern Europe, The Far East*, vol. III (Washington, DC, 1963), doc. 12. **37.** *FRUS 1943*, III, doc. 63. **38.** *FRUS 1943*, III, doc. 18. **39.** Susan Howson, 'Meade, James Edward (1907-95)', *Oxford Dictionary of National Biography*; James Meade, *Public Works in Their International Aspects* (London, 1933), reprinted in Susan Howson, ed., *The Collected Papers of James Meade: Employment and Inflation* (London and New York, 1988), 6-25; James Meade, *The Economic Basis of a Durable Peace* (London, 1940), 9-10, 179-81. **40.** James Meade, 'A proposal for an International Commercial Union', in S. Howson, ed., *The Collected Papers of James Meade, vol. III, International Economics* (London and New York, 1988), 27-35. **41.** TNA, FO371/31531, Dalton to Eden, 5 Nov. 1942 and Eden to Dalton, 17 Nov. 1942. **42.** TNA, FO371/31531, J. E. Coulson, 9 Nov. 1942. **43.** TNA, FO 371/31531, Report of the Committee on Post-War Commercial Policy, 6 Jan. 1943. **44.** TNA, FO 371/31531, Report of the Committee on Post-War Commercial Policy and Note of dissent by H. Henderson. **45.** TNA, FO371/31512, J. E. Coulson, 9 Nov. 1942. **46.** *Collected Writings of Keynes*, 26, Keynes to Waley and others, 'Overton committee draft report', 31 Dec. 1942, 251; Keynes to Eady and others, 'Sir H. Henderson's criticism of the Overton draft report on post-war commercial policy', 4 Jan. 1943, 253-4. **47.** *Collected Writings of Keynes*, 26, 4 Jan. 1943, 255; 'Post-war commercial policy: the report of the committee and the note by the President of the Board of Trade', 15 Jan. 1943, 256-60; Keynes to Waley, 'The report of the Overton committee on commercial policy', 1 Feb. 1943, 264; Keynes to Overton, 'Commercial policy', 12 Feb. 1943, 268. **48.** TNA, FO371/31512, minute 4 Dec. 1942; FO371/31531, Gladwyn Jebb, 14 Jan. 1943; minute 15 Jan. 1943; Report of the Committee on Post-War Commercial Policy, 6 Jan. 1943 and Note by the President of the Board of Trade [H. Dalton] on the Report of the Committee on Post-War Commercial Policy, 9 Jan. 1943. **49.** TNA, FO371/35358, Richard Law speech to first plenary meeting at Washington on monetary and economic problems, 20 Sept. 1943. **50.** TNA, FO371/35358, Report on commercial policy discussions in Washington, 20 Sept. to 16 Oct. 1943, 21 Oct. 1943. **51.** TNA, FO371/45680, minute by J. E. Coulson, 16 April 1945; *FRUS: Diplomatic Papers, 1944, General: Economic and Social Matters*, vol. II (Washington, DC, 1967), docs. 21, 42, 45; Skidelsky, *Keynes: Fighting for Britain*, 327. **52.** *FRUS 1944*, II, doc. 30; *FRUS: Diplomatic Papers, 1944, The British Commonwealth and Europe*, vol. III (Washington, DC, 1965), docs. 17, 19, 23; Hull,

Memoirs, II, 1476–7. **53.** *FRUS 1944*, III, doc. 29. **54.** *FRUS 1944*, II, doc. 42; Dean Acheson, *Present at the Creation: My Years in the State Department* (New York, 1969), 55, 64; Susan Aaronson, 'How Cordell Hull and the postwar planners designed a new trade policy', *Business and Economic History*, 2nd ser., 20 (1991), 174, 176, 178. **55.** *FRUS: Diplomatic Papers, 1945, The British Commonwealth, The Far East*, vol. VI (Washington, DC, 1969), doc. 13. **56.** Michael J. Devine and Nathan Giles, 'Stettinius, Edward Reilly Jr', *American National Biography*. **57.** *FRUS 1945*, VI, docs. 10, 15, 17. **58.** TNA, FO371/45680, Article VII, summary of discussion held at Board of Trade on 9 Aug. 1945, 15 Aug. 1945; CP(45)116, 19 Aug. 1945, Article VII of the mutual aid agreement: commercial policy. Memo by the President of the Board of Trade; *FRUS 1945*, VI, docs. 19, 28. **59.** Edgerton, *Britain's War Machine*, 281; Marcelo de Paiva Abreu, 'Britain as a debtor: Indian sterling balances 1940–53', *Economic History Review* 70 (2017), 586–8; J. Gallagher and A. Seal, 'Britain and India between the wars', *Modern Asian Studies* 15 (1981), 412–14; B. Tomlinson, 'India and the British empire, 1935–1947', *Indian Economic and Social History Review* 13 (1976), 344, 348; Catherine R. Schenk, *The Decline of Sterling: Managing the Retreat of an International Currency, 1945–1992* (Cambridge, 2010), 39; National Archive of Australia, A9790 control 4232(1), Note of conversation between the Chancellor and Chifley, nd. **60.** Abreu, 'Britain as a debtor', 588–91. **61.** TNA, T236/61, F. E. Harmer to F. Lee, 8 Nov. 1944. **62.** TNA, T236/473, Cobbold to Trend, 11 Sept. 1946. **63.** TNA, T236/61, Lucius Thompson-McCausland to Frank Lee, 7 Nov. 1944. **64.** *FRUS 1943*, III, docs. 52, 59, 61; FRUS *1944*, III, docs. 4, 10, 12, 13, 15; Blum, *Morgenthau Diaries: Years of War*, 126, 131–9; Kenneth M. Right, 'Dollar pooling and the sterling area, 1939–1952', *American Economic Review* 44 (1954), 573–5; US National Archives and Records Administration (NARA) RG43 International trade 1934–56: 698 International Trade Organization 1933–50, Box 3, A. I. Bloomfield to M. B. Northrop, Sterling area dollar pool, 1 June 1945 and American policies and the British balance of payments, 25 April 1945; Committee on American trade problems in the sterling area: blocked sterling balances, 22 Aug. 1945 and 7 Sept. 1945. **65.** TNA, T236/441, JSM Washington to Cabinet offices, 22 Nov. 1945. **66.** Richard S. Sayers, *Financial Policy, 1939–1945* (London, 1956), 254–5; *FRUS 1944*, III, doc. 29; *FRUS 1945*, VI, docs. 43, 64, 71, 90. **67.** TNA, T236/441, W. Eady to Chancellor, Washington talks, 23 Nov. 1945; *FRUS 1945*, VI, doc. 90. **68.** Ikenberry, 'A world economy restored', 300, 314.

6. 'A FIRM FOUNDATION'

1. League of Nations [Ragnar Nurkse], *International Currency Experience*, quoted in John G. Ruggie, 'International regimes, transactions, and change: embedded liberalism in the postwar economic order', *International Organization* 46 (1992), 392. **2.** *United Nations Monetary and Financial Conference, Proceedings and Documents*, US Department of State, International Organizations and Conference Series (Washington, DC, 1948), vol. I, 81. **3.** Robert Skidelsky, *John Maynard Keynes: Fighting for Britain, 1937–46* (London, 2000), 140, 150, 344; Alec Cairncross, ed., *The Robert Hall Diaries, 1947–53* (London, 1989), 147, 256. **4.** Skidelsky, *Keynes: Fighting for Britain*, 148–9. **5.** Barry Eichengreen, Arnaud Mehl and Livia Chiţu, *How Global Currencies Work: Past, Present and Future* (Princeton, NJ, and Oxford, 2018), 118–19; Catherine R. Schenk, *The Decline of Sterling: Managing the Retreat of an International Currency* (Cambridge, 2010), 22–7, 30. **6.** Raymond Mikesell, 'The Bretton Woods debates: a memoir', Essays in International Finance No. 192, Department of Economics, Princeton, 1994, 3–4. **7.** Speech to Lords, 16 May 1944, from *The Collected Writings of John Maynard Keynes, Vol. 26, Activities 1941–1946*, ed. D. Moggridge (Cambridge, 1980), 5. **8.** For an overview, D. E. Moggridge, *Maynard Keynes: An Economist's Biography* (London and New York, 1992), ch. 26. **9.** Skidelsky, *Keynes: Fighting for Britain*, 191–2; Keynes, *A Treatise on Money: Volume II, The Applied Theory of Money* in *The Collected Writings of John Maynard Keynes, Vol. 6*, ed. D. Moggridge (Cambridge, 1971), 262, 267–9, 272, 274–7, 303, 314–15, 348–61. **10.** Skidelsky, *Keynes: Fighting for Britain*, 194–9; *The Collected Writings of John Maynard Keynes, Vol. 25, Activities 1940–1944*, ed. D. Moggridge (Cambridge, 1978), Keynes to Harold Nicholson, 20 Nov. 1940, 1-2; ibid., Proposals to counter the German 'New Order', 1 Dec. 1940, 7-10 and draft statement, 11-16, 23-4; S. G. Gross, 'Gold, debt and the quest for monetary order: the Nazi campaign to integrate Europe in 1940', *Contemporary European History* 26 (2017), 290-91, 309.   **11.** James Meade, *The Economic Basis of a Durable Peace* (London, 1940), 9-10, 179-81.   **12.** *Collected Writings of Keynes, 25*, Postwar currency policy, 8 Sept. 1941, 21-33 and Proposals for an International Currency Union, 8 Sept. 1941, 33-40; ibid., Proposals for an international currency union, 18 Nov. 1941, 48-9, 52-3.   **13.** *Collected Writings of Keynes, 25*, Postwar currency policy, 27-8, 30.   **14.** J. H. Williams, 'Currency stabilization: the Keynes and White plans', *Foreign Affairs* 21 (1943), 647-9.   **15.** *Collected Writings of Keynes, 25*, Keynes to Norman, 19 Dec. 1941, 98-9.   **16.** Skidelsky, *Keynes: Fighting for Britain*, 203-9; *Collected Writings of Keynes, 25*, Keynes to Harrod, 16 Dec. 1941, 86 and Proposals, 18 Nov. 1941, 55, 60, 61-2.   **17.** The National Archive (TNA), T247/116, 'Mr Keynes's proposal for an international currency union', R. G. Hawtrey, 15 Oct. 1941; letter to Keynes, unsigned and undated [25 Nov. 1941]; S. D. Waley, 'A few queries on Mr Keynes' proposals for an International Currency Union, Sept. 1941; T247/67, memos by H. D. Henderson, 7 and 17 April 1942; T247/116, Post-war external policy: suggestions for reconciliation, H. D. Henderson, 24 Nov. 1941; T247/221, 'The nineteen thirties', H. D. Henderson; Anglo-American economic cooperation, H. D. Henderson, 3 Sept. 1941; T247/122, H. D. Henderson to Keynes, The Sterling area, 23 Oct. 1941; Bank of England memo on post-war trade and financial policy, 22 Oct. 1941; *Collected Writings of Keynes, 25*, Proposals for an International Currency Union, 44, 57; Keynes to Henderson: Your note on the Anglo-American discussions, 9 May 1942, 153-7; Skidelsky, *Keynes: Fighting for Britain*, 210-18.   **18.** *Collected Writings of Keynes, 25*, Proposals for an international currency union, 18 Nov. 1941, 42-66.   **19.** Skidelsky, *Keynes: Fighting for Britain*, 218-27; *Collected Writings of Keynes, 25*, Keynes to Harrod, Your memorandum on forthcoming US conversations, 19 April 1942, 146-51; TNA, T247/67, Forthcoming conversation with the United States on economic questions, nd; T247/116, Meeting with the Board of Trade etc on 1 Dec. 1941 to discuss the Keynes plan, 29 Nov. 1941; Harrod to Hopkins, 4 and 18 Dec. 1941; T247/117, Anglo-American Investment Board, R. Harrod, 12 Jan. 1942.   **20.** *Collected Writings of Keynes, 25*, 'Proposals for an international currency union', 15 Dec. 1941, 69-94.   **21.** TNA, T247/116, Phillips to Keynes, 18 Dec. 1941, Hopkins to Phillips, 5 Jan. 1942, Keynes to Phillips, 13 Jan. 1942; marginal note by Dennis Robertson, 30 Dec. 1941 on Keynes to Robertson, 29 Dec. 1941; Skidelsky, *Keynes: Fighting for Britain*, 184.   **22.** *Collected Writings of Keynes, 25*, 'Plan for an International Currency (or Clearing) Union', Jan. 1942, 108-39 and J. Keith Horsefield, ed., *The International Monetary Fund 1945-1965: Twenty Years of International Monetary Cooperation: Volume III, Documents* (Washington, DC, 1969), 'Proposals for an international (or clearing union), 11 Feb 1942', 3-18.   **23.** Skidelsky, *Keynes: Fighting for Britain*, 224-8; TNA, T247/119, Note of a meeting on 25 Feb. 1942: Treasury draft of note for Sir George Chrystal's committee on monetary, financial and trade policy after the war; *Collected Writings of Keynes, 25*, Minutes of a meeting of the War Cabinet committee on Reconstruction Problems, 31 March 1942, 139-42 and Keynes to Hopkins and Wilson Smith, 22 April 1942, 142-3.   **24.** TNA, T247/67, American conversations: outline of strategy, 30 June 1942; T247/94, D. Robertson to J. M. Keynes, 10 May 1942.   **25.** FDR Presidential Library, Berle papers, Box 65, Postwar speech, 15 Dec. 1942; untitled and undated paper to President, Secretary and Under-Secretary; similar ideas are in Box 211, Possible study of post war, A. A. Berle, nd.   **26.** FDR Presidential Library, Berle papers, Box 58, memorandum A. A. Berle, 28 Sept. 1942; J. D. Coppock, Harry S. Truman Library and Museum, Oral History Interview, at https://trumanlibrary.gov/library/oral-histories/coppockj.   **27.** Letter in *New York Herald-Tribune*, 31 March 1946, quoted in Richard N. Gardner, *Sterling-Dollar Diplomacy: Anglo-American Collaboration in the Reconstruction of Multilateral Trade* (Oxford, 1956), 76.   **28.** Sarah Binder and Mark Spindel, *The Myth of Independence: How Congress Governs the Federal Reserve* (Princeton, NJ, 2017), 84, 122.   **29.** *UN Monetary and Financial Conference*, II, 1227.   **30.** Liaquat Ahamed, *Lords of Finance: The Bankers Who Broke the World* (New York, 2009), 492; J. P. Young, Harry S. Truman Library and Museum, Oral

History Interview, at https://trumanlibrary.gov/library/oral-histories/youngjp; Mikesell, 'Bretton Woods', 55; R. F. Harrod, *The Life of John Maynard Keynes* (London, 1951), 557.   31. *Collected Writings of Keynes*, 25, Keynes to Eady, 3 Oct. 1943, 356; see also Lionel Robbins, *Autobiography of an Economist* (London, 1971), 198.   32. Skidelsky, *Keynes: Fighting for Britain*, 242–3, 256–63; Mikesell, 'Bretton Woods', 56–7; Christopher Andrew and Vasili Mitrokhin, *The Sword and the Shield: The Mitrokhin Archive and the Secret History of the KGB* (New York, 1999), 104, 106, 130, 142; John Haynes and Harvey Klehr, *Venona: Decoding Soviet Espionage in America* (New Haven, CT, 2000), 138–45; Benn Steil, *The Battle of Bretton Woods: John Maynard Keynes, Harry Dexter White and the Making of a New World Order* (Princeton, NJ, 2013), 39, 49, 50, 53, 55, 108, 128, 136–7, 155, 197–9, 273–4, 291, 293–9. James Boughton, the official historian of the IMF, rightly comments that Steil 'gets the history consistently wrong', and that the claim that Bretton Woods was skewed to the Soviets is 'dangerously misleading': James Boughton, 'Harry Dexter White and the history of Bretton Woods', Institute of New Economic Thinking, 9 Nov. 2013.   33. Eric Helleiner, *Forgotten Foundations of Bretton Woods: International Development and the Making of the Postwar Order* (Ithaca, NY, 2014), 11–12, 50–51, chs. 2 and 3, 100–113; Skidelsky, *Keynes: Fighting for Britain*, 239–40; Mikesell, 'Bretton Woods', 5–6; Warren F. Kimball, *The Juggler: Franklin Roosevelt as Wartime Leader* (Princeton, NJ, 1991), 88, 92, 95.   34. Helleiner, *Forgotten Foundations*, 109–13; Horsefield, ed., *IMF, 1945–65, III*, 78.   35. Helleiner, *Forgotten Foundations*, 45–50, 121, 123, 133, 141–6; idem, 'The Southern side of "embedded liberalism": America's unorthodox money doctoring during the early post-1945 years', in Marc Flandreau, ed., *Money Doctors: The Experience of International Financial Advising, 1850–2000* (London, 2003), 250–55.   36. Helleiner, *Forgotten Foundations*, 107; Skidelsky, *Keynes: Fighting for Britain*, 243–5, 323; Horsefield, ed., *IMF, 1945–65, III*, 37–82, omitting the proposals on the Bank; *Foreign Relations of the United States (FRUS): Diplomatic Papers, 1942, General, The British Commonwealth, The Far East*, vol. I (Washington, DC, 1960), doc. 148; Gardner, *Sterling-Dollar Diplomacy*, 73–7, 84; Mikesell, 'Bretton Woods', 5–10; Williams, 'Currency stabilization', 647–9; Elizabeth McIntyre, 'Weighted voting in international organizations', *International Organization* 8 (1954), 487–8.   37. *FRUS 1942*, I, doc. 148; Mikesell, 'Bretton Woods', 6–7; Skidelsky, *Keynes: Fighting for Britain*, 245–6; J. Morton Blum, *From the Morgenthau Diaries: 3, Years of War, 1941–45* (Boston, MA, 1967), 232–3. The published version is in Horsefield, ed., *IMF, 1945–65, III*, 83–96, 'Preliminary draft outline of a proposal for an International Stabilization Fund of the United & Associated Nations', 10 July 1943.   38. Skidelsky, *Keynes: Fighting for Britain*, 246–7; *Collected Writings of Keynes, 25*, Keynes to Hopkins, 3 Aug. 1942, 158; Keynes to Phillips, 3 Aug. 1942 covering Notes on the memo for post-war currency arrangements transmitted by Sir F. Phillips, 159–67. The draft sent to the US is in ibid., 'Proposal for an international clearing union', 168–95; *FRUS 1942*, I, doc. 160.   39. Skidelsky, *Keynes: Fighting for Britain*, 247–8; *FRUS 1942*, I, docs. 162, 163, 164.   40. Horsefield, ed., *IMF, 1945–1965, III*, 'Tentative draft proposals of Canadian experts for an international exchange union, 12 July 1943', 103–18; M. Bordo, T. Gomes and L. Schembri, 'Canada and the IMF: trailblazer or prodigal son?', Bank of Canada Discussion Paper 2009-1, January 2009.   41. Horsefield, ed., *IMF, 1945–1965, III*, 'Suggestions regarding international monetary relations, May 1943', 97–102; see also Bordo, Gomes and Schembri, 'Canada', 3.   42. J. H. Williams, 'The monetary doctrines of JM Keynes', *Quarterly Journal of Economics* 45 (1931); idem, 'The crisis of the gold standard', *Foreign Affairs*, 10 (1932); idem, 'The world's monetary dilemma: internal versus external monetary stability', *Proceedings of the Academy of Political Science* April (1934), 62–8; idem, 'The adequacy of existing currency mechanisms under varying circumstances', *American Economic Review* 27, supplement (1937), 151–68, presented to the American Economic Association in December 1936; idem, 'Currency stabilizations', 655; Max Harris, *Monetary War and Peace: London, Washington, Paris, and the Tripartite Agreement of 1936* (Cambridge, 2021), 236; Horsefield, ed., *IMF, 1945–1965, III*, 119–23; A. E. Bourneuf, 'Prof. Williams and the Fund', *American Economic Review* 34 (1944); R. F. Mikesell, 'The key currency proposal', *Quarterly Journal of Economics* 59 (1945); R. Opie, 'Anglo-American economic relations in war-time', *Oxford Economic Papers* 9 (1957); Michele

Alacevich, Pier Francesco Asso and Sebastiano Nerozzi, 'Harvard meets the crisis: the monetary theory and policy of Lauchlin B. Currie, Jacob Viner, John H. Williams and Harry D. White', *Journal of the History of Economic Thought* 37 (2015), 391; Pier Francesco Asso and Luca Fiorito, 'A scholar in action in interwar America: John H. Williams' contribution to trade theory and Bretton Woods', in Robert Leeson, ed., *American Power and Policy* (Basingstoke, 2009), 180–242.   43. Skidelsky, *Keynes: Fighting for Britain*, 248–50; *Collected Writings of Keynes, 25*, Phillips to Keynes, 8 Jan. 1943, 204–5; FDR Presidential Library, Sumner Welles papers, Box 191, Postwar general, Pasvolsky to sec of state, 20 Jan 1943; Memo of conversation, economic studies concerning post-war developments, 12 March 1943; FDR Presidential Library, Berle papers, Box 214, Memo of conversation, White letter to Sir Frederick re stabilization fund proposal, 24 March 1943; White to Phillips, 23 March 1943; *FRUS: Diplomatic Papers, 1943, General*, vol. I (Washington, DC, 1963), docs. 888, 889, 890, 894, 896.   44. *FRUS 1943*, I, docs. 894, 898, 903, 906; Gardner, *Sterling-Dollar Diplomacy*, 77; Skidelsky, *Keynes: Fighting for Britain*, 252–3. The British scheme was published as a White Paper, Cmd 6437, *Proposals for an international clearing union, April 1943*, reprinted in Horsefield, ed., *IMF, 1945–65, III*, 19–36; see also *Collected Writings of Keynes, 25*, 459–68.   45. Mikesell, 'Bretton Woods', 24. The White scheme was revised after these discussions: Horsefield, ed., *IMF, 1945–65, III*, 'Preliminary draft outline', revised 10 July 1943, 83–96.   46. *FRUS 1943*, I, docs. 920 and 921; FDR Presidential Library, Berle papers, Box 69, Memo of a meeting on the international stabilization fund in Mr White's office, June 2 1943; Memo of a meeting on the international stabilization fund in Mr White's office, June 23, 1943; Box 70, Memo: summary of discussions with the British monetary experts, June 24 1943.   47. Skidelsky, *Keynes: Fighting for Britain*, 110, 305–6; Gardner, *Sterling-Dollar Diplomacy*, 111; Anand Chandavarkar, 'A fresh look at Keynes: Robert Skidelsky's trilogy', *Finance and Development* 38 (2001); S. Howson and D. Moggridge, eds., *The Wartime Diaries of Lionel Robbins and James Meade* (Basingstoke, 1990), 251.   48. Skidelsky, *Keynes: Fighting for Britain*, 302–5, 310–18; *Collected Writings of Keynes, 26*, Keynes to Opie, 7 Dec 1943, 393–4.   49. *Joint Statement by Experts on the Establishment of an International Monetary Fund* was printed as British White Paper Cmd 6519 in April 1944: it is reproduced in Horsefield, ed., *IMF, 1945–1965, III*, 128–35; Skidelsky, *Keynes: Fighting for Britain*, 320; *Collected Writings of Keynes, 25*, 338–92.   50. Blum, *Morgenthau Diaries: Years of War*, 246–9.   51. Skidelsky, *Keynes: Fighting for Britain*, 326–33; TNA, T247/27, 'Currency plans: memorandum by the Bank of England', 31 Jan. 1944; Note by Lord Catto: International Monetary Fund, 24 Jan. 1944; Memorandum by Lord Catto: International Monetary Fund, 16 Feb. 1944.   52. *Collected Writings of Keynes, 25*, Keynes to Chancellor of the Exchequer, 23 Feb. 1944, 410–13.   53. TNA, T247/27, Monetary conversations, S. D. Waley, 17 Jan. 1944; 'Article VII: summary of present strategic position', W. Eady, 19 Jan. 1944; 'Currency scheme', Eady to Padmore, 25 Jan. 1944; W. Eady to R. Hopkins, 3 April 1944; Skidelsky, *Keynes: Fighting for Britain*, 307, 327–33.

7. 'AN INTEGRATED PROGRAM'

1. US National Archives and Records Administration (NARA) RG43 International trade, 698 ITO, Box 19, Plenary sessions, plenary second meeting: informal economic discussions, 21 Sept. 1943.   2. Louis Rasminsky, 'International credit and currency plans', *Foreign Affairs* 22 (1944), 603.   3. Alvin H. Hansen and Charles P. Kindleberger, 'The economic tasks of the post-war world', *Foreign Affairs* 20 (1942), 469, 473; Alvin H. Hansen, 'World institutions for stability and expansion', *Foreign Affairs* 22 (1944), 249; Alvin Hansen, *Full Recovery or Stagnation?* (New York, 1938) and *Fiscal Policy and Business Cycles* (New York, 1941), 82, 117, 185, 261, 300.   4. NARA RG43 International trade, 698 ITO, Box 19, Plenary second meeting: informal economic discussions, 21 Sept. 1943.   5. For more detail, Martin Daunton, 'Nutrition, food, agriculture and the world economy', in Naomi Lamoreaux and Ian Shapiro, eds., *The Bretton Woods Agreements* (New Haven, CT, 2019), 145–72.   6. *Foreign Relations of the United States (FRUS): Diplomatic Papers, 1943, General*, vol. I (Washington,

DC, 1963), doc. 729.   7. E. F. Penrose, *Economic Planning for the Peace* (Princeton, NJ, 1953), 120.   8. S. Howson and D. Moggridge, eds., *The Wartime Diaries of Lionel Robbins and James Meade* (Basingstoke, 1990), 52; Robert Mabro, 'Edith Elura Tilton Penrose, 1914–96', *Oxford Dictionary of National Biography*.   9. Franklin D. Roosevelt, 'Statement on the Atlantic Charter Meeting with Prime Minister Churchill, August 14, 1941', online in Gerhard Peters and John T. Woolley, *The American Presidency Project*; Craig Alan Wilson, 'Rehearsal for United Nations: the Hot Springs conference', *Diplomatic History* 4 (1980), 265, 267.   10. Amartya Sen, *Poverty and Famine: An Essay on Entitlement and Deprivation* (Oxford, 1981), ch. 6.   11. Geoffrey H. Bourne, *Starvation in Europe* (London, 1943), 35, 129–31.   12. Ruth Jachertz and Alexander Nützenadel, 'Coping with hunger? Visions of a global food system, 1930–1960', *Journal of Global History* 6 (2011), 105–7.   13. Adam Tooze, *The Wages of Destruction: The Making and Breaking of the Nazi Economy* (London, 2006), 476–85, 538–49.   14. Lizzie Collingham, *The Taste of War: World War Two and the Battle for Food* (London, 2011).   15. S. N. Broadberry, *The Productivity Race: British Manufacturing in International Perspective, 1850–1990* (Cambridge, 1997), table 5.1, 64.   16. Historical Statistics of the United States, Millennial Online edition, table Da15.   17. Michael Tracy, *Government and Agriculture in Western Europe, 1880–1988*, 3rd edn (Hemel Hempstead, 1988).   18. P. N. Rosenstein-Rodan, 'Problems of industrialisation of eastern and south-eastern Europe', *Economic Journal* 53 (1943), 202–11; *idem*, 'The international development of economically backward areas', *International Affairs* 20 (1944), 157–65.   19. Nick Cullather, 'The foreign policy of the calorie', *American Historical Review* 112 (2007), 350.   20. Patricia Clavin, 'The Austrian hunger crisis and the genesis of international organization after the First World War', *International Affairs* 90 (2014), 265–78; Jachertz and Nützenadel, 'Coping with hunger?', 102–3; Frank Trentmann, 'Coping with shortage: the problem of food security and global visions of coordination, *c.* 1890s–1950', in Frank Trentmann and Flemming Just, eds., *Food and Conflict in Europe in the Age of the Two World Wars* (Basingstoke, 2006), 14, 27–8.   21. Cullather, 'Foreign policy of the calorie', 338–40, 351–2, 355, 361–2; David F. Smith, 'Nutrition science and the two world wars', in David F. Smith, ed., *Nutrition in Britain: Science, Scientists and Politics in the Twentieth Century* (London, 2013), 153; Dana Simmon, 'Starvation science: from colonies to metropolis', in Alexander Nützenadel and Frank Trentmann, eds., *Food and Globalization: Consumption, Markets and Politics in the Modern World* (Oxford and New York, 2008), 173–9.   22. Michael Worboys, 'The discovery of colonial malnutrition between the wars', in David Arnold, ed., *Imperial Medicine and Indigenous Societies* (Manchester, 1988), 210–12; John Boyd Orr, *Food, Health and Income: Report of a Survey of Adequacy of Diet and Income in Relation to Income* (London, 1936); Collingham, *Taste of War*, 350–53; James Vernon, *Hunger: A Modern History* (Cambridge, MA, 2007), 124–39; Charles Webster, 'Healthy or hungry thirties?', *History Workshop Journal* 13 (1982), 110–29.   23. Vernon, *Hunger*, 106; David Arnold, 'The "discovery" of malnutrition and diet in colonial India', *Indian Economic and Social History Review* 31 (1994), 11–19; Worboys, 'Discovery', 213–14.   24. Patricia Clavin, *Securing the World Economy: The Reinvention of the League of Nations, 1920–46* (Oxford, 2013), 165; Sunil Amrith and Patricia Clavin, 'Feeding the world: connecting Europe and Asia, 1930–1945', *Past & Present* supplement 8 (2013), 41–7; Kenneth J. Carpenter, 'The work of Wallace Aykroyd: international nutritionist and author', *Journal of Nutrition* 137 (2007), 873–8; R. Passmore, 'Wallace Ruddell Aykroyd', *British Journal of Nutrition* 43 (1980), 245–8; Arnold, 'The "discovery"', 12–19.   25. Sunil Amrith, 'Food and welfare in India c. 1900–1950', *Comparative Studies in Society and History* 50 (2008), 1010–35; Amrith and Clavin, 'Feeding the world', 43; Vernon, *Hunger*, 113–15, 144; Worboys, 'Discovery', 216–22; Arnold, 'The "discovery"', 22–5; Alison Bashford, *Global Population: History, Geopolitics and Life on Earth* (New York, 2014), 413, 416.   26. Henry A. Wallace, 'Foundations of the peace', reprinted in Russell Lord, ed., *Democracy Reborn: Selected from Public Papers* (New York, 1944), 181, 183–5, 187–9.   27. John Boyd Orr, *Fighting for What? To 'Billy Boy' and All the Other Boys Killed in the War* (London, 1942), v, ix, 1–2, 22, 26, 30–41, 49–53, 58.   28. Sean Turnell, 'Monetary reformers, amateur idealists and Keynesian crusaders: Australian economists' international advocacy, 1925–50', Ph.D. thesis, Macquarie University, 1999, 140–41.   29. Wilson,

'Rehearsal', 265–74, 278, 280. **30.** F. D. Roosevelt, 'Annual message to Congress on the State of the Union', 6 Jan. 1941 in Peters and Woolley, *American Presidency Project*; *FRUS 1943*, I, doc. 746; Wilson, 'Rehearsal', 279; *United Nations Conference on Food and Agriculture, Hot Springs, Virginia, 18 May–3 June 1943. Final Act and Section Reports* (Washington, 1943), 5–31. **31.** *Documents on Australian Foreign Policy (DAFP), vol. 7, 1944*, docs. 199, 272; Tim Rowse, *Nugget Coombs: A Reforming Life* (Cambridge, 2002), 120–24; Turnell, 'Monetary reformers', 137–45; Jachertz and Nützenadel, 'Coping with hunger?', 107–8; John Boyd Orr, *As I Recall* (London, 1966), 157–61. **32.** Boyd Orr, *As I Recall*, 161–4, 166–71; Passmore, 'Aykroyd', 248–9; Collingham, *Taste of War*, 483; *DAFP, 9, 1946*, doc. 267; Amy L. Staples, *The Birth of Development: How the World Bank, Food and Agriculture Organization and World Health Organization Changed the World, 1945–1965* (Kent, OH, 2006), 84–9; *idem*, 'To win the peace: the FAO, Sir John Boyd Orr, and the World Food Board proposals', *Peace and Change* 28 (2003), 495–523. **33.** Harry S. Truman Presidential Library, Joseph D. Coppock papers, Box 2, Proposals for a World Food Board, J. Coppock, 26 Aug. 1946; Boyd Orr, *As I Recall*, 171–8; Collingham, *Taste of War*, 483–4; Staples, *Birth of Development*, 91–3. **34.** Boyd Orr, *As I Recall*, 179, 191–5, 202–3, 205–6, 210–11; TNA, PREM8/195, CP(46)374, 11 Oct. 1946: Cabinet. International Commodity Policy. Memo by the President of the Board of Trade and the Minister of Food, 11 Oct. 1946 and cover note by J. M. Fleming, 14 Oct. 1946; Collingham, *Taste of War*, 484. **35.** Jachertz and Nützenadel, 'Coping with hunger?', 110–12; Staples, *Birth of Development*, 96–9. **36.** Amrith and Clavin, 'Feeding the world', 30, 36. **37.** For example, Fiona Gordon-Ashworth, *International Commodity Control: A Contemporary History and Appraisal* (London, 1984), 72–3, 194–6, 235–7; A. McFadyean, *The History of Rubber Regulation, 1934–1943* (London, 1944). **38.** Gordon-Ashworth, *International Commodity Control*, 84–8; Edward S. Mason, *Controlling World Trade: Cartels and Commodity Agreements* (New York, 1946) and review by Arthur R. Upgren, *American Economic Review* 38 (1948), 438–41; United Nations, *International Cartels: A League of Nations Memorandum* (New York, 1947). **39.** J. M. Keynes, 'The policy of government storage of food-stuffs and raw materials', *Economic Journal* 48 (1938), 449–60; Robert W. Dimand and Mary Ann Dimand, 'J M Keynes on buffer stocks and commodity price stabilization', *History of Political Economy* 22 (1990), 113–23. **40.** *The Collected Writings of John Maynard Keynes, Vol. 27, Activities 1940–1946*, ed., D. Moggridge (Cambridge, 1980), 3–19. **41.** Franklin D. Roosevelt, 'Statement on Inter-American Economic Cooperation', 21 June 1940 in Peters and Woolley, *American Presidency Project*; *FRUS: Diplomatic Papers, 1940, The American Republics*, vol. V (Washington, DC, 1961), docs. 434, 438, 439, 446–469; *FRUS: Diplomatic Papers, 1941, The British Commonwealth, the Near East and Africa*, vol. III (Washington, DC, 1959), doc. 64; Rosemary Thorp, 'The Latin American economies, 1939–c. 1950', in Leslie Bethell, ed., *The Cambridge History of Latin America, vol. VI: Latin America since 1930: Economy, Society, Politics. Part I Economy and Society* (Cambridge, 1994), 120–21. **42.** *FRUS: Diplomatic Papers, 1940, The British Commonwealth, the Soviet Union, the Near East and Africa*, vol. III (Washington, DC, 1958), doc. 123; *FRUS 1941*, III, docs. 64, 65. **43.** *Collected Writings of Keynes*, 27, surplus policy, 20–23 and Keynes to Acheson, 4 June 1941, 23–6; *FRUS 1941*, III, doc. 66. **44.** *FRUS 1941*, III, doc. 70; *The Collected Writings of John Maynard Keynes, Vol. 25, Activities 1940–1944*, ed. D. Moggridge (Cambridge, 1978), 24–5; *Collected Writings of Keynes*, 27, 'War Cabinet: Official committee on export surpluses draft international wheat agreement, memo by JMK', 18 Aug. 1941, 31–6; 'The wheat conference: JMK to R. Hopkins and H. Wilson Smith', 3 Sept. 1941, 37–40. **45.** Robert Skidelsky, *John Maynard Keynes: Fighting for Britain, 1937–46* (London, 2000), 234–6; *Collected Writings of Keynes*, 27, 105–11 for correspondence on the first drafts; 'The international control of raw materials', 14 April 1942, 112–33; International regulation of primary products, Aug. 1942, 135–66; War Cabinet Committee on Reconstruction Problems. The international regulation of primary products, 168–94, on the outcome, 196; TNA, T247/9, R. Harrod, 'Note on "The international regulation of primary products"', 15 June 1942; Dimand and Dimand, 'Keynes on buffer stocks', 118–22. **46.** NARA RG43 International trade, 698 ITO, Box 18, Informal economic discussions, subcommittee on commodity policy, first to fifth meetings, 22–29 Sept. 1943; Boris

C. Swerling, 'Buffer stocks and international commodity problems', *Economic Journal* 63 (1953), 778–90; R. S. Porter, 'Buffer stocks and economic stability', *Oxford Economic Papers* ns 2 (1950), 95–116.   **47.** NARA RG43 International trade, 698 ITO, Box 25, Memo of dissent of the Department of Agriculture from the report of the committee on commodity agreements; Interim report of the special committee on commodity agreements and methods of trade, 10 Sept. 1943.   **48.** NARA RG43 International trade, 698 ITO, Box 18, Subcommittee on international commodity arrangements. Commodities paper no. 1, The international regulation of primary products, L. Robbins, 22 Sept. 1943; Final report, Joint statement on international commodity policy, 19 Oct. 1943; Box 25, Report on commodity arrangements, 19 Sept. 1944; Views on commodity arrangements expressed at the food conference, 22 July 1943; Box 54, Memo: international commodity agreements in relation to the problem of international economic organization, L. R. Edminister, 14 Dec. 1944; *Collected Writings of Keynes*, 27, editorial notes, 199.   **49.** Jasmien Van Daele, 'Engineering social peace: networks, ideas and the founding of the International Labour Organization', *International Review of Social History* 50 (2005), 435–66; Gerry Rodgers, Eddy Lee, Lee Swepston and Jasmien Van Daele, *The International Labour Organization and the Quest for Social Justice, 1919–2009* (Geneva, 2009), 4–9, 12–20; ILO constitution 1919, available on the ILO website.   **50.** Full list of conventions on ILO website; Rodgers *et al.*, *International Labour Organization*, 171–80.   **51.** Susan Estabrook Kennedy, 'Perkins, Frances' and Sylvia B. Larson, 'Winant, John Gilbert', in *American National Biography*.   **52.** Sandrine Kott, 'Fighting the war or preparing for peace? The ILO during the Second World War', *Journal of Modern European History* 12 (2014), 361, 365–71; Rodgers *et al.*, *International Labour Organization*, 150–52, 154–5, 207–9.   **53.** NARA RG43 International trade, 698 ITO, Box 19, Informal economic discussions, subcommittee on employment policies, 14 Oct. 1943 and 'The possibility of creation an international agency for the promotion of policies conducive to high employment', 4 Oct. 1943; Box 20, Report on organizational aspects of plans for postwar international economic cooperation, 23 Dec 1943.   **54.** Turnell, 'Monetary reformers', 149–53; Sean Turnell, 'Australia's "employment approach" to international postwar reconstruction: calling the bluff of multilateralism', *History of Economics Review* 36 (2002), 116–7; *DAFP, 7, 1944*, docs. 21, 28, 78, 85, 99, 113.   **55.** *DAFP, 7, 1944*, docs. 114, 117, 121, 122, 123, 127, 129, 134, 136, 138, 140, 142, 144, 145, 146; ILO, *Resolutions Adopted by the 26th Session of the ILO Conference Philadelphia April–May 1944* (Montreal, 1944); Declaration of Philadelphia, at https://www.ilo.org/legacy/english/inwork/cb-policy-guide/declarationofPhiladelphia1944. pdf; Turnell, 'Monetary reformers', 154–5; Rodgers *et al.*, *International Labour Organization*, 43–5, 47, 53.   **56.** Kott, 'Fighting the war', 370–76; Rodgers *et al.*, *International Labour Organization*, 6, 209.   **57.** Turnell, 'Monetary reformers', 159–67; *DAFP, 7, 1944*, docs. 158, 194, 224, 225, 226, 227, 231, 233, 235, 242; *DAFP, 9, 1946*, doc. 212.

8. 'THE THRESHOLD OF THE FUTURE'

1. *Proceedings and Documents of the United Nations Monetary and Financial Conference: Bretton Woods, New Hampshire, July 1 to July 22 1944* (Washington, DC, 1948), 1225, 1226.   **2.** Marriner S. Eccles Document Collection, available at https://fraser.stlouisfed.org /archival-collection/marriner-s-eccles-papers-1343, Box 36, folder 11 item 3, E. A. Goldenweiser, Federal Reserve, 'Bretton Woods', Director of Research and Statistics, Board of Governors of the Federal Reserve System, Remarks made at joint meeting of directors of Federal Reserve Bank of Cleveland and branches, 22 Nov. 1944.   **3.** Warren F. Kimball, *The Juggler: Franklin Roosevelt as Wartime Leader* (Princeton, NJ, 1991), 85, 186, 191.   **4.** *The Collected Writings of John Maynard Keynes, Vol. 26, Activities 1941–1946*, ed. D. Moggridge (Cambridge, 1980), Keynes to Hopkins, 25 June 1944, 61.   **5.** *Collected Writings of Keynes*, 26, Keynes to Hopkins, 30 June 1944, 67–9; Raymond Mikesell, 'The Bretton Woods debates: a memoir', Essays in International Finance No. 192, Department of Economics, Princeton, 1994, 33–4; Robert Skidelsky, *John Maynard Keynes: Fighting for Britain, 1937–46* (London, 2000), 343–6; Marriner S. Eccles Document Collection, Box 36, folder 11 item 2, E. A. Goldenweiser, 'Issues at Bretton Woods', 29 July 1944. On the US Treasury position at Atlantic City, see 'Questions and answers on the International Monetary Fund', 10 June 1944 in J. Keith Horsefield, ed., *The International Monetary Fund 1945–1965: Twenty Years of International Monetary Cooperation: Volume III, Documents* (Washington, DC, 1969), 136–82. **6.** Goldenweiser, 'Bretton Woods'. **7.** J. Morton Blum, *From the Morgenthau Diaries: 3, Years of War, 1941–45* (Boston, MA, 1967), 250; *Collected Writings of Keynes, 26*, Keynes to Catto, 4 July 1944, 81–2. **8.** Mikesell, 'Bretton Woods', 34. **9.** Goldenweiser, 'Bretton Woods'; Blum, *Morgenthau Diaries: Years of War*, 273–4; Richard N. Gardner, *Sterling-Dollar Diplomacy: Anglo-American Collaboration in the Reconstruction of Multilateral Trade* (Oxford, 1956), 111–12; Armand van Dormael, *Bretton Woods: Birth of a Monetary System* (London, 1978), 174, 198–9; Benn Steil, *The Battle of Bretton Woods: John Maynard Keynes, Harry Dexter White and the Making of a New World Order* (Princeton, NJ, 2013), 218–21; on Keynes's role, see D. E. Moggridge, *Maynard Keynes: An Economist's Biography* (London and New York, 1992), ch. 28. **10.** Oscar Sanchez-Sibony, 'Capitalism's fellow traveller: the Soviet Union, Bretton Woods and the Cold War, 1944–56', *Comparative Studies in Society and History* 56 (2014), 295–7. **11.** Goldenweiser, 'Bretton Woods'; Mikesell, 'Bretton Woods', 41–2; Skidelsky, *Keynes: Fighting for Britain*, 356; Blum, *Morgenthau Diaries: Years of War*, 258–65; Raymond Mikesell, 'Negotiating at Bretton Woods', in Raymond Dennett and Joseph E. Johnson, eds., *Negotiating with the Russians* (Boston, MA, 1951), 112; Elizabeth Borgwardt, *A New Deal for the World: America's Vision for Human Rights* (Cambridge, MA, and London, 2005), 252. A full list of all delegates is given in Kurt Schuler and Mark Bernkopf, 'Who was who at Bretton Woods?', Center for Financial Stability, 1 July 2014. **12.** FDR Presidential Library, Berle papers, Box 69, Memo on a meeting on the international stabilization fund in Mr White's office, May 5 1943; Morgenthau Diary, Book 749, 1–3 July 1944, Bretton Woods, 1 July 1944, Instructions of American delegates, Fund; Goldenweser, 'Issues' and 'Bretton Woods'; J. G. Crawford, *Australian Trade Policy 1942–46* (Canberra, 1968), 9–10; Sean Turnell, 'Monetary reformers, amateur idealists and Keynesian crusaders: Australian economists' international advocacy, 1925–50', Ph.D. thesis, Macquarie University, 1999, ch. 7. **13.** Stuart Macintyre, *Australia's Boldest Experiment: War and Reconstruction in the 1940s* (Sydney, 2015), 367, 369. **14.** Eric Helleiner, *Forgotten Foundations of Bretton Woods: International Development and the Making of the Postwar Order* (Ithaca, NY, 2014), 184–200; Rana Mitter, *China's War with Japan, 1937–1945: The Struggle for Survival* (London, 2013), chs. 17 and 18; Jung Chang, *Big Sister, Little Sister, Red Sister: Three Women at the Heart of Twentieth-Century China* (London, 2019), 71, 149, 205–7, 231, 296–7; Claude Buss, *War and Diplomacy in Eastern Asia* (New York, 1941), 148, 384–92, 405–6, 414–19; Alan Bollard, *Economists at War: How a Handful of Economists Helped Win and Lose the World Wars* (Oxford, 2019), 32–62. **15.** Helleiner, *Forgotten Foundations*, 221; Goldenweiser, 'Issues'; *Collected Writings of Keynes, 26*, Keynes to Catto, 4 July 1944, 80 and Statement by Lord Keynes on behalf of the delegation of the United Kingdom at meeting of Commission I, 86–7; Aditya Balasubramanian and Srinath Raghavan, 'Present at the creation: India, the global economy and the Bretton Woods conference', *Journal of World History* 29 (2018), 71–2, 80, 83–8; B. R. Tomlinson, *The Political Economy of the Raj 1914–47: The Economics of Decolonisation* (Cambridge, 1979); G. Balachandran, *John Bullion's Empire: Britain's Gold Problem and India between the Wars* (London, 1996), 47–65; The National Archives (TNA), T247/5, W. Eady, 1 Jan. 1944 and Keynes, 11 Jan. 1945; E. F. Penrose, *Economic Planning for the Peace* (Princeton, NJ, 1953), 55. **16.** Balasubramanian and Raghavan, 'Present at the creation', 88–91, 93; V. S. Krishna, *Bretton Woods and After* (New Delhi, 1946); B. T. Ramadive, *The Sterling Balances Betrayed* (Bombay, 1948). **17.** Horsefield, ed., *IMF 1945–1965, III*, 187; Helleiner, *Forgotten Foundations*, 159, 254. **18.** Helleiner, *Forgotten Foundations*, 156–72. **19.** Ibid., 114, 118; Mikesell, 'Bretton Woods', 39–40, 61–2. **20.** *The Economist*, 21 Feb. 1948, quoted in Craig Murphy, *Emergence of the NIEO Ideology* (Boulder, CO, 1984), 11. **21.** Paul Volcker and Toyoo Gyohten, *Changing Fortunes: The World's Money and the Threat to American Leadership* (New York, 1992), 14; Gottfried Haberler, 'Currency depreciation and the International Monetary Fund', *Review of Economic Statistics* 26 (1944), 180–81; Mikesell, 'Bretton Woods', 18; Marriner S. Eccles

Document Collection, Box 36, 'Bankers' Association Reports on Bretton Woods', Alice Bourneuf, 28 Feb. 1945. **22.** *The Collected Writings of John Maynard Keynes, Vol. 25, Activities 1940–1944*, ed. D. Moggridge (Cambridge, 1978), Keynes section of 'The proposal for an International Monetary Fund', annex A of the Washington Conversations Article VII, Memorandum by the Minister of State, 7 Feb. 1944, 404–5; Sidney Dell, 'On being grandmotherly: the evolution of IMF conditionality', Essays in International Finance No. 144, Department of Economics, Princeton, 1981, 1–2. **23.** Horsefield, ed., *IMF 1945–65, III*, 132, 190; Dell, 'On being grandmotherly', 2–4, 6; *Proceedings and Documents*, II, 1212–13; Walter Lippmann, 'Bretton Woods', *Washington Post*, 6 July 1944; Goldenweiser, 'Issues'. **24.** Dell, 'On being grandmotherly', 7–8; Kenneth W. Dam, *The Rules of the Game: Reform and Evolution in the International Monetary System* (Chicago, IL, 1982), 105–8; J. Keith Horsefield, *The International Monetary Fund 1945–1965: Twenty Years of International Monetary Cooperation: Volume I, Chronicle* (Washington, DC, 1969), 69–77; Sarah Babb, 'Embeddedness, inflation, and international regimes: the IMF in the early postwar period', *American Journal of Sociology* 113 (2007), 142–4. **25.** Michael Bordo and Harold James, 'Haberler versus Nurkse: the case for floating exchange rates as an alternative to Bretton Woods?', NBER Working Paper 8545, Oct. 2001; Gottfried Haberler, *Prosperity and Depression: A Theoretical Analysis of Cyclical Movements* (Geneva, 1937), esp. 441–51; *idem*, 'The choice of exchange rates after the war', *American Economic Review* 75 (1945), 209; *idem, Currency Convertibility* (New York, 1954), 24–5. **26.** Douglas Irwin, 'The missing Bretton Woods debate over flexible exchange rates', in Naomi Lamoreaux and Ian Shapiro, eds., *The Bretton Woods Agreements* (New Haven, CT, 2019), 62–3, 64–5, 68; Anthony M. Endres, 'Frank Graham's case for flexible exchange rates: a doctrinal perspective', *History of Political Economy* 40 (2008), 133–62; Frank Graham and Charles Whittlesey, 'Fluctuating exchange rates, foreign trade and the price level', *American Economic Review* 24 (1934), 401–16; Frank Graham, 'Fundamentals of international monetary policy', Essays in International Finance No. 2, Department of Economics, Princeton, 1943; Charles Whittlesey, *International Monetary Issues* (New York, 1937). **27.** Ragnar Nurkse, *The International Currency Experience* (Geneva, 1944); Lionel Robbins, *Economic Planning and the International Order* (London, 1937), 287–91; F. Hayek, *Monetary Nationalism and International Stability* (London, 1937); Irwin, 'The missing Bretton Woods debate', 57, 61, 65–8; Bordo and James, 'Haberler versus Nurkse'. **28.** Milton Friedman, 'The case for flexible exchange rates', in his *Essays in Positive Economics* (Chicago, IL, 1953), 203. **29.** J. Viner, 'The international economic organization of the future', in *idem, Toward International Organization* (New York, 1942), 129–30; Irwin, 'The missing Bretton Woods debate', 64. **30.** James Meade, 'Financial policy and the balance of payments', *Economica* 15 (1948), 101–15; Frank Graham, 'Exchange rates: bound or free?', *Journal of Finance* 4 (1949), 21; Friedman, 'Case for flexible exchange rates' was drafted in 1950. **31.** Harry D. White, *The French International Accounts, 1880–1913* (Cambridge, MA, 1933), 311–12. **32.** Steil, *Battle of Bretton Woods*, 134–5 from White's draft of March 1942; Horsefield, ed., *IMF, 1945–1965, III*, 46 for April draft. **33.** 'National self-sufficiency', *New Statesman and Nation*, 8 and 15 July 1933, in *The Collected Writings of John Maynard Keynes, Vol. 21, Activities 1931–1939*, ed. D. Moggridge (Cambridge, 1978), 236. **34.** Bertil Ohlin, 'International economic reconstruction', in *International Economic Reconstruction* (Paris, 1936), 90, quoted in Eric Helleiner, *States and the Re-emergence of Global Finance from Bretton Woods to the 1990s* (Ithaca, NY, 1994), 37. **35.** *Collected Writings of Keynes*, 25, Keynes to Harrod, 'Your memo on forthcoming US conversation', 18 April 1942, 148–9; *Collected Writings of Keynes*, 26, House of Lords debate 23 May 1944, 16–17; Helleiner, *States and the Re-emergence*, 25–38. **36.** Horsefield, ed., *IMF, 1945–1965, III*, 193–4. **37.** A. Bloomfield, 'Postwar control of international capital movement', *American Economic Review* 30 (1946), 687. **38.** Helleiner, *States and the Re-emergence*, 39–41. **39.** Jacob Viner, *Two Plans for International Monetary Stabilization* (New Haven, CT, 1943), 27 and 'International finance in the post-war world', *Journal of Political Economy* 55 (1947), 100. **40.** Erin E. Jacobsson, *A Life for Sound Money: Per Jacobsson, His Biography* (Oxford, 1979), 165–6, 178–85; Gianni Toniolo, *Central Bank Cooperation at the Bank for International Settlements, 1930–1973* (Cambridge, 2005), 214, 256–9, 550. **41.** Helleiner, *States and the Re-emergence*,

53–4; Toniolo, *Central Bank Cooperation*, 267–76, 279–82; Jacobsson, *Life for Sound Money*, 186–92. **42.** Helleiner, *Forgotten Foundations*, 100–113; David Ekbladh, *The Great American Mission: Modernization and the Construction of the American World Order* (Princeton, NJ, 2010), 17. **43.** Helleiner, *Forgotten Foundations*, 114–16. **44.** FDR Presidential Library, Berle papers, Box 70, Memo, A. A. Berle, 15 Aug. 1943; Proposal for an international investment agency, 28 Sept. 1943. **45.** Helleiner, *Forgotten Foundations*, 116–17; Skidelsky, *Keynes: Fighting for Britain*, 307. **46.** Helleiner, *Forgotten Foundations*, 118; Skidelsky, *Keynes: Fighting for Britain*, 340. **47.** Gardner, *Sterling-Dollar Diplomacy*, 117–18; Skidelsky, *Keynes: Fighting for Britain*, 319, 339. **48.** Blum, *Morgenthau Diaries: Years of War*, 272; *Collected Writings of Keynes*, 25, Notes by Lord Keynes on the US proposals for a Bank of Reconstruction and Development, 7 March 1944, 419–27; *Collected Writings of Keynes*, 26, Bank for Reconstruction and Development, 9 June 1944, 52–3. **49.** Blum, *Morgenthau Diaries: Years of War*, 271–3. **50.** *Collected Writings of Keynes*, 26, Opening remarks by Lord Keynes at the first meeting of the second commission on the Bank for Reconstruction and Development, 3 July 1944, 72–3. **51.** Blum, *Morgenthau Diaries: Years of War*, 274–7. **52.** Devesh Kapur, John P. Lewis and Richard Webb, *The World Bank: Its First Half Century: Volume I, History* (Washington, DC, 1997), 60–61. **53.** Helleiner, *Forgotten Foundations*, 119; Alvin H. Hansen and Charles P. Kindleberger, 'The economic tasks of the post-war world', *Foreign Affairs* 20 (1942), 474. **54.** Gardner, *Sterling-Dollar Diplomacy*, 118; Mikesell, 'Bretton Woods', 40, 61–2; Roy Harrod, *The Life of John Maynard Keynes* (London, 1951), 580; Articles of Agreement of the IBRD; *Proceedings and Documents*, II, 1620. **55.** Volcker and Gyohten, *Changing Fortunes*, 8–9. **56.** Penrose, *Economic Planning*, 60. **57.** *Proceedings and Documents*, I, 1116–17; Borgwardt, *New Deal*, 127–8. **58.** *Documents on Australian Foreign Policy (DAFP)*, vol. 7, 1944, docs. 327, 337, 345, 361, 374, 381, 384; Turnell, 'Monetary reformers', 171–8; *Foreign Relations of the United States (FRUS): Diplomatic Papers, 1945, General: Political and Economic Matters*, vol. II (Washington, DC, 1967), doc. 667. **59.** Turnell, 'Monetary reformers', 175–6; *FRUS 1945*, II, docs. 668, 669; US National Archives and Records Administration (NARA), RG43 International trade, 698 ITO, Box 53, Exchange of notes between Australian and US governments regarding an international conference on employment: Australian note on holding of full employment conference, 30 Jan. 1945; US reply to Australian note on full employment conference, 13 March 1945. **60.** *DAFP, 8, 1945*, doc. 62.

9. 'A FINANCIAL DUNKIRK'

1. *The Collected Writings of John Maynard Keynes, Vol. 25, Activities 1940–1944*, ed. D. Moggridge (Cambridge, 1978), Proposals to counter the German 'new order', 1 Dec. 1940, 9–10. **2.** Keynes, HL Deb 5th ser. vol. 138, 18 Dec. 1945, cols. 792, 793–4. **3.** Warren F. Kimball, *The Juggler: Franklin Roosevelt as Wartime Leader* (Princeton, NJ, 1991), 10, 13, 17, 19, 85, 99, 127, 186–7, 199. **4.** *The Collected Writings of John Maynard Keynes, Vol. 26, Activities 1941–1946*, ed. D. Moggridge (Cambridge, 1980), Keynes to White, 24 May 1944, 27; Keynes to L. Pasvolsky, 24 May 1944, 28–9. **5.** Eric Rauchway, *The Money Makers: How Roosevelt and Keynes Ended the Depression, Defeated Fascism and Secured a Prosperous Peace* (New York, 2015), 210–13; Louis Rasminsky, 'International credit and currency plans', *Foreign Affairs* 22 (1944), 590. **6.** Richard N. Gardner, *Sterling-Dollar Diplomacy: Anglo-American Collaboration in the Reconstruction of Multilateral Trade* (Oxford, 1956), 129–31; Raymond Mikesell, 'The Bretton Woods debates: a memoir', Essays in International Finance No. 192, Department of Economics, Princeton, 1994, 43; Walter Lippmann, 'Bretton Woods and Senator Taft', *Washington Post*, 13 July 1944; Elizabeth Borgwardt, *A New Deal for the World: America's Vision for Human Rights* (Cambridge, MA, and London, 2005), 129–30; James T. Patterson, 'Alternatives to globalism: Robert A. Taft and American foreign policy, 1939–45', *The Historian* 36 (1974), 678; Rauchway, *Money Makers*, 204–6. **7.** Robert Skidelsky, *John Maynard Keynes: Fighting for Britain, 1937–46* (London, 2000), 182, 184, 190; J. H. Williams, 'Currency stabilization: American and British attitudes', *Foreign Affairs*

22 (1944), 233–47.   8. Llewellyn H. Rockwell Jr, 'Biography of Henry Hazlitt (1894–1993)', at http://mises.org/about/3233; Mark Thornton, 'Anderson, Benjamin McAlester', *American National Biography*; Skidelsky, *Keynes: Fighting for Britain*, 253; Rauchway, *Money Makers*, 204; Benjamin M. Anderson, *Economics and the Public Welfare: Financial and Economic History of the United States, 1914–1946* (Princeton, NJ, 1949), 495, 581, 582, 584–8, 594; Benjamin M. Anderson, 'International currency: gold versus bancor or unitas'. Speech delivered before the Chamber of Commerce of the State of New York, 3 Feb. 1944, *Vital Speeches of the Day*, 1 April 1944, 379–80.   9. *Foreign Relations of the United States (FRUS): Diplomatic Papers, 1943, General*, vol. I (Washington, DC, 1963), doc. 915.   10. 'Aldrich recovery program discards Bretton proposals', *Washington Post*, 16 Sept. 1944; 'Aldrich proposes new money plan', *New York Times*, 16 Sept. 1944.   11. Pier Francesco Asso and Luca Fiorito, 'A scholar in action in interwar America: John H. Williams' contributions to trade theory and international monetary reform', *Quaderni* 430 (2004), 3–5, 13–31; J. H. Williams, 'Currency stabilization: the Keynes and White plans', *Foreign Affairs* 21 (1943), 656–7 and 'International monetary problems: the post-war monetary plans', *American Economic Review* supplement, 34 (1944), 372–84; *idem*, 'International monetary plans: after Bretton Woods', *Foreign Affairs* 23 (1944), 53; *idem*, 'International trade theory and policy: some current issues', *American Economic Review* supplement, 41 (1951); Raymond F. Mikesell, 'The key currency proposal', *Quarterly Journal of Economics* 59 (1945), 563–76.   12. 'ABA studies plan of Bretton Woods', *New York Times*, 24 Sept. 1944; 'Bretton Woods plans "complex and unclear"', Burgess tells ABA', *New York Times*, 28 Sept. 1944; Rauchway, *Money Makers*, 171, 205–6, 210–14; Benn Steil, *The Battle of Bretton Woods: John Maynard Keynes, Harry Dexter White and the Making of a New World Order* (Princeton, NJ, 2013), 253–4; Marriner S. Eccles Document Collection, available at https://fraser.stlouisfed.org/archival-collection/marriner-s-eccles-papers-1343, Box 34, folder 12 item 3, Burgess to White, 9 June 1944; Box 36, folder 12 item 2, E. A. Goldenweiser, 'Meeting with the bankers on Bretton Woods', 6 Jan. 1945; Box 36, folder 13 item 2, Bankers' Association Reports on Bretton Woods', Alice Bourneuf, 28 Feb. 1945; American 'Bankers' Association, *Practical International Financial Organization*, 20–21, quoted in Borgwardt, *New Deal*, 129; J. Morton Blum, *From the Morgenthau Diaries: 3, Years of War, 1941–45* (Boston, MA, 1967), 253–4.   13. Asso and Fiorito, 'Scholar in action', 25.   14. Rasminsky, 'International credit', 599–600.   15. Marriner S. Eccles Document Collection, Box 36, folder 11 item 3, E. A. Goldenweiser, Federal Reserve, 'Bretton Woods', Director of Research and Statistics, Board of Governors of the Federal Reserve System, Remarks made at joint meeting of directors of Federal Reserve Bank of Cleveland and branches, 22 Nov. 1944.   16. FDR Presidential Library, OF 5549, Cutting of W. Lippmann, 'The bankers and Bretton Woods', *New York Herald Tribune*, 17 March 1945; Mikesell, 'Key currency proposal', 573.   17. Marriner S. Eccles Document Collection, Box 36, folder 18 item 3, 'Poll of economists on the recommendation of the economists' committee on the Bretton Woods Program', 12 Feb. 1945; Rauchway, *Money Makers*, 225; Borgwardt, *New Deal*, 131–3.   18. Rauchway, *Money Makers*, 209–26, 228; Mikesell, 'Bretton Woods', 45; Borgwardt, *New Deal*, 91; Amy L. Staples, *The Birth of Development: How the World Bank, Food and Agriculture Organization and World Health Organization Changed the World, 1945–1965* (Kent, OH, 2006), 18–19; 'Selling the CIO', *Wall Street Journal*, 28 March 1945, 5.   19. The National Archives (TNA), FO371/45680, meeting Lauchlin Currie and R. Law, 13 March 1945; Eady to Keynes, 20 March 1945.   20. Michael F. Hopkins, ed., *British Financial Diplomacy with North America, 1944–46*, Camden 5th ser. vol. 62 (Cambridge, 2021), Brand to Hopkins, 15 June 1944, 121.   21. TNA, T236/436, 'Our financial problem in the transition': Memo by Lord Keynes, 16 May 1944; *The Collected Writings of John Maynard Keynes, Vol. 24, Activities 1944–1946*, ed. D. Moggridge (Cambridge, 1978), 'The problem of our national finance in transition', 12 June 1944, 34–65.   22. *Collected Writings of Keynes*, 26, 'Article VII conversations on commercial policy', Keynes, 12 June 1944, 305–10; Hopkins to Anderson, 14 June 1944, 310–11; Keynes to Hopkins, 14 June 1944, 311–12.   23. Skidelsky, *Keynes: Fighting for Britain*, 378–92; Hopkins, ed., *British Financial Diplomacy*, Brand to Chancellor, 23 Aug. 1944, 126–7; TNA, T236/436, Overseas financial arrangements in Stage III, J. M. Keynes, 18 March 1945; *Collected Writings of Keynes*, 24, 'Overseas financial

policy in stage III', May 1945, 256–95; R. H. Brand to Keynes, 5 April 1945, 306–10; Keynes to Brand, 24 April 1945, 315; Brand to Keynes, 25 April 1945, 319–20; Brand to Keynes, 14 May 1945, 332; Hopkins, ed., *British Financial Diplomacy*, Brand to Keynes, 23 June 1945, 172. **24.** TNA, T236/437, The present overseas financial position of UK, Keynes, 20 July 1945; *Collected Writings of Keynes, 24*, 'The present overseas financial position of UK', 13 Aug. 1945, 377–411; Skidelsky, *Keynes: Fighting for Britain*, 379–407. **25.** *FRUS: Diplomatic Papers, 1945, The British Commonwealth, The Far East,* vol. VI (Washington, DC, 1969), docs. 33, 48, 49, 51, 57; Skidelsky, *Keynes: Fighting for Britain*, 398–401; TNA, FO371/45698, J. E. Coulson, 16 Aug. 1945; Financial negotiations and commercial policy: Memo prepared in the Treasury and the Board of Trade, 3 Sept. 1945. **26.** Diary entry for 27 Aug 1945 quoted in Richard Toye, 'Churchill and Britain's "financial Dunkirk"', *Twentieth Century British History* 15 (2004), 334. **27.** *Collected Writings of Keynes, 24*, 'Our overseas financial prospects', 13 Aug. 1945, 410; Dean Acheson, *Present at the Creation: My Years in the State Department* (New York, 1969), 28; David James Gill, *The Long Shadow of Default: Britain's Unpaid War Debts to the United States, 1917–2020* (New Haven, CT, 2022), 168–73; Harry S. Truman, *Memoirs, vol. II* (New York, 1955), 475–6; Skidelsky, *Keynes: Fighting for Britain*, 401–3. **28.** *Collected Writings of Keynes, 24*, Meeting of ministers, 23 Aug. 1945, 420–25; Proposals for financial arrangements in the sterling area and between US and UK to follow after Lend Lease, 427–51; *FRUS 1945*, VI, doc. 50. **29.** Quoted in Gill, *The Long Shadow*, 180. The details of the negotiations are covered in Skidelsky, *Keynes: Fighting for Britain*, 407–52 and Gill, *The Long Shadow*, 175–87. **30.** Hopkins, ed., *British Financial Diplomacy*, Harmer diary, 30 Aug. 1945, 43 and 9 Oct. 1945, 79; also Brand to Keynes, 9/10 Jan. 1945, 137. **31.** Skidelsky, *Keynes: Fighting for Britain*, 415; TNA, T236/438, P. L. J. Bareau, UK Treasury delegation, 29 Sept. 1945; George Gallup, 'US public still not "sold" on Britain's request for loan', *Washington Post*, 30 Sept. 1945. **32.** TNA, FO371/45680, minute by Coulson, 3 July 1945 and Hall-Patch, 10 July 1945; FO 371/45698, Hall-Patch, 3 Aug 1945. **33.** S. Howson and D. Moggridge, eds., *The Wartime Diaries of Lionel Robbins and James Meade* (Basingstoke, 1990), entry 27 September and 1 Oct 1945, 222, 224, 225; Skidelsky, *Keynes: Fighting for Britain*, 416. **34.** *Collected Writings of Keynes, 24*, Keynes to Dalton, 1 Oct. 1945, 514. **35.** Quoted in Skidelsky, *Keynes: Fighting for Britain*, 417. **36.** *Collected Writings of Keynes, 24*, Keynes to Dalton, 26 Sept. 1945, 502–3 and 'Terms of Assistance', 503–8; Eady to Keynes, 3 Oct. 1945, 524–5; Keynes to Dalton, 4 Oct. 1945, 525–8. **37.** Ben Pimlott, ed., *The Political Diary of Hugh Dalton* (London, 1986), entry for 7 Dec. 1945, 365. **38.** *Collected Writings of Keynes, 24*, Eady to Keynes, 3 Oct. 1945, 524–5; Eady to Keynes, 6 Oct. 1945, 536 and editorial note 537–8; R. Bullen and M. E. Pelly, eds., *Documents on British Policy Overseas, Series I, Vol. III* (London, 1986), Dalton to Keynes, 8 Oct. 1945, 200; Skidelsky, *Keynes: Fighting for Britain*, 419–21. **39.** Skidelsky, *Keynes: Fighting for Britain*, 419–25; *Collected Writings of Keynes, 24*, editorial note, 546; Keynes to Eady, 12 Oct. 1945, 538–42; Keynes to Dalton, 18 Oct. 1945, 547–9 and 20 Oct. 1945, 557–63; Hopkins, ed., *British Financial Diplomacy*, diary entries 17 Oct. 1945, 84; 27 Oct. 1945, 88; 28 Oct. 1945, 90; *FRUS 1945*, VI, doc. 81. **40.** *FRUS 1945*, VI, docs. 72, 86; Bullen and Pelly, eds., *Documents on British Policy Overseas*, Dalton to Keynes, 8 Oct. 1945, 200 and Keynes to Dalton, 12 Oct. 1945, 216–17. **41.** *Collected Writings of Keynes, 24* Keynes to Eady, 12 Oct. 1945, 540–42; Hopkins, ed., *British Financial Diplomacy*, Harmer diary, 7 Nov. 1945, 96; 8–19 Nov. 1945, 97–100; 20 Nov.–6 Dec. 1945, 101–3; Skidelsky, *Keynes: Fighting for Britain*, 426–41; TNA, T236/441, GEN89/13, 22 Nov. 1945, Cabinet: Washington financial talks. Memo by the Chancellor of the Exchequer, H. Dalton, 22 Nov. 1945; GEN89/6th meeting Financial and Commercial Policy, 23 Nov. 1945; Eady to Keynes 22 Nov. 1945; *FRUS 1945*, VI, doc. 5. **42.** TNA, T236/442, CM(45) 57th conclusions minute 3 confidential annex 29 Nov. 1945; Cabinet offices to JSM Washington: Baboon 338, from Prime Minister, Chancellor of the Exchequer and President of the Board of Trade, 3 Dec. 1945; T236/443, Baboon 349, 5 Dec. 1945, personal from Prime Minister for Bridges; Nabob 465, 5 Dec. 1945 from Prime Minister and Chancellor for ambassador, Bridges, Keynes and all members of the delegation; *FRUS 1945*, VI, docs. 93, 95; Skidelsky, *Keynes: Fighting for Britain*, 438–53; *Collected Writings of Keynes, 24*, 598, 600–604. **43.** 'Financial Agreement between His Majesty's Government in the United Kingdom and the Government of the United States', 6 Dec. 1945, in Skidelsky, *Keynes: Fighting for Britain*, 453–8; *FRUS 1945*, VI, doc. 49.   **44.** Hopkins, ed., *British Financial Diplomacy*, Brand to Eady, 19 Dec. 1945, 195, 196, 198.   **45.** Toye, 'Churchill and Britain's "financial Dunkirk"', 335; Hugh Dalton, *High Tide and After: Memoirs 1945–1960* (London, 1962), 73, 74–5, 85.   **46.** TNA, FO371/45699, GEN89/2, Cabinet commercial policy: commercial policy and the lend lease negotiations at Washington: Memo by the President of the BOT, 13 Sept. 1945; Note on GEN89/2 and CP(45)116, Coulson, 13 Sept. 1945; GEN89/1st meeting, Financial Negotiations and Commercial Policy, 14 Sept. 1945; minute J. E. Coulson, 14 Sept. 1945; telegram from Helmore, 19 Sept. 1945.   **47.** *FRUS 1945*, VI, doc. 63; Cmd 6709, *Proposals for consideration by an international conference of trade and employment as transmitted by the Secretary of State of the United States of America to His Majesty's Ambassador at Washington, 6 Dec. 1945*, 2–3.   **48.** Attlee, HC Deb 5th ser. vol. 416, 6 Dec. 1945, cols. 2662–70.   **49.** *Collected Writings of Keynes*, 26, Joan Robinson to Keynes, 14 Sept. 1944, 132; also D. H. Robertson to Keynes, 22 May 1944, 23–4; House of Lord Debates, 23 May 1944, 12, 16, 17, 18.   **50.** *Collected Writings of Keynes*, 26, Joan Robinson to Keynes, 14 Sept. 1944, 132; Thomas Balogh, 'The monetary plan: effect on sterling area: a critical survey', *The Times*, 10 May 1944.   **51.** *Collected Writings of Keynes, 26*, Keynes to D. H. Robertson and W. Eady, 'Monetary and commercial bilateralism', 31 May 1944, 25.   **52.** *Collected Writings of Keynes, 26*, 'Notes for the Chancellor on Bretton Woods', 15 Feb. 1945, 190–92; 'The monetary plan: convertibility of sterling. A reply from Lord Keynes', *The Times*, 20 May 1944.   **53.** HC Deb vol. 417, 12 Dec. 1945, cols. 463–6, 469; 13 Dec. 1945, cols. 642, 646; Toye, 'Churchill and Britain's "financial Dunkirk"', 340–45; for Keynes's assessment, *Collected Writings of Keynes*, 24, Keynes to Halifax, 1 Jan. 1946, 625–8.   **54.** HC Deb vol. 416, 6 Dec. 1945, col. 2672; HC Deb vol. 417, 12 Dec. 1945, col. 461.   **55.** Skidelsky, *Keynes: Fighting for Britain*, 428, 433–4; HC Deb vol. 416, 6 Dec. 1945, cols. 2662–84; HC Deb vol. 417, 12 Dec. 1945, cols. 421–558 and 13 Dec. 1945, cols. 641–739; the Bill is at HC Deb vol. 417, cols. 739–48; Toye, 'Churchill and Britain's "financial Dunkirk"', 329–31, 334, 337–45; *Collected Writings of Keynes*, 24, Keynes to Halifax, 1 Jan. 1946, 625–8; *FRUS 1945*, VI, doc. 99. The agreements were published in Cmd 6708, *Financial Agreement between the Governments of the United States and United Kingdom dated 6 December 1945 with a joint statement regarding settlement for Lend Lease, reciprocal aid, surplus war property and claims* and Cmd 6885, *Articles of Agreement of the International Monetary Fund and of the International Bank for Reconstruction and Development, 27 December 1945*. The Articles of the IMF are in J. Keith Horsefield, ed., *The International Monetary Fund 1945–1965: Twenty Years of International Monetary Cooperation: Volume III, Documents* (Washington, DC, 1969), 185–214.   **56.** Keynes, HL Deb vol. 138, 18 Dec. 1945, cols. 792, 793–4.   **57.** 'Text of speech by Prime Minister Attlee', *New York Times*, 14 Nov. 1945; Gardner, *Sterling-Dollar Diplomacy*, 237.   **58.** Toye, 'Churchill and Britain's "financial Dunkirk"', 330, 346–54; Gardner, *Sterling-Dollar Diplomacy*, 238–9, 241; Gill, *The Long Shadow*, 189–98.   **59.** Gardner, *Sterling-Dollar Diplomacy*, 250–51; 'Alternatives to loans', *Washington Post*, 15 Nov. 1945.   **60.** TNA, T236/474, 'The consideration by Congress of the Anglo-American financial agreement', British Embassy Washington, 15 Aug. 1946; Skidelsky, *Keynes: Fighting for Britain*, 390, 451.   **61.** Hopkins, ed., *British Financial Diplomacy*, Brand to Eady, 29 March 1945, 141–2.   **62.** *Collected Writings of Keynes, 26*, 'Bretton Woods', 14 June 1945, 197; Keynes to Treasury, 7 March 1946, 212; Keynes to Kahn, 13 March 1946, 217; 'The Savannah conference on the Bretton Woods final act', 27 March 1946, 220–34; Blum, *Morgenthau Diaries: Years of War*, 269–70; Mikesell, 'Bretton Woods', 60.   **63.** John G. Ruggie, 'International regimes, transactions and change: embedded liberalism in the postwar economic order', *International Organization* 36 (1982), 392–5; Dani Rodrik, *The Globalization Paradox: Why Global Markets, States and Democracy Can't Coexist* (Oxford, 2011), xvii.   **64.** Quinn Slobodian, *Globalists: The End of Empire and the Birth of Neoliberalism* (Cambridge, MA, 2018), 117–19.   **65.** Quoted in Giuliano Garavini, *After Empires: European Integration, Decolonization, and the Challenge from the Global South, 1957–1986* (Oxford, 2012), 63.   **66.** G. John Ikenberry, 'Rethinking the origins of American hegemony', *Political Science*

Quarterly 104 (1989), 376. **67.** *Collected Writings of Keynes*, 25, 'Proposals to counter the German "new order"', 1 Dec. 1940, 9-10; *Collected Writings of Keynes*, 26, 'Germany's contribution to the cost of keeping the peace of the world', 21 Dec. 1942, 340-41; 'Recommendations of the British Interdepartmental Committee on Reparations and Economic Security', 28 Sept. 1943, 348-73. **68.** FDR Presidential Library, Berle papers, Box 214, diary, 5 Nov. 1943; Memo, 21 Nov. 1942; Hopkins papers, Box 333, Memo, Lubin to Hopkins, 14 Sept. 1944 covering 'Germany: general objectives of United States economic policy with respect to Germany', ECEFP D-36/44, Aug. 14 1944; Blum, *Morgenthau Diaries: Years of War*, 331-2. **69.** Blum, *Morgenthau Diaries: Years of War*, 332-4, 339-45, 354-5, 376; Harry S. Truman Library and Museum, Oral History Interview with John Parke Young, at https://trumanlibrary.gov/library /oral-histories/youngjp; John L. Chase, 'The development of the Morgenthau plan through the Quebec conference', *Journal of Politics* 16 (1954), 324-59. **70.** *Collected Writings of Keynes*, 24, Keynes to Anderson, 4 Oct. 1944, 133-5. **71.** Blum, *Morgenthau Diaries: Years of War*, 350, 355, 361-2. **72.** Ibid., 349, 369-72; Henry Morgenthau, 'Post-war treatment of Germany', *Annals of the American Academy of Political and Social Science* 246 (1946), 126; Peter Clarke, *The Last Thousand Days of the British Empire* (London, 2007), 60-66; Skidelsky, *Keynes: Fighting for Britain*, 363-4. **73.** Blum, *Morgenthau Diaries: Years of War*, 376, 378, 382; Cordell Hull, *The Memoirs of Cordell Hull*, vol. II (New York, 1948), 1614-17; FDR Presidential Library, Hopkins papers, Box 333, Presidents of Engineering Societies to Sec of State, 2 Oct. 1944 covering 'Program for industrial control of postwar Germany', 29 Sept. 1944; Steven Casey, 'The campaign to sell a harsh peace for Germany to the American public, 1944-48', *History* 90 (2005), 62-92. **74.** *Collected Writings of Keynes*, 26, Keynes to Anderson, 'The dismemberment of Germany', 26 Feb. 1945, 384-5. **75.** Blum, *Morgenthau Diaries: Years of War*, 394-5; FDR Presidential Library, Morgenthau papers, Box 910, Book 810, Meeting with Mr Morgenthau, Mr Stettinius and other officers of the Departments of Treasury and State, 17 Jan. 1945; Skidelsky, *Keynes: Fighting for Britain*, 362. **76.** Hull, *Memoirs*, II, 1619-22; Blum, *Morgenthau Diaries: Years of War*, 390-91; Henry L. Stimson and McGeorge Bundy, *On Active Service in Peace and War* (New York, 1948), 581. **77.** *FRUS: Diplomatic Papers, 1945, European Advisory Commission, Austria, Germany*, vol. III (Washington, DC, 1968), docs. 343, 344, 350, 351. **78.** Morgenthau, 'Post-war treatment of Germany', 128. **79.** Robert Murphy, *Diplomat Among Warriors* (London, 1964), 251. **80.** Michael J. Hogan, *The Marshall Plan: America, Britain and the Reconstruction of Western Europe, 1947-1952* (Cambridge, 1987), 30; Alan S. Milward, *The Reconstruction of Western Europe, 1945-51* (London, 1984), 1-55; Nicholas Balabkins, *Germany Under Direct Controls: Economic Aspects of Industrial Disarmament 1945-48* (New Brunswick, NJ, 1964), 107, 124, 128; Dennis L. Bark and David R. Glass, *A History of West Germany, Vol. 1: From Shadow to Substance* (Oxford, 1989), 179; Henry C. Wallich, *Mainsprings of the German Revival* (New Haven, CT, 1955), 348. **81.** *FRUS 1945*, VI, doc. 101. **82.** *FRUS: Diplomatic Papers, 1946, General; the United Nations*, vol. I (Washington, DC, 1972), docs. 639, 641, 643, 644, 647, 649, 650, 659, 660, 661, 662, 663, 668, 674, 679, 680, 683, 684, 685, 687, 688, 698, 699, 703, 704; NARA RG43 International trade, 698 ITO, Box 55, Procedure on commercial policy, Harry Hawkins, 17 Feb. 1945.

10. 'HAPPIER RELATIONS BETWEEN ALL COUNTRIES'

1. US National Archives and Records Administration (NARA), RG43 International trade, 698 ITO, Box 55, Harry Hawkins to W. Clayton, 30 April 1945. **2.** The State Department's position is explained in NARA RG43 International trade, 698 ITO, Box 3, 'Notes on the urgent need to prepare a plan for a permanent International Trade Organization and to give it high priority in international trade negotiations', E. F. Penrose, 17 Oct. 1944. **3.** NARA RG43 International trade, 707 Conference on Trade and Employment, Box 146, Box 147, Meeting of the American delegation to the Havana Trade Conference, 17 Nov. 1947. **4.** NARA RG43 International trade, 707 Conference on Trade and Employment, Box 146, Official report of the US delegation to the UN conference on trade and employment, Havana, Cuba, 17 Nov. 1947-24 March 1948, Nov. 1948, Annex B, Speech by W. Clayton at the fourth plenary session, 27 Nov. 1947.   5. Marguerite Dupree, ed., *Lancashire and Whitehall: The Diary of Sir Raymond Street, vol. II, 1939–1957* (Manchester, 1987), 414.   6. Harry S. Truman Presidential Library, Joseph D. Coppock papers, Box 1, Coppock to Acheson, nd.   7. *Documents on Australian Foreign Policy (DAFP), vol. 8, 1945*, doc. 75.   8. The National Archives (TNA), T236/439, Eady to Bridges, 16 Aug. 1945.   9. TNA, FO371/52983, telegram Washington to Board of Trade, 20 April 1946.   10. Harry S. Truman Presidential Library, Joseph D. Coppock papers, Box 2, Clayton to Henry Wallace, 25 March 1946.   11. Henry Wallace, *Sixty Million Jobs* (New York, 1945), 8, 10 and see also his *The Century of the Common Man* (New York, 1943); J. C. Culver and J. Hyde, *American Dreamer: The Life and Times of Henry A. Wallace* (New York, 2002), 367–73, 379–80, 388–90; John W. Malsberger, *From Obstruction to Moderation: The Transformation of Senate Conservatism, 1938–1952* (Selinsgrove, PA, 2000), 131–2.   12. Material is collected in United States Congress, *Senate Committee on Labor and Public Welfare, Selected Readings in Employment and Manpower Policy*, vol. 6: *Looking Ahead to the Post-war Economy and the Concept of Full Employment in Congress* (Washington, DC, 1965), 'Assuring full employment in a free competitive economy, 22 Sept. 1945', 2390–423; s.380, 'A Bill to establish a national policy and program for ensuring continuing full employment in a free competitive economy, through the concerted efforts of industry, agriculture, labor, State and local governments, and the Federal Government'; G. J. Santoni, 'The Employment Act of 1946: some history notes', *Federal Reserve Bank of St Louis* (Nov. 1986), 8–10.   13. Harry S. Truman, 'Annual message to the Congress on the State of the Union, 5 Jan 1949', online in Gerhard Peters and John T. Woolley, *The American Presidency Project*; Alonzo L. Hamby, *Beyond the New Deal: Harry S. Truman and American Liberalism* (New York, 1977).   14. Mark R. Wilson, *Destructive Creation: American Business and the Winning of World War II* (Philadelphia, PA, 2016); Kiran Klaus Patel, *The New Deal: A Global History* (Princeton, NJ, 2016), 264–8, 288; Charles S. Maier, 'The politics of productivity: foundations of American international economic policy after World War II', *International Organization* 31 (1977), 607–33, quotes at 613, 615; Robert M. Collins, *The Business Response to Keynes, 1929–64* (New York, 1981) and review by Jim F. Heath, 'American business and commercial Keynesianism', *Reviews in American History* 11 (1983), 143–7; Margaret Weir, 'Ideas and politics: the acceptance of Keynes in Britain and the United States', in Peter A. Hall, ed., *The Political Power of Economic Ideas: Keynesianism Across Nations* (Princeton, NJ, 1989), 78; Charlie Whitham, 'The Committee for Economic Development, foreign trade and the rise of American corporate liberalism, 1942–48', *Journal of Contemporary History* 48 (2013), 845–71.   15. D. K. Pickens, 'Keyserling, Leon', *American National Biography*; D. K. Pickens, 'Truman's Council of Economic Advisers and the legacy of the New Deal', in W. F. Levantrosser, ed., *Harry S. Truman: The Man from Independence* (Westport, CT, 1986); Edmund F. Wehrle, *Between a River and a Mountain: The AFL-CIO and the Vietnam War* (Ann Arbor, MI, 2005), 3, 24–5, 59–60.   16. Maier, 'Politics of productivity', 630.   17. Tony Judt, *Postwar: A History of Europe since 1945* (London, 2005), 86–9; Michael J. Hogan, *The Marshall Plan: America, Britain and the Reconstruction of Western Europe, 1947–1952* (Cambridge, 1987), 30.   18. Harry S. Truman Library and Museum, Online collection on Truman and the Marshall Plan: Truman to Hoover, 18 Jan. 1947; Hoover to Truman, 19 Jan. 1947; The President's Economic Mission to Germany and Austria, Report No. 1. German Agriculture and Food Requirements, 26 Feb. 1947; The President's Economic Mission to Germany and Austria, Draft Report No. 3. The Necessary Steps for Promotion of German Exports, so as to relieve American taxpayers of the burdens of relief and for economic recovery of Europe, 18 March 1947.   19. Warren F. Kimball, *The Juggler: Franklin Roosevelt as Wartime Leader* (Princeton, NJ, 1991), 92, 99, 100, 191, 193, 194; Anne Deighton, *The Impossible Peace: Britain, the Division of Germany and the Origins of the Cold War* (Oxford, 1990), 5–8, 35, 52, 53, 79, 80, 101–2, 105, 108, 120, 134, 135, 136, 166.   20. Harry S. Truman, 'Special message to the Congress on Greece and Turkey: the Truman doctrine', 12 March 1947, in Peters and Woolley, *The American Presidency Project*.   21. Deighton, *The Impossible Peace*, provides a detailed account.   22. *Foreign Relations of the United States (FRUS), 1948, Germany and Austria*, vol. II (Washington, DC, 1973), doc. 470; JCS 1779, 11 July 1947, Directive to the Commander in Chief of United States Forces of Occupation regarding the military government of Germany.   23. *FRUS: Diplomatic Papers, 1945, General: Political and Economic Matters*, vol. II (Washington, DC, 1967), doc. 682.   24. *FRUS 1945*, II, docs. 671, 678.   25. *FRUS 1946, General: The United Nations*, vol. I (Washington, DC, 1972), docs. 645, 704; Harry S. Truman Library and Museum, Blaisdell papers, Box 7, 'Russian view on the trade and employment conference: statement to conference of economic counselors and advisors by Thomas Whitney, American embassy in Moscow', 31 Jan. 1946; extracts from Soviet writings in NARA RG43 International trade, 698 ITO, Box 8; Francine McKenzie, 'GATT and the Cold War: accession debates, institutional development and the western alliance, 1947–1959', *Journal of Cold War Studies* 10 (2008), 84–5; *idem, GATT and Global Order in the Postwar Era* (Cambridge, 2020), 66–7. On state trading, see Jacob Viner, 'Conflicts of principle in drafting a trade charter', *Foreign Affairs* 25 (1947), 623–6.   26. William L. Clayton, 'GATT, the Marshall Plan, and OECD', *Political Science Quarterly* 78 (1963), 494, 496–8.   27. Timothy Healey, 'Will Clayton, negotiating the Marshall Plan and European economic integration', *Diplomatic History* 35 (2011), 229–30, 233, 242–51; Harry S. Truman Library and Museum, Blaisdell papers, Box 6, Thomas Blaisdell to Ted Geiger, 17 March 1947; Box 7, 'Program on European economic organizations', 15 Nov. 1946; NARA RG43 International trade, 698 ITO, Box 55, The ITO in relation to the European Recovery Program, nd; Box 8, ITO and the European Recovery Program, nd; 707 Conference on Trade and Employment, Box 147, Meeting of the American delegation to the Havana trade conference, 17 Nov. 1947.   28. Joseph Bohling, 'Colonial or continental power? The debate over economic expansion in interwar France, 1925–32', *Contemporary European History* 26 (2017), 217–41; Healey, 'Will Clayton', 248, 250.   29. Attlee, HC Deb 5th ser. vol. 416, 6 Dec 1945, cols. 2662–70.   30. TNA, PREM8/495, Gen179/6, 9 June 1947, World dollar shortage.   31. TNA, PREM8/495, TN(P)(47)61, 15 May 1947, Trade Negotiations Committee, second session of the preparatory committee on trade and employment; Geneva negotiations, letter from Helmore to Clayton, 14 May 1947; BT11/3646, Record of conversation between Cripps and Clayton, 12 July 1947; FO371/62305, Discussion between President of the Board of Trade and Mr Clayton, 16 July 1947; Harry S. Truman Library and Museum, Oral History Interview with John Leddy at http://trumanlibrary.gov/oralhist/leddyj.htm; *FRUS 1947, General: The United Nations*, vol. I (Washington, DC, 1973), docs. 473, 487; Dupree, ed., *Lancashire and Whitehall*, 408–9, 414.   32. *Documents on Canadian External Relations (DCER), vol. 13, 1947*, doc. 686.   33. *FRUS 1947*, I, doc. 495; *DCER, 13, 1947*, doc. 686.   34. *FRUS 1947*, I, docs. 487, 488, 489, 490, 495, 496, 501, 502, 503; *DCER, 13, 1947*, doc. 686; Harry S. Truman Library and Museum, Oral History Interview, Winthrop Brown at https://truman library.gov/library/oral-histories/brownwg; TNA, FO371/62321, Edmund Hall-Patch, 7 Oct. 1947; PREM8/490, CP(47)230, 9 Aug. 1947, The trade negotiations at Geneva: Memorandum by the Prime Minister; CP(47)245, 27 Aug. 1947, Cabinet: Trade negotiations in Geneva. US requests on tariffs and preferences. Memorandum by the President of the Board of Trade; CP(47)266, 24 Sept. 1947, Memo by the President of the BOT; CM(47) 77th conclusions, meeting of Cabinet, 25 Sept. 1947; Thomas W. Zeiler, *Free Trade, Free World: The Advent of GATT* (Chapel Hill, NC, 1999), 113–24, 197.   35. Harry S. Truman Library and Museum, Oral History Interview with John Leddy.   36. Harry S. Truman Library and Museum, Oral History Interview with John Leddy; NARA RG43 International trade, 698 ITO Box 55, 'Trade agreements and the proposed conference on trade and employment', J. M. Leddy, nd; 'Methods and procedures for the expansion of international trade', W. A. Brown to Haley, 17 Feb. 1945; 'Procedure on commercial policy', Harry Hawkins, 17 Feb. 1945; Box 60, 'United States post-war commercial policy – proposed multilateral convention on commercial policy', nd; The "nuclear" approach', J. M. Leddy, 11 April 1945; 'The "nuclear" approach to a postwar commercial policy', Clayton to Fowler, 31 Dec. 1944; TNA, CAB66/62/2, WP(45)97, 24 Feb. 1945, War Cabinet: Commercial policy: article VIII, note by the Chancellor of the Exchequer – Article VIII. Resumption of informal discussions with American officials, Annex I: Commercial policy; *FRUS: Diplomatic Papers, 1945, The British Commonwealth, The Far East*, vol. VI (Washington, DC, 1969), docs. 35, 36, 38, 42, 46; Joanne Gowa and S. Y. Kim, 'An exclusive country club: the effects of the GATT/WTO on trade, 1950–94', *World Politics* 57 (2005), 455–9, 462, 476–7; Joanne Gowa and Raymond Hicks, 'The most-favored nation rule in principle and practice: discrimination in the GATT', *The Review of International Organizations* 7 (2012), 248–51, 263–5; Zeiler, *Free Trade*, 50; E. F. Penrose, *Economic Planning for the Peace* (Princeton, NJ, 1953), 105–9. **37.** Dupree, ed., *Lancashire and Whitehall*, 408. **38.** Gowa and Kim, 'Exclusive country club', 60; William A. Brown, *The United States and the Restoration of World Trade: An Analysis and Appraisal of the ITO Charter and the General Agreement on Tariffs and Trade* (Washington, DC, 1950), 131–3; Zeiler, *Free Trade*, 121–2; McKenzie, *GATT and Global Order*, 45. **39.** NARA RG43 International trade, 698 ITO, Box 1, Meeting with non-governmental advisers on ITO, 5 May 1948, morning session; Harry S. Truman Presidential Library and Museum, Joseph D. Coppock papers, Box 2, Robert Schmaetzel to Coppock, 6 Jan. 1948. **40.** *The Collected Writings of John Maynard Keynes, Vol. 24, Activities 1944–1946*, ed. D. Moggridge (Cambridge, 1978), Keynes to Anderson, 31 Oct. 1944, 153–4; TNA, FO371/62309, Geneva (UK delegation) to Foreign Office, 31 July 1947; FO371/62312, Geneva (UK delegation) to Foreign Office, 16 Aug. 1947; Kimball, *Juggler*, 115, 118–20, 122; Odd Arne Westad, *The Cold War: A World History* (London, 2017), 344–5. **41.** NARA RG43 International trade, 698 ITO, Box 3, 'Preparation of paper for ECEPP on voting in ITO', 17 Oct. 1947; Box 5, US position on voting under the Charter, preliminary rough draft, 20 Oct. 1947; Box 10, Suggested US position with regard to weighted voting and other provisions to protect the interests of the US in the ITO charter, 31 March 1947; Box 13, 'US position on voting under the ITO Charter', L. Weiss, 24 Oct. 1947; 'Why didn't the United States obtain a provision for weighted voting in the ITO?', nd; Elizabeth McIntyre, 'Weighted voting in international organizations', *International Organization* 8 (1954), 488–92; TNA, PREM8/1416, CP(48)84, Cabinet, Havana Trade Conference, Memorandum by the President of the Board of Trade, H. Wilson, 12 March 1948; *DCER, 14, 1948*, docs. 581 and 582. **42.** Dupree, ed., *Lancashire and Whitehall*, 316. **43.** Zeiler, *Free Trade*, 23; Richard Toye, 'The Labour Party's external economic policy in the 1940s', *Historical Journal* 43 (2000), 190, 195, 204, 215. **44.** *FRUS: Diplomatic Papers, 1944, General: Economic and Social Matters,* vol. II (Washington, DC, 1967), doc. 8, see also docs. 5 and 14. **45.** Anthony M. Endres and Grant A. Fleming, *International Organizations and the Analysis of Economic Policy, 1919–1950* (Cambridge, 2002), 105–32, Meade quote at 126. **46.** TNA, T236/702, 'International employment policy', nd, with cover letter from Meade, 24 June 1946. **47.** TNA, T236/702, P. J. Grigg to S. D. Waley, 11 July 1946; G. Bolton to S. D. Waley, 15 July 1946 and Washington to Foreign Office no. 461 REMAC, 6 Sept. 1946. **48.** TNA, T236/702, 'International full employment', R. W. B. Clarke, 18 July 1946. **49.** TNA, T236/703, S. D. Waley to B. Trend, 14 and 18 Oct. 1946; T236/704, S. D. Waley to P. J. Grigg, 28 Oct. 1946. **50.** TNA, T236/703, International employment policy, note prepared by the Treasury, the Board of Trade and the Economic Section, nd; PREM8/195, CM(46) 84th conclusions, 3 Oct. 1946; CP(46)364, 30 Sept. 1946: Cabinet. International employment policy. Memo by the Lord President of the Council. The tension is outlined in Viner, 'Conflicts of principle', 621–3. **51.** *Employment Policy*, May 1944, Cmd6527, 3. **52.** NARA RG43 International trade, 698 ITO, Box 40, Edward R. Stettinius to Senator James E. Murray, 22 Jan. 1945; Harry S. Truman Library and Museum, Oral History Interviews with John Leddy and Winthrop Brown. **53.** Ira Katznelson, *Fear Itself: The New Deal and the Origins of Our Time* (New York, 2013), 363, 370–72, 380, 402. **54.** Employment Act, 1946; Santoni, 'The Employment Act of 1946', 11–12; J. Bradford De Long, 'Keynesianism, Pennsylvania Avenue style: some economic consequences of the Employment Act of 1946', *Journal of Economic Perspectives* 10 (1996), 41–53. **55.** Commonwealth of Australia, *Full Employment in Australia* (Canberra, 1945); Stuart Macintyre, *Australia's Boldest Experiment: War and Reconstruction in the 1940s* (Sydney, 2015), 134–7, 202, 237–70, 284–7, 291, 294, 296–7; Shirley Jenkins, 'Australia plans full employment', *Far Eastern Survey* 14 (1945), 240–42; Tim Rowse, 'Full employment and the discipline of labour: a chapter in the history of Australian social democracy', *The Drawing Board: An Australian Review of Public Affairs* 1 (2000), 1–13; Tim Rowse, *Nugget Coombs: A Reforming Life* (Cambridge, 2002), 108–10. **56.** National Archive of Australia, A9790 control 4232(1), H. T. Armitage [governor, Commonwealth Bank] to secretary of the Treasury, 15 March 1946: US trade and employment proposals. Restrictions to safeguard the balance of payments; *FRUS 1947*, I, doc. 486;

Zeiler, *Free Trade*, 97–8, 100–103.   **57.** TNA, T236/704, United Nations, Economic and Social Council, Preparatory committee of the international conference on trade and employment, Committee I, summary record of meetings, second meeting, part two, 21 Oct. 1946, E/PC/T/CI/7, 22 Oct. 1946.   **58.** TNA, T236/704, E/PC/T/C1/7, 22 Oct. 1946; Preparatory committee of the international conference on trade and employment, observations by the Cuban delegation, E/PC/T/CI/10, 28 Oct. 1946.   **59.** Nicolas Lamp, 'Lawmaking in the multilateral trading system', Ph.D. thesis, London School of Economics, 2013, 133–4.   **60.** John Toye and Richard Toye, *The UN and Global Political Economy: Trade, Finance and Development* (Bloomington, IN, 2004), 29–30, 35.   **61.** TNA, T236/704, No. 102, Eager, 28 Oct. 1946.   **62.** NARA RG43 International trade, 698 ITO, Box 53, Minutes of the meeting of the committee on international cooperation with respect to employment, 10 April 1946; TNA, T236/704, E/PC/T/CI/7, 22 Oct. 1946; T236/705, United Nations Economic and Social Council, Preparatory committee of the international conference on trade and employment, Report of Committee I, London E/PC/T/16 19 Nov. 1946.   **63.** TNA, T236/704, International employment policy – proposed amendments to undertakings (1) to (5) in annex A of the UK paper; United Nations Economic and Social Council, Preparatory committee of the international conference on trade and employment, report of the subcommittee, London E/PC/T/CI/11 4 Nov. 1946.   **64.** TNA, BT64/484, TN(48)5, 14 June 1948, Trade Negotiations Committee: The Havana Trade Conference; NARA RG43 International trade, 698 ITO, Box 6, Memorandum for Mr Wilcox: Changes from suggested Charter – economic development, S. J. Rubin, 9 Feb. 1948; *DCER, 14, 1948*, doc. 582.   **65.** NARA RG43 International trade, 698 ITO, Box 6, Desirability of economic development, R. Terrill, 10 and 11 Feb. 1948.   **66.** *DAFP, 10, 1946*, doc. 95; NARA RG43 International trade, 698 ITO, Box 12, Report of discussions on draft charter for an ITO held at Commonwealth Bank, Sydney, 30–31 Aug. and 2 Sept. 1946; National Archive of Australia, A9913 control 274(b), document B: The case in support of the industrial development amendment to the charter for an ITO.   **67.** TNA, FO317/53050, TN(46)60, 11 Nov. 1946, Trade Negotiations Committee: Indian industrial development and attitude of India towards United States proposals: note by the India Office; T236/704, United Nations, Economic and Social Council, Preparatory committee of the international conference on trade and employment, Committee I, summary record of meetings, second meeting, first part, 21 Oct. 1946, E/PC/T/CI/4, 21 Oct. 1946; NARA RG43 International trade, 707 Conference on Trade and Employment, Box 147, C. Wilcox to W. Clayton, 'Issues at Habana conference', 30 Sept. 1947.   **68.** NARA RG43 International trade, 698 ITO, Box 30, Wilcox to Brown, 25 Nov. 1947; 707 Conference on Trade and Employment, Box 144, Tactics and behavior at the UN conference on trade and employment, Habana, 21 Nov. 1947–22 March 1948, J. Robert Schaetzel, March 1948; Box 150, Memo of conversation, 3 Dec. 1947; *FRUS 1948, General: The United Nations*, vol. I, part 2 (Washington, DC, 1976), docs. 135, 147.   **69.** *CER, 14, 1948*, docs. 581, 582.   **70.** NARA RG43 International trade, 707 Conference on Trade and Employment, Box 149, Willard L. Beaulac to Sec of State, commenting on 'Analysis of Latin American Proposals, Tactics and Behavior at the United Nations Conference on Trade and Employment', 1 July 1948.   **71.** TNA, FO371/62284, 62286, 62287, 62288, 62302; Glenn J. Dorn, '"Bruce plan" and Marshall plan: the United States' disguised intervention against Peronism in Argentina, 1947–50', *International History Review* 21 (1999), 331–51; Robert A. Potash, *The Army and Politics in Argentina 1945–1962: Peron to Frondizi* (London, 1980), 53–77; Joseph Page, *Peron: A Biography* (New York, 1983); Eduardo Crawley, *A House Divided: Argentina 1880–1980* (New York, 1985); David Rock, *Authoritarian Argentina* (Berkeley, CA, 1993); Paul Lewis, *The Crisis of Argentine Capitalism* (Chapel Hill, NC, 1990).   **72.** NARA RG43 International trade, 698 ITO, Box 6, Argentina: Attitude toward ITO Charter and Habana conference, W. F. Gray, 14 Nov. 1947; 707 Conference on Trade and Employment, Box 150, Reaction to Molinari's speech, 4 Dec. 1947 and airgram 5 Dec. 1947; Richard Toye, 'Developing multilateralism: the Havana Charter and the fight for the International Trade Organization, 1947–48', *International History Review* 25 (2003), 291.   **73.** TNA, BT11/5206, ninth plenary meeting, 1 Dec. 1947.   **74.** NARA RG43 International trade, 707 Conference on Trade and Employment, Box 147, Coppock to J. R. Schaetzel 1 Dec. 1947.   **75.** NARA RG43 international

trade, 707 Conference on Trade and Employment, Box 146, Official report of the US delegation to the UN conference on trade and employment, Habana, Nov. 1948: annex D, statement
by Clair Wilcox, 23 Dec. 1947. **76.** TNA, PREM8/1416, Prime Minister, Havana Trade
Conference, memorandum by the Chancellor of the Exchequer and the President of the Board
of Trade, EPC(48)16, 10 March 1948; CP(48)84, Cabinet, Havana Trade Conference, memorandum by the President of the Board of Trade, H. Wilson, 12 March 1948; *DCER, 14, 1948,*
docs. 581, 582; *FRUS 1948,* I, pt 2, docs. 172, 173; Toye, 'Developing multilateralism', 291–2,
296–301; Healey, 'Will Clayton', 251; Kerry Chase, 'Multilateralism compromised: the mysterious origins of GATT Article XXIV', *World Trade Review* 5 (2006), 1–30. **77.** NARA
RG43 International trade, 698 ITO, Box 1, Meeting with non-governmental advisers on ITO,
5 May 1948, morning session; Box 7, The Havana Charter for an International Trade Organization: An Appraisal, National Association of Manufacturers, April 1949; Box 14, NFTC
meeting: ITO Charter – investment provisions, L. Weiss, 8 Nov. 1948; Investment clauses in
Geneva draft charter, 21 Nov. 1947; Box 16, Investment provisions for ITO charter, nd; Box
55, An international investment code: proposals likely to be advanced by underdeveloped
countries, J. P. Young, 8 April 1947; Attitude of other countries toward investment and an
International Investment Code, 9 April 1947. **78.** NARA RG43 International trade, 698
ITO, Box 25, Summary of third meeting of coordinating committee, 13 Feb. 1948. **79.**
NARA RG43 International trade, 698 ITO, Box 30, Wilcox to Brown, 25 Nov. 1947. **80.**
NARA RG43 International trade, 698 ITO, Box 14, ITO chapter III – economic develop-
ment and reconstruction, 1 May 1949. **81.** *FRUS 1948,* I, pt 2, doc. 135. **82.** Harry
S. Truman Presidential Library and Museum, Clayton papers, Box 76, Statement by William
Clayton at Havana, 23 March 1948. **83.** *FRUS 1948,* I, pt 2, docs. 164, 166, 167; TNA,
PREM8/1416, EPC(48)16 8 March 1948: Cabinet. Economic Policy Committee. Havana
Trade Conference: memorandum by the Chancellor of the Exchequer and the President of the
Board of Trade, and Note to Prime Minister, 10 March 1948; CP(48)84, Cabinet, Havana
Trade Conference, memorandum by the Board of Trade, H. Wilson, 12 March 1948;
CP(49)114, Cabinet, Havana Charter for an International Trade Organization, memorandum
by the President of the Board of Trade, 10 May 1949; *DCER, 14, 1948,* 581, 582. **84.** Richard Toye, 'The Attlee government, the imperial preference system and the creation of the
GATT', *English Historical Review* 118 (2003), 914, 918, 938–9. **85.** *FRUS 1948,* I, pt 2,
docs. 134, 153. **86.** TNA, T236/709, Non-discrimination and ITO, Clarke to Rowe-Dutton
and Trend, 13 Feb. 1948. **87.** Harry S. Truman Presidential Library and Museum, Clayton
papers, Box 72, Clayton to Percy Chubb, 11 March 1949. **88.** Material on the Committee
for the ITO is in Harry S. Truman Presidential Library and Museum, Clayton papers, boxes
72 and 76; quotes from Box 72, Jack Biggers, Libbey-Owens-Ford Glass Co. to William Batt,
5 April 1949 and Henry P. Bristol to Clayton, 5 April 1949; Box 76, Philip Courtney to Clayton, 3 March 1949. See also Philip Cortney, *The Economic Munich: The ITO Charter,
Inflation or Liberty, the 1929 Lesson* (New York, 1949), 17, 100–116; NARA RG43 International trade, 698 ITO, Box 3, Excerpts from statements by business spokesmen on the ITO,
24 Dec. 1948; Box 6, Basic criticisms of the Havana Charter, 15 Sept. 1948; *FRUS 1948,* I, pt
2, doc. 132. **89.** Harry S. Truman, 'Special Message to the Congress Transmitting the Charter for the International Trade Organization', 28 April 1949 and 'Annual Message to the
Congress on the State of the Union', 4 Jan. 1950, in Peters and Woolley, *American Presidency
Project*; Toye, 'Developing multilateralism', 282–305 for an overview. **90.** Zeiler, *Tree Trade,*
78–88, 137, 154, 157, 160; Harry S. Truman Library and Museum, Oral History Interviews
with Leddy and Stinebower. **91.** William Diebold, 'The end of the ITO', Essays in International Finance No. 16, Department of Economics, Princeton, 1952, 1; Zeiler, *Free Trade,*
153–64. **92.** *FRUS 1950, National Security Affairs: Foreign Economic Policy,* vol. I (Washington, DC, 1977), doc. 85; Acheson quoted in Zeiler, *Free Trade,* 196. **93.** Diebold, 'End of
the ITO', 14–24; *FRUS 1947,* I, doc. 455. **94.** Zeiler, *Free Trade,* 79–83, 161–4. **95.** Ibid.,
84–8, 125, 165–70; Thomas W. Zeiler, *American Trade and Power in the 1960s* (New York,
1992), 177. **96.** *FRUS 1950,* I, docs. 270, 272, 273, 274. **97.** TNA, T236/707 L. P.
Thompson-McCausland to R. W. B. Clarke, 27 Feb. 1947. **98.** Zeiler, *Free Trade,* 1. **99.**
Harry S. Truman Library and Museum, Oral History Interview with Winthrop Brown. **100.**

McKenzie, *GATT and Global Order*, 17–18, 54–61.   101. Harry S. Truman, 'Letter to Gordon Gray Regarding His Appointment as Special Assistant to the President', 3 April, 1950; 'Statement by the President in Response to the Gray Report on Foreign Economic Policy', 12 Nov. 1950; 'Letter to Members of the Public Advisory Board for Mutual Security Requesting a Study of Foreign Trade Policies', 13 July 1952, in Peters and Woolley, *American Presidency Project*; *Report to the President on Foreign Economic Policies* (Washington, DC 1950).   102. McKenzie, 'GATT and the Cold War', 79, 82, 88–109; *idem, GATT and Global Order*, 62–3, 68–88.   103. Douglas Irwin, 'The GATT's contribution to economic recovery in post-war western Europe', NBER Working Paper 4944 (1994), 27–9.   104. *FRUS 1950*, I, doc. 299; Zeiler, *Free Trade*, 108.   105. *FRUS 1952–54, General: Economic and Political Matters*, vol. I, pt 1 (Washington, DC, 1983), doc. 16.   106. Dwight D. Eisenhower, 'Special message to the Congress on foreign economic policy', 30 March 1954, and 'Special message to the Congress recommending the renewal of the Reciprocal Trade Agreements Act', 7 April 1953, in Peters and Woolley, *American Presidency Project*.

11. 'CONVERTIBLE CURRENCIES IN THE FREE WORLD'

1. Harry S. Truman Presidential Library, Office files of Gordon Gray, Box 7, 'Statement on dollar shortage by staff of the ECA', 9 June 1950. 2. Alec Cairncross, ed., *The Robert Hall Diaries, 1947–53* (London, 1989), 60.   3. Catherine R. Schenk, *The Decline of Sterling: Managing the Retreat of an International Currency 1945–1992* (Cambridge, 2010), 22–7, 30; Barry Eichengreen, Arnaud Mehl and Livia Chiţu, *How Global Currencies Work: Past, Present and Future* (Princeton, NJ, and Oxford, 2018), 118–19; Adam Tooze, 'Reassessing the moral economy of post-war reconstruction: the terms of the West German settlement in 1952', *Past & Present*, supplement 6 (2011), 47–70; Mark Mazower, Jessica Reinisch and David Feldman, eds., *Post-War Reconstruction in Europe: International Perspectives, 1945–49* (Oxford, 2011), 4.   4. Timothy Healey, 'Will Clayton, negotiating the Marshall Plan and European economic integration', *Diplomatic History* 35 (2011), 235–40, 246–7.   5. J. M. Keynes, 'The balance of payments of the United States', *Economic Journal* 56 (1946), 172, 185.   6. Thomas Balogh, *The Dollar Crisis: Causes and Cure. A Report to the Fabian Society* (Oxford, 1949), 9; Hugh Gaitskell, 'The sterling area', *International Affairs* 28 (1952), 172; Richard Law, *Return from Utopia* (London, 1950), 136; David Goldsworthy, ed., *The Conservative Government and the End of Empire, 1951–1957* (London, 1994), 46–7; Tim Rooth, 'Economic tensions and conflict in the Commonwealth, 1945–c.1951', *Twentieth-Century British History* 13 (2002), 121–43.   7. *Foreign Relations of the United States (FRUS): Diplomatic Papers, 1945, The British Commonwealth, The Far East*, vol. VI (Washington, DC, 1969), docs. 43, 64, 71, 90; Aditya Balasubramanian and Srinath Raghavan, 'Present at the creation: India, the global economy, and the Bretton Woods conference', *Journal of World History* 29 (2018), 83–9, 92–3; Marcelo de Paiva Abreu, 'Britain as a debtor: Indian sterling balances 1940–53', *Economic History Review* 70 (2017), 591–4; Richard Sayers, *Financial Policy, 1939–45* (London, 1956), 254–5.   8. The National Archives (TNA), T236/439, From Sec of State and Chancellor of the Exchequer, nd.   9. Winston S. Churchill, *The Second World War, Vol. IV: The Hinge of Fate* (London, 1953), 181, quoted in Abreu, 'Britain as a debtor', 588.   10. TNA, T236/51, Sterling balances of the sterling area, S. D. Waley to Rowe-Dutton and Eady, 23 March 1946; note to Keynes, 30 March 1946; Memo: cancellation of colonial sterling balances, nd; PREM8/195, H. Dalton to Prime Minister, 9 Jan. 1946.   11. Jawaharlal Nehru, *The Discovery of India* (London, 1946), 561 quoted in Abreu, 'Britain as a debtor', 591.   12. Quoted in B. R. Tomlinson, 'India and the British empire, 1935–47', *Indian Economic and Social History Review* 13 (1976), 345 from Hugh Dalton, *High Tide and After: Memoirs 1945–1960* (London, 1962), 83.   13. TNA, T236/2698, SB(49)12(revised) Working Party on sterling balances: report.   14. Abreu, 'Britain as a debtor', 597–602.   15. Harry S. Truman Presidential Library, office file of Gordon Gray, Box 11, Economic and political objectives of the US with respect to the sterling area, nd; The UK and the sterling area: summary of postwar economic developments, 7 July 1950.   16. TNA, CAB129/38/18, CP(50)18,

22 Feb. 1950: Cabinet, The Colombo Conference: memo by the Secretary of State for Foreign Affairs, covering 'Commonwealth meeting on foreign affairs', Colombo, Jan. 1950: summary of proceedings; PREM8/1187, Cabinet. Working Party on sterling balances. Report, Treasury, 4 Nov. 1949; EPC(50)40, 'Sterling balances and south-east Asia: memorandum submitted jointly by the working parties on the sterling area and on development in south and south-east Asia', 18 March 1950; Sterling balances: memo by the Chancellor of the Exchequer EPC(50)40, J. M. Fleming, 27 March 1950; EPC(50) 11th meeting, 28 March 1950; EPC(50)58, 23 May 1950, Cabinet Economic Policy Committee: the sterling balances, memo by the Chancellor of the Exchequer; Memo to PM, sterling balances, 24 May 1950; R. Hall, Sterling balances, EPC (50)58, 24 May 1950; T236/2640, SA(50)4 (Final), Working Group on the sterling area: the sterling balances, 14 April 1950; T236/2641, ED(SA)(50)5, SA(50)9, 3 March 1950: Cabinet Official committee on economic development in south and south-east Asia. Working party on the sterling area. South and South-East Asia: note by the Treasury, 3 March 1950; *FRUS 1950, Western Europe*, vol. III (Washington, DC, 1977), doc. 704.   17. Harry S. Truman Presidential Library and Museum, office file of Gordon Gray, Box 7, European recovery, the past two years, W. Diebold, 2 May 1950; US National Archives and Records Administration (NARA), RG59 Department of State, Great Britain, Box 4778, Memo: sterling balances, Henry R. Labourisse to Webb, 13 Feb. 1950; Box 4779, Memo of conversation, Acheson to Stinebower and Labourisse, 5 May 1950; Memo of conversation, Foreign Office, 17 May 1950; Box 4769, Douglas to Secretary of State, 4 Nov. 1950.   18. Cmnd 237, *The United Kingdom's Role in Commonwealth Development, July 1957*; V. K. R. V. Rao, 'The Colombo plan for economic development', *Lloyds Bank Review* 21 (1951), 12–32; Political and Economic Planning, 'The sterling area: I, History and mechanism', *Planning* 18 (1951), 65; G. Krozewski, *Money and the End of Empire: British Economic Policy and the Colonies, 1947–58* (Basingstoke, 2001), 65; J. Tomlinson, 'The Commonwealth, the balance of payments and the politics of international poverty: British aid policy, 1958–1971', *Contemporary European History* 12 (2003), 416–17; Rooth, 'Economic tensions', 140–43; TNA, CAB129/48, C(51) 51, 20 Dec. 1951, Colombo plan: note by the Secretary of State for Foreign Affairs, the Chancellor of the Exchequer, the Secretary of State for Commonwealth Relations, and the Minister of State for Colonial Affairs; PREM11/21, C(52)3, 5 Jan. 1952: Cabinet. Commonwealth Finance Ministers meeting: memo by Chancellor of the Exchequer, R. A. Butler, 5 Jan. 1952; BT213/96, United Kingdom investment in the sterling Commonwealth. On Australia, see *Documents on Australian Foreign Policy (DAFP), vol. 24: Australia and the Colombo Plan, 1949–1957*, docs. 11, 16.   19. *FRUS 1947, The British Commonwealth, Europe*, vol. III (Washington, DC, 1972), docs. 1, 6, 11, 25, 26, 34, 35, 36; C. C. S. Newton, 'The sterling crisis of 1947 and the British response to the Marshall Plan', *Economic History Review* 37 (1984), 391–2, 397, 408; TNA, T236/2395, TP(L)(49)55 revise, 11 Aug. 1949, Cabinet. European Economic Cooperation Committee. Subcommittee on inter-European trade and payments. The future of bilateral negotiations.   20. John Rentoul, '"I've got a typewriter and a bottle of gin": Sir Richard "Otto" Clarke, titan of the civil service', *Independent*, 22 July 2015; Cairncross, ed., *Robert Hall Diaries*, 8 July 1952, 237.   21. TNA, T236/436, Towards a balance of payments, first draft, R. W. B. Clarke, 11 May 1945; T236/437, Financial policy in stage III, W. Eady, 25 June 1945; Brand to Eady and Keynes, 20 July 1945; Stage III, Clarke to Eady, 27 June 1945; the argument was developed in TNA T236/2400, Clarke to Playfair, Rowe-Dutton and Brittain, 'Currency unions with USA', 24 Aug. 1949; T236/2725, Clarke to Wilson Smith, Anglo-American discussions, 29 June 1949; Making one world work, Clarke, 4 July 1949.   22. TNA, T232/88, telegram from FO to Washington, Exchange rates, 1 April 1949; Ambassador (Franks) to Chancellor, 6 April 1949; Chancellor to British Ambassador in Washington, 6 April 1949; Ambassador to Chancellor, 8 April 1949; Exchange rates and OEEC, E. E. Hall-Patch, 7 April 1949; OEEC Paris (UK delegation) to FO, 12 April 1949; FO (Wilson Smith) to Washington (Caine), 14 April 1949; FO to Washington, 15 April 1949; Washington (Bolton) to FO (Wilson Smith) and Governor of the Bank of England, 12 May 1949; Washington to FO, International Monetary Fund: Devaluation, 18 May 1949; T232/89, The future of sterling, R. L. Hall, 1 June 1949; H. Wilson Smith, Devaluation, 15 June 1949; E. E. Bridges, draft minute, nd;

T232/90, R. L. Hall, Caliban: note on memo by the Governor of the Bank of England, nd; EPC: The dollar situation. Forthcoming discussions with USA and Canada: draft memo by the Chancellor of the Exchequer [Wilson Smith], 30 June 1949, record of a conversation at the Foreign Office, 4 July 1949; PREM8/976, Cobbold to PM, 3 Aug. 1949 and memo 23 June 1949; PREM8/1178, Economic situation. Note by the Permanent Secretary of HM Treasury, EEB, 26 July 1949; CM(49) 50th conclusions, 28 July 1949; CP(49)175, 23 Aug. 1949: Cabinet: The economic situation – Washington talks and note by R. F. Bretherton and J. M. Fleming, 25 Aug. 1949; CM(49) 53rd conclusions: confidential annexe 29 Aug. 1949 and amended paper CP(49)185, 29 Aug. 1949, Cabinet: The economic situation; *FRUS 1949, Western Europe*, vol. IV (Washington, DC, 1974), docs. 431, 432, 433, 436, 440, 441, 444, 458; Schenk, *Decline of Sterling*, 68–79.   23. *FRUS 1949*, IV, docs. 455, 458 also 218, 222, 225, 226, 228, 230, 241, 245, 251, 433; Harry S. Truman Presidential Library and Museum, Office file of Gordon Gray, Box 19, The adjustment problem resulting from trade liberalization and productivity improvement, 29 May 1950; Trade liberalization in Europe, nd; TNA, T232/90, record of a conversation, E. Roll, 12 July 1949.   24. Alfred Mierzejewski, *Ludwig Erhard: A Biography* (Chapel Hill, NC, 2005), 18–26; Charles P. Kindleberger and F. Taylor Ostrander, 'The 1948 monetary reform in western Germany', in M. Flandreau, Carl-Ludwig Holtfrerich and Harold James, eds., *International Financial History in the Twentieth Century* (Cambridge, 2003), 192–5; Michael L. Hughes, 'Hard heads, soft money? West German ambivalence about currency reform, 1944–1948', *German Studies Review* 21 (1998), 309–27; Uwe Fuhrmann, *Die Entstehung der Sozialen Marktwirtschaft, 1948/9* (Konstanz and Munich, 2017); the Ahlen programme is at https://ghdi.ghi-dc.org/sub_document.cfm?document _id=3093.   25. Hughes, 'Hard heads, soft money?', 320, 322.   26. Fuhrmann, *Die Entstehung der Sozialen Marktwirtschaft*; the Düsseldorf guidelines are at https://ghdi.ghi-dc.org/sub _document.cfm?document_id=3094.   27. Wilhelm Röpke, *The German Question* (London, 1946), 191–2; idem, *A Humane Economy: The Social Framework of the Free Market* (London, 1960), 4–7, 30–32, 35, 121, 123–6; idem, *International Economic Disintegration* (London, 1942), 3–6, 71–7, 213–16, 239–44, 252–5, 261–5; Henry Hazlitt, *Will Dollars Save the World?* (New York, 1947), 62.   28. Quinn Slobodian, 'The world economy and the color line: Wilhelm Röpke, apartheid and the White Atlantic', in Jan Logemann and Mary Nolan, eds., *More Atlantic Crossings? European Voices in the Postwar Atlantic Community*, Bulletin of the German Historical Institute, Supplement 10 (2014), 61–87; Quinn Slobodian, *Globalists: The End of Empire and the Birth of Neoliberalism* (Cambridge, MA, 2018), 22, 149, 152–4, 156–7, 169–72; Rolf Ptak, 'Neoliberalism in Germany: revisiting the ordoliberal foundations of the social market economy', in Philip Mirowski and Dieter Plehwe, eds., *The Road from Mont Pèlerin* (Cambridge, MA, 2009), 125; Ben Jackson, 'At the origins of neo-liberalism: the free economy and the strong state, 1930–1947', *Historical Journal* 53 (2010), 130, 132, 138–41, 151.   29. Tooze, 'Reassessing the moral economy', 47–70; Adam Tooze, *The Wages of Destruction: The Making and Breaking of the Nazi Economy* (London, 2006), 673–4; Jerome Roos, *Why Not Default? The Political Economy of Sovereign Debt* (Princeton, NJ, 2019), 304; John Gimbel, *Science, Technology and Reparations: Exploitation and Plunder in Post-War Germany* (Stanford, CA, 1990).   30. Ken Dyson, *State, Debt and Power* (Oxford, 2014), 214, 216; Gregori Galofre-Via, Christopher M. Meissner, Morton McKee and David Stuckler, 'The economic consequences of the 1953 debt agreement', *European Review of Economic History* 23 (2019), 1, 2, 25; Kindleberger and Ostrander, '1948 monetary reform', 188.   31. Woodrow Wilson Center Digital Archive, telegram from Nikolai Novikov, Soviet Ambassador to the US, to the Soviet leadership, 27 Sept. 1946.   32. Oscar Sanchez-Sibony, *Red Globalization: The Political Economy of the Soviet Cold War from Stalin to Khrushchev* (Cambridge, 2014), 59; idem, 'Capitalism's fellow traveler: the Soviet Union, Bretton Woods, and the Cold War', *Comparative Studies in Society and History* 56 (2014), 294–5, 298; William Traubman, *Stalin's American Policy: From Entente to Détente to Cold War* (New York, 1982); Scott D. Parrish, 'The turn towards confrontation: the Soviet reaction to the Marshall Plan, 1947', in Scott D. Parrish and Mikhail M. Narinsky, 'New evidence on the Soviet rejection of the Marshall Plan, 1947: two reports', Working Paper 9 of the Cold War International History Project, Woodrow Wilson Center, March 1994, 3, 5, 9–11.   33. *FRUS*

1947, III, docs. 135, 153; Benjamin Grob-Fitzgibbon, *Continental Drift: Britain and Europe from the End of Empire to the Rise of Euroscepticism* (Cambridge, 2016), 67; Anne Deighton, *The Impossible Peace: Britain, the Division of Germany and the Origins of the Cold War* (Oxford, 1990), 189–91. **34.** Deighton, *Impossible Peace*, 219–35. **35.** Statement by Molotov, Paris, 2 July 1947, from Department of State, *A Decade of American Foreign Policy: Basic Documents, 1941–49* (Washington, DC, 1985), 807–9. **36.** *FRUS 1947*, III, doc. 198; Sanchez-Sibony, 'Capitalism's fellow traveler', 298–301; Parrish, 'The turn towards confrontation', 27–40; Mikhail M. Narinsky, 'The Soviet Union and the Marshall Plan', in Scott D. Parrish and Mikhail M. Narinsky, 'New evidence on the Soviet rejection of the Marshall Plan, 1947: two reports', Working Paper 9 of the Cold War International History Project, Woodrow Wilson Center, March 1994, 43–51; Geoffrey Roberts, 'Moscow and the Marshall Plan: politics, ideology and the onset of the Cold War, 1947', *Europe-Asia Studies* 46 (1994), 1371–86. **37.** *FRUS 1947*, III, doc. 233. **38.** Special message to the Congress on the threat to freedom in Europe, 17 March 1948, online in Gerhard Peters and John T. Woolley, *The American Presidency Project*; Michael J. Hogan, *The Marshall Plan: America, Britain and the Reconstruction of Western Europe, 1947–1952* (Cambridge, 1987), 47–134; Alan S. Milward, *The Reconstruction of Western Europe, 1945–51* (London, 1984), 56–89. On the situation in Europe, see Norman M. Naimark, *Stalin and the Fate of Europe: The Postwar Struggle for Sovereignty* (Cambridge, MA, 2019). Data are from The George Marshall Foundation, 'Marshall plan payments in millions to European Economic Cooperation countries' (1952). The total of individual entries differs from the stated total; the percentages are based on the former. **39.** NARA RG43 International trade, 698 ITO, Box 15, telegram 30 July 1947 for Clayton from Lovett, quoting London telegram from Marshall, 25 July 1947, to Secretary and Lovett; TNA, PREM8/980, European Economic Cooperation (London Committee), The continuing organisation, 2 March 1948; EPC(48) 9th meeting, 4 March 1948; TNA, T232/196, T. L. Rowan (Washington) to E. A. Hitchman (Treasury), 15 Nov. 1949; Hitchman to Rowan, 26 Nov. 1949; Note on 'integration', 29 Dec. 1949; R. L. Hall to Rowan, 'Integration', 3 Jan. 1950 covering Note on integration, 5 Jan. 1950; Rowan to Hall, 20 March 1950. **40.** TNA, PREM8/495, Note of a meeting on 24 June 1947 in the Chancellor's room; T236/808, European integration (GEN191/4), R. W. B. C. to Trend, 31 July 1947. **41.** Grob-Fitzgibbon, *Continental Drift*, 42–3, 68–75; Sven Beckert, 'American danger: United States empire, Eurafrica and the territorialization of industrial capitalism, 1870–1950', *American Historical Review* 127 (2017), 1168; Joseph Bohling, 'Colonial or continental power? The debate over economic expansion in interwar France, 1925–32', *Contemporary European History* 26 (2017), 218–22. **42.** Grob-Fitzgibbon, *Continental Drift*, 101–2, 105–9, 113, 115–16. **43.** Ibid., 125–9; Frances Lynch, 'France and European monetary integration: from the Schuman plan to EMU', *Contemporary European History* 3 (2004), 119 and *France and the International Economy: From Vichy to the Treaty of Rome* (London, 1997), 214; Schuman declaration 9 May 1950 at Europa.eu; Monnet quote from 'Jean Monnet: the unifying force behind the European Union' on EU website; Frederic J. Fransen, *The Supranational Politics of Jean Monnet: Ideas and Origins of the European Community* (Westport, CT, 2001), 89. **44.** Cairncross, ed., *Robert Hall Diaries*, 20 June 1950, 119; Grob-Fitzgibbon, *Continental Drift*, 134–51; Attlee, HC Deb 5th ser. vol. 477, 5 July 1950, col. 472; TNA, CAB128/17/34, Cabinet 34(50), 2 June 1950 and CAB129/40/20, CP(50) 120, 2 June 1950: Integration of French and German coal and steel industries, Report by Committee of Officials. **45.** Grob-Fitzgibbon, *Continental Drift*, 151. **46.** Harry S. Truman Presidential Library and Museum, office file of Gordon Gray, Box 6: National Advisory Council Staff Committee to National Advisory Council, European Payments Union, 28 June 1950; TNA, T236/1944, ER(L)(49)320, 24 Nov. 1949: Cabinet. European Economic Cooperation Committee. The future of intra-European payments; TP(L)(49)76, 7 Nov 1949: Cabinet. European Economic Cooperation Committee. Subcommittee on intra-European trade and payments. Intra-European Trade and Payments: some propositions and a project. Note by the Economic Section. The EPU is covered by Jacob J. Kaplan and Gunther Schleiminger, *The European Payments Union: Financial Diplomacy in the 1950s* (Oxford, 1989) and Barry Eichengreen, *Reconstructing Europe's Trade and Payments: The European Payments Union*

(Manchester, 1993). **47.** S. G. Gross, 'Gold, debt and the quest for monetary order: the Nazi campaign to integrate Europe in 1940', *Contemporary European History* 26 (2017), 291, 304–9. **48.** TNA, FO371/87110, Franks to Chancellor, 13 April 1950; NARA RG59 Department of State, Great Britain, Box 4779, Memo of conversation, 13 April 1950. **49.** *FRUS 1949*, IV, doc. 258; *FRUS 1950*, III, doc. 349; NARA RG59, Department of State, Great Britain, Box 4768, F. P. Bartlett to ambassador, Memo: British attitude toward economic integration of western Europe, 16 March 1950; Box 4779, Memo of conversation, 9 Oct. 1950; TNA, CAB134/225, EPC(50)10, Cabinet Economic Policy Committee: A new scheme for intra-European payments: memorandum by the Chancellor of the Exchequer, 7 Jan. 1950. The British position is in FO371/87110, 87113 and 87114, Agreement on the establishment of a European Payments Union, 19 Sept. 1950; Albert Hirschman, 'The European Payments Union: negotiations and issues', *Review of Economics and Statistics* 33 (1951), 49–55. **50.** Harry S. Truman Presidential Library and Museum, office file of Gordon Gray, Box 7, ECA views on British EPU proposal, Hoffman, 5 April 1950; *FRUS 1949*, IV, docs. 259, 261, 267. **51.** Letter from H. Ansiaux to P. van Zeeland, Brussels, 27 March 1950, Archives historiques des Communautés européennes, Florence, Depots, DEP. Organisation de coopération et de développement économiques. OECD. European Payments Union/European Monetary Agreement. **52.** *FRUS 1950*, III, doc. 349. **53.** Ibid., docs. 333, 703. **54.** Ibid., doc. 458; NARA RG59 Department of State, Great Britain, Box 4783, 'Britain's susceptibility to foreign exchange crises and its implications for the US', Samuel D. Berger, 2 March 1950. **55.** *FRUS 1950*, III, doc. 492; NARA RG59, Department of State, Great Britain, Box 4769, 'Psychological aspects of US foreign economic policies', Winthrop G. Brown, 30 Oct. 1952. **56.** Kaplan and Schleiminger, *The European Payments Union*, 35–7, 49–53, 61, 63– 79; P. M. Williams, ed., *The Diary of Hugh Gaitskell 1945–1956* (London, 1983), 181; *Documents on Canadian External Relations (DCER)*, vol. 15, 1949, docs. 565, 574, 578, 579. **57.** Kaplan and Schleiminger, *The European Payments Union*, 61, ch. 4; R. Toye and T. Geiger, 'Britain, America and the origins of the European Payments Union: a reassessment', Working Paper, University of Exeter, 2008. **58.** NARA RG59 Great Britain, Box 4783, 'Britain's susceptibility to foreign exchange crises and its implications for the United States', Samuel D. Berger, 2 March 1950; Milward, *Reconstruction*, 472–3; C. S. Maier, 'The making of "pax Americana": formative moments of United States ascendancy', in R. Ahmann, A. Birke and M. Howard, eds., *The Quest for Stability* (Oxford, 1994), 417–18; Newton, 'Sterling crisis', 391–2, 408; Barry Eichengreen, *Global Imbalances and the Lessons of Bretton Woods* (Cambridge, MA, 2007), ch. 4. **59.** Barry Eichengreen and J. Braga de Macedo, 'The European Payments Union: history and implications for the evolution of the international financial architecture', OECD Development Centre, Paris, March 2001; Eichengreen, *Reconstructing Europe's Trade and Payments*. **60.** *FRUS 1952–54, General: Economic and Political Matters*, vol. I, pt 1 (Washington, DC, 1983), doc. 108. **61.** Raymond Mikesell, 'The Bretton Woods debates: a memoir', Essays in International Finance No. 192, Department of Economics, Princeton, 1994, 60; TNA, T236/5716, L. Bolton to Harcourt, 11 May 1955. **62.** NARA RG59 Department of State, Great Britain, Box 4768, 'The long-run economic problem of the United Kingdom', Stinebower, 26 Dec. 1951; 'The British economic position', C. F. Baldwin, 10 Nov. 1950. **63.** TNA, T236/2311, Methods of devaluation, E. Rowe Dutton, 3 Sept. 1948; J. M. Fleming to Playfair, 3 March 1950; 'Variable rates', G. Bolton, 18 Aug. 1949; T236/3940, Clarke to Wilson Smith, 21 Sept. 1948. **64.** TNA, T236/2311, Playfair to Clarke, 4 March 1950. **65.** HC Deb 5th ser. vol. 468, 29 Sept. 1949, cols. 336, 338. **66.** TNA, T236/3240, 'Inconvertible sterling', G. Bolton, 16 Feb. 1952; 'Plan for "overseas sterling"', G. F. Bolton, 16 Feb. 1952; 'Plan for "overseas sterling"', R. W. B. Clarke, 19 Feb. 1952. **67.** Accounts of the plan are in Peter Hennessy, *Having It So Good: Britain in the 1950s* (London, 2006), 199–217; S. J. Procter, 'Floating convertibility: the emergence of the Robot plan, 1951–52', *Contemporary Record* 7 (1993), 24–43; J. Bulpitt and P. Burnham, 'Operation Robot and the British political economy in the early 1950s: the politics of market strategies', *Contemporary British History* 13 (1991), 1–31. **68.** TNA, T236/3240, 'Convertibility', R. W. B. Clarke, 25 Jan. 1952; 'Septuagesima plus', R. W. B. Clarke, 12 Feb. 1952; Clarke to Hall, 24 Feb. 1952; T236/3241, 'ESP: causes and consequences', R. W. B. Clarke, 26 Feb. 1952. 69. TNA, T236/3240, R. Hall to E. Plowden, 22 Feb. 1952; 'External action', R. Hall, 23 Feb. 1952. 70. TNA, T236/3244, Supplementary notes, L. Robbins, 1 July 1952. 71. TNA, T236/3240, 'Septuagesima plus – or Greek Kalends', 13 Feb. 1952; T236/3241, E. E. Bridges to Chancellor, 26 Feb. 1952; External action, E. Plowden, 26 Feb. 1952; Cobbold to Chancellor, 13 and 24 Feb 1952; T236/3243, 'Robot', W. Eady to L. Rowan, 17 April 1952. 72. Cairncross, ed., *Robert Hall Diaries*, 23 Feb. and 4 March 1952, 206. 73. TNA, T236/2725, Clarke to Wilson Smith, Anglo-American discussions, 29 June 1949; 'Making one world work', R. W. B. Clarke, 4 July 1949; T236/3243, External sterling plan, 4 April 1952; W. Eady to L. Rowan, 'Robot', 17 April 1952. 74. Cairncross, ed., *Robert Hall Diaries*, 25 March 1952, 212; TNA, T236/3243, Prices under a two-world system: note by the Economic Section, 10 April 1952; E. N. Plowden to Chancellor of the Exchequer, External sterling plan, 8 April 1952. 75. TNA, T236/3240, EPU, 22 Feb. 1952; 'Septuagesima plus', 12 Feb 1952. 76. Nigel Lawson, 'Robot and the fork in the road', *Times Literary Supplement*, 21 Jan. 2005, 11–13; Sam Brittan, *The Treasury Under the Tories, 1951–1964* (Harmondsworth, 1964), 177. 77. TNA, T236/3240, E. Bridges to E. Plowden, 22 Feb. 1952; T236/3241, Third draft of memo by Chancellor of the Exchequer, 26 Feb. 1952; Notes of a meeting of ministers, 27 Feb. 1952; PREM11/1437, 'Setting the pound free', Cherwell to Prime Minister, 18 March 1952. Cabinet decisions are in CAB128/40/1 and 2; CAB128/40/1, CC(52) 23rd, 24th, 25th conclusions, 28 and 29 Feb. 1952; P. Burnham, 'Britain's external economic policy in the early 1950s: the historical significance of Operation Robot', *Twentieth-Century British History* 11 (2000), 379–408; Hennessy, *Having It So Good*, 205–6. 78. TNA, PREM11/22, CC(52) 92nd conclusions, minute 1, 3 Nov. 1952; CAB129/59/6, C(53)56, 10 Feb. 1953, 'A collective approach to freer trade and currencies: memorandum submitted to the United States administration by HMG in the UK'; Kaplan and Schleiminger, *The European Payments Union*, 168–71. 79. TNA, PREM11/884, Cherwell to Churchill, 13 March 1953; *FRUS 1952–54, Western Europe and Canada*, vol. VI, pt 1 (Washington, DC, 1986), doc. 368. 80. TNA, PREM11/884, CC(53) 20th conclusions, minute 3, 17 March 1953; Cairncross, ed., *Robert Hall Diaries*, 14 Jan. 1953, 260–61; Catherine Schenk, *Britain and the Sterling Area: From Devaluation to Convertibility in the 1950s* (London, 1994), 122–3; B. W. Muirhead, 'Britain, Canada and the collective approach to freer trade and payments, 1952–57', *Journal of Imperial and Commonwealth History* 20 (1992), 114; Kaplan and Schleiminger, *The European Payments Union*, 171–81. 81. Schenk, *Decline of Sterling*, 25, 27, 32, 35, 80, 83, 91, 95–6, 115, 207, 225. 82. TNA T236/4304, Problems of the sterling area: report by a working party of the Treasury and Bank of England, 25 June 1956, discussed in undated and unsigned memorandum; PREM11/2307, Peter Thorneycroft to Prime Minister, 'The sterling area', 21 Nov. 1957. 83. Kaplan and Schleiminger, *The European Payments Union*, 182–4; TNA, PREM11/2671 covers the decision to restore convertibility.

12. 'DAMN IT, WE'RE A BANK'

1. *Proceedings and Documents of the United Nations Monetary and Finance Conference, Bretton Woods, New Hampshire, July 1–22 1944*, vol. I (Washington, 1948), opening remarks by Secretary Morgenthau, 80–81. 2. Devesh Kapur, John P. Lewis and Richard Webb, *The World Bank: Its First Half Century, Volume 1: History* (Washington, DC, 1997), 70–77. 3. Ibid., 76–84. 4. Amy L. Staples, *The Birth of Development: How the World Bank, Food and Agriculture Organization and World Health Organization Changed the World, 1945–1965* (Kent, OH, 2006), 38–40, 40–41, 46–63. 5. Bertil Ohlin, 'International economic reconstruction', in *International Economic Reconstruction* (Paris, 1936), 82, 90; United Nations Department of Economic Affairs, *International Capital Movements during the Interwar Period* (Lake Success, NY, 1949). 6. *The Collected Writings of John Maynard Keynes, Vol. 15, Activities 1906–1914*, ed. D. Moggridge (Cambridge, 1978), 'Great Britain's foreign investments', 57; 'Proposals for an International Currency (or Clearing) Union', 11 Feb. 1942 in J. Keith Horsefield, ed., *The International Monetary Fund 1945–1965: Twenty Years of*

International Monetary Cooperation: Volume III, Documents (Washington, DC, 1969), 13 and 'Proposals for an International Clearing Union', April 1943, 32.   7. Ragnar Nurkse, 'International investment today in the light of nineteenth-century experience', *Economic Journal* 64 (1954), 744–58.   8. Hans W. Singer, 'The distribution of gains between investing and borrowing countries', *American Economic Review* 40 (1950), 473–85; Richard Jolly, obituary of Singer, *Guardian*, 1 March 2006.   9. NARA RG43 International trade, 698 ITO, Box 38, 'Control over American private foreign investment, working draft 14 Feb. 1946'; 'US policy toward control and disclosure of American private foreign investment', 13 Dec. 1945 and 'Committee on Foreign Economic Investment Policy and NAC D-103, 24 April 1946'; 'United States Foreign Investment Policy', 18 July 1946.   10. NARA RG43 International trade, 698 ITO, Box 7, 'The Havana Charter for an International Trade Organization: An Appraisal', National Association of Manufacturers, Economic Policy Division Series No. 9, April 1949; Box 14, 'Investment clauses in Geneva draft Charter, 21 Nov. 1947, appendix D: memorandum on importance of encouraging foreign investments'; Box 38, 'United States Foreign Investment Policy', 18 July 1946.   11. P. N. Rosenstein-Rodan, 'Problems of industrialisation of eastern and south-eastern Europe', *Economic Journal* 53 (1943), 145–71, 202–11; *idem*, 'The international development of economically backward areas', *International Affairs* 20 (1944), 157–65.   12. Michele Alacevich, 'Early development economics debates revisited', *Journal of the History of Economic Thought* 33 (2011); *idem*, *The Political Economy of the World Bank: The Early Years* (Palo Alto, CA, 2009), 80; Kapur *et al.*, *World Bank*, 13; Ragnar Nurkse, 'The conflict between "balanced growth" and international specialization', in *idem*, *Equilibrium and Growth in the World Economy* (Cambridge, MA, 1961), 241, 243–4, 247, 257; Ragnar Nurkse, 'Growth in underdeveloped countries: some international aspects of the problem of economic development', *American Economic Review* 42 (1952), 571–83; Ragnar Nurkse, *Problems of Capital Formation in Underdeveloped Countries* (Oxford, 1953), 11, 13, 15, 24–30, 83–5, 87, 89; Jeremy Adelman, *Worldly Philosopher: The Odyssey of Albert O. Hirschman* (Princeton, NJ, and Oxford, 2013), 328–31; D. John Shaw, *Sir Hans Singer: The Life and Work of a Development Economist* (Basingstoke, 2002), 134–8.   13. Kapur *et al.*, *World Bank*, 8.   14. Robert Garner, *This Is the Way It Was* (Chevy Chase, MD, 1972), 163–4 quoted in Alacevich, *Political Economy*, 32.   15. R. Konkel, 'The monetization of global poverty: the concept of poverty in World Bank history 1944–1990', *Journal of Global History* 9 (2014), 280–83; Michele Alacevich, 'The World Bank and the politics of productivity: the debate on economic growth, poverty and living standards in the 1950s', *Journal of Global History* 6 (2011), 53–74; *idem*, 'The World Bank's early reflections on development: a development institution or a bank?', *Review of Political Economy* 21 (2009), 227–44; *idem*, 'Not a knowledge bank: the divided history of development economics and development organizations', *Social Science History* 40 (2016), 627–56.   16. Alacevich, *Political Economy* covers Colombia in depth, quotations at 41, 129, 144; Roger J. Sandilands, 'Currie, Lauchlin', *American National Biography*; Roger J. Sandilands, *The Life and Political Economy of Lauchlin Currie: New Dealer, Presidential Adviser, and Development Economist* (Durham, NC and London, 1990); Kapur *et al.*, *World Bank*, 111, 130; Arturo Escobar, *Encountering Development: The Making and Unmaking of the Third World* (Princeton, NJ, 1995), 25–6; Lauchlin Currie, *The Role of Economic Advisers in Developing Countries* (Westport, CT, 1981), 61. On espionage, see Christopher Andrew and Vasili Mitrokhin, *The Sword and the Shield: The Mitrokhin Archive and the Secret History of the KGB* (New York, 1999), 107, 130, 142 and John Earl Haynes and Harvey Klehr, *Venona: Decoding Soviet Espionage in America* (New Haven, CT, 2000), 43, 145–50.   17. Adelman, *Worldly Philosopher*, 260–74, 298–309, 321–3, 333, 338–49, 437, 450–51; Alacevich, *Political Economy*, 70–73, 83–103; *idem*, 'Early development economics debates', 146–71; *idem*, 'World Bank's early reflections', 232; *idem*, 'Visualizing uncertainties, or how Albert Hirschman and the World Bank disagreed on project appraisal and what this says about the end of "high development theory"', *Journal of the History of Economic Thought* 36 (2014), 137–68; Albert Hirschman, *The Strategy of Economic Development* (New Haven, CT, 1958), 5, 51–2; Albert Hirschman, 'Foreign aid: a critique and a proposal', in *idem A Bias for Hope: Essays on Development in Latin America* (New Haven, CT, 1971), 203, 205; Amartya Sen, review in *Economic Journal* 70 (1960),

590–94.   18. Kapur *et al.*, *World Bank*, 6–8, 86, 109.   19. Alacevich, 'The World Bank', 67; Kapur *et al.*, *World Bank,* 110–17, 130–35; Edward S. Mason and Robert E. Asher, *The World Bank since Bretton Woods* (Washington, DC, 2008), 151–2; Escobar, *Encountering Development*, 39–40; W. Arthur Lewis, *The Theory of Economic Growth* (London, 1955), 264–5.   20. Frederick Cooper, 'Reconstructing empire in British and French Africa', *Past & Present* supplement 6 (2001), 196, 199; Christopher Bayly and Tim Harper, *Forgotten Wars: The End of Britain's Asian Empire* (London, 2007).   21. Nicholas J. White, 'Reconstructing Europe through rejuvenating empire: the British, French, and Dutch experiences compared', *Past & Present* supplement 6 (2011), 216.   22. Cooper, 'Reconstructing empire', 199.   23. White, 'Reconstructing Europe', 211–12, 215, 220–22; Cooper, 'Reconstructing empire', 204.   24. White, 'Reconstructing Europe', 215, 222.   25. Ibid., 213–14, 218–19.   26. Frances Lynch, *France and the International Economy: From Vichy to the Treaty of Rome* (London, 1997), 186, 189, 197–8; White, 'Reconstructing Europe', 212–13, 217–18, 221–2, 225, 226–7; Fanny Pigeaud and Ndongo Samba Sylla, *Africa's Last Colonial Currency: The CFA Franc Story* (London, 2021) and Rakmane Idrissa, 'Countries without currency', *London Review of Books* 43, 2 Dec. 2021.   27. Joanna Lewis, *Empire State-Building: War and Welfare in Kenya, 1925–52* (Oxford, 2000), 2–4; Ronald Hyam, *Britain's Declining Empire: The Road to Decolonisation, 1918–1968* (Cambridge, 2007), 162; Veronique Dimier and Sarah Stockwell, 'Introduction: new directions in the history of business and development in post-colonial Africa', in Dimier and Stockwell, eds., *The Business of Development in Post-Colonial Africa* (Cham, 2020), 4–7, 11–14; Jacques Marseille, 'The phases of French colonial imperialism: towards a new periodization', *Journal of Imperial and Commonwealth History* 13 (1985), 127–41; White, 'Reconstructing Europe', 222–3, 225–7.   28. White, 'Reconstructing Europe', 227, 234; Cooper, 'Reconstructing empire', 200–203; Frederick Cooper, *Citizenship between Empire and Nation: Remaking France and French Africa, 1945–60* (Princeton, NJ, 2014); L. Bartels, 'The trade and development policy of the European Union', *European Journal of International Law* 18 (2007), 718.   29. White, 'Reconstructing Europe', 219–220.   30. Ibid., 228–36; Cooper, 'Reconstructing empire', 204–6; Cooper, *Citizenship*, 202–10, 211, 263–4; Frederick Cooper, *Decolonization and African Society: The Labor Question in French and British Africa* (Cambridge, 1996).   31. *Foreign Relations of the United States (FRUS) 1952–54, General: Economic and Political Matters*, vol. I, pt 1 (Washington, DC, 1983), docs. 22, 26; for an overview, Anthony M. Endres and Grant A. Fleming, *International Organizations and the Analysis of Economic Policy, 1919–1950* (Cambridge, 2002), 213–33.   32. *Documents on Australian Foreign Policy (DAFP), vol. 16: 1948–1949 Australia and the Post War World: Beyond the Region*, docs. 228, 229, 230, 236, 239, 240, 241, 242, 244, 248.   33. John Toye and Richard Toye, 'How the UN moved from full employment to economic development', *Commonwealth and Comparative Politics* 44 (2006), 21–2; John Toye and Richard Toye, *The UN and Global Political Economy: Trade, Finance and Development* (Bloomington, IN, 2004), 93–4; *DAFP, 16, 1948–49*, doc. 249.   34. Endres and Fleming, *International Organizations*, 227–32; Toye and Toye, *UN and Global Political Economy*, 97–9; Jacob Viner, 'Full employment at whatever cost', *Quarterly Journal of Economics* 64 (1950), 385–407; Henry C. Wallich, 'United Nations report on full employment', *American Economic Review* 40 (1950), 876–83. Walt Rostow was more sympathetic, while noting the problems of American politics: 'The United Nations report on full employment', *Economic Journal* 60 (1950), 323–50.   35. Toye and Toye, 'How the UN moved', 23–6, 28 and *UN and Global Political Economy*, 98, 100, 102–4; Charles P. Kindleberger, 'Economists in international organizations', *International Organization* 9 (1955), 346.   36. Escobar, *Encountering Development*, 3; W. Arthur Lewis, 'Economic development with unlimited supplies of labour', *Manchester School* 22 (1954), 139–91; Robert L. Tignor, *W. Arthur Lewis and the Birth of Development Economics* (Princeton, NJ, 2006); Toye and Toye, 'How the UN moved', 31–4; P. T. Bauer, 'Lewis' theory of economic growth', *American Economic Review* 46 (1956), 632–41.   37. *FRUS 1952–54*, I, pt 1, docs. 70, 71.   38. President Eisenhower, 'The chance of peace', address delivered before the American Society of Newspaper Editors, 16 April 1953, online in Gerhard Peters and John T. Woolley, *The American Presidency Project*.   39. *FRUS 1952–54*, I, pt 1, docs. 82, 83, 84, 90.   40. *FRUS 1952–54*, I, pt 1, docs. 22,

26, 28.   41. Kapur *et al.*, *World Bank*, 136.   42. *FRUS 1952–54*, I, pt 1, docs. 73, 77, 81, 85, 86, 88, 89, 92, 94, 95.   43. Ronald A. Manzer, 'The United Nations Special Fund', *International Organization* 18 (1964), 766–89.   44. *FRUS 1952–54*, I, pt 1, doc. 95; Kapur *et al.*, *World Bank*, 137–8; Konkel, 'Monetization of global poverty', 268.   45. Alison Bashford, *Global Population: History, Geopolitics and Life on Earth* (New York, 2014), 267.   46. Ibid., 272–3, 286, 301–3.   47. Staples, *Birth of Development*, 104–8, 117–19, 121; Ruth Jachertz and Alexander Nützenadel, 'Coping with hunger? Visions of a global food system, 1930–1960', *Journal of Global History* 6 (2011), 113–17.   48. Nick Cullather, *The Hungry World: America's Cold War Battle Against Poverty in Asia* (Cambridge, MA, 2010), 28–9, 43–5, 56, 61–3; Mark Mazower, *Governing the World: The History of an Idea* (London, 2012), 143–4, 147–9; Warren F. Kuehl and Lynne K. Dunn, *Keeping the Covenant: American Internationalists and the League of Nations, 1920–1939* (Kent, OH, 1997), 22, 83, 145, 167, 168; Sunil S. Amrith, 'Internationalising health in the twentieth century', in Glenda Sluga and Patricia Clavin, eds., *Internationalisms: A Twentieth-Century History* (Cambridge, 2017), 248–50.   49. Amrith, 'Internationalising health', 248, 255–61; Sunil S. Amrith, *Decolonizing International Health: India and Southeast Asia, 1930–65* (Basingstoke, 2006), 3–7, 11–19.   50. Cullather, *Hungry World*, 49–50, 52–4, 56–63.   51. R. P. Dore, 'Land reform and Japan's economic development', *Developing Economies* 3 (1965), 487–96; T. Kawagoe, 'Agricultural land reform in postwar Japan: experiences and issues', World Bank Policy Research Working Papers no. 2111, Nov. 1999; Cullather, *Hungry World*, 102–3.   52. Inhan Kim, 'Land reform in South Korea under the US military occupation, 1945–48', *Journal of Cold War Studies* 18 (2016), 97–129; C. Clyde Mitchell, 'Land reform in South Korea', *Pacific Affairs* 22 (1949), 144–54; Cullather, *Hungry World*, 100–106.   53. David Ekbladh, *The Great American Mission: Modernization and the Construction of an American World Order* (Princeton, NJ, and Oxford, 2010), 153–5, 164–5, 173, 182–4, 188–9, 190–91, 197, 201–2, 202–3, 204, 210, 212, 221, 223–5; D. Wurfel, 'Agrarian reform in the Republic of Vietnam', *Far Eastern Survey* 26 (1957); David Elliott, *The Vietnamese War: Revolution and Social Change in the Mekong Delta, 1930–1975* (London, 2003); Douglas C. Dacey, *Foreign Aid, War and Economic Development: South Vietnam 1955–1975* (Austin, TX, 1986); E. E. Moise, *Land Reform in China and North Vietnam* (Chapel Hill, NC, 1983); R. Prosterman, 'Land reform in South Vietnam: a proposal for turning the tables on the Vietcong', *Cornell Law Review* 53 (1967); R. Prosterman, 'Land to the tiller in South Vietnam: the tables turned', *Asian Survey* 10 (1970); Cullather, *Hungry World*, 94–106, 203.   54. Cullather, *Hungry World*, 76–9, 92.   55. Ekbladh, *Great American Mission*, 40–42, 49, 58–63, 65–8, 71–2, 74–6, 81, 97, 100; Cullather, *Hungry World*, 108–33.   56. Harry S. Truman, Inaugural Address, 20 Jan. 1949, in Peters and Woolley, *American Presidency Project*.   57. Ekbladh, *Great American Mission*, 78–9, 90, 111–13.   58. Ibid., 159–61.   59. Bashford, *Global Population*, 270–71, 321–2, 335–8.   60. Ibid., 259–61, 331–3; UNESCO, *UNESCO and its Programme: III, The Race Question* (Paris, 1950), 8; Garland E. Allen, 'Julian Huxley and the eugenical view of human evolution', in C. K. Waters and A. Van Helden, eds., *Julian Huxley: Biologist and Statesman of Science* (Houston, TX, 1982), 206–7, 221; D. Hubback, 'Julian Huxley and eugenics', in M. Keynes and G. A. Harrison, eds., *Evolutionary Studies: A Centenary Celebration of the Life of Julian Huxley* (London, 1989); J. Huxley, *Man in the Modern World* (London, 1947), 68–9; J. Huxley, *Essays in Popular Science* (London, 1926), ix.   61. Bashford, *Global Population*, 274–8, 287–9, 305–10, 317–20, 327, 336; Cullather, *Hungry World*, 66–7.   62. Bashford, *Global Population*, 16–17, 181–210, 278–83, 289–93, 320; Cullather, *Hungry World*, 187–8.   63. Escobar, *Encountering Development*, 30, 35, 38, 41, 43–5, 52–3, 73–4.   64. On ECOSOC, see Australian views at *DAFP, 16, 1948–49*, docs. 226, 229; UN oral history, interview with Manuel Pérez-Guerrero, 27–28 April 1983.

13. 'A COMMON DETESTATION OF COLONIALISM'

1. *Africa-Asia Speaks from Bandung*, Indonesian Ministry of Foreign Affairs (Djakarta, 1955), 22–3.   2. Frantz Fanon, *The Wretched of the Earth*, English edn (New York, 1963),

102. **3.** Christopher Bayly and Tim Harper, *Forgotten Wars: The End of Britain's Asian Empire* (London, 2007). **4.** The Charter is available on the United Nations website. **5.** Mark Mazower, *No Enchanted Palace: The End of Empire and the Ideological Origins of the United Nations* (New Haven, CT, 2009), 7–9, 12–14. **6.** Ibid., 17–18, 20–21, 28–30, 59–65, 151–85; Mark Mazower, *Governing the World: The History of an Idea* (London, 2012), 197–9, 204, 212. **7.** Mazower, *No Enchanted Palace*, 185. **8.** Speech at the opening of the Bandung conference, 18 April 1955, *Africa-Asia Speaks from Bandung*, 24–5. **9.** Nehru's speech to the Bandung conference political committee, reprinted in G. M. Kahin, *The Asia-Africa Conference* (Ithaca, NY, 1956), 64–72. **10.** Mazower, *No Enchanted Palace*, 187–8. **11.** Richard Rathbone, 'Nkrumah, Kwame (1909? –1972)', *Oxford Dictionary of National Biography*; K. Nkrumah, *Neo-colonialism: The Last Stage of Imperialism* (London, 1965), ix; J. Ayodele Langley, *Pan Africanism and Nationalism in West Africa 1900–45: A Study in Ideology and Social Classes* (Oxford, 1973); R. L. Tignor, *W. Arthur Lewis and the Birth of Development Economics* (Princeton, NJ, 2006), chs. 4 and 5. **12.** Odd Arne Westad, *The Cold War: A World History* (London, 2017), 262. **13.** Final Communiqué, 24 April 1955 from *Asia-Africa Speaks from Bandung*, 161–9; Westad, *The Cold War*, 271. **14.** Westad, *The Cold War*, 326–30; Rex Mortimer, *Indonesian Communism under Sukarno: Ideology and Politics, 1959–1965* (Ithaca, NY, 1974); Matthew Jones, 'US relations with Indonesia, the Kennedy–Johnson transition, and the Vietnam connection, 1963–65', *Diplomatic History* 26 (2002), 249–81. **15.** Westad, *The Cold War*, 262, 271–4, 281; Sergey Radchenko, 'The Sino-Soviet split', in Melvyn Leffler and Odd Arne Westad, eds., *The Cambridge History of the Cold War, vol. II: Crises and Détente* (Cambridge, 2010), 350–57. **16.** Fanon, *The Wretched of the Earth*; George Padmore, *Africa and World Peace* (London, 1937); *idem, Pan Africanism or Communism? The Coming Struggle for Africa* (London, 1956). **17.** Rahul Mukherji, 'Introduction: the state and private initiative in India', in Rahul Mukherji, ed., *India's Economic Transition: The Politics of Reforms* (New Delhi, 2007), 2–5; Jagdish Bhagwati, 'What went wrong?', in Mukherji, ed., *India's Economic Transition*, 35, 37–9; Frederick Cooper and Randall Packard, 'Introduction', in Cooper and Packard, eds, *International Development and the Social Sciences* (Berkeley, CA, 1997), 11; Sugata Bose, 'Instruments and idioms of colonial and national development: India's historical experience in comparative perspective', in Cooper and Packard, eds, *International Development*, 48. **18.** A. Rudra, *Prasanta Chandra Mahalanobis: A Biography* (Oxford, 1996). **19.** Government of India Planning Commission, 'The first five year plan: a draft outline', 1951, 7–11; *Jawaharlal Nehru's Speeches, vol. 3, March 1953–August 1957* (New Delhi, 1958), 1–4, 97–8, 100–101, 102; Jawaharlal Nehru, *India's Foreign Policy: Selected Speeches, September 1946–April 1961* (New Delhi, 1961), 257–8; Madhav Khosla, ed., *Letters for a Nation: From Jawaharlal Nehru to his Chief Ministers, 1947–1963* (Gurgaon, Haryana, 2014), letter dated 22 Dec. 1952 and letter dated 3 March 1953; Ramachandra Guha, *India After Gandhi: The History of the World's Largest Democracy* (London, 2007), 206–7, 210–11. **20.** Government of India Planning Commission, *Second Five Year Plan 1956* (Delhi, 1956), 6–10; A. H. Hanson, *The Process of Planning: A Study of India's Five Year Plans, 1950–1964* (London, 1966), 122–70; Bose, 'Instruments and idioms', 54; Sukhamoy Chakravarty, *Development Planning: The Indian Experience* (Oxford, 1987), 3, 12–18, 20–21; Guha, *India After Gandhi*, 207–10; Nick Cullather, *The Hungry World: America's Cold War Battle Against Poverty in Asia* (Cambridge, MA, 2010), 148, 186. **21.** Daniel Klingensmith, 'Building India's "modern temples": Indians and Americans in the Damodar Valley Corporation, 1945–60', in K. Sivaramakrishnan and Arun Agrawal, eds., *Regional Modernities: The Cultural Politics of Development in India* (New Delhi, 2003), 122–42; *Nehru's Speeches*, 3, 3. **22.** Cullather, *Hungry World*, 77, 183–6; *Nehru's Speeches*, 3, 100–101; Guha, *India After Gandhi*, 216–17. **23.** Cullather, *Hungry World*, 77–8, 91–2. **24.** Milton Friedman, 'Mahalanobis's plan', 15 Feb. 1956, reprinted in *The Statesman*, 22 Nov. 2006; Milton Friedman, 'A memorandum to the Government of India, 1955', in Parth J. Shah, ed., *Friedman on India* (New Delhi, 2000), 27–43 quoted in Guha, *India After Gandhi*, 222–3. **25.** Bose, 'Instruments and idioms', 45, 52–3. **26.** Julia Lovell, *Maoism: A Global History* (London, 2019), 26–59. **27.** Yang Jisheng, *Tombstone: The Great Chinese Famine, 1958–62* (New York, 2013), 18, 87, 90–95, 99, 100; Lovell, *Maoism*, 127–9; Frank

Dikötter, *Mao's Great Famine: The History of China's Most Devastating Catastrophe* (London, 2010), 7–9, 13–14, 19, 27.   **28.** Yang, *Tombstone*, 71–3, 123–5; Dikötter, *Mao's Great Famine*, 25–8.   **29.** Dikötter, *Mao's Great Famine*, 56–61, 144.   **30.** Yang, *Tombstone*, 20–21, 166, 168, 326–31; Dikötter, *Mao's Great Famine*, 38–41, 46–54, 63, 128–9.   **31.** Dikötter, *Mao's Great Famine*, 67–70, 85–9, 99, 100–103; Yang, *Tombstone*, 331, 389–90.   **32.** Dikötter, *Mao's Great Famine*, 324–34; Yang, *Tombstone*, 394–430.   **33.** Yang, *Tombstone*, 436–7, 500–505; Dikötter, *Mao's Great Famine*, 122, 335–7.   **34.** Yang Jisheng, *The World Turned Upside Down: A History of the Chinese Cultural Revolution* (New York, 2021), xxi–xxxii, 80, 517; Frank Dikötter, *The Cultural Revolution: A People's History 1962–1976* (London, 2016), xi–xviii, 18, 20–26, 55, 180, 235; Lovell, *Maoism*, 6, 142; Roderick MacFarquhar and Michael Schoenhals, *Mao's Last Revolution* (Cambridge, MA, 2006), 92–3.   **35.** Dikötter, *Cultural Revolution*, xvii; Yang, *World Turned Upside Down*, xxix–xxxi.   **36.** Dikötter, *Mao's Great Famine*, 73–83, 113–14, 133.   **37.** Jung Chang and Jon Halliday, *Mao: The Unknown Story* (London, 2006), 560–63, 688, 693–5; Lovell, *Maoism*, 20–24.   **38.** Adeeb Khalid, *Central Asia: A New History from the Imperial Conquest to the Present* (Princeton, NJ, 2021), 199–202, 236–40, 272–3, 277–8, 332–4; see also Terry Martin, *The Affirmative Action Empire: Nations and Nationalism in the Soviet Union, 1923–1939* (Ithaca, NY, 2001), Jonathan Brunstedt, *The Soviet Myth of World War Two: Patriotic Memory and the Russian Question in the USSR* (Cambridge, 2021) and Krista A. Goff, *Nested Nationalism: Making and Unmaking Nations in the Soviet Caucasus* (Ithaca, NY, 2021).   **39.** Khalid, *Central Asia*, 379–82; Odd Arne Westad, *The Global Cold War: Third World Interventions and the Making of Our Times* (Cambridge, 2005), 67–9; Westad, *The Cold War*, 279–81.   **40.** Oscar Sanchez-Sibony, *Red Globalization: The Political Economy of the Soviet Cold War from Stalin to Khrushchev* (Cambridge, 2014), 132–4, 138, 247–8; Jeremy Friedman, *Shadow Cold War: The Sino-Soviet Competition for the Third World* (Chapel Hill, NC, 2015), 29–30, 36, 39–40, 57–8, 63, 82–3.   **41.** Sergey Mazov, *A Distant Front in the Cold War: The USSR in West Africa and the Congo, 1956–1964* (Washington, DC, and Stanford, CA, 2010), 7, 63–7, 72–5, 132–3, 135, 185–7, 188–90, 192, 193–6, 256–7; Friedman, *Shadow Cold War*, 77–82, 108–9; Sanchez-Sibony, *Red Globalization*, 235–40.   **42.** Tignor, *W. Arthur Lewis*, 142–53, 161–78; Mazov, *Distant Front*, 6–9, 14–15, 247, 252, 253, 255–7; Westad, *The Cold War*, 282–3; Alessandro Iandolo, *Arrested Development: The Soviet Union in Ghana, Guinea and Mali, 1955–68* (Ithaca, NY, and London, 2022); Sanchez-Sibony, *Red Globalization*, 228–35.   **43.** Friedman, *Shadow Cold War*, 2, 5–14, 23, 62, 63, 86, 123; Lovell, *Maoism*, 33–4, 48, 109, 130–31, 133–4, 137–8, 141–2; on US response, Michael E. Latham, *Modernization as Ideology: American Social Science and 'Nation Building' in the Kennedy Era* (Chapel Hill, NC, 2000), 3, 27.   **44.** Friedman, *Shadow Cold War*, 44–6.   **45.** Sanchez-Sibony, *Red Globalization*, 4–5, 21, 109, 123, 125–7, 131, 140–41, 168–9, 174–5, 185–6, 192, 202, 205–7, 241–4; Friedman, *Shadow Cold War*, 148.   **46.** Westad, *Global Cold War*, 71; Westad, *The Cold War*, 281; Friedman, *Shadow Cold War*, 99–100, 104–5, 108–10, 114, 124–5, 128, 129, 131, 146, 148–9.   **47.** Westad, *The Cold War*, 248–9.   **48.** Friedman, *Shadow Cold War*, 59, 124–5, 128, 150, 155–6, 163–4, 178.   **49.** Lovell, *Maoism*, 147–50, 154, 188, 216–20, 222, 226, 227, 255–9, 306–7, 349, 384–5, 390, 396, 412, 415, 417.   **50.** Charles Kindleberger, 'Planning for foreign investment', *American Economic Review* 33 (1943) supplement, 349; *idem*, 'International monetary stabilization', in Seymour E. Harris, ed., *Postwar Economic Problems* (New York, 1943).   **51.** W. Arthur Lewis, *Economic Survey 1919–39* (London, 1949), 196.   **52.** D. John Shaw, *Sir Hans W. Singer: The Life and Work of a Development Economist* (Basingstoke, 2002), 51–8; John Toye and Richard Toye, *The UN and Global Political Economy: Trade, Finance and Development* (Bloomington, IN, 2004), 116–20.   **53.** Edgar J. Dosman, *The Life and Times of Raúl Prebisch 1901–1986* (Montreal and Kingston, 2008), 37–8, 43, 49, 53, 58, 61, 69, 77, 79, 81, 82, 89, 95, 99.   **54.** Hernán Santa Cruz, 'The creation of the United Nations and ECLAC', *Cepal Review* 57 (1995), 24–5; Toye and Toye, *The UN and Global Political Economy*, 58, 137–40.   **55.** For this and previous paragraph, Dosman, *Prebisch*, 211, 219, 220, 222–4, 227, 231–4; John Toye and Richard Toye, 'The origins and interpretation of the Prebisch–Singer thesis', *History of Political Economy* 35 (2003), 437–67; Toye and Toye, *The UN and Global Political Economy*, ch. 5, 'The early terms of trade controversy'; UN Department of Economic Affairs, *The Economic Development of Latin America and its Principal Problems*, United Nations E/CN.12/89/rev1 (Lake Success, NY, 1950), 5–7, 10, 14. **56.** John Pincus, *Trade, Aid and Development: The Rich and Poor Nations* (New York, 1967), 13–14; Toye and Toye, *The UN and Global Political Economy*, 131–4. **57.** Byung-Nak Song, *The Rise of the Korean Economy*, 2nd edn (Hong Kong, 1997); Song-Chiu Suk, *Growth and Structural Changes in the Korean Economy 1910–40: The Korean Economy under Japanese Occupation* (Cambridge, MA, 1978); Mitsuhiko Kimura, 'The economics of Japanese imperialism in Korea, 1910–39', *Economic History Review* 48 (1995), 555–74; Atul Kuhli, *State-Directed Development: Political Power and Industrialisation in the Global Periphery* (Cambridge, 2004); Randall S. Jones, *The Economic Development of Colonial Korea* (Ann Arbor, MI, 1984); K. Nakajima and T. Okazaki, 'The expanding empire and spatial distribution of economic activity: the case of Japan's colonization of Korea during the pre-war period', *Economic History Review* 71 (2017), 593–616. **58.** W. Elliot Brownlee, Eisaku Ide and Yasunori Fukagai, eds., *The Political Economy of Transnational Tax Reform: The Shoup Mission to Japan in Historical Context* (Cambridge, 2013); J. D. Savage, 'The origins of budgetary preferences: the Dodge line and the balanced budget norm in Japan', *Administration and Society* 34 (2002), 261–84. **59.** Thomas A. Bissell, *Zaibatsu Dissolution in Japan* (Berkeley, CA, 1954); Hidemasa Morikawa, *The Rise and Fall of Family Enterprise Groups in Japan* (Tokyo, 1992); M. Schaller, *Altered States: The United States and Japan since the Occupation* (Oxford, 1997); Chalmers A. Johnson, *MITI and the Japanese Miracle* (Stanford, CA, 1982); R. Komiya, 'Direct foreign investment in post-war Japan', in P. Drysdale, ed., *Direct Foreign Investment in Asia and the Pacific* (Canberra, 1972). **60.** Michele Alacevich and Pier Francesco Asso, 'Money doctoring after World War II: Arthur I. Bloomfield and the Federal Reserve Missions to South Korea', *History of Political Economy* 41 (2009), 249–70. **61.** David Ekbladh, *The Great American Mission: Modernization and the Construction of an American World Order* (Princeton, NJ, and Oxford, 2010), 121–35. **62.** Ibid., 115–16, 135–47. **63.** Ibid., 147–52. **64.** Stephen Haggard, Byung-Kook Kim and Chung-In Moon, 'The transition to export-led growth in South Korea, 1954–1966', *Journal of Asian Studies* 50 (1991), 850–73; Stephen Haggard, *Pathways from the Periphery: The Politics of Growth in the Newly Industrializing Countries* (Ithaca, NY, 1990); see also Robert Wade, 'East Asia's economic success: conflicting perspectives, partial insights, shaky evidence', *World Politics* 44 (1992), 270–320; Jeff Frieden, 'Third-world indebted industrialization: international finance and state capitalism in Mexico, Brazil, Algeria, and South Korea', *International Organization* 35 (1981), 424–8; Byung-Kook Kim and E. F. Vogel, *The Park Chung Hee Era: The Transformation of South Korea* (Cambridge, MA, 2013); Kyung Moon Hwang, *A History of Korea* (London, 2010); Alice Amsden, *Asia's Next Giant: South Korea and Late Industrialization* (New York, 1989).

14. 'COMPETITIVE COOPERATION'

1. JFK Presidential Library, Herter papers, Box 9, The GATT trade negotiations: report by the Director General, 3 Jan. 1966. **2.** Lyndon B. Johnson, 'Remarks upon signing the Kennedy Round trade negotiations proclamation', 16 December 1967, online in Gerhard Peters and John T. Woolley, *The American Presidency Project*. **3.** John F. Kennedy, Inaugural Address, 20 Jan. 1961, in Peters and Woolley, *American Presidency Project*; *Economic Report of the President Transmitted to Congress, February 1974, Together with the Annual Report of the Council of Economic Advisers* (Washington, 1974), table C93. **4.** John W. Evans, *The Kennedy Round in American Trade Policy: The Twilight of the GATT?* (Cambridge, MA, 1971), 134; Thomas Zeiler, *American Trade and Power in the 1960s* (New York, 1992), 30, 32–3. **5.** John F. Kennedy, 'Special message to the Congress on gold and the balance of payments deficit', 6 Feb. 1961, in Peters and Woolley, *American Presidency Project*. **6.** John F. Kennedy, 'Special message to the Congress: program for economic recovery and growth', 2 Feb. 1961, in Peters and Woolley, *American Presidency Project*. **7.** The best account is Lucia Coppolaro, *The Making of a World Trading Power: The European Economic Community (EEC) in the*

GATT Kennedy Round Negotiations, 1963–67 (London, 2013). **8.** Declassified Documents Record System (DDRS), Memo of conversation, Brussels negotiations Kennedy Round, 28 Dec. 1963, comment by George Ball. The distinction between diversion and creation rests on Jacob Viner, *The Customs Union Issue* (New York, 1950). **9.** Frederick Cooper, *Citizenship between Empire and Nation: Remaking France and French Africa, 1945–60* (Princeton, NJ, 2014), 264–8. **10.** Frances Lynch, *France and the International Economy: From Vichy to the Treaty of Rome* (London, 1997), 128–30; *idem*, 'De Gaulle's first veto: France, the Rueff plan and the free trade area', *Contemporary European History* 9 (2000), 111–35. **11.** Giuliano Garavini, *After Empires: European Integration, Decolonization and the Challengers from the Global South, 1957–1986* (Oxford, 2012), 45, 48–9; Lynch, *France and the International Economy*, 128–30, 177–80, 186–206; Frances Lynch, 'France and European monetary integration: from the Schuman Plan to Economic and Monetary Union', *Contemporary European History* 13 (2004), 119; Evans, *Kennedy Round*, 45–6; Convention of Association between the European Economic Community and the African and Malagasy States Associated with that Community, and annexed documents, signed at Yaoundé on 20 July 1963; Quinn Slobodian, *Globalists: The End of Empire and the Birth of Neoliberalism* (Cambridge, MA, 2018), 183. **12.** Francine McKenzie, *GATT and Global Order in the Postwar Era* (Cambridge, 2020), 110–14. **13.** Ibid., 107–10. **14.** Ibid., 114–29. **15.** Ibid., 88–93. **16.** The National Archives (TNA), FO371/172342, J. A. M. Marjoribanks, 22 May 1963. **17.** Evans, *Kennedy Round*, 115. **18.** Slobodian, *Globalists*, 183, 200–201; Evans, *Kennedy Round*, 117–20; G. Haberler, Roberto de Oliveira Campos, J. E. Meade and J. Tinbergen, *Trends in International Trade: A Report by a Panel of Experts* (Geneva, 1958), quotes at 11, 119. **19.** Slobodian, *Globalists*, 201, 214–16. **20.** Evans, *Kennedy Round*, 1, 8–20; Zeiler, *American Trade*, 34–6. **21.** Zeiler, *American Trade*, 38–46, 248–9. **22.** Ibid., 48, 52–3; A. E. Eckes, 'The Kennedy Round reconsidered', in *idem*, ed., *Revisiting US Trade Policy: Decisions in Perspective* (Athens, OH, 2000), reminiscence of Michael Blumenthal, 49–50. **23.** John F. Kennedy, 'Special message: program for economic recovery and growth', and 'Special message on gold and the balance of payments deficit'. **24.** *Foreign Relations of the United States (FRUS) 1961–63*, vol. IX, *Foreign Economic Policy* (Washington, DC, 1995), docs. 3, 4, 227, 228, 229, 230; Zeiler, *American Trade*, 54–6, 589, 64; Eckes, 'Kennedy Round reconsidered', 50. **25.** Harry S. Truman Presidential Library and Museum, Clayton papers, Box 126, Clayton to Humbert H. Humphrey, 29 Dec. 1958; to Anderson, 14 Aug. 1959; to Charles P. Taft, 22 Oct. 1959; Box 169, 'A new look at foreign economic policy in light of the Cold War and the existence of the Common Market in Europe', William Clayton and Christian Herter to Sub-committee on Foreign Economic Policy of the Joint Economic Committee, Congress of the US, 87th Congress 1st session, 1961. **26.** John F. Kennedy, 'The president's news conference', 8 Nov. 1961, in Peters and Woolley, *American Presidency Project*; Zeiler, *American Trade*, 64–5. **27.** John F. Kennedy, 'Address in New York City to the National Association of Manufacturers', 6 Dec. 1961, in Peters and Woolley, *American Presidency Project*. **28.** John F. Kennedy, 'Annual message to the Congress on the state of the union', 11 Jan. 1962, in Peters and Woolley, *American Presidency Project*. **29.** John F. Kennedy, 'Address at Independence Hall, Philadelphia', 4 July 1962, in Peters and Woolley, *American Presidency Project*; Zeiler, *American Trade*, 152–4. **30.** Lucia Coppolaro, 'Trade and politics across the Atlantic: the European Economic Community and the USA in the GATT negotiations of the Kennedy Round, 1962–67', Ph.D. thesis, European University Institute, 2006, 9, 42, 56, 67–9, 71–2, 73–4, 99, 110–11. **31.** John F. Kennedy, 'Special message to the Congress on foreign trade policy', 25 Jan. 1962, in Peters and Woolley, *American Presidency Project*; Joanne Gowa and S. Y. Kim, 'An exclusive country club: the effects of the GATT/WTO on trade, 1950–94', *World Politics* 57 (2005), 460. **32.** John F Kennedy, 'Special message on foreign trade policy'. **33.** Zeiler, *American Trade*, 73–89, 98–102, 122–9, 144–52. **34.** Ibid., 134–40. **35.** JFK Presidential Library, Herter papers, Box 16, 'TEA and agriculture: the sense of Congress, prepared for C. A. Herter trip to Geneva and Brussels, Jan.–Feb. 1965'; George W. Ball papers, Box 4, Weiss–Ball, 14 Aug. 1962, 11.30 a.m.; Box 8, Dillon–Ball, 4 Jan. 1962, 7.30 p.m.; Martin–Ball, 5 Jan. 1962, 10.25 a.m.; Murphy–Ball, 7 May 1962, 12.30 p.m.; Zeiler, *American Trade*, 87–8, 156; Alfred E. Eckes, *Opening America's Market: US Foreign Trade Policy* *since 1776* (Chapel Hill, NC, 1995), 187–90; Eckes, 'Kennedy Round reconsidered', 51.   **36.** JFK Presidential Library, George W. Ball papers, Box 8, Dillon–Ball, 7 May 1962, 10.55 a.m.; Gottlied–Ball, 11 July 1962, 5.45 p.m.; McNamara–Ball, 17 Aug. 1962, 12.40 p.m.; Duggan–Ball, 7 Sept. 1962, 3.10 p.m.; Arthur Dean–Ball, 26 Sept. 1962, 4.05 p.m.; McNamara–Ball, 5 Oct. 1962; Sharon–Ball, 8 Nov. 1962, 6.10 p.m.; Clark Clifford–Ball, 13 Nov. 1962, 3.20 p.m.; Dungan–Ball, 13 Nov. 1962, 6.10 p.m.   **37.** JFK Presidential Library, George W. Ball papers, Box 8, Gossett–Ball, 27 Feb. 1963, 6.25 p.m.; Donna Lee, *Middle Powers and Commercial Diplomacy: British Influence at the Kennedy Round* (Basingstoke, 1999), 45.   **38.** JFK Presidential Library, George W. Ball papers, Box 8, Kaysen–Ball, 28 Feb. 1963, 4.10 p.m.; *FRUS 1961–63*, IX, doc. 263.   **39.** JFK Presidential Library, George W. Ball papers, Box 8, Bundy–Ball, 10 May 1963, 10.50 a.m.; Blumenthal–Ball, 11 May 1963, 10.15 a.m.   **40.** Lee, *Middle Powers*, 45–8; Steve Dryden, *Trade Warriors: USTR and the American Crusade for Free Trade* (New York, 1995), 92–3; TNA, FO371/172313, J. A. M. Marjoribanks, 15 Oct. 1963; FO371/178092, J. A. M. Marjoribanks, 11 May 1964; C. H. Johnston, 11 May 1964.   **41.** Lee, *Middle Powers*, 48–9; TNA, FO371/172315, Paris to Foreign Office, 29 Nov. 1963.   **42.** 'Press conference by President de Gaulle, Paris (14th January 1963)', available at www.cvce.eu.   **43.** Zeiler, *American Trade*, 162; Coppolaro, 'Trade and politics', 66, 74.   **44.** Ernest H. Preeg, *Traders and Diplomats: An Analysis of the Kennedy Round of Negotiations under the General Agreement on Tariffs and Trade* (Washington, DC, 1970), 36–7; JFK Presidential Library, Herter papers, Box 1, C. A. Herter to President, meeting with Sicco Mansholt, 6 April 1963; Coppolaro, 'Trade and politics', 180, 199, 205.   **45.** Lee, *Middle Powers*, 31; Julian Jackson, *A Certain Idea of France: The Life of Charles de Gaulle* (London, 2018), 564–9; Charles de Gaulle, *Memoirs of Hope: Renewal 1958–62, Endeavour 1962–* (London, 1971), 184; Luuk van Middelaar, *The Passage to Europe: How a Continent Became a Union* (London, 2013), 4, 56, 58–9; Perry Anderson, *Ever Closer Union? Europe in the West* (London, 2021), 160.   **46.** TNA, FO371/172328, A. Rumbold, Paris, to Patrick Reilly, Foreign Office, 17 Aug. 1963; FO371/172313, The Kennedy Round and the related problem of the EEC common agricultural policy, British embassy, Paris, 23 Oct. 1963; T171/758, GB(64)32 14 Oct. 1964, Treasury General Briefing: The future of the Kennedy Round. Annex: Kennedy Round: Background; FO1108/1, Piers Dixon, 12 March 1964.   **47.** JFK Presidential Library, Herter papers, Box 15, Thomas L. Hughes to Secretary, 'De Gaulle looks at Europe', 8 Jan. 1964; McKenzie, *GATT and Global Order*, 133–4.   **48.** *FRUS 1961–63*, IX, docs. 18, 22; John F. Kennedy, 'Special message to the Congress on balance of payments', 18 July 1963, in Peters and Woolley, *American Presidency Project*.   **49.** *FRUS 1961–63*, IX, doc. 32.   **50.** Ibid., docs. 32, 67.   **51.** Ibid., doc. 68.   **52.** Ibid., docs. 27, 32, 34.   **53.** Ibid., docs. 30, 32.   **54.** JFK Presidential Library, George W. Ball papers, Box 1, Bundy–Ball, 9 Aug. 1962, 1 p.m.; Kaysen–Ball, 19 April 1963, 10.50 a.m.; Kaysen–Ball, 1 April 1963, 5.40 p.m.; Heller–Ball, 20 March 1963, 12 noon.   **55.** *FRUS 1961–63*, IX, doc. 24.   **56.** Ibid., doc. 20.   **57.** Kennedy, 'Special message on balance of payments'; Jacqueline Best, 'Hollowing out Keynesian norms: how the search for a technical fix undermined the Bretton Woods regime', *Review of International Studies* 30 (2004), 397–9; Jeffrey M. Chwieroth, *Capital Ideas: The IMF and the Rise of Financial Liberalization* (Princeton, NJ, and Oxford, 2010), 123–4; Eric Helleiner, *States and the Re-emergence of Global Finance from Bretton Woods to the 1990s* (Ithaca, NY, 1994), 85–6; FRUS 1961–63, IX, doc. 79.   **58.** *FRUS 1961–63*, IX, doc. 32.   **59.** LBJ Presidential Library, Bator papers, Box 16, Moral suasion, the business community and the improvement of the US balance of payments, Commerce, 16 Feb. 1965; CEA, Balance of payments program, Graham Ashley, 11 Jan. 1965; Lyndon B. Johnson, 'Special message to the Congress on international balance of payments', 10 Feb. 1965, in Peters and Woolley, *American Presidency Project*.   **60.** Helleiner, *States*, 86–7; US National Archives and Records Administration (NARA) RG59 State, Bureau of European Affairs, Box 5, US balance of payments, Comments on S/P balance of payments paper, Abraham Katz to John Leddy, 12 Aug. 1967.   **61.** *FRUS 1961–63*, IX, doc. 32.   **62.** TNA, FO371/172342, UK position on the Kennedy Round, R. Burgess Watson, 16 March 1963; GATT Policy committee meeting, A. T. Lamb, 19 March 1963; FO371/172313, The Kennedy Round and the related problem of the EEC common agricultural policy, 23 Oct. 1963.   **63.**

TNA, FO371/178090, The Kennedy Round: the position on 31 Dec. 1963, 2 Jan 1964; PREM13/1869, Kennedy Round C(67)12, Burke Trend, 30 Jan. 1967; 'Rostowiana', Balogh to Wilson, 22 March 1967; Kennedy Round C(67)53, Burke Trend to Prime Minister, 17 April 1967; T171/758, GB(64)32, 14 Oct. 1964, Treasury General Briefing: the future of the Kennedy Round; T312/1742, Kennedy Round: preliminary impressions, J. F. Slater, 19 May 1967; Kennedy Round: preliminary impressions, N. Jordan-Moss, 19 May 1967; Kennedy Round: preliminary impressions, Frank Figgures, 24 May 1967; Lee, *Middle Powers*, 95–6, 109.   **64.** JFK Presidential Library, Herter papers, Box 10, Bohlen to Secretary of State, 25 Feb. 1963.   **65.** TNA, FO371/171398, Pierson Dixon (Paris) to P. Reilly (FO), 6 Nov. 1963; FO1108/1, Dixon, 12 March 1964.   **66.** *FRUS 1961–63*, IX, doc. 271.   **67.** JFK Presidential Library, Herter papers, Box 10, Memo for the president, C. Herter, The Trade Negotiations, 27 Nov. 1963.   **68.** *FRUS 1964–68*, vol. VIII, *International Monetary and Trade Policy* (Washington, DC, 1998), doc. 287.   **69.** TNA, BT241/372, A. Clones to Earl W. Kintner, Pending anti-dumping legislation and some probable effects on British imports, 3 July 1963; Memo re WHEC: Effect of the proposed Humphrey–Walter amendments to the Anti-dumping Act of 1921; see also BT241/376 and 377; FO371/164433, Kennedy Round, F. C. Mason, 8 Nov. 1962 and J. A. M. Marjoribanks, 8 Nov. 1962.   **70.** TNA, FO371/183387, The Kennedy Round, Edgar Cohen to Michael Stewart, 31 Aug. 1965; NARA RG59 Kennedy Round, Box 1, Office of the Special Representative for Trade Negotiations, Additional guidelines for US delegation to GATT working party on tariff reductions, TEC-D-4, 16 April 1963; *FRUS 1961–63*, IX, doc. 278; TNA, FO371/172313, The 'Kennedy round': situation and prospects at 1 Nov. 1963, Tariff Division, 6 Nov. 1963; FO371/172328, J. E. Chadwick (Washington) to P. Reilly (Foreign Office), 14 May 1963; FO371/172336, L. E. M. Taylor, UK delegation, to European Communities, Brussels, 4 June 1963; McKenzie, *GATT and Global Order*, 132; Lee, *Middle Powers*, 40–41, 59–61, 64–5; B. Norwood, 'The Kennedy Round: a try at linear trade negotiations', *Journal of Law and Economics* 12 (1969), 297–319.   **71.** JFK Presidential Library, Herter papers, Box 5, An appraisal of the proposal of the EEC for agricultural negotiations in the Kennedy Round, I. R. Hedges, 4 Jan. 1965; Status of the Kennedy Round, 5 Jan. 1965; Box 9a, Trade negotiations: another look at strategy. Memo for Governor Herter, Mr Roth, 16 Dec. 1963, Irwin Hedges; *FRUS 1964–68*, VIII, docs. 242, 243, 270.   **72.** Zeiler, *American Trade*, 164; NARA RG 59 Kennedy Round, Box 3, C. P. Worthington to Blumenthal, 3 May 1965: Your request: an 'essay' on agriculture; TNA, CAB148/40, Cabinet: Defence and Overseas Policy (Official) Committee, Washington talks, Dec. 1964. The Kennedy Round. Note by the Board of Trade, 26 Nov. 1964; Coppolaro, 'Trade and politics', 6–7; JFK Presidential Library, Herter papers, Box 1, D. Gale Johnson to Herter, 'Trade negotiation issues involving agriculture – some preliminary comments and questions', 17 Jan. 1963.   **73.** Zeiler, *American Trade*, 167, 186; JFK Presidential Library, Herter papers, Box 7, Components of a strategy for the Kennedy Round, draft 10 Dec. 1963, Ball to Herter, 10 Dec. 1963; TNA, FO371/171398, Common agricultural policy and the Kennedy Round, Paris to FO, 23 Nov. 1963; A. C. Buxton, 3 Dec. 1963; FO371/172323 Frank Roberts to Patrick Reilly, 23 Aug. 1963; A. T. Lamb, 30 Aug. 1963; The Kennedy Round and the related problem of the EEC common agricultural policy, British embassy, Paris, 23 Oct. 1963; Coppolaro, 'Trade and politics', 148; Preeg, *Traders and Diplomats*, 151–6; *FRUS 1964–68*, VIII, docs. 268, 276.   **74.** JFK Presidential Library, Herter papers, Box 5, Atlantic affairs conference, 15–16 May 1964; Box 8, Visit of Chancellor Erhard of Germany, Dec. 28–29 1963, 26 Dec. 1963.   **75.** Coppolaro, 'Trade and politics', 159, 179, 205, 237, 264, 322, 358–9; LBJ Presidential Library, Bator papers, Box 1, Memo for the president, Bator and Bundy, 20 July 1964; Box 11, Acheson to Bundy, 24 Oct. 1964 and Memo for Bundy, 26 Oct. 1964; Kennedy Round strategy, 27 Oct. 1964; TNA, FO371/172312, UK delegation to EFTA, Geneva to FO, 9 Oct. 1963; FO371/178092, The Kennedy Round, F. C. Mason, 14 July 1964; FO371/183387, J. A. M. Marjoribanks (UK delegation to European communities) to Michael Stewart, 7 Oct. 1965; Zeiler, *American Trade*, 183–9; *FRUS 1964–68*, VIII, doc. 255; NARA RG59 Kennedy Round, Box 6, Memo of conversation Sicco Mansholt and Ambassador Tuthill, 6 July 1965; JFK Presidential Library, Herter papers, Box 15, US Department of State research memo. A study of two hypotheses: French withdrawal from or non-participation in the

NOTES TO PAGES 391–5

Common Market, Thomas L. Hughes to Secretary, 6 Nov. 1964.   76. LBJ Presidential Library, Bator papers, Box 12, draft, Impact of EEC crisis on the Kennedy Round, nd.   77. LBJ Presidential Library, Bator papers, Box 11, Acheson to Bundy, 24 Oct. 1964, covering Memo for Bundy, 26 Oct. 1964.   78. NARA RG59 State Subject numeric files: Central foreign policy files 1964–66 Economic, Box 979, Action circular: Kennedy Round and the Trade Expansion Act 14 May 1965; Box 972, Kennedy Round: Memo of conversation, ambassadors Roth and Blumenthal's discussions with the EEC, 11 Jan. 1966; RG59 Kennedy Round, Box 3, Memo of conversation: community situation, 13 Sept. 1965; LBJ Presidential Library, Bator papers, Box 12, draft, 'Impact of EEC crisis on the Kennedy Round', nd; TNA, BT303/247, P. W. Ridley (Washington) to D. Carter (BOT), 8 Feb. 1966; Coppolaro, 'Trade and politics', 9, 264.   79. FRUS 1964–68, VIII, docs. 287, 288, 289, 290, 292; NARA RG59 Kennedy Round, Box 4, The EEC crisis, agriculture and the Kennedy Round, John M. Leddy and Anthony Solomon to Ball and Mann, 30 July 1965; Agricultural negotiations – a strategy for completing the Kennedy Round, 27 July 1965; The agricultural negotiations – a summary, nd; The agricultural negotiations, 28 July 1965; USDA position on September 16: counterarguments, 4 Aug. 1965; Tabling of US agricultural offers in the Kennedy Round negotiations on Sept. 16, Anthony Solomon to Secretary, 10 Aug. 1965; LBJ Presidential Library, Bator papers, Box 2, Memo for the President: agriculture in the Kennedy Round, F. M. Bator, 10 Aug. 1965.   80. On the 'Luxembourg compromise', see material in www.cvce.eu; FRUS 1964–68, VIII, docs. 316, 317.   81. NARA RG59 Kennedy Round, Box 11, J. Robert Schaetzel to Leddy, 30 Jan. 1967.   82. NARA RG59 Kennedy Round, Box 11, Memo S. H. Rogers to Hinton, 27 Jan. 1967.   83. TNA, PREM13/1869, UK Mission Geneva (E. Melville) to FO, 14 April 1967; Washington (P. Dean) to FO, 10 May 1967.   84. FRUS 1964–68, VIII, doc. 335.   85. LBJ Presidential Library, Bator papers, Box 12, Memo for the president: scheduling Kennedy Round decisions, Francis Bator, 28 April 1967; Memo for the president, action item for tomorrow's meeting on the Kennedy Round, F. Bator, 21 Feb. 1967 and Memo for the president, American selling price system of custom valuation, W. Roth, 15 Feb. 1967.   86. Irwin Hedges, 'Kennedy Round agricultural negotiations and the World Grains Agreement', Journal of Farm Economics 49 (1967), 1332–41; Lyndon B. Johnson, 'Statement by the president upon signing the Food for Peace Act, 1966', 12 Nov. 1966, in Peters and Woolley, American Presidency Project; Kristin L. Ahlberg, Transplanting the Great Society: Lyndon Johnson and Food for Peace (Columbia, MS, 2008); NARA RG59 Kennedy Round, Box 8, Food aid, 7 July 1966; Blumenthal to Hedges, 27 April 1966; Memo of conversation Kennedy Round, 21 April 1966; Box 11, Food aid in the Kennedy Round, 21 Feb. 1967; Memo, Grains agreement, Hinton to Leddy, 23 Feb. 1967; Kennedy Round grains agreement – food aid, 16 Feb. 1967; Memo for A. Solomon and J. Leddy, Kennedy Round grains, 16 March 1967, Eugene W. Rostow; Preeg, Traders and Diplomats, 155–8; Orville Freeman, 'Malthus, Marx and the North American breadbasket', Foreign Affairs 45 (1967), 579–93.   87. DDRS, 'Notes on key European Issues', 21 April 1967.   88. FRUS 1964–68, VIII, doc. 346.   89. LBJ Presidential Library, Bator papers, Box 12, 'Political and economic consequences of Kennedy Round failure', D. R. Hinton, 10 May 1967.   90. LBJ Presidential Library, Bator papers, Box 5, Memo for the president, Talking points on Kennedy Round, Francis Bator, 11 May 1967; FRUS 1964–68, VIII, doc. 351.   91. LBJ Presidential Library, National Security Council Histories, Box 52, The Kennedy round crisis, April–June 1967 collects the documents together.   92. FRUS 1964–68, VIII, doc. 367; Lyndon B. Johnson, 'Special message to the Congress transmitting multilateral trade agreement concluding the Kennedy Round of trade negotiations', 27 Nov. 1967, in Peters and Woolley, American Presidency Project; Eckes, Opening America's Market, 197; J. M. Finger, 'Effects of the Kennedy Round tariff concessions on the exports of developing countries', Economic Journal 86 (1976), 94–5; Hedges, 'Kennedy Round agricultural negotiations', 1335–40; McKenzie, GATT and Global Order, 135–6.   93. TNA, T312/1742, Kennedy Round: preliminary impressions, N. Jordan-Moss, 19 May 1967; C(67)81, The Kennedy Round, J. F. Slater, 8 June 1967.   94. William A. Lovett, Alfred E. Eckes and Richard L. Brinkman, US Trade Policy: History, Theory and the WTO (London, 1999), 81–2.   95. Lovett, Eckes and Brinkman, US Trade Policy, 82–3; Howard P. Marvel and Edward J. Ray, 'The Kennedy Round: evidence on the regulation of international trade in the United States', *American Economic Review* 73 (1983), 190–97; Zeiler, *American Trade*, 236–42, 257, 259. 96. Jack Metcalf, speech on HJ Res 90, 4 May 2000, *Congressional Record* 146, no. 54. 97. Eckes, 'Kennedy Round reconsidered', 77, 79, 83; Coppolaro, 'Trade and politics', 6–7, 398–9. 98. *FRUS 1964–68*, VIII, doc. 283; NARA RG59 State, Bureau of European Affairs, Box 6, Future work program of the GATT, William E. Culbert to A. Solomon, 7 Sept. 1967; Preeg, *Traders and Diplomats*, 201; McKenzie, *GATT and Global Order*, 137–40. 99. *FRUS 1964–68*, VIII, doc. 318. 100. LBJ Presidential Library, Roth papers, Box 2, Memo: pizzazz for the trade program, William Roth, 3 Oct. 1966. 101. *FRUS 1964–68*, VIII, docs. 330, 333; Lyndon B. Johnson, 'Remarks in Punta del Este at the public session of the meeting of American chiefs of state', 13 April 1967, in Peters and Woolley, *American Presidency Project*.

15. 'PROGRESS TOWARDS SELF-SUSTAINING GROWTH'

1. Quoted in Giuliano Garavini, *After Empires: European Integration, Decolonization, and the Challenge of the Global South, 1957–1986* (Oxford, 2012), 41–2. 2. US National Archives and Records Administration (NARA) RG59 Kennedy Round, Box 10, 'From aid to cooperation: development strategy for the next decade', statement by Eugene V. Rostow, Under-Sec of State for political affairs and chairman of the US delegation to the second UNCTAD, New Delhi, 5 Feb. 1968. 3. Richard N. Gardner, 'The United Nations Conference on Trade and Development', *International Organization* 22 (1968), 100–104; Arturo Escobar, *Encountering Development: The Making and Unmaking of the Third World* (Princeton, NJ, 1995), 81 denies there was a 'radical critique'. 4. Odd Arne Westad, *The Global Cold War: Third World Interventions and the Making of Our Times* (Cambridge, 2005), 4–5. 5. Ibid., 27, 31–2, 40, 68, 72, 107–8. 6. Michael E. Latham, *Modernization as Ideology: American Social Science and 'Nation Building' in the Kennedy Era* (Chapel Hill, NC, 2000), 51–3; Nils Gilman, *Mandarins of the Future: Modernization Theory in Cold War America* (Baltimore, MD, and London, 2003), 181–3. 7. Jeremy Adelman, *Worldly Philosopher: The Odyssey of Albert O. Hirschman* (Princeton, NJ, and Oxford, 2013), 321–2. 8. Latham, *Modernization as Ideology*, 55, 57–8; Gilman, *Mandarins of the Future*, 156–60. 9. Ann T. Keene, 'W. W. Rostow', *American National Biography*; Gilman, *Mandarins of the Future*, 158, 160–65; John Toye and Richard Toye, *The UN and Global Political Economy: Trade, Finance and Development* (Bloomington, IN, 2004), 168–72. 10. W. W. Rostow, *The Stages of Economic Growth: A Non-Communist Manifesto* (New York and Cambridge, 1960), 167 and passim; Gilman, *Mandarins of the Future*, 160–5, 190–202. 11. Gilman, *Mandarins of the Future*, 179; Latham, *Modernization as Ideology*, 16. 12. Gilman, *Mandarins of the Future*, 43. 13. Gilman, *Mandarins of the Future*, 43, 196–7; W. W. Rostow, 'Guerrilla warfare in the underdeveloped areas', *Department of State Bulletin* 45 (1961), 234; 'Statement by Mr Rostow', *Department of State Bulletin* 46 (1962), 234. 14. Latham, *Modernization as Ideology*, 55–6; Nick Cullather, *The Hungry World: America's Cold War Battle Against Poverty in Asia* (Cambridge, MA, 2010), 141–2. 15. Latham, *Modernization as Ideology*, 55; Gilman, *Mandarins of the Future*, 69. 16. JFK Presidential Library, digital identifier JFKNSF-338-010, National Security Action Memorandum no. 182, 'Counterinsurgency doctrine', 24 Aug. 1962, cover letter to 'US overseas internal defense policy', also in *Foreign Relations of the United States (FRUS) 1961–63*, vols. VII, VIII, IX, *Arms Control; National Security Policy; Foreign Economic Policy*, Microfiche Supplement (Washington, DC, 1997), doc. 279. 17. *FRUS 1961–63*, vol. IX, *Foreign Economic Policy* (Washington, DC, 1995), doc. 94. 18. Latham, *Modernization as Ideology*, 84–7; Gilman, *Mandarins of the Future*, 165, 174–180. 19. *FRUS 1961–63*, IX, doc. 124. 20. *FRUS 1964–68*, vol. IX, *International Development and Economic Defense Policy; Commodities* (Washington, DC, 1997), doc. 23. 21. Ibid., doc. 47. 22. *FRUS 1961–63*, IX, docs. 120, 124, 164. 23. Ibid., doc. 95. 24. Latham, *Modernization as Ideology*, 74–7. 25. Edgar J. Dosman, *The Life and Times of Raúl Prebisch 1901–1986* (Montreal and Kingston, 2008), ch. 14 on return to Argentina and ch. 15 on ECLA; Raul Prebisch, 'Soviet challenge to American leadership: America's role in helping

under-developed countries', in Committee for Economic Development, *Problems of United States Economic Development*, vol. I (Washington, DC, 1958), 48, 50, 55 and copy of the original typescript provided by Richard Toye.   26. Dosman, *Prebisch*, 324–33, 342.   27. Ibid., 341.   28. Anabel Gonzalez, 'Can customs union members negotiate bilateral free trade agreements? Yes, with caution', Peterson Institute for International Economics, 15 April 2021.   29. Latham, *Modernization as Ideology*, 69, 78–81.   30. John F. Kennedy, 'Address at a White House reception for members of Congress and for the diplomatic corps of the Latin American republics', 13 March 1961, online in Gerhard Peters and John T. Woolley, *The American Presidency Project*.   31. Latham, *Modernization as Ideology*, 82–3, 87.   32. Dosman, *Prebisch*, 365–75; Toye and Toye, *The UN and Global Political Economy*, 175–6.   33. W. W. Rostow, *Eisenhower, Kennedy and Foreign Aid* (Austin, TX, 1985), 157–9.   34. *FRUS 1951, Asia and the Pacific*, vol. VI, pt 2 (Washington, DC, 1977), docs. 427, 428, 432, 434; Harry S. Truman, 'Special message to Congress on the famine in India', 12 Feb. 1951; Dwight D. Eisenhower, 'Statement by the president upon signing the Agricultural Trade Development and Assistance Act of 1954', 10 July 1954; and 'Remarks of Senator John F. Kennedy, Corn Palace, Mitchell, SD', 22 Sept. 1960, all in Peters and Woolley, *American Presidency Project*; Ruth Jachertz and Alexander Nützenadel, 'Coping with hunger? Visions of a global food system, 1930–1960', *Journal of Global History* 6 (2011), 117–18; Amy L. Staples, *The Birth of Development: How the World Bank, Food and Agriculture Organization and World Health Organization Changed the World, 1945–1965* (Kent, OH, 2006), 109–11; Cullather, *Hungry World*, 134–58; D. Merrill, *Bread and the Ballot: The United States and India's Development 1947–1963* (Chapel Hill, NC, 1990), ch. 7.   35. John F. Kennedy, 'Special message to Congress on foreign aid', 22 March 1961, in Peters and Woolley, *American Presidency Project*.   36. Public Law 87-195 Act for International Development, 1961 was amended as Foreign Assistance Act 1961; see *FRUS 1964–68*, IX, doc. 20.   37. John F. Kennedy, 'Special message to the Congress on free world defense and assistance programs', 2 April 1963, in Peters and Woolley, *American Presidency Project*.   38. John F. Kennedy, 'Address in New York City before the General Assembly of the United Nations', 25 September 1961, in Peters and Woolley, *American Presidency Project*.   39. Resolution 1710(XVI), United Nations Development Decade: a programme for international economic cooperation, 19 Dec. 1961.   40. *FRUS 1961–63*, IX, doc. 193; UN resolution A/RES/1710(XVI); Diego Cordovez, 'The making of UNCTAD: institutional background and legislative history', *Journal of World Trade Law* 1 (1967), 255–6; Gardner, 'UNCTAD', 103.   41. Gardner, 'UNCTAD', 102; Richard N. Gardner, 'GATT and the United Nations Conference on Trade and Development', *International Organization* 18 (1964), 688.   42. N. Lamp, 'Law-making in the multilateral trade system', Ph.D. thesis, London School of Economics, 2013, 23–5, 86–7, 121–3, 219–21.   43. Francine McKenzie, *GATT and Global Order in the Postwar Era* (Cambridge, 2020), 184–90.   44. Ibid., 192–4.   45. Ibid., 194–8.   46. Ibid., 213–14.   47. Alfred E. Eckes, ed., *Revisiting US Trade Policy: Decisions in Perspective* (Athens, OH, 2000), 28–9.   48. James Boughton and Domenico Lombardi, 'The role of the IMF in low income countries', in Boughton and Lombardi, eds., *Finance, Development and the IMF* (Oxford, 2009), 5; Harold James, 'Bretton Woods and the debate about development', in Boughton and Lombardi, eds., *Finance, Development*, 40.   49. Ivana Ancic, 'Belgrade: the 1961 non-aligned conference', *Global South Studies*, 17 Aug. 2017; Cordovez, 'The making of UNCTAD', 256–8; UN resolution A/RES/1707(XVI).   50. Toye and Toye, *The UN and Global Political Economy*, 185.   51. ECOSOC E/CN14/STC/16, Cairo Declaration of developing countries, 14 Sept. 1962; J. Toye and R. Toye, 'From new era to neo-liberalism: US strategy on trade, finance and development in the United Nations, 1964–82', *Forum for Development Studies* 1 (2005), 152–5; Toye and Toye, *The UN and Global Political Economy*, 187–8; Cordovez, 'The making of UNCTAD', 258–62.   52. Craig Murphy, *The Emergence of the NIEO Ideology* (Epping, 1984), 59.   53. Cordovez, 'The making of UNCTAD', 262–7; Toye and Toye, *The UN and Global Political Economy*, 188.   54. The National Archives (TNA), BT241/1348, L. E. Chasanovitch, 'Dr Raul Prebisch', 25 June 1964; Gardner, 'UNCTAD', 101; Toye and Toye, *The UN and Global Political Economy*, 204.   55. UN General Assembly 18th session, 1897 (XVIII) United Nations Conference on Trade and Development, Annex, Joint Declaration of the Developing Countries made at the 18th session of the General Assembly. 56. Toye and Toye, *The UN and Global Political Economy*, 158–9, 225; *Proceedings of the United Nations Conference on Trade and Development, Geneva 23 March–16 June 1964, Vol. II, Policy Statements* (New York, 1964), 'Report by the Secretary General of the Conference: Towards a New Trade Policy for Development', 5–64 and Prebisch's opening statement, 76–81. 57. McKenzie, *GATT and Global Order*, 199–204. 58. Cordovez, 'The making of UNCTAD', 254, 273–9; Dosman, *Prebisch*, 421–4; McKenzie, *GATT and Global Order*, 204–12; Gardner, 'UNCTAD', 104–6. 59. NARA RG59 State, FT3 Economic: Foreign Trade, UNCTAD, Box 961, 'Meeting with the Australian Ambassador on UNCTAD Special Procedures Committee, 23 Sept. 1964; 'UNCTAD – US attitude toward and planning for the work of the new institutional machinery', Dean Rusk, 28 Oct. 1964. Enclosure: 'The United Nations Trade and Development Board and periodic conference on trade and development'; Box 962, Gardner to Cleveland, 16 June 1964; Gardner, 'GATT and UNCTAD', 698–9; Robert S. Walters, 'International organizations and political communication: the use of UNCTAD by less developed countries', *International Organization* 25 (1971), 818–35; Cordovez, 'The making of UNCTAD', 281–313, 323–5; Gardner, 'UNCTAD', 105–6; Thomas G. Weiss, *Multilateral Development Diplomacy in UNCTAD: The Lessons of Group Negotiations 1964–84* (Basingstoke, 1986), 5, 59, 98–9; Sidney Dell, 'An appraisal of UNCTAD III', *World Development* 1 (1973), 2. 60. Toye and Toye, *The UN and Global Political Economy*, 210; Interoffice memorandum, C. Eckenstein to R. Prebisch, 16 Aug. 1965 from UNCTAD archive, courtesy of Richard Toye. 61. Gardner, 'UNCTAD', 106–7, 124; Toye and Toye, *The UN and Global Political Economy*, 211–13; Walters, 'International organizations', 821–2. 62. NARA RG59 State, FT3 Economic: Foreign Trade, UNCTAD, Box 962, telegram Ball, 9 July 1964; LBJ Presidential Library, National Security Files, Box 293, 'UNCTAD', Ball to Bundy, 3 March 1964; Memo for the president, UNCTAD, G. Ball, 30 March 1964; *FRUS 1961–63*, IX, doc. 290. 63. Charles P. Kindleberger, 'Economists in international organizations', *International Organization* 9 (1955), 347; LBJ Presidential Library, Bator papers, Box I, UNCTAD strategy paper, 19 March 1964; *FRUS 1961–63*, IX, doc. 290. 64. JFK Presidential Library, George Ball papers, Box 8, Bundy–Ball, 20 Oct. 1963, 10.30 a.m.; *FRUS 1961–63*, IX, doc. 290. 65. *Compensatory Financing of Export Fluctuations: A Report by the International Monetary Fund on Compensatory Financing of the Fluctuations in Exports of Primary Exporting Countries* (Washington DC, 1963) and *Compensatory Financing of Export Fluctuations: Developments in the Fund's Flexibility. A Second Report by the International Monetary Fund on Compensatory Financing of the Fluctuations in Exports of Primary Producing Countries*, September 1966, in J. Keith Horsefield, ed., *The International Monetary Fund, 1945–1965: Twenty Years of International Monetary Cooperation: Volume III: Documents* (Washington, DC, 1969), 442–57 and 469–96; Toye and Toye, *The UN and Global Political Economy*, 220–24. 66. Gardner, 'GATT and UNCTAD', 696. 67. A. E. Eckes, 'Is GATT dead? A retrospective', in Eckes, ed., *Revisiting US Trade Policy*, 29. 68. NARA RG59 State, FT3 Economic: Foreign Trade. UNCTAD. Box 962, Report of the US delegation to the UNCTAD, Geneva March 23–June 16 1964, submitted to the Secretary of State, John M. Leddy, Chairman of the delegation; NARA RG59 Kennedy Round, Box 10, US strategy for UNCTAD II: a discussion paper, 12 Oct. 1966. 69. Joint Declaration of the seventy-seven developing countries made at the conclusion of the United Nations Conference on Trade and Development, Geneva, 15 June 1964; First ministerial meeting of the Group of 77, Charter of Algiers, Algiers, 10–25 October 1967. 70. NARA RG59 Kennedy Round, Box 10, US strategy for UNCTAD II: a discussion paper, 12 Oct. 1966; Blumenthal to Roth, 1 Oct. 1965. 71. LBJ Presidential Library, Bator papers, Box 11, draft statement for Assistant Sec Solomon before Subcommittee of Joint Economic Committee, 10 Sept. 1965; Under-Secretary [Ball] to Secretary, 17 Feb. 1965; Tom Mann to Secretary, 'Suggested new initiatives to aid new dynamics to Alliance for Progress and promote economic integration in Latin America', 9 Feb. 1965. 72. *FRUS 1964–68*, vol. VIII, *International Monetary and Trade Policy* (Washington, DC, 1998), docs. 18, 22. 73. John W. Evans, *The Kennedy Round in American Trade Policy: The Twilight of the GATT?* (Cambridge, MA, 1971), 121–2. 74. NARA RG59 Kennedy Round, Box 11, J. Robert Schaetzel to Eugene Rostow, 5 Sept. 1967; Box 12, Memo, John Leddy and

A. M. Solomon to Under Secretary, 'Trade preferences', 13 May 1968; LBJ Presidential Library, Roth papers, Box 2, Generalized preferences for LDCs: proposal and strategy, 16 May 1966; Thomas Zeiler, *American Trade and Power in the 1960s* (New York, 1992), 200, 203–5, 214.   75. Lyndon B. Johnson, 'Statement by the president at an informal meeting with the American chiefs of state at Punta del Este, Uruguay, 12 April 1967', in Peters and Woolley, *American Presidency Project*.   76. Quinn Slobodian, *Globalists: The End of Empire and the Birth of Neoliberalism* (Cambridge, MA, 2018), 214–16.   77. *FRUS 1969–76*, vol. IV, *Foreign Assistance, International Development, Trade Policies, 1969–72* (Washington, DC, 2001), docs. 191, 198, 200, 209, 210, 214, 215, 216, 218; Toye and Toye, 'From new era to neo-liberalism', 155, 163–6.

16. 'TRYING TO LIVE WITH AN ANOMALY'

1. *Foreign Relations of the United States (FRUS) 1969–76*, vol. III, *Foreign Economic Policy; International Monetary Policy, 1969–72* (Washington, DC, 2001), doc. 161.   2. Ford Presidential Library, Burns papers, Box B24, 'A foreign economic perspective', Peter G. Peterson, 27 Dec. 1971.   3. Barry Eichengreen, Arnaud Mehl and Livia Chiţu, *How Global Currencies Work: Past, Present and Future* (Princeton, NJ, and Oxford, 2018), 119.   4. Paul Volcker and Toyoo Gyohten, *Changing Fortunes: The World's Money and the Threat to American Leadership* (New York, 1992), 20, 25.   5. Peter Peterson, *The United States in the Changing World Economy: A Foreign Economic Perspective* (Washington, DC, 1971), 16; Charles Coombs, *Arena of International Finance* (New York, 1976), x.   6. Catherine R. Schenk, *The Decline of Sterling: Managing the Retreat of an International Currency, 1945–1992* (Cambridge, 2010), 79; *FRUS 1969–76*, III, doc. 26.   7. Peterson, *United States*, 17; *FRUS 1969–76*, III, doc. 26.   8. Statement to the Joint Economic Committee of the 87th Congress, 28 Oct. 1959, reprinted in Robert Triffin, *Gold and the Dollar Crisis: The Future of Convertibility* (New Haven, CT, 1960), 3–14.   9. *FRUS 1961–63*, vol. IX, *Foreign Economic Policy* (Washington, DC, 1995), doc. 6.   10. *The Monetary Merry-Go-Round: The Global Financial System in Crisis*, Lombard Street Research and Churchill Archives Centre, 17 Nov. 2008, 14.   11. Eric Helleiner, *States and the Re-emergence of Global Finance from Bretton Woods to the 1990s* (Ithaca, NY, 1994), 55–8, 61–2, 76–7; Jeffrey M. Chwieroth, *Capital Ideas: The IMF and the Rise of Financial Liberalization* (Princeton, NJ, and Oxford, 2010), 109–12, 119–20.   12. Jeffrey M. Chwieroth, 'Normative change from within: the International Monetary Fund's approach to capital account liberalization', *International Studies Quarterly* 52 (2008), 137; J. Keith Horsefield, ed., *The International Monetary Fund 1945–1965: Twenty Years of International Monetary Cooperation: Volume III, Documents* (Washington, DC, 1969), 246.   13. The National Archives (TNA), T295/413, The Hong Kong and Persian Gulf gaps, nd; Leakages through Hong Kong, nd; T295/109, PM to Chancellor, 9 Oct. 1966; T295/441, The resident sterling gap, 31 Oct. 1968; Catherine Schenk, 'The re-emergence of Hong Kong as an international financial centre, 1960–78: contested internationalization', in Youssef Cassis and Laure Quennouëlle-Corre, eds., *Financial Centres and International Capital Flow in the Nineteenth and Twentieth Centuries* (Oxford, 2011), 230.   14. Maurice Obstfeld and Alan M. Taylor, *Global Capital Markets: Integration, Crisis, and Growth* (Cambridge, 2004), 52–3, 55.   15. J. Best, 'Hollowing out Keynesian norms: how the search for a technical fix undermined the Bretton Woods regime', *Review of International Studies* 30 (2004), 399–400.   16. US National Archives and Records Administration (NARA) RG56 Treasury, Widman, Box 4, Tentative outline for the research project entitled 'The Euro-dollar market and the efficacy of monetary policy in a world of capital mobility', Peter B. Clark to Wilson F. Schmidt, 17 June 1971.   17. John Connally, 'Address to the international meeting of the American Bankers Association', 28 May 1971, in *Department of State Bulletin* 65, 12 July 1971; *FRUS 1969–76*, III, doc. 156.   18. Daniel J. Sargent, *A Superpower Transformed: The Remaking of American Foreign Relations in the 1970s* (New York, 2015), 109–11.   19. *The Monetary Merry-Go-Round*, 15.   20. Barry Eichengreen, 'From benign neglect to malignant preoccupation: US balance of payments policy in the 1960s', NBER Working Paper 7603 (2000);

Coombs, *Arena*, ix. **21.** TNA, PREM11/4766, message from PM to Chancellor, nd; LBJ Presidential Library, Bator papers, Box 16, Memo for the president from the Council of Economic Advisers, 'International monetary reform and related problems', Walter Heller, 18 March 1961; Coombs, *Arena*, 21; Best, 'Hollowing out', 383–7, 390–93. **22.** Kazuhiko Yago, 'A crisis manager for the international monetary system? The rise and fall of the OECD Working Party 3, 1961–80', in Matthieu Leimgruber and Matthias Schmelzer, eds., *The OECD and the International Political Economy since 1948* (Cham, 2017), 185–96, 201–2; C. Fred Bergsten, *Dilemmas of the Dollar: The Economics and Politics of the United States* (New York, 1975), 449–51. **23.** TNA, PREM13/250, Brief for Washington, Balogh to PM, 4 Dec. 1964; PREM13/251, Record of meeting between the PM and the US Ambassador, 26 July 1965; T171/758, GB(64)30, 13 Oct. 1964, Treasury General Briefing: The problem of international liquidity; LBJ Presidential Library, Bator papers, Box 7, Memo to Council from Frank W. Schiff: 'Meeting of CEA consultants on international monetary reform, May 10 1965', 20 May 1965. **24.** Gianni Toniolo, *Central Bank Cooperation at the Bank for International Settlements, 1930–1973* (Cambridge, 2005), 402. **25.** Coombs, *Arena*, viii, x–xiv, 193. **26.** LBJ Presidential Library, Bator papers, Box 22, untitled paper, Nov. 1968. **27.** General de Gaulle's press conference, 4 Feb. 1965, in Yale University Library Digital Repository, Henry Kissinger Papers, Box 286, folder 9; Harold James, *International Monetary Cooperation since Bretton Woods* (Washington, DC, and New York, 1996), 169; *FRUS 1964–68*, vol. VIII, *International Monetary and Trade Policy* (Washington, DC, 1998), doc. 36; Julian Jackson, *A Certain Idea of France: The Life of Charles De Gaulle* (London, 2018), 652. The phrase 'exorbitant privilege' captured de Gaulle's argument but was coined by his finance minister, Valéry Giscard d'Estaing: see Barry Eichengreen, *Exorbitant Privilege: The Rise and Fall of the Dollar* (New York, 2011), 4. **28.** LBJ Presidential Library, Bator papers, Box 9, 'The dollar as seen from Europe': talk delivered by Otmar Emminger, New York, 7 Oct. 1965. **29.** James, *International Monetary Cooperation*, 212. **30.** *FRUS 1969–76*, III, doc. 153. **31.** LBJ Presidential Library, papers of William McChesney Martin, Box 43, George Ball, State, Memo for the president, A fresh approach to the gold problem, George Ball, 24 July 1962. **32.** JFK Presidential Library, George W. Ball papers, Box 1, telecon, Walter Lippmann–Ball, 22 Sept. 1962, 9.25 a.m.; Box 5, telecon, Lippmann–Ball, 29 June 1962 11.50 a.m.; Eichengreen, Mehl and Chiţu, *How Global Currencies Work*, 118–19. **33.** Jacques Rueff, *The Times*, 27, 28 and 29 June 1961; Jacques Rueff, *The Monetary Sin of the West* (New York, 1972); J. Rueff and Fred Hirsch, 'The role and rule of gold: an argument', Essays in International Finance No. 47, Department of Economics, Princeton, 1965; C. S. Chivvis, 'Charles de Gaulle, Jacques Rueff and French international monetary policy under Bretton Woods', *Journal of Contemporary History* 41 (2006), 701–20. **34.** Chivvis, 'Charles de Gaulle', 711; De Gaulle, press conference, 4 Feb. 1965; Jackson, *Certain Idea of France*, 500–503, 639, 652; M. Daou, 'Jacques Rueff and the liberal social order: a liberal interventionist', *Journal of the History of Economic Thought* 41 (2019), 573–91. **35.** TNA, PREM13/2050, Paris to FO, International monetary system, 5 April 1968. **36.** TNA, PREM11/4201, David Ormsby-Gore, Washington to PM, 11 July 1962. **37.** NARA RG56 Treasury, Monetary Reform, Box 11, VG/LIM/69-11, The issues facing US international monetary policy, C. Fred Bergsten, 5 Feb. 1969; Effects of gold price rise, VG/LIM/69-35, Willis, 4 March 1969; Ford Presidential Library, Burns papers, Box B34, R. Solomon and R. Bryant to Burns, Repercussions for the president of an international financial crisis, 8 Dec. 1970; JFK Presidential Library, National Security Files, Box 289A, Reasons for Ministers' endorsement of a stable gold price and fixed exchange rates, 13 Nov. 1963; LBJ Presidential Library, Fowler papers, Box 83, Comment on gold in South Africa, 30 July 1968; *FRUS 1969–76*, III, doc. 160; TNA, PREM11/3284, L(61)6 revise 30 Jan. 1961. International economic problems: The international monetary problem and the price of gold. Memo by Treasury. **38.** J. F. Kennedy, 'Special message to Congress on gold and the balance of payments deficit', 6 Feb. 1961, online in Gerhard Peters and John T. Woolley, *The American Presidency Project*; Robert V. Roosa, *Monetary Reform for the World Economy* (New York, 1965), 17–22. **39.** LBJ Presidential Library, Bator papers, Box 16, Memo for the president from the Council of Economic Advisers, International monetary reform, 18 March 1961;

Coombs, *Arena*, 19–21.　40. Coombs, *Arena*, ix, 5, 20, 21, 71–2, 80, 188, 192–3.　41. Ibid., 68, 199–200.　42. NARA RG59 State, Bureau of European Affairs, Box 5, Memo of conversation, 'The international monetary system', 14 Dec. 1967; Francis J. Gavin, *Gold, Dollars and Power: The Politics of International Monetary Relations, 1958–1971* (Chapel Hill, NC, and London, 2004), 168–70.　43. Federal Open Market Committee, 'Memorandum of discussion', 14 March 1968; LBJ Presidential Library, Bator papers, Box 53, The gold crisis, Nov. 1967–March 1968; Henry Fowler papers, Box 83, 'The two-tier gold system: a temporary or permanent solution?', Otmar Emminger, Aug. 1968; Gavin, *Gold, Dollars and Power*, 166, 184–5.　44. TNA, PREM11/4193, 'World monetary systems', 5 May 1961 and 'Prof. Triffin's proposals', 29 June 1962.　45. TNA, PREM11/4201, Macmillan to Ormsby-Gore, 3 July 1962; Macmillan to Poole, 21 Oct. 1962; Macmillan to Maudling, 1 Sept. 1962.　46. TNA, PREM11/4201, Maudling (Colonial Office) to Macmillan, 22 July 1962; PREM11/4766, Washington to FO: text of Chancellor's speech, 19 Sept. 1962.　47. James, *International Monetary Cooperation*, 166.　48. TNA, PREM11/4201, International liquidity, Chancellor to PM, 15 May 1963; *FRUS 1961–63*, IX, doc. 61.　49. TNA, PREM11/4193, 'World monetary systems', 5 May 1961; 'Mr Bernstein's proposals', 29 June 1962; PREM11/4201 P. de Zuleta to PM, 29 June 1962; James, *International Monetary Cooperation*, 160–65; Helleiner, *States and Re-emergence*, 96. The various plans were explained in *The Economist*, 6 May 1961.　50. LBJ Presidential Library, Henry Fowler papers, Box 59, Memo of conversation: international liquidity, 25 Feb. 1966.　51. Rinaldo Ossola, 'On the creation of new reserve assets: the Report of the Study Group of Ten', *Banco Nazionale del Lavoro* 18 (1965), 272–92.　52. TNA, T171/758, GB(64)30, 13 Oct. 1964, Treasury General Briefing: The problem of international liquidity.　53. Coombs, *Arena*, 189.　54. *FRUS 1964–68*, VIII, doc. 64; LBJ Presidential Library, Bator papers, Box 2, Memo for the Secretary of the Treasury, F. M. Bator, 23 Aug. 1965; Box 7, Major issues for the US in proposals for reserve creation, 23 April 1965; *Guidelines for Improving the International Monetary System: Report of the Subcommittee on International Exchange and Payments of the Joint Economic Committee Congress of the United States, 89th Congress 1st session* (Washington, DC, 1965).　55. James, *International Monetary Cooperation*, 169–70; Margaret Garritsen de Vries, ed., *The International Monetary Fund 1966–1971: The System under Stress. Vol. I, Narrative* (Washington, DC, 1976), 54.　56. Volcker and Gyohten, *Changing Fortunes*, 44; James, *International Monetary Creation*, 167.　57. LBJ Presidential Library, Fowler papers, Box 58, International monetary arrangements, Fowler to Schiller, 6 June 1967; *FRUS 1964–68*, VIII, doc. 119.　58. *FRUS 1964–68*, VIII, docs. 136, 141, 145; the documents are in Margaret Garritsen de Vries, ed., *The International Monetary Fund 1966–1971: The System under Stress. Vol. II, Documents* (Washington, DC, 1976).　59. TNA, PREM13/2050, telegram, international liquidity, meeting of ministerial Group of Ten, 29 Aug. 1967; PREM13/3151, International monetary reform summary, 20 Oct. 1967; Volcker and Gyohten, *Changing Fortunes*, 45; Coombs, *Arena*, 202–3.　60. J. E. Meade, 'Bretton Woods, GATT and the balance of payments: a second round', *Three Banks Review* 16 (1952), 3–22; *idem*, 'The case for variable exchange rates', *Three Banks Review* 27 (1955), 3–27, quote at 6.　61. M. Friedman, 'The case for flexible exchange rates', reprinted in his *Essays in Positive Economics* (Chicago, IL, 1953), 157–203.　62. Milton Friedman, *Capitalism and Freedom* (Chicago, IL, 1962), ch. 4; Milton Friedman and Robert Roosa, *The Balance of Payments: Free versus Fixed Exchange Rates* (Washington, DC, 1967), 4, 11–13, 15–18, 20, 22–3, 71–2, 76–7, 83, 90–91, 94, 118–20, 183; George N. Holm, ed., *Approaches to Greater Flexibility of Exchange Rates: The Bürgenstock Papers* (Princeton, NJ, 1970) showed that most still agreed with Roosa in favouring limited flexibility, with only 7 of 34 participants supporting floating.　63. TNA, PREM11/4201, Maudling (Colonial Office) to Macmillan, 22 July 1962.　64. TNA, T312/1485, Bank of England, Floating rates, 13 Jan. 1961; J. A. Downie, Floating rates, 18 Jan. 1961; DHFR to Hubback, Exchange rate policy, 23 June 1961.　65. TNA, T312/1636, FU(66)10, Fixed or flexible rates, W. S. Ryrie, 22 Sept. 1966.　66. Richard Roberts, '"Unwept, unhonoured and unsung": Britain's import surcharge, 1964–66, and currency crisis management', *Financial History Review* 20 (2013), 209–29, quotes at 221; Scott Newton, 'The two sterling crises of 1964 and the decision not to devalue', *Economic History Review* 62 (2009),

73–98; *idem*, 'The sterling devaluation of 1967: the international economy and post-war social democracy', *English Historical Review* 125 (2010), 912–45; Alec Cairncross and Barry Eichengreen, *Sterling in Decline: The Devaluations of 1931, 1949 and 1967* (Oxford, 1983). 67. Robert Leeson, *Ideology and the International Economy: The Decline and Fall of Bretton Woods* (London, 2003), 64–9; Milton Friedman, 'A proposal for resolving the US balance of payments problem: confidential memorandum to president-elect Nixon', in Leo Melamed, ed., *The Merits of Flexible Exchange Rates: An Anthology* (Fairfax, VA, 1988), 429–38. 68. *FRUS 1969–76*, III, note 2 to doc. 115. 69. Roosa, *Monetary Reform*, 26–32, 128, 129; Friedman and Roosa, *Balance of Payments*, 30, 38–9, 40, 42, 46–7, 50–53, 62. 70. TNA, T295/904, 'Enquiry into the position of sterling January 1966–February 1968', vol. II, 203. 71. John H. Williamson, 'The crawling peg', Essays in International Finance, No. 50, Department of Economics, Princeton, 1965. 72. Bundesarchiv, B136-3336, Hans von der Groeben (EC Commission) to State Secretary Dr Karl Karsten, 19 Sept. 1969. 73. NARA RG56 Treasury, Monetary Reform, Box 11, Hubert Ansiaux to William McChesney Martin, 8 Sept. 1969. 74. Otmar Emminger, 'The D-mark in the conflict between external and internal equilibrium, 1948–75', Essays in International Finance No. 122, Department of Economics, Princeton, 1977, 1–3, 51–3; William Glenn Gray, 'Floating the system: Germany, the United States and the breakdown of Bretton Woods', *Diplomatic History* 31 (2007), 295–323. 75. TNA, T267/36, Treasury Historical Memorandum 30: The collapse of the Bretton Woods system, 1968–1973, 31–2; NARA RG56 Treasury, Monetary Reform, Box 11, VG/WG/70-32, Recapitulation of views: wider margins, 3 March 1970; Memo from George H. Willis to Volcker, Limited exchange rate flexibility – conversations with some executive directors on progress of discussions in IMF and approach in forthcoming deputies' meeting, 3 April 1970; F. Lisle Widman to Volcker, Limited exchange rate flexibility, 2 June 1970, Position paper on limited exchange rate flexibility, draft 15 April 1970 [William Dale]; Position paper on limited exchange flexibility, draft 15 Sept. 1970, G. H. Willis to Volcker; and in general Boxes 11 and 14; *FRUS 1969–76*, III, doc. 148; de Vries, ed., *IMF 1966–71*, *II*, 'The role of exchange rates in the adjustment of international payments, Sept 1970: Part II, Implications for policy', 273–330. 76. Gavin, *Gold, Dollars and Power*, 185. 77. *FRUS 1964–68*, VIII, doc. 190. 78. Hendrik S. Houthakker, 'The breakdown of Bretton Woods', in Werner Sichel, ed., *Economic Advice and Economic Policy: Recommendations from Past Members of the CEA* (New York, 1978), 61. 79. TNA, T318/192, Leslie O'Brien, Bank of England to Douglas Allen, 6 May 1968. 80. TNA, T318/192, telegram to certain missions and dependent territories, 12 Sept. 1968, 'The Basle facility and the sterling area'; PREM13/2053, Sterling negotiations, general description, Treasury 13 Sept. 1968; The Basle scheme and the sterling area, 1 July 1968; T318/253, Report of the Sterling Area Working Party, Feb. 1969; Schenk, *Decline of Sterling*, 273–313; *FRUS 1964–68*, VIII, doc. 200; Eichengreen, Mehl and Chiţu, *How Global Currencies Work*, 119; Michael Oliver and Arran Hamilton, 'Downhill from devaluation: the battle for sterling, 1967–72', *Economic History Review* 60 (2007), 490–97. 81. Schenk, *Decline of Sterling*, 120, 124–6, 132, 135–7, 206–7, 238–40, 272. 82. *FRUS 1964–68*, VIII, docs. 208, 214, 215, 216, 217, 219, 221; TNA, PREM13/2055, telegram from Paris to FO, 'France and the franc', 24 Nov. 1968, Personal message, PM to president, 20 Nov. 1968; TNA, PREM13/2586, Record of a conversation between the PM, Foreign and Commonwealth Secretary, Chancellor of the Exchequer and German ambassador, 20 Nov. 1968. 83. M. D. Bordo, 'The Bretton Woods international monetary system: a historical overview', in M. D. Bordo and B. Eichengreen, eds., *A Retrospective on the Bretton Woods System* (Chicago, IL, 1993), 78; *FRUS 1969–76*, III, doc. 116; Gray, 'Floating the system', 300–303.

17. 'BENIGN NEGLECT'

1. US National Archives and Records Administration (NARA) RG56 Treasury, Monetary Reform, Box 11, VG/LIM/69-31, Realignment of exchange rates, RCB/RS, 3 March 1969. 2. NARA RG56 Treasury, Monetary Reform, Box 11, 'The situation of the key currencies',

Otmar Emminger, Geneva, 1970.   3. Association for Diplomatic Studies and Training: Foreign Affairs and History Project. Ambassador Winston Lord, interviewed by Charles Stuart Kennedy and Nancy Bernkopf Tucker, 28 April 1998; Margaret MacMillan, *Nixon and Mao: The Week That Changed the World* (New York, 2007).   4. Richard Nixon, Remarks to top personnel at the Department of the Treasury, 14 Feb. 1969, online in Gerhard Peters and John T. Woolley, *The American Presidency Project*.   5. Allen J. Matusow, *Nixon's Economy: Booms, Busts, Dollars and Votes* (Lawrence, KS, 1998), 16; *Foreign Relations of the United States (FRUS) 1969–76*, vol. III, *Foreign Economic Policy; International Monetary Policy, 1969–72* (Washington, DC, 2001), doc. 38.   6. Robert P. Bremner, *Chairman of the Fed: William McChesney Martin and the Creation of the American Financial System* (New Haven, CT, 2004), 123, 144, 261; Matusow, *Nixon's Economy*, 1, 9–12, 18–20; Jeffrey E. Garten, *Three Days at Camp David: How a Secret Meeting in 1971 Transformed the Global Economy* (New York, 2021), 101; James L. Butkiewicz and Scott Ohlmecher, 'Ending Bretton Woods: evidence from the Nixon tapes', *Economic History Review* 74 (2021), 940.   7. Charles Coombs, *Arena of International Finance* (New York, 1976), 205; Matusow, *Nixon's Economy*, 142; Garten, *Three Days*, Part II on 'the cast'.   8. Matusow, *Nixon's Economy*, 142; *FRUS 1969–76*, III, doc. 1; Harold James, *International Monetary Cooperation since Bretton Woods* (Washington, DC, and New York, 1996), 212; Robert Leeson, *Ideology and the International Economy: The Decline and Fall of Bretton Woods* (London, 2003), 67, 69–71.   9. NARA RG59 State, Bureau of European Affairs, Box 4, '"Benign neglect" and the balance of payments', Emmett M. Coxson to Katz, nd; on Nixon Doctrine, Richard Nixon, 'Informal remarks in Guam with newsmen', 25 July 1969, and 'Address to the nation on the war in Vietnam', 3 Nov. 1969, in Peters and Woolley, *American Presidency Project*.   10. Coombs, *Arena*, 209, 211–12.   11. William L. Silber, *Volcker: The Triumph of Persistence* (New York and London, 2012), 56–7; Matusow, *Nixon's Economy*, 142–3; Paul Volcker and Toyoo Gyohten, *Changing Fortunes: The World's Money and the Threat to American Leadership* (New York, 1992), 63.   12. NARA RG56 Treasury, Widman, Box 2, 'Your September 19 memorandum on trade policy', Widman to Petty, 23 Sept. 1968; 'Some personal observations on the world payments problem', Widman to Petty, 28 Jan. 1969; Box 4, 'Observations growing out of the Wednesday consultants' meeting', Widman to Petty, 27 Nov 1970.   13. 'The President's news conference of February 6 1969', in Peters and Woolley, *American Presidency Project*.   14. Matusow, *Nixon's Economy*, 119.   15. Ibid., 119–23.   16. *FRUS 1969–76*, III, docs. 12, 48.   17. Ibid., docs. 10, 15.   18. Ibid., docs. 54, 62.   19. Ibid., doc. 60.   20. NARA RG56 Treasury, Monetary Reform, Box 11, VG/LIM/69-11, The issues facing US international monetary policy, C. Fred Bergsten, 5 Feb. 1969.   21. *FRUS 1969–76*, III, docs. 119, 129, 130, 131; NARA RG56 Treasury, Widman, Box 3, 'Notes on international finance policy discussions, May 16–17 1969', F. Lisle Widman; RG56 Treasury, Monetary Reform, Box 11, VG/LIM/69-30, Memo for members of the Volcker group, 'The three principal options', Hendrik S. Houthakker, 28 Feb. 1969; VG/LIM/69-31, Realignment of exchange rates, RCB/RS 3 March 1969; VG/LIM/69-37, 10 March 1969, Strategy for improving international monetary arrangements: a paper approved by the Volcker group; VG/LIM/69-38, 10 March 1969, Strategy for improving international monetary arrangements: a paper approved by the Volcker group, Part II and second draft at VG/LIM/69-47, 17 March 1969; VG/LIM/69-48, Summary of a possible US approach to improving international monetary arrangements, 17 March 1969; Silber, *Volcker*, 62–7.   22. *FRUS 1969–76*, III, doc. 131.   23. NARA RG56 Treasury, Widman, Box 3, Suspension of dollar convertibility, Widman to Petty, 3 Nov. 1969.   24. *FRUS 1969–76*, III, doc. 138.   25. Kenneth Dyson and Ivo Maes, 'Intellectuals as policy-makers: the value of biography in the history of European Monetary Union', in Dyson and Maes, eds., *Architects of the Euro: Intellectuals in the Making of the European Monetary Union* (Oxford, 2016), 3; Ivo Maes and Eric Bussière, 'Robert Triffin: the arch monetarist in the European integration debates?' in Dyson and Maes, eds., *Architects*, 37, 41–4; Ivo Maes, *Robert Triffin: A Life* (Oxford, 2021), 71–2, 79–86, 89–98, 109, 121–2, 129, 151–66; Robert Triffin, *Europe and the Money Muddle: From Bilateralism to Near Convertibility* (New Haven, CT, 1957), 288–9; *idem*, *Gold and the Dollar Crisis*, rev. edn (New Haven, CT, 1961), 87–93, 120–44.   26. Katja Seidel, 'Robert Marjolin: securing the common market through economic and monetary union', in Dyson and Maes, eds., *Architects*, 53, 58–71. 27. 'Declaration by the Commission on the occasion of the achievement of the customs union on 1 July 1968', *Bulletin of the European Communities* no. 7 (1968), 5–8; Commission Memorandum to the Council on the co-ordination of economic policies and monetary co-operation within the Community, submitted on 12 Feb. 1969, COM(69)150, *Bulletin of the European Communities Supplement* no. 3 (1969); Valéry Giscard d'Estaing, 'La monnaie unique pour l'Europe', *Communauté européenne*, April 1969, 17–19 available in English on www.cvce.eu; Maes and Bussière, 'Triffin', 44–5, 50; Seidel, 'Marjolin', 71–2; David Howarth, 'Raymond Barre: modernizing France through European monetary cooperation', in Dyson and Maes, eds., *Architects*, 75–88. 28. Integral text of the final communiqué of the conference of the heads of state or government on 1 and 2 December 1969 at The Hague, available on www .cvce.eu. 29. Emmanuel Mourlon-Druol, *A Europe Made of Money: The Emergence of the European Monetary System* (Ithaca, NY, 2012), 22–3; Jean Lecerf, 'Why a European currency?' *Communauté européenne* 123 (Oct 1968); Pierre Werner, 'Politique monetaire européenne', *Bulletin de documentation* 6 (1969), 17–19; Elena Danescu, 'Pierre Werner: a visionary European and consensus builder', in Dyson and Maes, eds., *Architects*, 97, 99–103, 108. 30. Danescu, 'Pierre Werner', 103–14; Report to the Council and the Commission on the realisation by stages of Economic and Monetary Union in the Community 'Werner Report', supplement to Bulletin 11 – 1970 of the European Communities, 26. Report by the Commission to the Council, 30 Oct. 1970, *Bulletin of the European Communities* no. 11 (Nov. 1970), 15–18; Resolution of the Council and the representatives of the governments of the member states, 22 March 1971, *Official Journal of the European Communities*, 18 April 1972. 31. NARA RG59 State, Bureau of European Affairs, Box 4, 'Some possible implications for the United States of the proposed monetary and economic union of the EEC', A. I. Bloomfield, Jan 1971; 'Comment on Prof. Bloomfield's paper on the effects on the US of EEC monetary integration', Donald C. Templeman, 22 Feb. 1971; Ford Presidential Library, Burns papers, Box B114, Werner report (1), Comments on the Werner report, Charles Siegman to R. Solomon, 6 Nov. 1970; NARA RG56 Treasury, Widman, Box 3, 'United States position with respect to European monetary unity', draft, F. L. Widman, 17 March 1970. 32. NARA RG56 Treasury, Widman, Box 4, World balance of payments problem, Widman to Volcker, 25 Jan. 1971; Box B65, R. Solomon, draft 21 March 1971. 33. Barry Eichengreen, Arnaud Mehl and Livia Chiţu, *How Global Currencies Work: Past, Present and Future* (Princeton, NJ, and Oxford, 2018), 159–60. 34. Shinji Takagi, *Conquering the Fear of Freedom: Japanese Exchange Rate Policy since 1945* (Oxford, 2015), 27–35; Philip H. Trezise, 'The realities of Japan–US economic relations', *Pacific Community* 1 (1970), 363. 35. Eichengreen, Mehl and Chiţu, *How Global Currencies Work*, 158, 160; Oral History interviews with Kikuchi Kiyoaki, Yusuke Kashiwagi and Toyoo Gyohten from the National Security Archive, US–Japan Special Documentation Project: US foreign policy and relations with Japan, 1969–1977; Thomas Zeiler, Working Paper 1, 'US foreign economic policy and relations with Japan, 1969–77' and Hiroshi Ando, Working Paper 3, 'Change in Japan: a comparison of Japan's response to international monetary crisis in 1971 and 1973', from The Nixon Shocks and US–Japanese Relations 1969–1976, Conference organized by the National Security Archive and the Woodrow Wilson Center for Scholars, 1996; Bai Gao, *Economic Ideology and Japanese Industrial Policy: Developmentalism from 1931 to 1965* (Cambridge, 1997), 225–79; Mikio Sumiya, ed., *A History of Japanese Trade and Industry Policy* (Oxford, 1994), 452–67, 507–14; Tadashi Sasaki, 'Japan's recent monetary situation', *Pacific Community* 1 (1970), 612–19; Tadaski Ino, 'Japan's twenty-year experience with a fixed rate yen', in George N. Halm, ed., *Approaches to Greater Flexibility of Exchange Rates* (Princeton, NJ, 1970), 357–63; Tadaski Ino, *Dollar Shokku Kaisaroku* [A Memoir of the Dollar Shock] (Tokyo, 1986); Ushio Shiotu, *Kasumigaseki ga Furueu Hi: Tsuuka Senso no Jyu-ni Nichi Kan* [The Days That Shook Kasumigaseki: Twelve Days of Monetary War] (Tokyo, 1983); Hiroshi Makino, *Nichibei tsuka gaiko no kikaku bunseki: Nikuson shokku kara sumisononian gai made* [A Comparative Analysis of US–Japan Currency Diplomacy: From the Nixon Shock to the Smithsonian] (Tokyo, 1999), 116–17; James Babb, *Business and Politics in Japan* (Manchester, 2001), ch. 8; Fukuda, Upper House, Finance Committee, 27 March 1971; Bank of

Japan, *Nippon Ginko Hyakunen-Shi* [Bank of Japan: The First Hundred Years], vol. 6 (Tokyo, 1986), 307–9; Taizo Hayashi, 'From the failure of the "Alpha Operation" to the yen float: memories of the yen policy during the turbulent era', *Kinyu-Zaisei Jijyo*, 31 Jan and 7 Feb. 1982; *Asahi Shimbun*, 16 July 1969, 3 March 1970; *Asahi Evening News*, 15 May, 16 July, 28 and 30 Aug. 1971; *Japan Times*, 15 April 1971; *Japanese Economic Journal*, 20 April 1970; Kamekichi Takahashi, 'Kokumin Keizai teki Mainasu' ['Loss for the national economy'], in Koizumi and Tachi, eds., *Yen no Jitsuryoku* [The Real Strength of the Yen] (Tokyo, 1970); Robert Angel, *Explaining Economic Policy Failure: Japan in the 1969–1971 International Monetary Crisis* (New York, 1991), 272–4; *Japan Economic Journal*, 27 April and 1 June 1971; *Japan Times*, 17 June 1971. I am grateful to Dr Hiroki Shin for assistance. **36.** Joanne S. Gowa, *Closing the Gold Window: Domestic Politics and the End of Bretton Woods* (Ithaca, NY, and London, 1983), 13, 23, 88–9, 95, 99–103, 107, 110–17, 122. **37.** Nixon Presidential Papers, Federal government – organizations, Department of Treasury: Box 2, Memo for secretaries, 18 Jan. 1971; NSC subject files, EEC Box 322, Fred Bergsten to Kissinger, Alternatives to the common market, 11 Dec. 1970; Matusow, *Nixon's Economy*, 131–3; Daniel J. Sargent, *A Superpower Transformed: The Remaking of American Foreign Relations in the 1970s* (New York, 2015), 100–101; Peter G. Peterson, *Education of an American Dreamer: How a Son of Greek Immigrants Learned His Way from a Nebraska Diner to Washington, Wall Street and Beyond* (New York, 2009), 96–100, 136; idem, *The United States in the Changing World Economy: I, A Foreign Economic Perspective* (Washington, 1971); Richard Nixon, 'Remarks to midwestern news media executives attending a briefing on domestic policy in Kansas City, Missouri', 6 July 1971, in Peters and Woolley, *American Presidency Project*. **38.** *FRUS 1969–76*, III, docs. 158, 159; Henry Kissinger, *The White House Years* (London, 1979), 951. **39.** Matusow, *Nixon's Economy*, 117; Butkiewicz and Ohlmecher, 'Ending Bretton Woods', 928. **40.** Robert H. Ferrell, ed., *Inside the Nixon Administration: The Secret Diary of Arthur Burns, 1969–1974* (Lawrence, KS, 2010), 41, 43, 47. **41.** Bremner, *Chairman of the Fed*, 263. **42.** Matusow, *Nixon's Economy*, 14–18; Bremner, *Chairman of the Fed*, 266–7, 270–73. **43.** Matusow, *Nixon's Economy*, 25–33; Bremner, *Chairman of the Fed*, 266–7, 271–8. **44.** Matusow, *Nixon's Economy*, 59. **45.** Sarah Binder and Mark Spindel, *The Myth of Independence: How Congress Governs the Federal Reserve* (Princeton, NJ, 2017), 145, 149–64; Peter Conti-Brown, *The Power and Independence of the Federal Reserve* (Princeton, NJ, 2016), 181, 190–7; Allan Sproul, 'The Accord', *Federal Reserve Bank of New York, Monthly Review* 46 (1964), reprinted in Lawrence S. Ritter, ed., *Selected Papers of Allan Sproul* (New York, 1980), 51–73. **46.** Ferrell, ed., *Inside the Nixon Administration*, 39. **47.** Matusow, *Nixon's Economy*, 60–61. **48.** Ibid., 62–7. **49.** Ibid., 72–9. **50.** Ibid., 80–81, 83. **51.** Ibid., 143. **52.** Ferrell, ed., *Inside the Nixon Administration*, 47–8. **53.** William Glenn Gray, 'Floating the system: Germany, the United States and the breakdown of Bretton Woods', *Diplomatic History* 31 (2007), 308–9. **54.** NARA RG56 Treasury, Monetary Reform, Box 5, 'Inflation and the world monetary system', Otmar Emminger lecture at Per Jacobsson Foundation, 16 June 1973; Ford Presidential Library, Burns papers, Box B65, conversation with Dr Klasen, 5 May 1971 and telephone call from Dr Karl Klasen, 10 May 1971; RG56 Treasury, J. Connally, Box 1, Wallich to Connally, 23 July 1971; Bundesarchiv, B136-3332, Capital inflows and potential reactions, 9 June 1971; Memo on Cabinet meeting, 21 June 1971; *FRUS 1969–76*, III, docs. 151, 155; Otmar Emminger, 'The D-mark in the conflict between internal and external equilibrium', Essays in International Finance No. 122, Department of Economics, Princeton, 1977, 22–31; Butkiewicz and Ohlmacher, 'Ending Bretton Woods', 929, 930. **55.** Catherine R. Schenk, *The Decline of Sterling: Managing the Retreat of an International Currency* (Cambridge, 2010), 138–46, 151–3. **56.** Michael Oliver and Arran Hamilton, 'Downhill from devaluation: the battle for sterling, 1967–72', *Economic History Review* 60 (2007), 505. **57.** The National Archives (TNA), PREM15/53, Cromer to Prime Minister, 1 Sept. 1970 covering 'Proposals regarding United Kingdom participation in a European monetary system', August 1970 and response by W. S. Ryrie; PREM15/1271, Cromer to Douglas-Home, 9, 11 and 13 May 1971; Bank of England Archive, C43/425, 'Some possible consequences of the Americans formally going off gold', J. L. Sangster, 19 July 1971; 'Possibility of US going off gold', 13 Aug. 1971. **58.**

Matusow, *Nixon's Economy*, 134–7, 145; John Connally, 'Address to American Bankers Association', 28 May 1971. **59.** Matusow, *Nixon's Economy*, 139, 145–6; Garten, *Three Days*, 140. **60.** Matusow, *Nixon's Economy*, 141, 145–6; *FRUS 1969–76*, III, docs. 157, 158; Butkiewicz and Ohlmacher, 'Ending Bretton Woods', 930. **61.** Garten, *Three Days*, 147–8; Butkiewicz and Ohlmacher, 'Ending Bretton Woods', 931–2. **62.** Garten, *Three Days*, 148–54; Butkiewicz and Ohlmacher, 'Ending Bretton Woods', 932–5. **63.** Matusow, *Nixon's Economy*, 147; Ford Presidential Library, Burns papers, Box B65, 'Exchange rate realignment and related matters', W. Dale – cover note by R. Solomon to Burns, 9 Aug. 1971; Box B73, 'A proposal for a US initiative on international monetary reform', R. Solomon, 26 July 1971; Garten, *Three Days*, 155; Butkiewicz and Ohlmacher, 'Ending Bretton Woods', 932. **64.** Matusow, *Nixon's Economy*, 147; Butkiewicz and Ohlmacher, 'Ending Bretton Woods', 932, 935; Coombs, *Arena*, 215; Sargent, *Superpower Transformed*, 112; *Action now to strengthen the dollar*, Joint Economic Committee Report, August 1971; *FRUS 1969–76*, III, docs. 166, 167; Garten, *Three Days*, 157–8, 161–2, 164–5. **65.** Ferrell, ed., *Inside the Nixon Administration*, 53; Ford Presidential Library, Burns papers, Box B100, Burns to Connally, 19 May 1971; Box K31, Note on Camp David weekend, 13–15 Aug. 1971, 16 Aug. 1971; Matusow, *Nixon's Economy*, 149–54, 157; Garten, *Three Days*, 166–212. **66.** Volcker and Gyohten, *Changing Fortunes*, 78; William Safire quoted in Paul Volcker, *Keeping At It: The Quest for Sound Money and Good Government* (New York, 2018), 72. **67.** Ferrell, ed., *Inside the Nixon Administration*, 49, 52, 53, 55. **68.** Matusow, *Nixon's Economy*, 154–5; Garten, *Three Days*, 213–41; Richard Nixon, 'Address to the nation to outline a new economic policy: the challenge of peace', 15 August 1971, in Peters and Woolley, *American Presidency Project*; Executive Order 11615 providing for stabilization of prices, rents, wages and salaries, 15 Aug. 1971 and Proclamation 4074, Imposition of supplemental duty for balance of payments purposes, 15 Aug. 1971. **69.** Volcker and Gyohten, *Changing Fortunes*, 79–80; Matusow, *Nixon's Economy*, 156–64; Garten, *Three Days*, 147–8, 245, 247; Richard M. Nixon, *RN: The Memoirs of Richard Nixon* (New York, 1978), 521. **70.** Garten, *Three Days*, 238–9, 248, 250. **71.** TNA, PREM15/309, Cromer to Foreign Secretary, International monetary situation, 15 Aug. 1971. **72.** Sargent, *Superpower Transformed*, 128–9. **73.** *The Economist*, 18 Sept. 1971, 75. **74.** Ford Presidential Library, Burns papers, Box B100, 'The international monetary and trading situation – a proposed approach', 1 Sept. 1971. **75.** Garten, *Three Days*, 246.

18. 'MUSIC WITHOUT ANY MIDDLE C'

1. Ford Presidential Library, Burns papers, Box B65, Ralph Bryant to Arthur Burns, 'Checklist of issues to be resolved in coming weeks', 17 Aug. 1971. **2.** Ford Presidential Library, Burns papers, Box B24, 'A foreign economic perspective', Peter Peterson, 27 Dec. 1971. **3.** The National Archives (TNA), PREM15/1458, Cromer to Edward Heath, 18 Feb. 1973. **4.** Ford Presidential Library, Burns papers, Box B65, 'Stage management of a US suspension of gold sales and purchases: a checklist of questions', R. Bryant to R. Solomons, 6 Aug. 1971; International negotiations: Objectives, issues and conclusions, 18 Aug. 1971; Box B100, The international monetary and trading situation – a proposed approach, 1 Sept. 1971, which refers to US National Archives and Records Administration (NARA), RG56 Treasury, Monetary Reform, Box 6, International monetary issues – the setting and the options, 30 Aug. 1971; Robert H. Ferrell, ed., *Inside the Nixon Administration: The Secret Diary of Arthur Burns, 1969–1974* (Lawrence, KS, 2010), 57–8. **5.** TNA, PREM15/309, 'Note for the record: meeting with Mr Paul Volcker at the home of the US economic minister in London', A. D. Neale, 17 Aug. 1971; Note of a meeting in the Chancellor of the Exchequer's room, Treasury, 16 Aug. 1971. For the American memorandum on the meeting, *Foreign Relations of the United States (FRUS) 1969–76*, vol. III, *Foreign Economic Policy; International Monetary Policy, 1969–72* (Washington, DC, 2001), doc. 170. **6.** Paul Volcker and Toyoo Gyohten, *Changing Fortunes: The World's Money and the Threat to American Leadership* (New York, 1992), 81; James L. Butkiewicz and Scott Ohlmacher, 'Ending Bretton Woods: evidence from the Nixon tapes', *Economic History Review* 74 (2021), 937; Jeffrey E. Garten, *Three Days at Camp David: How a Secret Meeting in 1971 Transformed the Global Economy* (New York, 2021), 258–9, 262; Ford Presidential Library, Burns papers, Box B65, International negotiations: Objectives, issues and conclusions, 18 Aug. 1971; TNA, PREM15/309, telegram from Selby, 17 Aug. 1971, International currency situation.   7. NARA RG56 Records of Secretary Shultz, Box 7, 'Co-ordinating Group: Planning the negotiations for the new economic policy abroad', Peter G. Peterson, 20 Sept. 1971; Garten, *Three Days*, 271–3.   8. *FRUS* 1969–76, III, doc. 174; Butkiewicz and Ohlmecher, 'Ending Bretton Woods', 937–8; Garten, *Three Days*, 266–7, 275; Henry Kissinger, *The White House Years* (London, 1979), 957.   9. Luke Nichter, *Richard Nixon and Europe: The Reshaping of the Postwar Atlantic World* (Cambridge, 2015), 88; Kissinger, *White House Years*, 956.   10. Harold James, *International Monetary Cooperation since Bretton Woods* (Washington, DC, and New York, 1996), 222; William L. Silber, *Volcker: The Triumph of Persistence* (New York and London, 2012), 92–3; Garten, *Three Days*, 261.   11. Silber, *Volcker*, 98, 108–9; Ferrell, ed., *Inside the Nixon Administration*, 56, 65.   12. *FRUS* 1969–76, III, doc. 195; obituary of Connally, *New York Times*, 16 June 1993.   13. TNA, PREM15/310, William Neild to Armstrong, The dollar crisis, summitry and European policy, 5 Nov. 1971; Silber, *Volcker*, 108, 195.   14. TNA, PREM15/310, Cromer, International monetary situation, 4 Nov. 1971; PREM15/1271, Cromer to Douglas Allen, Treasury, 9 Nov. 1971.   15. Ferrell, ed., *Inside the Nixon Administration*, 64–6.   16. TNA, PREM15/309, Note for the record, meeting with Mr Paul Volcker at the home of the US economic minister in London on Monday 16 August, A. D. Neale, 17 Aug. 1971; James, *International Monetary Cooperation*, 221–3, 225.   17. TNA, PREM15/812, Cromer to Edward Heath, 26 Jan. 1972; Cromer to Anthony Barber, 4 April 1972; International Monetary Reform, Cromer to Chancellor, 8 May 1972; D. J. Mitchell to Alan Neale, International monetary reform: forum, 11 May 1972; PREM15/1271, Cromer to FCO, 13 May 1972; NARA RG56 Treasury, Monetary Reform, Box 6, Record of discussion, Treasury consultants, 10 Nov. 1972; James, *International Monetary Cooperation*, 244.   18. NARA RG56 Treasury, Monetary Reform, Box 4, The furor over fora, W. C. Cates to Volcker, 24 Feb. 1972; *FRUS* 1969–76, III, doc. 171; TNA, T267/36, Treasury Historical Memorandum No. 30, The collapse of the Bretton Woods system 1968–1973, 39–40.   19. NARA RG56 Treasury, Monetary Reform, Box 5, Inflation and the world monetary system, lecture at Per Jacobsson Foundation, 16 June 1973; TNA, T318/473, The Federal Republic's handling of the dollar crisis: Ambassador at Bonn to Secretary of State for Foreign and Commonwealth Affairs, 12 June 1972; Bundesarchiv, B136-11608, Pohl to Brandt, 20 Aug. 1971; B136-7355, Weinstock report, 9 Sept. 1971: Thoughts on the current debates over monetary policy; B136-3332, Results of Council of Europe meeting 19/20 Aug. 1971; B136-7355, Results of Council of Ministers Meeting, 13 Sept. 1971.   20. Silber, *Volcker*, 94, 98.   21. Charles Coombs, *Arena of International Finance* (New York, 1976), xiii.   22. Ferrell, ed., *Inside the Nixon Administration*, 65.   23. NARA RG56 Records of Secretary Shultz, Box 7, Co-ordinating Group: Planning the negotiations for the new economic policy abroad, Peter Peterson, 20 Sept. 1971; Negotiating the new economic policy abroad, Peter G. Peterson, 23 Sept. 1971; Peter Peterson to John Connally, Negotiating the new economic policy abroad – work group, 26 Oct. 1971 covering Draft paper: negotiating the new economic policy abroad, 25 Oct. 1971; *FRUS* 1969–76, III, docs. 177, 184.   24. TNA, PREM15/310, International monetary situation, Cromer, 7 Nov. 1971.   25. Garten, *Three Days*, 269–70; TNA, T267/36, Treasury Historical Memorandum, 41, quoting BIS Annual Report for 1971–72.   26. *FRUS* 1969–76, III, doc. 195.   27. TNA, T318/473, The Federal Republic's handling of the dollar crisis: Ambassador at Bonn to Secretary of State for Foreign and Commonwealth Affairs, 12 June 1972.   28. Garten, *Three Days*, 277–8; *FRUS* 1969–76, III, docs. 190, 197, 201.   29. *FRUS* 1969–76, III, docs. 210, 211; TNA, T267/36, Treasury Historical Memorandum, 44–6; Silber, *Volcker*, 99–101; Volcker and Gyohten, *Changing Fortunes*, 85–6; Catherine R. Schenk, *The Decline of Sterling: Managing the Retreat of an International Currency, 1945–1992* (Cambridge, 2010), 324–5; James, *International Monetary Cooperation*, 236; Garten, *Three Days*, 279–82.   30. TNA, T318/473, The Federal Republic's handling of the dollar crisis: Ambassador at Bonn to Secretary of State for Foreign and Commonwealth Affairs, 12

June 1972.   31. Daniel J. Sargent, *A Superpower Transformed: The Remaking of American Foreign Relations in the 1970s* (New York, 2015), 117, quoting Kissinger to Kraft telecon., 29 Nov. 1971.   32. Kissinger, *White House Years*, 959–62; Harry R. Haldeman, *The Haldeman Diaries: Inside the Nixon White House* (New York, 1994), 383–5; Allen J. Matusow, *Nixon's Economy: Booms, Busts, Dollars and Votes* (Lawrence, KS, 1998), 176–7; NARA RG56 Records of Secretary Shultz, Box 7, Memo for the President: Monetary issues aiming at the Azores meeting, J. Connally, 10 Dec. 1971; *FRUS 1969–76*, III, doc. 220; Richard Nixon, 'Joint statement following meetings in the Azores with President Pompidou of France, Dec. 14 1971', online in Gerhard Peters and John T. Woolley, *The American Presidency Project*; Butkiewicz and Ohlmecher, 'Ending Bretton Woods', 940.   33. NARA RG56 Records of Secretary Shultz, Box 7, 'The approach to Japan – next steps', 24 Aug. 1971; Thomas Zeiler, 'US foreign policy and relations with Japan, 1969–1977', Working Paper 1 for the Nixon Shocks and US–Japanese Relations 1969–1976 Conference organized by the National Security Archive and the Woodrow Wilson Center for Scholars, 1996, and Hiroshi Ando, 'Change in Japan: a comparison of Japan's response to international monetary crisis in 1971 and 1973', Working Paper 3; Tadashi Sasaki, 'Japan's recent monetary situation', *Pacific Community* (July 1970), 612–19; Bank of Japan, *Nippon Ginko Hyakunen-Shi* [Bank of Japan: The First Hundred Years], vol. 6 (Tokyo, 1986), 307–9; Taizo Hayashi, 'From the failure of the "Alpha Operation" to the yen float: memories of the yen policy during the turbulent era', *Kinyu-Zaisei Jijyo*, 31 Jan. and 7 Feb. 1982; Yusuke Kashiwagi oral history interview conducted by Makoto Iokibe, Masayuki Tadokoro and Yoshiko Kajo, 29 Feb. 1996, available at https://nsarchive2.gwu.edu/japan/kashiwagiohinterview.htm. Thanks to Dr Hiroki Shin for research assistance.   34. Silber, *Volcker*, 108; Paul Volcker, *Keeping at It: The Quest for Sound Money and Good Government* (New York, 2018), 79; Matusow, *Nixon's Economy*, 177–8; James, *International Monetary Cooperation*, 236–8; *FRUS 1969–76*, III, doc. 221; Richard Nixon, 'Remarks announcing a monetary agreement following a meeting of the Group of Ten, Dec. 18 1971', in Peters and Woolley, *American Presidency Project*.   35. Sargent, *Superpower Transformed*, 118.   36. Coombs, *Arena*, xiii, 225.   37. TNA, PREM15/812, Brian Reading to Armstrong, 'Back to square one?', 6 Jan. 1972.   38. NARA RG56 Treasury, Monetary Reform, Box 4, Nathaniel Samuels to Paul Volcker, 22 and 24 Feb. 1972; Development of proposals for US positions in future discussions of international monetary reform, P. Volcker, 22 Feb. 1972; Memo for Paul A. Volcker from Nathaniel Samuels, 'A start toward negotiating international monetary reform', 22 Feb. 1972.   39. Volcker and Gyohten, *Changing Fortunes*, 103.   40. *FRUS 1969–76*, III, doc. 223.   41. *FRUS 1969–76*, III, doc. 224.   42. Barry Eichengreen, *The European Economy since 1945: Coordinated Capitalism and Beyond* (Princeton, NJ, 2007), 247–8; TNA, T267/36, Treasury Historical Memorandum, ch. 5; James, *International Monetary Cooperation*, 239–40. Resources on the tunnel and snake are available at www.cvce.eu.   43. Silber, *Volcker*, 108–9; Volcker and Gyohten, *Changing Fortunes*, 118; Volcker, *Keeping at It*, 82–3.   44. Volcker and Gyohten, *Changing Fortunes*, 105; Silber, *Volcker*, 109–10; Transcript of a recording of a meeting between President Nixon and H. R. Haldeman in the Oval Office, 23 June 1972, 10.04 to 11.39 am, 11, 12, at https://www.nixonlibrary.gov/sites/default/files/forresearchers/find/tapes/watergate/trial/exhibit_01.pdf.   45. TNA, T295/868, PMVP(71)3, 13 May 1971: Visit of the Prime Minister to Paris 19–21 May 1971, Future of sterling.   46. TNA, T295/868, FMV(72)3, Jan. 1972 and revise March 1972, Visit of the president of France to the United Kingdom 19 and 20 Feb. 1972, Monetary questions: Brief by the Treasury.   47. Anthony Barber, HC Deb., ser. 5, vol. 833, 21 March 1972, col. 1354.   48. Peter Jay, 'A half-hearted jump at the four big hurdles', *The Times*, 22 March 1972, 25.   49. Schenk, *Decline of Sterling*, 337; Milton Friedman's article in *Newsweek*, 24 July 1972 reprinted in *idem*, *An Economist's Protest: Columns on Political Economy* (Glen Ridge, NJ, 1972), 216–17.   50. William Glenn Gray, 'Floating the system: Germany, the United States and the breakdown of Bretton Woods', *Diplomatic History* 31 (2007), 317, 319.   51. Sargent, *Superpower Transformed*, 121–2; *FRUS 1969–76*, III, docs. 234, 236; NARA Nixon Presidential Papers, Box 356, Robert Hormats to Kissinger, 'Report on international monetary situation', 22 Aug. 1972.   52. TNA, CAB130/532, GEN57(72)5th meeting, Cabinet International monetary situation, 26 June 1972; TNA, PREM15/1518, Sterling exchange rate, Anthony Barber to PM, 1 Dec. 1972; PREM15/1457, Refixing the sterling exchange rate, A. D. Neale, 6 Oct. 1972; Barber to PM, 11 Oct. 1972. **53.** NARA RG56 Treasury, Monetary Reform, Box 4, Proposal for a new international negotiating forum, S. Y. Cross, 21 Jan 1972; Memo for Paul A. Volcker from Nathaniel Samuels: 'A start toward negotiating international monetary reform', 22 Feb. 1972; Organization for negotiations on monetary reform, 6 March 1972 and 20 March 1972; Notes on meeting of deputies (G10) at Bank of England, 23 April 1972; Memo of conversation: The OECD as an international forum, 25 April 1972; Paul Volcker to Emile van Lennep, 'Suggestions for internal organization of OECD in support of international economic negotiations', 8 May 1972; 'An overview of institutional arrangements for negotiations of reform of the international monetary and trading system', 8 May 1972; Box 6, Record of discussion, Treasury consultants' meeting, 10 Nov. 1972; Box 8, folder MR8/10 Organizational; RG56 Treasury, Briefing books, international monetary discussions 1967–74, Box 9, 'Institutional change in the IMF and GATT', Kenneth W. Dam, 7 Sept. 1972; Matthias Schmelzer, *The Hegemony of Growth: The OECD and the Making of the Economic Growth Paradigm* (Cambridge, 2016), 1–2, 10–19, 28–33; *FRUS 1969–76*, III, docs. 91, 210, 225, 227, 229. **54.** Alexandre Kafka, 'The International Monetary Fund: reform without reconstruction?' Essays in International Finance No. 118, Department of Economics, Princeton, 1976, 19. **55.** J. Marcus Fleming, 'Reflections on the international monetary reform', Essays in International Finance No. 107, Department of Economics, Princeton, 1974, 9–10; Margaret Garritsen de Vries, ed., *The International Monetary Fund 1972–1978: Cooperation on Trial. Vol. I, Narrative* (Washington, DC, 1985), 265–9. **56.** *The Monetary Merry-Go-Round: The Global Financial System in Crisis*, Lombard Street Research and Churchill Archive Centre, 17 Nov. 2008, 18. **57.** *FRUS 1969–76*, III, doc. 239; discussion of indicators in NARA RG56 Treasury, Monetary Reform, Box 7, MR8/4 Reserve/trigger mechanism; Ford Presidential Library, Burns papers, Box B73, The US proposal for using reserves as an indicator of the need for balance of payments adjustments, 9 Nov. 1972; Liquidity and reserve assets: US views, 10 Jan. 1973; Box B74, Some comments on the nature of reserve assets in the context of a reformed international monetary system, 11 Jan. 1973. **58.** Volcker and Gyohten, *Changing Fortunes*, 114–15, 120; NARA RG56 Treasury, Briefing books, international monetary discussions 1967–74, Box 9, 'International balance of payments: adjustment process incentives', draft M. Bradfield, 8 Sept. 1972. **59.** *FRUS 1969–76*, III, doc. 236. **60.** *FRUS 1969–76*, vol. I, *Foundations of Foreign Policy, 1969–1972* (Washington, DC, 2003), doc. 122; *FRUS 1969–76*, III, doc. 230; NARA RG56 Treasury, Monetary Reform, Box 6, Record of discussion Treasury consultants' meeting, 10 Nov. 1972; 'US views on major issues of monetary reform', for release 27 Aug. 1973; Sargent, *Superpower Transformed*, 119–23; Silber, *Volcker*, 112–13. **61.** Sargent, *Superpower Transformed*, 123; NARA RG56 Treasury, Monetary Reform, Box 5, Donald McGrew, US Treasury rep. Paris, to Volcker, 18 Dec. 1972; Memo of conversation, 31 May 1973; Box 6, Japanese views on monetary reform, Leddy, 16 Feb. 1973; NARA RG56 Treasury, Briefing books, international monetary issues, Box 8, A sketch of a world monetary system, nd. **62.** Ford Presidential Library, Burns papers, Box N1, Nixon to Burns, 28 Jan. 1972; Ferrell, ed., *Inside the Nixon Administration*, 73. **63.** Matusow, *Nixon's Economy*, chs. 7 and 8; quote from Stein at 186. **64.** Volcker and Gyohten, *Changing Fortunes*, 105–6. **65.** *FRUS 1969–76*, III, doc. 240; *FRUS 1969–76*, vol. XXXI, *Foreign Economic Policy, 1973–1976* (Washington, DC, 2009), doc. 5; Silber, *Volcker*, 113–18; Volcker and Gyohten, *Changing Fortunes*, 106–11; Ando, 'Change in Japan'. **66.** Gray, 'Floating the system', 319–23. **67.** Butkiewicz and Ohlmecher, 'Ending Bretton Woods', 942. **68.** *FRUS 1969–76*, XXXI, doc. 16. **69.** Ibid. **70.** Ibid., docs. 16, 17. **71.** Ibid., docs. 31 and 35 editorial note. **72.** Communiqué issued by the G10 and the European Economic Community, Paris, 16 March 1973, available at www.cvce.eu; Sargent, *Superpower Transformed*, 127. **73.** Silber, *Volcker*, 118–21; Volcker and Gyohten, *Changing Fortunes*, 113–14. **74.** *Economic Report of the President transmitted to the Congress January 1973, together with the Annual Report of the Council of Economic Advisers* (Washington, DC, 1973), 128; Eric Helleiner, *States and the Re-emergence of Global Finance from Bretton Woods to the 1990s* (Ithaca, NY, 1994), 111; Butkiewicz and Ohlmecher, 'Ending Bretton Woods', 939. **75.** Eric Helleiner, 'Explaining the globalization of financial markets: bringing states back in', *Review of International Political Economy* 2 (1995), 321–4, 335; Helleiner, *States and Re-emergence*, 109, 113–15; Denis Healey, *The Time of My Life* (London, 1989), 423; Sargent, *Superpower Transformed*, 129–30. **76.** TNA, T355/78, PCC(73)2, 19 March 1973, Treasury Policy Coordinating Committee: 'Joining the Community float: Economic Policy Implications and further draft of 29 March 1973'; PREM15/1519, Barber to PM, 10 April and 19 June 1973; Armstrong to PM, 21 June 1973; Kiyoshi Hirowatari, *Britain and European Monetary Cooperation 1964–1979* (Basingstoke, 2015), 73–7. **77.** TNA, PREM15/1459, Note of a meeting at 10 Downing Street on 2 March 1973; Record of a meeting held at Chequers, 4 March 1973; Armstrong to Chancellor, 10 March 1973; Heath to Chancellor, 12 March 1973; Note by R. A. Armstrong, 13 March 1973; Hirowatari, *Britain and European Monetary Cooperation*, 54–6, 61–2. **78.** TNA, T355/78, 'Rejoining the EEC snake: support facilities', 17 April 1973; T355/84, 'Sterling agreements and the Basle facility', Bank of England, 9 July 1973; PREM15/1427, Barber to PM, Sterling agreements, 9 July 1973; Alec Douglas-Home to PM, 12 July 1973; telegram Douglas-Home on sterling agreements, 6 Sept. 1973; PREM15/1518, 'Sterling and sterling agreements', nd; G. Toniolo, *Central Bank Cooperation at the Bank for International Settlements, 1930–1973* (Cambridge, 2005), 423–6; Schenk, *Decline of Sterling*, 347–56, 378–93. **79.** Emmanuel Mourlon-Druol, *A Europe Made of Money: The Emergence of the European Monetary System* (Ithaca, NY, and London, 2012), 25; James, *International Monetary Cooperation*, 240–43, 256; Valéry Giscard d'Estaing, *Le Pouvoir et la Vie*, extract and translation at www.cvce.eu. **80.** Kafka, 'The International Monetary Fund', 23–5; James, *International Monetary Cooperation*, 235. **81.** *IMF Annual Report, 1975*, 33. **82.** Raymond F. Mikesell and Henry N. Goldstein, 'Rules for a floating-rate regime', Essays in International Finance No. 109, Department of Economics, Princeton, 1975, 1. **83.** Coombs, *Arena*, 237–8. **84.** Healey, *Time of My Life*, 109; James, *International Monetary Cooperation*, 266–7; Peter I. Hajnal, *The G8 System and the G20: Evolution, Role and Documentation* (Aldershot, 2013), 12–13 for a list of meetings and 230–31 for success. **85.** James, *International Monetary Cooperation*, 255–7; de Vries, *IMF 1972–78, I*, 253–71 and ed., *VOL. III, Documents*, 155–96; Tom de Vries, 'Jamaica, or the non-reform of the international monetary system', *Foreign Affairs* 54 (1976), 585–8; IMF, *International Monetary Reform: Documents of the Committee of Twenty* (Washington, DC, 1974), 79. **86.** Guidelines in *IMF Annual Report, 1974*, 114–16; de Vries, *IMF 1972–78, I*, 297–301; Louis W. Pauly, *Who Elected the Bankers? Surveillance and Control in the World Economy* (Ithaca, NY, 1997), 101–2. **87.** William E. Simon, *A Time for Truth* (New York, 1978), 221; Robert Solomon, *The International Monetary System, 1945–1981* (New York, 1982), 270; Pauly, *Who Elected the Bankers?*, 102–5; James, *International Monetary Cooperation*, 268–9; de Vries, *IMF 1972–78, II*, 739–46; FRUS 1969–76, XXXI, docs. 87, 93, 98, 107; de Vries, 'Jamaica', 588–9; Volcker and Gyohten, *Changing Fortunes*, 141. **88.** FRUS 1969–76, XXXI, docs. 112, 114, 116, 118, 121, 122, 123, 124, 125, 257; de Vries, *IMF 1972–78, II*, 745–7 and *III*, 301–3; Volcker and Gyohten, *Changing Fortunes*, 141–3; Sargent, *Superpower Transformed*, 190–92; James, *International Monetary Cooperation*, 269–70; TNA, PREM16/838, E. E. Tomkins to James Callaghan, 25 Nov 1975. **89.** FRUS 1969–76, XXXI, doc. 128; Margaret Garritsen de Vries, *The IMF in a Changing World, 1945–85* (Washington, DC, 1986), 158–68. **90.** De Vries, *IMF 1972–78, II*, 747–71 and *III*, 317–76, 379–427; de Vries, 'Jamaica', 592–6; FRUS 1969–76, XXXI, docs. 128, 129; Pauly, *Who Elected the Bankers?*, 105–6; James, *International Monetary Cooperation*, 370–73; Kafka, 'The International Monetary Fund', 3–13; de Vries, 'Jamaica', 577, 589; Sargent, *Superpower Transformed*, 193–4; George N. Halm, 'Jamaica and the par-value system', Essays in International Finance No. 120, Department of Economics, Princeton, 1977, 4–15; *IMF Annual Report, 1976*, 43–6. **91.** Gerald M. Meier, 'The "Jamaica Agreement", international monetary reform, and the developing countries', Stanford Graduate School of Business, Research Paper 306, April 1976; NARA RG56 Treasury, Monetary Reform, Box 9, 'Special interests of developing countries in international monetary reform', Manmohan Singh, 22 May 1973; 'Effects of advanced country exchange rate flexibility on developing country commodity price and economic uncertainty', W. R. Cline, 22 Dec. 1972; 'Analysis of LDC concern that increased exchange rate flexibility among the major currencies would increase the risks and costs of external debt and reserve management', J. T. Donnelly, 20 Dec. 1972; Halm, 'Jamaica and the par value system', 13.   **92.** *FRUS 1969–76*, XXXI, docs. 147, 148, 149, 150; Sargent, *Superpower Transformed*, 194–5.   **93.** Pauly, *Who Elected the Bankers?*, 107–15.   **94.** Robert Triffin, 'Jamaica: "Major revision" or fiasco?', in Edward M. Bernstein *et al.*, 'Reflections on Jamaica', Essays in International Finance No. 115, Department of Economics, Princeton, 1976, 45, 48, 49.   **95.** Kafka, 'The International Monetary Fund', 18–22.   **96.** Ford Presidential Library, National Security Adviser: International economic affairs staff files, Box 4, 'Strengthened coordination of economic and monetary policies among industrialized countries', Ernest H. Preeg to Hartman, 15 Sept. 1975; Wilfred Ethier and Arthur I. Bloomfield, 'Managing the Managed Float', Essays in International Finance No. 112, Department of Economics, Princeton, 1975, 3–5; de Vries, *IMF 1972–78*, I, 3–4.   **97.** Nixon Presidential Papers, NSC subject files, EEC Box 322, 'Results of your meeting with Dahrendorf', C. Fred Bergsten to Kissinger, 16 Oct. 1970.   **98.** Richard Nixon, 'Special message to the Congress on United States trade policy', 18 Nov. 1969, in Peters and Woolley, *American Presidency Project*; *FRUS 1969–76*, vol. IV, *Foreign Assistance, International Development, Trade Policies, 1969–1972* (Washington, DC, 2001), docs. 181, 188, 189, 194, 195, 205.   **99.** 'The Trade Act of 1971: a fundamental change in United States foreign trade policy', *The Yale Law Journal* 80 (1971), 1419 note 7.   **100.** *FRUS 1969–76*, IV, doc. 237.   **101.** Ibid., docs. 237, 238, 239, 241.   **102.** *FRUS 1969–76*, III, docs. 49, 53, 55, 195; *FRUS 1969–76*, IV, docs. 248, 256; Nixon Presidential Papers, Box 401, Memo of conversation: launching of President's Commission on Trade and Investment, 6 April 1970; Box 402, Memo for Kissinger from Ernest Johnson, The Williams Commission Report, 2 Aug. 1971.   **103.** *FRUS 1969–76*, III, docs. 56, 64, 94.   **104.** Schmelzer, *Hegemony of Growth*, 296.   **105.** *FRUS 1969–76*, III, docs. 100, 103; *FRUS 1969–76*, IV, docs. 264, 277; Ford Presidential Library, Burns papers, Box B116, 'Timing of trade legislation', Office of the Special Representative for Trade Negotiations; 'Thoughts on trade legislation and the European trip', Kenneth A. Guenther, nd; 'Trade legislation: pros and cons of major options', W. R. Pearce, 14 Dec. 1972.   **106.** *FRUS 1969–76*, IV, docs. 280, 285, 286, 287.   **107.** *FRUS 1969–76*, XXXI, doc. 153; NARA RG56 Treasury, Records of Secretary Shultz, Box 6, Talking points on the Trade Reform Act 1973, Peter M. Flanigan, 7 Feb 1973; Memo from Flanigan to Kissinger, US–European economic relations, Economic objectives, 27 Feb. 1973.   **108.** NARA RG56 Treasury, Records of Secretary Shultz, Box 6, Memo for President from Peter Flanigan, The trade bill, 5 March 1973; Box 2, Tariff authority to be requested, 27 March 1973; *FRUS 1969–76*, XXXI, docs. 154, 156, 168; *Annual Report of the Secretary of the Treasury on the State of the Finances for the Fiscal Year Ended June 30, 1973* (Washington, DC, 1973), 336, 406–8; M. G. Harvey and R. A. Kerin, 'Multinational corporations versus organized labor: divergent views on domestic employment', *California Management Review* 18 (1976), 5–13; Irwin Ross, 'Labor's big push for protectionism', *Fortune*, 1 March 1973.   **109.** Thomas W. Zeiler, *American Trade and Power in the 1960s* (New York, 1992), 247.   **110.** *FRUS 1969–76*, XXXI, docs. 191, 192, 195, 200, 201.   **111.** Giuseppe La Barca, *The US, the EC and World Trade: From the Kennedy Round to the Start of the Uruguay Round* (London, 2016), 41–2.   **112.** Ministerial meeting, Tokyo, 12–14 Sept. 1973: Declaration.   **113.** Ford Presidential Library, CEA Greenspan files, Box 46, 'US leadership in trade matters and managing the multilateral trade negotiations', nd; *FRUS 1969–76*, IV, doc. 268; Zeiler, *American Trade*, 247; Daniel Drezner, *US Trade Strategy: Free versus Fair*, Critical Policy Choices 7, Council on Foreign Relations (New York, 2006), 13; La Barca, *US, EC and World Trade*, 56, 68–70, 73, 77–81; Guy F. Erb, 'The Trade Reform Act of 1974', *Challenge* 18 (1975), 60–61; Todd Allee, 'The role of the United States: a multilevel explanation for decreased support over time', in Amrita Narlikar, Martin Daunton and Robert M. Stern, eds., *The Oxford Handbook on the World Trade Organization* (Oxford, 2012), 242–3.   **114.** *FRUS 1969–76*, XXXI, doc. 236.   **115.** Ibid., docs. 224, 225, 226, 228, 229, 230, 233.   **116.** Carter Presidential Library, CEA, Charles L. Schultze subject files, Box 44, International Economics: issues and options [76 transition material], Economic summit notes, 12-1976, 'A trade policy strategy for 1977', C. Fred Bergsten, 14 Dec. 1976; 'An early economic summit?', C. Fred

Bergsten, 13 Dec. 1976; La Barca, *US, EC and World Trade*, 81–106; Francine McKenzie, *GATT and Global Order in the Postwar Era* (Cambridge, 2020), 232–3, 237, 240–54, 257–262; Thomas W. Zeiler, 'The expanding mandate of the GATT: the first seven rounds' in Narlikar, Daunton and Stern, eds., *Oxford Handbook on the WTO*, 113–18. 117. *FRUS 1969–76*, XXXI, docs. 236, 240; *FRUS 1977–80*, vol. III, *Foreign Economic Policy* (Washington, DC, 2013), docs. 133, 163 and also 4, 9, 45, 68, 89, 170, 173, 177, 180, 183, 185, 189, 191, 199, 216, 219, 220, 223. 118. McKenzie, *GATT and Global Order*, 214–23; Amrita Narlikar, 'Fairness in international trade negotiations: developing countries in the GATT and WTO', *The World Economy* 29 (2006), 1015–18; John Croome, *Reshaping the World Trading System: A History of the Uruguay Round* (London, 1999), 9–10.

19. 'A TRADE UNION OF THE POOR'

1. Giuliano Garavini, *After Empires: European Integration, Decolonization, and the Challenge of the Global South, 1957–1986* (Oxford, 2012), 98, 114, 121. 2. Nils Gilman, 'The New International Economic Order: a reintroduction', *Humanity* 6 (2015), 1, 3–4; John Toye and Richard Toye, *The UN and Global Political Economy: Trade, Finance and Development* (Bloomington, IN, 2004), ch. 10; for an overview, see Craig Murphy, *The Emergence of the NIEO Ideology* (Boulder, CO, 1984). 3. Quinn Slobodian, *Globalists: The End of Empire and the Birth of Neoliberalism* (Cambridge, MA, 2018), 221; *idem*, 'The world economy and the color line: Wilhelm Röpke, apartheid and the white Atlantic', in Jan Logemann and Mary Nolan, eds., *More Atlantic Crossings? European Voices in the Postwar Atlantic Community* (Washington, DC, 2014), 65. 4. Resolution adopted by the General Assembly, 2626 (XXV), International development strategy for the second United Nations development decade, 24 Oct 1970, 39–49; Murphy, *Emergence*, 79, 91–5. 5. Jeremy Friedman, *Shadow Cold War: The Sino-Soviet Competition for the Third World* (Chapel Hill, NC, 2015), 182; Resolutions of the Third Conference of Non-Aligned States, September 1970. 6. UN Oral History: interview with Manuel Peréz-Guerrero. 7. Murphy, *Emergence*, 111. 8. Fourth conference of heads of state or government of non-aligned countries, Economic Declaration, Algiers, 5–9 September 1973. 9. Andre Gunder Frank, *The Development of Underdevelopment* (New York, 1966); *idem, Capitalism and Underdevelopment in Latin America* (New York, 1967); Nils Gilman, *Mandarins of the Future: Modernization Theory in Cold War America* (Baltimore, MD, and London, 2003), 205, 208, 224–7, 234–9; Michael E. Latham, *Modernization as Ideology: American Social Science and 'Nation Building' in the Kennedy Era* (Chapel Hill, NC, 2000), 5. 10. Friedman, *Shadow Cold War*, 183, 193–203, 207–9, 217–21; *Chairman Mao's Theory of the Differentiation of the Three Worlds Is a Major Contribution to Marxism–Leninism* (Beijing, 1977). 11. Giuliano Garavini, *The Rise and Fall of OPEC in the Twentieth Century* (Oxford, 2019), 31–2, 47, 53–4, 59–60, 73, 77, 87–9, 111–25, 133–4, 136, 153, 159, 178, 180–84, 187, 193, 203–9, 217–18, 221. 12. Ibid., 251–3, 255; J. Toye and R. Toye, 'From new era to neo-liberalism: US strategy on trade, finance and development in the United Nations, 1964–82', *Forum for Development Studies* 1 (2005), 169; Murphy, *Emergence*, 1. 13. Garavini, *After Empires*, 123, 187; Toye and Toye, 'From new era', 169; Request for the convening of a Special Session of the General Assembly: letter dated 30 Jan. 1974, addressed to the Secretary General by the Permanent Representative of Algeria to the UN. 14. *Foreign Relations of the United States (FRUS) 1969–76*, vol. XXXI, *Foreign Economic Policy, 1973–1976* (Washington, DC, 2009), doc. 257. 15. Daniel J. Sargent, *A Superpower Transformed: The Remaking of American Foreign Relations in the 1970s* (New York, 2015), 165–75; Garavini, *Rise and Fall of OPEC*, 266–71; Victor McFarland, 'The NIEO, interdependence and globalization', *Humanity* 6 (2015), 217–18; Robert O. Keohane and Joseph Nye, *Power and Interdependence: World Politics in Transition* (Boston, MA, 1977); Zbigniew Brzezinski, *Between Two Ages: America's Role in the Technetronic Era* (New York, 1970). 16. Sargent, *Superpower Transformed*, 131, 157–9, 186–8; Garavini, *After Empires*, 195, 197; *FRUS 1969–76*, vol. XXXVII, *Energy Crisis, 1974–1980* (Washington, DC, 2012), doc. 9; see also *FRUS 1968–76*, vol. XXXVI, *Energy Crisis, 1969–1974*

(Washington, DC, 2011), docs. 295, 299, 305, 306, 311, 314, 315, 319; Henry Kissinger, *Years of Upheaval* (London, 1982), 722–9, 896–925; Margaret Garritsen de Vries, ed., *The International Monetary Fund 1972–1978: Cooperation on Trial. Vol. I, Narrative* (Washington, DC, 1985), 336–41; *Documents on British Policy Overseas (DBPO)*, ser. 3, vol. 4, nos. 499, 501, 503, 505, 516, 519, 536, 539, 542, 544, 547, 549, 550, 553, 555, 557; Final Communiqué of the Washington Conference, 13 Feb. 1974; The National Archives (TNA), PREM 16/49, Record of a conversation between the PM and the Federal German Chancellor, 1 Dec. 1974; A. Graham to Armstrong, 'Petrodollars', 23 Oct. and 20 Nov. 1974.   **17.** Henry Kissinger, 'Address to the sixth special session of the UN General Assembly', *International Organization* 28 (1974), 573–83; Sargent, *Superpower Transformed*, 179.   **18.** *FRUS 1969–76*, XXXI, docs. 257, 258, 291; Sargent, *Superpower Transformed*, 176–83, 190, 197; Henry Kissinger, *Years of Renewal* (London, 1999), 697–700.   **19.** Resolution adopted by the General Assembly, 3201 (S-VI), Declaration on the establishment of a new international economic order, 1 May 1974; McFarland, 'NIEO', 217–18.   **20.** Resolution adopted by the General Assembly, 3281 (XXIX), Charter of economic rights and duties of states, 12 Dec. 1974; Murphy, *Emergence*, 117–18; Garavini, *Rise and Fall of OPEC*, 213–15, 227–8.   **21.** Gamani Corea, *Taming Commodity Markets: The Integrated Programme and the Common Fund* (Manchester, 1992), 29; Murphy, *Emergence*, 94–5.   **22.** Gilman, 'NIEO', 4–7; Adom Getachew, *Worldmaking After Empire: The Rise and Fall of Self-Determination* (Princeton, NJ, 2019), 2, 12, 145; Murphy, *Emergence*, 77–80.   **23.** Gamani Corea, 'UNCTAD and the New International Economic Order', *International Affairs* 53 (1977), 177–87; *idem, Taming Commodity Markets*, 29–31.   **24.** Vanessa Ogle, 'State rights against private capital: the "new international economic order" and the struggle over aid, trade and foreign investment', *Humanity* 5 (2014), 220; Slobodan, *Globalists*, 220; Murphy, *Emergence*, 101; Charles Lipson, *Standing Guard: Protecting Foreign Capital in the Nineteenth and Twentieth Centuries* (Berkeley, CA, 1985), 98; Lauge N. Skovgaard Poulsen, *Bounded Rationality and Economic Diplomacy: The Politics of Investment Treaties in Developing Countries* (Cambridge, 2015), 36–7, 60, 88–9, 118; Jonathan Bonnitcha, Lauge N. Skovgaard Poulsen and Michael Waibel, *The Political Economy of the Investment Treaty Regime* (Oxford, 2017), 12–13, 19, 21, 211–12; Stephan Krasner, *Defending the National Interests: Raw Material Investment and US Foreign Policy* (Princeton, NJ, 1978), 144–6.   **25.** Gilman, 'NIEO', 7 quoting the *Wall Street Journal*, 17 July 1975; Ogle, 'State rights', 221 referring to Daniel Moynihan, 'The United States in opposition', *Commentary*, March 1975; *FRUS 1969–76*, XXXI, docs. 290, 291, 294; Roger B. Porter, *Presidential Decision Making: The Economic Policy Board* (Cambridge, 1983).   **26.** *FRUS 1969–76*, XXXI, docs. 124, 292, 293, 294, editorial note 295; Kissinger, *Years of Renewal*, 677–8.   **27.** A/Res/3362(S-VII), Resolution adopted by the General Assembly of the United Nations on the report of the ad hoc committee of the seventh special session during its seventh special session, 16 September 1975.   **28.** Declaration of Rambouillet, 17 Nov. 1975; Garavini, *After Empires*, 131, 152, 153, 157, 160, 192, 193, 200–207, 242.   **29.** Sargent, *Superpower Transformed*, 165, 166, 176; *FRUS 1969–76*, XXXI, doc. 150; *FRUS 1969–76*, vol. XXXVIII, *Part 1, Foundations of Foreign Policy, 1973–1976* (Washington, DC, 2012), doc. 46.   **30.** Sargent, *Superpower Transformed*, 182; Toye and Toye, 'From new era', 172–3; *FRUS 1969–76*, XXXI, docs. 301, 302, 304.   **31.** UNCTAD, TD/RES/93(IV), 10 June 1976, resolution adopted by the conference, integrated programme for commodities, Nairobi, 5 May 1976; TNA, CAB 134/4025, UNCTAD IV, 21 June 1976; Toye and Toye, 'From new era', 173–4; Overseas Development Institute, Briefing papers, The integrated programme for commodities, No. 1, July 1982.   **32.** Jahangir Amuzegar, 'A requiem for the North–South conference', *Foreign Affairs* 56 (1977), 136–59; Ford Presidential Library, National Security Adviser: International economic affairs staff files, Robert Hormats, Box 11, Summary report on Hormats briefing 9/9/76, 16 September 1976; telegrams on CIEC meetings dealing with debt and indexation – Rogers to Greenwald, 'Consultation with France, FRG and UK on CIEC', Aug. 1976; US National Archives and Records Administration (NARA), RG 56 Treasury, Records relating to monetary reform, 1968–78, Box 1, 'June session of the Financial Affairs Commission', W. H. Witherell, nd; 'The Financial Affairs Commission: Scope paper for the second half', W. Witherell, 29 June 1976; 'Further US comments on G19 paper on oil exporting country international investments: the issues of exchange rate risk and political risk', 10 June 1975; OECD/IEA, 'Producing country positions: note by the secretariat', 27 June 1975; 'General orientation for the conference on international economic cooperation', R. A. Sorenson, 5 Nov. 1975; 'US objectives for the CIEC', Andy Safir to Niehuss, 24 Nov. 1975; Strategy paper consumer–producer conference, 13 March 1975; Box 2, 'PRM 8 – track III, US relations with the developing countries, the next twelve months', draft, 6 Sept. 1977; Talking points: Opec assets, protection against political risks, W. H. Wetherell, 4 June 1976; OECD, temporary working party of the economic policy committee: 'Indexation of oil prices, provisional report by the working party', 3 Dec. 1975; Indexation, 7 Aug. 1975.   **33.** *FRUS 1977–80*, vol. III, *Foreign Economic Policy* (Washington, DC, 2013), doc. 253.   **34.** Ibid., docs. 257, 272, 275, 295, 296, 310, 313, 314, 315, 318, 321, 328.   **35.** Ibid., doc. 330.   **36.** Club of Rome, 'The predicament of mankind: quest for structured responses to growing world-wide complexities and uncertainties: a proposal'; Jan Tinbergen, Anthony J. Dolman and Jan van Ettinger, *Reshaping the International Order: A Report to the Club of Rome* (New York, 1976); *North–South: A Programme for Survival. Report of the Independent Commission on International Development Issues* (Cambridge, MA, 1980); Ogle, 'State rights', 223–5; Garavini, *After Empires*, 234–40.   **37.** David Ekbladh, *The Great American Mission: Modernization and the Construction of an American World Order* (Princeton, NJ, and Oxford, 2010), 223–5; M. Alacevich, 'Visualizing uncertainties, or how Albert Hirschman and the World Bank disagreed on project appraisal and what this says about the end of "high development theory"', *Journal of the History of Economic Thought* 36 (2014), 137–68.   **38.** J. Kraske with W. H. Becker, William Diamond and L. Galambos, *Bankers with a Mission: The Presidents of the World Bank, 1946–1991* (Oxford, 1996), 153–6, 184–5; Matthew Wright, 'The Pearson Commission, aid diplomacy and the rise of the World Bank, 1966–1970', Ph.D. thesis, Durham University, 2016; J. Gibson, *Jacko: Where Are You Now? A Life of Robert Jackson* (London, 2006).   **39.** Ekbladh, *Great American Mission*, 252–6; Martha Finnemore, 'Redefining development at the World Bank', in Frederick Cooper and Randall Packard, eds, *International Development and the Social Sciences* (Berkeley, CA, 1997), 210–14; Michele Alacevich, 'The World Bank's early reflections on development: a development institution or a bank?', *Review of Political Economy* 21 (2009); Kraske *et al.*, *Bankers with a Mission*, 159–212.   **40.** Gunnar Myrdal, *Asian Drama: An Inquiry into the Poverty of Nations* (New York, 1968); Michael Lipton, *Why Poor People Stay Poor: Urban Bias in World Development* (Cambridge, MA, 1977); R. Jolly, 'A short history of IDS: a personal reflection', IDS Discussion Paper 388, Jan. 2008; Sugata Bose, 'Instruments and idioms of colonial and national development: India's historical experience in comparative perspective', in Cooper and Packard, eds, *International Development*, 54–6.   **41.** Hollis Chenery *et al.*, *Redistribution with Growth: Policies to Improve Income Distribution in Developing Countries in the Context of Economic Growth: A Joint Study Commissioned by the World Bank's Development Research Center and the Institute of Development Studies, University of Sussex* (London, 1974), xvi, 3; Dudley Seers and Leonard Joy, *Development in a Divided World* (London, 1971).   **42.** Robert McNamara, *The McNamara Years at the World Bank: Major Policy Addresses of Robert S. McNamara, 1968–1981* (Baltimore, MD, 1981), Address to the Board of Governors, Washington, 29 Sept. 1969, 74–93; Address to the Board of Governors, 27 Sept 1971, 140–47; Address to the Board of Governors by Robert S. McNamara, President, World Bank Group Nairobi, 24 Sept. 1973, 237–40; Address to the Board of Governors, 25 Sept. 1972, 211; John L. Maddux, *The Development Philosophy of Robert S. McNamara* (Washington, DC, 1981); Robert L. Ayres, *Banking on the Poor: The World Bank and World Poverty* (Cambridge, MA, 1983); R. Konkel, 'The monetisation of global poverty: the concept of poverty in World Bank history, 1944–1990', *Journal of Global History* 9 (2014), 289–91.   **43.** *McNamara Years*, McNamara to Board of Governors, Washington, 29 Sept. 1969, 74–5; 27 Sept. 1971, 140–43, 152–66; 25 Sept. 1972, 211, 217–28; Address to the UN Conference on Trade and Development, 14 April 1972, 171–7; to the UN Conference on the Human Environment, 8 June 1972, 193–4; to the Board of Governors, 25 Sept. 1972, 223, 24 Sept. 1973, 233, 238–40, 30 Sept. 1974, 268 and 1 Sept. 1975, 308–9; at University of Chicago, 2 May 1979, 558.   **44.** Finnemore, 'Redefining development', 217; Konkel, 'Monetisation', 291–300; Morris

D. Morris, 'A physical quality of life index', *Urban Ecology* 3 (1978), 225–40; World Bank, *The Assault on World Poverty: Problems of Rural Development, Education and Health* (Baltimore, MD, 1975). **45.** Amy L. Staples, *The Birth of Development: How the World Bank, Food and Agriculture Organization and World Health Organization Changed the World, 1945–1965* (Kent, OH, 2006), 104–8, 117–19; Ruth Jachertz and Alexander Nützenadel, 'Coping with hunger? Visions of a global food system, 1930–1960', *Journal of Global History* 6 (2011), 113–17. **46.** Donella H. Meadows, Dennis L. Meadows, Jørgen Randers and William W. Behrens III, *The Limits to Growth: A Report for the Club of Rome's Project on the Predicament of Mankind* (New York, 1972); Gabriel Cunha, 'The road to servomechanisms: the influence of cybernetics on Hayek from the sensory order to the social order', Center for the History of Political Economy Working Paper 2015-11 (2015). **47.** Rachel Carson, *Silent Spring* (Boston, MA, 1962); Alvin Toffler, *Future Shock* (New York, 1970); Matthias Schmelzer, *The Hegemony of Growth: The OECD and the Making of the Economic Growth Paradigm* (Cambridge, 2016), 238–49, 253–68, 271. **48.** Stephen J. Macekura, *Of Limits and Growth: The Rise of Global Sustainable Development in the Twentieth Century* (Cambridge, 2015), 1, 3–5; Slobodian, *Globalists*, 231–3; Elke Seefried, 'Towards *The Limits to Growth*? The book and its reception in West Germany and Britain, 1972–3', *Bulletin of the German Historical Institute London* 33 (2011), 3–37; Wilfred Beckerman, 'Economists, scientists and environmental catastrophe', *Oxford Economic Papers* 24 (1972); *idem, In Defence of Economic Growth* (London, 1974); Henry C. Wallich, 'To grow or not to grow', *Newsweek*, 13 March 1972, 102–3 and *New York Times*, 2 April 1972; Josh Eastin, Reiner Grundmann and Aseem Prakash, 'The two limits debates: "Limits to Growth" and climate change', *Futures* 43 (2011), 16–26; Christopher Freeman and Marie Jahoda, eds., *World Futures: The Great Debate* (London, 1978). **49.** Ekbladh, *Great American Mission*, 227, 230–37, 244–52; Macekura, *Of Limits and Growth*, 6–9. **50.** Schmelzer, *Hegemony of Growth*, 268–9, 273–90, 301, 308–12, 317–20. **51.** Tinbergen *et al., Reshaping*; Garavini, *After Empires*, 234. **52.** *The Global Report to the President: Entering the Twenty-First Century: A report prepared by the Council on Environmental Quality and the Department of State*, Gerald O. Barney, Study Director (Washington, DC, 1980), quote at 1. **53.** Alison Bashford, *Global Population: History, Geopolitics and Life on Earth* (New York, 2014), 289–93; Nick Cullather, *The Hungry World: America's Cold War Battle Against Poverty in Asia* (Cambridge, MA, 2010), 66–7, 87–8, 187. **54.** W. S. Gaud, 'The green revolution: accomplishments and apprehensions', address to the Society of International Development, 8 March 1968; Cullather, *Hungry World*, 233–8. **55.** Gregg Easterbrook, 'Forgotten benefactor of humanity', *The Atlantic*, January 1997; Cullather, *Hungry World*, 230–31, 239–43, 247, 250–51; Amartya Sen, *Poverty and Famines: An Essay on Entitlement and Deprivation* (Oxford, 1983). **56.** Arturo Escobar, *Encountering Development: The Making and Unmaking of the Third World* (Princeton, NJ, 1995), 105, 113–23. **57.** Quoted in Bashford, *Global Population*, 293–4. **58.** Paul Ehrlich, *The Population Bomb* (New York, 1968); Garrett Hardin, 'The tragedy of the commons', *Science*, 13 Dec. 1968, 1243–8; *idem*, 'The cybernetics of competition: a biologist's view', *Perspectives in Biology and Medicine* 7 (1963), 58–84. **59.** Bashford, *Global Population*, 330, 336, 338, 341, 364. **60.** Susan Greenhalgh, 'Science, modernity and the making of China's one-child policy', *Population and Development Review* 29 (2003), 163–96; *idem, Just One Child: Science and Policy in Deng's China* (Berkeley, CA, 2008); Bashford, *Global Population*, 330.

20. 'EXPANSION OF ECONOMIC FREEDOM'

1. Reagan Presidential Library, Jerry Jordan files, Box 1, Memo for Ed Meese, Don Regan, Richard V. Allen, Murray Weidenbaum, from Martin Anderson, 'Cancún summit', 11 Aug. 1981. **2.** R. C. O. Matthews, C. H. Feinstein and J. C. Odling-Smee, *British Economic Growth, 1856–1973* (Oxford, 1982), 31, 545–7. **3.** S. N. Broadberry, *The Productivity Race: British Manufacturing in International Perspective, 1850–1990* (Cambridge, 1997), 64; *idem, Market Services and the Productivity Race 1850–2000: British Performance in International Perspective* (Cambridge, 2006), 21; Peter Temin, 'The golden age of European growth reconsidered', *European Review of Economic History* 6 (2002), 3–22. **4.** See B. Eichengreen and J. Braga de Macedo, 'The European Payments Union: history and implications for the evolution of the international financial architectures', OECD Development Centre, Paris, March 2001, http://docentes.fe.unl.pt/~jbmacedo/oecd/triffin.html. **5.** Temin, 'Golden age', 4. **6.** Richard Vinen, *The Long '68: Radical Protest and Its Enemies* (London, 2018), 319–34; Florence Sutcliffe-Braithwaite, Aled Davies and Ben Jackson, 'Introduction: a neoliberal age?', in Aled Davies, Ben Jackson and Florence Sutcliffe-Braithwaite, eds., *The Neoliberal Age? Britain since the 1970s* (London, 2021), 14. **7.** E. Robinson, C. Schofield, F. Sutcliffe-Braithwaite and N. Thomlinson, 'Telling stories about post-war Britain: popular individualism and the "crisis" of the 1970s', *Twentieth Century British History* 28 (2017), 268–304; Florence Sutcliffe-Braithwaite, *Class, Politics, and the Decline of Deference in England, 1968–2000* (Oxford, 2018), 4–11, 146, 172, 203–9; Ben Jackson, 'Intellectual histories of neoliberalism and their limits', in Davies, Jackson and Sutcliffe-Braithwaite, eds., *Neoliberal Age?*, 59–60; Avner Offer, 'British manual workers: from producers to consumers, *c.* 1950–2000', *Contemporary British History* 22 (2008), 537–71. **8.** Andrew Glyn and Bob Sutcliffe, *British Capitalism, Workers and the Profits Squeeze* (Harmondsworth, 1972), 66–8; Andrew Glyn, *Capitalism Unleashed: Finance, Globalisation and Welfare* (Oxford, 2008); Gérard Duménil and Dominique Lévy, *Capital Resurgent: Roots of the Neoliberal Revolution* (Cambridge, MA, 2004), 21–8. **9.** Overview of western Europe in Barry Eichengreen, *The European Economy since 1945: Coordinated Capitalism and Beyond* (Princeton, NJ, 2007), chs. 4 and 7; Eric Helleiner, *States and the Re-emergence of Global Finance from Bretton Woods to the 1990s* (Ithaca, NY, 1994), 125. **10.** J. R. Hicks, *The Crisis in Keynesian Economics* (Oxford, 1974). **11.** Daniel Stedman Jones, *Masters of the Universe: Hayek, Friedman and the Birth of Neoliberal Politics* (Princeton, NJ, 2012), 215–16; Jackson, 'Intellectual histories', 57–9; Sutcliffe-Braithwaite, Davies and Jackson, 'Introduction: a neoliberal age?', 3; Rob von Horn, 'Reinventing monopoly and the role of corporations: the roots of Chicago law and economics', in Philip Mirowski and Dieter Plehwe, eds., *The Road from Mont Pèlerin: The Making of the Neoliberal Thought Collective* (Cambridge, MA, 2009), 229. **12.** 'Thatcher, Hayek and Friedman', www.margaretthatcher.org; F. Sutcliffe-Braithwaite, 'Neoliberalism and morality: the making of Thatcherite social policy', *Historical Journal* 55 (2012). **13.** Robert Triffin, 'Gold and the dollar crisis: yesterday and tomorrow', Essays in International Finance No. 132, Department of Economics, Princeton, 1978, 13. **14.** Duncan Needham, 'The evolution of monetary policy (goals and targets) in Western Europe', in Stefan Battilossi, Youssef Cassis and Kazuhiko Yago, eds., *Handbook of the History of Money and Currency* (Singapore, 2018); D. Needham, 'Britain's money supply experiment, 1971–73', *English Historical Review* 130 (2015), 89–122; Simon Mee, *Central Bank Independence and the Legacy of the German Past* (Cambridge, 2019), 7–8; Andreas Beyer, Vitor Gaspar, Christina Gerberding and Otmar Issing, 'Opting out of the great inflation: German monetary policy after the breakdown of Bretton Woods', NBER Working Paper 14596, Dec. 2008; O. Issing, 'Monetary targeting in Germany: the stability of monetary policy and of the monetary system', *Journal of Monetary Economics* 39 (1997), 67–79; M. J. M. Neumann, 'Monetary targeting in Germany', in I. Kuroda, ed., *Towards More Effective Monetary Policy* (Basingstoke, 1997); M. J. M. Neumann, 'Monetary stability: threat and proven response', in Deutsche Bundesbank, *Fifty Years of the Deutschemark: Central Bank and Currency in Germany since 1948* (Oxford, 1999), 269–306. **15.** Sarah Binder and Mark Spindel, *The Myth of Independence: How Congress Governs the Federal Reserve* (Princeton, NJ, 2017), 171–80. **16.** Arthur Burns, 'The anguish of central banking', Per Jacobsson Lecture, Belgrade, 30 Sept. 1979. **17.** Binder and Spindel, *Myth of Independence*, 166. **18.** Burns, 'Anguish', 9, 13, 15–16. **19.** Presidential Papers of Jimmy Carter, Office of the Chief of Staff Files, Box 103, Inflation work plan, 22 June 1978; Box 126, White Paper, The president's anti-inflation program, 24 Oct. 1978; Office of the Special Adviser on Inflation, Box 34, Memo for the president, 'Taking stock on anti-inflationary policy', Alfred E. Kahn, 5 Nov. 1979; Helleiner, *States and Re-emergence*, 123–4; W. Carl Biven, *Jimmy Carter's Economy: Policy in an Age of Limits* (Chapel Hill, NC, 2002), 95–101, 123–9, 185–207; Gottfried Haberler, 'Reflections on the U.S. trade deficit and the floating dollar', in William Fellner, ed., *Contemporary Economic Problems* (Washington, DC, 1978), 212;

L. Hollerman, 'Locomotive strategy and United States protectionism: a Japanese view', *Pacific Affairs* 52 (1979), 193–209. 20. Paul Volcker and Toyoo Gyohten, *Changing Fortunes: The World's Money and the Threat to American Leadership* (New York, 1992), 145–6, 151; William L. Silber, *Volcker: The Triumph of Persistence* (New York and London, 2012), 53; Biven, *Jimmy Carter's Economy*, ch. 11; David E. Lindsey, Athanasios Orphanides and Robert H. Rasche, 'The reform of October 1979: how it happened and why', *Federal Reserve Bank of St Louis, Review*, March/April, Part 2 (2005), 194. 21. Lindsey, Orphanides and Rasche, 'The reform of October 1979', 205, 207, 208; Silber, *Volcker*, 178; Volcker and Gyohten, *Changing Fortunes*, 164–7, 176. 22. Presidential Papers of Jimmy Carter, Box 26, Ray Moore to Carter, 26 Feb. 1980. 23. Presidential Papers of Jimmy Carter, Box 68, Interest rates/the Fed, 10 March 1980. 24. Presidential Papers of Jimmy Carter, Box 38, Charlie Schultze to Bill Miller, Jim McIntyre, Fred Kahn, 'Notes for Quadriad meeting of September 19', 18 Sept. 1980. 25. Binder and Spindel, *Myth of Independence*, 167, 189–97. 26. Meg Jacobs, *Pain at the Pump: The Energy Crisis and the Transformation of American Politics in the 1970s* (New York, 2016), 6–9; Vanessa Ogle, 'State rights against private capital: the "new international economic order" and the struggle over aid, trade and foreign investment', *Humanity* 5 (2014), 212; for an overview, Daniel T. Rodgers, *Age of Fracture* (Cambridge, MA, and London, 2012). 27. Rodgers, *Age of Fracture*, 44, 69, 72. 28. Edmund Dell, *A Hard Pounding: Politics and Economic Crisis, 1974–1976* (Oxford, 1991), 12; for an overview, Mark Wickham-Jones, *Economic Strategy and the Labour Party: Politics and Policy Making, 1970–83* (London, 1996). 29. Douglas Wass, *Decline to Fall: The Making of British Macro-Economic Policy and the 1976 IMF Crisis* (Oxford, 2008), xii, xv, 35, 41–2, 87–8. 30. Joel Barnett, *Inside the Treasury, 1974–1979* (London, 1982), 49. 31. Catherine R. Schenk, *The Decline of Sterling: Managing the Retreat of an International Currency, 1945–1992* (Cambridge, 2010), 368–75. Details are in HM Treasury, Papers on the 1976 Sterling Crisis released under FOI request. The 1976 IMF crisis is covered in detail in Wass, *Decline to Fall* and in K. Burk and A. Cairncross, *Goodbye Great Britain: The 1976 IMF Crisis* (New Haven, CT, 1992); Mark D. Harmon, *The British Labour Government and the 1976 IMF Crisis* (Basingstoke, 1997); Kevin Hickson, *The IMF Crisis of 1976 and British Politics* (London, 2005); Richard Roberts, *When Britain Went Bust: The 1976 IMF Crisis* (London, 2016). 32. *Report of the 75th Annual Conference of the Labour Party* (London, 1976). 33. Ibid. 34. Helleiner, *States and Re-emergence*, 124. 35. *Labour's Programme for Britain: Annual Conference 1976* (London, 1976); The National Archives (TNA), CAB128/60/3, CM(76) 25th Conclusions, Minute 3, 7 Oct. 1976; CAB129/93/7, CP(76)117, 29 Nov. 1976, 'Cabinet. The Real Choices facing the Cabinet: memorandum by the Secretary of State for Energy'; see analysis in CP(76)116/6, 30 Nov. 1976: 'Cabinet. The case for and against import controls. Note by the Central Policy Review Staff'. 36. TNA, PREM16/803, 'The IMF negotiations: a compromise package', Bernard Donoghue to PM, 25 Nov. 1976. 37. TNA, PREM16/800, PM to president, 12 Nov. 1976. 38. TNA, PREM16/800, Note on conversation with Herr Pohl at 11.45 a.m. on Monday Nov. 8 in Brussels, Derek Mitchell, 9 Nov. 1976. 39. US National Archives and Records Administration (NARA), RG56, Treasury, monetary reform, Box 2, Memo for the president from secretary of the treasury William Simon, 15 Nov. 1976; Memo for the president: alternative proposals for dealing with United Kingdom sterling balances, 17 Dec. 1976. 40. TNA, CAB129/193, CP(76)123, 30 Nov. 1976, 'Cabinet. Economic Policy and the IMF Credit. Memorandum by the Chancellor of the Exchequer'. 41. TNA, CAB128/60/11, CM(76) 33rd conclusions, 23 Nov. 1976; CAB128/60/12, CM(76) 34th conclusions, 25 Nov. 1976; CAB128/60/13, CM(76) 35th conclusions, 1 Dec. 1976; CAB128/60/14, CM(76) 36th conclusions, 2 Dec. 1976; CAB128/60/15, CM(76) 37th conclusions, 6 Dec. 1976; CAB128/60/16, CM(76) 38th conclusions, 7 Dec. 1976; CAB128/60/17, CM(76) 39th conclusions, 7 Dec. 1976; CAB128/60/20, CM(76) 41st conclusions, 14 Dec 1976; Burk and Cairncross, *Goodbye Great Britain*; Harmon, *British Labour Government*; Hickson, *IMF Crisis of 1976*; Roberts, *When Britain Went Bust*; Wass, *Decline to Fall*. 42. Nigel Lawson, *The New Conservatism: Lecture to the Bow Group* (London, 1980); *idem*, *The View from Number 11: Memoirs of a Tory Radical* (London, 1992), 8–9 and ch. 7; Adrian Williamson, *Conservative Policymaking and the Birth of Thatcherism*

1964–1979 (Basingstoke, 2015), 108–10; Martin Chick, *Changing Times: Economics, Policies and Resource Allocation in Britain since 1951* (Oxford, 2020), 44–6, 78–9; Helleiner, *States and Re-emergence*, 124, 144–5; David Edgerton, 'What came between new liberalism and neoliberalism? Rethinking Keynesianism, the welfare state and social democracy', in Davies, Jackson and Sutcliffe-Braithwaite, eds., *Neoliberal Age?*, 42, 45; Sutcliffe-Braithwaite, Davies and Jackson', 'Introduction: a neoliberal age?', 5–6; Martin Daunton, 'Creating a dynamic society: the tax reforms of the Thatcher government', in Marc Buggeln, Martin Daunton and Alexander Nützenadael, eds, *The Political Economy of Public Finance: Taxation, State Spending and Debt since the 1970s* (Cambridge, 2017), 32–56. **43.** Rodgers, *Age of Fracture*, 3–12; Avner Offer and Gabriel Söderberg, *The Nobel Factor: The Prize in Economics, Social Democracy and the Market Turn* (Princeton, NJ, 2016), 2–13; Avner Offer, *Understanding the Private–Public Divide: Markets, Governments and Time Horizons* (Cambridge, 2022), 2–10; Sutcliffe-Braithwaite, Davies and Jackson, 'Introduction: a neoliberal age?', 12; Jackson, 'Intellectual histories', 58–67; Mark Blyth, *Great Transformations: Economic Ideas and Institutional Change in the Twentieth Century* (Cambridge, 2002); Edgerton, 'What came between new liberalism . . .?', 43–6; Jim Tomlinson, 'The failures of neoliberalism in Britain since the 1970s: the limits on "market forces" in a deindustrialising economy and a "New Speenhamland"', in Davies, Jackson and Sutcliffe-Braithwaite, eds., *Neoliberal Age?*, 94–6; Peter Sloman, 'Welfare in a neoliberal age: the politics of redistributive market liberalism', in Davies, Jackson and Sutcliffe-Braithwaite, eds., *Neoliberal Age?*, 75–82; Peter Sloman, *Transfer State: The Idea of a Guaranteed Income and the Politics of Redistribution in Modern Britain* (Oxford, 2019), 14–23. **44.** Vanessa Ogle, 'Archipelago capitalism: tax havens, offshore money and the state, 1950s–1970s', *American Historical Review* 122 (2017), 1457–8; Layna Mosley, 'Room to move: international financial markets and national welfare states', *International Organization* 54 (2004), 737, 776; Layna Mosley, *Global Capital and National Governments* (Cambridge, 2003), 2–3, 9–10, 12–14, 17, 20–23; Duane Swank, *Global Capital, Political Institutions and Policy Change in Developed Welfare States* (Cambridge, 2002), 5–8, 275–283; Jim Tomlinson, 'The strange survival of "embedded liberalism": national economic management and globalization in Britain from 1944', *Twentieth Century British History* 32 (2021), 495–503; Ben Clift, 'Social democracy and globalization: the cases of France and the UK', *Government and Opposition* 37 (2003), 467–500; T. Iversen and T. Cusack, 'The causes of welfare state expansion: deindustrialization or globalization?', *World Politics* 52 (2000), 313–49; Jeffrey M. Chwieroth and Andrew Walter, *The Wealth Effect: How the Great Expectations of the Middle Class Have Changed the Politics of Banking Crises* (Cambridge, 2019), xvi–xviii, 4–13, 22; Helleiner, *States and Re-emergence*, 203–5; Nita Rudra, *Globalization and the Race to the Bottom in Developing Countries: Who Really Gets Hurt?* (Cambridge, 2008), 47, 74, 75, 107, 213–18. **45.** Giuliano Garavini, *The Rise and Fall of OPEC in the Twentieth Century* (Oxford, 2019), 255, 266, 271, 272, 285; idem, *After Empires: European Integration, Decolonization, and the Challenge from the Global South, 1957–1986* (Oxford, 2012), 239–40, 246–7. **46.** Document de travail remis par M. François Mitterrand, Président de la République à l'ouverture de la Conférence Nord-Sud de Cancún au Mexique, jeudi 22 octobre 1981, https://www.elysee.fr /francois-mitterrand/1981/10/22/document-de-travail-remis-par-m-francois-mitterrand -president-de-la-republique-a-louverture-de-la-conference-nord-sud-de-cancun-au-mexique -jeudi-22-octobre-1981; Margaret Thatcher, *The Downing Street Years* (London, 1993), 168–70; J. Toye and R. Toye, 'From new era to neo-liberalism: US strategy on trade, finance and development in the United Nations, 1964–82', *Forum for Development Studies* 1 (2005), 175–8; Ogle, 'State rights', 224; Garavini, *After Empires*, 257–8. **47.** Garavini, *Rise and Fall of OPEC*, 301, 302, 308, 361. **48.** Jeremy Friedman, *Shadow Cold War: The Sino-Soviet Competition for the Third World* (Chapel Hill, NC, 2015), 213, 218, 219, 221. **49.** Nils Gilman, 'The New International Economic Order: a reintroduction', *Humanity* 6 (2015), 7–11. **50.** Ogle, 'State rights', 212. **51.** Thomas G. Weiss, *Multilateral Development Diplomacy in UNCTAD: The Lessons of Group Negotiations, 1964–84* (Basingstoke, 1986), 41–2, 83–5. **52.** Toye and Toye, 'From new era', 175. **53.** Quinn Slobodian, *Globalists: The End of Empire and the Birth of Neoliberalism* (Cambridge, MA, 2018), 223–5, 235, 240–42, 245–7,

250–62.   54. Ibid., 182–93, 200, 204–17, 253; Luuk van Middelaar, *The Passage to Europe: How a Continent Became a Union* (New Haven, CT, 2013), 27; Thomas Horsley, *The Court of Justice of the European Union as an Institutional Actor: Judicial Lawmaking and its Limits* (Cambridge, 2018), 3–16; Perry Anderson, *Ever Closer Union? Europe and the West* (London, 2021).   55. Matthias Schmelzer, *The Hegemony of Growth: The OECD and the Making of the Economic Growth Paradigm* (Cambridge, 2016), 324–8.   56. Anne Krueger, 'The political economy of the rent-seeking society', *American Economic Review* 64 (1974), 291–303.   57. Sheldon Garon, *Beyond Our Means: Why America Spends While the World Saves* (Princeton, NJ, and Oxford, 2012).   58. R. Konkel, 'The monetisation of global poverty: the concept of poverty in World Bank history, 1944–1990', *Journal of Global History* 9 (2014), 249–300; Schmelzer, *Hegemony of Growth*, 311–12; Louis W. Pauly, 'New therapies from contemporary money doctors: the evolution of structural conditionality in the Bretton Woods institutions', in Marc Flandreau, ed., *Money Doctors: The Experience of International Financial Advising 1850–2000* (London, 2003), 284, 288; Mahbub ul Haq, *Reflections on Human Development* (New York, 1995), cover.   59. Stephen J. Macekura, *Of Limits and Growth: The Rise of Global Sustainable Development in the Twentieth Century* (Cambridge, 2015), 8–9; Arturo Escobar, *Encountering Development: The Making and Unmaking of the Third World* (Princeton, NJ, 1995), 192–7; Schmelzer, *Hegemony of Growth*, 321, 328–35.   60. M. S. Morgan and M. Bach, 'Measuring development – from the UN's perspective', *History of Political Economy* 50 (2018), 193–210; United Nations, *A World that Counts: Mobilising the Data Revolution for Sustainable Development* (New York, 2014); S. Macekura, 'Whither growth? International development, social indicators and the politics of measurement, 1920s to 1970s', *Journal of Global History* 14 (2019), 261–79; *idem*, 'Development and economic growth: an intellectual history', in Iris Borowy and Matthias Schmelzer, eds., *History of the Future of Economic Growth: Historical Roots of Current Debates in Sustainable Growth* (London, 2017), 110–28; https://www.un.org/millenniumgoals/global.shtml.

21. 'MARKET FUNDAMENTALISM'

1. Quoted in Paul Blustein, *The Chastening: Inside the Crisis that Rocked the Global Financial System and Humbled the IMF* (Oxford, 2001), 49.   2. Joshua Cooper Ramo, 'The three marketeers', *Time*, 15 Feb. 1999.   3. George Soros, *The Crisis of Global Capitalism: Open Society Endangered* (New York, 1998), xxvi.   4. Maurice Obstfeld and Alan M. Taylor, *Global Capital Markets: Integration, Crisis, and Growth* (Cambridge, 2004), 52–3, 55.   5. Dani Rodrik, *The Globalization Paradox: Why Global Markets, States, and Democracy Can't Coexist* (Oxford, 2011), xvi–xix.   6. Jacques J. Polak, 'Monetary analysis of income formation and payments problems', Staff Papers (International Monetary Fund) 6, 1 (1957), 1–50; Jacques J. Polak, 'The IMF monetary model at forty', IMF Working Paper WP/97/49 (April 1997), 4–5; Sarah Babb and Ariel Buira, 'Mission creep, mission push and discretion in sociological perspective: the case of IMF conditionality', in A. Buira, ed., *The IMF and the World Bank at Sixty* (London, 2005); Manuel Guitián, *Fund Conditionality: Evolution of Principles and Practices* (Washington, DC, 1981), 2–8; Sarah Babb, 'Embeddedness, inflation, and international regimes: the IMF in the early postwar period', *American Journal of Sociology* 113 (2007), 144–5, 151–2; Harold James, *International Monetary Cooperation since Bretton Woods* (Washington, DC, and New York, 1996), 141–2; Ngaire Woods, *The Globalizers: The IMF, the World Bank and Their Borrowers* (Ithaca, NY, and London, 2006), 40–42; Sidney Dell, 'On being grandmotherly: the evolution of IMF conditionality', Essays on International Finance No. 144, Department of Economics, Princeton, 1981, 9–11; Joseph Gold, 'Mexico and the development of the practice of the International Monetary Fund', *World Development* 16 (1988), 1129–30.   7. Dell, 'On being grandmotherly', 12–13, 20; Ben Clift and Jim Tomlinson, 'When rules started to rule: the IMF, neo-liberal economic ideas and economic policy change in Britain', *Review of International Political Economy* 19 (2011), 477–500.   8. IMF, First amendment to the Articles of Agreement, 28 July 1969 in Margaret Garritsen de Vries, ed., *The International Monetary Fund 1966–1971: The System under Stress. Vol. II,*

Documents (Washington, DC, 1976), 97–141; Polak, 'The IMF monetary model', 9; Dell, 'On being grandmotherly', 13–14; Guitián, *Fund Conditionality*, 13–16; Babb, 'Embeddedness', 144.   9. Louis W. Pauly, 'New therapies from contemporary money doctors: the evolution of structural conditionality in the Bretton Woods institutions', in Marc Flandreau, ed., *Money Doctors: The Experience of International Financial Advising 1850–2000* (London, 2003), 276–9, 296; Harold James, 'From grandmotherliness to governance: the evolution of IMF conditionality', *Finance and Development* (Dec. 1998), 45; Jacques J. Polak, 'The changing nature of IMF conditionality', Essays in International Finance No. 184, Department of Economics, Princeton, 1991, 1–5, 18, 19; Nitsan Chorev and Sarah Babb, 'The crisis of neoliberalism and the future of international institutions: a comparison of the IMF and WTO', *Theory and Society* 38 (2009), 465–6; Guitián, *Fund Conditionality*, 19–20; Alexandre Kafka, 'Some IMF problems after the Committee of XX', in Jacob A. Frenkel and Morris Goldstein, eds., *International Financial Policy: Essays in Honor of Jacques J. Polak* (Washington, DC, 1991).   10. Polak, 'Changing nature', 24–7, 39–40.   11. Babb and Buira, 'Mission creep', 62, 66.   12. Guitián, *Fund Conditionality*, 3; James, 'Grandmotherliness', 45–6.   13. Babb and Buira, 'Mission creep', 65 quoting Joseph Gold, *Interpretation: The IMF and International Law* (The Hague, 1996), 484; Joseph Stiglitz, *Globalization and its Discontents* (New York, 2002), 34–6, 55, 66, 84–5, 196–7.   14. Dell, 'On being grandmotherly', 24–6, 28.   15. G. Bird, 'A suitable case for treatment? Understanding the ongoing debate about the IMF', *Third World Quarterly* 22 (2001), 829–30; S. Dell, 'The question of cross conditionality', *World Development* 16 (1988), 557–8; Polak, 'Changing nature', 12–13.   16. John Williamson, 'What Washington means by policy reform', in John Williamson, ed., *Latin American Adjustments: How Much Has Happened?* (Washington, DC, 1990).   17. John Williamson, 'What should the Bank think about the Washington consensus?', *World Bank Research Observer* 15 (2000), 251–64; John Williamson, 'Did the Washington consensus fail?' Speech at the Center for Strategic and International Studies, Washington, DC, 6 Nov. 2002; William Becker, oral history interview with John Williamson, 31 Jan. and 1 Feb. 2006, World Bank; Soros, *Crisis of Global Capitalism*, xxvi; James M. Boughton, 'The IMF and the force of history: ten events and ten ideas that have shaped the institution', IMF Working Paper WP/04/75 (2004), 18; Narcis Serra, Shari Spiegel and Joseph Stiglitz, *Washington Consensus Reconsidered: Towards a New Global Governance* (Oxford, 2008); Daniel Yergin and Joseph Stanislaw, *The Commanding Heights: The Battle for the World Economy* (New York, 2002), 237; Nancy Birdsall, Augusto de la Torre and Felipe Valencia Caicedo, 'The Washington consensus: assessing a damaged brand', Center for Global Development Working Paper 211 (2010).   18. Robert A. Packenham and William Ratcliff, 'What Pinochet did for Chile', Hoover Institution, 30 Jan. 2007; Jeffrey A. Frieden, *Debt, Development, and Democracy: Modern Political Economy and Latin America, 1965–1985* (Princeton, NJ, 1991), 142–77; Odd Arne Westad, *The Cold War: A World History* (London, 2017), 362.   19. Frederick Cooper and Randall Packard, 'Introduction', in Cooper and Packard, eds., *International Development and the Social Sciences* (Berkeley, CA, 1997), 21; Kathryn Sikkink, 'Development ideas in Latin America: paradigm shift and the Economic Commission for Latin America', in Cooper and Packard, eds., *International Development and the Social Sciences*, 228–56; idem, *Ideas and Institutions: Developmentalism in Brazil and Argentina* (Ithaca, NY, 1991); ECLAC, *Changing Production Patterns and Social Equity: The Prime Task of Latin American and Caribbean Development in the 1990s* (Santiago, 1990), 12–15; ECLAC, *Social Equity and Changing Production Patterns: An Integrated Approach* (Santiago, 1992).   20. Jeffrey Chwieroth, 'Testing and measuring the role of ideas: the case of neoliberalism in the International Monetary Fund', *International Studies Quarterly* 51 (2007), 5–30; idem, 'Neoliberal economists and capital account liberalization in emerging markets', *International Organization* 61 (2007), 443–63; idem, 'Normative change from within: the International Monetary Fund's approach to capital account liberalization', *International Studies Quarterly* 52 (2008), 129–58; idem, *Capital Ideas: The IMF and the Rise of Financial Liberalization* (Princeton, NJ, 2010), 40–51; Woods, *The Globalizers*, 53–6; Roger E. Backhouse, 'The rise of free market economics: economists and the role of the state since 1970', *History of Political Economy* 37 (2005), 355–92; Gerald G. Helleiner, 'The Refsnes seminar: economic theory and North–South negotiations',

World Development 9 (1981), 539–55; Susan Strange, 'IMF: money managers', in Robert W. Cox and Harold Karan Jacobson, eds., *The Anatomy of Influence: Decision Making in International Organizations* (New Haven, CT, and London, 1974), 269; Adam Tooze, 'The gatekeeper', *London Review of Books* 43, 22 April 2021, 7; Avner Offer and Gabriel Söderberg, *The Nobel Factor: The Prize in Economics, Social Democracy and the Market Turn* (Princeton, NJ, 2016), 25–36. 21. Mariana Mazzucato, *The Entrepreneurial State: Debunking Public vs Private Sector Myths* (London, 2013). 22. Madrid Declaration, https://www.elibrary.imf.org/view/book/9781498337625/ch015.xml; Boughton, 'The IMF and the force of history', 17–19; Chwieroth, *Capital Ideas*, 194–5. 23. Sachs, quoted in Blustein, *Chastening*, 152. 24. Charles Gore, 'The rise and fall of the Washington consensus as a paradigm for developing countries', *World Development* 28 (2000), 795–9. 25. Offer and Söderberg, *Nobel Factor*, 11–12, 24–5, 29, 35–6, 149–50. 26. Ford Presidential Library, Burns papers, Box B64, Blumenthal to President, 'The International Monetary Fund and conditionality', 22 Sept. 1977. 27. Woods, *The Globalizers*, 56–83, on Mexico 84–103. 28. Ibid., 30, 208; Nigel Gould-Davies and Ngaire Woods, 'Russia and the IMF', *International Affairs* 75 (1999), 2. 29. World Bank, *Governance and Development* (Washington, DC, 1992) and *Governance: The World Bank's Experience* (Washington, DC, 1994); IMF, *Good Governance: The IMF's Role* (Washington, DC, 1997); IMF, 'The role of the IMF in governance issues: guidance note', approved by Executive Board, 25 July 1997; Woods, *The Globalizers*, 3, 77, 106, 108–9, 122, 123, 183. 30. James, 'Grandmotherliness', 46–7. 31. IMF, Guidelines on Conditionality, 25 Sept. 2002. 32. Ngaire Woods, 'The challenge of good governance for the IMF and the World Bank themselves', *World Development* 28 (2000), 823–41. 33. Robert Picciotto and Rachel Weaving, 'A new project cycle for the World Bank?', *Finance and Development* 31 (1994), 42–3. 34. Woods, 'Challenge of good governance', 828. 35. Paul Volcker and Toyoo Gyohten, *Changing Fortunes: The World's Money and the Threat to American Leadership* (New York, 1992), 143. 36. Eric Helleiner and Bessma Momani, 'Slipping into obscurity? Crisis and reform at the IMF', Centre for International Governance Innovation, Working Paper 16 (2007), 2, 3; Eric Helleiner and Geoffrey Cameron, 'Another world order? The Bush administration and HIPC debt cancellation', *New Political Economy* 11 (2006), 125–40; Chwieroth, *Capital Ideas*, 6. 37. Eric Helleiner, *States and the Re-emergence of Global Finance from Bretton Woods to the 1990s* (Ithaca, NY, 1994), 91–5; OECD Code of Liberalization of Capital Movements, art. 1(a). 38. Helleiner, *States and Re-emergence*, 96–8; Chiewroth, *Capital Ideas*, 121, 125–8, 134–5. 39. George F. Bolton, *A Banker's World: The Revival of the City, 1957–1970: Speeches and Writings of Sir George Bolton* (London, 1970), 112, 115, 123; Seung Woo Kim, 'The Euromarket and the making of the transnational network of finance, 1959–79', Ph.D. thesis, University of Cambridge, 2018, 88; Oscar Sanchez-Sibony, 'Capitalism's fellow traveller: the Soviet Union, Bretton Woods and the Cold War, 1944–58', *Comparative Studies in Society and History* 56 (2014), 313–14; *idem, Red Globalization: The Political Economy of the Soviet Cold War from Stalin to Khrushchev* (Cambridge, 2014), 73. 40. Quoted in Kim, 'Euromarket', 89–90; on Moscow Narodny Bank, ibid., 80–103. 41. Helleiner, *States and Re-emergence*, 89; John D. Turner, *Banking in Crisis: The Rise and Fall of British Banking Stability, 1800 to the Present* (Cambridge, 2014), 175, 181, 188. 42. Helleiner, *States and Re-emergence*, 82; Vanessa Ogle, 'Archipelago capitalism: tax havens, offshore money and the state, 1950s–1970s', *American Historical Review* 122 (2017), 1447–8; Catherine Schenk, *The Decline of Sterling: Managing the Retreat of an International Currency, 1945–1992* (Cambridge, 2010), 236–8. 43. R. Alton Gilbert, 'Requiem for Regulation Q: what it did and why it passed away', Federal Reserve Bank of St Louis, 1986. 44. Schenk, *Decline of Sterling*, 206. 45. Ibid., 225–33; J. Green, 'Anglo-American development, the Euromarkets and the deeper origins of neoliberal deregulation', *Review of International Studies* 42 (2016), 439–41, 444; Gary Burn, 'The state, the City and the Euromarket', *Review of International Political Economy* 6 (1999), 225; Aled Davies, *The City of London and Social Democracy: The Political Economy of Finance in Britain 1959–79* (Oxford, 2017), 143–5, 179–80; *idem*, 'The roots of Britain's financialised political economy', in Aled Davies, Ben Jackson and Florence Sutcliffe-Braithwaite, eds., *The Neoliberal Age? Britain since the 1970s* (London, 2021), 299–318; Florence Sutcliffe-Braithwaite, Aled Davies and Ben Jackson, 'Introduction: a neoliberal age?', in Davies, Jackson and Sutcliffe-Braithwaite, eds., *Neoliberal Age?*, 16–17, 19; Eric Helleiner, 'Explaining the globalization of financial markets: bringing states back in', *Review of International Political Economy* 2 (1995), 320–21; Helleiner, *States and Re-emergence*, 84.   **46.** Carlo Edoardo Altamura, *European Banks and the Rise of International Finance: The Post-Bretton Woods Era* (Abingdon and New York, 2017), 201; Daisuke Ikemoto, 'Not Maggie's fault? The Thatcher government and the re-emergence of global finance', seminar paper, Centre for Financial History, Cambridge; idem, 'Re-examining the removal of exchange control by the Thatcher government in 1979', Political Studies Association conference, 2016; The National Archives (TNA), T639/5, Lawson to Chancellor of the Exchequer, 'Dismantling exchange control', 4 Oct. 1979 and Howe to Prime Minister, 'Exchange control', 11 Oct. 1979.   **47.** Davies, 'The roots of Britain's financialised political economy', 301, 302.   **48.** Helleiner, *States and Re-emergence*, 90–91.   **49.** Schenk, *Decline of Sterling*, 231; Helleiner, *States and Re-emergence*, 85–8; Chwieroth, *Capital Ideas*, 123–4.   **50.** Schenk, *Decline of Sterling*, 229–33.   **51.** Helleiner, 'Explaining', 330, 334, 336; Helleiner, *States and Re-emergence*, 112–14; Susan Strange, *States and Markets: An Introduction to International Political Economy* (London, 1988), 31; Davies, *City of London*, 143–4; Green, 'Anglo-American development', 441–2.   **52.** Green, 'Anglo-American development', 426; Ogle, 'Archipelago capitalism', 1449–51; Helleiner, *States and Re-emergence*, 138–9.   **53.** Helleiner, *States and Re-emergence*, 196–8, 201–5.   **54.** Jeffrey A. Frieden, 'Invested interests: the politics of national economic policies in a world of global finance', *International Organization* 45 (1991), 425–51.   **55.** Avner Offer, 'Narrow banking, real estate and financial stability in the UK, *c.* 1870–2010', in Nicholas Dimsdale and Anthony Hotson, eds., *British Financial Crises since 1825* (Oxford, 2014), 170; Green, 'Anglo-American development', 425, 431, 434, 439–41, 444; Jeremy Green, *The Political Economy of the Special Relationship: Anglo-American Development from the Gold Standard to the Financial Crisis* (Princeton, NJ, 2020), 2–15, 42–4, 271–5; Gérard Duménil and Dominique Levy, *Capital Resurgent: Roots of the Neoliberal Revolution* (Cambridge, MA, 2004), 211.   **56.** Margaret Garritsen de Vries, *The International Monetary Fund, 1972–78, Cooperation on Trial, Vol. I: Narrative and Analysis* (Washington, DC, 1985), 192; Ogle, 'Archipelago capitalism', 1433–4, 1455–7.   **57.** Schenk, *Decline of Sterling*, 225–35.   **58.** Daniel J. Sargent, *A Superpower Transformed: The Remaking of American Foreign Relations in the 1970s* (New York, 2013), 112.   **59.** Robert H. Ferrell, ed., *Inside the Nixon Administration: The Secret Diary of Arthur Burns, 1969–1974* (Lawrence, KS, 2010), 41; Helleiner, *States and Re-emergence*, 104–5; Gianni Toniolo, *Central Bank Cooperation at the Bank for International Settlements, 1930–1973* (Cambridge, 2005), 465–9; Press communiqué of the Ministerial meeting of the Group of Ten, 18 Dec. 1971.   **60.** Altamura, *European Banks*, 89–98; de Vries, *IMF 1972–78, I*, 192–3; Helleiner, *States and Re-emergence*, 106–11; TNA, T318/399, OFSG(71)17, 'Overseas Finance Steering Group: Some international monetary questions. Summary of UK position', 21 May 1971; OFSG(71)15, 21 May 1971: 'Overseas Finance Steering Group. The Eurodollar market', A. H. Lovell and M. Hedley-Miller.   **61.** Helleiner, *States and Re-emergence*, 144–5.   **62.** Sargent, *Superpower Transformed*, 139–40.   **63.** Guitián, *Fund Conditionality*, 17–18; Tom Cutler, 'Recycling petrodollars to the Third World: a critique of the IMF oil facility', *World Affairs* 139 (1976/77), 189–205; James, *International Monetary Cooperation*, 316, 341; de Vries, *IMF 1972–78, I*, chs. 17 and 18 on oil facility.   **64.** Denis Healey, *The Time of My Life* (London, 1989), 419; *Foreign Relations of the United States (FRUS) 1969–76*, vol. XXXVII, *Energy Crisis, 1974–80* (Washington, DC, 2012), doc. 9; William E. Simon, *A Time for Truth* (New York, 1978), 221.   **65.** Declassified Document Reference System, 'US Policy and objectives on international investment', Peter M. Flanigan, 24 April 1974.   **66.** Margaret Garritsen de Vries, ed., *The International Monetary Fund 1972–78: Cooperation on Trial, Vol. III: Documents* (Washington, DC, 1985), 381–2; Helleiner *States and Re-emergence*, 110–11; TNA, PREM16/49, S. A. Robson to Bridges, 22 Nov. 1974; Charles Goodhart, *Basel Committee on Banking Supervisions: A History of the Early Years 1974–1997* (Cambridge, 2011), 31.   **67.** *FRUS 1977–80*, vol. III, Foreign Economic Policy (Washington, DC, 2013), doc. 23; Altamura, *European Banks*, 100, 106–10, 114–15, 119–20, 122, 128, 178–81; idem, 'European banks and the rise of international finance after Bretton Woods (1973–1982)', *Uppsala*

Studies in Economic History 101 (2015), 228; Volcker and Gyohten, *Changing Fortunes*, 191–3, 197.   **68.** Helleiner, 'Explaining', 324–31, 335; Helleiner, *States and Re-emergence*, 135–8; Ogle, 'Archipelago capitalism', 1433–4, 1449–51; Altamura, *European Banks*, 195–204.   **69.** Helleiner, 'Explaining', 331–2; Helleiner, *States and Re-emergence*, 171–6, 188–91.   **70.** Louis W. Pauly, *Who Elected the Bankers? Surveillance and Control in the World Economy* (Ithaca, NY, 1997), 116–28; Helleiner, 'Explaining', 332–3, 336; Helleiner, *States and Re-emergence*, 182–5; Altamura, *European Banks*, 204–8, 211, 228–33, 239.   **71.** 'Tietmeyer proposal: Financial Stability Forum convened to promote cooperation in supervision of financial markets', *IMF Survey* 28 (March 1999), 69–71.   **72.** Joseph P. Joyce, *The IMF and Global Financial Crisis: Phoenix Rising?* (Cambridge, 2013), 67–9, 143–8.   **73.** Offer and Söderberg, *Nobel Factor*, 84–8; Erin E. Jacobsson, *A Life for Sound Money: Per Jacobsson – His Biography* (Oxford, 1979), 160, 299, 402.   **74.** Helleiner, *States and Re-emergence*, 198–201; Volcker and Gyohten, *Changing Fortunes*, 201; Peter Haas, 'Introduction: Epistemic communities and international policy coordination', *International Organization* 46 (1992), 1–35.   **75.** Altamura, *European Banks*, 128, 203, 233.   **76.** James Boughton, 'Northwest of Suez: the 1956 crisis and the IMF', *IMF Staff Papers* 48 (2001), 425–46; *idem*, 'From Suez to Tequila: the IMF as crisis manager', *Economic Journal* 110 (2000), 279–81; Frank Southard, 'The evolution of the International Monetary Fund', Essays in International Finance No. 135, Department of Economics, Princeton, 1979, 25–7; Markus K. Brunnermaier, Harold James and Jean-Pierre Landau, *The Euro and the Battle of Ideas* (Princeton, NJ, and Oxford, 2016), 291.   **77.** Babb, 'Embeddedness', 146; Frieden, *Debt, Development and Democracy*, 62 and *idem*, 'Third world indebted industrialization: international finance and state capitalism in Mexico, Brazil, Algeria and South Korea', *International Organization* 35 (1981), 407–8.   **78.** Frieden, 'Indebted industrialization', 410–18.   **79.** Helleiner, *States and Re-emergence*, 176–9; Stephen Haggard and Sylvia Maxfield, 'The political economy of financial internationalisation in the developing world', *International Organization* 50 (1996), 37–8, 55–6, 60.   **80.** Joyce, *The IMF*, 55–7, 70; Jeffrey Sachs, 'Introduction', in Jeffrey Sachs, ed., *Developing Country Debt and Economic Performance* (Chicago, IL, 1989), 24–6; Jeffrey Sachs and Harry Huizinga, 'US commercial banks and the developing country debt crisis', *Brookings Papers on Economic Activity* 18 (1987), 555–608; Joseph Gold, 'Mexico and the development of the practice of the International Monetary Fund', *World Development* 16 (1988), 1130–34; Boughton, 'From Suez to Tequila', 16–18; Pauly, *Who Elected the Bankers?*, 117–19; Volcker and Gyohten, *Changing Fortunes*, 206; Woods, *The Globalizers*, 88–90.   **81.** Dani Rodrik, 'The limits of trade policy reform in developing countries', *Journal of Economic Perspectives* 6 (1992), 88, 89, 90, 96, 97; Woods, *The Globalizers*, 49, 90–98; Frieden, *Debt*, 83–8.   **82.** Boughton, 'From Suez to Tequila', 18–20; Pauly, *Who Elected the Bankers?*, 120–25; Woods, *The Globalizers*, 95, 97; Ian Vasquez, 'The Brady plan and market-based solutions to debt crisis', *Cato Journal* 16 (1996), 233–43.   **83.** Boughton, 'From Suez to Tequila', 4, 5–6, 7; Woods, *The Globalizers*, 99–103.   **84.** Offer and Söderberg, *Nobel Factor*, 238–9, 244.   **85.** Allan H. Meltzer, *Why Capitalism?* (New York, 2012), 22 and *idem*, 'Capital flight and reflight', in R. Dornbusch, J. H. Makin and D. Zlowe, eds., *Alternative Solutions to Developing Country Debt Problems* (Washington, DC, 1989), 71.   **86.** IMF, *Signaling by the Fund: A Historical Review* (Washington, DC, 2004), 13 quoted by Joyce, *The IMF*, 70.   **87.** Steven Radelet and Jeffrey Sachs, 'The onset of the East Asian financial crisis', NBER Working Paper 6680, Aug. 1998, 9–40.   **88.** Joyce, *The IMF*, 115–19; Radelet and Sachs, 'East Asian financial crisis', 40–54; Woods, *The Globalizers*, 5; Martin Feldstein, 'Refocusing the IMF', *Foreign Affairs* 20 (1998), 24–32.   **89.** Feldstein, 'Refocusing', 27.   **90.** Brunnermeier, James and Landau, *Euro and Ideas*, 292 quoting Friedman in the *Wall Street Journal*, 13 Oct. 1998; Woods, *The Globalizers*, 49–50, 52; Allan Meltzer, *Report of the International Financial Institution Advisory Commission* (Washington, DC, 2000); Allan H. Meltzer, 'The Report of the IFI Advisory Commission: comments on the critics', *CESifo Forum* 1 (2000), 9–17; Christian Weller, 'Meltzer report misses the mark', *Economic Policy Institute* Issue Brief 141, 13 April 2000.   **91.** Adam Tooze, *Crashed: How a Decade of Financial Crises Changed the World* (London, 2018), 7; Barry Eichengreen, Asmaa El-Ganainy, Rui Estever and Kris James Mitchener, *In Defense of Public Debt* (New York, 2021), 149–53.   **92.** 'Crisis in emerging market economies: the road to recovery', Michel Camdessus to the European-American Business Council, New York, 15 Sept. 1998.   93. Carlo Edoardo Altamura, 'Global banks and Latin American military dictators 1974–82', *Business History Review* 95 (2021), 309–10; Maurice Obstfeld and Alan M. Taylor, 'Globalization and capital markets', in Michael D. Bordo, Alan M. Taylor and Jeffrey G. Williamson, eds., *Globalization in Historical Perspective* (Chicago, IL, 2003), 173–5; Jerome Roos, *Why not Default? The Political Economy of Sovereign Debt* (Princeton, NJ, and Oxford, 2019), 1–4, 10–14, 16.   94. Noel Maurer, *The Empire Trap: The Rise and Fall of US Intervention to Protect American Property Overseas, 1893–2013* (Princeton, NJ, 2013), 386–99, 422–32; Andrew Hurrell, *On Global Order: Power, Values and the Constitution of International Society* (Oxford, 2007), 62–3; Madeleine Lynch Dungy, *Order and Rivalry: Rewriting the Rules of International Trade After the First World War* (Cambridge, 2023), ch. 7.   95. Vanessa Ogle, 'State rights against private capital: the "New International Economic Order" and the struggle over aid, trade, and foreign investment, 1962–1981', *Humanity* 5 (2014), 219–21; Lauge N. Skovgaard Poulsen, *Bounded Rationality and Economic Diplomacy: The Politics of Investment Treaties in Developing Countries* (Cambridge, 2015), xiii–xvi, 1–21; Maurer, *The Empire Trap*, 399–422, 108; Alexis Rieffel, 'The role of the Paris Club in managing debt problems', Essays in International Finance No. 161, Department of Economics, Princeton, 1985.   96. Mervyn King, 'Reform of the International Monetary Fund', speech at the Indian Council for Research on International Economic Relations, New Delhi, India, 20 Feb. 2006, 3.   97. Announcement of the ministers of finance and central bank governors of France, Germany, Japan, the UK and the US (the Plaza Accord), 22 Sept. 1985; Volcker and Gyohten, *Changing Fortunes*, 228–30, 234–5, 241–3, 245–6, 259; Pauly, *Who Elected the Bankers?*, 27–9.   98. 'Statement of the G6 finance ministers and central bank governors (Louvre Accord)', Paris, 22 Feb. 1987; Volcker and Gyohten, *Changing Fortunes*, 260, 268–71, 281–3.   99. Volcker and Gyohten, *Changing Fortunes*, 276–7.   100. Martina Larionova and John K. Kirton, eds., *The G8–G20 Relationship in Global Governance* (Aldershot, 2015) discusses the role of the two bodies.   101. Joyce, *The IMF*, 164–7.   102. Blustein, *Chastening*, 50; Chwieroth, 'Normative change', 129–58; Chwieroth, *Capital Ideas*, 13, 20–21, 55, 147, 151–4, 167, 170–71, 177, 179–82, 184, 187–8, 201; Stanley Fischer, 'Capital account liberalization and the role of the IMF' in Stanley Fischer *et al.*, 'Should the IMF pursue capital account convertibility?', Essays in International Finance No. 207, Department of Economics, Princeton, 1998, 1, 8–10.   103. Jacques Polak, 'The articles of agreement of the IMF and the liberalization of capital movements', in Fischer *et al.*, 'Should the IMF pursue capital account convertibility?', 49–50; Brunnermaier, James and Landau, *Euro and Ideas*, 290–91; Chwieroth, *Capital Ideas*, 202–7, 212–13, 215–16, 222, 226–7, 232–3, 239, 241–3.   104. Dani Rodrik, 'Who needs capital account convertibility?', in Fischer *et al.*, 'Should the IMF pursue capital account convertibility?', 56, 65.   105. Pauly, *Who Elected the Bankers?*, 40–41.   106. Joyce, *The IMF*, 135–9, 161–7.   107. Raghuram Rajan, 'Has financial development made the world riskier?', in *The Greenspan Era: Lessons for the Future. A 2005 Economic Symposium held by the Federal Reserve Bank of Kansas City, Jackson Hole Economic Policy Symposium*, 313–69; Raghuram Rajan, 'The Greenspan era: lessons for the future', speech at Jackson Hole, 27 Aug 2005 available at https://www.imf.org/en/News/Articles/2015/09/28/04/53/sp082705; transcript of Summers' remarks in 'Grasping Reality' by Brad DeLong, https://delong.typepad.com/sdj/2010/10/it-does-not-seem-to-me-that-charles-ferguson-has-gotten-it-right.html; Remarks by Governor Ben S. Bernanke at the meeting of the Eastern Economic Association, Washington, DC, 20 Feb. 2004, 'The great moderation'; Joyce, *The IMF*, 163–4.   108. Bank for International Settlements, 77th Annual Report, 2007, 145 quoted in Joyce, *The IMF*, 163.

22. 'RULES-BASED SYSTEM'

1. United States National Security Strategy, September 2002, quoted in Daniel W. Drezner, *US Trade Strategy: Free versus Fair*, Council on Foreign Relations (Washington, DC, 2006), 21.   2. Francine McKenzie, *GATT and Global Order in the Postwar Era* (Cambridge, 2020),

160–61; Ernest H. Preeg, *Traders in a Brave New World: The Uruguay Round and the Future of the International Trading System* (Chicago, IL, 1995), 83-4, 124; Andrew Hurrell, *On Global Order: Power, Values, and the Constitution of International Society* (Oxford, 2007), 240.   3. Giuseppe La Barca, *The US, the EC and World Trade: From the Kennedy Round to the Start of the Uruguay Round* (London, 2016), 103–5.   4. Preeg, *Traders in a Brave New World*, 33, 48-51; La Barca, *US, EC and World Trade*, 131–6; McKenzie, *GATT and Global Order*, 222-3.   5. Ronald Reagan, 'Remarks at a White House meeting with business and trade leaders', 23 Sept. 1985, online in Gerhard Peters and John T. Woolley, *The American Presidency Project*.   6. La Barca, *US, EC and World Trade*, 135-7.   7. Ronald Reagan, 'Remarks announcing his candidacy for the Republican presidential nomination', 13 Nov. 1979, in Peters and Woolley, *American Presidency Project*.   8. Reagan Presidential Library, Edward Stucky files, Box 4, Memo for the president: Bilateral trade talks, Donald T. Regan, 17 Sept. 1985; Michael Mussa files, Box 4, Memorandum for the president from the Economic Policy Committee, 'Canadian free trade agreement', 31 March 1987.   9. Ronald Reagan, 'Address to a joint session of parliament in Ottawa', 6 April 1987; see also 'Address before a Joint Session of Congress on the State of the Union', 25 Jan. 1988 in Peters and Woolley, *American Presidency Project*.   10. Reagan Presidential Library, Michael Mussa files, Box 4, Memorandum for the president from the Economic Policy Council, 'Canadian free trade agreement', 31 March 1987.   11. Preeg, *Traders in a Brave New World*, 108, 128-31, 164-5; McKenzie, *GATT and Global Order*, 162-3.   12. McKenzie, *GATT and Global Order*, 141-5, 161-71; Fred Bergsten, 'Globalizing free trade: the ascent of regionalism', *Foreign Affairs* 75 (1996), 106, 108.   13. John Croome, *Reshaping the World Trading System: A History of the Uruguay Round* (London, 1999), 8-27; Ernest H. Preeg, 'The Uruguay Round negotiations and the creation of the WTO', in Amrita Narlikar, Martin Daunton and Robert M. Stern, eds., *The Oxford Handbook on the World Trade Organization* (Oxford, 2012), 123; La Barca, *US, EC and World Trade*, 190-92; McKenzie, *GATT and Global Order*, 165-70; Reagan Presidential Library, Michael Mussa files, Box 3, 'International trade'.   14. Julie Hatch and Angela Clinton, 'Job growth in the 1990s: a retrospect', *Monthly Labor Review* (Dec. 2000), 4, 5; US international trade in goods and services from United States Census Bureau website, May 1990.   15. R. H. Wade, 'What strategies are viable for developing countries today? The WTO and the shrinking of "development space"', *Review of International Political Economy* 10 (2003), 621-44.   16. Amrita Narlikar, 'Fairness in international trade negotiations: developing countries in the GATT and WTO', *The World Economy* 29 (2006), 1018-23; Amrita Narlikar, 'Collective agency, systemic consequences: bargaining coalitions in the WTO', in Narlikar, Daunton and Stern, eds., *Oxford Handbook on the WTO*, 186-9; La Barca, *US, EC and World Trade*, 195-6; Preeg, 'Uruguay Round', 123-5; Preeg, *Traders in a Brave New World*, 55-63, 244-51; McKenzie, *GATT and Global Order*, 268-71; L. Alan Winters, 'The road to Uruguay', *Economic Journal* 100 (1990), 1297-302.   17. Croome, *Reshaping*, 32-6, 382-92; *Financial Times*, 22 Sept. 1986 cited in Preeg, 'Uruguay Round', 124.   18. McKenzie, *GATT and Global Order*, 225-7.   19. Croome, *Reshaping* provides a detailed narrative; Preeg, *Traders in a Brave New World* for an account by an insider.   20. Paul Blustein, *Misadventures of the Most Favored Nations: Clashing Egos, Inflated Ambitions, and the Great Shambles of the World Trade System* (New York, 2009), 30; Preeg, 'Uruguay Round', 124-5; Winters, 'Road to Uruguay', 1301-2.   21. *Journal of Commerce*, 12 Dec. 1988, cited in Preeg, 'Uruguay Round', 126.   22. Croome, *Reshaping*, 172-3.   23. Preeg, 'Uruguay Round', 126; Bruce E. Moon, *Dilemmas of International Trade*, 2nd edn (Boulder, CO, 2000), 107; Croome, *Reshaping*, ch. 5.   24. Croome, *Reshaping*, ch. 6; Preeg, 'Uruguay Round', 127-9; McKenzie, *GATT and Global Order*, 165-70.   25. Preeg, 'Uruguay Round', 129, 130; Croome, *Reshaping*, 328-80; McKenzie, *GATT and Global Order*, 271-82.   26. 'The Uruguay round' on the WTO website provides details; Croome, *Reshaping*, 381; Preeg, 'Uruguay Round', 133-4; Moon, *Dilemmas*, 107; William R. Cline, 'Evaluating the Uruguay Round', *The World Economy* 18 (1995), 1-23.   27. Preeg, 'Uruguay Round', 124.   28. Colin Hines, *Localization: A Global Manifesto* (London and Sterling, VA, 2000), x; Amrita Narlikar, *The World Trade Organization: A Very Short Introduction* (Oxford, 2005), 23; Ricardo Wahrendorff Caldas, *Brazil in the Uruguay Round of the GATT: The*

Evolution of Brazil's Position in the Uruguay Round, with Emphasis on the Issues of Service (Aldershot, 1998), 3–4, 5, 26–7, 111, 125–41, 231, 232; Michael Northrop, 'The Uruguay Round: a GATTastrophe', *Alternatives: Global, Local, Political* 18 (1993), 171–200; J. Michael Finger and Julio J. Nogués, 'The unbalanced Uruguay Round outcome: the new areas in future World Trade Organization negotiations', *The World Economy* 25 (2002), 321, 326–7, 337; J. Michael Finger, 'A diplomat's economics: reciprocity in the Uruguay Round negotiations', *World Trade Review* 4 (2005); Narlikar, 'Fairness', 1019–21. **29.** Rajeev Anand, 'Uruguay Round text in perspective', *Economic and Political Weekly*, 2 May 1992, 967–70; Narlikar, 'Fairness', 1021–2. **30.** Quinn Slobodian, *Globalists: The End of Empire and the Birth of Neoliberalism* (Cambridge, MA, 2018), 240, 281. **31.** John Jackson, 'The crumbling institutions of the liberal trade system', *Journal of World Trade Law* 12 (1978) and *Restructuring the GATT System* (New York, 1990); Narlikar, *The World Trade Organization*, 24; Blustein, *Misadventures*, 31, 32, 36; Gilbert R. Winham, 'The World Trade Organization: institutional building in the multilateral trade system', *World Economy* 21 (1998), 351, 353–4, 356–7, 365; McKenzie, *GATT and Global Order*, 170, 228; Judith Goldstein, 'Trade liberalization and domestic politics', in Narlikar, Daunton and Stern, eds., *Oxford Handbook on the WTO*, 78–80; Thomas Bernauer, Manfred Elsig and Joost Pauwelyn, 'Dispute settlement mechanism – analysis and problems', ibid., 485–506; Alan O. Sykes, 'The dispute settlement mechanism: ensuring compliance?', ibid., 560–84; Amrita Narlikar, Martin Daunton and Robert M. Stern, 'Introduction', ibid., 9. **32.** Claus-Dieter Ehlermann and Lothar Ehring, 'Decision-making in the World Trade Organization: is the consensus practice of the World Trade Organization adequate for making, revising and implementing rules on international trade?' *Journal of International Economic Law* 8 (2005), 51–65; R. H. Steinberg, 'In the shadow of law or power? Consensus-based bargaining and outcomes in the GATT/ WTO', *International Organization* 56 (2002), 339–74. **33.** Preeg, 'Uruguay Round', 132–6; Kendall Stiles, 'Negotiating institutional reform: the Uruguay Round, the GATT and the WTO', *Global Governance* 2 (1996), 145; Northrop, 'The Uruguay Round', 175. **34.** Raymond Vernon, 'The WTO: a new stage in international trade and development', *Harvard International Law Journal* 36 (1995), 332–40. **35.** Amrita Narlikar, 'The ministerial process and power dynamics in the World Trade Organization: understanding failure from Seattle to Cancún', *New Political Economy* 9 (2004), 413–28; John S. Odell, 'The Seattle impasse and its implications for the World Trade Organization', in Daniel L. M. Kennedy and James D. Southwick, eds., *The Political Economy of International Trade Law* (Cambridge, 2002), 403, 427–9; Robert Baldwin, 'Failure of the WTO ministerial conference at Cancún', *World Economy* 29 (2006), 681–2. **36.** Robert E. Hudec, 'The GATT legal system: a diplomat's jurisprudence', *Journal of World Trade Law* 4 (1970), 615–65; Finger, 'A diplomat's economics', 27. **37.** Richard Blackhurst, 'The role of the director general and the secretariat', in Narlikar, Daunton and Stern, eds., *Oxford Handbook on the WTO*, 143–5. **38.** Blustein, *Misadventures*, 47. **39.** Goldstein, 'Trade liberalization'; Blustein, *Misadventures*, 45–7. **40.** Marion James, 'Defining the borders of the WTO agenda', in Narlikar, Daunton and Stern, eds., *Oxford Handbook on the WTO*, 176; Druscilla Brown, 'Labour standards and human rights', ibid., 698; Blustein, *Misadventures*, 65–8. **41.** Blustein, *Misadventures*, 60–64, 68–9; Odell, 'Seattle impasse', 400–429. **42.** Lori Wallach and Michelle Sforza, *Whose Trade Organization? Corporate Globalization and the Erosion of Democracy* (Washington, DC, 1999), 3, 7; idem, *The WTO: Five Years of Reasons to Resist Corporate Globalization* (New York, 1999); Lori Wallach, 'Slow motion coup d'état: global trade agreements and the development of democracy', *Multinational Monitor* 26 (2005), 16; Blustein, *Misadventures*, 57–60; website of People's Global Action. **43.** R. Dragusanu and N. Nunn, 'The effects of Fair Trade certification: evidence from coffee producers in Costa Rica', NBER Working Paper 24260, Jan. 2018, revised June 2019. **44.** Blustein, *Misadventures*, 68–74, 75–6; UNDP, *Human Development Report 1999: Globalization with a Human Face* (New York, 1999), 12; William J. Clinton, Executive Order 13141: Environmental review of trade agreements, 16 Nov. 1999 in Peters and Woolley, *American Presidency Project*. **45.** Blustein, *Misadventures*, 78–81; Narlikar, 'Fairness', 1022. **46.** Oxfam Briefing Paper 9: 'Eight broken promises. Why the WTO isn't working for the world's poor'. **47.** Mike Moore, Director General of the

WTO, 'Preparations for the fourth WTO ministerial conference', Paris, 9 Oct. 2001. 48.
Ibid.; John S. Odell, 'Breaking deadlocks in international institutional negotiations: the WTO,
Seattle and Doha', *International Studies Quarterly* 53 (2009), 293–4; Blustein, *Misadventures*,
4. 49. Doha WTO Ministerial Conference 2001: Ministerial Declaration, adopted 14
November 2001; Blustein, *Misadventures*, ch. 5 on Doha meeting. 50. Dani Rodrik, 'The
global governance of trade as if development really mattered', Report submitted to UNDP,
July 2001; Gerald K. Helleiner, 'Markets, politics and the global economy: can the global
economy be civilized?' *Global Governance* 7 (2001), 243–63; Matthias Schmelzer, *The
Hegemony of Growth: The OECD and the Making of the Economic Growth Paradigm*
(Cambridge, 2016), 330. 51. Blustein, *Misadventures*, 18, quoting Michael Moore, *A World
Without Walls: Freedom, Development, Free Trade and Global Governance* (New York,
2003), 110. 52. For the full list, see www.wto.org. 53. Amrita Narlikar and Brendan Vick-
ers, 'Introduction', in their *Leadership and Change in the Multilateral Trading System*
(Dordrecht, 2009), 3, 5, 9; Narlikar, 'Collective agency', 189–97, 207; Amrita Narlikar, *Inter-
national Trade and Developing Countries: Bargaining Coalitions in the GATT and WTO*
(London, 2003); R. Blackhurst, 'Reforming WTO decision making: lessons from Singapore to
Seattle', Stanford Center for International Development, Working Paper 63, Aug. 2000. 54.
Rudolf Adlung, 'Trade in services in the WTO: from Marrakesh (1994), to Doha (2001),
to . . . (?)', in Narlikar, Daunton and Stern, eds., *Oxford Handbook on the WTO*, 370–
93. 55. Odell, 'Seattle impasse', 403–6; Statement of Robert Zoellick, US Trade
Representative, to Committee on Finance of the US Senate, 9 March 2004. 56. Blustein,
Misadventures, 134–7; Drezner, *US Trade Strategy*, 14–16, 20, 21. 57. Baldwin, 'Failure',
677–88; Amrita Narlikar and Rorden Wilkinson, 'Collapse of the WTO: a Cancun postmor-
tem', *Third World Quarterly* 25 (2004), 447–60; Amrita Narlikar and Diana Tussie, 'The G20
at the Cancun ministerial: developing countries and their evolving coalitions', *The World
Economy* 27 (2004), 947–66; Andrew Hurrell and Amrita Narlikar, 'A new politics of confrontation? Brazil and India in multilateral trade negotiations', *Global Society* 20 (2006),
415–33; Blustein, *Misadventures*, 147–56. 58. Barry Eichengreen, Yung Chul Park and
Charles Wyplosz, eds., *China, Asia and the New World Economy* (Oxford, 2008), 'Introduction', xvii–xix and chapters by Richard Baldwin, 'The spoke trap: hub-and-spoke bilateralism
in East Asia', Yung Chul Park and Inkyo Cheong, 'The proliferation of FTAs and prospects of
trade liberalization in East Asia', and Cédric Dupont and David Huang, 'Containing the PTA
wildfire'; Baldwin, 'Failure', 685; Robert Baldwin, 'Preferential trading arrangements', in Narlikar, Daunton and Stern, eds., *Oxford Handbook on the WTO*, 643–7. See also the websites
of the organizations for more detail. 59. Blustein, *Misadventures*, 174–6, 178–80; Statement
of Robert B. Zoellick, US Trade Representative, before the Committee on Ways and Means of
the House of Representatives, 26 Feb. 2003. 60. WT/L/579, 2 Aug. 2004: Decision adopted
by the General Council on 1 Aug. 2004; WTO news, 'Round-the-clock meetings produce
historic breakthrough', 31 July 2004; Blustein, *Misadventures*, 182–91, 194–8. 61. Quoted
by Amrita Narlikar and Piet van Houten, 'Know the enemy: uncertainty and deadlock in the
WTO', in Amrita Narlikar, ed., *Deadlocks in Multilateral Negotiations: Causes and Solutions*
(Cambridge, 2010), 142. 62. Blustein, *Misadventures*, 224, 248; Alasdair R. Young, 'Transatlantic intransigence in the Doha Round: domestic politics and the difficulty of compromise',
in Narlikar, ed., *Deadlocks*, 128–41. 63. Blustein, *Misadventures*, 249–52, 265–7; Brendan
Vickers, 'The role of the BRICs in the WTO: system-supporters or change agents in multilateral trade?', in Narlikar, Daunton and Stern, eds., *Oxford Handbook on the WTO*, 261,
263–4, 268. 64. Blustein, *Misadventures*, 8–10; Tod Allee, 'The role of the United States: a
multilevel explanation for decreased support over time', in Narlikar, Daunton and Stern, eds.,
Oxford Handbook on the WTO, 246. 65. Allan Beattie, 'Retread required', *Financial Times*,
30 Nov. 2009; Allee, 'Role of the United States', 243–9. 66. As argued in Ricardo Melendez-
Ortiz, Christopher Bellmann and Miguel Rodríguez Mendoza, eds., *The Future of the WTO:
Confronting the Challenges* (Geneva, 2012); Peter Kleen, 'So alike and yet so different: a
comparison of the Uruguay Round and the Doha Round', Jan Tumlir Policy Essays 2, Brus-
sels, 2008. 67. Narlikar, *The World Trade Organization*, 35, 86–92; John H. Jackson and
Alan O. Sykes, *Implementing the Uruguay Round* (Oxford, 1997), 465; Blackhurst, 'Role of

the director general and the secretariat', 145–9; Sam Laird and Raymundo Valdes, 'The trade policy review mechanism', in Narlikar, Daunton and Stern, eds., *Oxford Handbook on the WTO*, 463–84.   **68.** Winham, 'World Trade Organization', 364, 366; Bernauer, Elsig and Pauwelyn, 'Dispute settlement mechanism', 485–506; Sykes, 'The dispute settlement mechanism', 560–84, Gregory Shaffer and Joel Trachtman, 'WTO judicial interpretation', in Narlikar, Daunton and Stern, eds., *Oxford Handbook on the WTO*, 535–59; Mitsuo Matsushita, 'The dispute settlement mechanism at the WTO: the appellate body – assessment and problems', ibid., 507–34.   **69.** The cases are covered in Narlikar, Daunton and Stern, eds., *Oxford Handbook of the WTO*, 170, 306, 443–7, 449–50, 453–5, 513–16, 521–5, 538–9, 541, 546–7, 552, 554–5, 573–4, 666, 724–6, 732, 798; Hurrell, *On Global Order*, 109.   **70.** Kathryn Lavelle, 'Participating in the governance of trade: the GATT, UNCTAD and WTO', *International Journal of Political Economy* 28 (2003); Robert E. Hudec, 'The adequacy of WTO dispute settlement remedies: a developing country perspective', in B. Hoekman, A. Mattoo and P. English, eds., *Development, Trade and the WTO* (Washington, DC, 2002); C. L. Davis, 'Do WTO rules create a level playing field?, in J. S. Odell, ed., *Negotiating Trade: Developing Countries in the WTO and NAFTA* (Cambridge, 2006), 219–20, 251–4.   **71.** Thomas Cottier, 'The role of domestic courts in the implementation of WTO law: the political economy of separation of power and checks and balances in international trade regulation', in Narlikar, Daunton and Stern, eds., *Oxford Handbook on the WTO*, 607–31; Marion Jansen, 'Defining the borders of the WTO agenda', ibid., 161–83; Robert Howse, 'Regulatory measures', ibid., 441–2.

23. 'SETTING THE BIRD FREE'

1. Richard Baum, *Burying Mao: Chinese Politics in the Age of Deng Xiaoping* (Princeton, NJ, 1996), 152.   **2.** Yegor Gaidar, *Days of Defeat and Victory* (Seattle, WA, 1999), 67.   **3.** Charles S. Maier, 'Two sorts of crisis? The "long" 1970s in the West and the East', in Hans Gunter Hockerts, ed., *Koordinaten deutscher Geschichte in der Epoche des Ost-West Konflikts* (Munich, 2004), 58–9.   **4.** Isabella M. Weber, *How China Escaped Shock Therapy: The Market Reform Debate* (London and New York, 2021), 1–3.   **5.** Roderick MacFarquhar and Michael Schoenhals, *Mao's Last Revolution* (Cambridge, MA, 2006), 47, ch. 22 on Deng; Baum, *Burying Mao*, 3–5; Ezra Vogel, *Deng Xiaoping and the Transformation of China* (Cambridge, MA, 2011); Yang Jisheng, *The World Turned Upside Down: A History of the Chinese Cultural Revolution* (New York, 2021), xxviii–xxix.   **6.** 'Uphold the four cardinal principles', 30 March 1979, from *Selected Works of Deng Xiaoping, Vol. II, 1975–1982* (Beijing, 1994).   **7.** Vogel, *Deng Xiaoping*, 453–5; Julian Gewirtz, *Unlikely Partners: Chinese Reformers, Western Economists and the Making of Global China* (Cambridge, MA, 2011), 10.   **8.** Vogel, *Deng Xiaoping*, 424–5, 453–5; Maurice Meisner, *The Deng Xiaoping Era: An Enquiry into the Fate of Chinese Socialism, 1978–84* (New York, 1996), 209–13; Barry Naughton, *Growing Out of the Plan: Chinese Economic Reform 1978–1993* (Cambridge, 1995), 176–9; Weber, *How China Escaped*, 1, 7–11, 13, 119, 178–9, 184, 221, 260–68.   **9.** Jeffrey Sachs, *The End of Poverty: Economic Possibilities for Our Time* (New York, 2005), 157–60.   **10.** Frank Dikötter, *The Cultural Revolution: A People's History 1962–1976* (London, 2016), xvii; Yang, *World Turned Upside Down*, xxix–xxx.   **11.** Meisner, *Deng Xiaoping Era*, 222–31; Weber, *How China Escaped*, 161–5; Sachs, *End of Poverty*, 160.   **12.** Meisner, *Deng Xiaoping Era*, 231; Vogel, *Deng Xiaoping*, 390, 440–49.   **13.** Yasheng Huang, *Capitalism with Chinese Characteristics* (Cambridge, 2008), xiii–xv, 73, 79, 80, 98.   **14.** David Harvey, *A Brief History of Neoliberalism* (Oxford, 2005), 135, 138; Sachs, *End of Poverty*, 161; Naughton, *Growing Out of the Plan*, 11; Meisner, *Deng Xiaoping Era*, 274–84.   **15.** Branko Milanović, *Capitalism, Alone: The Future of the System that Rules the World* (Cambridge, MA, 2019), 123–4; Chenggang Xu, 'The fundamental institutions of China's reform and development', *Journal of Economic Literature* 49 (2011), 1076–1151; Frank Dikötter, *China After Mao: The Rise of a Superpower* (London, 2022), xiv–xvi.   **16.** Baum, *Burying Mao*, 151–3, 161, 164–6, 178, 207, 209, 211, 213.   **17.** Yang Jisheng, *Tombstone: The Great*

Chinese Famine, 1958–62 (New York, 2013), 20, 297; Frank Dikötter, *Mao's Great Famine: The History of China's Most Devastating Catastrophe* (London, 2010), 191–3, 230–31, 237, 238; Matthew C. Klein and Michael Pettis, *Trade Wars are Class Wars: How Rising Inequality Distorts the Global Economy and Threatens International Peace* (New Haven, CT, 2020), 112–13; Eduardo Jaramillo, 'China's hukou reform in 2022: do they mean it this time?', blog post on Center for Strategic and International Studies website, 20 April 2022.   18. Meisner, *Deng Xiaoping Era*, 242–54, 319, 329, 321–3.   19. Naughton, *Growing Out of the Plan*, 13–16; Gewirtz, *Unlikely Partners*, 7–9.   20. Baum, *Burying Mao*, 143, 156–63; Vogel, *Deng Xiaoping*, 427–31, 434.   21. Gewirtz, *Unlikely Partners*, 11; Naughton, *Growing Out of the Plan*, 179–80; Vogel, *Deng Xiaoping*, 464–6; Baum, *Burying Mao*, 169–74; Weber, *How China Escaped*, 176–8.   22. Baum, *Burying Mao*, 95, 169–70.   23. Naughton, *Growing Out of the Plan*, 7–10, 18–21, 181–7.   24. Weber, *How China Escaped*, 185–92.   25. Vogel, *Deng Xiaoping*, 456–61; Gewirtz, *Unlikely Partners*, 9, 74–5, 109–12, 134, 178–80; Weber, *How China Escaped*, 121–2, 135–46.   26. Gewirtz, *Unlikely Partners*, 12, 135–55, 160, 168–71; Weber, *How China Escaped*, 193–200; J. Kornai, *The Shortage Economy* (Amsterdam, 1980).   27. Weber, *How China Escaped*, 184, 200–221.   28. Baum, *Burying Mao*, 214, 218–20; Vogel, *Deng Xiaoping*, 469–73; Meisner, *Deng Xiaoping Era*, 376–9, 392–5; Weber, *How China Escaped*, 227–30.   29. Vogel, *Deng Xiaoping*, 470–73, 595–636; Baum, *Burying Mao*, 223, 226–310; Andrew Nathan, 'The Tiananmen papers', *Foreign Affairs* 80 (2001), 2–48; James Miles, *The Legacy of Tiananmen: China in Disarray* (Ann Arbor, MI, 1997); Weber, *How China Escaped*, 225–6, 230–43, 247–58; Gewirtz, *Unlikely Partners*, 209–14; Julian Gewirtz, *Never Turn Back: China and the Forbidden History of the 1980s* (Cambridge, MA, 2022).   30. Suisheng Zhao, 'Deng Xiaoping's southern tour: elite politics in post-Tiananmen Square China', *Asian Survey* 33 (1993), 739–56; Baum, *Burying Mao*, 319–22, 328–30, 334, 341–4, 352, 374; Vogel, *Deng Xiaoping*, 664–90; Dikötter, *China After Mao*, 87.   31. Huang, *Capitalism with Chinese Characteristics*, xv–xvii, 69–71, 103–5, 110–18, 123–4, 129, 151–4, 159–60, 164–71, 239, 280–82; Weber, *How China Escaped*, 268–9; Julia Lovell, *Maoism: A Global History* (London, 2019), 432–3.   32. Klein and Pettis, *Trade Wars*, 101–30; Adam Tooze interview with Michael Pettis and Matthew Klein, *Phenomenal World*, 13 June 2020; https://data.worldbank.org/indicator/NE.CON.PRVT.ZS?locations=CN-US accessed 26 July 2022; US Census: foreign trade balances; Investopedia web site: Shobhit Seth, 'Why China buys US debt with Treasury bonds', 30 Dec. 2021.   33. Francine McKenzie, *GATT and Global Order in the Postwar Era* (Cambridge, 2020), 97–100; WTO successfully concludes negotiations on Chinese entry, Press/243, 17 Sept. 2001, on WTO website; WTO/L/432, 23 Nov. 2001, Accession of the People's Republic of China; Robert Zoellick, 'Whither China? From membership to responsibility', Remarks to the National Committee on US–China Relations, 21 Sept. 2005; Barry Naughton, *The Chinese Economy: Transitions and Growth* (Cambridge, MA, 2007), 410–12; Reihan Salam, 'Normalizing trade relations with China was a mistake', *The Atlantic*, 8 June 2018; Paul Blustein, *Schism: China, America and the Fracturing of the Global Trading System* (Waterloo, Ontario, 2019), 65–6; Dikötter, *China After Mao*, 235–6.   34. Blustein, *Schism*, 65–6, 132, 139, 154, 172.   35. Vogel, *Deng Xiaoping*, 473–6; Sachs, *End of Poverty*, 157–8, 162–4; Naughton, *Growing Out of the Plan*, 16–18, 24–5, 311–20.   36. Sachs, *End of Poverty*, 109–26; Jeffrey Sachs, 'Building a market economy in Poland', *Scientific American* 266, 3 (March 1992), 36; J. Kornai, 'The Hungarian reform process: visions, hopes and reality', *Journal of Economic Literature* 24 (1986); *idem*, *The Road to a Free Economy* (New York, 1990).   37. David Lipton and Jeffrey Sachs, 'Creating a market economy in eastern Europe: the case of Poland', *Brookings Papers on Economic Activity* 1 (1990); Jeffrey Sachs, *Poland's Jump to the Market Economy* (Cambridge, MA, 1993), xiii, 29, 34, 84–92; Kornai, *Road*, 58.   38. Sachs, *End of Poverty*, 115–16, 128–9.   39. Johanna Bockman, *Markets in the Name of Socialism: The Left-Wing Origins of Neoliberalism* (Stanford, CA, 2011), 191–97, 200, 202, 207, 209; Joseph Stiglitz, 'More instruments, broader goals: moving towards the post-Washington consensus', UN University World Institute for Development Economics Research (WIDER), Annual lecture, Helsinki, 7 Jan. 1998, 7, 18–24; Joseph Stiglitz, *Whither Socialism?* (Cambridge, MA, 1994).   40. Mark Harrison, 'The Soviet Union after 1945: economic recovery and political repression', *Past and*

Present Supplement 6 (2011), 104, 107–10, 115, 118, 120; Vladimir Kontorovich, *Reluctant Cold Warriors: Economists and National Security* (New York, 2019); xv, 25–47; Sachs, *End of Poverty*, 163. **41.** Marc Edele, *The Soviet Union: A Short History* (Hoboken, NJ, 2018), 195–7; Donald Filtzer, *Soviet Workers and Stalinist Industrialization: The Formation of Soviet Production Relations, 1928–1941* (London, 1986); *idem, Soviet Workers and Late Stalinism: Labour and the Restoration of the Stalinist System after World War II* (Cambridge, 2002), 245–65; *idem, Soviet Workers and De-Stalinization: The Consolidation of the Modern System of Soviet Production Relations 1953–64* (Cambridge, 1992), 1–10; Kontorovich, *Reluctant Cold Warriors*. **42.** Edele, *Soviet Union*, 197–8; Alena Ledeneva, *Russia's Economy of Favours: Blat, Networking and Informal Exchange* (Cambridge, 1998). **43.** Yegor Gaidar, *State and Evolution: Russia's Search for a Free Market* (Seattle, WA, 2003), 71–4; the quote is from Vitaly Naishul, 'The highest and last stage of socialism', *Sinking in the Quagmire* (Moscow, 1991). **44.** Sachs, *End of Poverty*, 130, 132, 163–4; Oscar Sanchez-Sibony, *Red Globalization: The Political Economy of the Soviet Cold War from Stalin to Khrushchev* (Cambridge, 2014), 184–92; Michael Ellman and Vladimir Kontorovich, eds., *The Disintegration of the Soviet Economic System* (London and New York, 1992), 'Overview', 11; Edele, *Soviet Union*, 198–201; Donald Filtzer, *Soviet Workers and the Collapse of Perestroika: The Soviet Labour Process and Gorbachev's Reforms* (Cambridge, 1998), 6–11; Chris Miller, *The Struggle to Save the Soviet Economy: Mikhail Gorbachev and the Collapse of the USSR* (Chapel Hill, NC, 2016). **45.** Vogel, *Deng Xiaoping*, 423; Miller, *Struggle*, 174–6; Edele, *Soviet Union*, 201–4; Kristina Spohr, *Post Wall Post Square: Rebuilding the World After 1989* (London, 2019), 387–9. **46.** Edele, *Soviet Union*, 192–3, 201–9; Ellman and Kontorovich, eds., *Disintegration*, 2–22; Spohr, *Post Wall*, 391–6. **47.** Edele, *Soviet Union*, 209–12. **48.** Nigel Gould-Davies and Ngaire Woods, 'Russia and the IMF', *International Affairs* 75 (1999), 2, 4–5; Ngaire Woods, *The Globalizers: The IMF, the World Bank and Their Borrowers* (Ithaca, NY, and London, 2006), 104–12. **49.** Gaidar, *Days of Defeat*, 67–9. **50.** Ibid., 74–7. **51.** Sachs, *End of Poverty*, 133, 135, 137–41, 146–7; Spohr, *Post Wall*, 400–402; Stephen Hayes, *The Brain: Paul Wolfowitz and the Making of the Bush Doctrine* (New York, 2005); Chris Dolan, *In War We Trust: The Bush Doctrine and the Pursuit of Just War* (Aldershot, 2005); Woods, *Globalizers*, 110–12, 135–6. **52.** Gaidar, *Days of Defeat*, 81–3. **53.** Laurence Cockcroft, *Global Corruption: Money, Power and Ethics in the Modern World* (London and New York, 2012), 26–32; Gaidar, *Days of Defeat*, 168–71. **54.** Woods, *Globalizers*, 112–19, 122–5. **55.** Gaidar, *State and Evolution*, 59–62; Sachs, *End of Poverty*, 143–5; Woods, *Globalizers*, 119–22. **56.** Gaidar, *Days of Defeat*, 151–3; Woods, *Globalizers*, 105; Joel Hellman, Geraint Jones and Daniel Kaufmann, 'Seize the state, seize the day: an empirical analysis of state capture, corruption and influence in transition', World Bank Policy Research Working Paper 2444, 2000; Marshall Goldman, *The Privatization of Russia: Russian Reform Goes Astray* (New York, 2004); Daniel Triesman, '"Loans for shares" revisited', NBER Working Paper 15819, March 2010; Woods, *Globalizers*, 121, 136. **57.** David Stuckler and Sanjay Basu, *The Body Economic: Why Austerity Kills* (London, 2013), 21–40; David Stuckler, Lawrence King and Martin McKee, 'Mass privatization and the post-communist mortality crisis: a cross-national analysis', *Lancet* 73 (2009), 403; Sachs, *End of Poverty*, 134–6, 146–7. **58.** Gould-Davies and Woods, 'Russia and the IMF', 19; Anders Åslund, *Russia's Crony Capitalism: The Path from Market Economy to Kleptocracy* (New Haven, CT, 2019), 70–72; Woods, *Globalizers*, 30, 125–32. **59.** McKenzie, *GATT and Global Order*, 94–7; WTO website. **60.** Baum, *Burying Mao*, 18–20, 307–10, 313–15. **61.** Ramachandra Guha, *India After Gandhi: The History of the World's Largest Democracy* (London, 2007), 692; Howard L. Erdman, *The Swatantra Party and Indian Conservatism* (Cambridge, MA, 1967), 65–78, 193–7. **62.** Rahul Mukherji, 'Introduction: the state and private initiative in India', in Rahul Mukherji, ed., *India's Economic Transition: The Politics of Reforms* (New Delhi, 2007), 6–10. **63.** Ibid., 10–11; Gyan Prakash, *Emergency Chronicles: Indira Gandhi and Democracy's Turning Point* (Princeton, NJ, 2019), 92–108, chs. 6 and 7; Sagarika Dutt, *India in a Globalised World* (Manchester, 2006), 171. **64.** Mukherji, 'Introduction', 11. **65.** V. Dagli, *Report of the Committee on Control and Subsidies* (New Delhi, 1979); Tata interview in the *Times of India*, 12 July 1981, quoted in Guha, *India After Gandhi*, 693; Shankar

Acharya and Rakesh Mohan, 'Introduction', in Acharya and Mohan, eds., *India's Economy: Performance and Challenges: Essays in Honour of Montek Singh Ahluwalia* (New Delhi, 2010), 1-3; Mukherji, 'Introduction', 11-13. **66.** Isher Judge Ahluwalia and I. M. D. Little, 'Introduction', in Ahluwalia and Little, eds., *India's Economic Reforms and Development: Essays for Manmohan Singh* (New Delhi, 1998), 2; Manmohan Singh, *India's Export Trends and the Prospects for Self-Contained Growth* (Oxford, 1964); Speech by Dr Manmohan Singh, Minister of Finance, introducing the budget for the year 1991/92, Lok Sabha Debates, 24 July 1991, cols. 271-330. **67.** Guha, *India After Gandhi*, 694-9; Ahluwalia and Little, 'Introduction', 4-5; Sachs, *End of Poverty*, 178-9; Jagdish Bhagwati, 'What went wrong?', in Mukherji, ed., *India's Economic Transition*, 47-8; Rahul Mukherji, 'Economic transition in a plural policy: India', in Mukherji, ed., *India's Economic Transition*, 118, 123-6, 129-32. **68.** Ashutosh Varshney, 'Mass politics or elite politics? Understanding the politics of India's economic reforms', in Mukherji, ed., *India's Economic Transition*, 147-9, 154-8, 163-4. **69.** Baldev Raj Nayar, 'The limits of economic nationalism in India: economic reforms under the BJP-led government, 1998-9', in Mukherji, ed., *India's Economic Transition*, 202-3, 208-11, 217-21. **70.** Branko Milanović, *Global Inequality: A New Approach for the Age of Globalization* (Cambridge, MA, and London, 2016), 3, 5, 10-11, 18-22, 26, 30-32, 39-41, 45, 93-9, 103, 106, 109-10, 119, 127-8, 130-31. **71.** Weber, *How China Escaped*, 2.

24. 'EUROFANTASIES'

1. Rudiger Dornbusch, 'Euro fantasies', *Foreign Affairs* 75 (1996), 117. **2.** Milton Friedman, 'Canada and flexible exchange rates', in *Revisiting the Case for Flexible Exchange Rates: Proceedings of a Conference Held by the Bank of Canada, November 2000*, 419. **3.** Joaquín Almunia, Commissioner for Economic and Monetary Affairs, in *EMU@10: Successes and Challenges after Ten Years of Economic and Monetary Union*, DG Economic and Monetary Affairs, European Commission, 2008, iii. **4.** Treaty establishing the European Economic Community, 25 March 1957, article 105(2); Council decision on the Rules governing the Monetary Committee, 18 March 1958; Memorandum of the Commission on the Action Programme of the Community for the Second Stage, COM(62)300 final, 24 Oct. 1962; Walter Hallstein, 'Customs union and free trade area', *Bulletin of the European Economic Community*, No. 1, Feb. 1959, 5-12; Katja Seidel, 'Robert Marjolin: securing the Common Market through Economic and Monetary Union', in Kenneth Dyson and Ivo Maes, eds., *Architects of the Euro: Intellectuals in the Making of European Monetary Union* (Oxford, 2016), 61-2. **5.** Harold James, *Making the European Monetary Union: The Role of the Committee of Central Bank Governors and the Origins of the European Central Bank* (Cambridge, MA, 2012), 62-3; Emmanuel Mourlon-Druol, *A Europe Made of Money: The Emergence of the European Monetary System* (Ithaca, NY, and London, 2012), 22. **6.** Dornbusch, 'Euro fantasies', 123. **7.** Giandomenico Majone, *Rethinking the Union of Europe Post-Crisis: Has Integration Gone Too Far?* (Cambridge, 2014), 29. **8.** Kenneth Dyson and Ivo Maes, 'Intellectuals as policy-makers', in Dyson and Maes, eds., *Architects of the Euro*, 19-22. **9.** Ibid., 19-20; Charles Kindleberger, *A Financial History of Western Europe* (London, 1984), 117; Markus K. Brunnermaier, Harold James and Jean-Pierre Landau, *The Euro and the Battle of Ideas* (Princeton, NJ, and Oxford, 2016), 2-5, 27-8, 40-55, 59-67, 74-6, 80, 82; Harold James, 'Monetary and fiscal unification in nineteenth-century Germany: what can Kohl learn from Bismarck?', Essays in International Finance No. 202, Department of Economics, Princeton, March 1997; Manfred J. M. Neumann, 'Monetary stability: threat and proven response', in Deutsche Bundesbank, ed., *Fifty Years of the Deutsche Mark: Central Bank and the Currency in Germany since 1948* (Oxford, 1999), 303-4; Ernst Baltensperger, 'Monetary policy under conditions of increasing integration, 1979-1986', ibid., 501-9; Simon Mee, *Central Bank Independence and the Legacy of the German Past* (Cambridge, 2019), 7-28. **10.** Brunnermeier, James and Landau, *Euro and Ideas*, 2-5, 27, 40-55, 67-82; Dyson and Maes, 'Intellectuals', 20. **11.** David Howarth, 'Raymond Barre: modernizing France through European monetary cooperation', in Dyson and Maes, eds., *Architects of the Euro*, 77-8,

89–92. 12. The National Archives (TNA), CAB134/2602, AEO(F)(70)5, 9 Nov. 1970, Cabinet. Official Committee on the Approach to Europe, Sub-committee on financial and monetary aspects: Economic and monetary union; PREM15/53, 'Proposals regarding United Kingdom participation in a European monetary system', Cromer, Aug. 1970 and 'Note', W. S. Ryrie, 23 Oct. 1970; T328/654, Ministerial committee: An approach to Europe, Nov. 1970; Kiyoshi Hirowatari, *Britain and European Monetary Cooperation, 1964–79* (Basingstoke, 2015), 40, 78–80. 13. Seidel, 'Robert Marjolin', 72; Mourlon-Druol, *Europe Made of Money*, 24–9, 33–6, 54, 57, 58, 62, 72–4, 87–9, 99; James, *Making the EMU*, 94–5. 14. Mourlon-Druol, *Europe Made of Money*, 31–64, 90–93; Marjolin report, at Commission of the European Communities: DG for Economic and Financial Affairs, Brussels, 8 March 1975 II/675/3/74-Efin, Report of the Study Group 'Economic and Monetary Union 1980', Brussels, March 1975. 15. Ashoka Mody, *Eurotragedy: A Drama in Nine Acts* (New York, 2018), 55–6, 67 quoting Robert Marjolin, 'Europe in search of its identity', Russell C. Leffingwell Lectures, Council on Foreign Relations, New York, Sept. 1980 and Robert Marjolin, *Architect of European Unity: Memoirs 1911–86* (London, 1989). 16. Paul Wallace, *The Euro Experiment* (Cambridge, 2016), 40; James, *Making the EMU*, 24, 27; Mourlon-Druol, *Europe Made of Money*, 8–10, 19–20. 17. Mourlon-Druol, *Europe Made of Money*, 100–103, 113–16. 18. N. Piers Ludlow, 'Roy Jenkins: the importance of top-level politics', in Dyson and Maes, eds., *Architects of the Euro*, 120–38; Meeting of the Commission at La Roche-en-Ardenne, 16–18 Sept. 1977: 'The prospect of monetary union, note distributed by the president'; Roy Jenkins, 'Europe's present challenge and future opportunity', Jean Monnet lecture, 27 Oct. 1977; MacDougall report is Commission of the European Communities: Report of the Study Group on the Role of Public Finance in European Integration, Vol. 1, General Report, Brussels, April 1977; Mourlon-Druol, *Europe Made of Money*, 110–13, 116–31, 134–41. 19. Mourlon-Druol, *Europe Made of Money*, 134–41, 147–51; Roy Jenkins, *Life at the Centre* (London, 1991), 467, 469; Ludlow, 'Roy Jenkins', 133, 136–8; Commission of the European Communities: DG for Economic and Financial Affairs, II-G/8.9.1977, 'A progress report on convergence and EMU'; Commission of the European Communities: DG for Economic and Financial Affairs, II-C/AL.eg./20.2.1978, 'Note: arguments for improving exchange rate cooperation in the community'. 20. Mourlon-Druol, *Europe Made of Money*, 143–6. 21. Ibid., 151–9, 164–8; Jenkins, *Life at the Centre*, 476–8; James, *Making the EMU*, 152–5. 22. Mourlon-Druol, *Europe Made of Money*, 188–95, 198–227; Conclusions of the Bremen European Council, 6–7 July 1978, *Bulletin of the European Communities*, No. 6, 1978. 23. TNA, PREM16/1634, European currency arrangements, D. W. Healey, 22 June 1978. 24. TNA, PREM16/1636, European monetary system and the choice for the UK, Gordon Richardson, Bank of England, 31 Oct. 1978. 25. TNA, PREM16/1636, Donoghue to PM, 9 Oct. 1978; PREM16/1637, Healey to PM, 'EMS: UK stance in the coming weeks', 13 Nov. 1978; CAB128/64/20, Cabinet: Conclusions of a meeting of the Cabinet, 23 Nov. 1978; CAB129/204/14, CP(78)114, 31 Oct. 1978, Cabinet: European Monetary System: Memorandum by the Chancellor of the Exchequer; CAB129/204/15, CP(78)115, 30 Oct. 1978, Cabinet: European Monetary System: Memorandum for Parliament. Note by the Chancellor of the Exchequer; CAB129/204/21, CP(78)121, 22 Nov. 1978, Cabinet: European Monetary System. Note by the Chancellor of the Exchequer; CAB129/204/22, CP(78)122, 28 Nov. 1978, Cabinet: European Monetary System: Memorandum by the Chancellor of the Exchequer; Jenkins, *Life at the Centre*, 477, 483–4; House of Commons Expenditure Committee, *The European Monetary System: First Report* (London, 1978); J. Statler, 'British foreign policy to 1985: the European Monetary System from conception to birth', *International Affairs* 55 (1979), 220–22; Denis Healey, *The Time of My Life* (London, 1989), 439–40; Hirowatari, *Britain and European Monetary Cooperation*, 170–74. 26. Neumann, 'Monetary stability', 297–9; Peter Bernholz, 'The Bundesbank and the process of European monetary integration', in *Fifty Years of the Deutsche Mark*, 734, 740; James, *Making the EMU*, 174–6, 274; Mourlon-Druol, *Europe Made of Money*, 230, 238–41. 27. Resolution of the European Council on the establishment of the EMS, Brussels, 5 Dec. 1978, from *Bulletin of the European Communities*, No. 12, Dec. 1978; Mourlon-Druol, *Europe Made of Money*, 250–61. 28. James, *Making the EMU*, 179–80, 207–9; Nigel Lawson, *The View from Number 11: Memoirs of a Tory Radical* (London, 1992), 662.   **29.** Resolution on the EMS as an aspect of the international monetary system, 17 April 1980, *Official Journal of the European Communities*, C 117, 12 May 1980, 56–9.   **30.** Committee for the Study of Economic and Monetary Union, *Report on Economic and Monetary Union in the European Community* (Luxembourg, 1989); Perry Anderson, *Ever Closer Union? Europe in the West* (London, 2021), 162.   **31.** Dermot Hodson, 'Jacques Delors: vision, revisionism, and the design of EMU', in Dyson and Maes, eds., *Architects of the Euro*, 213–14, 217–19, 227–8, 230–32.   **32.** James, *Making the EMU*, 228–9.   **33.** Bernholz, 'Bundesbank', 775; James, *Making the EMU*, 230, 241–2.   **34.** James, *Making the EMU*, 249; Lamfalussy appendix to Werner report: 'Macro-coordination of fiscal policies in economic and monetary union in Europe'; Ivo Maes, 'Alexandre Lamfalussy: a Cassandra about financial stability', in Dyson and Maes, eds., *Architects of the Euro*, 233–4, 243–5.   **35.** Conclusions of the Madrid European Council, *Bulletin of the European Communities*, No. 6, June 1989, 11; Margaret Thatcher, *The Downing Street Years* (London, 1993), 708; Thatcher, HC Deb 6th ser. vol. 155, 29 June 1989, cols. 1109–24; Major, HC Deb 6th ser. vol. 159, 2 Nov. 1989, col. 491. The British response to Delors and rejection of a single currency is in HM Treasury, *An Evaluating Approach to Economic and Monetary Union* (London, 1989).   **36.** Speech to the College of Europe, 20 September 1988, available on Margaret Thatcher Foundation website; Thatcher, *Downing Street Years*, 707–8.   **37.** Speech by Nigel Lawson, 25 Jan. 1989, Royal Institute for International Affairs.   **38.** Nicholas W. C. Woodward, *The Management of the British Economy, 1945–2001* (Manchester, 2004), 178–80; Dennis Kavanagh, *Thatcherism and British Politics: The End of Consensus?* (Oxford, 1987), 301–2.   **39.** Thatcher, HC Deb 6th ser. vol. 181, 22 Nov 1990, col. 451.   **40.** Mary Elise Sarotte, 'Eurozone crises as historical legacy: the enduring impact of German unification 20 years on', Working Paper, International Institutions and Global Governance Program, 2010; Wallace, *Euro Experiment*, 12–13; Brunnermeier, James and Landau, *Euro and Ideas*, 8; Lawson, *View from Number 11*, 662–3.   **41.** Commission of the European Communities, DG for Economic and Financial Affairs, 'One Market, one money: an evaluation of the potential benefits and costs of forming an economic and monetary union', *European Economy* 44 (Oct 1990), 9, 63; Mody, *Eurotragedy*, 71.   **42.** Martin Feldstein, 'The political economy of the European economic and monetary union', *Journal of Economic Perspectives* 11 (1997), 23–42; *idem*, 'Europe's monetary union: the case against EMU', *The Economist*, 13 June 1992; Barry Eichengreen, 'European monetary integration', *Journal of Economic Literature* 31 (1993), 1321–57; *idem*, 'Costs and benefits of European monetary unification', University of California Berkeley, Working Paper 90-150, 1990; Michael Bordo and Finn E. Kydland, 'The gold standard as a rule', NBER Working Paper 3367, May 1990.   **43.** Treaty on European Union, *Official Journal of the European Communities*, C191 [s1], 29 July 1992; on the flaws, see James, *Making the EMU*, 16–20.   **44.** Brunnermeier, James and Landau, *Euro and Ideas*, 7, 85–7, 96–9, 116, 135–7, 145; Barry Eichengreen, 'The political economy of fiscal policy after EMU', CIDER Working Paper C92-004, 1992; Anderson, *Ever Closer Union?*, 162–3.   **45.** Mody, *Eurotragedy*, 11, 89–90; Reuven Glick and Michael Hutchinson, 'Budget rules and monetary union in Europe', *FRBSF Weekly Letter* 92-32, 18 Sept. 1992; Charles Bean, 'Economic and monetary union in Europe', *Journal of Economic Perspectives* 6 (1992), 48, 51; Jean-Paul Fitoussi *et al.*, *Competitive Disinflation: The Mark and Budgetary Politics in Europe* (Oxford, 1993), 14–15; Brunnermeier, James and Landau, *Euro and Ideas*, 9, 157–8; Wallace, *Euro Experiment*, 47, 55; Maurice Obstfeld, 'EMU: ready or not?', NBER Working Paper 6682, 1998; Eichengreen, 'The political economy of fiscal policy'.   **46.** Mody, *Eurotragedy*, 9; Dieter Nohlen and Philip Stover, *Elections in Europe: A Data Handbook* (Baden Baden, 2010), 525, 674.   **47.** Vernon Bogdanor, 'Why the people should have a vote on Maastricht', *Independent*, 9 June 1993; *idem*, 'Futility of a House with no windows', *Independent*, 26 July 1993.   **48.** James, *Making the EMU*, 357–63; M. Zurlinden, 'The vulnerability of pegged exchange rates: the British pound in the ERM', *Federal Reserve Bank of St Louis Economic Research* 75 (1993).   **49.** Barry Eichengreen, 'Designing a central bank for Europe: a cautionary tale from the early years of the Federal Reserve System', NBER Working Paper 3840, 1991.   **50.** James, *Making the EMU*, 15, 285–6; Harold James, 'Karl-Otto Pöhl: the pole position', in Dyson and Maes, eds., *Architects of the Euro*, 170–71, 174–90; Wallace, *Euro Experiment*, 64–5; Maastricht Treaty, Protocol on the Statutes of the ECSB and of the ECB, article 2. **51.** Tommaso Padoa-Schioppa quoted in James, *Making the EMU*, 8; Fabio Masini, 'Tommaso Padoa-Schioppa: EMU as the anchor stone for building a federal Europe', in Dyson and Maes, eds., *Architects of the Euro*, 200–207. **52.** Dani Rodrik, 'How democratic is the euro?', Project Syndicate, 11 June 2018; Yanis Varoufakis, *And the Weak Suffer What They Must?* (London, 2016). **53.** Friedman, 'Canada', 419. **54.** Brunnermeier, James and Landau, *Euro and Ideas*, 80; Bernholz, 'Bundesbank', 770. **55.** Conclusions of the Madrid European Council, 15–16 Dec. 1995, *Bulletin of the European Union*, No. 12, Dec 1995, 11–12, 27–8; Presidency conclusions, Amsterdam European Council, 16–17 June 1997; Declaration by the council (Ecofin) and the ministers meeting in that Council issued on 1 May 1998, *Official Journal of the European Communities*, L 139, 11 May 1998, 28–9; Resolution of the Amsterdam European Council on the Stability and Growth Pact, 17 June 1997; Wallace, *Euro Experiment*, 25, 49–53; Willem Buiter *et al.*, 'Excessive deficits: sense and nonsense in the Treaty of Maastricht', *Economic Policy* 8 (1993), 57, 60–61, 87–8. **56.** Wim Duisenberg, 'The past and future of European integration: a central banker's perspective', Per Jacobsson Foundation, 26 Sept. 1999; James, *Making the EMU*, 18. **57.** Kenneth Dyson and L. Quaglia, *European Economic Governance and Policies, Vol. I: Commentary on Key Historical and Institutional Documents* (Oxford, 2010), 491–4. **58.** David Marsh, *The Euro: The Politics of the New Global Currency* (New Haven, CT, 2009), 186, 190–99; Wallace, *Euro Experiment*, 61–2; James, *Making the EMU*, 17–18. **59.** Commission of the European Communities, Report from the Commission – Convergence Report 2000. **60.** Mody, *Eurotragedy*, 112. **61.** Martin Feldstein, 'EMU and international conflicts', *Foreign Affairs* 76 (1997), 72; Feldstein, 'Political economy', 25. **62.** Quoted in Martin Holmes, ed., *The Eurosceptical Reader* (Basingstoke, 1986), 42–9. **63.** HC Deb 6th ser. vol. 299, 27 Oct. 1997, cols. 583–8, Statement by the Chancellor of the Exchequer on economic and monetary union; HC Deb 6th ser. vol. 326, 23 Feb. 1999, cols. 179–84, Statement by Tony Blair on euro; discussion by Ed Balls in John Rentoul, 'Ed Balls: Tony Blair never really wanted to join the Euro', *Independent*, 3 March 2017. **64.** Ed Balls, 'Euro-monetarism: why Britain was ensnared and how it should escape', Fabian Society Discussion Paper 14, 1992. **65.** Helen Thompson, 'Will it hold?', *London Review of Books*, 21 June 2018, 19; Martin Sandbu, *Europe's Orphan: The Future of the Euro and the Politics of Debt* (Princeton, NJ, and Oxford 2017), ch. 10 implausibly argues for the success of the euro and that a better outcome would have been possible if Britain had been a member. **66.** Jeffry Frieden, 'The euro: who wins? Who loses?', *Foreign Policy* 112 (1998), 38. **67.** Robert Mundell, 'A theory of optimum currency areas', *American Economic Review* 51 (1961), 657–65; Ronald McKinnon, 'Optimum currency areas', *American Economic Review* 53 (1963), 712–25; Peter B. Kenñen, 'The theory of optimum currency areas: an eclectic view', in Robert Mundell and Alexander Swoboda, eds., *Monetary Problems of the International Economy* (Chicago, IL, 1969), 41–60. **68.** Tamim Bayoumi and Barry Eichengreen, 'Shocking aspects of European monetary unification', NBER Working Paper 3949, 1992; Barry Eichengreen, 'Is Europe an optimum currency area?', NBER Working Paper 3579, 1991; Feldstein, 'Political economy', 33–6; Wallace, *Euro Experiment*, 34, 36, 37. **69.** Mody, *Eurotragedy*, 6–7, 48–9 quoting Sam Brittan, 'The politics of monetary union', *Financial Times*, 16 Nov. 1970 and Nicholas Kaldor, 'The dynamic effects of the Common Market', 1971, reprinted in Nicholas Kaldor, *Further Essays on Applied Economics* (London, 1978). **70.** Ronald McKinnon, 'EMU as a device for collective fiscal retrenchment', *American Economic Review* 87 (1997), 227–9; Barry Eichengreen, 'Déjà vu all over again: lessons from the gold standard for European monetary unification', CIDER Working Paper C94-032, 1994; James Browne, Paul Johnson and David Phillips, 'The budget of the European Union: a guide', Institute for Fiscal Studies Briefing Note BN181, April 2016, 6. **71.** Xavier Sala-i-Martin and Jeffrey Sachs, 'Fiscal federalism and optimum currency areas: evidence for Europe from the United States', NBER Working Paper 3855, 1991; Barry Eichengreen, 'One money for Europe? Lessons from the US currency union', *Economic Policy* 5 (1990), 165–6; Maurice Obstfeld and Giovanni Peri, 'Regional non-adjustment and fiscal policy', *Economic Policy* 13 (1998), 205–59. **72.** Brunnermeier, James and Landau, *Euro* and Ideas, 100–102, 103–4. **73.** Martin Wolf, *The Shifts and the Shocks: What We've Learned – and Have Still to Learn – from the Financial Crisis* (London, 2014), 60–73; Dani Rodrik, *Straight Talk on Trade: Ideas for a Sane World Economy* (Princeton, NJ, and Oxford, 2018), 64; for a different view, see Sandbu, *Europe's Orphan*, 9–11, 35–9, 268–70. **74.** Michael D. Bordo and Lars Jonung, 'The future of EMU: what does the history of monetary unions tell us?', NBER Working Paper 7365, 1999; Lars Jonung and Eoin Drea, 'The euro: it can't happen. It's a bad idea. It won't last. US economists on the euro, 1989–2002', *Economic Papers* 395 (Dec. 2009); Jeffrey A. Frankel and Andrew Rose, 'The endogeneity of the optimum currency area criteria', NBER Working Paper 5700, 1996; Frieden, 'The euro'; Hugh Rockoff, 'How long did it take the United States to become an optimal currency area?' NBER Historical Working Paper 0124, 2000; Feldstein, 'Political economy'; Obstfeld, 'EMU: ready or not?' **75.** C. Fred Bergsten, 'The dollar and the euro', *Foreign Affairs* 76 (1997), 83–95. **76.** Barry Eichengreen, 'Will emu work?' April 1998 from his website; Tamim Bayoumi and Barry Eichengreen, 'Ever closer to heaven: an optimum currency area index for European countries', *European Economic Review* 41 (1997), 761–70; Barry Eichengreen, *Global Imbalances and the Lessons of Bretton Woods* (Cambridge, MA, 2007), 7, 25–7, 123–4, 135, 137–40, 145–7. **77.** Quoted in Wallace, *Euro Experiment*, 1 from *Le Figaro*, 23 Jan. 2009; Jean-Claude Trichet, President of the European Central Bank, 'The euro@10: achievements and responsibilities', remarks at the European Parliament, 13 Jan. 2009. **78.** James, *Making the EMU*, 381. **79.** Adam Tooze, *Crashed: How a Decade of Financial Crises Changed the World* (London, 2018), 14–15, 188, 329–30. **80.** Mody, *Eurotragedy*, 115. **81.** Dyson and Maes, 'Intellectuals', 5–6; Michael Bordo and Harold James, 'The European crisis in the context of the history of previous financial crises', NBER Working Paper 19112, 2013, abstract and 27.

25. 'BEHAVING BADLY'

1. Joseph Stiglitz, 'Lessons from the global financial crisis of 2008', *Seoul Journal of Economics* 23 (2010), 322–3. **2.** Wolfgang Schäuble, 'Why austerity is only cure for the eurozone', *Financial Times*, 5 Sept. 2011. **3.** Remarks by Governor Ben S. Bernanke at the meetings of the Eastern Economic Association, Washington, DC, 20 Feb. 2004, 'The great moderation', https://www.federalreserve.gov/boarddocs/speeches/2004/20040220/. **4.** Lawrence H. Summers, 'The United States and the global adjustment process', speech at the third annual Stavros S. Niarchos Lecture, Peterson Institute for International Economics, 23 March 2004. **5.** Adam Tooze, *Crashed: How a Decade of Financial Crises Changed the World* (London, 2018), 5–7, 75–9, 239, 241. **6.** The episode is recounted in Michael Lewis, *The Big Short: Inside the Doomsday Machine* (New York, 2010) and the film of 2015 directed by Adam McKay. See also the documentary *Inside Job* (2010), directed by Charles Ferguson which exposed the complicity of some economists. For a brief account, see Stiglitz, 'Lessons', 321–39. **7.** Tooze, *Crashed*, 7–8, 256, 261. **8.** Ibid., 2. **9.** Stiglitz, 'Lessons'. Paul Krugman had warned of 'Crony capitalism, USA' in *The Great Unravelling: From Boom to Bust in Three Scandalous Years* (New York, 2003). **10.** Paul Krugman, 'The Great Recession versus the Great Depression', *New York Times*, 20 March 2009. **11.** Barry Eichengreen and Kevin O'Rourke, 'A tale of two depressions', 6 April 2009, with updates 4 June 2009 and 8 March 2010, at https://voxeu.org/article/tale-two-depressions-what-do-new-data-tell-us-february-2010-update. **12.** Michael Hirsh, 'The reeducation of Larry Summers', *Newsweek*, 20 Feb. 2009. **13.** Barry Eichengreen, *The Hall of Mirrors: The Great Depression, the Great Recession, and the Uses and Misuses of History* (New York, 2016), 6–7, 284, 301; Miguel Almunia, Agustín Bénétrix, Barry Eichengreen, Kevin O'Rourke and Gisela Rua, 'The effectiveness of fiscal and monetary stimulus in depressions', 18 Nov. 2009, at http://www.voxeu.org/article/effectiveness-fiscal-and-monetary-stimulus-depressions. **14.** Chris Giles, Ralph Atkins and Krishna Guha, 'The undeniable shift to Keynes', *Financial Times*, 29 Dec. 2008; Eichengreen, *Hall of Mirrors*, 340–42. **15.** George Parker and Bertrand Benoit, 'Berlin hits out at "crass" UK strategy', *Financial Times*, 10 Dec. 2008; Daniel Pimlott, 'G20 agrees $1,100bn to fight crisis', *Financial Times*, 2 April 2009; Philip Stephens, 'Summit success reflects a different global landscape', *Financial Times*, 2 April 2009; Giles, Atkins and Guha, 'Undeniable shift'; Chris Giles, 'Large numbers hide big G20 divisions', *Financial Times*, 2 April 2009; Tooze, *Crashed*, 268–73; Eichengreen, *Hall of Mirrors*, 10.   16. Chris Giles, 'UK bank chief urges caution', *Financial Times*, 25 March 2009; Evidence to House of Commons Treasury Committees: Bank of England February 2009 Inflation Report, Oral and Written Evidence, Tuesday 24 March 2009, Q97; Tooze, *Crashed*, 268–73; Mervyn King, *The End of Alchemy: Money, Banking and the Future of the Global Economy* (London, 2016), 11, 29–33, 325–6, 328–33, 335, 367, 369.   17. Alan S. Blinder, *After the Music Stopped: The Financial Crisis, the Response, and the Work Ahead* (New York, 2013), 226–7; Tooze, *Crashed*, 277–81, 290.   18. Alberto Alesina, Carlo Favero and Francesco Giavazzi, *Austerity: When It Works and When It Doesn't* (Princeton, NJ, 2019) provides an overview of work over the previous two decades, including Alberto Alesina and Silvia Ardagna, 'Tales of fiscal adjustment', *Economic Policy* 13 (1998), 487–545; *idem*, 'Large changes in fiscal policy: taxes versus spending', NBER Working Paper 15438, Oct. 2009; IMF, 'Will it hurt?', in *World Economic Outlook: Recovery, Risk and Rebalancing* (Washington, 2010), 113; Ben Clift, *The IMF and the Politics of Austerity in the Wake of the Global Financial Crisis* (Oxford, 2018), 130–31; Robert Lucas, 'The industrial revolution – past and future', *The Region: 2003 Annual Report of the Federal Reserve Bank of Minneapolis* (2004); Mark Blyth, *Austerity: The History of a Dangerous Idea* (New York, 2013), 173–6 and Iyanatul Islam and Anis Chowdhury, 'Revisiting the evidence on expansionary fiscal austerity: Alesina's hour?', Vox CEPR policy portal, 28 Feb. 2012; Eichengreen, *Hall of Mirrors*, 7, 9–10, 282, 284, 332–3; Martin Wolf, *The Shifts and the Shocks: What We've Learned – and Have Still to Learn – from the Financial Crisis* (London, 2014), 31, 266–72; Barry Eichengreen, Asmaa El-Ganainy, Rui Esteves and Kris James Mitchener, *In Defense of Public Debt* (New York, 2021), 190–92.   19. Tooze, *Crashed*, 274, 348–54, 468.   20. Wolfgang Schäuble, 'A comprehensive strategy for the stabilization of the Economic and Monetary Union', speech to Brussels Economic Forum, 18 May 2011.   21. Carmen Reinhart and Kenneth Rogoff, 'Growth in a time of debt', NBER Working Paper 15639, Jan. 2010; Carmen Reinhart and Kenneth Rogoff, *This Time is Different: Eight Centuries of Fiscal Folly* (Princeton, NJ, 2009); Tooze, *Crashed*, 347.   22. George Osborne, 'Mais Lecture: A new economic model', 24 Feb. 2010.   23. *The Path to Prosperity: Restoring America's Promise. Fiscal Year 2012 Budget Resolution, House Committee on the Budget, Chairman Paul Ryan Wisconsin*; Martin Wolf, 'The radical right and the US state', *Financial Times*, 12 April 2011.   24. Carmen Reinhart and Kenneth Rogoff, 'Debt, growth and the austerity debate', *New York Times*, 25 April 2013; *idem*, 'Why we should expect low growth amid debt', *Financial Times*, 27 Jan. 2010; J. Cassidy, 'The Reinhart–Rogoff controversy: a summing up', *New Yorker*, 26 April 2013.   25. Thomas Herndon, Michael Ash and Robert Pollin, 'Does high debt consistently stifle economic growth? A critique of Reinhart and Rogoff', Political Economy Research Institute, University of Massachusetts Amherst, Working Paper series no. 322, April 2013, at www.peri.umass.edu/fileadmin/pdf/working_papers/working_papers_301-350/WP322.pdf; Martin Daunton, *Trusting Leviathan: The Politics of Taxation in Britain, 1799–1914* (Cambridge, 2001); *idem, Just Taxes: The Politics of Taxation in Britain, 1914–1979* (Cambridge, 2002); Eichengreen, *Hall of Mirrors*, 10; Nick Crafts, 'Reducing high public debt ratios: lessons from UK experience', *Fiscal Studies* 37 (2016), 201–23; Eichengreen *et al., In Defense*.   26. Blyth, *Austerity*, 5, 7, 13–16.   27. The G20 Toronto Summit Declaration, 26–27 June 2010; Tooze, *Crashed*, 354; Wolf, *Shifts and the Shocks*, 257.   28. Wolf, *Shifts and the Shocks*, 257.   29. Eleva Bolva, Tidiane Kinda, Priscilla Muthoora and Frederick Toscani, 'Fiscal rules at a glance', IMF, April 2015; X. Debrun, L. Moulin, A. Turrini, J. Ayuso-i-Casals, M. S. Kumar and C Fuest, 'Tied to the mast? National fiscal rules in the European Union', *Economic Policy* 23 (2008), 297–362; Charles Wyplosz, 'Fiscal rules: theoretical issues and historical experiences', in Alberto Alesina and Francesco Giavazzi, eds., *Fiscal Policy After the Financial Crisis* (Chicago, IL, 2013); Tooze, *Crashed*, 96–7, 286–9, 355.   30. Paul Krugman, 'The third depression', *New York Times*, 28 June 2010.   31. Olivier Blanchard and Carlo Cottarelli, 'Ten commandments for fiscal adjustment in advanced economies', IMF Blog, 24 June 2010; A. Berg and J. D. Ostry, 'Inequality and unsustainable growth: two sides of the same coin?', IMF Staff Discussion Note SDN/11/09, April 2011; IMF, 'Will it hurt?', 93–124; Jonathan D. Ostry, Andrew Berg and Charalambos Tsangarides, 'Redistribution, inequality and growth', IMF Staff Discussion Note SDN/14/02, February 2014; Jonathan D. Ostry, Prakash Loungani and Davide Furceri, 'Neoliberalism: oversold?', *Finance and Development* 53 (2016), 38–41; Clift, *IMF and the Politics of Austerity*, 1–26, 130–32, 151–77, 206–7. **32.** Clift, *IMF and the Politics of Austerity*, 26, 151; Olivier Blanchard and Daniel Leigh, 'Growth forecasts and fiscal multipliers', NBER Working Paper 18779, Feb. 2013, 1, 3, 17; IMF, 'Are we underestimating short-term fiscal multipliers?', in IMF, *World Economic Outlook: Coping with High Debt and Sluggish Growth* (Washington, DC, 2012); Olli Rehn, letter to Michael Noonan and other European finance ministers, Brussels, 10 Feb. 2013, at http://ec.europa.eu/archives/commission_2010-2014/rehn/documents/cab20130213_en.pdf; Ashoka Mody, *Eurotragedy: A Drama in Nine Acts* (New York, 2018), 287–90. **33.** Tooze, *Crashed*, 7, 243, 246, 248, 251, 252; Eichengreen *et al.*, *In Defense*, 203. **34.** Milton Friedman and Anna Jacobson Schwartz, *A Monetary History of the United States, 1867–1960* (Princeton, NJ, 1963), 301, 407–19; Eichengreen, *Hall of Mirrors*, 114–16; Ben S. Bernanke, *The Courage to Act: A Memoir of a Crisis and its Aftermath* (New York and London, 2015), 29–30, 33–6, 65, 387–9, 416–21. **35.** Tooze, *Crashed*, 15–17, 210; Eichengreen, *Hall of Mirrors*, 8, 182–3; Eichengreen and O'Rourke, 'Tale of two depressions', 6 April 2009. **36.** Brad DeLong, quoted by Bernanke, *Courage to Act*, 310. **37.** Eichengreen, *Hall of Mirrors*, 188, 190, 284. **38.** The argument went back to Ron Paul and Lewis Lehrman, *The Case for Gold: A Minority Report of the US Gold Commission* (Washington, DC, 1982); 'Ron Paul on gold standard and paper money's moral hazard', CNBC, 23 April 2012; Will Weissert, 'Ron Paul gives new life to gold standard issue', *Huffington Post*, 18 Jan. 2012. See the websites of the Mises Institute and Liberty Fund for reprints of leading books on the gold standard and engagement with the present debates. Ludwig von Mises, *On the Manipulation of Money and Credit: Three Treatises on Trade Cycle Theory*, ed. Percy L. Greaves Jr (Indianapolis, IN, 2011); Friedrich Hayek, *Prices and Production* (London, 1931); *idem*, *Monetary Theory and the Trade Cycle* (London, 1932), quote at 21. **39.** Blinder, *After the Music Stopped*, xvii, 343–64; Ron Paul, *End the Fed* (New York, 2009), 141; John Taylor, *Getting Off Track: How Government Actions and Interventions Caused, Prolonged and Worsened the Financial Crisis* (Stanford, CA, 2009). **40.** Joseph Stiglitz, 'It's folly to place all our trust in the Fed', *Financial Times*, 18 Oct. 2010; Office for National Statistics, 'Labour market economic commentary: February 2020', at ons.gov.uk; Anne Case and Angus Deaton, *Deaths of Despair and the Future of Capitalism* (Princeton, NJ, and Oxford, 2020), 7. **41.** Atif Mian and Amir Sufi, *House of Debt: How They (and You) Caused the Great Recession. And How We Can Prevent It From Happening Again* (Chicago, IL, 2014), 23, 25, 31, 39, 43–5, 51, 59, 70–71, 122, 134, 152–3; Wolf, *Shifts and the Shocks*, 263. **42.** Tooze, *Crashed*, 1–13, 73–4, 110, 116, 155, 165–9, 197–9, 206–7, 210–19; Blinder, *After the Music Stopped*, 269–70; Benn Steil, 'Central bank currency swaps tracker', Council on Foreign Economic Relations, 5 Nov. 2019; Ben Bernanke, *The Federal Reserve and the Financial Crisis: Lectures by Ben S. Bernanke* (Princeton, NJ, 2013), does not mention swaps; they are mentioned, though not stressed, in his *Courage to Act*, 157, 163, 183–4, 207–8, 278, 294, 300, 307, 347, 410 and in Bernanke, Timothy F. Geithner and Henry M. Paulson Jr, *Firefighting: The Financial Crisis and its Lessons* (New York, 2019), 42–3, 196. **43.** Tooze, *Crashed*, 202–3, 215, 218–19, 482–4. **44.** Ibid., 15; Tamim Bayoumi, *Unfinished Business: Unexplored Causes of the Financial Crisis and the Lessons Yet to be Learned* (New Haven, CT, 2017), 1, 10–11, 71. **45.** Tooze, *Crashed*, 9. **46.** Blinder, *After the Music Stopped*, 343–64. **47.** Eichengreen, *Hall of Mirrors*, 250–52, 315, 318; Tooze, *Crashed*, 281; Bernanke, *Courage to Act*, 389–90, 407–9; Blinder, *After the Music Stopped*, 320–42. **48.** Blinder, *After the Music Stopped*, 343; Jeffrey M. Chwieroth and Andrew Walter, *The Wealth Effect: How the Great Expectations of the Middle Class Have Changed the Politics of Banking Crises* (Cambridge, 2019), xv–xviii, 4–10, 22. **49.** 'Treasury Deputy Secretary Lawrence H. Summers testimony before the Senate Committee on Agriculture, Nutrition and Forestry on the Commodity Futures Trading Committee Concept Release', 30 July 1998. **50.** Tooze, *Crashed*, 81–7; Bayoumi, *Unfinished Business*, 133–4, 146–51, 207; John Eatwell and Lance Taylor, *Global Finance at Risk* (Cambridge, 2000), 26, 203–4; Joseph P. Joyce, *The IMF and Global Financial Crisis: Phoenix Rising?*

(Cambridge, 2013), 67–9, 143–8. **51.** Sebastian Mallaby, *The Man Who Knew: The Life and Times of Alan Greenspan* (London and New York, 2016), 64, 68–9, 378, 444–5, 450–51, 454–5, 469–70, 497–8, 504–7, 553–6, 558–9, 627, 631–2, 640, 632–5, 654–5, 656–7, 660, 663–4, 666, 667, 669, 675, 678–84; Jennifer Burns, *Goddess of the Market: Ayn Rand and the American Right* (New York, 2009), 142–3, 149–50, 269–71. **52.** Wolf, *Shifts and the Shocks*, 146. **53.** Ibid., 117; Ben S. Bernanke, 'Modern risk management and banking supervision', Remarks at Stoner Graduate School of Banking, Washington, 12 June 2006. **54.** Hyam Minsky, *Stabilizing an Unstable Economy* (New York, 1986); idem, *Can "It" Happen Again?* (New York, 1982). **55.** Joseph E. Stiglitz, *Globalization and its Discontents* (New York, 2002); idem, *The Roaring Nineties: A New History of the World's Most Prosperous Decade* (New York, 2003); idem, *Making Globalization Work* (New York, 2006); Wolf, *Shifts and the Shocks*, xvi–xvii, 2, 5–6, 12, 147, 191–2. **56.** Financial Services Authority, 'The Turner Review: a regulatory response to the global banking crisis', March 2009. **57.** Andrew Baker, 'Restraining regulatory capture? Anglo-America, crisis politics and trajectories of change in global financial governance', *International Affairs* 86 (2010), 647–8, 651; Simon Johnson, 'A quiet coup', *The Atlantic*, May 2009; Paul Collier, 'Goldilocks and the bear: the aftermath of the financial crisis', *Times Literary Supplement*, 16 Nov. 2018, 8. **58.** Wolf, *Shifts and the Shocks*, 147; Avner Offer, *Understanding the Private–Public Divide: Markets, Governments, and Time Horizons* (Cambridge, 2022), 40, 44. **59.** Tooze, *Crashed*, 298–311; Jonathan Tepper with Denise Hearn, *The Myth of Capitalism: Monopolies and the Death of Competition* (Hoboken, NJ, 2019), 182; Blinder, *After the Music Stopped*, 268–319; Baker, 'Restraining regulatory capture?', 648, 654, 663; Wolf, *Shifts and the Shocks*, 232–3; A. Haldane and V. Madouros, 'The dog and the frisbee', Federal Reserve Bank of Kansas City, 36th economic policy symposium, Jackson Hole, 31 Aug. 2002. **60.** Warren Clarke, 'Creating the Financial Stability Forum: what role for existing institutions?', *Global Society* 28 (2014), 195–216; *Report of the Financial Stability Forum on Enhancing Market and Institutional Resilience*, April 2008; Tooze, *Crashed*, 269–70, 311; Randal K. Quarles, 'Global financial cooperation as a legacy of Bretton Woods', in The Bretton Woods Committee, *Revitalizing the Spirit of Bretton Woods*, July 2019, 137–9; Jean-Claude Trichet, 'Financial architecture', ibid., 148–9; Howard Davies and David Green, *Global Financial Regulation: The Essential Guide*, rev. edn (Cambridge, 2010), xv, xvii–xx, xxxv–xxxvi, 214–25; 'Report to the G20 Los Cabos Summit on strengthening FSB capacity, resources and governance', at http://www.fsb.org/history/; Peter Isard, *Globalisation and the International Financial System: What's Wrong and What Can Be Done* (Cambridge, 2005), 106–12. **61.** Tooze, *Crashed*, 311–13, 316–17; Wolf, *Shifts and the Shocks*, 233. **62.** Tooze, *Crashed*, 454–6, 460, 462. **63.** Tracey Samuelson, 'Why do so many people love Glass–Steagall?' at http://www.marketplace.org/2016/01/05/world/glass-steagall; Kevin Cirilli, 'Sanders backs reviving Glass–Steagall', *The Hill*, 17 July 2015, at http://thehill.com/policy/finance/248407-sanders-backs-reviving-glass-steagall; Richard Eskow, 'Wall Street: five reasons Glass–Steagall matters', 16 Nov. 2015 on Bernie Sanders website; Robert Reich, 'Why Hillary Clinton is wrong for refusing to resurrect Glass–Steagall', *In These Times*, 9 Oct. 2015; Simon Johnson, 'Resurrecting Glass–Steagall', Project Syndicate, 29 Oct. 2015; Robert Hockett, 'Clinton and Summers are wrong on Sanders's Glass–Steagall proposals', 5 Jan. 2016, at http://thehill.com/blogs/pundits-blog/finance/264675-clinton-and-summers-are-wrong-on-sanderss-glass-steagall-proposal. **64.** Article 104b of the Maastricht and article 125 of the Lisbon treaties. **65.** Paul Wallace, *The Euro Experiment* (Cambridge, 2016), 82–3; Ashoka Mody and Damiano Sandri, 'The Eurozone crisis: how banks and sovereigns came to be joined at the hip', *Economic Policy* 27 (2012), 201–6, 225–7; M. Ehrmann, M. Fratzscher, R. S. Gurkaynak and E. T. Swanson, 'Convergence and anchoring of the yield curves in the euro area', *Review of Economics and Statistics* 93 (2011), 350–64; Tooze, *Crashed*, 322, 323, 325, 329, 343–5; Markus K. Brunnermaier, Harold James and Jean-Pierre Landau, *The Euro and the Battle of Ideas* (Princeton, NJ, and Oxford, 2016), 90–91, 337–9. **66.** Tooze, *Crashed*, 325, 331–5, 358, 366, 368, 370–71; Brunnermeier, James and Landau, *Euro and Ideas*, 12–13. **67.** Tooze, *Crashed*, 336, 344–5, 358, 366; Brunnermeier, James and Landau, *Euro and Ideas*, 20–22, 287–312, 328; Harold James, *Making the European Monetary Union: The Role of the Committee of Central Bank Governors and the*

Origins of the European Central Bank (Cambridge, MA, 2012), 13; Clift, *IMF and the Politics of Austerity*, 123, 126–8.   68. Milton Friedman, 'The euro: monetary unity and political disunity', Project Syndicate, 28 Aug. 1997.   69. Brunnermeir, James and Landau, *Euro and Ideas*, 24–7, 328; Tooze, *Crashed*, 337–45.   70. Tooze, *Crashed*, 361–4.   71. Ibid., 376–8, 381–4, 397–8, 402, 408, 413, 414, 416, 417, 418.   72. Ibid., 423–33, 436–8; Dani Rodrik, *Straight Talk on Trade: Ideas for a Sane Economy* (Princeton, NJ, and Oxford, 2016), 64.   73. Sebastian Edwards, *American Default: The Untold Story of FDR, the Supreme Court, and the Battle over Gold* (Princeton, NJ, and Oxford, 2018), 205–6; Wallace, *Euro Experiment*, 9–10, 21–2, 99, 151–3, 156–7, 160–61, 171–3; Wolfgang Schäuble, 'Why Europe's monetary union faces its biggest crisis', *Financial Times*, 11 March 2010; Brunnermeir, James and Landau, *Euro and Ideas*, 9.   74. Wallace, *Euro Experiment*, 3, 15–16, 189–97; Brunnermeir, James and Landau, *Euro and Ideas*, 5, 122–4, 191, 263, 313, 320, 354–7; Tooze, *Crashed*, 437–46.   75. Wallace, *Euro Experiment*, 175, 192–5; Brunnermeir, James and Landau, *Euro and Ideas*, 9, 358–9; 'Germany's judges give the ECB a grudging nod', *Financial Times*, 21 June 2016.   76. Tooze, *Crashed*, 365–6; Wallace, *Euro Experiment*, 17–18, 28, 206; Brunnermeier, James and Landau, *Euro and Ideas*, 314, 318, 334, 358–9, 361, 364.   77. Mehreen Khan and Paul McClean, 'Dijsselbloem under fire after saying Eurozone countries wasted money on "alcohol and women"', *Financial Times*, 21 March 2017.   78. Stefano Battilossi, 'Structural fiscal imbalances, financial repression and sovereign debt sustainability in southern Europe, 1970s–1990s', in Marc Buggeln, Martin Daunton and Alexander Nützenadel, eds., *The Political Economy of Public Finance: Taxation, State Spending and Debt since the 1970s* (Cambridge, 2017), 263–6; Tooze, *Crashed*, 101, 323–4; Wolf, *Shifts and the Shocks*, 75; Mody, *Eurotragedy*, 259–62; IMF Greece: Staff report on request for stand-by arrangement, IMF country report 20/220, Washington, 5 May 2010 and Minutes of Executive Board meeting, 9 May 2010: Greece – request for stand-by arrangement, Washington 20 Sept. 2010; Eichengreen *et al.*, *In Defense*, 192–8; Rui Pedro Esteves and Ali Coşkun Tunçer, 'Eurobonds past and present: a comparative review on debt mutualization in Europe', *Review of Law and Economics* 12 (2016), 659–88; *idem*, 'Feeling the blues: moral hazard and debt dilution in Eurobonds before 1914', *Journal of International Money and Finance* 65 (2016), 46–68.   79. Wolf, *Shifts and the Shocks*, 85–6.   80. Wallace, *Euro Experiment*, 3.   81. Joseph Stiglitz, *The Euro and its Threat to the Future of Europe* (London, 2017), xxxiv–xxxvi; Gideon Rachman, 'Germany faces a machine from hell', *Financial Times*, 13 Feb. 2012.   82. Nadia Sabitova and Chulpan Shavaleyeva, 'Oil and gas revenues of the Russian Federation: trends and prospects', *Procedia Economics and Finance* 27 (2015), 426.   83. Anders Åslund, *Russia's Crony Capitalism: The Path from Market Economy to Kleptocracy* (New Haven, CT, 2019), 3–9, 37, 68–70, 73, 76, 89, 94–6, 99, 130, 212–13; see also Karen Dawisha, *Putin's Kleptocracy: Who Owns Russia* (New York, 2014); Zeke J. Miller, 'World leaders cancel G8 summit in Russia after Ukraine crisis', *Time*, 24 March 2014; 'German foreign minister against excluding Russia from G8', Reuters, 2 March 2014; Stephen Kotkin, 'True believer', *Times Literary Supplement*, 9 Sept. 2022, 19.   84. 'Russia's economy is staggering, but still on its feet', *Financial Times*, 19 Aug. 2022.   85. Gyan Prakash, *Emergency Chronicles: Indira Gandhi and Democracy's Turning Point* (Princeton, NJ, 2019), 381; Christophe Jaffrelot, 'What "Gujarat model"? Growth without development and with socio-political polarisation', *South Asia: Journal of South Asian Studies* 38 (2015), 820–38.   86. P. R. Ramesh, 'We will use every provision in the Constitution to push reforms', *Open*, 8 Jan. 2015; website of NITI Aayog at http://niti.gov.in.   87. Prakash, *Emergency Chronicles*, 5, 6, 382–3; Ramachandra Guha, *India After Gandhi: The History of the World's Largest Democracy* (London, 2007), 701–14; Amartya Sen, 'Theory and practice of development', in Isher Judge Ahluwalia and I. M. D. Little, eds., *India's Economic Reforms and Development: Essays for Manmohan Singh* (New Delhi, 1998), 82–3; Amartya Sen and Jean Drèze, *An Uncertain Glory: India and its Contradictions* (London, 2013), 37–41.   88. Vijay Joshi, *India's Long Road: The Search for Prosperity* (New York, 2017), 6–8.   89. Quoted in James Kynge, 'Chaos v control: China's Communists and a century of revolution', *Financial Times*, 25 June 2021; David Runciman, *The Confidence Trap: A History of Democracy in Crisis from World War I to the Present* (Princeton, NJ, and Oxford, 2013), 320–23.   90. Matthew Klein, 'Beijing is tanking the domestic economy – and helping the world', *Financial Times*, 17 Aug. 2022; FT film, 'Evergrande: China's Lehman moment?' March 2022. **91.** Kevin O'Rourke and Jeffrey G. Williamson, *Globalization and History: The Evolution of a Nineteenth-Century Atlantic Economy* (Cambridge, MA, 1999), 13–15, 29, 35, 40, 55, 60, 74–5, 91, 93, 105, 113, 145, 163, 166, 167, 169, 177, 181, 183, 283–7; Harold James, *The End of Globalization: Lessons from the Great Depression* (Cambridge, MA, 2001), 4. **92.** James, *End of Globalization*, 4–7, 13, 15, 198–9, 203–24. **93.** Branko Milanović, *Global Inequality: A New Approach for the Age of Globalization* (Cambridge, MA, and London, 2016), 20. **94.** Ibid., 3, 10–45; François Bourguignon, *The Globalization of Inequality* (Princeton, NJ, 2015), 2–7; Thomas Piketty and Emmanuel Saez, 'Income inequality in the United States, 1913–1998', *Quarterly Journal of Economics* 118 (2003), 1–39; F. Alvaredo, A. Atkinson, T. Piketty and E. Saez, 'The top 1 percent in international and historical perspective', *Journal of Economic Perspectives* 27 (2013), 3–20. **95.** Thomas Piketty, *Capital in the Twenty-First Century* (Cambridge, MA, 2014). **96.** Thomas Piketty, *Capital and Ideology* (Cambridge, MA, 2020), 31–2; Martin Daunton, 'Creating a dynamic society: the tax reforms of the Thatcher government', in Buggeln, Daunton and Nützenadel, eds., *Political Economy*, 32–56. **97.** Jim Tomlinson, 'De-industrialization not decline: a new meta-narrative for post-war British history', *Twentieth Century British History* 27 (2017), 76–99; *idem*, 'Brexit, globalisation and de-industrialisation', Vox CPR portal, 21 April 2017; M. Goos and A. Manning, 'Lousy and lovely jobs: the rising polarisation of work in Britain', *Review of Economics and Statistics* 89 (2007), 124–5; Elhanan Helpman, *Globalization and Inequality* (Cambridge, MA, 2018); Carl Benedikt Frey, *The Technology Trap: Capital, Labor and Power in the Age of Automation* (Princeton, NJ, 2019); Jonathan Haskel and Stian Westlake, *Capitalism without Capital: The Rise of the Intangible Economy* (Princeton, NJ, 2018); Carles Boix, *Democratic Capitalism at the Cross-roads: Technological Change and the Future of Politics* (Princeton, NJ, 2019); Tepper and Hearn, *Myth of Capitalism*, 217, 224, 228–30, 241–8. **98.** Joseph Stiglitz, *The Price of Inequality: How Today's Divided Society Endangers Our Future* (New York, 2012). **99.** See its website at https://www.attac.org/en/overview. **100.** http://www.putpeoplefirst.org.uk and http://www.putpeoplefirst.org.uk/wp-content/uploads/2009/03/ppf-policyplatform.pdf; http://www.brettonwoodsproject.org/. **101.** Piketty, *Capital and Ideology*, ch. 17. **102.** David Goodhart, *The Road to Somewhere: The New Tribes Shaping British Politics* (London, 2017); Maria Sobolewska and Robert Ford, *Brexitland: Identity, Diversity and the Reshaping of British Politics* (Cambridge 2020); Piketty, *Capital and Ideology*, 37–9. **103.** Donald J. Trump, Inaugural address, 20 Jan. 2017, online in Gerhard Peters and John T. Woolley, *The American Presidency Project*. **104.** Michael Kenny and Nick Pearce, *Shadows of Empire: The Anglosphere in British Politics* (Cambridge, 2018), 151–66. **105.** Matthew C. Klein and Michael Pettis, *Trade Wars are Class Wars: How Rising Inequality Distorts the Global Economy and Threatens International Peace* (New Haven, CT, 2020); Atif Mian, Ludwig Straub and Amir Sufi, 'The saving glut of the rich', NBER Working Paper 26941, 2020; *idem*, 'Indebted demand', NBER Working Paper 26940, 2020. **106.** Branko Milanović, *Capitalism, Alone: The Future of the System That Rules the World* (Cambridge, MA, 2019), 5.

26. 'MESSY MULTILATERALISM'

1. Miguel d'Escoto Brockmann, 'Foreword', *Report of the Commission of Experts of the President of the United Nations General Assembly on Reforms of the International Monetary and Financial System*, 21 Sept. 2009, 9. **2.** Online in Gerhard Peters and John T. Woolley, *The American Presidency Project*. **3.** WTO, *Report on G20 trade measures (May 2010 to Oct. 2010)*; Paul Blustein, *Misadventures of the Most Favored Nations: Clashing Egos, Inflated Ambitions, and the Great Shambles of the World Trade System* (New York, 2009), 11. **4.** G. John Ikenberry, *Liberal Leviathan: The Origins, Crisis and Transformation of the American World Order* (Princeton, NJ, 2011), xii, xv, 6, 7, 9, 10, 338–42, 344–8, 357–60. **5.** Daniel W. Drezner, *The System Worked: How the World Stopped Another Great Depression* (New York, 2014), 14, 23, 25–7, 77–9, 100, 106–8, 147–50, 152–5, 175. **6.** Quoted in Steve

Le Vine, 'Obama and the G20: is it 1933 all over again?', Bloomberg Businessweek, 30 March 2009. **7.** Barry Eichengreen, *The Hall of Mirrors: The Great Depression, the Great Recession, and the Uses and Misuses of History* (New York, 2016), 11. **8.** Adam Tooze, 'Reimagining the IMF', *Finance and Development* 56 (June 2019), 30; Chris Giles and Andrew Balls, 'BOE chief urges radical shake-up of IMF', *Financial Times*, 20 Feb. 2006. **9.** Mark Mazower, *Governing the World: The History of an Idea* (London, 2012), xiii. **10.** Krishna Guha, 'IMF must reform to remain relevant', *Financial Times*, 26 Feb. 2008; Quentin Peel, 'Political will for IMF reform is lacking', *Financial Times*, 16 March 2009; Edward Luce and Alan Beattie, 'IMF reforms at risk, warns Boutros-Ghali', *Financial Times*, 21 April 2009; Alan Beattie, 'Retread required', *Financial Times*, 30 Nov. 2009; Markus K. Brunnermaier, Harold James and Jean-Pierre Landau, *The Euro and the Battle of Ideas* (Princeton, NJ, and Oxford, 2016), 295–6; Joseph P. Joyce, *The IMF and Global Financial Crisis: Phoenix Rising?* (Cambridge, 2013), 1–3, 17. **11.** Krishna Guha, 'IMF refuses to rule out use of capital controls', *Financial Times*, 2 Nov. 2009. **12.** IMF, *The Liberalization and Management of Capital Flows: An Institutional View* (Washington, DC, 2012); J. D. Ostry, A. R. Ghosh, K. Habermeier, M. Chamon, M. S. Qureshi and D. B. S. Reinhardt, 'Capital inflows: the role of controls', IMF Staff Position Note SPN10/04, 19 Feb. 2010; José Antonio Ocampo, *Reseting the International Monetary (Non)System* (Oxford, 2017), ch. 4; Paulo Nogueira Batista Jr, 'The IMF, capital account regulation, and emerging market economies', in *Regulating Global Capital Flows for Long-Run Development: Pardee Center Task Force Report*, March 2012, 93–102; Jonathan D. Ostry, Prakash Loungani and Davide Furceri, 'Neoliberalism: oversold?', *Finance and Development* 53 (2016), 38–41; Alan Rappeport, 'IMF reconsiders capital controls opposition', *Financial Times*, 22 Feb. 2010; Alan Beattie, 'IMF study looks at capital controls', *Financial Times*, 13 April 2010; K. Brown, 'Emerging Asia toys with capital controls', *Financial Times*, 1 July 2010; S. Johnson, 'Controls on currencies "doomed"', *Financial Times*, 17 Oct. 2010; Ilene Grabel and Ha-Joon Chang, 'Why capital controls are not all bad', *Financial Times*, 25 Oct. 2010; C. Oliver, 'South Korea may need more capital controls', *Financial Times*, 2 Dec. 2010; Alan Beattie, 'Tensions rise in currency wars', *Financial Times*, 9 Jan. 2011; Alan Beattie, 'IMF drops opposition to capital controls', *Financial Times*, 3 Dec. 2012. **13.** Gita Gopinath, 'Rethinking macroeconomic policy: international economy issues', Peterson Institute for International Economics, 10 Oct. 2017. **14.** Paul Volcker, 'Toward a more cooperative international monetary system: some remarks', in Atish R. Ghosh and Mahvash S. Qureshi, eds., *From Great Depression to Great Recession: The Elusive Quest for International Monetary Cooperation* (Washington, DC, 2017), 215–17. **15.** IMF, 'Toward an integrated policy framework', 8 Oct. 2020. **16.** Christine Lagarde, 'A new global economy for a new generation', 23 Jan. 2013 at www.imf.org; Christine Lagarde, 'An overhaul of the international tax system can wait no longer', *Financial Times*, 11 March 2019. On a mandate for dealing with corruption, see Frank Vogl and William Rhodes, 'Bank–Fund: facing the rising challenge of corruption', in Bretton Woods Committee, *Revitalizing the Spirit of Bretton Woods*, July 2019, 336–46; Jennifer Rankin, 'IMF steps up fresh bailout criticism over debt relief pledge', *Guardian*, 17 July 2015; Ivan Tulley, 'IMF: no cash now for Greece because Europe hasn't provided debt relief', *Wall Street Journal*, 25 May 2016; David Lipton, 'Foreword', in Ghosh and Qureshi, eds., *From Great Depression*, vii. **17.** Alexander E. Kentikelenis, Thomas H. Stubbs and Lawrence P. King, 'IMF conditionality and development policy space, 1985–2014', *Review of International Political Economy* 23 (2016), 544, 546; Rebecca Ray, Kevin P. Gallagher and William Kring, 'IMF austerity since the global financial crisis: new data, same trend, similar determinants', Boston University Global Development Policy Center, Global Economic Governance Initiative Working Paper 11/2020. **18.** Pascal Lamy, 'Crisis is opportunity to restore coherence in global economic governance', 8 Dec. 2010 and 'Lamy calls for addressing macro-economic imbalances through cooperation', 19 Nov 2010, both on WTO website; Pascal Lamy, 'Global governance requires localising global issues', in Ricardo Meléndez-Ortiz, Christine Bellmann and Miguel Rodriguez Mendoza, eds., *The Future of the WTO: Confronting the Challenges* (Geneva, 2012), 152–5. **19.** 'Azevêdo launches "rolling set of meetings" aimed at delivering success in Bali', 9 Sept. 2013, WTO website. **20.** Quoted in Shawn Donnan, 'WTO up in the air', *Financial Times*, 2 Dec. 2013. **21.** Amrita Narlikar, 'New powers in the club: the challenges of global governance', *International Affairs* 86 (2010), 717–28; *The Future of the WTO: Addressing Institutional Challenges in the New Millennium: Report by the Consultative Board to the Director General Supachai Panitchpakdi* (Geneva, 2004). **22.** Shawn Donnan, 'WTO approves global trade deal', *Financial Times*, 7 Dec. 2013; Shawn Donnan, 'Global deal shows "coming alive" of WTO', *Financial Times*, 8 Dec. 2013; 'Bali breathes life into global trade', *Financial Times*, 8 Dec. 2013; Larry Elliott, 'How deal in Bali brought WTO back from the brink', *Guardian*, 19 Dec. 2013; 'The Doha round dies a merciful death', *Financial Times*, 21 Dec. 2015; World Trade Organization Ministerial Conference. Ninth Session, Bali, 3–6 Dec. 2013, Ministerial Declaration and Decisions, and Nairobi Ministerial Declaration adopted 19 Dec. 2015. **23.** Jagdish Bhagwati, *Termites in the Trading System: How Preferential Agreements Undermine Free Trade* (Oxford, 2008); Robert Zoellick, 'Questions for the world's next trade chief', *Financial Times*, 1 April 2013; Gary Clyde Hufbauer and Jeffrey J. Schott, 'Will the World Trade Organization enjoy a bright future?', Peterson Institute for International Economics Policy Brief 12-11, May 2012. **24.** Donnan, 'WTO up in the air'; Shawn Donnan, 'Pascal Lamy questions US-led regional trade talks', *Financial Times*, 18 July 2013; Zaki Laïdl, 'Trade deals show power politics is back', *Financial Times*, 31 March 2013; Philip Stephens, 'Transatlantic pact promises bigger prize', *Financial Times*, 14 Feb. 2013; M. Fratzscher, 'EU–US free trade deal could be costly', *Financial Times*, 21 Feb. 2013; Adam Thomson, 'WTO must adapt to remain relevant', *Financial Times*, 5 April 2013; European Commission, Final Report of the EU–US High Level Working Group on Jobs and Growth, 11 Feb. 2013. **25.** George Parker, Vanessa Houlder and James Politi, 'EU–US trade talks launched amid French fury with Brussels', *Financial Times*, 17 June 2013; Shawn Donnan, 'World Trade Organisation's Pascal Lamy defends Doha talks round', *Financial Times*, 18 July 2013; Christian Oliver, Shawn Donnan and Anne-Sylvvaine Chassany, 'Europe and France in race to keep TTIP on track', *Financial Times*, 31 May 2016; Leo Cendrowicz, 'Europeans fight US trade deal with fear of McHospitals, fracking under the Eiffel Tower', *Daily Beast*, 22 April 2015; Karel De Gucht, 'Foreword', in Jean-Federic Morin, Tereza Novotnà, Frederic Ponjaert and Mario Tella, eds., *The Politics of Transatlantic Trade Negotiations: TTIP in a Globalized World* (Farnham, 2015), xvii; Transatlantic trade and investment partnership (TTIP) – trade – European Commission: EU negotiating texts in TTIP, 14 July 2016 and Council Decisions of 15 April 2019; T. J. Bollyky and A. Bradford, 'Getting to yes on transatlantic trade', *Foreign Affairs*, 10 July 2013; Susanne Kraatz, 'The transatlantic trade partnership and labour', European Parliament Think Tank, 1 Dec. 2014; S. Jeffries, 'What is TTIP and why we should be angry about it', *Guardian*, 13 Aug. 2015; Lee Williams, 'What is TTIP? And six reasons why the answer should scare you', *Independent*, 6 Oct. 2015; European Commission, Final Report High Level Working Group on Jobs and Growth, 11 Feb. 2013; Max Otte, 'Vollige Entmachtung der Politik', 3Sat, 8 April 2016. **26.** Shawn Donnan, 'Follow "#TPP" to discover the trade netherworld', *Financial Times*, 18 Dec. 2013; 'Days to stop the corporate death star', at https://secure.avaaz.org/campaign/en/stop_ttip_4; 'Stop the corporate death star', at https://secure.avaaz.org/campaign/en/stop_the_corporate_death_star_d/. **27.** Alex Newman, 'Trade agenda: full story' and 'Stop the globalists' trade agenda' at https://www.jbs.org/action-projects/stop-the-free-trade-agenda. **28.** European Council decision, 15 April 2019. **29.** Adam Tooze, *Crashed: How a Decade of Financial Crises Changed the World* (London, 2018), 206–8. **30.** Program on Negotiation, Harvard Law School, 'Renegotiation lessons from the NAFTA talks', 5 July 2021 at www.harvard.edu. **31.** 'Brazilian President calls on UN to take role in responding to financial crisis', 23 Sept. 2008 at https://news.un.org/en/story/2008/09/274112. **32.** Report of the Commission of Experts of the President of the United Nations General Assembly on Reforms of the International Monetary and Financial System, 21 Sept. 2009; Harvey Morris, 'UN's turbulent priest refuses to go quietly', *Financial Times*, 7 June 2009. **33.** Summit on financial markets and the world economy, Washington, 14–15 Nov. 2008, at https://georgewbush-whitehouse.archives.gov /infocus/financialmarkets/; Colin I. Bradford, Johannes F. Linn and Paul Martin, 'Global governance breakthrough: the G20 summit and the future agenda', Brookings Institute, 17 Dec. 2008; Andrew F. Cooper, 'The G20 as an improvised crisis committee and/or a contested "steering committee" for the world', *International Affairs* 86 (2010), 741–57; Richard Haass, 'The case for messy multilateralism', *Financial Times*, 5 Jan. 2010; Anthony Payne, 'How many Gs are there in "global governance" after the crisis? The perspective of the "marginal majority" of the world's states', *International Affairs* 86 (2010), 729–40; C. Schenk, 'Lessons from history', in Paula Subacchi and John Driffill, eds., *Beyond the Dollar: Rethinking the International Monetary System* (London, 2010), 22; G20 website, https://www.G20.org/about-the-G20.html; Martina Larionova and John K. Kirton, eds., *The G8–G20 Relationship in Global Governance* (Aldershot, 2015) discusses the role of the two bodies.   34. Martin Wolf, 'Currencies clash in new age of beggar-my-neighbour', *Financial Times*, 29 Sept. 2010.   35. Robert Skidelsky, *Keynes: The Return of the Master* (London, 2009), 184; Robert Skidelsky, 'A golden opportunity for monetary reform', *Financial Times*, 9 Nov. 2010; Jamil Anderlini, 'China calls for new reserve currency', *Financial Times*, 24 March 2009.   36. Gavyn Davies, 'A novel G20 proposal from Tim Geithner', *Financial Times*, 22 Oct. 2010; Christian Oliver, Song Jung-a, Alan Beattie and Chris Giles, 'US pushes plan on exchange rates', *Financial Times*, 23 Oct. 2010; Martin Wolf, 'Current account targets are a way back to the future', *Financial Times*, 2 Nov. 2010; Tooze, *Crashed*, 266–8.   37. Alan Beattie and Song Jung-a, 'Doubts grow on prospects for G20', *Financial Times*, 19 Oct. 2010; Alan Beattie, 'International economy: a display of disunity', *Financial Times*, 22 Oct. 2010; 'Seoul searching', *Financial Times*, 8 Nov. 2010; Gideon Rachman, 'The world's seven pillars of friction', *Financial Times*, 8 Nov. 2010; Yao Yang, 'Beijing can afford to stand firm in Seoul', *Financial Times*, 9 Nov. 2010; Chris Giles, ' "Seoul consensus" to establish nine pillars for growth', *Financial Times*, 10 Nov. 2010; Alan Beattie, 'Deep fractures change hopes of G20 breakthrough', *Financial Times*, 10 Nov. 2010; Chris Giles, Alan Beattie, Christian Oliver, 'Leaders warn on Doha deadlock', *Financial Times*, 11 Nov. 2010; Christian Oliver, Chris Giles and Alan Beattie, 'Forget summit failures, look at the G20 record', *Financial Times*, 12 Nov. 2010; 'G20 show how not to run the world', *Financial Times*, 12 Nov. 2010; Chris Giles, Alan Beattie and Christian Oliver, 'G20 shuns US on trade and currencies', *Financial Times*, 12 Nov. 2010.   38. Brent Scowcroft, 'A world in transformation', *The National Interest* 119, special issue: The crisis of the old order (2012), 8.   39. Ian Bremmer and Nouriel Roubini, 'A G-zero world: the new economic club will produce conflict not cooperation', *Foreign Affairs* 90 (2011), 2.   40. C. Fred Bergsten, *The United States and the World Economy* (Washington, DC, 2005); *idem*, 'A partnership of equals', *Foreign Affairs* 87 (2008), 57–69; *idem*, 'Two's company', *Foreign Affairs* 88 (2009), 169–70; Niall Ferguson, *The Ascent of Money: A Financial History of the World* (New York, 2008); Geoffrey Garrett, 'G2 in G20: China, the United States and the world after the global financial crisis', *Global Policy* 1 (2010), 29–39; Martin Wolf, *The Shifts and the Shocks: What We've Learned – and Have Still to Learn – from the Financial Crisis* (London, 2014), 10.   41. Peter Temin and David Vines, *The Leaderless Economy: Why the World Economic System Fell Apart and How to Fix It* (Princeton, NJ, 2013), 2–3, 246–55.   42. George Magnus, 'China and the US are too intertwined to keep up the trade war', *Financial Times*, 8 June 2019.   43. Robert Zoellick, 'Modernizing multilateralism and markets', Peterson Institute for International Economics, 6 Oct. 2008.   44. Eric Helleiner, 'A Bretton Woods moment? The 2007–2008 crisis and the future of global finance', *International Affairs* 86 (2020), 619–36.   45. Haass, 'The case for messy multilateralism'; Cooper, 'G20', 756–7.   46. T. Shanmugaratnam, 'We need a new, more co-operative international order', *Financial Times*, 11 Oct. 2018; *idem*, 'Building the new cooperative international order', in Bretton Woods Committee, *Revitalizing the Spirit of Bretton Woods*, July 2019, 48–54; Making the Global Financial System Work for All: Report of the G20 Eminent Persons Group on Global Financial Governance, Oct 2018; Gillian Tett, 'The business case against Bretton Woods', *Financial Times*, 25 July 2019.   47. James Boughton, 'A new Bretton Woods', *Finance and Development* 46 (2009), 44–6 offers some thoughts but is too optimistic that inclusivity will work.   48. M. Wolf, 'The folly of Donald Trump's bilateralism in global trade', *Financial Times*, 14 March 2017; Robert Zoellick, 'The US will be the loser from Trump's focus on trade deficits', *Financial Times*, 24 May 2018.   49. Chad P. Brown and Melina Kolb, 'Trump's trade war timeline: an up-to-date guide', updated 21 June 2022, Peterson Institute for International Economics.   50. https://www.bbc.co.uk/news

/business-46395379. **51.** 'WTO report shows trade restrictions among G20 continuing at historic high levels', 24 June 2019 at https://www.wto.org/english/news_e/news19_e /trdev_24jun19_e.htm; WTO, *Report on G20 trade measures mid-October 2018 to mid-May 2019*, 24 June 2019, 28 at https://www.wto.org/english/news_e/news19_e/g20_wto_eport _june19_e.pdf. **52.** Chris Giles and Robin Harding, 'G20 relief but experts say trade "ceasefire" might be temporary', *Financial Times*, 1 July 2019; James Politi, Benedict Mander and Andres Schipani, 'Divided G20 vows to overhaul global trade', *Financial Times*, 1 Dec. 2018; Robin Harding, Alan Beattie and James Politi, 'Early talks reveal G20 members' frustration with China and the US', *Financial Times*, 20 June 2019. **53.** US Department of the Treasury Press Releases, 5 Aug. 2019: Treasury designates China as a currency manipulator; Demetri Sevastopulo and Coby Smith, 'US Treasury official labels China as currency manipulator', *Financial Times*, 6 Aug. 2019; Tom Mitchell and Xinnig Liu, 'Why China's managed float of renminbi has drawn US ire', *Financial Times*, 6 Aug. 2019. The decision was reversed in 2020: James Politi and Brendan Greeley, 'US lifts China "currency manipulator" tag ahead of trade deal', *Financial Times*, 14 Jan. 2020. **54.** Shawn Donnan, 'US says China WTO membership was a mistake', *Financial Times*, 19 Jan. 2018; 2017 Report to Congress on China's WTO Compliance: USTR, January 2018; 2018 Report to Congress on China's WTO Compliance: USTR, February 2019. **55.** Jeffrey Schott and Euijin Jung, 'The United States wins more WTO cases than China in US–China trade disputes', Peterson Institute of International Economics, 22 Nov. 2019; *idem*, 'In US–China trade disputes, the WTO usually sides with the United States', Peterson Institute of International Economics, 12 March 2019. **56.** Shawn Donnan, 'WTO faces an identity crisis as Trump weighs going it alone', *Financial Times*, 6 Dec. 2017; Alan Beattie, 'US bullying on trade deals undermines global rule book', *Financial Times*, 4 March 2019. **57.** Chris Giles, 'Merkel defends global order with veiled swipe at Trump', *Financial Times*, 23 Jan. 2019. **58.** Ted Posner, 'Do we really need fast track?', International economic law and policy blog, 20 Dec. 2013 at http://worldtradelaw. typepad.com/ielblog/2013/12/do-we-really-need-fast-track; Edward Luce, 'Obama cannot lead from behind on trade', *Financial Times*, 8 Dec. 2013; Donnan, 'Follow "#TPP"'; Aime Williams, FT Trade Secrets Newsletter, 30 June 2021; Karen Hansen-Kuhn and Sharon Anglin Treat, 'Good riddance? Fast-track fades away', *The Hill*, 30 June 2021. **59.** James Politi and Chris Giles, 'Christine Lagarde urges world to "de-escalate" trade disputes', *Financial Times*, 1 Oct. 2018. **60.** David Miliband, 'Beyond development: rethinking aid in an era of fragile states', *Revitalizing the Spirit of Bretton Woods*, 368–75.

27. FAIR CAPITALISM AND GLOBALIZATION

1. *The Collected Writings of John Maynard Keynes, Volume 21: Activities 1931–39. World Crises and Politics in Britain and America* (Cambridge, 1971), 239. **2.** Adam Tooze, *Shutdown: How Covid Shook the World's Economy* (London, 2021), 88, 107–9, 111–12, 127–30, 141–9. **3.** Evangelos Kontopantelis *et al.*, 'Excess years of life lost to COVID-19 and other causes of death by sex, neighbourhood deprivation, and region in England and Wales during 2020: a registry-based study', *PLOS Medicine* 19, 15 Feb. 2022; David Spiegelhalter and Anthony Masters, *Covid by Numbers: Making Sense of the Pandemic with Data* (London, 2021). **4.** Denys Dukhovnov and Magali Barbieri, 'County-level socio-economic disparities in Covid-19 mortality in the USA', *International Journal of Epidemiology* 51 (2022), 419. **5.** Peter Hennessy, *A Duty of Care: Britain Before and After Covid* (London, 2022); Hilary Cooper and Simon Szreter, *After the Virus: Lessons from the Past for a Better Future* (Cambridge, 2021). **6.** Tooze, *Shutdown*, 11–16, 129–30, 132, 292–4. **7.** Address to the 74th session of the UN General Assembly by António Gutteres, and remarks by presidents Jair Bolsonaro and Donald Trump, 24 Sept. 2019. **8.** Tooze, *Shutdown*, 32–4. **9.** Tooze, *Shutdown*, 63, 65–6, 242–4; 'G20 must rise to the challenge of global crisis', *Financial Times*, 5 July 2021. **10.** Stephen D. King, *Grave New World: The End of Globalization, The Return of History* (New Haven, CT, 2017), 225; Dani Rodrik, *Straight Talk on Trade: Ideas for a Sane World Economy* (Princeton, NJ, and Oxford, 2018), 14, 47, 202–12, 218–27, 233–5;

Dani Rodrik, *One Economics, Many Recipes: Globalization, Institutions and Economic Growth* (Princeton, NJ, 2007), 8–9, 195–6, 199–200, 203, 205; Mervyn King, *The End of Alchemy: Money, Banking and the Future of the Global Economy* (London, 2016), 351–2; Martin Wolf, 'Capitalism and democracy: the strain is showing', *Financial Times*, 30 Aug. 2016; Lawrence Summers, 'Voters deserve responsible nationalism, not reflex globalism', *Financial Times*, 10 July 2016; Claire Jones and Alex Barker, 'Do more to help globalisation's losers, say champions of liberalism', *Financial Times*, 13 Sept. 2016; Kevin O'Rourke, 'Capitalism: worries of the 1930s for the 2020s', *Oxford Review of Economic Policy* 27 (2021), 661. **11.** Robert Kuttner, *Can Democracy Survive Global Capitalism?* (New York, 2018), xiv, xxii, 307; Tooze, *Shutdown*, 292–4. **12.** Alan Beattie, 'WTO in for the long haul on ecommerce talks', *Financial Times*, 9 May 2019; Bertlesmann Stiftung, *Revitalizing Multilateral Governance at the World Trade Organization: Report of the High-Level Board of Experts on the Future of Global Trade Governance* (Berlin, 2018). **13.** Sam Fleming and Chris Giles, 'EU risks trade fight over carbon border tax adjustment', *Financial Times*, 16 Oct. 2019. **14.** For example, Bernhard Hoekman, 'Proposals for WTO reform: a synthesis and assessment', in Amrita Narlikar, Martin Daunton and Robert M. Stern, eds., *The Oxford Handbook on the World Trade Organization* (Oxford, 2012), 743–75; Steven Bernstein and Erin Hanna, 'The WTO and institutional (in)coherence in global economic governance', in Narlikar, Daunton and Stern, eds., *Oxford Handbook on the WTO*, 778–808; Ngozi Okonjo-Iweala, 'WTO members must intensify cooperation', *Financial Times*, 2 March 2021; Alan Beattie, 'The WTO's marathon exercise in staying alive', *Financial Times*, 17 June 2022. **15.** For example, Martin Wolf, *The Shifts and the Shocks: What We've Learned – and Have Still to Learn – from the Financial Crisis* (London, 2014), 193–222. **16.** Jonathan Aldred, *Licence to be Bad: How Economics Corrupted Us* (London, 2019), 246–61; Mark Carney, *Value(s): Building a Better World For All* (London, 2021), 5; Michael J. Sandel, *What Money Can't Buy: The Moral Limits of Markets* (New York, 2012), 4–15; Kay quote from Philip Mirowski, *Never Let a Serious Crisis Go to Waste: How Neoliberals Survived the Financial Meltdown* (London, 2013), 3; Robert Skidelsky, *Money and Government: A Challenge to Mainstream Economics* (London, 2018). **17.** Willem Buiter, 'The unfortunate uselessness of most "state of the art" academic monetary economics', 6 March 2009 at https://voxeu.org/article/macroeconomics -crisis-irrelevance. **18.** King, *End of Alchemy*, 3, 11, 370; also Skidelsky, *Money and Government*, pt IV. **19.** John Kay and Mervyn King, *Radical Uncertainty: Decision-Making for an Unknowable Future* (London, 2020), xiv–xvi; Paul Collier and John Kay, *Greed is Dead: Politics After Individualism* (London, 2021), xiii, xx–xxiii, 3–4, 7, 8, 14, 47; Michael J. Sandel, *The Tyranny of Merit: What's Become of the Common Good?* (New York, 2020), 212, 226–7; *idem*, *What Money Can't Buy*, 203. **20.** Joseph Stiglitz, 'Crime shouldn't pay', *Times Literary Supplement*, 7 June 2019; David Vines and Samuel Wills, 'The rebuilding macroeconomic theory project: an analytical assessment', *Oxford Review of Economic Policy* 34 (2018), 1–42; *idem*, 'The rebuilding macroeconomic theory project, Part II: Multiple equilibrium, toy models and policy models in a new macroeconomics paradigm', *Oxford Review of Economic Policy* 36 (2020), 427–97; Martin Guzman and Joseph Stiglitz, 'Towards a dynamic disequilibrium theory with randomness', *Oxford Review of Economic Policy* 36 (2020), 621–74; Robert Shiller, *Narrative Economics: How Stories Go Viral and Drive Economic Events* (Princeton, NJ, 2019); Paul Collier, Diane Coyle, Colin Mayer and Martin Wolf, 'Capitalism: what has gone wrong, what needs to change, and how it can be fixed', *Oxford Review of Economic Policy* 37 (2021), 647. **21.** Anne Case and Angus Deaton, *Deaths of Despair and the Future of Capitalism* (Princeton, NJ, 2020), 11, 13–14, 209–10, 230–44, 256–7; Joseph E. Stiglitz, *The Price of Inequality: How Today's Divided Society Endangers our Future* (London, 2013), ch. 2. **22.** Mariana Mazzucato, *The Value of Everything: Making and Taking in the Global Economy* (London, 2018); Brett Christophers, *Who Owns the Economy and Who Pays for It?* (London, 2020), xx–xxxi, 32–3, 36–7, 40, 42, 47, 92–3, 378–80, 386–405. **23.** Milton Friedman, 'The social responsibility of business is to increase its profit', *New York Times*, 13 Sept. 1970; Tim Wu, *The Curse of Bigness: Antitrust in the New Gilded Age* (New York, 2018), 16, 17, 33, 77, 82, 83–92, 103, 106, 109. **24.** Roosevelt Institute, 'Joseph Stiglitz on "ersatz capitalism" and moral bankruptcy', Roosevelt Institute, 20 Jan. 2010;

Lawrence Mishel and Jessica Schieder, 'CEO compensation surged in 2017', Economic Policy Institute, 16 Aug. 2018 (epi.org/152123), 1. **25.** Thomas Philippon, *The Great Reversal: How America Gave Up on Free Markets* (Cambridge, MA, 2019), 9, 10, 48–51, 97, 103, 107, 110, 122–5, 137, 141-3, 147, 151, 174–5; *idem*, 'The case for free markets', *Oxford Review of Economic Policy* 37 (2021), 707–19. **26.** *IMF World Economic Outlook. April 2019: Growth Slackens, Precarious Recovery*, ch. 2 on 'The rise of corporate market power and its macroeconomic effects'. **27.** Kevin P. Gallagher and Richard Kozul-Wright, *A New Multilateralism for Shared Prosperity: Geneva Principles for a Global Green New Deal* (Boston, MA, 2019), 12; Kevin P. Gallagher and Richard Kozul-Wright, 'Crocodile capitalism and the multilateral system crisis', *Financial Times*, 10 April 2019; Jason Furman and Peter Orszag, 'Slower productivity and higher inequality: are they related?', Peterson Institute for International Economics, Working Paper 18-4, June 2018. **28.** Jonathan D. Ostry, Andrew Berg and Charalambos G. Tsangarides, 'Redistribution, inequality and growth', IMF Discussion Note, April 2014, 4; Era Dabla-Norris, Kalpana Kochhar, Nujin Suphaphiphat, Frantisek Ricka and Euridiki Tsounta, 'Causes and consequences of income inequality: a global perspective', IMF Staff Discussion Note, June 2015, 4, 6–9; Stiglitz, *The Price of Inequality*, chs. 5 and 6; Richard Wilkinson and Kate Pickett, *The Spirit Level: Why Equality is Better for Everyone* (London, 2009); Michael Marmot, *The Health Gap: The Challenge of an Unequal World* (London, 2015). **29.** John Harwood, 'Democratic Sen Elizabeth Warren: "I am a capitalist" – but markets need to work for more than just the rich', CNBC, 24 July 2018; Business Roundtable, 'Statement on the Purpose of a Corporation', 19 Aug. 2019; letter from Elizabeth Warren to Jamie Dimon and Doug McMillon, 17 Sept. 2020. See also Dominic Barton, 'Capitalism for the long term', *Harvard Business Review* (March 2011). **30.** Naomi Rovnick, 'Bridgewater's Dalio warns US inequality risks social conflict', *Financial Times*, 5 April 2019; Andrew Edgecliffe-Johnson, 'Why American CEOs are worried about capitalism', *Financial Times*, 22 April 2019; Andrew Ross Sorkin, 'Bridgewater's Ray Dalio tops the list of hedge fund manager compensation', *New York Times*, 30 April 2019. **31.** Sam Long, 'The financialization of the American elite', *American Affairs*, 20 Aug. 2019; 'Big business is beginning to accept broader social responsibilities', *The Economist*, 22 Aug. 2019; Council of Institutional Investors Responds to Business Roundtable Statement on Corporate Purpose at https://www.cii.org/aug19_brt_response. **32.** British Academy, *Principles for Purposeful Business: How to Deliver the Framework for the Future of the Corporation: An Agenda for Business in the 2020s and Beyond* (London, 2019); Colin Mayer, *Prosperity: Better Business Makes the Greater Good* (Oxford, 2018), 2, 230–32; Rebecca M. Henderson, 'Changing the purpose of the corporation to rebalance capitalism', *Oxford Review of Economic Policy* 37 (2021), 838–50; Colm Kelly and Dennis J. Snower, 'Capitalism recoupled', *Oxford Review of Economic Policy* 37 (2021), 851–63; Pope Francis, Encyclical letter, *Laudato Si': Care for Our Common Home*, 24 May 2015, paras 124-9, 195; Andrew Edgecliffe-Johnson, 'The war on woke capitalism', *Financial Times*, 27 May 2022. **33.** Case and Deaton, *Deaths of Despair*, 12, 147. **34.** Brett Christophers, *Rentier Capitalism: Who Owns the Economy, and Who Pays for It* (London and New York, 2020), xxvi, 277–8. **35.** Stiglitz, *The Price of Inequality*, 104; Case and Deaton, *Deaths of Despair*, 8. **36.** Jannick Damgaard, Thomas Elkjaer and Niels Johannesen, 'The rise of phantom investments', *Finance and Development* 56 (2019), 12–13. **37.** Brad Setser, 'The global con hidden in Trump's tax reform law, revealed', *New York Times*, 6 Feb. 2019. **38.** Andrew Hill, Mehreen Khan and Richard Waters, 'The global hunt to tax Big Tech', *Financial Times*, 2 Nov. 2018; Mark Bou Mansour, 'IMF support for radical overhaul of international tax rules welcomed by Tax Justice Network', 10 March 2019, at https://www.taxjustice.net/2019/03/10/imf-support-for-radical-overhaul-of-international-tax-rules-welcomed-by-tax-justice-network/; Christine Lagarde, 'An overhaul of the international tax system can wait no longer', *Financial Times*, 10 March 2019; Ernesto Crivelli, Ruud De Mooij and Michael Keen, 'Base erosion, profit shifting and developing countries', IMF Working Paper/15/118, May 2015; IMF, 'Corporate taxation in the global economy', Policy Paper 19/006, 2019; 'IMF Executive Board reviews corporate taxation in the global economy', 10 March 2019; Benjamin Carton, Emilio Fernandez-Corugedor and Benjamin Hunt, 'Corporate tax reform: from income to cash flow taxes', IMF Working

Paper/19/13; Martin Wolf, 'The world needs to change the way it taxes companies', *Financial Times*, 7 March 2019; IMF, 'Spillovers in international corporate taxation', 9 May 2014; Republican Party, *A Better Way: Our View for a Confident America*, June 2016; The Platform for Collaboration on Tax, PCT Progress Report 2021. The best account of tax havens is Vanessa Ogle, 'Archipelago capitalism: tax havens, offshore money, and the state, 1950s–1970s', *American Historical Review 122 (2017)*, 1431–58. **39.** James Politi, Aime Williams, Chris Giles, Sam Fleming and Miles Johnson, 'US removes stumbling block to global deal on digital tax', *Financial Times*, 26 Feb. 2021; Chris Giles, 'IMF proposes "solidarity tax" on pandemic winners and wealthy', *Financial Times*, 7 April 2021; James Politi, 'Janet Yellen calls for global minimum corporate tax', *Financial Times*, 5 April 2021; 'Biden's global tax plan is not without its challenges', *Financial Times*, 12 April 2021; 'Biden's global tax plans are brave and bold', *Financial Times*, 9 April 2021; 'A grand bargain: how the radical US corporate tax plan would work', *Financial Times*, 8 April 2021; Martin Sandbu, 'The good, the bad and the ugly of the global tax reform deal', *Financial Times*, 4 July 2021; Chris Giles, Emma Agyemang and Aime Williams, '136 nations agree to biggest corporate tax deal in a century', *Financial Times*, 8 Oct. 2021; Alex Cobham, 'G20 could improve on "one-sided" global tax reform', *Financial Times*, 11 June 2021; Chris Giles, Leila Abboud and Emma Agyemang, 'Global tax deal backers battle to win over holdout centres', *Financial Times*, 29 June 2021; Glenn Hubbard, 'Governments should tax cash flows, not global corporate income', *Financial Times*, 9 June 2021; Chris Giles and Delphine Strauss, 'G7 tax deal is "starting point" on road to global reform', *Financial Times*, 6 June 2021; Mary McDougall, 'Germany to push ahead with minimum business tax deal in Europe', *Financial Times*, 6 Sept. 2022; Rebecca Kysar, 'US must follow Europe's lead on global minimum tax – or be left behind', *Financial Times*, 19 Dec. 2022. **40.** Jim Tomlinson, 'The strange survival of "embedded liberalism": national economic management and globalization in Britain from 1944', *Twentieth Century British History* 32 (2021), 501; T. Clark and Andrew Dilnot, *Long-Term Trends in British Taxation and Spending* (London, 2000), 8; Andrew Glyn, 'The assessment: how far has globalization gone?', *Oxford Review of Economics* 20 (2004), 10. **41.** Emanuel Saez and Gabriel Zucman, *The Triumph of Injustice: How the Rich Dodge Taxes and How to Make them Pay* (New York, 2019), x–xvi; Thomas Piketty, *Capital in the Twenty-First Century* (Cambridge, MA, 2014), 506–7; idem, *Capital and Ideology* (Cambridge, MA, 2020), 452–3; Jens Beckert, *Inherited Wealth* (Princeton, NJ, 2008), 189–93; Michael J. Graetz and Ian Shapiro, *Death by a Thousand Cuts: The Fight over Taxing Inherited Wealth* (Princeton, NJ, 2005); Stuart Adam and Helen Miller, 'Taxing work and investment across legal forms: pathways to well-designed taxes', Institute of Fiscal Studies, 26 Jan. 2021. **42.** Chris Giles, 'IMF proposes "solidarity tax" on pandemic winners and wealthy', *Financial Times*, 7 April 2021; IMF, *Fiscal Monitor*, April 2021, 27. **43.** Piketty, *Capital and Ideology*, 679. **44.** Saez and Zucman, *Triumph of Injustice*, xiv–xvi, 195; Piketty, *Capital*, 515; Edgecliffe-John, 'Why American CEOs are worried'; Tim Bond, 'A wealth tax is the buffer rich nations need', *Financial Times*, 8 Feb. 2021; Martin Wolf, 'Why rigged capitalism is damaging liberal democracy', *Financial Times*, 18 Sept. 2019; Arun Advani, Emma Chamberlain and Andy Summers, *Final Report, Wealth Tax Commission: A Wealth Tax for the UK* (London, 2020). **45.** Lauren Fedor and James Politi, 'Democrats' proposed billionaires tax collapses after resistance from moderates', *Financial Times*, 28 Oct. 2021. **46.** Martin Wolf, 'We must accept higher taxes to fund health and social care', *Financial Times*, 29 Nov. 2021. **47.** Adam Tooze, 'Should we be scared of the coronavirus debt mountain', *Guardian*, 27 April 2020; Barry Eichengreen, Asmaa El-Ganainy, Rui Esteves and Kris James Mitchener, *In Defense of Public Debt* (New York, 2021), 210, 223; A. B. Atkinson, *Inequality: What Can Be Done?* (Cambridge, MA, 2015), 172–8; see also *World Economic and Financial Surveys. Fiscal Monitor 2018. Monitoring Public Wealth* (Washington, DC, 2018). **48.** Raghuram Rajan, 'Communities, the state, and markets: the case for inclusive localism', *Oxford Review of Economic Policy* 37 (2021), 811–23; Paul Collier, *The Future of Capitalism: Facing the New Anxieties* (London, 2018), 3, 19, ch. 7; Robert Putnam, *Our Kids: The American Dream in Crisis* (New York, 2015), 242–60; Collier and Kay, *Greed is Dead*, 138–50; Carney, *Value(s)*, 454–514; Case and Deaton, *Deaths of Despair*, 245–62; Dani Rodrik and Stefanie Stantcheva, 'Fixing capitalism's good jobs problem',

Oxford Review of Economic Policy 37 (2021), 824–37; Carl Benedikt Frey, *The Technology Trap: Capital, Labor and Power in the Age of Automation* (Princeton, NJ, 2019), 346–54; Charles Boix, *Democratic Capitalism at the Crossroads: Technological Change and the Function of Politics* (Princeton, NJ, 2019), 204–15. **49.** Minouche Shafik, 'Capitalism needs a new social contract', *Oxford Review of Economic Policy* 37 (2021), 758–72; *idem*, *What We Owe Each Other: A New Social Contract* (London, 2021). **50.** Stephen G. Cecchetti and Enisse Kharroubi, 'Why does financial sector growth crowd out real economic growth?', BIS Working Paper 490, Feb. 2015. **51.** Thomas Philippon and Ariell Reshef, 'Wages and human capital in the US financial industry, 1909–2006', NBER Working Paper 14644, Jan. 2009. **52.** Gillian Tett, 'Five surprising outcomes of the financial crash', *Financial Times*, 6 Sept. 2018; Wolf, *Shifts and the Shocks*, 10–11. **53.** Gita Gopinath, 'Rethinking international macroeconomic policy', in Olivier Blanchard and Lawrence H. Summers, eds., *Evolution or Revolution? Rethinking Macroeconomic Policy after the Great Recession* (Cambridge, MA, 2019), 294. **54.** Sheldon Garon, *Beyond our Means: Why America Spends While the World Saves* (Princeton, NJ, and Oxford, 2012), 332–55; Christophers, *Rentier Capitalism*, 47, 92; James D. G. Wood, 'Can household debt influence income inequality? Evidence from Britain, 1966–2016', *British Journal of Politics and International Relations* 22 (2019), 25, 36–9; Jonathan Haskel and Stian Westlake, *Capitalism without Capital: The Rise of the Intangible Economy* (Princeton, NJ, 2018), 166, 218–21. **55.** Raghuram Rajan, *Fault Lines: How Hidden Fractures Still Threaten the World Economy* (Princeton, NJ, and Oxford, 2011), ch. 8. **56.** King, *End of Alchemy*, 260, 270–81, 288–9, 367–8. **57.** Damgaard, Elkjaer and Johannesen, 'The rise of phantom investments'; Thomas Elkjaer and Jannick Damgaard, 'How digitalization and globalization have remapped the global FDI network', Sept. 2018 at http://www.oecd.org/iaos2018/programme/IAOS-OECD2018_Elkjaer-Damgaard.pdf; Tamim Bayoumi, *Unfinished Business: Unexplored Causes of the Financial Crisis and the Lessons Yet to be Learned* (New Haven, CT, 2017), 178; Wolf, *Shifts and the Shocks*, 285–8. **58.** Tooze, *Shutdown*, 301–2; Maurice Obstfeld, 'The global capital market reconsidered', *Oxford Review of Economic Policy* 37 (2021), 690–706. **59.** Colby Smith and Robin Wigglesworth, 'Why the coming emerging markets debt crisis will be messy', *Financial Times*, 12 May 2020. **60.** Asian Infrastructure Investment Bank website; 'US anger at Britain joining Chinese investment bank AIIB', *Guardian*, 13 March 2015; https://findchina.info/china-does-not-control-aiib-says-bank-chief; Smith and Wigglesworth, 'Why the coming emerging markets debt crisis will be messy'; Colby Smith, 'Belt and Road or debt trap?', *Financial Times*, 24 July 2018; Farhan Bokhari and Kiran Stacey, 'Pakistan hits back at US resistance to IMF bailout', *Financial Times*, 31 July 2018; *idem*, 'Pakistan gains guarantee of China's financial backing', *Financial Times*, 13 Aug 2018; 'China's reputation as development financier on the line', *Financial Times*, 10 Sept. 2018; Farhan Bokhari and Stephanie Findlay, 'Pakistan unveils austerity budget in bid to secure IMF loan', *Financial Times*, 11 June 2019; Steve Johnson, 'Frontier market debt at 15 year high', *Financial Times*, 8 March 2019; James Kynge, Kathrin Hille, Benjamin Parkin and Jonathan Wheatley, 'China reckons with its first overseas debt crisis', *Financial Times*, 21 July 2022; Daniel Drach, A. T. Kingsmith and Duan Qi, *One Road, Many Dreams: China's Bold Plan to Remake the Global Economy* (London, 2019); Bruno Maçães, *Belt and Road: A Chinese World Order* (London, 2018); Bertil Lintner, *The Costliest Pearl: China's Struggle for India's Ocean* (London, 2019); Eichengreen *et al.*, *In Defense*, 204–5. **61.** Tooze, *Shutdown*, 157–64, 252–65, 268; Eichengreen *et al.*, *In Defense*, 199–205; Martin Wolf, 'The looming threat from long financial covid', *Financial Times*, 15 Feb. 2022. **62.** Jim Brunsden and Mehreen Khan, 'Brussels sets out plan for euro to challenge dollar dominance', *Financial Times*, 3 Dec. 2018; Sam Fleming, 'Currency warrior: why Trump is weaponizing the dollar', *Financial Times*, 1 July 2019; Gita Gopinath, 'The elusive benefits of flexible exchange rates', Project Syndicate, 4 Dec. 2017; Alan Beattie, 'The EU's halfhearted attempts to globalise the euro', *Financial Times*, 21 Jan. 2021; European Commission, 'The European economic and financial system: fostering openness, strength and resilience', 19 Jan. 2021. **63.** Barry Eichengreen, Arnaud Mehl and Livia Chiţu, *How Global Currencies Work: Past, Present and Future* (Princeton, NJ, and Oxford, 2018), 6–8, 11, 129, 133, 158–69, 170–74, 179, 181–94; Fred Bergsten, 'The dollar and the euro', *Foreign Affairs*

76 (1997), 83; Alexandre Tanzi, 'Dollar loses to euro as payment currency for first time in years', Bloomberg, 19 Nov. 2020; Steve Johnson, 'Rise of the renminbi is "story of the next cycle"', *Financial Times*, 26 April 2019; Gopinath quoted in Fleming, 'Currency warrior'; Paola Subacchi, 'Who is in control of the international monetary system?', *International Affairs* 86 (2010), 667, 668, 675–6; Paola Subacchi and John Driffil, *Beyond the Dollar: Rethinking the International Monetary System* (London, 2020), ix–x.   **64.** Justin Yifu Lin, *Against the Consensus: Reflections on the Great Recession* (Cambridge, 2013), xxvi–xxix.   **65.** 'Poorer countries need more global assistance', *Financial Times*, 1 March 2021; Jonathan Wheatley, 'IMF prepares to bolster developing countries' finances', *Financial Times*, 5 April 2021; Tooze, *Shutdown*, 132–3, 162–4.   **66.** Gavyn Davies, 'Bitcoin has ambitions for gold's role', *Financial Times*, 10 Jan. 2021; BIS, 'Central bank digital currencies: foundational principles and core features', 2020; Yuan Yang and Hudson Lockett, 'What is China's digital currency plan?', *Financial Times*, 25 Nov. 2019; Henny Sender, 'China's new digital currency takes aim at Alibaba and Tencent', *Financial Times*, 4 Aug. 2020; Rana Foroohar, 'Bitcoin's rise reflects America's decline', *Financial Times*, 14 Feb. 2021.   **67.** Eichengreen, Mehl and Chiţu, *How Global Currencies Work*, 8, 10–13; Rana Foroohar, 'Key US commission heralds coming capital wars', *Financial Times*, 21 Nov. 2021; *idem*, 'China, Russia and the race to a post-dollar world', *Financial Times*, 27 Feb. 2022; Robin Harding, 'Toppling the dollar as reserve currency risks harmful fragmentation', *Financial Times*, 10 March 2022; Ruchir Sharma, 'A post-dollar world is coming', *Financial Times*, 28 Aug. 2022; Christopher O'Brien and Chris Boone, 'Beijing and Washington grapple with crypto in their own unique fashion', *Fortune*, 3 Dec. 2021; Nicholas Mulder, *The Economic Weapon: The Rise of Sanctions as a Tool of Modern War* (New Haven, CT, 2022), 11, 13.   **68.** Ed Crookes, 'Janet Yellen calls for US carbon tax', *Financial Times*, 10 Sept. 2018; Raghuram Rajan, 'A fair and simple way to tax carbon emissions', *Financial Times*, 17 Dec. 2019; Tim Harford, 'The climate won't wait: we need a carbon tax now', *Financial Times*, 29 Oct. 2021; Gillian Tett, 'A carbon price should be top of the wish list at the climate talks', *Financial Times*, 28 Oct. 2021; Alice Hancock and Javier Espinoza, 'Brussels agrees details of world-first carbon border tax', *Financial Times*, 18 Dec. 2022; Michael E. Mann, *The New Climate War: The Fight to Take Back Our Planet* (London and New York, 2021), 107–20; IMF, *Fiscal Monitor: How to Mitigate Climate Change* (Washington, DC, 2019), viii; IMF, *World Economic Outlook: Global Manufacturing Downturn, Rising Trade Barriers, Oct. 2019* (Washington, DC, 2019), 25, 188.   **69.** Matthias Schmelzer, *The Hegemony of Growth: The OECD and the Making of the Economic Growth Paradigm* (Cambridge, 2016), 295–7; Steven Bernstein, *The Compromise of Liberal Environmentalism* (New York, 2001); Mann, *New Climate War*; on pricing carbon, see William Nordhaus, *The Climate Casino: Risk, Uncertainty, and Economics for a Warming World* (New Haven, CT, 2013) and *idem*, *The Spirit of Green: The Economics of Collisions and Contagions in a Crowded World* (Princeton, NJ, 2021) versus Nicholas Stern, *The Economics of Climate Change* (Cambridge, 2007) and discussion by John Broome, 'The ethics of climate change', *Scientific American*, June 2008; Daniela Gabor and Isabella Weber, 'COP26 should distance itself from carbon shock therapy', *Financial Times*, 8 Nov. 2021; Piketty, *Capital and Ideology*, 668–9.   **70.** Partha Dasgupta, *Natural Capital: Valuing the Planet* (New Haven, CT, 2015); *The Economics of Biodiversity: The Dasgupta Review* (London, 2021), 5.   **71.** Geoff Mann, 'Reversing the freight train', *London Review of Books*, 18 August 2022, 27–30 discusses recent books on degrowth: Per Espen Stoknes, *Tomorrow's Economy: A Guide to Creating Healthy Green Growth* (Cambridge, MA, 2022); Jason Hickel, *Less is More: Degrowth Will Save the World* (London, 2021); Tim Jackson, *Post Growth: Life After Capitalism* (Cambridge, 2021); Giorgos Kallis, Susan Paulson, Giacomo D'Alisa and Federico Demaria, *The Case for Degrowth* (Cambridge, 2020).   **72.** Thomas Piketty, 'Our manifesto to save Europe from itself', *Guardian*, 9 Dec. 2018.   **73.** Emmanuel Macron, 'Initiative pour l'Europe – Discours d'Emmanuel Macron pour une Europe souveraine, unie, démocratique', 26 September 2017.   **74.** Yale Program on Climate Change Conversation, 'The Green New Deal has strong bipartisan support', 14 Dec. 2018; https://apps.npr.org/documents/document .html?id=5729033-Green-New-Deal-FINAL; US Presidential Twitter Feed, 9 Feb. 2019; Emily Holden, 'What is the green new deal and is it technically possible?', *Guardian*, 29 Dec.

2018; Emily Holden and Lauren Gambio, 'Green new deal: Ocasio-Cortez unveils bold plan to fight climate change', *Guardian*, 7 Feb. 2019. **75.** Camilla Hodgson, 'World Bank under fire for being "missing in action" on climate change', *Financial Times*, 13 Dec. 2021; Camilla Hodgson and Aime Williams, 'World Bank head under pressure to quit over climate change doubts', *Financial Times*, 22 Sept. 2022; Valdis Dombrovskis, 'We must not miss this chance to reform the WTO', *Financial Times*, 25 Nov. 2021; Jake Hess, 'Working at the World Bank, I can see how it is failing humanity in the climate crisis', *Guardian*, 28 Oct. 2021. **76.** Paris agreement at COP21; COP26 The Glasgow Climate Pact; Fiona Harvey, Damian Carrington and Adam Morton, 'Second COP26 draft text', *Guardian*, 12 Nov. 2021. **77.** Aime Williams, 'Global climate leaders push for overhaul of IMF and World Bank', *Financial Times*, 24 Sept. 2022; UN Climate Press Release, 'COP27 reaches breakthrough agreement on new "loss and damage" fund for vulnerable countries', 20 Nov. 2022; Aime Williams and Camilla Hodgson, 'The World Bank prepares for a new "green mission"', *Financial Times*, 21 Feb. 2023. **78.** *The Australian*, 15 Oct. 2019 and Scott Morrison, Lowy lecture, 3 Oct. 2019; 'NSW's ambitious plan to become renewable superpower', *Sydney Morning Herald*, 9 Nov. 2020. **79.** Kate Brown, 'Child's play: the global quest for a Green New Deal', *Times Literary Supplement*, 7 June 2019; the approach was recommended by Elinor Ostrom, 'A polycentric approach for coping with climate change', *Annals of Economics and Finance* 15 (2014), 97–134. **80.** Adam Tooze, 'Is this the end of the American century?', *London Review of Books*, 4 April 2019; *idem*, *Shutdown*, 215–30. **81.** Steven Levitsky and Daniel Ziblatt, *How Democracies Die: What History Reveals About Our Future* (London, 2019), 8–9, 13, 20, 67, 99, 102, 106, 143, 146, 174. **82.** Tooze, *Shutdown*, 105, 131–2, 135–41, 222–4, 227, 229, 270–75. **83.** Nigel Pain and Patrice Ollivaud, 'The American Rescue Plan is set to boost global growth', OECD, 17 March 2021; Myles McCormick, 'Biden throws weight of US government behind clean energy', *Financial Times*, 3 April 2021; Tooze, *Shutdown*, 288–91, 299–300; The White House, 'American Families Plan'; Martin Wolf, 'Policy errors of the 1970s echo in our times', *Financial Times*, 14 June 2022; Tommy Stubbington, Colby Smith, Martin Arnold and Katie Martin, 'Time for strong medicine', *Financial Times*, 17 June 2022; Chris Giles, 'Leading economies at risk of falling into high-inflation trap, BIS says', *Financial Times*, 26 June 2022; Martin Wolf, 'Inflation is a political challenge as well as an economic one', *Financial Times*, 12 July 2022; John Plender, 'The Great Reversal into a higher inflation environment', *Financial Times*, 8 Sept. 2022. **84.** 'A historic moment in US stimulus', *Financial Times*, 8 March 2021; James Politi, 'How Biden walked a political tightrope to pass $1.9tn stimulus', *Financial Times*, 11 March 2021; Tooze, *Shutdown*, 300–301; Mary McDougall, 'Joe Biden tax proposals fall short of OECD standards for minimum rate', *Financial Times*, 9 Aug. 2022; Emiliya Mychasuk, 'A guide to the US climate, health and tax package', *Financial Times*, 12 Aug. 2022; Rana Foroohar, 'New rules for business in a post-neoliberal age', *Financial Times*, 9 Oct. 2022; 'Trade rift between EU and US grows over green industry and jobs', *Financial Times*, 30 Oct. 2022. **85.** Macron, 'Initiative pour l'Europe'; Anne-Sylvaine Chassany and Guy Chazan, 'Eurozone reform: solving the Franco-German puzzle', *Financial Times*, 29 June 2018. **86.** Ashoka Mody, *Eurotragedy: A Drama in Nine Acts* (Oxford, 2018). **87.** Adam Tooze, *Crashed: How a Decade of Financial Crises Changed the World* (London, 2018), 610, 613; *idem*, *Shutdown*, 177–83; Claire Jones, 'German court hears case against ECB bond buying', *Financial Times*, 30 July 2019; Philip Stephens, 'The EU's fate rests on Germany's identity crisis', *Financial Times*, 21 May 2020; Mehreen Kahn, 'What next in Karlsruhe v ECB?', *Financial Times*, 6 May 2020. **88.** Tooze, *Shutdown*, 134, 184–9, 279–83, 302; Eichengreen *et al.*, *In Defense*, 205, 207; Jeffrey Sachs, 'The world needs a prosperous and properly funded Europe', *Financial Times*, 19 Feb. 2020; Tobias Buck, 'German economists urge Berlin to ditch balanced budget rule', *Financial Times*, 2 Oct. 2019; Guy Chazan, 'Doubts grow over Germany's balanced budget rule', *Financial Times*, 28 April 2019; *idem*, 'The minds behind Germany's Shifting Fiscal Stance', *Financial Times*, 9 June 2020; Ben Hall, Sam Fleming and Guy Chazan, 'Is the Franco-German plan Europe's "Hamiltonian" moment?', *Financial Times*, 21 May 2020. **89.** Sylvie Kauffmann, 'A new Europe is emerging from the tragedy of Ukraine', *Financial Times*, 6 March 2022; Marton Dunai, 'Bad blood between Hungary and Ukraine undermines EU unity on Russia', *Financial Times*, 1 Jan.

2023.   90. Tooze, *Shutdown*, 18–19, 201–2, 209–13, 295–6.   91. Ibid., 296–7; Joe Miller, 'Volkswagen faces union and shareholder calls to examine China human rights allegations', *Financial Times*, 17 June 2022.   92. Martin Wolf, 'Donald Trump and Xi Jinping's battle over globalisation', *Financial Times*, 24 Jan. 2017; Nicholas R. Lardy, *The State Strikes Back: The End of Economic Reform in China?* (Washington, DC, 2019), tables 2.1 and 2.2; Sun Yu and Tom Mitchell, 'Chinese local government funds run out of projects to back', *Financial Times*, 17 Oct. 2019; Tom Mitchell and Yuan Yang, 'Xi challenged over direction of China's economic reforms', *Financial Times*, 17 Dec. 2018; Lucy Hornby, 'Xi versus Deng, the family feud over China's reforms', *Financial Times*, 15 Nov. 2018; Tooze, *Shutdown*, 297–8.   93. Tooze, *Shutdown*, 135; M. Ayhan Kose, Peter Nagle, Franziska Ohnsorge and Naotaka Sugawara, *Global Waves of Debt: Causes and Consequences* (Washington, DC, 2020), 152; Megan Greene, 'Ignoring China's disastrous "three Ds" could be a global risk', *Financial Times*, 6 Sept. 2022.   94. Matthew C. Klein and Michael Pettis, *Trade Wars are Class Wars: How Rising Inequality Distorts the Global Economy and Threatens International Peace* (New Haven, CT, 2020), 101–30; Edward White, 'Xi Jinping's last chance to revive the Chinese economy', *Financial Times*, 5 Oct. 2022.   95. Tim Besley, 'Is cohesive capitalism under threat?', *Oxford Review of Economic Policy* 37 (2021), 720–33; Kuttner, *Can Democracy Survive?*, xv, 283, 296–304, 307–8.   96. Mulder, *Economic Weapon*, 13.   97. Gideon Rachman, 'Worlds apart: how decoupling became the new buzzword', *Financial Times*, 13 Dec. 2019; Rana Foroohar, 'Coronavirus is speeding up the decoupling of global economies', *Financial Times*, 23 Feb. 2020; Faroohar, 'New rules'; Martin Sandbu, 'Brad DeLong: "The US is now an anti-globilisation outlier"', *Financial Times*, 24 Nov. 2022; J. Bradford DeLong, *Slouching Towards Utopia: An Economic History of the Twentieth Century* (London, 2022), 530–32.   98. Martin Wolf, 'Globalisation is not dying, it's changing', *Financial Times*, 13 Sept. 2022.

Index

Page numbers in **bold** refer to illustrations; those in *italics* refer to figures.

Abs, Herman 284, 286
Access to Covid-19 Tools
    Accelerator (ACT)
    795
Acheson, Dean 34, 51, 127,
    159
    at Bretton Woods 193–4
    and European economic
        co-operation 282
    and foreign economic
        policy 267–8, 273
    on GATT (Kennedy
        Round) 391
    and Lend Lease 126, 130
    and Marshall Plan 274
    on Soviet Union 249
    and UK dollar holdings
        140–41
    and White's stabilization
        fund 161
Act for International
    Development (US,
    1961) 411–12
Afghanistan
    Helmand Valley Authority
        333
    Soviet invasion and war
        in 583, 682
Africa 319, 339, 551, 584
    and Bretton Woods
        institutions 235
    British investment in
        316–17
    French empire in 317,
        318–19
    and 'green growth' 821
    and Non-Aligned
        Movement 342
    relations with EEC 371
African Economic
    Community, Abuja
    Treaty (1991) 633

Afro-Asian Peoples' Solidarity
    Organization
    Conference (Guinea,
    1960) 355
Agnew, Spiro 480
Agricultural Adjustment
    Act (AAA) (US,
    1933) 34, 35, 39,
    45, 53–4, 181
agricultural production, and
    nutrition 84–5, 114,
    327
Agricultural Trade
    Development and
    Assistance Act (US,
    1954) 393, 410–411
agriculture
    application of science and
        technology to 327–8,
        561–3
    China 86, 98, 99–100,
        348–9
    and Doha Round 654
    EEC/US negotiations
        (GATT) 392, 393–4
    employment in 322–3,
        567–8
    GATT and 369–70, 636,
        638–9
    and green revolution 552,
        562–3
    and land reform 329–31
    plant genetics 563
    reduced tariffs 640
    rural co-operatives 86, 100
    Soviet collectivization 7,
        93, 94–5
    subsidies 636, 638
    US 380
    see also food supply
Aldrich, Winthrop 216–17
Alesina, Alberto 737

Alfonzo, Juan Pablo Pérez
    537, 543–4
Algeria 317, 355, 538
Allende, Salvador 600
Alliance for Progress
    (Kennedy) 409–12
Allied Maritime Transport
    Council (1917) 13
Almunia, Joaquín 697
Alphand, Hervé 162
Alternative Economic
    Strategy, protectionism
    and capital controls
    580–81
Amato, Giuliano 709
Amazon rainforest 794,
    818, 821
American Arbitration
    Association 624
American Bankers'
    Association (ABA)
    217, 482, 483
American Economic
    Association 219, 572
American Federation of Labor
    (AFL) 184, 185, 246
American Relief
    Administration 174
American Selling Price
    380, 395
    EEC objection to 389,
    393, 524–5
Amery, Leo 105, 127, 139–40
Amin, Samir 536
Anderson, Benjamin 216
Anglo-German Payments
    Agreement (1934)
    69, 73
Anglo-Irish Bank,
    nationalized 753
Ansiaux, Hubert 455
Appleby, Paul 54, 183

Aranha, Oswaldo 108
arbitration, creditor–debtor
    nations 624–5
Argentina 61, 624
    agricultural exports 106,
      107, 173, 358
    and Cairns group 637
    Central Bank of
      Argentina 358
    and hyperinflation 591
    IMF loan 775
    and ITO negotiations
      256, 263–4
Armenia 683
Aron, Raymond 443
ASEAN (Association of
    South-East Asian
    Nations) xxxii, 633,
    653
Asia
    and Bretton Woods
      institutions 235
    and British sterling
      balances 279
    colonial empires 337, 339
    export-led growth
      360–64
    shift of power to 833
    see also China; East Asia;
      India; Japan; South
      Korea
Asia-Pacific Economic
    Cooperation group
    636, 653
Asian Free Trade Area 652
Asian Infrastructure
    Investment Bank 814
Association of African
    States, Yaoundé
    Convention (1963)
    371
Atatürk, Kemal 98–9
Atkinson, Tony 809
Atlantic Charter (1941)
    128–9, 172–3
Attlee, Clement 226,
    239, 252
    and American loan
      agreement 229, 231,
      232–3
    rejection of ECSC
      294–5
Auriol, Vincent 78, 79
austerity 734, 737, 738,
    739–40
    and increase in inequality
      741, 742, 743, 752,
      809–10
Australia 173

aim of full employment
    114, 186, 210, 211,
    259–60
borrowing 111–12
at Bretton Woods 195
and climate change 823
economic development
    model 110–115
and ILO 187, 228
and IMF 188
and ITO 262
Melbourne Agreement
    (1930) 112
Mutual Aid agreement
    (with US) (1942) 195
and post-Second World
    War reconstruction
    91, 114–15
and utilization of
    resources 114–15,
    138
Austrian Business Cycle
    Research Institute 82
Austrian School of
    economics 81, 83,
    743
Austro-Hungarian empire
    13, 14
authoritarianism
    banks' links with 623–4
    China 762, 770, 773, 828
    liberal democratic alliance
      against 60, 62, 74–5
    Russia 695, 773
    see also Communism;
      nationalism
AVAAZ movement,
    denouncement of
    TTIP and TTP
    780–81
Avenol, Joseph 77, 100
Aykroyd, Wallace 175, 178
Aylwin, Patricio 601
Azevêdo, Roberto 778–9,
    786–7
Azores, meeting of Nixon
    and Pompidou 502–3

Baker, James 818
balance of payments
    adjustments 150
    American 273, 276,
      367–9, 368, 385–8;
      problems of 436–7,
      440–41, 467–70,
      793, 816
    and global liquidity 434
    stabilization fund and
      160

    variations 433
Ball, George 366, 377, 380,
    384, 396
    and GATT (Kennedy
      Round) 381
    on UNCTAD 421–2, 424
    and US balance of
      payments crisis
      440–41
Balls, Ed 718–19
Balogh, Thomas 277
Baltic republics 683
Banca d'Italia 705
Bancor, super-national bank
    money 153, 162, 817
Bandung Conference (1955)
    336, 340–43, 400
    Bandung Declaration 342
Bangladesh 638
Bank of England
    Apocalypse Now
      memorandum 615
    and capital exports
      (1920s) 22
    and Eurodollar market
      609–10
    money supply targets 573
    quantitative easing 742
    view of stabilization fund
      166
Bank of International
    Settlements see BIS
banks
    and deregulation 571,
      582, 610, 746, 748
    Keynes's proposal for
      international clearing
      bank 149–55
    links with authoritarian
      regimes 623–4
    and moral hazard 615,
      629
    and move towards free
      markets 515
    need for better financing
      813
    post-crisis regulation
      751–3
    regional development 326
    swap networks for
      bailouts 744–5, 745
    US risk-taking 614–15,
      732, 747, 748–9
    see also central banks
Banque de France 23, 77,
    80, 700, 713
Baran, Paul, The Political
    Economy of Growth
    536

Barber, Anthony 482, 506
Bareau, Paul 223, 224
Barnett, Joel 579
Barre, Raymond 472–3, 700, 705
Barroso, José Manuel 758, 780
Barshefsky, Charlene 645, 647
Baruch, Bernard 222–3
Basel agreement, with UK 457–8, 516
Basel Committee on Banking Supervision (1974) 615
  Basel II rules 748
  Basel III rules 752
Basel Concordat (1975) 615
Batista, Fulgencio 406
Batista, Paulo Nogueira 776
Bator, Francis 392–3, 394
Bean, Charles 714
Beaverbrook, Lord 127
Beckerman, Wilfred 559, 590
Bedjaoui, Mohammed 544
Belarus 683
Bell, David E. 405
Bella, Ahmed Ben 355
Bengal, famine 173
Benn, Tony 580–81
Bergsten, Fred 466–7, 524, 525
  on China 676
  on euro 723
  on regional trade agreements 636
  and suspension of convertibility 467–8
Berle, Adolf 54–5, 110, 121, 410
  and international financial scheme 155, 157, 162
  opposition to Bretton Woods 216
Berlin, blockade (1948–9) 289
Berlin Wall, fall of (1989) 659, 712
Bernanke, Ben 601, 630
  and inflation 748, 749
  and monetary policy 742, 743
  and mortgage relief 746
  and swap networks 744
Bernstein, Edward 145, 159, 446
Beteta, Ramón 263

Bevin, Ernest 21, 248–9, 288
  and Communist threats 279, 288
  on Keynes's clearing union scheme 154
  view of European integration 292–3
Bezos, Jeff 804
Bhagwati, Jagdish 636, 778
Bidault, Georges 287, 288, 292
Biden, Joe 788, 795
  and China 828
  and climate change 821
  and corporation tax 806
  economic nationalism 832
  economic stimulus plans 825–6
  mid-term elections (2022) 793
  and pandemic 792
bilateral agreements
  foreign investment 545, 624–5
  Germany 70, 72, 74, 108
  and multilateralism 254–5
  trade 11, 14, 62, 132, 148, 652–3
  see also 'most favoured nation' principle
BIS (Bank of International Settlements) (1930) xxi, xxxii, 29, 204–6, 432
  Basel arrangements with UK 457–8
  'Basel consensus' 32, 33
  and Eurodollar market 612–13
  growing influence of 438–9
  and post-crisis regulation 751–2
  relations with Third Reich 204–5
  role in financial liberalization 615–16, 811
  and swap networks 745
  view of US 500
  and World Monetary and Economic Conference (1933) 32
Black, Eugene 308–10, 325, 326
Blair House Accord (1992) 639
Blair, Tony 718–19

Blanchard, Olivier 740–41
Blessing, Karl 71
Blinken, Antony 760
Bloomfield, Arthur 203–4, 208, 324, 362
Blumethal, Michael 390, 424, 603
  and GATT (Kennedy Round) 381–2, 392, 394, 395–6
Blyth, Mark 739
Bogdanor, Vernon 715
Böhm, Franz 286
Bolsonaro, Jair 794, 822
Bolton, George 200, 258, 300–301, 608
Bombay Plan 106, 196
Boothby, Robert 229, 231
Borah, William 52, 65
Bordo, Michael 725
Borlaug, Norman 328, 532, 561, 562
Bose, Subhas Chandra 103–4
Bose, Sugata 346–7
Boughton, James 599
Boumédiène, Houari 539, 544–5
Bourne, G. H., Starvation in Europe 173
Bowles, Chester 346
Boxer Rebellion (1899–1901) 97
Boyd Orr, John 176, 333, 334
  and FAO 178–9, 327
  Food, Health and Income (1936) 174
Brady, Nicholas 619, 620
Brand, Robert 145, 219, 220–21, 227, 233
Brandt, Willy 481, 552
  and EEC further integration 511, 702
  North-South: A Programme for Survival 583
  and realignment of currencies 501–2
Brasseur, Maurice 424
Brauer, Max 100
Brazil 107–9, 263, 358, 408
  Amazon rainforest 794, 818, 821
  and Cairns group 637
  and climate change 822
  and Doha Round 654
  and Germany 108–9
  and hyperinflation 591
  primary exports 106, 107

Brazilian Landless Workers
    Movement 646
Bremmer, Ian 784
Bretton Woods Agreement
    189–212, 305
  American criticism of
    216–17
  asymmetry of 433
  call by developing
    countries for reform
    (2022) 822
  capital transfers (Article
    VI) 203–4
  dependency on dollar
    433–4
  end of (1973) 513–14
  and 'key currency' plan
    217–18
  and models of
    development 364
  and post-war European
    reconstruction 215
  and post-war monetary
    system 209, 246–7,
    433
  ratification 211–12,
    215–19, 226–7,
    229–33
  tensions in regime
    432–41, 456–7
  US attempts to preserve
    465–6
  weakness of institutions
    437–8
Bretton Woods conference
    (1944) xxii, xxiii,
    xxv, 119, 189, 190,
    191, 193–206
  and BIS 204–6
  and employment policies
    210
  as 'Grand Design' 167–8
  less developed countries
    at 106, 115–16
  member countries 146
  negotiations xxxi, 145
  preparatory conference
    (Atlantic City) 146,
    191–3
  and stabilization fund
    198
  and Tripartite Agreement
    principles 79–80
  US–UK domination
    145–6
Brexit 768
Brezhnev, Leonid 356
Briand, Aristide 14
British Empire 339

American suspicion of
    123–4, 319
  and development schemes
    316–17, 319
  and local African
    government 320
  nationalist leaders 319
  and political identity 318
  and support in Second
    World War 123
  see also imperial
    preference
Brittan, Leon 639–40, 645
Brittan, Samuel 721
Brockmann, Miguel
    d'Escoto 771, 782
Brown, Edward (Ned) 193,
    207
Brown, Gordon xvii–xviii,
    610, 719, 736
Brown, Winthrop 253, 270,
    371–2
Bruce, Stanley Melbourne
    84–5, 111–12, 114
Brüderle, Rainer 783
Brundtland, Gro Harlem
    590
Brüning, Heinrich 27
Bryan, William Jennings 20,
    34–5
Bryant, Ralph 493
Brzezinski, Zbigniew 540
Buffett, Warren 807
Buiter, Willem 798
Bukharin, Nikolai 92–3,
    94–5
Bundesbank (Germany)
  and ECB 715–16
  and European economic
    convergence
    699–700, 713
  and European Monetary
    System 708, 709–10
  monetary targets for
    stability 573
Bunning, Jim 654
Burgess, W. Randolph 217
Burke, James 527
Burma 139
Burns, Arthur 453, 478–9,
    492, 493
  on Connally 477–8, 497,
    498
  on Eurodollar market
    613
  and monetary policy
    510–511, 573–4
  and monetary system
    reforms 509, 512

and Nixon 464, 479–80,
    488
  and suspension of
    convertibility 486–7
  view of interdependence
    policy 542
  and Volcker report 468
Bush, George H. W. 635,
    659, 683, 684
Bush, George W. 651–2,
    733, 782, 807
Bush, Prescott 380
Business Roundtable (US)
    803
Butler, Richard 'Rab' 302,
    303, 304
Byrnes, James 248, 249

C20 (Committee of Twenty)
  and currency realignment
    508–9
  'Outline of Reform' paper
    (1974) 519
Cairncross, Alec 669
Cairns group (agricultural
    exporters) 637
Cairo, conference on
    Problems of
    Developing Countries
    (1962) 416
Callaghan, James 522–3,
    579, 582
  and Carter 581
  rejection of membership
    of EMS 706–7
  and Social Contract
    579–80, 581
Cambodia 400
  Khmer Rouge 356
Camdessus, Michel 597
  and capital account
    liberalization 627–8
  and euro 725
  on good governance 604
  and Mexican rescue
    package 619–20
  rejection of 'Asian tiger'
    economic models
    622–3
  and Russia 684, 688
Cameron, David 739
Campbell, W. K. H. 100
Campbell-Bannerman,
    Henry 12
Campos, Roberto de Oliveira
    315, 373, 414
Canada
  agricultural production
    183

and Cairns group 637
on Latin America 263
and NAFTA 635
proposed international
exchange union 162
at Rambouillet summit
520
Trump's trade war with
786
Cancún summit (1981)
583–4
capital
free movement of xix
and global integration
xxiv
capital account
liberalization
IMF and 627–30, 775–6,
795
and incentivization of risk
630
and moral hazard 615,
629
capital controls 202–4,
434–5, 627, 813–14
bankers' opposition to
204, 515
IMF and 434–5, 627,
776, 813–14
Keynes's view of 149–50
US view of 466–7,
514–15
capital flows 22, 202–3,
813–16
and foreign investment
435, 813
and interest rates 436
speculative 607
and surveillance of gross
776
and tax avoidance 813
capitalism
demands for fairness
767–8
dynamic xx–xxi
and economic growth
567–8
rentier 799–800
see also 'crony capitalism'
Capper, Arthur 63–4
carbon taxes
border tax 818, 821,
828
and emissions trading
system 818–19
proposed 818–19, 821
Cardoso, Fernando 536
Carson, Rachel, Silent
Spring 558

cartels, for basic
commodities 180
Carter, Jimmy 540, 575, 705
report on economic
growth and
environment 561
review of US development
policies 550–51
and tariff reductions 530
Case, Anne 800, 804
Cassel, Gustav 24
Castro, Fidel 400, 407
Catchings, Waddill 36–7
Catto, Lord 166, 205
Center for International
Studies (CIS), and
modernization theory
401–2
central banks
and Basel Committee on
Banking Supervision
(1974) 615
capital requirements 616
and efforts to shore up
Bretton Woods 439,
518
and inflation targeting
748–9
and international
oversight 523
interventions (global
financial crisis and
pandemic) 797, 812
and monetary targets 573
and swap networks 745,
745
see also banks
Chamberlain, Joseph
11–12, 18
Chamberlain, Neville
18–19, 56, 74
and Anglo-American
trade agreement 74
and Australia 114
and currency
stabilization 76
and imperial preference
73, 74
and Lausanne conference
(1932) 27–8
and leaving gold
standard 42
and payment of war debt
41–2, 49
Chayanov, Alexander 92, 94
Chen Yun 659, 669, 671
Chenery, Hollis 534, 554,
555
Cheney, Dick 685

Chernobyl nuclear plant
disaster 682
Chernomyrdin, Viktor 686
Chiang Kai-shek 99, 195,
196
'Chicago School' of
economics 450, 571,
600–601
Chifley, Ben 114
Chile 107, 263, 591
application for IBRD
loan 308–9
nationalization of mines
545
under Pinochet 600–601
China 662–77, 828–31
and Asian Infrastructure
Investment Bank 814
authoritarianism of Xi
Jinping 762, 770,
773, 828
and Bretton Woods
conference 191,
195–6
and Bretton Woods
institutions 235; and
GATT 271, 673–5;
member of World
Bank 669; and WTO
651, 675–7, 788, 831
and call for New
International
Economic Order
536–7
carbon emissions 818
corruption 666, 667
and Covid-19 795, 829
Cultural Revolution
349–51, 356
dissolution of communes
665
economic disequilibrium
824
Economic and Finance
Commission 659
economic shift (from
1990s) xxiii, 429,
591; adoption of
capitalist methods
662; dual-pricing
667, 669; economic
development model
91, 97–101, 345,
623, 661; gradualism
667–8; inflation 667,
671; internal
development 584,
661, 662; 'pillar'
industries 672; and

China (*cont.*)
price liberalization 670, 671;
privatizations 672;
reliance on exports 666, 673, 793, 829–30; 'socialist market economy with Chinese characteristics' 672; special economic zones 665–6; state enterprises 665, 668–9; town and village enterprises (TVEs) 664–5, 672; trade surplus 673
and EU 757
financial system: and risk of next financial crisis 763, 816, 830; weakness of 762, 816, 830
fiscal policy after global financial crisis 741–2, 745, 828
geopolitics: annexation of Tibet 355; Belt and Road Initiative 770, 814, 829, 830; and influence in Third World xxx, 354–6, 815, 815; loans to developing countries 814–16; nationalist 770; and South China Seas 831
global power 784, 816
Great Famine 349
Great Leap Forward 347–9
household consumption 673, 674, 769, 793
household incomes 672–3
household production 663–4
household savings 667, 673, 830
hukou (household registration) 666–7, 672, 673, 830
human rights: abuses 788, 831; agreements 675
League of Nations advice 86, 99–100
modernization under Sun Yat-sen 98–9
Nationalist economic policy 100

one child policy 564
political reform 670
power of local elites 830
property market 762–3, 816, 829–30
and Regional Comprehensive Economic Partnership 781
relations with Russia 770, 831–2
relations with Soviet Union 343, 351
silver-based currency xx, 100–101
social problems 666, 762, 829–30
social unrest 667, 671
Three Gates Gorge, Yellow River 348
Tiananmen Square (1989) 659, 671
treaty ports 97
and United States: economic imbalance 732; Nixon and 463; purchase of US treasury bonds 673, 674, 676; relations with US 626–7, 673, 675–6, 831; US investment in 828; US trade deficit 673, 675, 793; US trade war 658
war with India 342, 356
Xinjiang province 355, 829
Yangtze Valley Authority 332, 347
Chinese Communist Party (CCP)
continuing control of 663, 666, 667, 672, 695, 762
Long Live Leninism! (1960) 351
Xi Jinping and 829
Chinese Development Finance Corporation 99
Christian Democrat party (CDU) (Germany), Ahlen programme for reform 284, 285
Churchill, Winston
and American loan agreement 231, 232

and Atlantic Charter 128–9
and IMF 166
and India 105, 139, 278
'iron curtain' speech 232, 248
and Lend Lease 130–31
and Morgenthau 237–8
and Operation Robot 303
and return to gold standard 20–21
and Roosevelt 42, 123
at Yalta 238
CIA (Central Intelligence Agency), and CIS 402
'Citizens for Democracy', India 691
City of London
American banks in 607, 610–611
deregulation ('Big Bang') reforms 582, 610
Eurodollar market 595, 608–10
and European economic convergence 700–701
influence of 589
recycling of petrodollars 565, 585, 589
relations with Wall Street 595, 611–12
and restrictions on American foreign investment 387
self-regulation 609–10
and Soviet bloc dollar holdings 608
and sterling area 304–5, 459
Clarke, 'Otto' (R. W. B.) 258, 266–7
on British relations with Europe 291–2
on floating exchange rate 300, 301, 302–3
and 'one world' policy 281, 302–3
and Operation Robot 301
Clausen, Alden W. ('Tom') 587
Clavin, Patricia 28
Clayton, William L. 159
on buffer stocks 182–3
and Cripps 252–3
and Havana Charter 265–6
and ITO **242**, 267

on Marshall Aid 291
and post-war conditions
in Europe 250–51
proposal for European
customs union
251–2
and proposed American
loan 221–2, 225
on sterling area 141
and trade policy 229,
244, 377
and UN Conference on
Trade and
Employment 241,
243
Clemenceau, Georges 26
Clémentel, Étienne 13
Clift, Ben 740
climate change
emissions trading 819–20
as existential crisis xviii,
xxv, 794, 818
funding for vulnerable
countries 822
and green 'new deal'
818–24
local level action 823
need for global co-
operation 821–2,
823–4
reduced energy
consumption 821
see also ecology; energy;
environment
Climate Leadership Council
(US) 819
Clinton, Bill 635, 647
and China 675
and Russia 688–9
trade policy 639, 644–5
Clinton, Hillary 747, 752,
781
Club of Rome
and development 551–2
population and resources
558, 818
Reshaping the
International Order
(1976) 561
The Limits to Growth
(1972) 558–9
Cobbold, Cameron 140
Cobden, Richard 12
Cobden-Chevalier Treaty
(1860) 11
Codex Alimentarius
Commission 656–7
Cold War xxii, xxx,
xxxiv, 97

effect on US economic
policy 268, 305,
324–5
end of 659
revived (1979) 583–4
and UN development
policies 320, 324,
335
and views of modernity
356–7
see also Russia; Soviet
Union
Colijn, Hendrikus 31, 47
Collado, Emilio 110, 159,
180–81, 308
collective action
on climate change 821–2,
823–4
and pandemic 792, 808
problems of xxvii–xxviii
Collier, Paul 799, 810–811
Colm, Gerhard 283
Colm–Goldsmith–Dodge
Plan for German
currency reform
283–4
Colombia 260–61
Colonial Development
Corporation 318
Colonial Development and
Welfare Act (UK,
1945) 318
Combined Food Board
(1942) 173
COMECOM, Soviet
economic bloc 289
Commission on
International Labour
Legislation 183
Committee of European
Economic Co-
operation 290
Committee on External
Economic Policy
(UK) 167
Committee of Twenty see
C20
commodities
and call for changes to
terms of trade
357–60, 546
falling prices 89, 106,
107, 111
international agreements
on 180, 549
post-First World War
schemes 179–80
price fluctuations 373,
545

proposal for buffer stocks
175–6, 181–2, 549
proposed international
price management
545
Commodity Credit
Corporation (US) 54
Commonwealth
Colombo conference of
foreign ministers
(1950) 279, 280
Economic Conference
(1952) 280
Communism
and capitalism xxx, 403
China 99
Cuba 400
Soviet 289, 290, 352–3
as threat 279, 288
US horror of 324–5, 331,
409–10
see also Chinese
Communist Party
(CCP)
Communist bloc, dollar
holdings 608
competition
corporations and
800–804
and profits 802
regulation of 801
Condliffe, J. B. 81
Conference of European
Economic
Co-operation (Paris,
1947) 288–90
Conference on International
Economic
Cooperation
(1975–7) 550, 551,
552
conflict zones, and extreme
poverty 789
Congress of Industrial
Organizations (CIO)
218
Congress Party of India
101–2, 103, 104–5,
262, 690–91
economic liberalization
694, 760–61
post-independence
planning 343–5
Connally, John 477–8, 483,
505
aggressive nationalism
495, 498
and Camp David meeting
(1971) 462, 486

Connally, John (*cont.*)
  on capital flows 435
  and currency realignment
    497–500
  and demand for foreign
    action on US deficit
    482–3
  dislike of IMF 499, 507
  on Eurodollar market 613
  pressure for suspension of
    convertibility 484–6
Conservative governments
  1951–5 (Churchill)
    299–300
  1979–7: 582
  from 2015: 739, 792,
    793, 809
  see also Thatcher,
    Margaret
Conservative Party (UK)
  scepticism about EU 711
  support for ECSC 294–5
  and tariff reform 12
Conservative-Liberal
    Democrat coalition
    government
    (2010–15) 738
consumer protection, and
    non-tariff barriers
    526
consumerism, rise of 569
consumption
  energy 543–4, 820
  maintained by credit 588,
    769
  need to increase 84–5
Cook, Tim 804
Coombs, Charles 433, 465,
    503, 510
  on central banks 439, 518
  on Connally 499–500
  and gold price 444–5
  and SDR 449
Coombs, H. C. 114–15,
    210, 262
COP21, Paris (2015) 781,
    822
COP26, Glasgow (2021)
    xxxi, 822
COP27, Cairo (2022) 822
Copenhagen, food conference
    (1946) 178
Copland, Douglas 111, 113
Cordovez, Diego 420
Corea, Gamani 544, 545
Coronavirus Aid, Relief and
    Economic Security
    Act (CARES) (US,
    2020) 825

corporations
  and competition 800–804
  earnings differentials 801,
    801
  multinational 595, 608,
    657–8
  profit-shifting 804, 805,
    806, 813
  and shareholders 800
  and social responsibility
    803
  taxation of 805–6
Cost of Living Council (US)
    488
Coughlin, Charles Edward
    35, 45
Couzens, James 39
COVAX 795
Covid-19 pandemic xviii,
    xxiv–xxv, 769, 789
  and collective action 792,
    808
  economic impact 791–2,
    807–8
  inadequacy of WHO 795
  provision of vaccines 792
Cox, James M. 31, 39
credit
  household reliance on
    588, 595, 729, 769,
    812
  Keynes's proposal for
    international
    provision 149–52
  over-extension 630
credit cards, profitability
    588, 812
Crimea, Russian invasion
    (2014) 759
Cripps, Stafford 226, 228
  and African development
    316
  and Clayton 252–3
  and devaluation 282
  and India 105
  and ITO 266
Cromer, Rowland Baring,
    earl of 452, 490, 493
  on Connally 497–8
  criticism of IMF 498
  and European Monetary
    System 482–3, 701
  on G10 500
  'crony capitalism' 605
  India 762
  in South Korea 364, 604
  in US 605, 623, 750–51
Crosbie, John 635, 641
Cuba 157–8, 400

at Bretton Woods 197
  multilateralism 260
  relations with US 61
  Soviet missile crisis 367,
    410
currencies
  call for single
    supranational 817
  cryptocurrencies 813, 818
  fluctuations after Bretton
    Woods *518*
  foreign exchange reserves
    442
  future of 816–18
  manipulation of 783
  new Deutsche Mark
    (1948) 284
  realignment negotiations
    497–500, 501–11
  renminbi (China) 676,
    775, 817
  rouble 685, 687
  silver-based xx, 20,
    100–101
  Tripartite Agreement, US,
    UK and France
    (1936) 60, 75–81
  see also Bretton Woods;
    devaluations; dollar;
    euro; exchange rates;
    gold standard;
    monetary system; sterling
currency blocs
  after 1933 conference 48
  risk of retreat into 818,
    831, 832
currency convertibility xxiii,
    19–20, 200–202,
    272–3
  American commitment to
    275–6
  EEC reaction to US
    suspension 470–75,
    490
  and problem of US
    balance of payments
    431–2, 467–70
  sterling 301–2, 303, 304
  US suspension of 470,
    485–91
  see also exchange rates
currency instability 19–25,
    146–7
currency warfare, 21st
    century 626–7
Currie, Lauchlin 313–14,
    315
customs unions

compared with free trade areas 370
proposals for European 251–2, 292
Czechoslovakia
Communist regime 289, 290
and GATT 271
and Paris conference (1947) 288

Daane, Dewey 611
Dagli, Vadilal 691
Dale, William 456, 485
Dalio, Ray 803–4
Dalton, Hugh 133–4, 166, 205, 224–5, 226–7
dams and irrigation projects 306, 315–16, 331–3
China 348
India 345
Soviet Union 315
Dasgupta, Partha 820
Davies, Howard 747–8
Davis, Kingsley 334, 563
Day, Edmund 32, 33
de Gaulle, Charles
on Bretton Woods 439
and British membership of EEC 379, 382–3, 388, 458, 459
and G10 438
and gold 443
and view of EEC 383–4
de-financialization, need for 811–13
de-industrialization 569, 587–8, 766
effect on jobs 810–811
Deaton, Angus 800, 804
Debré, Michel 318–19, 443
debt
and deflation 37, 53
ECB rules on 714–15, 716, 722, 754, 758, 827–8
G20 Debt Service Suspension Initiative 815–16
loan refinancing 814
relationship to growth 738–9
structural 739
and taxation 809
see also financial crises; war debt
debt restructuring 814
developing countries 606, 619–20

ECB opposition to 754, 755, 758
debt sustainability
Chinese lending risk 816
global financial crisis 738
debt-to-GDP ratio, and net worth of public assets 809
decolonization 367
and new members of GATT 373
deficit finance 736
theory of 84, 246
deflation
Australian plan (1930–31) 112–13
and balance of payments 436, 448–9, 451, 468, 609
and debt 37, 53
Keynes on 21, 570
UK policy 578–9, 580
and unemployment 23, 112, 707, 729
Dell, Sidney, UN 417
DeLong, Bradford 743, 832
Delors, Jacques 708–10, 711
democracy
and multilateralism 795–6
and nationalism xxviii
social 603
see also embedded liberalism; liberal democracies
Democratic Party (US)
and green new deal 821
and market liberalism 573–4, 578, 651–2
Southern 17–18, 64, 259, 269, 477
views of trade 8, 16
Deng Xiaoping 347–8, 349, 660
and CCP 663, 672, 762
and household enterprises 665
and market reform 662–3, 671–2
'planned commodity economy' 668
rapid price liberalization 670, 671
rehabilitation (1977) 350–51, 662
Denmark 714, 715, 719
dependency theory 536–7, 539

deregulation 571, 746, 811–12
City of London 582, 610
and financial crises 747–53
Deutsche Mark 284
flotation 459–60, 480–81
devaluations
competitive 449
of dollar (1934) 50–53
of dollar (1970s) 503, 511
of franc (1936) 79
of franc (1958) 370, 471
of sterling (1949) 281–2, 298
of sterling (1967) 445, 452, 457–8
of zloty (1990) 678
see also revaluation
developing countries
at Bretton Woods 115–16
and call for economic development policies 211, 235
and capital liberalization 583
criticism of concept of sustainable development 590
debt: Chinese loans to 814–16, 815; to official creditors 815; and restructuring 619–20
and GATT 240, 373–4, 413–14; discontent with Kennedy Round 395, 397; and North-South imbalance in Uruguay Round 640–41; and Tokyo round 530–31, 631; and Uruguay Round 636–7, 638
and Generalized System of Preferences 422
and IMF Compensating Financing Facility 522
and IMF conditionality 598, 814
and ITO 261–2
and management of floating rates 522
need for modernization 335–6

developing countries (*cont.*)
  and New International
    Economic Order 529,
    534–9; collective
    self-reliance 544; and
    interdependence
    540–42; and
    sovereign equality
    543
  private enterprise 407,
    408
  and reciprocity 636–7,
    641
  resistance to multilateral
    institutions xxx, 235,
    336, 774
  and SDRs 817–18
  and shallow
    multilateralism
    xxii–xxiv
  Soviet aid for 352–3
  and tariff preferences
    424–5
  trade: call for better terms
    of 357–60, 371;
    export earnings
    fluctuations 416, 422
  and UNCTAD 415–26
  US support pledged to
    367
  view of intellectual
    property agreements
    637, 638
  and WTO 642–3, 647;
    and Doha
    Development Agenda
    649–50
  see also G-77; Third
    World
development
  community 331–2
  dangerous stage of 402,
    405
  and dependency theory
    536–7
  equated with
    industrialization 323,
    336
  imperial projects 316–20
  institutional changes in
    approach 552–4
  and Malthusian visions
    326–36, 557–8
  North-South dialogue
    548–52
  post-war consideration of
    239–40
  programmes for 169, 171,
    324, 326

rural 554–7
Special UN Fund for
  Economic
  Development
  (SUNFED) 323–6
  see also IBRD; IMF; UN
  Conference on Trade
  and Development
  (UNCTAD)
development aid
  dependent on self-help
    406
  and differing approaches
    to IBRD loans
    312–15
  and military assistance
    404, 406
  and overseas capital
    investment 310–313
  Soviet provision 352–3
  and technology 324, 326,
    332–5
  US criteria for 405–6
development banks 811
Dewey, Thomas 238
Diebold, William 279–80
Dijsselbloem, Jeroen 757–8
Dikötter, Frank 350, 664
Dillon, Douglas 374, 385,
    386, 387, 444
Dimon, Jamie 803
Direct Action Network
    646
Dispute Settlement Board
    (WTO) 655–6
distributive justice
  global institutions and
    xxxiii–xxxiv, 555
  NIEO and 637, 638
  redistributive taxation
    808–9
  Uruguay Round failure
    on 641
Dodd, Norris 179
Dodd–Frank Act (Wall
  Street Reform and
  Consumer Protection
  Act) (US, 2010) 751,
  752
Dodge, Joseph 283, 361
Doha Round (WTO)
    651–5, 795
  agriculture negotiations
    651, 654
  Cancún meeting (2003)
    652
  effect of 2008/9 global
    financial crisis 654
  failure of 654–5, 774, 779

'framework agreement'
  (2004) 653
  non-tariff barriers 651
  and services 651
  and tariffs 651
Dole, Robert 643
'dollar pool' 140
dollar (US)
  Bretton Woods
    dependence on
    433–4
  crisis of confidence in
    (1970–71) 476–7,
    479–80, 485–6
  devaluation (1934) 50–53
  devaluation (1971) 503
  devaluation (1973) 511
  dominance of 816–17
  fixed against gold 369,
    377, 444
  and global financial crisis
    745
  and renminbi 817
  as reserve currency xix,
    376, 441
  speculation against 507
  stabilization of (1933)
    45–7
  stabilization of (1936)
    75–81
Domestic Credit Expansion,
  condition of IMF
  loans 596
domestic policies
  economic planning 86–7
  and international
    trade-offs xxviii–xxix,
    202
  in 'shallow multilateralism'
    796, 832–3
Dornbusch, Rudiger 697, 698
Douglas, Lewis 36
Draghi, Mario 756–7, 827
Dragoni, Carlo 86, 100
Drezner, Daniel 773
Dubos, René 560
Duffy, Michael 638
Duisenberg, Wim 703, 717
Dulles, Allen 404
Dulles, John Foster 325
Dunkel, Arthur 636–7,
    638–9
Dutt, Romesh Chunder 102
Dyson, Kenneth 725

Eady, Wilfrid 219, 244
East Africa, groundnuts
    scheme 317
East Asia

financial crisis (1997)
620–23
industrializing countries
584
see also South Korea
East Asian Free Trade
Agreement 653
ECB (European Central
Bank) 714, 715–17
and eurozone crisis 754,
755, 756–7
and fiscal rules 714–15
as lender of last resort in
EU 757
and loss of monetary
sovereignty 725
Outright Monetary
Transactions
(OMTs) 757
Pandemic Emergency
Purchase Programme
827
rejection of QE 754, 757
rules on debt 714–15,
716, 722, 754, 758,
827–8
support from US Federal
Reserve 742–3
Eccles, Marriner 479
Echeverría, Luis 535
ecology
and development
concerns 334–5, 557
effect of climate change
on 789
see also environment
Economic Commission for
Latin America
(ECLA) [and
Caribbean (ECLAC)]
(UN) xxxii, 358,
400, 410
Economic Cooperation Act
(US, 1948) 290
Economic Cooperation
Administration
(ECA) 246, 290–91,
297, 470
economic development
89–116
Australia 110–115
China 91, 97–101
India 91, 101–6
and post-war global
economy 115
Soviet model 91–7
economic growth
debate on limits of
552–65

and inequality 802
per capita income 765
post-war 567–8
slowing of 564–5, 568–9
social worth of assets 820
and welfare provision
560–61
economic planning, national
level 86–7
economic theory 84, 571–2,
798
dependency theory 536–7
and modernization theory
401–6
need for new perspectives
798–800, 833
and theory of three
worlds 536–7
The Economist
on IMF 415, 491
on Uruguay Round 640
on World Monetary and
Economic
Conference 56
ECOSOC *see* UN
Economic and Social
Council (ECOSOC)
Eden, Anthony 73, 127, 303
Edgerton, David 122
education
India 692, 693, 761
and levelling up 811
EEC (European Economic
Community) 295,
367, 633
Associated Overseas
Countries 425
British applications to
join 382, 457–8,
481–2
central bank governors'
committee 698, 703,
708
Common Agricultural
Policy 369, 384, 389,
455, 636, 708
and currencies: collective
float 512, 515, 517;
Economic and
Monetary Union
(EMU) 702, 708–10;
European Common
(Currency) Unit
(ECU) 702, 706;
European Monetary
System (EMS)
706–8; negotiations
on realignment 499,
500–502; role of

sterling 481–2; the
'snake' (currency
band) 505, 515, 517,
705–6, 708
Delors report 708–10
economists *v.* monetarists
debate 698–701,
707–8
European Monetary
Co-operation Fund
703, 706
European Unit of Account
702
on excess liquidity 447
exchange rate: flexible
455, 698; mechanism
(ERM) 712, 715
and former European
colonies 371, 425
institutional structure
383, 586
and interdependence 540
Maastricht Treaty (1992)
713–16
Marjolin report 701–3,
721
Monetary Committee 703
monetary zone 429, 706
moves towards
integration 501–2,
511–12, 698,
710–711; proposals
for economic and
monetary union
473–5, 698, 701–8,
712–13
and proposed Atlantic
Alliance 378–9
as protectionist threat
374, 388, 394
and regional development
initiatives 547–8
trade: common external
tariff 389; customs
union 697–8;
membership of WP3
and G10 438; share
of world trade 636
US: and American tariffs
530; criticism of
American policies
440–41, 705–6;
criticism of American
Selling Price 524;
relations with
369–71, 377, 432;
and US suspension of
convertibility 470–75,
490, 496, 499–502

EEC (European Economic Community) (*cont.*)
see also EU (European Union); European Community; GATT, Kennedy Round
Eggleston, Frederic 243–4
Egypt
Aswan Dam 333, 352
sterling balance (1945) 139
war with Israel 538
Ehrlich, Paul, *The Population Bomb* 563
Eichengreen, Barry 568, 714, 715
on global financial crisis 733–4, 736, 774
Einzig, Paul 608
Eisenhower, Dwight D. 273, 304, 323–4, 371, 406–7
'embedded liberalism' xxii, xxiii, 234–6
crisis of 564
Emminger, Otmar 440, 461, 481, 669
on Eurodollar market 613
and European Monetary System 708
and gold market 445
and OECD 438
and outflow of dollars to Germany 480, 499
employment
to create demand 179
ECOSOC and 320–23
full 169, 183–8, 259–61;
Australian commitment to 114, 186, 210, 211, 259–60
labour market changes 766–7
migrants and 811
need for reform 810–811
precarious 603, 729, 791–2, 802, 810–811
and trade 229, 244–5
UK 258–9, 451, 766–7
working from home 810
see also unemployment
energy
consumption 543–4, 820, 821
and environment 335
phasing out of fossil fuels 19, 822
solar power 821

switch to renewables 819, 821
and windfall tax on profits 808–9
see also oil
energy crisis (2022) (after Russian invasion of Ukraine) 793, 821, 828, 831
environment
and climate change 789
continuing concern for 590
and development concerns 334–5, 543, 557, 559–60
green revolution 552, 562–3
impact of pesticides on 558, 562
and WTO dispute 657
see also climate change; ecology
Erhard, Ludwig 383, 452
and Common Agricultural Policy 390
and currency reforms 283–4
and EEC/US tariffs 390
and German economic reform 284–5
Essen, Germany 214
Essential Commodities Reserves Act (1938) 180
EU (European Union) (from 1993) 713–14
banks' exposure to US mortgage debts 744–5, 753
budget 705, 709, 721, 827
and China 829, 831
Council of Ministers 724
and Doha Round 651, 654
economic disequilibrium 824
and emissions trading system 819, 828
European Financial Stabilization Facility 755
and eurozone crisis (2008–13) 719, 753–8
fiscal rules 714–15, 721–2
IMF and 724–5

Lisbon Treaty (2007) 724, 755
national institutional variations 721, 724
need for banking union 756
NextGen recovery fund (2020) 827–8
north-south imbalance within 722, 757–8
relations between eurozone and other members 719–20
reliance on Russian energy supplies 828, 831
and Russia 685, 831
single currency *see* euro
single market 589
Stability and Growth Pact 716–17
structural weaknesses 720, 724
and supra-nationality 778
Trump's trade war with 786
and US global corporation taxation 806
and US protectionism 826
view of Eurodollar market 613–14
see also EEC; euro; European Central Bank; European Commission; eurozone
EU-China Comprehensive Agreement on Investment 829
eugenics 333–4
euro (EU single currency) 589, 698, 705–6, 717–18
adoption 720
convergence criteria 714–15, 717
measures to preserve 756–7
as reserve currency 723–4
see also eurozone; eurozone crisis
Eurocurrency Market Control Act, proposed 615
Eurodollar market 607, 608–10
London 355, 595, 608–10
US 608–9, 610–613

Europe
labour migration to
Americas xx
post-war economic crisis
213, 214, 215,
247–8, 272–3
proposals for integration
287–95
Schuman plans for
federation 293–5
US proposals for customs
union 251–2, 292
wartime food shortages
173
see also EEC; EU; France;
Germany; Marshall
Aid
European Bank for
Reconstruction and
Development
(EBRD) 684
European Coal and Steel
Community (ECSC)
293–5, 372
European Commission
and dollar pricing 816–17
One Market, One Money
(1990) 713
and profit-shifting 806
regulation of competition
801
European Community
and GATT 639
and WTO 641
see also EEC; EU
European Council, and
banking union 756
European Court of Justice
586, 756, 757
European Defence
Community,
proposed 303
European Free Trade Area
(EFTA) 382
European Monetary
Authority, proposed
471
European Parliament,
powers of 724
European Payments Union
(EPU) 276, 295–9,
367
as model for international
monetary reform 471
proposed European
Reserve Fund 471–2
European Recovery
Programme see
Marshall Plan

eurozone
comparison with US
system 721–3
design flaws 720–21,
754–5, 826–7
effect of pandemic on 827
expulsion from 756, 826
prospects for 723–4, 817,
826–8
as sub-optimal currency
area 720–26, 758,
817
eurozone crisis (2008–13)
719, 753–8
sovereign debts 753
and 'troika' of IMF, EU
and ECB 754, 755,
774
Evans, F. E. 121
'ever-normal granary',
concept of 175–6, 181
Evergrande, Chinese
property company
763, 830
exchange rates
in 1930s xix, xxii
and collapse of Bretton
Woods system
517–18
and devaluations 50–53,
433
floating 300–305, 429,
449–54, 494–531;
attempts to manage
519–24, 625–6
fluctuations after Bretton
Woods 518
margins of flexibility
454–6
pegged (1940s-1973) xxii,
200–202, 433
stabilization fund and
160
and Tripartite
Agreement 80
US view of flexibility
512–15
see also currency
convertibility; gold
standard
export earnings fluctuations,
developing countries
416, 422
export-led growth 360–64,
408
China 666, 673, 793, 829
East Asian model 364,
591, 638, 761
Latin America 107, 359

export-led industrialization
363–4, 556–7, 585
Extinction Rebellion
movement 819
Ezekiel, Mordecai 54

'fair trade', US use of term
525–6
Fairtrade groups 646–7
Falconer, Crawford 654
famines 173, 563
China 348–9
Fanon, Frantz, The
Wretched of the
Earth 337, 343
Federal Open Market
Committee 575, 577
Federal Reserve see US
Federal Reserve
Federal Reserve Act (US,
1977) 574
Federal Union 87
Feis, Herbert 17, 39, 40, 43
Feldstein, Martin 621–2,
713, 718
Ferguson, Niall 784
Ferrari Aggradi, Mario 495
finance, international
and national regulation
812
political influence 750, 814
power of 589, 744–5
remuneration 811–12
and vested interests 813
finance ministers, and global
governance 519
financial crises
1982 Mexican debt
617–20
1997 East Asia xxiv,
620–23
see also eurozone crisis
(2008–13); global
financial crisis
(2007–8)
Financial Crisis Inquiry
Commission (US)
751
financial derivatives, US
market in 732
financial markets
inherent instability 749
and 'invisible earnings'
610
liberalization of 607–12
need for improved
regulation 751–3
see also Eurodollar
market

Financial Services Authority (UK) 610, 747–8
Financial Stability Forum 751
Financial Stability Oversight Council (US) 751
Financial Times
  on Biden's spending plans 826
  on Doha Round 654–5, 779
  on EU single currency 721
  on G20 783
  on WTO 797
financialization xxiv, 587–8
  need for de-financialization 811–13
  and pandemic 793
  and risk 729, 812, 813
  of trade 612
  of US elite 804
First World War
  breakdown of economic order xviii–xix, 763
  economic co-operation of allies xxi, 13
  postwar food shortages 174
  and trade 10–12
  see also reparations; war debt
Fisher, Irving 37, 50, 75
Flanigan, Peter 527, 528
Fleming, Marcus 508
Food and Agriculture Organization (FAO) (1945) xxii, 179, 308, 794, 818
  and disposal of surpluses 416
  establishment 178
  and global population growth 326–7
  and Hot Springs conference (1943) 171–9
Food and Nutrition Policy and Planning programme (MIT) 563
Food for Peace Act (US, 1966) 393, 411
food safety, WTO disputes and 656–7
food stamps, United States 170, 175
food supply 173, 174, 175

and green revolution 552, 562–3
  see also agriculture; nutrition
Ford Foundation, and community development 331, 346
Ford, Gerald 522, 545, 546
  fast-track authority for tariff reduction 529
  and leadership of West 548
  Trade Reform Act (1974) 529–30
Ford, Henry 16
foreign exchange reserves 442, 442
foreign investment 264–5
  from 1980s 595
  American 311–12, 387
  bilateral treaties 624–5
  British (pre-1914) 310–311
  and capital flows 435, 813
  China 665–6
  in Latin America 617
  private 310, 311
Foreign Securities (Johnson) Act (US, 1934) 48–9, 122–3
Fosdick, Raymond 328
Foster, William Trufant 36–7
Foundation for Economic Education 216
Fowler, Henry 448
France
  and 1973 oil shock 517
  and Allied occupation of Germany 249
  and Arab oil producers 539
  and Clayton's customs union 251
  colonies 317, 318–19
  and currencies: pressure on franc (1968–9) 459; proposals for currency stabilization 162; and proposed flotation of Deutsche Mark 481; and realignment of currencies (1971) 501–2
  and developing countries 547, 583

and ECSC 293–4
Europe: British applications to join EEC 481–2; and Common Agricultural Policy 384, 389; and economic convergence 700, 705–6, 707–8; and euro convergence criteria 717; and proposed customs union 13; and single currency 712
and GATT 372; agriculture negotiations 639; Kennedy Round 'empty chair' crisis 384, 391
and gold standard 45, 77; gold as basis for monetary stability 442–4, 447; leaves (1914) 23; return to (1928) 23, 32
IBRD loan 307
income distribution 765
Marshall Aid 291
Popular Front government (1936) 77
proposed imperial customs union 370
Second World War: fall of (1940) 122; and German reparations 26–7
and tariffs xx, 389
taxation: and corporation tax 806; demand for tax on financial transactions 767; taxation of digital companies 806
and Tripartite Agreement (1936) 76–9
and UNCTAD 419
and US 379; and American Trade Expansion Act 388–9; and US suspension of convertibility 469
and World Monetary and Economic Conference (1933) 44
Frank, Andre Gunder, *The Development of*

Underdevelopment 536
Frankfurter, Felix 37
Franklin Bank 615
Franks, Oliver 296
free trade
  British commitment to 11–13
  changing attitudes to 515, 646
free trade areas
  compared with customs unions 370
  see also NAFTA
Freedom from Hunger Campaign (1959) 327
French National Committee of Liberation 162
Frieden, Jeffry 720
Friedman, Milton 571, 572, 697
  Capitalism and Freedom (1962) 450
  and China 668
  on corporations 800
  criticism of IMF 622
  on ECB 716
  on euro 754
  on exchange rates 201–2, 432, 449–51, 452–3, 512
  and income support benefits 582
  on Indian development programmes 346–7
  and Nixon 452–3
  and suspension of convertibility 484
  on US domestic monetary policy 478
  on wage and price controls (1971) 489
Friends of the Earth 559
Fukuda, Takeo 476
Full Employment Act (US, 1946) 244–5, 258
Full Employment and Balanced Growth Act (US, 1978) 574
Funk, Walther 148–9, 150, 295–6
Furtado, Celso 314, 536

G-77 (group of developing countries)
  Algiers meeting (1967) 423
  divisions among 585

Manila meeting 548–9, 551
  origins in UNCTAD 421, 423
  on Uruguay Round 640
  see also Non-Aligned Movement
G7 (G8) group of countries 520, 606, 626
  and austerity 739
  and Financial Stability Forum 615–16
  and international oversight 523
  Russian membership 688–9, 759
G10 432, 438
  and Basel Committee on Banking Supervision (1974) 615
  London meeting (1971) 499
  Paris meeting (1973) 513–14
  proposal for Composite Reserve Unit 446–7
  proposals for liquidity creation 447–8
  Washington meeting (1971) 500, 507
G20 778, 782–5
  2009 summit (London) xvii–xviii, xxxi, 730, 733–4
  and austerity policy 739
  and currency manipulation 783
  Debt Service Suspension Initiative 815–16
  divisions within 783–4
  Eminent Persons Group 785
  and Financial Stability Board 751–2
  and IMF funding 775
  lack of influence 783–4
  membership 782–3
  and profit-shifting 806
  protests at 767
  Seoul meeting (2010) 783–4
  and Trump's attack on multilateralism 787
Gaidar, Yegor 659, 684–5
  Soviet economic reforms 681, 685–6
Galbraith, J. K. 385, 386, 387–8
Gandhi, Indira xxv, 690–91

Gandhi, Mahatma 105, 340
  vision for development 102–3, 344, 345–6
Gandhi, Rahul 760
Gandhi, Rajiv 691–2
Gandhi, Sanjay 691
Gardner, Richard 413
Garner, Robert 308–9, 313, 314
Gaspar, Vítor 806
Gates, Bill 804
Gates Foundation 795
GATT (General Agreement on Tariffs and Trade) (1947) xxii, 240, 255, 365, 777
  Dillon Round 374
  failure of 'group' negotiations 585
  Generalized System of Preferences 531
  Geneva Round 240, 252–5, 376
  and industrial trade preferences 425
  and International Trade Centre 419
  Kennedy Round 371, 388–97, 424; agricultural negotiations 393–4; geopolitical influences 395–6; industrial negotiations 393–4; negotiating teams 381–4; shortcomings 395; tariff reductions 389–90, 394–5, 396, 424
  membership 271–2, 372–3, 414–15
  'most favoured nation' principle 11
  need for dispute settlement mechanism 638
  negotiations on 252–5
  'Quad' group 640, 641, 643
  and quantitative restrictions 414, 419
  readmission of China 673–5
  and reciprocity 413–14
  relation to IMF xxxii–xxxiii
  review (1954–5) 371–2
  Russian membership 689

GATT (General Agreement on Tariffs and Trade) (*cont.*)
services and intellectual property 587, 637, 638
Soviet Union and 235
tariff negotiations 253
Tokyo round (1973) 528–31, 631, 633
trade agreements 253–5, 270–72; regional 633, 636
Trade Policy Review Mechanism 639, 641
trade rounds 375
transformation into World Trade Organization (1995) xxxi, 586
TRIMS agreement 637, 638, 640
TRIPS agreement 637, 638, 640, 676
and UN Development Decade 413–15
and WTO 633, 641
see also Uruguay Round; WTO
Gaud, William 562
Gazprom 686, 759
Geithner, Tim 746–7, 751, 783
General Arrangements to Borrow (IMF) 446
G10 and 438
General Strike (1926) 21
Generalized System of Preferences 422, 424–5, 531
call for extension 536, 547
'Genevan liberals', at GATT 585–6
Georgia 683
Georgieva, Kristalina xxv, 822
Germany
and Brazil 108–9
Bundesbank Act (1957) 573
and China 829
and corporation tax 806
'debt brake' 740, 755
dependence on Russian energy supplies 828
and ECB 757, 827–8
and EPU 299
and European economic convergence 699–700, 705–6, 707–8

and eurozone crisis 754–5, 758
household savings 588
inter-war period 6, 69; hyperinflation (1921–3) 23, 27; and over-valuation of Reichsmark 67, 69; rearmament (1934) 68–70; recession (1929) 27; relations of Third Reich with BIS 204–5; Schachtian economic policy 67–72; trade bloc (south-east and central Europe) 59, 70; trade with Britain (1930s) 68
low domestic consumption 769
and oil prices 517, 541
post-war: Allied occupation 248–9, 288; American policy 180, 236–9; Bizone division 288; conditions 247–8, 284; economic rise xxvii; Marshall Plan 275–6, 286; new currency (1947) 249, 283–4
and realignment of currencies (1971) 501–2
reunification 639, 685, 712, 716
Second World War 7, 122, 195
social market economy 285–6, 575
unification (1871) 699
war debt settlements 286–7
and war debts and reparations (First World War) 25, 26, 67
and World Monetary and Economic Conference (1933) 44
see also Bundesbank; West Germany
Ghana
Akosombo Dam 333, 354
cocoa 317, 353–5
Soviet aid to 354

Gilder, George, *Wealth and Poverty* 578
Gilman, Nils 533
Giscard d'Estaing, Valéry xix, 440, 696
and European integration 701, 705–6
and international monetary reform 472–3, 510
and joint float of European currencies 512
and oil prices 541
Rambouillet summit 520, 548
and Volcker 499
Glass, Carter 109
Glass-Steagall Act (1933 US) 751
repeal (1999) 747, 752
global economic order
disequilibrium 793–4
and distributive justice xxxiii–xxxiv, 555
and economic theory 571–2
effect of Chinese economic growth on 676–7, 694–5, 759, 784, 816
and EU 725–6
post-global financial crisis discussions 781–6
pre-First World War xix–xx, 763
structural changes (1980s) 595
see also Bretton Woods; G20; GATT; globalization; IMF; World Bank; WTO
global financial crisis (2007–8) xxiv, 630, 654, 689, 729, 770
austerity 734, 737, 738, 739–40
comparison with Great Depression 733–4, 747, 773, 774
and debt sustainability 738
dominant narratives of 799–800
effect on global trade 773–4
'expansionary fiscal contraction' 737, 743

fiscal sustainability
740–41
and global influence of
China 759
monetary interventions
742–5
origins 732–3
partial recovery 734, 735
proposals for fiscal
stimulus 736–7, 739,
740
regulatory response to
750–53
stagnant wages 734,
743–4
swap networks 744–5
and weak regulation
747–53
global income distribution
694, 695
Global South
divergence within 583
see also developing
countries; Third
World
Global Trade Watch 646
globalization
and de-globalization
831–3
dropped (1930s) xxviii
and inequality 764–9
integration of supply
chains xxiv, 595,
657, 766, 831–2
potential backlash 763,
764
views of 763–4
Glyn, Andrew 570
Goebbels, Joseph 67
Goerdeler, Carl 69–71, 72,
283
gold
as basis of monetary
stability 442–4, 447
Keynes's plan to
de-monetize 150–51
London market for 444–5
market price of 444, 521
price against dollar
(1934) 51–2
as reserve asset 521, 522
US sale of (1933) 50–52
see also gold standard
Gold Act (US, 1900) 51
Gold, Joseph 598
Gold Reserve Act (US,
1934) 51–2
Gold Stabilization Act (US,
1934) 163

gold standard 19–25
after 1933 conference 48
France and 23, 32, 45, 77
League of Nations and
24–5
and prices 20, 21–2
problems of xix–xx,
22–4, 149
and reparations and war
debts 24–5
and wages 21
gold window, Nixon's
closure of 469–70,
485–91, 494
Goldenweiser, E. A. 189,
193, 218
Goldsmith, Raymond 283
Gompers, Samuel 183, 184
'good governance', IMF and
604–6
Goodhart, Charles 614
Gopinath, Gita 776, 812,
817
Gorbachev, Mikhail 659,
660
and democratic reforms
682–3
detente with West 683
economic reforms 681–3
glasnost (openness) 682
perestroika (reform) 681
Gore, Al 821, 822
Gore, Charles 602–3
Göring, Hermann 69–70
Gossett, William 381
Government of India Act
(1935) 105
Graduate Institute of
International Studies,
Geneva 83, 87
Graham, Frank 201, 202
grain prices 111, 393
Great Britain see United
Kingdom
Great Depression xxv, 6
comparison with global
financial crisis 733–4,
747, 773, 774
economic effects of 5–6
effect on trade policies
14–15
League of Nations study
on causes 82, 83–4
politics of 5–10
response of primary
producers to 91
Greece
and euro convergence
criteria 717

famine 173
northern European
criticism of 758
sovereign debt crisis 753,
754
Syriza Party 756
Green, Jeremy 611
green 'new deal' 818–24
Greenspan, Alan 522, 593,
628, 748–9
Gregory, Theodore 196
Grigg, James 20, 104, 258
growth see economic
growth; export-led
growth
Gucht, Karel De 779
Guevara, Che 399
Guffey, Roger 577
Guinea
and OPEC 538
Soviet aid to 353
Guitián, Manuel 597–8, 626
Gulick, Luther 152
Guterres, António 794
Gutt, Camille 200
Gyohten, Toyoo 626

Haass, Richard 785
Haberler, Gottfried 81, 83,
198, 360
on exchange rates 517
and New International
Economic Order
534, 586
Prosperity and
Depression (1937)
201
report on GATT 373–4,
414
and US balance of
payments 464–5
Halifax, Lord 223
Hall, Robert 275, 282, 321
and sterling convertibility
301–2, 303, 304
Hallstein, Dr Walter 366,
383, 697–8
Hansen, Alvin 75, 152, 169,
171, 208
and full employment
244–5
Haq, Mahbub ul 554, 560,
590
Hardin, Garrett, 'tragedy of
the commons' 563–4
Harmer, Frederic 223
Harriman, Averell 249–50,
296, 354
Harrison, George 45, 75

Harrod, Roy 182, 193, 209
  on Keynes's clearing
    union 152–3, 154
Hartke, Vance 527
Havana conference
    (1947–8) (UN
    Conference on Trade
    and Employment)
    239–40, 241, 243,
    255
  and foreign investment
    312
  Havana Charter 242,
    265–6
  Latin American demands
    263–5
  see also International
    Trade Organization
Hawkins, Harry 65, 126,
    241, 243, 254
Hawley, Willis 15
Hayashi, Taizo 476
Hayek, Friedrich von 82,
    86, 572
  Constitution of Liberty
    571
  on exchange rates 201
  need for international
    rules 585–6
  The Road to Serfdom
    86–7
Hazlitt, Henry 216
Healey, Denis 519, 541,
    579, 582
Heath, Edward 482, 506,
    516, 552, 578
hedge funds 814
hegemonic stability
    xxviii–xxix
Helleiner, Eric 785
Henderson, Hubert 145,
    151–2
Hennessy, Peter 792
Herriot, Édouard 28, 34, 38
Herstatt Bank 615
Herter, Christian 377,
    381–2, 389
Hicks, John 570–71
Highly Indebted Poor
    Countries, loans
    written off 606
Hindenburg, Paul von 67
Hirschman, Albert 314–15,
    553, 601
Hitler, Adolf 27, 38, 44,
    58, 67
Hobson, John 12, 22, 36,
    768–9
Hoffman, Paul 245–6, 331

and ECA 246, 290–91
and EPU 296
and Marshall Plan 274
and South Korea 362
Hofstadter, Richard 9
Hollande, François 780
Homburg plan, for German
    economic recovery
    283
Home Owners' Loan
    Corporation (US) 54,
    746
Hong Kong 435, 788, 831
Hoover, Herbert 32, 174
  on European post-war
    recovery 247–8
  and German economic
    crisis (1931) 27
  and gold standard 23
  and tariffs 15, 16
Hoover Institution 600
Hopkins, Harry 165
Hormats, Robert 496, 520,
    545–6
Hot Springs conference
    (1943) 168, 171–9
  and agriculture 173–4
  food shortages 173
Houthakker, Hendrik 457
Howe, Geoffrey 582, 610
Huawei, US action against
    828
Hugenberg, Alfred 38
Hull, Cordell 8, 9
  and alliance against
    authoritarianism
    74–5
  and Brazil 108, 109
  and China 100
  on free trade 646
  on Germany 72, 74, 238
  and IBRD 206
  and import substitution
    107
  and post-war economic
    policy 132–3, 155
  and proposed
    International Trade
    Organization 228
  and Reciprocal Trade
    Agreements Act 57,
    61–6
  relations with UK 73–4,
    125, 129–30
  and tariffs 16–17, 60
  and World Monetary and
    Economic
    Conference (1933)
    34, 39–40, 42–3

human behaviour, and
    rationalism 601, 680,
    750, 798
Human Development Index
    590
human rights
  Atlantic Charter and 129
  China 675, 788, 831
Humphrey, Hubert 574
Hungary
  economic reform model
    667, 669–70
  IMF and 775
  right-wing populism 773,
    828
Huxley, Julian 333–4, 559
hyper-globalization 629
  inequalities of 649–50,
    694

Ibarra, David 599
IBRD (International Bank
    for Reconstruction
    and Development)
    159, 307–36
  dams and irrigation
    projects 306,
    315–16, 331–3
  and development 424,
    542
  establishment (at Bretton
    Woods) 206–9, 233
  funding 309
  loans: criteria for 309–10;
    distribution of
    (1946–61) 315;
    limitations on 197–8,
    207–8; types
    (project/programme)
    312–15
  missions 313–14, 315–16
  and reconstruction of
    war-hit areas 307
  and regional development
    banks 326
  and UNCTAD 419
  see also World Bank
identity politics 764, 768,
    794–5
  US 824
Ikenberry, John 773
ILO (International Labour
    Organization) xxi,
    xxxii, 29, 85
  and labour standards
    184–5, 645
  Philadelphia conference
    (1944) 115, 168,
    210; Declaration of

Philadelphia (1944)
186–7
post-war marginalization
of 187–8
IMF (International
Monetary Fund)
(1944) xxii, xxx,
xxxii
amendment of Articles
521–2, 596, 607,
614, 628
and capital account
liberalization
627–30, 775–6, 795
and capital controls
434–5, 627, 813–14
and carbon pricing 819
China and 101
and collapse of EMS
724–5
Compensatory Financing
Facility 422, 424,
446, 522, 547
on 'crony capitalism' 364,
750
establishment 166, 233,
625
and eurozone crisis 754,
755–6
and exchange rates 775;
flexibility 455–6,
517–18; management
of floating rates
519–24, 626
and export earnings
fluctuations 416, 422
funds xxxi, 606, 606; and
conditionality
199–200, 596–7,
603–4, 777; and
cross-conditionality
599; debt re-
scheduling 606,
619–20, 774, 797;
for development 197;
General
Arrangements to
Borrow 446; Special
Drawing Rights
448–9, 547, 817–18,
822; 'stand-by
agreements' 596,
597; structural
adjustment lending
587, 591–2, 597–8
and global corporation
taxation 806
and global financial crisis
740–41, 774–7

and 'good governance'
604–6, 688
governance structure and
voting system 775;
Council of Economic
Advisers 437, 515;
inaugural meeting of
Board of Governors
144; Interim
Committee 593, 602,
627–8
'Guidelines on
Conditionality'
(2002) 605
on income inequality 802,
808
and India 691
Madrid declaration
(1994) 602
and market liberalism
593, 595, 596–606
and Mexico 618–20
and petrodollars 614
policy: changing 585,
776–7, 797; focus on
growth 597;
Integrated Policy
Framework 776; 'one
size fits all' approach
601–3; and Plan X
reforms 509–10
problems of: budgetary
crisis (2003) 606;
criticisms of 415,
437, 498, 621–2;
declining influence
625–30, 774, 794;
failure of leadership
432, 460, 491, 498;
limitations of 795;
political interference
621–2; US
domination 498–9,
775, 817; weakness
of 299, 437, 507
reaction to US suspension
of convertibility 490
relationship to GATT
and IBRD
xxxii–xxxiii
response to pandemic
808
and risks of financial
liberalization 812
role: in banking system
616–17; changing
522, 523–4;
stabilization role
198–200, 299

and Russia 604, 661, 684,
685, 686
and South Korea 591–2,
594, 602, 621–3
superseded by G7 626
and taxation of
transactions 806
and UK Labour
government (1976)
580, 581
and UNCTAD 418–19
World Economic Outlook
(2010) 737
World Economic Outlook
(2019) 802
imperial preference (British)
xxx, 18–19, 70, 127,
264
American hostility to xxx,
19, 73, 125–6, 138,
213, 215
modified (1937) 74
imperialism, as obstacle to
change 535–6
import-substitution
industrialization 107,
108, 110, 359, 407–8
India 343–4
shift from 359, 360, 418,
691, 692
South Korea 362
income disparity 588, 765,
766
global 694, 695
IMF on 802, 808
and need for
redistribution 831
UK 765, 766–7
US 765, 767, 802
see also inequality
India xx, 101–2, 542,
690–95
American assistance for
410–411
Bengal famine (1942–3)
105
Bharatiya Janata Party
(BJP) 693–4, 760–62
Bombay Plan (1944)
105–6, 690
and Bretton Woods 106,
196–7
bureaucracy 693, 694
'Citizens for Democracy'
691
community projects
345–6; model
villages 346; village
co-operatives 86, 690

INDEX

India (*cont.*)
crony capitalism 762
Damodar Valley 333, 345
deficiency diseases 175
democratic modernization 404
and Doha Round 654
economic development 91, 101–6, 260, 343–7, 661, 662; five-year plans 344–5; land reform 331, 345; move from import-substitution 343–4, 691, 692; new industries 692; *swadeshi* (home-grown consumption) 693, 694
economic growth 692–3, 761, 762
economic liberalization 692–4, 760, 761–2
food self-sufficiency 562
foreign exchange crisis (1991) 692
Forum of Free Enterprise 690
and global financial crisis 760
and globalization 693–4
IMF loans 691, 692
independence (1947) 105, 106, 316, 339
industrial licences 691
infrastructure 692, 694, 761–2; education 692, 693, 761; poor sanitation and health 175, 761
and ITO 262–3
National Extension Service 345
National Institution for Transforming India 760
National Planning Commission 103, 105–6
nationalism 101–2; Hindu nationalism 693–4, 760–61
nationalizations 690–91
Naxalite Maoist guerrillas 356
Planning Commission 690, 760
social and religious divisions 693, 760

and South Africa 340
and sterling balances 139, 277–9
Swatantra Party 690–91
voluntary sterilization 564, 691
war with China 342, 356
and WTO 651
Indian Institutes of Technology 692
Indian National Army 104
individualism
and community 799
and inequality 800
rise of 569
Indo-China, French colonies 317
Indonesia
and Cairns group 637
green revolution 563
and IMF 597
Maoist Communists 342, 356
industrialization
critiques of 102
development equated with 323, 336
East Asia 360
export-led 363–4, 556–7, 585
India 103
Soviet Union and 7, 92, 93–4, 353
see also de-industrialization; import-substitution industrialization
industry, structural relationship to primary products 89, 91
inequality
corporate earnings differentials 801, *801*
effects of 587–8, 805
global financial crisis and 796–7; austerity 741, 742, 743, 752, 809–10; QE 742, 743–4, 746, 752, 765
and globalization 649–50, 694, 764–9
health 791–2
India 760
and individualism 800
and 'levelling up' 810–811
pandemic and 791–2

and political power 767–8
protest movements against 747, 752, 767–8
and rise of populist nationalism 768, 773–4, 786–9
and trade wars 768–9
inflation
1960–2020: 577
1970s xxiii, 429
apparent control of (2000s) 731
central banks' focus on 748–9
and energy crisis 793
and interest rates 435–6
and monetary policy 565, 570
and risk of recession 582
UK 507
US 478, 575–6
and wage demands 569–70
information technology 595, 608
and digital business 805–6
India 692
and labour market changes 767
and trade expansion 657
inheritance tax 55, 807, 807
Inkeles, Alex and David Smith, *Becoming Modern . . .* (1974) 401
insecticides, ecological effects of 329
Institute of Development Studies, Sussex University 554–5
Redistribution with Growth (with World Bank) 555
Institute of Fiscal Studies 807
Institute for International Economics 599
Institute of International Finance 748, 752, 816
institutions, international agreements xxxi
calls for reforms 509–10, 774, 778–9, 822
developing countries and xxii–xxiv, xxx, 235, 336, 774

and internationalism xxii, 86–7
limitations of 437–8, 794, 795–6
negotiations xxxiii
and networks 785–6, 797
post-First World War xxi
pre-First World War xix–xx
representation in xxxii–xxxiv
Second World War and xxii
supranational xxxi–xxxii, 86
see also Bretton Woods; FAO; GATT; IBRD; ILO; IMF; UN; WHO; World Bank; WTO
intellectual property rights
Doha Round 651
Non-Agricultural Market Access 651
TRIPS (GATT) 637
WTO and 642
Inter-American Conference on Problems of War and Peace (1945) 110
Inter-American Development Bank 326, 553
Inter-American Economic Conference, Rio de Janeiro (1942) 158
Inter-American Economic Conference, Bogotá (1949) 265
Inter-American Financial and Economic Advisory Committee 180–81
Inter-American Trading Corporation, proposed 181
Inter-Asian Relations Conference (1947) 341
interdependence 577
and development 540–42
Interest Equalization Tax (IET) (US, 1963) 386–7, 436
interest rates
effect of gold standard on 22
and inflation 435–6, 575

and short-term financial flows 436
International Association for Labour Legislation (1900) 183–4
International Center for Maize and Wheat Improvement 532, 561
International Centre for Settlement of Investment Disputes 553, 624, 756
International Chamber of Commmerce 29, 624
International Conference on Nutrition, National Development and Planning (1971) 563
international conferences
negotiations xxix, xxx–xxxi, xxxiii
see also Bretton Woods; Havana; Lausanne; Paris; UN Climate Change; World Monetary (London)
International Development Association 547, 553
International Finance Corporation 547
International Financial Institution Advisory Commission (US) 622
International Institute of Agriculture, Italy (1905) xix, 85, 86
International Labour and Socialist Conference (Berne, 1919) 183
International Meeting on Cooperation and Development (Cancún, 1981) 583–4
International Resources Bank, proposed 549
International Rice Research Institute 561
International Telegraph Union (1865) xix
International Trade Centre 419
International Trade Organization 256–65, 777–8
failure of 270, 272

Havana Charter: drafting 256–65; signing 242, 265–6
proposed (1947–8) 115, 228, 240
voting rights 256
International Wheat Conference (1942) 176
internationalism 600
and institutions xxii, 86–7
League of Nations and 82–3
United States and 109, 218
Iran
at Bandung 342
Islamic Republic 584
Iran–Iraq war 584
Iraq
at Bandung 342
External Development Fund 538
invasion of Kuwait 639
oil 538, 545
and UN Development Decade 413
Ireland
banking crisis 753, 755
referendum on Maastricht 715
Islamic Development Bank 815
Israel, Egyptian attack (1973) 538
Istel, André 162
Italy
debt 753, 827
and Ethiopia 59
and euro convergence criteria 717
fascism 6, 86
International Institute of Agriculture (1905) xix
at Rambouillet summit 520

Jackson, John 396
Jackson, Julian 641
Jackson, Tim 820
Jacobsson, Per 32–3, 204–5, 415, 437, 446, 607, 616
Jamaica Accord (1976) 521–2
James, Harold 724, 725, 763–4

Japan 6
   at Bandung 342
   and China 831
   compared with US 575,
      588
   and Comprehensive
      Economic
      Partnership for East
      Asia 653
   and currencies:
      management of
      floating rates 519;
      and realignment
      502–3, 511; and US
      suspension of
      convertibility 470,
      475–6
   economy xxiii, xxix;
      export-led growth
      361–2; policy 361,
      476
   and GATT (Kennedy
      Round) 395
   household savings 588
   income distribution 765
   and India 104
   invasion of Manchuria
      (1931) 59, 99
   land reform 330
   Ministry of International
      Trade and Industry
      361–2
   modernization (from
      1868) 98, 360
   Second World War 124,
      139, 195; American
      occupation 360–61
   tariffs and import
      controls 361–2
   US trade deal (1969) 466
   zaibatsu and keiretsu
      business groups 361
Jay, Peter 506
Jebb, Gladwyn 292
Jenkins, Roy 703–5, 706
Jews, and German economic
   policy 70, 71
Jha, L. K. 414, 417
John Birch Society, on global
   trade agenda 781
Johnson, Boris 792, 809
Johnson (Foreign Securities)
   Act (US, 1934) 48–9,
   122–3
Johnson, Hiram 48
Johnson, Lyndon 269, 368,
   456, 497
   and GATT 365, 393,
      394–5

and multilateralism 396
preferences for developing
   countries 397
at Punta del Este (1967)
   425
tax on foreign investment
   387
and Vietnam War 398
Johnson, Simon 750
Jones, Jesse 51
Jones, Marvin 176
Joshi, Vijay 761–2
Judt, Tony 718
'just in time' delivery 657

Kafka, Alexandre 315, 508,
   522, 523, 617
Kahn, Richard 454–5
Kaldor, Nicholas 451–2, 721
   'National and
      International
      Measures for Full
      Employment' 321
Kantor, Mickey 639–40
Karnataka State Farmers
   Union 646
Kashiwagi, Yusuke 476, 503
Katznelson, Ira 18
Kay, John 798, 799
Kemmerer, Edwin 50, 110
Kennan, George 248, 250,
   288, 289–90
Kennedy, David 463, 467,
   470
Kennedy, John F. 269, 366
   and aid for India
      410–411
   and Alliance for Progress
      409–12
   and anti-Communist
      policy 409–10
   and balance of payments
      368–9, 386–7
   and CIS modernization
      theory 401–2
   and GATT negotiations
      372
   inaugural address (1961)
      365, 367
   Latin American task force
      408
   and price of gold 444
   and proposed Atlantic
      Alliance 378–9
   State of the Union
      Address (1962) 378
   and Trade Expansion Act
      375–81
   trade policy 375–7

and UN Development
   Decade 412
Kennedy, Joseph 232–3
Kennedy, Paul xvii, 773, 833
Kenya, and WTO 651
Kenyatta, Jomo 319
'key currency' plan 217–18
Keynes, John Maynard 24,
   37, 144, 145, 169,
   791
   Bretton Woods 146–7,
      193–4; Atlantic City
      meeting 191–3; and
      ratification 229–30,
      231–2
   on capital flows 202–3
   and commodities schemes
      180, 181–2
   and direct foreign
      investment 435
   The Economic
      Consequences of Mr
      Churchill 21
   The Economic
      Consequences of the
      Peace xviii–xix, 25–6
   and Funk 148–9, 150
   General Theory of
      Employment, Interest
      and Money (1936)
      82, 570–71
   on Harry Dexter White
      156–7, 161–2
   and IBRD 207–8, 233–4
   and IMF 198–9, 233–4,
      596
   and imperial preference
      18, 220
   and India 196
   and internationalism 793
   on Lloyd George 26
   on mercantilism 59
   and post-war Germany
      215, 236
   and post-war monetary
      reform 143, 145,
      149; and clearing
      union plan 149–55,
      162, 163–4; proposal
      for new monetary
      system 53, 82; on
      return to gold
      standard 20–21,
      147–8; and role of
      international bank
      149, 150–51
   'Proposals to counter the
      German "new
      order"' 213

and protectionism 203,
793
and scheme for German
bonds (1919) 25
*Tract on Monetary
Reform* (1923)
20–21
Treatise on Money (1930)
147–8, 149
and US 123, 132, 223;
negotiation of
American loan
220–23, 224–6; on
Roosevelt 47, 51;
view of terms of
Lend Lease 126–8
on World Monetary and
Economic
Conference 56
Keynesianism
China and 668
commercial 246
end of in UK 581
in response to global
financial crisis 736
Keyserling, Leon 246
Khmer Rouge, Cambodia
356
Khrushchev, Nikita 351,
352, 356
and Mao 348
relations with West 355,
416
support for liberation
movements 355
Kimball, Warren 62, 131
Kindleberger, Charles xxix,
169, 171, 208, 322,
357
King, Alexander 551, 558
King, Mervyn 625, 736, 774
on economic thinking
798, 799
proposals on banking
813
Kirchner, Cristina Fernández
de 733
Kissinger, Henry
and China 461, 463
and economic policies: on
capital controls 466;
ignorance of
economics 498; and
realignment of
currencies 502; and
suspension of
convertibility 469
on interdependence
540–42[policy of

'divide and rule' for
LDCs 546–7
and Nixon's foreign
policy 496
and trade policy 528; and
commodities
agreements 549; and
protectionism 525
view of European
integration 513–14
and Volcker working
group on
international
monetary issues 465
Klarman, Seth 803
Klein, Matthew 768–9
Kohl, Helmut 678, 712–13,
718
Kondratiev, Nikolai 92, 94
Korea
division (1953) 362
early industrialization
360
see also South Korea
Korean War 270–71, 289,
400
Kornai, János 669–70,
678–9
Kosygin, Alexei 356
Krishna, V. S. 197
Kristol, Irving 545
Krueger, Anne 587, 589
Krugman, Paul 601, 733,
740
Kubitschek, Juscelino, Brazil
406–7
Kumar, Veerendra 645
Kung Hsiang-hsi 195
Kuomintang (Chinese
Nationalist Party) 97,
98, 99
Kure, Bunji 476
Kuwait, Iraq invasion 639

La Follette, Robert 15
Labour governments (UK),
1929–31: 23
Labour governments (UK),
1945–51 (Attlee) xxii
American view of 223–4,
225
and Bretton Woods 212,
230
and European co-
operation 290,
294–5
and European Payments
Union 296, 297–8
full employment 179

and ITO 257
Labour governments (UK),
(1964–70) 451–2
application to join EEC
457–8
devaluation of sterling
457–8
Labour governments (UK),
(1974–9) 578–82
Alternative Economic
Strategy 580–81
and Social Contract
578–9, 581
Labour Party (UK) 12,
184
Conference (1976) 579
and EEC 711
labour relations
Germany 699
and loss of bargaining
power 729, 811
UK 21, 507, 516, 581
US 802
see also strikes
labour standards
and capital 811
and UN Human
Development Report
647
in US trade deals 788–9
WTO and 644–5
see also ILO
Ladejinsky, Wolf 330
Laffer, Arthur 517
Lagarde, Christine v, xxv,
789, 790
at ECB 827
on inequality 776–7
laissez-faire, compared to
bilateralism 132
Lall, K. B., India 373
Lamfalussy, Alexandre 710
Lamont, Thomas 16, 25,
153
Lamy, Pascal 650, 654,
777–8, 779–80
land tenure, Africa 319
Lang, Jack 112, 113
Laos 400
Larosière, Jacques de 434,
520, 616–17,
618–19, 716
Latin America xxii–xxiv, 91,
339, 367
1982 debt crisis 617
and Alliance for Progress
409–12
and Bretton Woods
197–8, 235

Latin America (*cont.*)
  Cartagena debtors
    meeting (1984) 619
  economic development
    106–10; import
    substitution 106–7,
    617
  economic policies 591,
    600–601
  foreign investment 617
  and IBRD 208, 209,
    309–10
  and ITO 263–5
  need for common market
    408
  private enterprise 407,
    408
  role of state 600–601
  and UNCTAD 551
  and US Good Neighbor
    Policy 61–2, 106,
    109–10, 115, 159
Lausanne, world economic
  conference (1932)
  27–8
Law, Richard 132, 133
Lawson, Nigel 303, 581
  and City of London 610
  on Delors' vision of EU
    711–12
  on EMS 708
  and ERM 712
Le Pen, Marine 827
League of Nations
  (1920) xxi
  and cartels 180
  and China 86, 99–100
  and currency stability
    76, 81
  Depression Delegation
    83–4
  Economic Committee 14,
    24, 81
  Economic and Financial
    Organization (EFO)
    (1923) 24, 29, 76
  economists at 81–8
  Financial Section 81
  and food security 174, 175
  and Gold Delegation
    group 24–5, 81
  international monetary
    conference (Brussels,
    1920) 24
  and Lausanne conference
    (1932) 28
  and taxation of
    multinational
    corporations 805

World Economic
  Conference (1927) 14
Leddy, John 254, 259, 423
Leddy, Margaret Potter 415
Lee, Frank 145
Lehman Brothers, failure
  732, 733
Leigh-Pemberton, Robin
  710
Leith-Ross, Frederick 180,
  181
Lend Lease Act (1941 US)
  116, 120, 123–4
  Article VII: 127–8,
    129–31, 163
  call for renewal of 222–3
  terminated (1945) 222–3
  terms imposed (the
    'consideration')
    124–31
  UK view of terms 126–8
Lenin, V.I., New Economic
  Policy (1921) 92
Lennep, Emiel van 559
less developed countries *see*
  developing countries
Levitsky, Steven 824
Lewis, Michael, *The Big
  Short* 814
Lewis, W. Arthur 89,
  315–16
  and Ghana 354
  and India 345
  'Measures for the
    Economic
    Development of
    Under-Developed
    Countries' (1951)
    322–3
  and terms of trade 357
Li Fuchun 349
liberal democracies, alliance
  against
  authoritarianism 60,
  62, 74–5
Liberal Party (UK), and free
  trade 12, 13
'liberal world federation',
  proposed 87
liberation movements 355
  popular support for 533
Libya, oil 538, 545
licences
  banking 812
  and corporate power 801
  to limit access 800
Lighthizer, Robert 787
Lilienthal, David 306, 331,
  332–3

Lim, Edwin 669
Lin, Justin Yifu 784, 817
Lindemann, Frederick (Lord
  Cherwell) 237
  and Operation Robot
    303, 304
Linlithgow, Lord 105
Lippmann, Walter 35, 176,
  218
  Colloquium in Paris
    (1938) 83
  on IMF 200
  *Inquiry into the Principles
    of the Good
    Society* 83
  and Tripartite Agreement
    79
  on World Monetary and
    Economic
    Conference 43
Lipton, David 678–9
liquidity, global 441–57
  and floating exchange
    rates 449–54
  G10 proposals for
    creation 447–8
  and IMF Special Drawing
    Rights 448–9
  and US economy 434
Lisbon Treaty (2007) 724,
  755
  deficiencies 757
Liu Shaoqi 349, 350
Lleras Restrepo, Carlos 197,
  260–61
Lloyd George, David 26
lobbying, political 801
Lobokova, Lydia (Lady
  Keynes) 47
Lomé Convention (1975)
  547
London
  Anglo-American talks
    (1942–3) 163–4
  trade meeting (1946) 240
London Chamber of
  Arbitration 624
'London Club', and
  creditor–debtor
  disputes 625
London Conference (1933)
  see World Monetary
  and Economic
  Conference
London Food Board (1942)
  173
London Imperial Conference
  (1937) 74
Long, Huey 55

Long, Russell 528, 529
Lothian, Lord 122, 123
Louvre Accord (1987) 626
Loveday, Alexander 29, 76,
    81, 83, 84, 85–6
Lucas, Robert 737
Lula da Silva, Luiz Inácio
    781–2
Lyttleton, Oliver 300

Maastricht Treaty (1992)
    713–16
  and convergence criteria
    714–15
  deficiencies 722, 757
  labour mobility 722
  no provision for exit from
    euro 756
  referenda on 715
  see also EU
McCarthy, Eugene 381
McCloy, John 307–8, 309
McCormick, David 775
McCracken, Paul 463, 480,
    484
MacDonald, Ramsay 38, 49
  at World Monetary and
    Economic
    Conference 30, 34,
    41, 47
MacDougall, Donald 705,
    721
McDougall, Frank 84, 86,
    114
  on agriculture 175, 176,
    178
Machado, Gerardo 61
McKinley, William 20
McKittrick, Thomas 204
McMahon, Kit 436
Macmillan, Harold 382,
    437, 445
McNamara, Robert 381,
    554, 555–7
  as president of World
    Bank 552, 553, 554
MacNeill, Jim 561, 590
Macron, Emmanuel 792,
    821, 827
MacSharry, Ray 639
Madrid declaration (IMF,
    1994) 602
Madrid, Miguel de la 618
Maes, Ivo 725
Mahalanobis, P.C. 344–5
Maier, Charles 245–6, 568
Maine, Henry, Village-
    Communities ... 102
Majone, Giandomenico 698

Major, John 710–711, 712
Makins, Roger 295
malaria, eradication
    programme 329
Malaya 279, 317
Malaysia 621, 637
malnutrition, World Bank
    programme on 556
Malpass, David 822
Mann, Thomas 408
Mansholt, Sicco 390
Mantenga, Guido 783
Mao Zedong 354–5
  Cultural Revolution
    349–51
  Great Famine 349
  Great Leap Forward
    347–9
Maoism, spread of 351, 356
Marcos, Ferdinand 549
Marjolin, Robert 470,
    471–2, 701–3, 705
market fundamentalism 599
market liberalism
  adopted by UK 582–3
  IMF and 593, 595,
    596–606
  rise of 567–92
  see also neo-liberalism
Markey, Edward 821
Marshall, George 249, 274,
    287
Marshall Plan (Marshall Aid)
    236, 246, 250–51,
    273, 274, 308
  and European integration
    287–95
  and restoration of
    German economy
    275–6, 286
  Truman and 269
Martin, William McChesney
    386, 455, 463–4
  and gold price 444
  and US domestic
    monetary policy 478,
    574
Marx, Karl 91–2
  and Friedrich Engels, The
    Communist
    Manifesto 403
Masani, Minoo 690
mass production 568
Maudling, Reginald 445–6,
    451
Mayo, Robert 463
Mazower, Mark 339, 774
Meade, James 81, 84, 165,
    278

The Economic Basis of a
    Durable Peace 149
  on exchange rates 202,
    449
  and GATT 373, 414
  on multilateralism
    257–8
  plans for post-war
    commercial union
    133–4
  and post-war monetary
    reform negotiations
    145
Meaney, George 246,
    489–90
Means, Gardiner 54
Meltzer, Allan 620, 622
Menzies, Robert 113–14
mercantilism 59
Mercosur, Southern
    Common Market
    (South America) 408,
    633
Merkel, Angela xxv, 740,
    772, 788
  and ECB 757
  and eurozone crisis 754,
    755, 756, 758, 827
  and global financial crisis
    736, 738
  and IMF 754
  and pandemic 792
Messersmith, George 329
Mestmäcker, Ernst-Joachim
    586
Metal Reserves Company
    181
Metcalf, Jack 395
Mexican Agricultural
    Program 328
Mexico 62, 107, 329
  and Bretton Woods 197
  debt crisis (1982) 601,
    603, 617–20
  IMF loans to 618–20
  International Center for
    Maize and Wheat
    Improvement 532,
    561
  and ITO 263, 265
  Nacional Financiera 618
  Trump's trade war with
    786
Meyer, Eugene 307, 308
Microsoft 767
Middelaar, Luuk van 586
Middle East
  conflict in (1967) 445
  oil production 537

Midland Bank, offshore
    dollar market 608
migrants, populist
    opposition to 811
Mikesell, Raymond 157,
    193, 218, 299, 518
Miksch, Leonhard 284–5
Milanović, Branko 694,
    695, 764
Miliband, David 789
Millennium Development
    Goals (2000) 591
Millikan, Max 401–2, 403
Millikin, Eugene 269
Mills, Wilbur 380, 466, 525
Milward, Alan 298
Minsky, Hyman 749
Mises Institute 743
Mises, Ludwig von 82–3, 86
Mitterand, François 583,
    712–13
Mizuta, Mikio 503
modernity, conflicting views
    of 400–401
modernization, theory of
    401–6, 426
Modi, Narendra 760–62
    and Hindu nationalism
    760–61
Mody, Ashoka 758, 827
Moley, Raymond 8–10, 34,
    36, 49–50
    as Assistant Secretary of
    State 39–40
    at World Monetary and
    Economic
    Conference 43, 45–6,
    47
Molinari, Diego Luis,
    Argentina 198, 264
Mollet, Guy 370
Molotov, Vyacheslav 288–9
monetary system,
    international
    Atlantic City discussions
    191, 192–3
    Keynes's proposals
    147–55
    Plan X (1972) 509–10
    and post-Bretton Woods
    reform negotiations
    504–18
    reforms 143–86
    White's proposals 109,
    147
    see also Bretton Woods;
    Tripartite Agreement
Mönick, Emmanuel 77–8
Monnet, Jean 13, 99, 317

Action Committee for the
    United States of
    Europe 470, 471
    and ECSC 293–4
monopolies 800–801
Monroe Doctrine 61, 62
Mont Pèlerin Society (1947)
    83, 216, 582–3
Montevideo, Treaty of
    (1960) 408
Moore, Hugh 333
Moore, Mike 645–6, 647,
    650, 675
Moore, Ray 576
Moore, Lt-Col Sir Thomas
    230
Moret, Clément 45
Morgenthau, Henry 17, 37,
    51
    Bretton Woods 143, 146,
    189, 193–4, 209,
    629; ratification
    218–19
    and China 100–101
    demand for German
    deindustrialization
    236–7, 238, 239
    on development 307
    and 'dollar pool' 140–41
    and France 77–8
    and IBRD 206, 207
    and proposed Inter-
    America Bank (IAB)
    109
    on Soviet Union 97, 157
    and stabilization of
    currencies 57, 75–6
    and Tripartite Agreement
    76, 77–9, 80
    and wartime support for
    Britain 123, 125, 126
    and White's stabilization
    fund 155–6, 158–9,
    160–61, 166
    and World Monetary and
    Economic
    Conference (1933)
    46
Morgenthau, Henry, Snr 40
Morrison, Scott 822–3
Morse, Jeremy 508
mortgage finance 609, 812
    reliance on 729
    US 588, 595, 732–3,
    746–7, 812
Moscow Narodny Bank 608
'most favoured nation'
    principle 11, 14,
    47–8, 651, 675

developing countries and
    396, 417, 530–31
    and free trade areas 264,
    372
    League of Nations and 81
    and liberalization of trade
    62–3, 779
    and principal supplier 65,
    254
    see also bilateral
    agreements
Mottley, Mia 822
Moynihan, Daniel Patrick
    545, 546
Mudaliar, Ramaswami 105
Müller-Armack, Alfred
    286
Mulroney, Brian 635
multilateral-bilateralism, on
    trade agreements
    254–5, 266
multilateralism 228
    Bretton Woods
    institutions and
    234–5
    Carter administration and
    551
    and democracy 795–6
    GATT and 252
    and growing regionalism
    633, 634–6, 652–3,
    777–81
    and ITO negotiations
    256–7
    networks 785–6, 797
    proposals for new
    structures 783–6
    and reform of institutions
    774
    resistance of developing
    countries to xxx,
    235, 336
    US commitment to 260,
    272–3, 275, 396–7,
    653, 771, 773
    see also 'shallow
    multilateralism'
multinational corporations
    595, 608, 657–8
    profits and labour income
    803
    taxation of 805–6
    see also corporations
Musk, Elon 818
Myrdal, Gunnar 235, 554

Nader, Ralph 646
NAFTA (North American
    Free Trade

Agreement) xxxii,
633, 635, 636, 639
opposition to 635, 645,
646
success of 653
Trump and 781, 786
Nairobi, UNCTAD session
(1976) 547, 548–9
Nansen, Fridtjok 174
Naoroji, Dadabhai 101–2
Narayan, Jayaprakash 691
Nasser, Gamal Abdel 338,
342, 343
Nath, Kamal 653–4
nation states
and international
co-operation xxii,
xxvii–xxviii, 87
see also domestic policies
National Advisory Council
on International and
Monetary and
Financial Problems
(USA) 233–4
National Labor Relations
Act (US, 1935) 55
National Recovery
Administration
(NRA) (US) 39, 54
National Security
Memorandum 182
(US, 1962) 404–5
nationalism
and democracy xxviii
and economic tensions
xx–xxi, xxv–xxvii,
768
populist 768, 773–4,
786–9, 794–5
responsible 796–7, 832
and welfare state 235
see also authoritarianism;
internationalism
Nationalities Act (1948),
Commonwealth
citizenship 318
NATO (North Atlantic
Treaty Organization)
268, 270
Nixon and 526
and Russia 684
Nehru, Jawaharlal 115, 338,
411, 690
and Bandung conference
341
and economic planning
104, 344, 345–6
and Non-Aligned
Movement 342

and South Africa 340
and sterling balances 278
view of economic
development 103,
104, 344–6
Nehru, R. K. 260
neo-colonialism, non-
aligned hostility to
341–3
neo-liberalism xxiii, xxiv,
565
adoption of 571–2
and global financial crisis
(2007–8) 729
negotiated 591–2
political considerations
589–90
and response to pandemic
792–3
see also market liberalism
Nepal, Maoist insurrection
356
Netherlands, colonies 317
Neutrality Act (US, 1935)
49
Neutrality Act (US, 1937),
'cash and carry'
provision 49, 73, 74,
122–3
New Deal, Roosevelt's 54–5,
313
New Delhi, second
UNCTAD session
(1968) 425
New International
Economic Order
(NIEO) (1974) xxiii,
xxx, 235, 429,
542–52
Cancún summit (1981)
583–4
conference (1977) 586
Declaration 542–3
demand by developing
countries for 529,
534–9
and distributive justice
637, 638
end of 565, 583–92
and GATT 631
and mutual co-operation
544–5
sovereign equality 543,
544
New York Times
on Connally 503
on Nixon's New
Economic Policy 489
on Volcker 575

New Zealand, and Cairns
group 637
Nicaragua 309
Niemeyer, Otto 22, 112
NIEO see New
International
Economic Order
Nixon Doctrine 464
Nixon, Richard xxiii, 513,
553
and Camp David meeting
(August 1971) 462,
486–7
and China 461, 463
and Connally 477–8,
484–5
Council on International
Economic Policy
(CIEP) 476–7, 500
dislike of economics 463,
476, 513
and easing of monetary
policy 510–511,
574
and exchange rates 481,
505
fast-track authority for
tariff reduction 527,
528
focus on re-election 453,
464, 488, 505, 510,
527
and Friedman 452–3
New Economic Policy
488–9
political strategy 461–70
and Pompidou 502
suspension of dollar
convertibility 429,
469–70, 485–91,
494–5, 496
and trade policy 465–6,
524–5, 527–8
wage and price controls
487, 488, 489–90
Watergate scandal 496,
527
Nkrumah, Kwame 116,
319, 338
and Bandung conference
341
Neo-colonialism 341
and Non-Aligned
Movement 342
and Soviet aid 353–4
Non-Aligned Movement
(1961) xxx, 342–3
Algiers meeting (1973)
535–6

Non-Aligned
    Movement (*cont.*)
  Lusaka meeting (1970)
    535
  and UN resolutions on
    trade 415–16
  see also G77
non-tariff barriers (NTBs)
    631, 633
  Doha Round 651
  quantitative restrictions
    264, 414
  US use of 525–6
Nordhaus, William 820
Norman, Montagu 22, 45,
    150
North Atlantic Free Trade
    Area, proposed 477
North Korea, land reform
    330
North Vietnam, land reform
    330
North–South dialogue
    548–52
  Cancún summit (1981)
    583–4
*North–South: A Programme
    for Survival* (1980)
    552
Notestein, Frank 333
Novikov, Nikolai 287, 288
Nurske, Ragnar 81, 201,
    310–311, 312–13
nutrition 169, 172
  and agricultural
    production 84–5, 114
  and food security 174–5
  and welfare provision 85,
    177
  see also food supply
Nutrition Research
    Laboratories,
    Coonoor, India 175
Nyerere, Julius 535, 538–9,
    544

Obama, Barack 779, 828
  2009 G20 summit
    xvii–xviii
  and Doha Round 654
  and global financial crisis
    734, 736, 743,
    750–51
O'Brien, Leslie 457
Obstfeld, Maurice 813–14
Ocasio-Cortez, Alexandria
    821
Occupy Movement 747,
    767–8, 814

OECD (Organization of
    Economic
    Cooperation and
    Development) xxxii,
    291, 419, 432
  as alternative forum to
    IMF 437–8
  Code of Liberalization of
    Capital Movements
    607
  and Committee of Twenty
    (C20) 508–9
  and economic growth
    558–9, 560–61
  and Keynesian working
    party 587
  'polluter must pay'
    principle 819
  rules on international
    taxation 805–6
  Working Party 3 initiative
    437–8
Ogle, Vanessa 612
Ohlendorf, Otto 283
Ohlin, Bertil 81, 83, 203
oil
  criticism of over-
    consumption 543–4
  European dependence on
    Russia 793, 821
  falling prices 565, 584
  and formation of OPEC
    537–8
  nationalization of western
    interests 545
  political economy of 537–9
  price rises 539, 539, 545,
    760
  production in North Sea
    and Alaska 584
  proposal of Common
    Trust 540
  proposed 'oil facility'
    613–14
  research on reducing
    dependency on 540
  see also climate change;
    energy; 'oil shock';
    OPEC
oil companies 537–8, 808–9
'oil shock' (crisis) (1973)
    xxiii, 429, 515, 517
  and artificial fertilizers
    562
  economic effects of 568–9
  effect on environmental
    strategy 560
oil shock (second, 1979)
    615

Okonjo-Iweala, Ngozi xxv,
    790, 797
'one world' policy 281
OPEC (Organization of
    Petroleum Exporting
    Countries) 426, 533,
    537–9, 584
Operation 'Pan-America',
    proposed 407
Operation Robot, on
    sterling convertibility
    301–3, 451
'ordo-liberalism', Germany
    286
Organization of American
    States (OAS), Punta
    del Este meeting
    (1961) 397, 410
Organization for European
    Economic Co-
    operation (OEEC),
    and Marshall Plan
    270, 291
Ormsby-Gore, David
    443–4
O'Rourke, Kevin 733–4,
    736, 763
Ortoli, François-Xavier 702,
    705
Osborn, Fairfield 334–5
Osborne, George 738, 741
Ossola, Rinaldo 438, 447
Ostrom, Elinor 823
Ostry, Jonathan 741
Ostry, Sylvia 641
Ottawa Conference (1932)
    114
Otte, Max 780
outsourcing, of production
    657
Oxfam (Oxford Committee
    for Famine Relief)
    173, 647

Padmore, George 343
Padoa-Schioppa, Tommaso
    716
Pakistan 339
  debts to China 815
  and IMF 775, 797
Palme, Olof 552
Pan-Africanism 343
Pan-American conference,
    Montevideo
    (1933) 61
Panitchpakdi, Supachai
    645–6, 653
Paris, Conference of
    European Economic

Co-operation (1947) 288–90
'Paris Club' 625, 814
Paris Economic Conference (1916) 13
Park Chung-hee 363
Pasvolsky, Leo 63, 132, 339
Patiño, Alfonso 416–17
Patriotic Millionaires 808
Paul, Ron 743
Paul VI, Pope 564
Paye, Jean-Claude 587
Pearl Harbor, Japanese attack on (1941) 7
Pearl, Morris 808
Pearson, Lester 553
Peccei, Aurelio 551
Peek, George 63, 65
Pennsylvania Central Railway, bankruptcy 479
Penrose, E. F. 172, 197, 209–10
People's Global Action 646
People's Party, United States 20
Peréz-Guerrero, Manuel 535
Perkins, Frances 185
Perón, Juan 263–4, 358, 359
Petersen, Howard 377
Petersmann, Ernst-Ulrich 585
Peterson Institute for International Economics, on median family incomes 802
Peterson, Peter 431, 433, 493, 495
  Institute for International Economics 599–600
  on internationalism 600
  and Nixon 500–501
  view of US economy 477
  and World Bank commission on aid 552
petrodollars, recycling 515, 572, 595, 613–14
  Latin America 589
  second oil shock (1979) 615
  through City of London 565, 585, 589
  through Wall Street 565, 585, 589
Pettigrew, Pierre 648

Pettis, Michael 768–9
Philippines 309, 331, 563
Phillips, Sir Frederick 123, 145, 153–4
Physical Quality of Life Index (World Bank) 557
Pierre-Brossolette, Claude 510
Piketty, Thomas
  on carbon tax 820, 821
  on inequality 764–5, 766, 767–8, 808
Pinochet, General Augusto 600–601
Pittman, Key 36, 39, 40, 47, 100
Planned Parenthood Foundation of America 335
Plaza Accord (1985), on exchange rates 625
Plowden, Edwin 303
Pöhl, Karl-Otto 708, 710, 715–16
Polak, Jacques 83–4, 596, 597, 628
Poland 7, 122, 591
  economic transition 678–9, 685
  and GATT 271, 372–3
  membership of EU 679
  and Paris conference (1947) 288
  right-wing populism 773, 828
Pompeo, Mike 788
Pompidou, Georges 469, 502, 504–5, 506, 511
  and realignment of currencies 499, 501–2
population
  birth control 327, 329, 333
  birth rate reduction 327, 329, 544
  and development policies 326–36, 552
  Malthusian concerns over 326–36, 557–8
  planning policies 555–6
  and resources 558, 561–4, 818
Portillo, José López 618
Portugal, sovereign debt crisis 753
Potsdam conference (1945) 239, 248

poverty 631
  and failing states 789
  focus on 554–7
  monetized 557
  reduction 694
  rising (1980s) 590
  and UN Millennium Development Goals 591
  WTO and 647
Powell, Jerome 825
Prebisch, Raúl 89, 91, 116
  and development policy 407–8, 553
  and ECLA 407, 410
  and GATT 419–20
  and terms of trade 357–9
  The Economic Development of Latin America . . . 358–9
  and UNCTAD 417, 418
Preobrazhensky, Yevgeni 92, 94
price liberalization
  China 670, 671
  Russia 684, 685–6
prices
  controls (US) 487, 488, 489–90
  gold standard and 20, 21–2
  primary commodity fluctuations 89, 106, 107, 111, 373, 545
  Roosevelt's monetary policy and 53–4
  see also commodities; gold; oil
Princeton Office of Population Research 333
private enterprise, Latin America 407, 408
privatization
  in China 672
  in Poland 678–9
  Russia 684–5, 686–7
Problems of Developing Countries, conference (1962) 416
  Cairo Declaration 416
productivity 568
  American emphasis on 245–6
  falling 570, 802
profit-shifting 804, 805, 806, 813

profits
  and competition 802
  at expense of labour 802,
    803
  falling 570
  and productivity 802
  for public benefit 804
  taxation of 800, 808–9
property markets
  China 762–3, 816,
    829–30
  Ireland 753
  UK 810–811
  US 732–3, 743–4
Prosterman, Roy 330–31
protectionism xvii
  in Alternative Economic
    Strategy 580–81
  and capital flows 202–3
  Keynes and 203, 793
  regulations as disguised
    645, 647, 657, 823
  Trump and 768, 781, 787
  United States 14–18, 65,
    524–30, 634–7, 826
  see also imperial
    preference; tariffs
protest groups 559, 752
  Occupy movement 747,
    767–8, 814
  at Seattle 632, 646–7
Public Citizen group 646
public health
  India 761
  and overpopulation 334
  Rockefeller Foundation
    and 328
  WHO smallpox
    programme 329
  see also WHO
Puerto Rico summit (1976)
  522–3, 548
Puhl, Emil 204
Put People First movement
  767
Putin, Vladimir 688–9
  anti-democratic
    nationalism 759
  authoritarianism 695
  rents from state
    companies 759,
    762
Putnam, Robert 811

Qing dynasty, China 97
Quantitative Easing (QE)
  742–3, 774
  and asset prices 792
  criticisms of 743–4

and inequality 742,
  743–4, 746, 752, 765
rejected by ECB 754, 757
quantitative restrictions
  (non-tariff barriers)
  264
  GATT and 414

racism, in views of
  development 534
Rainforest Alliance 646
Rajagopalachari,
  Chakravarti 343, 690
Rajan, Raghuram, IMF
  630, 725, 732, 810,
  812–13
Rajchman, Ludwik 99
Rambouillet summit (1975)
  520, 548
Rand, Ayn 748
Randall, Clarence B. 273,
  304, 325
Rao, Narasimha 692–3
Rappard, William 83, 87
Rasminsky, Louis 169,
  217–18, 607
Rato, Rodrigo de 629–30
Reagan, Ronald xxiii, 565,
  566
  at Cancún 584
  and market liberalization
    577–8
  trade policy 634–5
Reciprocal Trade
  Agreements Act
  (RTAA) (1934) 57,
  60, 61–6, 74–5,
  252–3
  Kennedy and 377–8
  and low tariffs 64–5
  renewal (1948) 266,
    268–70
  renewals (from 1945) 66,
    133, 374–5
reciprocity
  developing countries and
    636–7, 641
  in trade deals 394–5,
    413–14, 415–16
Reconstruction Finance
  Corporation (US) 51
Regional Comprehensive
  Economic
  Partnership 781
regionalism 633, 634–6,
  652–3
  banks and 326
  supranational institutions
    xxxii

WTO and 777–81, 797
Rehn, Olli 741
Reich, Robert 752
Reinhart, Carmen 738, 815
rentier capitalism 799–800
  and competition policies
    804
  financial sector 812
  and profit 800
reparations and war debts
  25–8
  and gold standard 24–5
  suspension of debt
    payments to America
    (1933) 48–9
  and World Monetary and
    Economic
    Conference 41–2
Republican Party (US)
  support for tariffs 8, 15,
    64, 65
  and taxation of wealth
    809
resources
  commitment to full
    employment of
    114–15, 138
  see also commodities
Reuss, Henry 485–6
Reuther, Alan 644
revaluation 79, 439, 465,
  482, 783
  Deutsche Mark 460, 469,
    476, 480, 502
  yen 475, 476, 502, 503,
    511
Rey, Jean 383
Rhee, Syngman 362
Rhodesia (Zimbabwe),
  copper 317
Ricardo, David 799–800
Richardson, Gordon 615,
  706
Rio Declaration (1992) 819
risk
  banks and 614–15, 747,
    748–9
  and financialization 729,
    812, 813
  incentivized 630, 732,
    752
Robbins, Lionel 83, 87, 224,
  302
  on exchange rates 201
  on food production 172
  and Keynes 145, 165
Robertson, Dennis 145, 154
Robinson, Joan 229–30
Rockefeller, David 540

Rockefeller Foundation 82, 335
  and Graduate Institute 83
  Population Council 334
  and scientific development programmes 328–9, 561–2
Rockefeller, John D. 328–9
Rockefeller, John D. III 334
Rockefeller, Nelson 110, 159, 329
Rodney, Walter 536
Rodrik, Dani xxv, 629, 649
  on global–national balance 796
  'shallow multilateralism' xxii, 234, 629
Roessler, Frieder 585
Rogers, Will 42
Rogoff, Ken 738
Roman Catholic Church, and birth control 557, 564
Romania, and GATT 271
Rome, Treaty of (1957) 295, 369–70, 698
  and GATT 372
Romer, Christina 737
Romney, Mitt 743
Roosa, Robert, G10 387, 438–9
  and capital flows 435
  and Eurodollar market 611
  and floating exchange rates 453–4
  and gold price 444–5
  and OECD 438
Roosevelt, F. D. 4, 5, 9, 166, 177
  anti-colonialism 19, 213
  and Brains Trust 8–10
  and Brazil 108
  and China 101
  Commonwealth Club speech (1932) 54
  concept of pan-American trusteeship 124
  criticisms of 49–50
  death (1945) 243
  and Good Neighbor Policy 62, 159, 213
  Hot Springs conference 171–2, 176
  increased executive power 63–4, 65–6
  inheritance tax 55, 807
  monetary policy 35–8, 50–56; abandonment

of gold standard xxi, 34, 45–6, 51;
  devaluation of dollar 50–53; stabilization of dollar 45–7, 75; and White's stabilization fund 161
  and New Deals 7, 54–5, 60
  on post-war Germany 237, 238–9
  and trade policy 8–9, 60, 74, 243–4
  and Tripartite Agreement 79
  and UK: and Lend Lease 123, 130–31; opposition to imperial preference 128–9, 213; proposed 'cash and carry' scheme with UK 73, 74; and Sterling Area 140; support in Second World War 123
  view of Soviet Union 97, 157
  and war debts 48–9
  and World Monetary and Economic Conference (1933) xvii, 32, 34–5, 42–3, 46–7
Rooth, Ivar 616
Roper, Daniel 57
Röpke, Wilhelm 86, 285–6, 534, 571
Rosenstein-Rodan, Paul 174, 312, 313, 326
Rosneft, oil company 759
Rostec armaments company 759
Rostow, Eugene 399, 402
Rostow, Walter 385, 402–4
  and Bretton Woods system 456–7
  and Latin America 408
  The Process of Economic Growth 402
  The Stages of Economic Growth 402
  and Vietnam War 398, 404
Roth, William 382, 393, 394, 396
Roubini, Nouriel 784
Rowan, Leslie 301

Rubber Reserve Company 181
Rubio, Marco 804
Rueff, Jacques 81, 84, 370, 442–3
Ruggie, John, 'embedded liberalism' xxii, 234
Runciman, Walter 73–4
rural development 554–7
Rusk, Dean 385, 392, 396–7, 405–6
Ruskin, John 102
Russia 683–9
  authoritarianism 695, 773
  contrast with China 689, 770
  debt 685, 686–7
  dependence on oil and gas revenues 759, 760
  economic crisis (1998) 687, 688
  economic stagnation 662, 695, 759
  fall in male life expectancy 687–8
  and global financial crisis 759–60
  IMF and 604, 684, 685, 686, 687
  inflation 686
  invasion of Crimea 759
  invasion of Ukraine xviii, xxiv–xxv, 760, 769, 793, 831
  kleptocracy of oligarchs 686, 687, 759, 762
  membership of G7 (G8) 688, 759
  membership of WTO 689
  military spending 759
  and Polish economic model 685
  price liberalization 684, 685–6
  privatization 684–5, 686–7
  return to state capitalism 759
  rouble as common currency 685, 687
  sudden transition to market economy 592, 661, 677–8
  see also Soviet Union
Russian Revolution (1917) 26, 91
Ryan, Paul 738
Rykov, Alexei 92–3, 94–5

Saavedra Lamas, Carlos 61
Sachs, Jeffrey 602, 678–9,
    685
Saez, Emmanuel 764, 808
Safire, Bill 487–8
Salinas de Gortari, Carlos
    618, 635
Salman, Mohammad 537
Salter, Arthur 13, 14, 29, 56
Samuel, Frank 320
Sandel, Michael,
    'contributive justice'
    799
Sanders, Bernie 752–3, 821
Santa Cruz, Hernán 358
Santelli, Rick 746
Sargent, Daniel 490, 510
Sarkozy, Nicolas 736, 744,
    754, 755
Sartre, Jean-Paul 351
Sasaki, Tadashi 475, 503
Saudi Arabia, petrodollars
    613
Saudi Development Fund
    538
Savannah, Georgia, IMF
    inaugural meeting
    144, 233
savings, household 588,
    589, 667
Scalia, Antonin 800–801
Schacht, Hjalmar 58, 59, 71,
    699
    at Bretton Woods 195
    and German economic
        policy 67–72, 152
    relations with Hitler 71–2
    and World Monetary and
        Economic
        Conference 38–9
Schaetzel, Robert 392
Schäuble, Wolfgang 731,
    738, 754
Schiller, Karl 459–60,
    480–81, 499, 501,
    507
Schlesinger, Arthur 332
Schlesinger, James 431, 540
Schmelzer, Matthias 558,
    587
Schmidt, Helmut 507, 511,
    522, 696
    and development 548
    and European integration
        701
    and European single
        currency 705–6
    and management of
        floating rates 519

Schmitt, Kurt 67
Scholz, Olaf 827–8
Schuman, Robert 293–4
Schuster, George 104, 105
Schweitzer, Pierre-Paul 456,
    490, 498–9
Scowcroft, Brent 784
Sculling, James 112
Seattle, WTO ministerial
    meeting (1999)
    645–7
    protests 632, 646–7
Second World War xxiii, 74,
    122–3, 191, 222
    and return to
        internationalism xxii
Seers, Dudley 554
Seldon, Arthur 569
Sen, Amartya 563, 761
Sen, Binay Ranjan 327, 557
Senghor, Léopold Sédar
    318–19, 370
Seoul consensus (G20 2010)
    783–4
service sector
    Doha Round 651
    GATT agreement on 587,
        637, 638
    and globalization 832,
        832
    UK 767
    wages 810
    WTO and 642
Sforza, Michelle 646
'shallow multilateralism'
    xxii–xxiv, 234, 629,
    796
    and balance with national
        policies 796, 832–3
Shanghai Cooperation
    Organization 831
Shanmugaratnam, Tharman
    785
Shann, E. O. G. 56, 112–13
Share our Wealth Society
    (US) 55
shareholders 800, 803, 804
    and stakeholders 804
Shastri, Lal Bahadur 690
Shiller, Robert 799
Shore, Peter 718
Short, Dewey 122
Shoup, Carl 361
Shroff, Ardeshir Darabshaw
    106, 196, 690
Shultz, George 453, 492,
    505, 577
    and capital controls 467,
        514–15

and carbon tax 819
    and financial markets
        613
    and floating exchange
        rates 484, 487, 496,
        512–13, 514, 519
    and interdependence 540
    and monetary policy
        479–80, 509, 511
    and trade policy 527–8
Silver Purchase Act (US,
    1934) 100
silver-based currencies xx,
    100–101
Simon, William 519, 521,
    545, 581
Singer, Hans 311–13, 357,
    358, 554
Singh, Manmohan 522,
    692–3, 694, 760
smallpox, eradication
    programme 329
Smith, Adam 59
Smith, Al 8
Smithsonian Institute,
    Washington,
    agreement on
    realignment of
    currencies 502–4
Smoot, Reed 14–15
Smoot-Hawley Tariff Act
    (US, 1930) 14–16,
    18, 65, 253
Smuts, Jan 339–40
social changes, from 1960s
    569, 572
Social Contract (UK, 1976)
    579–80, 582
social democracy, rejected
    by Washington
    consensus 603
social policies, combined
    with neo-liberalism
    591, 600–601
social rights, WTO disputes
    and 656–7
Soong Tse-ven 99, 101
Soros, George 593, 599, 807
South Africa 339–40
South Korea 360, 364, 542
    American occupation
        360–61, 362
    chaebol business groups
        363–4, 621
    Economic Planning Board
        363
    export-led
        industrialization
        363–4

IMF intervention (1997) 591–2, **594**, 597, 602, 621–3
import-substituting industrialization 362
land reform 330, 331
South Vietnam, land reform 330–31
South-East Asia, Communist 'menace' 279
South-East Asian Command, Second World War 124
sovereign wealth funds 809
Soviet Union 677–89
   black market 680–81
   borrowings and debt 682
   and Bretton Woods conference 191, 194
   collapse (1989) xxiii, 429, 591, 639, 659, 661; disintegration 683–4
   collective farms 90, 93, 94–5, 677, 689; destruction of kulaks 93, 94, 96
   command economy xxii, 7, 91–7, 677–8, 680–81
   Communist Party 682, 689; ideology 351–4
   and concept of modernity 400–401
   Congress of People's Deputies 682, 683
   corruption 681
   defence industries 679–80
   and Eastern Europe 288
   fall in oil revenues 682
   famine 95–6
   forced industrialization 7, 93–4
   forced labour 680
   and GATT 235
   and IBRD 208, 235
   and ILO 187
   and IMF 194, 235
   and influence in 'Third World' xxx
   infrastructure schemes 333; dams and irrigation projects 315
   invasion of Afghanistan 584
   and need for modernization 336
   New Economic Policy 92–3

relations with China 343, 351
   Russian nationalism 352; independence movements 683
   'shock therapy' transition 661, 677–8
   trade: call for world trade organization 413; and COMECOM economic bloc 289; international 355, 416; view of ITO 250
   wage reforms 681
   and West: American attitude to 157, 232–3, 248–50, 268; Cold War xxii, xxx, xxxiv; and post-war Europe 287–9, 290; Western perception of 96–7
   see also Russia
Spain, sovereign debt crisis 753
Special Drawing Rights (IMF) 448–9
Special UN Fund for Economic Development (SUNFED) 323–6, 419
Sprague, Oliver 45
Sri Lanka
   failure of green revolution 562–3
   Hambantota International Port 815
stabilization fund
   and voting rights 159–60, 162
   White's proposal for 155–61
stagflation 429
   as crisis of capitalism 568
   effect on environmentalism 560
   risk of 793
stakeholders 804
Staley, Eugene 331–2
Stalin, Joseph 289, 323
   and agricultural reform 93, 94, 95–6
   campaign of terror 96, 680
   and New Economic Policy 92–3

and post-war Germany 238, 239, 249
   and rapid industrialization 93–4
   show trials 94–5
   at Yalta 238
statistics, use of 86
Stedman Jones, Daniel 571
Steil, Benn 157
Stein, Herbert 486, 512
Steinbrück, Peer 736
Steiwer, Frederick 64
Stepanov, Mikhail Stepanovich 194
sterling
   1976 crisis 578–9
   call for devaluation (1949) 281–2
   convertibility 299–305; as condition of American loan 280
   decline 441–2, 457–9
   devaluation (1967) 445, 452, 457
   as major reserve currency 145–6, 273, 298, 432, 481–2
sterling area 140, 298
   decline of 458–9
   end of 516
   and European Payments Union 296
   viability of 304–5
sterling balances 276–82
   Second World War 139–42
   US view of 140–41
Stern, Nicholas 820
Stettinius, Edward 138, 245
   on employment and trade 211
   and full employment 258–9
Stiglitz, Joseph 598, 601
   and climate change 821
   on economic equilibrium 799
   on 'ersatz capitalism' 801
   on euro 758
   on fiscal expansion 743
   on global financial crisis 731
   on privatization 679
   UN Commission of Experts 782
   on US financial market 749
Stilwell, General Joseph 196

Stimson, Henry L. 9, 61, 237, 238
Stinebower, Leroy 299
Stockholm school of economics 81
Stoppani, Pietro 29, 33, 76–7, 80–81
Strakosch, Henry 24
Strauss-Kahn, Dominique 740, 754, 755, 775
Street, Raymond 254–5, 257
strikes
    France (1968) 569
    General (UK, 1926) 21
    UK coal miners' 516
    UK 'winter of discontent' (1978–9) 582
    see also labour relations
structural adjustment lending, by World Bank and IMF 587, 591–2, 597–8
sub-prime mortgages, US market 732
Sudan, development schemes 317
Sukarno 116, 337, 338, 339, 341, 342
Summers, Larry 601, 732
    on Biden's stimulus plans 825
    on global financial crisis 734, 738, 746, 747, 752
    on IMF financial liberalization 628, 630
    on responsible nationalism 796
Sun Yat-sen 97, 196, 347
    and Kuomintang 97, 98
    and modernization 98, 99
Sunak, Rishi 793
Sunrise Movement (US) 821
supranational institutions xxxi–xxxii, 86
    see also institutions
Supreme Court (US), ruling on gold clause (1934) 52–3
sustainable development 560
    defined 590
    WTO and 647
Sustainable Development Goals (2015) 591
Sutcliffe, Bob 570
Sutherland, Peter 640, 644, 778

swap networks, to bail out banks 744–5, 745
Sweden
    rejection of EU membership 719
    Unemployment Commission 84

Taft, Robert 193, 216, 232, 290
Tai, Katherine 788–9
Taiwan 271, 330, 788, 831
Tan Zhenlin 349
tariff reform, Britain 11–12
tariffs
    average levels 272
    preferential 424–5
    proposed removal (Doha) 651
    US reductions 252–3, 269–70
    see also GATT; protectionism
Tariki, Abdullah 537
Tata, J. R. D. 691
tax avoidance 813
tax regimes 804–10
    need for reform 808–10
taxation
    base erosion 806
    of corporations 805–6
    cuts 578
    of financial transactions 767
    of foreign investment 387
    of income from capital 806, 809
    inheritance 55, 807, 807
    national insurance (UK) 809
    need for international co-ordination 806
    and profit-shifting 804, 805, 806, 813
    of profits 800
    progressive 806–7
    redistributive 808–9
    shift from income to sales 805
    of wealthy 803
    windfall (on energy profits) 808–9
technology
    application in agriculture 327–8, 561–3
    and development 324, 326, 332–5
    and labour market changes 766–7

South Korean use of 364
    see also information technology
Tennessee Valley Authority 315, 331–2
    Wilson Dam 306
terrorism 647, 648
textile industry
    cotton prices 182
    GATT and 639
    trade restrictions 414, 638
    US 380, 466
Thailand, currency collapse (1997) 621
Thakurdas, Purshottamdas 196
Thatcher, Margaret xxiii, xxv, 565, 705
    Bruges speech (1988) 711
    at Cancún 584
    and Delors report 710–711
    and European single market 589, 633
    and Hayek 571
Third World
    American influence xxx
    China and xxx, 354–6
    influence of Maoism 351
    influence of Soviet Communism 352–3
    racism in views of 534
    see also developing countries; G77; Non-Aligned Movement
Thomas, Elmer 34, 35–6, 50
Thorneycroft, Peter 305
three worlds theory 536–7
Tiananmen Square, 1989 protests 659, 671
Tibet, annexed by China 355
Tietmeyer, Hans 615–16
Tinbergen, Jan 81, 83
    ECOSOC Committee on Development Planning 553
    and GATT 373, 414
    report on reform of international economic system 551–2
    and Reshaping the International Order (1976) 561
Tito, Josip Broz 338, 342

Tobey, Charles 193, 218
Tobin, James 385, 434, 438, 669, 670
Tofler, Alvin, *Future Shock* 558
Tooze, Adam 69, 286, 742
  on DSSI 816
  on eurozone crisis 753–4
  on Fed swap lines 744
  on pandemic 792, 795
Touré, Ahmed Sékou 353
trade
  effect of crises on 14–15, 773–4
  and employment 229, 244–5
  financialization 612
  global goods and services 831–2, 832
  global merchandise exports 657, 658
  and liquidity 441–57
  multilateral 244
  need for rules 641–2
  world trade and production 6
  WTO definition 647
  see also EEC; GATT; International Trade Organization; WTO
trade agreements
  bilateral 11, 14, 62, 132, 148, 652–3
  multilateral-bilateralism 254–5, 266
  plurilateral 779–80
  and reciprocity 394–5, 413–14, 415–16
  regional 633, 634–6, 652–3
  US 65
  see also multilateralism
Trade Agreements Act (US, 1979) 634
Trade Agreements Extension Acts (1955, 1958) 374
trade blocs 62, 633
  German 59
Trade and Competitiveness Act (US, 1988) 638
trade cycles, League of Nations work on 84
Trade Expansion Act (TEA) (US, 1962–7) 374–81, 388
trade liberalization 612, 613, 633
trade policy

changes after end of Bretton Woods 524–31
  Clinton's 639, 644–5
  Kennedy's 375–7
  Nixon's 465–6, 524–5, 527–8
  Reagan's 634–5
  Roosevelt 8–9, 60, 74, 210–211, 243–5
  Trump's 786–8
  US–UK discussions (from 1942) 131, 132–8
  see also free trade; protectionism
trade relations xx
  pre-First World War 10–12
  and warfare 59
  World Monetary and Economic Conference on 47
  see also GATT
trade, terms of, and demands of primary producers 357–60, 373, 418, 549
trade unions
  power curtailed 582
  UK 153, 154
  USA 55, 644
  wage demands to combat inflation 569–70
trade-related investment measures (TRIMS) (GATT) 637
Trades Union Congress, and Labour government 578, 579
'tragedy of the commons' xxviii, 563–4, 794
Trans-Pacific Partnership (TTP) 779, 780–81
Transatlantic Trade and Investment Partnership (TTIP) 779–81
  criticisms of 780, 781
transport, costs 657
Treadway, Allen 65
Trezise, Philip 475
Trichet, Jean-Claude 724, 742–3, 754
Triffin, Robert 159, 470, 523
  on global liquidity 434
  and gold reserves 445
  and international monetary system 430, 470–71, 573

on US suspension of convertibility 491
Trilateral Commission (US) 540
'trilemma' of economic policies xix, xxi
  Bretton Woods trade-off 202
Trip, L. J. 31
Tripartite Agreement: US, UK and France (1936) 60, 75–81, 143, 162
  daily gold standard 80
  France and 76–9
Trotsky, Leon 92
Trowbridge, Alexander 395
Truman Doctrine, on European bloc 287
Truman, Harry S. 243–4, 245, 332
  foreign economic policy 271–2, 273, 275
  and Havana Charter 267, 268
  and JCS1067 directive (on Germany) 239, 248
  National Security Council paper NSC-68 268
  ratification of Bretton Woods 219
  and renewal of RTAA 269
  and Soviet Union 248, 249, 290
  termination of Lend Lease (1945) 222–3
Trump, Donald J. 771, 795, 824
  on climate change 821, 822
  corporation tax 805
  economic nationalism v, xxiv, 658, 734, 768
  fight with WTO 788
  and IMF 817
  and NAFTA 781, 786
  rejection of multilateralism 787, 788, 794
  review of Dodd-Frank Act 752
  trade war with China 658, 786–8, 828
  and TTIP 781
  withdrawal from Paris agreement 781, 822
Truss, Liz 793, 808

Tugwell, Rexford 8–9, 34, 36, 40, 43, 55
Tumlir, Jan 586
Turkey 98–9, 775
Turner, Adair 749–50

Ukraine 352, 683
  famine (1932–3) 96
  Russian invasion xviii, xxv, 760, 769, 793, 831
UN Climate Change Conferences
  COP21 (Paris) 781, 822
  COP26 (Glasgow) xxxi, 822
  COP27 (Cairo) 822
UN Conference on Environment and Development (Rio Earth Summit, 1992) 590
  and 'Southern consensus' 602
UN Conference on the Human Environment (Stockholm, 1972) 560
UN Conference on Trade and Development (UNCTAD) xxxii, 235, 420–21, 802
  challenge to multilateral institutions 418–19
  Charter of Economic Rights and Duties of States 535, 543
  first conference (Geneva, 1964) 416–17, 422–3
  as forum for developing countries 336, 415–26, 631
  Joint Declaration 417–18
  Manila meeting (1979) 551
  membership 400, 420
  Nairobi session (1976) 547, 548–9
  and New International Economic Order 235, 535
  and terms of trade 91, 116, 183, 422–5
  Trade and Development Board 420
  see also G-77
UN Development Decade, First (1960s) 412–15

UN Development Decade, Second (1970s) 533, 534–5
UN Development Programme, Human Development Index 590
UN Economic Commission for Latin America [and the Caribbean] (ECLAC) 591, 600
UN Economic and Social Council (ECOSOC) xxxii, 229, 308, 413
  Committee on Development Planning 553
  developing countries and 336
  and employment 320–23
  and 'fuzzy loans' 323–6
  and International Finance Corporation 325–6
UN Educational, Scientific and Cultural Organization (UNESCO), and population control 333–4
UN Human Development Report (1999) 647
UN Industrial Development Organization, 'Guidelines for Project Appraisal' 553
UN Korean Reconstruction Agency (UNKRA) 362–3
UN Monetary and Financial Conference (1944) v, 190
  see also Bretton Woods conference
UN Relief and Rehabilitation Administration (UNRRA) 308
under-employment, in agriculture 322–3
unemployment
  and deflation 23, 112, 707, 729
  Great Depression 6
  and inflation policies 570, 582
  US 480
  see also employment
United Kingdom

  abolition of exchange controls (1979) 582, 610
  and Anglo-German Payments Agreement (1934) 69, 73
  Basel agreement 457–8, 516
  bilateral trade treaties (nineteenth century) 11
  Bretton Woods: Anglo-American discussions before 161–7; and ratification 212, 215–27, 229–33
  capital exports (1920s) 22
  and corporation tax 806
  and currency stabilization 76
  de-industrialization 766–7
  economic relations with Australia 112, 115
  economy: crisis (1974–9) 578–82; labour relations 507, 516; recession (1980) 582; 'stop-go' cycle 451–2
  and ECSC 293–5
  and employment 258–9
  and Europe 291–5; applications to join EEC 382, 457–8, 481–2; 'Black Wednesday' (1992) 715; Brexit 768; and Delors report 710–711; and EEC collective float 515–17; and European economic convergence 700–701; exchange rate mechanism 712, 715; and Maastricht 715; and membership of EEC 382–3, 458–9, 505; membership of EEC 'snake' 506–7, 515, 517; membership of EFTA 382; opt-out from single currency 714, 719; rejection of EMS 706–7
  flotation of pound 505–7

and GATT (Kennedy
Round) 382–3, 388,
389
and German trade policy
(1930s) 72–3
global financial crisis,
austerity 738
gold standard 20–21, 23;
leaves (1931) xxi,
23–4, 32
and Havana Charter
(ITO) 266–7
and IMF 200
IMF and BIS loans
457–8, 516, 581
income inequality 765,
766–7
and India 101, 104–6,
115, 196
Interdepartmental
Committee on
Reparations and
Economic Security
(1943) 236
and ITO 266
labour market changes
766–7
Marshall Aid 291
North Sea oil revenues
610
post-war identity 276
post-war trade policies
228–9
relations with France
505–6
Second World War 74;
debts 48, 49, 287;
informal talks on
policy (1942) 133;
resources in 122–3;
wartime payments in
sterling 122
sterling: balances 139–42,
276–82; valuation
against dollar
(1934) 53
and UNCTAD 417
and US 121, 133;
Anglo-American
trade agreement
(1938) 74; and
Kennedy's proposed
Atlantic Alliance 379;
post-war assistance
219–27, 229–33,
287; terms of Lend
Lease 126–8, 129–31
view of globalization 767,
768

view of Smithsonian
agreement 503–4
and World Monetary and
Economic
Conference (1933)
32, 41
see also British empire;
Conservative
governments;
imperial preference;
Labour governments
United Nations
Charter of Economic
Rights and Duties of
States 535, 543
Charter preamble 339
Commission of Experts
on Reform of the
International and
Monetary System
(2009) 782
Convention on the
Recognition and
Enforcement of
Foreign Arbitral
Awards 624
Convention on the
Settlement of
Investment Disputes
624
Economic Commission
for Latin America 91
Expanded Programme of
Technical Assistance
324, 326
General Assembly: (2008)
781–2; resolution on
International
Development
Strategy (1970) 533
and international
organizations xxxii
membership of newly-
independent
countries 340, 400
Millennium Development
Goals (2000) 591
Security Council 194
Special Assembly on
Man's Right to
Freedom from
Hunger 327
Special sessions 540–41,
547
Sustainable Development
Goals (2015) 591
and UN Development
Decade (1960s)
412

and UN Development
Decade (1970s) 533,
534–5
see also UN Economic
and Social Council
(ECOSOC); UN
institutions
United States xx, 170, 175
agriculture 380, 393–4
American Families Plan
825
American Jobs Plan 825,
828
American Rescue Plan
(2021) 825
American Selling Price
380, 389, 393,
524–5
antagonism towards
'socialism' 545
balance of payments 368,
385–8; deficit 367–9,
433–4, 436, 461,
786, 793; problems
of 436–7, 440–41,
467–70, 816; surplus
273, 276
Bretton Woods: Anglo-
American discussions
before 161–7; and
Bretton Woods
failures 456–7;
ratification 211–12;
and suspension of
exchange rates
system xxiii, 467–8
and carbon pricing
819–20
chemical industry 380
and China 626–7, 673,
675–6, 787–8,
828–9, 831–2; and
Chinese membership
of WTO 676–7; and
Chinese silver-based
currency 100–101;
demand for
revaluation of
renminbi 676, 775,
783, 787; economic
imbalance 673, 675,
732, 793
civil rights 400, 569
Commission on Foreign
Economic Policy 273,
304, 325
Committee on Long-Run
International
Payments 447–8

United States (*cont.*)
and commodity
production 182–3
and competition policy
801
and concept of modernity
400
consumer credit 588, 769
corporations: tax 805;
view of 800–801
creation of Federal
Reserve 715
crony capitalism 605,
623, 750–51
Department of Labor
187
and developing countries
xxx, 17–18, 64;
demands of 550;
level of aid 555; and
notion of
interdependence
541–2; policy of
'divide and rule'
546–7
economic ambitions 121,
131
economic disequilibrium
824
economy: comparative
purchasing power
662; need for growth
(1960s) 376–8; and
post-war reforms
125–6
and Eurodollar market
608–9, 610–613, 615
and Europe: and
European integration
schemes 289–91,
371, 372, 377–8,
512–14; and
European war debts
25, 41–2, 48–9; and
post-war European
reconstruction 213,
215, 235–6, 247–9;
proposals for
customs union
251–2, 292; relations
with EEC 369–71,
377, 432; tensions
with 448, 457, 526;
view of proposals for
economic and
monetary union
474–5
failure to ratify Havana
Charter 266–8

fast-track presidential
authority 527, 528,
529, 635, 639, 788–9
financial sector: bankers'
risk-taking 614–15,
732, 747, 748–9,
752; deregulation
746
food stamps 54, 170, 175
foreign policy 271–2,
324–5, 525
and full employment
258–9
and GATT: acceptance of
268–9, 270–72;
Kennedy Round
388–97
and Germany: and
German war debt
286; JCS1067
directive 239, 248;
JCS1779 directive
249; post-war 236–9;
pre-war 69, 72, 180
and Ghana 354
global financial crisis:
Affordable
Refinancing Program
746; American
Recovery and
Reinvestment Act
(2009) 736–7;
Economic Stimulus
Act (2008) 736–7;
Home Affordable
Modification
Program 746; origins
of 729; property
market 732–3,
743–4; regulatory
response to 750–51
and gold embargo 34
and gold price 444–5
and gold standard xx,
xxi, 10, 21–2, 23
Good Neighbor Policy
(Latin America) 62,
106, 108, 109–10,
115, 180
Great Depression 5
and Green New Deal 821
horror of Communism
324–5, 331, 409–10
household consumption
674
household savings 588,
793
and IBRD 206–7, 208–9
and IMF 198–200

income inequality 765,
766, 767, 802
inflation: from 1970s
429; 2020s 825–6
Inflation Reduction Act
821, 826
influence over IMF and
IBRD 233–4
interest rates 436;
lowered 480; rises
435
international influence
397, 784; extension
of American values
60, 62; failure of
leadership xxix, 8,
324, 773–4
and internationalism 109,
218
and ITO 256
Job Development Act
(1971) 488
labour market changes
767
and land reform 329–30
link between military and
economic aid 404–5,
411
military expenditure
368–9
modernization theory
401–6
and monetary policy:
1930s 9, 35–8,
50–56; 1970s
510–511, 573–4
and monetary system: and
Keynes's proposed
clearing union
151–2, 154–5, 165;
proposal for
international
conference (1965)
447–8; and White's
stabilization fund
165
mortgage finance 588,
595, 732–3, 746–7
National Association of
Manufacturers 377
National Security Council
paper NSC-68 268
National Security Strategy
(2002) 631
Nixon's New Economic
Policy 488–9
and Nixon's policy of
benign neglect
464–5

Office of the Special
Representative for
Trade Negotiations
380–81
Point Four programme
346
and Poland 678
Policy Planning Council
405–6
politics: limit to role of
state 740; lobbying
and campaign
financing 801, 824;
polarization 770,
773–4, 824–6
and post-war financial
stability 155–6,
272–3
poultry market 380
pressure for protectionism
14–18, 65, 269–71,
395, 524–30, 634–7,
654
proposals for
International Trade
Organization 228–9
relations with France 502,
519–20
and Russia 685
Second World War 122,
123, 124
single currency compared
with euro 704,
721–3
and Soviet Union 157,
232–3, 243, 248–50,
528; and Soviet
influence in Third
World 354
Supreme Court 52, 53,
800, 824
suspicion of capital
development funding
without oversight
324–5
Tariff Commission 269
tax system 807, 809;
corporation tax 805
and taxation of global
profits 806
Tea Party movement 740,
746, 747
Temporary Loans
Guarantee Program
746
textile industry 380, 466
trade xxii, 63–4, 133;
commitment to
multilateralism

272–3, 275, 396–7,
653, 771, 773;
employment linked
with trade policy
210–211, 244–5;
Foreign Trade and
Investment Bill
527–8; import tax
(1971) 489, 503;
principles of
post-war 138, 228–9,
243–4; Trump's
policy 786–8
Trade Agreements Act
(1979) 634
Trade and
Competitiveness Act
(1988) 638
Trade Expansion Act
(TEA) (1962)
374–81, 524
Trade Reform Act (1974)
529–30, 673
trade unions 55, 644–5
Troubled Assets Relief
Program 746
and UK 74, 124, 319–20;
and British relations
with Europe 297–8;
hostility to imperial
preference xxx, 19,
73, 125–6, 138, 213,
215, 253;
misunderstanding of
Britain 280–81, 305;
and post-war Britain
215, 219–23, 226–7,
232–3; and sterling
balances 279–80;
view of UK sterling
area 140–41, 298
and UN Development
Decade 413
and UNCTAD 420,
421–2, 424
unemployment 480
US National Security
Strategy (2017)
828
view of flexible exchange
rates 512–15
view of India 277–8
view of Non-Aligned
Movement 343
wage and price controls
(1971) 487, 488,
489–90
and World Monetary and
Economic

Conference (1933)
28, 32, 34–8
and WTO 643; disputes
656–7
see also Democratic
Party; dollar;
Marshall Plan;
Republican Party;
Roosevelt, Franklin;
US Federal Reserve
Universal Postal Union
(1874) xix
Uruguay 263
Uruguay Round (GATT)
636–41
Dispute Settlement
Understanding 640
Marrakesh agreement
(1994) 640–41, 642
North-South imbalance
640–41
Punta del Este Declaration
(1986) 637–8
Trade Policy Review
Mechanism 640
US Committee on Foreign
Investment Policy
311–12
US Congress
and liberalization of trade
63–4
and post-war trade
agreements 133
and Roosevelt's monetary
policy 52
US Federal Reserve 715,
723
autonomy of 479, 514
and Biden's stimulus
plans 825
and BIS 205–6
and global financial crisis
824–5
as global lender of last
resort 744–5
and New Deal 156
Open Market Committee
445
and pandemic 791,
824–5
and quantitative easing
742–3
Regulation Q (1933)
608–9, 612
relations with Treasury
478–9
sale of gold 444
use of monetary targets
573

US Federal Reserve Bank of
New York 217
US Treasury bonds
Chinese purchase of 673,
674, 676
sale of (post-pandemic)
791
USAID 412

Van Rompuy, Herman 756
van Zeeland, Paul 163
Vandenberg, Arthur 66,
232, 269
Vansittart, Robert 72–3
Vargas, Getúlio 108–9
Venezuela, and ITO
negotiations 264
Versailles Peace Conference,
and League of
Nations xxi
Versailles, Treaty of (1919)
xviii, 13
and proposed economic
schemes 13–14
and threat of
Bolshevism 26
Vienna Chamber of
Commerce 82
Vietnam War 367, 398, 400,
426
villages
China (TVEs) 664–5, 672
India 86, 346, 690
study of 102, 554–5
Viner, Jacob 51, 75, 125
on capital controls 204
on exchange rates 202
on terms of trade 359–60
on trade and employment
321–2
Vnesheconombank (Russian
bank company) 759
Vocke, Wilhelm 71
Vogt, William, Road to
Survival 334–5
Volcker, Paul 492, 497, 565
on Bretton Woods 209,
432–3
and capital flows 467,
776
on central banks 616
and control of inflation
574–7
on exchange rates 625–6
on IMF 498, 605–6
and Japan 511
and negotiations on
currency realignment
499, 502, 504

and Plan X for monetary
reform 508–9
as president of Federal
Reserve of New York
574–7
on regional trade
agreements 636
and SDR 448–9
and 'social compact' 576
and suspension of
convertibility 468–9,
481, 483–4, 487–8,
494–5
Volcker Working Group
461, 465, 468–9
von Mises, Ludwig 216
von Neurath, Konstantin 44

wages
gold standard and 21
post-war restraint 568
and price controls 487,
488, 489–90, 569–70
service sector 810
stagnation 734, 743–4
Wagner, Robert 55, 218,
245
Wall Street
Crash (1931) 27
political influence of
bankers 434, 589,
750
relations with City of
London 595, 611–12
Wallace, Henry 54, 244
and 'ever-normal granary'
175–6, 181–2
Sixty Million Jobs (1945)
244
Wallach, Lori 646
Wallich, Henry 322, 559–60
Walters, Alan 712
Wanniski, Jude 578
war debt
First World War 25–8,
41–2, 48–9
Second World War 286–7
Warburg, James 10, 34, 36,
45, 50, 79
The Money Muddle
(1934) 50
Warburg, Paul 24, 36
Ward, Barbara 560
Warren, Elizabeth 751,
752–3, 803, 821
Warren, George 37, 46, 50,
51–2
Washington Consensus 429,
599–600

rejection of social
democracy 603
Wass, Douglas 578
wealth distribution
and reward for
innovation 804
Roosevelt and 54–5
see also income disparity;
inequality
Weaver, Warren 335, 561–2
Weber, Isabella 672, 694–5
Weidmann, Jens 757
Weizsäcker, Jakob von 827
welfare
benefits to tackle poverty
582
national provision of 763,
765
and neo-liberalism 582
social spending on 568
welfare reforms, equated
with Bolshevism 82
welfare state
costs as barrier to growth
587
as form of nationalism
235
Welles, Sumner 176
Wells, H. G. 39–40, 56
Wen Jiabao 673, 757
Werner, Pierre 392, 473–4,
703
West Germany 288, 471
and American monetary
expansion 440
and flexible exchange
rates 455
flotation of Deutsche
Mark 459–60,
480–81
and French expansionary
policies 459–60
Marshall Aid 291
outflow of dollars to
(1971) 480–81
and US suspension of
convertibility 469
see also Germany
Westad, Odd Arne 400
Wheat Executive (1916) 13
Wheeler, Burton 35, 36
White, Harry Dexter 53, 76,
144
Atlantic City meeting 192
at Bretton Woods 194–5
and call for abolition of
BIS 205
on capital flows 202
and Cuba 110

and direct foreign investment 435
and economic development 171, 239–40
and IBRD 206–7
and IMF 199, 200
international monetary system 109, 145, 217; and proposed stabilization fund 155, 156–61, 163
and Keynes 156–7, 194
and Latin America 115, 157–8
and Soviet Union 97, 157
White, Nicholas 318
Whittlesey, Charles 201
WHO (World Health Organization) 308, 328–9, 794, 795
and birth control 333, 564
response to Covid pandemic 795
and Rockefeller Foundation funding 328
Soviet Union and 328–9
Widman, Lisle 456, 465–6, 470, 474–5
Wilcox, Clair 253, 255, 265, 266
Wilgress, Dana 371–2
Williams, Eric 536
Williams, John H. 32, 33, 217, 236
proposal on currency stabilization 162–3
Williamson, Jeffrey 763
Williamson, John 455, 599–600
Wilson, Harold 243, 251, 266, 438, 579
and development initiatives 548
and membership of EEC 388
Wilson, Woodrow 16, 25
Fourteen Points (1917) 17
national determination 7–8
Winant, John 172, 185
Witteveen, Johannes 579, 613–14
Wolf, Martin 749, 809
Wolfowitz, Paul 685
women
role in economic policy-making xxv
role as producers 336
Woods, George 553

World Bank (International Bank for Reconstruction and Development) (IBRD) (1944) xxii
changing policy 552–3, 585
and China: on Chinese loans 815, 816; conference with (1985) 669–70
and climate change 822
Commission on International Development 553
conditional loans xxxi; cost-benefit analysis for projects 553; structural adjustment lending 587
development funding 547; and rural development aid 556, 557
and 'good governance' 688
limitations of 795
limited approach of 552, 794
and market reforms (1980s) 587
and neo-liberalism 589–90
and Physical Quality of Life Index 557
population planning projects 556
Redistribution with Growth (with IDS) 555
relationship to IMF xxxii
report on Uruguay Round 640–41
and Russia 684, 686
The Assault on World Poverty 557
see also IBRD
World Commission on Environment and Development, Our Common Future (1986) 590
World Development Report (1990) 590
World Economic Conference (Geneva, 1927) 14
World Food Board, proposed 178, 549

World Food Plan 327
World Monetary and Economic Conference (London, 1933) xvii, xix, 3, 28, 30, 40–49, 824
agenda 29–31, 33
China and 99
and commodities 179
failure of xxi, xxxi, 44, 47–9, 56–7
and gold standard 33–4
preparations 31–40
Preparatory Commission of Experts 31–2
sub-commissions 31–2, 47–8
US delegation 39
World Trade Center, New York, 11 September 2001 attacks 647
World Wildlife Fund 559
WTO (World Trade Organization) (1995) 586, 633, 641–9
agenda 643–4
Bali meeting (2013) 778–9
calls for reform 778–9
Cancún meeting (2003) 652
and carbon trading 797
Chinese membership 675–7, 787–8
choice of director general 644, 645–6
coalitions within 650
country reviews 655
cross retaliation permitted 642, 657
decision-making 642, 647, 650
and democratic national regulations 657
and development 643–4, 647–8
and dispute settlement 642, 655–7
Doha Development Agenda (from 2001) xxxi, 649–58, 779, 786
Five Interested Parties 653
Geneva meeting (2009) 654–5
and global financial crisis 773
and investment 643, 645, 652

WTO (World Trade
        Organization) (*cont.*)
    legal mechanisms xxxi, 644
    limited powers of 794
    normative view of world
        economy 649
    and poverty 647
    regionalism versus
        multilateralism
        777–81, 797
    rules-based system 642,
        655, 773
    Seattle meeting (1999)
        645–7
    secretariat 655
    Singapore meeting (1996)
        645, 652
    Transitional Safeguard
        Mechanism (for
        China) 676
    see also Doha Round
Wyndham White, Eric 365,
        371–2, 414, 419, 420

and Kennedy Round 391,
        394, 396
    on Latin American
        common market 408
    UN 270, 271

Xi Jinping 762, 829, 830
Xu Zhangrun 762

Yago, Kazuhiko 438
Yalta conference (1945),
        agreement on
        Germany 238–9
Yaoundé Convention (1963)
        371, 547
Yavlinsky, Grigory 685
Yellen, Janet 601, 806, 817,
        819
Yeltsin, Boris 683, 684–5,
        686–7, 688
Yeo, Ed 520
Young, Owen 27

Yuan Shikai 97
Yugoslavia, membership of
        GATT 372
Yukos Oil Company 759

Zambia, nationalization of
        mines 545
Zhao Ziyang 663–4, 668–9,
        670–71
Zhou Enlai 342, 347
Ziblatt, Daniel 824
Zimbabwe, copper 317
Zinoviev, Grigory 92
Zoellick, Robert 647–8,
        651–2
    on China 675, 784
    Doha Round 651
    proposal for global
        economic order 784–5
    on WTO 653, 779
Zuckerberg, Mark 818
Zumwalt, Elmo 540

A NOTE ABOUT THE AUTHOR

Martin Daunton is Emeritus Professor of Economic History at the University of Cambridge, where he was Master of Trinity Hall and on two occasions the head of the School of the Humanities and Social Sciences. He has been the president of the Royal Historical Society, a Commissioner of Historic England, a trustee of the National Maritime Museum, and the chair of the Leverhulme Trust Research Awards Advisory Committee. He has held visiting professorships in Japan and Australia and is a visiting professor at Gresham College.